ECONOMIC ENVIRONMENT OF BUSINESS

Based on the Latest Syllabi of MBA, BBA, B.Com., MFC, MBE, M.Com. and Various Academic and Professional Courses of all Indian Universities, Business Schools and Management Institutes

ECONOMIC ENVIRONMENT OF BUSINESS

An Insightful Analysis of

New Economic Policy of the BJP Government
Indian Economy: Macroeconomic Indicators and Projections
The Maiden Economic Survey of Modi Government
The Budget 2015-16
The Recommendations of the 14th Finance Commission
A New Method of Calculating India's GDP
(a) National Manufacturing Policy
(b) The 'Make in India' initiative
(c) Special Economic Zones (SEZs)
(d) National Investment and Manufacturing Zones (NIMZs)
Land Acquisition, Rehabilitation and Resettlement Act (2014)
India's Inclusive Growth Stake on FDI

Sampat Mukherjee MSc (LSE)
Ex-Faculty, Calcutta University (Postgraduate Deptt.)
and ICFAI University

New Central Book Agency (P) Ltd
LONDON
HYDERABAD ERNAKULAM BHUBANESWAR
NEW DELHI KOLKATA PUNE GUWAHATI

NCBA

REGD OFFICE
8/1 Chintamoni Das Lane, Kolkata 700 009, India
email: ncbapvtltd@eth.net

OVERSEAS
NCBA (UK) Ltd, 149 Park Avenue North, Northampton, NN3 2HY, UK
email: ncbauk@yahoo.com

EXPORT
NCBA Exports Pvt. Ltd, 212 Shahpur Jat, New Delhi 110 049
email: ncbaexports@ncbapvtltd.com

BRANCHES

212 Shahpur Jat
New Delhi 110 049
email: ncbadel@ncbapvtltd.com

House No. 3-1-315, 1st Floor
Nimboliadda, **Kachiguda, Hyderabad** 500 027
email: ncbahydb@ncbapvtltd.com

Shop Nos. 3 & 4, Vinayak Towers
681/B Budhwar Peth, Appa Balwant Chowk
Pune 411 002
email: ncbapune@ncbapvtltd.com

GSS Shopping Complex, 1st Floor
Opposite College Post Office, Convent Road
Ernakulam 682 035
0484-4021054/53

Shop No. 15, Bharati Towers, Ground Floor
Forest Park
Bhubaneswar 751 001
email: ncbabub@ncbapvtltd.com

Radhamayee Complex (Second Floor)
Opp. SBI, Panbazar, Jaswanta Road
Guwahati 781 001
email: ncbaguwahati@ncbapvtltd.com

ECONOMIC ENVIRONMENT OF BUSINESS • Sampat Mukherjee

First Published: 2014
With Additions: 2015

PUBLISHER AND TYPESETTER
New Central Book Agency (P) Ltd
8/1 Chintamoni Das Lane, Kolkata 700 009

PRINTER
New Central Book Agency (P) Ltd
Web-Offset Division, Dhulagarh, Sankrail, Howrah

COVER DESIGNER
Soumen Paul

PROOF CHECKING
Samiran Bhattacharya

PROJECT TEAM
Swapan Sarkar, Somenath Ganguly, Pradip Biswas, Prodip Baidya and Prabhat Jas

ISBN 978 81 7381 938 4

Price ₹ 495.00

Contents

Preface ix-xi

PART I

Introducing the Subject

1. Business Environment: Meaning and Scope 1-35
   1A: Strategic Management 25
2. Macroeconomic Environment: Certain Key Issues 36-63
   2A: The Balance of Payments and National Income 62
3. Corporate Governance 64-73
4. Social Responsibility of Business 74-81
5. The Use of Growth Models in Indian Planning 82-93
6. Indian Economic Reforms — Structural Adjustments and Growth 94-104

PART II

Analysis of Certain Broad Aggregates

7. The Circular Flow of Income and National Income Accounting 107-139
   7A: Saving, Investment and Current Account Balance 139
8. The Sources and Uses of National Income 140-158
   8A: Saving, Investment and Financial System 153
9. The Keynesian Model of Income Determination 159-184
   9A: Integration of the Goods Market and the Money Market in the Complete Keynesian Model (CKM) 181
10. Income Determination in Extended Models 185-214
11. The Consumption Function 215-233
12. The Theory of Multiplier 234-247
13. The Theory of Investment and the Acceleration Principle 248-266
14. Employment and Unemployment 267-288
    14A: The Measurement of Unemployment and Underemployment in India 286

PART III

Business Cycles and Fiscal Policy

15. Theories of Business (Trade) Cycles 291-313
    15A: Advanced Treatment of Samuelson's Model 311
16. Fiscal Policy for Economic Stabilisation 314-320

PART IV

The Role of Money in the Macroeconomy

17. The Theories of Demand for Money 323-343
18. The Supply of Money and its Determinants 344-366
19. Money Market Equilibrium 367-380
20. Monetary Policy for Economic Stabilisation 381-390
21. Monetary Policy in a Developing Economy with Particular Reference to India 391-401

PART V

The Synthesis of Monetary Analysis and Income Analysis

22. The IS-LM Curve Model 405-435
    22A: The IS-LM Curve Model for an Open Economy 431

PART VI

Macroeconomic Instability

23. Inflation and Unemployment: The Great Trade-Off 439-458
24. Inflation: Causes, Consequences and Remedies 459-483

PART VII

International Business Environment

25. Theories of International Trade: Ricardian and Heckscher-Ohlin 487-509
26. The Multiplier in an Open Economy 510-519
    26A: Numerical Examples on Open Economy Multiplier 517
27. International Linkages and the Mundell-Fleming Model 520-531
28. Free Trade vs Protection 532-541
29. Trade Strategy for India: Import Substitution vs Export Promotion 542-551
    29A: Recent Trade Liberalisation and Growth in Developing Countries 551
30. India's Foreign Trade 552-561
    30A: Special Economic Zones (SEZs) in India 559
31. Foreign Exchange 562-585
32. International Financial Institutions: The IMF and the World Bank 586-592
33. The Balance of Payments and the Performance of India's External Sector 593-614
    33A: India's Balance of Payments and External Sector Reforms 606
34. Foreign Investment and Multinational Corporations (MNCs) 615-638

34A: Foreign Capital Flows and Macroeconomic Stability in India 633
34B: FDI in Multi-Brand Retail Sector 635
34C: Franchising—An Emerging Business Venture in India 637

35. Globalisation and its Impact on the Indian Economy 639-647

36. India and the WTO 648-656
36A: WTO and Agriculture 655

PART VIII

MACROECONOMIC PROBLEMS, POLICIES AND PLANNING

37. India's Fiscal Situation and Fiscal Policy 659-691

38. Fiscal Deficit and Economic Growth 692-702
38A: Fiscal Deficit and Economic Growth in India 698

39. Financial Sector Reforms 703-733
39A: India's Capital Market 718

40. Industrial Policy 734-747
40A: Note on the Industrial Licensing System 746

41. The Public Sector and the Issue of Privatisation 748-760
41A: PSU Disinvestment—Endemic Problems 759

42. Industrial Sickness in India 761-769

43. Consumer Protection 770-780

44. Planning in India 781-814
44A: The Twelfth Five Year Plan (2012-17) 810

45. Global Financial Crisis, Eurozone Crisis and their Impact on Indian Economy 815-823

46. Environment, Climatic Change and Sustainable Environment 824-846
46A: Economic Externalities 837

Epilogue: New Economic Policy of the BJP Government **847**

Bibliography **849**

Index **851-853**

Preface

In 1982 the then Institute of Cost and Works Accountants of India (ICWAI) introduced a new subject in their intermediate course, viz., the economic environment of business. The author wrote a book on the subject entitled *'Economic Environment of Business'*. It was published in 1984 and was recommended as a text by the Cost Institute. The book had gone into seven editions before the subject was dropped from the ICWAI curriculum after a few years.

Now that the same subject has been introduced in various universities and management institutes induced and inspired the author to rewrite this book. In the past few years, the subject called 'Economic Environment of Business' or, in short, Business Environment, has been introduced in M.Com, MBA, MFC, MBE courses of all Indian universities and for PGDBM of IIMs and other management institutes offering various management courses.

No doubt there is wide variation in the courses of different universities and management institutes. However, there is a common theme in all the courses, viz., integration of macroeconomic analysis with India's business environment. The objective is to make an insightful analysis of the macroeconomic environment of not only industrialised countries of the world but also of India's changing economy.

A study of this subject (having great practical relevance) will enable budding entrepreneurs, future managers and business executives to gain a thorough understanding of business environment and enable them to take rational and correct decisions by studying the current macroeconomic problems facing the country as also the policy measures adopted by the Government of India from time to time to solve the problem.

This book deals not only with India's domestic business environment but also with international business environment. The reason is easy to find out. A clear and thorough understanding of this topic is absolutely essential due to rapid globalisation of the Indian economy. This is why an in-depth analysis of international business environment has been made in this title.

For conceptual clarity and clear exposition of the subject, the title has been divided into seven different parts:

Part I deals with the nature of the overall business environment and its various aspects. In this part the various components of business environment have been clearly discussed. The focus is on various macroeconomic issues of contemporary relevance, viz., economic growth, inflation, employment and unemployment, the balance of payments and foreign exchange. These topics have been explained in detail for the benefit of both students and practising managers. Two related issues — corporate governance and social responsibility of business— have been discussed in detail because of their strategic importance in determining the macroeconomic environment of business. In fact, it was lack of good corporate governance on the part of companies and banks and non-bank financial institutions which often led to financial crisis and corporate collapse in the recent past. In addition, the role of Planning in India, the use of growth models in Indian Planning as also various structural adjustment programmes and economic reforms initiated in India since July 1991 (mainly at the insistence of the IMF and the World Bank—the two sister organisations) have been discussed at length.

Part II deals with the theory of income and employment determination in the context of the simple Keynesian two-sector model as also the extended models such as the three-sector model (with government) and the four-sector (open economy) model with foreign trade (exports and imports). In addition, various numerical problems have been solved in a few chapters. Finally, attempts have been made to evaluate India's business environment in the context of the Keynesian analysis of investment multiplier, investment behaviour of firms, consumption behaviour of households, determinants of employment, and causes of inflation as also monetary and fiscal policies.

Part III of the title deals with short-term economic fluctuations (business cycles) which characterise all free market economies as also the role of fiscal policy for stabilising the economy. Two interesting concepts have been discussed in this context — the balanced (unit) budget multiplier and automatic (built-in) stabiliser.

Part IV deals with the monetary sector of the economy. The focus is on the demand for and the supply of money as also on monetary equilibrium. In this part the role of monetary policy — both in the short run and in the long run — has been discussed. In the short run it is used to achieve economic stability, mainly price stability, which implies the absence of inflation and deflation. In the long run, monetary policy seeks to promote faster economic growth.

Part V is concerned with the great neo-classical synthesis, or the synthesis of monetary analysis and income analysis, by using the IS-LM model. It shows that the goods market and money market can be in equilibrium at the same time. This is known as macroeconomic general equilibrium. When the economy reaches this point, equilibrium national income and equilibrium rate of interest are simultaneously determined. By using this famous Hicks-Hansen model the author has examined, in detail, how government intervention, through appropriate use of monetary and fiscal policies, affects the macroeconomic environment of business.

In Part VI the author has discussed macroeconomic instability. And, in this context, the thorny issue of trade-off between the two social evils — inflation and unemployment — has been critically examined. Furthermore, the problem of inflation has been discussed with special reference to India, with focus on the rise in food and asset prices.

In Part VII the author has discussed various theoretical and applied aspects of the international environment of business such as theories of international trade, gains from trade, balance of payment deficit, foreign exchange crisis, etc. This part also deals with international linkages and the Mundell-Fleming model which explores the implications of capital flows in an open economy under alternative exchange rate regimes. In this part the author has also discussed India's trade policies such as import substitution and export production and the trends of India's export and import trade.

In the last part, i.e., Part VIII, the author has discussed some important aspects of India's business environment, viz., India's fiscal policy, fiscal deficit and fiscal consolidation, disinvestment and privatisation of public sector units, financial sector reforms and India's present industrial policy, declared in July 1991. The last two chapters of this part analyse (1) the nature of the world financial crisis of 2008 which originated in the USA due to sub-prime housing crisis, their gradual spread to the entire world and, ultimately, hit the Indian economy quite hard, and (2) various environmental issues including sustainable development.

The best possible attempt has been made to make the title as comprehensive as possible so that it covers the syllabi of various Indian universities and management institutes. The whole subject has been explained in a simple, lucid language so that a wide cross-section of students are able to understand the subject easily and quickly without much endeavour.

The author is thankful to his publisher, Mr. Amitabha Sen, for his supportive role and collaborative endeavour. Thanks also go to his students Rubena Bose, Avisek Roy, Soham Dasgupta, Dia Mukherjee, Archisman Dutta and Suchaita Sinha for making computer entry, as also to Somenath Ganguly and all the staff members of the New Central Book Agency who have directly and indirectly extended their corporative effort in this project.

Thanks also go to Prof. Amitava Ghose of St. Xavier's College, Kolkata, Mr. Dipak Dasgupta of IBD, Mr. Sanjay Jhunjhunwala, Chairman of the Mani Group, Sambit Mukherjee and Sachi Pan for their indirect support for this ambitious (if not over-ambitious) project.

Any suggestion(s) for further improvement of the title will enable the author to make it less imperfect than it is in its first edition. Students and subject teachers (or esteemed colleagues) may feel free to get in touch with the author personally and give necessary feedback. It will be a great favour to the author and a thrilling experience for him and the publisher.

15 June 2014 Sampat Mukherjee
Kolkata
Cell: 09 1635 65580
09 7481 81503

Special Topics included in the Title

1. Long-run Consumption Function
2. Tobin's *Q*-Theory of Investment
3. Advanced Treatment of Samuelson's Multiplier-Accelerator Interaction Model of Business Cycles
4. Global Financial Crisis and its Impact on India
5. Eurozone Crisis (or Sovereign Debt Crisis)
6. Interim Budget for 2014-15
7. India's Balance of Payments and External Sector Reforms
8. Foreign Direct Investment (FDI) in India's Retail Trade
9. The World Trade Organisation and India's Agriculture
10. Structural Adjustment Programme in the Context of Globalisation
11. Corporate Governance in India
12. Social Responsibility and Corporate Ethics

Part-I

Introducing the Subject

1. Business Environment: Meaning and Scope
2. Macroeconomic Environment: Certain Key Issues
3. Corporate Governance
4. Social Responsibility of Business
5. The Use of Growth Models in Indian Planning
6. Indian Economic Reforms, Structural Adjustments and Growth

CHAPTER 1

Business Environment: Meaning and Scope

> *Microeconomic decision making by the firm has nevertheless to be made within the broader macroeconomic environment.*
> C. I. Savage and J. R. Small

PREVIEW

A business firm or an organisation is not an isolated entity. So it does not operate in a vacuum. It has to face an external environment on which it depends in a number of ways. For rational and judicious decision making a business organisation has to take note of its link and relationship with its environments. As Iam Brookes and J. Weatherston have nicely put it, "Whether it is a financial institution, a university or a multinational chemical manufacturer, no organisation exists within a vacuum. It is very likely, for example, to have a number of compettitors, to be subject to government restrictions, obliged to comply with national regulations and subject to fluctuation in the fortunes of the local, national or global economy. The business environment comprises an array of 'forces' acting upon organisations, often with far-reaching implications."[1]

A business firm is often described as **an open system**. This means that it not only affects but is also affected by external events and various factors which together constitute its external environment. A business firm is also affected by various internal factors, i.e., forces external to and beyond the control of the firm. In this context we may refer to three respective roles of three levels of management — top, middle and lower. The top management is generally concerned with the external environment. In contrast, middle-level and lower-level managements are mainly concerned with the internal environment. Thus business environment encompasses all those external and internal factors which have both a direct and an indirect bearing on a business firm or its management at all levels.

A business organisation is not only a part of industry to which it belongs, but also a part of the broader economy and the larger society. The relation of a business firm with its environment can be

1. *The Business Environment* (Prentice Hall, 2nd edn., 2000). p. 4

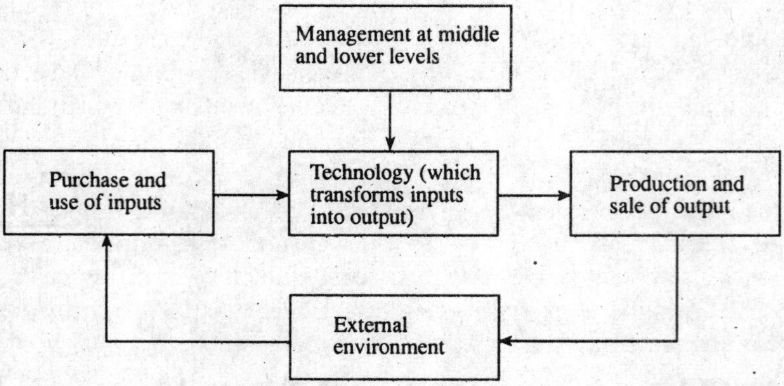

Fig. 1.1: The Business System in Terms of Input-Output Relationship

clearly understood from Fig. 1.1, in which we present the firm as a system which is based on input-output relationship.

The task of management is to acquire inputs from the external environment and transform them into output (economic goods and services) for sale to consumers, other business firms, governments at different levels and the rest of the world (through exports). A more extended and realistic model of operational management brings into focus how the process of conversion of inputs into output is planned, organised, monitored and controlled by production managers. The organisation and management of the conversion process is affected both by internal and external environment of the firm. The external environment is also known as the general environment and the internal environment as the task environment. We now discuss the nature of external environment of business against this backdrop.

EXTERNAL ENVIRONMENT

The word 'environment' is a general concept which embraces the totality of external environmental forces which may influence any aspect of organisational activity. Hence 'the business environment' is a broad and all-embracing term which encompasses any and all influences which are external to the organisation in question.

The organisational environment includes all elements outside the organisation's boundaries which have the potential to affect the organisation. Things happening all the time in the external environment exert much influence on organisational behaviour and performance.

Task Environment and General Environment: The external environment has two main components (or layers): the task environment and the general environment. The task environment includes customers, competitors, suppliers and the labour market. The general environment includes technological, socio-cultural, legal-political, international and national dimensions.

The external environment consists of all those factors which are external to and beyond the control of a firm and its management. It includes shareholders, competitors, customers, the society at large (the general public), various laws passed by the governments at different levels (central, state and local), different types of regulations, and the current state of technology as also expected changes therein. The external environment has both micro and macro components. In the language of Philip Kotler," The micro-environment consists of actors in the company's immediate environment that affects the performance of the company. These include the suppliers, marketing intermediaries, competitors, customers and the public".[1]

1. *Marketing Management* [illegible] Delhi, 1998), p. 127

Since production and sales of goods and services are two main activities of a firm, the micro-environment of business includes three main types of players whose decisions and actions have a direct bearing on the day-to-day functioning of a firm, viz., (i) the input suppliers, (ii) the competitors and (iii) various intermediaries in the whole chain of distribution. While (i) affect a firm's production, (ii) affect its sales.

Macro-environment of human has a much broader canvass

In contrast, the micro-environment has several broad components. It includes various economic and non-economic forces which are quite diverse in nature, viz., demographic, technological, natural and socio-cultural. These factors jointly affect input suppliers and customers (as also competitors and distributors). We now describe the micro and macro aspects of external environment of a business in detail.

EXTERNAL ENVIRONMENT: MICRO-ASPECTS

Different micro-economic forces have different but important effects on a firm's operations. For example, since large firms make bulk purchase of raw materials, they get price concessions from the suppliers of such materials. Small firms do not enjoy this advantage.

Similarly, a firm is in a position to initiate a price war if its rival(s) is (are) small in size and has (have) no market power. If its rival(s) is (are) large and strong, it will hesitate to cut the price(s) of its product(s) for fear of retaliation from powerful rival(s) which has (have) market power, i.e., capacity to exert influence on price.

We now make a broad overview of the important components of the micro-environment of business as also the forces operating in such an environment. The various components of such environment are shown in Fig. 1.2.

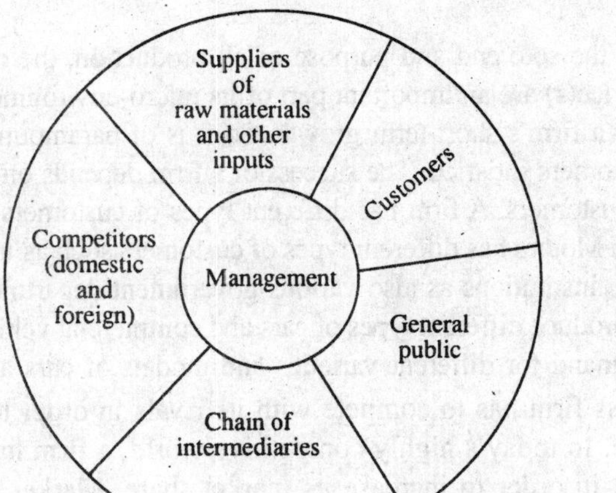

Fig. 1.2: The Main Components of Micro-Environment

(i) *Suppliers of Inputs*

The suppliers of inputs such as raw materials and components constitute a strong force behind the external environment of business. The smooth and efficient functioning of a firm requires an assured supply of raw materials and other inputs. Otherwise it is not possible for a firm to ensure uninterrupted production. If a firm faces uncertainty regarding the supply of raw materials, it has to keep sufficient inventories. However, this raises a firm's cost of production and thus reduces its margin of profit.

In order to ensure a regular and smooth supply of raw materials (and other inputs) some firms adopt a business strategy, called backward vertical integration and set up their own plants for producing raw materials. For instance, the Aluminium Company of America (ALCOA) once owned bauxite from which aluminium is made. The Tata Group has its own iron ore mines as also captive power plants so that there is an assured and timely supply of power and its production activities do not suffer. However, it is not possible for mini steel plants to create such facilities. Furthermore, it is not judicious on the part of a firm such as '*X*' to rely on a single supplier of inputs. The reason is easy to find out. If there is a sudden disruption of production of an input supplier's plant due to strike or lockout, firm *X*'s production schedule will be adversely affected. Thus in order to reduce risk and uncertainty, business firms buy inputs from a number of suppliers, and not just from a single supplier.

Focus on Terminology: Vertical Integration

A firm is said to be vertically integrated if it transfers internally, from one department to another, a commodity that could be sold in the market without major adoption. Most firms carry out some function or manufacture some tool or part that could, without major adoption, be purchased from another firm. However, no firm is totally vertically integrated since all firms purchase some inputs or services which they themselves could manufacture.

Vertical integration is likely to have at least *three* potential anti-competitive consequences. (i) Firstly vertical integration might leave no independents and thereby require new firms (rivals) in an industry to operate at two or more stages of production. This is likely to raise entry barriers. (ii) Secondly, vertically integrated firms can squeeze independents by raising supply prices of raw materials and intermediate goods and/or reducing prices of final goods. (iii) Thirdly, vertically integrated firms can foreclose markets to their independent rivals.

(ii) *Customers*

Since consumption is the sole end and purpose of all production, the customers who buy and use a firm's product(s) and service(s) are an important part of its micro-environment. No doubt sale of product or a service is crucial for a firm's short-term growth. So it is of paramount importance for a firm or its managers to keep the customers satisfied. The success of a firm depends on how it responds to the wants, needs and desires of its customers. A firm has different types of customers. For example, an automobile manufacturer like the Tata Motors has different types of customers such as individuals, private companies, public sector units, public institutions as also various government departments (at the central, state, and local levels). So it has to produce different types of cars and commercial vehicles to meet existing (present) and changing (future) demand for different varieties and models of cars and vehicles.

In addition, a business firm has to compete with its rivals in order to attract customers and thus increase its market share. In today's highly competitive world, a firm has to spend huge amounts of money on advertisement in order to increase its market share. Market share can be increased both by retaining existing customers and creating new buyers of its product(s). Market share can be increased not only by selling existing products in large numbers but also by introducing new products as also new models of existing products.

In the context of present trend towards increasing globalisation and liberalisation what is of paramount importance to the success of a domestic firm is customer satisfaction. Otherwise customers may go for imported goods and services. Therefore in order to survive and grow, a firm has to make a constant and a conscious effort to improve its product availability so as to ensure customer satisfaction.

(iii) *Chain of Intermediaries*

In the area of marketing a chain of intermediaries plays a crucial role. In fact it is through its channel of distribution that a firm distributes and sells its product to final buyers. Such intermediaries include various selling agents, merchants such as distribution firms, wholesalers and retailers. They perform various useful functions such as storing and stocking of goods as also transferring goods from producing to distant consuming centres for purchase by final users. Various agencies such as market research firms, consulting firms and advertising agents assist a firm in promoting and selling its products to eager buyers in target markets.

Case Example: Relationship Marketing

Saturn prides itself on the notion that it manufactures a superior automotive product, and provides superior service. Part of this superior service involves listening better to its customers and responding to their suggestions. During early summer, for example, thousands of Saturn owners typically respond to the company's invitation to attend a 3-day picnic at company headquarters in Spring Hill, Tennessee, USA. Not only is it a way to thank owners for their business, but it is a proven means of building customer loyalty. Mail-order merchants Cabela's, L. L. Bean, and Lands' End, among others, deploy impressive computer capabilities to track and anticipate customer needs better. At Cabela's, for example, customers that order camping equipment and hiking boots are good candidates for the company's camping and outdoor gear catalogue. Lands' End customers who order chinos and other casual attire also receive specialised catalogues. At L. L. Bean, which ensures the company's unconditional 100 percent satisfaction guarantee, keeps valued customers coming back. At Fed Ex, highly profitable customers get special attention.

Car companies, mail-order merchants, airlines (with frequent flyer programmes), and hotels with repeat business customers are obvious candidates for effective relationship marketing. The untapped potential for relationship marketing lies in new and innovative applications. For example, if a company wants to sell detergent, it might obtain a database of large families and offer them a bargain price. While a typical product promotion effort would stop there, relationship marketing goes further. Relationship marketing would suggest the firm to offer such families a free washer or dryer if they remained a loyal customer for, say, 5 years. Because the mark-up on detergent is substantial, such a long-term promotion could be highly beneficial for both the customer and the company.

The logic behind relationship marketing is simple. It costs much more to get a new customer than it does to keep a current one. So the retention of valued customers is key to long-term success.

In truth, marketing is a crucial link between a firm and the ultimate buyers of its product. A dislocation of this link is likely to do considerable damage to a firm. If a firm cannot ensure timely delivery of its product(s), rivals will take away a portion of its established business. And if this trend continues for sometime, a firm will lose most, if not all, of its customers, in which case its long-term survival will be threatened. Sometimes retailers (who meet customers directly) refuse to sell those products of a firm which provide very low retail margins. Progressive organisations should take note of this reality. In short, a business firm must take care of its intermediaries if it has to survive in today's highly competitive global market.

(iv) *Competitors*

Business firms have to face not only price competition while selling their products, but various non-price competition as well. Competition is conspicuous by its absence in case of public utility concerns which are found in generation and distribution of electricity, railway service and distribution of cooking gas. Most real life markets are of two main types, viz., monopolistic competition and differentiated oligopoly. In these two types of market firms compete with one another not only on the basis of price but also on other (non-price) aspects of competition, such as competitive advertising and sponsored cricket or football matches for promoting the different varieties and models of their products. And each firm tries to prove the superior quality of its product(s).

We are all aware of the intense competition between Coca-cola and Pepsi-cola which goes by the name *cola war*. These two firms often engage in price war to expand the size of their respective markets. There is also severe competition between Nirma and Surf washing powders, between Nestle and Amul chocolates and also among the manufacturers of varieties of colour T.V sets.

In fact, there is competition not only among the products of different firms but also among different products offered for sale by the same firm.

Focus on Terminology: Non-Price Competition

There are different ways in which firms can compete against each other. In monopolistic competition and oligopoly there is not only price competition among firms but quality rivalry as well. Such quality rivalry is an important aspect of what is called non-price competition. Non-price competition includes the following:

(i) ***Physical product differentiation*** : Sellers may attempt to differentiate technically similar products by altering the quality and design, and by improving their performance. All these efforts are intended to secure buyer allegiance by causing buyers to treat these products as, in some way, better than those of competitors.

(ii) ***Product differentiation by selling techniques*** : Competition in selling efforts includes media advertising, general sales promotion (free trial offers, discount coupons), personal sales promotions (through representatives) and the creation of distribution outlets (channels). These activities are directed at stimulating demand by emphasising real and imaginary product attributes (qualities) relative to those of competitors.

(iii) ***New brand competition*** : In a dynamic world characterised by constant changes in technology and tastes and preferences of buyers, a firm's existing products often become obsolete. A supplier is thus obliged to introduce new brands or redesign existing ones in order to remain competitive.

Given the enormous cost, it usually pays to promote only those products which consumers are likely to buy again and again or to speak more of to their friends and relatives. Where the quantity differences between (among) competing goods are small, advertising may have a significant influence on which brand a consumer actually chooses. Market incentives do not always lead to the amount of advertising that is the best from a society's point of view. True enough, strong competition among firms may sometimes lead them to spend huge sums on advertising.

This type of competition among different brands of a product is known as 'intra-firm competition or product-product competition'. For example, there is not only competition among products of different automobile manufacturers but also competition among the different products (or even different models of the same product) offered by Maruti Udyog Ltd.

Desired Competition

In recent years we find a new type of competition, called desired competition as different goods and services compete for consumers' limited budget. For example, a firm producing colour TV sets faces competition not only from its rivals belonging to the same industry but also from manufacturers of air-conditioners, cars, etc. The reason is that different goods meet diverse desires of the customers.

Greater Intensity of Competition

Due to increasing globalisation and liberalisation of the Indian economy since July 1991, the Indian economy has been integrated with the global economy. As a result India's business environment has become highly competitive. Indian firms have now to compete not only with their domestic counterparts but also with their foreign rivals, from whom they obtain imports. In the same way, leading US firms now face intense competition from their Japanese counterparts in such products as motor cars, cameras and various electronic goods.

Of late we find fierce (cut-throat) competition between Indian and Chinese products both in domestic and international markets. It is important to note that in order to meet or match competition Indian firms have to reduce cost by raising labour productivity so that Indian products become internationally competitive. An improvement in the quality of Indian products is equally vital.

(v) *The General Public*

Finally, the public at large is a strong force in the micro-environment of business. The term 'Public' is a broad one. It refers to any group which has an interest—actual and potential—in or impact on a company's ability to achieve its objective. The term ' Public' includes non-government organisations, environmentalists, media groups, local groups, pressure groups such as chambers of commerce and trade associations and citizens' associations (or forums such as the Forum of Free Enterprise). All these groups and associations exert considerate influence on the environment of firms.

In the context we cite a few examples.

Example 1

In 2003-04 a consumer protection firm from Delhi revealed an alarming fact that cold drinks such as Coca-cola, Pepsi-cola, Limca and Fanta contained a substantial quantity of pesticides which posed threat to human health and human life. This led to a sharp drop in the sale of soft drinks in spite of various advertisements given by superstars like Amir Khan, Shah Rukh Khan and others to disprove the allegation. So Indian laws had to be amended to ensure that these drinks do not contain pesticides beyond European safety standards.

Example 2

Environmentalists have been campaigning against polluting industries which cause various types of health hazards in the form of air and sound pollution as also contamination of water which is a cause of skin disease. This is why many industries have been forced to relocate in rural areas.

Example 3

Women in some Indian villages strongly protested against the setting up of liquor shops in their localities. The main reason is that excessive consumption of liquor by poor people is one of the causes of rural poverty and rural indebtedness.

Example 4

Many consumer forums and groups are now strongly campaigning against those cigarette manufacturers which are inducing people to smoke through persuasive advertising.

All these examples make it quite clear that the pressures created by various types of public exert strong influence on the functioning of business firms and make them socially responsive. Many Indian firms are now modifying their behaviour and responsibilities due to public awareness and pressure.

EXTERNAL ENVIRONMENT: MACRO-ASPECTS

Business firms also face diverse external forces when they operate within the macroeconomic environment. The macro-environment creates both opportunities and poses threats. It determines the opportunities which can be exploited by a firm for promoting its business and thus increasing its market share. It also poses threats by imposing various types of restrictions on business expansion and business growth. Thus the macro-environment of business exerts both favourable and adverse influence on a firm. However, main forces operating in the macro-environment are beyond the control of a firm or its management. This means that the firm has to adjust itself in the light of changing external environment or adopt itself to external forces.

The external macroeconomic forces are listed in Fig. 1.3 and may now be discussed one by one.

(i) Economic Environment

Economic forces consist of the general economic conditions and trends such as unemployment, inflation, exchange rates, interest rates and economic growth which may affect the performance of a firm or an organisation.

The economic environment of business mainly includes the nature and type of economic system of the country under consideration, the structure of economy (i.e., the interrelationship among its various sectors), the phase of the business cycle (i.e., whether the economy is speeding up as it does in times of recovery and prosperity or is slowing down as it does at times of recession or depression) as also monetary, fiscal, foreign trade, foreign investment and exchange rate policies of the government. The economic policies of the government have both positive and negative aspects. These create both opportunities and pose threats to a firm by imposing various types of restrictions on its operations.

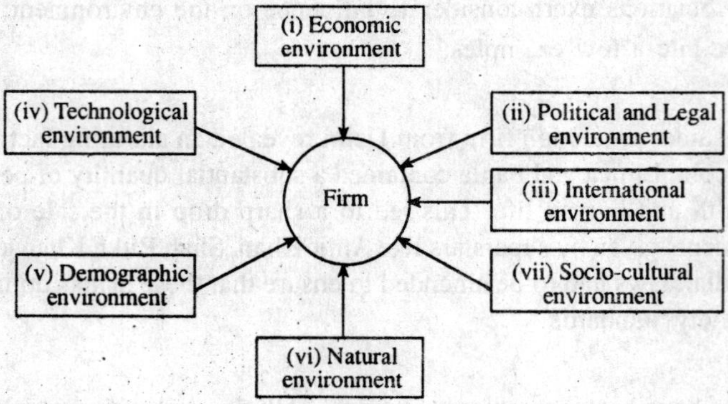

Fig. 1.3: Macro-Environment of Business

The type of economic system, i.e., whether a country has a capitalist or a socialist or a mixed economic system, determines the scope of doing business as also economic freedom enjoyed by the firms. In fact, the economic system of a country provides the institutional framework within which a firm has to operate. For example, upto June 1991, the Indian economy was a mixed economy with control. It had a strong bias towards the public sector. So the sphere of operations of the private sector was considerably restricted.[1]

Various important industries were exclusively reserved for the public sector. Private firms were allowed to enter industries producing consumer goods. In addition, the operation of the private sector was exclusively controlled by the government through the licensing policy[2] as also various acts such as *the Essential Commodities Act* (1951), *the Supply of Goods Act* (1955), *the MRTP Act* (1969), *the Factories Act* (1948) and so the Competition Act (2002) on. In addition various export-import restrictions were imposed on the private sector industry through import tariffs and foreign exchange control. Import tariffs were imposed to raise revenue as also to encourage domestic production of various import-substitute items. The basic objective was to pursue inward-looking (import-substitution) strategy of industrial growth.

However, there has occurred significant changes in economic policies of the Government since 1991. Such changes have changed the whole macroeconomic environment of business of India. Various types of structural reforms were carried out at the insistence of IMF during a five-year period (1991-96). The industrial licensing system has virtually been abolished. This means that the private sector can now produce a wide range of goods and services without obtaining licence.

Most industries except those, which were of strategic importance to the nation and which were earlier reserved for the public sector, have been thrown open to the private sector. Import duties have been substantially reduced as per the directives of the World Trade Organisation (WTO). Consequently domestic industries have now to face intense competition from imported products. At the same time various incentives have been given to promote exports. The rupee has been made partially convertible, i.e., on current account. In short, various economic and structural reforms carried out since July 1991 have changed India's business environment quite considerably. There has been a virtual metamorphosis, so to say.

1. In fact, the private sector of India was excessively controlled by the Government before the implementation of the economic reform measures and adoption of the policy of liberalisation in the context of globalisation (i.e., greater integration of the Indian economy without rest of the world).
2. The licensing system was introduced through the enactment of the Industries (Development and Regulation) Act, 1951.

(ii) The Socio-Cultural Environment

Socio-cultural forces are influences and trends originating in a country's, a society's, or a culture's human relationships and values that may affect an organisation. The members of a community or society exerts influence on business firms. People have now become conscious of the fact that the activities of business firms may lead to degradation of the physical environment and impose huge social costs in the form of deforestation, and various types of pollution.

In addition, business practices may go against the cultural ethos, and the value systems of a society. For example, aggressive advertisements by business firms do considerable damage to a country's culture and tradition.

So it is in the rightness of things for businesses to take into account the socio-cultural implications of their decisions. This means that they have to take into consideration the impact of their actions on the whole society. When a firm takes into consideration various social interests and society groups while making decisions it is said to be socially responsive or responsible. Social responsibility of business refers to the obligation or the self-enforced duty of a firm to protect various interest groups in society as also to serve society as much as possible and in the best possible way. By doing so a business firm seeks to promote social welfare.

Now-a-days most business managers understand the importance of good corporate governance. The importance of corporate governance should be judged not only by its capacity to increase productivity of a company's resources (especially manpower) and thus profits earned by it but also by the extent to which it is engaged in welfare-promoting activities.

The modern view is that social responsibility of business refers to the ability of a corporate form of business or a company to relate its operations and policies to the social environment in such a way that it is mutually beneficial to the company and the society at large. It may be noted that social responsiveness (responsibility) of business is related to ethical behaviour of corporate firms. The term 'ethics' is concerned with what is good or bad, right or wrong, fair or unfair, moral or immoral. This means that if the performance of business managers is judged solely by the amount of profits they make for their owners (the shareholders), it is not possible or proper to expect socially responsive behaviour on their part.

(iii) The Political and Legal Environment

Political-legal forces are changes in the way politics shaped laws and laws shape the opportunities or threats to an organisation. The day-to-day functioning and performance of business is largely, if not entirely, influenced by the economic policy of the government. After independence GOI declared that India was going to have a socialistic pattern of society. It implied that the public sector was to play a pivotal role in India's economic development. At the same time the expansion of the private sector had to be held in check by a suitable industrial policy. In such a regulated environment private firms had to function under various types of restrictions which together gave directions for the functioning of business firms. Thus *the Industries (Development and Regulation) Act*, 1951, *the Industrial Policy Resolution* (1956), *the Foreign Exchange Regulation Act* (1973), *the MRTP Act* (1969) were passed to control the private sector as much as possible. In addition, the role of foreign direct investment (through the multinational corporations) was restricted to a few areas. However, since July 1991, various structural reform programmes have been undertaken by the GOI following the adoption of a policy of liberalisation, privatisation and deregulation and the consequent move towards a free market economy.[1]

1. It may be noted that the collapse of socialism in Soviet Union, China and several East European countries in 1989 brought about a change in economic philosophy of the GOI about the respective roles of that private and the public sectors in India's industrial development.

In order to encourage the expansion of the private sector, the industrial licensing system has been virtually scrapped. The size of the public sector has been greatly contracted (entrenched). In addition, the GOI has been encouraging greater foreign investment — both direct and portfolio — in order to step up the overall rate of capital formation.[1] And the FERA has been replaced by the Foreign Exchange Management Act (FEMA).

All these measures led to a sea change in Indian business environment — virtually a structural transformation.

(iv) The Technological Environment

Technology refers different types of machines and production processes used by a firm. It shows how inputs are converted or transformed into output. Technological forces are new developments in methods for transforming resources into goods or services.

Focus on Terminology: Technology
In the broadest sense, the term 'technology' refers to the method of carrying out any activity which incorporates recurring acts, as well as the use of tools or implements. In a narrow sense technology refers to the method of pursuing activities on a given minimum level of mechanical, engineering, or scientific sophistication. Moreover, the concept of technology can be used to describe a reservoir of knowledge or it may be restricted to knowledge applied to actual procedures.

The success of a business firm depends to a large extent as the nature of technology used by it in production of goods and services. If a firm's technology improves over time, productivity of its resources increases. As a result its unit cost falls.

The use of superior or improved technology by a firm determines its competitive strength and determines its competitive advantage in both domestic and international markets. This is why C. K. Prahalad called the modern age by the name *the new age of innovation*.

To put it from the other side, if a firm is unable to improve the technology it uses, it will not only fall behind in the competitive growth race, but its very survival will be threatened as well. If a firm operates in a highly protected domestic market, and acts like a monopolist, it has hardly any incentive to improve its technology. It can survive for some time by using the same old technology but it cannot survive forever. Technological environment affects the success of a firm and its capacity to survive, grow and diversify in a highly competitive environment.

Two Case Examples

In this context we may first site the example of Indian automobile industry up to 1984. When Maruti cars were first introduced in that year there existed only two car manufacturers, viz., the Hindustan Motors Ltd (HML) (which produced Ambassador cars) and the Premier Automobiles Ltd (PAL) (which produced Fiat cars). These companies managed to survive for long without making much changes in their product designs. And due to absence of competition there was virtually no pressure on them to improve their production technology or to introduce new models of cars. However, as soon as Maruti Udyog Ltd. started car production by using superior technology, prices of cars fell[2] and consumers could make choice from a wide variety of cars. With economic liberalisation many new car manufacturers entered the Indian automobile industry. Now they are producing a wide variety of cars and changing their models almost every year by using improved technology and HML and PAL are struggling for survival.

In addition, following trade liberalisation many textile mills in India have become sick. They survived so long as GOI protected them from foreign competition by imposing high tariffs on imported

1. This has been done by raising the asset limits of foreign companies operating in India.
2. This happened due to significant improvement in car manufacturing by using modern (superior) technology.

cotton textiles. Many other firms have closed down because they could not withstand competition from cheap imports.

(v) The Demographic Environment

Demographic forces are influences on an organisation arising from changes in the characteristics of a population, such as age, gender, or ethnic origin. The demographic environment includes not only quantitative aspects of its people such as size of a country's population, the annual rate of growth of population, life expectancy of its people, as also the distribution of its people in rural and urban areas. It also includes qualitative aspects of population such as the level of education, skill and efficiency of its labour force. All these have direct and indirect bearing on the functioning of a firm. Since a firm recruits all new workers from the external labour market, demographic factors are an integral part of a firm's business environment. The skill, ability and efficiency of a firm's labour force determine the extent to which it will be able to achieve its mission.

Economic Insight: Population Growth and Technological Progress
Technological progress and population growth are interrelated. If there are more people, then there are more scientists, inventors and engineers to contribute to technological advance, which benefits everyone. Thus having more people induces faster technological progress.

Since the labour force of a country keeps on changing all the time, there is likely to be changes in a firm's work force. So a firm has to make necessary adjustments to these changes in meeting its needs for different types of labour. This is done through personnel management, manpower planning and human resource development. The firm has to make adequate provision for worker welfare so as to prevent the emergence of an adverse industrial relations situation.

Supply and Demand Sides

The demographic environment affects a firm from both the demand side and the supply side. It affects the supply of labour to a firm as also the demand for its product.

The supply of skilled workers to a firm depends on the level of human resource development in a country, which, in its turn, is a part of a firm's demographic environment.

On the other hand the size of the population as also its geographical (spatial) distribution determine the demand for manufactured goods. Most people in India, for instance, live in rural areas. And their main occupation is farming which largely depends on monsoon. Thus if there is good monsoon in a particular year, the income of the rural people increases. Consequently there is be an increase in the demand for industrial goods. Thus industrial growth depends on agricultural prosperity.

Inducement of Foreign Investors

India is a vast country and the size of its population is really gigantic. This is why many foreign companies were induced to invest in India during the period of economic reforms. These companies are now profitably exploiting the large Indian market for manufactured goods.

The Age Composition of People and Pattern of Demand

In addition, the pattern of demand for industrial (manufactured) goods depends not just on the size of the population but also on the age composition of the people. When there is rapid growth of population in a country, the number of children in total population is fairly high. So there is high demand for such products as baby food and children's toys. On the other hand, if a country experiences zero rate of growth of population, the size of its population will be fairly stable. In such a country the proportion of elderly people in total population will be high. So there will be more demand for medicines mainly life-savings drugs, dentures and walking sticks. This means that business firms have to take into account the relevant demographic factors while formulating marketing strategies as also while carrying out production plans.

Choice of Techniques

The choice of technique of production by a firm also depends on its demographic environment. In a labour-abundant country like India, the wage rate is low. So business firms are supposed to choose labour-intensive technique of production so as to minimise cost per unit. But in practice we observe that in spite of low price of labour, most firms use capital-intensive technique of production. There are various reasons for this such as stringent labour laws, low labour productivity,[1] as also various types of incentives and concessions given to firms for investment in physical assets such as plant, equipment and machinery. There is also transfer of modern capital-intensive technology through multinational corporations. This has created unemployment, especially among the youth. As a result there is more and more government and public pressure on the business firms to create more employment opportunities in India's labour-surplus economy.

However, there is an offsetting consideration. In order to take advantage of cheap labour in India, Korea and China , many foreign companies are setting up manufacturing plants and production centres in these countries.

In short, demographic factors play a crucial role in determining the functioning as also the profitability of business firms. The reason is that such factors affect the productivity of labour and management.

(vi) The Natural Environment

The natural environment of business includes various geographical factors such as land, minerals, deposits like as coal, iron ore, bauxite, etc., rivers (as also port facilities), oil reserves and forest resources.[2] It also includes ecological factors such as weather and climatic conditions. These are of strategic importance for various types of business activities for at least two reasons.

Firstly, natural environment is the main source of supply of raw materials and energy which are used by business firms in their production processes. In fact, the nature and pattern of production depends largely on the natural resource endowment of a region or a country.

Secondly, the availability of minerals such as iron ore, coal, etc. in a region influences the location of certain industries. In fact, industries with high material contents are set up near the sources of raw materials mainly to save transport cost. For example, most steel plants are set up near coal mines. Similarly, the availability of raw materials such as sugarcane determines the location of sugar industry. These are known as weight-losing industries.

The Demand for Goods

The pattern of demand for industrial goods is also determined by the natural environment. For example, those areas such as Mumbai and Chennai where temperature is high throughout the year there is steady demand for air conditioners, soft drinks and icecream. So business firms set up plants in these areas to produce such goods. Similarly, the demand for products such as wollen garments, building materials, etc. is influenced by weather and climatic conditions. Moreover, perishable goods like flowers, fruits, vegetables, etc. require adequate storage facilities, particularly in those areas where the weather is hot and humid. In addition, seasonal products also require changes in design as also in the type of packaging facilities.

It may be noted that an abundant availability of natural resources is just a necessary but not a sufficient condition for carrying out production activities within a firm smoothly as also for business

1. In fact, in most cases we find that cheap labour is inefficient labour.
2. Differences in natural resource endowments account for some of the differences in standards of living around the world.

growth. For example, Japan is a glaring example of a resource poor country which has achieved some sort of economic miracle in the post Second World War period (1939-45). In contrast, India has an abundant supply of natural resources. In spite of that India has not succeeded in achieving the desired rate of economic growth. The main reason is that India could not utilise its natural resources fully and effectively mainly due to lack of adequate financial resources and investible capacities of most Indian firms. This is why India remains poor and underdeveloped even after 63 years of planning. India's story is one of wasted opportunities.

In short, the rate of business growth in particular and economic growth in general depends not just on the availability of natural resources. It also depends on the state of technology which largely determines a country's ability to make effective use of its natural resources.

Ecological Effects of Business Activities

Till the 1970s most businesses did not take note of the serious ecological effect of their activities. Being solely guided by the motive of profit maximisation they have destroyed non-renewable natural resources such as forests and mineral reserves indiscriminately and thus they did considerable damage to the environment. Due to their indifferent attitude they caused air, water and sound pollution which posed health hazards for the people. By generating external diseconomies they imposed external costs on the members of society.

Of late, businesses have become aware of the adverse effects of the depletion of non-renewable resources and pollution created by business activities on society, mainly due to the efforts of environmentalists and international organisations like the UN and the World Bank as also the people of a country and its government. And various laws have been passed from time to time for protecting the environment through conservation of natural resources and prevention of different types of pollution. These laws have made business firms more responsive to the needs of society. Many firms have installed pollution control equipment. Others have cut their volumes of production for reducing the level of pollution. So environmental protection laws have imposed costs on business firms. This cannot be avoided if economic development has to be sustainable and a healthy environment for humans has been created.

(vii) The International Environment

International environment is constituted by such forces as changes in economic, political, legal and technological forces at the global level which may affect an organisation. The international dimension of the external environment represents events originating in foreign countries as well as opportunities for Indian companies in other countries. International dimension represents a context which influences all other aspects of the external environment. The international environment provides new competitors, customers, and suppliers and shapes social, technological, and economic trends as well.

Today, every company has to compete on a global basis. The global environment represents a complex, ever-changing, and uneven playing field compared with the domestic environment. As R. L. Daft has put it, "Managers who are used to thinking only about the domestic environment must learn new rules to remain competitive. When operating globally, managers have to consider legal, political, socio-cultural and economic factors not only in their home countries but in other countries as well."[1]

THE INTERNAL ENVIRONMENT

Since both external and internal factors determine the business environment, we may now pass on to the internal environment of business. The internal environment includes such factors[2] as the value system, the mission and objectives of a firm, its management structure, quality of its human

1. *New Era of Management* (9th Edition, 2011, South-Western), p. 66
2. These are a firm's performance indicators.

resources, physical assets, state of technology and changes therein, financial (liquidity) position and capital structure (the ratio of fixed to variable capital or the degree of operating leverage).

These internal factors are largely controllable. The reason is that the firm can change or modify these factors with a view to improving its operational efficiency and thus its profitability. The various components of an organisation's internal environment are shown in Fig. 1.4.

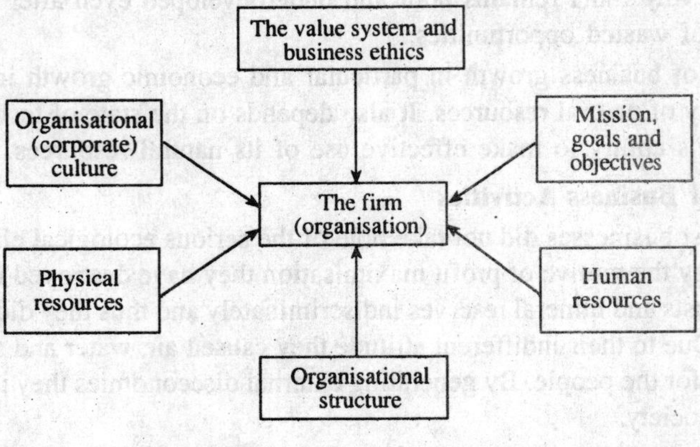

Fig. 1.4: Internal Environment

(i) The Value System

The value system of an organisation refers to its ethical beliefs. Ethics may be defined as a system of right and wrong. Business ethics assists managers in deciding when an act is moral or immoral, socially desirable or not. Ethical behaviour gives a guidance to an organisation and enables it to achieve its mission and objectives.

Focus on Terminology: Morality and Ethics
Morality is concerned with the norms, values, and beliefs embedded in social processes which define right and wrong for an individual or a community. Ethics is concerned with the study of morality and the application of reason to elucidate specific rules and principles which determine right and wrong for a given situation. Ethics rationalises morality. Andrew Crane and Dirk Mallen

The behaviour of an organisation towards its employees , customers and society at large is largely determined by its value system. The value system of the original promoters of a firm exerts considerable influence on the choice of business (i.e., the type of business in which the firm likes to be engaged) as also the adoption of business policies and practices.

Ethical behaviour in business is critical. When business firms, large and small, are charged with various infractions, and when employees of those firms are under some legal investigation, there is a concern raised about moral behaviour in business.

Due to its value system a business may refuse to produce certain articles which hamper human health such as liquor, cigarettes or harmful drugs. Similarly US firms do not employ child labour in factories and establishments.

The success of an organisation depends to a large extent on its value system. The reason is that the value system is crucially important in reputation building which is so important for the long-run viability of a business firm. For instance, the value system of Tata group of industries has all along been its self-imposed obligation to adopt morally just and fair business policies and practices. It was thought that this would promote the interests of customers, employees, shareholders and the whole society.

Commentary: Importance of Business Ethics

At present consumers and pressure groups are increasingly demanding that firms seek out more ethical and ecologically sounder ways of doing business. The media is also keeping a constant spotlight on corporate abuses and malpractices. And even firms themselves are now increasingly recognising that being ethical may prove to fruit-bearing or, at least, good for business.

The value of an organisation guides its corporate culture. A good corporate culture helps an organisation to achieve its objectives in an environment of fairness, honesty, transparency and courtesy towards its customers, employees, vendors and society at large. Thus, by exerting considerable influence on its corporate culture, the value system of an organisation determines its behaviour towards its customers, employees, shareholders and its attitude towards the society at large.

(ii) Mission, Goals and Objectives

Goals and objectives provide organisations with a blueprint that determines a course of action and aids them in proposing for changes in the future. A goal can be defined as a future state that an organisation strives to achieve. For each goal that an organisation sets it also sets objectives. An objective is a short-term target with measurable results. Organisations that do not have clearly defined goals and objectives will have trouble coordinating activities and forecasting future events.

An organisational mission is an organisation's reason for existence. It often reflects the values and beliefs of top managers in an organisation. A mission statement is the broad definition of the organisation's mission. It is sometimes referred to as creed, purpose, or statement of corporate philosophy and values.

Business Focus: The Mission Statement

A company's mission statement is a key indicator of how an organisation views the claims of its stakeholders.

The Mission

The *mission* describes what it is that the company does. An organisation's mission statement is formulated by fixing a definition of its business. Such definition should answer three questions: 'What is our business? What will it be? What should it be? An answer to the first question is the key to the mission statement. In terms of this question, a company should define its business in terms of three dimensions: who is being satisfied (what customer groups), what is being satisfied (what customer needs), and how customer needs are being satisfied (by what skills, knowledge, or competences). Fig. 1.5 illustrates these dimensions.

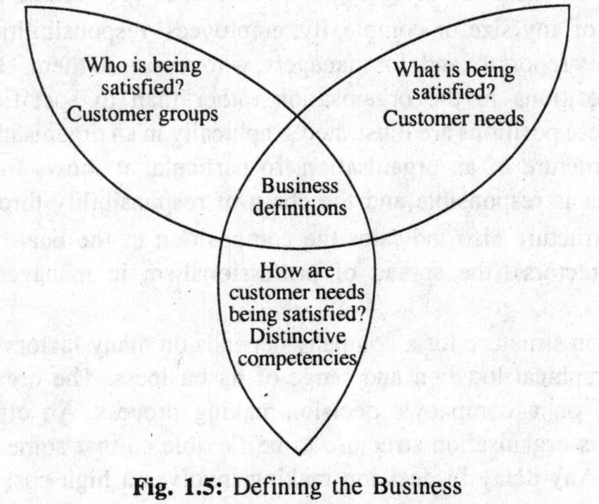

Fig. 1.5: Defining the Business

A good mission statement inspires employees and provides a focus and direction fot setting lower-level objectives. It is supposed to guide employees in making decisions and establishing what the organisation does. Mission statements are crucial for organisations to prosper and grow.

A mission statement includes descriptions of an organisation's target market, the geographical domain, its concern for survival, growth and profitability, the company philosophy and the organisation's desired public image. For example:

Our mission is to become the favourite family dining restaurant in every neighbourhood in which we operate. This will be accomplished by serving a variety of delicious tasting and generally healthy food at moderate prices. Our restaurants will be clean. Our guests will be served by friendly and knowledgeable people that are dedicated to providing excellent customer service.

This mission statement describes the target market which is families and its geographical domain is neighbourhood. It clearly states how the business expects to be profitable by offering excellent customer service by friendly and knowledgable people.

An organisation's mission statement guides and influences its business decisions and various activities, mainly production, distribution, and sale. The choice of a firm's business domain, adoption of business strategy and policies and path of business growth and diversification are all influenced and guided by its overall mission. For example, the mission of Reliance Industries Ltd. has been to become a world-class company and to achieve global dominance. Similarly, the mission of Microsoft has been to become a knowledge-based international company.

Commentary: Mission Statement and its Importance

An organisation's mission statement is the purpose of or reason for its existence. A well-conceived mission statement defines the fundamental, unique purpose that sets a company apart from others of its type and identities, the scope of the company's operations in terms of products offered and markets served. It promotes a sense of shared expectations in employees and communicates a public image to important stakeholder groups in the company's internal (task) environment.

(iii) Organisational Structure

Organisational structure refers to the way people and jobs in an organisation are arranged so that the work of an organisation can be performed. When a work group is very small and face-to-face conversation is frequent, formal structure is not necessary. But in a large organisation decisions are to be made about the delegation of the various tasks and the sharing of various responsibilities. Procedures are thus established for assigning responsibilities for various functions.

In an organisation of any size or complexity, employees' responsibilities are defined, including what they do, whom they report to, and, for managers, who reports to them. Over time these definitions are used to assign positions in the organisation rather than to specific individuals. Often the relationships among these positions are illustrated graphically in an organisation chart. An organisation chart illustrates the structure of an organisation. In particular it shows for which functions of the business, each manager is responsible and the chain of responsibility throughout the organisation.

The organisation structure also indicates the composition of the board of directors (as also the number of outside directors), the spread of professionalism in management and the pattern of shareholding.

The best organisation structure for a company depends on many factors such as the work it does, its size, and the geographical location and range of its business. The organisation structure exerts considerable influence on a company's decision-making process. An efficient functioning of an organisation requires its organisation structure to be flexible so that some critical (crisis) decisions can be taken quickly. Any delay in decision making involves a high cost to an organisation.

The highest decision-making authority in an organisation is its board of directors. It takes overall policy decisions regarding the growth of the firm and monitors and oversees (supervises) its overall functioning (operation). This means that the *efficiency* and *effectiveness* of the board of directors is of strategic importance for the efficient functioning of an organisation and for achieving its objectives and goals (in the context of mission statement).

In truth, there is not much spread of professionalism of management in Indian firms and industries. This is why various unethical business and trade practices are followed. And in this context many experts have suggested that the number of external and independent directors has to be increased to ensure smooth and transparent working of the board of directors in India.

The sad truth is that many corporate enterprises in India are managed by the family members of their promoters. This is not at all conducive to the efficient operation of those firms. It is high time there was spread of professionalism in these enterprises.

The pattern of shareholding has also one important implication for business firms as also their managers. In a number of Indian firms the majority of shares is held by the promoters of the company themselves because they have a controlling interest. In some other organisations the pattern of shareholding is very much diversified and diffused among the public.

In India the public financial institutions such as the IFCI, IDBI, UTI, LIC, GIC, etc. hold a large portion of shares in some leading corporate enterprises. So it is quite obvious that the nominees of these financial institutions take part in major policy decisions in these enterprises, i.e., they play an active role in making decisions on business policies.

The shareholders elect directors who together constitute the board of directors. The board then appoint the top managers who take various types of business decisions. However, most shareholders do not attend the annual general meeting (AGM) to cast their votes. Instead they give proxy votes. Of course, things have changed of late. The shareholders have come to exert considerable influence on corporate affairs particularly in developed countries. The bankruptcy of leading firms such as Enron and World Com. have created not only an awareness among the shareholders about their duties but also mistrust in management. Quite recently shareholders have taken legal action against directors and managers either for ignoring the interests of shareholders or for cheating them by skipping dividends for a number of years consecutively. This is why now there is deep concern throughout the world about the importance of proper corporate governance of business firms.

(iv) Corporate Culture and Style of Management

An organisational (or a corporate) culture is the set of key values, beliefs, understandings and norms that members of the organisation share. It consists of the generally agreed-on statements people would make about how to perceive, interpret, and feel about the way the organisation operates, that is, 'how we do things here'. In other words, organisational culture includes the values, customs, rituals, attitudes and norms shared by the members of an organisation, which have to be learnt, accepted and adopted by the new members of the organisation.

Organisational cultures are dynamic, especially under turbulent conditions. This means that culture can be a 'moving target' for employees and leaders who are aware of its importance. Culture gives employees more explicit guidance.

Corporate culture exerts much influence on the style of functioning of top managers. These two are important determinants of the internal environment of the company.

Corporate culture is of two main types, viz., (i) closed and threatening and (ii) open and participatory. In the first type of corporate culture only top-level managers take part in the decision-making process. The reason is that top-level managers have no confidence in their subordinates. In addition, the former do not trust the latter either. So secrecy prevails throughout the organisation. But there is hardly any sense of involvement and belongingness among middle- and lower-level managers in corporate affairs.

In contrast, in an open and participatory culture, most business decisions are taken at lower levels of management. The reason is easy to find out. Top-level managers have enough trust and high confidence in their subordinates. Easy and free communication between top-level management and managers at middle and lower levels is a rule rather than an exception. In this culture top management support workers and an atmosphere conducive to worker participation in management is created.

Commentary: Environment and Culture
The external environment of business exerts considerable influence on its internal culture. A major internal element for helping organisations adapt to the environment is culture. Corporate culture is an important part of the internal organisational environment and includes the key values, beliefs, understandings and norms that the members of the organisation share. Cultures can vary widely across organisations. However, organisations belonging to the same industry often show similar cultural characteristics because they are operating in similar environments. In the opinion of management expert R. L. Daft, "The internal culture should embody what it takes to succeed in the environment. If the external environment requires extraordinary customer service, the culture should encourage good service; if it calls for careful technical decision making, cultural values should reinforce managerial decision-making."

Healthy and Unhealthy

A related point may also be noted here. A strong corporate culture alone does not ensure business success unless the culture encourages healthy adaptation to the external environment. A strong culture alone is not enough because an unhealthy culture may encourage the organisation to match resolutely in the wrong direction. Healthy cultures help companies adapt to the environment.

(v) The Style of Top Management

The style of top management refers to the nature and pattern of its functioning. It is inseparably linked up with corporate culture. Some top-level managers believe in giving orders and instructions to lower-level managers without consulting them or communicating with them. They want their instructions to be strictly followed. This is known as autocratic style of management which is not at all conducive to the smooth functioning of an organisation. The reason is that it acts as a serious obstacle to the adaptability and flexibility of the organisation which is absolutely essential in the context of the changing external environment of business.

(vi) The Quality of Human Resources

The quality of a firm's labour power (human resources) is an important component of its internal environment. The survival and growth of an organisation depends largely, if not entirely, on the skill, efficiency, ability (competence) and attitude of commitment of its employees. The reason is that the most important resource of an organisation is its people.

However, employees differ on all these traits (attributes). In a large organisation it is virtually impossible for top management to deal or interact with all employees. This is why most companies divide employees into different groups. The top-level managers do not pay much attention to the technical details of a task or sub-task performed by a group. Instead it encourages cooperation and cohesion among different groups for promoting the overall interest of the company. This ensures efficient management of human resources.[1]

1. The selection of different types of people to meet the present and future manpower needs of an organisation is done through manpower planning.

Since the most important resource of an organisation is its people in most progressive organisations special course is offered to managers to enable them learn the art of selecting and efficiently managing human resources as also to undertake another important activity, viz., human resource development.

(vii) Labour Unions

Labour (trade) unions also determine the internal environment of a firm. Through collective bargaining (i.e., bargaining between a union and the employees or top management) unions fix wages and determine working conditions of different types of employees. The smooth functioning of an organisation presupposes the prevalence of harmonious relations between management and the union(s).

This is possible when both sides reach a consesnus on wage fixation and related issues. This means that both sides accept the terms of any wage contract.

Sometimes there is need for restructuring and modernising an organisation for increasing labour productivity, reducing cost and raising profitability. This becomes a reality only when there is cooperation among the workers.

(viii) Physical Resources

Physical resources such as plant, equipment, machines, etc., determine how much output a firm is able to produce. Not only the quantity, buy also the quality of such resources is equally vital in determining a firm's volume of output.

(ix) The State of Technology

The state of technology of a firm also determines, to a large extent, its production efficiency. If by using modern technology a firm can raise labour productivity and reduce its cost per unit, it will have a competitive advantage over its rivals.

In today's dynamic world, or new age of innovation, a firm has to develop new products and processes (new methods of production) so that it can gain sustainable competitive advantage. This requires adequate investment on research and development (R & D). Thus a firm's competitive advantage depends on its capacity to undertake R & D activities.

(x) Marketing Capabilities

Finally, a firm's internal environment consists of its marketing capabilities. In fact, according to P. F. Drucker, a business has only two functions, viz., innovation and marketing. And now-a-days there is need for innovative marketing.

A company's internal environment is largely influenced by its **marketing mix** which refers to the factors controlled by a company that can influence consumers' buying of its products. The potential profitability of a particular marketing mix and its acceptability to its market are assessed by marketing research.

Comments

In recent years unprecedented growth of information technology has fostered rapid technological progress and has increased the relative importance of human resources as also intellectual capital. And knowledge is the only factor of production which is not subject to diminishing returns.

Human capital is inextricably linked to productivity[1]. Productivity is determined in part by natural resources but in a modern economy, productivity is more affected by technology, specialisation and skills, all of which are a function of human capital. The success stories of Microsoft company and Infosys Technologies narrate the importance of human resources and intellectual capital than physical resources.

1. As J. M. Keynes once commented, "In the long-run, productivity is everything."

BUSINESS ENVIRONMENT AND MANAGEMENT STRATEGY

The external environment of business determines to a large extent the formulation and implementation of management strategy and policy. Management strategy is defined as the set of decisions made and activities undertaken to achieve corporate goals. After an insightful analysis and evaluation of the environment, a manager implements a set of policies or adopts a course of action which helps to achieve the organisation's mission and goals. From a scanning and evaluation of the external environment, management can identify the opportunities presented as also the threats posed by the external environment. This, in its turn, enables a firm to identify the strengths and weaknesses of the firm as brought into focus by its internal environment. The analysis of strengths(S) and opportunities(O) on the one hand and weaknesses(W) and threats(T) on the other of the business environment comes under the heading 'SWOT analysis'. For many years, the SWOT analysis has been used. However, this kind of analysis is static and seldom leads to the development of distinct alternative strategies based on it. Therefore, the TOWS Matrix has been introduced for analysing the competitive situation of the company. This is a modern tool for analysis of the situation.

The TOWS Matrix is a conceptual framework for a systematic analysis that facilitates matching of the external threats and opportunities with the internal weaknesses and strengths of the organisation.

Harold Koontz has suggested that companies should identify their strengths and weaknesses, as well as the opportunities and threats in the external environment, but combining these factors may require distinct strategic choices. To systematise these choices, the TOWS Matrix has been proposed where all abbreviations have the same meaning as in SWOT analysis. However the TOWS model starts with the threats (T in TOWS) because in many situations, a company undertakes strategic planning as a result of perceived crisis, problem, or threat. The TOWS Matrix has considerable significance as far as the formulation of an optimal course of action to achieve organisational goals is concerned.

The external environment of a firm is likely to present various growth opportunities for a firm. But often a firm is not able to exploit those opportunities mainly due to various internal weaknesses.

The external environment may also pose threats to the survival of a firm. For example, competitors may make huge and aggressive advertising campaigns or start a destructive price war to throw a firm out of business.

There is a need to scan and evaluate the various environment factors (which present opportunities and pose threats) in the light of internal factors such as physical resources, existing production technology, efficiency and effectiveness of management, technological improvement, the quality of its human resources and marketing skills. The strength of these factors determines the ability of an organisation to take advantage of the opportunities and to meet the threats successfully. Economic reforms introduced by the GOI since July 1991 in the context of liberalisation, privatisation and globalisation changed the business environment of the country almost completely. The domestic economy has become more competitive due to greater and greater competition from foreign firms and imported products. No doubt, some Indian firms have changed their product lines in order to remain competitive and survive in the long run. At the same time some inefficient firms lost money, became sick and closed their businesses.

However, some firms such as Reliance Industries Ltd., Infosys Technologies, Ranbaxy Laboratories, and WIPRO have identified the opportunities created by economic liberalisation and have become truely global. They have, therefore, set up businesses abroad and are examples of Indian multinational corporations (MNCs).

Meeting Global Competition

Now every company has to compete on a global basis. High quality, and cheap automobiles from Korea and Japan have permanently changed the American automobile industry. In cell phones US-based companies face stiff competition from Korea's Samsung and Finland's Nokia. For many US companies, such as Google domestic markets have become saturated and.the only potential for growth lies overseas. Google's mission is to reach ever the most far-flung corners of the globe.

China and India are likely to engage as super powers ere long

Perhaps the most dramatic change in the international environment in recent years is the shift of economic power to China and India. These two countries together have the population, brain power, and necessary dynamism to transform the global economy of the 21 century.

Competition from Chinese Products

A related point may also be noted here. Mainly due to their technological superiority some Chinese firms discovered the opportunities for the sale of various types of light consumer goods and they grabbed the opportunity immediately. As a result the Indian market has been flooded with cheap Chinese products. However, it is important to note that some Indian firms have succeeded in meeting the challenge thrown by Chinese products.

Japan's Penetration of the US Market

We are all aware of the entry of Japanese products in the US market. Japanese firms have captured the market in a big way. This is because there is high demand for Japanese goods such as small fuel-efficient cars and cameras in the USA. This is attributable to high quality and low prices of Japanese products made possible by superior Japanese technology and conducive (entrepreneur-friendly) business environment. The existence of such an environment is made possible due to positive attitude of the Japanese Government. As Philip Kotler writes, "The Japanese government and companies work hard to identify attractive global markets. They favour industries that require high skills, high labour intensity and only small quantity of natural resources. Candidates include consumer electronics, cameras, watches, motor cycles and pharmaceuticals. They prefer product markets that are in a state of technological evolution. They like product markets where consumers around the world would be willing to buy the same product designs. They look for industries where the market leaders are complacent or under-financed." [1]

Final Comments: The Response of Management to the External Environment

In the ultimate analysis it seems that business managers respond to changes in external business environment in any two ways — proactively or reactively. A proactive response refers to taking corrective activities, or introducing necessary changes in business policy in anticipation of changes in the external environment of business. In contrast, a reactive response refers to taking corrective actions or making appropriate changes in business decision in the context of the changing external environment of business. Since it is not possible for a business firm to react instantaneously to unpredictable changes in external environment, it is absolutely essential for it to adopt methods of anticipating changes through proper forecasts , i.e., prediction of the future course of business activity on the basis of current and past trends. Thus an efficient enterprise does not prepare itself for the war in war time but in peace time. Otherwise it will have to chase the dark cat in darkness. This means that no progressive organisation can wait for its products to be obsolete and for its sale to fall to a very low level (like that of Hindusthan Motors). This implies that forecasting the future course of business activities assumes significance in the context of proactive business policy which induces a firm to react actively rather than passively to its changing environment. This implies that proaction is an integral component of the planning process of an organisation.

It may, however, be noted that forecasting the business environment is problematic due to change and complexity. Yet many methods exists and are widely used to do the best of the so-called bad job.

---

1. Globalisation is essentially external liberalisation.

KEY POINTS

1. ***Organisational environment*** **:** The organisational environment includes all elements existing outside the boundaries of the organisation. But all these elements have the potential to affect the organisation. The relationship between organisation and environment is not clear-cut, as information flows from the environment to the organisation but also from the organisation to the environment. Events in the external environment are considered important influences on organisational behaviour and performance.

2. ***External environment*** **:** There are a number of interrelated forces acting upon organisation which emanate from the external environment of the organisation. The external enviornment has two components. The task environment includes customers, competitors, suppliers and the labour market. The general environment has technological, socio-cultural, economic, legal-political, international, and national dimensions.

3. ***Internal environment*** **:** An organisation has an internal environment which includes the elements within the boundaries of the organisation. For the purpose of analysis these forces can be placed in distinct catagories, but in reality they form an interrelated and complex whole.

4. ***Corporate culture*** **:** A major internal element for helping an organisation to adapt to the environment is culture. Corporate culture is an important part of the internal organisational environment. It includes the key values, beliefs, understandings, and norms that the members of the organisation share.

5. ***Diverse influence of environment on organisations*** **:** Business organisations are of different types due to differences in their objectives or legal status. And the environment influences different types of organisations in different ways.

KEY TERMS

Globalisation	External environment
Task environment	Internal environment
Economic environment	Non economic environment
Technological environment	Legal environment
Domestic environment	International environment
Balance of payment	Organisational environment
Exchange rate	Corporate culture

ASSIGNMENTS

1. What do you mean by business environment? What are its different components?
2. Distinguish between economic and non-economic environment of business giving examples of different sub-components of each.
3. How does a business firm react to changes in its external environment actively?
4. How does international environment of a business differ from its domestic environment?
5. "The long-term success of an organisation lies in converting a threat into an opportunity." Critically examine this view.
6. Highlight the different macroeconomic aspects of a firm's external environment.
7. Make a brief review of the different components of a firm's internal environment.
8. Show how the current account of BOP affect the country's national income.
9. Does the BOP of a country always balance?
10. Discuss the affects of globalisation on India's capital flows.
11. Show the affect of exchange rate change on India's balance of payments.

1A STRATEGIC MANAGEMENT

While studying business environment, it is of paramount importance to understand the concept of strategic management. The reason is simple. Strategic planning and management are based on an insightful analysis of strengths and weaknesses of the company as also its opportunities and threats.

There is a fundamental difference between strategic management and general (routine) management.

What is Strategy?

Although the word *strategy* comes from the Greek word *strategus*, meaning a command of an army, it was introduced in business literature in 1952 by William Newmann. He saw strategy as a plan for achieving organisational goals. The increasing pace of environmental change over the last six decades has forced management to make their strategies explicit and to change them quite frequently.

Strategy and Tactic

In the early 1990s, strategy was identified as the means an organisation uses to achieve its objectives. In 1995 R.M. Grant defined *strategy* as 'the overall plan for deploying resources to establish a favourable position, while a *tactic* is a scheme for a specific action'. In his view, the task of strategy is to determine how the firm will deploy its resources within its environment and satisfy its long-term goals and how it will organise itself to implement that strategy.

Other Definitions of Strategy

In 1998 P. Field and C. Gilligen added a competitive dimension and defined strategy as 'the broad statement of the way in which the organisation sets out to achieve its objectives. Included within this would be a series of decisions on the markets in which the organisation will operate, the type of products/ services it will offer and the bases of competitive stance.' In 1998 Henry Mintzberg and J.B. Quinn proposed five definitions of strategy from a multi-angular view — as plan, ploy, pattern, position and perspective. They also looked at some of the interrelationships among them.

Four Ingredients

To be very specific successful strategies have four key elements:

1. They are directed towards unambiguous long-term goals.
2. They are based on insightful understanding of the external environment.
3. They are based on in-depth (comprehensive) self-knowledge by the organisation or individual of internal capabilities.
4. They are implemented with coordination and effective harnessing of the capabilities to achieve the competitive position targeted.

Three Levels of Strategy

Modern writers on management define strategy in terms of three organisational levels: the corporate, business and functional. This hierarchical relationship is presented in Fig. 1A.1.

(i) Corporate Strategy

Strategy describes 'a company's overall direction in terms of its general attitude toward growth and the management of its various business and product lines to achieve a balanced portfolio of products and services. Additionally, it is (a) the pattern of decisions regarding the types of business in which a firm should be involved, (b) the flow of financial and other resources to and from its divisions, and (c) the relationship of the corporation to key groups in the environment'. The key groups refer to various stakeholders such as customers, suppliers, government, NGOs and the community at large.

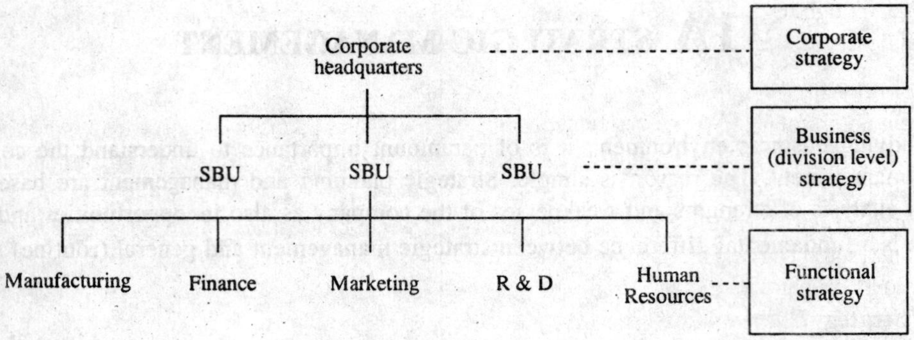

Fig 1A.1: Hierarchy of Strategy

(ii) Business Strategy

Business strategy is also known as competitive strategy. It is normally 'developed at divisional level and emphasises improvement of the competitive position of a corporation's products or services in the specific industry or market segment served by that division'. While corporate strategy asks what industry the company should be in, business strategy asks how the company or its strategic business units (SBUs) should compete or cooperate in each industry.

Business Focus: Strategic Business Units (SBUs)
Strategic business units, or SBUs refer to organisational groups composed of discrete, independent, product-market segments served by a firm. These units are to be identified by a firm first and then given primary responsibility and authority to manage their own functional areas. An SBU may be of any size or level, but it must have (1) a unique mission, (2) identifiable competitors, (3) an external market focus, and (4) control of its business functions.

A related point may also be noted here. Business strategies should also integrate various functional activities to achieve divisional objectives.

(iii) Functional Strategy

Functional strategy is essentially concerned with maximising productivity of organisational resources. Within the constraints imposed by corporate and business strategies functional departments such as production (operations), marketing, finance and R & D develop strategies to pull together their various activities and competencies to generate synergic effects and improve the overall performance of the organisation. One such strategy is outsourcing.

Business Focus: Outsourcing
In Kotler's view outsourcing refers to buying more goods and services from outside domestic or foreign vendors. Simply put, it refers to subcontracting of services and operations to an outside vendor, i.e, using suppliers outside the company to provide goods and services.

It may be noted that the three levels of strategy form a hierarchy of strategy development within any large corporation. They interact closely all the time and must be well integrated for corporate success.

The Strategy-Making Process and the Planning Framework

There is a fundamental difference between strategy (as an outcome) and the process by which strategy is developed, approved, implemented, and evaluated. This process of strategy making has been described as 'budgeting', 'long-range planning', 'strategic planning' and 'strategic management'. Since these terms carry a similar meaning, they are often used interchangeably.

Strategic Planning

Strategic planning is the process which defines the long-run objectives of a company and the means by which these objectives are to be achieved. Planning horizons may, however, vary from one company to another and from industry to industry.

Comparison with Strategic Planning: Strategic planning is different from *strategic thinking*. As D. West and others have put it, 'Whereas strategic thinking involves creative and entrepreneurial insights into a company and its environment, strategic planning has often degenerated into frameworks for the systematic and comprehensive analysis of known options'.[1] In their view, strategic thinking is 'a shaping process in which a reflective conversation with a situation takes place in order to reduce complexity of such a situation, while strategy making is a process of continuous adaptation between the industry environment and organisational capabilities'.[2]

Following Mintzberg, we present below a comprehensive framework of strategic planning and its related components in Fig. 1A.2. It illustrates the two dimensions of external environment and organisational capabilities.

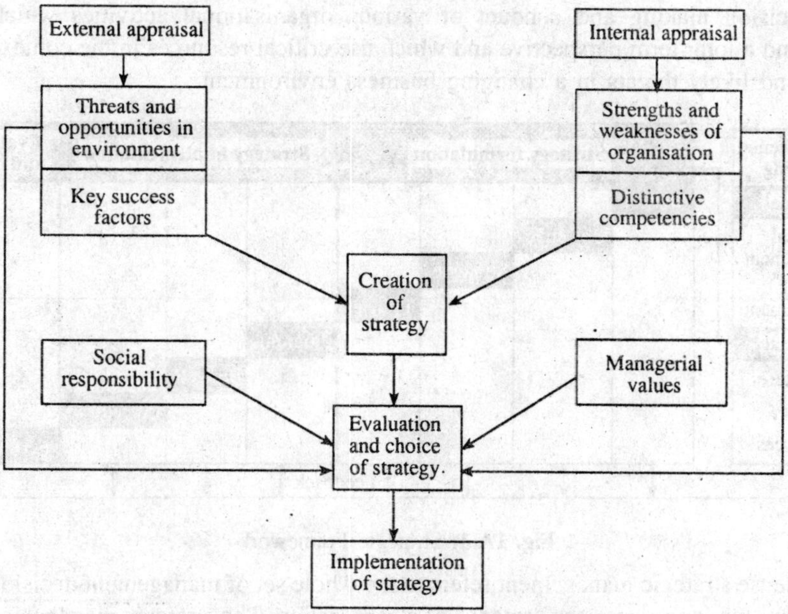

Fig. 1A.2: Strategic Planning Process

It may be noted that strategic planning is done by top management and determines the major goals of the organisation and policies, procedures, strategies and resources it will need to achieve them. While policies are broad guidelines for action, strategies determine the most efficient way to use organisational resources.

At the strategic planning stage, top managers of the company decide which customers to serve, when to serve them, what products or services to sell, and the geographic areas in which to operate (for meeting and matching competition).

1 and 2. Op. cit, p.46

A related point may be noted in this context. In today's rapidly changing environment, strategic planning is becoming more and more difficult day by day for a very simple reason. Changes are occurring very fast. So plans which are formulated just a few months into the future are often becoming obsolete. This is why many companies are now making short-term plans which are more flexible than their long-term counterparts. The reason is that short-term plans allow for quick responses to customer needs and requests. The goal is to be flexible so that the company can be responsive to the market.

Strategic planning refers to the process of determining the major goals of the organisation and the policies and strategies for acquiring and deploying resources to achieve those goals

Strategic Management

Strategic management involves and brings into focus the importance of strategic implementation, evaluation and control. The rationale behind strategic management is that the planning cycle is not adequate enough to deal with rapid rate of change which can occur in the environment facing the firm. Therefore, in order to cope with strategic surprises and fast-developing threats and opportunities, a firm's planning decisions need to be made outside the planning cycle.

In the language of William Gulock, 'Strategic management is that set of decisions and actions which lead to the development of an effective strategy or strategies to help achieve corporate objectives'.[1] It involves decision making and conduct of various organisational activities which have wider ramifications and a long-term perspective and which use critical resources in the context of perceived opportunities and likely threats in a changing business environment.

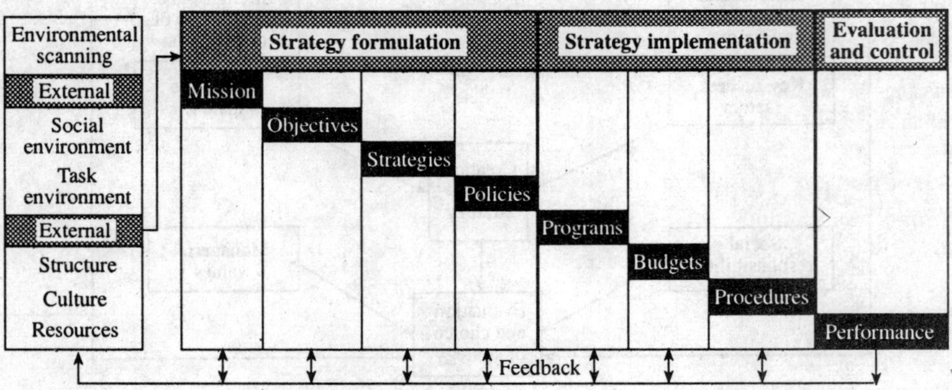

Fig. 1A.3: Strategic Framework

In a broad sense strategic management refers to the whole set of management decisions and actions which determines the long-range performance of a corporation. The strategic management process has four basic elements as shown in Fig. 1A.3., viz., (i) environmental scanning, (ii) strategy formulation, (iii) strategy implementation and (iv) evaluation and control.

The strategic management process starts when executive members evaluate their current position with respect to mission, goals and strategies. Then they scan the organisation's internal and external environment and identify strategic factors which require change. Internal or external events may indicate a need to redefine the mission, or goals to formulate new strategy at either the corporate, business or functional level. The final stage of the strategic management process is implementation of the new strategy.

We now discuss the process involved in strategic management one by one:

1. *Business Policy and Corporate Strategic Management* (McGraw-Hill, 1972), p. 19

1. Formulation of Mission Statement

The strategic management process starts with the formulation of mission. An organisation's mission is the purpose of a reason for the organisation's existence. A well-conceived mission statement defines the fundamental, unique purpose which sets a company apart from other firms of its types and identifies the scope of the company's operations in terms of products offered and markets served. It promotes a sense of shared expectations in employees and communicates a public image to important stakeholder groups in a company's task environment.

Mission statement expresses the purpose of the organisation

An organisation's mission is its purpose or reason for being. Determining the mission is the responsibility of top management and the board of directors. It is up to them to formulate a mission statement, which expresses the purpose of the company (i.e., the reason for its being). 'Only a clear definition of the mission and purpose of the organisation makes possible clear and realistic objectives,' said Peter Drucker. Whether the organisation is for-profit or non-profit, the mission statement identifies the goals or services the organisation provides and will provide. Sometimes it also gives the reasons for providing them (to make a profit or to achieve humanitarian goals, for example).

Business Focus: A Few Examples from the Real World of Business

Amazon. Com's Mission Statement: 'Use the Internet to offer products that educate, inform and inspire. We decided to build an online store that would be customer-friendly and easy to navigate and would offer the broadest possible selection. We believe that a fundamental measure of our success will be the shareholder value we create over the *long-term.*'

Coca-Cola: Our mission is: To refresh the world—in mind, body and spirit;

To inspire moments of optimism—through our brands and actions; and to create value and make a difference—everywhere we engage.

Ford: Our vision: To become the world's leading company for automotive products and services.

Our mission: We are a global, diverse family with a proud heritage, passionately committed to providing outstanding products and services.

2. Environmental Scanning and Evaluation

Environmental scanning and evaluation are of considerable importance for strategic management. This is usually done by SWOT analysis. It includes a search for strategies, weaknesses, opportunities and threats which affect organisational performance.

Main Focus: SWOT Analysis

An organisation's internal environmental strengths and weaknesses and external environmental opportunities and threats are determined through a SWOT analysis (SWOT stands for strengths, weaknesses, opportunities and threats). In a SWOT analysis the internal environmental factors analysed for strengths and weaknesses are management, mission, resources, systems processes and threats to customers, competitors, suppliers, labour force, shareholders, society, technology, the economy and the government.

Internal strengths and weaknesses

Strengths are positive internal characteristics which the organisation can exploit to achieve its strategic performance goals. Weaknesses are internal characteristics that might inhibit or restrict the performance of the organisation.

External opportunities and threats

Threats are characteristics of the external environment which may prevent the organisation from achieving its strategic goals. *Opportunities* are characteristics of the external environment which have no potential to help the organisation achieve or exceed its strategic goals.

The task environment is most relevant for strategic behaviour and includes the behaviour of competitors, suppliers, customers and the external labour market. The general environment includes technological developments, the macro-economy, legal-political and international events, natural resources and socio-cultural changes. It thus exerts an indirect influence on the organisation. Additional factors which might reveal opportunities or threats include pressure groups like chambers of commerce, trade associations or trade unions, interest groups, creditors and potential competitors. Even in today's highly liberalised, privatised and globalised business environment in India, the Government is exerting much influence on the level of economic activities to ensure that the goals of planning, viz., faster economic growth with distributional justice are achieved. So a business firm is constrained to scan and analyse its external environment before formulating its strategy of growth (through expansion of its production capacity) or diversification of its product line or even markets. In truth, the main focus of organisational planning is to develop strategies to take advantage of the company's strengths and minimise its weaknesses in order to exploit opportunities and avoid threats.

While the task environment exerts direct influence on the organisation, general environment exerts only indirect influence on it

Business Focus: Scanning the Environment

Large global enterprises expend huge resources and devote time regularly scanning their environment. Their objective is to identify forces which will have a major influence on them. To be more specific, they will be looking for changes in the environment that could have an impact on their operations in terms of helping or hindering them from achieving their objectives such as profit and growth. Industrial firms and commercial enterprises may also set their own target with regard to market share or becoming the leading brand. This simply means that firms will be particularly sensitive to those environmental forces which are likely to affect their ability to achieve their objectives. To be more specific, the amount of profit a firm is likely to earn depends largely on its ability to generate sales revenue and control costs. So the firm has to identify external forces which generate major opportunities to increase revenue or to cut costs. At the same time, production managers will also try to identify strong threats which might reduce revenues and increase costs.

Due to increasing volatility and turbulence in the external environment, firms must prepare themselves for the unexpected. This is done through impact analysis, i.e., an analysis of the impact of external forces or forces which are beyond its control. If a firm does this early, it will have time to consider a range of responses to exploit the opportunities and defuse the threats.

The Indian Example

In the present Indian scenario it seems that managers of corporate enterprises have to keep in view the following microeconomic factors and policies before formulating corporate strategies.

1. Public expenditure on infrastructure building, i.e., power plants, highways, ports, etc.
2. The magnitude of fiscal deficit of GOI and the public sector borrowing requirement which affect the availability of loanable funds for the private sector as also the market rate of interest.
3. The current rate of economic growth and expected future growth.
4. Trends of exports and imports and the balance of trade situation.
5. Inflows and outflows of financial capital, both direct and portfolio (FDI and FPI).
6. Monetary policy of the RBI.
7. Fiscal policy of the GOI (i.e, policy relating to taxation, public expenditure and borrowing).

Microeconomic Factors

It is also necessary to identify, scan and evaluate selected microeconomic factors which are likely to affect various individual enterprises. The micro-scanning of the environment on a selective basis is as important as macro-scanning on a general basis.

Importance of Scanning in a Globalised Environment

In addition, in the context of globalisation there are wider opportunities for Indian firms to trade with other countries. As Philip Kotler and others have put it, "Technological advances in transportation, shipping and communication have made it easier for companies to market in, and consumers to buy from, almost any country in the world. International travel has continued to grow as more people and players are making other countries"[1]

Business Focus: The Global Environment and Business
In an era of globalisation a company's performance depends on a whole range of forces in the global environment. As L. Hamilton and P. Webster have put it, "Factors such as the state of the global economy, events in the foreign currency markets, changes in the price of oil, and the activities of foreign competitors, can have effects on important competitiveness, sales, costs and profits.'

Financial globalisation has created tremendous opportunities for Indian firms to invest their surplus funds in other countries. At the same time Indian firms are being threatened by high import tariffs imposed on other countries as also subsidies provided by them to their domestic export-oriented firms (as in China and Korea). So while scanning and evaluating the environment at the time of formulation of the long-term strategies, Indian firms have to take note of these diverse external forces.

Setting Objectives in Specific Terms

Research shows that if goals are made more difficult people may achieve them less often than they would with easy goals. People also do better when the objectives are specific rather than general.

These are the kinds of matters addressed in the activity known as management by objectives (MBO). First suggested by P. F. Drucker in 1954 MBO has spread largely because of the appeal of its emphasis on converting objectives into specific ones for all members of an organisation. For example, a statement like maximisation of profits does not give any clear direction to management. A more specific objective is this: the company has to make a net profit of 10% per annum now and in the next 5 years. Drucker suggested that corporate objectives should be challenging but attainable. So there is no point in setting overambitious and unrealistic objectives.

Satisfying rather than Maximising

During the 1950s Herbert Simon proposed that managers could not act truly logically for a very simple reason. Their rationality was bounded by so many restrictions. Called *bounded rationality*, the concept suggests that the ability of decision makers to be rational is limited by numerous constraints, such as complexity, time, and money and their cognitive capacity, values, skills, habits and unconscious reflexes.

Because of such diverse constraints, managers avoid making an exhaustive search for the best alternative. Instead, they follow what Simon calls *the satisfying model*, that is, managers seek alternatives until they find one which is just satisfactory, not optimal. For example, a company's target may be to earn 10% which, it seems, is the maximum it can earn. However, it may be well satisfied by being able to earn 7% or a little more, but not less than this. However, satisfying can sometimes lead to suboptimal decisions.

Choice of an Appropriate Strategy

In the next step of the strategic management process a corporation has to choose an appropriate corporate strategy. A company has the following alternative strategies to choose from:

1. Carrying on the same type of business or giving it up and venture out in a new area which seems to be more profitable.

---

1. *Marketing Management* (Pearson, 15th edition, 2013), p.13

2. In case a company decides to continue its operation in the same line of business, it has to decide whether to grow by expanding its scale of operation (or size). In case it decides to grow, it has to take the next important decision, i.e., whether to expand its existing line of business or set up new business establishments or take over or acquire or merge with other establishments in the same industry.

Corporate Growth Through Product Diversification Strategy

While adopting growth strategy through diversification of the product line, top-level managers have to exercise choice. They have to decide whether to diversify in related areas or unrelated areas. The first type of diversification can be achieved through either horizontal or vertical integration. And the second type of diversification can be achieved through conglomerate merger.

Business Focus: Industry Convergence

Industry boundaries are gradually disappearing as companies recognise new opportunities at the interaction of two or more industries. The computing and consumer electronics industries are gradually coming close to each other. For example, Apple, Sony and Samsung release a stream of entertainment devices from MP3 players to plasma TVs and camcords. According to Kotler, digital technology has fuelled this massive convergence.[1]

In case of the former the company has to plan to produce a wider variety of goods while keeping its sphere of operations unchanged, i.e., while staying within the confines of its current businesses. The main rationale behind the strategy is to minimise the risk of doing business. In other words, risk reduction can be achieved through product diversification. Thus in bad times even if the demand for one or two products falls, the overall turnover of a diversified company such as Maruti Udyog Ltd does not fall much.

This policy is comparable to judicious management of an investor's wealth portfolio. No rational investor wants to put all the eggs in the same basket.

Backward and Forward Integration

A company can achieve growth through two types of integration—backward and forward. For example, the acquisition of a printing press by a publishing house is an example of backward integration. Thus backward integration occurs between a manufacturing enterprise and an input supplier. By comparison, a company can acquire its distribution channels. This is an example of forward integration. For example, Maruti Udyog Ltd can use up its own distribution network by acquiring Jalan Distributor. Forward integration occurs between a manufacturer and its product distributor.

A company may also integrate with a foreign firm. This is an example of globalisation of a company.

Advantages of Integration

1. By strengthening (widening) the existing marketing network, integration increases the sales turnover of a company.

2. By increasing demand and stimulating production of its goods and services integration enables firms to achieve cost reduction by being able to enjoy economies of scale associated with mass production. Cost reduction can also be achieved by producing inputs rather than buying the same from the market. This benefit is enjoyed by a firm through backward integration.

3. Through proper integration a company can exercise improved control over its environment.

4. By taking over other firms, a firm can achieve product differentiation. This enables the firm to increase its turnover by being able to meet the customers' needs in a better way. An increase in product variety leads to an increase in sales revenue.

---

1. Kotler, op.cit, p.13

Implementation of a Strategy

The formulation of a strategy is not enough. Its effective implementation is equally vital. This calls for changes in the following aspects of the organisation.

(i) **Leadership and motivation**

The primary function of a leader is to get things done through and with the help of others. It is the task of management to play the leadership role which consists of the leader's ability to influence the other members of the organisation such as middle and low-level managers as also supervisory personnel and to mould them properly and change their behaviour in a desired way so that they accomplish their tasks properly. The involvement of departmental managers in strategy formulation makes implementation of strategy easier. Employee motivation plays a very important role in the process.

(ii) **Organisation structure**

Organising refers to arranging tasks, people and other resources to accomplish the work. Organisational structure refers to a formal system of task and reporting relationship that coordinates and motivates an organisation's members so that they can work together to achieve the organisation's goals. With growth through diversification or integration there is need for a change in organisational structure so that the required needs are met. Organisation consists of authority-responsibility relationship among managers and their substitutes inside a department. It also involves the issue of the degree of centralisation and decentralisation, i.e., who makes the important decisions in an organisation for performing various tasks to be performed while implementing strategies.

(iii) **Technology**

Technology transforms inputs into output. For implementing a strategy for producing a new product, top management has to assign, classify and reallocate jobs according to the skill, ability and competence of various employees. It is also necessary to make appropriate changes in the physical facilities. Managers have also to take note of the fact that "the digital revolution has created an Information Age that promises to lead to the accurate levels of production move targeted communication and more relevant pricing."[1]

(iv) **Human resources**

Implementation of strategy may require recruitment of new personnel, selection and training of working staff, inter-departmental transfer and promotion as also retrenchment of some employees (who do not have the required marketable skills in the new environment). However, given the outdated, yet comprehensive and stringent, labour laws, this is quite difficult.

Business Focus: India's Outdated Labour Laws

Labour unrest indirectly has adversely affected Honda Motor, Hyundai Motor, Air India, Kingfisher Airlines, Bosch, Appollo Tyres, Hitachi, Dr. Reddy's as also banks and coal mines. Both public and private sector enterprises have been hard hit by industrial disputes. Perhaps the worst sufferer has been Maruti Udyog Ltd. which was hit by the strike of July 18, 2012. The resultant lockout continued for 28 days at the Manser plant. And India lost 9,60,089 worker days in the first five months of 2012.

Indian labour laws are still outdated. There are at present 45 Central labour laws and 205 State laws. Since the laws are very complex and extremely rigid most companies now hire contract workers who are outside the purview of the laws. The need to grow and diversify at a rapid rate has made companies less responsive to workers. And outsourcing has added to the plight of the workers who now find it virtually impossible to form unions.

One of the main provisions of the Contract Workers Abolition and Regulation Act of the GOI stipulates that companies cannot outsource workers where there is need for permanent (and not casual) workers. But there is no provision for equal pay for equal work in the Act. However, most companies have been violating norms regarding contract labour. And it is apprehended that inequality among workers will immediately lead to unrest.

1. For further details and an insightful analysis see R. L. Daft: *Foundations of Management* (South-Western, 9th edn, 2011), p. 37

So a more pragmatic and down-to-earth strategy is retraining of existing staff for accomplishing new tasks required by the needed strategy which is being implemented. A comprehensive model of

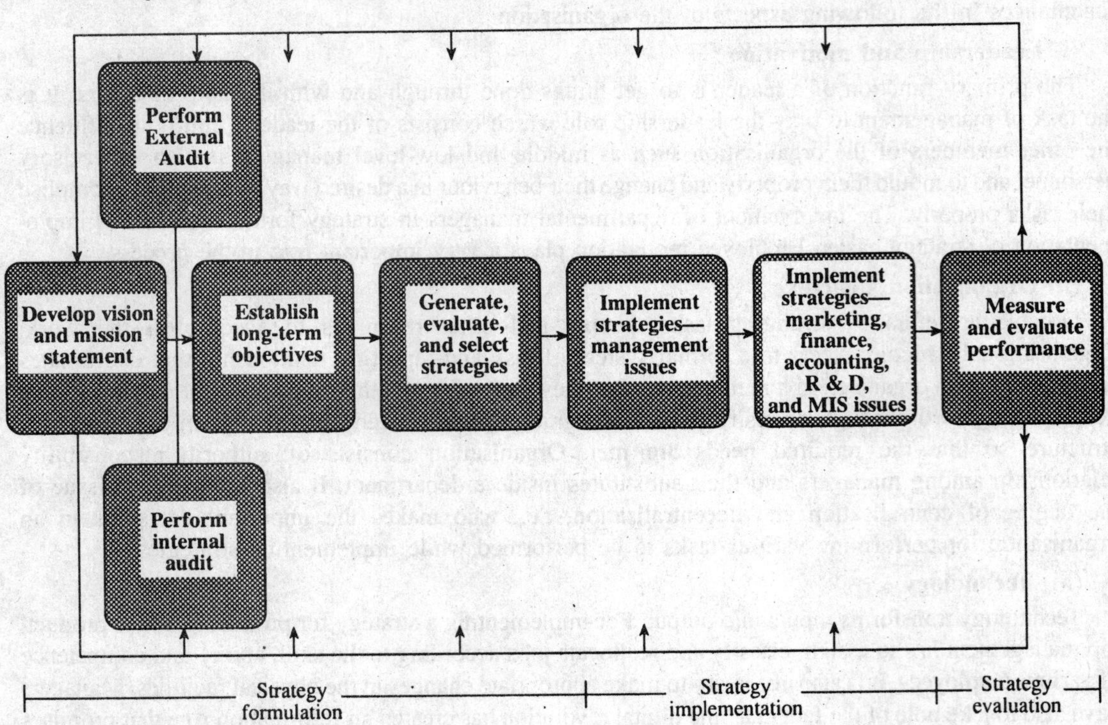

Fig. 1A.4: A Comprehensive Strategic Management Model

Source: Fredd R. David, "How Companies Define Their Mission," *Long Range Planning* 22, no. 3 (June 1988): 40.

strategic management is presented in Fig. 1A.4. It lays down the whole strategic management framework and furnishes necessary details.

Importance of Strategic Management

Professional managers are now becoming increasingly aware of the importance of strategic management for achieving higher growth and profitability of the business enterprise. An efficient and effective strategic management is of paramount importance for smooth functioning and steady growth of an organisation. It is important for other reasons also such as satisfying the shareholders (the investors) by making them feel safe and secure and ensuring job security to employees. For example, some enlightened Indian companies such as the Tata Chemicals and Infosys pay workers handsomely, protect their jobs in turbulent times and give them both monetary rewards and non-monetary incentives so that they show improved performance.

When the mission of a company and its objectives are defined in clear and specific terms, managers at lower levels as also employees put forth the maximum effort toward the attainment of organisational objectives. In addition, strategic management enables a firm to respond to changing business environment and tide over any type of difficult situation as and when it arises and is able to earn more profit.

However, strategic planning and management creates a serious problem—the emergence of a bureaucracy of 'managers' at different levels of the organisation. The bureaucratic managers are likely to lose touch with reality. They seem to remain completely detached from the various different markets the enterprise is striving to serve in the best possible way. Furthermore, too much emphasis on unnecessary details and completion of various formalities in strategic management is likely to slow down the whole decision-making process. Managers can strive to make rational decisions by setting realistic targets but they may resist the innovative endeavours or activities and exploration of profitable business opportunities.

Strategic management, in general, leads to improved performance far more often than it results in no change or in even poorer performance.

CHAPTER 2

Macroeconomic Environment: Certain Key Issues

The economic well-being of consumers, rich or poor, is affected by movement in interest rates, exchange rates, the rate of inflation, and other macroeconomic variables. Businesses can gain or lose large amounts of money when their environment changes, regardless of how well they are managed. Being prepared for such macroeconomic futures can have considerable value.

M. Bruda and C. Wyplosz

Economic growth contributes most to poverty reduction when it expands the employment, productivity and wages of poor people and when public resources are channeled to promoting human development.

A virtuous cycle of economic growth and human development arises when growth is labour-using and employment-generating and when human skills and health improve rapidly.

UNDP: **Human Development Report** (1997)

In the last chapter we have discussed the nature and scope of business environment. In this chapter we discuss some major macroeconomic issues which are taken into consideration by firms while taking different business decisions. Some major macroeconomic issues are the annual rate of inflation, external value of the country's currency (or the foreign exchange rate) and the balance of payments position of the country. All these issues have important bearing on a firm's decision-making process. The issues may now be discussed one by one.

ECONOMIC GROWTH

Meaning

Economic growth refers to a sustained or a continuous increase in the national and per capita incomes of a country. To be more specific, economic growth refers to the annual rate of increase of real per capita income (PCI)[1] of a country. In other words, it refers to the growth of output per head of population in real terms. The main objective of achieving faster economic growth is to raise the standard of living of the people of a country. This is why the rate of economic growth is taken as the most important indicator of the performance of an economy.

1. Real PCI refers to PCI adjusted for price inflation. If the rate of inflation exceeds the nominal rate of increase of PCI, real rate of increase in PCI will be negative.

A related point has to be noted in this context. Since economic growth is essentially a long-term phenomenon, a short-term rise in PCI, which occurs in the expansionary phase of a business cycle, cannot be called economic growth in true sense. The concept of economic growth becomes meaningful if and only if the increase in PCI is sustained over a period of time.

It may be noted that unless gross national product (GNP) or net national product (NNP) increases faster than the annual rate of growth of population, PCI will not increase. So economic growth refers to a continuous increase in both GNP and output per head or PCI. While GNP (or national income) measures the value of total output of goods and services produced by an economy in an accounting year, PCI measures how much of the total value of output an average person gets for consumption and saving. In other words, PCI indicates the share of an average person in a country's aggregate output of goods and services.

The standard of living of a country indicates the extent to which its people can acquire and enjoy certain basic things of life such as food, clothing, shelter, education, medical care and recreation. It depends not only on PCI but also on the pattern of income distribution. Those who get less than the PCI of a country are said to be living below the poverty line.

In Table 2.1 we make an international comparison of growth rates. It as interesting to note that developing countries are growing faster than the developed countries. Moreover, China and India, which are often cited as the two models of globalisation, are also the two fastest growing nations in the world today.

Table 2.1: GNP Per Capita, Growth Rate and Population in Some Developed and Developing Countries

Country	Population (millions)	GNP Per Capita (US dollars)	Growth Rate of GNP		
	2009	2009	1980-90	1990-00	2000-09
Developed Countries					
U.S.A	307	46,360	3.0	2.0	2.0
Australia	22	43,770	3.5	3.3	3.3
U.K.	62	41,378	3.2	2.0	2.0
Canada	34	41,980	3.4	2.0	2.0
Japan	128	38,080	4.1	1.1	1.1
Developing Countries					
India	1,155	1,230	5.8	7.9	7.9
China	1,331	3,650	10.2	10.9	10.9
Pakistan	170	1,000	6.3	5.2	5.2
Bangladesh	162	580	4.3	5.9	5.9
Sri Lanka	20	1,990	4.2	5.8	5.8

Source: World Bank: *World Development Report,* 2013

It may be noted that in the past two centuries (starting from the Industrial Revolution in England) today's developed countries achieved much faster growth than most developing countries. This is why the income gap between the two groups of countries widened over time. Now the developing countries are trying to catch up with the developed countries by surpassing their growth rates. And the main objective of developing countries, is to improve the living standards of their people.

Some countries even experienced virtual stagnation. This implies a negligible rate of growth of PCI.

Economic Insight: The Convergence Hypothesis

Economic convergence refers to a tendency for two or more economies to become increasingly similar. This may, for example, be in respect of per capita incomes, real growth rates, inflation rates and interest rates. In the context of economic growth, convergence implies that poorer countries converge in living standards with their richer counterparts owing to the tendency of the former to grow faster than the latter.

Economic Growth and Economic Development

Economic development is growth plus change

While economic growth refers to an increase in real PCI over time, economic development is a much broader term and has both economic and non-economic determinants. Economic development is said to occur when an increase in PCI is accompanied by various changes in the structure of the economy as also in the occupational pattern (distribution) of the labour (work) force.

An economy experiences structural changes when the share of the agriculture in both national product and employment declines and that of industries and services increases. Until 1970s, many countries adopted a strategy of rapid industrialisation so as to achieve the much needed structural transformation. The structural changes are often brought about by appropriate institutional and technological changes. As C. P. Kindleberger writes, "Economic growth means more output and economic development implies more output and changes in the technical and institutional arrangements by which it is produced." [1] Thus economic development implies economic growth plus structural change such as the transformation of a predominantly agricultural economy into a highly industrialised nation. So economic growth can occur in the absence of structural change, but economic development cannot take place.

Economic Insight: Structural Change

The interrelationships existing among different sectors of the economy at a fixed point in time define the structure of an economy. But over a period of time we find a change in such interrelationships. This implies structural change. For example, structural change occurs when there is a fall in the share of agriculture in GDP and total employment of a country and there is a corresponding increase in the share of industry and services at the same time.

As an economy grows over time, we find that there is shift of the labour force from agriculture (where productivity is low) to industry and services (where productivity is high). Consequently there occurs a change in the sectoral composition of GDP. The share of agriculture in GDP falls mainly due to a change in the pattern of consumption of the people as their income increases. Income increases due to shift of the labour force from less productive agriculture to more productive industries and services. With economic growth people eat more food. With economic development people consume less food and more of other things, i.e., those things that they always wanted to consume but could not afford. However, economic development is not to be equated with industrialisation. Two other things make the concept of economic development really meaningful, viz., human development and an improvement in the physical quality of life of the people. Thus while economic growth has only *quantitative dimension* economic development has *qualitative dimension* as well.

Economic development has both quantitative and qualitative dimensions

The Trickle-Down Hypothesis (Theory)

Upto the 1970s it was believed that with economic growth and structural change there would occur an automatic improvement in the standard of living of the people. It was felt that the benefits of

1. *Economic Development* (McGraw-Hill, Kogakusha, 1980), p. 2.

development would trickle down to the poor, the needy and the unemployed. The trickle-down theory simply suggests that accumulation of wealth by the rich eventually results in the improvement of the quality of life of the poor.

THE MODERN VIEW OF ECONOMIC DEVELOPMENT

Upto the early 1970s, no special attention was paid to eliminate mass poverty and unemployment and to reduce growing inequalities in the distribution of income and wealth among different sections of society. No doubt, during the 1960s and 1970s most developing countries succeeded in achieving their target growth rates. But the trickle- down effect of economic growth in the form of creation of adequate employment opportunities, rise in wages and an improvement in the pattern of income distribution was conspicuous by its absence. Instead during these two decades, the problems of poverty, unemployment and income inequality became more and more serious in India even in the presence of positive PCI growth. For instance, according to V. M. Dandekar and N. Rath, 40% of India's rural population lived below the poverty line in 1968-69. According to another study made by B. S. Minhas, 37% of India's rural population lived below the poverty line in 1967-68. The trend of growing unemployment and inequality in the distribution of income was observed in many other countries at comparable levels (or similar stages) of development.

Redistribution with Growth

Faster economic growth by itself cannot generate sufficient employment opportunities and reduce inequality in the distribution of income and wealth. Much depends on the pattern of the growth process as measured by the composition of aggregate output, how growth is financed and how benefits from growth are distributed among different sections of society.

Even when GDP increases new employment may not be generated. For instance, if in a labour surplus economy, capital-intensive techniques of production are used, the level of employment, instead of increasing, is likely to fall. And, if with economic growth, the level of employment falls and inequality and poverty increase, then growth will be anti-developmental in nature. However, if with an increase in PCI, unemployment, poverty and inequality decline over time, then only economic development becomes really meaningful.

The Quality of Life

According to the *World Development Report* (1991) of the World Bank, for economic development to occur in the true sense there has to be an improvement in the quality of life of the people. This happens when people live in a clean environment, get adequate and nutritious food, maintain good health and get minimum education. According to the Report: "The challenge of development is to improve the quality of life. Especially in the world's poor countries, a better quality of life generally calls for higher incomes. But it involves much more. It encompasses as ends in themselves better education, higher standards of health and nutrition, less poverty, a cleaner environment and more equality of opportunity. "

According to Amartya Sen, an improvement in the quality of life consists of an enlargement of opportunities of people for achievement of their goals and freedom of human choices. This new concept of development includes the achievement of freedom from servitude, dependence, ignorance, illiteracy as also enjoyment of human rights.

The Capabilities Approach

According to the *Human Development Report* (1994): "Human beings are born with certain potential capabilities. The purpose of development is to create an environment in which all people can expand their capabilities, and opportunities can be enlarged for both current and future generations. Wealth is important for human life, but to concentrate on it exclusively is wrong for two reasons. First, accumulating wealth is not necessary for the fulfilment of some important human choices. Secondly, human choices extend far beyond economic well-being."

In one of his latest book on development, Amartya Sen writes: "Economic growth cannot be sensibly treated as an end in itself. Development has to be more concerned with enhancing the lives we lead and the freedoms we enjoy."[1]

Economic Growth and Poverty Alleviation

Fiscal and structural adjustment reforms accelerated economic growth in many developing countries in the past few decades. In spite of this we find widespread poverty in developing countries. So the question arises: does faster economic growth lead to a fall in the incidence of poverty?

According to a study made by the World Bank, economic growth has led to a reduction in absolute poverty where it has been accompanied by more equal distribution of assets, especially land. Developing countries with a more equal distribution of assets, mainly land, grow faster than countries with a less equal distribution of assets. A more equal distribution of assets is good for at least one reason. Land can be used as a collateral to obtain credit which is so essential for investment, and investment is crucial for growth. In countries with a very unequal distribution of assets, many people find it difficult or virtually impossible to invest, even in their own health or education.[2]

In this context we may cite the examples of East Asian countries which had fairly equal distribution of land and which aggressively pursued economic growth. And they succeeded in achieving dramatic reductions in poverty. By contrast, distribution of land in Latin American countries has generally been less equal. As a result growth has been slower and less consistent, and the incidence of poverty has remained quite high. This means that to achieve human development and to reduce poverty, faster economic growth is just a necessary and not a sufficient condition. According to the World Development Report (2004) human welfare is unlikely to increase unless poor people have wide access to affordable, better quality services in education and health care, as also improved quality of water, sanitation and electricity, which constitute the minimum essential things of life. This is why the World Bank adopted the 'minimum' or the 'basic' needs approach to economic development in the 1980s.

According to D. Goulet, people can escape poverty if and only if they are free from illness, illiteracy and ignorance. This is not possible without improvements in the above types of services.

No doubt there has occurred a decline in the incidence of poverty in India of late. But this is not attributable to faster economic growth. Various special programmes such as employment guarantee programme, promotion of literacy, strengthening of the public distribution system to supply foodgrains at subsidised prices and to keep inflation under control have conjointly contributed to the reducton of the incidence of poverty in India.

Total Factor Productivity and Economic Growth

Economic growth is of two types — extensive and intensive. Extensive growth occurs due to an increase in the supply of resources such as natural resources (land), human resources (manpower/labour) and physical capital (such as machines, plants and equipment). Intensive growth occurs due to an increase in the efficiency (productivity) of resources. This is made possible by technological progress.

Growth economists like R. Denison, J. E. Meade and R. M. Solow make use of the concept of aggregate production function to find out the separate contributions and relative importance of various sources of growth. The following type of aggregate production function has been used to do growth accounting exercise, i.e., to measure the separate contributions of different factors to economic growth:

$$Y = AF(N, K, L)$$

1. Sen: *Development as Freedom* (Oxford 2001).
2. An example of the mechanism through which wealth may trickle down to the poor is borrowing and lending in the capital market. This is possible if land is used as a collateral. When the capital market is imperfect, as more capital is accumulated in an economy more funds become available to the poor for investment purposes.

where Y = gross domestic product (GNP)

A = an efficiency parameter showing the effect of technological progress (or total factor productivity),

N = the quantity of natural resources,

L = the size of the labour force and

K = the size of physical stock of capital.

In the study of economic growth natural resources are treated as constant. So we ignore N here. At the same time human capital is now-a-days treated as a separate factor of production which makes substantial contribution to economic growth.[1]

So we can rewrite the production function as:

$$Y = AF(L, K, H)$$

where H is the quantity of human capital.

Productivity

The contribution of a resource to the output of goods and services is its productivity. Productivity is the ratio of output produced to the quantity of inputs used in the production process. Productivity is the efficiency with which we convert inputs into output of goods and services.[2] Upto the first half of the 1950s, economists used to measure productivity of a single factor of production such as labour or capital. Due to the appearance of the Solow model of economic growth in two parts (in 1956 and 1957), economists now use a new concept called total factor productivity (TFP) to measure the overall productivity of resources, i.e., the productivity of all inputs fallen together. TFP refers to the ratio of output produced to the quantities of all inputs used.

In short, TFP is essentially an index of overall productivity of resources of a country. And technological progress is measured by the annual rate of increase in TFP.

Economic growth depends on two factors: (i) an increase in the supply of factors of production, and (ii) technological progress, i.e., the rate at which technology is improving over time. Technological progress increases the productivity of inputs or resources, i.e., its gets reflected in an increase in TFP. This point is illustrated Fig. 2.1.

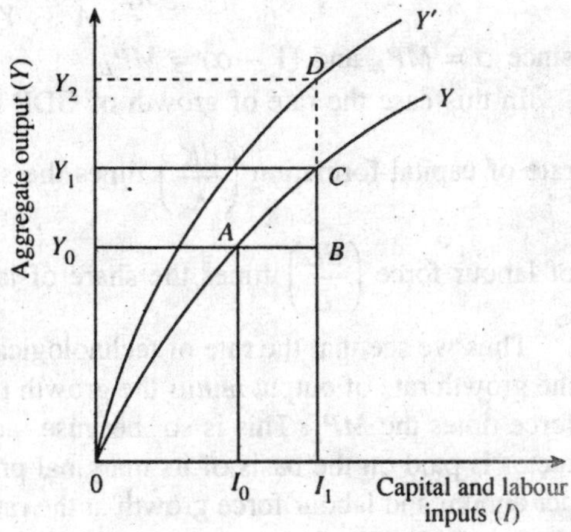

Fig. 2.1: Graphical Illustration of Economic Growth

Here we measure factor inputs (I) on the horizontal axis and aggregate output (Y) on the vertical axis. The economy is initially at point A of the aggregate production function Y. By using I_0 amount of inputs it is producing an output of Y_0. Now if the supply (use) of input increases from I_0 to I_1, aggregate output will increase from Y_0 to Y_1, as is shown by a movement along the same aggregate production function from point A to C. But if there is an

1. It may be noted that human capital is the total of skills embodied within an individual: education, intelligence, charisma, creativity, work experience and entrepreneurial vigour. In this context a quote from the Nobel Laureate Gary S. Becker is important: "While all forms of capital — physical capital such as machinery and plants, financial capital and human capital — are important, human capital is the most important. Indeed, in a modern economy, human capital is by far the most important form of capital in creating wealth and achieving growth."
2. The more productive we are, the richer we are, The reason is simple: the more we produce per day, the more we consume. Since an average American (or Japanese) worker produces more output per day than an average Indian worker, per capita consumption level in America (or Japan) is higher than that in India.

increase in TFP due to technological improvement, the whole production function will shift upward from Y to Y'. As a result there will be an increase in productivity of inputs and aggregate output will increase from Y_1 and Y_2. This additional increase in output is attributable to technological progress which amounts to an increase in TFP.

Thus we see that if, along with an increase in the supply of resources, TFP also rises, then aggregate output (Y) would grow much faster than the rate at which the use of resources is increasing. Thus economic growth has two main sources:

(i) an increase in the use of labour, capital (as also other factor inputs) and

(ii) an increase in TFP.

While the former leads *to extensive growth*, the latter ensures *intensive growth.*

According to the neo-classical economists like J. E. Meade and R. M. Solow we can do growth accounting exercise by using the following production function:

$$Y = AK^{\alpha}L^{1-\alpha}$$

where α is the share of capital in total output and $1 - \alpha$ is the share of labour. In the context of economic growth the above equation may be converted into the following form:

$$\frac{dY}{Y} = \frac{dA}{A} + \alpha\frac{dK}{K} + (1-\alpha)\frac{dL}{L}$$

$$\text{or,}\quad \frac{dA}{A} = \frac{dY}{Y} - \alpha\frac{dK}{K} - (1-\alpha)\frac{dL}{L}$$

$$\text{or,}\quad \frac{dA}{A} = \frac{dY}{Y} - MP_K.\frac{dK}{K} - MP_L.\frac{dL}{L}$$

since $\alpha = MP_K$ and $(1 - \alpha) = MP_L$

In this case the rate of growth of GDP is equal to the rate of technological progress (A) *plus* the rate of capital formation $\left(\frac{dK}{K}\right)$ times the share of capital in total output (α) and the rate of growth of labour force $\left(\frac{dL}{L}\right)$ times the share of labour in total output $(1 - \alpha)$.

Thus we see that the rate of technological progress (or increase in TFP) is the difference between the growth rate of output *minus* the growth rate of capital times the MP_K and the growth rate of labour force times the MP_L. This is so because according to the neo-classical theory of distribution every factor is paid on the basis of its marginal product. Suppose, for example, capital stock grows by 4% per annum and labour force growth at the rate of 2% and capital's share of output is 25% and labour's share is 75%. We also assume that TFP increases at the rate of 2% per annum. Thus by applying the growth accounting formula we get:

$$\frac{dY}{Y} = 2 + 0.25(4) + 0.75(2)$$

$$= 2 + 1.00 + 1.50 = 4.5$$

This means that the GDP will grow at the rate of 4.5% per annum. In other words, if 2.5% of GDP is accounted for by the increase in the stock of capital and the growth in labour force, then the remaining 2% of the growth rate has to be the result of technological progress. This is why it is called the **residual factor of growth**. However, the effect of technological progress cannot be always measured. This is why it is also called a **measure of our ignorance**. Since this growth accounting exercise was first done by Solow in 1957, the residual factor of growth (*dA/A*) is popularly known as the Solow residual.

Criticisms of the Growth Accounting Approach

The growth accounting approach has been criticised on the ground that there is an interrelationship among different variables (or sources of growth). For example, the increase in labour productivity and labour income together determine the rate of household saving. This, in its turn, determines the rate of capital formation. Similarly, the rate of saving largely determines the extent to which people make investment in human capital to enhance their future earning and in the process they make a contribution to society's output of goods and services by raising the productivity of resources. Moreover, capital formation (both physical and human) and technological progress are interrelated. The reason is that new knowledge remains embodied in new machines.

A related point may be noted here. Productivity is determined partly by natural resources — it is easier to grow wheat in Punjab than in West Bengal. But in a modern economy, productivity is more affected by technology, specialisation and skills, all of which are a function of human capital.

In the post Second World War period, Japan achieved an economic miracle by raising its TFP which led to higher and higher growth rates over time. Now-a-days we also hear of the Chinese miracle. China has raised its TFP by using modern, improved (or superior) technology which led to improvements in product quality, and fall in costs of production and prices of products. China has succeeded in capturing the global market due to the adoption of cost-effectiveness strategy. In contrast, the U.S. economy lost its predominant position in the world economy from 1973 to the mid-1990s mainly due to productivity slowdown which led to some sort of deindustrialisation. In fact, the differences in growth rates among nations can be explained in terms of differences in the rates of physical and human capital formation as also differences in their rates of increase in TFP.

Importance of Productivity

In the long run productivity is everything. American workers produce more output than Mexican workers because the former are better educated, healthier and have better access to capital and technology.

Productivity growth is what improves our standard of living. If our productivity grows at 2% a year, then we will become 2% richer every year. Why? Because we can take the same inputs and produce 2% more output. Or, we could make the same amount of output with 2% fewer factor inputs.

Productivity growth makes us richer, regardless of what is going on in the rest of the world. If productivity grows at 4% in Japan and 2% in India then both countries are growing richer.

Natural Resources as a Limit to Growth

An important source of productivity and economic growth is natural resources. Natural resources are inputs in the production that are provided by nature, such as agricultural land, forests, rivers and mineral deposits. Natural resources are of two types: renewable (like forest) and non-renewable (like crude oil).

The population of the world is much larger today than what it was five years ago. To meet the needs and wants of people more and more resources of the world are to be used. In the past few decades, most countries of the world have achieved an improvement in the living standards of their people.

Differences in natural resource endowments are responsible for some of the differences in the standards of living around the world. The USA achieved growth in the initial stage by using its large supply of land well suited for agriculture. At present Kuwait and Venezuela are rich simply because they have huge resources of crude oil. However, in the process of achieveing faster economic growth and improved living standards they have already used up huge amounts of natural resources. So the question has been raised in the late 1960s as to whether the trend of faster economic growth and improved living standards will continue in the future or the depletion of natural resources — sooner or later — will set a limit to economic growth. In 1972 a group of economists belonging to the Club of Rome convincingly argued that the exhaustion of non-renewable natural resources such as crude oil and minerals would set a limit to world economic growth. It was feared that either there would be a slowdown in the rate of economic growth with the passage of time or economic growth would ultimately come to halt as soon as the non-renewable (and finite) natural resources get exhausted. The reason is that an acceleration in the rate of economic growth year after year will eventually lead to exhaustion of fixed stock of natural resources. When this stage eventually appears, economic growth will suddenly come to a grinding halt (or a dead end). As a result the standards of living will deteriorate in the face of growing population.

No doubt, the above argument makes enormous good sense. A shortage of natural resources is likely to set a limit to economic growth. In this context we refer to two offsetting factors, viz, technological progress and discovery of substitutes.

(i) *Technological progress* : Technological progress increases the productivity of existing resources. This means that the same output can be produced by using fewer inputs. And if there is improvement in the use of natural resources due to technological progress, resources can be saved. For example modern fuel efficient cars save petrol and diesel. Power saving bulbs and heating equipment are now widely used. In addition, some non-renewable resources are used more than once through recycling.

(ii) *Discovery of substitutes* : Due to shortage of certain raw materials, their prices rose. This led to the discovery and use of substitutes. For example, now-a-days synthetic materials are used as substitutes of jute goods. Gas is used instead of petrol in cars and three-wheelers. Now plastic, instead of tin, is used to make food containers. Cooking gas is used by most households instead of coal and wood. Telephones now use fiber-optic cables which are made from sand. Plastics are used in making spectacles instead of glass. We also find the use of ethanol as substitute for gasoline.

So there is no genuine reason to apprehend that economic growth will ultimately come to a halt due to shortage of natural resources. After all, the famous proverb —'necessity is the mother of invention', like many other proverbs, contains an element of truth. In short, natural resources are not necessary for making a country highly productive in turning out goods and services. Japan is a glaring example of a resource-poor country which has achieved high rate of economic growth by importing natural resources.

The East Asian Miracle

During 1966-1990, four Asian countries, viz., Hong Kong, Singapore, South Korea and Taiwan have achieved very high rates of growth. This is why such economies are called Tiger economies or Asian tigers. The rate of growth of these countries varied between 5.7% to 6.8% per annum during the reference period, as Table 2.2 shows. In contrast, India's growth rate during this period varied between 2% to 2.5%.

Table 2.2: Economic Growth in Asian Tigers (Per cent per annum)

	Hong Kong (1966-1991)	Singapore (1966-1990)	South Korea (1966-1990)	Taiwan (1966-1990)
Growth in GDP per capita	5.7	6.8	6.8	6.7
Change in labour force participation (%)	38 → 49	27 → 51	27 → 36	28 → 37
Change in secondary or higher education (%)	27.2 → 71.4	15.8 → 66.3	26.5 → 75.0	25.8 → 67.6
TFP growth (%)	2.3	0.2	1.7	2.6

Source: Stiglitz and Walsh: *Economics* (4th edn, 2011, Norton)

These countries did not apply any "special tricks" to achieve such high rates of economic growth. The only truth is that their economic fundamentals were correct. The following points may be noted in this context:

(i) *Extensive growth* : All the countries relied on the increase in the supply and use of resources to achieve high rate of growth. So they achieved extensive rather than intensive growth. These countries made more effective use of their labour force, saved and invested more, increased their physical stock of capital, put special efforts to train and educate their labour force and to build more human capital. The increase in TFP (which measures the effect of technological progress) played a secondary role in the process. In fact, the increase in TFP has not been really significant or noteworthy. And in Singapore it was marginal. In spite of that Singapore achieved a growth rate of 6.8% per annum.

(ii) *Greater labour force participation* : In all these countries the labour force participation rate increased steadily, implying the use of more and more inputs in the production of goods and services. The main reason for this has been the entry of more and more women in the labour force and greater and greater participation of woman in the production process.

(iii) *Investment in human capital* : However, the main focus in all these countries was on investment in human capital. So the stock of human capital increased very fast. In fact, the educational level of these countries was quite comparable to those of most Western industrialised countries.

Economic Insight: Human Capital Formation and Technological Progress
Human capital formation and technological progress are interrelated. The reason is that the application of modern technology requires an educated work force. The East Asian countries achieved an economic miracle by laying stress on knowledge capital. It is the only factor of production which is not subject to diminishing returns. In contrast, India's Green Revolution achieved only partial success during the same period of time (1965-90) because most Indian farmers were illiterate and did not know how to use modern technology.

(iv) *Outward-looking policy* : Unlike India and other less developed countries (LDCs), the best Asian countries adopted an outward-looking economic policy (i.e., the policy of export promotion) to achieve faster economic growth and they succeeded in achieving export-led growth.

(v) *Laissez-faire policy* : Only in Singapore the government played an important role in controlling and regulating the private sector and in giving proper guidelines to investors and thus succeeded in directing the flow of investible resources into desirable channels. In addition, Singapore relied on foreign direct investment (FDI) mainly for ensuring transfer of modern technology from the Western countries.

But the other three countries adopted the policy of *laissez faire*, i.e., non-intervention by the government in most economic matters. The main stress was on promoting competition which was supposed to act as a driving force behind faster economic growth. And the operation of market forces enabled these countries to achieve high rates of growth, which were unprecedented in economic history.

The remarkable achievement of the Asian countries is no doubt praiseworthy on the basis of current and past trends which predict that these countries will soon catch up with most Western industrialised countries of the world. In fact, the PCI of Singapore has already reached the level of the rich industrialised countries of the world. It may, however, be noted that since 1991 China and India have also achieved a high rate of economic growth. In fact, in the past few years these two countries have become the fastest growing economies of the world. India's annual growth rate increased from 6.2% during the period 1992-2006, increased to 8% during the period 2006-2010 and increased to around 8.5% in the next three years (2011-13).

INFLATION

Another factor which determines the macroeconomic environment of a country is the annual rate of inflation. While economic growth is a major yardstick of macroeconomic performance of an economy, a low rate of inflation is an indicator of macroeconomic stability.

Inflation refers to a phenomenon of constantly rising prices of commodities and factors of production. It refers to a persistent rise in the prices of food, fuel, cloth, as also rise in house rents, interest rates, wages, etc.[1]

Inflation is not just a national problem. It is a global problem. It is the most important cause of concern of people all over the world. The reason is that in times of inflation most people are forced

1. An exactly opposite phenomenon is deflation. This is not to be confused with disinflation. A disinflationary situation arises when the government of a country tries to bring the inflation under control or the inflation rate down or at least to suppress it by adopting corrective monetary and fiscal measures.

to live under severe hardship due to fall in their real incomes and purchasing power. As a result their standard of living deteriorates. Inflation redistributes income in undesirable ways. It makes the rich people richer and the poor people poorer.

Inflation discourages businesses to make investment in those projects which are productive. The investible surplus of rich people go into wrong and socially undesirable channels such as the purchase of gold, diamonds, silver as also in real estate. Inflation also encourages unproductive and socially harmful activities such as the speculation, hoarding and black marketing. For all these reasons inflation has been described by the past President of America, Richard Nixon as "public enemy number two".

The Measurement of Inflation

Inflation is the rate of change of the general price level over a certain period of time. And the general price level in the current period is the result of inflation in the past. The rate of inflation is used by economists and policymakers to measure the value (purchasing power) of money and thus the cost of living in an economy. The formula given below is generally used to measure the annual rate of inflation:

$$\pi = \frac{P_t - P_{t-1}}{P_{t-1}}$$

where π is the rate of inflation, P_t is the price level in the current year and P_{t-1} was the price level in the last year.

Suppose the consumer price index (CPI) in India in April 2013, was 300 and rose to 330 in March 31, 2014. So the rate of inflation in 2013-14 will be:

$$\pi = \frac{330 - 300}{300} \times 100\% = \frac{30}{300} \times 100\% = 10\%$$

The people of a country produce and consume a large number of goods and services. The aggregate price index is prepared by constructing weighted price index. And different weights are attached to different goods depending on their relative importance in consumers' budget. The rate of inflation is measured by using the weighted price index.

In India the wholesale price index (WPI) is constructed by taking 1993-94 as the base year and is used to measure inflation. However, the WPI which shows the general price level at the end of each fiscal year fails to truly indicate the rise in cost of living. For this reason separate consumer price index (CPI) for agricultural labourers and industrial workers (with base 1982 =100) at the end of each fiscal year are constructed to measure the actual rate of inflation as accurately as possible. In constructing the CPI, the prices of a standard basket of goods which a representative consumer, industrial worker or agricultural labourer consumes are taken into account.

Causes of Inflation

Inflation, like disease, has many causes. We will discuss the nature, causes, consequences and control of inflation in a later chapter. Here we make a brief review of the causes of inflation.

(i) *The classical view* : The classical economists believed in the Quantity Theory of Money (QTM). And according to the theory, an increase in the money supply is always inflationary in its effect. Since the general level is determined by the quantity of money in the economy, the rate of inflation depends on the rate of growth of the money supply.

(ii) *The Keynesian view demand-pull inflation* : Keynes criticised the QTM and argued that an increase in the money supply did not always lead to inflation. He argued that inflation occurs, from the demand side, when there is inflationary gap in the economy which refers to the excess of desired expenditure on goods and services over available output at the current price level.

(iii) *The monetarists' view of inflation* : According to Keynes, inflation arises due to real forces such as continuous increase in consumption, investment or government expenditure(demand) which is independent of any increase in the supply of money. In contrast the monetarists, led by Milton

Friedman, explain the emergence of excess demand and the resultant inflation in terms of an increase in the money supply. In their view, inflation is always and everywhere a purely monetary phenomenon. It occurs when there is a more rapid increase in the quantity of money than in output of goods and services. Friedman argues that when the central bank of a country increases the supply of money then there arises an excess supply of real money balances (i.e., nominal balances deflated by the price index) with the public over their demand for such balances. As a result the money market equilibrium can be restored if the public reduce their money holdings by increasing their expenditure on goods and services. Thus the excess of real balances results in the increase in aggregate demand for goods and services. In the absence of a proportionate increase in aggregate output, the extra money supply generates an excess demand for goods and services and thus creates inflation. Thus, according to the monetarists, an excessive increase in the money supply is always and everywhere the main cause of inflation.

Inflation is always a monetary phenomenon

(iv) *The modern view—cost-push inflation* : Keynes argued that inflation occurs only when an economy reaches the state of full employment. But post-Keyensian economists have argued that inflation may occur from the supply side (even at less than full employment) if cost-push pressures arise in the economy. In other words, inflation is likely to occur if aggregate supply falls due to cost-push pressures.

There are three variants of cost-push inflation, viz., (i) wage-push (ii) profit-push and (iii) supply shock. According to the wage-push version of cost-push theory, inflation occurs if wages rise faster than labour productivity. This happens when trade unions demand and succeed in getting higher wage even when if there is no excess demand for labour. An employer passes on the rise in wages to consumers in the form of higher prices. But this is just the beginning and not the end of the process.

There are three variant of cost-push inflation

Economic Insight: The Wage-Price Spiral

An important factor which feeds the inflationary process is the wage-price spiral. It is a cumulative destabiliser. The process operates as follows. A rise in prices reduces real wages and so the cost of living rises and workers demand higher wages as compensation. If the wage demand is conceded, entrepreneurs find that their costs of production are rising. So they are constrained to raise the prices of their products to maintain their profit margin or, at least, avoid losses. This just adds fuel to the existing inflationary fire. A further rise in prices raises the cost of living further and workers demand still higher wages. This is how wages and prices

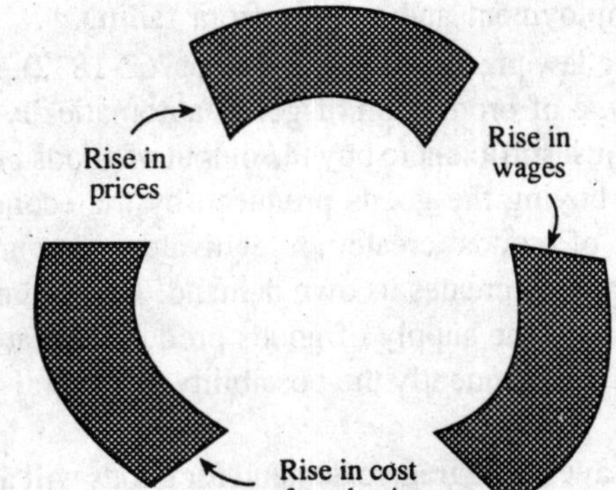

Fig. 2.2: The Wage-Price Spiral

chase each other and the inflationary process becomes self-perpetuating rather than self-destroying. See Fig. 2.2. which is self-explationatory. If left unchecked, mild inflation at the beginning may ultimately turn out to be hyperinflation, i.e., inflation at a quite high rate since wages and prices chase each other very fast.

Profit-push inflation occurs due to the pricing practices adopted by large oligopolistic and monopolistically competitive firms. These firms adopt cost-push (or mark-up) pricing policies. They add either a fixed or a variable margin of profit every time cost increases. As a result prices rise faster than costs.

Cost-push inflation occurred in the early 1970s mainly due to rise in the price of crude oil. This is an example of international supply shock. Since then oil prices have increased from time to time, depending on the international demand-supply situation. As a result prices of petrol, diesel and cooking gas were raised at periodic intervals. This has pushed up the rate of inflation.

Cost-push inflation also occurs due to domestic supply shock such as rise in prices of raw materials, strike in a major industry, power crisis, shortage of a critical wage goods such as wheat and rice due to a natural calamity (such as drought or flood) or bottlenecks like non-availability of transport facilities due to, say, shortage of railway wagons. An increase in food prices leads to a rise in cost of living, wages of industrial workers, and prices of products.

EMPLOYMENT AND UNEMPLOYMENT

Another important macroeconomic issue is the determination of the level of employment in the economy as also the causes of involuntary unemployment. Involuntary unemployment prevails if a large number of workers are willing at work at the prevailing (market) wage rate but are unable to get jobs. In times of low economic activity such as depression (or recession), the level of output falls since a large number of people become involuntary unemployed. In this context it is interesting to note the classical and Keynesian views on employment.

Say's Law of Markets and Automatic Full Employment

The classical economists[1] believed in automatic full employment. In their view, a free enterprise or market-based economy would always reach the state of full employment, in which there would exist no involuntary idleness of resources including manpower. According to them if there was any lapse from full employment, then some forces would work automatically to restore it. The classicists' view was based on their strong belief in the Say's Law of Markets.

According to the Say's Law, there is always enough desired expenditure (aggregate demand) to purchase the full-employment level of output (GDP). The classicists ruled out the possibility of deficiency of aggregate demand or purchasing power which was likely to cause unemployment. Even where there was deficiency of aggregate demand, prices and wages move up or down in such a way as to prevent aggregate output, employment and income from falling.

The Say's Law of Markets is the law presented by J.B.Say (1767-1832), a French economist. The law is based on the fact that any type of production of goods automatically increases the incomes of the factors of production, which are just sufficient to buy the output of goods produced by them. Incomes earned by the factors are spent on buying the goods produced by the economy. This means that the production of goods create an equivalent amount of purchasing power. Therefore, supply creates its own demand. This is the essence of the Say's law. This means that the supply of goods produced creates demand for it which is exactly equal to the value of output. Consequently the possibility of general overproduction (glut) and unemployment is ruled out.

The Say's Law states that supply creates its own demand

In short, according to the Say's Law, the aggregate demand for goods will always be just be sufficient to ensure that all resources are fully employed. The factors which participate in the production process and earn income therefrom spend a major portion of it on consumer goods and save the residue. Since saving is converted into investment (which is another form of expenditure), there is no leakage

1. All those economists who made their respective contributions to macroeconomics before the publication of Keynes's revolutionary book: *The General Theory* are known as the classical economists.

(subtraction/withdrawal) from the circular flow of income. Therefore the proposition that supply creates its own demand holds.

According to the classical theory, changes in rate of interest ensure saving-investment equality. If saving increases (falls) rate of interest falls. As a result the demand for investment increases (falls) and the process continues until and unless the level of investment is once again equated to the new level of saving and the Say's Law continues to hold. This, in its turn, ensures full employment of resources in the economy. Changes in the rate of interest ensure that the withdrawal from the circular flow of income in the form of saving automatically comes back to it in the form of investment and the smooth flow of output and income continues.

Wage-Price Flexibility and Automatic Full-Employment

The classicists also thought that any deficiency of demand would disappear sooner or later due to changes in the overall (aggregate) price level. Suppose, due to increase in the savings of the people, aggregate expenditure falls. As a result prices of goods would decline and the quantity of goods demanded would increase. So the entire output would be sold, i.e., the markets would be cleared, at lower prices though (since the producers would reduce prices of their products so as to avoid excessive accumulation of undesired inventories). Hence the level of production and employment would remain unaffected. This is known as the self-correcting mechanism of a free market (or the capitalist) economy. Furthermore, producers will now pay low wages in the face of falling prices of their products. As a result, the demand for labour will increase. So all workers who are willing to work at lower wages will be absorbed and full employment will be restored.

Voluntary Unemployment

Some workers may, however, decide against working at lower wages. So they would prefer to remain unemployed, voluntarily though. Thus the classical economists ruled out the possibility of involuntary unemployment. Only voluntary unemployment could exist in the classical world.

However, there may be temporary unemployment in the classical world due to too high a real wage (i.e., money wage divided by the price level). However, the real wage would fall immediately and the labour market would be cleared due to the classical assumption of wage-price flexibility.

However, A. C. Pigou pointed out that the real wage might be too high due to trade union pressure and government intervention in the labour market. These two forces might artificially keep the wage rate high. And Pigou expressed the view that if wage rates were cut, then demand for labour would increase, the labour market would be cleared and sooner or later full employment would be restored. This view was challenged by J. M. Keynes who brought about some sort of revolution in economic thinking, known as the Keynesian revolution. We may now briefly discuss the Keynesian view on employment and unemployment.

Keynesian Employment and Unemployment

In the context of the great world trade depression (1929-33), Keynes challenged the Say's Law, and argued that in times of declining economic activities demand creates its own supply. He also criticised Pigou's view that a general cut in wages in times of depression would restore full employment.

Keynes argued that investment expenditure by entrepreneurs would not necessarily be equal to the desired saving of the people as has been postulated by the classical economists. These are two reasons for the divergence between saving and investment. Firstly, saving and investment are generally made by two different sections of the society. The major portion of saving originates from the household sector (i.e., from families). But most of the investment activities are carried out by business firms. Secondly, the motives for saving and investment are diverse. Households save for various personal reasons. But businesses make investment only for making profits. For these two reasons investment will not be automatically equal to saving at the full-employment level of output (income). So the problem of deficiency of demand (purchasing power) may arise even in a capitalist economy and this may cause involuntary unemployment.

Keynes also challenged Pigou's view regarding the impact of an all-round cut in wages on output and employment. In his view, a cut in wages in a particular industry would not affect the demand for the product of that industry. The reason was that most of the demand for the product of an industry came from the persons employed in other industries. However, when an all-round cut in wages was made, the aggregate demand for output of goods and services would fall because workers would now have less income and, therefore, would spend less on all goods and services. As a result, a smaller output would be produced and less workers would be employed.

According to Keynes the level of employment would be determined by aggregate demand and aggregate supply. He also showed that full employment was not the only possibility in a capitalist economy. Such an economy could reach equilibrium even at less-than-the-full-employment level of output. Such an equilibrium is known as *underemployment equilibrium.* According to Keynes, deficiency of aggregate demand could cause involuntary unemployment and unutilised (idle) production capacity. In a later chapter of this book we will explain the Keynesian theory of income and employment.

Employment and Unemployment in India

It may be noted at the outset that the Keynesian type of cyclical unemployment does not exist in India. Such unemployment is transitory (short-term) in nature and is associated with business cycle movements. In India we find long-term or chronic unemployment and underemployment. If a worker is capable of working for 8 hours a day but remains employed for any 4 hours, he is said to be underemployed. The reason is that he works for lesser than normal hours. So undevelopment gets reflected in lower intensity of work.

The main causes of unemployment in India are the following:

1. *Shortage of physical capital* : The main cause of labour redundancy or joblessness in densely populated (labour-surplus) countries like in India is the shortage of physical capital with which to absorb the growing labour force. For this reason, India failed to create sufficient gainful (productive) employment opportunities during the entire plan period.

2. *The use of capital-intensive techniques of production* : The use of capital-intensive techniques of production in the organised sector of the industry, mostly imported from the industrially developed countries of the West, is another cause of unemployment in India. Due to globalisation of the Indian economy, Indian firms are now facing more and more competition from foreign firms and imported products. So they have been forced to reduce cost and improve product quality in order to survive and grow by closely competing with their foreign counterparts. So more and more Indian firms have been constrained to use capital-intensive techniques in order to remain competitive.

3. *Factor market distortions* : Factor market distortions in India have also encouraged the use of capital-intensive techniques of production. This means that the factor prices in India do not reflect true scarcity or abundance of factors. It sounds like a paradox that in a labour-surplus and capital-scarce country like India, the wage rate is high but the cost of capital is low.

The wage rate is high due to institutional pressures in the form of strong trade unions and capital is relatively cheap due to various fiscal concessions offered by the central government such as liberal depreciation, investment allowance as also availability of institutional finance at low rates of interest for investment purposes. Due to the use of highly capital-intensive techniques of production in most industries, labour productivity has been increasing no doubt, but the rate of employment generation has slowed down considerably. This is not an encouraging trend.

4. *Mechanisation of agriculture* : Growing mechanisation of various types of agricultural operations in most Indian States has reduced employment opportunities by lowering the employment elasticity of output growth. This elasticity is expressed as follows:

$$E_m = \frac{\text{\% increase in employment}}{\text{\% increase in output}}$$

Here, E_m is the coefficient of employment elasticity. If 3% increase in agricultural output leads to a mere 1% increase in employment, then E_m will be 0.33.

5. *Land hunger* : There is land hunger in most rural areas of India due to undue concentration of land holdings in few hands. Most farmers do not have adequate amount of land even for getting self-employment opportunities.

6. *Deficiency of infrastructure* : Another cause of unemployment in India is inadequate availability of infrastructural facilities in the form of roads, highways, bridges, power plants, tele-communication network, irrigation dams, etc. And acute shortage of infrastructure acts as an obstacle to economic growth and employment generation. [In a later chapter of this book, we will explain in detail the various causes of unemployment and suggest some strategies which can be adopted to solve India's unemployment problem].

Growing of Employment in India: a Case of Jobless Growth

A declared objective of planning in India is to generate adequate employment opportunities not only for the huge backlog of the unemployed but also to the new annual entrants into the labour force. Various economic reforms initiated in India since July 1991 envisaged that the acceleration of economic growth would automatically create adequate employment opportunities. The total growth rate of employment (on usual principal status) which was 2% per annum during the period 1983-84 to 1993-94 fell to about 1.57% per annum during the post-reform period (1993-94 to 1999-2000). However, it recorded a higher growth rate of 2.48% per annum during 1999-2000 and 2004-05. The organised sector employment which grew at the annual rate of 1.2% during 1983-84 and 1994-95 recorded less than half of that growth (0.44%) during the post-reform period (1994-2000). However, the growth rate picked up from 5.4% during the 11-year period (from 1983-94 to 2004-05) to 6.7% during the next 6-year period (from 1994 to 2000). The higher output growth failed to generate adequate employment opportunities during this period. In fact, during 1993-94 and 2004-05 there was a negative growth in employment in the public sector. In fact, whereas in the organised public sector employment declined at the rate of 0.80% per annum in the organised private sector employment increased at the rate of 0. 61% per annum. Thus the growth in employment in the organised private sector was not sufficient to make up for the loss of jobs in the public sector. Consequently there was surplus labour in the organised sector during 1999-2000 and 2004-2005 in spite of high rate of economic growth. The much lower growth of employment opportunities is attributable to the recent fall in employment elasticity of output in the organised private sector. This happened mainly due to an increase in capital intensity, i.e., growing use of capital-intensive techniques of production both in the organised sector of industry as also in agriculture. This means that fewer and fewer people have derived benefit from the growth process in the organised private sector during the whole post-reform period.

There was a full backlog of unemployed of 35 million persons at the beginning of the Tenth Plan (in April 2002) and an additional 35 million persons were expected to join the labour force during the five-year period (2002-07). But the Tenth Plan aimed at creating employment for only 50 million persons, 30 million jobs from the normal growth process and additional 20 million from special employment schemes. According to the 61st NSS round about 47 million persons were employed during 2000 and 2005. Since there was hardly any growth in employment in the organised sector, all the new employment opportunities were created in the unorganised sector.

It is a pity that despite growth in employment in the 10th Plan period (through the unorganised sector though), the unemployment rate (on the usual principal status) was higher at 3. 06% of the labour force in 2004-05 compared to 2.78% in 1999-2000. Furthermore, the average daily status of unemployment rate also increased from 7.3% in 1999-2000 to 8.3% in 2004-05. Thus there is no denying the fact that the employment situation deteriorated due to rapid growth of the labour force. However, lack of employment growth in the organised sector despite higher growth in GDP shows almost complete failure of the strategy of employment generation. We may now briefly discuss some employment generation strategies which have been adopted by both the Central and the State governments in India during the plan period.

Strategies to Reduce Unemployment

The following measures should be adopted to solve India's unemployment problem:

1. ***The use of labour-intensive techniques of production*** : If sufficient employment opportunities are to be created in both rural and urban areas, it is necessary for both the organised and the unorganised sectors of the economy to adopt labour-intensive techniques of production. So the GOI should make appropriate use of monetary and fiscal measures to discourage the use of capital-intensive techniques of production. However, some output loss is inevitable if more labour-intensive techniques are used. The reason is that productivity of labour is low in India. In fact, there is always a conflict between output and employment objectives of planning. However, considering the present state of the Indian economy and the seriousness of the unemployment problem, the economy should sacrifice some output growth for creating more employment. Thus there is an output-employment trade-off.

There is a conflict between output and employment objectives of planning

2. ***Making more investment for rural infrastructure building*** : One major reason for the slow growth of employment in rural areas has been *capital starvation* of agriculture. Both private and public sector investments in agriculture declined during the reform period (starting from July 1991). This is why employment opportunities in agriculture have not increased much. Instead there has occurred an increase in rural unemployment. So there is need to make more investment in rural infrastructure (in the form of irrigation dams, roads, flood control systems and power generation) and development of a strong rural marketing network. Such investment not only generates direct employment but indirect unemployment through the multiplier effect due to various linkages—both backward and forward.

It is gratifying to note that quite recently the Government of India made provision for stepping up of investment in agriculture and rural infrastructure as part of its Common Minimum Programme (CMP). This measure is likely to generate enough employment opportunities in the rural sector where the majority of Indian people live. Agriculture is still the main employment provider in India in spite of a steady fall in the share of agriculture in GDP.

The decision by the GOI to provide more credit to farmers at concessional rates of interest from nationalised commercial banks is likely to ensure that the small and medium farmers are able to buy fertilisers, HYV seeds and other inputs make provision for irrigation facilities themselves. This measure is likely to raise agricultural productivity and reduce the magnitude of underemployment and disguised unemployment.

3. ***Agricultural diversification*** : There is also the need for diversification of agriculture. This can be achieved by making a partial shift from crop production to production of vegetables as also to other activities such as horticulture, floriculture, animal husbandry, pisciculture, etc. These activities are highly labour-intensive in nature and, at the same time, highly income-yielding endeavour. In addition agro-processing industries have a large employment potential because they can export a major portion of their output. So they will not be constrained to reduce production and employ less labour due to saturation of the domestic market. The export market is virtually unlimited.

4. ***Changes in monetary and fiscal policies*** : In order to encourage the use of more and more labour-intensive technology and thereby to generate more employment opportunities, most of the existing fiscal and monetary concessions given at present for the use of capital must be withdrawn. This step has to be taken even if labour productivity falls and some output is lost.

5. ***The growth of services sector*** : The services sector has a tremendous employment potential in India. Therefore the growth of the sector has to be encouraged. During the period 1933-94 to 1999-

2000, the employment elasticity of output growth in the services sector was 0.50. This was higher than that of the construction sector. Two main services, viz., software services and business process outsourcing (BPO) have virtually unlimited employment potential particularly for India's educated youth. Other services such as transport and communication, finance, insurance, trade, hotels and restaurants have also considerable employment potential. However, since the services sector is a derived sector of the economy, the growth of employment opportunities in this sector depends crucially on the growth of agricultural and industrial sectors.

6. *Investment in social infrastructure* : Investment in social infrastructure refers to investment in education and health care which conduces to human capital formation and thereby contributes to the growth of output and generates more and more employment opportunities. The setting up of more schools, technical training institutes, hospitals, health care clinics, in both rural and urban areas will create primary employment. When these institutions start functioning, more secondary and tertiary employment will be created for both educated and technically qualified as also for uneducated and unskilled persons. Therefore, there is need for a higher allocation of resources in government budgets and in five year plans for developing social infastructure, as has been suggested by Amartya Sen.

THE BALANCE OF PAYMENTS

No country in today's world is completely self-sufficient. So it has to import various goods and services to meet the needs and wants of its people. It has to import those items which it needs but cannot produce cheaply (at low cost) or cannot produce at all. In other words, no country can meet all its requirements for domestic production. However, to import necessary goods and services it needs adequate foreign exchange which it acquires by exporting other goods and services; and the home country's exports become foreign countries' imports.

In addition, there are inflows and outflows of financial capital from one country to another or to the rest of the world. Capital flows are of two types — international portfolio investment (IPI) by institutional investors and non-resident Indians (NRIs) and foreign direct investment (FDI) through multinational corporations.

Every member of the IMF has to keep an official record of all its economic transactions, i.e., transactions with the rest of the world. The balance of (international) payments (BOP) is a systematic record of all external economic transactions of a country for a certain period, usually an accounting year.

The BOP account is prepared with a view to measuring the various components of a country's external economic transactions such as all receipts and payments on account of goods and services exported and imported as also capital inflows into and outflows from the country. The main purpose of keeping official records of all these transactions is to judge the present international status of a country. This helps the government to adopt appropriate monetary and fiscal measures on the one hand and trade and exchange rate policies on the other.

The Balance of Trade and the Balance of Payments

The balance of (visible or merchandise) trade of a country is the difference between the value of its exports and that of its imports of goods or visible items only. Goods exported and imported are known as visible items of trade. The reason is that the movement of goods is open and visible and can be checked, inspected and verified by the customs authorities.

If the value of a country's exports of goods is exactly equal to the value of such imports, then its balance of trade is said to be in balance. If the value of exports exceeds that of imports, the country is said to have a surplus in its balance of trade. In contrast if the value of imports exceeds that of its exports, there is said to exist a deficit in its balance of trade.

Two Main Components of BOP

There are two main components of a country's BOP, viz., (i) current account and (ii) the capital (financial) account. The balance of current account is a broader concept than the balance of trade. It includes four main items: (i) exports and imports of goods (visible items), (ii) export and import of services (invisible items) such as transport and communication, insurance, banking, etc., (iii) investment income (e.g., interest and dividend on foreign investment) and (iv) net unilateral (unconditional/one-sided) transfers such as gifts, donations, charities, etc.

India has to make payments to the rest of the world for its imports of goods but also for Indians travelling in foreign countries, as also for banking, insurance, aviation and shipping services provided by foreign countries. In addition, India has to pay royalties to foreign firms for printing Indian editions of foreign books, consultancy fees to foreign engineers and technicians employed in various Indian projects, educational, training and medical expenditure of Indians in foreign countries and interest and dividends on foreign investment in India. For India these are all debit items, since the transactions involve payments to the rest of the world. In the same way foreign countries import goods from India, as also various types of services[1] for which they make payments to India. These are credit items for India,[2] since India receives payment for these items from the rest of the world.

India's Current Account Balance

India's current account balance during the period 2003-04 to 2009-2010 as presented in Table 2.3.

Table 2.3: India's Balance of Payments on Current Account

(in billion US $)

Sl. No. Items	2007-08	2008-09	2009-10	2010-11	2011-12	2012-13
1. Exports	166.2	189.0	182.2	256.2	309.8	306.6
2. Imports	257.6	307.6	300.6	383.5	499.5	592.2
3. Trade Balance	–91.5	–118.6	–118.4	–127.3	–189.9	–195.7
	(–7.4)	(–9.8)	(–8.6)	(–7.8)	(–10.1)	(–10.8)
4. Invisibles (Net)	75.7	89.9	79.9	79.3	111.6	64.9
(i) Non-factor Services	38.9	49.6	35.7	44.1	64.1	–
(ii) Investment Income	–5.1	–4.0	–8.0	–17.9	–16.0	–
(iii) Private Transfers	41.7	44.6	52.3	53.1	63.5	–
5. Goods and Services Balance	–52.6	–69.0	83.0	–83.2	–125.7	–130.7
6. Current Account Balance (Net)	–15.7	–28.7	–38.4	–48.1	78.2	–87.8
	(–1.3)	(–2.4)	(–2.8)	(–2.7)	(–4.2)	(4.8)

Source: GOI—*Economic Survey* (2013-14)

(**Note:** Figures in brackets show the item as per cent of GDP at market prices)

From Table 2.3, we find that the most important item in the current account is the balance of trade, i.e., the difference between exports and imports. In all the four years India ran a deficit in its balance of trade. The balance on current account showed a surplus for three consecutive year (2001 to 2004). In fact, due to surplus in invisible items, the current account showed a surplus in 2003-04. However, the surplus was converted into a deficit in 2004-05 and the trend continued in 2006-07. The current account deficit represents net capital inflows (i.e., net foreign investment) in India in an accounting year. [The recent trends in India BOP are discussed in detail in a later chapter.]

1. Many construction workers from India and Bangladesh go to other countries in search of higher incomes.
2. Of late software service exports have emerged as an important foreign exchange earner for India.

Now the question arises: is a deficit in the current account necessarily bad for a developing country? The truth is that it is not bad provided it is kept within safe and manageable limits. If India runs a trade deficit due to import of capital goods in order to build up adequate production capacity, it will be good for the country in the long-run. The reason is that India will be able to achieve faster economic growth. This is why many developing countries import huge amounts of capital goods in the initial stages of industrialisation even by running a current account deficit.

India's Capital Account of the BOP

India's capital account of the BOP is presented in Table 2.4. Two main items of the account are borrowing of financial capital from foreign countries and lending such capital to foreigners. Foreign borrowing is of two main types: (i) external assistance and (ii) external commercial borrowing. External assistance refers to aid from foreign countries at concessional rate(s) of interest and long repayment periods. External commercial borrowing refers to borrowing by both the GOI and the private sector from the world financial market at the market rates of interest.

Table 2.4: India's Balance of Payments on Capital Account (in billion US $)

Sl. No.	Items	2007-08	2008-09	2009-10	2010-11	2011-12	2012-13
A.	External Assistance (Net)	2.1	2.6	2.9	4.93	2.3	–
B.	Commercial Borrowing (Net)	22.6	7.0	2.8	11.8	10.3	–
C.	Non-Resident Deposits (Net)	0.2	–4.3	N.A.	3.18	11.9	–
D.	Foreign Investment (Net) of which	43.3	3.5	51.2	44.18	39.3	–
(i)	FDI net	15.9	17.5	18.8	7.1	22.1	–
(ii)	Portfolio Investment (Net)	27.4	–15.0	32.4	37.2	17.2	–
(iii)	Other capital flows (Net)	39.7	–9.7	–13.1	–10.36	–	–
	Capital Account Total (Net)	107.9	8.6	53.4	59.7	67.8	–
	Use of Exchange Reserves*	–92.2	+20.1*	–13.4*	(–13.1)	(+12.8)	–3.8

* Also includes errors and omissions

Source: GOI—*Economic Survey* (2013-14)

Non-resident deposits are another important item of the capital account. These deposits arrive in India when non-resident Indians (NRIs) keep their surplus funds in Indian banks for getting higher rates of interest than can be obtained from their places of work.

Another important item in the capital account is investment made by foreigners in India. Foreign investment as noted earlier in this chapter is of two types, viz., (i) international portfolio investment (IPI) which is made by foreign institutional investors (FIIs)[1] and NRIs by purchasing shares and debentures of Indian companies, and (ii) foreign direct investment (FDI) which is made by foreign companies or multinational corporations (MNCs) which set up plants and factories on their own or in financial collaboration with Indian subsidiaries.

In 2006-07 the net inflow of foreign direct investment in India was US $ 15. 541 million. In the same year net external commercial borrowing was negative (–16155 million US dollars). Another important source of external funds in India is remittance made by Indians working abroad. The capital account balance is presented in Table 2.4 for a five-year period (2002-03 to 2006-07). We see that the capital account surplus increased from 10,640 to 46,372 million US dollars during the reference period. The capital account showed a surplus in each year.

1. FIIs include banks, investment companies, insurance companies and mutual funds.

The inflow of foreign capital is volatile in nature. In 2008-09 due to global financial crisis, foreign institutional investors sold shares of Indian companies in large volumes. As a result there was huge outflow of capital from India.

Distinction between Current Account and Capital Account

The current account shows receipts and payments for currently produced goods and services. It also includes interest earned or paid on financial investment as also unilateral transfers in the form of gifts and donations. The capital account, on the other hand, deals with capital inflows (receipts) and outflows (payments). These transactions arise when India borrows funds from abroad or makes investment abroad. Inflow of funds implies that India is a debtor to the rest of the world (ROW) and outflow of funds implies that India is a creditor to the ROW.

The current account of the BOP has a direct bearing on the level of national income of the country. For instance, when India sells its currently produced goods and service abroad, the producers of those items earn income from abroad. So there is an increase in the flow of income in India and this constitutes an injection into (or addition) to India's circular flow of income. On the country, when India imports goods and services by utilising its foreign exchange, money goes out of the country. This leads to a fall in the flow of income in India and is thus a leakage (or subtraction) from the circular flow of income. By comparison, the capital account only affects the volume of assets which India holds in the ROW.

Determinants of the BOP

One of the basic propositions of the theory of balance of payments is that any deficit in the current account is to be covered (financed) by a surplus in the capital account. To be more specific, any deficit in India's current account has to be covered by using the accumulated foreign exchange reserves of the RBI, if any, or capital inflows (in the form of external assistance, external commercial borrowing or deposits of NRIs). In this context we may note that various factors affect the BOP of a country, viz., national income of India and that of India's trading partners, the prices of goods and factors, the supply of money, the rate of interest, and so on. All these factors together determine, both directly and indirectly, the volume of exports and imports and the demand for and the supply of foreign exchange (currencies). Various real forces operate behind these factors such as the aggregate production function, the state of technology, tastes and preferences of consumers, the existing pattern of income distribution, expectations of economic agents, etc. If there is a change in any of these variables with no offsetting change in other variables, disequilibrium in the BOP is likely to arise.

The main cause of disequilibrium in the BOP of a country is the imbalance between exports and imports of goods and services, i.e., deficit or surplus in the current account. When, for some reason, exports of goods and services fall short of imports, disequilibrium in the BOP is likely to arise. The volume of exports may be small due to inadequate exportable surplus (which is the difference between domestic production and domestic consumption). To be more specific, exports may be small due to low domestic production and high domestic consumption or due to high costs and prices of exportable goods due to domestic inflation or overvalued exchange rate.[1] When the prices of goods are high in India, its exports fall and its imports rise. If this is not matched by adequate compensating capital inflow, disequilibrium in BOP arises.

Does the Balance of Payments Always Balance?

It is often said that the balance of payments of a country always balances. This simply means that the deficit in the current account has to be offset (covered) by generating a surplus in the capital account of an equivalent amount so the sum of the two accounts is zero. A country can generate surplus in the capital account by selling financial assets such as shares, bonds and debentures of companies or foreign exchange as also real assets such as gold or even by external borrowing. If a country sells its

1. Overvalued exchange rate leads to fall in exports and rise in imports.

assets or borrows externally, then there is an inflow of financial capital into the country. Due to such capital inflows, the capital account of the BOP shows a surplus which enables a country to cover the deficit in the current account. This is exactly what has happened in India in the first two decades of economic resources (1991-2011). Thus the accounting relation between these two components of the BOP of a country is written as

Current Account Deficit + Capital (Financial) Account Surplus = 0.

From this basic equation we can make a very important prediction:

If a country does not have adequate foreign exchange reserves or it has no assets to sell to pay for its imports or if it is unable to borrow from foreign countries (due to lack of creditworthiness) it will have to reduce its imports. This will, in its turn, reduce the productive capacity of the economy. As a result the rate of economic growth will fall. Thus just a rise in exports raises national income and employment and acts as an engine of growth, a cutback in imports acts as a hindrance to growth.

India faced this type of situation in may 1991 when its foreign exchange reserves fell to such a low level that these were just sufficient to pay for three weeks' worth of imports. As a result foreigners were unwilling to lend money to India or give adequate aid to enable the country to tide over the difficult situation. In fact, due to almost complete loss of confidence of foreign investors, there occurred a huge outflow of financial capital from India.

In fact, in 1991 India was constrained to mortgage and sell a portion of her gold stock to the bank of England and the Central Bank of Japan in order to acquire the necessary foreign exchange to pay for its needed imports. India had also to accept the stringent conditions of the IMF for getting assistance so as to be able to tide over the crisis situation. It was in such a critical situation that, largely at the insistence of the IMF, India had to adopt several reform measures which really worked wonders. Foreign exchange reserves showed steady increase and the BOP position became comfortable.

The Effect of Globalisation on Capital flows

The globalisation of the Indian economy has an important implication as far as inflows of financial capital into India are concerned. Financial capital is the most mobile of all assets. It has always an extra temptation to go abroad in search of higher returns. Thus if the rate of interest in India is higher than that in other countries, all other things remaining the same, there is likely to occur a large inflow of financial capital into India. This principle can be explained by using the following simple relation:

$$BP = NX(Y_d, Y_f, e_r) + B_i + T_r + FAB\ (i_d - i_f) \qquad \ldots \quad (1)$$

where BP is the balance of payments, NX is net exports (or the balance of visible trade), which is a function of three variables, i.e., domestic income (Y_d), foreign income (Y_f) and the real exchange rate (e_r) or the terms of trade, B_i is the balance of invisibles (i.e., export of services-import of services), T_r is the net unilateral transfers (i.e., unilateral receipts — unilateral payments) and FAB is financial account balance which the difference between capital inflow and capital outflow and is a function of the difference between domestic rate of interest (i_d) and foreign rate of interest (i_f).

The above equation can be simplified as:

$$BP = CAB + FAB \qquad \ldots \quad (2)$$

where CAB is current account balance and FAB is financial account balance.

From the above equation we can predict that an increase in domestic income due to faster rate of industrial growth, or a fall in the real exchange rate (or appreciation of the rupee) will adversely affect the balance of trade or net exports by increasing imports. FAB shows net foreign investment. If the rate of interest in India (i_d) is higher than that in a foreign country such as the USA (i_f), there will occur huge capital inflows into India. So a deficit in the current account is likely to be offset, partly or fully, by a surplus in the capital account. Such capital inflows occurred in India in 2003-04 and 2004-05. In these two years large capital inflows into the Indian economy led to huge accumulation of foreign exchange reserves, which exceeded \$100 billion in Dec. 2003 and increased further to \$119 billion in July 2004 and $144 billion in March 2005. The trend of increasing foreign exchange reserves continued in the net three years. Consequently, in Sept. 2007 India's foreign exchange reserves increased to $2.47 billion.

[In a later chapter we will discuss in detail India's BOP problems and GOI's trade policies during the reform period(1991-2011).]

THE EXCHANGE RATE

Another macroeconomic issue related to the balance of payments of a country is the foreign exchange rate.

The exchange rate is a relative price. It is the price of a nation's currency in terms of a foreign currency. In other words, it is the rate at which one country's currency is exchanged for that of another country. At present (May 2014) one US dollar is exchanged for Rs. 64. Thus Rs. 64 for one dollar is the rate of exchange of the rupee in terms of dollars.

Exchange rate changes affect the prices of exports and imports and thus their volumes. Since the foreign exchange market is a real-life example of a competitive market, the foreign exchange rate is determined by the demand for and the supply of a foreign country (such as the dollar) in short run. It is influenced by the demand for imports and exports of goods and services as also inflows and outflows of financial capital between two trading countries.

Fixed and Floating Exchange Rate

There are two main types of exchange rate systems, viz., the fixed exchange rate system and the flexible (freely floating) exchange rate system. Under the fixed exchange rate system, the rate of exchange between the domestic currency and any foreign currency is fixed by the government of the home country or its central bank. This type of exchange rate system prevailed in the world under the Bretten Woods (IMF) system since 1944. Under the system the exchange rate is pegged (fixed) at a certain rate. In the Brentten Woods system, the US dollar played a key role. This system collapsed in the mid-1970s when it could not defend the dollar by maintaining its fixed price in terms of gold.

On the other hand, the exchange rate system under which the external value of a country's currency is allowed to move up or down through the market forces of demand and supply is called a flexible (or freely floating) exchange rate. At present most countries of the world (including India) have this type of exchange rate system.

Devaluation and Depreciation

Under the fixed exchange rate system, a country can officially reduce the external value of its currency in terms of another currency. Such a situation exists when all other (usual) methods of reducing a deficit in the current account have either failed or proved to be partially effective. In that case it has to obtain the official permission of the IMF to devalue its currency.[1] The rupee was devalued three times after independence — in 1949, 1966 and 1991. In July 1991, the rupee was devalued in terms of the US dollars by 20% in two instalments, within a week, by the architect of India's reforms, viz., Dr. M. Singh.

While a country suffering from current account deficit devalues its currency, a country enjoying surplus in the current account officially raises the external value of its currency. Such a measure is called currency *revaluation*. In contrast, under the flexible exchange rate system there occur automatic upward or downward movements in the exchange rate due to changes in market forces. These movements are known as currency depreciation or appreciation.

1. Incidentally, the currency of a country is devalued only when it is found to be overvalued. The rupee is said to be overvalued in terms of the US dollar if there is an excess demand for dollars in India at the official rate of exchange.

Since March 1993 India adopted flexible exchange rate system and made rupee partially convertible into a foreign currency, i.e., convertible only on current account (and not capital account).[1] At present, the rupee can appreciate or depreciate every day due to changes in demand for and supply of it.

Purchasing Power Parity

However, in the long run, the rate of exchange between two currencies is determined by their relative purchasing power in their domestic economies, as has been predicted by the purchasing power parity theory. The theory of purchasing power parity, developed by Gustav Cassel, is based on a law, called the Law of One Price (LOOP).

This law simply states that the price of an internationally traded good is the same throughout the world when denominated in the currency of a particular country.

[In a later chapter we will discuss how the rate of exchange between two currencies is determined. We will also highlight the factors which lead to exchange rate changes.]

The Exchange Rate, the Balance of Payments and Capital Movements

Exchange rate changes directly affect a country's balance of payments position. When there is either devaluation or depreciation of a country's currency, its exports become cheaper in foreign countries and its imports become expensive. As a result exports increase and imports fall. This is known as an expenditure-switching measure. So there is a fall in deficit in the balance of payments. It has to be noted that the devaluation (depreciation) affects only the current account of a country's balance of trade; it has no effect on the capital (financial) account. This is why most countries suffering from balance of trade deficit devalue their currencies.

In addition, inflow of foreign exchange in various forms such as exports, foreign direct investment, and international portfolio investment by foreign institutional investors lead to appreciation of the domestic currency. It also leads to an increase in the money supply in the economy and, therefore, generates inflation from the demand side.

In fact, the appreciation of the rupee against the dollar in 2007-2008 occurred due to huge inflows of capital in to India. The rupee rose from Rs. 45 per dollar in Jan. 2007 to Rs. 39. 5 per dollar in Sept. 2007, showing 11. 5 % appreciation. The appreciation was partly caused by rising software exports but largely by huge inflows of funds through FIIs. Such funds were pumped into the Indian economy to take the advantage of the then stock market boom in India. There occurred additional foreign exchange inflows through the NRIs who deposited their funds in Indian banks to earn higher rates of interest. FDI also increased in India in 2006-07 and 2007-08. And this led to further injection of financial capital into the Indian economy.

No doubt, the RBI bought some dollars from the market at periodic intervals to prevent the appreciation of the rupee. But the appreciation of the rupee in 2007-08 could not be prevented since the RBI could not buy the required amount of dollars. So the large inflows of dollars could not be fully offset. The RBI undertook partial sterilisation by selling government securities to banks and keeping the proceeds from such sales in a special account not to be used by the Government. This is known as the market stabilisation scheme (MSS). The objective was to prevent excessive increase in the money supply and to keep price inflation under control.

However, since April, 2008, there occurred net outflows of capital from India due to slowdown of the US economy. Consequently FIIs withdrew more than $13 billion from the Indian market till November 30, 2008.

The Conflict between Internal Balance and External Balance

An important fact emerges from our above discussion. There is often a conflict between external balance (i.e., exchange rate stability) and internal balance (i.e., domestic price stability). The RBI has

1. If the currency of a country is convertible in the capital account also, it is called a fully convertible currency.

been trying to achieve a pragmatic compromise between the two. If, in order to ensure exchange rate stability, the RBI buys large quantity of dollars, it will be pumping a large sum of rupees into the economy. This will lead to a huge increase in the money supply, which, in its turn, will cause inflation by overheating the economy. If, in order to bring inflation under control it does not buy dollars from the market and permits free inflows of dollar into the Indian economy, the rupee will appreciate. Thus the RBI has to strike a balance between buying dollars from the market as to ensure price stability on the one hand and to prevent excessive appreciation of the rupee on the other.

A related point may also be noted in this context. An appreciation of the rupee makes imports cheaper. As a result imports rise, but exports fall. A fall in exports and a rise in imports adversely affect the balance in the current account. However, there is an offsetting consideration. Larger imports add to aggregate supply and help in controlling inflation. On the other hand, too much depreciation of the rupee makes imports costlier, especially of crude oil and so adversely affects the current account balance.

KEY POINTS

1. *Economic growth* : Economic growth refers to a sustained, or a continuous increase in a country's national and per capita incomes. Economic development is a broader term and refers to economic growth plus *structural change*. In short economic development is growth *plus* change. While economic growth has a quantitative dimension, economic development has a qualitative dimension also. It is just possible to describe the process of development; it is not possible to measure it.

2. *Sources of economic growth* : There are three main sources of economic growth, viz., (i) the growth of the labour force, (ii) capital accumulation and (iii) technological progress, called the residual factor of economic growth. The separate contribution of each factor to overall economic growth is measured by adopting the growth accounting approach. Of late, economists have laid stress on human capital formation as an important, and in some Asian countries, as perhaps the most important source of economic growth.

3. *Inflation* : Inflation refers to a phenomenon of constantly rising prices of commodities and factors of production. The opposite situation is known as deflation. There are two main causes of inflation, viz., an increase in aggregate demand and a fall in aggregate supply due to rise in cost of production.

4. *Employment and unemployment* : The classical economists, who believed in the 'Say's law of markets, assumed automatic full employment. This was supposed to prevail due to another reason—wage-price flexibility. The classical economists admitted the possibility of voluntary unemployment. However, Keynes introduced the concept of involuntary unemployment which, he believed, would occur in a capitalist economy, at periodic intervals, due to deficiency of demand (or purchasing power).

5. *Unemployment in India* : Neither classical theory nor Keynesian theory can explain the prevalence of chronic unemployment in labour-surplus countries like India. In such countries there is the problem of both seasonal unemployment and disguised unemployment. These are attributable to rapid growth of population and inadequate functioning of the saving-investment process. Although India has achieved satisfactory growth since the adoption of various economic reform measures the rate of employment generation has slowed down. And India has achieved virtually jobless growth. In other words, India's economic growth has been anti-developmental in nature. Of course, various measures have been adopted by the both Central and State Governments to create new employment opportunities during the plan period, especially since July 1991.

6. *The Balance of Payments* : The balance of payments (BOP) is an official record of all economic transactions between the members of India and the rest of the world in an accounting year. It has two main components: the current account and the capital account. And the BOP of country is conveniently defined as credit and debit transactions of a country with foreign countries and international institutions on (i) Current Account and (ii) Capital Account. Various items are included in the BOP account of a country. It is said that any deficit in the current account is offset by a surplus in the capital account. This is why the BOP of a country always balances at least in an accounting sense, though not in an economic sense.

7. *Exchange rate* : Exchange rate is a relative price such as the price of the Indian rupee in terms of a foreign country such as the US dollar. It affects the BOP of a country. Two main exchange rate systems of today are the fixed exchange rate and the floating exchange rate.

8. *Devaluation* : Devaluation refers to an official reduction in the external value of a country's economy in terms of another country under the fixed exchange rate system. The opposite term is revaluation. Currency depreciation refers to an automatic fall in the external value of a country's currency through the market forces of demand and supply under the flexible exchange rate system. The opposite term is currency appreciation. However, in the long run, the rate of exchange between two countries is determined by their relative purchasing power in their domestic economies.

KEY TERMS

Economic growth	Economic development
Total function productivity	Economic structure
Convergence hypothesis	Structural change
Devaluation	Human development
Depreciation	Physical quality of life of people (PQLP)
Real exchange rate	Market stabilisation scheme
Purchasing power parity	Internal balance
Stabilisation	External balance
Fixed exchange rate	Floating exchange rate

ASSIGNMENTS

1. Make a brief review of certain contemporary macroeconomic issues.
2. What is economic growth? What are its sources?
3. What is total factor productivity?
4. What is the difference between economic growth and economic development?
5. What is the main objective of achieving faster economic growth?
6. What is convergence hypothesis?
7. What do you mean by economic structure? What is structural change?
8. What do you mean by (a) human development and (b) an improvement in the physical quality of life of people?
9. What is price inflation? Briefly discuss the factors which cause inflation in a country like India.
10. The balance of payments of a country always balances. Critically examine the statement.
11. How do exchange rate changes affect a country's international competitiveness as also its balance of payments?
12. How are business firms affected by the growth and stagnation of the country?
13. What is devaluation? How does it differ from currency depreciation? How does devaluation affect a country's balance of payments?
14. Write short notes on the following:
    (a) real exchange rate,
    (b) purchasing power parity,
    (c) sterlisation,
    (d) market stabilisation scheme,
    (e) internal balance and external balance, and
    (f) fixed and floating exchange rate systems.
15. What are the items to be included in the BOP of a country? How does the BOP position of a country affect its national income, saving and investment?

2A THE BALANCE OF PAYMENTS AND NATIONAL INCOME

The components of the balance of payments may be classified into groups that show some important relationships between internal and external expenditure flows. These relationships are useful in organising some of the macroeconomic variables in an economy that is assumed to engage in international transactions (an *open economy*) rather than the *closed economy.*

In an open economy the demand for a country's output is increased by the foreign demand for exports and decreased by the domestic demand for imports. The components of the demand for a country's domestic output are as follows:

total domestic output = domestic consumption
+ domestic investment
+ exports
– imports . . . (1)

total domestic output – domestic consumption
– domestic investment
= exports – imports . . . (2)

Saving is output (which equals income) minus domestic consumption. Therefore, the equality between saving and investment for a closed economy must be amended by substituting saving in equation (2):

domestic saving – domestic investment = exports – imports . . . (3)

Not all the increase in domestic wealth caused by domestic investment will be owned by the residents. Foreigners may demand some of the new securities, thereby causing *capital inflow*, a foreign purchase of new domestic securities. Likewise, some domestic savers may buy foreign securities, reducing the demand for new domestic securities and thereby causing a *capital outflow*, a domestic purchase of foreign securities. The net capital outflow is the difference between capital outflows and capital inflows. Domestic saving can exceed domestic investment by the net capital outflow:

domestic saving – domestic investment = net capital outflow . . . (4)

Because the right-hand sides of equations (3) and (4) both equal the same quantity, they may be set equal to each other, to form a third relationship to show the following overall equilibrium condition for the balance of payments:

exports – imports = net capital outflow . . . (5)

This is the identity for equilibrium in the balance-of-payments statement.

Suppose that desired imports exceed exports and the net capital outflow is zero. The conditions in equation (5) are thus not met, and something must change. The country may lose reserves, paying for the imports until the reserves run so short that the country must borrow from abroad. At some point, if the deficit in the merchandise (trade) balance is chronic, the exchange rate of the currency must fall.

How is the rest of the world paid for this deficit in the balance of payments? The deficit country may use its international reserves (say US dollars and gold) until they are exhausted. It may raise the price of imports to domestic residents by imposing *tariffs*—taxes on imports (though there is still the question of how the government spends the proceeds from the tariffs). The country may contract its money supply and/or run a fiscal surplus to induce a lower domestic income and a consequent lower domestic demand for foreign imports. Part, and sometimes most, of the adjustment may come through a devaluation of the country's currency. This can occur through market forces under floating exchange rates.

Income Changes and the Trade Balance

Economic models of international trade are frequently formulated so that (1) the trade balance (exports *minus* imports) depends primarily on changes in income and (2) capital flows depend primarily on differences in real interest rates between the domestic economy and foreign economies.

Consider first the balance of trade; assume there are no capital flows. Let B be the trade balance, X be exports, M be imports, and P be the price of imports, all in terms of domestic currency. Then

$$B = X - PM \qquad \ldots \quad (6)$$

Suppose that huge imports (say, of oil) cause imports to exceed exports, so that B is negative. This trade balance is shown along QQ in Fig. 2A.1, drawn on the assumption that expenditures depend only on real income. The hypothetical size of different trade balances at each level of income before huge imports of foreign oil were demanded is given along QQ. Because the demand at a given *real* income is for a real amount of goods the line QQ is drawn on the basis of a given set of prices in equation (6). After huge imports of oil are demanded, the trade balance is shown along $Q'Q'$. The higher real income is, the greater will be the demand for goods and services, including imports. Both $Q'Q'$ and QQ, therefore, slope upward. At a real income of $0A$, the trade balance is zero before huge oil imports are demanded. After they are demanded, the trade deficit is AF at that level of income.

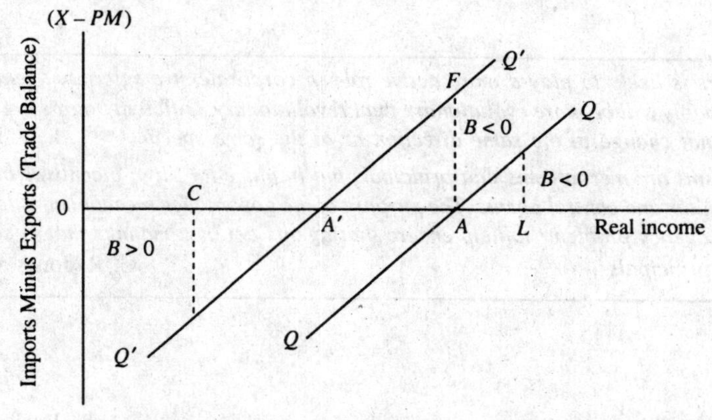

Fig. 2A.1: Trade Deficit and Trade Surplus as a Function of Income

The assumption underlying the shift in the curves in Fig. 2A.1 is that the increased demand for imported oil does not depend on real income. Instead, it depends on a reduction in oil production in India, causing a switch to imported oil. At each level of real income there is a greater demand for imports. A rise in the price of imports (changed in equation (6) to units of domestic currency) also means that the same quantity of imports demanded will cost more. Curve QQ shows that the higher the domestic demand for goods and services is, the greater will be the demand for imports. If the demand increases, the curve will shift to $Q'Q'$. These curves are comparable to the aggregate demand curves of macroeconomic in the sense of excess demand for domestic goods and services that is reflected in the demand for foreign goods and services.

One way to achieve equilibrium in the trade balance is to reduce real income. An engineered recession will reduce the demand for imports. In Fig. 2A.1 a real income level of $0C$ will produce a positive balance in the trade account, and a level of real income of $0A$ will reduce the trade balance to zero. This approach can be costly in terms of unemployment and substantially reduced real incomes.

Taxes on imports (tariffs) and subsidies on exports are direct ways to improve the trade balance if it is in deficit. But they can also be costly, as they change the allocation of goods available in the economy from what is desired for efficient production. In addition, these steps invite retaliatory measures from other countries, resulting in a reduction in world trade. Consequently, world income and, in many cases, the income of the domestic country will fall.

CHAPTER 3

Corporate Governance

> *The board of directors is likely to play a more active role in corporate strategic management in the future. However, change probably will be more evolutionary than revolutionary. Different boards are at different levels of maturity and will not change in the same direction or at the same speed.* J. D. Hunger: Strategic
>
> *Governance mechanisms are mechanisms that principals put in place to align incentives between principals and agents and to monitor and control agents. The purpose of the governance mechanism is to reduce the scope and frequency of the agency problem: to help ensure that agents act in a manner that is consistent with the best interest of their principals.*
> G. R. Jones and C. W. L. Hill

PREVIEW

Corporate governance refers to the manner in which organisations, particularly limited companies, are managed, and the nature of accountability of the managers to the owners. The issue has gained much importance after the publications of the Cadbury Report in 1992, which set a code of practice later in corporate into the combined Code on Corporate Governance. There is also a stock exchange requirement for limited companies to state their compliance with this code or to explain any departure from it.

The whole issue of corporate governance arose from the agency problem. Principals (owners of a corporation) put governance mechanisms inside an organisation to monitor agents (i.e., the senior managers and particularly the chief executive officer), evaluate their performance and, if necessary, take corrective action. The board of directors is one such governance mechanism. The reason is that one of the functions of the board is to monitor and evaluate senior managers on behalf of stakeholders. The term 'governance' is used to refer to the form and style in which a company is governed by the law, by its own statutes, and by custom. This can vary from country to country and period to period. The state in France, banks in Germany and shareholders in the USA in the governance of corporations are uniquely powerful.

The term corporate governance is used to refer to the duties and responsibilities of a company's board of directors in managing the company and their relationship with the shareholders of the company. In general salaried professional managers have acquired substantial powers in respect of the affairs of the company they run on behalf of their shareholders. However, directors have not always had the best interest of shareholders in mind when performing their managerial functions. And this has led to attempts to make directors more accountable for their policies and actions. It is against this backdrop that we discuss the whole issue of corporate governance.

Corporate governance refers to the selection of senior offices of the organisation and their conduct and relationships with owners, employees and other stakeholders. The governance system concerns the monitoring systems of a corporation and consists of incentives, safeguards and dispute resolution processes used to perform the controlling and coordinating functions of management.

Corporate governance is the responsibility of a firm's board of directors. The basic idea behind corporate governance is to have more demanding standards of behaviour.

Focus on Terminology: Director and Board of Directors
A director is one of a group of persons entrusted with the overall direction of a corporate enterprise. A board of directors is a group of individuals who are elected by the ownership of a corporation to have oversight and guidance over management and who look out for shareholders' interests.

While management runs the company and overseas day-to-day operations, it is the board of directors which 'governs' the corporates by overseeing management and representing the interest of the firm's shareholders. According to strategist F.R. David, the act of oversight and direction is referred to as governance. The US National Association of Corporate Directors defines governance as 'the characterisation of ensuring that long-term strategic objectives and plans are established and that the proper management structure is in place to achieve those objectives, while at the same time making sure that the (organisational) structure functions to maintain the corporation's integrity, reputation and responsibility to its various constituencies'. This broad scope of responsibility for the board shows how boards are being held accountable for the overall performance of the firm.

By law, a corporation of any size must have a board of directors elected by its shareholders. The directors have a fiduciary duty to the shareholders, who are the corporation's owners, and directors as well as corporate officers can be held liable for failing to meet their fiduciary duties to stockholders.

KEY GOVERNANCE ISSUES

The board of directors must mediate and resolve conflicts when shareholders and managers disagree. Key issues include takeovers and controls, executive compensation, capital structure, top management succession, board nomination, and shareholder rights.

One of the most difficult governance duties of the board of directors is the removal of the firm's chief executive officer (CEO). This becomes necessary when a passive board gets into trouble by relying on an influential CEO. This is likely to happen when the board, representing the interests of the shareholders, disagrees with the strategic direction being pursued by the CEO.

One measure of good governance is whether the company has the right CEO, who can maximise the company's performance. A part of the governance function of the board of directors is to select the firm's CEO. Another is to endorse the CEO's strategy if it is the right one.

Another difficult time for boards comes when the firm become the target of a takeover attempt. It is vitally important at such a time that the board members have a clear sense of the value of the firm and the board is enabled to fully evaluate takeover offers. During a takeover it is the board's responsibility to accept or reject offers, and in so doing it must represent the interest of shareholders when negotiating the sale of the firm.

Active Governance

The central idea of corporate governance is an engaged board of directors — not an advisory board, but a monitoring board. While boards should actively address matters relating to ownership issues, boards in fact are either active or passive. A passive board is one which is led by a strong CEO who is also the chairperson of the board. Boards can also be made passive by not having the right information provided to them in a comprehensive form.

Boards can take several steps to ensure that they are active rather than passive. One is to have a non-executive chairperson, that is, having a separate chairperson and CEO. Other factors contributing to good governance include having all outside directors except the president and the CEO, and staffing all the committees with independent outside directors.

The Basic Concept

Corporate governance seeks to deal with the problems faced by shareholders, improve the performance of a corporate organisation as much as possible and promote the interests of other stakeholders such as employees, consumers and lenders or financiars.

Due to separation of ownership from management in a large corporation there is always a conflict of interest between the two groups — the principal (the shareholders) and the agent (the managers).

Corporate governance is essentially a way of tackling the principal-agent problem

This means that corporate governance is a way of tackling the principal-agent problem. The shareholders supply external funds to a corporation. But the fund is controlled by top management under the overall guidance and supervision of the board of directors. And the directors may pursue their own interests by misusing corporate assets in various ways such as undertaking very risky or less rewarding projects and misappropriating funds raised from investors.

The essence of good corporate governance has been summed up in the following words by Mr. Justice A Pasayat; "Corporate financiers (whether they are individuals or financial institutions, or even governments) need assurances that their investment will be protected from misappropriation and used as intended for the agreed corporate objective. These assurances are at the heart of what effective, corporate governance is all about." The objective of a corporation is maximisation of the shareholders' wealth, or value of their shares subject to the protection of interests of other stakeholders such as factor suppliers, consumers and the public at large.

To protect investors from misappropriation of funds by management of a corporation as also to achieve the main objective of a corporation, viz., maximisation of long-term wealth of shareholders (i.e., the value of their shares), it is absolutely essential to adopt certain good principles of corporate governance. Three main principles are: (i) transparency in the transactions of a corporation with stakeholders, (ii) accountability and responsibility for the decisions taken, and (iii) keeping correct and accurate accounts and maintaining fairness in treatment of shareholders. Only by adopting these principles a corporation can attain its objectives. Corporate governance is affected by the relationships among various participants in the process. The shareholders, especially those who can hold the major portion of shares, have a controlling position in the organisation. They are in a position to influence corporate behaviour. Similarly institutional investors (such as banks, insurance companies, investment companies, housing finance companies and mutual funds) are having more and more say now-a-days in the corporate governance of some large companies. Creditors also want to play an active role in corporate governance. Likewise employees can also get involved in governance matters. And this is likely to lead to an improved performance of the corporation and realisation of its long-term objective, i.e., maximisation of the value of the corporation and thus shareholders' wealth.

The main focus of a good corporate governance is on the voluntary adoption of an ethnical code of conduct as far as business decision-making and financial transactions within a corporate enterprise are concerned. This is supposed to lead to improved operational efficiency of the corporation and conduce to its long-term success, within the legal framework provided by the government so that a corporate enterprise does not indulge in corrupt practices and deceive the shareholders and customers.

The board of directors and top management play a crucial role in corporate governance. They are the central figure in any corporate governance scheme. And it is the accountability and transparency in their dealings with shareholders and other stakeholders that underlie good corporate governance. The practices of good corporate governance are expressed as ethical codes of conduct and are essentially self-imposed and self-regulated. This means that the principles of a good corporate governance should be non-binding on a corporation.

The Need for and Importance of Corporate Governance

The need for corporate governance has arisen in recent years mainly due to growing concern about two things: (i) the non-compliance of financial reporting standards, and (ii) lack of accountability by boards of directors and management of corporations. As a result investors have made huge financial losses. And due to absence of good corporate governance and the adoption of corrupt practices by management of a corporation as also its financial consultancy firms, international giants like Enron, World Com (USA), Xerox (Japan) have virtually collapsed. The failure of these multinational corporations (MNCs) or international giants bring into focus the importance of a good corporate governance structure. In such a structure there should exist a clear separation (division) of power between the board of directors and management so that management is free to manage an organisation and the board of directors is at liberty to give policy directions and monitor the activities of management. Such an organisational structure (with clear division of power) is likely to ensure appropriate governance processes and procedures. The need for good corporate governance was realised by the Securities and Exchange Board of India (SEBI). This is why a number of committees, such as the Kumar Mangalam Birla Committee, Naresh Chandra Committee and Narayana Murthy Committee were appointed by it. Good corporate governance is important for the following reasons:

(i) ***Investor protection*** : Investors and shareholders of a corporation need protection due to lack of adequate standards of financial reporting and accountability. In the past many companies raised capital from the market by artificially raising the prices of their shares by presenting a bright picture of their present performances and future profit prospects. The investors suffered huge financial losses due to unscrupulous management of corporations which showed sub-optimal performance — much worse than that reported at the time of raising capital. According to Ranjan Kumar, "Bad governance was also exemplified by allotment of promoters' shares at preferable prices disproportionate to market value". This had adversely affected the interests of minority shareholders, who had no controlling power. Indian investors always seek to invest in companies which have a good record of adopting the practices of good corporate governance. For raising India's growth rate, more and more investment is needed. So it is necessary to encourage people to make adequate investment in corporate stocks. This can be achieved to a large extent by protecting the investors from fraudulent practices of corporate management as also the board of directors.

(ii) ***Paying heed to investors' grievances*** : Corporate governance is one way to listen to the complaints of investors. Most Indian companies pay hardly any attention to timely dissemination of required information to investors.

(iii) ***Attracting capital and improving corporation's performance*** : Good corporate governance enables corporations to attract sufficient capital by winning the confidence of investors. Investors are willing to invest in companies which have a good record of corporate governance. Good corporate governance also enables a corporation to improve its operational efficiency.

(iv) ***Attracting the much-needed foreign capital*** : Foreign investors are eager to invest in Indian companies if and only if they are convinced that the basic principles of good corporate governance will be implemented. Foreign firms go into joint venture projects with well-governed companies. If India is to reap the full benefits of the global capital markets, and if it is to attract long-term capital, corporate governance arrangement must be credible and well understood across national borders. And large inflows of foreign capital will surely make a positive contribution to India's economic growth by accelerating the overall rate of capital formation.

(v) ***Improving the health of the stock market*** : Good corporate governance is indispensable for improving the health of the stock market and making it vibrant. A healthy stock market is one which does not give any scope for insider trading and thus protects the investors. Insider trading refers to dealing in company share with a view to making a profit or avoiding a loss by getting price-sensitive information by insiders such as the managing director, the company secretary, professional advisors and other employees. Such information is not made publicly known.

Even if the SEBI has prohibited such insider trading nothing really has happened. The prohibition of insider trading by passing law is not very effective. The main reason is that the legal process of punishing the offender is a lengthy one. In addition, the conviction rate is very low. So an effective way of tackling the problem is to encourage companies to impose self-regulation and self-control and take preventive measure(s). This is inseparably linked up with corporate governance. According to S. Parekh, "Corporate governance is a means by which the company signals to the market that effective self-regulation is in place and that investors are safe to invest in securities. In addition to prohibiting inappropriate actions (which might not necessarily prohibited) self-regulation is also considered an effective means of creating shareholder value. Companies can always regulate their directors and officers beyond what is prohibited by law". Governments have traditionally taken less interest in the minutest (i.e., very small and unimportant) details of corporate governance, apart from ensuring that directors did not break the law and companies did not behave is a monopolistic fashion.

Comments

The effective implementation of good corporate governance practices is likely to increase investor confidence in corporate enterprises which will increase the flow of investment in them so as to help them expand and diversify. This means that good corporate governance brings a number of benefits to companies and enables them to thrive and prosper.

In addition, in the context of economic liberalisation and globalisation there is a growing realisation in market-based economies like India that such a business environment has to be created which is conducive to investor confidence so that both domestic and foreign investors get the necessary incentives to make adequate investment in corporate enterprises. This is likely to raise the rate of capital formation and ensure self-sustaining growth of the economy.

The application of the principles of good corporate governance is likely to increase investor confidence. In fact, studies show that investor confidence has increased in those companies which have a record of good corporate governance.

In addition, the principles and practices of good corporate governance stimulate business, instead of doing any damage to it. In fact, under a good governance structure companies follow ethical code of business conduct voluntarily. This leads to an increase in the volume of investment. It also helps to increase the (rate of) return on investment.

Current Trend

Today, boards of directors are composed mainly of outsiders who are becoming more involved in the management of an organisation. Boards of directors are now becoming much more closely involved with management decision-making. Due to Enron and World Com scandals, the CEOs and boards are under the legal obligation to personally certify financial statements; any loan to a company's own executives and directors is illegal. And there is faster reporting of insider stock transactions.

In this context F.R. David writes, " Just as directors are beginning to place more emphasis on staying informed about an organisation's health and operations, they are also taking a more active role in ensuring that publicly issued documents are accurate representations of the firms's status. It is becoming widely recognised that a board of directors has legal responsibilities to stockholders and society for all company activities or corporate performance and for ensuring that a firm has an effective strategy". David also sounds a note of caution for corporate directors in the following words, "Failure to accept responsibility for auditing or evaluating a firm's strategy is considered a serious breach of a director's duties. Stockholders, government agencies and customers are filing legal suits against directors for fraud, omissions, inaccurate disclosures, lack of due diligence and culpable ignorance about a firm's operations with increasing frequency. Liability insurance for directors has become exceptionally expensive and has caused numerous directors to resign." It is high time directors took note of these harsh realities and acted accordingly.

PRINCIPLES OF GOOD CORPORATE GOVERNANCE

OECD Guidelines

Good corporate governance contributes to growth of a company and its financial stability. The OECD Principles of Good Governance or guidelines for governments were issued in 1999 and updated in 2004. These principles are applicable to corporations also. Six such principles are the following:

1. Ensuring the basis for an effective corporate governance framework

The corporate governance framework (CGF) should clearly articulate the division of responsibilities among different supervisory, regulatory and enforcement authorities.

2. The rights of shareholders and key ownership functions

The CGF should protect and facilitate the exercise of shareholders' rights.

3. The equitable treatment of shareholders

The CGF should ensure the equitable treatment of all shareholders, including minority and foreign shareholders. All shareholders should have the opportunity to obtain effective redress for violation of their rights.

4. The role of stakeholders in corporate governance

The CGF should recognise the rights of stakeholders established by law or through mutual agreements and encourage active cooperation between corporations and stakeholders in creating wealth, jobs and sustainability of financially sound enterprises.

5. Disclosure and transparency

The CGF should ensure that timely and accurate disclosure is made on all material matters regarding the corporation, including the financial situation, performance, ownership and governance of the company.

6. The responsibilities of the board

The CGF should ensure the strategic guidance of the company, the effective monitoring of management by the board, and the board's accountability to the company and the shareholders.

The above principles make enormous good sense. However, subject to various government regulations, corporations must enjoy sufficient freedom as far as their operations are concerned, so that they can serve the interests of shareholders and other stakeholders in the best possible way, of course, within the framework of free markets for both goods and securities. In the context of developing countries like India we may refer to the following three principles of corporate governance:

1. Recognition of the rights of shareholders and giving fair treatment to them

Perhaps the first basic principle of corporate governance is that it should protect the rights of shareholders. And the corporation must give fair and almost equal treatment to all stakeholders including minority shareholders and foreign shareholders. In addition, all shareholders must get the opportunity to redress their grievances relating to the violation of their rights, especially the access to information through proper disclosure of facts and figures. Last, but not the least, the CGF should recognise the rights of shareholders in creating value, generating employment and ensuring financial stability as far as the sound functioning of an enterprise is concerned.

2. Corporate transparency

The principle of corporate transparency requires accurate and timely disclosure of information by a corporation on such matters as its financial status, performance and pattern of ownership. Inefficiency and lack of transparency in corporate governance often lead to scandals and frauds and thus distort the image of a company. These also hamper its smooth functioning as also the functioning of stock markets and thus obstruct the smooth flow of funds needed for long-term investment which is crucial for achieving sustained growth. The outbreak of corporate scandal disease — Enron, World Com, Tyco — that tore through corporate America in 2002 forced the US Government to pass the Sarbanes-Oxley Act. This set up the Public Company Accounting Oversight Board to keep a close and watchful eye on auditors, and made independent audit committees compulsory for listed firms. It obliged CEOs and chief financial officers to certify the company's account and promised to send them to jail if these proved false.

Transparency in the conduct of business by corporation is an absolute necessity for effective corporate governance. This is why for making the operation of corporate enterprises effective and transparent several initiatives have been taken by firms all over the world in recent years, such as code of conduct, self-imposition of rules of business ethics by corporations to furnish complete information, disclosure of the position of the company as also its financial performance (in terms of profits and losses) and pattern of ownership to its shareholders and other stakeholders.

Importance: Transparency is important for at least two reasons. First, the board of directors and top management of a corporation are supposed to provide prior information to the shareholders on business transactions. This is supposed to make the firm more conscious of their duties and responsibilities and ensure that their transactions are fair and not in the interest of the board. This is likely to reduce the chance of their committing frauds and damaging the interest of shareholders, financiers and investors. On the basis of such information the investors are able to decide in which company to put their funds to get good return. This also enables companies to attract both domestic and foreign capital. Thus transparency in corporate governance helps to promote long-term investment and thus ensure sustained growth of the corporate enterprise.

Business Focus: Fourteen Principles of Good Governance

Business Week recently evaluated the boards of most large US companies and provided the following fourteen principles of good governance:

1. No more than two directors are current or former company executives.
2. No directors do business with the company or accept consulting or legal fees from the firm.
3. The audit, compensation and nominating committees are made up solely of outside directors.
4. Each director owns a large equity stake in the company, excluding stock options.
5. At least one outside director has extensive experience in the company's core business and at least one has been CEO of an equivalent-size company.
6. Fully employed directors sit on no more than four boards and retirees sit on no more than seven.
7. Each director attends at least 75% of all meetings.
8. The board meets regularly without the presence of management and evaluates its own performance every year.
9. The audit committee meets at least four times a year.
10. The board is frugal on executive pay, diligent in CEO succession, oversight responsibilities and prompt to act in times of trouble.
11. The CEO is not the chairperson of the board.
12. Shareholders have considerable power and information to choose and replace directors.
13. Stock options are treated as a corporate expense.
14. There are no interlocking directorships (where a director or CEO sits on another director's board).

Source: Louis Lavelle, "The Best and Worst Boards", *Business Week* (Oct, 7, 2002), pp. 104-110

Corporate Accountability

The CGF should be such as to ensure effective monitoring of management by the board as also the responsibility of board and top management to the shareholders and other stakeholders for any transactions made and productive activities undertaken by the company. It is in this context that corporate accountability assumes importance.

The principle of accountability refers to the assignment of responsibilities to specified persons or groups within the corporation for performing certain tasks. The basic objective is to achieve certain preconceived results and holding such persons or groups responsible for accomplishing the assigned tasks properly.

Focus on Terminology: Accountability
Normally in management accountability refers to an employee's responsibility for the exercise of certain duties and the requirement to report to his superiors on his (her) performance. In recent years, many managers have attempted to strengthen lines of accountability so as to achieve improvements in the job performance of their subordinates. One approach to this has been the creation of various separate profit centers. The profit performance of these sub-units of the organisation can be closely monitored by organisational leaders, thereby increasing the accountability of those working in the profit centres.

The accountability of a corporation to it shareholders, financiers and investors is of considerable importance for winning investor confidence. In general the board of directors and top managers are accountable to shareholders and others (who have financial stake in a corporation) for any wrong doing as far as disclosure, financial reporting and business decisions taken by them are concerned. Since the board members and top managers control and supervise the corporate enterprise and have sufficient authority to get things done properly, they are expected to adopt sound principles and codes of good governance and be fair and honest in their dealings with the shareholders and investors. They are supposed to observe established standards of financial honesty and integrity.

Conclusion

Good corporate governance should provide incentives for the board and management to pursue objective that are in the interest of the company and its shareholders. Good practice of corporate governance is likely to boost a company's share price and, by leading to better credit ratings, can reduce cost of debt. It can raise debt capital at low cost. A Harvard/Wharton study showed that US firms with better governance had faster sales growth and were more profitable than their peer groups. But most agree that there is no single model good corporate governance. Even in a world dominated by MNCs, it is difficult is expect a corporate governance system, as it is rooted in domestic laws and habits.

In spite of all these, things have swung in favour of the shareholders in recent years. Investors have more influence over management than they ever had. They would like to have more say in the selection of directors who, they believe, should be able to hire and fire management.

Despite the existence of governance mechanisms and comprehensive measurement and control systems, a degree of information asymmetry will always remain between principals and agents and there is always an element of trust involved in the relationship. Unfortunately, not all agents are worth of this trust. A minority will deliberately mislead principals for personal gain, sometimes behaving unethically or breaking laws in the process. The interests of principals and of agents are not always the same; they diverge and some agents may take advantage of information of asymmetries to promote their own interests as much as possible at the expense of principals and to encourage behaviours that the principals would never condone. Hence there is the need for more appropriate and effective governance mechanisms in the future.

The Future

Experts feel that the board of directors is likely to play a more active role in corporate management in the future. However, change probably will be more evolutionary than revolutionary. Different boards are at different levels of maturity and will not change in the same direction or at the same speed. Three current trends which are likely to continue in the future are the following:

1. ***Pressure for improving corporate performance*** : Institutional investors, such as mutual funds, pension funds and insurance companies likely to put more and more pressure on top management to improve corporate performance. This is more so in view of the fact that institutions are likely to hold more than 50% of the shares of public companies in near future.

2. ***Increase in shareholdings of top management*** : Shareholders are likely to demand that directors and top managers own more than token amounts of stocks in the corporation. This is likely to improve corporate performance.

3. ***Increase in the power of outside directors*** : Outside or non-management directors will continue to increase their numbers and power in publicly held corporations as CEOs loosen their grip on boards. Shareholders are likely to put extra pressure for the chairman of the board to be selected from the outside directors.

James Worthy and Robert Neuschel neatly summarised the importance of the board of directors and its likely future in their study on corporate governance thus:

Boards of directors will be importantly concerned with helping to achieve the balance (between the degree of freedom necessary for business to function profitably and the need for society to preserve other freedoms and institutions) in the years ahead. More and more, society will expect the board to provide the fine line between achieving the economic objectives of the corporation and meeting the broadest needs of society.

KEY POINTS

1. ***Meaning*** : Corporate governance refers to the manner in which organisations, particularly public limited companies or corporations, are managed and the nature of accountability of the managers to the owners.

The focus is on the duties and responsibilities of a company's board of directors in managing the company and their relationship with its shareholders. Normally salaried professional managers have acquired substantial powers in respect of affairs of the company they run on behalf of their shareholders. However, directors do not always promote the best interests of shareholders when performing their managerial functions. And his has led to attempts to make directors more accountable for their policies and actions.

2. ***Origin of the concept and practice*** : In the World Com, Tyco and Enron due to bankruptcies and scandals, the firms' boards of directors were sued by shareholders for mismanaging their interests. New accounting rules in the USA and Europe now enhance corporate governance codes and require much more extensive financial disclosure among publicly held companies.

3. ***Stock exchange requirement*** : There is stock exchange requirement for listed companies to state their compliance with the code of corporate governance or to explain any departure from it.

KEY TERMS

Director	Board of directors	Stock options
Due diligence	Investor protection	Principal-agent problem
Corporate accountability	Corporate transparency	Investor confidence
Outside director	Incentives	Ethical code of conduct

ASSIGNMENTS

1. What is the basic concepts of corporate governance? What are the essentials of a good governance system?
2. Present the OECD principles of good governance. To what extent are these applicable in the private corporate sector?
3. Suggest some practical guideline for improving the system of corporate governance in India?
4. What is corporate accoutability? How does is affect corporate governance?
5. Outline 14 principles of good governance as presented by *Business Week* in the context of most large US companies.
6. Analyse the need for and the importance of corporate governance.

CHAPTER 4

Social Responsibility of Business

> *Businesses do indeed have responsibility beyond simply making a profit. This is based on a number of distinct, but related, arguments, many of which tend to be couched in terms of enlightened self-interest, i.e., the corporate takes on social responsiblities insofar as doing so promotes its own self-interest.*
>
> Andrew Crane & Dirk Matten

Corporate social responsibility (CSR) or social responsibility of business (SRB) is essentially a business philosophy which stresses the need for firms to behave as good corporate citizens, not merely obeying the law but conducting their production and marketing activities in a manner which avoids causing environmental pollution or exhausting the world's finite resources.

In the opinion of Niall Fitzerald, former CEO, Unilever, "Corporate social responsibility is a hard-edged business decision. Not because it is a nice thing to do or because people are forcing us to do it ... because it is good for our business."

DEFINITION

The definition of CSR as suggested by the World Business Council for Sustainable Development goes as follows:

CSR is "the continuing commitment by business to behave ethically and contribute to economic development while improving the quality of life of the workforce and their families as well as of the local community and society at large."

More succinctly, Mallen Baker says that it's "about how companies manage the business processes to produce an overall positive impact on society."

So CSR is essentially about sustaining a business's licence to operate, by managing its relationship with powerful constituencies — customers, staff and the community at large. The basic idea behind CSR is "managing one's reputation".

It is against this backdrop that we study the issue of social responsibility of business, with particular reference to India.

SRB or CSR implies the obligations of management of a business enterprise to society so that the interests of diverse groups are preserved. It is believed that the objective of managers is not just the maximisation of profit or shareholders' value but also to serve and protect the interests of all stakeholders, viz., workers, customers, factor suppliers and the society at large. The social responsibility of a corporation can only be judged by how it responds to meet the needs of society.

Since a corporation acquires its capital and other resources from society for production of goods and services, it should, therefore, use the resources for the benefit of society. This means that businesses should maximise their profit subject to their working in a society in a responsive manner so as to promote the interests of the members of society. It also means that activities of corporations should not do any harm to various stakeholders and the public at large. According to N.R. Narayana Murthy, "A corporation's foremost social responsibility is to create maximum shareholder value, working in a way which is fair to all its stakeholders—workers, consumers, the community, government and the environment". He further wrote that, "Working in harmony with the community and environment around us and by not cheating our customers and workers, we might not gain anything in the short run, but in the long run it means greater profits and higher shareholder value".

SRB is the expectation that a business will strive to improve the welfare of society. From a business perspective this translates into the public expecting business to take active steps to make society better by virtue of the business being in existence.

In this context we refer to carrol's models of CSR.

Carrol's Model of CSR

In 1979 Archie Carrol presented the 'Four-Part model of CSR'. And the model is illustrated in Fig. 4.1 in the context of his comprehensive definition of CSR. In his language, 'CSR includes the economic, legal, ethical and philanthropic expectations placed on organisations by society at a given point in time'.

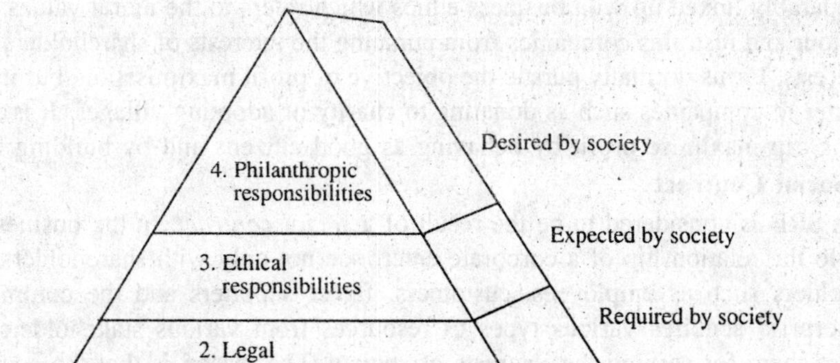

Fig. 4.1: Carrol's Four-Part Model of CSR

To Carrol CSR is a multi-layered concept, which can be differentiated into four interrelated aspects — economic, legal, ethical and philanthropic responsibilities. 'True' social responsibility requires melting of all four levels consecutively.

(i) ***Economic responsibilities*** : The first layer of CSR forms the basis of the other three. Economic responsibilities consist of satisfying shareholders by giving them a reasonable return, making employees happy by paying them fair wages and creating a safe place for them to work and satisfying customers by supplying quality products at fair (or reasonable) prices.

(ii) ***Legal Responsibility*** : Business should abide by the law and 'play by the rules of the game'. Satisfaction of legal responsibility is *required* of all corporations seeking to be socially responsible.

(iii) ***Ethical responsibility*** : Corporations should do what is right, just and fair even outside the legal framework (i.e., even when they are complied to do so by the legal or regulatory framework of business). Companies are now under growing pressure from consumers, the general public and employees to reduce greenhouse gas emissions, leading to a number of voluntary initiatives. Ethical responsibilities therefore consist of what is generally *expected* by society beyond economic and legal expectations.

(iv) ***Philanthropic Responsibility*** : Finally, at the top of the pyramid, the fourth level of CSR looks at the philanthoropic responsibilities of corporations. It incorporates activities which are within the corporations discretion to improve the quality of life of employees, local communities and ultimately society at large. This aspect of CSR embraces various issues such as charitable donations, the provision of recreation facilities for employees and their families, support for local schools or even sponsoring sports and art events.

In truth, philanthropic responsibilities are merely desired of corporations without being expected or required. So they are less important than the other three categories.

Merits and Drawback

The advantage of the four-part model of CSR is that its structures the various social responsibilities into different dimensions. However, the main drawback (limitation) of the model is that it fails to address the problem of what should happen when two or more responsibilities are in conflict.

SOCIAL RESPONSIBILITY AND BUSINESS ETHICS

SRB is inseparably linked up with business ethics which refers to the moral values which governs business behaviour and restrains companies from pursuing the interests of shareholders at the expense of all other interests. Firms normally pursue the objective of profit maximisation, but in practice other values also matter to companies such as donating to charity or adopting villages. It is said that in the long term, firms can maximise profit by behaving as good citizens and by building reputations.

SRB and Social Contract

Now-a-days SRB is considered to be the result of a *social contract*. In the business world social contract refers to the relationship of a corporate enterprise not only with shareholders, but also with various stakeholders such as employees, customers, factor suppliers and the community at large. A business enterprise acquires various types of resources from various stakeholders. So it has an obligation to use them for serving the interests of society. The reason is that the society at large is affected by the various activities of a business firm. SRB implies that corporate managers promote the interests of not only the shareholders or the owners of the firm but that of all shareholders as well. In this context we refer to three key ideas of P.F. Drucker which now underlie the organisation and practice of management—that workers should be treated as assets, that the corporation could be considered a human community and that there is no business without a customer. In Fig. 4.2 we show that the interests of different stakeholders are to be served by a corporate enterprise.

We will now discuss in detail how the interests of various stakeholders are to be served by a corporation.

1. Responsibility to Shareholders

We noted earlier in this chapter that a corporate enterprise has to recognise the rights of shareholders and protect their interests. It should give due importance to the shareholders' rights to get correct

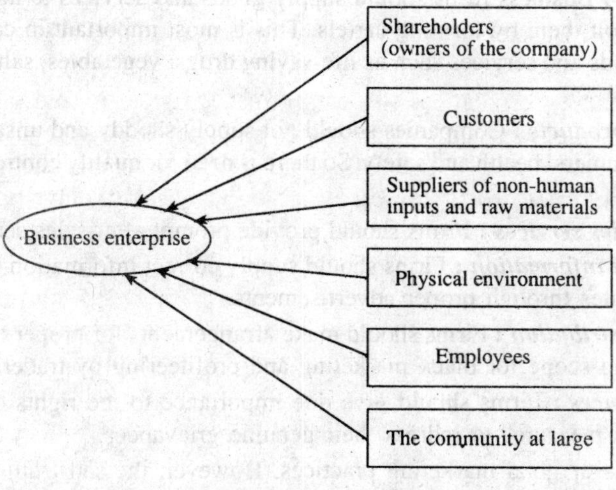

Fig. 4.2: The Responsibility of a Corporation towards Stakeholders and the Community at Large

information as also their voting rights and rights to ask questions at the annual general meetings. It is absolutely essential for a corporate enterprise to observe the best code of conduct in its dealings with the shareholders. However, while pursuing the objective of profit maximisation, the corporate board and management should protect the interests of employees, customers and other stakeholders.

2. Responsibility to Employees

Perhaps the most important resource of an organisation is its people and its success depends to a large extent on the morale of its employees. Employers make valuable contribution to a firm's value creation. So the dealings of the corporation with its employees have to be good and fair so that a healthy industrial relation prevails within the organisation and labour productivity increases. A corporation must recognise the rights of workers or employees to freedom of association and collective bargaining. Furthermore, it should not discriminate among its various employees.

Perhaps the most important responsibility of a corporation towards its employees is the payment of fair wage as also the provision of a healthy and favourable working condition. It should recognise the need for promoting labour welfare. Special care has to be taken to serve women workers. In addition, a corporation should make arrangements for proper training and education of the workers so as to increase their skill levels.

However, it is a pity that very few companies in India follow most of these good practices. While the business managers generally complain about low labour productivity, hardly any positive measure has been adopted so far to take care of the problems faced by workers even in the organised sector of industry.

3. Responsibility to Customers

Modern companies must take responsibility to protect the interests of customers in undertaking their productive activities. Referring to the importance of customers in a business, P.F. Drucker writes, "The customer is the foundation of a business and keeps it in existence. The customer alone gives employment. To meet the wants and the needs of a customer, the society entrusts wealth-producing resources to the business enterprise".

This implies that a business firm should recognise the rights of customers and be aware about the needs and wants and produce goods and services for satisfying them. A business firm has to discharge the following responsibilities to its customers:

(i) *Charging fair price* : Business firms should supply goods and services to the customers at fair prices and should not exploit them by forming cartels. This is most important in case of firms which supply highly essential goods and services such as life-saving drugs, vegetables, salt, sugar, electricity, etc.

(ii) *Supplying quality products* : Companies should not supply shoddy and unsafe products which may do damage to the consumers' health and safety. So there is need for quality control before launching a consumer good.

(iii) *Providing after-sales services* : Firms should provide prompt after-sales service to customers.

(iv) *Furnishing correct information* : Firms should supply correct information to customers about product quality and attributes through proper advertisements.

(v) *Ensuring proper distribution* : Firms should make arrangements for proper distribution of their products so that there is no scope for black marketing and profiteering by traders.

(vi) *Redressing grievances* : Firms should give due importance to the rights of customers to be heard and adopt necessary measures to redress their genuine grievances.

These are the essentials of good marketing practices. However, the sad truth remains that most business enterprises in India do not adopt the above practices. Consequently consumers are dissatisfied or disappointed in most cases. Of course, in recent years we find a growing awareness among consumers about their rights. The organised movement led by R. Nader in 1973 in the USA to protect consumer rights (which is known as consumerism) has been the result of a long neglect by business enterprises of their responsibilities to serve consumers. In addition, due to the indifferent attitude of the business enterprises to consumer rights, the Government of India has passed the Consumer Protection Act (1986). The objective of this Act is to protect the rights of the consumers and prevent exploitation of consumers by businesses.

4. Responsibility for Protecting the Environment

In their attempts to maximise profit, business firms pollute the physical (natural) environment in various ways. One special responsibility of business is that in its effort to maximise profits, it should not pollute the physical environment or do any irreparable damage to it.

So business enterprises must ensure that they reduce air and water pollution which they generate through their production processes by dumping toxic wastes into rivers and lakes. Environmental pollution is a great health hazard. It is a cause of various types of respiratory and skin diseases. Since the pollution of environment imposes cost on society or generates negative externalities, these should be minimised.

Now-a-days we find climatic changes and global warming due to huge emissions of carbon dioxide and other pollutants. So it is absolutely essential for corporate enterprises to adopt high standards of environmental protection and implement these standards effectively.

Of late, many countries including India have passed laws to protect the environment. But it is a pity that these have not been taken seriously and strictly enforced. Hence it is of paramount importance that governments of different countries take stringent measures to enforce environmental laws. Otherwise the physical environment cannot be protected.

5. Responsibility to Society at Large

Business enterprises have the following responsibilities to society at large:

1. To take proper (or effective) measures to reduce the levels of different types of pollution and adopt environment-friendly production technology.
2. To create adequate opportunities so as to reduce the incidence of mass poverty.
3. To give due respect to the rights of workers and other employees, adopt necessary and appropriate measures to ensure their safety and security and to improve their working conditions.

4. To provide quality health care service to their employees.
5. To make adequate investment in research and development (R & D) to make product and process innovations and thus to improve total factor productivity through technological upgradation.
6. To abstain from paying excessive remuneration to promoters and senior executives so as to avoid resentment by workers.
7. To prevent the formation of cartels that keep prices high.
8. To take affirmative action and to provide jobs to SCs, STs and weaker sections of society such as OBCs. The private corporate sector should give preference to minorities in providing jobs.
9. To resist the lust to pay bribes to officials so as to avoid corrupt practices. This is why the Anti-corruption Bill has been passed in India in 2011 after a prolonged period of debate on the issue.

Economic Insight: Three Case Examples

We now present a few instances of social irresponsibility of business in the Indian context.

1. The Bhopal Gas Tragedy

On December 2, 1984, in the pesticide factory of Union Carbide India Limited, a multinational company, located in Bhopal, Madhya Pradesh, there was a leakage of a poisonous gas. As a result of this some 3,000 people died and about 2 lakh people were injured. Some of them because permanently crippled and some became blind. Investigations showed that this tragic incidence occurred due to the non-installation of adequate safety measures under the factory premises. The management of the company did not admit its mistake and negligence. However, the company got involved in several court cases and the prices of its shares fell by 34.5% overnight. Ultimately the company was held responsible by the court of law, and the court ordered the company to pay a compensation of $650 million to the victims.

2. The Uphaar Fire Tragedy

On June 13, 1997, 59 people died and more than 200 people were seriously injured in the Uphaar cinema hall in South Delhi. This happened due to a fire breakout from the transformers installed in the premises on the hall. This incidence occurred because some seats were installed at the emergency exit points, by violating the provisions of the Cinema Act. The management had also violated the safety norms prescribed by the government authority for the installation of transformers. After a long legal battle of 10 years, a sessions court held the owners (Ansal Brothers), managers of the Hall and the (DESU) officials who gave the permission to violate the safety norms to be followed in case of cinema halls responsible and sentenced them. Due to their negligence and unlawful practices, their customers' lives were at great risk.

3. Satyam Fraud

The billion-dollar fraud at Satyam raised serious questions about how Indian companies define and discharge corporate responsibilities. In January 2009, Satyam Computer Services, India's fourth largest information technology outsourcing company, revealed that it lied about nearly $1 billion of non-existent cash on its books.

India's massive IT outsourcing industry was under pressure after the Satyam scandal and a disclosure by Wipro that the World Bank banned it in 2008 for four years for providing improper benefits to bank staff. In fact, in 2008 it was blacklisted by the World Bank for eight years for similar charges.

India's top property companies including DLF and Unitech also felt the heat. So they went under real pressure to focus on corporate governance and transparency if they were to rebuild their old reputation by convincing public of their ethical credentials.

Comments

The socially responsive behaviour of firms or corporation changes over time. In the 1970s village adoption was a high priority in India. During the early 1990s the public was very much concerned with the quality of the environment. Many firms responded by engaging in recycling and striving to lower their quantity of wastes.

The stakeholder approach to social responsibility demonstrates some of the complexities associated with the inclusion of socially responsible issues into a firm's strategies. A stakeholder is anyone with a stake in the organisation's existence. Highly visible stakeholders are stockholders, employees, customers and the local community. Decisions to be responsible and to maximise the return to stockholders could require closing an unprofitable plant. However, the employees and the local community could view this as not a socially responsible act since the move would not improve their well-being.

In India some businesses have begun to behave in a more socially responsible manner, partly because their managers want to do so, and partly because of fear of environmental and consumer pressure groups and the media, and concern for their public image.

It is argued that socially responsible behaviour can pay off in the long run, even where it involves some short-term sacrifice of profit. No doubt, there is some evidence of the beneficial impact of CSR on corporate profits as also on employee benefits. But this is not yet too much convincing. There is ample evidence to prove the cost of negligence, with tremendous reputational damage, from negative CSR.

Climatic change is a serious issue in many Western countries and could drive home the public sentiment. The largest UK advertising agencies predict a wave of green marketing campaigns as business strategy to brandish their environmental credentials. They believe that consumers will punish companies not seen to be green.

Tomorrow's world, a pro-CSR business lobby, fears that CSR would go in one of the two ways. In one future, it would be an expression of values, with companies free to say that they cared only for shareholders, and with the market seeing clearly where organisations stood. That would be "conviction CSR". In the other, social pressures would force compliance and companies would win applause for saying the right things in their reports — "compliance CSR". The consumer would surely be able to sniff out which was which.

KEY POINTS

1. ***Social responsibility of business*** **:** In one sense, the conkcept of corporate social responsibility (CSR), like business ethics, means distinguishing rights from wrongs and doing rights. It means being a good corporate citizen. CSR can be defined as management's obligation to make choices and take actions which will contribute to the welfare and interest of society as well as the organisation. CSR refers to the notion that corporations are expected to go above and beyond following the law and making a profit.

2. ***Arguments in favour of social responsibility*** **:** Six arguments in favour of corporate social responsibility are the following:

(i) Business is created by members of society and it makes use of society's resources. So business has to discharge certain obligations to the society and its various stakeholders with which it has constant interaction.

(ii) In the long run self-interested behaviour of the business (i.e., profit maximisation) induces it to assume various social responsibilities.

(iii) If businesses follow socially responsible policies, there will be need for less government control and regulation of business.

(iv) Businesses have always to discharge moral obligations which are beyond the scope of law.

(v) By fulfilling its social obligations a business firm can improve its public image considerably. This is likely to pay rich dividends in the long run.

(vi) Now consumers have also become much conscious of their rights. Various consumer organisations can force businesses to behave in a socially desirable way.

3. ***The top of the pyramid*** **:** The responsibilities of an organisation in today's corporate world should take the following priorities:

(i) Be a good corporate citizen (Philanthropic responsibility)

(ii) Be ethical in its practices (ethical responsibility)

(iii) Obey the law (legal responsibility)

(iv) Make a profit (economic responsibility)

KEY TERMS

Business ethics	Corporate social responsibility	Shareholders
Sustainability	Air pollution	Water pollution
Soil pollution	Green management	Accountability
Social responsiveness	Social audit	Environmental audit

ASSIGNMENTS

1. What is meant by corporate social responsibility?
2. "Business should be socially responsible". Explain.
3. What is the relation between social responsibility and business efficiency?
4. What is the relation between social responsibility of business and social contact?
5. Discuss briefly how the diverse interest of various stakeholders are to be served by a corporation.
6. What is the role of business in protecting the physical environment?
7. What is the responsibility of business to society at large?
8. How has the practice of CSR changed over time?

Chapter 5

The Use of Growth Models in Indian Planning

> *Industrialisation produces steel, it produces power. They are the base. Once you have got the base, it is easy to build. The strategy governing planning in India is to industrialise and that means the basic industries being given the first place.*
> Jawaharlal Nehru

Two growth models have been used in India during the plan period, viz., the Harrod-Domar model and the Mahalanobis Model. The Harrod-Domar is based on the static Keynesian model of income determination. It is often treated as a dynamic version of the simple Keynesian model. However, the model includes the acceleration principle which was completely ignored by Keynes. However, this model was developed to address the problems of cyclical fluctuations and secular stagnation in advanced capitalist countries of the world and suggest the adoption of appropriate stabilisation (monetary and fiscal) policies. But it does not have much practical prevalence in formulating policies for achieving faster economic growth and all-round development in developing countries like India.

The Mahalanobis model was based on one Soviet model known as the Feldman model. This is why economists often refer to the Feldman-Mahalanobis model. We start with the Harrod-Domar model.

HARROD-DOMAR MODEL OF ECONOMIC GROWTH

The Harrod model of economic growth is a dynamic extension of Keynes' static equilibrium analysis. In Keynes' *General Theory*, in a two-sector closed economy without government, national income attains its equilibrium value when desired saving is equal to desired investment (or leakages from the circular flow of income are equal to injections into it). Initially H. Harrod and then E. Domar extended the basic Keynesian static model to study the dynamic problems and issues of growth in a capitalist economy. These two models appeared separately. However, since they contain the same basic theme, they are often lumped together and presented as the Harrod-Domar growth model. Here we discuss each model separately.

Keynes ignored the concept of induced investment. But both Harrod and Domar considered induced investment and analysed its effect on economic growth.

The Harrod Model

To be specific, Harrod asked the following two questions:

(i) If change in income induced investment, what has to be the rate of growth of income for desired investment to equal desired saving so as to ensure and maintain a *dynamic* (moving) equilibrium in a growing economy over time?

(ii) Is there is any guarantee that this required rate of growth will prevail? If not, what will happen?

In a static Keynesian theory if equilibrium between saving and investment is disturbed, the economy gets adjusted automatically and a new equilibrium is reached through the Keynesian multiplier process. If growth equilibrium is disturbed will it be self-correcting or self-perpetuating? Moreover, will this equilibrium rate of growth equal to the maximum rate of growth that the economy is capable of sustaining, given the rate of growth of its productive capacity? If not, in which direction will the economy move? These are the fundamental questions raised and answered by Harrod as far as the performance of a capitalist economy is concerned.

To tackle these questions, Harrod distinguished three different growth rates: the actual growth rate (g), the warranted growth rate (g_w) and the natural growth rate (g_n). The actual growth is rate is expressed as

$$g = s/v \qquad \ldots (1)$$

where s is the saving rate or the average propensity to save (S/Y) and v is the incremental capital-output ratio, that is, the ratio of extra capital required to prove one extra unit of output ($\Delta K/\Delta Y = I/\Delta Y$). This expression for the actual growth rate (1) expresses the accounting identity that savings equals investment. We can verify this if we substitute the expressions for s and v into (1)—that is, $s/v = (S/Y)/(I/\Delta Y) = \Delta Y/Y$ given $S = I$, where $\Delta Y/Y$ measures the growth of output.

In other words, the warranted growth rate is the rate that induces just enough investment to match planned saving and therefore keeps a society's capital fully utilised so that manufacturers are willing to carry on investment in the future at the same rate as they did in the past. How is this rate determined? Plans to save are given by the Keynesian savings function:

$$S = sY \qquad \ldots (2)$$

where s is the *APS*. This gives the potential supply of investment goods. The demand for investment is given by *the acceleration principle*, where α is the accelerator coefficient measured as the amount of extra capital or investment *required* to produce a unit of output, determined by technological conditions. Thus:

$$\alpha = \Delta K/\Delta Y = I/\Delta Y \qquad \ldots (3)$$

The demand for investment, given by the accelerator principle, is then

$$I = \alpha\Delta Y \qquad \ldots (4)$$

For planned saving to equal planned investment, therefore, we have

$$sY = \alpha\Delta Y \qquad \ldots (5)$$

and the required rate of growth for a dynamic equilibrium is

$$\Delta Y/Y = s/\alpha = g_w \qquad \ldots (6)$$

This is the warranted rate of growth, g_w. For dynamic equilibrium, output must grow at this rate so that indeed expenditure on consumption goods equals their production. And only at this rate will entrepreneurs be satisfied with what they are doing, so that they have no reason to their investment plans.

Now suppose there is a departure from this equilibrium rate. What happens in such a situation? The condition for equilibrium in terms of equations (1) and (6) is that $g = g_w$. First suppose that the actual growth rate exceeds the warranted rate. It is easily seen that if $g > g_w$ then $v < \alpha$, which means that actual investment falls below the level required to meet the increase in output. There will be a shortage of equipment, a depletion of stocks and an incentive to invest more. The actual growth rate will then deviate even further from the warranted rate. Conversely, if the actual growth rate falls short of the warranted rate, $g < g_w$, then $v > \alpha$, and there will be a surplus of capital goods and investment will fall, causing the actual growth rate to deep even further below the equilibrium rate. Thus, as Harrod points out, a departure from equilibrium, instead of being self-correcting, will be self-perpetuating. This is essentially the short-term trade cycle problem in Harrod's growth model.

The Domar Model

Evsey Domar also arrived at Harrod's central conclusion. Domar recognised that investment has a dual aspect: it increases demand *via* the Keynes multiplier. It also increases supply *via* its effect on expanding capacity or through the acceleration effect. The question Domar asked, therefore, is what rate of growth of investment must prevail in order for supply to grow in line with demand (at full employment)? The required rate of growth of investment can be found out in the following way. A change in the level of investment increases demand by

$$\Delta Y_d = \Delta I/s \quad \ldots \quad (7)$$

and investment itself increases supply by

$$\Delta Y_s = I\sigma \quad \ldots \quad (8)$$

where σ is the productivity of capital or the flow of output per unit of investment ($\Delta Y/I$). For $\Delta Y_d = \Delta Y_s$ we must have

$$\Delta I/s = I\sigma \quad \ldots \quad (9)$$

or

$$\Delta I/I = s\sigma \quad \ldots \quad (10)$$

This means investment has to grow at a rate equal to the product of the savings ratio and the marginal product of capital. With a constant savings-investment ratio, this also implies output growth at the rate $s\sigma$. If $\sigma = I/\alpha$ (at full employment), then the Domar result for equilibrium growth is the same as that of Harrod.

Natural Rate of Growth

Now we define the natural rate of growth (g_n). It is the rate of growth of productive capacity or the long-run full employment equilibrium growth rate. It also sets the upper limit to the actual growth rate, which brings cumulative expansion in the Harrod model to a dead end. If $g > g_w$, g can continue to diverge from g_w only until it is equated to g_n, when the labour force has been fully absorbed. With fixed coefficient production functions, full employment of labour clearly requires $g = g_n$. And full employment of labour and capital requires.

$$g = g_w = g_n \quad \ldots \quad (11)$$

a state of affairs that is often called a 'golden age'. However, there is nothing in the Harrod model that would automatically ensure this desirable outcome.

Divergence between the two growth rates

What happens if the warranted growth rate diverges from the natural rate. If $g_w > g_n$ there will be a chronic tendency towards depression because the actual rate of growth will never be sufficient to stimulate investment demand to match the amount of saving at full-employment equilibrium. There is too much capital and too much saving. If $g_w < g_n$, there will be a possibility of demand-pull inflation since the actual rate of growth would tend to exceed that necessary to induce investment to match saving. Inflationary pressure, however, will be accompanied by growing structural unemployment because the growth of capital falls short of the growth of the effective labour force with unchanged techniques of production. This is known as the knife-edge problem of the Harrod model.

Relevance for Developing Countries

In most developing countries the natural rate of growth usually exceeds the warranted rate. This has two main consequences. First, it means that the labour force is growing faster than capital accumulation, implying growing unemployment. Second, it implies that business derives to invest are stronger than household derives to save, and therefore there is an inherent inflationary pressure in the economy.

In Fig. 5.1 economic growth is measured on the vertical axis, and the investment and savings ratios on the horizontal axis. Growth and the investment ratio are related through α. The savings ratio is independent of the growth rate. Fig. 5.1 shows a situation in which the natural growth rate (g_n) exceeds the warranted growth rate (g_w). To equalise g_n and g_w we can bring down g_n to g_w by reducing the rate of growth of the labour force. We can shift the S/Y curve rightwards through monetary and fiscal policies (and also by external borrowing) to raise g_w to g_n, or we can pivot the I/Y curve inwards by reducing α through the use of more labour-intensive techniques of production.

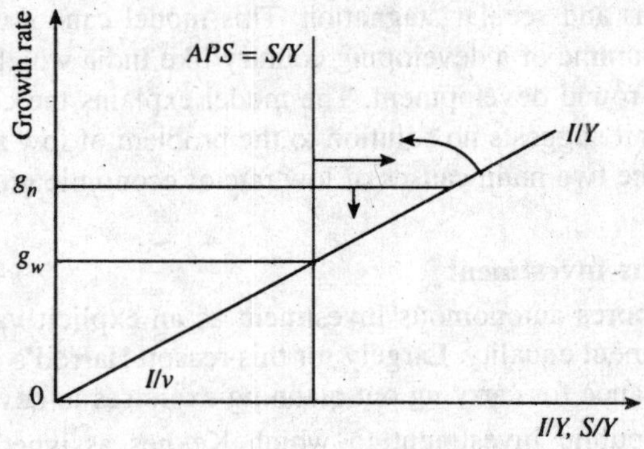

Fig. 5.1: Converge of g_w to g_n

Thus Harrod framework is extremely useful for development planning. If for instance, India sets a target rate of growth of, say, 10% per annum and the required capital-output ratio is 3, it knows that it has to save and invest 30% of GDP if the target growth rate is to be attained. If domestic saving is less than 30% of GDP there is an investment-savings gap to fill, which might be bridged by foreign borrowing.

The Relevance of the Harrod-Domar Model for Indian Planning

Since the Harrod-Domar model lays much stress on the role of capital formulation and capital-output ratio in determining the rate of economic growth, it has great practical relevance in setting growth target(s) and raising the rate of saving and investment to reach the target. This is why it has been extensively used in Indian planning to achieve the required rate of investment. However, the Harrod-Domar model has certain major pitfalls. This is why it is not fully relevant for carrying out planning exercises in a developing country like India. The following points may be noted in this context:

1. Little operational significance of ICOR

Since the Harrod-Domar model is based on the concept of incremental capital-output ratio (ICOR) it has hardly any relevance for development planning. Due to various types and degrees of shortages, structural bottlenecks and market imperfections, the productivity of capital shows considerable fluctuations in India. In addition, it is virtually impossible to arrive at an accurate and valid estimate of ICOR in such conditions. So the model cannot explain the actual mechanism through which a country like India can achieve self-sustaining growth.

2. Inability to show sectoral trend

The overall ICOR fails to show interrelationship among various sectors of the economy such as agriculture, industry and services and predict sectoral trends and interrelations and sectors. This is more so in view of the fact that the key growth variables are highly aggregative in nature. In fact, the process of economic development is essentially linked with various diverse changes — both structural and institutional. However, their highly aggregative nature prevents them from being used as a tool in detailed quantitative policy making and conceals many structural aspects of the problems associated with a steady rate of growth.

3. Irrelevance in LDCs

Since the Harrod-Domar model is based on the Keynesian model of income and employment determination, the former is useful only for formulating stabilisation policy and not for promoting faster economic growth. For instance, in Harrod's model, any deviation of actual (warranted) growth rate from natural growth rate indicates that an advanced capitalist economy is subject to periodic business cycle fluctuations and secular stagnation. This model cannot therefore serve as a guide to the industrialisation programme of a developing country like India which is striving to achieve faster economic growth and all-round development. The model explains the consequences of low demand in advanced countries but it suggests no solution to the problem of low savings and low productivity of investment which are the two main causes of low rate of economic growth in developing countries like India.

4. Neglect of autonomous investment

Harrod completely ignores autonomous investment as an explicit variable in his formulation of 'warranted' saving-investment equality. Largely for this reason Harrod's concept of warranted growth rate has no practical relevance for carrying out planning exercises in developing countries like India.

Harrod also ignored public investment to which Keynes assigned a key role in stimulating aggregate demand and in creating jobs and incomes. However, autonomous investment, both private and public, is of strategic importance to developing countries like India.

5. Constancy of saving ratio and capital-output ratio

The Harrod-Domar model assumes that the average propensity to save and the capital-output ratio are constant. But these are likely to change in the long-run.

6. Capital-labour substitution and economic efficiency

Finally the Harrod-Domar model is based on fixed coefficient production function of the Leontief type. However, R. M. Solow had pointed out that if the aggregate production function permits smooth capital-labour substitution, then the economy can make necessary adjustment easily and quickly and achieve steady growth (through improved efficiency in the use of resources).

Conclusion

In spite of these limitations, the Harrod-Domar model is useful for fixing the overall targets of savings, investment and income as also in testing the consistency of various plan objectives and targets. For this reason the model has been used by Indian planners. For instance, in India's First Five Year Plan (1950-51-1955-56), the rate of marginal savings was planned to be raised above its average rate. The planners sought to maximise the current rate of capital formation and, therefore, the growth rate of the economy through this measure. Thus the Harrod-Domar model served as a guideline for Indian planners and enabled them to determine the target rate of growth of the economy on the basis of savings and investment trends.

THE MAHALANOBIS GROWTH MODEL AND THE STRATEGY OF DEVELOPING HEAVY INDUSTRIES

In 1953 P. C. Mahalanobis presented a heavy industry model of development. His basic objective was to show the strategic importance of capital formation in the process of economic growth. The model suggested that the rate of economic growth could be accelerated in the long-run only by allocating a major portion of investment outlay in heavy industries, i.e., industries producing capital goods. The Mahalanobis strategy of development was adopted in India initially during the Second Plan period (1956-1961) but the strategy was not abandoned completely till March 1978, when the Fifth Plan (1974-79) was prematurely terminated one year earlier in 1979. We may now discuss the Mahalanobis model in detail.

The Mahalanobis Growth Model

The Mahalanobis model of industrialisation provides a strong rationale for achieving faster growth by developing heavy industries. In fact, the model was strongly biased in favour of heavy industries. The model identifies the rate of growth of investment in the economy with the rate of growth of output in the capital goods producing sector. This, in its turn, depends on the proportion of total investment allocated to the sector and output-capital ratio in the sector. Given the output-capital ratio in the heavy industries sector he proves that the higher the proportion of total investment allocated to the sector, the faster will be the rate of growth of output of capital goods. So the future rate of growth of investment will be higher than its current rate and thus the long-term rate of economic growth. This implies that the proportion of total investment allocated to industries producing capital goods each year is the most important determinant of long-term economic growth.

The model has two versions — the two-sector model and the four-sector model. We start with the two-sector model.

The Mahalanobis Two-Sector Model

In the basic two-sector Mahalanobis model the economy is divided into two sectors — the sector producing consumption goods (C) and the sector producing capital goods (K).

Let I_0 stand the initial rate of investment and λ_K and λ_C the proportion of total investment allocated to the two sectors, respectively.

Therefore $\lambda_K + \lambda_C = 1$.

Let β_C and β_K stand for marginal output-capital ratio (or ratio of incremental income to incremental investment, i.e., $\Delta Y/\Delta I$) in the two sectors, respectively.

Let Y_0, C_0 and I_0 denote national income, consumption and investment, respectively in the initial year of a plan and Y_1, C_1 and I_1 denote the same three variables in the terminal year of the plan.

In this model, net investment in any year, say, 't' has two components. So we can write

$$I = \lambda_K I_t + \lambda_K I_t$$

where $\lambda_K I_t$ is the amount going to the capital goods producing sector and $\lambda_C I_t$ is the amount allocated to sector producing consumption goods.

Let ΔI_t stand for the increase in investment (i.e., net addition to society's stock of capital) and ΔC_t for the increase in the supply of consumer goods in any period 't' which depends on the net investment made in the previous period ($t - 1$). Now, if β_K and β_C are predetermined variables, we can write the relationship between investment and the resultant increase in output of capital goods as follows

$$I_t - I_{t-1} = \Delta I_t = \beta_K \lambda_K I_{t-1} \quad \ldots \quad (1)$$

This means that investment in period 't' is the increase in output of capital goods. Note that ΔI_t is positive if $I_t > I_{t-1}$. The increase in output of capital goods ($\beta_K \lambda_K I_{t-1}$) in period '$t$' is the product of three things:

(i) Investment in period $t - 1$ (i.e., I_{t-1}), (ii) the proportion of investment allocated to the capital goods producing sector (λ_K), and (iii) the output-capital ratio in the capital goods producing sector (β_K).

The model takes into account only the physical aspect of investment, which depends on the proportion of investment allocated to capital goods producing sector (λ_K) and output-capital ratio of this sector (β_K). In the same way for the consumer-goods producing sector we can write

$$C_t - C_{t-1} = \Delta C_t = \beta_C \lambda_C I_{t-1} \quad \ldots \quad (2)$$

as also

$$\Delta I_{t-1} = \beta_K \lambda_K I_{t-2}$$

Since income in period t is the sum of consumption and investment, we can write:

$$Y_t = I_t + C_t$$

$$\text{or, } Y_t = \beta_K \lambda_K I_{t-1} + \beta_C \lambda_C I_{t-1}$$

Now, through little manipulation, we get the final equation of the Mahalanobis two-sector model:

$$Y_t = Y_0 \left[1 + \alpha_0 \frac{\beta_C \lambda_C + \beta_K \lambda_k}{\lambda_K + \beta_K} (1 + \lambda_K \beta_K)^{t-1} \right] \quad \ldots (3)$$

where α_0 is the initial rate of investment expressed as percentage of income (i.e., I_0/Y_0).

The model assumes that $\beta_C > \beta_K$. So it may apparently seem that the growth of output (income) will be faster if more investment is made in the consumption goods producing-sector. But in this case the higher rate of income growth can be achieved only in the short run. As equation (3) shows, after a certain period of time, the larger the investment allocated to the consumption goods producing-sector (λ_K), the higher will be the income growth.

The Rationale of the Model

According to the Mahalanobis model the rate of the economic growth depends upon the rate of physical capital formation (or real investment). The faster the rate of capital formation the higher the rate of economic growth. The rate of economic formation, in its turn, depends on the capacity of the economy to produce capital (investment) goods, and not on the rate of savings, as has been predicted earlier by the Harrod-Domar model. A large volume of savings will go waste if a closed economy does not have the capacity to produce a large volume of capital goods.

The Role of Public Sector in the Model

The production of capital goods requires huge amount of initial investment. The private sector cannot undertake investment on such a huge scale. So it logically follows that only the government can take the lead in this direction by setting up a large number of public sector enterprises. This is why there was so much stress on the expansion of the public sector in the Indian plans from 1956 onwards. And the Second Industrial Policy Resolution, announced by the G.O.I in the same year declared that the public sector would gradually reach the commanding heights of the economy. And five integrated steel plants (under the management of the Steel Authority of India — SAIL), and several heavy engineering and chemical units were set up in the public sector since such industries are essentially input-supplying industries. Huge investment was also made in infrastructure building to lay the foundation for industrialisation and economic development.

Thus if a large investment was not made in basic and heavy industries, the country would remain import dependent for steel, and various types of machines (capital goods). Since in the initial years of planning, it was not possible for India to earn efficient foreign exchange by raising exports adequate capital goods could not be imported to step up the developmental effort.[1]

This would slow down the rate of real capital formation and thus the rate of economic growth. This meant that without adequate investment in heavy industries, it would not be possible to achieve rapid economic growth with self-reliance. So the maximum priority had to be accorded to heavy industries in India's development strategy and planning for industrialisation.

Employment Aspect of the Model

The model predicts that gainful employment in both agriculture and industry can be created only by increasing the production of capital and intermediate input goods such as various types of steel, machines, etc. This means that high priority has to be accorded to capital goods producing industry for achieving the goal of high employment.

1. Thus the model implicity assumed slow growth or virtual stagnation of exports. This provided the rationale for a sudden shift in investment pattern from agriculture to capital goods producing industries.

Import-Substituting Industrialisation

The Model laid stress on the development of heavy industries for another important reason – to reduce import of capital goods as much as possible and enable the country to achieve import substituting industrialisation. This means that the model emphasised inward-looking strategy of industrial development (more so due to its assumption of export pessimism).

The stress in the model was on domestic production of import-substitute items

However, there is an offsetting consideration. If India's export can be raised to a high level, sufficient foreign exchange can be earned. This can be fruitfully utilised to import various types of capital goods. In that case the rate of investment (capital formation) can be pushed up even without giving high priority to basic and heavy industries.

The Mahalanobis Model and India's Development Strategy during the Plan Period

The strategy of developing heavy industries first, as suggested by the Mahalanobis model, was first put into effect in India at the time of the Second Five year Plan. This Plan was based on a strategy which gave maximum priority to basic and heavy industries. By building up economic and social overhead, through the exploration and development of minerals and the development of basic industries like steel, machine building, coal and heavy chemicals, India sought to achieve the main objectives of the Second Plan, viz., (i) faster economic growth, (ii) employment generation, and (iii) economic self-sufficiency as also self-reliance.[1]

And to quote the Second Five Year Plan, "Rapid industrialisation and diversification of the economy is thus the core of development. But if industrialisation is to be rapid enough, the country must aim at developing basic industries and industries which make machines to make the machines needed for further development".

In India's Second Plan there was a clear shift of priorities from agriculture to industry and within the industrial sector from light to heavy industries. The basic logic of the model is that the rate of growth of investment is identified with domestic production of capital goods. It was also thought that profits made by the heavy industries sector would be ploughed back for further development of the sector so that more and more machines could be produced.

The Mahalanobis Four-Sector Model

Mahalanobis realised that since the basic and heavy industries are highly capital-intensive in nature, their long-run employment potential is limited. This is why he presented a four-sector model in which he kept the capital goods production-sector intact but divided the capital goods production-sector into the sub-sectors: C_1 representing factory enterprises using machanised techniques for producing consumer goods; C_2 representing the small-scale and household enterprises for producing consumer goods; and C_3 representing the provision of services.

It was sector C_2 which was supposed to ensure an increased supply of consumer goods to meet their growing demand as also to create adequate employment opportunities due to their highly labour-intensive character. In keeping with this approach the Second Plan imposed restrictions on the capacity creation in the factory sector engaged in the production of manufactured articles. However, for the cottage and household enterprises, adequate investment was not allocated. In addition, no genuine effort was made to improve labour productivity in such enterprises. For these two reasons these enterprises could neither create adequate employment opportunities nor produce a large amount of consumer (wage) goods.

The strategy of the Second Plan was continued in the Third Plan (1961-66) also. One of the basic objectives of this Plan was to achieve self-sufficiency in foodgrains and increase agricultural production to meet the requirements of industry and exports.

1. It was thought that the achievement of these goods would enable the planners to set up a vibrant economy.

The heavy industry bias prevailed in the development strategy of both the Fourth Plan (1969-74) and the Fifth plan (1974-78).

An Overall Evaluation of The Model

The main drawbacks of the Mahalanobis model are the following:

1. Non-equivalence of saving and investment

Investment cannot be equated with savings

One serious drawback of the Mahalanobis model is that it identifies investment with savings. But in ready there is often imbalance between the two. It investment exceeds savings, there will emerge an inflationary gap in the economy. This will cause the general price level to rise. So it is not judicious to show the equivalence of the two, as the model has done.

The planners may allocate more resources to heavy industries. This is supposed to lead to more physical investment and, as a result, the society's stock of capital will increase. But there is no guarantee that total saving will rise enough to match the higher level of investment. The reason is that aggregate saving has three components, viz., household saving, corporate (business) saving and government saving. And each type of saving has its own determinants. The Mahalanobis model envisaged higher level of physical investment. But the model completely ignored the issue of generation of adequate savings to match the higher level of investment[1]. This is why the GOI had to rely on deficit financing which were inflationary in its effect.

Economic Insight: Determinants of Saving

Aggregate saving in a mixed economy depends on the optimising behaviour of households and firms as the policy of the government. Household saving depends on the propensity to consume which, in its turn, depends on various subjective and objective factors, as mentioned by Keynes. Corporate saving depends on corporate policies relating to depreciation, distribution of dividends and retained earnings (undistributed profits). Government saving depends on its budgetary surplus (excess of revenue—both from tax and non-tax sources—over expenditure). This, in its turn, depends on the government's policy regarding taxation as also its consumption and investment expenditures. Government saving also depends on the trading surplus of public sector units, which, in its turn, depends on the optional efficiency and profitability of such units.

2. The wage goods model

By criticising the Mahalanobis model, C.N. Valik and P.R. Brahmanand presented an alternative model known as the wage goods model of development and suggested a strategy of development which accorded maximum priority to agriculture and industries producing wage goods (or mass consumption goods). According to this model, national income growth and employment generation are determined by the supply of wage goods. It is so because the root cause of both open and disguised unemployment in less developed countries (LDCs) like India is the shortage of wage goods, which acts as a constraint on industrialisation and economic growth. The reason is that when the disguisedly unemployed people are employed in productive work and are paid wages, the demand for wages goods (mainly foodgrains) will increase. And unless an adequate amount of wage goods is produced and supplied in the market, the surplus labour[2] of LDCs cannot be absorbed. Since in this model wage goods play a key role in employment generation, the model suggests a development strategy which accords top priority to agriculture for supplying adequate foodgrains to workers.

Thus in the Mahalanobis model, the stress is on fixed capital in determining income and employment in the long run. Capital goods are the creators of consumption and intermediate goods and thus help to generate employment in a number of other industries, indirectly though. By comparison in the Vakil Brahmanand model the main focus is on the supply of wage goods, which are a form of 'circulating capital'. The reason is that corn is required to produce corn.

1. Thus the Mahalanobis model had an inherent inflationary potential.
2. Surplus labour includes those who are disguisedly unemployed as also those who are openly unemployed.

3. Neglect of agriculture

The Mahalanobis model completely neglected agriculture and thus did not give any importance to the supply of wage goods in the process of economic growth. Largely due to this food prices started rising sharply from the beginning of the Second Plan. In fact, the stress on the development of heavy industries led to large increase in money income. As a result the demand for wage goods increased quite sharply. But the supply of such goods could not be increased proportionately due to almost complete neglect of agriculture. As a result India had to face the problem of food inflation. The same problem exists even now due to undue emphasis on industrial growth and almost complete neglect of agriculture in the entire reform process.

In truth, the most unfortunate consequence of India's wrong and biased economic policies has been the appalling neglect of agriculture and rural development. The failure of present development strategy to step up public investment for agricultural development has accentuated the problem of unemployment in rural areas.

4. Failure to create adequate employment opportunities

Another serious drawback of the Mahalanobis development strategy was its failure to create adequate employment opportunities in a labour-surplus country. The pattern of industrialisation was based on the adoption of imported capital-intensive technology. So a few large-scale industries were set up in urban areas. But their employment potential was limited.

Not much stress was given to the production of fertilisers, steel, cement, etc. which were required by the farm sector after the adoption as a new agriculture strategy in the mid-1960s. This could have served two purposes at the same time — an increase in the supply of foodgrains (so as to make the country self-sufficient in food) and employment generation.

5. Need for import of machines

In a capital-scarce country, allocation of a large proportion of investment to industries producing machines left very little funds for agriculture and rural industries which have a tremendous employment potential due to their labour-intensive nature. This means that in the initial stages of development Indians planners could have done better by importing some capital and intermediate goods and thus gain comparative advantage in the production of such goods in the long-run. Some financial resources would be saved in the process which could be more fruitfully utilised for the development of agriculture and rural (mainly agro-based) industries[1] in which there is hardly any gestation lag.

6. Form of machines

The production of capital goods is not enough. The form of capital which is created is crucially important as far as employment generation is concerned. Since agriculture and small-scale industries have tremendous employment potential what is needed in India is production of those small and simple types of machines and tools which are used in agriculture and small-sector industries. The production of such machines on a large scale will promote the growth of these two sectors.

7. Production of intermediate goods

Furthermore, it is necessary to step up the production of certain intermediate goods such as fertilisers, pesticides, cement, power, etc. which help in modernising agriculture, raise agricultural productivity and expand employment opportunities in rural areas.

In short, if the problem of growing unemployment is to be solved, there is need to revise the Mahalanobis strategy of development. In the new strategy, agriculture has to play a key role in absorbing surplus labourers and employing them productivity on a long-term basis.

1. In such industries factories can be set up quickly and production can be started immediately.

8. High ICOR and low growth rate

Another major drawback of the Mahalanobis strategy of development was that with its heavy industry bias, it chose the pattern of investment in which the incremental capital output ratio was high. Since the major portion of investment was allocated to the capital goods producing sector with a high ICOR, the overall ICOR which is a weighted average of sectoral ratios was also high. Since economic growth varies directly with the saving ratio and inversely with the ICOR (as the Harrod-Domar model suggests), the choice of the pattern of investment with a bias in favour of heavy industries and a bias against agriculture implied a low rate of growth of the economy.

9. Huge foreign exchange requirement

The Mahalanobis development strategy had another major weakness. It heavily depended upon large imports of capital goods (machines and equipment), materials and even food. This is why India had to face a serious foreign exchange crisis in 1956, even if India received huge foreign aid from the USA and other countries. Thus there was a logical inconsistency in the model since it was framed in the context of a closed economy or stagnant exports. The Mahalanobis strategy made India dependent as foreign aid, with all its adverse consequences.

10. Neglect of exports

Due to low priority assigned to agriculture and consumer goods industries, which had high export potential, India's exports virtually stagnated. The Mahalanobis model has been criticised on the ground that it has completely ignored India's comparative advantage and gains to be derived from trade and specialisation in its areas of relative efficiency.

11. Import of foodgrains and waste of scarce foreign exchange

Due to rapid growth of population and inadequate increase in the supply of food, there was a severe food crisis from 1956. This was the direct result of neglect of agriculture in India's development strategy. So a huge amount of food had to be imported to feed India's growing population even by utilising scarce foreign exchange. This could well be fruitfully utilised to import capital goods (which would lead to an expansion of the economy's production capacity).

At the beginning of the Fifth Plan, i.e., in 1974, India's foreign exchange reserves were largely used to import foodgrains to meet the current consumption needs of the people. So very little foreign exchange was left to import capital equipment and materials to raise the rate of capital formation or to step up the country's investment effort.

12. Inward-looking development strategy

Finally the Mahalanobis strategy of development involved import-substitution type of industrialisation. Due to the adoption of this inward-looking strategy or all-round import-substitution strategy in order to build up basic and heavy industries, India's dependence on imports increased considerably.

Thus in the Mahalanobis strategy hardly any consideration was given to the alternative policy of development of industries which had large employment potential. The planners failed to take into account the point that the country could earn sufficient foreign exchange through exports. This would enable the country to import necessary capital goods without depending on foreign aid or without external borrowing. This was how the country could achieve economic self-reliance, which was one of the declared objectives of planning.

Conclusion

In short, the Mahalanobis strategy involved neglect of agriculture and rural development, more so due to scarcity of resources. It also neglected the development of export-oriented industries and thus deprived the country from deriving the gains from specialisation and exchange.

KEY POINTS

1. ***Use of two growth models in Indian planning*** **:** Two growth models were used in Indian planning, viz., the Harrod-Domar model and the Mahalanobis model. The Mahalanobis model was used during the second plan period and the H-D model in the Third Plan Period as also in formulating subsequent plans.

2. ***The Harrod-Domar model*** **:** The Harrod-Domar model is a major model of economic growth independently developed by R. Harrod and E. Domar in the 1940s. The models use the concepts of the warranted rate of growth (determined by the rate of capital formation) and the natural rate of growth (determined by the rate of population growth).

If the 'actual' rate of growth exceeds (or falls short of) the 'warranted' rate, income will be raised more (or lowered more) than is appropriate for maintaining equilibrium, causing a cumulative deviation from the equilibrium path.

Since the Harrod-Domar model lays much stress on the role of capital formation and capital-output ratio in determining the rate of economic growth, it has great practical relevance in setting growth target(s) and raising the rate of saving and investment to reach the target.

3. ***The Mahalanobis model*** **:** The Mahalanobis model appeared in 1953. It formed the basis of India's second five year plan (1956-61) which propounded the view that a shift to investing in machines to make capital goods, viz., heavy industry, instead of investment in light industry would eventually produce a higher level and a faster rate of growth of consumption. The model has been criticised for neglecting supply constraints, other than a shortage of capital and for ignoring the fact that many industries supply both intermediate and final goods.

KEY TERMS

Heavy industries
Light industries
Wage goods model
Consumer goods
Capital goods
Knife-edge problem
Economic self-reliance

Natural rate of growth
Warranted rate of growth
Accleration effect
Multiplier effect
Inward-looking strategy
Export pessimism
Economic self-sufficiency

ASSIGNMENTS

1. Discuss the role of the public sector in the context of the Mahalanobis model adopted during India's Second Five Year Plan.
2. What is the practical relevance of the Harrod-Domar model in the context of India's planning for economic development?
3. Describe the role of capital accumulation in India's development plans in the 1950s. Explain how this development strategy ran into difficulties in the late 1960s. How did the development strategy change as a result?

CHAPTER 6

Indian Economic Reforms, Structural Adjustments and Growth

While the case for economic reforms may take good note of the diagnosis that India has too much government interference in some fields, it ignores the fact that India also has insufficient and ineffective government activity in many other fields, including basic education, health care, social security, land reforms and the promotion of social change. This inertia too contributes to the persistence of widespread deprivation, economic stagnation and social inequality.

Jean Dreze and Amartya Sen

THE RATIONALE OF ECONOMIC REFORMS

An unanswered question faced by planners and policymakers in developing countries like India is whether further economic growth can be promoted by relying on the planning system (which is basically a system of managing and controlling the economy and determining the pattern of resource allocation) or by relying on the market system (in which the private sector and foreign investors are allowed to play a dominant role). Economists has long debated on the issue. In the 1950s and 1960s, most developing countries, including India, relied on the planning system and controlled and regulated the private sector excessively. It was widely believed that state intervention was absolutely essential to break the spreading vicious circle of poverty and underdevelopment and to initiate the process of economic development. However, since the early 1980s, it became quite clear that the then strategies of development with excessive regulation and control of the private sector and more reliance on the public sector were acting as serious obstacles to India's economic growth by creating various types of inefficiencies. Consequently the growth rate in developing countries slowed down. In addition, these countries faced large fiscal deficit which created two major problems—a high rate of inflation and a huge deficit in the balance of payments which, in its turn, led to high external indebtedness. At this time few noted economists advised the developing countries to adopt the policy of economic liberalisation to overcome these problems. It was felt that various liberalisation measures would promote faster economic growth, slow down the rate of price inflation and improve the balance of payments position. They convincingly argued that if markets were left free and private sectors (including foreign investors) were allowed to play a pivotal role in the economy, a competitive business environment would be created and it would promote both productive and allocative efficiency. This would be possible if direct controls (through the licensing system) were removed and the public sector and the planning system were assigned a secondary rather than a primary role in the country's economic development. Those who advocated the policy of economic liberalisation suggested two other measures, which were (i) import liberalisation by drastically cutting down the tariff rates and (ii) provision of various incentives to foreign investors and giving them wider scope to operate in India.

Immediately after Independence, India adopted the mixed economy principle in which private and public sectors were supposed to exist side by side and take decisions. However, the dominant role was to be played by the public sector and the planning system. The mixed economy principle achieved quite some success in the first two decades of planning (1951-1971). However, during the 1970s and 1980s, the following shortcomings of the principle gradually become visible:

1. Inefficient operation of public enterprises: The public sector was expected to generate adequate resources so as to make the economy grow faster than in the pre-Independence period. However, just the opposite thing happened. Most public sector enterprises incurred losses mainly due to operational inefficiency and required constant budgetary support in order to survive. So they became a burden on the Exchequer. In fact, one of the causes of mounting fiscal deficit of the Government of India during the entire plan period has been the staggering losses of public sector enterprises.

2. Increase in the money supply and price inflation: Macroeconomic imbalances, both internal and external, emerged and gradually assumed serious proportions. No doubt, national income grew at the rate of 5% per annum during the 1980s and the industrial sector grew at the rate of 8%. But due to the emergence of macroeconomic imbalances, these trends could not be maintained for long. The growing deficits[1] in the successive budgets of the Government had to be covered by deficit spending. As a result the money supply increased which generated a high rate of inflation. In fact, the annual rate of inflation was 17% in 1991. This forced the Government to reduce its expenditure and fiscal·deficit so as to achieve measurable price level stability.

3. BOP deficit and foreign exchange crisis: Due to rising imports and sluggish exports, a huge deficit appeared in the balance of payments. As a result foreign exchange reserves fell to very low levels. In order to overcome the deficit initially, the Government had to resort to excessive commercial borrowing at high rates of interest. But the economic condition did not improve much. In fact in May, 1991, India's foreign exchange reserves were just sufficient to meet the import needs of three weeks.

In fact, India's external economic position was so critical in 1991 that India lost its creditworthiness to the rest of the world. In order to avoid such an embarrassing situation and to earn (win) the confidence of external lenders, the Government had to sell a part of its accumulated gold stock. In fact, a certain portion of the stock was even pledged with the Bank of England in order to acquire same foreign exchange needed to meet its external obligations. In addition, the dwindling reserves compelled India to approach the IMF for loans so as to be able to tide over the foreign exchange crisis.

4. Excessive control over the private sector: In addition, excessive control and regulation destroyed the initiative and energy of the private entrepreneurs and ultimately proved to be counter-productive. This is why India's economic policies have been criticised at both domestic and international levels by both economists and policymakers.

Critics of controls and regulations have put forward the following arguments in favour of economic liberalisation, deregulation of the private sector and for assigning it an important role in India's economic growth:

(i) *Inefficient allocation of resources*: Industrial licensing and controls replaced efficient allocation of resources which could be achieved by relying on the market system. The licensing system

1. Budgetary deficits occurred mainly due to sharp increase in non-plan revenue expenditure of the Government and slower rate of generation of revenue, both from tax and non-tax sources.

introduced arbitrary bureaucratic controls on the allocation of resources among competing uses. In fact, excessive regulation of the private sector had resulted in inefficient allocation of resources in industries.

(ii) *Loss of initiative and enterprise* : The industrial licensing system destroyed private initiative and enterprise and led to loss of incentives to invest in productive and socially desirable ventures. It prevented the emergence of a healthy and competitive business environment in which firms would strive to reduce cost and improve product quality in order to achieve sustainable competitive advantage.

Consequently entrepreneurs were eager to earn *monopoly rent* by cornering licences rather than to earn genuine profits by setting up those ventures in which they could show their skill and efficiency. In fact, the licensing and control regime was held largely responsible for low productivity and high capital-output ratio in Indian industries.

(iii) *Obstacles to capacity creation and optimal plant utilisation* : The industrial licensing system prevented the creation of additional production capacity and its optimal utilisation. The reason is that the industrial units which tried to increase output beyond the licensed capacity were penalised.

(iv) *Regional imbalance* : The industrial licensing system failed to achieve one of its major objectives, viz., promoting balanced regional development. In fact, during the licensing regime, regional imbalance increased.

5. Increase in concentration of economic power: One of the objectives of industrial licensing policy was reduction of undue concentration of wealth and economic power in private hands. But in reality, exactly the opposite thing happened. The same industrial house applied for multiple licences from different branch offices located at different places and succeeded in acquiring as many licences as possible since licences were issued on a "first-come-first-serve" basis.

The Washington Consensus, Development Policy and Structural Adjustment Reforms

Various economic reform measures introduced in India in 1991 under the pressure of the IMF and the World Bank constituted what is now called Washington Consensus. John Williamson and other officials of the World Bank and the IMF reached the consensus after some debate and discussion with key US government agencies. Surprisingly enough, the Washington policy package was completely silent on the issue of poverty alleviation and reduction of income inequality. It was felt that if appropriate fiscal and structural reform measures were adopted, a developing country would achieve rapid growth and poverty would therefore be automatically eradicated.

Economic Insight: The Washington Consensus

Stabilise, privatise, liberalise, globalise and balance your budget, claimed the Washington consensus. The term was coined by John Willamson in 1989 to describe (and, of course, prescribe) a set of policy recommendations for developing countries. According to the World Bank, IMF and the US Treasury, the key to development was deregulation and fiscal discipline.

(i) ***Stabilise*** : keep inflation down, reduce trade deficits and keep the money supply in check.

(ii) ***Privatise*** : turn public goods, such as electricity, over to private companies to improve efficiency.

(iii) ***Liberalise*** : open your orders to free trade and attract foreign direct investment (FDI).

(iv) ***Deregulate*** : don't limit competition or try to keep players out of the market.

(v) ***And stick to fiscal discipline*** : Don't let government spend more than it brings in. Low-income countries which took IMF loans were forced to satisfy conditions, known as structural adjustment policies, stabilise, privatise and so on.

This consensus followed a free market approach to economic development. It contains a 12-point policy programme for developing countries with a view to promoting faster economic growth in such countries as also to help them achieve price stability, overcome trade deficit and solve the problems of external indebtedness.

The 12-Point Programme: The twelve elements of the Washington action plan are the following:

1. Fiscal adjustment: Developing countries should take steps to reduce fiscal deficit by curtailing unnecessary government expenditure. One way of doing this is to drastically reduce explicit and implicit subsidies.

2. Tax reforms: Tax rates should be cut substantially to promote both household saving and business investment with a view to promoting a higher rate of economic growth, as has been suggested by the supply side economics. Reduction of tax rates would also generate larger revenue for the government, depending on the elasticity of the tax system. At the same time, the tax base has to be broadened by plugging the loopholes of the existing tax system.

3. Deregulation: Industrial licensing should be scrapped. In addition, restrictive measures in the form of the Monopolies and Restrictive Trade Practices (MRTP) Act, now the Competition Act, and the Foreign Exchange Regulation Act (FERA), now the Foreign Exchange Management Act (FEMA) should be abolished so that the private sector can achieve automatic expansion.

4. Trade liberalisation: Import tariff rates should be drastically cut to promote free multilateral trade. In addition, quantitative restrictions on imports should be done away with in a phased manner.

5. Competitive exchange rate system: Developing countries like India should devalue their overvalued currencies and ultimately move to a flexible exchange rate system[1]. In addition, they should make their currencies more convertible so as to remove obstacles to freer trade and greater capital mobility.

6. Privatisation: There should be disinvestment of public sector enterprises. This can be done either by making outright sale of a public sector unit (PSU) to the private sector or by selling a portion of the stocks and shares of such an unit to private enterprises in order the reduce the Government's stake in it.

7. Removal of barriers to foreign investment: Since economic growth in developing countries could be accelerated through larger foreign direct investment (FDI), all barriers to the free flow of such capital should be eliminated. This would attract FDI in developing countries, more so if they made their currencies fully convertible, i.e., convertible on both the current account and the capital account. Incidentally, rupee has been made partially convertible during the reform period.

8. Financial sector reforms: There is need for reforms in both the money and the capital markets. There is also need for reform in the insurance sector.

9. Protection of private property rights: Suitable legal measures should be adopted to protect private property rights. Otherwise people will lose incentives to work hard, save, invest and take risk.

10. Amendment of labour laws: At present many loss-making companies are not allowed to close down their operations just to prevent job loss. Therefore labour laws should be amended so as to make it easy for a new private enterprise to enter an industry or for an old firm to leave the industry. There is no point in keeping a sick firm alive just for giving job protection.

11. Change in the pattern of investment in the public sector: The public sector should make investment in those areas where it has comparative advantage such as health care, education and infrastructure. Since in such activities social benefits exceed private benefits, there is likely to be underinvestment in the absence of state participation. The public sector should not get involved in constructing luxury hotels and shopping malls. These activities can be easily left for the private sector to perform more efficiently.

12. Opening up new areas to the private sector: Finally, newer and newer areas should be left open to the private sector. The government of a country may even encourage private-public partnership in infrastructure building. This has become a reality in several developing Asian countries of late.

1. The rupee is said to be overvalued in terms of the US dollar if there is excess demand for dollar in India at the current official rate of exchange between the two currencies.

STRUCTURAL ADJUSTMENT PROGRAMMES

According to the New Economic Policy (NEP), 1991, the Government of India was to cut its expenditure drastically so as to reduce fiscal deficit with a view to achieving price level stability. Perhaps the most important element of NEP is the adoption of structural adjustment reforms which sought to transform India's mixed economy into a free market economy. This implies that the private sector would now be guided by the free play of the market forces, that is, by the forces of demand and supply of commodities and factors of production. In other words, this implies an expansion of the private sector and a contraction of the public. This is exactly the opposite of what was sought to be achieved in 1956 (expansion of the public sector and contraction of the private). So we now have a full circle.

Under the NEP the private sector was assigned a pivotal role in promoting economic growth by fostering competition and promoting efficiency. The NEP was adopted for initiating far-reaching structural reforms. The main objective has been to remove excessive direct controls and regulations on industries and to establish a free market.

We may now make a review of the various economic reforms undertaken in India since 1991 under the NEP or structural adjustment programme at the insistence of the IMF and the World Bank.

1. Dereservation of Industries for the Public Sector

The NEP clearly indicates the Government of India's intention to invite the private sector to participate in the key areas of the economy which were so long reserved for the public sector. This is why the number of industries reserved for the public sector has been reduced drastically to only 6, mainly on security and strategic grounds.

The NEP threw open core industries such as iron and steel, electricity, air transport, ship-building, heavy machinery, heavy chemicals, heavy engineering as also telecommunication cables and instruments for the private sector. The resources for the public sector will now be used for the development of strategic, high technology and infrastructural industries as also for social sectors such as education and health, so as to achieve poverty alleviation and improve the physical quality of life of the people.

2. Abolition of the Industrial Licensing System

The first step towards liberalisation was taken by the Government by abolishing all industrial licensing, irrespective of the level of investment (in fixed assets such as plant, equipment and machinery) except for 15 industries. The two main reasons are as follows. Firstly, such industries are of strategic importance for the safety and the security of the country. Secondly, these industries help in the protection of the physical environment. Even for these industries, the licensing procedure has been simplified to a considerable extent. For getting licence, a firm has to follow only certain guidelines relating to their location. The objective is to ensure that polluting industries are not set up in major urban centers.

3. Privatisation of Public Sector Enterprises

The NEP declares that the Government will not operate commercial enterprises. So it decided to undertake a programme of disinvestment of PSUs. The Government can either sell its enterprises to the private sector or a part of the equity of any PSU to the private companies or in the open market. This is why the disinvestment policy of the Government is also known as the policy of privatisation. The funds raised in this process can be used to restructure and strengthen potentially viable PSUs. A portion of the resources may also be used to service public debt at least partly, i.e., the repayment of debt interest along with a portion of the original debt (i.e., the principal amount). These resources will also enable the Government to cover its fiscal deficit.

The Reasons for Privatisation and Disinvestment of PSUs

There are *three* main reasons for the disinvestment of PSUs:

(i) *Reducing fiscal deficit* **:** The Government needs resources to reduce its fiscal deficit.

(ii) *Improving operational efficiency* **:** Since a number of existing PSUs are incurring huge losses mainly due to operational inefficiency, disinvestment will enable PSUs to improve their operational efficiency.

(iii) *Investment in economic and social infrastructure* **:** The resources acquired through disinvestment can be used for investment in building roads, highways, power plants, etc., as also in education, health and for the implementation of various poverty alleviation programmes.

Economic Insight: Public Sector Reforms in a Mixed Economy

The IMF and the World Bank suggested two types of reforms for the member countries in the early 1990s. They have recommended market reforms for post-socialist countries and public sector reforms for developing countries. As part of its policy of economic reforms, the Government of India started reforms in PSUs. The main elements of such reforms are the following:

(i) ***Disinvestment:*** Disinvestment of Government equity in all non-strategic PSUs to 26%, or lower, if necessary.

(ii) ***Restructuring:*** Those PSUs which are potentially viable are to be restructured and revived.

(iii) ***Exit policy:*** Those PSUs which cannot be revived or nursed back to health would have to be closed down so that there is no future (further) pressure on the Exchequer.

In the past two decades, the Government of India has succeeded in evolving a fair, transparent and equitable procedure for disinvestment in selected PSUs. The success achieved in the sale of minority stakes in some PSUs is shown in Table 6.1.

Table 6.1: Disinvestment of Equity in Public Sector Enterprises

Target	Realisation	Cumulative
1991-92	2000-01	2009-10
2,500	3,038	3,038
10,000	1,871	20,354
N.A	4,260	57,684

N.A: Not available

Source: *Statistical Outline of India* (TECS) 2012-13, p. 124.

Two important points may be noted in this context.

(i) During the four-year period, from 1999 to 2003, disinvestment in PSUs was mainly through sale of Government equity to strategic private partners.

(ii) However, in the year 2003-04, the policy of disinvestment through the sale of Government's shares of various public enterprises in the open market was adopted.

4. Welcoming private foreign investment

The Government has liberalised its policy relating to private foreign investment. To welcome such investment, it granted automatic permission to private foreign investors to hold 51% of total equity in 34 high priority industries (which also include power generation and petroleum refining) subject to the fulfilment of certain norms. This facility will be available to those firms that are able to finance the import of capital through foreign equity. This is, no doubt, a notable departure from the earlier policy of case-by-case approval of foreign investment. In addition, the Government has given an extra incentive to the foreign investors — a guaranteed return of 16% on foreign investment in priority sectors. The Government is also planning to allow automatic clearance for foreign financial and technical collaborations with Indian firms.

5. Transfer of Foreign Technology

According to the NEP, for a few selected high technology and high investment priority industries, firms will receive automatic permission to sign foreign technology agreements subject to certain clear-cut and specific guidelines. The objective is to minimise the delay and reduce the uncertainty related to the transfer of technology associated with the inflow of private foreign capital.

6. Trade Liberalisation

With a view to opening up the economy, quantitative restrictions on imports have been removed. In addition, to promote competitiveness, efficiency and globalisation of the Indian economy import duties have been reduced to 20% (excluding agricultural and dairy products) with effect from January, 9, 2004. The basic idea behind this move was that with the cheapening of imported goods, Indian firms would be eager to improve their operational efficiency and reduce cost so that their products could compete closely with their foreign counterparts. If this expectation materialises, India's exports will increase.

7. Currency Convertibility and Free Floating of the Indian Rupee

Since March, 1993, the rupee has been made partially convertible. In other words, the rupee became convertible on the current account. This means that for the purpose of export-import trade, foreign travel and higher studies abroad, an Indian can convert rupees into dollars and dollars into rupees in the foreign exchange market at the market determined rate, which is liable to change in response to changes in the demand and supply conditions. In June 1991, the rupee was devalued by 20%. But now, with market determined exchange rate, the rupee can depreciate or appreciate depending on market movements, i.e., changes in supply and demand conditions. So we now have a floating exchange rate.

A Critical Review of Economic Reforms or NEP

Thanks to economic reforms, at present we have a mixed economy with much orientation towards a free market and private sector. This point requires little elucidation.

More than two decades have passed since we initiated economic reforms in July 1991. Now the pertinent question is whether these reforms have ensured the intended results, which are faster and sustained economic growth, price stability, reduction of poverty and unemployment and improvement in the balance of payments position (which gets reflected in an increase in foreign exchange reserves). Here is the scorecard:

1. Increase in Exports and Foreign Exchange Reserves

During the six year period, 1991-97, India's export increased steadily. The average annual rate of growth of exports was 11.7%. However, during the Ninth Plan period (1997-2002) the rate of growth of exports fell to 6% per annum mainly due to global recession. However, since 2002 India's exports again increased substantially. In fact, during the Tenth plan period (2002-07), exports grew at the rate of 20% or more per annum.

In short, external sector reforms led to steady growth of exports. This is why in spite of growth of imports (due to removal of various trade restrictions) India's current account balance improved considerably. And during three years consecutively — 2001-02, 2002-03 and 2003-04 — there occurred net investment abroad by Indians. However, since 2004-05, the current account surplus had been converted into a deficit. It was 1.2% in 2005-06 and 1.1% in 2006-07. As a result there occurred net inflow of capital which was good for India since it enabled the country to cover the excess of domestic investment over domestic saving. Due to the adoption of various liberalisation measures, both exports and imports increased. There also occurred huge inflow of foreign exchange due to remittances by non-resident Indians (NRIs). Consequently there was a huge increase in India's foreign exchange reserves — from US $42.3 billion in 2000-01 to US $279.6 billion in 2009-10. India's foreign exchange (forex) reserves increased from £11,416 crores in 1990-91 Rs. 168,783 crores in 2000-01 and to Rs. 1,283,865 crores in 2008-09 and in Nov. 26, 2010 total forex reserves were Rs. 11,342,061 crores ($294 bn.) of which foreign currency assets were Rs. 1,213,279 crores ($265.3 bn.).

2. Partial Control of Inflation

In India the annual rate of inflation (ROI) is measured by the wholesale price index (WPI). The ROI came down from 17% in August 1991 to 3.6% in 2001-02 to 3.4% in 2002-03. However, it increased to 5.5% in 2003-04 and 6.5% in 2004-05. The average annual rate of inflation (with 1993-94 as the base year) was 4.4% in 2005-06 and around 5.4% in 2006-07. All these figures make one thing very clear — the rate of inflation was brought under control, thanks to the adoption of prudent monetary policy by the RBI. However, there was an offsetting factor. Even during the reform period, the fiscal deficit of the Government was quite high, except for a few years. This created inflationary pressures in the economy. Thus the monetary policy of the RBI and the fiscal policy of the Government worked at cross purposes. While fiscal policy generated inflationary forces in the economy, monetary policy succeed in offsetting, to a large extent, the inherent inflationary potential of growing fiscal deficit.

However, inflationary pressures got built up in 2006-07 and 2007-08 in spite of the adoption of contractionary monetary policy and restrictive fiscal policy which were supposed to hold inflation in check. But, the rate of inflation came down marginally due to the adoption of supply-side measures by the Government. At present India is facing the new problem of food inflation as also asset price inflation.

It may be noted that the current inflation is not due to the adoption of economic reforms since July, 1991. It is the result of imbalance between the aggregate demand and aggregate supply. [We will discuss in detail the causes of price inflation in India during the plan period in a different chapter.]

3. Economic Growth

In the decades after economic reforms, India's growth rate, as measured by the annual rate of increase in GDP, has picked up. The overall growth rate as also the sectorwise trends are presented in Table 6.2.

Table 6.2: Average Annual Growth Rate

	1981-82 to 1990-91	1991-92 to 2000-01 2002-07	The Tenth Plan (Average)	2005-06	2006-07	2007-08
Agriculture	3.6	3.2	2.5	5.9	3.8	2.5
Industry	7.1	6.4	8.6	10.6	11.5	9.4
Services	6.7	7.8	9.28	10.9	11.3	10.2
GDP at factor cost	5.6	6.1	7.8	9.4	9.6	8.7

Source: 1. Dr Shankar Acharya, Growth has slowed, *Economic Times*, 22 May, 2001
2. GOI, *Economic Survey*, 2005-06, 2006-07 and 2007-08

Since economic reforms largely neglected the agricultural sector, agricultural growth rate has been the lowest. In contrast, the industry and services sectors grew much faster. The overall growth rate picked up from 5.6% in the pre-reform period (1981-82 to 1991-91) to 6.1% after 10 years of reform (1991-92 to 2001-02). However, the rate of industrial growth slowed down during 1997 to 2002 due to global recession and sluggish demand conditions, attributable to the following two factors: (i) decline in public sector investment and (ii) slowdown of the rate of agricultural growth.

Thereafter it increased to 7.8% during the Tenth Plan period (2002-07), to 9.4% in 2005-06 and to 9.6% in 2006-07. Then it fell to 8.7% in 2007-08. The higher average growth rate attained was largely attributable to higher domestic investment which exceeded one-third of India's GDP in 2007-08. Privatisation and liberalisation of the Indian economy largely contributed to this growth rate.

Thanks to the adoption of various reform measures, India became one of the fastest growing nations of the world. Only China was able to surpass India's overall growth rate. However, due to the global financial crisis (2008-09), which was triggered by sub-prime mortgage crisis in the USA and which spread to other countries due to contagion effect, hit the Indian economy very hard. It led to huge outflow of financial capital from India, leading to a crash of India's stock exchange. It also caused the depreciation of rupee and adversely affected India's export earnings as also real investment. Consequently the rate of growth in the economy slowed down.

4. Unemployment

At the all-India level, the rate of unemployment on current daily status basis rose to 8.3%% in 2004-05. In spite of faster economic growth during the reform period, there is a high rate of unemployment in India at present. This poses a serious threat to India's economic stability. The main cause of such high rate of unemployment is the use of labour-saving techniques of production. The use of capital-intensive techniques of production by most domestic and foreign enterprises or multinational corporations (MNCs) operating in India not only displaces labour already employed but also reduces the number of jobs which can be created with new investment.

Another cause of unemployment in India is the growing competition from the imported products faced by domestic industries which forced many firms to reduce their volume of production levels. The third cause of unemployment is job loss in the public sector due to large-scale disinvestment.

5. Poverty Alleviation

Economic reforms along with stabilisation have resulted in the slowdown in the rate of decline in the poverty ratio in spite of an increase in the rate of GDP growth. The percentage of people living below the poverty line fell from 36 in 1993-94 to 27.44 in 2004-05. This shows a modest 0.74% annual drop in the overall incidence of poverty. This is much less than the reduction in the poverty ratio achieved during the pre-reform period. In fact, the percentage of people living below the poverty line dropped from 51.3 in 1977-78 to 38.9 in 1987-88. This shows a 2.2% decline in the poverty ratio per annum.

6. Inequality

Inequality is a measure of relative poverty. During the reform period, inequality in the distribution of income and wealth increased mainly due to the assignment of a very important role to the private sector, big business houses and MNCs in India's industrial economy. This has gone against the move towards a socialistic pattern of society as declared by the Directive Principles of India's State Policy.

7. Volatility in Exchange Rate and Economic Instability

Economic reforms created volatility in the external value of the rupee which adversely affected the economy. During the reform period, the Government allowed free movements of capital into and out of the country and switched over to market-determined exchange rates and made the rupee partially convertible. Since 2003-04, there occurred huge inflows of financial capital into India, mainly due to portfolio investment through foreign institutional investors (FIIs). This caused appreciation of the rupee which adversely affected India's exports. In addition, huge inflows of dollars got converted into rupees. This led to a sharp increase in the money supply, which, in its turn, generated inflationary pressures in the economy. Along with it, injection of a huge amount of funds by FIIs caused an artificial rise in the prices of shares.

However, 2008-09, the trend was reversed. There was an acute liquidity crisis in the US banking system due to excessive sub-prime housing loans made by the US banks.[1]

In short, globalisation, along with liberalisation of capital flows and market-determined exchange rates and convertibility of the rupee has created a lot of volatility in exchange rate and was fraught with various risks and dangers.

Economic Reforms and Market Failures

The advocates for economic reforms argue in favour of the contraction of the public sector since it breeds operational inefficiency. The failure of the public sector in achieving its goals and thus in promoting faster economic growth is known as *government failure*.

However, they failed to take note of the market failures which are also a fact of life, much like government failures. In the words of J. Stiglitz, "New liberal ideologies assume perfect markets, perfect information and a host of other things which even the best performing market economies cannot satisfy." So what is called for is a balanced approach to government and market since both play a complementary role in promoting a common goal: faster economic growth with distributive justice. Thus the debate on "market vs state" is largely sterile. In truth, due to market failure, it is not possible to rely on the private sector alone to promote sustained economic growth and create adequate employment opportunities in India's labour-surplus economy.

However, markets should be left free to promote maximum social welfare. At the same time it is absolutely essential to regulate markets by the government if the objective of growth with distributive justice is to be achieved.

In truth, the market-based economy of India is not self-correcting and self-regulating. There is, therefore, need for effective control and regulation of the private sector by the Government for achieving self-sustaining growth with price stability and high employment.

It is of paramount importance for India to step up public sector investment in infrastructure. Otherwise sustained economic growth cannot be achieved. It is also necessary for the Government to make adequate investment in social sectors such as education and health care. The Government should also spend money on poverty alleviation programmes since the private sector has hardly any incentive to make such investment. For alleviating poverty, the Government should undertake various rural public works programmes and thus increase its own expenditure. This will serve two purposes at the same time, viz., (i) utilisation of accumulated food stock and (ii) generation of adequate employment opportunities for the poorer and weaker sections of society. The Government is justified in incurring a moderate fiscal deficit for three purposes, viz., investment on economic infrastructure and social sectors as also for creating guaranteed employment opportunities for the poor and needy. The Government is also justified in meeting its investment expenditure by market borrowing. But it should not borrow for meeting its consumption expenditure.

In this context Amartya Sen has rightly cautioned that the closer integration of Indian economy with the global economy may be held in check and India's planned programme of industrialisation and economic development may be thwarted by backwardness in basic education, elementary health care, gender inequality and poor implementation of various land reforms measures. While the architect of India's economic reforms, Dr. M. Singh initiated the correction of governmental overactivity in some fields, the need of the hour is to correct the government underactivity in other areas. Therefore, there is a need for public discussion and debate on these crucial issues.

1. Many people could not pay back their housing loans and wanted to sell their houses. As a result housing prices fell to a very low level and there were just a few buyers of houses. The reason was simple. Most people thought that the prices of houses would fall further. In such a situation, FIIs sold shares of Indian companies held by them. This led to net outflow of capital from India and the rupee started depreciating in terms of the US dollar (and other key currencies).

KEY POINTS

1. ***Need for economic reforms*** **:** It was necessary for the Government of India to undertake various types of reform programmes from July 1991 due to various shortcomings of the mixed economy principles during the 1970s and 1980s: (i) inefficient operation of public enterprises; (ii) increase in the money supply and price inflation, (iii) BOP deficit and foreign exchange crisis, (iv) excessive control over the private sector and (v) increase in the degree of concentration of wealth and economic power in private hands.

2. ***The Washington Consensus*** **:** The term 'Washington consensus' was coined by economist John Williamson in 1989 to describe a set of policy recommendations for developing countries like India. His main focus was on stabilisation, privatisation and liberalisation. Low income countries like India which took IMF loans were forced to satisfy certain conditions, known as structural adjustment policies: stabilisation, privatisation and deregulation. In fact the Washington Action Plan presented a 12-point programme.

3. ***Structural adjustment programmes*** **:** At the insistence of the IMF India adopted various structural adjustment programmes and announced a new economic policy (NEP) in July 1991. The various economic reform measures undertaken by India are the following: (i) dereservation of industries for the public sector, (ii) abolition of the industrial licensing system, (iii) privatisation of public sector enterprises, (iv) welcoming private foreign investment, (v) inviting foreign technology, (vi) trade liberalisation, (vii) currency convertibility and free floating of the Indian rupee.

4. ***Effect of reforms*** **:** Economic reforms generated both favourable and adverse effects. Favourable effects are: (i) increase in exports and foreign exchange reserves, (ii) partial control of inflation, (iii) increase in growth rate. The adverse effects are: (i) an increase in unemployment rate, (ii) increase in the incidence of absolute poverty, (iii) increase in degree of inequality, (iv) volatility in exchange rate and economic instability.

KEY TERMS

Market failure	Government failure
Structural adjustment reforms	Economic reforms
Washington Consensus	Social infrastructure
Globalisation	Currency convertibility
Floating exchange rate	Economic self-sufficiency
Private-public partnership	Economic self-reliance
Delicensing	Privatisation
Liberalisation	Deregulation
Underactivity of government	Overactivity of government

ASSIGNMENTS

1. Highlight the crises of Indian planning during the 1970s and 1980s.
2. Discuss briefly the rationale of economic reforms in India since July 1991.
3. Write an explanatory note on public sector reforms in a mixed economy.
4. List the twelve elements of the Washington Action Plan.
5. Make an overall assessment of structural adjustment programmes undertaken by the Government of India during the reform period.
6. Make a critical review of economic reforms. Do you support the view of the critics that reforms should be disutilised?

Part-II

Analysis of Certain Broad Aggregates

7. The Circular Flow of Income and National Income Accounting
8. The Sources and Uses of National Income
9. The Keynesian Model of Income Determination
10. Income Determination in Extended Models
11. The Consumption Function
12. The Theory of Multiplier
13. The Theory of Investment and the Acceleration Principle
14. Employment and Unemployment

CHAPTER 7

The Circular Flow of Income and National Income Accounting

> *In the statistical measurement of national income the question reduces itself to what commodities and services should be excluded because, by and large, they do not contribute to the goal of economic activity — satisfaction of consumers' wants.*
>
> Simon S. Kuznets
>
> National Income: A Summary of Findings

THE CONCEPT OF NATIONAL INCOME

The three main factors of production, viz., land, labour, capital employed by the fourth factor, viz, organiser or entrepreneur together produce a certain amount of goods in an economy per period, usually an accounting year. This is known as Gross Domestic Product (GDP) of a country which is slightly different from its Gross National Product (GNP). GNP is another name of the country's national income (NI) because production of goods and services generates an equivalent amount of income per period. National income is the pure monetary value of all final goods and services produced by an economy in an accounting year. Three points may be noted at the outset.

1. Monetary Measure

National Income is a monetary measure, not a physical measure. The reason is that if we add up the different goods and services valued in an economy, the end result will be a meaningless jumble. So money is used as the measuring rod of every single item which is produced in an economy and is, therefore, called the unit of account.

2. Adjustment for Price Level Changes

In order to find out changes in the values of output from one year to the next, we have to adjust national income for price level changes. This adjustment becomes necessary in times of inflation (or deflation). Value is the product of price and quantity. If the value of society's output increases in a year, it may be either due to an increase in price or an increase in quantity. If adjustment is made for price level changes (i.e:, inflation or deflation), we can find out how much physical output has increased over a period of time.

3. Avoidance of Double (Multiple) Counting

Sometimes national income accountants count the same item twice or thrice. The reason is that the output of one industry (such as coal) is used as an input in various other industries (such as steel, automobile, furniture, etc.). So the same item may pass through different stages of production before reaching the market and be sold as a final good. This creates a problem, known as double (multiple) counting. The problem can be avoided by including only the money value of final goods in national income and excluding the value of raw materials and intermediate goods.

THREE INTERPRETATIONS OF THE CONCEPT OF NATIONAL INCOME

In fact, there are three different interpretations of the concept of national income. It is the total value of final goods produced. It is the total flow of incomes generated in the production process. And it is the total of final expenditure, i.e., different types of expenditure on final goods. It may be noted that every unit of output sold in the market generates an equivalent amount of income. Similarly, every expenditure, made on goods and services generates an equivalent amount of income (since any form of expenditure always generates some income). So the national income accounting system of a country shows the equivalence of three final figures — the value of output of goods and services, the value of income and the value of expenditure.

A SIMPLE TWO-SECTOR ECONOMY

To explain the above ideas we take the case of a simple two-sector economy. The two sectors are households and business firms. Households are the consumers and suppliers of productive factors and business firms are the producers. Firms receive various factors of production to produce different goods and services. The owners of the factors are given reward in terms of money for their respective contributions to the production process. So factor incomes such as rent, wages, interest and profits arise from the production of goods and services. The sum of factor incomes is equal to the total revenue or sales value of net output (i.e., gross output minus depreciation or the wear and tear of capital) because factor payments are made from such sales value. In other words, total sales revenue received by producing units goes to factor suppliers in the form of rent, wages, interest and profits. The recipients of these factor incomes spend their earnings on the society's output of goods and services. In other words, incomes earned become equal to expenditures made.

The sales value of aggregate output is equal to the sum of all factor payments

Initially income flows from firms to households because households supply the factor inputs to firms and firms buy the inputs by paying money. The money paid out by firms comes back to the firms in the form of expenditure which households make on the goods produced and sold by firms.

Thus it is clear that national income = national product = national expenditure. Alternatively stated, there are three ways of arriving at an estimate of the national income of a country, viz.,

(i) the sum of the money values of all final goods and services produced in an economy in an accounting year;

(ii) the sum of all factor incomes, in cash or in kind, earned by the factors of production; and

(iii) the sum of expenditures made by consumers as also net investment expenditure made by firms.

In a two-sector economy total final expenditure has two components: (a) household consumption and (b) business investment. In a three-sector economy, to be considered later, total final expenditure has another component, viz., government expenditure on goods and services (but not transfer payments). In an open economy, with foreign trade (i.e., exports and imports), total final expenditure also includes net exports which are the difference between total exports and total imports.

There is no doubt that the sum of all factor incomes, the sum of the money value of all products and the sum of all final expenditures will yield the same result. Thus the routes are different but the destination is the same. Thus the question arises why do we look at national income from three different angles. The answer to this question is plain and simple. The three different ways of presenting a country's national income highlights three different economic activities, viz., production of goods and services, distribution of factor incomes and expenditure of income earned on final goods and services produced.

THE CIRCULAR FLOW OF INCOME

A study of the different methods of measuring a country's national income starts with a simple model which is called the Circular Flow Model of National Income or the Circular Flow Model of the Economy. It is so called because production is a continuous process. So is the flow of factor services from households to business firms (or supply firms) and the flow of income from firms to households in exchange. The flow of income leads to another flow, viz., the expenditure flow. Households spend their money on various goods and services. So there is a flow of expenditure from households to firms and there is a flow of goods and services from firms to households. These three types of flows— of factors of production, of money and of goods and services—are shown by the circular flow model of the economy. The three types of flows are the following:

(i) Households supply factor inputs to firms. This is a direct flow from households to firms.

(ii) Firms pay money to households against the factor inputs that they receive. This is a reverse flow.

(iii) Households use the money to make purchases of consumption goods from business firms. This is a direct flow. And business firms supply consumption goods to households. This is a reverse flow and the process is complete. In Fig. 7.1, we present a simple circular flow diagram for a two-sector economy.

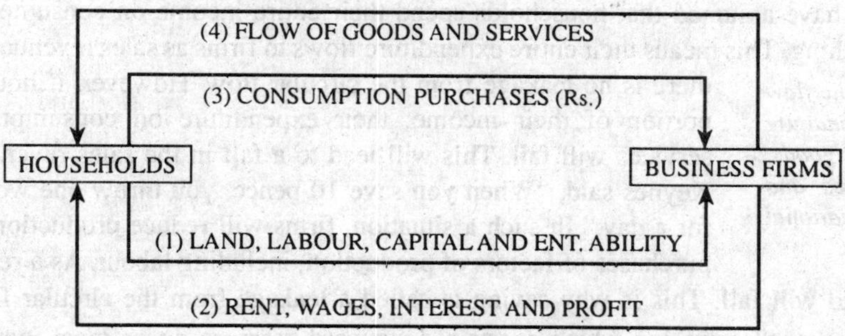

Fig. 7.1: Circular Flow of Income and Expenditure in a Two-Sector Economy

Four flows are shown in the diagram—two direct flows, viz., (1), (3) and two reverse flows, viz., (2) and (4).

In the lower part of this figure we see direct flow of factors of production from households to business firms (1). Firms purchase the factors and make payments to households in the form of rent, wages, interest and profits. These money payments are indicated by the reverse flow (2).

In the upper part of the figure we see that households spend their income by purchasing consumption goods from firms. They make the payments in rupees. This is how firms derive their revenues from the sale of goods and services. This is direct flow of money from households to firms (3). And firms supply goods and services to households against money payments. This is a reverse flow (4).

Thus the above circular flow diagram shows two types of flows:

(i) two direct flows — (1) and (3) and

(ii) two reverse flows — (2) and (4).

Three types of flows occur between the two sectors, viz., flows of factors of production, money and goods and services. Money flows twice—once from firms to households in the form of factor payments and from households to firms in the form of consumption expenditure.

The circular flow does not remain constant at all times. It is high in a year of prosperity (growing) and low in a year of recession or depression or declining economy activity.

The circular flow continues period after period and shows how the economy functions. This circular flow diagram also shows how national income circulates.

Assumptions

We have drawn the circular flow diagram and explained it by making certain restrictive assumptions.

1. First, we have assumed that households spend their entire income. They do not save anything.
2. Similarly, we have assumed that firms do not save any portion of their profits.
3. We have assumed that the government does not play any role in the economy. It does not collect any taxes from households and firms. It does not pay any subsidies to them either. In addition, the government does not buy any goods and services from the private sector.
4. We assume that the economy is closed. It does not export anything to other countries and it does not import anything from them either.

In Fig. 7.1 we have explained the circular flow model of a closed economy with no saving and no role of the government on the basis of the above assumption.

We may now relax the assumptions one by one. First we extend the two-sector circular flow model by taking into account saving and investment. Then we will proceed further.

THE CIRCULAR FLOW OF INCOME WITH SAVING AND INVESTMENT

Saving reduces the flow of household expenditure on consumption goods, business revenues and thus the size of national income

So long we have assumed that households spend their entire income on consumption goods and do not save anything. This means their entire expenditure flows to firms as sales revenue. Consequently, there is no leakage from the circular flow. However, if households save a portion of their income, their expenditure on consumption goods and services will fall. This will lead to a fall in the sales revenue of firms. As Keynes said, "When you save 10 pence, you throw one worker out of job for a day." In such a situation, firms will reduce production and thus their purchases of factors of production, including labour. As a result the income of the household will fall. This is why saving is called a leakage from the circular flow of income.

What is a leakage? Anything which exerts a downward pressure on national income is called a leakage from the circular flow of income.

Since saving leakage is offset by investment injection, the flow of expenditure and thus income does not diminish

However, national income will not fall if savings return to the circular flow in the form of investment spending. Usually households save and businesses invest. Households are called surplus-generating units and businesses deficit-spending units. These two units do not interact directly. There is a set of institutions such as banks, post offices, insurance companies, etc. which collect the savings of the households and make loans to business firms. Here we assume that one household does not borrow from any other household. Households are the savers and businesses are the investors. Businesses borrow funds from financial institutions for buying machines, setting up factories and expanding the size of existing factories. They do this for expanding their capacity to produce more goods and services and make more profits. Since household savings are converted into investment expenditure by businesses, the flow of expenditure and thus income does not diminish even if there is saving leakage.

In Fig. 7.2 we illustrate the circular flow of income with saving and investment. We now see that the saving of the household sector flows to the business sector in the form of loans and advances. This is how saving is balanced by investment and the circular flow of money income continues. Although savers and investors are two different groups of people, saving is equated to investment by a well-functioning financial system.

Just as saving is a leakage from the circular flow of income, investment is an injection into the circular flow.

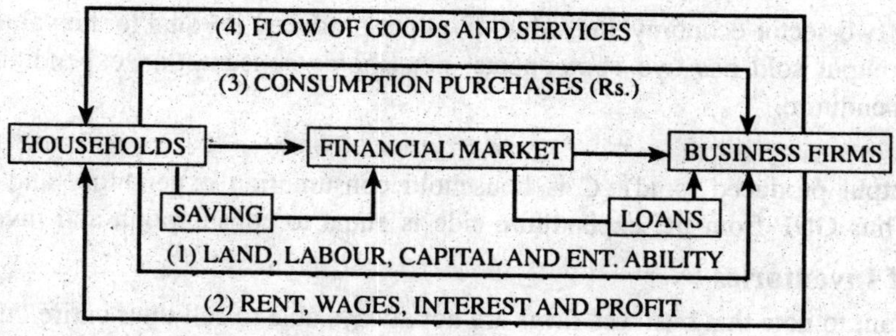

Fig. 7.2: Circular Flow of Income and Expenditure with Savings and Investment

What is an injection? Anything which exerts an expansionary pressure on national income is called an injection.

For the circular flow of money to continue, withdrawal of money in the form of saving has to be balanced (offset) by injection of money in the form of investment.

Any imbalance between planned saving and planned investment will cause national income to rise or fall. Only when the two are equal will the circular flow of income continue at the same rate. How is saving equated to investment?

According to the classicists every imbalance between saving and investment gets corrected through changes in the rate of interest. However, this view has been refuted by Keynes. According to Keynes, actual saving of an economy is always equated to actual investment. This is known as saving-investment equality (identity), since it always holds. But planned (desired) saving is not aways equal to planned (desired) investment. There are two reasons for this. Firstly, savers and investors are two different groups of people. Some people save and others invest. The major portion of saving comes from the household sector but investment is made by business firms. Secondly, the motives for saving and investment are different. Households save for certain personal reasons such as maintaining the same consumption level after retirement, children's education, daughters' marriage, etc. But business firms make investment for making profits. For these two reasons there can be divergence between planned saving of the household sector and planned investment of the business sector. This implies that the circular flow of income will not continue at the same rate period after period. But the divergence gets corrected through income changes. National income keeps on increasing or falling until and unless such divergence disappears. Since in a free enterprise economy income may not rise or fall to the desired extent through market forces, the government has to take appropriate measures to maintain a steady level of income. This virtually amounts to controlling economic fluctuations (business cycles) and stabilising the economy. This point will be discussed in detail in a later chapter in the context of the Keynesian theory of income determination.

SAVING-INVESTMENT IDENTITY (EQUALITY) IN NATIONAL INCOME ACCOUNTS

Two components of aggregate expenditure are consumption and investment

We have already noted that in a two-sector economy without government and foreign trade, planned saving of the household sector may differ from planned investment of the business sector for two reasons. However, in national income accounts, we consider actual (realised) saving and actual (realised) investment. These two are always equal in an accounting sense and their equality is known as saving-investment equality. We now prove this equality in a simple way.

In a simple two-sector economy, the value of output produced is equal to the value of output sold. The value of output sold has two components: households consumption expenditure and business investment expenditure.

$$Y \equiv C + I \qquad \ldots (1)$$

where Y is output produced (sold), C is household consumption expenditure and I is investment expenditure. Thus GNP from the expenditure side is equal to consumption and investment.

Treatment of Inventories

Inventories are taken as a part of business investment

It is important to note that business firms are not always able to sell their entire output. Sometimes they are left with unsold stocks. This is added to the inventories of goods. In national income accounts an increase in inventories of goods is taken as a part of actual investment. It is assumed that the owners of the firms have themselves purchased a portion of their output for future sales.

DIVISION OF TOTAL OUTPUT BETWEEN CONSUMPTION AND SAVING

Saving is that part of national income which is not spent on consumption goods

We now look at national income (GNP) from the side of its disposition. In the absence of taxes, national income is largely spent on consumption goods and partly saved. According to Paul Samuelson, consumption and saving are mirror image concepts because any part of national income which is not spent on consumption goods is automatically saved. Thus saving is a residue. So from the side of disposition of national income we have

$$Y \equiv C + S \qquad \ldots (2)$$

where S is saving.

Now by combining (1) and (2) we get

$$C + I \equiv C + S \qquad \ldots (3)$$

The value of output sold is equal to aggregate expenditure on goods and services produced

This identity shows that the value of output produced (sold), i.e., $C + I$ is identically equal to the division of national income into consumption and saving. In equation (3) C on the left side is the demand for consumer goods and C on the right hand side is the supply of consumer goods. Thus if we assume that the goods market is in equilibrium the C on the l.h.s of (3) will be equal to C on the r.h.s. Therefore we cancel C from both sides and rewrite (3) as follows:

$$I \equiv S \qquad \ldots (4)$$

This proves that in a simple two-sector economy, investment is identically equal to saving.[1]

THE CIRCULAR FLOW OF INCOME WITH GOVERNMENT

The government affects the economy in four main ways: (1) taxing, (2) spending, (3) borrowing and (4) purchasing goods and services from households and firms. The government spends money on public goods such as social capital or infrastructure (which consists of roads, highways, bridges, power plants, railways, etc.) but also merit goods like defence, education, etc. In addition government, in developing countries like India, buy food from farmers for distribution through fair price (ration) shops. Moreover, most of the medicines distributed through government hospitals are purchased from the private firms. These different types of government expenditure add to the money flows which are shown in Fig. 7.3.

Here we see that the government purchases of goods and services from the private sector— both firms and households — represent flow of money spending on various goods and services. Government

1. For the sake of simplicity, we assume that only households save. But in reality business firms also save. This is done from their undistributed (retained) profits. In our study of national income accounting we refer to private saving which is the sum of household saving and business saving.

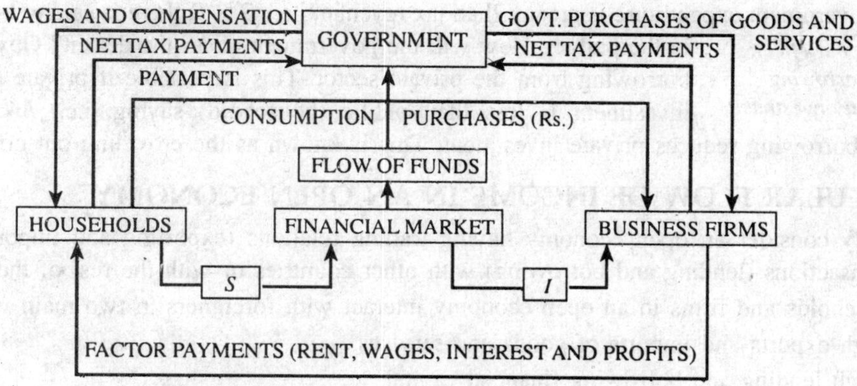

Fig. 7.3: The Circular Flow of Income in a Three-Sector Economy

expenditure is financed in three main ways, viz., taxes, sale of assets (in the form of disinvestment of public sector units), and borrowing either from the private sector by selling bonds (called market borrowing) or from the central bank (called deficit financing).

Firstly, the government tries to cover its current expenditure from net tax revenue, which is the difference between tax revenue less transfer payments received by people from the government in the form of unemployment compensation, pensions, interest on government bonds, etc.

A rise in the rate of interest due to government borrowing causes private investment to fall

However, if the tax revenue of the government is not enough to cover its current expenditure fully, the government has to borrow from the private sector. This is indicated in the Fig. 7.3 by the upward pointing arrow which shows flow of loanable funds from the financial market to the government. When the government competes with the private sector to borrow funds, the demand for loanable funds increases and the consequent shortage of funds leads to a rise in the market rate of interest. A rise in the rate of interest implies an increase in the cost of loanable funds. As a result both households and business firms reduce their borrowing for consumption and investment purposes. Two things happen due to a rise in the rate of interest. First, households consume less and save more. Second, business firms make less investment. So private investment falls. Thus a rise in the rate of interest has two effects — one is favourable to the economy but the other is not.

Thus government activities affect the economy in more ways than one. Total expenditure flow in an economy has now three components, as shown below

$$E = C + I + G \qquad \ldots (5)$$

where E is total expenditure, C is consumption, I is investment and G is government expenditure.

Total income (Y) is now divided into three parts, as shown below

$$Y = C + S + T \qquad \ldots (6)$$

Since aggregate expenditure has to be equal to income received (Y), by combining equations (5) and (6), we get

$$C + I + G = C + S + T \qquad \ldots (7)$$

Since the demand for consumption goods, shown on the l.h.s., is equal to the supply of consumption goods shown on the r.h.s., we cancel C from equation (7) and get

$$I + G = S + T \qquad \ldots (8)$$

If we transfer T to the l.h.s and I to the r.h.s., we get

$$G - T = S - I \qquad \ldots (9)$$

Now if government expenditure is greater than tax revenue, i.e., $G > T$, there is said to be a deficit in the budget. How will the government cover the deficit? Obviously by borrowing from the private sector. This is possible if private (business) investment is less than public (household) saving, i.e., $I < S$. Thus government borrowing reduces private investment. This is known as the crowding out effect.

The crowding out effect: government borrowing reduces private investment

THE CIRCULAR FLOW OF INCOME IN AN OPEN ECONOMY

We finally consider an open economy having trading relations (exporting and importing) and financial transactions (lending and borrowing) with other countries or with the rest of the world.

The households and firms in an open economy interact with foreigners in two main ways:

(i) through exports and imports of goods and services

(ii) through lending and borrowing financial capital.

That portion of goods and services produced within the domestic territory but sold to foreigners is called exports. Exports are the excess of domestic production over domestic consumption. By contrast, that portion of the output of goods and services produced abroad but consumed by domestic households and used by firms is called imports. Fig. 7.4 shows the additional money flows which occur in an economy when its interactions with the rest of the world are taken into consideration.

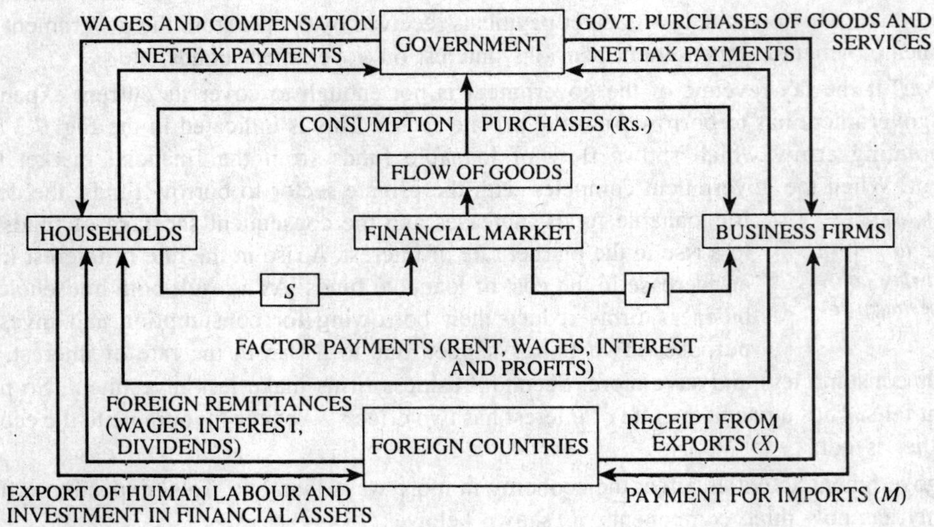

Fig. 7.4: The Circular Flow of Income in a Four-Sector Economy

Individuals do not directly export goods and services. Only business firms do. There is inflow of money from foreign countries to domestic firms when they export a portion of their goods and services, shown by the symbol (X). Similarly there is outflow of money from domestic firms to foreign countries when the former import certain goods and services (and is shown by the symbol M). If exports (X) are equal to imports (M) there is said to be a trade balance. If exports are greater (less) than imports, there is a trade surplus (deficit).

A trade surplus makes a country a lender in the international financial market

In an open economy there is an additional flow. If a country has a trade surplus (i.e., if $X > M$), it will lend its surplus funds to foreigners and thus receive foreign financial assets such as fixed interest bonds or equity shares[1]. Thus a surplus country is a lender and a deficit country is a borrower in the international financial market.

1. This is now happening on a much larger scale than before due to the integration of the world's capital (financial) markets.

In fact, when exports exceed imports, there is net capital inflow in a country. So domestic savers will now lend their surplus funds to foreigners in order to acquire foreign financial assets.

On the contrary, if imports exceed exports, there is a trade deficit. In this case domestic households and firms will borrow from foreigners to pay for the excess of imports over exports. So foreigners will acquire domestic financial assets and there is net capital outflow from the country.

In an open economy net exports are an additional component of total final expenditure

The circular flow which occurs in an open economy includes a new item called net export which is the difference between export and import and is expressed as $X - M$. The minus sign implies that imports are to be subtracted from the total final expenditure since imports represent expenditure on foreign goods. Thus in an open economy

$$Y = C + I + G + X - M$$
$$= C + I + G \pm NX \qquad \ldots \quad (10)$$

where $NX = X - M$ = net export. This can be positive or negative.

Since national income can be consumed on domestic and foreign goods, saved or paid in taxes to the government, we have:

$$Y = C + I + G + X = C + S + T + M$$

or, $I + G + X = S + T + M$, ignoring C

or, $I + G + X - M = S + T$

or, $I + G + NX = S + T$, ignoring the negative sign from NX for simplicity ... (11)

Thus, from (11) we see that in an open economy the sum of private investment (I), government purchases net of transfers (G) and net exports (NX) must equal the sum of savings and taxes. National income of a country now includes another component, called factor income from abroad. Such income may be received by Indians from foreign countries in the form of wages, salaries, interest and dividends, as shown in the l.h.s. of the bottom part of Fig. 7.4. These incomes are received for supplying factor services to foreigners in the form of labour power and financial capital which includes both debt capital on which interest is earned and risk capital from which dividend comes.

NATIONAL INCOME AND NATIONAL PRODUCT

National income refers to the sum of all incomes earned by the people of a country through their contribution to the production process. This not only includes income earned within the domestic territory of a country but also any income earned abroad. And, as we have already noted, national income is related to national product since production of goods and services is the source of all incomes. In a two-sector economy national income is equal to national product (ignoring government and depreciation of fixed capital). The owners of the four factors, viz., land, labour, capital and enterprises derive their incomes in the form of rent, wages, interest and profits by making their respective contributions to the production of goods and services. In fact, from the money value of national output produced and sold, factor payments are made. The sum of all factor payments is a country's national income. This part is illustrated in Fig. 7.5.

Households supply the productive factors to businesses and get paid in terms of money. This is shown in the bottom half of Fig. 7.5. It we add the money incomes of the four factors taking part in the production process we arrive at national income. Since incomes earned by productive factors are, in fact, different components of costs of production, national income (GNI) is measured at factor cost. For example, total wage bill is income to the labourers. But from the business firms' point of view, wage payment constitutes cost of production, viz., labour cost or variable cost, as is taught in microeconomics.

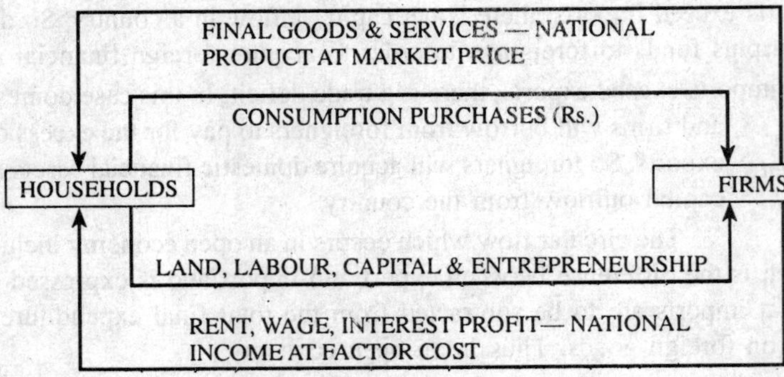

Fig. 7.5: The Equivalence of National Income and National Product

On the other half, if we add up the money value of all final goods produced by business firms and sold to households in the top half of the diagram, we arrive at another final figure, viz., gross national product (GNP). It is measured at market price. In fact, GNP is the collection of various final goods and services produced in an economy in an accounting year. And if we multiply the quantity of each good or service produced by its market price, we arrive at the total value of final goods and services which is indeed national product (or national income from the output side).

The equivalence of national income and national product can be shown by another diagram. See Fig. 7.6.

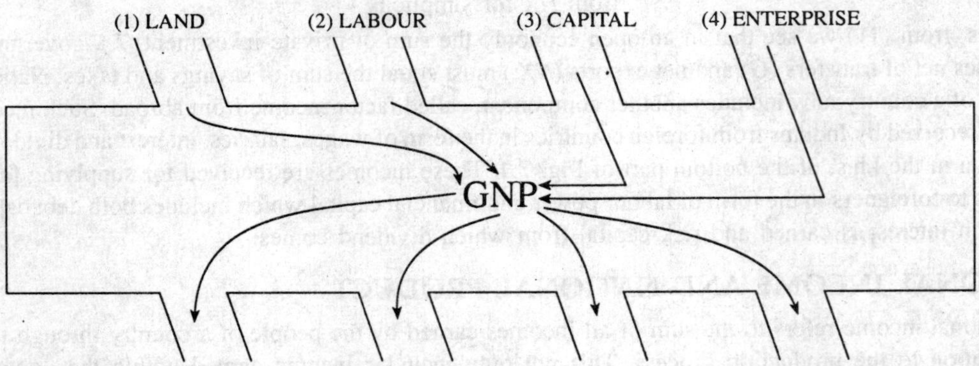

Fig. 7.6: The Equivalence of National Income and National Output

In the top half of Fig. 7.6, we see that the four factors make their respective contributions to GNP. In fact, GNP is the joint contribution of all four factors.[1] And national output is paid out in the form of rent, wages, interest and profits as is shown in the bottom part of the diagram. If we add up these factor incomes, we arrive at a final figure, called national income. Thus from one side national income is the total value of all final goods produced in an economy. From another side, it is the total of all factor incomes. This equivalance is shown more clearly in Fig. 7.7.

Thus, the gross value of output produced in an economy is identically equal to gross income received by the factor owners. This shows the apparent equivalence of national output and national income. However, we will see later in this chapter that an adjustment has to be made to arrive at national income from national product. The reason is that national product is measured at market price and national

1. In fact, long ago William Petty said, "Land is mother of output which is produced by society and labour is the father."

National product	=	The total money value of all final goods and services produced in an economy per annum	=	1. Wages and compensation 2. Rent 3. Interest 4. Profits and dividends	= NI

Fig. 7.7: The Equivalence of National Product and National Income

income is measured at factor cost. There is discrepancy between the two measures due to indirect taxes and subsidies which distort market prices of goods and services.

THEORY AND REALITY

In reality, there is divergence between national output and national product for at least two reasons. These are the following:

NI is less than national product for two reasons: (i) depreciation and (ii) indirect taxes

1. Depreciation: In reality, firms set aside a portion of their output to make provision for depreciation, i.e., wear and tear of fixed capital. Depreciation refers to the loss of value of fixed capital due to its contribution to the production process. The amount of depreciation expenditure is not available for distribution among factors in the form of income.

2. Indirect taxes: The government also collects a portion of society's output in the form of indirect (commodity) taxes. So income received by factor owners is reduced by the amount of taxes they pay on the goods and services which they purchase.

So the basic point to note is that an increase in the output of goods and services will lead to an increase in national income only if no provision is made for depreciation and no indirect tax is imposed on commodities.

But in reality, these do not happen. In fact, there are various concepts of national income. We now turn to these concepts and discuss them one by one.

VARIOUS CONCEPTS OF NATIONAL INCOME

The key concepts associated with national income accounting are gross national product (GNP), gross domestic product (GDP), net national product (NNP), national income (NI), net factor income from abroad (NFIFA), personal income (PI) and personal disposable income (PDI). We may now discuss these concepts one by one.

Gross National Product (GNP)

The GNP is the most important measure of a country's annual output of goods and services. In modern terminology, it is equal to an economy's aggregate supply. GNP is the total money value of all final goods and services produced in an economy in an accounting year. It may be expressed as follows:

GNP is a monetary measure and not a physical measure

GNP = price of bread × quantity of bread + price of orange × the quantity of orange + price of cars × the number of cars produced + price of haircuts × the number of haircuts done and so on.

Four points may be noted in this context :

1. Measurement at market prices: Since different goods and services have different units of measurement, money is used as the common measuring rod (yardstick). Thus GNP can be defined as a collection of goods and services reduced to a common basis by being measured in terms of money.

Since GNP is a monetary measure, if we are to accurately measure the changes in the volume of output, between two years, say 2012 and 2013, new GNP has to be adjusted for the annual rate of inflation.

2. Avoidance of double counting: Recall that (p. 24) while measuring GNP accounting it is necessary to count all goods and services produced in an accounting year only once, not twice or several times. No doubt many goods pass through different stages of production before reaching final buyers. As a result parts and components of various goods such as TV sets, cars, refrigerators, mobile phones, etc. are bought and sold a number of times. To avoid such double or multiple counting, it is necessary to include only final goods and exclude all purchases involving intermediate goods and raw materials.

The final goods are those which are not used for further production, i.e., production of any other good and is destroyed after consumption or use. By contrast, an intermediate good is one which is used for further production, i.e., production of final goods and services. Intermediate goods are excluded from GNP simply because the money value of all final goods itself includes the money value of all intermediate goods (and, of course, raw materials). For example, if we calculate the market value of cars produced, we need not calculate the value of tyres and tubes, paint, steel, glass, etc., which have gone into the production of a final good — the finished car. If, through mistake, we calculate the market value of all the parts and components of cars, along with the market value of cars, there will be counting of the same item twice or a number of times and we will arrive at any exaggerated value (inflated figure) of GNP.

If we include raw materials and intermediate goods while calculating national income, we will overestimate it

3. Time period: Since GNP has a time dimension (i.e., so much per period), it is a flow variable. GNP is a measure of the total value of goods and services produced in an economy in an accounting year. Therefore two things are to be excluded from GNP:

(i) purchase and sale of old goods such as old houses, factories, cars, refrigerators and other second hand goods. [Such second hand goods may be both consumption goods and capital goods like machines, or even steel or automobile assembly plant.]

(ii) purchase and sale of financial assets such as fixed interest bonds or equity shares.

The reason is easy to find out. The above two transactions do not involve any current production of goods and services. Recall that GNP is the market value of all currently produced goods and services in an accounting year.

4. Net factor (property) income from abroad: GNP is the total market value of goods and services produced by the normal residents of a country. These residents may be owners of domestic and foreign companies. No doubt, many foreign companies have set up production units in India such as KFC, McDonalds, Sony, Ford, Marks and Spencer and so on. These companies are largely owned by foreigners but carry on business in India. They produce various goods and services from their plants located within India's domestic territory. They generate income for Indians who work in such companies. At the same time such companies repatriate a portion of their profits to their countries of origin— the USA, Japan, the UK etc. Just as Indians earn income from foreign companies located within India's domestic territory, foreigners earn incomes from Indian companies located in foreign countries. Thus on the one hand we receive factor income from abroad and, on the other hand, we make payments to foreigners. The difference between the two is known as net factor income from abroad (NFIFA). It has the following four components[1]:

The difference between what Indians earn for supplying factors of production to foreigners and what foreigners earn for supplying their factors to India is NFIFA

(i) Net compensation (consisting of wages, salaries, bonus to employees, etc.) which is the income of labour or the suppliers of the human factor.

1. Here we use the term 'net' to refer to the point that it is the difference between what we receive from foreigners for supplying our factors to them and what they receive from us for supplying their services to us.

(ii) Net income from property, i.e., rent and interest.

(iii) Net income from entrepreneurship, i.e., from risk taking and uncertainty bearing and includes profits and distributed dividends.

(iv) Net undistributed dividends or net retained earnings of the Indian companies carrying on business in foreign countries.

A few examples will make the concept of NFIFA clear.

(i) Many Indians who are working in Gulf countries send a portion of their incomes to India for the maintenance of their family members.

(ii) If an Indian buys a share from an American company and earns a dividend of say, $ 1,000 in the current year, it will be a part of India's national income or GNP.

(iii) If a German engineer works in India in a certain project such as construction of a bridge or a new railway network, he will receive income from India. And he may send a certain portion of his income to Germany for the maintenance of his family there.

(iv) If Mr. L. Mittal sends a portion of profits earned from his steel plants located in the UK, to India, it will be part of India's factor income (earned from abroad).

Transition from GDP to National Income

The following steps are involved in arriving at national income from GDP process:

Step 1: Deduct depreciation to arrive at NDP at market price.

Step 2: Subtract indirect taxes and add subsidies to arrive at NDP at factor cost.

Step 3: Add net factor income from abroad to NDP_{FC} to arrive at NNP_{FC} which is indeed national income.

FIVE MAIN COMPONENTS OF GNP

It may now be noted that GNP has the following four components:

(i) ***Household consumption expenditure*** **(*C*):** The value of final consumer goods and services produced in a year and consumed by domestic households. This is denoted by the symbol *C*. This is the largest component of GNP in any country.

(ii) ***Gross private investment*** **(*I*):** The money value of all new capital goods produced in India in an accounting year such as machines, transport equipment, structures, as also new factories set up within a year. To these we have to add the inventories of goods such as raw materials (paint), semi-finished goods (such as chasis) as also inventories of consumer goods such as cars produced but not sold in the current year. All these come under the broad heading gross private investment (*I*).

(iii) ***Government purchase of goods and services*** **(*G*):** The value of goods and services produced by the central government (not state or local governments), denoted as *G*.

(iv) ***Net exports*** **(*X-M*):** Net exports (*NX*) are equal to the difference between the value of goods exported by India (in an accounting year) and the value of goods imported by it.

(v) ***Net factor income from abroad*** **(*NFIA*):** It is the difference between the factor incomes earned from abroad less factor payment made to foreigners in an accounting year. Factor incomes are earned by Indians from abroad in various ways. Indian workers employed abroad earn wages and salaries. Similarly many Indian individuals and corporations have acquired foreign assets—both physical and financial. They have acquired factories, buildings, offices, commercial space, etc. located abroad. They have also invested in foreign bonds, stocks, etc. and deposited money in foreign banks. From these they earn rent, interest and dividends. Indian companies also earn profits from the factories they have set up in foreign territories. Factor incomes are paid to foreigners because both foreign individuals and companies from the USA, Japan, Germany and other countries have not only been employed by Indians in their enterprises located in India but also because foreigners have acquired real assets in the form of property such as factories, office buildings, land as also financial assets such as bonds and shares of Indian companies. Two types of income accrue to them from such factors, viz., rent and interest. Foreigners also earn profits from the enterprises which they have set up in India.

The difference between the two—factor incomes earned from abroad and factor payments made to foreign—is NFIFA. This is the last component of GNP.

GROSS DOMESTIC PRODUCT (GDP)

The difference between GNP at market price and GDP at factor cost arises due to NFIFA

Gross domestic product is the total money value of all final goods and services produced by both resident Indians as also non-resident Indians within India's own domestic territory. It does not include NFIFA. If NFIFA is zero, which is highly unlikely, the two will be equivalent.

So it is important to note the following:

$$GNP_{MP} = GDP_{MP} - NFIFA$$

$$\text{or, } GDP_{MP} = GNP_{MP} + NFIFA$$

If NFIFA is negative then GNP will be less than GDP

It is interesting to note that in most countries NFIFA is just 0.5% or so of GDP. Therefore there is not much difference between the two except in case of Kuwait. If NFIFA is negative, then we arrive at a surprising result: GNP is less than GDP.

A simple example will make the point clear. Suppose GDP of India now is Rs. 1,000 crore at market price and NFIFA is Rs. 100 crore.

Then GNP = GDP – NFIFA
= Rs.1,000 cr. – Rs.100 cr.
= Rs.900 cr.

If by coincidence, GDP = GNP, then NFIFA must be zero.

Economic Insight: NFIFA and NX

A related point may be noted in this context. NFIFA is not to be equated with net exports (i.e., difference between exports and imports) which are a part of both GNP and GDP. India's exports are a part of India's GDP which are sold to foreign buyers. But exports are not the same thing as factor income earned from abroad. By contrast, imports are the value of output of foreigners purchased by Indians. Therefore imports are not a part of India's GDP or GNP either. We include net exports in both GDP and in GNP. Thus net exports are different from NFIFA.

Thus we arrive at GDP by adding up the first four components of GNP.

$$GDP = C + I + G + NX$$

where $NX = (X - M)$

In Fig. 7.8 we show four different concepts of national product.

NET NATIONAL PRODUCT (NNP) AT MARKET PRICE

NNP or national income at market price is GNP minus depreciation

If we subtract depreciation or consumption of fixed capital from GNP at market price, we arrive at net national product at market price. Depreciation refers to the wear and tear of fixed capitals, such as plants, equipment and machinery due to their use in the production of various goods and services. If no provision is made for annual depreciation, a society's stock of capital will completely disappear after some time and the flow of goods and services cannot be maintained.

NATIONAL INCOME (NI) [AT FACTOR COST] OR NNP_{FC}

National income is measured at factor cost, by adding the incomes of the four factors—land, labour, capital and organisation—which make their respective contributions to current year's net production. Although rent, wage, interest and profit are incomes of the productive factors, from the producing units'

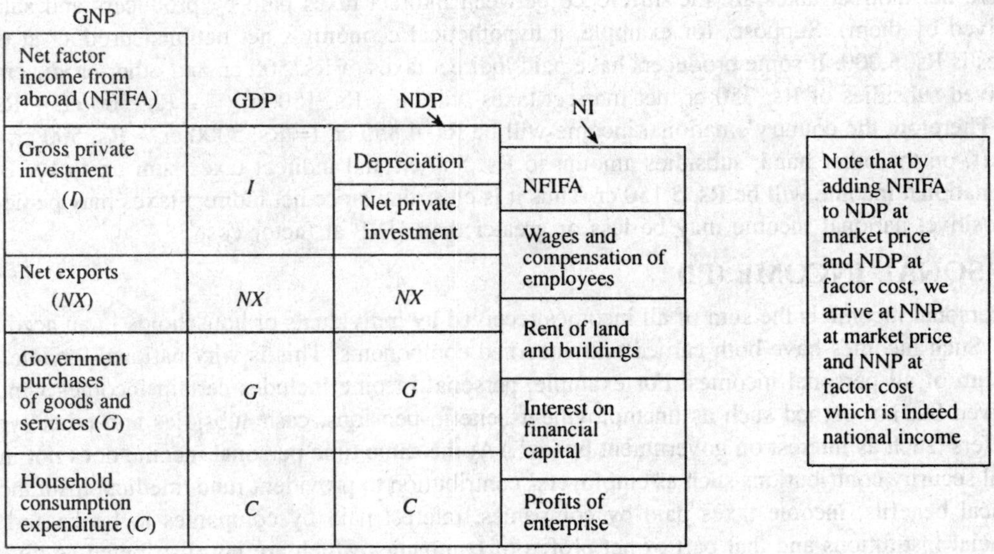

Fig. 7.8: Different Concepts of Income

point of view, these are factor payments or factor costs. For example, wage is the income of the labourer.

In fact, NNP at factor cost is called national income

But for the company making wage payment, it is wage (labour) cost. In a broad sense, i.e., from a society's point of view, national income at factor cost, or simply national income shows the cost incurred by society in terms of payments made to various economic resources used to produce NNP. In this context, we may note the difference between two measures of national income, viz., the market price measure and the factor cost measure.

Net Indirect Business Taxes and Factor Cost Adjustment

There is a divergence between national income at market price and national income at factor cost due to the fact that the market price of almost everything which is produced and sold includes indirect business taxes, i.e., indirect taxes paid by the producers to the government less subsidies received by them. Indirect taxes and subsidies create distortions by causing market price of output to be different from the factor incomes generated through the production process. It may be noted that indirect taxes such as sales tax or VAT cause the market prices of the taxed goods and services to exceed their true costs. By comparison, subsidies[1] (negative taxes) cause market prices of the subsidised items to fall below their true costs. A simple example will make the point clear. Suppose the sales (retail) price of an electric fan is Rs. 495. It includes a VAT

National income is calculated by subtracting net indirect taxes from NNP

of 10% or Rs. 45. (The ex-factory price was Rs. 450). This means that even if the fan is sold at Rs. 495, the factors of production employed (or used) in the production and distribution of it would receive only Rs. 450 per fan. By contrast, a per unit subsidy causes the market price to be less than the factor cost. Suppose there is a subsidy of Rs. 25 on cooking gas cylinder and it sells at Rs. 350. In this case even though the consumers pay Rs. 350 for cylinder, the factors employed in the production and distribution of gas cylinder will receive Rs. 375 (= Rs. 350 + Rs. 25). This means the value of a gas cylinder would be equal to its ex-factors price plus the unit subsidy paid on it. From this it follows that national income at factor cost or, simply, national income is equal to NNP at market price ± net indirect taxes (i.e., indirect taxes paid by producers less subsidies received by them). Thus we can write

National income at factor cost = NNP at market price – indirect taxes + subsidies

or, National income = NNP ± net indirect taxes

1. Subsidies are a form of fiscal handout paid to certain sections of society at the cost of the taxpayers.

(where net indirect taxes are the difference between indirect taxes paid by producers and subsidies received by them). Suppose, for example, a hypothetical economy's net national product at market prices is Rs. 5,000. If some producers have paid indirect taxes of Rs. 500 cr. and other producers have received subsidies of Rs. 350 cr, net indirect taxes will be – Rs. 150 cr. (= – Rs. 500 cr. + Rs. 350 cr.). Therefore the country's national income will be Rs. 4,850 cr. (= Rs. 5000 cr. – Rs. 500 cr. + 350 cr.). If, on the other hand, subsidies amount to Rs. 500 cr. and indirect taxes sum up to Rs. 350 cr. then national income will be Rs. 5,150 cr. Thus it is clear that since net indirect taxes may be negative or positive, national income may be less or greater than NNP at factor cost.

PERSONAL INCOME (PI)

Personal income is the sum of all incomes received by individuals or households in an accounting year. Such incomes have both earned and unearned components. This is why national income is not the sum of all personal incomes. For example, personal income includes certain incomes which are received but not earned such as unemployment benefit, pensions, cash subsidies and other types of transfers (such as interest on government bonds[1].) At the same time personal income does not include social security contributions such as employers' contribution to provident fund, medical insurance and medical benefits, income taxes paid by companies, interest paid by companies to banks and other financial institutions and that part of net profits of companies which are not distributed as dividends among the shareholders (i.e., undistributed profits or retained earnings of corporations). The reason is that these do not represent any income earned or received by households. So we cannot arrive at national income just by adding up all personal incomes. In moving from national income to personal income we have to include those incomes which are received but not earned and subtract those incomes which are earned but not received. And an exactly opposite procedure has to be followed if we are to move from personal income to national income.

Fig. 7.9 shows how we arrive at personal income from national income. We also refer to another concept of income, viz., personal disposable income in this context. It is shown in this figure and explained below.

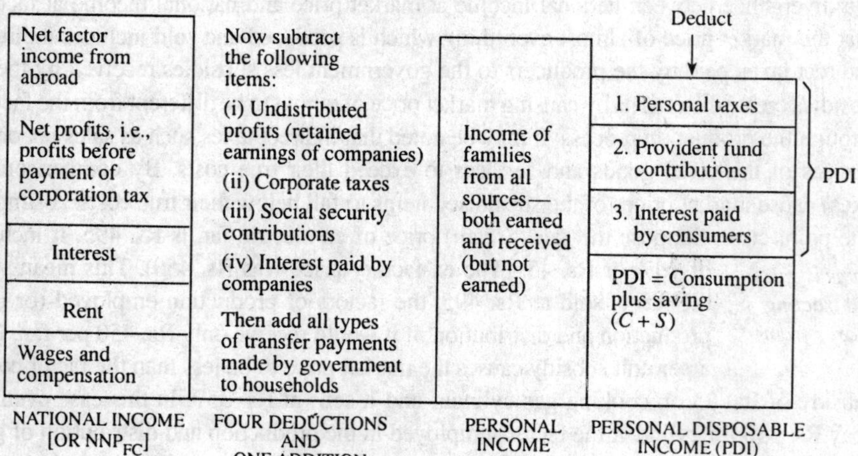

Fig. 7.9: From National Income to Personal Disposable Income

1. It may be noted that interest on corporate bonds and debentures is a part of a country's national income because it represents a payment for borrowing financial capital or acquiring loanable funds (which is a factor of production). By contrast, the government pays interest on its bonds by imposing taxes on people. So there is transfer of money from taxpayers to bondholders but no extra output is produced in the process. In fact, the same individual may be a taxpayer and a bondholder at the same time.

Thus we see that

Personal income = National income – social security contributions – corporate income taxes – interest paid by corporates – undistributed corporate profits (retained earnings) + transfer payments received from private and household sectors.

It may be noted that households receive transfer payments from both private sources and from the government. For example, an individual may receive a gift of Rs. 10,000 from his father who is also a resident of India. This is a part of personal income but not a part of India's national income[1]. The same statement is true in case of capital gains (and, of course, loss). If an individual sells shares in the stock exchange and makes a capital gain of Rs. 10,000 this will be a part of his personal income but not a part of India's national income. The reason is that there is transfer of money from the seller to the buyer of certain stocks.

Similarly an individual may receive unemployment compensation or pension from the government. These are examples of government transfer. These are all included in personal income.

Personal Disposable Income

Personal disposable income is that part of personal income which is available to household after paying taxes and fulfilling certain contractual obligations such as making provident fund contributions and paying interest on house loan or car loan.

PDI is equal to consumption plus saving

The term 'disposable' implies that households can dispose of their income as they wish. And disposable personal income is largely spent on consumption goods and partly saved, as shown in Fig. 7.9. And what is not spent on consumption goods is automatically saved. So saving is a residue. It is that part of personal income which is not spent on consumption goods. This is why Paul Samuelson calls consumption and saving the mirror image concepts. This means that at a fixed level of PDI more consumption means less saving and *vice-versa*.

In short

PDI = PI – personal taxes and all other deductions made from PI in the form of provident fund contributions and interest payments made by consumers.

Normally, we ignore all those deductions which are very small in magnitude and say that PDI = PI – personal taxes (such as income and property taxes[2]).

THE MEASUREMENT OF NATIONAL INCOME

Since the production of various goods and services lead to the generation of different types of incomes and incomes earned are spent on the goods and services produced, there are three alternative methods of arriving at an estimate of a country's national income. All the three methods yield the same result. So the methods are different no doubt but the result is the same. We may now discuss these methods one by one and show their equivalence later.

THE OUTPUT OR THE VALUE ADDED METHOD

The output method or the value added method is also known as the product method. When this method is used, an economy is divided into three different sectors or segments, viz., (i) the primary sector which includes agriculture and allied activities such as forestry, fishing and mining, (ii) the

1. However, if an individual receives a gift of £ 2,000 from his father who is a non-resident Indian (say, a doctor working in the U.K), this will be a part of India's national income. If £ 1 = Rs. 90, then Rs. 180,000 will be added to India's national income but £ 2,000 must be deducted from UK's national income in order to avoid double counting at the international land. The reason is that there are certain international accounting standards.
2. Note that indirect taxes and subsidies are considered in the context of national income at market price and direct taxes are considered in the context of national income at factor cost. While calculating PDI, we consider only direct taxes.

secondary sector, which includes manufacturing (of all types—large, medium and small) and construction and (iii) the tertiary sector which includes all types of service-rendering activities such as education and health care, trade and commerce, transport and communication, insurance, banking and tourism. Then net value added at factor cost by each producing unit also as well as for each industry and sector is calculated. Initially, the gross value of output of each producing unit limit is calculated by multiplying the value of output produced of a good or service by its market price. For example, if a firm produces 10 electric fans and the market price of a fan is Rs. 500, then the market value of its output is Rs. 5,000. This is done for each item which is produced or each type of service which is rendered.

However, in order to avoid double or multiple counting, we have to calculate the net value added at factor cost by each producing unit such as a bakery. This is done by subtracting the following three items from the gross value of output:

1. Cost of raw materials purchased and used such as flour, fuel, etc. This is known as intermediate consumption.
2. Depreciation of capital goods such as oven (also called consumption of fixed capital).
3. Net indirect taxes, i.e., taxes paid less subsidies received by producers.

By adding up the value added figures of all producing units or enterprises belonging to a particular sector or industry, we arrive at net value added at factor cost of each industry or sector, such as the automobile industry or the large manufacturing sector. Then we add up net value added at factor cost by all industries or sectors to arrive at net domestic product at factor cost (NDP_{FC}). Finally, if we add net factor income from abroad to NDP_{FC}, we arrive at NNP_{FC} or, simply, national income.

This method is widely used in those countries where the government takes a census of production every year. However, in many LDCs data of production of the organised sector are available. But data on agriculture and unorganised sectors of industry are not available. This is why two other methods of estimating national incomes are used.

The sectoral distribution (composition) of national income indicates the state of development of the economy as also the occupational pattern of the work force

However, the most important advantage to be secured from this method is that it clearly indicates the sectoral composition (division) of national income, i.e., the relative importance of the three sectors — primary, secondary and tertiary, in national income. And the sectoral composition of national income indicates the state of development of an economy. The larger the contribution of agriculture in particular and the primary sector in general to the national income of a country, the more economically backward the country is supposed to be. And economic development implies a fall in the relative contribution of the primary sector to national income and a corresponding increase in the share of the secondary and tertiary sectors. The sectoral distribution of income also indicates the occupational pattern of the population.

Precautions

Certain precautionary measures are to be taken while measuring national income from the output side. There are some inclusions and a few exclusions also.

A. Inclusions

(i) *Imputed rent* : Imputed rent values of owner-occupied houses should be included for a very simple reason. Those who stay in their own houses receive a flow of service — housing service and they are both tenants and landlords at the same time. Though the beneficiaries do not make any payment to outsiders, the value of the services they receive can be counted from the rents paid on similar houses in the locality. Such income is known as notional rent.

(ii) *Value of production for self-consumption* : The production of goods for self-consumption as in subsistence agriculture has to be valued at the prevailing market price. So there is need for imputation of the value of output on the basis of present market prices of such goods which are sold and not consumed or partly consumed and partly sold.

(iii) *Brokerage* : If an individual has purchased a share last year and sells it in the current year, the brokerage fee which he pays this year will be a part of India's national income.

B. Exclusions

(i) *Transactions involving old goods* : The sale and purchase of second-hand goods has to be excluded from the market value of output to avoid double counting. For example, if an individual has purchased a car last year (when it was produced) it was included in last year's GNP. But if he sells the same car this year, it will not be a part of this year's output. Hence it has to be excluded from GNP.

(ii) *Do-it-your-exercise* : The value of services rendered by housewives such as cooking, nursing, washing clothes, etc. and other works of the family are to be excluded. For example, if a person coaches his son or cleans his own car, the value of his services can be imputed no doubt. In spite of this such services are to be excluded while estimating national income from the output side. The reason is that the correct imputation of such services is not possible. However, the fact remains that if an individual stops driving his own car and keeps a driver, India's national income will increase.

(iii) *The value of intermediate goods* : The cost of raw materials and intermediate goods used in the production of final goods has to be excluded. Otherwise there would be double or multiple counting.

THE INCOME (FLOW OF EARNINGS) METHOD

The income method looks at national income from the distribution side

Just as the output or the value added method shows the sectoral composition of national income and the occupational pattern of the population, the income method enables us to study how national income gets divided into four main types of factor incomes. According to this method national income is the total income earned by the people of a country through their contribution to the production of goods and services. The following five main types of incomes are earned by the people of a country:

1. ***Income from labour***— wages/salaries and other types of compensation (as also employers' contribution to provident fund) or health insurance,
2. ***Income from real property*** — rent of land and buildings,
3. ***Income from financial assets (loanable funds)*** — interest,
4. ***Income from personal and intellectual capital*** — consultancy fees and royalty of books and musical cassette (CDs) and
5. ***Income from entrepreneurship***—profits (which include dividends, undistributed profits and corporation income tax).

National income is sum of rent, wages, interest and profit as also the incomes of self-employed persons

Such income has several components and is known as mixed income[1]. This type of income is an important component of national income in developing countries like India. The reason is a large number of people are included in household production (as in small-scale and cottage industries as also in family farms) and various unorganised enterprises (such as selling tea, fast food or cigarettes on the pavement). Since the owners of such enterprises do all types of work themselves in their respective units, it is difficult to separate wages for the work done by them from rent, interest and profits earned by them for risk-taking, for using out their property and supplying their

1. Take, for example, the income of the owner of a shop. Suppose she has opened the shop in her own house. She is doing all types of job herself without employing any person. She has invested Rs. 50,000 from her personal saving. And she is taking the risk of business. So her income includes the opportunity costs of all resources supplied by her (such as implicit rent, implicit wage and implicit interest) plus her explicit profits.

own funds as also for risk-taking. Therefore the incomes earned by them contain wage, rent, interest and profits. Such incomes are called mixed income of self-employed persons or proprietors' income.

Now the question here is: how to measure different types of factor incomes (which are factor payments from the side of the producing units)? The income earned by each factor is calculated by multiplying the number of units of each factor employed by all the producing units by its price per unit. To do this, we have to identify the different producing units and collect data on the number of units of each factor employed by each producing unit and the factor payments made by each such unit. Suppose there are 10 identical firms in an economy and each employs 5 workers per day at a daily wage of Rs. 20. So each firm makes a wage payment of Rs. 100 and total wage payment per day is Rs. 1,000. This means that the income from labour will be Rs. 1,000 per day. If all the workers work for 300 days a year, then total annual wage income will be Rs. 3 lacs. In the same way we can calculate rent of land and buildings, interest on loans and profit (which is a residue — surplus left with enterpreneurs after making all contractual factor payments).

By adding up the factor payments made by all producing units in the current year, we arrive at domestic income at factor cost which is also known as net domestic product at factor cost (NDP_{FC}). To this we have to add net factor income earned from abroad (NFIFA) to arrive at net national product at factor cost (NNP_{FC}) which is indeed national income.

In Fig. 7.10 we show different components of income and other related aggregates by using the income method. Note that the income approach is also known as the flow of earnings approach to national income estimation.

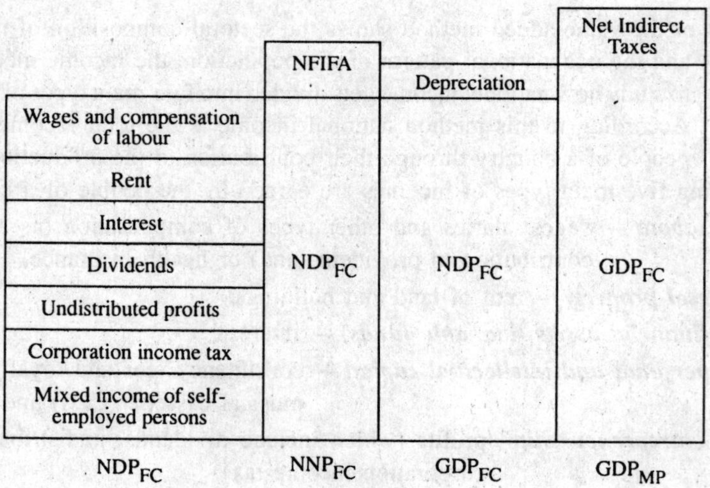

Fig. 7.10: Income (Flow of Earnings) Approach to National Income

EQUIVALENCE OF VALUE ADDED AND FACTOR PAYMENTS

It may be noted that the sum of value added is equal to the sum of all factor incomes. All factor payments are made from the value additions made by producing units. This shows the equivalence of national output and national income. And we can show that the net value of output produced in an economy in an accounting year is identically equal to the net flow of income generated from the production process.

Inclusions and Exclusions

Certain precautions are to be taken while measuring national income by using the income approach. This becomes clear if we note the following points:

A. Inclusions

1. ***Notional rent*** **:** Imputed or notional rent of owner-occupied houses is included in national income. The reason is that these houses provide a flow of services to the owners. Notional rent can be calculated from rents of similar houses or buildings in the locality.

2. ***Self-consumption*** **:** The income equivalent of the value of current output used for self-consumption (such as consumption of wheat by subsistence farmers) has to be estimated and included in national income.

3. ***Personal taxes*** **:** Two types of personal taxes, viz., income tax and capital gains tax are included. If an individual in India buys a share and sells it at a higher price within the same financial year, then 15% capital gains tax has to be paid.

B. Exclusions

1. ***Transfer incomes*** **:** All types of transfer incomes (including interest earned from government bonds) are to be excluded because these are not associated with the current production of goods and services.

2. ***Illegal income(s)*** **:** Since it is not possible to officially estimate illegal incomes such as income from gambling, smuggling, black marketing, money laundering, etc., these should be excluded.

3. ***Windfall gains*** **:** Since windfall gains are essentially unearned incomes, they are also excluded from national income.

4. ***Corporate income tax*** **:** There is no need to separately include corporate income tax (which is essentially a tax on corporate profits). The reason is that it is included as a part of profits (which have three components, as mentioned earlier).

5. ***Other taxes*** **:** Various other taxes are paid by individuals from their past savings or accumulated wealth and not from their current income. Examples of such taxes are death duties (abolished in India in 1985), gift tax, wealth tax and tax on lotteries. These are excluded from national income.

6. ***Second-hand goods*** **:** The receipts from the sale of second-hand goods are to be excluded. The reason that the money received by selling old goods such as used cars or furnitures are not part of current year's production. So receipts from the sale of such goods do not represent payment for factors of production which have made their respective contributions to current year's output of goods and services.

THE EXPENDITURE METHOD

According to the expenditure method national income is calculated by adding up all types of expenditures made by households, business firms and government(s). The total of these three types of expenditure is known as total domestic expenditure (TDE). If we add net exports to TDE, we arrive at total final expenditure (TFE). It may be noted that net exports represent two things—foreigners' expenditure on Indian goods (which constitutes India's exports) and India's expenditure on foreign goods (which constitutes India's imports). So the four components of TFE are the following:

1. ***Consumption*** **:** This is expenditure of individuals and households on consumption goods, called final private consumption expenditure. It is denoted by the symbol C, which includes expenditure on both durable and non-durable goods.

2. ***Investment*** **:** This is business expenditure on fixed capital as also on inventories (i.e., stocks of finished goods). It is a broad term and is also called gross domestic capital formation or gross domestic investment and denoted by I. It has two main components, viz., (i) gross fixed capital formation, and (ii) addition to the stocks of finished goods (i.e., goods which have been produced in the current year but not sold within the same year and carried on for future sales).

3. ***Government purchase of goods and services*** **:** These represent government expenditure on currently produced goods and services, but not transfer expenditure. Examples of such expenditure are

FCI purchase of foodgrains from farmers for distribution through ration (fair price) shops, purchase of medicines for distribution through government hospitals and purchase of books by national (public) libraries. The government also purchases steel and cement for road construction. All these purchases are made for satisfying wants of all people of the country, called social (collective) wants.

4. *Net exports* : The expenditure made by foreigners on Indian goods is called exports (X). Similarly the expenditure made by households, enterpreneurs and Government of India on foreign goods is called imports (M). The difference between exports and imports is net exports ($X–M$).

By adding up these four types of expenditure we arrive at final expenditure on GDP at market price (GDP_{MP}). Thus

$$GDP_{MP} = C + I + G + X - M$$
$$= C + I + G \pm NX$$

where all the terms have their usual meaning. Now if we deduct depreciation, D, i.e., consumption of fixed capital, from GDP_{MP}, we arrive at NDP_{MP}.

Again if we subtract net indirect business taxes (i.e., indirect taxes paid by business firms *less* subsidies received by them) we arrive at NDP_{FC}. Finally, if we add NFIFA to NDP_{FC}, we arrive at NNP_{FC} which is another name of national income[1].

In Fig. 7.11, we illustrate the expenditure method of measuring national income.

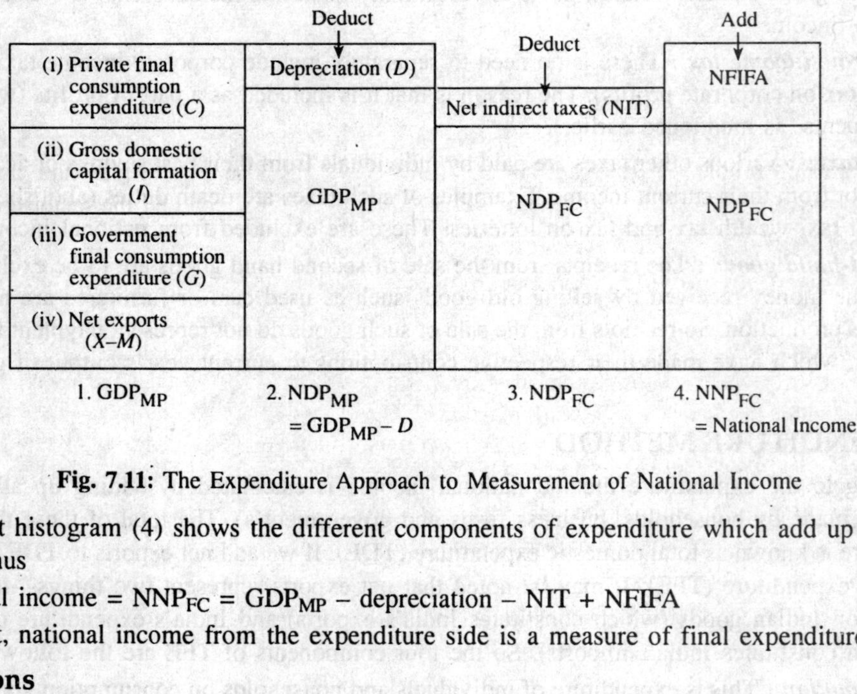

Fig. 7.11: The Expenditure Approach to Measurement of National Income

The last histogram (4) shows the different components of expenditure which add up to national income. Thus

National income = $NNP_{FC} = GDP_{MP}$ – depreciation – NIT + NFIFA

In short, national income from the expenditure side is a measure of final expenditure on GNP.

Precautions

Even in case of the expenditure method certain precautions are to be taken so as to arrive at an accurate measure of national income. So the following points are to be noted in this context:

A. Exclusions

1. *Second-hand goods* : The expenditure on old goods should not be included because they do not correspond to the current year's production of goods and services.

1. It may be noted that if we add NFIFA to any concept of domestic product, we arrive at the corresponding national product.

2. ***Purchase of existing shares*** **:** The purchase of existing shares and securities from other people and not from businesses (at the stage of their initial public offering) has to be excluded from total final expenditure. The reason is that shares are just financial claims and do not represent expenditure on currently produced goods and services.

3. ***Transfer expenditures*** **:** Transfer expenditure made by the government in the form of unemployment benefits, retirement pensions, and interest on government bonds is not to be included. The reason is that these are not associated with any current production of goods and services. Those who receive such benefits from the government do not provide anything to the government in exchange.

4. ***Expenditure on raw materials and intermediate goods*** **:** As in the product method, expenditure on raw materials such as flour, raw cotton, fertiliser, oil, coal, etc. used by producing units should be excluded. The objective is to avoid double (multiple) counting. This means that for estimating national income from the expenditure side, we have to include only expenditure on final goods and services.

DIFFICULTIES IN THE MEASUREMENT OF NATIONAL INCOME

There are various conceptual (theoretical) and practical problems associated with the measurement of a country's national income. Some of those difficulties (problems) are the following:

1. ***Treatment of non-market transactions*** **:** Some transactions do not occur through the markets. For example, work done by housewives within their families such as washing clothes, cooking food, coaching children and looking after elderly persons remain unpaid because they do not enter the market. Such non-market transactions are excluded from national income. Another example is production of wheat by the members of a farmer's family for their own consumption (as is found in subsistence farming) and not for sale through the market (as is found in commercialised agriculture). However, the value of wheat or any farm output consumed at home is included in national income. But, this type of accounting practice gives rise to certain anomalies. For example, if an individual, who was driving car over the years, suddenly keeps a full-time driver, then India's national income will rise. But if a working lady marries her driver, she will not pay any salary to her husband and India's national income will fall (since the driver will do the same job as before but without receiving any payment in cash).

In the first case, the value of national income would increase, but in the second case it would fall, although in each case the real amount of services performed remains the same.

2. ***Treatment of final goods*** **:** We have mentioned that national income, from the output side, includes only the money value of all final goods (and services) produced in an economy in an accounting year. We have also noted that final goods are those which are not used in further production of other goods and are destroyed after consumption. However, in reality it becomes difficult at times to draw a distinction between a raw material (or an intermediate good) and a final good. For example, paint used by a commercial artist for his artwork which he sells in the market is a raw material and has to be excluded from GDP_{MP}. However, suppose he is left with some surplus paint with which he paints his house or car. In this case it is a final good and is a part of GDP_{MP}.

The cost of providing government services is included in national income

3. ***Treatment of government activities*** **:** The government has to pay wages and salaries and incur other expenses for performing various administrative functions such as maintenance of law and order, defending the country from foreign aggression, providing economic and social infrastructure in the form of roads, highways, education and healthcare. Since there is no market for the services provided by the government, the convention is to calculate the cost of providing such services and include this in national income. In fact, government expenditure on such public goods and services gives rise to final consumption of such goods and services by all members of society collectively. So the contribution of general government services has to be equal to the amount of wages and salaries paid by government.

Government expenditure has two components, viz., consumption expenditure on final goods and investment expenditure (capital formation)

As for investment by government there is no difference between private investment on setting up factories or buying new machines and government investment on infrastructure building.

4. ***Treatment of income generated by foreign firms*** : The production of goods and services by foreign companies operating in India and incomes therefrom have to be included in India's national income. However, any remittance made by foreign companies or multinational corporations (MNCs) in the form of interest, dividends, royalties or technical consultancy fees are to be deducted from India's national income because these represent incomes earned by foreigners from India.

SPECIAL (ADDITIONAL) PROBLEMS FACED BY DEVELOPING COUNTRIES

National income accountants face some special problems when they estimate national income of developing countries like India. Some of these difficulties are the following:

1. ***Non-monetary (or non-market) transactions*** : A major portion of output produced by most developing countries is for self-consumption. Such output does not come to the market. For example, agriculture in India is largely a subsistence occupation. Farmers produce food mainly for consumption by their family members. Subsistence farmers do not sell their output in the market. So it is difficult for national income accountants to estimate the value of output of subsistence farmers.

2. ***Lack of reliable information*** : Most producers in developing countries are illiterate. They have no clear idea of the volume and value of their output. They do not keep accounts of their output on a regular basis. For this reason it is very difficult to get reliable information about output produced by millions of small farmers. This is not only true for agriculture, but also of small-scale and cottage industries, petty trade and personal services (like more of plumbers, housekeepers and domestic maids). In such countries output of the unorganised sector constitutes a major portion of total output of goods and services.

3. ***Lack of clear-cut classification of economic activities*** : There is no clear-cut classification of economic activities in developing countries because the same person remains engaged in two or more activities during the same accounting year. For example, the teacher of a primary school may remain engaged in rice trade. He may also participate in farming. He may cultivate his own land during summer and winter when his school remains closed. Due to such overlapping activities it is difficult to estimate national income in developing countries.

It is virtually impossible to calculate the output of the unorganised sector

4. ***Output of unorganised sector*** : In developing countries production units in agriculture, small-scale and cottage industries and indigenous banking remain scattered all over the country. All these activities fall under the unorganised sector. It is not easy to calculate the exact volume or value of output produced by self-employed persons such as subsistence farmers and owners of small or very small (tiny) enterprises. The task is not only extremely difficult, but virtually impossible to accomplish.

5. ***Lack of separate consumption data*** : Separate data on consumption expenditure are not available in developing countries like India because such data are not collected. This is why the expenditure method of measuring national income cannot be applied in such countries.

6. ***Underground economy*** : Certain legal transactions are deliberately concealed. These are not officially disclosed in order to evade taxes. Such transactions are said to occur in an underground economy.

Conclusion

Perhaps the most serious problem associated with the measurement of national income in developing countries is lack of reliable and adequate data. An accurate estimate of national income in such countries is not possible due to inadequacy and unreliability of data. In addition, data regarding production in agriculture and allied activities such as forestry and fishing, household enterprises such as small-scale and cottage industries are not available. Even data on the organised sector is not only inadequate but unreliable also. For all these reasons it is very difficult to gather correct information about consumption, saving and investment expenditure of both rural and urban people.

Due to lack of accurate data and reliable information, it is difficult to arrive at a proper estimate of national income of developing countries

NOMINAL AND REAL GNP

Nominal GNP is expressed in terms of money. It is the total money value of all final goods and services produced in an economy in an accounting year. It is calculated by using the current market prices of all final goods and services produced. However, in times of inflation, nominal GNP fails to give a true indication of the performance of the economy. The reason is that nominal GNP may increase due to a rise in prices of goods and services, even if the quality of final goods and services produced remains constant. However, an increase in the quality of goods and services produced is a true indicator of economic growth or the performance of the economy of a country over a period of time. So it is necessary to eliminate the effect of price changes from the nominal GNP in the current year. This will give us an estimate of the true increase in the output of final goods and services produced. For this reason, economists use the price index of a certain base year to correctly estimate the real value of output of all final goods and services produced in an economy in an accounting year. In India, for example, the year 1999-00 is now taken as the base year. Thus if real GNP for 2003-2004 is calculated by using the base year price index, we arrive at national income at constant prices.

National income at constant prices is calculated by using the price index of a certain base year

A simple example will now be helpful in explaining how market prices of a base year are used to calculate GNP for the current year. Suppose a single hypothetical economy produces only four final goods, viz., bread, steel, petrol and cars. The prices of these goods in the current year 2012-13 and base year 1999-00 are presented in columns (3) and (5) of Table 7.1. The quantities of these final goods produced in the current year are shown in column (2).

Table 7.1: Estimation of Real GNP for a Hypothetical Economy

1	2	3	4	5	6
Final Goods	Quantities produced in 2012-13	Market prices in 2012-13 (Rs.)	The value of final goods at current market prices (2012-13)	Market prices in the base year (1999-00)	The value of final goods at base year prices (1999-00)
1. Bread (pounds)	20	7	140	10	70
2. Steel (tonnes)	15	5	75	8	120
3. Petrol (gallons)	10	3	30	2	20
4. Cars (rupees)	5	1,000	5,000	500	2,000
			5,245		2,210

In column (4), we show nominal GNP for the current year which is Rs. 5,245. We arrive at this figure by multiplying the quantities of four final goods produced by their respective market prices of the current year (2012-13). If we add up the market prices we arrive at nominal GNP for the current year which is Rs. 5,245.

By comparison, for estimating real GNP for the current year (2012-13), we multiply the quantities of final goods produced in the current year by their respective base year (1999-00) prices. The estimates are shown in col. (6). Now if we add up the money values of the four final goods (each one evaluated at its base year price) we arrive at the real GNP (which is another name of GNI at constant prices), for the current year. From Table 7.1 we see that it is Rs. 2,210 — much less than nominal GNP of Rs. 5,245. The discrepancy has occurred due to the fact that market prices have risen between the base year and the current year. It is quite obvious that there is no difference between real GNP and nominal GNP for the base year (1999-00).

IMPORTANCE OF GNP

It is to be noted that it is a real GNP rather than nominal GNP which is the true indicator of the performance of the economy. Three points may be noted in this context:

1. Indicator of welfare: National income is indicator of welfare. The reason is that an improvement in the standard of living and the level of welfare of a country depends on an increase in the availability of real goods and services over a period of time.

2. Economic growth: Economic growth is measured by calculating the percentage change in real GNP in a year. If nominal GNP increases by 5% in a year, but the price level has also increased by 5%, there will be no increase in real GNP. This means that country under consideration has not achieved economic growth in the true sense.

3. Measurement of inflation: Finally by using both the concepts, viz., nominal GNP and real GNP, we can measure the rate of inflation of a period of time. This measure of rate of inflation is known as GNP deflator which is expressed as follows:

$$\text{GNP deflator} = \frac{\text{Nominal GNP of a year}}{\text{Real GNP of the same year}} \times 100$$

$$\text{or, Real GNP} = \frac{\text{Nominal GNP}}{\text{GNP Deflator}} \times 100$$

A simple example will make the concept clear. Suppose nominal GNP for the current year is Rs. 1,250 cr. and real GDP is Rs. 1,140 cr.

Therefore

$$\text{GNP Deflator} = \frac{\text{Rs. }1{,}250\text{ cr.}}{\text{Rs. }1{,}140\text{ cr.}} \times 100 = 110.$$

$$\text{or, Real GNP} = \frac{\text{Rs. }1{,}250\text{ cr.}}{110} \times 100$$

$$= \text{Rs. } 1{,}140 \text{ cr.}$$

This means that if there is 10% inflation in an economy between the base year (when the price index was 100) and the current year (when the price index is 110), an increase in nominal GNP does not get reflected in a proportionate increase in real GNP. The increase in real GNP is less than that of nominal GNP due to price inflation.

If there is 27.5% inflation over an 13-year period (say, between the base year 1999-00 and the current year 2012-13), then also we can calculate the annual rate of inflation. In this case it is 27.5% ÷ 13 = 2.15% (approx.) per annum.

Finally, it may be noted that if there is no inflation in the economy over a certain period, there will be no divergence between nominal GNP and real GNP and the GDP deflator will be 100 (which is the same as the base year price index).

NATIONAL INCOME (GNP) AND SOCIAL WELFARE

It may be recalled that national income, or GNP is the total money value of all goods and services produced in an economy in a year. Since goods and services satisfy human needs and wants, national income is often used as a measurement of social welfare. Welfare is the perception of the feeling of happiness derived from want satisfaction. So it may apparently seem that the higher the level of national income, the higher the level of satisfaction or economic welfare. A more reliable indicator of welfare is per capita income (or income per head). And economic growth or the rate of material progress of a nation is measured by the annual rate of increase of per capita income. However, there are several limitations of both national and per capita incomes as a measure of economic welfare. The following points may be noted in this context:

1. *From GNP to NEW* : National income includes certain things which do reduce social welfare. Mention may be made of certain harmful effects which result from increase in output of goods and services such as air, sound (noise) and water pollution. We may also mention traffic hazards and various disamenities of urban life such as accidents, traffic jams, violence, corruption, strikes, bandhs, hartals, etc. All these reduce social welfare. The different forms of pollution are treated as costs of economic growth. These are to be deducted from national income to arrive at a measure of economic welfare.

By contrast, certain things are excluded from national income but these raise social welfare. Examples are personal services rendered by members of families such as cooking food, gardening, driving, washing clothes, coaching children and looking after elderly persons. The value of such non-market activities (also called 'do-it-your-exercise') raise welfare. So these are to be included in national income. People also derive satisfaction from leisure as they do from consumption of goods and services. So the value of leisure has also to be added to national income so that it can be used as a true indicator of welfare.

If we make these adjustments (i.e., minuses and pluses) we arrive at net economic welfare (NEW.) from GNP. This term was populared by James Tobin and W. D. Nordhaus. However, critics have commented that in practice measuring all these things is virtually impossible. So arriving at NEW from GNP is like measuring the immeasurable.

2. *Regrettable costs* : A modern-day government has to incur huge expenditure on police forces, on army, and on law courts in order to maintain the law and order situation in the country as also to defend the country from foreign aggression. Modern economists consider the major portion of such expenditure as wasteful. The reason is that expenditure on these things represent outlay on regrettable necessities. Such expenditure does not lead to an increase in economic welfare. So such expenditure is to be excluded from national income in order to arrive at a true measure of NEW.

We make a transition from GNP to NEW as follows:

Prima facie, we have to deduct depreciation from real GNP to arrive at real NNP (or national income at constant price). Then we have to make the following four adjustments of which the first two are deductions and the next two are additions.

Deductions from Real NNP	Additions to Real NNP
1. Costs of environmental pollution (or negative externality).	3. The value of leisure enjoyed by people (due to shorter working hours).
2. Regrettable costs.	4. Value of all non-market activities (such as the work done by the housewives and personal services rendered within the family).

Economic welfare depends not just on the size of national income but also on how it is divided between rich and poor

3. *Distribution of national product* : Even NEW does not truly indicate the welfare enjoyed by the people of a country. An important factor which does not get reflected in broad aggregates such as national income or national product but affects economic welfare is the pattern of distribution of national income. The distribution of society's output or GNP among different sections of society depends on the distribution of income. If with an increase in national and per capita incomes, the rich gets richer and the poor gets poorer, then social welfare will not be promoted.[1]

In fact, the pattern of production is governed by the pattern of demand and the pattern of demand, in its turn, is determined by the pattern of income distribution. If income is inequitably distributed, there will be maximum demand for and production of luxury goods such as costly cars, jewellery, dress matches, watches, diamonds, etc. Such goods meet the demand of a very small section of the population. On the other hand, there will be inadequate production of essential items of consumption such as cheap food, cheap cloth and other items of mass consumption, also known as wage goods. In this case, scarce resources will be diverted from the production of necessities (meant for consumption by the masses) to luxuries (which are consumed by a small percentage of the people). So there will be a shortage of essential consumer goods and more and more people will go below the poverty line. Thus an increase in national income and per capita income is not enough for making people happy. An equitable distribution of income is equally vital for promoting economic welfare. In short, economic welfare depends on two things: (1) faster economic growth and (2) an equitable distribution of income.

4. *Composition of national output* : The composition of national output is also an important determinant of economic welfare. Many countries are now spending huge amounts of money on national defence. As a result GNP is increasing no doubt but there is less and less increase in actual welfare of the people. By contrast, if an increase in GNP is due to increase in the production of mass consumption goods, economic welfare will increase even if there is a small increase in national and per capita incomes.

5. *Quality of products* : Economic welfare also depends on the quality of goods produced and not just the value of output produced. Due to improvement of technology, there is a constant improvement in the quality of products. But this does not get reflected in GNP. For example, now people pay high prices for the cars they buy, compared to the prices paid by people in the past. However, the high prices do not just reflect the effect of inflation but the costs of improving the quality of products. An individual gets much safer and fuel efficient cars by paying higher prices. This makes him better-off.

6. *Methods of production* : If an increase in GNP is brought about by forcing workers to work beyond their normal capacity (say, 12 to 16 hours a day instead of 8 hours), their health will deteriorate and their efficiency will decline. Moreover, many child workers may be illegally employed and forced to work for long hours. For these reasons an increase in GNP will lead to a fall in social welfare.

Finally, if more and more capital-intensive techniques of production are used to increase the output of goods and services, the country will be achieving a satisfactory rate of economic growth no doubt. But there is a cost of such growth. More and more workers will be unemployed and underemployed. And these have both economic and social costs. Therefore an increase in national income will lead to a fall in economic welfare.

Conclusion

So an increase in national income does not necessarily imply (or lead to) an increase in social welfare. In spite of this national (per capita) income is taken as a rough and ready indicator of economic welfare (due to absence of a more reliable guage of well-being).

1. This is why the World Bank had suggested a strategy for developing countries in 1974 known as *redistribution with growth.*

KEY POINTS

1. *National income (NI)* : NI is the total of income received by the people of a country for their contribution to the production of goods and services. This not only includes incomes earned within the domestic territory of a country but also any income earned abroad.

2. *Measurement of national income* : There are three approaches to the measurement of national income of a country, viz., the output (value added) method, the income (flow of earnings) method and the expenditure (total spending method). All the approaches yield the same result.

3. *Double counting and value added* : Since the output of one producing unit is used as input in various other units the same item is counted twice or thrice as it passes through various stages of production and distribution. As a result the problem of double (multiple) counting arises. The problem can be avoided by using the value added figure of each producing unit. National income from the output side is calculated by adding up the value added figures of all producing units. This is known as GNP which is the sum of value added by different sectors per annum. Value added is the difference between output value and imput value.

4. *Final goods and intermediate goods* : GNP is the total market value of final goods and services produced in a year. It excludes the cost of raw materials and intermediate goods used in the production of final goods. While intermediate goods are used for further production of other goods, final goods are destroyed after consumption or use.

5. *Income method* : According to the income method national income is the sum of six types of factor incomes: (i) wages and compensation of employees, (ii) rent of land and building, (iii) interest on financial capital, (iv) profits (which include dividends, undistributed profits or retained earnings and corporate taxes), (v) mixed income of self-employed persons and (vi) net factor income earned from abroad.

6. *Equivalence of output method and income method* : National output (GNP) is identically equal to gross national income (GNI) because the revenue earned from output produced and sold is paid out to factors of production in the form of incomes. In fact, the sum of value added is equal to the sum of all factor incomes. However, national income from the output side (or GNP) is measured at market price and GNI is measured at factor cost. If we subtract depreciation (capital consumption) we arrive at NNP and NNI. By subtracting indirect taxes from NNP and adding subsidies to it, we get NNI which is indeed national income at factor cost. Transfer income (i.e., income received but not earned) has to be deduced while measuring national income. While the output method shows the sectoral composition (distribution) of national income, the income method indicates how national income is divided among the four main factors of production making their respective contributions to national income. Thus the income method looks at national income from the distribution side.

7. *The expenditure approach* : Income is earned from production of goods and services and is spent on various goods and services. There are four main components of total expenditure, viz., household consumption, private business investment, government purchase of goods and services and net exports (exports—imports). We can show the equivalence of national income and expenditure also. So it turns out that national output = national income = total final expenditure (on both domestically produced and foreign goods).

8. *Other concepts of income* : Two other concepts of income are personal income, i.e., income of individuals and households and personal disposable income which is personal income less personal taxes paid. Personal disposable income is largely spent on consumption goods and partly saved. Personal income includes transfer income but not undistributed profit of companies. National income is not the sum of all personal incomes.

9. *Difficulties of measuring national income* : There are various conceptual (theoretical) and practical problems associated with the measurement of national income such as household production, final goods and intermediate goods, illegal transactions, unpaid jobs by housewives, transactions in the unofficial economy and so on. There are additional difficulties of measuring national income of developing countries like India mainly due to production for self-consumption, lack of clear-cut classification of economic activities and lack of reliable, adequate and accurate data about some key macroeconomic variables.

10. *National income and economic welfare* : An increase in national and per capita incomes does not necessarily lead to an increase in economic welfare. Much depends on the pattern of income distribution, the composition of output, and the quality of output produced.

KEY TERMS

National Income	Gross national product GNP
Gross domestic product GDP	Net factor income earned from abroad NFIFA
Transfer income	Net exports
Personal income	Disposable income
Net Economic Welfare (NEW)	Regrettable waste
Economic welfare	Net indirect taxes
Total domestic expenditure	Total final expenditure
Double (multiple) counting	Depreciation
Value added	GNP deflator
Consumer price index	Real GNP
Real GDP	Underground economy
Income received but not earned	Intermediate goods
Final goods	Inventories

ASSIGNMENTS

1. How is the circular flow of income measured?
2. Present a simple two-sector circular model of an economy (i) without *S* and *I*, and (ii) with *S* and *I*. How will the model be affected if we incorporate the government and the external sector in our analysis?
3. What will be the effect of the following on India's national income:
   (a) Mr. A receives a cash gift of Rs. 10,000 from his father who is also a resident of India.
   (b) Mr. B receives a gift of £ 2,000 from his father who is a non-resident Indian.
   (c) Mr. C sells shares in the stock exchange and makes a capital gain of Rs. 5 lakhs, from which he pays a broker's commission of Rs. 25,000.
   (d) Aggregate inventories of Indian companies go down by Rs. 2 crores in the current year. [**Hint:** Sales from inventories]
   (e) Mr. D receives a dividend of $ 1,500 from an American multinational corporation.
4. How are saving and investment treated in national income accounts? In this context, draw a distinction between *S-I* equality (identity) and *S-I* equilibrium.
5. We know that savers and investors are two different groups of people. Can you think of a person who is saving and investing at the same time?
   [**Hint:** A self-sufficient farmer who sets aside a portion of his wheat every year (season) to be used as seed next year (season) from which more wheat can be produced.]
6. When does the budget of the government show a deficit? How does a budget deficit affect the circular flow of income?
7. Present a circular flow diagram to show that the net value of output produced in an economy in an accounting year is identically equal to net flow of income generated from the production process.
8. Using a circular flow diagram of the economy show that the sum of private investment and government expenditure equals the sum of saving and tax.
9. What do you mean by injections into and leakages from the circular flow of income? Why is saving called a leakage and investment called an injection? How do they affect the circular flow of income and expenditure in an economy?
10. If business investment is less than household saving, will the circular flow of income be affected? If so, how? Be explicit in your assumptions and statements that you made while answering the question.
11. How do exports and imports and inflows and outflows of financial capital affect the circular flow of income?

12. Explain the statement that in an open economy, the sum of private investment, government spending and net exports must equal to sum of saving and taxes. Identify leakages and injections from this extended model.

13. Which of the following transactions are included in the GDP, and by how much does each raise GDP?
   (i) You buy a used bicycle paying Rs. 2,000.
   (ii) Your grandmother receives a pension of Rs. 50,000 for the year.
   (iii) You sell a poster to your roommate for Rs. 25.
   (iv) Maruti manufactures 2,000 automobiles at a cost of Rs. 2,50,000 each. Unable to sell 500 of them, it holds them as inventories.

14. The following is information from the national income accounts (in rupees) for a hypothetical country.

GNP	4,800
Gross investment	800
Net investment	300
Consumption	3,000
Government purchase of goods and services	960
National income	3,850
Wages and salaries	2,920
Proprietors' income	320
Dividends	100
Net interest	260
Government budget surplus	30
Social security contribution	380
Personal interest income	380
Government transfers to persons	520
Personal tax and non-tax payments	600

Find out:
   (i) Net Exports;
   (ii) Disposable Personal Income; and
   (iii) Private Savings.

15. Study the following table; then answer the questions.

Stages of production	Sales receipt (Rs. lac)	Cost of intermediate goods (Rs. lac)
Coal	2	0
Steel	5	2
Manufactured autos	8	5
Sold autos	9	8

   (i) Find out the value added for each stage.
   (ii) What is the intermediate good for steel production?

(iii) If automobiles are the only final goods produced in this economy, what would GDP via the expenditure approach be?

(iv) What would be GDP via the income approach?

16. Define GNP and GDP. Is the distinction between GNP and GDP significant?
17. Present the circular flow explication to show the linkage among households, firms and the government.
18. Explain the basic macroeconomic identity and show why the total investment, domestic and foreign, must always be equal to total saving of an economy.
19. What adjustments are required to calculate disposable personal income from GNP?
20. How far GDP can be considered as a measure of economic well-being?
21. What is meant by underground economy? What problems does an underground economy pose in the calculation of GDP?

[**Hint:** The term 'underground economy' is used to refer to economic activities not officially recorded and sometimes illegal. Such an economy includes a variety of economic activities unreported or unaccounted for in national income (product) account. Examples include legal activities such as garage sales and illegal activities such as smuggling drug sales, unauthorised gambling and sales of country liquor.

Since economic activities in an underground economy are not included in official statistics the activities which are undertaken in such an economy go largely unnoticed. The broadest definition of the underground economy includes legal activity that is not officially disclosed, illegal economic activities and home production (including subsistence farming). In India, the underground economy is as stronger as, if not stronger than, the official economy. So India is said to have a parallel economy.

The presence of an underground economy creates two problems:

(i) Firstly there is widespread tax evasion. So the government loses its potential tax revenue and its budget deficit increases.

(ii) Secondly, the official figure of GDP is much less than its true figure.]

22. Define GNP and GDP. Is the distinction between GNP and GDP significant?
23. Present the circular flow explication to show the linkage between households, firms and the government.
24. Explain the basic macroeconomic identity and show why the total investment, domestic and foreign, must always be equal to total saving of an economy.
25. What adjustments are required to calculate disposable personal income from GNP?
26. How far GDP can be considered as a measure of economic well-being?
27. What is meant by underground economy? What problems does an underground economy pose in the calculation of GDP?

7A SAVING, INVESTMENT AND CURRENT ACCOUNT BALANCE

In an open economy, the difference between total saving (private and government) and investment equals the current account balance. This point is proved as follows:

The equilibrium condition of national income in an open economy is:

$$S + T + M = I + G + X \qquad \ldots \quad (1)$$

where all the terms are standard. Equation (1) can be rewritten as follows:

$$S + (T - G) - I = X - M$$

where S = private saving and $(T - G)$ = government saving which can be negative. If $X < M$ the country is saving less than what it is investing domestically. If $X > M$, the country is saving more than what it is investing domestically (and hence it can invest overseas via a capital outflow, with the capital account deficit being equal to the current account surplus).

A. The Concept of Twin Deficits

Many countries including the USA are now suffering from two types of deficit, viz., budget deficit and trade deficit. This point is explained by using the standard national income accounting identity:

$$I + G + X = S + I + M$$

$$\text{or, } I - S + (G - T) = (M - X)$$

$$\text{or, } I + (G - T) - S = (M - X)$$

Here $(G - T)$ is negative government saving and $(M - X)$ is trade deficit defined as the excess of imports over exports. These two deficits together constitute twin deficits.

B. Saving and Savings

It is important to distinguish between saving and savings. Saving is the setting aside of surplus funds, that is, what an individual does not spend. Savings refers to the actual accounts, like an individual's savings account, in such he does it. The level of 'saving', not 'savings', is what is really important for an individual and for the economy as a whole.

Saving is income what is not spent. So it is $Y - C$. It is a *flow* as it represents how much is saved over a given period of time. For example, a person may save Rs. 500 a week whereas savings is a *stock* concept and represents an accumulation of past saving. If the person had savings of Rs. 20,000 initially, he would now have Rs. 20,500.

CHAPTER 8

The Sources and Uses of National Income

Consumption, saving, and investment play a central role in a nation's economic performance. High consumption relative to income spells low investment and slow growth; high saving leads to high investment and rapid growth.

P. A. Samuelson and W. D. Nordhaus

As we noted in the last chapter, the key macroeconomic variable is gross domestic product (GDP). It can be looked at from two sides. In one sense it is a measure of a country's total amount of goods and services. In another sense it is a measure of a country's total income. This is why it is so important. Countries with high GDP have more of the most desirable things of life such as food, cloth, shelter, healthcare, education and entertainment. However, a large GDP is no guarantee that all the people of a country enjoy a high standard of living or are happy. But with our present state of knowledge of the macroeconomy, we can only say that GDP is a part measure of happiness.

There is constant interaction among households, firms and governments

In this chapter, we present a simple circular flow model of the economy to explain the various interactions among economic agents. Fig. 8.1 presents a comprehensive picture of the economy in terms of functioning of real economies. Here we show linkages among three sectors of a closed economy, viz., the household sector, the firm (business) sector and the government sector. The focus is on the flow of money among the various markets such as the markets for goods and services, the markets for factors of production and financial markets (also called markets for loanable funds).

Households sell their labour and capital to the business firms and receive income. Then they spend their income after paying taxes to the government. They also save a portion of their after-tax (disposable) income through the financial markets. Firms derive revenue by selling goods and services. The revenue is used to buy factors of production from households. Households borrow funds from the market for loanable funds to buy durable goods. Firms borrow to buy capital goods such as machines and equipment or to set up plants and factories. The government collects revenue from both households and firms through taxes. Tax revenue is used to buy various things from business firms and households such as cars, electricity, labour and capital. If the government's tax revenue is greater than its spending, there is said to be a surplus in the budget. This surplus is known as government (public) saving. This saving is negative if there is a deficit in the budget, i.e., if government spending exceeds government revenue. Now we shall present a simple model to explain the various interactions among economic agents in terms of Fig. 8.1.

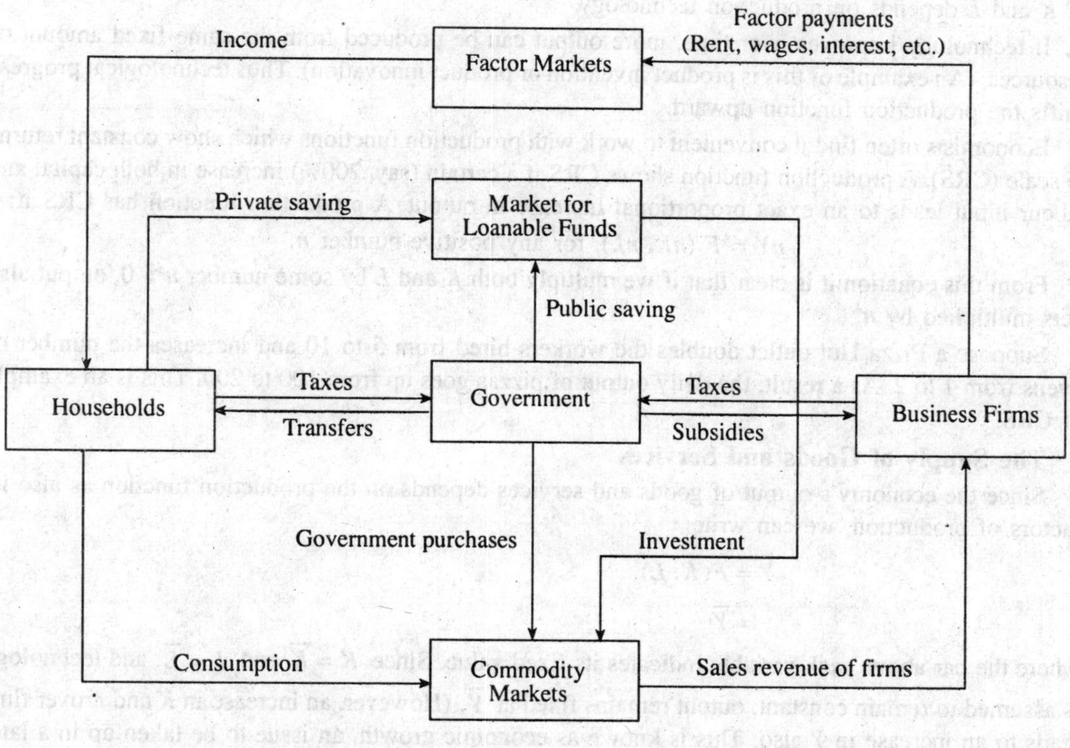

Fig. 8.1: The Circular Flow Model of a Three-Sector (Closed) Economy

THE DETERMINANTS OF AN ECONOMY'S AGGREGATE OUTPUT

An economy's GDP, i.e., its total output of goods and services depends on: (1) the factors of production (or the quantity of inputs) and (2) its aggregate production function (which is a technical relation showing how inputs are converted into output by using existing technology).

The Factors of Production

The factors of production are called inputs or economic resources because they are scarce. However, they have alternative uses. For analytical simplicity we assume the economy makes use of only two factors of production, viz., labour (the human factor) and capital (the man-made resource). Labour refers to human effort of any kind and is a flow variable. It is measured by the time people spend in the workplace to turn out various economic goods and services. Capital is a stock variable. It refers to such things as the workers' tool(s) or the farmers' tractor or a retailer's calculator or an accountant's computer.

Labour and capital are the two main factors of production

Here we assume that our hypothetical economy is endowed with a fixed amount of capital (denoted by K) and labour (denoted by L). We assume that the economy does not keep any of its resources idle. In other words, it fully utilises its existing stock of capital and labour. In other words, we rule out the possibility of unemployment of labour or idle capacity in factories.

The Aggregate Production Function

The aggregate production function is written is:

$$Y = F(K, L)$$

where Y is the output or GDP, K is capital input and L is labour input.

The production function states that output Y depends on the amount of capital and labour used in the production process. How much output an economy is capable of producing from a given amount of K and L depends on production technology.

If technology improves over time, more output can be produced from the same fixed amount of resources. (An example of this is product invention or product innovation). Thus technological progress shifts the production function upward.

Economists often find it convenient to work with production functions which show constant returns to scale (CRS). A production function shows CRS if a certain (say, 200%) increase in both capital and labour input leads to an exact proportional increase in output. A production function has CRS if:

$$nY = F(nK, nL), \text{ for any positive number } n.$$

From this equation it is clear that if we multiply both K and L by some number $n > 0$, output also gets multiplied by n.

Suppose a Pizza Hut outlet doubles the workers hired from 5 to 10 and increases the number of ovens from 1 to 2. As a result, the daily output of pizzas goes up from 100 to 200. This is an example of CRS.

The Supply of Goods and Services

Since the economy's output of goods and services depends on the production function as also its factors of production, we can write:

$$Y = F(\overline{K}, \overline{L})$$
$$= \overline{Y}$$

where the bar above each variable indicates its fixed value. Since $K = \overline{K}$ and $L = \overline{L}$, and technology is assumed to remain constant, output remains fixed at $\overline{Y}$. (However, an increase in K and L over time leads to an increase in Y also. This is known as economic growth, an issue to be taken up in a later chapter).

DISTRIBUTION OF NATIONAL INCOME AMONG FACTORS OF PRODUCTION

Factor pricing and output distribution are interrelated

National income is equivalent to total output of goods and services, which are produced jointly by the factors of production and the production function. However, there is no such thing as free lunch in economics. So each factor of production has to be paid on the basis of its contribution to the society's output. According to the standard neo-classical theory of distribution, developed by J. B. Clark, Philip Wicksteed and others, factor prices, together with quantities of factors supplied in various factor markets, determine factor payments, i.e., how much of national income goes to workers and how much to the suppliers of capital. Here we assume fixed supplies of factors. So factor rewards are determined only by factor prices, an issue to which we turn now.

Factor Prices

Factor prices refer to the wage of workers and the rent of the owners of capital. In Fig. 8.2 we see that the price of factor (P_F) is determined by the forces of demand and supply. Since the quantity of the factor remains fixed the supply curve S_F is a vertical straight line. The total return to the factor is the price of the factor (P_F) multiplied by the quantity of the factor and is indicated by the shaded area.

So the demand for a factor plays a crucial role in determining how a factor is compensated. Since the demand for a factor arises from the demand for numerous firms that use capital and labour, we may now examine how a profit-maximising firm takes decisions regarding how much of these factors to employ or hire.

The Decisions of a Competitive Firm

The neo-classical theory of distribution is based on the assumption that a typical firm is competitive. This means that it is a very small part of the market and thus acts as a price-taker. It has to take the prices of its inputs and outputs as given. In other words, it cannot exert any influence on prices of factors that it buys or the commodity that it sells. Being a small firm it can sell as much as it likes without cutting the price of its product. On the contrary, if it stops selling its product, it cannot cause the price of its product to rise. Similarly, the representative firm can hire as many workers as it likes at the market wage rate. It need not pay more to hire extra workers. But if it pays less than the market wage, it will lose all its workers who will join other firms.

A competitive firm is a price-taker

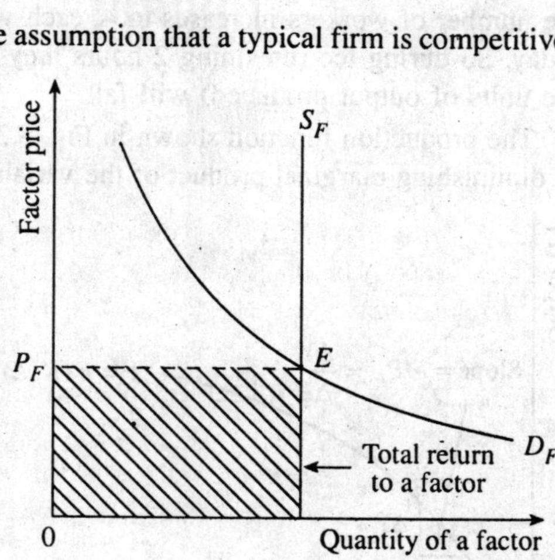

Fig. 8.2: Returns to a Factor

In order to produce its output a typical firm hires both capital and labour from the households. It sells its output *Y* at a price *P*, hires workers at a wage *W* and rents capital at a rate *T*.

The objective of the firm is to maximise profits, i.e., to make the difference between its total revenue (*TR*) and total cost (*TC*) as large as possible. *TR* is what comes to the firm from sale of its output in the market. *TC* is what goes out of the firm in factor payments. If cash inflows exceed cash outflows, the firm is profitable.

Total revenue is $P \times Y$, i.e., price times the units of output sold. Total cost is the sum of labour costs and capital costs. Labour cost equals $W \times L$, the wage rate times the units of labour hired. Capital costs equal $T \times K$, the rental price of capital *T* times the amount of capital. So we get:

$\pi = TR - TC$ where π = total profit, *TR* = total revenue and *TC* = total cost.

The above equation can be written as:

$$\pi = PY - WL - TK$$

So three determinants of profits are the price of the product (*P*), factor prices (*W* and *T*) and the quantities of the two factors (*K* and *L*) purchased or hired. So a competitive firm has to decide how many units of *L* and *K* to hire in order to maximise profits, taking *P*, *W* and *T* as fixed.

A Competitive Firm's Demand for Factors

Factors of production are demanded by a firm because they are productive. By using these factors a firm can produce its profit-maximising quantity of output. In order to find out the firm's profit-maximising quantities of labour and capital, we have to introduce another neo-classical concept, viz., the marginal product. We start with the marginal product of labour.

THE MARGINAL PRODUCT OF LABOUR

In economics the term 'margin' always refers to anything extra. So the marginal product of labour is the addition made to the total product of a firm by one extra worker, when *K* remains fixed. If, for example, three workers using a machine produce 30 units of output and 4 workers using the same machine produce 36 units of output, we say that the marginal product of labour (MP_L) is 6.

The neo-classical production function shows diminishing marginal returns

One property of the production function is that it shows diminishing marginal product. The reason is that productivity of labour depends, among other things, on the availability and usage of complementary factor(s) such as capital (and land). In the above example each of the 3 workers can work for 8 hours a day (if the machine is in operation for 24 hours). If the number of workers increases to 4, each worker will be able to use the machine for only 6 hours a day. So during the remaining 2 hours they will have to sit idle and their productivity (in terms of the units of output produced) will fall.

The production function shown in Fig. 8.3 exhibits diminishing returns. Diminishing returns refer to diminishing marginal product of the variable factor (labour). If, with the employment of any extra worker, total product increases at a decreasing rate, we say that the production function is showing diminishing returns (to labour).

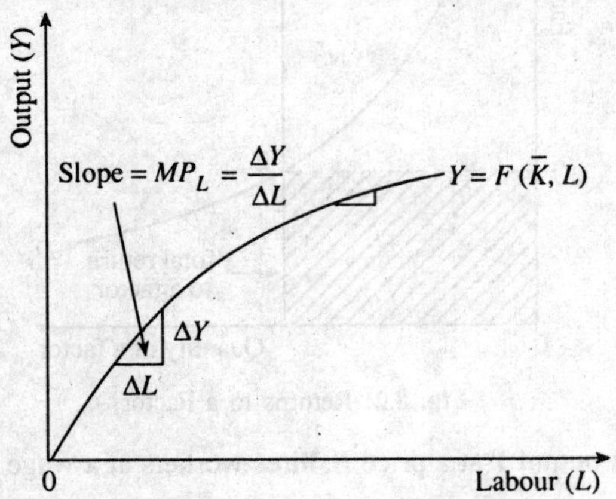

Fig. 8.3: Diminishing MP_L

In Fig. 8.3 the slope of the production function is $MP_L = \Delta Y/\Delta L$. It is clear that as L increases, MP_L falls. In other words, each extra worker gradually makes less and less contribution to the total product of the firm.

The Demand for Labour

A profit-maximising firm hires an additional unit of labour when, by doing that, it makes extra profit. So it always compares the extra revenue which is earned by selling the output produced by the last worker with the wage that has to be paid to the same worker. The extra revenue generated by an extra worker depends on two variables: the MP_L and the price of the product of the firm. The product of the two ($P \times MP_L$) is called the marginal revenue product (MRP_L) of the firm. For example, if P = Rs. 10, and MP_L = 6 units, MRP_L = Rs. 10 × 6 = Rs. 60. The cost of hiring a worker is the wage rate W. So long as W is less than Rs. 60, the firm makes more profits by hiring an extra worker. Thus the extra benefit that a firm can earn by hiring an extra worker is:

$$\Delta\pi = \Delta R - \Delta C$$

$$= MRP_L - W,$$ where 'Δ' denotes any change in a variable.

A firm will hire an extra worker so long as $MRP_L > W$. However, MRP_L has two components: a price component and a physical component. Under perfect competition in the product market, the price component remains constant. But the physical component (MP_L) falls due to diminishing returns. This leads to a fall in MRP_L. When $MRP_L = W$, no further worker is hired since no extra profit can be made by doing that.

So a profit-maximising competitive firm's demand function is determined by the following condition:

$$P \times MP_L = W$$

$$\text{or, } MP_L = W/P$$

Here, W/P is the real wage rate, which is measured in units of goods rather than in terms of money. The main prediction of neo-classical theory of factor demand is that the firm hires labour up to the point at which MP_L = the real wage rate.

Suppose the price of pizza is Rs. 10 and a worker gets Rs. 60 per day. The real wage rate is 6 pizzas per day. So a profit-maximising firm will go on hiring workers so long as each extra worker would produce at least 6 pizzas per day. When MP_L falls to 6 pizzas or even less, the firm does not find it profitable to hire any extra worker.

Fig. 8.4 (p. 145) shows that the MP_L depends on the amount of labour. The MP_L curve slopes downward from left to right due to diminishing MP_L. The firm hires labour up to the point where the MP_L is equal to the real wage. Here MP_L is the demand for labour at the real wage rate (W/P). So the MP_L curve is also the firm's demand for labour curve.

THE MARGINAL PRODUCT OF CAPITAL AND THE DEMAND FOR CAPITAL

The above rule for optimal purchase of labour also applies to capital. This means that, in order to maximise profits, a competitive firm will go on renting capital until the marginal product of capital (MP_K) falls to equal the real rental price:

$$MP_K = T/P$$

Like the real wage rate, the rental price of capital is measured in units of goods rather than in terms of money.

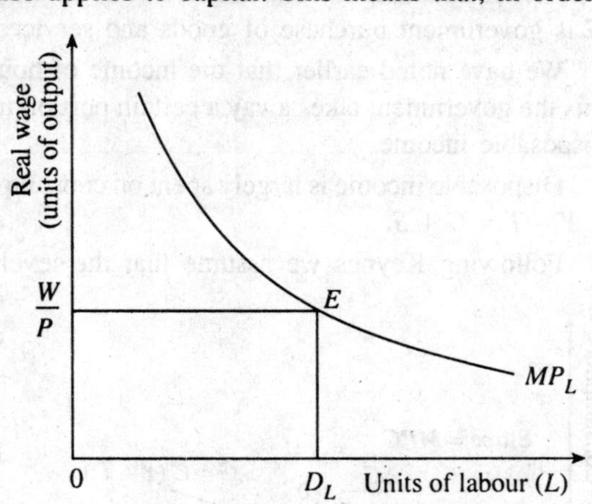

Fig. 8.4: The MP_L Curve as the Demand Curve for Labour

The Distribution of National Income

If all firms in the economy are competitive and seek to maximise profits, then each factor of production is paid on the basis of its marginal product, i.e., $W/P = MP_L$ and $T/P = MP_K$. So the total real wage payment is $MP_L \times L$ and the total real return to capital is $MP_K \times K$.

The economic profit (π) of firms is therefore:

$$\pi = Y - (MP_L \times L) - (MP_K \times K)$$

$$\text{or, } Y = (MP_L \times L) + (MP_K \times K) + \pi$$

This means that total income is divided among the three factors in the form of real wage, real rental, and economic profit.

Thus if each factor is paid according to its marginal product, the total product gets exhausted in factor payments. So economic profit is zero. This is known as the Euler's theorem. The theorem holds under three assumptions:

1. Perfect competition in output and factor markets;
2. Constant returns to scale production function;
3. Profit-maximising behaviour of the business firms.

If the theorem holds then,

$$F(K, L) = (MP_L \times L) + (MP_K \times K)$$

So economic profit is zero.

In the real world, most firms own rather than rent capital they use. Since the owners of the firm are also the owners of capital, economic profit and the return to capital are often added together. This combined return to capital is called accounting profit.

$$\text{Accounting profit} = \text{Economic profit} + (MP_K \times K)$$

Since economic profit is zero under the above three assumptions, profit in national income accounts is largely the return to capital.

THE DETERMINANTS OF THE DEMAND FOR GOODS AND SERVICES

Now, in terms of the circular flow diagram of Fig. 8.1, we examine the disposition of the country's goods and services.

For the sake of simplicity, here we assume a closed economy having no trading relation with the rest of the world. This means that net exports ($X - M$) are zero.

In a closed economy goods and services are used in three ways. So we write the three components of GDP in the form of national income accounts identity:

$$Y = C + I + G$$

The three components of *GDP*, viz., *C*, *I* and *G* have already been identified in ch. 2. Recall that *C* refers to consumption expenditure of households, *I* is investment expenditure of business firms and *G* is government purchase of goods and services for public purposes.

We have noted earlier that the income of households equals the output of the economy *Y*. From this the government takes away a certain portion in taxes (*T*). The difference between the two is called disposable income.

Disposable income is largely spent on consumption goods and partly saved. Thus disposable income $= Y - T = C + S$.

Following Keynes we assume that the level of consumption depends directly on the level of disposable income. Thus, if disposable income increases, consumption will also increase since

$$C = C(Y - T)$$

This equation is called the consumption function. Here *C* is a function of disposable income.

A key concept is marginal propensity to consume (*MPC*). It is the ratio of the change in *C* to one rupee increase in disposable income. It lies between zero and one. Thus, if disposable income increases by one rupee, *C* rises by less than one rupee. If $MPC = 0.80$, then, for every rupee increase in disposable income, *C* increases by 80 paise.

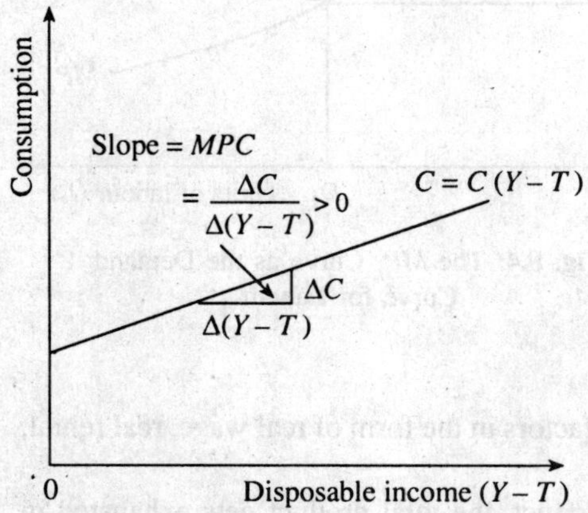

Fig. 8.5: A Simple Linear Consumption Function

Fig. 8.5 presents a simple consumption function. It shows how much *C* increases when disposable income rises by one rupee. The slope is *MPC*, i.e., the ratio of the change in *C* to a change in disposable income. [We will explain the consumption function presented in Fig. 8.5 in further detail in a later chapter.]

INVESTMENT

Investment refers to expenditure on capital goods such as machines, plant, equipment, etc. While households make investment by buying durable goods like houses, firms buy capital goods to produce both consumption and capital goods as also to make provision for the wear and tear of capital.

The main determinant of the demand for investment good is the interest rate. It is the cost of funds borrowed to buy investment goods. Investment has both return and cost sides. If the return from an investment (measured by the revenue earned by selling goods and services in the future) exceeds the cost of the investment (measured in terms of interest paid on borrowed funds), then the investment will be profitable. A rise in the rate of interest reduces investment demand since some potentially profitable projects will no longer appear to be lucrative. So the demand for investment goods will fall.

Investment mainly depends on the rate of interest

Economists draw a distinction between two types of interest rate, viz., the nominal rate and the real rate. Real interest (*r*) is nominal interest (*i*) minus the rate of inflation. The volume of investment depends on real rate of interest because it measures the true cost of borrowing funds needed to finance an investment project. If there is no inflation in the economy, the two rates are the same.

In short, investment is a function of the real rate of interest (*r*):

$$I = I\ (r)$$

Fig. 8.6 shows the investment function. It slopes downward because as *r* increases, the volume of investment falls. A simple example will make this very important point clear. Suppose, $r = 10\%$

and there are four investment projects whose prospective rates of return are 16%, 14%, 12% and 11%. Now all the projects are economically feasible because each one yields a positive return. Now if r increases to 12%, only the first two projects will remain profitable. The third one will not yield any net return (and may be called a marginal, i.e., no-profit-no-loss) project and the fourth one is unprofitable. So a profit-maximising firm will at best undertake the first three projects. It will decide against accepting the last project which is now a losing proposition.

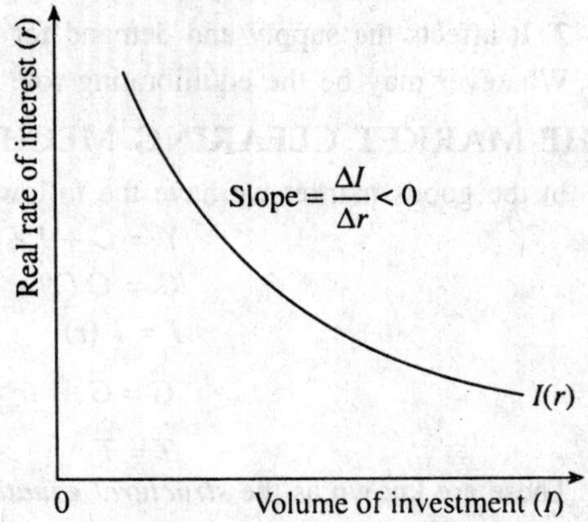

Fig. 8.6: The Investment Function

GOVERNMENT PURCHASE

Government purchases various types of goods and services produced by the private sector. For example, the Food Corporation of India (FCI) purchases foodgrains from farmers for distribution through fair price (ration) shops. The Railway Board purchases wagons. The central, state and local governments buy cars, stationery, books, etc. Most of the medicines distributed through government hospitals are purchased from private companies.

There is another type of government expenditure, called transfer payments. Such payments are made to households. For example, payments are made to needy families, retired people, the unemployed persons, the holders of government bonds and the freedom fighters. Transfer payments are not included in G because those who receive such payments do not provide anything to the government in exchange. There is no *quid pro quo* (or exchange of favour) in case of such transactions.

Transfer payments affect the demand for goods and services

Transfer payments are the opposite of taxes. They increase the disposable income of the households just as taxes reduce it. Thus disposable income remains unchanged if increased transfer payments are made by imposing additional taxes. This means that disposable income now includes both the negative impact of taxes and the positive impact of transfer payments. Therefore transfer payments also affect the demand for goods and services.

If government purchases equal taxes less transfer payments, then $G = T$, where T is the net tax revenue (i.e., gross tax revenue *minus* transfer payments). In such a situation the government budget is said to be in balance. If G exceeds T, there is said to be a deficit in the budget which is funded by selling bonds in the financial markets. This is known as market borrowing. Taxation and borrowing are two usual methods of financing government spending.

Here we treat both government purchases and taxes as exogenous variables in the sense that they are beyond the control of private economic agents. So we take them as constant during the observation period:

$$G = \overline{G}$$

$$T = \overline{T}$$

Three endogenous variables in this simple model are consumption, investment and the real rate of interest. These are affected by fiscal (budgetary) policy.

THE EQUILIBRIUM IN THE GOODS MARKET

In the classical model (ch. 4), we find price adjustment because Y is assumed to remain fixed at the full employment level. The most important price is the real rate of interest. It brings the supply and demand for goods and services into equilibrium.

Note that the real rate of interest plays two crucial roles in this model:

1. The rate of interest affects the supply and demand for goods and/or services.
2. It affects the supply and demand for loanable funds.

Whatever may be the equilibrating role of the rate of interest, the end result is the same.

THE MARKET CLEARING MECHANISM

In the goods market we have the following demand equations:

$$Y = C + I + G$$
$$C = C\,(Y - T)$$
$$I = I\,(r)$$
$$G = \overline{G}$$
$$T = \overline{T}$$

These are known as the *structural equations*, because they describe the structure of the economy.

The supply equations of the model are the following:

$$Y = F(\overline{K}, \overline{L})$$
$$= \overline{Y}$$

Now by combining the two sets of equations and through substitution we get:

$$Y = C(Y - \overline{T}) + I(r) + \overline{G}$$

Since Y remains fixed due to fixed supplies of K and L and unchanged production function and G and T remain fixed because these two exogenous variables are set by fiscal policy, the above equation is written as:

$$\overline{Y} = C(\overline{Y} - \overline{T}) + I(r) + \overline{G}$$

This equation simply states that the supply of output Y equals its demand, which is the sum of C, I and G.

Now we see that r, the only variable not determined in the last equation, plays a key role here. If r is very high, investment is too low, and the demand for output falls short of supply. The converse is also true. So it logically follows that when r reaches its equilibrium level, the demand for goods and services equals the supply. This quite surprising but very interesting conclusion can be tested and verified by considering the functioning of the financial market.

EQUILIBRIUM OF THE MARKET FOR LOANABLE FUNDS

Since the interest rate is both the cost of borrowing and the return to lending in financial markets, it is easy to understand how the market for loanable fund operates and attains equilibrium. Let us rewrite the national income accounts identity as:

$$Y - C - G = I$$
$$\text{or,}\quad S = I$$
$$\text{since}\quad S = Y - C - G$$

Here S is the national saving which is obtained by subtracting C and G from Y. We can simply call it saving. Thus saving equals investment in this model.

National saving has two broad components — private saving and government (public) saving:

$$(Y - T - C) + (T - G) = I,$$

where $(Y - T - C)$ is private saving and $(T - G)$ is budgetary surplus or government saving.

The meaning of the above equation becomes clear in terms of the circular flow diagram of Fig. 8.1 which reveals that the inflow of funds into the financial sector (private and public saving) equals the outflow of funds from the financial sector (investment).

To clearly understand the equilibrating role of the financial market, we substitute the consumption function and the investment function into the national income accounts identity:

$$Y - C(Y - T) - G = I(r)$$

Moreover, $G = \overline{G}, T = \overline{T}$ and $Y = \overline{Y}$, for reasons already explained. So we write

$$\overline{Y} - C(\overline{Y} - \overline{T}) - \overline{G} = I(r)$$

or, $\overline{S} = I(r)$

Thus, from the left hand side of this equation we see that national saving depends on *Y, G* and *T* whose values remain fixed. So *S* also assumes a fixed value. The right hand side of the equation shows that investment depends on *r*.

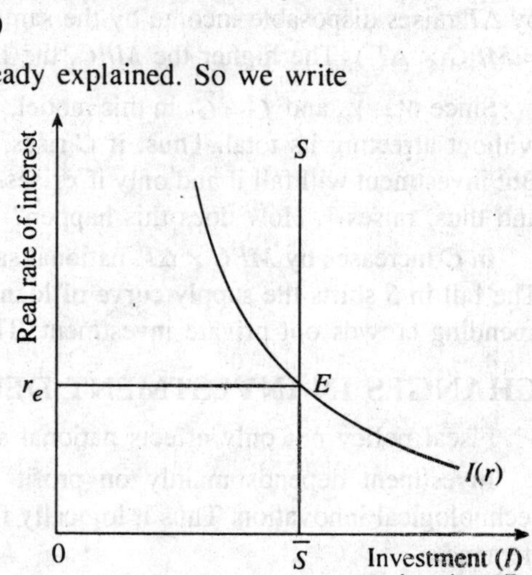

Fig. 8.7: Interest Rate Determination by *S* and *I*

Fig. 8.7 shows equilibrium in the market for loanable funds. The price of loanable funds is the rate of interest. The saving curve is a vertical straight line since it has no relation to *r*. The downward sloping investment schedule intersects the vertical *S* schedule at *E* to determine the equilibrium rate of interest (r_e) at which the households' desire to save is balanced by business firms' desire to invest. If $S > I$, *r* falls. If $S < I$, *r* increases.

EXPANSIONARY FISCAL POLICY AND CROWDING-OUT EFFECT

(a) *An Increase in G*

We shall now see that expansionary fiscal policy reduces national saving and raises *r*. Suppose the government increases its purchase by an amount ΔG. Since *Y* remains fixed, an increase in *G* leads to an increase in *I* since *C* remains unchanged in this model where $Y - T$ remains unchanged.

Why does *I* fall ? Simply because an increase in *G* creates shortage of funds in financial markets. As a result, *r* increases which induces a fall in *I*. This is known as fiscal crowding out, which we may now explain.

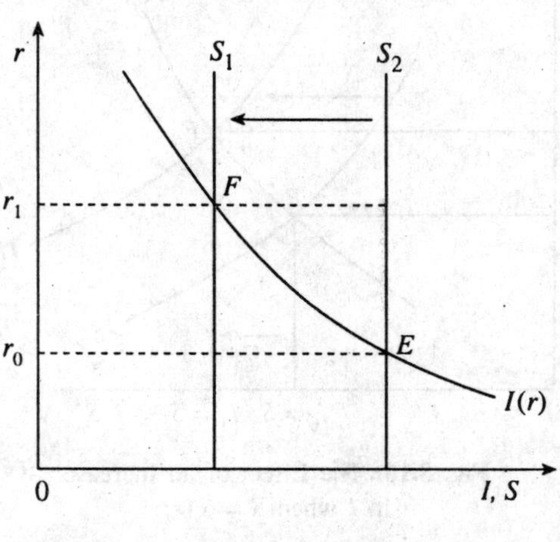

Fig. 8.8: A Fall in National Saving Due to Fiscal Crowding Out

Since the increase in *G* is not financed by an increase in *T*, there is a deficit in the budget which is funded by borrowing, i.e., by reducing public saving. (Just as an increase in *T* leads to an increase in public saving, an increase in budget deficit leads to a fall in public saving). Since private saving remains constant, government borrowing leads to a fall in national saving. Fig. 8.8 shows that a fall in national saving leads to a fall in the supply of loanable funds and its supply curve shifts to the left. At the equilibrium *r*, the demand for loanable funds exactly matches the supply. The new supply schedule intersects the original demand schedule at point *F*, which lies to the left of point *E*. So the equilibrium real rate of interest rises from r_0 to r_1, just because the government has increased its purchases, an interesting result indeed.

(b) *A Cut in T*

We shall now see that a cut in taxes can also crowd out private investment. Note that a cut in taxes by ΔT raises disposable income by the same amount. As a result C falls by MPC times ΔT, (i.e., $\Delta C = MPC \times \Delta T$). The higher the MPC, the larger is the drop in C for the same cut in taxes.

Since $Y = \overline{Y}$, and $G = \overline{G}$, in this model, a policy of tax cut will just alter the composition of output without affecting its total. Thus, if C rises, I has to fall. There is no other possibility in this world. But investment will fall if and only if r rises. In this model, a tax cut crowds out (obstructs) investment and thus, raises r. How does this happen?

In C increases by $MPC \times \Delta T$, national saving S which equals $Y - C - G$ falls by the same amount. The fall in S shifts the supply curve of loanable funds to the left. As a result, r rises and government spending crowds out private investment. The same process, illustrated in Fig. 8.8, works here.

CHANGES IN INVESTMENT DEMAND

Fiscal policy not only affects national saving, it also leads to changes in investment demand.

Investment depends mainly on profit prospects. Profit prospect improves when there is any technological innovation. Thus it logically follows that technological innovation increases investment demand.

Promotion of Investment

Tax cuts promote investment

The government may raise personal taxes and use the extra revenue to give tax concessions to business firms desirous of making investment in new capital. This fiscal boost will make more investment projects profitable and will increase the demand for investment goods just as a technological innovation promotes investment in plant, equipment and machinery.

In Fig. 8.9 we see that the investment demand curve I_0 shifts upward to I_1 due to fiscal concessions given by the government. Since the supply of loanable funds (savings) remains constant, the volume of investment remains unchanged. So only one outcome is possible: r rises from r_0 to r_1.

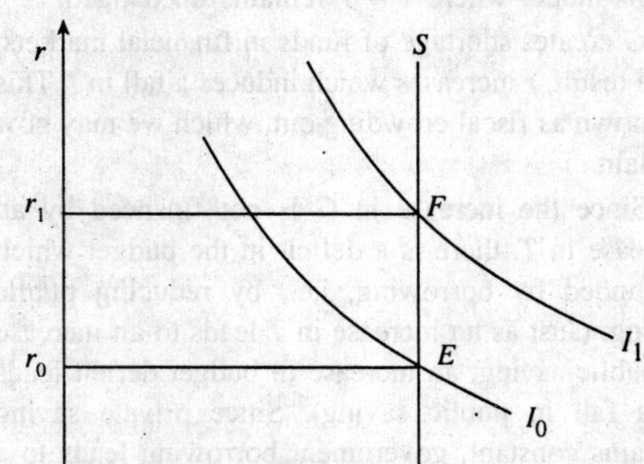

Fig. 8.9: The Effect of an Increase in I on r

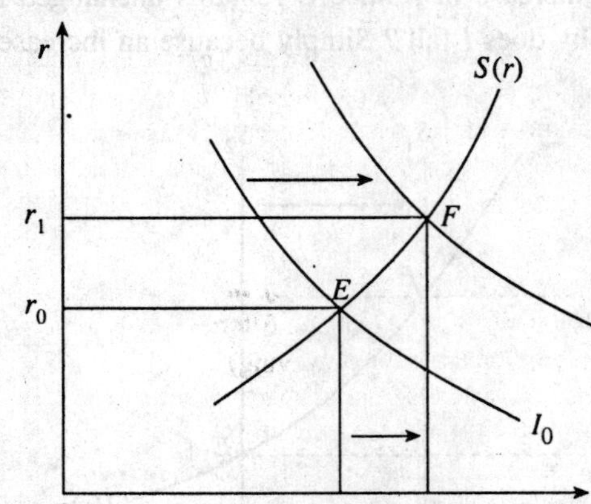

Fig. 8.10: The Effect of an Increase in I when $S = S(r)$

The above conclusion will be modified if we examine the functioning of the model more closely. So long we assumed that C depends on Y. But it is quite reasonable to assume that C also depends on r. We know that $S = Y - C$ and S depends on r. So if r rises, S will increase but C will fall. So the saving curve is likely to be upward sloping like the one shown in Fig. 8.10. In such a situation, an increase in investment demand and a rightward shift of the investment demand curve leads to an increase in both the volume of investment and *r* because a rise in *r* reduces *C*, increases *S* and makes more funds available for use by the business firms.

ESSENTIALLY A GENERAL EQUILIBRIUM MODEL

The simple model presented in this chapter shows various types of interactions among the different markets of the economy, viz., the market for factors of production, the market for goods and services and financial markets (or the market for loanable funds). This explains the production and allocation of the economy's goods and services, and distribution of factor incomes. Commodity prices bring the balance between demand and supply. Factor prices equilibrate the markets for labour and capital. The interest rate brings the supply of goods and services in line with their demand. This amounts to ensuring equilibrium in the market for loanable funds. On the basis of this model, we shall present another general equilibrium model of the economy, viz., the *IS-LM* curve model in a later chapter. This model seeks to integrate the classical (neo-classical) model with the Keynesian model (to be presented in the next chapter). This is why the *IS-LM* curve model presents what Paul Samuelson calls 'the great neoclassical synthesis.'

This chapter lays the foundation for the IS-LM model

KEY POINTS

1. *Determinants of total output* : An economy's total output of goods and services depends on the availability and use of its existing stock of capital and labour (the two main factors of production) and technology. Output increases if the supply (availability) of one of the factors of production (or both) increases. Technological change has the effect of increasing society's output because it raises the productivity of existing resources.

2. *The profit-maximisation rule* : A profit-maximising firm operating in a competitive environment takes decisions regarding optimal output by following the marginalist rule of profit maximisation. It continues to hire labour until marginal product of labour equals the real wage rate (i.e., nominal wage rate deflated by the price level), and marginal product of capital equals its real rental price. If each factor is paid according to its marginal product and the production function shows CRS, all output gets exhausted in making factor payments, leaving neither a surplus nor a deficit at the end. This follows from a mathematical theorem, known as the Euler's theorem or the product exhaustion theorem of microeconomics.

3. *Uses of output in a closed economy* : In a closed economy the total output is used for three purposes, viz., consumption by households, investment by both firms and households and government purchases of privately produced goods and services. Consumption varies directly with disposable income (i.e., income received *less* taxes paid). Investment varies inversely with the real rate of interest. Government purchases and taxes are exogenous (policy) variables and are determined by the decisions of the fiscal authorities. These are not influenced by the behaviour of economic agents.

4. *The role and behaviour of interest rates* : The supplies of various goods and services are brought into balance by interest rate changes. Alternatively stated, interest rates also equilibrate the market for loanable funds. The supply of loanable funds (saving) is brought into line with its demand (investment). An increase in government purchases or a cut in taxes leads to a fall in national saving. As a result, *r* rises and *I* falls. The real rate of interest (*r*) may rise if investment demand increases. Investment demand is likely to increase if the government reduces the corporation tax rate and gives incentives for production of new capital goods. If a rise in *r* stimulates saving, the volume of investment will also rise in spite of a rise in *r*. But in this case *r* rises by less than the amount by which investment increases assuming fixed supply of loanable funds.

KEY TERMS

Production function	Factors of production	Real wage
Real rental price of capital	Marginal product of capital	Marginal product of labour
Loanable funds	Constant returns to scale	Factor prices

Competitive market	Consumption function	Marginal propensity to consume
Disposable income	Crowding out effect	National saving
Private saving	Government saving	Investment
Structural equality	Exogenous variables	Endogenous variables
Market borrowing		

ASSIGNMENTS

1. How is aggregate output determined?
2. How does a profit-maximising competitive firm take decision regarding optimum purchase of capital and labour?
3. If a production function shows constant returns to scale, and the markets are competitive, payment of each factor on the basis of its marginal product will exhaust the total product. True or false?
4. What are the determinants of consumption and investment?
5. How does the real interest rate adjust to equilibrate the supply and demand for the country's output?
6. How does fiscal policy affect consumption, investment and the interest rate?
7. What is the difference between government purchases and transfer payments? Give examples of each.
8. Can the same production function show increasing returns to scale and decreasing returns to scale? If so, why?
9. What happens to the real rental price of capital in each of the following cases:
   (a) Immigration from Bangladesh increases the size of the labour force.
   (b) A portion of capital stock is destroyed by flooding in a major industrial belt.
   (c) Technology improves over time.
10. Suppose Y = Rs. 5,000, G = Rs. 2,000, T = Rs. 2,000, C = Rs. 500 + 0.6 $(Y - T)$, I = Rs. 2,000 – 100r.
    (a) Compute national saving.
    (b) What is r?
    (c) What happens to national saving and r if G increases to Rs. 2,500?

8A SAVING, INVESTMENT AND FINANCIAL SYSTEM

> *In many ways, financial markets are like other markets in the economy. In one way, however, financial markets are special. Financial markets, unlike most other markets, serve the important role of linking the present and the future.*
>
> N. G. Mankiw

Two basic units of an economic system are the households and business firms. They can be placed into two broad categories, viz., surplus-generating units (SGUs) and deficit-spending units (DSUs). The SGUs spend less than they earn. Thus they save a portion of their incomes.

On the other hand, the DSUs spend more than they earn and they have to borrow to meet the deficit (excess of current expenditure over current income). In most cases it is found that the DSUs cannot

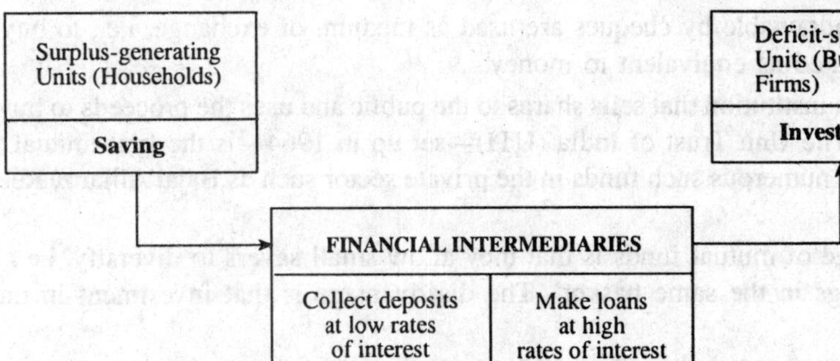

Fig. 8A.1: Financial Intermediaries

directly borrow from the SGUs because there is no direct link or flow of information between the two. But there are certain institutions which work as financial intermediaries or institutions. Such institutions receive fund from savers and lend them to borrowers. These include depository institutions such as mutual funds like the Unit Trust of India (UTI) and insurance companies. They collect the saving of the SGUs for making loans to DSUs in order to enable the latter to meet the excess of expenditure over income. Fig. 8A.1 shows that the savings of SGUs are collected by financial institutions for investment in DSUs. In this way, the saving of the households is converted into investment of firms. Herein lies the role of financial intermediaries.

THE FINANCIAL SYSTEM

In every economy some people save and others invest. The financial system of a country helps to match the saving of one person with the investment of another person. Thus it plays a very important role in a modern economy. It moves the economy's scarce financial resources from savers (the surplus-generating units) to borrowers (the deficit-spending units). In fact, savers are lenders and investors are borrowers.

The financial system consists of those institutions that help coordinate the lending activities of savers with the borrowing activities of investors. Financial institutions are of two types — financial markets and financial intermediaries.

(a) Financial Markets

Financial markets are those institutions through which savers can *directly* supply funds to borrowers. The two most important components of the financial markets are the *bond market* and the *stock market*. A company can borrow directly by selling *bonds* to the public. A bond is essentially a certificate of indebtedness. It specifies the obligations of the borrower to the holder of the bond. The sale of bonds to raise funds is called *debt finance.*

Companies can also raise funds for investment by selling stocks. A stock is a claim to partial ownership in a firm (or a company) and, thus, a claim to the profits of the firm. The sale of stock to raise funds is called *equity finance.*

(b) Financial Intermediaries

Financial intermediaries are institutions through which savers can *indirectly* provide funds to borrowers. Such intermediaries play an important role in the financial system of a country by standing between savers (lenders) and investors (borrowers).

The two most important financial institutions are banks and mutual funds. A *bank* is a financial intermediary in the sense that it is a dealer in loans and a dealer in debts. The primary function of banks is to accept deposits from savers at low rates of interest and make loans from such savings to investors at higher rates of interest.

Bank deposits withdrawable by cheques are used as medium of exchange, i.e., to buy goods and services. They are treated as equivalent to money.

A mutual fund is an institution that sells shares to the public and uses the proceeds to buy a portfolio of stocks and bonds. The Unit Trust of India (UTI)—set up in 1964—is the first mutual fund of the country. Now there are numerous such funds in the private sector such as Bajaj Allianz, Reliance, Tata, Kotak Mahindra, etc.

The main advantage of mutual funds is that they allow small savers to diversify, i.e., reduce risk by 'not putting all eggs in the same basket'. The disadvantage is that investment in mutual funds involves market risk.

In this context, we may refer to the flow of funds account. This is illustrated in the following box.

Flow of Funds

Flow of funds refers to a set of accounts that describe the sources and uses of saving in the economy. The accounts provide a means for analysing financial flows between economic sectors (such as households, businesses, and governments) and into and out of financial instruments (such as mortgages, corporate debentures, and bank loans).

Framework of Flow-of-Funds Accounts

Flow-of-funds accounts are an integral part of the economic accounts of a nation, and they are usually tied explicitly to the national income accounts. These latter accounts show receipts and outlays by sectors and by type of final product. The difference between receipts and outlays for each sector is a source of funds (saving). A second source of funds is borrowing. For each sector of the economy and for the economy as a whole, total saving must be equal to total investment, and, broadly speaking, investment takes to forms—purchases of tangible assets and net acquisition of financial assets. Thus, the flow-of-funds accounts are sometimes expressed as a system that provides the details underlying the following basic framework:

Sources of funds		Uses of funds
Saving (= receipts less outlays) Borrowing		Purchases of tangible assets Net acquisition of financial assets
Total	=	**Total**

A second, equivalent framework for the flow-of-funds accounts is derived from the perspective of a balance sheet. A balance sheet for an economic sector shows the accumulated amount (or stock) of assets and liabilities at a moment in time, with assets *less* liabilities measuring the net worth of the sector. The flow-of-funds accounts show the changes (flows) of assets and liabilities over a specified period, highlighting flows of financial assets and liabilities. Under this framework, a generalised flow-of-funds statement for a sector would include the following broad elements:

1. Gross saving (from the national income accounts),
2. Gross investment,
3. Investment in tangible assets (from the national income accounts),
4. Net investment in financial assets,
5. Acquisition of financial assets *less* increase in financial liabilities,
6. Borrowing,
7. Change in other liabilities and
8. Discrepancy.

The heart of the flow-of-funds accounts lies in items 4 through 7, with added detail showing the types of financial assets and liabilities acquired by different sectors. The discrepancy (item 8) is the difference between measured gross saving and measured gross investment (item 1 *less* item 2). In theory, the discrepancy is equal to zero. In practice, however, the discrepancy for a specific sector may be significant relative to the size of gross saving or investment. The size of the discrepancy depends in part on the quality of the data available to measure the various flows. The absence of capital gains and losses as a source of funds in national income accounts also introduces a measurement problem, as investment for a sector no doubt reflects such gains and losses. A measure of flows into and out of financial institutions such as banks, life insurance companies, and pension funds allows for analysis of their contribution to economic activity and for examination of changes in the relative importance of banks and other depository institutions, other types of financial institutions, and open market financing.

SAVING AND INVESTMENT IN A CLOSED ECONOMY

Since saving and investment are important determinants of long-run growth in GDP and the consequent improvement in standards of living it is important to know how financial markets coordinate the economy's saving and investment.

For analytical simplicity we start with a closed economy where GDP (denoted by Y) is written as

$$Y = C + I + G \qquad \ldots \quad (1)$$

where all the terms have their usual meaning. Here we assume that export (X) is zero and import (M) is also zero.

Now we subtract C and G from both sides of this equation and get

$$Y - C - G = I \qquad \ldots \quad (2)$$

The left hand side of this equation is saving, which is a residue, i.e., the portion of income which is left after consumption and government purchases. So we can write

$$S = I \qquad \ldots \quad (3)$$

Thus, saving equals investment. This equation can also be written as

$$S = Y - C - G$$

$$\text{or,} \quad S = (Y - T - C) + (T - G) \qquad \ldots \quad (4)$$

where T is the tax that the government collects from households *minus* the amount it returns to households through transfer payments (such as social security in the form of unemployment compensation and/or pension).

From equation (4) we see that national saving has two parts: (i) private saving $(Y - T - C)$, and (ii) public (government) saving $(T - G)$. Private saving is that part of income which households have left with them after paying taxes and buying consumption goods. Public saving is the excess of tax revenue of the government after purchases of goods and services. If T exceeds G, there is said to exist a *surplus* in the budget and this is public saving. So if there is a deficit in the budget, public saving is negative. This is exactly what was found in India up to 2002-03: national saving was *less than* private saving due to negative public saving attributable to budget deficit. However, things changed since then. In 2005-06 India's gross domestic saving rate was 31.2% of GDP of which the contribution of the household sector was 21.8%, of the corporate sector 7.4% and of the public sector 2%.

The equation $S = I$ implies that for the economy as a whole, saving must be equal to investment. This is ensured by the financial system. The bond market, the stock market, banks and insurance companies and mutual funds collect the nation's saving and direct it to the nation's investment.

MEANING OF SAVING AND INVESTMENT

Saving is that portion of an individual's disposable income which is not spent on consumption goods. It is a residue, i.e., excess of $Y - T$ over C. Investment refers to the purchase of new capital, such as plant, equipment, machinery, structures, etc. If Ram, for instance, borrows from the Life Insurance Corporation of India or Allahabad Bank to build a new house, he adds to India's investment. Similarly, when Tata Chemicals Ltd. sells some stocks and uses the funds raised to set up a new factory, it also adds to India's investment.

In every economy some people save and others invest. Moreover, Ram's saving may be greater than his investment. So he will deposit the surplus in a bank. John's saving may be less than his investment and he can borrow the shortfall from a bank. Banks thus enable one person's saving to finance another person's investment.

Alternative Measures of Saving

Saving looks different to the household sector than to the nation as a whole. In national income accounts, saving is the difference between disposable income (excluding capital gains) and consumption. The *balance sheet measure* of saving calculates the change in real net worth (that is, assets *less* liabilities—corrected for inflation) from one year to the next; this measure includes real capital gains.

The difference in the two measures of saving has an important implication. While consumers may feel richer due to stock market boom, an economy is actually richer only when its productive tangible and intangible assets increase.

Market for Loanable Funds

The term 'loanable funds' refers to all income that people decide to save and lend out after meeting their consumption needs. The market for loanable funds is the one in which savers supply funds and those who want to borrow for investment purposes demand funds. All savers go to the market to deposit their surplus resources and all borrowers go to this market to borrow the excess of investment over saving. In this market there is one rate of interest, which is both the return to saving and the cost of borrowing.

Supply and Demand for Loanable Funds

Loanable funds are supplied by people who want to save and lend their saving. The demand for loanable funds is generated by borrowers — households and firms — who wish to buy durable goods (such as cars or computers) or make investments in houses, factories, etc. Capital markets balance saving and investment. The demand for capital arises from the fact that indirect or roundabout methods of production are productive; by abstaining from consumption today, society can consume more in the future. On the other hand, people must be willing to abstain from consumption in order to accumulate financial assets, lending funds to firms that make the productive investments which are likely to generate profits. These two forces of demand and supply are brought into balance by the interest rate which ensures that society's accumulation of capital just matches the amounts that people are willing to save by curtailing (i.e., abstaining from) current consumption.

Simply put, the interest rate is the price of a loan. It represents the amount that borrowers pay for loans and the amount that lenders receive on their saving. In Fig. 8A.2 the interest rate (6%) equates the supply and the demand for loanable funds. The supply of such funds is equal to saving (both private and government). The demand for such funds comes from both households and firms who want to borrow for purposes of investment. The rate of interest, like the price of a commodity, moves up or down to balance the economy's supply of such funds with its demand. A high interest rate encourages people to save more and therefore, increases the supply of loanable funds. But it makes borrowing to finance capital projects more costly. Thus it discourages investments and reduces the quantity of loanable funds demanded.

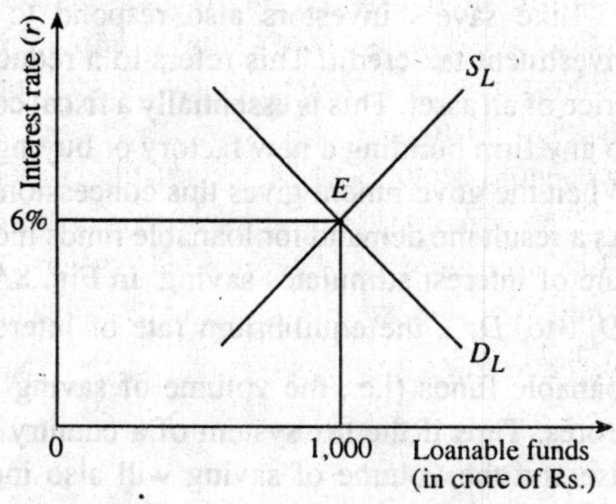

Fig. 8A.2: The Market for Loanable Funds

Effects of Taxes on Saving and Investment

When high taxes are imposed in one sector, resources will flow into more lightly taxed areas. For example, since there is double taxation in case of corporate capital, people's savings will flow out of the corporate sector and into lightly taxed sectors like food or housing financed by tax-deductible interest payments. If risky investments are taxed unfavourably investors may prefer safer investments. The inefficiency results both from the divergence of taxes across sectors and from the existence of high taxes.

Effect of Taxes on the Rate of Interest

Looked at from the other side, it is anybody's observation that people respond favourably to incentives. An example of such incentive is tax cut. If the government reduces the rate of personal income tax, people will save more even at the existing rate of interest by curtailing current consumption.

A tax cut increases personal saving

So the supply of loanable funds will increase and its supply curve will shift to the right, as shown in Fig. 8A.3. As a result the equilibrium rate of interest will fall and the lower rate of interest will stimulate investment. And, in this case, the equilibrium quantity of loanable funds saved and invested rises from Rs. 1,000 crores to Rs. 1,200 crores.

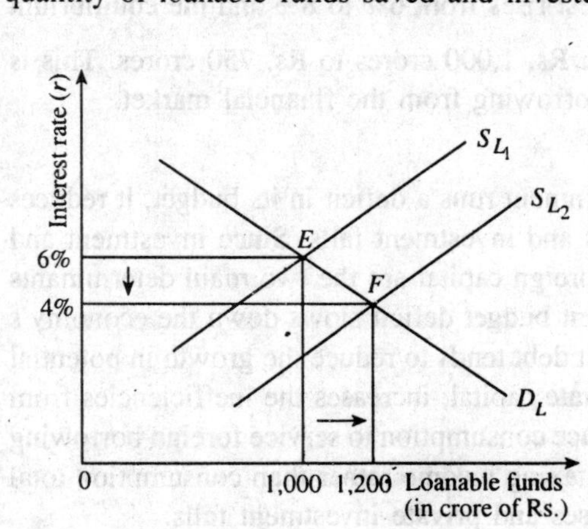

Fig. 8A.3: The Effect of an Increase in the Supply of Loanable Funds

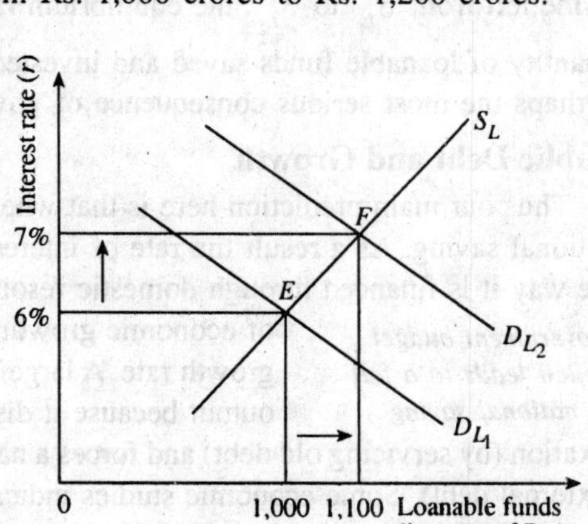

Fig. 8A.4: An Increase in the Demand for Loanable Funds

Effect of Investment Incentive on the Rate of Interest

Like savers investors also respond to incentives. An example of investment incentive is the investment tax credit. This refers to a reduction in tax liability equal to some portion of the purchase price of an asset. This is essentially a fiscal concession offered to certain investors. It gives tax advantage to any firm building a new factory or buying any capital good such as a new machine or an equipment. When the government gives this concession by passing a law, firms get extra incentive to invest more. As a result the demand for loanable funds increases and the equilibrium rate of interest rises. This higher rate of interest stimulates saving. In Fig. 8A.4 when the demand curve for loanable funds shifts from D_{L_1} to D_{L_2}, the equilibrium rate of interest rises from 6% to 7%, and the equilibrium quantity of loanable funds (i.e., the volume of saving and investment) rises from Rs. 1,000 crores to Rs. 1,100 crores. Thus if the tax system of a country gives encouragement to investors, the rate of interest will rise and the volume of saving will also increase.

Effect of Government Budget Deficit on the Rate of Interest

If the government spends more than it collects in taxes, there is a deficit in the budget which is equivalent to negative public saving. The government finances this deficit by borrowing in the bond market. The accumulation of past government borrowing is called government debt.

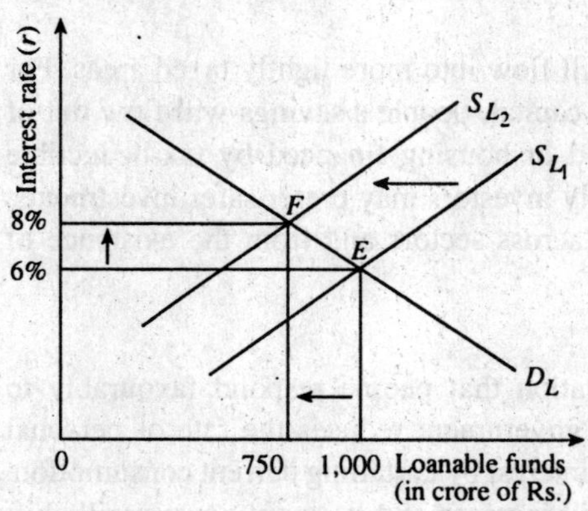

Fig. 8A.5: The Effect of Government Budget Deficit

The budget deficit of the government lowers national saving. As result the supply of loanable funds falls and the shortage of such funds raises the equilibrium rate of interest and reduces the borrowing of the households for the purpose of investment. This is known as the crowding out (capital displacement) effect. As P. A. Samuelson has put it: "The effect of government debt is that people will accumulate government debt instead of private capital and the nation's private capital stock will be displaced by public debt". In Fig. 8A.5 the supply curve of loanable funds shifts to the left from S_{L_1} to S_{L_2}, the equilibrium rate of interest rises from 6% to 8% and the equilibrium quantity of loanable funds saved and invested falls from Rs. 1,000 crores to Rs. 750 crores. This is perhaps the most serious consequence of government borrowing from the financial market.

Public Debt and Growth

Thus our main prediction here is that when the government runs a deficit in its budget, it reduces national saving. As a result the rate of interest increases and investment falls. Since investment and the way it is financed through domestic resources and foreign capital are the two main determinants of economic growth, government budget deficit slows down the economy's growth rate. A large government debt tends to reduce the growth in potential output because it displaces private capital, increases the inefficiencies from taxation (by servicing old debt) and forces a nation to reduce consumption to service foreign borrowing (external debt). Some economic studies indicate that by taxing income rather than consumption total saving is discouraged. As a result the rate of interest rises and private investment falls.

Government budget deficit leads to a fall in national saving

CHAPTER 9

The Keynesian Model of Income Determination

> *I believe myself to be writing a book on economic theory which will largely revolutionise — not at once but in the course of the next ten years — the way the world thinks about economic problems.*
>
> J. M. Keynes

PREVIEW

In this chapter we examine how, according to the Keynesian theory, the level of employment is determined in a free market-based capitalist economy in the short run when the size of the labour force and capital stock remain constant and the state of technology (which shows how inputs can be converted into output) also remains unchanged. In addition, Keynes assumed that the price level remains unchanged. Thus, under these restrictive assumptions, the level of income depends on the level of employment in a static framework. Since income is a function of employment, both are determined simultaneously. So in the simple Keynesian model, like the level of employment, the level of income is determined by aggregate demand and aggregate supply. If employment increases, national income will also increase. In this chapter we analyse determination of national income in the context of a simple two-sector economy, with a fixed price level. We start with the key concept of the model, viz., aggregate demand.

In Keynes's model income and employment are the mirror image concepts

AGGREGATE DEMAND AND AGGREGATE EXPENDITURE

Aggregate demand refers to the total desired expenditure of households and firms at various level of national income per period. So we will use the terms 'aggregate demand' and 'aggregate expenditure' synonymously in this chapter.

VARIABLE PRICE LEVEL VS. FIXED PRICE LEVEL

In a later chapter, we will be discussing the modern concepts of aggregate demand and aggregate supply by assuming that prices are variable. At that stage, we will be deriving the aggregate demand curve from aggregate desired expenditure schedule. In this chapter, we take the price level as fixed, as assumed by Keynes and study macroeconomic equilibrium by using Keynes's concept of aggregate demand and aggregate supply.

THE CONCEPT OF AGGREGATE DEMAND (WITH A CONSTANT PRICE LEVEL)

In a two-sector closed economy without Government and foreign trade aggregate demand has two components: (i) household demand for consumption goods and (ii) business demand for capital goods or investment demand. By aggregate demand Keynes means how much expenditure the households and businesses are making on consumption and investment, respectively per period. So we can write:

Aggregate demand = Consumption demand + investment demand

$$\text{or, } AD = C + I \quad \ldots (1)$$

where AD stands for aggregate demand, C for household consumption and I for business investment. Accordingly we can rewrite equation (1) as

$$AE = C + I \quad \ldots (2)$$

where AE is aggregate expenditure. Now we discuss each component of aggregate demand one by one.

CONSUMPTION DEMAND (*C*)

In the short-run, consumption demand depends on two main factors: (i) the level of national income, and (ii) the propensity to consume[1]. The propensity (tendency) to consume is likely to remain constant in the short run. So as income increases, consumption demand also increases. This means that consumption demand depends on income or is a function of income. The functional relation between income and consumption is shown by the Keynesian consumption function. It can be either linear with a constant slope (the slope is *MPC*) or non-linear with a declining slope. For analytical simplicity, we assume here a linear short-run consumption function which takes the following form:

$$C = a + bY \quad \ldots (3)$$

Here C is consumption, Y is income, b is *MPC* and a (the intercept of the consumption function) stands for autonomous consumption. Even if income is zero, consumption cannot be zero because of this autonomous component. This represents subsistence consumption, i.e., the minimum amount an individual has to consume in order to survive even when his income is zero. The second component of equation (3) shows induced consumption. It depends on income (Y).

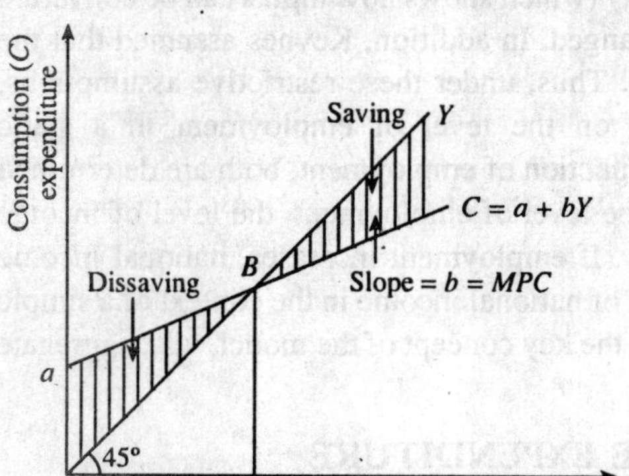

Fig. 9.1: The Keynesian Short-run Consumption Function

In Fig. 9.1 we present a simple Keynesian short-run consumption function. Here we measure disposable national income on the horizontal axis and consumption expenditure on the vertical axis. Here we have drawn a 45° income line which acts as a guideline. This line has an important property. If we drop a perpendicular from any point on the line, we see that national income = consumption expenditure. But this does not happen at all points. We see that the consumption line $C = a + bY$ (which represents a linear consumption function) intersects the income line at point B. Point B is called the break-even point in the theory of consumption. If income reaches a minimum level, $Y_{min.}$ (shown on the horizontal axis), the entire income is consumed. However,

1. The propensity to consume is of two types: marginal and average. The marginal propensity to consume (*MPC*) is the ratio of the change in C to the change in Y which brings it about and is written as $\Delta C/\Delta Y$ where 'Δ' denotes any change. The *MPC* measures the slope of the consumption function. It is the key concept in the Keynesian theory of income (output) determination. Average propensity to consume is the ratio of total consumption to total income (C/Y).

if income is less than this, C exceeds Y. This means that saving is negative. Such negative saving is called dissaving. If, on the other hand, Y exceeds $Y_{min.}$, $Y > C$, and S is positive. So national income has to reach a minimum level for any saving to occur. The vertical distance between the income line and the consumption line shows the level of saving at each level of income. The reason is that like employment and income, C and S are mirror image concepts. We know that $Y = C + S$ or $S = Y - C$ (in the absence of G, T and M). So if Y remains constant and C increases or falls, S will increase or fall. After all S is a residue. It is that portion of Y which is not spent on currently produced goods and services.

We also see from Fig. 9.1 that the vertical distance (or the gap between Y and C) increases as Y increases. This means that as Y increases, C increases no doubt, but not proportionately or S increases more than proportionately. The reason is that at low levels of income people consume more and at high levels of income, they save more.

MOVEMENT VS. SHIFT

In the short-run the consumption function does not change. There is just movement along the same consumption function. As Y increases, C also increases. But the consumption function does not shift to a new position. The reason is that, apart from national income, consumption depends on various other factors such as the tastes and preferences of consumers, the pattern of income distribution in the economy, the size of the population, the age and sex composition of the people and so on. These factors, which cause shift of the consumption function, remain constant in the short-run. This means that in the short-run, consumption demand depends only on national income (or on disposable income).

INVESTMENT DEMAND (*I*)

No doubt, household consumption expenditure is the most important component of aggregate demand. The second most important component of aggregate demand is investment. It plays a crucial role in the determination of the equilibrium level of national income. It also causes short-run fluctuations in the level of income, or business cycles. Investment demand depends on two main factors: (1) the marginal efficiency of capital (*MEC*) and (2) the rate of interest (r). Since in the short-run, the rate of interest normally remains constant, any fluctuations in the level of income occurs due to changes in *MEC*. *MEC*, in fact, refers to the rate of return the business people expect to earn from new investment, i.e., from the purchase or acquisition of new capital goods such as machines or equipment. The *MEC*, in its turn, depends on two factors (1) the prospective rate of return from an asset over its economic life (which depends on the annual rate of depreciation)[1] and (2) the replacement costs of old capital goods (or purchase price of new capital goods). In the short-run, the replacement costs of old machines remain firmly constant. But profit expectations of business firms fluctuate every now and then. And this causes fluctuations in *MEC*, which, in turn, causes investment fluctuations[2].

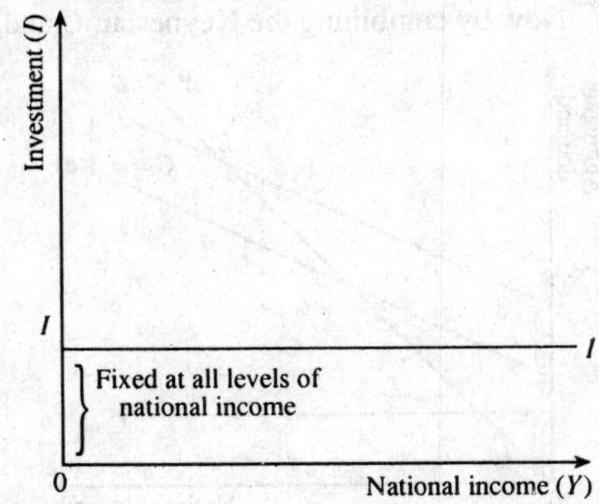

Fig. 9.2: Autonomous Investment

1. If the annual rate of depreciation of a machine is 10%, its economic life is 10 years. If the rate of depreciation is 20%, it is 5 years and if $33^1/_2$%, then only 3 years. Depreciation refers to consumption of fixed capital.
2. This has an important policy implication. If the government of a country seeks to achieve a target level of real GNP, investment has to be stepped up to the desired level by giving business firms various types of incentives such as tax cut, investment tax credit, investment subsidy, and loans at concessional rates of interest through public sector banks and public financial institutions.

AUTONOMOUS VS. INDUCED INVESTMENT

Investment is of two types — (a) autonomous (or independent of income) and (b) induced (or dependent on income). Keynes assumed that all investment is autonomous and hence independent of national income or its rate of change. In Keynes's theory, investment depends on *MEC* and *r*. In Fig 9.2. we show the Keynesian investment demand schedule *II* which is horizontal. This means that investment remains constant at all levels of national income, i.e., whether national income is high or low. So its slope is zero.

Economic Insight: Theory and Reality

In reality, investment is partly autonomous and partly induced. In a later chapter, when we discuss the various theories of investment, we will be referring to induced investment. In fact, that part of total investment, which occurs due to an increase in national income, is called induced investment. From this emerges a very important theory of investment, called the acceleration theory which was ignored by Keynes. This theory was presented in 1917 by J. M. Clark on the basis of the initial work done by A. Aftalion. According to this theory anything which increases consumer demand such as national or per capita income improves the profit prospect of entrepreneurs. So they get an incentive to invest more. If, for example, the demand for textiles increases and more profits are made by textile producers, they will buy more textile producing machines. After all the demand for capital goods is a derived or indirect demand.

In fact, a rise in income improves the *MEC* and thus affects investment demand indirectly. See the sequence below:

Rise in national (per capita) income → rise in demand for consumer goods → improved profit prospects → increase in *MEC* → more investment in new capital goods.

THE COMBINED *C* + *I* SCHEDULE

Now by combining the Keynesian *C* and *I* functions, presented in Fig. 9.1 and Fig. 9.2, we present the combined $C + I$ schedule in Fig. 9.3. This is known as the aggregate demand curve or, in modern terminology, the aggregate desired expenditure schedule (curve).

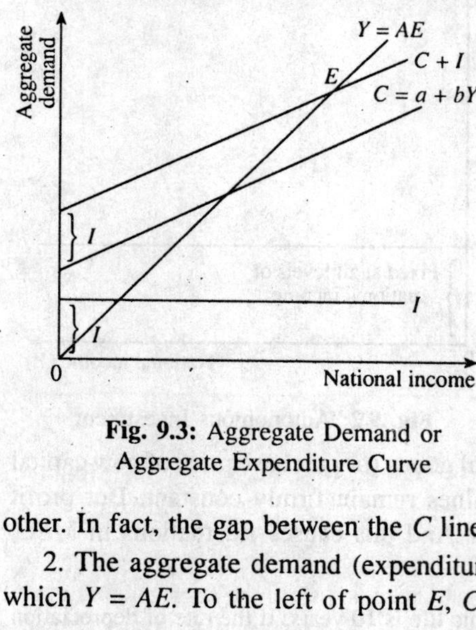

Fig. 9.3: Aggregate Demand or Aggregate Expenditure Curve

We proceed in four steps:

1. First we draw the 45° income line *Y*.
2. Then we draw the consumption line *C*.
3. In the next step we draw the investment line *I*.
4. Finally we superimpose the investment line on the consumption line to arrive at the combined $C + I$ line.

Two points are to be noted here:

1. Since the investment line is horizontal, implying a fixed amount of investment at all levels of income, the consumption line and the $C + I$ line are parallel to each other. In fact, the gap between the *C* line and the $C + I$ line measures fixed autonomous investment.

2. The aggregate demand (expenditure) schedule, $C + I$, intersects the income line at point *E* at which $Y = AE$. To the left of point *E*, $C + I > Y$ and to the right of point *E*, $Y > C + I$.

AGGREGATE SUPPLY

By aggregate supply Keynes means the total money value of (final) goods and services produced in an economy per year at constant prices. Two components of aggregate supply are the following:

1. the output of all final consumer goods and services; and
2. the output of producer or capital (investment) goods.

Capital goods are the creators of other goods. For example, textile producing machines are used to produce textiles (or consumer goods). Machines are also used to produce other machines (or capital goods). For these reasons capital goods are also called producer goods.

NATIONAL PRODUCT

In fact, aggregate supply is another name of *GNP*. Both represent the total market value of all final goods and services produced in an economy per annum. In another sense, *GNP* is the same as national income. The reason is that aggregate supply or money value of all final goods and services produced and sold is distributed among the various factors of production as rent, wages, interest and profits as rewards for their respective contributions to *GNP*.

THE SHORT-RUN PRODUCTION FUNCTION

Much like his predecessors (like classicists), Keynes derived his aggregate supply function from the short-run aggregate production function which is expressed as

$$Y = F(L, \overline{K}, \overline{T}) \qquad \ldots (4)$$

where *Y* is *GNP*, *L* is labour input (which is the only variable factor), $\overline{K}$ is the fixed stock of capital, and $\overline{T}$ stands for unchanged technology. Thus the aggregate production function may also be written as:

$$Y = F(L) \qquad \ldots (5)$$

This means that in the short-run more output can be produced only by employing more labourers (or using more labour inputs), so long as the economy has unutilised resources (mainly manpower) and of course, excess production capacity.

Since Keynes assumed that the size of the labour force remains constant in the short-run, the level of employment (or the utilisation of the labour force) increases (falls) only if the demand for labour increases (falls). After all the Keynesian model is a demand-determined model.

THE AGGREGATE SUPPLY CURVE

Since the aggregate price level is assumed to remain constant in the short-run, the Keynesian aggregate supply curve relates the level of aggregate output to national income[1]. In fact, while drawing this supply curve money wages and productivity of labour are also assumed to remain constant[2]. These assumptions together imply that more output will be produced and supplied at the given price level if aggregate demand increases. Thus aggregate demand sets the tune and aggregate supply dances at it.

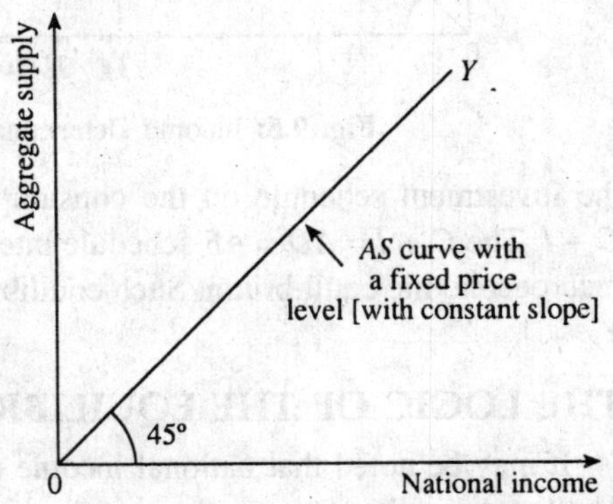

Fig. 9.4: The Keynesian Short-run Aggregate Supply Curve

1. Modern economists present a different type of *AS* curve. They relate the real *GNP* to the aggregate price level through the *AS* curve and use the curve along with the *AD* curve to explain two types of inflation, viz., demand-pull and cost-push.
2. The productivity of labour remains constant when $MP_L = AP_L$ and labour cost also remains constant when the nominal wage rate and productivity of labour remain constant. These assumptions have important implications for the nature and slope of the aggregate supply curve.

In Fig. 9.4 we draw the Keynesian short-run aggregate supply curve as a 45° line $0Y$ since aggregate supply or national product is always equal to national income. Due to constant marginal cost and average cost of production, the value of aggregate output increases at the constant rate along the 45° line.

The 45° line shows two things:

1. It shows that even at constant prices, varying amounts of output (of both consumer and capital goods) will be offered for sale in response to changes in aggregate demand. If aggregate demand rises, more output will be offered for sale until and unless the state of full employment of resources is reached. When full employment is reached, a society's actual output will be equal to its potential output. At this stage, no further increase in production and in aggregate supply is possible.

2. Since national income is the same thing as national product, the 45° line represents national income in nominal (money) terms.

THE EQUILIBRIUM LEVEL OF NATIONAL INCOME

In Fig. 9.5 we put forth both the aggregate demand and aggregate supply curves to show how the equilibrium level of national income is determined in the two-sector model of Keynes. Here we proceed in four steps. First we draw the aggregate supply curve schedule $0Y$ which is the 45° line. Then we draw the consumption schedule C. Next we draw the investment schedule I. Finally we superimpose

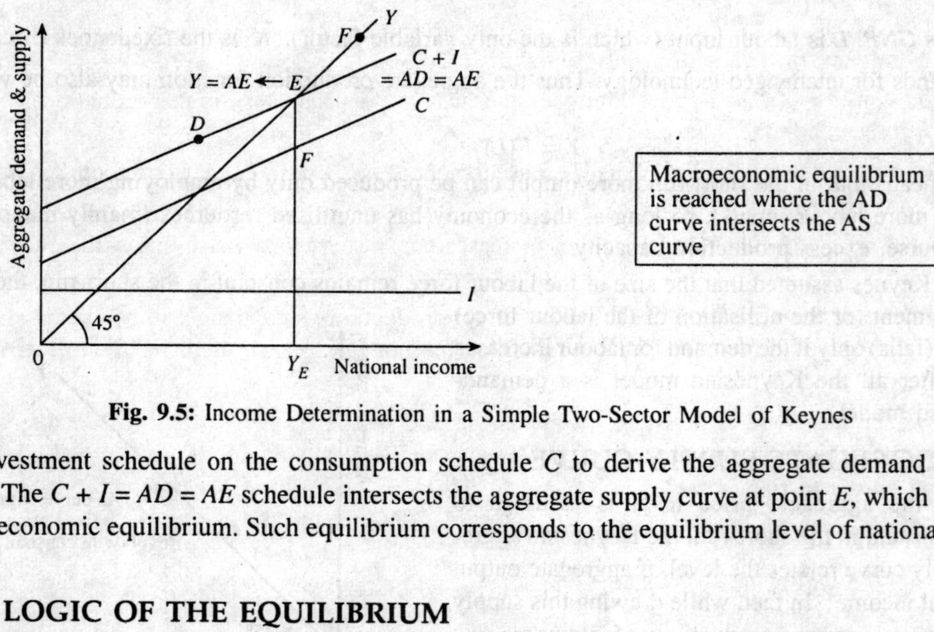

Fig. 9.5: Income Determination in a Simple Two-Sector Model of Keynes

the investment schedule on the consumption schedule C to derive the aggregate demand schedule $C + I$. The $C + I = AD = AE$ schedule intersects the aggregate supply curve at point E, which indicates macroeconomic equilibrium. Such equilibrium corresponds to the equilibrium level of national income Y_E.

THE LOGIC OF THE EQUILIBRIUM

It may be noted that national income cannot be in equilibrium if it is less than or greater than Y_E. The reason is that at any other level of income either AD will exceed AS (as at point D) or AS will exceed AD (as at point F) as shown in Fig. 9.5. Why does this discrepancy occur? It occurs due to unplanned (undesired) changes in inventories. A simple example will make the point clear.

Unplanned changes in investment play an important role in Keynesian theory of income determination

Table 9.1 presents data for a hypothetical economy. An equilibrium will be reached in this economy when output produced or income received (Y) is equal to its planned (desired) expenditure, i.e., $C + I$. When this happens desired saving is also equal to desired investment. Here we assume that $MPC = \frac{4}{5}$ and a fixed level of autonomous investment of Rs. 100 crores takes place at all levels of income.

Table 9.1: An Illustration of the Keynesian Theory of Income Determination

(Figures in Rs. crores)

Y	C	S	I	$C + I$	Changes in Stock	Tendency of Income to
100	80	20	100	180	– 80	Expand
200	160	40	100	260	– 60	”
300	240	60	100	340	– 40	”
400	320	80	100	420	– 20	”
500	400	100	100	500	0	Remain unchanged
600	480	120	100	580	+ 20	Contract

Total expenditure in this economy has two components: spending on consumer goods (C) and spending on investment (capital) goods (I). Thus total expenditure is $C + I$. From Table 9.1 we see that total desired (planned) expenditure is equal to income received at the level of Rs. 500 crores. When national income reaches this level:

$$Y = C + I = \text{Rs. 500 crores}$$

$$\text{and } S = I = \text{Rs. 100 crores}$$

Three points are to be noted in this context:

1. When $C + I > Y$, $I > S$ and Y increases (because the expansionary forces on national income are stronger than the contractionary forces).
2. When $Y > C + I$, $S > I$, and Y falls (because the contractionary pressure exerted on Y is stronger than the expansionary pressure).
3. When $Y = C + I$, $S = I$ and Y neither increases nor decreases (because this is the equilibrium state).

If sales plan of business firms are fulfilled but not production plans, there will be excess demand and Y will increase. If production plans are fulfilled but not sales plans, there will be excess supply and Y will fall.

Thus we see that there is divergence between AS and AD since the two plans of business firms do not always coincide. As a result there are unplanned changes using inventories, which cause national income and output to rise or fall.

THE PRINCIPLE OF EFFECTIVE DEMAND

From Fig. 9.5 we see that aggregate demand is equal to aggregate supply only at point E and not at any other level of national income. The aggregate demand corresponding to this equilibrium level of national income is called **effective demand**. The reason is that it is that level of aggregate demand which determines national income by being equal to aggregate supply. This is known as the Keynesian principle of effective demand. In Fig. 9.5, effective demand is equal to EY_E which is in turn, equal to equilibrium output produced and supplied ($0Y_E$). This means that income received is equal to both desired and actual expenditure, leaving neither a deficit (excess demand) nor a surplus (excess supply). So there is no pressure on national income to rise or fall. Since it is aggregate demand which determines the equilibrium value of national income, we present the equilibrium condition of national income in terms of the Keynesian principle of effective demand as follows:

Effective demand refers to not only desired expenditure but actual expenditure as well

$$Y = AED \quad \ldots (6)$$

where $AED = C + I$. So we can write

$$Y = C + I$$

where all the terms have usual meaning.

Importance of the Concept

Thus in the Keynesian model the level of employment and national income are determined simultaneously by aggregate effective demand. If aggregate effective demand rises, more output will be produced. So more workers will be employed and more income will be generated. Thus it logically follows that unemployment occurs due to deficiency of effective demand or purchasing power. And the solution to the problem lies in increasing effective demand. Therefore demand creates its own supply and not the other way round as the classicists had thought.

EQUILIBRIUM AT LESS-THAN-FULL EMPLOYMENT (OR UNDEREMPLOYMENT EQUILIBRIUM)

The classical economists equated macroeconomic equilibrium with full employment. They believed in the Say's law and wage-price flexibility which together ensured full employment in a self-adjusting free market-based capitalist economy. So the attainment of full employment was automatic in the classical model.

This view was challenged by Keynes. Keynes pointed out that national income may attain its equilibrium level (value) even at less-than-full employment. The reason is that there is always the possibility of involuntary unemployment in a capitalist economy due to deficiency of aggregate demand and downward rigidity of the nominal wage rate (which prevents smooth functioning of the labour market). The concept of underemployment equilibrium is illustrated in Fig. 9.6. Here the economy reaches initial equilibrium at point E. The equilibrium value of national income corresponding to this macroeconomic equilibrium (at which $AD = AS$) is Y_E. But this is not the full employment level of income. The economy is capable of producing more output and generating more employment and income in the process if aggregate demand increases. But, in this case, there is deficiency of aggregate demand due to inadequate investment demand. If investment demand can be increased by ΔI, there will be a parallel upward shift of the aggregate demand schedule to $C + I'$ where $I' = I + \Delta I$, i.e., original investment plus the needed increase in investment. The new aggregate demand schedule intersects the aggregate supply schedule at point F which is indeed the full employment point, at which actual output (income) is equal to potential output (income) of Y_F. Thus while at point E, the economy is in underemployment equilibrium, at point F it attains full employment.

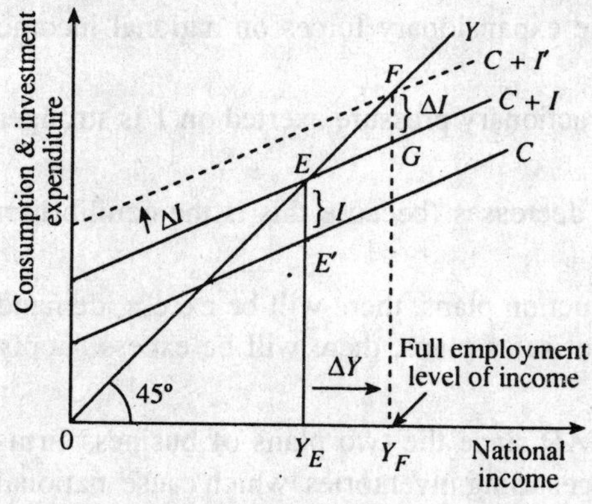

Fig. 9.6: Underemployment Equilibrium Due to Inadequate Investment Demand

DIVERGENCE BETWEEN S AND I

However, there is no guarantee that desired saving will always be equal to desired investment. There are two reasons for this. Firstly, savers and investors are two different groups of people. Some people save, while others invest. For example, the major portion of saving originates from the household sector (families). Of course companies also save by retaining a portion of their after-tax profits. Retained earnings provide internal funds for undertaking new investment activities. However, corporate saving is a very small proportion of total saving. But investment activities are carried out only by business firms. Households are unlikely to know how much business firms are planning to invest. And businesses are unlikely to know how much households are planning to save.

Secondly the motives for saving and investment are different. Individuals save for certain personal motives such as children's education and marriage as also for medical treatment. Some people save because they have a chance of being unemployed.[1] Others save certain amounts for maintaining their current living standards even after retirement, when their income suddenly falls. And some people save in order to buy durable goods such as cars, houses or even gold and jewellery. Household saving decision is governed by two main factors — income (which affects the capacity to save) and the rate of interest (which affects the desire to save). By contrast business people invest in plant and machinery for making profits. And their decision to invest in fixed asset is mainly governed by the marginal efficiency of capital (or the yield) and the rate of interest[2].

For these two reasons, there can be divergence between the planned saving of the household sector and planned investment of the business sector. Although saving, like consumption is a stable function of income, investment is a volatile component of aggregate demand. If, for some reason, there is a fall in the profit expectations of business firms, investment will fall. And this will lead to a fall in employment and equilibrium national income. This point will become clear when we study the saving- investment approach to national income determination later in this chapter.

INFLATIONARY GAP

It may also be noted that if aggregate demand exceeds the full employment level of output, there will be excess demand pressure in the economy. More output will be demanded by households and businesses than the economy is able to produce by utilising all its resources (including manpower) with its existing (unchanged) technology. In such a situation only one outcome is possible —a rise in the prices of goods and services. This type of situation occurs if there is an improvement in profit prospects and businesses make more investment. In Fig. 9.6, if investment exceeds $I' = I + \Delta I$, then the economy will face the problem of demand-pull inflation which occurs due to a rise in aggregate demand at full employment. In such a situation, national income will increase beyond $0Y_F$ only in nominal (money) terms and not in real terms. Thus full employment is taken as the economy's inflation threshold. The end of full employment is the beginning of inflation. True inflation starts only when output expansion comes to an end as soon as all the resources are fully employed and the economy's actual output exceeds the full employment output.

Keynes pointed out that for such inflation to occur there must be an inflationary gap in the economy. This concept may now be explained.

Classical economists believed that the root cause of inflation was continuous rise in the money supply. But modern discussion of inflation goes in terms of what Keynes called 'inflationary gap'. It is a situation in which aggregate demand in the economy is greater than the aggregate supply of resources coming forward to the market. The consequences are persistently rising prices (and disequilibrium in the balance of payments).

Suppose the total value of output in a country in a particular period is Rs. 900 crores. The government now takes away Rs. 150 crores in taxes to meet its own expenditure. So the private sector is left with Rs. 750 crores for its own expenditure — consumption and investment. From the national income analysis we know that the value of money income of the country is always equal to the net value of output. Here also the total money income of the people (Rs. 750 crores) is equal to the net value of output (Rs. 900 crores – Rs. 150 crores = Rs. 750 crores) at current prices. As long as expenditure is equal to income there is no pressure on prices and no inflation. Prices remain virtually stable.

Suppose now the government injects Rs. 200 crores of money in the economy (either by borrowing from banks or by printing new money) to finance its own expenditure. This expenditure is made on factors of production. They earn incomes of an equivalent amount. So money income of the people

1. This is known as precautionary saving.
2. Of course in the long run, investment depends on population growth and technological progress as the Solow model of growth shows.

rises to Rs. 950 crores (Rs. 750 crores + Rs. 200 crores). The government may now tax a part of the income (say, Rs. 50 crores). A part of the increased (disposable) income will be saved and a part spent. Suppose people save Rs. 50 crores and spend Rs. 100 crores. So the net money income available for expenditure is (Rs. 950 – Rs. 100) = Rs. 850 crores. So there is an increase over the previously available income amounting to (Rs. 850 crores – Rs. 750 crores =) Rs. 100 crores. The excess represents the inflationary gap, which will put an upward pressure on prices. If there is no corresponding increase in output, the price rise will continue until the value of output and the level of income become equal.

INCOME DETERMINATION THROUGH SIMPLE ALGEBRA

The process of determination of equilibrium level of national income will become clear if we use simple algebra. We know that national income (Y) is equal to consumption demand (C) plus investment demand (I). So we can write

$$Y = C + I \quad \ldots (1)$$

We also know that the simple Keynesian short-run consumption function is the following:

$$C = \bar{a} + bY \quad \ldots (2)$$

In equation (2), a is autonomous consumption which remains fixed at all levels of income. So we put a bar on it to indicate its fixed value. Here b is the constant slope of the consumption function and represents the marginal propensity to consume (MPC). It is expressed as $b = \frac{\Delta C}{\Delta Y}$. Thus total consumption demand has two components—autonomous consumption spending (a) and induced consumption spending (bY).

Keynes also assumed that all investment is autonomous and hence independent of income. It may be denoted by the symbol I_a. Thus we get the following three structural equations[1] for our simple two-sector economy:

$$Y = C + I \quad \ldots (1) \text{ definitional identity}$$

$$C = \bar{a} + bY \quad \ldots (2) \text{ consumption function}$$

$$I = \bar{I}_a \quad \ldots (3) \text{ autonomous investment}$$

Now if we substitute the values of C and I in equation (1), we have:

$$Y = \bar{a} + bY + \bar{I}_a$$

$$\text{or, } Y - bY = \bar{a} + \bar{I}_a$$

$$\text{or, } Y(1-b) = \bar{a} + \bar{I}_a$$

$$Y = \frac{1}{1-b}(\bar{a} + \bar{I}_a)$$

$$\text{or, } Y = \frac{1}{1-b}(\bar{A}) \quad \ldots (3)$$

where $\bar{A} = \bar{a} + \bar{I}_a$, i.e., total autonomous expenditure (= autonomous of consumption spending + autonomous investment expenditure).

The equilibrium value of national income is found by multiplying autonomous expenditure by the autonomous expenditure multiplier

Equation (4) shows the equilibrium value of national income when aggregate demand equals aggregate supply. Total autonomous expenditure $\bar{A}$ or aggregate demand equals the income generated through the production of goods and services.

1. Structural equations represent the structure of the economy.

Equation (4) also shows that the equilibrium value of national income (Y) can be found out by multiplying autonomous expenditure $\overline{A}$ by the autonomous expenditure multiplier $\frac{1}{1-b}$. [Since b is MPC and $1 - b$ is the marginal propensity to save (MPS), the autonomous expenditure multiplier, as we will see in a later chapter, is the reciprocal of the MPS].

Economic Insight: Structural Form and Reduced Form Equations

A structural form equation is expressed in terms of both exogenous and endogenous variables. Suppose we have the following three equations which describe the structure of the economy:

$$C = a + bY \quad \ldots (1)$$

$$I = \overline{I} \text{ and} \quad \ldots (2)$$

$$Y = C + I \quad \ldots (3)$$

Here Y is expressed in terms of endogenous variable C and exogenous variable I. But a reduced form equation is expressed only in terms of exogeneous variables and not any endogenous variables such as

$$Y = \frac{1}{1-b}(a + \overline{I}) \quad \ldots (4)$$

The endogenous variable C disappeared from equation (4) through substitution.
Here equation (4) is a reduced form equation, in which Y is expressed only in terms of exogenous variable I and two parameters a and b and in terms of no endogenous variable(s).

It may finally be noted that if either autonomous investment I_a increases or the MPC increases, national income will rise. Students can check this result by using hypothetical data on A and b.

The following numerical examples will clearly illustrate how the equilibrium level of national income is determined.

NUMERICAL EXAMPLES

Problem 1: Suppose in a simple hypothetical economy, autonomous investment (I) is Rs 100 crores and the consumption function is

$$C = 50 + 0.8Y$$

(a) Find out the equilibrium level of income. (b) Now suppose autonomous consumption falls by 10 and autonomous investment increases by 20. What will happen to equilibrium value of Y? (c) What happens if MPC falls to 0.5 at the original value of a and I_a?

Solution: (a) The equilibrium level of income is found by substituting C and I in Y:

$$Y = C + I$$

$$= 50 + 0.8Y + 100$$

$$\text{or, } Y - 0.8Y = 150$$

$$\text{or, } Y(1 - 0.8) = 150$$

$$\text{or, } Y = \frac{150}{0.2} = 150 \times 5 = \text{Rs 750 crores.}$$

(b) Now = $40 + 0.8Y + 120$

or, $Y - 0.8Y = 160$

or, $Y(1 - 0.8) = 160$

or, $Y = \frac{160}{0.2} = 160 \times 5 =$ Rs 800 crores.

(c) Now $Y = 50 + 0.5Y + 100$

or, $Y - 0.5Y = 150$

or, $Y(1 - 0.5) = 150$

or, $Y = \frac{150}{0.5}$ = Rs 150 × 2 = Rs 300 crores.

Problem 2: Find out the equilibrium level of income when I_a = Rs 200 crores and $C = 0.75Y$

Solution: We know that $Y = C + I$

$$= 0.75Y + 200$$

or, $Y - 0.75Y = 200$

or, $Y(1 - 0.75) = 200$

$$Y = \frac{200}{0.25} = 200 \times 4 = \text{Rs 800 crores.}$$

Problem 3: What will be the equilibrium level of income if $C = 15 + 0.7Y$ and $I = 25 + 0.1Y$, i.e., investment, like consumption, has an induced component. What happens if b increases to 1.1?

Solution: In this case, we assume that investment, like consumption, also depends on income. However, the method of calculating the equilibrium value of Y will remain the same. So we write

$$Y = C + I$$

$$= 15 + 0.7Y + 25 + 0.1Y$$

or, $Y - 0.8Y = 40$

or, $0.2Y = 40$

or, $Y = \frac{40}{0.2} = 40 \times 5$ = Rs 200 crores

Now if b increases to 1.1, we have

$$Y = 15 + 1.1Y + 25 + 0.1Y$$

or, $Y - 1.2Y = 40$

or, $-0.2Y = 40$

or, $Y = \frac{40}{-0.2}$ = – Rs 200 crores

Thus we get a negative value of Y which is absurd. The *MPC* is positive but less than 1. It cannot exceed 1. Otherwise Y will be negative.

NATIONAL INCOME AND EMPLOYMENT

In the Keynesian model, equilibrium levels of employment and national income are determined simultaneously through aggregate demand and aggregate supply (which together ensure macroeconomic equilibrium). In the Keynesian model employment is a function of output and output is equal to income. The relation between income and employment is dictated by the aggregate production function $Y = F(L)$ since capital stock (K) and the state of technology (T) remain constant. This means the larger the number of workers employed, the higher is the level of output and national income. This point is illustrated by the aggregate production function $Y = F(L)$ in Fig. 9.7(a). The curvature of the function indicates diminishing returns to labour.

In Fig. 9.7(b) we show how the equilibrium value of national income is determined. Suppose the economy is initially at full employment at point F which corresponds to aggregate output at Y_F, as shown in both panels of the diagram. Now if due to sudden fall in *MEC*, investment demand falls by

ΔI the combined $C + I$ schedule will shift downward to $C + I'$ where $I' = I - \Delta I$ (or $I' < I$ by ΔI). Now the aggregate demand curve intersects the aggregate supply curve $0Y$ at point E. So a new macroeconomic equilibrium is established but at a lower level of output or national income (Y_E). This level of income in panel (a) corresponds to a lower level of employment L_E in panel (b). Thus E represents underemployment equilibrium or equilibrium at less-than-full employment.

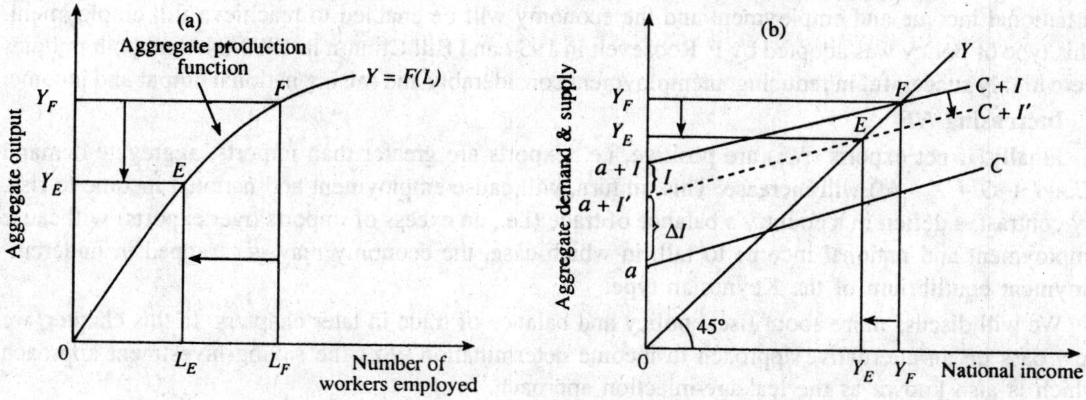

(a): The Determination of Employment by Aggregate Production Function

(b): The Determination of Equilibrium Value of National Income

Fig. 9.7: The Theory of Involuntary Unemployment

An economy gets stuck in such a situation due to fall in investment demand. Thus deficiency of demand is the main cause of such involuntary unemployment in the Keynesian model of income determination. Such unemployment is called by modern economists cyclical unemployment. Therefore equilibrium does not necessarily imply full employment as the classicists had thought. Equilibrium may occur even at less than full employment, as Keynes had postulated. Such involuntary unemployment cannot be automatically eliminated through the free play of the market forces.

The deficiency of demand causes involuntary unemployment in the Keynesian model

MEASURES TO INCREASE NATIONAL INCOME AND EMPLOYMENT

Since national income, from the spending side, has four main components, there are four ways of increasing national income, viz., increasing C, I, G and NE.

Increasing C

Consumption (C) can be increased by cutting taxes. A tax cut will lead to an increase in disposable income and an increase in C. As a result the short-run consumption function will shift upward causing the combined $C + I$ schedule to shift upward parallely (assuming constant MPC) and the economy will be enabled to reachieve full employment. This type of policy was adopted in the famous Kenedy budget of the USA in 1964 as also in the budget of 2003, presented by President George Bush (which announced a drastic tax cut).

Increasing I

Investment can be increased in two ways. Firstly, the central bank can increase the supply of money. As a result Y will increase. This will induce business people to invest more. Secondly, the government can provide various types of incentives to investors in the form of tax cuts, investment tax credit and subsidies on investment. Tax cuts increase corporate profit, and make more funds available for investment. If I increase, the $C + I$ schedule will shift upward. As a result employment and national income will increase.

Increasing *G*

It was Keynes who first suggested the policy of increasing government spending in times of depression and unemployment. If the government spends more on public works or on slump clearance, government spending (*G*) will add to private spending $C + I$ and thus increase aggregate demand (which, in a three-sector economy, to be studied later in this chapter, is $C + I + G$). This will lead to an increase in national income and employment and the economy will be enabled to reachieve full employment. This type of policy was adopted by F. Roosevelt in 1934 and Bill Clinton in 1993-94. And both policies were highly successful in reducing unemployment considerably and raising national output and income.

Increasing *NE*

Finally, if net exports (*NE*) are positive, i.e., exports are greater than imports, aggregate demand $(C + I + G + X - M)$ will increase. This, in turn, will cause employment and national income to rise. By contrast, a deficit in a country's balance of trade (i.e., an excess of imports over exports) will cause employment and national income to fall, in which case, the economy may get trapped in underemployment equilibrium of the Keynesian type.

We will discuss more about fiscal policy and balance of trade in later chapters. In this chapter, we now pass on an alternative approach to income determination, viz., the saving-investment approach which is also known as the leakage-injection approach.

THE S-I APPROACH TO NATIONAL INCOME DETERMINATION

There is an alternative method of determining equilibrium value of national income, known as the *S-I* approach. It explains how national income is determined by desired (planned or intended) saving and desired investment. This method is illustrated in Table 9.2 and Fig. 9.8.

Table 9.2: Income Determination by the (*S-I* Approach)

Y	*C*	*S*	*I*	Effect on *Y*
100	80	20	100	*Y* increases
200	160	40	100	*Y* increases
300	240	60	100	*Y* increases
400	320	80	100	*Y* increases
500	400	100	100	$Y = Y_E$
600	480	120	100	*Y* falls

From Table 9.2 we see that investment (*I*) remains constant at 100 but *S* increases as *Y* increases. So long as $I > S$, *Y* will increase since the injection into the circular flow of income through investment will exceed the leakage from the flow through(*s*).

Table 9.3: Saving-Investment Balance in a Two-Sector Economy

Planned income	Planned consumption	Planned saving	Planned investment	Unplanned investment	Realised investment (Planned & implemented)	Planned expenditure
400	370	30	50	−20	30	420
500	450	50	50	0	50	500
600	530	70	50	+20	70	580

Table 9.3 presents a consumption function, from which saving plans can be obtained. Assuming that planned investment is autonomous and that all household plans are realised, an equilibrium level of income can be calculated.

When income is 500 the consumption spending is 450 and saving is 50. At this level of income autonomous planned investment is 50, thereby bringing total planned expenditure (consumption + investment) equal to the level of output (or income). With planned saving and investment being equal, the economy is in equilibrium— there are no forces at work changing the level of output or income.

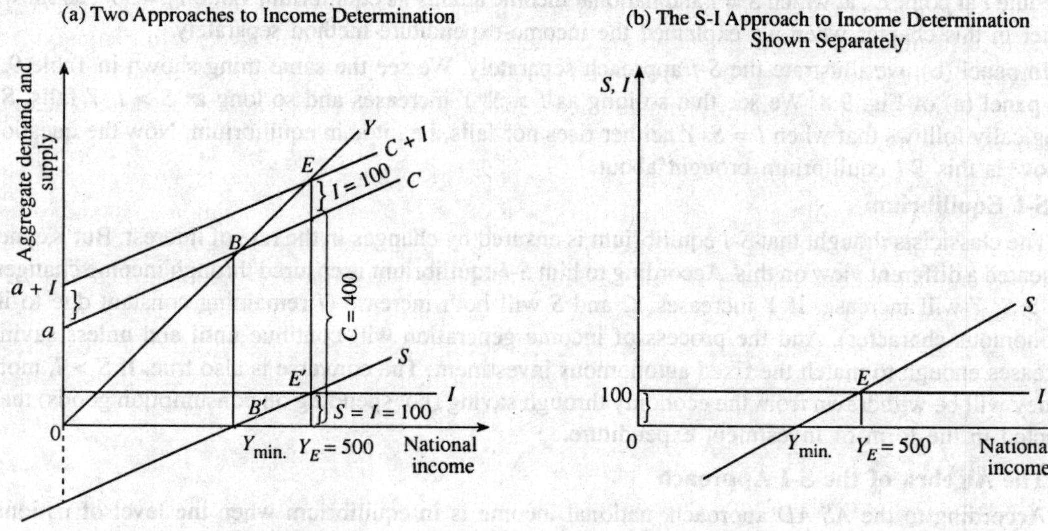

Fig. 9.8: Income Determination in a Two-Sector Economy

However, at the higher level of income (600), planned saving exceeds planned investment, resulting in planned expenditure falling below planned income. As the rate of production exceeds the rate of sales by 20, the level of stock will rise, thereby resulting in a rise in unplanned investment. Any stock changes are regarded as changes in investment. At this stage realised investment, made up of planned and unplanned investment, will still be equal to realised saving, but the discrepancy between the intentions of savers and investors will result in the level of income falling back until it reaches the equilibrium level of 500.

If income were 400 the consumption schedule would indicate that 370 would be consumed and 30 saved. With planned investment exceeding planned saving, planned expenditure would exceed planned income, resulting in a fall in the value of stocks (inventories). The fall in stocks can be regarded as unplanned disinvestment, giving a realised investment figure of 50 – 20 = 30 (which is the same as actual saving).

It may be noted that anything which exerts an expansionary pressure on *Y* is called a **leakage** and anything which exerts a contractionary pressure on it is called an **injection**. The reason is that if *S* increases, *C* will fall. Therefore, the combined *C* + *I* schedule will shift downward and *Y* will fall. As Keynes said in the early 1930s, "if you save 5 pence, you throw one worker out of job for the day". Thus, from Table 9.2 we see that so long as *I* > *S*, *Y* increases and when *I* = *S*, *Y* remains constant at 500. It neither increases, nor falls. It is in equilibrium. By comparison if *S* > *I*, *Y* will fall and will come back to 500, i.e., its equilibrium value.

The *S-I* approach is illustrated in two parts of Fig. 9.8. In part (a) we present two approaches to income determination, viz., (a) the income-expenditure approach (according to which *Y* = *C* + *I*), and (b) the saving-investment approach (according to which *S* = *I*). Although the two approaches are different, they are interrelated. In fact by using Fig. 9.8, we have achieved synthesis between the two approaches. In other words, the *S-I* approach is a logical deduction from the income-expenditure approach. In panel (a), we derive the saving function *S* from the income line *Y* and consumption function.

In fact, the vertical distance between Y and C measures S at each level of income (since $Y = C + S$ and $S = Y - C$). The saving schedule starts from point B' which corresponds to the break-even point B. This shows that income has to reach a minimum level for any saving to occur. The saving schedule which shows the positive relation between Y and S is upward sloping. It intersects the autonomous investment schedule I at point E', at which $S = I$ and national income attains its equilibrium value $Y_E = 500$, as shown earlier in this chapter when we explained the income-expenditure method separately.

In panel (b), we illustrate the *S-I* approach separately. We see the same thing shown in Table 9.2 and panel (a) of Fig. 9.8. We see that so long as $I > S$, Y increases and so long as $S > I$, Y falls. So it logically follows that when $I = S$, Y neither rises nor falls, i.e., it is in equilibrium. Now the question is how is this *S-I* equilibrium brought about.

S-I Equilibrium

The classicists thought that *S-I* equilibrium is ensured by changes in the rate of interest. But Keynes presented a different view on this. According to him *S-I* equilibrium is ensured through income changes. If $I > S$, Y will increase. If Y increases, C and S will both increase (I remaining constant due to its autonomous character). And the process of income generation will continue until and unless saving increases enough to match the fixed autonomous investment. The converse is also true. If $S > I$, more money will be withdrawn from the economy through saving (not spending on consumption goods) than injected in the form of investment expenditure.

The Algebra of the S-I Approach

According to the *AS-AD* approach, national income is in equilibrium when the level of national income is equal to effective demand. Thus we get

$$Y = AD \quad \ldots (1)$$

From this equation, we arrive at the other condition of national income equilibrium, i.e.,

planned saving = planned investment

We know that in a simple two-sector Keynesian model $Y = C + I$. So we can write

$$AD = C + I$$

$$\text{or, } Y = C + I$$

We know that

$$C = Y - S \quad \ldots (2)$$

Now the linear saving function corresponding to the linear consumption function $C = a + bY$ is $S = -a + (1 - b)Y$ where $1 - b = MPS$

Since $Y = C + S$

$$\Delta Y = \Delta C + \Delta S \quad \text{or} \quad \frac{\Delta Y}{\Delta Y} = \frac{\Delta C}{\Delta Y} + \frac{\Delta S}{\Delta Y}$$

or $1 = MPC + MPS$ or, $1 = b + (1 - b)$

or $MPC + MPS = 1$ or, $MPS = 1 - MPC = 1 - b$

Now substituting $Y - S$ in equation (2), we get

$$Y = Y - S + I$$

$$\text{or, } Y - Y + S = I$$

$$\text{or, } S = I$$

Thus national income is in equilibrium when desired saving is equal to desired investment.

Now we present the equilibrium condition of national income in terms of autonomous expenditure, as we have done earlier. So the saving function is

$$S = -a + (1 - b)Y$$

$$\text{and } I = \bar{I}$$

In equilibrium $I = S$

or $\bar{I} = -a + (1 - b)\,Y$

or $(1 - b)\,Y = \bar{I} + a$

or $Y = \dfrac{1}{1-b}\,(\bar{I} + a) = \dfrac{1}{1-b}\,(\bar{A})$

where $\bar{A} = \bar{I} + a$.

Here, as noted earlier, $\dfrac{1}{1-b}$ is the autonomous expenditure multiplier and b is MPC and $(1 - b)$ is MPS. Thus, as noted earlier, the equilibrium value of national income is found by multiplying the autonomous expenditure multiplier by autonomous expenditure.

NUMERICAL PROBLEM

Problem 4: Find the equilibrium level of income when $S = -50 + 0.20Y$ and I = Rs 100 crores.

Solution: National income reaches equilibrium when

$$S = I \quad \ldots (1)$$

Given $S = -50 + 0.20Y$ and

I = Rs 100 crores

we arrive at the following by substituting the values of S and I in equation (1)

$-50 + 0.20Y = 100$

or, $0.20Y = 100 + 50 = 150$

or, $Y = \dfrac{150}{0.20}$ = Rs 150 × 5 = Rs 750 crores.

We can check the result by using the other formula: $Y = \dfrac{1}{1-b}(I + a)$

Here $b = 1 - 0.20 = 0.80$, $a = 50$ and $I = 100$

$$Y = \frac{1}{1-0.80}(100+50)$$

$$= \frac{1}{0.20}\,(150) = \text{Rs } 750 \text{ crores.}$$

THE RELATION BETWEEN S AND I

According to classical economists saving is equal to investment only when the money market is in equilibrium.[1] The money market has no relation to real economy due to the classical dichotomy which implies neutrality of money. This equilibrium is brought about by changes in the interest rates. Keynes, however, did not agree and argued that saving and investment are not always equal. Keynes challenged the view which generated a serious controversy which was resolved by modern economists.

According to modern economists, there are two senses in which the terms 'saving' and 'investment' are used. In one sense S and I are always equal whether they correspond to the equilibrium level of Y or not. In another sense, S and I are equal only when national income attains its equilibrium value.

Recall that saving is that part of income which is not spent on consumption goods and can be positive, zero or negative. Investment is expenditure on capital goods. It is a flow concept which is

1. There may be divergence between S and I if the excess of investment expenditure over saving is incurred by borrowing money from banks which is financed through creation of new credit.

positive. It refers to the change in the stock of capital of an economy per year: $I_t = K_t - K_{t-1}$ or $I_t = \Delta K$. Therefore $I_t > 0$ if $\Delta K > 0$ or $K_t > K_{t-1}$. Investment may be gross or net. Gross investment *less* depreciation is net investment.

Now-a-days saving and investment are made by two classes of people. However, we can think of a wheat farmer who saves and invests at the same time. He sets aside a portion of output to be used as seed next year. In this sense, wheat is both a consumption good and a capital good (a form of circulating capital).

Let us take another example. Suppose the farmer's annual income is Rs 15,000 and he spends Rs 10,000 on consumer goods and spends another Rs 2,000 on the construction of a tubewell for his field and Rs 3,000 for buying a husking machine. His saving will be Rs 15,000 – Rs 10,000 = Rs 5,000. His expenditure of Rs 5,000 on the tubewell and machine will be his saving on one hand and investment on the other assuming that he does not deposit any part of his saving in banks to earn interest and he does not borrow fund to buy the machine or construct the tubewell either. However, this is true of an individual but not for the economy as a whole. For the economy as a whole, saving may differ from investment.

Modern economists point out that since savers and investors are two different groups of people and the motives for S and I are diverse, there can be divergence between S and I.

According to Keynes, actual saving is always equal to actual investment during a year. Actual saving is called *ex-post* (realised) saving and actual investment is called *ex-post* (realised) investment. The actual figures of S and I are presented in the national income accounts of a country.

However, according to modern economists the concepts of S and I are to be used in another sense. Such S and I are known as desired S and desired I. Desired S is also known as *ex-ante* or planned or intended saving. Similarly, desired I is also known as *ex-ante* or planned or intended investment.

A. SAVING-INVESTMENT EQUALITY

According to Keynes, saving and investment are equal in the *ex-post* (actual) sense. This can be proved as follows:

Since a country's national income is earned by producing and selling two types of goods: (i) consumer goods, (ii) capital goods, national income is the total market value of both types of goods. So we can write

$$\text{National income} = C + I$$

$$\text{or, } Y = C + I \qquad \ldots \quad (1)$$

where Y is national income, C is consumption demand and I is investment demand.

Equation (1) represents national income from the output or income side. From the expenditure side, national income is largely spent on consumption goods and partly saved. So we can write

$$\text{National income} = \text{Consumption} + \text{saving}$$

$$\text{or, } Y = C + S \qquad \ldots \quad (2)$$

By combining the above two equations, we see that

$$\text{Consumption} + \text{saving} = C + I \qquad \ldots \quad (3)$$

Now if we cancel C from both sides, we get the following equation:

$$\text{Saving} = \text{Investment}$$

$$\text{or, } S = I$$

In Keynes's view, investment is that part of national output (income) which arises from the production of goods ($I = Y - C$). Similarly saving is that part of national income which is not spent on consumption ($S = Y - C$). Hence, actual or *ex-post* S is always equal to actual I. This identity follows from the standard national income accounting system of a country.

As we have noted for an individual saving may differ from investment. But for the community as a whole saving is equal to investment. But this is not true as far as *ex-ante S* and *I* are concerned. This point may now be explained further.

Following Keynes, modern economists have pointed out that *ex-ante* (anticipated or desired) *S* is not always equal to *ex-ante I*. This point is explained by referring to inventories (i.e., goods produced in the current year but not sold in the same year). And unplanned (undesired) changes in inventories play an important role in the Keynesian theory of income determination based on the *S-I* approach. This point may now be explained.

Let us suppose, at a certain arbitrarily chosen level of income *ex-ante S* exceeds *ex-ante I*. This means that aggregate expenditure $(C + I)$ will not be sufficient to absorb all the goods and services produced at that level of income. So business firms will find that their unplanned (undesired) investments are increasing. The problem arises due to deficiency of aggregate demand. Since prices remain fixed in the Keynesian model, the unplanned income in stocks will be cleared. In such a situation actual (*ex-post*) investment equals planned investment *plus* unplanned increase in inventories and actual investment will, of course, be equal to actual saving. Now since businesses do not want to hold these extra undesired inventories, a cut back on production in the next period is inevitable.[1]

By contrast, if at another arbitrarily chosen level of income, planned investment exceeds planned saving, aggregate expenditure $(C + I)$ will exceed planned output of goods and services. Since sales exceed this output, there will be a unplanned fall in inventories. Consequently actual investment (which equals planned investment *minus* unplanned running down of inventories) will be equal to actual saving in the same period. This, in its turn, will stimulate production in the next period. As a result national income and employment will rise. Thus, in the *ex-post* or realised sense, *S* and *I* are always equal. This is known as *S-I* equality or *S-I* identity, which is different from *S-I* equilibrium, a concept to which we turn now.

S-I EQUILIBRIUM

We have noted that planned *S* may differ from planned *I* for two reasons: (i) savers and investors are two different groups of people and (ii) the motives for saving and investment are different. However, the divergence between the two cannot last for long. They are brought into equality by changes in national income. Let us see how this happens. If in a particular year planned *I* exceeds planned *S*, the level of national income rises. As *Y* increases, both *C* and *S* will increase. And the process of increase in *Y* continues until and unless planned *S* is brought into balance with planned *I*. By contrast, if planned *S* exceeds planned *I*, the income contractionary process will start. As *Y* falls, both *C* and *S* fall. And the process of income contraction will continue until and unless desired *S* is brought into balance with desired *I*.

Due to income changes there is a tendency for ex-ante S and ex-ante I to be equal

Now we present the views of two great economists in this context.

View 1: According to Paul Samuelson in Keynes' theory of income determination, investment calls the tune and saving dances at it.

View 2: According to R. G. Lipsey, there is no reason why saving will always be equal to some randomly chosen level of investment. However, if there is any divergence between the two, it will get corrected sooner or later through income changes and the process of income change will continue until and unless the level of saving is equated to a fixed level of investment.

The equality of planned *S* with planned *I* is known as *S-I* equilibrium because such equality is achieved only when *Y* is in equilibrium and not at other values of *Y*.

1. We have noted in the context of national income accounting that inventories are a part of business investment.

Thus while actual S is always equal to actual I, desired S has only a tendency to match desired I. This matching occurs only when Y is in equilibrium.

The balance between desired S and desired I is illustrated in Fig. 9.9.

Desired S = desired I at point E, which corresponds to the equilibrium value of national income (Y_E). If actual income is Y_1, $I > S$ and Y will increase and ultimately reach Y_E. Since I remains the same but S increases with an increase in Y, S will be equal to I. The converse is also true. If actual income is Y_2, $S > I$ and Y will fall and ultimately return to Y_E. Since I remains constant and S falls with a fall in Y, S-I equilibrium will be reached at point E.

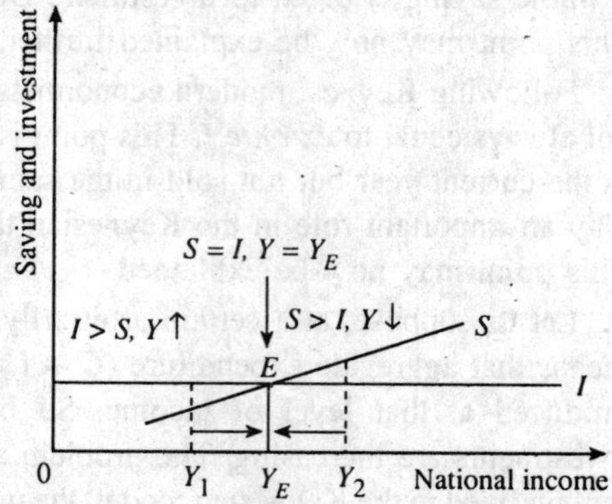

Fig. 9.9: *S-I* Equilibrium

Thus while actual (*ex-post*) S is always equal to actual (*ex-post*) I, planned (*ex-ante*) S will be equal to planned (*ex-ante*) I only when national income is in equilibrium. This means that S-I equality is not the same thing as S-I equilibrium.

KEY POINTS

1. ***Aggregate demand*** **:** While classical economists believed that supply creates its own demand Keynes argued that demand creates its own supply. So in Keynes's model national income is determined by aggregate effective demand, viz., consumption and investment (in a simple two-sector economy).

2. ***Full employment output*** **:** The Keynesian theory is based on the following two assumptions: (i) Firms are desirous of supplying all that is demanded at current prices up to full-employment output. (ii) Actual output cannot, for an obvious reason, exceed full-employment (capacity) output. Full-employment output is also known as the economy's capacity (potential) output.

3. ***Equilibrium condition*** **:** National income equilibrium is reached where there are no pressures for income to change, i.e., when income remains steady at a particular level. It has no tendency to rise or fall.

4. ***Income-expenditure approach*** **:** According to the income-expenditure approach national income is in equilibrium where aggregate planned expenditure is equal to actual output (i.e., actual national income). For levels of income greater than equilibrium, desired expenditure ($C + I$) is less than current output and output will fall. For levels of income less than equilibrium, desired expenditure is greater than current output and output will increase. The two terms 'national income' and 'national output' are used interchangeably. So Keynes's theory of income determination may also be called *the theory of output determination.*

5. ***Saving-investment (leakage-injection) approach*** **:** According to the leakage-injection approach equilibrium income occurs where leakage (desired saving) is equal to injection (desired investment). The reason is obvious. In a simple two-sector economy saving is the only leakage and investment is the only injection. Therefore saying that leakage equals injection is equivalent to saying that desired saving equals desired investment.

6. ***The equivalence of the two approaches*** **:** The two approaches are equivalent because they give us the same result. So saying that income = total desired expenditure is the same thing as saying that desired saving = desired investment or $E = Y$ implies $S = I$.

7. ***Saving-investment equilibrium*** **:** If the actual level of income is such that desired saving is not equal to desired investment, national income will tend to rise or fall. Income change will continue until saving is again equated to desired investment. When this happens national income reaches its equilibrium value. Income change is the mechanism through which the two desired values are equated.

8. ***Underemployment equilibrium*** **:** However, equilibrium level of income does not necessarily ensure full employment. National income equilibrium may also occur even at less-than full employment, i.e., equilibrium income may be less-than full employment (potential) income. If this happens there is involuntary idleness of resources, including manpower and the consequent waste (loss) of potential output.

KEY TERMS

Effective demand
Underemployment equilibrium
S-I equilibrium
Unintended changes in inventories
S-I approach
Full employment equilibrium
Saving-investment equality
Saving-investment controversy
Income-expenditure approach
Fix-price model

ASSIGNMENTS

1. Show how the equilibrium level of national income is determined in the simple Keynesian two-sector model. Does equilibrium always imply full employment?
2. Discuss the Keynesian theory of income determination by using the income-expenditure approach. Does the *S-I* approach yield the same result?
3. (i) Saving is always equal to investment.
   (ii) Saving is equal to investment only in equilibrium. How would you reconcile between the two statements?
4. Why does underemployment equilibrium occur in Keynes's model? Explain the causes of such disequilibrium.
5. Discuss the Keynesian concept of aggregate demand. How does it differ from the classical aggregate demand function?
6. What measures can be taken by the government to increase the level of income and employment? Can you think of a situation where national income rises in spite of constancy of investment?
7. (a) Find out the equilibrium level of income (Y_E) for an economy which has the following saving function $S = -20 + 0.25\ Y$ and investment function I = Rs 100 crores.
   (b) Also find out the level of C at Y_E.
   (c) Trace out the effect of an increase in investment by Rs 10 crores on Y and C.

[**Solution:** (a) In equilibrium $S = I$. So we can write

$$-20 + 0.25\ Y = 100$$
$$\text{or, } 0.25\ Y = 120$$
$$Y = 480$$

(b) $C = Y - S$

$$S = -20 + 0.25\ Y$$
$$= -20 + 0.25\ (480) = 100$$

and $C = 480 - 100 = 380.$

(c) If I increases by Rs 10 crores, the new level of I will be Rs 110 crores.

So we can write

$$S = I$$
$$\text{or, } -20 + 0.25\ Y = 110$$
$$\text{or } Y = 520$$

This is the new equilibrium level of income.

Now $S = -20 + 0.25\ Y$

$$= -20 + 0.25\ (520)$$
$$= 110$$

and $C = Y - S = 520 - 110$

$$= 410.]$$

8. Suppose an economy has the following consumption function: $C = 20 + 0.6Y$

If planned investment is Rs 50 crores, what will be the equilibrium level of Y and C at that income level?

[Solution: Following the income-expenditure approach we can write:

$Y = C + I$

or, $Y = 20 + 0.6\,Y + 50$

or, $Y - 0.6\,Y = 70$

or, $Y = 70 \times 2.5 = 175$

$C = Y - I = 175 - 50 = 125$]

9. For a hypothetical economy, we have

$C = 50 + 0.80\,Y$, and

$I = 25$ crores

(a) Find out the equilibrium level of income.

(b) Suppose the full-employment level of income is Rs 500 crores. How much extra investment is needed to reach the target?

[Solution: (a) $Y = C + I = 50 + 0.80Y + 25$

or $Y = 75 \times 5 = 375$

(b) To ensure full-employment level of income, investment at full-employment equilibrium has to be equal to saving at that level of income. With a target income of Rs 500 crores

$S_F = Y_F - C_F = Y_F - (50 + 0.80\,Y_F)$

$= 500 - 50 - (0.80 \times 500)$

$= 450 - 400 = 50$

Thus an additional investment of Rs 50 crores will be needed to achieve the full-employment level of income of Rs 500 crores.]

10. Suppose the consumption function is given by $C = 100 + 0.8Y$, while investment is given by $I = 50$.

(a) What is equilibrium level of income in this case?

(b) What is the level of saving in equilibrium?

[Solution: (a) $Y = 150 + 0.8Y$

or, $Y - 0.8Y = 150$

or, $0.2Y = 150$

or, $Y = \dfrac{150}{0.2} = 750$

(b) $S = -100 + 0.2Y$

Since $S = Y - C$ and $C = 100 + 0.8Y$

or, $S = -100 + 0.2\,(750)$

$= -100 + 150 = 50$]

11. Define Keynesian cross. Why is the Keynesian cross a stable equilibrium?

12. (i) What role does interest rate play in determining the Keynesian cross?

(ii) What role does unplanned inventory investment play in determining the Keynesian cross?

13. In a simple Keynesian model for a closed economy without government, there are two groups of income earners. Group 1 earns 800, while the income of Group 2 is Y-800, where Y denotes net domestic product. Average consumption propensities of Group 1 and 2 are 0.6 and 0.5 respectively. Investment function is given by $400 + 0.1Y$. Derive the aggregate saving function and the equilibrium amount of saving. Now suppose that there takes place a transfer of income from Group 1 to Group 2 of 100 units. How will it affect the aggregate saving function? Do you expect paradox of thrift here?

14. Explain the following puzzle: Saving depends positively on the interest rate, investment depends negatively on the interest rate, and saving equals investment. How does an increase in money supply that lowers the interest rate and thereby increases investment also increase saving? It would seem that, with the lower interest rate, saving would be lower. What is going on?

9A INTEGRATION OF THE GOODS MARKET AND THE MONEY MARKET IN THE COMPLETE KEYNESIAN MODEL(CKM)

ESTABLISHING LINKS BETWEEN THE GOODS MARKET AND THE MONEY MARKET

We noted in the main text that in the classical model the supply of money determines only the aggregate price level (and, of course, the nominal variables such as the nominal rate of interest). It has no effect on real variables such as aggregate real output (income) and the level of employment. In fact, it was Keynes who brought about some sort of synthesis of monetary analysis and income analysis by establishing a link between the money market and the goods market. Keynes was able to make an improvement over the classical approach by showing interest rate determination in the money market (through the interaction of the exogenously determined supply of money with the demand for money or liquidity preference). In contrast, the classicists explained interest rate determination in the capital market (through the saving-investment process).

In fact, it is the rate of interest which links the money market with the goods market in Keynes' complete macroeconomic model. Let us now study and analyse the model.

Any change in the money supply by the central bank in a normal situation leads to a change in the rate of interest, which alters the level of autonomous (income-independent) investment, assuming that the marginal efficiency of capital (MEC) or the expected rate of return on new investment remains unchanged. And in the Keynesian model such investment plays the key role in determining the level of employment and real income (GDP). To be more specific, an increase in the supply of money leads to a fall in the rate of interest and stimulates investment (since investment varies inversely with the rate of interest), with the MEC remaining unchanged. The higher level of investment generates a multiplier effect in respect of national income and employment. Thus, in the complete Keynesian model money plays an important role in exerting influence on real variables such as income and employment (except, of course, in times of deep depression or recession when the economy faces a liquidity trap situation or when MEC is very low).

Note that Keynes was mainly concerned with suggesting solutions to short-term economic fluctuations (or business cycles). And in normal times, monetary policy can be used to stabilise the economy.

However, according to Keynes, the effect of an increase in the money supply on employment and income depends on two crucial factors, viz., (1) interest elasticity of demand for money (or liquidity preference curve) and, (2) interest sensitivity of investment demand. The more elastic is the interest elasticity of demand for money and less elastic is the interest elasticity of autonomous investment, the less strong will be the effect of changes in the money supply on national income and employment. Keynes argued that in normal times monetary policy is quite effective in determining the level of employment and real income (GDP). However, Keynes admitted that in times of depression the demand for money would be highly (or even infinitely) elastic. In such a situation monetary policy would not be much effective. So he suggested that an expansionary monetary policy has to be supported by a positive fiscal policy to increase the level of aggregate demand and thus to stimulate the economy.

Empirical evidence in the post-Keynesian era revealed that even in times of recession the demand for money is not infinitely interest-elastic. But investment demand is fairly interest-elastic. Therefore modern Keynesian economists suggested the use of an appropriate mix of monetary policy and fiscal policy to achieve economic stability. In other words, by making appropriate use of monetary and fiscal measures it is possible to achieve high employment growth even in the absence of demand-pull inflation.

Graphical Representation of the Complete Keynesian Model (CKM)

In Fig. 9A.1 we present the complete Keynesian two-sector macroeconomic model with stress on the integration of the money market and the goods market. In panel (a) we show initial money market equilibrium at point E (where the demand curve for money or the liquidity preference curve M_d intersects the initial money supply curve) and the equilibrium rate of interest is r_1. In panel (b) we show the level of investment (I_1) corresponding to this interest rate. Now if the rate of interest falls from r_1 to r_2 due to an increase in the money supply from M_{s_1} to M_{s_2} in panel (a), the volume of investment increases from I_1 to I_2 in panel (b). In panel (c) we show the determination of the equilibrium level of national income at point E'' where income received (Y_1) is equal to the desired expenditure ($C + I_1$). Now due to an increase in investment from I_1 to I_2 in panel (b), the aggregate desired expenditure schedule in panel (c) shifts upward to $C + I_2$ where $I_2 = I_1 + \Delta I$. It now intersects the 45° income line at point F'' which is indeed the new equilibrium point for the economy and it corresponds to a higher level of income (Y_2).

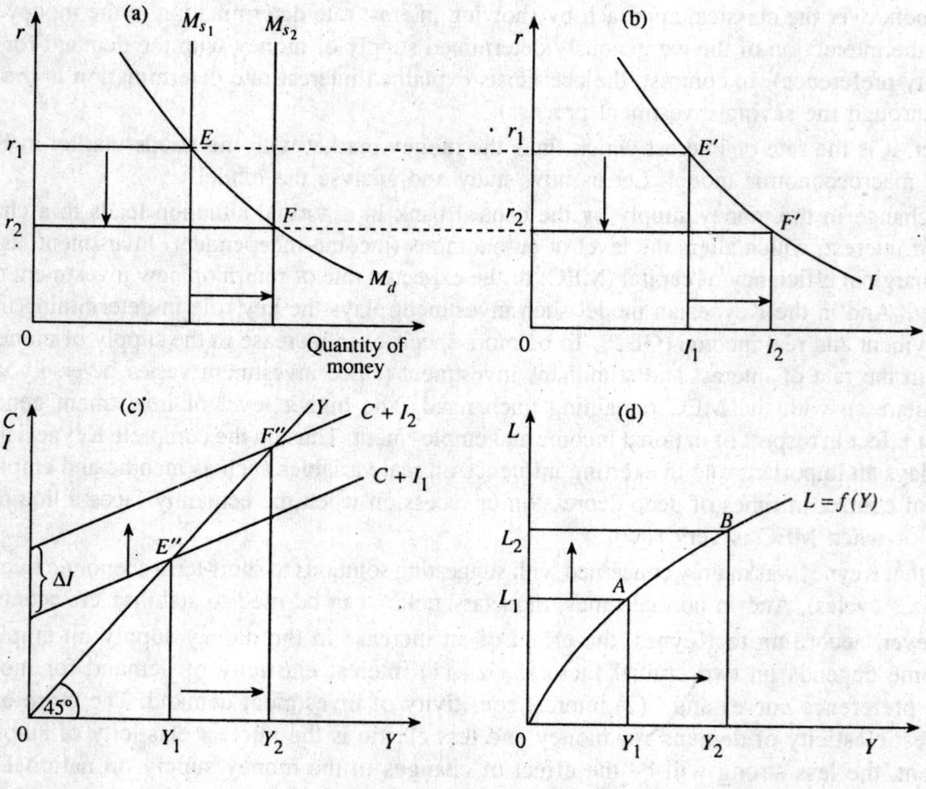

Fig. 9A.1: The Complete Keynesian Macroeconomic Model

Finally in panel (d) we show the relation between aggregate employment and aggregate income. In Keynes' model, aggregate employment (L) is a function of aggregate output (Y) and aggregate output, in its turn, depends on aggregate demand (desired expenditure — in this case $C + I$). Now at the initial level of income Y_1, the level of employment is L_1 (shown on the vertical axis). And when income increases to Y_2, the level of employment also increases to L_2.

Thus we see that it is through interest rate changes that Keynes was able to achieve an integration of the money market with the goods market. The complete Keynesian model (CKM) is presented in Fig. 9A.2.

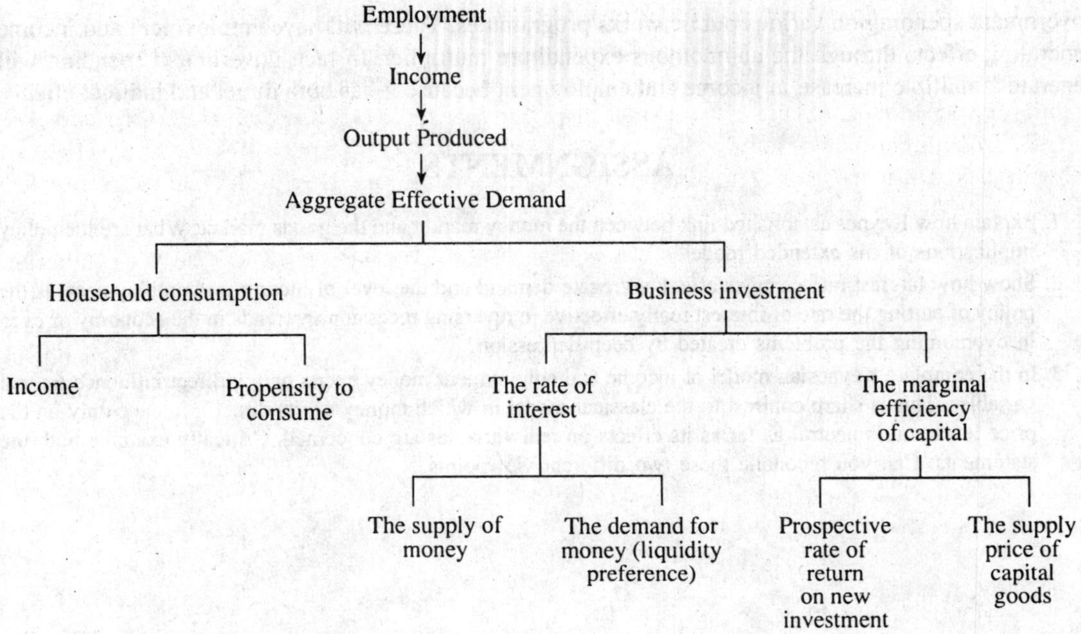

Fig. 9A.2: A Broad Overview of the CKM in terms of its Main Components

Policy Implications of CKM

We may now explore policy implications of Keynes' theory of income and employment determination. When an economy attains underemployment equilibrium (i.e., equilibrium at less-than-full employment), the Government may adopt monetary policy or fiscal policy to enable the economy achieve short-run stability. How expansionary monetary policy stimulates an economy which is initially in a situation of underemployment equilibrium is illustrated in Fig. 9A.3. The monetary transmission mechanism in Keynes' model is illustrated in this diagram below.

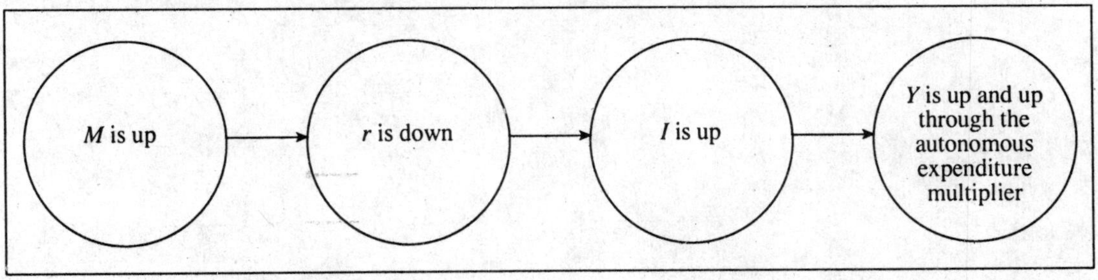

Fig. 9A.3: The Monetary Transmission Mechanism in Keynes' Model

However, since monetary policy is not much effective in times of depression due to low MEC and infinite elasticity of the demand for money (or liquidity preference) curve, a stimulative fiscal policy in the form of a cut in taxes or an increase in public spending (government expenditure) has to be used in addition to achieve the much needed macroeconomic stability. A policy of tax cut will stimulate investment by improving corporate profit prospects (or, in Keynes' terminology, by increasing the MEC or the yield on new investment). As a result the MEC curve or the investment demand curve will shift upward. This will lead to an upward shift of the combined $C + I$ schedule. Consequently national income and employment will increase. The same expansionary effect can be generated by increasing government spending on various public works programmes. These will have employment and income generating effects through the autonomous expenditure multiplier. In fact, government spending will generate a multiple increase in income and employment because it has both direct and indirect effects.

ASSIGNMENTS

1. Explain how Keynes established link between the money market and the goods market. What are the policy implications of his extended model?
2. Show how interest rate changes affect aggregate demand and the level of income and employment. Is the policy of cutting the rate of interest really effective in reversing recessionary trends in the economy or even in overcoming the problems created by deep depression?
3. In the complete Keynesian model of income and employment money exerts only indirect influence on real variables. This is sharp contrast to the classical model in which money exerts direct influence only on the price level and is neutral as far as its effects on real variables are concerned. Critically examine both the statements. Can you reconcile these two different viewpoints.

CHAPTER 10

Income Determination in Extended Models

The task of economic stabilisation requires keeping the economy from straying too far above or below path of steady high employment. One way lies inflation and the other lies recession. Flexible and vigilant fiscal policy and monitory policy will allow us to hold the narrow middle course.

J. F. Kennedy

In this chapter, we extend the basic Keynesian two-sector model of income determination to come closer to reality. We proceed in two steps. First, we discuss the Keynesian three-sector model with government. Then we discuss the four-sector (open economy) model with foreign trade and foreign investment, i.e., with exports, imports and financial transactions.

THE THREE-SECTOR MODEL OF INCOME DETERMINATION

Since the government plays a very important role in a modern economy, we now include the government in the analysis of income determination. The government is the third basic unit of an economy. Its basic objective is to create more jobs, promote faster economic growth and thus ensure maximum welfare. This is why it spends lots of money on construction of roads, bridges, schools, colleges, hospitals, etc. The expenditure of the government does not depend on national income or its rate of change. This is why in the Keynesian three-sector model of income determination, government expenditure is taken as autonomous and thus independent of income. To start with we assume that government spends money in the economy on various types of goods and services but does not impose any tax. We will relax the assumption later and extend the model further by taking into account the effect of the imposition of taxes on equilibrium national income. Here we consider several models.

Model 1: Income Determination with Government Expenditure but Without Taxes

We denote government expenditure by the symbol G. So in a three-sector economy, the equation for the equilibrium level of national income is written as:

$$Y = C + I + G$$

where Y is national income and output and $C + I + G$ represents aggregate demand (which now includes G, along with C and I).

Now the equilibrium condition of national income can be derived. We first express the equilibrium level of national income as follows:

$$Y = C + I + G \quad \ldots \quad (1)$$

Since the consumption function is $C = a + bY$ where a is autonomous consumption and b is MPC, equation (1) can be rewritten as:

$$Y = a + bY + I + G$$

$$\text{or } Y - bY = a + I + G$$

$$\text{or } Y(1 - b) = a + I + G$$

$$Y = \frac{1}{1-b}(a + I + G)$$

$$= \frac{1}{1-b}(A)$$

where $A = a + I + G$ = total autonomous spending (which includes autonomous consumption, private investment and government spending on goods and services).

Thus we see that the equilibrium value of national income can be calculated by multiplying autonomous expenditure A by the autonomous expenditure multiplier $\left(\frac{1}{1-b}\right)$.

Numerical Example

Table 10.1 gives an illustration of the Simple Keynesian Model of income determination (figures in Rs crores).

Table 10.1: An Illustration of the SKM of Income Determination

Income received (Y)	Consumption (C)	Saving (S)	T (tax)	Investment (I)—both intended and unintended	Govt. exp. (G)	Total desired expenditure $DE = C + I + G$	Saving plus tax $S + T$	$I + G$	Changes in inventories	Pressure on Y
100	80	15	5	90	10	180	20	100	–80	Y rises
200	160	30	10	90	10	260	40	100	–60	Y rises
300	240	45	15	90	10	340	60	100	–40	Y rises
400	320	60	20	90	10	420	80	100	–20	Y rises
500	400	75	25	90	10	500	100	100	0	$Y = Y_e$
600	480	90	30	90	10	580	120	100	20	Y falls

Here we assume that MPC is $^4/_5$. We also assume that $I = \bar{I} = 90$ and $G = \bar{G} = 10$ at all levels of income. Thus when Y is 100, $C + I + G$ is 180. So there is unintended inventory shortfall of 80. This will cause output to rise in order to meet the excess demand pressure. When output increases to 500, there is no unintended shortfall of inventories. Current output is just sufficient to meet current demand. Actual (realised) investment is equal to desired investment (which also includes desired inventory investment) and undesired inventory investment is zero.

If producers overreact to the excess demand pressure and produce an output of 600, there will be the problem of excess supply (surplus). So there is undesired accumulation of inventory of 20. This will cause output to fall to the equilibrium level (500).

Thus only when $Y = C + I + G$, national income attains its equilibrium value. At this level of income $S + T = I + G = 100$. So both the conditions of national income equilibrium are satisfied in the Keynesian model.

Graphical Illustration

In Fig. 10.1 we graphically illustrate how the equilibrium value of national income is determined in the Keynes' three-sector model. We proceed in five steps:

First we draw the 45° income line (which acts as the guideline). Then we draw the consumption line *C*. Next we draw the investment line *I*. Then we superimpose the *I* line on *C* line to arrive at the combined *C* + *I* line. Finally we add the fixed amount of government spending (*G*) to *C* + *I* to arrive at the aggregate demand schedule (*C* + *I* + *G*). The aggregate demand curve intersects the income line or the aggregate supply curve at point *E*. If we drop a perpendicular from *E* it touches the horizontal axis at point Y_E, which is indeed the equilibrium value of national income. The reason is that national income received (OY_E) is equal to the desired expenditure (EY_E). And the three components of aggregate demand (expenditure) are shown separately. We know that *G* is autonomous, i.e., independent of income. So the *C* + *I* + *G* line is parallel to the *C* + *I* line.

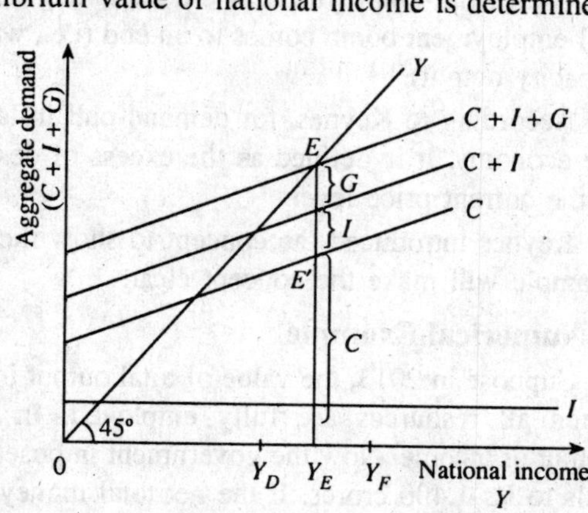

Fig. 10.1: Income Determination in Keynes' Three-Sector Model

Since $0Y_E$ is the equilibrium level of income, no other level of income can be treated as an equilibrium level of income. The reason is easy to find out. If actual income is less than $0Y_E$, say $0Y_D$, aggregate expenditure *C* + *I* + *G* will exceed aggregate supply. This means that the sales plans of the business firms are fulfilled but production plans are not. As inventories are exhausted, business firms will be eager to produce more to meet the extra demand pressure. As output increases, national income will rise and ultimately reach its equilibrium level ($0Y_E$). The converse is also true. If actual income (such as $0Y_E$) exceeds its equilibrium level, aggregate demand will fall short of aggregate supply. Due to such deficiency of demand[1], business firms will have unsold stocks of final goods. This unintended increase in inventories will force the firms to reduce production of goods. As production falls, national income will fall and come back to the equilibrium level ($0Y_E$).

Two related points may be noted in this context.

1. Balance between saving and autonomous spending

In the three-sector model aggregate saving (= *Y* – *C*) is equal to not only autonomous investment (*I*) but also government spending (*G*), i.e. at the equilibrium level of income *S* = *I* + *G*, since taxes are zero. In Fig. 10.1 it is measured by the vertical distance *EE′*.

2. Multiplier effect

Keynes pointed out that any increase in autonomous spending generates a multiplier effect. Thus like autonomous investment, government spending has also a multiplier effect.

Application of the Three-sector Model

We may now apply Keynes's three-sector model to study inflationary and deflationary gaps.

Inflationary and Deflationary Gaps

In the context of the three-sector model of income determination, we may refer to two important concepts, viz., inflationary and deflationary gaps. These two concepts may now be explained one by one.

Inflationary Gap

It was Keynes who first introduced the concept of 'inflationary gap' while discussing the theory of demand-pull inflation. According to Keynes, true inflation occurs only when the economy reaches

1. Demand is deficient when supply is excess.

the state of full-employment. In his view, 'full-employment' is the economy's inflation threshold. And the end of full-employment is the beginning of inflation; demand-pull inflation starts only when the full-employment boom comes to an end (i.e., when actual output or *GNP* = the potential or maximum capacity output).

According to Keynes, for demand-pull inflation to occur there has to exist an inflationary gap in the economy. It is defined as the excess of desired expenditure over full-employment output (*GNP*) at the current price level.

Keynes introduced the concept to show the factors which cause demand-pull inflation. A simple example will make the concept clear.

A Numerical Example

Suppose in 2013, the value of total output in a country is Rs 1,600 crores at the current price level when all resources are fully employed. In other words, this is the full-employment level of output or income. Now the government imposes a tax of Rs 200 crores. As a result disposable income falls to Rs 1,400 crores. If the net total money income of the people is Rs 1,400 crores, the income is equal to the value of output at the base year price level (which is 100). There is no inflationary pressure and the price level remains constant.

Now suppose the government increases its spending by Rs 600 crores by printing new currency notes. [This method of financing government spending is known as deficit financing]. So the money income of the people will increase to Rs 2,000 crores (= Rs 1,400 crores + Rs 600 crores). Now the government collects Rs 100 crores in taxes. So people's disposable income now is Rs 1,900 crores, out of which people save another Rs 200 crores. This means that net money income now available for expenditure is Rs 1,700 crores (= 2,000 – 100 – 200). This represents an increase over the previously available income by Rs 300 crores (= 1,700 – 1,400). This excess of desired expenditure over full-employment output indeed measures what Keynes called the inflationary gap. This extra money income will exert an upward pressure on the general price level. Since it is not possible to increase real output at full-employment, only money income will rise, real income remaining the same. This excess of desired expenditure due to an increase in money income will cause the price level to rise to the extent necessary to equalise the current income with the value of full-employment output. The money value of output will rise to Rs 1,700 crores, but the real value of output (= income) will remain constant at Rs 1,400 crores. Thus inflationary gap measures the excess of anticipated expenditure over available output at the base (i.e., pre-inflation) price level.

The inflationary gap can be narrowed (if not completely eliminated) in two ways: (i) by reducing money incomes and (ii) by increasing output. These points will be discussed in detail in a later chapter in the context of the theories of inflation.

Deflationary Gap

An exactly opposite type of situation is known as deflationary gap. This gap is created when there is an excess of full-employment output over desired expenditure at the current price level. This will cause the price level to fall so as to equalise the current income with the value of full-employment output.

Diagrammatic Illustration

These two concepts are illustrated in Fig. 10.2 and Fig. 10.3.

In Fig. 10.2 we show real income on the horizontal axis and desired (anticipated) expenditure in the vertical axis. Here Y_F is the full-employment level of output of Rs 1,600 crores. At this level of income aggregate saving = private investment + government spending. At this level of output income received $0Y_F$ = desired expenditure BY_F. Now if aggregate demand increases and the *AD* curve shifts upward from $(C + I + G)_1$ to $(C + I + G)_2$ nominal output (income) will no doubt rise from Y_F to

Y_A, but real output (income) will remain unchanged at the full-employment level ($0Y_F$). So the excess of nominal expenditure of AB over full-employment level of output will cause the price level to rise.

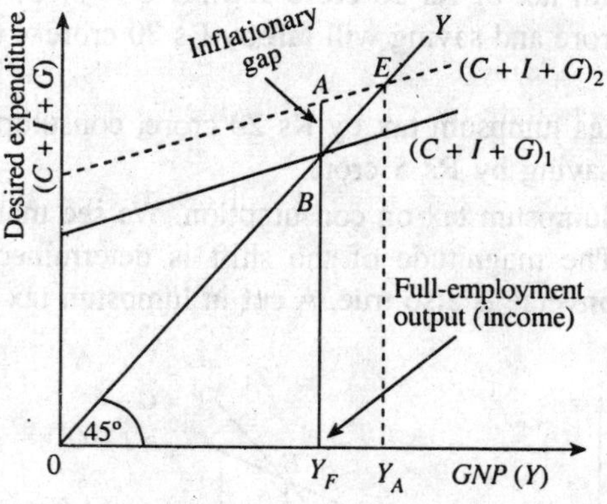

Fig. 10.2: Inflationary Gap

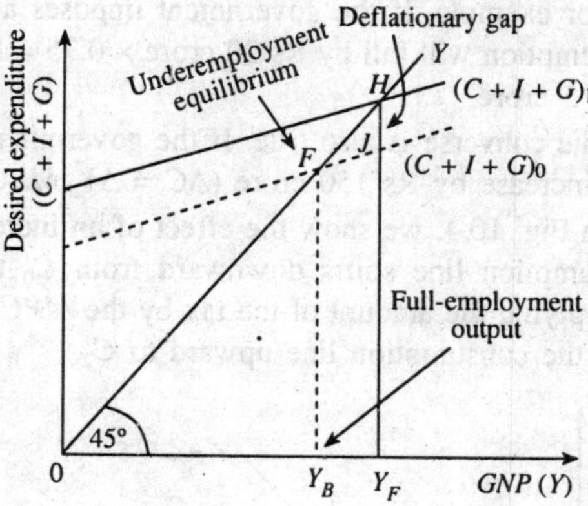

Fig. 10.3: Deflationary Gap

In Fig. 10.3, we show an exactly opposite type of situation. The economy is supposed to reach full-employment at point H, where output = income = $0Y_F$. Here as usual aggregate saving = investment + government spending. However, if there is deficiency of demand due to unemployment (or equilibrium at less than full-employment as at point F), the desired expenditure falls short of this output as shown by the vertical distance HJ. This deficiency of desired expenditure at full-employment output (= $0Y_F$) measures deflationary gap. This will cause the price level to fall.

It may also be noted that the decline in income is greater than the fall in demand caused by involuntary unemployment due to the working of the reverse multiplier process.

Model 2: Income Determination with Government Expenditure and a Lumpsum Tax (without transfer)

Since government expenditure is mainly financed by taxes, we have to take into account taxes also in our model of income determination. Let us suppose for simplicity that the government initially imposes a lumpsum tax (T), which does not rise or fall with income. Now if government expenditure (G) is equal to lumpsum tax (T), the budget of the government is said to be balanced ($G = T$). If however, G is greater than T, there will be a deficit in the budget. And if $T > G$, there will be a surplus in the budget.

Here we assume that the government budget is in balance ($G = T$). We also assume that the government does not make any transfer payments.

A lumpsum tax yields a fixed revenue at levels of national income, irrespective of the tax contribution of each individual. Suppose the government raises an extra revenue of Rs 20 crores by imposing such a tax. This will lead to a fall in the disposable income of the economy by the same amount. As a result people will reduce their consumption(C) and saving(S) at each level of national income. However, consumption will not fall exactly by the amount by which disposable income falls. The reason is that a fall in disposable income will lead to a fall in both consumption and saving. In fact, the amount by which consumption falls will be equal to the MPC times the lumpsum tax. Suppose disposable income falls by ΔY_d due to tax. Then fall in consumption ($-\Delta C$) will be:

$$-\Delta C = T.MPC \quad \ldots (1)$$

Since a lumpsum tax leads to a fall in disposable income, we can write

$$T = -\Delta Y_d \quad \ldots (2)$$

So equation (1) now becomes

$$-\Delta C = -\Delta Y_d.MPC$$

For example, if the government imposes a lumpsum tax of Rs 20 crore and $MPC = 0.75$, then consumption will fall by Rs 20 crore × 0.75 = Rs 15 crore and saving will fall by Rs 20 crore × 0.25 = Rs 5 crore.

The converse is also true. If the government reduces lumpsum tax by Rs 20 crore, consumption will increase by Rs 150 crore ($\Delta C = \Delta Y_d.MPC$) and saving by Rs 5 crore.

In Fig. 10.4, we show the effect of an increase in lumpsum tax on consumption. We see that the consumption line shifts downward from C_0 to C_1. The magnitude of the shift is determined by multiplying the amount of the tax by the *MPC*. The converse is also true. A cut in lumpsum tax will shift the consumption line upward to C_2.

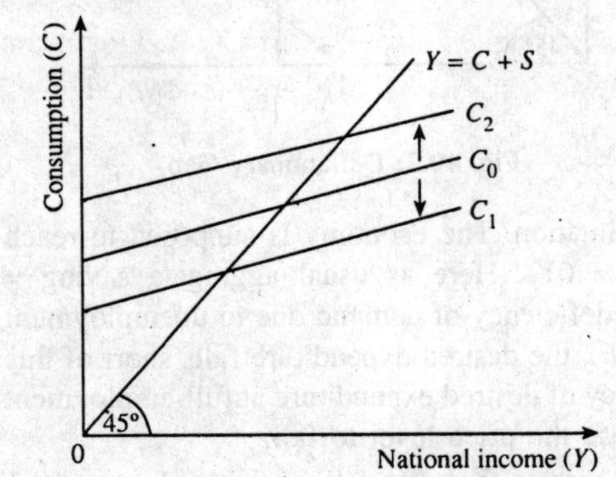

Fig. 10.4: Effect of a Lumpsum tax on Consumption Function

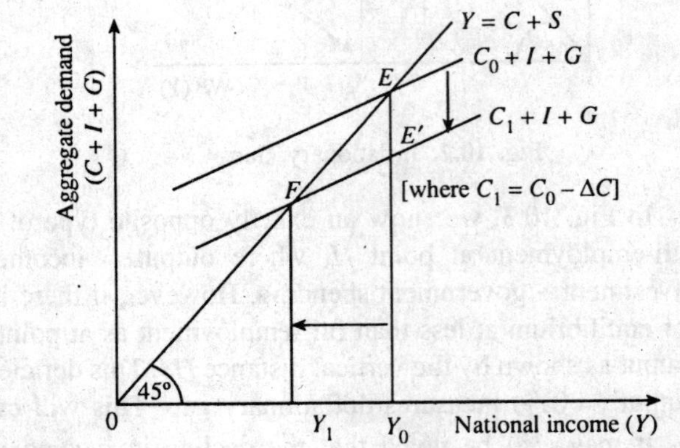

Fig. 10.5: Effect of Lumpsum tax on Equilibrium National Income

In Fig. 10.4 we show the effect of lumpsum tax Rs 20 crore on the equilibrium value of national income. Due to the lumpsum tax the consumption line shifts downward from C_0 to C_1 in Fig. 10.3. This gets reflected in Fig. 10.4 where the aggregate demand curve initially intersects the aggregate supply curve at point *E*. So the initial level of national income is $0Y_0$. Now, after the imposition of the lumpsum tax, the aggregate demand curve shifts downward from $C_0 + I + G$ to $C_1 + I + G$ where $C_1 = C_0 - \Delta C$. Here $\Delta C = MPC.T = b.T$. Thus the aggregate demand curve shifts downward exactly by the amount by which the consumption function shifts downwards due to a fall in Y_d caused by the lumpsum tax. This is shown by the vertical distance EE' which is equal to $-\Delta C = b.T$ where $b = MPC$. As a result, the economy reaches a new equilibrium point *F*. So national income falls from $0Y_0$ to $0Y_1$.

By comparison, a reduction in taxes increases disposable income of an economy and thus raises consumption spending. As a result national income rises not by the same amount (ΔC) but by a multiple of it, depending on the value of the multiplier. We now discuss this point in detail.

The Multiplier Effect

It is important to note here that the fall in the level of income ($-\Delta Y$) is not the same as the amount of lumpsum tax (T) imposed by the government, but a multiple of it. The extent to which income falls due to the imposition of a lumpsum tax depends on the value of the tax multiplier which is expressed as $\dfrac{-MPC}{1-MPC} = \dfrac{-b}{1-b}$, where b is the *MPC*.

We will explain how the tax multiplier formula is derived later in this chapter when we take into consideration another type of tax, viz., proportional tax which varies with national income.

Leakages and Injections

A related point may be noted in this context. While government expenditure increases national income, taxes reduce it. The reason is that government expenditure is an injection into the circular flow of income and taxes are a leakage from the flow. So in a three-sector model, there are two injections (I and G) and two leakages (S and T). National income attains its equilibrium value when the sum of injections is equal to the sum of leakages.

The Equilibrium Condition Expressed Algebraically

The equilibrium condition of national income may be expressed clearly in algebraic terms:

$$Y = AD = C + \bar{I} + \bar{G} \quad \ldots (1)$$

We put bars over I and G to indicate their fixed values (levels). Now the condition is written as

$$C = a + bY_d \quad \ldots (2)$$

where $Y_d = Y - T$ = disposable income i.e., the difference between national income (Y) and lumpsum tax (T). We know that a is the autonomous consumption and b is MPC. Now the consumption function is rewritten as:

$$C = a + b\,(Y - T)$$
$$= a + bY - bT$$

If we now substitute the value of C in income equation (1), we have

$$Y = a + bY - bT + \bar{I} + \bar{G}$$
$$\text{or, } Y - bY = a - bT + \bar{I} + \bar{G}$$
$$\text{or, } Y(1 - b) = a - bT + \bar{I} + G$$
$$\text{or, } Y = \frac{1}{1-b}\,(a - bT + \bar{I} + \bar{G}) = \frac{1}{1-b}(\bar{A}) \quad \ldots (3)$$

where $\bar{A}$ is fixed autonomous expenditure. Its value is constant since all the terms inside the bracket on the right hand side of equation (3) are constants.

Thus, once again, if we multiply fixed autonomous expenditure by the autonomous expenditure multiplier, we arrive at the equilibrium value of national income in a three-sector model with government expenditure (G) and lumpsum tax (T). The following example clearly illustrates the method of income determination.

EXAMPLE

Problem

Suppose we have the following data about a simple economy:

$$C = 10 + 0.75Y_d$$
$$I = 50$$
$$G = T = 20$$

where C is consumption, I is investment, Y_d is disposable income, G is government expenditure and T is lumpsum tax.

(a) Find out the equilibrium level of national income.

(b) What is the size of the multiplier ?

Solution

Substituting the values of C, I and G in Y we have

$$Y = a + bY_d + I + G$$
$$= 10 + 0.75\,(Y - 20) + 50 + 20$$
$$= 10 + 0.75\,Y - 15 + 50 + 20$$

or, $Y - 0.75\ Y = 65$

or, $Y\ (1 - 0.75) = 65$

or, $0.25\ Y = 65$

or, $Y = 65 \times 4 = 260.$

This is indeed the equilibrium value of Y in this model. The value of the autonomous expenditure multiplier in this case is $\frac{1}{1-MPC} = \frac{1}{1-b} = \frac{1}{1-0.75} = \frac{1}{0.25} = 4.$

Model 3: The Determination of National Income in a Three-Sector Economy with Taxes and Transfers

So long we have examined how national income is determined in a three-sector model with lumpsum taxes but without transfer payments. Now we extend the model to take into consideration the effect of transfer payments. We have already introduced the concept of transfer payments in our discussion of national income. Recall that transfer payments are basically welfare transfers. These are payments made by the government to certain sections of society at the cost of the taxpayers. These are one-sided payments since those who receive such payments do not provide anything to the government in exchange. In a modern mixed economy such payments are made to the unemployed, needy families, to the poverty-stricken people, and the retired persons.

Transfer payments are exactly the opposite of taxes. Just as taxes reduce the disposable income of the people, transfer payments increase it. So people have more money to spend on consumption of goods and services.

An important point has to be noted in this context. Transfer payments may be financed without imposing taxes. In this case such payments are autonomous like government purchase of goods and services.

But if transfer payments are financed by imposing a lumpsum tax, then transfer payments become a part of government expenditure (G). This means that if the government imposes an additional lumpsum tax to finance transfer payments, then the additional tax becomes a part of lumpsum tax (T) and disposable income will fall. In this case the process of income determination will be same as the one presented in Model 2 before.

However, here we treat transfer payment as autonomous expenditure and see how the analysis of income determination is modified.

Since transfer payments increase the disposable income of the people, such payments will lead to an increase in C. The extent to which C increases due to transfer payment depends on MPC. So we can now present our new model in terms of the following modified equations:

$$C = a + bY_d \quad \ldots \quad (1)$$

$$\text{and } Y_d = Y - T + TR \quad \ldots \quad (2)$$

where T is lumpsum tax and TR is transfer payments.

Now by substituting the value of Y_d from (2) in (1), we get the following consumption function:

$$C = a + b\ (Y - T + TR)$$

Now the national income equation becomes:

$$Y = C + I + G$$

$$= a + b\ (Y - T + TR) + I + G$$

$$= a + bY - bT + bTR + I + G$$

$$\text{or, } Y - bY = a - bT + bTR + I + G$$

$$\text{or, } Y\ (1 - b) = a - bT + bTR + I + G$$

$$\text{or, } Y = \frac{1}{(1-b)}\ (a - bT + bTR + I + G) \quad \ldots \ (3)$$

GOVERNMENT SPENDING MULTIPLIER

It may apparently seem that government spending multiplier and transfer payment multiplier will have the same value since both are injections into the circular flow. The reason is that if G increases by Rs 20, and $MPC = 0.75$, Y will increase by Rs 80. This means that an increase in govenment spending directly increases aggregate demand and by the full amount, i.e., aggregate demand rises exactly by the amount by which government spending increases. But if disposable income increases due to transfer payments, consumption demand does not increase by the full amount. It increases by less than the amount of increase in disposable income since MPC is less than 1. This point may be explained clearly by referring to equation (3). Let us suppose government spending increases by ΔG. As a result income increases. The new level of income is written as:

$$Y + \Delta Y = \frac{1}{1-b}\ (a - bT + bTR + I + G + \Delta G) \quad \ldots \ (4)$$

If we now subtract equation (3) from equation (4), we find out the absolute change in income which is written as:

$$\Delta Y = \frac{1}{1-b}(\Delta G)$$

$$\text{or, } \frac{\Delta Y}{\Delta G} = \frac{1}{1-b}.$$

This is indeed the government spending multiplier which is the same as investment multiplier in the two-sector model.

The reason is that according to Keynes, any increase in autonomous spending will have a multiplier effect. We discuss the logic of the multiplier in a later chapter. Here it suffices to note that there are two ways of interpreting this autonomous expenditure multiplier, or simply the multiplier.

1. The multiplier is the number by which an increase in the autonomous spending (in this case ΔG) has to be multiplied to find out the resulting increase in Y.

2. Alternatively, the multiplier is the ratio of two absolute changes, i.e., $\frac{\Delta Y}{\Delta G}$.

Now we consider transfer payments multiplier.

THE TRANSFER PAYMENTS MULTIPLIER

Now suppose the government increases its transfer payments by ΔTR (rather than its spending on goods and services). So we get the following income equation:

$$Y + \Delta Y = \frac{1}{1-b}(a - bT + bTR + b\Delta TR + G) \quad \ldots \ (5)$$

Now if we subtract equation (3) from equation (5), we get equation (6)

$$\Delta Y = \frac{1}{1-b}(b\Delta TR) \quad \ldots \ (6)$$

$$\text{or } \frac{\Delta Y}{\Delta TR} = \frac{b}{1-b} \quad \ldots \ (7)$$

This is indeed the transfer payments multiplier. Now, if we take the difference between the two multipliers, i.e., the government spending multiplier and transfer payments multiplier, we have

$$\frac{1}{1-b}-\frac{b}{1-b}=\frac{1-b}{1-b}=1$$

Suppose $\Delta G = 20$, $b = 0.75$.

So $\Delta Y = \frac{1}{1-0.75}(20) = 4(20) = 80$

If $\Delta TR = 20$, $b = 0.75$, then

$\Delta Y = \frac{0.75}{1-0.75}(20) = 3(20) = 60.$

Thus we see that the transfer payments multiplier is 3, while government spending multiplier is 4. So we arrive at an interesting result— the transfer payments multiplier is one less than the government spending multiplier.

A simple example will make the point clear.

Problem: Suppose an economy is represented by the following equations:

$C = 50 + 0.75Y_d$

$I = 100$

$G = T = 50$

$TR = 40.$

where all the terms have their usual meaning.

(i) Find out the equilibrium value of Y.

(ii) Calculate the government spending multiplier and the transfer payments multiplier. What is the difference between the two multipliers?

(iii) If the economy seeks to achieve a target income of Rs 1,000 crore, find out the increase in government spending needed to reach the target.

Solution

(i) We know that

$Y = C + I + G$

$= a + bY_d + I + G$

where Y_d = disposable income = $Y - T + TR$.

So the income equation has to be written as

$Y = a + b(Y - T + TR) + I + G$

Substituting the values of the parameters and variables, we have

$Y = 50 + 0.75\ (Y - 50 + 40) + 100 + 50$

or, $Y = 50 + 0.75Y - 7.5 + 150$

or, $Y - 0.75Y = 200 - 7.5$

or, $Y(1 - 0.75) = 192.5$

or, $0.25Y = 192.5$

or, $Y = 192.5 \times 4 = 770$

which is indeed the equilibrium value of Y.

(ii) In this case government spending multiplier (m_G) $= \frac{1}{1-b} = \frac{1}{1-0.75} = \frac{1}{0.25} = 4.$

Transfer payments multiplier (m_{TR}) $= \frac{b}{1-b} = \frac{0.75}{1-0.75} = 3.$

The difference between the two multipliers is equal to 1 as noted above [You can check this interesting result for any value of the *MPC*]

(iii) The equilibrium level of Y is 770. But the target level of Y is 1,000. So Y has to be increased by 230. We know that the increase in income (ΔY) is government spending multiplier (m_G) times the increase in government expenditure (ΔG). So we can write

$$\Delta Y = m_G \times \Delta G$$

or, $\Delta G = \dfrac{\Delta Y}{m_G}$, where m_G is the government spending multiplier.

$$= \frac{230}{4} = 57.5$$

This means that government expenditure has to be increased by Rs 57.5 crore if the objective of the government is to increase Y by Rs 230 crore. This target level of Y (i.e., Rs 1,000 crore) may be taken as the full employment level of Y.

PROPORTIONAL INCOME TAX AND THE EQUILIBRIUM LEVEL OF INCOME

We now assume that instead of a lumpsum tax which collects the same amount of money (in absolute terms), the government imposes a proportional income tax. Under the proportional income tax, the government collects a fixed proportion say 20% of the income. So if national income increases from say Rs 100 crore to Rs 110 crore within a year, the revenue of the government will increase from Rs 20 crore to Rs 22 crores. In this case consumption spending will not fall by the same amount at all levels of income, but by the same percentage of the level of income. As a result the consumption function rotates downwards from C_1 to C_2, with the intercept a (showing autonomous or income-independent consumption) remaining the same. The reason is that there is no parallel downward shift of the consumption function in this case. As shown in Fig. 10.6 the original consumption function is C_1 (before the imposition of the tax). The after-tax consumption function is C_2 which is flatter than C_1. This means that the slope of the consumption function falls, i.e., the *MPC* falls.

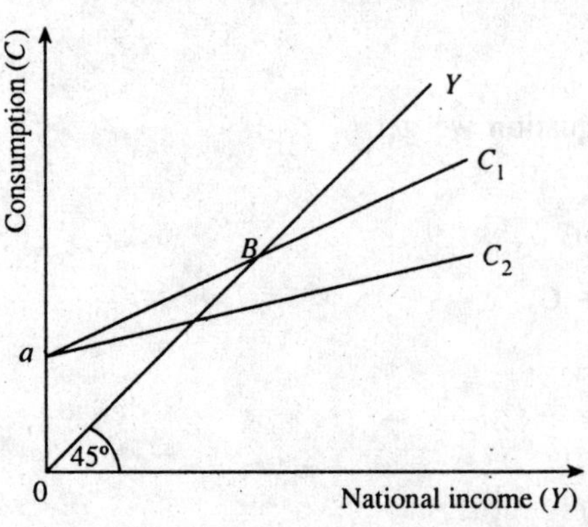

Fig. 10.6: The Effect of a Proportional (Personal) Income Tax on Consumption Function

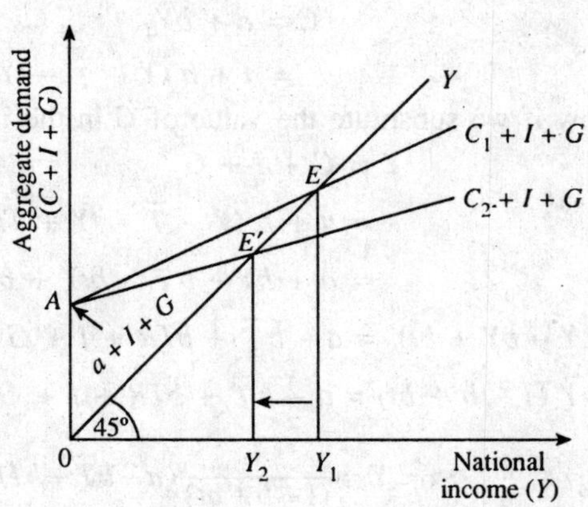

Fig. 10.7: The Effect of Proportional Income Tax on *AD* and *Y*

In Fig. 10.6 the vertical distance between that two consumption functions C_1 and C_2 shows the fall in consumption after the imposition of proportional income tax. The question now is how much does consumption fall in this case. The answer is that, at each level of income, consumption falls by the tax revenue (T) times the *MPC* (b). Now the tax revenue is the tax rate (t = 20%, in our example) times national income i.e., $T = tY$. So consumption falls by $\Delta C = t.Y.b$.

If Y = Rs. 100 crore, t = 20%, and b = 0.75, then ΔC = (Rs. 20 crore). (0.75) = Rs. 16.5 crore. And if Y = Rs. 80 crore, then consumption will fall by ΔC = (Rs. 16). (0.75) = Rs. 12 crore. This means that if Y increases (falls) the government collects more (less) revenue but consumption falls (rises).

It may also be noted that if the tax rate is increased from 20% to 30% consumption will fall at each level of income. If Y = Rs. 100 crore, t = 30% and b = 0.75, then ΔC = (Rs. 30 crore). (0.75) = Rs. 22.5 crore. The converse is also true. However, the revenue of the government will rise from $T = t.Y$ = 20% (Rs. 100 crore) = Rs. 20 crore to $T' = t'.Y$ = 30%. (Rs. 100 crore) = Rs. 30 crore. But if a lumpsum tax of Rs. 20 crore is imposed by the government, its tax revenue will remain the same, at all levels of income, although consumption demand will increase (fall) when income increases (falls).

In Fig. 10.7 we show the effect of proportional income tax on the equilibrium level of national income. We see that the economy is initially at point E, where aggregate demand ($C_1 + I + G$) is equal to aggregate supply and equilibrium national income is Y_1. Now as the consumption function rotates downward after the imposition of the proportional tax, the aggregate demand function also rotates downward (with point $A = a + I + G$ as a pivot).

Now the aggregate demand curve $C_2 + I + G$ intersects the aggregate supply curve at point E'. As a result national income falls from $0Y_1$ to $0Y_2$. So our main prediction here is the following:

All other things remaining the same, the higher the rate of proportional income tax, the greater is the fall in consumption and the larger is the fall in the equilibrium level of income.[1]

Algebraic Treatment of Model 3

We have noted that under the proportional tax, the revenue of the government is expressed as $T = t.Y$, where t is the tax rate and Y is national income. However, in reality the government may impose both a lumpsum tax and a proportional tax on income. Thus the tax function becomes

$$T = \overline{T} + tY \qquad \dots (1)$$

where $\overline{T}$ is the autonomous component of the tax function since it is not related to national income.

Now the equilibrium condition of national income has to be modified since the consumption function now takes the following form

$$C = a + bY_d$$
$$= a + b\,(Y - \overline{T} - tY + TR) \qquad \dots (2)$$

Now if we substitute the value of C in the income equation we get

$$Y = C + I + G$$
$$= a + b\,(Y - \overline{T} - tY + TR) + I + G$$
$$= a + bY - b\overline{T} - btY + bTR + I + G$$

or $Y - bY + btY = a - b\overline{T} + bTR + I + G$

or $Y(1 - b + bt) = a - b\overline{T} + bTR + I + G$

or $Y = \dfrac{1}{(1-b+bt)}(a - b\overline{T} + bTR + I + G)$

or $Y = \dfrac{1}{1-b(1-t)}(a - b\overline{T} + bTR + I + G)$

where $\dfrac{1}{1-b(1-t)}$ is the proportional tax multiplier.

---

1. It may also be noted that income falls by more than the amount by which consumption falls due to the reverse multiplier effect, a concept to be introduced in a later chapter. It may be noted that like I and G, C also has a multiplier effect (since it has an autonomous component). And, according to Keynes, any type of autonomous spending has a multiplier effect. And the multiplier works in both directions — positive and negative.

A simple example will be useful at this stage because we are gradually introducing some doses of realism in our analysis.

Problem: Suppose a closed economy is described by the following equations:

$$C = 20 + 0.75\ Y_d$$
$$I = 50$$
$$G = 100$$
$$TR = 60$$
$$t = 0.2.$$

(a) Write down the reduced form of the income equation.

(b) What is the numerical value of equilibrium income?

(c) What is the value of tax multiplier?

Solution: (a) The reduced form equation is one which is expressed only in terms of exogenous variables and parameters and not in terms of any endogenous variable. The reduced form of equation of national income is

$$Y = \frac{1}{1-b+bt}(a + bTR + I + G)$$

Here t, TR, I and G are all exogenous variables and a and b are parameters. No endogenous variable has appeared on the right hand side of this equation.

(b) If we substitute the values of the parameters and exogenous variables in the above reduced form equation, we get

$$Y = \frac{1}{1-0.75+0.75\times 0.2}(20 + 0.75\times 60 + 50 + 100)$$

$$= \frac{1}{1-0.60}(225)$$

$$= \frac{1}{0.40}(225)$$

$$= 225 \times \frac{100}{4} = 562.5 \text{ (approx)}$$

This is the equilibrium value of Y.

(c) The tax multiplier now is

$$mt = \frac{1}{1-b+bt} = \frac{1}{1-0.75+0.75\times 0.2}$$

$$= \frac{1}{1-0.60} = \frac{1}{0.40} = 2.5.$$

A DETAILED DISCUSSION OF TAX MULTIPLIER

After studying the multiplier effects of government spending (G) and transfer payments (TR), we may turn to a detailed discussion of the multiplier effects of change in tax. We have already studied the effects of two types of taxes on equilibrium national income, viz., lumpsum tax and proportional tax. Both types of taxes reduce Y, but in different ways as noted earlier. We will now see that both have a multiplier effect in the sense that a certain change in the tax rate or tax total will have a multiplier effect on Y. For analytical simplicity, we consider the multiplier effect of a lumpsum tax. It may be recalled that taxes are a leakage from the circular flow of income.

While a tax increase has an adverse effect on equilibrium Y, a tax increase has a favourable effect on it

So an increase in lumpsum tax will lead to a multiple drop in Y through the tax multiplier. The converse is also true. A tax cut will lead to a multiple increase in Y through the tax multiplier.

The reduced form equation of equilibrium national income for a three-sector economy with lumpsum taxes is written as

$$Y = \frac{1}{1-b}(a - bT + I + G) \quad \ldots \quad (1)$$

where T is lumpsum income tax. We know that an increase in tax will reduce consumption demand (as also saving) by reducing disposable income. The fall in consumption is the *MPC* times the tax, i.e., $\Delta C = b\Delta T$.

Now suppose national income rises by ΔY and the government imposes an additional lumpsum tax on this extra income. As a result the income equation (1) now becomes

$$Y + \Delta Y = \frac{1}{1-b}[a - b(T + \Delta T) + I + G]$$

$$= \frac{1}{1-b}[a - bT - b\Delta T + I + G] \quad \ldots \quad (2)$$

Now if we subtract equation (1) from (2) we get:

$$\Delta Y = \frac{1}{1-b}(-b\Delta T) \quad \ldots \quad (3)$$

Finally by dividing both sides of equation (3) by ΔT, we get:

$$\frac{\Delta Y}{\Delta T} = \frac{-b}{1-b} \quad \ldots \quad (4)$$

which is indeed the tax multiplier. It may be noted that the imposition of an additional lumpsum tax (ΔT) will reduce national income not by the same amount but by a multiple of it. Suppose, for example, that $b = 0.80$ and $\Delta T =$ Rs 20 crores.

So the tax multiplier is $\dfrac{\Delta Y}{\Delta T} = \dfrac{-b}{1-b} = \dfrac{-0.80}{1-0.80} = \dfrac{-0.80}{0.20} = -4$

The tax multiplier is negative because taxes act as a leakage from the circular flow of income. Thus if $\Delta T =$ Rs. 20 crores, ΔY will be – Rs 80 crores.

However, a cut in taxes will increase national income by the same amount since the multiplier will now be positive

$$\frac{\Delta Y}{\Delta T} = \frac{b}{1-b} = 4$$

and the multiplier effect will be favourable.

THE BALANCED BUDGET MULTIPLIER

An important theorem of macroeconomics is the balanced budget multiplier theorem, or the unit budget multiplier theorem. The multiplier is derived by assuming that the budget of the government is in balance, i.e., $G = T$. So an increase in government spending (ΔG) is financed by an equal increase in tax (ΔT). Here we consider the multiplier effect of an equal increase in G and T, assuming that the government imposes only lumpsum tax (T).

We know that if the government imposes a lumpsum tax, the equation of equilibrium national income is

$$Y = \frac{1}{1-b}(a - b\overline{T} + I + G) \quad \dots \quad (1)$$

where $\overline{T}$ is lumpsum tax which remains constant at all levels of income.

Now suppose the government increases its expenditure by (ΔG) and finances it by imposing lumpsum taxes of ΔT. So the budget of the government is in balance, i.e., $\Delta G = \Delta T$.

In this case two things will happen at the same time. National income will rise due to an increase in G. It will fall due to an increase in T. However, the net increase in Y will be positive since the government expenditure multiplier is greater than the tax multiplier.

So equation (1) now becomes

$$Y + \Delta Y = \frac{1}{1-b}[a - b(\overline{T} + \Delta T) + I + G + \Delta G] \quad \dots \quad (2)$$

where ΔY denotes the net increase in Y due to an equal increase in G and T.

Now if we subtract equation (1) from equation (2), we have

$$\Delta Y = \frac{1}{1-b}(-b\Delta T + \Delta G) \quad \dots \quad (3)$$

Since $\Delta G = \Delta T$, we can rewrite equation (3) as

$$\Delta Y = \frac{1}{1-b}(-b\Delta G + \Delta G)$$

$$\text{or } \Delta Y(1-b) = \Delta G(1-b)$$

$$\text{or } \Delta Y = \Delta G \quad \dots \quad (4)$$

Now if we divide both sides of equation (4) by ΔG, we get

$$\frac{\Delta Y}{\Delta G} = \frac{\Delta G}{\Delta G} = 1 \quad \dots \quad (5)$$

This is the balanced budget (or unit budget) multiplier. This means that if $\Delta G = \Delta T =$ Rs 20 crores Y will also increase by Rs 20 crore. In other words if the budget of the government remains balanced, i.e., if an additional G is financed by an additional T of the same amount, the net increase in national income will be exactly equal to the amount by which G and T increased in the first instance.

AN ALTERNATIVE PROOF

We can use an alternative method to prove that the balance budget multiplier (BBM) is always equal to 1. We know that the government expenditure multiplier $(m_G) = \frac{1}{1-b}$, where b is the *MPC*. We also know that lumpsum tax multiplier $(m_T) = \frac{-b}{1-b}$.

Now if we combine the two multipliers, we get the BBM:

$$m_G + m_T = \frac{1}{1-b} + \frac{-b}{1-b} = \frac{1-b}{1-b} = 1$$

Thus once again we prove that the BBM is always equal to one. The reason is that the government expenditure multiplier is always greater than the lumpsum tax multiplier by 1. For example, when $b = 0.80$, $m_G = 5$ and $m_T = 4$ and when $b = 0.50$, $m_G = 2$ and $m_T = 1$.

Now suppose $\Delta G = \Delta T =$ Rs. 20 crores and $b = 0.75$. In this case Y will increase by Rs. 80 crores, since $m_G = 4$. It will also fall by Rs. 60 crores since $m_T = 3$. So the net increase in income is $\Delta Y =$ Rs. 80 crores – Rs. 60 crores = Rs. 20 crores. This is exactly equal to the amount by which G and T increased initially.

Economic Insight: Situations Where the BBM ≠ 1

There are three situations when the BBM is not equal to 1.

1. If the *MPC* of taxpayers is less than that of other income recipients, BBM will be less than one, as Richard Musgrave has shown.
2. If investment has an induced component (i.e., if investment increases with Y), then BBM will be greater than one.
3. If all the components of aggregate demand expenditure have an import content, then BBM may be less than one, as has been suggested by R. Lipsey.

These three points are proved in the author's **Analytical Macroeconomics** (2nd edition, NCBA, 2009).

Example

Suppose an economy is described by the following equations:

$$C = 50 + 0.75Y$$
$$I = 60$$
$$G = 50$$
$$T = 50.$$

All the terms have their usual meaning and all figures are in crores of rupees.

Now answer the following questions:

(i) What is the equilibrium level of Y?

(ii) Suppose government spending increases by Rs. 30 crores. What will be effect of this on equilibrium Y?

(iii) Find out the tax multiplier as also the BBM.

(iv) Suppose $T = \overline{T} + tY = 50 + 0.20Y$

Find out the equilibrium value of Y.

Solution

(i) In equilibrium

$$Y = C + I + G$$
$$= a + bY_d + I + G$$
$$= a + b(Y - T) + I + G$$

Now it we substitute the numerical values of a, b, T, I and G in the previous equation, we get

$$Y = 50 + 0.75\ (Y - 50) + 60 + 50$$
$$= 50 + 0.75Y - 40 + 60 + 50$$

or $Y - 0.75Y = 120$

or $0.25Y = 120$

or $Y = 120 \times 4 = 480$ crores.

This is indeed the equilibrium value of Y.

(ii) Government expenditure multiplier $m_G = \dfrac{1}{1-b} = \dfrac{1}{1-0.75} = 4.$

If G increases by Rs. 30 crore, Y will increase by $\Delta Y = m_G \times \Delta G$

$$= 4 \times 30 \text{ crores}$$
$$= 120 \text{ crores}$$

(iii) Tax multiplier $= m_T = \dfrac{-b}{1-b} = \dfrac{-0.75}{1-0.75} = -3$

The $BBM = m_G + m_T$
$= 4 + (-3) = 1.$

(iv) When $T = 50 + 0.2Y$, then the equilibrium value of national income is

$$Y = \frac{1}{1-b+bt}(a - b\overline{T} + I + G)$$

$$= \frac{1}{1-0.75+0.15}(50 - 40 + 60 + 50)$$

$$= \frac{1}{0.40}(120)$$

$= 2.5\ (120) =$ Rs. 300 crores.

NATIONAL INCOME DETERMINATION IN AN OPEN ECONOMY

We may finally present the four-sector model of income determination by taking into account foreign trade, i.e., exports and imports. Now the economy has four sectors, viz., the household sector, the business sector, the government sector and the foreign trade (or the rest of the world) sector. We include the foreign trade in our analysis because exports like I and G, are injections into the circular flow of income and increase Y. By contrast, imports, like S and T, are leakages from the circular flow and reduce Y.

Exports represent that portion of a country's GDP which is not domestically absorbed by the households, firms and governments. When a country exports a portion of its output foreigners buy such output and spend money on it. So the exporting country earns foreign exchange. By comparison if a country needs more of certain things (such as crude oil, machinery, or fertilisers) that it cannot produce in adequate amount, then it has to meet this extra demand through imports.[1] The importing country spends money on foreign goods and foreigners' income goes up (since money goes out of the home country). In short, national income increases when a country exports certain goods and services and national income falls when it imports certain things. The difference between exports (X) and imports (M) is called net exports ($X - M$). So whether a country's national income will increase or fall due to exports and imports depends on its net exports (or balance of trade). If net exports ($NX = X - M$) are positive, then aggregate demand (expenditure) of a country will increase. But if net exports are negative, then its aggregate demand expenditure will fall.

In reality, when a country is able to achieve faster economic growth, its exports rise, provided the following two conditions are satisfied:

(i) The country is able to generate export surplus (after meeting its consumption needs).

(ii) There is sufficient demand for the products of the country in the world market.

This depends on various factors. But the supply of quality products and maintaining delivery schedules are most important. Thus if external demand conditions are favourable, exports of a country are likely to rise with economic growth and increase in national income. By comparison, imports normally increase with income. A developing country like India not only imports consumer goods like food but capital goods such as machinery. How much a country will import with an increase in its national income depends on the prospensity (tendency) to import.[2]

1. For example, the USA is a leading producer of motor cars in the world. But it imports cars from Japan since there is a high demand for small fuel-efficient Japanese cars in the USA.

2. More imports are not necessarily bad for a country. If India imports more capital goods in the initial stages of economic development, it will be able to build up additional production capacity and produce more goods and services in the future. However, more imports of consumer goods in times of rising income may create problems as had happened in Mexico in 1994.

However, in the Keynesian model of national income determination, exports and imports are treated as exogeneous, i.e., determined by forces outside the model. In other words exports and imports are treated as autonomous, i.e., independent of national income.

TDE and TFE

Earlier we noted that total domestic expenditure (*TDE*) has three components, viz., *C* and *I* and *G*. Now, in an open economy, we have to introduce a new concept called total final expenditure (*TFE*) or demand which includes net exports also. So we can now write the equation of the equilibrium level of national income as follows:

$$Y = C + I + G + (X - M) \qquad \ldots (1)$$

Since $C = a + b(Y - T)$, we get

$$Y = a + bY - bT + I + G + NX$$

$$\text{or } Y(1 - b) = a - bT + I + G + NX$$

$$\text{or } Y = \frac{1}{(1-b)}(a - bT + I + G + NX) \qquad \ldots (2)$$

This means that the equilibrium value of *Y* is calculated by multiplying the autonomous expenditure multiplier $\left(\frac{1}{1-b}\right)$ by the sum of all fixed autonomous expenditures shown on the right hand side of (2) inside the bracket. In the four sector-economy, aggregate saving ($S = Y - C$) has to be equal to the sum of private investment, government expenditure and net exports (i.e., $S = I + G + NX$).

The determination of the equilibrium level of national income is illustrated in Fig. 10.8.

Here we proceed in the following five steps:

1. First we draw the 45° income line *Y* and take this as the guideline.
2. Then we draw the consumption line *C*.
3. Next we add the fixed (autonomous investment) *I* to *C* to derive the combined $C + I$ schedule.
4. Next we add the fixed *G* to $C + I$ to arrive at the $C + I + G$ schedule.
5. Finally we add the fixed *NX* to $C + I + G$ to derive the aggregate demand curve $AD = C + I + G + NX$.

The *AD* curve shows total final expenditure in an open economy. It intersects the income line *Y* (or the aggregate supply curve) at point *E*. We drop a perpendicular from point *E* to find out the equilibrium value of *Y* which is $0Y_E$. And since $Y = AD$, $0Y_E = EY_E$. At the equilibrium level of income $Y - C = S = I + G + NX = EF$ as shown in the diagram.

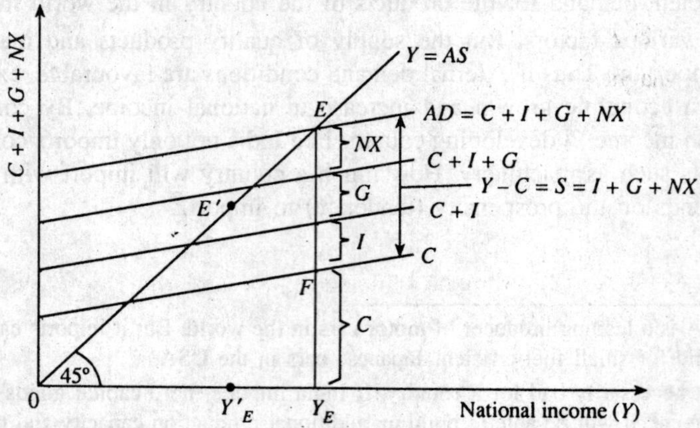

Fig. 10.8: Income Determination in an Open Economy

Here we assume that *NX* are positive. This is why the *AD* curve lies above the $C + I + G$ curve. But if *NX* were negative, the *AD* curve would lie below the $C + I + G$ curve, as is indicated by point E' and national income would be Y'_E which is less than Y_E.

Table 10.2 Illustrates how national income is determined in a four-sector model.

Table 10.2: An Illustration of Income Determination in a Four-Sector Model (Rs. Crores)

$Y = AS$	C	S	I	G	$I + G$	NX	$I + G + NX$	$AD = C + I + G + NX$	Changes in stocks	Effect on Y
100	80	20	10	20	30	5	35	115	–15	$Y\uparrow$
150	120	30	10	20	30	5	35	155	–5	$Y\uparrow$
175	140	35	10	20	30	5	35	175	0	$Y = Y_E$
200	160	40	10	20	30	5	35	195	+5	$Y\downarrow$

Here we assume that national income is initially 100. We also assume that $MPC = 0.80$. So consumption is 80, *S* is 20. Here $I + G + NX = 35$ at all levels of *Y*. Now since $AD > AS$ and $I + G + NX > S$, *Y* has to increase. Since $AD = 115$, there is an unintended fall in inventories of 15. This means that sales plans of firms are fulfilled, but production plans are not. As soon as the inventories are exhausted, output increases and national income increases to 150. Now $AD = 155$. So there is an unintended fall in inventories of 5, and, as a result, output increases once again and national income rises to 175. Now $AS = AD$, and change in stock is zero. So this is indeed the equilibrium value of *Y*. Now both the production and sales plans are fulfilled, and therefore no change in output is warranted. Thus three conditions are to be satisfied to ensure national income equilibrium, as noted earlier in this chapter.

1. $Y = C + I + G + NX$ (assuming $NX > 0$)
2. $S = I + G + NX$ (the only leakage = the sum of three injections, assuming away taxes)
3. No undesired change (accumulation or exhausion) in stocks.

However, if producers overreact to the excess demand pressure and the consequent exhaustion of stocks and produce an output of 200, they will be left with an unsold stock of 5 (since aggregate demand of 195 will now be less than aggregate supply of 200). In such a situation a cutback on production is inevitable. As production falls, national income will fall. The process will continue until and unless *Y* returns to 200 at which all the above three conditions of national income equilibrium are satisfied.

INDUCED IMPORTS AND INCOME DETERMINATION

Now we modify our analysis slightly and assume that only exports are autonomous, i.e., independent of national income. So take exports as fixed $(X = \bar{X})$. But imports have both autonomous and induced components so the import function now becomes:

$$M = \bar{M} + mY$$

where $\bar{M}$ denotes autonomous imports and *mY* stands for induced imports which depends on two factors—(i) the marginal propensity to import (*m*) and (ii) the level of national income (*Y*). Here *m* is the ratio of the increase in imports to the increase in national income (*Y*) (which brings it about) and is expressed as $\Delta M/\Delta Y$. Note that an increase (decrease) in *Y* leads to an increase (decrease) in imports and not vice-versa. Since *m* is assumed to remain constant, whether *Y* is high or low, as *Y* increases, *mY* will increase, depending on the fixed value of *m*.

The Equilibrium Condition of national income (Y)

Now the equilibrium condition of Y is written as:

$$Y = C + I + G + (X - M) \qquad \ldots (1)$$

where $C = a + b(Y - T)$ and

$$M = \bar{M} + mY.$$

By substituting the consumption function and import function in equation (1), we get

$$Y = a + b(Y - T) + I + G + [X - (\bar{M} + mY)]$$

$$\text{or, } Y = a + bY - bT + I + G + X - \bar{M} - mY.$$

$$\text{or, } Y - bY + mY = a - bT + I + G + x - \bar{M}$$

$$\text{or, } Y(1 - b + m) = a - bT + I + G + X - \bar{M}$$

$$Y = \frac{1}{1-b+m}(a - bT + I + G + X - \bar{M})$$

where the first term on the r.h.s of this equation $\frac{1}{1-b+m} = \frac{1}{s+m}$ is called the foreign trade multiplier or open economy multiplier. Since the value of this multiplier depends on both *MPC* and *MPI*, the open economy multiplier is less than the closed economy multiplier. Suppose $b = \frac{2}{3}$. So the closed economy multiplier will be 3. Now suppose 10% of Y leaks out in the form of imports. This implies that $m = \frac{1}{10}$. So the value of the open economy multiplier will be $= \frac{1}{\frac{1}{3} + \frac{1}{10}} = 2 \cdot 3$.

It may be noted that a change in any of the components of autonomous spending such as *C, I, G, X,* or $\bar{M}$ will lead to a multiple increase in Y through the foreign trade (open economy) multiplier $\frac{1}{1-b+m} = 2.3$ in our above example. Thus if exports increase by ΔX (= Rs. 20 cr.) national income will increase by $\Delta Y = \frac{1}{1-b+m}(\Delta X)$ = 2.3 (Rs. 20 cr.) = Rs. 46 cr.

EFFECT OF PROPORTIONAL INCOME TAX

We may now extend the four-sector model further by incorporating the effect of proportional income tax. A proportional tax will change the value of the foreign trade multiplier by affecting *MPC*. Suppose the tax function is $T = \bar{T} + tY$, where $\bar{T}$ is a constant lumpsum tax and t is proportional tax rate (which is a fixed percentage of national income). Now the foreign trade multiplier becomes:

$$m_0 = \frac{1}{1 - b(1-t) + m} = \frac{1}{1 - b + bt + m}$$

So the equilibrium income equation now becomes

$$Y = \frac{1}{1 - b(1-t) + m}(a - bT + I + G + X - \bar{M})$$

Now if exports increase by ΔX, national income will increase of ΔY through the foreign trade or open economy multiplier.

Example

Problem 1: Suppose an economy is described by the following equations:

$C = 14 + 0.60Y_d$

$I = 20 \qquad X = 15$

$G = 10 \qquad M = 5 + 0.10Y$

$T = 5$

(a) Find out the equilibrium value of income.

(b) Calculate net exports.

(c) What is the value of the open economy multiplier?

Solution

(a) $Y = C + I + G + NX$

or, $Y = (14 + 0.60\ Y_d) + 20 + 10 + 15 - (5 + 0.10Y)$

or, $Y = 14 + 0.60\ (Y - T) + 45 - 5 - 0.10Y$

or, $Y - 0.6Y + 0.1Y = 14 - 3 + 40 = 51$

or, $0.5Y = 51$

or, $Y = 102.$

(b) Net exports $(NX) = X - M$

$= 15 - (5 + 0.10Y)$

If we substitute the equilibrium value of Y, we get

$NX = 15 - (5 + 0.10 \times 102)$

$= 15 - 5 - 10.2 = -0.2$

This implies that there is a deficit in the balance of trade.

(c) The foreign trade multiplier $(m_0) = \dfrac{1}{1-b+m}$

Here $b = 0.60$ and $m = 0.10$. So $m_0 = \dfrac{1}{1-0.60+0.10} = \dfrac{1}{0.5} = 2$

So an increase in exports by Rs. 10 crores will lead to an increase in Y by Rs. 20 crores.

Problem 2: Suppose an economy is described by the following structural equations:

$C = 10 + b(Y - 40 - tY)$

$I = 50$

$X = 20$

$M = 5 + 0.1Y.$

Here we assume that (a) $MPC = 0.75$, (b) the budget of the government is in balance, (c) the proportional tax rate $t = 0.20$.

Now answer the following questions:

(a) Find out the equilibrium level of national income.

(b) What is the value of the foreign trade multiplier?

(c) What is the value of imports at equilibrium income?

(d) If equilibrium national income is less than the full-employment level of income by Rs. 100 crores, what should be the increase in government spending or in exports to attain the full-employment level of income?

(e) What will be the required increase in exports to attain the same target?

Solution

(a) The reduced form equation of the equilibrium level of income is

$$Y = \frac{1}{1 - b(1-t) + m}\{(a - bT) + I + G + X - \bar{M}\}.$$

Since the budget of the government is in balance we have $G = T = 40$. Now putting the values of the parameters and variables we have:

$$Y = \frac{1}{1 - 0.75(1 - 0.20) + 0.1}\{(10 - 40\times.75) + 50 + 40 - 20 - 5\}$$

$$= \frac{1}{1 - 0.75 + 0.15 + 0.10}(10 - 30 + 50 + 40 + 15)$$

$$= \frac{1}{0.5}(85)$$

$$= 2\ (85) = 170.$$

This is indeed the equilibrium value of Y.

(b) The foreign trade multiplier is

$$m_0 = \frac{1}{1 - b(1-t) + m} = \frac{1}{1 - 0.75(1 - 0.20) + 0.10}$$

$$= \frac{1}{1 - 0.75 + 0.15 + 0.10}$$

$$= \frac{1}{0.50} = 2.$$

(c) The equilibrium value of imports can be found out by putting the equilibrium value of national income 170 in the import function. Thus

$$M = 5 + 0.1 \times 170$$
$$= 22.$$

(d) The required increase in government expenditure to attain Rs 100 increase in income can be found out by multiplying the government expenditure multiplier by the increase in government expenditure

$$\Delta Y = m_G \times \Delta G$$

or, $100 = 2 \times \Delta G$

or, $\Delta G = \frac{100}{2} = 50.$

(e) Now since the value of the foreign trade multiplier is 2, the required increase in exports to achieve the same target will be

$$\Delta Y = m_0 \times \Delta X$$

or, $100 = 2 \times \Delta X$

or, $\Delta X = \frac{100}{2} = 50.$

So exports are to be increased by the same amount as government expenditure. This is an interesting coincidence.

USING NET EXPORTS FUNCTION TO DETERMINE THE EQUILIBRIUM VALUE OF INCOME

Net exports are influenced by national income, domestic price level and exchange rates

It may be noted that net exports of a country is not just influenced by its national income but also by the domestic price level as also by the exchange rate (i.e., the price of domestic currency in terms of foreign currency). In order to see how net exports are influenced by these three factors we have to discuss in detail the net exports function. This will enable us to find out the equilibrium value of national income by using an alternative (but more realistic) approach. We give Indian example to make the concept of net exports more clear.

The Net Exports Function

We know that net exports are the difference between exports and imports. How much India can export per annum depends on the decisions of foreigners to buy the goods and services produced in India. So exports are autonomous since these are exogenously determined. Exports influence national income in the same way as *I* or *G*.

By comparison, Indian imports depend more on decisions of Indian households, business firms and the government to buy goods and services (such as consumer goods, industrial raw materials, crude oil, machines and engineering goods) from foreign countries. Imports are a function of GDP and normally increase with an increase in national income.

Since exports are autonomous (hence independent of income) and imports rise with the GDP due to an induced component, net exports decrease as GDP increases. This means that desired net exports ($X - M$) are inversely related to GDP. Here we assume that the import function is of the following type:

$$M = \bar{M} + mY = 50 + 0.20Y$$

Here m is the marginal propensity to import. It is the ratio of the increase in import (M) to the increase in GDP (Y) which brings it about. We assume that $m = 0.20$. This means that 20% of any extra income earned within the country is spent on imported goods and services.

The data for exports and imports of a simple hypothetical economy are presented in Table 10.3. We see that exports remain constant at all levels of national income.

Table 10.3: The Net Exports Function (Rs. crores)

GDP (Y)	Exports (X)	Imports ($M = \bar{M} + 0.20Y$)	Net Exports ($X - M$)
0	700	50	650
1,000	700	250 (= 50 + 200)	450
2,000	700	450 (= 50 + 400)	250
2,750	700	600 (= 50 + 550)	100
3,250	700	700 (= 50 + 650)	0
3,750	700	800 (= 50 + 750)	– 100

A portion of imports remains fixed. But total imports increase with an increase in *Y* due to its induced component. We know that in a closed economy the equilibrium condition of national income is

$$S + I = I + G \quad \ldots (1)$$

i.e., the sum of leackages = sum of injections.

In an open economy the equilibrium condition has to be modified by including exports and imports. So we rewrite eqn. (1) in this modified (extended) form:

$$S + I + M = I + G + NX \quad \ldots (2)$$

Thus if $S + T = I + G$, i.e., the closed economy is in equilibrium, then $X = M$, i.e., exports have to be equal to imports for national income to attain its equilibrium value. This point is illustrated in Fig. 10.9.

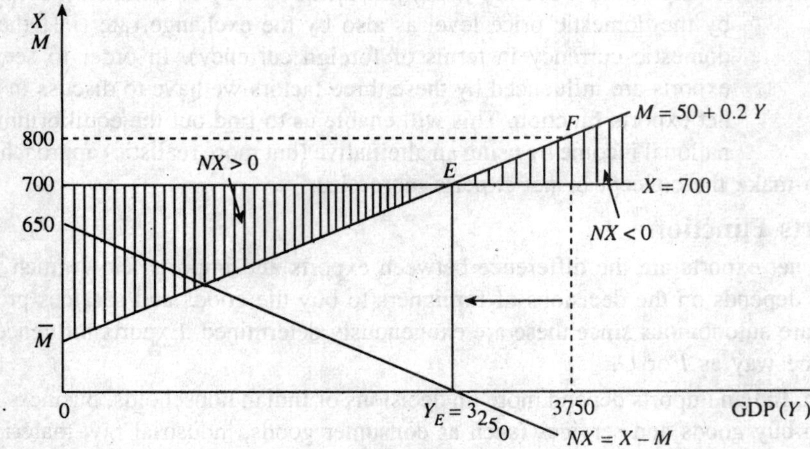

Fig. 10.9: Income Determination by the Net Exports Function

We see that when $Y = 0$, $X = 700$ and $M = 50$. So $X - M = 650$. So long as exports exceed imports, $(X > M)$ Y increases, since X are injections into the circular flow and M are leakages from it. As Y increases, imports rise (exports remaining constant). So long as $X > M$, NX will be positive and Y will continue to rise. When $M = X$ and $NX = 0$, national income attains its equilibrium value (Y_E). If $M > X$ at a higher level of Y, Y falls and comes back to the equilibrium level. Thus when Y temporarily increases to 3,750, imports rise to 800, exports remaining the same at 700. As a result, net exports are negative (– 100) and the net exports function goes below the horizontal axis. Consequently national income returns to the equilibrium level (3,250). It cannot be sustained beyond this level.

The net exports function $NX = X - M$ shows a negative value

Shift in Net Exports Function

We have seen that net exports function (NX) is related to national income. But this is not the whole truth. Net exports also depend on three other factors, viz., (1) income in foreign countries, (2) the price levels in different countries (which depend on the relative rates of inflation or deflation) and (3) exchange rate between currencies.

An increase in the intensity of export or import will shift the NX schedule

If exports increase due to the adoption of certain export-promotion policies, imports remain the same, the original net exports function of NX_1, shown in Fig. 10.10 will shift to the right to NX_2. Since, exports are autonomous and hence independent of Y, the two export schedules are parallel to each other. If autonomous exports rise by ΔX, GDP increases by ΔY from Y_E to Y_G. Due to the operation of the foreign trade multiplier, $\Delta Y > \Delta X$. The converse is also true. If autonomous exports fall by ΔX, there will be a parallel leftward shift of the original net export schedule to NX_3. Consequently Y will fall from Y_E to Y_F. And the fall in Y is a multiple of the fall in exports due to the operation of the reverse multiplier process.

There is a parallel rightward (leftward) shift of the net export schedule due to changes in autonomous exports, the propensity to import remaining the same

However, if exports remain constant but imports rise due to an increase in the marginal propensity to import from 0.20 to 0.25 (say), the net exports schedule which shows the difference between exports and imports will become sharper. As it shifts, its slope, which measures the marginal propensity to import, increases. This point is illustrated in Fig. 10.11, where national income falls from Y_E to Y_F due to an increase in induced imports, caused by a rise in the marginal propensity to import.

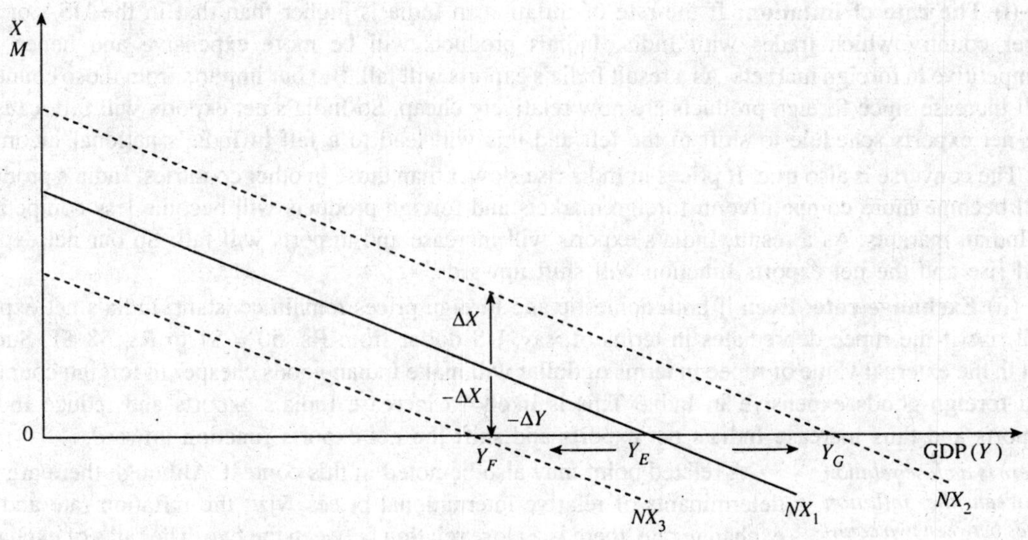

Fig. 10.10: Shifts of the Net Exports Function due to Change in Export Intensity

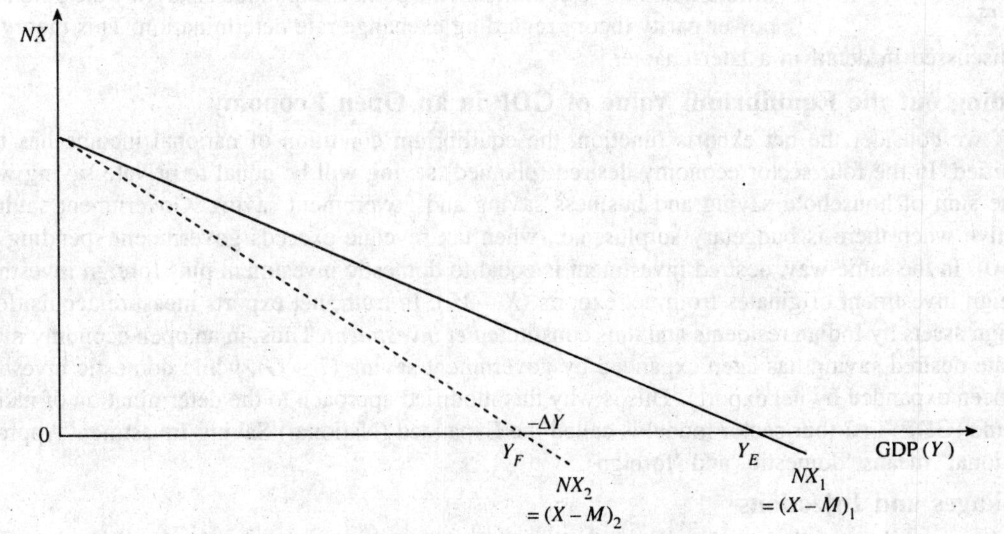

Fig. 10.11: Leftward Shift of the Net Exports Function

Factors leading to an Increase in Induced Imports

We may now explain the factors which cause a shift in net exports function.

1. Foreign income

If national income in foreign countries rises, foreigners will buy more of Indian goods. So India's exports (which are foreigners' imports) will increase. And the net exports function will shift upward and India's national income will rise. By contrast, if there is a recession in USA or in a country which trades with India, its national income will fall. So it will reduce imports and India's exports will fall. Therefore the net exports function will shift downward, causing India's national income to fall.

2. Relative price levels

Two factors cause changes in relative international prices and exert influence on India's exports and imports, viz., the rate of inflation and the exchange rate.

(i) **The rate of inflation:** If the rate of inflation in India is higher than that in the USA or any other country which trades with India, India's products will be more expensive and hence less competitive in foreign markets. As a result India's exports will fall. But our imports from those countries will increase since foreign products are now relatively cheap. So India's net exports will fall, causing the net exports schedule to shift to the left and this will lead to a fall in India's national income.

The converse is also true. If prices in India rise slower than those in other countries, India's products will become more competitive in foreign markets and foreign products will become less competitive in Indian markets. As a result, India's exports will increase and imports will fall. So our net exports will rise and the net exports function will shift upwards.

(ii) **Exchange rate:** Even if both domestic and foreign prices remain constant, India's net exports will rise if the rupee depreciates in terms of, say, US dollar from Rs. 50 = \$1 to Rs. 58 \$1. Such a fall in the external value of rupee in terms of dollar will make Indian goods cheaper in foreign countries and foreign goods expensive in India. This is likely to increase India's exports and reduce India's imports and thus increase India's net exports and shift the net exports function upward.

There is a close relation between the inflation rates between two countries and the exchange rate between their currencies

A related point may also be noted in this context. Although there are two determinants of relative international prices, viz., the inflation rate and the exchange rate, there is a close relation between the two. The rates of exchange between Indian rupee and US dollar is influenced by the relative rates of inflation in the two countries. This point is explained clearly by the purchasing power parity theory regarding exchange rate determination. This theory will be discussed in detail in a later chapter.

Finding out the Equilibrium Value of GDP in an Open Economy

If we consider the net exports function, the equilibrium condition of national income has to be modified. In the four sector economy desired (planned) saving will be equal to private saving which is the sum of household saving and business saving and government saving. Government saving is positive when there is budgetary surplus, i.e., when tax revenue exceeds government spending ($T - G > 0$). In the same way, desired investment is equal to domestic investment plus foreign investment. Foreign investment originates from net exports ($X - M$). In truth, net exports measure acquisition of foreign assets by Indian residents and thus constitute *net investment*. Thus, in an open economy model, private desired saving has been expanded by government saving ($T - G$), while domestic investment has been expanded by net exports. This is why this modified approach to the determination of national income (GDP) in a four-sector model is called the Expanded (National) Saving-Investment Approach. 'National' means 'domestic' and 'foreign'.

Leakages and Injections

Now in this expanded model there are three injections into the circular flow and three leakages from the flow. The leakages are saving (S), tax (T) and imports (M). The injections are investment (I), government spending (G) and exports (X). So national income will attain its equilibrium value when the sum of injections just equals the sum of leakages:

$$S + T + M = I + G + X$$

Rearranging this equation slightly we get

$$S + (T - G) = I + (X - M).$$

where ($T - G$) is government saving (budgetary surplus) and ($X - M$) is foreign investment (originating from net exports).

Fig. 10.12 shows how national income is determined in this expanded model. Here we measure national income on the horizontal axis and national saving and investment on the vertical axis. Now total saving is private saving (S_P) + government saving (S_t) or in terms of symbol,

$$S = S_P + S_G = S_P + (T - G)$$

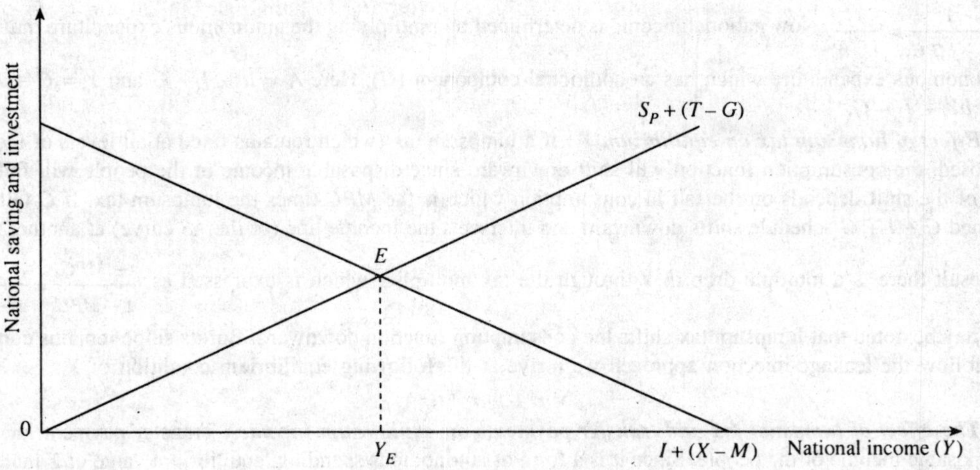

Fig. 10.12: The Determination of GDP

This means that as national income increases, national saving also increases. This is shown by the national saving curve $S_P + (T - G)$. Similarly total investment is shown by the downward sloping curve of $I + (X - M)$. Since net exports imply net acquisition of foreign assets or claims by Indian residents, the sum of domestic investment and net acquisition of foreign assets $I + (X - M)$ implies national asset acquisition or capital formation. The national investment function $I + (X - M)$ is downward sloping because the net exports function $(X - M)$ slopes downward, even if private investment (I) is autonomous.

National income attains its equilibrium value Y_E at point E where desired national saving $S_P + (T - G)$ equals desired national asset accumulation $I + (X - M)$. If actual income is less than Y_E, national asset formation will exceed desired national saving. This means that injections into the circular flow of income will exceed leakages from the circular flow. This means that planned aggregate expenditure will exceed national output (income received). Consequently, undesired inventories with producing units or firms will fall below the desired level. So the firms' production plans will have to be adjusted to meet the excess demand pressure. The economy will now be induced to increase output. Consequently national income will increase and will tend towards its equilibrium level Y_E. The converse is also true. If the level of income exceeds Y_E, national investment $[I + (X - M)]$ will be less than national saving $[S_P + (T - G)]$. As a result desired aggregate demand (expenditure) will be less than national output. Consequently unplanned inventories with the firm will exceed their desired level. So the firms will now be forced to reduce production consequently, national income will tend towards Y_E. Thus it logically follows that at income level Y_E, desired national saving is equal to desired national investment. Therefore firms have to plan to change their output levels. They will end up producing what they planned to produce. In such a situation national income will attain its equilibrium value with no tendency to move up or down.

KEY POINTS

1. *Government expenditure and national income* : In a three-sector model with government, there is one more leakage (in the form of tax) and one more injection (in the form of government expenditure). It may be noted that government expenditure generates multiplier effect in the same way private investment expenditure does. The reason is that both are autonomous. And, according to Keynes, any increase in autonomous spending has a multiplier effect. It may also be noted that government expenditure multiplier is the same as investment multiplier, i.e., $\frac{1}{1-MPC}=\frac{1}{1-b}$. Now national income is determined by multiplying the autonomous expenditure multiplier by autonomous expenditure which has an additional component (G). Here $A = a + I + G$ and $Y = C + I + G = a + bY + I + G$.

2. *Effect of lumpsum tax on equilibrium Y*: If a lumpsum tax (which remains fixed at all levels of income) is imposed, the consumption function will shift downward since disposable income of the people will fall. The extent of the shift depends on the fall in consumption which is the *MPC* times the lumpsum tax. If C falls, the combined $C + I + G$ schedule shifts downward and intersects the income line (or the *AS* curve) at another point. As a result there is a multiple drop in Y through the tax multiplier which is expressed as $\frac{-MPC}{1-MPC}=\frac{-b}{1-b}$.

It may be noted that lumpsum tax shifts the consumption function downward. But its slope remains constant. If we follow the leakage-injection approach we arrive at the following equilibrium condition of Y:

$$S + T = I + G$$

3. *The effect of lumpsum tax and transfer payments on equilibrium income*: Transfer payment increases the disposable income of the people. Since it is a form of autonomous spending, equilibrium value of Y increases. The transfer payment multiplier is expressed as $\frac{1}{1-b}$.

If we take the difference between the government expenditure multiplier and the transfer payment we get the following result:

$$\frac{1}{1-b}-\frac{b}{1-b}=\frac{1-b}{1-b}=1.$$

4. *The effect of proportional income tax on equilibrium income*: If a proportional income tax is imposed, the consumption function rotates clockwise, i.e., its slope falls. As a result the combined $C + I + G$ schedule becomes flatter. It intersects the income line (or AS curve) at a point to the left of the original equilibrium point. Consequently the equilibrium value of Y falls. The multiplier in this case is expressed as $\frac{1}{1-b(1-t)}$ where b is *MPC* and t is the tax rate (which is a fixed proportion of Y such as 2%).

5. *The Balanced Budget Multiplier*: If we combine the government expenditure multiplier with the tax multiplier, taking only lumpsum tax, we arrive at an interesting result called the balanced budget multiplier (*BBM*). It is expressed as:

$$\frac{\Delta Y}{\Delta G}+\frac{\Delta Y}{\Delta T}=\frac{1}{1-b}+\frac{-b}{1-b}=\frac{1-b}{1-b}=1.$$

Since its value is equal to 1, it is also called the unit budget multiplier. Thus if $\Delta G = \Delta T =$ Rs. 20 crores, Y will also increase by Rs. 20 crores. The *BBM* is usually equal to one since the government spending multiplier is greater than the lumpsum tax multiplier by 1. However, in some cases *BBM* may be greater or less than 1.

6. *Income determination in an open economy with foreign trade*: In an open economy with exports and imports, the equation for the equilibrium level of Y is the following:

$$Y = C + I + G + X - M$$

where X is exports, M is imports and $X - M = NX$ is net exports or the balance of trade. Since exports are autonomous, an increase in exports will have a multiplier effect through the export multiplier or the foreign trade multiplier (which is also known as the open economy multiplier). It is expressed as $\frac{1}{1-MPC+MPM}=\frac{1}{1-b+m}$, where m is the marginal propensity to import. It is the ratio of the increase in import to an increase in national income. The value of the open economy multiplier is less than that of closed economy since imports act as a leakage from the circular flow of national income.

If we incorporate proportional income tax (t) in the four-sector model, the value of the foreign trade multiplier has to be expressed as $\frac{1}{1-b(1-t)+m}$.

7. *Income determination by using the net exports function* : Imports are not fully induced. Imports may have an autonomous component also. So the import function is written as $M = \overline{M} + mY$, where $\overline{M}$ is autonomous import which has no relation to national income. National income is now determined where the upward sloping import function intersects the horizontal export function.

The net export function is downward sloping with respect to Y since as Y increases, imports rise (exports remaining constant). Therefore, NX falls.

If, the marginal propensity to import remains constant, but there is an increase (or decrease) in autonomous exports the NX function will shift upward (downward). As a result national income will increase (fall).

If however, the marginal propensity to import increases, but exports remain the same, then NX schedule will rotate clockwise. It will be the steeper, i.e., its slope will increase. In this case national income will fall

8. *Reasons for the shift of the NX function* : There are two main reasons for shifts of the NX function, viz., (1) foreign income and (2) relative international prices. Relative international prices are, in turn, influenced by two factors: (i) the rate(s) of inflation in domestic economy and in any foreign country (or countries) and (ii) the rate of exchange between the domestic currency (such as rupee) and any foreign currency (such as US dollar). If the rupee depreciates in terms of dollar, India's products will become more competitive in the world market and foreign products will become more expensive in India. If demand conditions are favourable (i.e., if the demand for exports and demand for imports are both fairly elastic), then exports will increase, imports will fall and the NX function will shift upward. As a result Y will increase.

There is, of course, a very close relation between the inflation rate and the exchange rate. The relation is clearly shown by the purchasing power parity theory regarding exchange rate determination.

9. *Net exports and the equilibrium value of Y* : As soon as we include net exports, our three-sector closed economy model of income determination gets extended. In this extended model, national income attains its equilibrium value when total saving (= private saving + government saving) = total investment (private investment + foreign investment). Government (public) saving is the same as budget surplus $(T - G)$ and foreign investment is the same as trade surplus $(X - M)$. Thus a country which generates trade surplus (by exporting more goods than it imports and saving a portion of its income) is able to acquire foreign assets by utilising the surplus. Since net exports mean acquisition of foreign assets by Indian residents, it is called foreign investment.

In this extended framework, national income equilibrium is attained when

$$S + (T - G) = I + (X - M).$$

where S is private saving, $(T - G)$ is government saving, and $(X - M)$ is net exports. This final model may be called the extended saving- investment approach to income determination.

KEY TERMS

Government expenditure	Proportional tax multiplier
Lumpsum income tax	Balanced budget multiplier
Lumpsum transfer payments	Foreign trade multiplier
Proportional income tax	Marginal propensity to import
Disposable income	Autonomous import
Inflationary gap	Autonomous export
Deflationary gap	Induced import
Government expenditure multiplier	Import function
Lumpsum tax multiplier	Foreign investment
Transfer-payments multiplier	Government saving
Reduced form equation	Private saving
Structural form equation	Imports as leakage
Inflation rate	Exports as injection
Exchange rate	Purchasing power parity
Net exports function	Private investment

ASSIGNMENTS

1. Show how national income is determined in a three-sector model with
   (a) lumpsum tax,
   (b) proportional income tax, and
   (c) lumpsum subsidy.
2. Show the net effect on national income of an equal increase in government spending and taxes.
3. Do you agree with the observation that if the budget of the government is in balance, the government is fiscally neutral? Can the balanced budget multiplier (*BBM*) ever be greater than or less than 1?
4. Discuss the theory of income determination in an open economy by applying the leakage(s)-injection(s) approach.
5. What is net exports function? Discuss briefly the two factors which determine net exports. Is there any relation between the inflation rate and the exchange rate? Explain clearly.
6. Why do imports act as leakages from the circular flow of income? Explain briefly.
7. Consider an economy described by the following equations:
   $Y = C + I + G$
   $Y = 5000$
   $G = 1000$
   $T = 1000$
   $C = 250 + 0.75\ (Y - T)$
   $I = 1000 - 50r.$
   (a) In this economy, compute private saving, public saving and national saving.
   (b) Find the equilibrium interest rate.
8. Suppose that the government increases taxes and government purchases by equal amounts. What happens to the interest rate and investment in response to this balanced-budget change? Does your answer depend on the marginal propensity to consume?
9. (i) In case of balanced budget, explain the relation of government with the financial market in a closed economy?
   (ii) In case of government budget deficit, explain the relation of private savings with investment in a closed economy?
10. The government raises taxes by Rs. 10 billion. If the marginal propensity to consume is Rs. 0.6, what happens to (i) national savings and (ii) investment?
11. In the Keynesian cross, assume that the consumption function is given by $C = 200 + 0.75\ (Y - T)$ Planned investment is 100; government purchases and taxes are both 100.
    (i) What is the equilibrium level of income?
    (ii) If government purchases increase to 125, what is the new equilibrium income?
    (iii) What level of government purchases is needed to achieve an income of 1,600?
12. Consider the following functions: $C = 50 + 0.8\ Y_D$; $I = 70$; $G = 200$; $TR = 100$; $t = 0.2$.
    (i) Suppose that 't' rises to 0.25. Calculate the change in the budget surplus. Would you expect the change in the budget surplus to be more or less if $C = 0.9$ instead of 0.8? Explain.
    (ii) Can you explain why the multiplier is 1 when $t = 1$.
13. Suppose marginal propensity to consume is 0.9 and tax rate is 0.3. Find out the multiplier? If investment decreases by Rs. 10 billion, by how much will GDP decline?
14. (i) Define fiscal policy.
    (ii) One percent increase in government purchase will cause a proportionate increase in aggregate output. Explain your agreement or disagreement to this statement.
15. Define tax multiplier. Explain the effect of tax cut on the equilibrium output.

CHAPTER 11

The Consumption Function

> *The amount of aggregate consumption depends mainly on the amount of aggregate income. The fundamental psychological law upon which we are entitled to depend with great confidence both a priori from our knowledge of human nature and from the detailed facts of experience is that men (and women, too) are disposed, as a rule and on an average, to increase their consumption as their income increases, but not by as much as the increase in their income.*
>
> J. M. Keynes

PREVIEW

The relation between income and consumption was of interest to economists for a long time. But the relation was first explained in a systematic way by J. M. Keynes in 1936. He related consumption to (disposable) income and developed the concept of consumption function on the basis of such relation.

The consumption function relates total consumption to the level of income or wealth and perhaps other variables. Consumption functions are sometimes defined for individual households, but their major role lies in determining total national consumption in a macroeconomic model.

The consumption function lies at the heart of Keynesian economics. The reason is that household consumption is the most important component of aggregate demand. So deficiency of consumption demand causes unemployment and depression.

Keynes pointed out that when income increases consumption also increases. But consumption also depends on another factor, known as propensity (tendency) to consume. The key concept is the marginal propensity to consume (henceforth *MPC*). It indicates how much consumption increases (ΔC) when income increases by a certain amount. (ΔY), other things being equal. One characteristic of the consumption function is the *MPC*. It is an important determinant of the stability of the economy in the simple Keynesian model of income determination. In general, the smaller the *MPC*, the more stable is the economy with respect to changes in government spending, investment, net exports, or money.

A related concept is average propensity to consume (*APC*) which is the ratio of total consumption to total income. To start with we have to note the difference between the amount of consumption and the consumption function. While the amount of consumption means the level of consumption at a certain level of income, the consumption function is a much broader concept. It is the whole schedule which relates the amount of consumption to different levels of income. Table 11.1 presents a simple consumption function schedule of the Keynesian type.

Table 11.1: A Consumption Schedule (Rs. Crores)

Income (Y)	Consumption (C)	Average propensity to consume ($APC = \frac{C}{Y}$)	Marginal propensity to consume ($MPC = \frac{\Delta C}{\Delta Y}$)
100	80	$\frac{80}{100} = 0{\cdot}80$	
110	88	$\frac{88}{110} = 0{\cdot}80$	$\frac{8}{10} = 0{\cdot}80$
120	96	$\frac{96}{120} = 0{\cdot}80$	$\frac{8}{10} = 0{\cdot}80$
130	104	$\frac{104}{130} = 0{\cdot}80$	$\frac{8}{10} = 0{\cdot}80$
140	112	$\frac{112}{140} = 0{\cdot}80$	$\frac{8}{10} = 0{\cdot}80$
150	120	$\frac{120}{150} = 0{\cdot}80$	$\frac{8}{10} = 0{\cdot}80$

The above schedule is an illustration of the consumption function. It shows how consumption demand increases (falls) with increase (decrease) in income. We see that when income is Rs. 100 cr consumption is Rs. 80 cr. If income increases to Rs. 110 cr, consumption increases to Rs. 88 cr. As income increases further to Rs. 150 cr., consumption increases to Rs. 120 cr. Thus we see that with a given consumption function, the level of consumption is different at different levels of income.

Since disposable income is largely spent on consumption goods and partly saved, consumption rises by less than the rise in income. Thus when income increases from Rs. 110 to Rs. 120 crore, consumption increases from Rs. 88 cr. to Rs. 96 cr. This means that when income increases by Rs. 10 cr., consumption increases by Rs. 8 cr. and saving increases by Rs. 2 cr. We find the same result for further increase in income.[1]

Consumption depends not only on income but also on the propensity to consume. Propensity to consume depends on such factors such as the rate of interest, the price level, the stock of wealth of the community and so on. Keynes assumed all these variables to remain constant in the short run. So the Keynesian consumption function is expressed as

$$C = f(Y) \quad \ldots (1)$$

where C is aggregate real consumption and Y is real disposable income (henceforth only income) of an economy. Here C depends on Y or is a function of Y. The causation works from right to left. If income (the independent variable) increases, consumption (the dependent variable) will also increase.

LINEAR AND NON-LINEAR CONSUMPTION FUNCTIONS

There are two possible shapes of the consumption function — a linear consumption function with a constant *MPC* and a non-linear consumption function with declining *MPC*. We will discuss the nature

1. The *MPC* is the ratio of the increase in consumption to the increase in income and is less than one. Keynes developed his multiplier theory on the basis of the hypothesis that consumption increases less than the increase in income.

and the characteristics of the two types of consumption function later in this chapter. Now we consider a linear consumption function of the following type:

$$C = a + bY \quad \ldots (2)$$

This is known as the Keynesian consumption function. Here *a* indicates autonomous (income-independent consumption and *b* is the slope of the consumpion function which is the *MPC*). The intercept term (*a*) appears because we are dealing with the short run. In the long-run the term disappears as we will see later in this chapter.

THE KEYNESIAN CONSUMPTION FUNCTION

The Keynesian consumption function is presented diagramatically in Fig. 11.1. Here we measure real income received on the horizontal axis and desired real consumption spending on the vertical axis. We first draw a 45° guideline. At each point of the line $Y = C + S$. This line shows how income is divided between consumption and saving at any level of income.

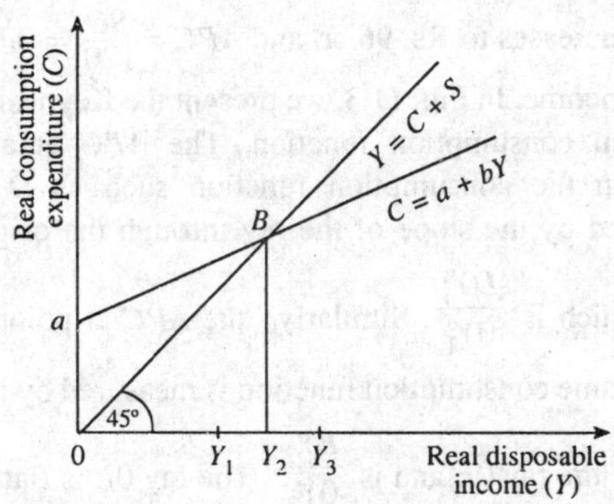

Fig. 11.1: The Keynesian Consumption Function

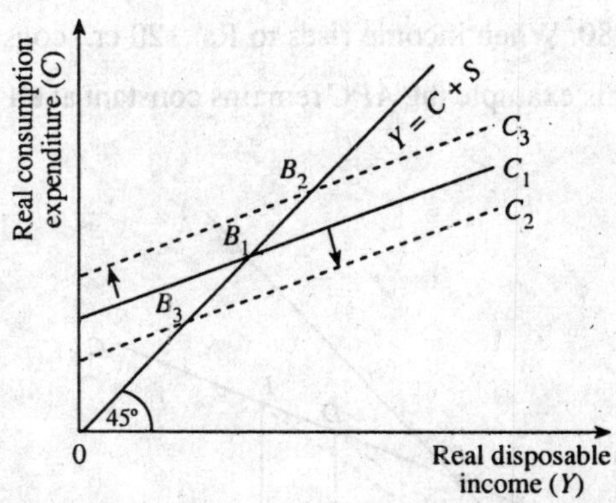

Fig. 11.2: Shifts in the Consumption Function

In Fig. 11.1 the line $C = a + bY$ is the linear short-run consumption function of the Keynesian type. We see that at a low level of income such as Y_1, consumption exceeds income. So saving is negative. Negative saving is called dissaving. Some people maintain themselves by utilising their past savings or by borrowing. When income reaches a minimum level such as Y_2, consumption is equal to income and saving is zero. And if income exceeds this level and is, say Y_3, consumption is less than income. And saving is positive.

This happens because at low levels of income people consume more than they earn. And at high levels of income they consume less than they earn.[1] Thus with an increase in saving, consumption does not increase as much as income increases. This means that saving increases with an increase in income.

Movement Versus Shift

It may by noted that when income increases, there is movement along the same consumption function. This means that consumption increases with an increase in income (*Y*). However, if there is an increase (decrease) in the propensity to consume, the whole consumption function will shift upward (downward). If the consumption function shifts upward (downward) from C_1 to C_3 (or from C_1 to C_2) in Fig. 11.2, more (less) is consumed at each level of income.

In fact, a parallel upward (downward) shift of the consumption function implies an increase (decrease) in the average propensity to consume (*APC*). But a change in the slope of the consumption

1. In an economy, some people save and others dissave. However, for the economy as a whole saving is positive because the negative dissaving of some people is more than offset by the positive saving of others. So for the economy as a whole, saving cannot be zero or negative.

function implies a change in the marginal propensity to consume (*MPC*) which is written as $\frac{\Delta C}{\Delta Y}$. However, to understand these points clearly, we have to clearly understand these two concepts and see the relation between the two in the short run.[1] The two concepts are different due to the presence of the term *a* in the consumption function which represents autonomous consumption.

THE APC AND THE MPC

We have already referred to the *APC* and *MPC*. If the consumption function is linear, the *MPC* remains constant but *APC* varies. If the consumption function is non-linear *MPC* also varies. Recall that the *APC* is the ratio of total consumption (*C*) to total income(*Y*) and is expressed as $APC = \frac{C}{Y}$. In Table 11.1 when income is Rs. 100 cr., consumption expenditure is Rs. 80 cr., so the *APC* is $\frac{80}{100}$ = 0·80. When income rises to Rs. 120 cr., consumption increases to Rs. 96 cr. and $APC = \frac{96}{120} = 0{\cdot}80$. In this example the *APC* remains constant at all levels of income. In Fig. 11.3, we present the Keynesian short-run consumption function. The *APC* at any point on the consumption function such as *D* is measured by the slope of the ray through the origin (0*D*) which is $\frac{DY_1}{0Y_1}$. Similarly, the *APC* at point *E* on the same consumption function is measured by the slope of the ray 0*E* and is $\frac{EY_2}{0Y_2}$. The ray 0*E* is flatter than 0*D*. This means that *APC* falls as income (*Y*) increases.

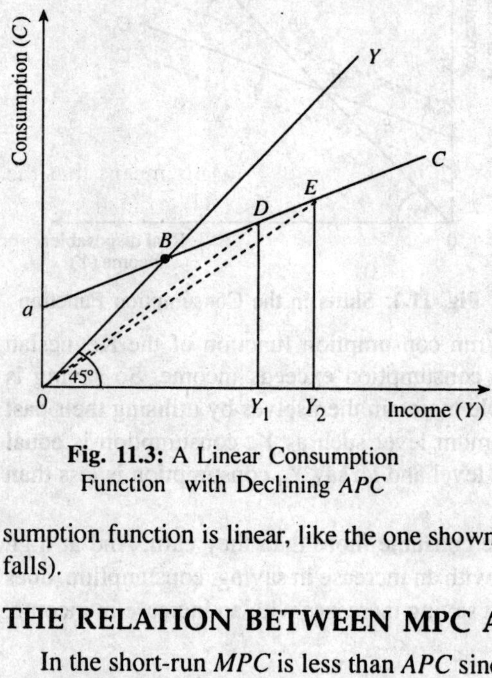

Fig. 11.3: A Linear Consumption Function with Declining *APC*

Recall that the *MPC* is the ratio of the change in consumption to the change in income which brings it about and is expressed as $MPC = \frac{\Delta C}{\Delta Y}$. It is indeed the slope of the whole consumption function. If the consumption function is linear, like the one shown in Fig. 11.3, the *MPC* remains constant (even if the *APC* falls).

THE RELATION BETWEEN MPC AND APC IN THE SHORT-RUN

In the short-run *MPC* is less than *APC* since *C* has an autonomous component. This very important proposition is proved as follows:

The consumption function is $C = a + bY$

So $$APC = \frac{C}{Y} = \frac{a}{Y} + b$$

and $$MPC = \frac{\Delta C}{\Delta Y} = b$$

Since $a > 0$ and $Y > 0$, $\frac{a}{Y} > 0$

1. In the next chapter when we discuss the long-run consumption function, we will see that there is no difference between *MPC* and *APC* because *C* does not have an autonomous component.

Therefore $\frac{a}{Y} + b > b$ or, $b < \frac{a}{Y} + b$

or, $MPC < APC$

Now we pass on to a different type of consumption function on which *MPC* falls.

The Value of MPC

The numerical value of the *MPC* is of considerable importance in macroeconomics. The *MPC* is greater than zero but less than one. In other words, it lies in between zero and one.

If, in an extreme situation, $MPC = 0$ then the whole increase in income would be saved and nothing would be spent on consumption goods. In this case the consumption function would coincide with the horizontal axis. By contrast, if, in another extreme situation, $MPC = 1$, the whole of any additional income earned would be spent on consumption goods and nothing would be saved. In this case the consumption function coincides with the 45° income line and the consumption line will be the same as the income line, with $\Delta C = \Delta Y$ and $\Delta S = 0$.

THE SAVING FUNCTION

Saving is that part of disposable income which is not spent on consumption goods. Since we know that $Y = C + S$, $S = Y - C$ where Y = disposable income, C = consumption expenditure and S = saving. Thus saving is a residue.

Since saving, like consumption, is also a function of income, the saving function is written as

$$S = g(Y)$$

In fact, C and S are called by Paul Samuelson as 'mirror image concepts'[1]. This means that the saving function is a replica of the consumption function. So we can derive the saving function from the consumption function. If we subtract the Keynesian linear consumption function $C = a + bY$ from income (Y), we get the following saving function:

$$S = Y - (a + bY)$$
$$= Y - a - bY = -a + Y - bY = -a + (1 - b)Y$$

Here $(1 - b)$ is the *MPS* since b is the *MPC*.

Suppose we have the following consumption function

$$C = 50 + 0{\cdot}75Y$$

Then the saving function will be

$$S = Y - 50 - 0{\cdot}75Y$$
$$= -50 + Y - 0{\cdot}75Y$$
$$= -50 + Y(1 - 0{\cdot}75)$$
$$= -50 + 0{\cdot}25Y$$

Here 0·25 is the *MPS*, since $Y = C + S$ and what is not consumed is saved, the sum of the two marginal propensities is always equal to one, i.e., $MPC + MPS = 1$ Or, $MPS = 1 - MPC$.

Thus if *MPC* increases, *MPS* will fall.

Now we pass on to two other important concepts, viz., average propensity to save (*APS*) and marginal propensity to save (*MPS*).

AVERAGE PROPENSITY TO SAVE (APS)

The *APS* is the ratio of total saving to total disposable income:

$$APS = \frac{\text{Saving}}{\text{Disposable income}} = \frac{S}{Y}$$

1. This means that, at a certain fixed level of income, if we know one (say C), we can find the other one (S).

Like the *APC*, *APS* also varies with income. Since *APC* falls as income increases, as noted earlier, *APS* will increase with increase in income. This happens because at low levels of income people consume more and at high levels of income they save more.

THE SUM OF APC AND APS

We can now show that the sum of the two average propensities is also equal to one. We know that $Y = C + S$. Now if we divide all the three terms by Y, we get $\frac{Y}{Y} = \frac{C}{Y} + \frac{S}{Y} = 1$, where $\frac{C}{Y}$ is *APC* and $\frac{S}{Y}$ is *APS*

or, $APC + APS = 1$

or, $APS = 1 - APC$

Thus if an economic society consumes 75% of its disposable income (i.e., $APC = 0{\cdot}75$), then it will save the remaining 25% of its disposable income. So its *APS* will be 0·25 (1 – 0·75 = 0·25).

In the lower panel (b) of Fig. 11.4 we derive the saving function from the income line and consumption function shown in the upper panel (a). When income is Y_{min}, income = consumption ($Y = C$) and saving (S) = 0. If income increases from Y_{min} to Y_2, i.e., by ΔY, consumption increases by ΔC in panel (a) and saving increases by ΔS in panel (b). The saving function starts from point B' which corresponds to point B in panel (a). Here B is called the break-even point. So the saving function is derived by taking the vertical difference between Y and C at different levels of Y.

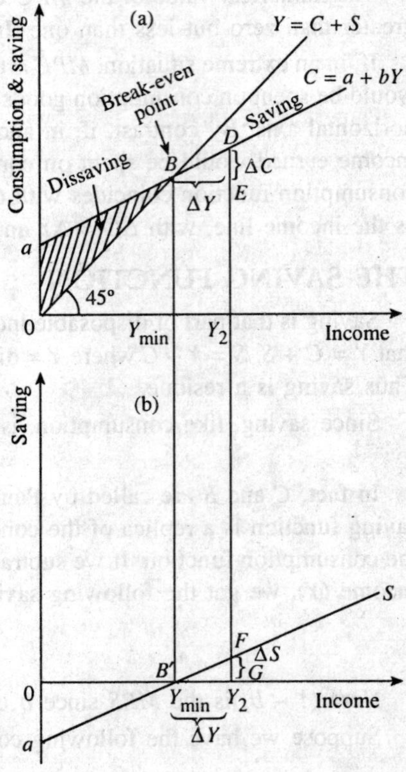

Fig. 11.4: The Derivation of the Saving Function

If income is less than Y_{min}, $C > Y$ and $S < 0$. This means that saving is negative. Negative saving is called dissaving. Thus upto point B the consumption function lies above the income line. If income exceeds the minimum level, the income line lies above the consumption function and saving is positive ($S > 0$). And as income increases consumption increases less than proportionately with income. So saving increases and the saving function is also upward sloping.

With an increase in income, not only the absolute amount of saving, but also the APS increases

As noted earlier *APC* falls with an increase in income. So it logically follows that *APS* increases with an increase in income (since the sum of the two is always equal to one).

THE MARGINAL PROPENSITY TO SAVE (MPS)

We know that *APS* is the proportion of income which is saved. By comparison, *MPS* shows how much of only extra disposable income earned is saved. Since like consumption (C), saving (S) is also a function of income, *MPS* is change in saving induced by a certain change in disposable income. It is defined as the ratio of the change in saving to change in income (Y). Thus we can express this as

$$MPS = \frac{\Delta S}{\Delta Y}$$

For example, if disposable income increases from Rs. 800 to Rs. 1,000 and as a result desired (planned) saving increases by Rs. 50.

$$MPS = \frac{50}{200} = \frac{1}{4} = 0{\cdot}25$$

Since any extra income earned is largely consumed and partly saved, the sum of the two marginal propensities is equal to one. We know that $Y = C + S$

$$\text{or, } \Delta Y = \Delta C + \Delta S$$

$$\text{or, } \frac{\Delta Y}{\Delta Y} = \frac{\Delta C}{\Delta Y} + \frac{\Delta S}{\Delta Y}$$

$$\text{or, } MPC + MPS = 1$$

$$\text{or, } MPS = 1 - MPC.$$

Thus if *MPC* increases, *MPS* will fall.

Just as *MPC* is the slope of the consumption function, *MPS* is the slope of the saving function. In panel (a) of Fig. 11.4 we see that as income increases from $0Y_{min}$ (say, Rs. 800 cr.) to $0Y_2$ (say Rs. 1,000 cr.), that is, ΔY = Rs. 200 cr., consumption increases by $DE = \Delta C$ (say Rs. 150 cr.), and in panel (b) saving increases by $FG = \Delta S$ (say Rs. 50 cr.). So the *MPS* is

$$\frac{\Delta S}{\Delta Y} = \frac{FG}{Y_{min}Y_2} = \frac{\text{Rs. 50 cr.}}{\text{Rs. 200 cr.}} = \frac{1}{4} = 0{\cdot}25$$

KEYNES ABSOLUTE INCOME HYPOTHESIS

Although the first Nobel Laureate economist Ragnar Frisch coined the term 'macroeconomics' in 1933, it was J. M. Keynes who truly built the foundation of modern macroeconomics in 1936. And the consumption function lies at the heart of Keynesian economics, as A. H. Hansen (the so called American Keynes) commented. In truth, the consumption function plays a very important role in the Keynesian theory of income determination. According to Keynes the level of consumption in a society depends on a number of factors—both objective (i.e., measurable such as the interest rate, the stock of wealth of an individual and also that of society) and subjective (i.e., psychological and not measurable). However, the most important factor affecting the consumption level of an individual as also of the whole society is the current level of income. Since the main factor influencing consumption demand in Keynes' theory is the absolute size of current income, his theory is known as **the absolute income hypothesis**.

The Keynesian short-run consumption function hypothesis is known as the absolute income hypothesis

Furthermore, Keynes presented a **psychological law of consumption**. According to the law, as income increases, consumption also increases, though not porportionately. Thus *MPC* is less than one:

$$0 < \frac{\Delta C}{\Delta Y} < 1.$$

Four points emerge from Keynes' absolute income hypothesis:

1. Role of absolute income

Consumption depends mainly on the absolute size of current income of an individual or society. Thus if absolute income increases, consumption expenditure will also increase. This implies that rich people will spend more on consumption goods than poor people.

2. Non-proportional relation

In the short-run consumption has an autonomous component. For this reason there is non-proportional relation between income(Y) and consumption(C).

3. Fall in *APC*

If the consumption function is linear, *APC* falls as income (Y) increases. But *MPC* remains constant.

4. The role of interest rate

In the short-run the rate of interest does not affect consumption demand.[1]

The Form of Keynesian Consumption Function

The Keynesian consumption function takes the following form

$$C = a + bY$$

where C is consumption, Y is disposable income, a is autonomous consumption (which is independent of Y) and b is MPC. So bY is induced consumption, that is, consumption which depends on income. Thus, in the short run C has two components[2] : autonomous and induced. We have already presented the Keynesian consumption function in Fig. 11.1.

Economic Insight: The Relation between *MPC* and *APC*

In the short-run since consumption has both autonomous and induced components, the MPC is less than APC. This may be proved as follows:

$$Y = a + bY$$

$$APC = \frac{a}{Y} + \frac{bY}{Y} = \frac{a}{Y} + b.$$

Since $a > 0$, and $Y > 0$, $\frac{a}{Y} > 0$.

Therefore $\frac{a}{Y} + b > b$, or, $b < \frac{a}{Y} + b$ or $MPC < APC$

Thus even if the consumption function is linear, with constant MPC, this relation holds.

MPC < APC in the short-run due to autonomous component of consumption

In Fig. 11.3, APC falls with an increase in income, as noted earlier. This means that the proportion of income saved increases as income increases. This result is also found in household budget studies.[3] Poor people spend a high proportion of income on consumption. But rich people save a much higher proportion of their income than poor people. This implies that as income increases, consumption increases less than proportionately and saving increases more than proportionately.

IMPLICATIONS FOR THE THEORY OF INCOME DETERMINATION

The assumption of declining APC has an important implication for the Keynesian theory of income determination. The Keynesian theory implies that as income continues to increase, larger and larger proportions of income is saved. Therefore investment has to increase sufficiently so that the additional saving is offset by an additional investment. Otherwise the contractionary pressure exerted on income by saving leakage will exceed the expansionary pressure exerted on income by investment injection. If adequate profitable investment opportunities for investment do not exist in the economy, aggregate demand (i.e., consumption plus investment) will fall short of the level required to produce the full employment level of output. So the economy will get stuck in a situation of underemployment equilibrium. Due to deficiency of demand (caused by inadequate investment expenditure) the economy

1. Of course, it affects consumption in the long run by shifting the consumption function to a new position.
2. We will see later that in the long run the autonomous component disappears from the consumption function and consumption is totally induced.
3. Thus cross-section data which show inter-individual differences in consumption support Keynes's absolute income hypothesis.

will stagnate. And A. H. Hansen and others developed the theory of secular stagnation or long-term sluggishness. The economy stagnates due to declining *APC*.

THE CONSUMPTION FUNCTION PUZZLE

The Keynesian absolute income hypothesis was empirically tested by the Nobel Laureate economist Simon Kuznets in the context of the U.S. economy for the period 1869-1938. Two sets of data were collected by him, viz., cross section data (on the basis of family budget studies) which show inter- individual differences in consumption per year (or over a short period of time) and time-series data which show the pattern of consumption over a long period of time. The Keynesian theory was found to be quite consistent with the cross section data and the relation between income and consumption was found to be non-proportional (with $MPC < APC$) in the short run. However, time-series data showed that in the long run the relation between income and consumption was proportional (with $MPC = APC$). This contradiction between Keynes' consumption function and Kuznets' empirical findings is known as the consumption function puzzle. Three main theories have been developed to resolve the conflict, viz., James Duesenberry's relative income hypothesis, F. Modigliani's life cycle hypothesis and M. Friedman's permanent income hypothesis. These are hypotheses regarding long-run consumption function and will be discussed in detail in the next chapter. Here we make a comparison between Keynes' (behaviour) consumption function and Kuznets' consumption function.

Comparing Keynes' Consumption Function with that of Kuznets'

For comparing Kuznets' consumption function (based on empirical evidence) with Keynes' consumption function (based on theory) we present the two functions side by side. In Fig. 11.5 we

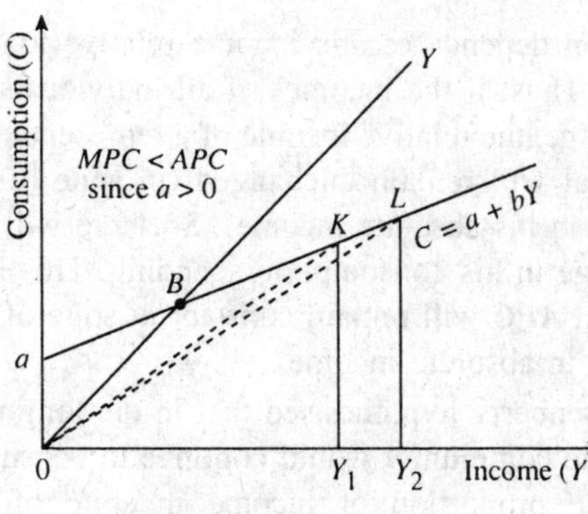

Fig. 11.5: The Keynesian Consumption Function with Falling *APC*

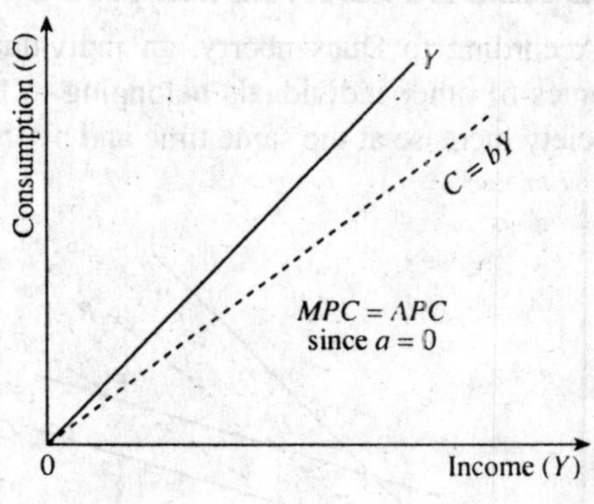

Fig. 11.6: Kuznets' Consumption Function with Constant *APC*

present the Keynesian consumption function once again. We see that in case of Keynesian short-run consumption function which takes the following form

$$C = a + bY \quad \ldots (1)$$

In this case *APC* falls with an increase in income. By comparison in Fig. 11.6 we find that the long-run consumption function takes the following form:

$$C = bY \quad \ldots (2)$$

since there is no autonomous consumption in the long run. As the intercept term does not appear in the long run, the consumption function starts from the origin, in which case $MPC = APC$. Over the period 1869-1933, the *MPC* was found to be 0·9 for the U.S. economy. Thus Kuznets found that there was no tendency for the *APC* to fall with an increase in disposable income. So the consumption function presented in equation (2) may be expressed as

$$C = 0.9Y \quad \dots (3)$$

Thus while *APC* falls in Keynes' short-run consumption function, it remains constant in Kuznets' long-run consumption function. Moreover, the propensity to consume is higher in the long run than in the short run because in the long run, the consumption function shifts upward. This means that more is consumed at each level of income. The reconciliation between the short-run consumption function and the long-run consumption function, as was done by post-Keynesian economists, will be studied in the next chapter.

Resolving Consumption Puzzle

The consumption puzzle has been explained by three economists by developing three different hypotheses. In 1949 James Duesenberry presented the **relative income hypothesis.** According to this hypothesis consumption expenditure depends on relative income, i.e., the ratio of current income to some previous peak income. In 1957, Milton Friedman presented the permanent income hypothesis according to which consumption of an individual depends on his permanent income rather than his current level of income. In 1958 F. Modigliani and Brumberg and in 1963 Ando and Modigliani presented the life cycle hypotheses of consumption. According to their hypothesis, an individual's consumption depends on his lifetime income, i.e., the expected income over his entire life (rather than his current income). These three hypotheses have proved that in short run $MPC < APC$. But in the long run, $MPC = APC$. There is no contradiction between these two results. We may now discuss the three hypotheses one by one.

THE RELATIVE INCOME HYPOTHESIS

According to Duesenberry, an individual's consumption depends on his income relative to the incomes of other individuals belonging to the community. Thus, if the incomes of all individuals in a society increase at the same time and by the same percentage, the relative income of a representative individual will remain unchanged (in spite of an increase in his absolute income). So there will be no change in his consumption spending. This implies that *APC* will remain constant in spite of an increase in absolute income.

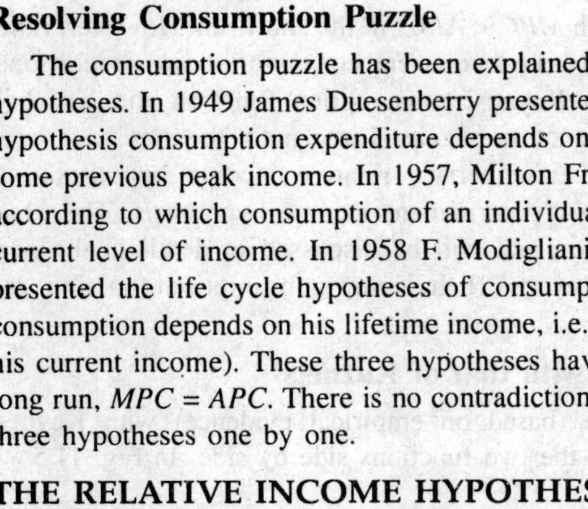

Fig. 11.7: Consumption as a Function of Relative Income

Duesenberry hypothesised that in the long run the whole community would continue to consume the same proportion of income in spite of an increase in its absolute income. This will happen if, of course, there is no change in the pattern of income distribution. The hypothesis suggests that as income increases, the consumption function shifts parellely so that the *APC* remains constant.

The hypothesis is illustrated in Fig. 11.7. Suppose family 1 has disposable income of Y_1 and it is spending Y_1E on consumption. Now suppose its disposable income increases to Y_2. Now its consumption will not rise to Y_2F which is equal to the consumption of family 2 (whose initial disposable income is Y_2), but to Y_2E', where E' lies on the same ray R_1 through the origin on which E lies. This means that the consumption spending of family 1 has to be increased in the same proportion as its income, i.e., $EY_1/0Y_1 = E'Y_2/0Y_2$. Therefore the *APC* remains constant.

In Fig. 11.7, the initial disposable income of family 2 is Y_2 and its consumption spending is Y_2F. Now its disposable income rises from Y_2 to Y_3 and as a result, its consumption spending increases to Y_3F', where F' lies on ray R_2 through the origin, on which F lies. This means the APC of family 2, $F'Y_3/0Y_3$, after increase in income is the same as $FY_2/0Y_2$, the initial APC. Thus APC remains constant in spite of a rise in the family's absolute income. The reason is that its relative income remains the same. If this is true for all families or households in an economy, the average consumption as a proportion of average income will also remain constant.[1] And if we join points E' and F', we get a new consumption function C', which lies above the original one (C).

Rationale

Duesenberry provides two explanations of his hypothesis. These are the following:

(i) ***The demonstration effect*** **:** Individuals or families try to emulate the consumption patterns of other members of society to which they belong. This is known as the demonstration effect of pure prestige or self-esteem.[2] Due to this effect APC does not fall as income increases. The reason is simple. If the income of all individuals (families) increase in the same proportion there will be no change in the pattern of income distribution. This implies that the APC, which depends on relative income, remains constant.

There is another reason for the operation of the demonstration effect. Suppose an individual lives in a community in which his money income of Rs. 5,000 is much lower than that of other members. So he will increase his consumption spending to keep up with the Joneses. On the other hand, suppose an individual's monthly income of Rs. 50,000 is much higher than the average income of persons in the same community. This family will spend a small proportion of its income on consumption since the demonstration effect will not operate in its case.

(ii) ***The ratchet effect*** **:** Ratchet effect refers to a tendency for a variable to be influenced by its own largest previous value. For example, consumption from any given income may be higher, the higher the previous peak consumption level.

This point is illustrated in Fig. 11.8. Suppose disposable income of a family steadily increases from zero to Y_2, at which its consumption spending is Y_2B. Now suppose due to economic recession, its disposable income falls to Y_1. But its consumption will not fall to Y_1A as the new consumption schedule C_{LR} would suggest. The family will now curtail its consumption spending only marginally to Y_1A' where point A' lies on the short-run consumption schedule C_{SR}. Since $Y_1A' > Y_1A$, the APC at income level Y_1 is Y_1A greater at A' than at B at the income level Y_2. The ray $0R$ through the origin at point A' has greater slope than that of $0B$. As the economy moves from recession to recovery and disposable income increases, the individual will move along his short-run consumption schedule C_{SR} from left to right until the consumption level BY_2 is reached at income level Y_2. If income increases further, the person will move along the long-run consumption function C_{LR} and maintain a proportional relation between Y and C. What is true of an individual is equally true of all other members of society. So the aggregate consumption function looks like that of an individual consumer.

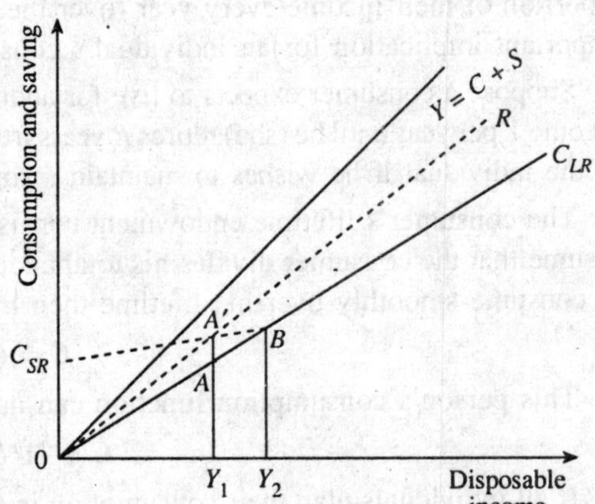

Fig. 11.8: The Ratchet Effect

1. Of course, both consumption and saving will increase in absolute terms with an increase in absolute income.
2. It is also known as the Duesenberry effect.

Thus the relative income hypothesis explains why average consumption function will be flatter than the cross-section (budget) studies would suggest. It also suggests that if the income of a community falls, its consumption expenditure does not fall much due to the ratchet effect. This explains why the aggregate consumption function is flatter than the family budget studies suggest.

THE LIFE CYCLE HYPOTHESIS

In the late 1950s and early 1960s Franco Modigliani and his coworkers Albert Ando and Richard Brumberg related consumption expenditure to demography. Modigliani, in particular, emphasised that income varies systematically over peoples' lives and that saving allows consumers to move income from early years of earning (when income is high) to later years after retirement when income is low. This interpretation of household consumption behaviour forms the basis of his **life cycle hypothesis**.

The life cycle hypothesis (henceforth LCH) represents an attempt to deal with the way in which consumers dispose off their income over time. In this hypothesis wealth is assigned a crucial role in consumption decision. Wealth includes not only property (houses, stocks, bonds, savings accounts, etc.) but also the value of future earnings. Thus consumers visualise themselves as having a stock of initial wealth, a flow of income generated by that wealth over their lifetime and a target (which may be zero) as their end-of-life wealth. Consumption decisions are made with the whole series of financial flows in mind. Thus, changes in wealth, as reflected by unexpected changes in flow of earnings or unexpected movements in asset prices, would have an impact on consumers' spending decisions because that would enhance future earnings from property, labour or both. The theory has empirically testable implications for the relation between saving and age of a person as also for the role of wealth in influencing aggregate consumer spending.

THE KEY PROPOSITION

The main reason that an individual's income varies over time is retirement. Since most people do not want their current living standard (as measured by consumption) to fall after retirement they save a portion of their income every year (over their entire service period). This motive for saving has an important implication for an individual's consumption behaviour.

Suppose a consumer expects to live for another T years, has initial wealth of W, and expects to earn income Y per year until he (she) retires R years from now. What should be the optimal level of consumption of the individual if he wishes to maintain a smooth level of consumption over his entire life?

The consumer's lifetime endowment consists of initial wealth[1] W and lifetime earnings RY. If we assume that the consumer divides his total endowment $W + RY$ equally among the T years and wishes to consume smoothly over his lifetime then his annual consumption will be:

$$C = (W + RY)/T \quad \ldots (1)$$

This person's consumption function can now be expressed as

$$C = (1/T)\ W + (R/T)\ Y$$

If all individuals plan their consumption in the same way then the aggregate consumption function will be the same as an individual consumer's consumption function. To be more specific, aggregate consumption depends on both wealth and life-time income. That is, the aggregate consumption function is

$$C = \alpha W + \beta Y \quad \ldots (2)$$

where the parameter α is the MPC out of wealth, and the parameter β is the MPC out of income.

1. For the sake of simplicity we assume the rate of interest to be zero. Otherwise, interest on savings would also be a part of his wealth.

Implications

Consumption depends on both wealth and income

Fig. 11.9 shows the relationship between consumption and income in terms of the life cycle hypothesis. For any initial level of wealth W, the consumption function looks like the Keynesian function. But the intercept αW which shows what would happen to consumption if income ever fell to zero, is not a constant, as is the term $\bar{a}$ in the Keynesian consumption function. Instead the intercept αW depends on the level of wealth. If W increases, the consumption line will shift upward parallely.

So one main prediction of the LCH is that consumption depends on wealth as well as income. This is shown by the intercept of the consumption function.

Solving the Consumption Puzzle

The LCH can solve the consumption puzzle in a simple way. According to this hypothesis, the *APC* is:

$$C/Y = \alpha(W/Y) + \beta \quad \ldots \quad (3)$$

Since wealth does not vary proportionately with income from person to person or from year to year, cross-section data (which show inter-individual differences in income and consumption over short periods) reveal that high income corresponds to a low *APC*. But in the long run wealth and income grow together, resulting in a constant *W/Y* and a constant *APC* (as time-series data show).

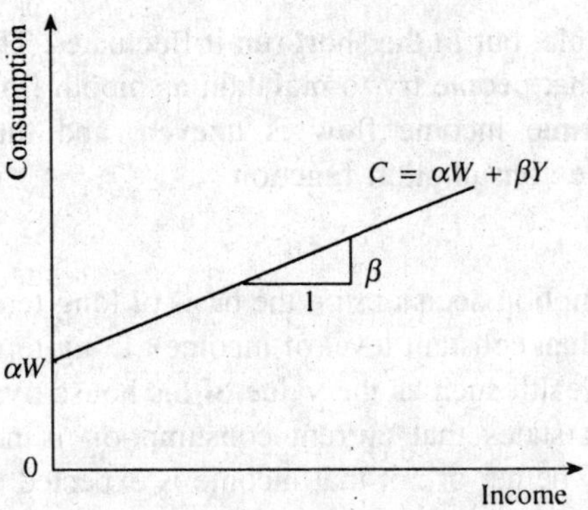

Fig. 11.9: The Life Cycle Consumption Function

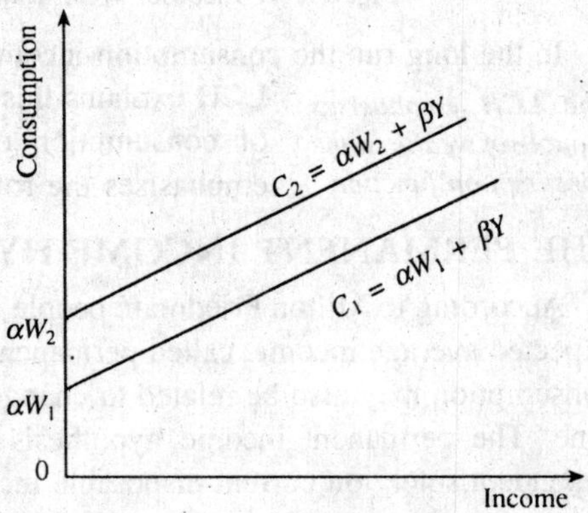

Fig. 11.10: Shift in Consumption Function Due to Change in Wealth

If wealth remains constant as in the short run the life cycle consumption function looks like the Keynesian consumption function. But in the long run, as wealth increases, say, from W_1 to W_2, the consumption function itself shifts upward, as shown in Fig. 11.10. This prevents the *APC* from falling as income increases. So the short-run consumption-income relation (which takes wealth as constant) will not continue to hold in the long run when wealth increases. This is how the LCH solves the consumption puzzle posed by Kuznets' studies.[1]

Other Predictions

Another important prediction of the LCH is that saving varies over a person's lifetime. The LCH helps to link consumption and saving with certain demographic considerations, especially with the age distribution of the population. The *MPC* out of lifetime income changes with age. If a person has no wealth at the beginning of his service life, then he will accumulate wealth over his working years and then run down his wealth after his retirement. Fig. 11.11 shows the consumer's income, wealth and consumption over his adult life.

1. *Macroeconomics* (5th edn., 1990), p. 279.

If a consumer smoothes consumption over his adult life (as is indicated by the horizontal consumption line), he will save and accumulate wealth during his working years and then dissave and run down his wealth after retirement. In other words, since people want to smooth consumption over their lives, the young — who are working — save, while the old — who have retired — dissave.

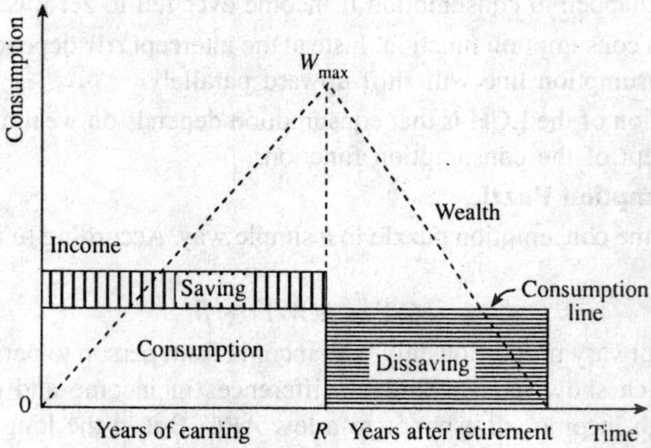

Fig. 11.11: Income, Wealth and Consumption over an Individual's Entire Life

In the long run the consumption-income ratio is very stable, but in the short run it fluctuates. The LCH explains this by pointing out that people try to maintain a smooth flow of consumption even if their lifetime income flow is uneven, and thus emphasises the role of wealth in the consumption function.

The LCH emphasises the role of wealth in the consumption function

THE PERMANENT INCOME HYPOTHESIS

According to Milton Friedman, people make their consumption decisions on the basis of long-term expected average income, called permanent income (rather than constant level of income). Long-term consumption may also be related to changes in a person's wealth such as the value of his house over time. The permanent income hypothesis (henceforth PIH) states that current consumption is not dependent solely on current disposable income but also on whether or not that income is expected to be permanent or transitory. The hypothesis argues that both income and consumption have two parts, viz., permanent and transitory.

Difference between Permanent Income (Y_P) and Transitory Income (Y_t)

Permanent income is that part of current income that people expect to persist into the future. Transitory income is that part of measured income that is unlikely to persist. Thus while Y_P is average income, Y_t is random deviation from the average.

In reality we find that different forms of income have different degrees of persistence.

For example, good education such as an MBA degree from IIM Ahmedabad or a PhD from MIT provides a permanently higher income, whereas good weather provides only transitorily higher income.

Suppose due to frost the apple crop of Kashmir is largely destroyed. This drives prices up. But farmers do not earn much due to supply shortage. At the same time good apple crop in Simla, due to favourable weather, raises the income of the farmers. Even if prices fall below normal levels, income goes up due to increased turnover.

Wages and compensation of permanent workers constitute permanent income. Interest on corporate debentures and gilt-edged (government) securities is permanent income. Dividends are transitory income with no negative components. Profits and capital gains are purely transitory income with both positive and negative components. In case of companies offering stock options to employees measured income has both permanent and transitory components.

There are three points of difference between these two types of income, as shown in Fig. 11.12.

1. Y_P is always positive, but Y_t can be zero or negative.

2. Y_P does not show fluctuation. It shows steady trend but Y_t shows short-run fluctuations.

3. Y_P shows greater persistence but Y_t may make its presence felt one year and may disappear next year.

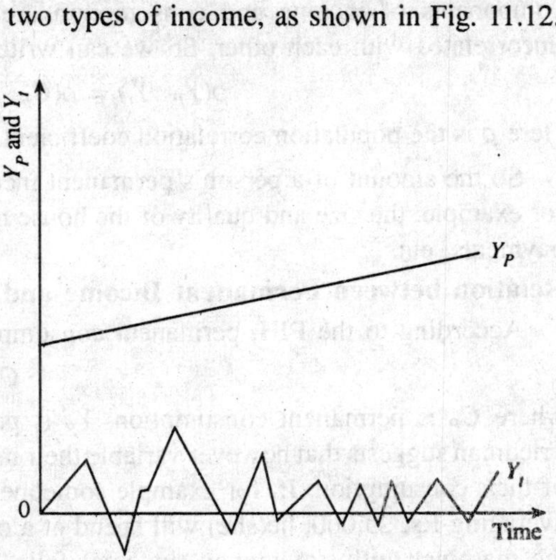

Fig. 11.12: Patterns of Income Changes

Similarity

Both may have earned and unearned components (such as rent) and windfall profit which is not the reward for genuine entrepreneurship (risk taking and uncertainty bearing).

Similarly, consumption has the same two components. Transitory consumption includes such things as additional holidays, clothes, etc. or any type of unplanned expenditure.

Sources of Permanent Income

Permanent income has two main sources, viz., labour income and capital income. Labour income is derived from human capital. It refers to income earned by selling labour services, i.e., skill, ability and efficiency of labour. Capital income is derived from non-human capital (wealth) or tangible assets such as loanable funds (saving), debentures, equity shares, real estate or even consumer durables (such as cars, refrigerators, generators, motor cars, television sets, etc.). Friedman treats the imputed value of the flow of services from consumer durables as part of a household's consumption.

In a broad sense, a person's permanent income comprises such things as his long-term earnings from employment (wages, and salaries), retirement pensions and income derived from the possession of capital assets (interest and dividends). The amount of a person's permanent income will determine his permanent consumption plans, for example, the size and quality of the house he(she) will buy and thus long-term expenditure as mortgage repayments, etc.

Transitory Income

Transitory income considers short-term temporary overtime payments, bonuses and windfall gains from winnings and inheritances, and short-term reductions in income arising from temporary unemployment and illness.

Measured Income

A third concept of income is measured income. The measured income of an individual (Y_m) has the above two components: permanent and transitory. So we can write:

$$Y_m = Y_p + Y_t \qquad \ldots \quad (1)$$

Similarly total measured consumption (C_m) has two components, viz., permanent (C_P) and transitory (C_t). So we can write:

$$C_m = C_P + C_t \qquad \ldots \quad (2)$$

Key Assumption

Friedman makes an important assumption which is the key to his hypothesis, viz., the transitory components of income and consumption are uncorrelated with their permanent components and uncorrelated with each other. So we can write:

$$\rho(Y_P, Y_t) = \rho(C_P, C_t) = \rho(Y_t, C_t) = 0 \qquad \ldots (3)$$

Here ρ is the population correlation coefficient between any two variables shown within the brackets.

So the amount of a person's permanent income will determine his permanent consumption plans, for example, the size and quality of the house he will buy and thus long-run expenditure on mortgage payments, etc.

Relation between Permanent Income and Permanent Consumption

According to the PIH, permanent consumption is proportional to permanent income:

$$C_P = kY_P \qquad \ldots (4)$$

where C_P is permanent consumption, Y_P is permanent income, and k is the proportionality factor. Friedman suggests that however variable their income, consumers will attempt to smooth out the pattern of their consumption. If, for example someone's income varies between zero and Rs. 50,000 a year, averaging Rs. 25,000, he(she) will spend at a constant rate equivalent to, say, Rs. 20,000. Given that the marginal utility of money (income) falls, with the increasing amounts of spending, it is quite judicious for an individual to transfer spending from good times (when income is high) to bad times (when income is low). This can be achieved by saving in some periods and 'dissaving' in others.

Implications of the PIH

The economic significance of the PIH is that in the short run the level of consumption may be higher (or lower) than that indicated by the level of current disposable income. The theory has the following three implications:

1. If one has a permanent increase in income, the *MPC* out of it will equal the *APC*.
2. A large increase in short-run incomes will not lead to corresponding increases in consumption. Any extra rupee a consumer gets will be treated not as a cause for quick spending spree, but as a temporary bonus (windfall) which should raise lifetime consumption by the value of the rupee spread over one's lifetime.
3. The hypothesis explains why high income households save more than low income households: the high income group is likely to contain the very people who are enjoying territory high incomes only temporarily so that they can save for the day when their income falls.

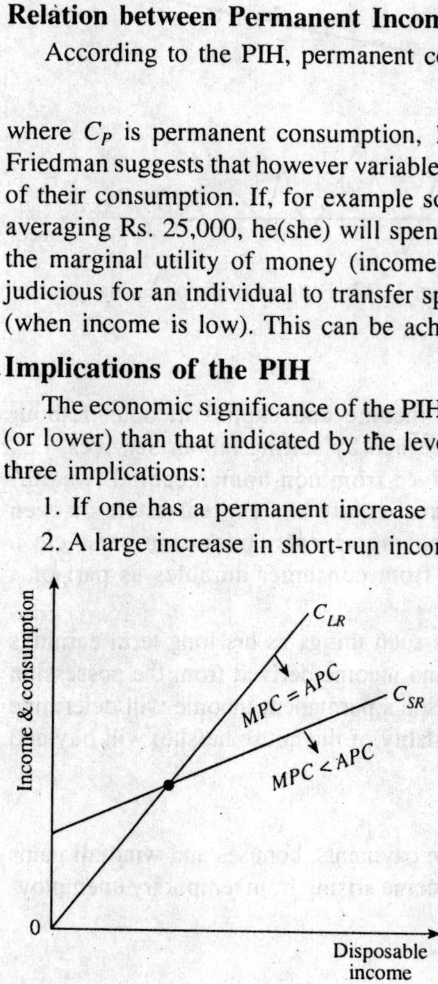

Fig. 11.13: *SRCF & LRCF*

Resolving the Consumption Puzzle

The PIH solves the consumption puzzle by suggesting that the Keynesian consumption function uses the wrong variable. According to PIH, consumption depends on Y_P; yet many studies relate consumption to current income (Y_m). This **errors-in-variables** problem explains various contradictory findings.

Here $APC = \dfrac{C_P}{Y_m} = \dfrac{kY_P}{Y_m}$

So the *APC* depends on ratio of Y_P to Y_m. When Y_m increases temporarily above Y_P, the *APC* temporarily falls. Similarly, when Y_m temporarily falls below Y_P the *APC* temporarily increases.

Therefore, $MPC \neq APC$ in the short run. But in the long-run there is an exact proportional relation between Y_P and C_P in which case $MPC = APC$. See Fig. 11.13 which is self-explanatory.

Consistency with Cross-Section Data

Friedman found that his formulation of the consumption function fits the facts better than the simple Keynesian function with current income. It is also consistent with time series data.

According to PIH the cross section data show combinations of Y_P and Y_t. Families with high Y_P have proportionately high consumption. If all variations in Y_m come from Y_P, the APC will be the same for all families. However, some of the variation in income originates from Y_t and households with high Y_t do not have higher consumption. Therefore, statistical studies show that high income families have, on average, lower APC.

The PIH is thus consistent with the cross-section data that high income families have low APC than that of low income families. A random sample of high income families at an arbitrarily chosen period of time is likely to contain a relatively large number of families who experience increase in transitory income. Since consumption depends only on permanent income the $APC = C/Y_m$, i.e., the ratio of total consumption to measured income will be low since $Y_t > 0$ and $Y_P < Y_m$ and $C/Y_m > C/Y_P$, on the other hand, a sample of families with low income for a certain period would contain a relatively large number of families experiencing negative transitory income. Thus in their case, the $APC = \left(\dfrac{C}{Y_P + Y_t}\right)$ will be fairly high since with $Y_t < 0$, $Y_m < Y_P$. So $\dfrac{C}{Y_m} < \dfrac{C}{Y_P}$.

Consistency with Time-Series Data

According to PIH year-to-year fluctuations in income are dominated by Y_t. Therefore, years of high income are supposed to be years of low APC. But over a long period of time the variation in income is due to rise or fall in Y_P. Hence, in long time-series, a constant APC is found, as was discovered by Simon Kuznets.

Comparison with LCH

The LCH relates saving to age composition of people and the PIH relates saving to two other things: (a) different income classes and (b) the time period under consideration—short run and long run.

Friedman's PIH relates total consumption to the income flow that would be obtained if current human and non-human wealth were converted into a real (constant-dollar) perpetuity. This income stream is called 'permanent income'. It is applied both to individual households and to the aggregate economy. In its strictest form, consumption is hypothesised to be a constant fraction of permanent income.

KEY POINTS

1. ***The concept of consumption function*** **:** The consumption function relates the amount of consumption to the level of disposable income, all other variables influencing consumption spending remaining constant.

2. ***Propensity to consume*** **:** Consumption demand depends not only on income but also on the propensity (tendency) to consume (PTC). PTC depends on the general price level, interest rates, stock of wealth and various subjective factors. In the short run economists hold all the variables constant and study income-consumption relation. PTC is of two types—marginal and average. MPC is the ratio of the change in consumption to the change in income ($\Delta C/\Delta Y$) and APC is the ratio of total consumption to total income (C/Y).

3. ***Autonomous and induced consumption*** **:** In the short run consumption has both autonomous (income-independent) and induced (income-dependent) components. Due to the autonomous component, $MPC < APC$.

4. ***Two possible shapes of the consumption function*** **:** There are two possible shapes of the short-run consumption function — linear and non-linear. If it is linear, APC falls as income increases. And if it is non-linear MPC falls with an increase in income.

5. ***Movements along the consumption function and shifts of the function*** **:** If there is a change in disposable income, there is movement along the same consumption function. This implies that consumption increases with an increase in income, though not proportionately. But if there is change in any other variable affecting the PTC the consumption function will shift upward or downward. This implies that consumption will increase even at the same level of income.

6. ***Saving function*** **:** Since disposable income is largely spent on consumption goods and partly saved, consumption and saving are called mirror image concepts. So the saving function can be derived from the consumption function, using the 45° income line as the guideline. Saving depends both on income and propensity to save which is of two types— marginal and average. *MPS* is the ratio of change in saving to change in income. *APS* is the ratio of total saving to total income. And all the factors which determine *MPC* (*APC*) also determine *MPS* (*APC*). If there is a change in any of the factors, the saving function will shift.

7. ***Keynes' theory of consumption*** **:** The Keynesian theory of consumption is known as the absolute income hypothesis. According to the hypothesis consumption depends on current absolute income. According to Keynes if income increases, consumption also increases though not proportionately. This is known as Keynes's fundamental psychological law of consumption.

8. ***Income-consumption relation*** **:** In the short run the relation between income and consumption is non-proportional due to the autonomous element of consumption. In the long run the relation is proportional since consumption has no autonomous component. This is why the intercept term of the short-run consumption function does not exist in the long-run consumption function. The long-run consumption function starts from the origin implying that $MPC = APC$.

9. ***Kuznets' consumption function*** **:** Simon Kuznets found that consumption function is of the following form:

$$C = bY$$

There is no contradiction between the Keynesian consumption function and the Kuznets' consumption function. While the former is consistent with cross-section data, the latter according with time-series data. The consumption puzzle created by the two sets of data was resolved by post-Keynesian economists like Milton Friedman and F. Modigliani.

10. ***Short-run vs. long-run consumption function*** **:** According to Keynes' absolute income hypothesis $MPC < APC$ in the short run since consumption has an autonomous component. Keynes's short-run consumption function hypothesis suggests that the *MPC* is between zero and one, that the *APC* falls as income rises, and that current income is the proximate determinant of consumption. Cross-section data (showing inter-individual differences in consumption spending) and short time-series confirmed Keynes' hypothesis. Simon Kuznets' post-Second World War period data were consistent with the view that consumption is a stable function of income, with an *MPC* less than one (and equal to *APC*). But they were not consistent with the consumption function derived from the annual (cross-section) data of the pre-Second World War (1939-45) period. Several studies of long time-series did not find any tendency for the *APC* to fall in the long run with an increase in income. So a paradoxical result was found. This has surprised economists and is known as the consumption puzzle. Some reconciliation of the two sets of data was obviously required.

11. ***Modigliani's life cycle hypothesis*** **:** The LCH suggests that income varies somewhat predictably over a person's life and that consumers both save and dissave (borrow) to smooth their consumption over their lifetimes. Modigliani postulates that consumption depends on both income and wealth.

12. ***Friedman's permanent income hypothesis*** **:** The PIH suggests that individuals experience both permanent and transitory fluctuations in their income. Since individuals can save and dissave, and because they want to smooth their consumption, consumption does not respond much to transitory income. Consumption depends primarily on permanent income.

KEY TERMS

Marginal propensity to consume (*MPC*)	Consumption function
Marginal propensity to save (*MPS*)	Saving function
Average propensity to consume (*APC*)	Movement along the consumption function
Average propensity to save (*APS*)	Shift of the consumption function

The multiplier	Absolute income hypothesis
Transitory consumption	Asset income
Permanent income	Measured income
Relative income	Transitory income
Measured consumption	Wealth
Permanent consumption	Cconsumption function puzzle

ASSIGNMENTS

1. What is consumption function? Discuss briefly the factors which affect short-run consumption behaviour?
2. What are the three possible shapes of the consumption function? Which one seems to be more realistic and why?
3. What is Keynes' fundamental psychological law of consumption? Discuss the importance of the consumption function in the theory of income and employment.
4. Distinguish between *MPC* and *APC*. Why does the consumption function remain stable in the short run and shift in the long run? Show the relation between *MPC* and *APC* in the short run and in the long run.
5. What is meant by consumption function puzzle? How has it been resolved?
6. Derive the saving function from Keynes' consumption function. Show that the sum of propensities to consume and save is always equal to one.
7. "The consumption function lies at the heart of Keynesian economics". Explain the statement.
8. Suppose you have the following data on disposable income for a hypothetical economy. Assume that $MPC = 0{\cdot}50$. Now complete the table and graphically derive the consumption and saving functions.

Y_d	C	S	APC	MPC	APS	MPS
1,000	1,250					
2,000						
3,000						
4,000						
5,000						

9. What are Keynes' basic conjectures about short-run income-consumption relation?
10. What is money illusion? Does money illusion affect an individual's consumption behaviour in the long run?
[**Hint:** Money illusion is rare in the long-run.]
11. What is relative income hypothesis? How does it explain the consumption puzzle? What are the shortcomings of the hypothesis?
12. Explain the cyclical behaviour of consumption in terms of RIH.
13. Do you think that 'in the presence of liquidity constraint, Keynes' AIH is more relevant than either PIH or LCH?
14. Explain the LCH of consumption. Make a comparison between the LCH and the PIH.
15. How does the RIH reconcile the secular consumption function with the cyclical consumption function?
16. Explain the PIH. In what sense it is an improvement over the AIH?
[**Hint:** By focusing on changes in rate of interest (*r*) and the wealth held by an individual and desired to add to one's wealth as crucial determinants of consumption. Friedman has made an important contribution to the theory of consumption.]
17. How does the PIH reconcile the fact that the *MPC* in the short run is lower than the *MPC* in the long run? Do you think that the short-run *MPC* of an individual, whose income is highly volatile, will be quite low? Explain your answer.
18. How does the PIH explain saving ratio across income groups and over a trade cycle?

CHAPTER 12

The Theory of Multiplier

The multiplier refers to changes in an economic variable which can bring about magnified changes in another performance-related economic variable. — Wiley Dictionary of Economics, p. 242

According to the simple Keynesian theory of income determination in a two-sector economy (without government and foreign trade), national income attains its equilibrium value when two different but interrelated conditions are satisfied, viz., (1) income received = desired expenditure, and (2) desired saving (S) = desired investment (I). When this happens national income remains unchanged at a certain level without a rise or a fall. However, if there is any change in the saving schedule or in the investment schedule, national income will rise or fall. If there is an upward shift of the saving schedule due to the change in average propensity to save (*APS*), real *GDP* or national income will fall and if there is a downward shift of the saving schedule, national income (Y) will rise, as shown in Fig. 12.1 panel (a).

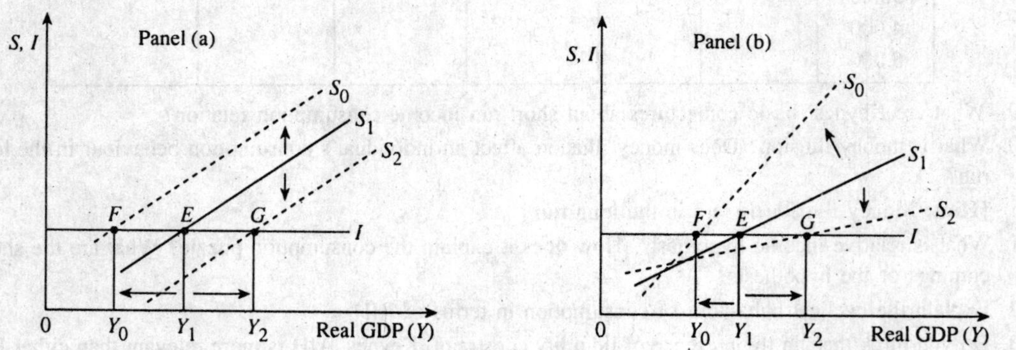

Fig. 12.1: Changes in Equilibrium Income

However, if there is a change in the marginal propensity to consume (*MPC*), there will be a corresponding change in the marginal propensity to save (*MPS*). If *MPC* falls and *MPS* rises the saving schedule will become steeper, i.e., its slope will increase as is shown by the new saving schedule S_0 in panel (b) of Fig. 12.1. It intersects the original investment schedule at point F and national income falls from Y_1 to Y_0. The converse is also true.

In Keynes's model all investment is autonomous and hence independent of national income. This is why the investment schedule is horizontal with zero slope. So the question of any change in the slope of the investment schedule does not arise.

However, if there is a fall in the rate of interest (r) or an increase in the marginal efficiency of capital (*MEC*), the investment demand schedule will shift upward and national income will rise, as shown in Fig. 12.2. The converse is also true. If the investment demand schedule shifts downward, national income will fall.

Since saving is a leakage from the circular flow of income, if *MPS* increases, Y falls. But since investment is an injection into the circular flow of income an increase in autonomous investment leads to an increase in Y. But by how much? In other words, what is the magnitude of income change? How much does Y change if I (investment) changes by a certain amount?

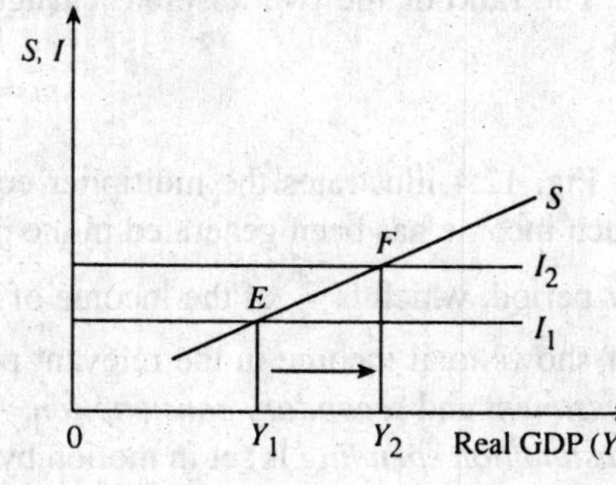

Fig. 12.2: Change in Equilibrium Income

In order to answer this question we have to refer to a concept known as the multiplier. The multiplier enables us to measure the magnitude of income change.

The concept of multiplier occupies a central place in the Keynesian theory of income and employment. It was first introduced by F. A. Kahn in 1932. Kahn's multiplier known as **employment multiplier**. In 1936 Keynes introduced the concept of **investment multiplier** or **autonomous expenditure multiplier**. According to Keynes any increase in autonomous spending has a **multiplier effect**. This means that increase in investment or government spending leads to an increase in Y not by the same amount but by a multiple of it due to a chain of secondary consumption spending and respending. This happens because in an interdependent economy one person's expenditure is another person's income. Thus an initial increase in investment leads to an increase in income of exactly the same amount. This is the direct effect of an increase in autonomous investment. But the increase in income in the initial round is not the end of the story. There is also the indirect effect of an income in autonomous investment through income changes in the next and subsequent rounds. So the total increase in income at the end of the income generation process is a multiple of the initial increase in autonomous spending (investment).

Graphical Representation of the Multiplier

The multiplier may also be illustrated graphically.

In Fig. 12.3 income is initially assumed to be in equilibrium at Rs. 80,000 cr. Now suppose autonomous investment increases by Rs. 1,000 cr. from Rs. 30,000 cr. to Rs. 31,000 cr. This may occur

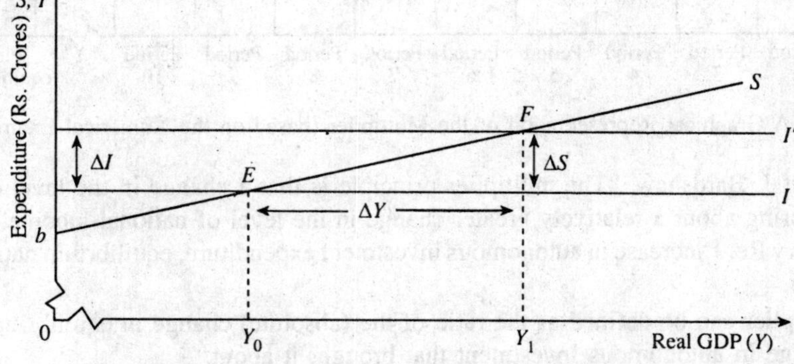

Fig. 12.3: The Multiplier In terms of the *S-I* Approach

if business firms increase their spending on new factories. This is shown by an upward shift of the investment curve from I to I'. Consequently national income increases by Rs. 5,000 cr.—from

Rs. 80,000 cr. to 85,000 cr. This increase in income—which is shown as ΔY—is larger than the increase in investment—which is shown by ΔI—which caused the increase in income.

The ratio of the two absolute changes is the multiplier, *m* or, we have

$$m = \frac{\Delta Y}{\Delta I} = \frac{\text{Rs.}5{,}000 \text{ cr.}}{\text{Rs.}1{,}000 \text{ cr.}} = 5.$$

Fig. 12.4 illustrates the multiplier concept graphically. The white bar in each period shows how much income has been generated in the previous period. The shaded bar shows the increase in income per period, which is $\frac{4}{5}$ of the income of the previous period. The total height of the two parts of each bar shows total income in the relevant period. Total income shown by the last bar is sum of *primary investment* and *secondary consumption*. According to P. A. Samuelson, "an endless chain of *secondary consumption spending* is set in motion by a primary investment spending. But, although it is an endless chain, it is a dwinding chain. And it eventually adds to a finite amount".

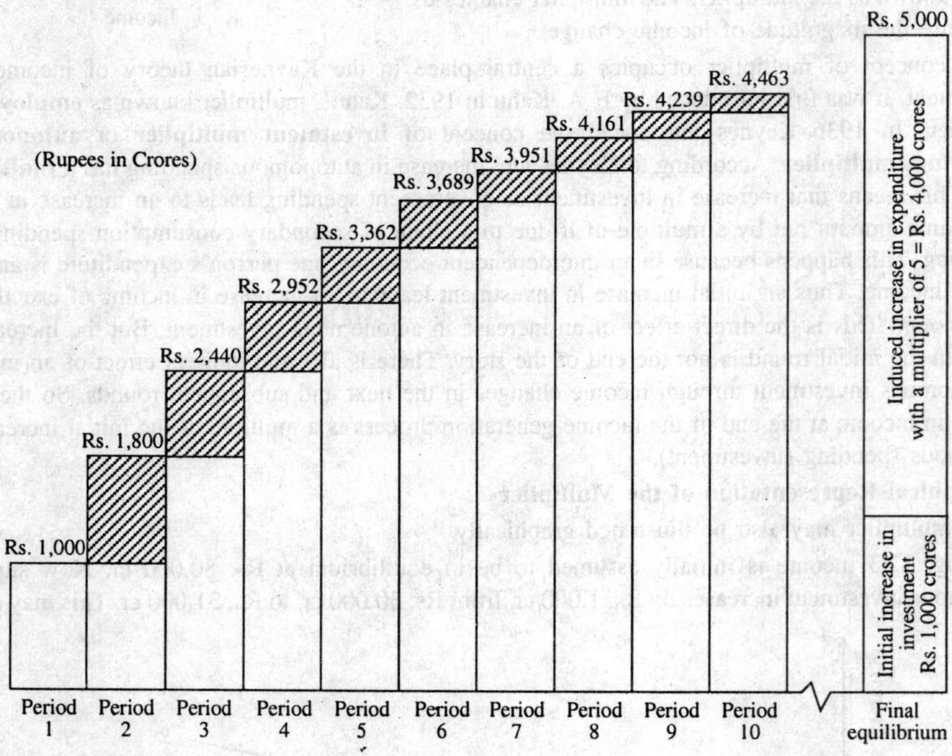

Fig. 12.4: A Graphical Representation of the Multiplier (based on the Numerical Example)

In the words of J. Bardshaw, "The multiplier principle is that a change in the level of injections (or withdrawals) bring about a relatively greater change in the level of national income." This again tells us that for every Re. 1 increase in autonomous investment expenditure, equilibrium national income increases by Rs. 5.

Thus the multiplier can be defined as the ratio of the (absolute) change in equilibrium income to the initiating change in autonomous investment that brought it about.

We may now consider Fig. 12.5. We see that the size of change in income brought about by a shift in the investment schedule from I to I' differs according to the slope of the saving curve. Here we present three saving curves with different slopes. The slopes of S_0, $S_1{}'$ and $S_2{}''$ are 0.40, 0.20, 0.133, respectively. The respective changes in equilibrium income in response to shift of the investment schedules from Rs. 30,000 cr. to Rs. 31,500 cr. are ΔY_1 = Rs. 2,500 cr., ΔY_2 = Rs. 5,000 cr. and ΔY_3 = Rs. 7,500 cr. The numerical values of the multiplier in these three cases are 2.5, 5 and 7.5, respectively. This shows that the flatter the saving schedule, the larger the value of the multiplier. It is because the slope of the saving schedule is the *MPS* and the reciprocal of the slope of the saving schedule gives us the value of the multiplier. Therefore, the flatter the saving schedule, the larger must be the increase in income before saving rises to equal the new level of investment.

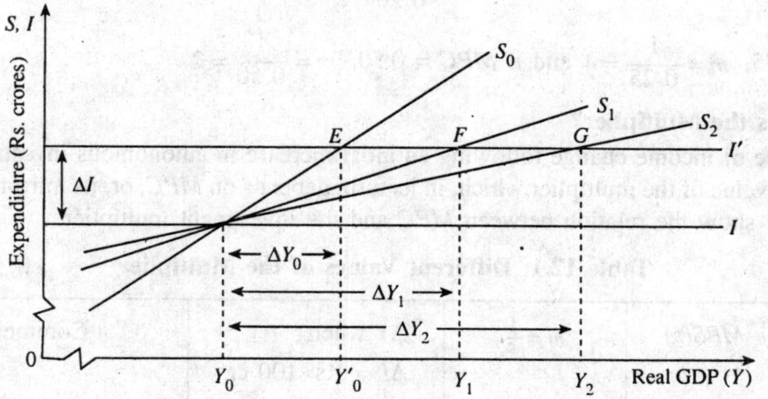

Fig. 12.5: Different Saving Functions and Different Values of the Multiplier

THE DERIVATION OF THE MULTIPLIER FORMULA

We can derive the multiplier formula from the simple Keynesian two-sector model of income determination.

We know that according to the income-expenditure approach to income determination, national income attains its equilibrium value when income received is equal to desired expenditure, which is the sum of *C* and *I*:

$$Y = C + I \qquad \ldots (1)$$

In the theory of multiplier, we are concerned with changes in *Y* induced by a direct change in *I* and indirect change in *C*. So if *Y* increases, *C* and *I* will both increase and we can rewrite the equation (1) as follows:

$$\Delta Y = \Delta C + \Delta I \qquad \ldots (2)$$

In the Keynesian model, investment is autonomous but consumption depends on income as is clear from the Keynesian consumption function:

$$C = a + bY \qquad \ldots (3)$$

where *a* is autonomous (income-independent consumption), and *bY* is induced consumption.

If *Y* increases, *C* will increase by *bY*, where *b* is the *MPC*. So we can write:

$$\Delta C = b\Delta Y$$

if we ignore *a* in the context of the multiplier theory.

Substituting (3) into (2) we have

$$\Delta Y = b\Delta Y + \Delta I$$

$$\text{or } \Delta Y - b\Delta Y = \Delta I$$

$$\text{or } \Delta Y(1 - b) = \Delta I$$

$$\text{or } \Delta Y = \frac{1}{1-b}(\Delta I)$$

$$\text{or } \frac{\Delta Y}{\Delta I} = \frac{1}{1-b} = \frac{1}{s}$$

where b is the *MPC* and s is the *MPS*. Thus the multiplier is the reciprocal of *MPS*.

The value of the multiplier will remain constant so long as *MPC* remains constant. If $MPC = 0.80$, $MPS = 0.20$ and the multiplier (m) is:

$$m = \frac{1}{0.20} = 5$$

If $MPC = 0.75$, $m = \frac{1}{0.25} = 4$ and if $MPC = 0.50$, $m = \frac{1}{0.50} = 2$.

How Large is the Multiplier?

The magnitude of income change following an intial increase in autonomous investment depends on the numerical value of the multiplier which, in its turn, depends on *MPC*, or, its mirror image, *MPS*. In Table 12.1 we show the relation between *MPC* and the investment multiplier.

Table 12.1: Different Values of the Multiplier

MPC(b)	*MPS(s)*	$m = \frac{1}{s}$	ΔY when ΔI = Rs. 100 cr.	Comments
0	1	1	Rs. 100 cr.	The multiplier effect is absent.
$\frac{1}{2}$	$\frac{1}{2}$	2	Rs. 200 cr.	The multiplier effect is present.
$\frac{3}{4}$	$\frac{1}{4}$	4	Rs. 400 cr.	The multiplier effect is stronger.
$\frac{4}{5}$	$\frac{1}{5}$	5	Rs. 500 cr.	The multiplier effect is much stronger.
1	0	Undefined	?	Income change cannot be specified.

Thus we see that if *MPC* increases and *MPS* falls, the value of the multiplier will increase and the same increase in investment will lead to further and further increases in *Y*. However, the concept of multiplier is meaningful if and only if *MPC* is greater than zero, but less than one. In other words, it must lie between 0 and 1 ($0 < MPC < 1$).

Assumptions of the Multiplier

The Keynesian multiplier theory is based on the following assumptions:

1. Constancy of *MPC*: The *MPC* is assumed to remain constant as income increases in various rounds due to a chain of secondary consumption spending and respending. This is a realistic assumption and gets strong support from empirical data. Consumption is found to be stable function of income at least in the short run.

2. A once-and-for all increase in investment: It is also assumed that there is a net increase in investment at the beginning of the income-generation process and there is no further (subsequent) increase in investment.[1]

1. Of course, this assumption can be modified to take into account the effects of continuous injections of investment.

3. No time lag: Keynes also assumed that there is no time lag between increase in investment and increase in income. In other words, an increase in investment leads to an instantaneous increase in income in the short run.

4. Existence of excess production capacity: Keynes also assumed that there exists excess capacity in the economy, particularly in industries producing consumer goods. Thus if the demand for such goods increases due to an increase in income, it will be possible to produce such goods in large amounts to meet the extra demand.[1]

Imports are a leakage from the circular flow of income or from the multiplier process

5. Closed economy: Keynes assumed that the economy is closed. In such an economy there is no export or import. In an open economy a portion of consumption spending leaks out in the form of imports and reduces the value of the multiplier. [This point will be discussed later in this chapter.]

Economic Insight: Real Multiplier Effect

Keynes's fixed price model also shows the real multiplier effect, i.e., in terms of an increase in the supply of goods and services. Since prices remain constant, and GDP is the product of prices and quantities of various goods and services produced in the economy, an increase in GDP and thus in national income can only be achieved by increasing the output of goods and services. We know that

$$\begin{aligned} \text{GDP} &= p_1q_1 + p_2q_2 + \cdots + p_nq_n \\ &= PQ = Y \end{aligned}$$

Thus if all the prices remain constant, then $PQ = Y$ can increase if the quantities $(q_1, q_2, \ldots, q_n)$ increase. However, if due to bottlenecks in the form of shortages of basic inputs like steel, power and coal, or inadequate availability of transport and communication facilities (such as shortage of wagons), or strike in some major industries output cannot be increased, then an increase in consumption demand will lead to a rise in prices only and the real multiplier effect will be largely lost.

LEAKAGES FROM THE MULTIPLIER PROCESS

In reality, various factors reduce the value of the multiplier. These are known as leakages from the multiplier.

1. Saving: Saving is the primary leakage from the multiplier. If *MPS* rises, the value of the multiplier will fall and the process of income generation will slow down. This point is illustrated in Fig. 12.6.

If the investment schedule shifts upwards from I_1 to I_2, Y will rise from Y_1 to Y_1', when the saving schedule is S_1. Now if the saving schedule becomes steeper (S_2) due to an increase in *MPS*, income will increase from Y_1 to Y_2.

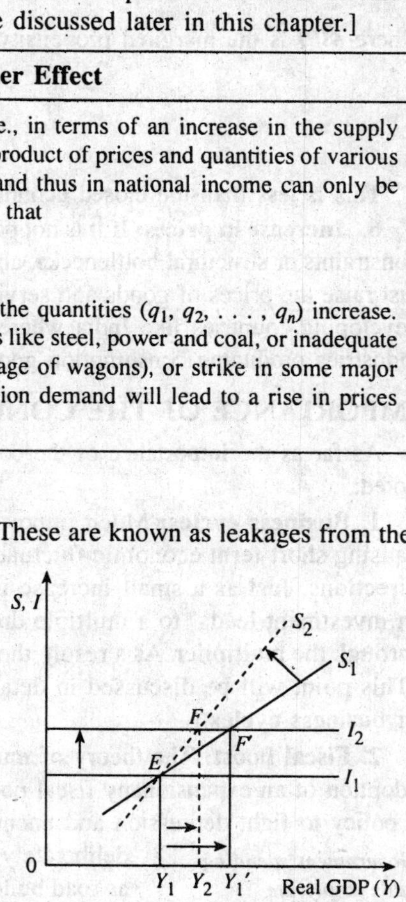

Fig. 12.6: The Effect of an Increase in *MPS* on Equilibrium Income

2. Debt repayment: In reality a portion of the extra income earned by people is used to repay past debt to banks, non-banking financial institutions or even private money-lenders. This portion thus leaks out of the circular flow of income since it is not spent on consumption goods.

3. Cash holding: If people hold a portion of their income in the form of idle cash balance (for precautionary and speculative purposes), there will be further leakage from the income stream. So consumption spending will not increase by the full amount of the increase in income and the multiplier effect will be partly lost.

1. If production capacity is being fully utilised, an increase in demand will lead to a rise in prices of such goods, with their output remaining constant.

4. Taxes: Taxes also act as leakage from the multiplier process. Taxes reduce the value of the multiplier by reducing disposable income and thus by reducing consumption expenditure in each round.[1]

5. Imports: Imports act as a further leakage from the multiplier. This is why the open economy multiplier is less than the closed economy multiplier. Suppose *MPC* for a closed economy is $\frac{2}{3}$. So the value of the multiplier is 3. Now if one-tenth of any extra income earned in the economy is spent on imports, i.e., if the marginal propensity to import (MPI) = $\frac{1}{10}$, then the value of the multiplier will fall. The open economy multiplier is written as

$$m_0 = \frac{1}{MPS + MPI}$$

where *MPI* is the marginal propensity to import

$$\text{So } m_0 = \frac{1}{\frac{1}{3} + \frac{1}{10}} = 2{\cdot}3$$

This is less than the closed economy multiplier (3).

6. Increase in prices: If it is not possible to increase the output of consumer goods due to capacity constraints or structural bottlenecks, an income in aggregate demand due to rise in money income will just raise the prices of goods and services and will not stimulate production. This is what happens in developing countries like India where there is hardly any unused idle capacity in agriculture or in industries producing consumption goods.

IMPORTANCE OF THE CONCEPT OF MULTIPLIER

As far as the importance of the concept of the multiplier is concerned, following points may be noted:

1. Business cycles: Much importance has been given by Keynes to the multiplier process in causing short-term economic fluctuations or business cycles. The multiplier process work in both directions. Just as a small increase in investment leads to a multiple increase in *Y* a small drop in investment leads to a multiple drop in *Y*. Thus investment fluctuations cause business cycles through the multiplier. As a result there are fluctuations in employment, output and the price level. [This point will be discussed in detail in a later chapter in the context of the Keynesian theory of business cycles.]

2. Fiscal boost: The theory of multiplier has also considerable practical relevance as far as the adoption of an expansionany fiscal policy is concerned. Keynes first suggested the adoption of such a policy to fight depression and unemployment. He specifically argued that the government should deliberately incur a deficit in the budget to spend more on public works such as road building, construction of hospitals, setting up of schools, expansion of irrigation facilities, etc. As a result aggregate expenditure ($C + I + G$) will increase and more jobs and incomes will be created. This, in its turn, will lead to an increase in demand for consumption goods and will stimulate private investment as well. As a result the economy will be enabled to reachieve full employment which is characterised by the absence of any involuntary idleness of resources including manpower.

Government spending adds to private spending in determining effective demand

3. Planning: The concept of multiplier has relevance for planners also. Suppose the Government of India plans to increase GDP by Rs. 200 crore in the current year by encouraging the private sector to investment. By how much should private investment increase so that the target can be reached? This

1. However, if the government spends the entire tax revenue the leakage through taxes can be offset.

depends on the value of the multiplier. If it is found to be 4, an increase in private investment of Rs. 50 crore will be enough. We know that

$$\Delta Y = m(\Delta I)$$

$$\text{or, } \Delta I = \frac{\Delta Y}{m}$$

Since ΔY = Rs. 200 crore, and $m = 4$, ΔI has to be $\frac{200}{4}$ = Rs. 50 crore. So the government should give necessary incentives to the private sector to make this extra investment.

EXAMPLES

Problem 1: Suppose the level of autonomous investment in an economy is Rs. 100 crore and the consumption function of the economy is $C = 50 + 0{\cdot}80Y$.

(a) Find out the equilibrium level of income.

(b) Find out the effect of an increase in investment by Rs. 20 crore on equilibrium income.

Solution: (a) We know that the equilibrium condition of national income for a two-sector economy is the following:

$$Y = C + I \qquad \ldots (1)$$

Here $C = 50 + 0{\cdot}80Y$ and I = Rs. 100 cr. Now substituting the values of C and I in (1), we get

$$Y = 50 + 0{\cdot}80Y + 100$$

$$\text{or, } Y - 0{\cdot}80Y = 150$$

$$\text{or, } 0{\cdot}20Y = 150$$

$$\text{or, } Y = 750$$

This is indeed the equilibrium level of income.

(b) In this case the value of the multiplier is $m = \frac{1}{1-0{\cdot}80} = \frac{1}{0{\cdot}20} = 5$

So if the investment increases by Rs. 20 crore the equilibrium national income will increase by Rs. 100 crore.

Problem 2: Suppose investment in a country increases by Rs. 200 crore and the consumption function is $C = 20 + 0{\cdot}75Y$. Find out the multiplier effect.

Solution: Here $m = \frac{1}{0.25} = 4$. So Y will increase by Rs. 800 crore (= 2 × Rs. 200 crore).

Problem 3: Suppose $MPC = 0{\cdot}80$. How much additional investment spending has to the made to increase Y by Rs. 5,000? What will be the increase in C and S?

Solution: Here $\Delta I = \frac{\Delta Y}{m}$ = Rs. $\frac{5{,}000}{5}$ = Rs. 1,000

Thus investment has to increase by Rs. 1,000 so that Y increases by Rs. 5,000. If ΔY = Rs. 5,000, $\Delta C = 0{\cdot}80 \times$ Rs. 5,000 = Rs. 4,000 and $\Delta S = 0{\cdot}20 \times$ Rs. 5,000 = Rs. 1,000. Thus investment is matched by saving and national income attains a higher equilibrium value.

Problem 4: Suppose I = Rs. 70; C = Rs. 60 + 0.80 Y. (a) Find the equilibrium level of income. (b) Find the equilibrium level of income when there is a Rs. 10 increase in autonomous planned investment (i.e., planned investment increases from Rs. 70 to Rs. 80). (c) Establish the multiplier effect of the Rs. 10 increase in autonomous spending.

Solution: (a)

$$Y = C + I$$

$$Y = \text{Rs. } 60 + 0.80\ Y + \text{Rs. } 70$$

$$Y - 0.80\ Y = \text{Rs. } 130$$

$$Y = \frac{\text{Rs.}130}{0.20} = \text{Rs.}650$$

(b) $$Y = C + 1$$

$$Y = \text{Rs. } 60 + 0.80\ Y = \text{Rs. } 80$$

$$Y = \frac{\text{Rs.}140}{0.20} = \text{Rs.}700$$

(c) The equilibrium level of income increases by Rs. 50 (from Rs. 650 to Rs. 700) as a result of a Rs. 10 increase in investment. There is a multiplier effect of 5 (that is, $\frac{\Delta Y}{\Delta I} = \frac{\text{Rs.}50}{\text{Rs.}10} = 5$) as a result of the increase in autonomous investment.

Problem 5: Suppose the equilibrium condition is given by $Y = \frac{(a+\bar{I})}{(1-b)}$ (a) Letting $\bar{A}$ represent fixed autonomous spending ($\bar{A} = a + \bar{I}$), find an expression that relates income changes to changes in autonomous spending. (b) What is the change in the equilibrium level of income when $\bar{C} = \text{Rs.}10, \Delta\bar{I} = +\text{Rs.}30$, and $b = 0.80$?

Solution: (a) Equilibrium income equals $\frac{\bar{A}}{(1-b)}$ where $\bar{A} = a + \bar{I}$. It, therefore, follows that

$\Delta Y = \frac{\Delta\bar{A}}{(1-b)}$. (b) $\bar{A}$ = (– Rs. 10 + Rs. 30) = + Rs. 20. $\Delta Y = \frac{\text{Rs.}20}{(1-0.80)}$; ΔY = Rs. 100.

Problem 6: (a) Derive the multiplier when the *MPC* is 0.90, 0.80, 0.75 and 0.50. (b) What is the relationship between the marginal propensity to consume and the investment multiplier? (c) Use the multiplier values found in (a) to establish what effect a Rs. 20 decrease in autonomous spending has upon equilibrium income.

Solution: (a) The multiplier (*m*) equals $\frac{1}{(1-b)}$; thus, *m* is 10 when the *MPC* is 0.90; 5 when *MPC* is 0.80; 4 when *MPC* is 0.75; and 2 when *MPC* is 0.50.

(b) There is a multiplier effect because consumption spending is related to the level of disposable income. Any change in income induces a change in aggregate consumption, with the magnitude of the change dependent on the value of the *MPC*. Thus, the value of the multiplier is directly related to the value of the *MPC*.

(c) The decline in income equals $\Delta\bar{I}(m)$. The decrease in equilibrium income is Rs. 200, Rs. 100, Rs. 80, and Rs. 40 respectively for the four values of *MPC*.

Problem 7: If investment falls Rs. 20 and the marginal propensity to consume is 0.60, what are (a) the change in the equilibrium level of income, (b) the change in autonomous spending, and (c) the induced change in consumption spending?

Solution: (a) The change in the equilibrium level of income equals $m\Delta\bar{I}$. Since $m = 2.5$, ΔY = Rs. 50.

(b) The Rs. 20 decline in investment is the change in autonomous spending.

(c) The induced change in spending is the difference between the change in the level of income and the change in autonomous spending. That is $\Delta Y - \Delta\bar{I} = \Delta C$. Induced spending falls by Rs. 30.

THE PARADOX OF THRIFT

The results obtained so far in this chapter have a surprising application. It is often observed that what is good for an individual (or from the micro-point of view) is not necessarily good for the society as a whole (or from the macro-point of view). When, for instance, an individual attempts to save more it is good for him. Thrift at the individual level may lead to wealth and prosperity, while dissaving may lead to ultimate bankruptcy. But if all individuals become desirous of saving more at the same time the result may be disastrous. There may be a fall in the actual saving of the community. This peculiar result is known as *the paradox of thrift* or *the paradox of saving*.

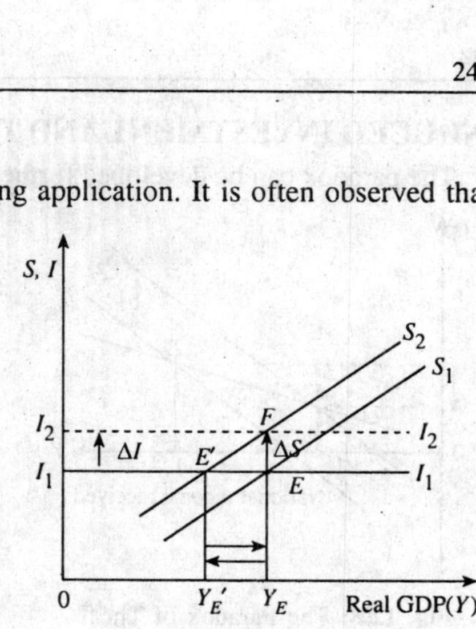

Fig. 12.7: Resolving the Paradox of Thrift

We have observed that if the saving curve shifts to the left there is a fall in national income. Suppose in Fig. 12.7 S_1 is the original saving curve. It now shifts to the left to S_2. The increase in thriftiness will lead to a fall in the equilibrium level of national income from Y_E to Y'_E in the Figure. This point has been explained by R. G. Lipsey and C. Harbury in the following words: "The upward shift in the saving schedule causes planned saving to exceed planned investment at the initial equilibrium level of income. National income falls and this induces a decline in planned saving. Income continues to fall until saving is again equal to investment."

However, we are assuming here that investment is autonomous. Here a fixed level of investment takes place at all levels of income. This has an important implication for the theory of income determination. In this case saving has to fall back to the original level so that it is again equated to the original level of investment. Thus attempts to save more are frustrated due to fall in income. And income continues to fall until everyone ends up saving exactly what they were saving before income change.

The opposite situation is one of a decrease in thriftiness or an increase in planned consumption spending. This will cause a downward shift of the saving function—e.g., from S to S'. Due to decreased desire to save on the part of households, desired leakage will be less than desired injection at the initial level of national income—Y_0. This will cause national income to rise. The income expansion process will continue until the actual volume of saving is again equated to its initial level but at a new, higher level of national income.

The paradox of thrift can be avoided if the extra saving of households flows into the market for loanable funds for investment purposes. In this case if the extra investment just offsets the extra saving, equilibrim national income will remain unchanged at Y_E, as shown in Fig. 12.7.

The upward shift of the saving schedule from S_1 to S_2 intially leads to a fall in income from Y_E to Y_E'. Now if the investment schedule shifts upward exactly by the same amount from I_1 to I_2, the new investment schedule I_2 will intersect the new saving schedule at point F, at which the extra saving is offset by the extra investment ΔI. Thus since at point E, $S = I$, and at point $F = S + \Delta S = I + \Delta I$ and national income returns to its intial level (Y_E).

However, according to modern economists this is unlikely to happen in times of recession or depression. The reason is that at such times the *MEC* is so low that no reduction in the rate of interest is sufficient to increase I to the desired level so as to fully offset the increase in S which caused Y to fall.

So the paradox can be avoided only through appropriate government intervention such as a cut in tax which increases disposable income and consumption expenditure or an increase in government spending.

INDUCED INVESTMENT AND THRIFT

The paradox can be developed further if we assume that investment is non-autonomous or induced. We now argue that investment increases with income. So the investment line now slopes upward (with positive rather than zero slope). The slope of the line measures the marginal propensity to invest which is expressed as $i = \frac{\Delta I_p}{\Delta Y}$. Here ΔI_p is the absolute change in induced private investment and ΔY is the absolute change in national income. In Fig. 12.8 we again consider the effect of an upward shift of the saving schedule. We are now able to explain the paradox fully in the sense that not only does increased saving bring about a lower level of income and investment but it also leads, ultimately, to less being saved. This effect is produced because people now have lesser ability to save at lower levels of national income. Their plan (or desire) to save more has been frustrated by the fall in income which a fall in saving causes. The paradox can be stated as follows:

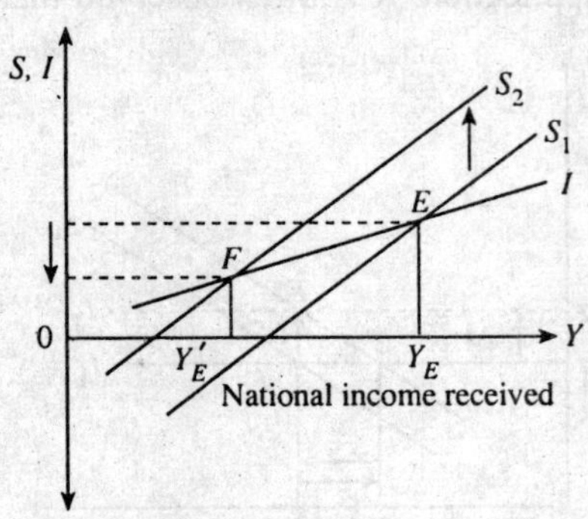

Fig. 12.8: The Paradox of Thrift with Induced Investment

An increased desire to save may lead to a fall in the actual saving of the community. (This simply means that sometimes the cure is worse than the disease.)

Keynes also pointed out that the effect of increase in thriftiness also depends upon the state of the economy. During inflation an increase in thriftiness or a decrease in consumption expenditure is desirable because it may act an anti-inflationary measure, by eliminating the excess demand pressure. If, on the other hand, the economy suffers from deep depression, with widespread unemployment, the consequence of an increase in thriftiness could be quite disastrous. It would take the economy into a cumulative (vicious) deflationary spiral. Thus if planners and policy-makers attempt to 'tighten our belts' during depression, the problem is likely to be more serious. In other words, the depression is likely to be made even worse. As J. M. Keynes himself commented: "When you save even five shillings you put a man out of work for a day".

THE KEYNESIAN EXPLANATION OF THE GREAT DEPRESSION

According to Keynes, the Great Depression of 1929 occurred due to the operations of the reverse multiplier. A fall in the autonomous investment due to a sharp fall in *MEC* (caused a widespread pessimism about business prospects and profits) led to a multiple drop in national income and employment. This point is illustrated in Fig. 12.9.

Here national income is originally in equilibrium at point *E* at which the aggregate desired expenditure schedule $(C + I)$ cuts the 45° income line $0Y$. Now if investment falls, the aggregate desired expenditure schedule shifts downward to $C + I'$. Here $I' = I - \Delta I$. The $C + I$ schedule intersects the income line at point *G*. As a result national income falls from Y_E to Y_E'. The fall in income is a multiple of the initial fall in investment due to the working of the reverse multiplier process. Thus a fall in investment, according to Keynes, is the root cause of great depression of October 1929 which lasted for four years (upto 1933). In the context of the depression, Keynes

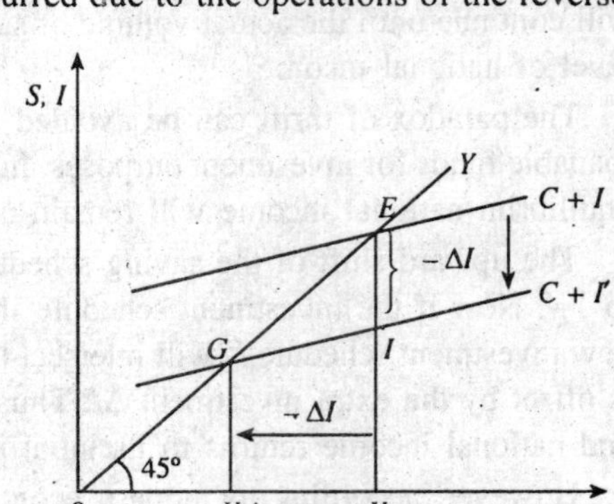

Fig. 12.9: The Working of the Reverse Multiplier in Times of Depression

suggested the adoption of an expansionary fiscal policy in the form of an increase in *G*. Keynes specifically suggested that the government should deliberately incur a deficit in the budget to create jobs and incomes. Most capitalist countries followed the Keynesian prescriptions and pumped huge amount of money in the economy and succeeded in reachieving full employment and high income growth. Thus the use of discretionary fiscal policy came into prominence for controlling business cycles and for stabilising most of the capitalist economies of the world.

THE WORKING OF THE MULTIPLIER IN DEVELOPING COUNTRIES

Keynes developed the multiplier principle in the context of advanced capitalist countries. According to Keynes four preconditions are to be fulfilled for making the multiplier process really effective. Firstly, there should exist sufficient excess production capacity in the economy. Secondly, there should not exist any shortage of raw materials and intermediate inputs. These should be readily available as and when required so that production does not suffer in times of increasing demand for goods and services.Thirdly, there should exist open unemployment in the economy. Finally, aggregate supply should be fairly elastic in the short-run so that prices do not rise when aggregate demand increases. If supply is fairly elastic then aggregate output will increase to meet growing demand for goods and services without putting any pressure on the price level.

In immediate post-Second World War period (1945 onwards) as also in the 1950s it was found that none of these conditions existed in developing countries.

Firstly, there did not exist any excess capacity in consumer goods industries.

Secondly, most unemployment in such countries was of a different nature. There was disguised unemployment and not open unemployment. It was difficult to measure the magnitude of such unemployment in a predominantly agricultural economy like India characterised by family farming. This type of unemployment problem could not be solved by adopting industrial policy.

Thirdly, there existed acute shortages of raw materials and intermediate inputs. Such bottlenecks made it difficult to increase production either in agriculture or in consumer goods industries.

Finally, aggregate supply was fairly inelastiic. The reason was that such economies were predominantly agricultural in nature and agriculture itself was characterised by low productivity and low supply elasticity. In such a situation public investment on agriculture and infrastructure building generated a different type of multiplier effect. There occurred a rise in prices rather than an increase in production of mass consumption goods. This is why V.K.R.V.Rao and others had opined that the multiplier principle, as enunciated by Keynes, does not work in diminishing unemployment or creating income in developing countries like India. In other words, the Keynesian multiplier works in India only in nominal terms, not in real terms.

THE CURRENT SITUATION

However, things have changed over the last few decades. Now the supply position in India has become more favourable than it was earlier. Due to industrial growth and diversification during the reform period (since July 1996), the aggregate supply situation has improved much. The supply of agricultural goods has also increased since the late 1960s due to the adoption of a new agricultural strategy which brought about the Green Revolution.

Moreover, at present due to deficiency of demand there is excess production capacity in a number of industries. In addition, the output of cement, power, steel, fertilisers has also increased quite significantly. So there is no real bottleneck in the economy. And due to urbanisation and industrialisation there has occurred huge migration of labour from rural to urban areas. So disguised unemployment of rural areas has been converted into open unemployment in urban areas.

For all these reasons the Keynesian multiplier principle is quite relevant in India and other developing countries today. According to the Harrod-Domar model of economic growth, investment not only creates new demand but also generates new production capacity in industrial and service sectors. Now if investment is made in a number of industries at a time such industries will grow simultaneously in two ways. One will create demand for the product of another and will buy inputs from others as Nurkse predicted. An increase in demand for products will lead to new investment and creation of additional production capacity. And the economy will be able to achieve self-sustaining growth.

So the Keynesian multiplier principle is quite relevant in India and other developing countries now. It can operate in such countries, if it is associated with carefully planned and designed pattern of investment so that Gunnar Myrdal's spread effects are generated.

KEY POINTS

1. ***Income change*** **:** If the actual level of income is such that desired saving is not equal to desired investment, national income will tend to rise or fall. Income change will continue until desired saving is again equated to desired investment. When this happens national income attains a new desired equilibrium value. Income change is the mechanism through which the two desired values are equated.

2. ***Equilibrium and full-employment*** **:** However, equilibrium level of income does not necessarily ensure full employment. National income equilibrium may also occur at less than full-employment, i.e., equilibrium income may be less than full employment (potential) income. If this happens there will exist involuntary idleness of resources, including manpower and the consequent waste (loss) of potential output.

3. ***Effect of thriftiness*** **:** When saving increases national income falls. More saving implies contraction of demand for goods and services and, in a demand-determined system (as that of Keynes), national income falls.

4. ***Expenditure multiplier*** **:** When investment increases national income rises. Keynes pointed out that any increase in autonomous spending will have a multiplier effect. Since investment is high-powered spending, a small increase in autonomous investment will lead to a multiple increase in national income. The multiplier, the reciprocal of the *MPS*, is the number by which change in autonomous investment has to be multiplied to find out the resulting change in national income. There are certain limitations of the multiplier which reduce the usefulness (practical application) of the concept.

KEY TERMS

Investment multiplier	Primary investment
Induced investment and thrift	Paradox of thrift
Leakages from the multiplier	Real multiplier effect
Discretionary fiscal policy	Secondary consumption spending

ASSIGNMENTS

1. Trace out the effect of an increase in autonomous spending on equilibrium level of income. What happens to equilibrium income if *MPC* rises or falls? Show graphically as also with the multiplier.
2. Saving is a leakage from the circular flow of income. At the same time the multiplier is the reciprocal of *MPS*. How would you reconcile these two apparently confusing statements?
3. What is the relation between the propensity to consume and the investment multiplier? What are the assumptions of the multiplier? What are the leakages from the multiplier?
4. "Even though the *MPC* is quite high in developing countries like India, an increase in government spending may have very little, if any, expansionary effect." —Discuss.
5. "An increased desire to save may lead to a fall in the actual saving of the community."— Explain this statement.

6. What is paradox of thrift? How can you resolve the paradox?
7. What is the significance of the Keynesian multiplier? Does the Keynesian multiplier process work in India in real terms?
8. Explain the Keynesian theory of investment multiplier. What are the limitations of the Keynesian theory?
9. Discuss the Keynesian theory of investment multiplier. What are the possible leakages from the multiplier mechanism?
10. How does an increase in investment cause a multiple increase in national income?
11. Find the value of the multiplier given the following:

    (a) $MPC = 0.40$ (b) $MPS = 0.25$ (c) $MPC = 0.67$ (d) $MPS = 0.50$ (e) $MPC = 0.90$ (f) $MPC = 0.75$.
12. Assume the initial equilibrium level of national income is Rs. 4,800 crores, and the $MPC = 0.9$. What will be the new equilibrium level of Y if I decreases by Rs. 100 crore from its initial level?
13. What will be the impact of an increase in investment of Rs. 100 crore on the equilibrium level of national income if the MPC is 80%?

    [**Hint:** The formula for calculation of the size of the multiplier is $m = \frac{1}{1-b}$, (where m = multiplier and $b = MPC$)

    So we can write, $m \frac{1}{1-0.8} = \frac{1}{0.2} = 5$.

    Thus, if autonomous investment increases by Rs. 100 crore the equilibrium level of national income will increase by Rs. 500 crore (= 5 × Rs. 100 crore).]
14. Suppose, in a country, investment increases by Rs. 100 and consumption is given by the equation $C = 10 + 0.6\,Y$ (where C = consumption and Y = income). Find out the resultant increase in nation income.
15. Trace out the effect of an increase in autonomous spending on equilibrium national income. Why does an increase in autonomous spending lead to a multiple increase in national income. Show graphically as also with the autonomous expenditure multiplier.
16. What is the relation between propensity to consume and investment multiplier. What happens to national income if MPC increases or falls?
17. The multiplier is the reciprocal of the MPS. But the multiplier effect is observed incase of an injection into the circular flow of income. We know that saving is a leakage from the circular flow. So how can the multiplier be related to saving? Explain your answer. Are you puzzled by the above statements?

CHAPTER 13

The Theory of Investment and the Acceleration Principle

Investment is the most volatile component of GDP. — N. G. Mankiw

IMPORTANCE OF INVESTMENT

In the short run the levels of employment and national income depend on aggregate demand. Aggregate demand has two components — household consumption and business investment. While consumption is a stable function of income in the short run, the level of income and employment depends on the volume of investment. And investment fluctuates sharply and causes short-term economic fluctuations or business cycles. According to Keynes, fluctuations in the levels of fixed business investment causes economic instability. Investment also affects economic growth in the long run, both directly and indirectly— by promoting technological progress which raises the productivity of resources or total factor productivity. And capital formation and technological progress are interrelated.

Investment fluctuations cause business cycles in the short run and an increase in investment leads to faster economic growth in the long run

MEANING OF INVESTMENT

Investment is of two main types — financial and real. Financial investment refers to purchase of financial (paper) assets such as shares, bonds, debentures, certificates of deposits, etc. by an individual. In this case there is just transfer of financial assets from one individual (the seller) to another individual (the buyer). Real investment refers to the addition to the stock of capital such as plant, equipment, tools, machines, structures, factories, etc. of a firm or of a country. In economics, investment refers to only real investment. Investment may be gross or net. Net investment is gross investment *less* depreciation. Net investment refers to the net addition to the stock of capital of a business firm. By adding up the volumes of investment by all the firms we arrive at aggregate investment which is more relevant for macroeconomic analysis than investment by a firm. An increase in aggregate net investment leads to an increase in aggregate demand which brings about an increase in aggregate output (income) and in the level of employment of an economy. Modern economists also include the increase in inventories of finished goods in investment. This point has already been mentioned in the context of national income accounting.

Types of Investment

Investment is of *three* main types:

1. Business fixed investment;

2. Inventory investment; and
3. Residential investment.

In this chapter we discuss the nature and determinants of the first two types of investment. We leave aside residential investment.

BUSINESS FIXED INVESTMENT

Business fixed investment refers to purchase or acquisition of new capital goods by business in the form of machines, tools, equipment, etc. for further production of goods and services. Since capital goods are durable goods, purchase of capital goods comes under the heading 'fixed investment.' The term 'fixed investment' implies that investment goods can be used in production for a fairly long period of time. By contrast inventories are held for short periods of time since production and sale do not coincide.

INVENTORY INVESTMENT

Although inventory investment is a very small part of total business investment, it is of considerable importance to the economy of a country because fluctuations of such investment cause business cycles.

That investment is the most volatile component of GDP is true. But it is not the whole truth. In a brief recession,[1] more than 50% of the fall in investment spending of the firms is due to a sharp decline in inventory investment.

Inventory investment tends to be closely related to changes in production. When higher levels of output are being produced, there are more goods in the pipeline. Filling up the pipeline to the higher level requires more inventory investment. Consequently, years of rapid GDP growth tend to be years of high inventory investment.

The name 'acceleration' model is derived from the fact that ΔY is the 'acceleration' of production. If Y (the rate of output) is high but is not increasing there will be no acceleration of investment. This means that inventory investment depends on the phase of the business cycle, i.e., whether the economy is speeding up or slowing down. The acceleration effect is very strong for inventory investment, because lags are less important for inventories than for fixed investment. The acceleration model explains a large proportion of the movements in investment. It partly accounts for the close association between investment and GDP. [We will discuss the principle again in this chapter in the context of fixed asset investment.]

AUTONOMOUS VS INDUCED INVESTMENT

Modern economists often draw a distinction between autonomous and induced investment. Keynes treated all investment as autonomous. Keynes ignored the concept of induced investment, because he was essentially concerned with the short-run problems of the macroeconomy. In his view, changes in national income affect investment only in the long run with which he was not concerned.

Autonomous investment refers to that investment which has no relation to national income or its rate of change. It depends on the expected rate of return on new investment and the cost of borrowing funds. So a fixed level of autonomous investment takes place at all levels of income as shown in panel (a) of Fig. 13.1. By contrast, any investment which depends on national income or its rate of change is called induced investment. Such investment increases with an increase in national income or real GDP, as shown in Panel (b) of Fig. 13.1. We see that if national income increases by ΔY induced investment increases by ΔI_i. The slope of the induced investment demand schedule (I_i) is ratio of the two absolute changes and is called the marginal propensity to invest (*MPI*).

1. It may be noted that during recession, inventory investment becomes zero or even negative because firms do not replenish their inventory as goods are sold.

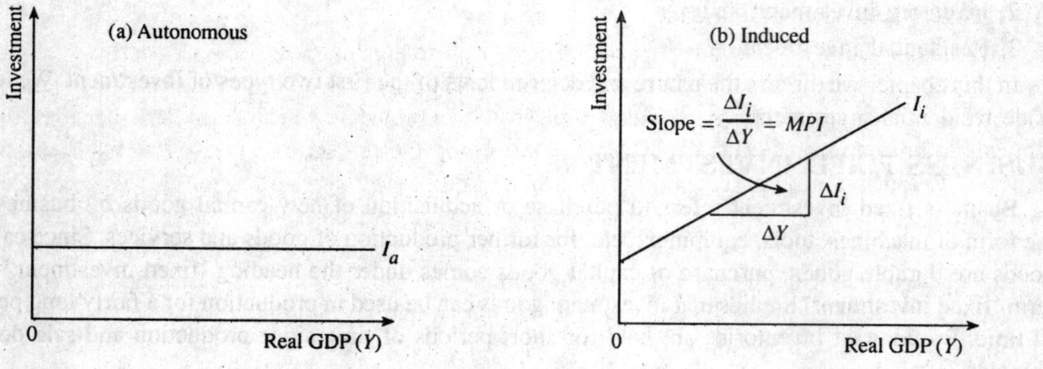

Fig. 13.1: Autonomous and Induced Investment

From the concept of induced investment, A. Aftalion and J. M. Clark have developed the accelerator theory or the acceleration principle of investment even before the publication of Keynes's revolutionary book in 1936.

Investment which depends on all other variables except national income (or its rate of change) is called autonomous investment while investment which depends on national income is called induced investment

Autonomous investment refers to investment expenditure which is not induced by changes in output. Examples of such investments are (a) government expenditure on infrastructure and (b) firms' expenditure on new plants to exploit an invention. 'Autonomous' means independent of income.

By contrast, induced investment depends on the rate of change of sales or of output of a firm. Thus if the demand for bread in India increases, the production of bread will become more profitable. Therefore bakers will buy more ovens. After all the demand for capital goods is derived (indirect) demand. Since capital goods are the creators of consumption goods, an increase in the demand for consumer goods will lead to an increase in demand for capital goods or investment demand.

DETERMINANTS OF FIXED INVESTMENT

Regarding determinants of fixed investment there are two theories, viz., the Keynesian theory and the neo-classical theory. These two theories may now be discussed one by one.

The Keynesian Theory of Investment

According to Keynes, investment depends on two main factors, viz., the expected rate of return on new investment or the marginal efficiency of capital (*MEC*) and the interest rate (*r*). Investment varies directly with *MEC* and inversely with *r*. So long as *MEC* > *r*, *I* will increase. However, as *I* increases, *MEC* will fall for two reasons: (i) an increase in the price of capital goods (such as machines) due to greater demand for such goods and (ii) a fall in the price of consumption goods due to an increase in the production and supply of such goods made possible by additional investment. At this stage we start with the Keynesian theory of investment.

According to the classical theory there are three determinants of business investment, viz., (i) cost, (ii) return and (iii) expectations. According to Keynes investment decisions are taken by comparing the marginal efficiency of capital (*MEC*) or the yield with the real rate of interest (*r*). So long as the *MEC* is greater than *r*, new investment in plant, equipment and machinery will take place. However, as more and more capital is used in the production process, the *MEC* will fall due to diminishing marginal product of capital. As soon as *MEC* is equated to *r*, no new investment will be made in any income-earning asset.

Marginal Efficiency of Capital

The *MEC* is the rate of discount which equates the present value of a series of cash flows obtainable from an income-earning asset like a machine over its entire economic life to the cost of the machine. The *MEC* is the rate of return at which a project is expected to break-even. This depends on the immediate profits (cash flows) expected from operating the project and the rate at which these are expected to decline through reduction in the price of output, or increases in the real wages or cost of raw materials and fuel. If all possible projects in an economy are arranged in descending order of their *MEC*, investors will accept those with *MEC* higher than *r* and reject those whose *MEC* is lower than *r*. The *MEC* is not the same as the marginal product of capital which is concerned only with the immediate effect of additional capital on possible output and not with how long the resulting profits can be expected to persist.

The *MEC* is the rate of return (profits) on an extra rupee worth of investment. The marginal efficiency of capital decreases as the amount of investment increases (as shown in Fig. 13.2). This is because initial investments are concentrated on the 'best' opportunities and yield high rates of return; later investments are less productive and generate less and less returns.

The amount of investment undertaken depends not only on expected returns but also on the cost of capital, that is, the interest rate. Investment will be profitable up to the point where the marginal efficiency of capital is equal to the cost of capital[1]. In Fig. 13.2 at an interest rate of 20% only $0I_1$ amount of investment is worthwhile. A fall in the interest rate to 10% increases the amount of profitable investment to $0I_2$.

It will be readily apparent from Fig. 13.2 that there is a link between the monetary side of the economy and the real economy: a fall in interest rate will stimulate more investment, which, in its turn, will result in a higher level of national income.

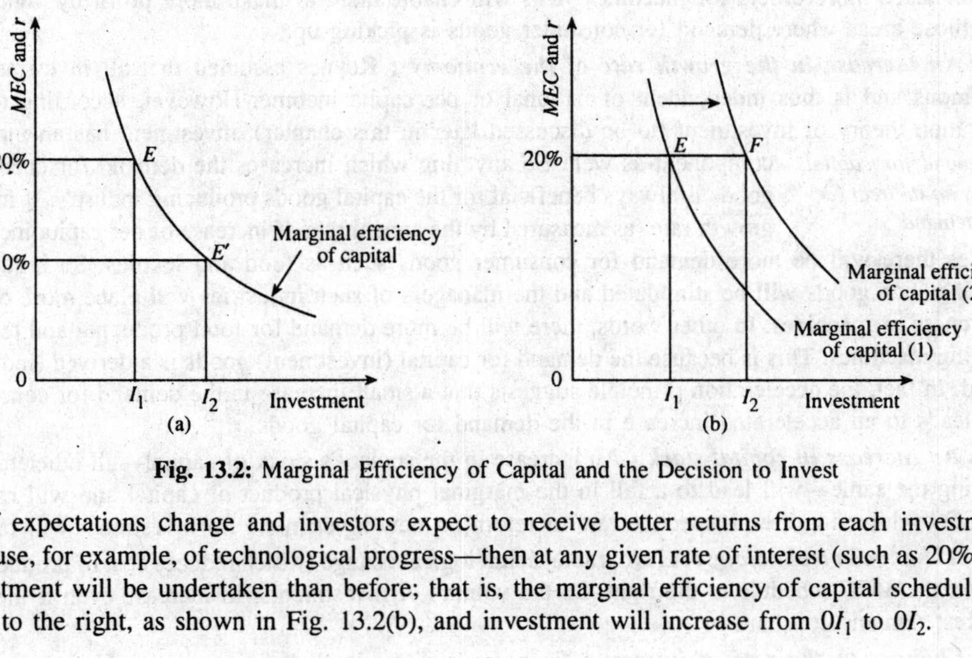

Fig. 13.2: Marginal Efficiency of Capital and the Decision to Invest

If expectations change and investors expect to receive better returns from each investment—because, for example, of technological progress—then at any given rate of interest (such as 20%) more investment will be undertaken than before; that is, the marginal efficiency of capital schedule[2] will shift to the right, as shown in Fig. 13.2(b), and investment will increase from $0I_1$ to $0I_2$.

---

1. If the supply price of capital goods changes over time it becomes necessary to draw a distinction between the marginal efficiency of capital (*MEC*) and marginal efficiency of investment (*MEI*).
2. Note that the *MEC* schedule is also known as the investment demand schedule.

The *MEC* is calculated by using the following formula:

$$C = \frac{R_1}{(1+e)} + \frac{R_2}{(1+e)^2} + \ldots\ldots + \frac{R_n}{(1+e)^n} \quad \ldots (1)$$

where C is the initial purchase price of the machine, R_1, R_2, etc. are the expected cash flows from the machine in the first, second and subsequent years and e is the *MEC* which acts as the balancing factor. It makes the two sides of the above equation equal. Here R_n is the expected cash flow from the machine in the last year which also includes the scrap value of the machine. It may be noted that e varies directly with r and inversely with C, i.e., the initial cost of purchasing the machine.

A simple method of calculating e for an infinitely durable capital good is available. In this case the economic life of the machine (which depends on the annual rate of depreciation) is not known. By little manipulation of equation (3) we get

$$e = \frac{R}{C} \quad \ldots (2)$$

The term R is called by Keynes the expected (prospective) rate of return on new investment (the machine) and C is the purchase price of the machine. If e exceeds r, an income-earning asset like a machine should be purchased or a project should be undertaken.

Factors Determining Investment

Anything which increases a firm's profit prospects by increasing R will increase its level of investment. On the other hand, if the purchase price of capital (C_0) increases, investment will fall. The following factors affect a firm's investment decisions:

(i) *Increased optimism among managers* : If business managers are more optimist about the future, they will place more orders for machines. This will enable them to make more profit by venturing out in those areas where demand for consumer goods is picking up.

(ii) *An increase in the growth rate of the economy* : Keynes assumed that all investment is autonomous and is thus independent of national or per capita income. However, according to the acceleration theory of investment (to be discussed later in this chapter), investment has an induced component as well. So anything which increases the demand for consumer goods is always beneficial for the capital goods producing industry. If India's growth rate (as measured by the annual rate of increase of per capita income) increases there will be more demand for consumer goods such as food and textiles. So industries producing such goods will be stimulated and the managers of such industries will place more orders for purchase of machines. In other words, there will be more demand for food-producing and textile-producing machines. This is because the demand for capital (investment) goods is a derived (indirect) demand. In fact, the acceleration principle suggests that a small increase in the demand for consumer goods leads to an accelerated increase in the demand for capital goods.

The demand for capital goods is an indirect (derived) demand

(iii) *An increase in capital stock* : An increase in the society's stock of capital—all other factors remaining the same—will lead to a fall in the marginal physical product of capital and will reduce the MEC by lowering the prospective rate of return on new investment. So investment will fall.

(iv) *A change in technology* : A favourable technological change (which reduces cost of production) will shift the *MEC* schedule to the right. So the volume of investment will increase even if the rate of interest remains constant.

(v) *Changes in the rate of interest* : Economists differ in their views about the interest rate sensitivity of investment. Some Keynesian economists argue that investment depends largely upon expected return and is not much sensitive to interest rate changes. This means that even large changes in interest rates have little effect upon investment (the marginal efficiency of capital curve being very steep). Thus the Keynesian economists claim that monetary policy will not be very effective in influencing the level of aggregate investment in the economy. In contrast the monetarists like Milton Friedman argue that investment is very much interest rate-sensitive. So even small changes in interest rates will have significant impact upon investment (the marginal efficiency of capital curve being quite flat). Thus, monetarists claim that monetary policy will be effective in influencing the level of investment. Empirical evidence tends to support the Keynesian view that interest rates have only a limited effect on investment.

However, the neo-classical economists such as Dale Jorgenson and his co-workers have abandoned the classical and the Keynesian theories of investment on the ground that both are unrealistic. They have developed an alternative theory of investment in terms of the profit-maximising behaviour of a firm under perfect competition. It is to this theory to which we will turn later in this chapter.

Synopsis for Learning: The Rate of Interest and Investment
A fall in the rate of interest will increase investment if investment demand is interest elastic. But this may not happen if *MEC* is lower than the rate of interest as is found in times of depression.

MOVEMENT VS. SHIFT OF THE INVESTMENT DEMAND SCHEDULE

Two points may be noted in this context. If *MEC* remains constant, but interest rate (r) falls, more fixed investment will take pace. In this case there will be movement along the *MEC* or investment demand schedule as shown in panel (a) of Fig. 13.3. This means that those projects which were not profitable earlier will now appear to be profitable. So firms will now accept those projects which were rejected earlier at a high rate of interest.

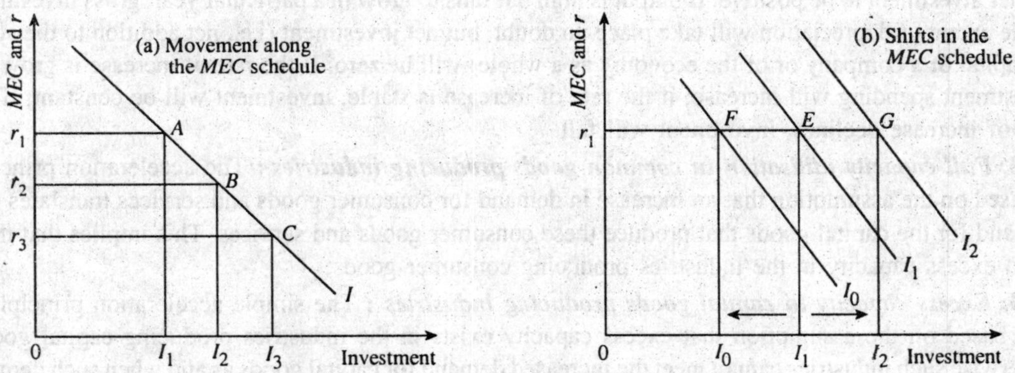

Fig. 13.3: Movement along the MEC Schedule and Shift of the Schedule

However, if, for some reasons, such as a fall in the supply price of capital goods or an increase in the profitability of new investment, *MEC* increases, the *MEC* schedule itself will shift to the right from I_1 to I_2 as shown in panel (b) and more fixed investment will take place even at the same rate of interest r_1. The converse is also true. If, for some reasons, the *MEC* falls and the *MEC* schedule shifts to the left from I_1 to I_0, less fixed investment will take place even at the same rate of interest (r_1).

In the short run, since r is sticky, investment depends more on *MEC* than on r. The reason is that *MEC* depends on business firm's expectations about future profitability of projects and such expectations keep on changing from time to time. This is why *MEC* is volatile and investment may fall sharply if *MEC* suddenly falls. While studying sensibility of investment, economists drew a distinction between marginal efficiency of capital and marginal efficiency of investment. We may discuss this issue in detail.

THE ACCELERATION PRINCIPLE

The acceleration principle refers to the relationship between increase in total output and the additional investment spending that occurs due to such output (income) increase. The theory postulates that the level of aggregate net investment depends on the expected change in output. The theory hypothesises that firms attempt to maintain a fixed ratio of desired capital stock to expected output. The principle states that an increase in income or output leads to an accelerated increase in investment. The acceleration principle is essentially a theory of investment which holds that the level of investment is accelerated only through the rate of increase in output (that is, gross domestic product or GDP). If GDP increases in period t, then net investment will increase by some fractional amount in period $t + 1$. Thus, net investment = accelerator × change in GDP. The acceleration effect is a kind of 'second round' multiplier that is directly linked to changes in investment spending brought on by the 'first-round' multiplier effect. In short, the acceleration principle explains why the increase in national income often results in a more than proportionate increase in investment spending and why the amount of investment spending depends not on the absolute level of business activity but on whether that level is increasing or decreasing.

Assumptions

The acceleration principle is based on the four assumptions:

1. *Proportional relation* : Investment is proportional to output or sale of consumer goods.

2. *Rate of change of output* : Investment depends not on the absolute level of output or demand but on the rate of increase in national income or in total demand. So it is not enough for national output (income) or sales level to be high. The level of output or sales must keep on increasing year after year for net investment to be positive. If output is high but fails to grow in a particular year, gross investment to the extent of depreciation will take place no doubt, but net investment (i.e., net addition to the stock of capital of a company or of the economy as a whole) will be zero. If the rate of increase is growing, investment spending will increase; if the rate of increase is stable, investment will be constant; if the rate of increase declines, investment will fall.

3. *Full capacity utilisation in common goods producing industries* : The acceleration principle is based on the assumption that an increase in demand for consumer goods and services translates into demand for the capital goods that produce these consumer goods and services. This implies that there is no excess capacity in the industries producing consumer goods.

4. *Excess capacity in capital goods producing industries* : The simple acceleration principle is also based on the assumption that excess capacity exists in the industries producing capital goods. Otherwise such industries cannot meet the increased demand for capital goods as and when such demand is created by the industries producing consumer goods.

Definition

The acceleration principle refers to the relationship between increases in total output and the additional investment spending that such increases encourage or induce. In brief, it explains why an increase in national output (income) often results in a proportionately larger increase in investment spending and why the amount of investment spending depends not on the absolute level of business activity but on whether that level is increasing or decreasing.

The acceleration principle refers to the accelerated effect on investment of a small change in demand for (output of) consumption goods

The Working of the Principle

The accelerator principle can work in both directions. As P. A. Samuelson puts it: "If sales fall below a certain level, gross investment may be zero for a long time; in fact, the firm might want to disinvest by selling off some of its machinery. On the contrary a tremendous increase in investment spending is possible as a result of a moderate increase in consumption sales." According to this principle, consumption has to keep on increasing for net investment to occur.

An example will help explain how the principle works. The accelerator is best explained if we assume that investment takes place both for replacement and for expansion. The example given below in Table 13.1 shows that (induced) investment depends on changes in output.

We assume that *the capital-output ratio* is 2 : 1, i.e., two units of capital are required to produce one unit of output. If the rate of output of a firm, say, is 50 units per year, 100 units of capital would be required to produce it. We also assume that 10 units of capital would have to be replaced each year. From year 3, however, the output rate goes up as shown. As output increases, new capital is required. Here when output increases by 20% from 50 to 60 between periods 2 and 3, gross investment demand increases by 200% from 10 to 30. Similarly, between periods 5 and 6, there is no increase in output. So gross investment drops down by 75% from 40 to 10. The name acceleration principle is given since net investment depends upon the *acceleration* or *deceleration* of output.

The acceleration principle bears out the fact that fluctuations in industries supplying capital goods are much greater than in the industries producing consumer goods. This is because the level of investment depends not on the absolute level of demand but on its rate of change. So investment may fall even when absolute demand is rising if the rate at which demand is increasing begins to fall.

Table 13.1: An Illustration of the Acceleration Principle

Year	Expected output (units)	Capital required (Rs.)	Replacement of old capital	Net investment (Rs.)	Gross investment (Rs.)
1	50	100	10	0	10
2	50	100	10	0	10
3	60	120	10	20	30
4	70	140	10	20	30
5	85	170	10	30	40
6	85	170	10	0	10

It is important to note also that investment is proportional to the change in total output. Given the change in total output, the amount of investment required can be calculated by multiplying the change in output by the capital-output ratio or the accelerator (also called the acceleration coefficient).

THE ACCELERATOR

A key element of the acceleration principle is the acceleration coefficient or the *accelerator*. This shows the amount of additional capital stock required to produce a unit increase in output. This is the coefficient which relates the level of investment to the change in output/sales. Thus, if I_t is investment in period t, and Y_t, Y_{t-1} are output or sales in periods t and $t - 1$, respectively, then we have: $I_t = v(Y_t - Y_{t-1})$, where v is the acceleration coefficient. Thus the value of v tells us strength of the effect that a change in output or sales will have on the level of investment. In our example of Table 13.1 when output increases from 50 to 60 and investment from 10 to 30 we have

$$I_t = v(Y_t - Y_{t-1})$$
$$\text{or, } 20 = v(10)$$
$$\text{or, } v = 2.$$

Note that v is also called *the incremental capital-output ratio* which is fixed over time.[1]

Since the value of v is greater than one there can occur a tremendous increase in investment expenditure caused by a moderate (marginal) increase in consumption spending. And it is a powerful factor causing economic instability, or business cycle(s).

1. Alternatively we can write this as $K_t - K_{t-1} = v(Q_t - Q_{t-1})$ where Q stands for output or sales. Or, $\Delta K_t = v(\Delta Q_t)$ or, $v = \Delta K/\Delta Q_t$, i.e., the incremental capital-output ratio.

As noted above the acceleration principle can work in both directions. If sales of the firm now drop below a certain level, gross investment would drop away to nothing for a long time; in fact, the firm might want to disinvest by selling off some of its machinery. On the contrary, a tremendous increase in investment spending is possible as a result of moderate increase in consumption sales. According to the acceleration principle, consumption has to keep on increasing period after period in order for net investment to be positive.

The simple accelerator, which is illustrated in Table 13.1, relates the level of *net investment* to the *rate of change* of output.[1] According to the simple accelerator with output growing continuously net additions to the capital stock are required. For net investment to take place at a *uniform level* over time, the rate of growth of output must stay constant. As soon as it declines, even if it remains positive, investment falls.

The acceleration principle also emphasises the extreme volatility of investment as compared with other components of aggregate demand. A simple example will make the point clear.

Qualifications

The acceleration principle is not free from defects. While criticising the principle both from the conceptual and practical points of view, the following qualifications have been suggested by modern economists:

(i) *Excess capacity* : Firms sometimes have excess production capacity. In such cases, it is unlikely that they will purchase new equipment as soon as there is an increase in demand. Firms are more likely to utilise any excess capacity fully before undertaking new investment to meet any increase in demand for their product.

(ii) *Time lag* : In certain circumstances, the capital goods supplying industries may not be able to respond immediately to increases in demand for capital goods. Investment may therefore be delayed. The reason is that such industries are characterised by delivery lags.

(iii) *Business outlook* : If the general business outlook is optimistic, businesses will be more inclined to think that an output increase will be permanent and will therefore be more inclined to invest, given the same output change, than if the business outlook is pessimistic.

(iv) *Capacity limits* : When a rapid rise in output leads to large planned investment, there are often physical limits to the rate at which actual investment can take place. The industries which produce capital goods themselves have capacity constraints.

(v) *Profits* : The accelerator principle, however, only provides a partial explanation of investment demand. Investment is also governed by present and future profits. Future profits are the main rationale behind investment and thus get much weight in the evaluation of new investment projects. It seems that any analysis of investment demand must include both profits and the acceleration principle, or some variant of it. Business firms usually prefer to expand internally, by using their own funds (i.e., retained profits). Therefore, we could expect profits to be a factor in the determination of investment. Investment usually varies directly with profits.

(vi) *Inventories* : Business investment in plant and equipment mainly depends on profit prospects and the rate of interest at which money is borrowed to purchase an asset. However, as noted above, usually inventory investment—i.e., investment in stocks of goods held by business to even out delivery and sales—varies proportionately with sales and output and, thus, fits the simple accelerator model quite well.

(vii) *Asymmetry* : The accelerator principle is asymmetric in its operation. When output falls, it cannot work in the same way it does when output rises.

1. Investment is change in capital stock. However, net investment means increase in capital stock over and above the requirement for depreciation. Thus gross investment = net investment + depreciation, or net investment = gross investment – depreciation.

(viii) *Learning from experience* : Business people often learn from experience. The implication is that they are unlikely to double their installed production capacity on the strength of one year's orders. On the contrary, if demand is falling, they might be willing to increase their inventories against a rise in demand in subsequent years.

(ix) *Capital-output ratio* : The capital-output ratio does not remain constant as assumed here. If demand rose it might be possible to obtain more output from the existing capital stock by varying other factors of production. For example, workers might undertake shift work or overtime to meet the extra demand. In such situation the capital-output ratio would fall.

(x) *Depreciation* : Apart from time, replacement of the capital stock may be a function of other factors as well. Suppose the rate of depreciation is 20% per annum, i.e., capital wears out after five years. Now if there is an increase in demand it may be possible to continue using old capital equipment even after it was decided to scrap it. Often the period over which a machine is depreciated is an accounting convenience and does not correspond to the physical life of the machine. Conversely, a machine or any capital good may become obsolete due to technologial progress even before it has physically depreciated.

(xi) *Other types of investment* : Moreover, the accelerator only applies to net or 'new' investment resulting from changes in national income or output. There are other forms of investment such as replacement investment and investment in new techniques or on research and development (R & D) which have no relation to GNP or its rate of change.

In short, the acceleration principle links the rate of change of aggregate demand to the level of new investment demand. And the principle works in both the directions. Just as a small increase in consumption demand leads to an accelerated increase in investment, a small drop in (or even a levelling-off of) sales leads to an accelerated drop in investment.

However, as R. G. Lipsey has pointed out, "the main insight which the accelerator theory provides is the emphasis on the role of net investment as a disequilibrium phenomenon — something that occurs when the stock of capital differs from what firms and households would like it to be".

Three general predictions of which can be made for the acceleration principle are the following:

1. For net investment to take place sales must rise rather than remain unchanged even at high levels.
2. For net investment to remain constant, sales must be rising by a constant amount every year.
3. The amount of net investment will be a multiple of the increase in sales because the accelerator is greater than one.

THE NEO-CLASSICAL THEORY OF INVESTMENT

The modern approach to business investment is based on Dale Jorgenson's approach known as the neo-classical model of investment. Jorgenson's model provides the micro-foundation of the social investment function. For analysical convenience, we classify an economy's firms into two broad categories, viz., (i) production firms that produce goods and services using capital owned by other firms by paying lease rental and (ii) rental firms, which buy capital and lease (rent) it to the producing units.

The Rental Price of Capital

The focus of attention in Jorgenson's model is on the typical production firm. The firm, operating in a pure competitive model, is guided by the neo-classical marginalist rule of profit maximisation. The key concept in the neo-classical model is the rental price of capital. A profit-seeking firm compares the cost and benefit of each unit of capital while taking decision on how much of capital to lease in by paying a fixed rental per period. Let us, for instance, take the case of a construction company which has got the contract to build a multi-storeyed house within a year's time. It requires an earthmoving equipment for three months. There is no point in buying this machine at a high cost. It gains by hiring this machine from another company (the rental firm) by paying a lease rental. The rental price of capital is the periodic payment that has to be made by the construction company to the leasing firm (which specialises in leasing out the machine) for a certain period to hire the earthmoving equipment. The construction company obtains the equipment by paying a rental of *R* per period and it sells its output at a price of *P*. So the real cost of a unit of capital to the production firm is *R/P*. The real benefit of a unit of capital to a producing firm is its marginal product. The marginal product of capital (*MPK*) is the addition made to the total product of the firm by one extra unit of real capital. So long as the *MPK* exceeds the rental price of capital, a firm makes extra profit by hiring and using an extra unit of capital. However, as more and more capital is used, *MPK* falls and a production firm maximises profit by equating *MPK* with the real rental price. In other words, a profit-maximising firm rents capital up to the point where the *MPK* continues to fall and ultimately becomes to equal to the real rental price.

Economic Insight: Three Determinants of Equilibrium Rental Price

There are three determinants of equilibrium real rental price of capital, viz., (1) the stock of capital; (2) the amount of labour employed; and (3) the state of technology. This point may be explained by referring to the Cobb-Douglas production

$$Y = AK\alpha L\beta$$

where *Y* is output, *K* is capital, *L* is labour, *A* is a parameter measuring the level of technology (called efficiency parameter) and α is a parameter between zero and one that measures capital's share of output. The marginal product of capital is

$$MPK = \alpha A(L/K)\beta.$$

In equilibrium the real rental price equals the *MPK*. So we get

$$R/P = \alpha A(L/K)\beta$$

From this equation, it is quite obvious that

1. The lower the stock of capital, the higher is *R/P*.
2. The greater the amount of labour employed, the higher is *R/P*.
3. The more improved the technology, the higher is *R/P*.

So it logically follows, that anything which reduces society's stock of capital (such as a war or a natural calamity such as an earthquake), or increases the level of employment (such as an increase in the level of aggregate demand), or improvement in technology (a scientific discovery) will have a favourable effect on the equilibrium *R/P*.

Fig. 13.4 shows the equilibrium in the rental market for capital. The demand curve of capital is *MPK* curve. It slopes downward from left to right because as more and more units of capital are used *MPK* falls. In other words, *MPK* is low when the level of capital is high. The aggregate supply of real capital remains fixed in the short run. So the supply curve of capital indicating the amount of capital available in the economy (per period) is a vertical straight line. The real rental price of capital is $(R/P)_0$. This is indeed the equilibrium rental price because it is the rate which brings the demand for capital (determined by *MPK*) in line with the fixed supply.

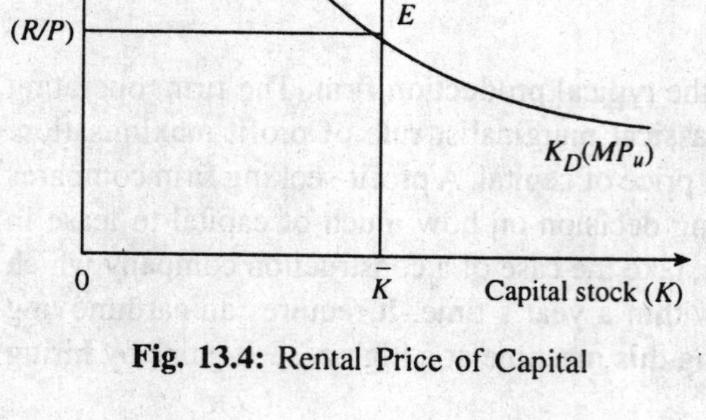

Fig. 13.4: Rental Price of Capital

The Cost of Capital

The benefit of the rental firm from owning capital is the revenue it gets from renting it to the production firms. It receives the real rental price of capital R/P for each unit of capital it owns and rents out.

There are three types of costs owning and renting out a unit of capital:

1. *Interest on loan* : When a rental firm borrows funds to buy a unit of capital for the purpose of renting it out, it has to pay interest on the loan. The interest cost iP_K where i is the nominal interest rate and P_K is the purchase price (acquisition cost) of a unit of capital.

2. *Capital loss* : It is quite possible for the price of capital (the firm is renting out) to fall, in which case it loses. The reason is that the market value of the firm's capital has fallen. The cost of this loss is $-\Delta P_K$.

3. *Depreciation* : The rate of depreciatin of capital is another component of the cost of owning and renting out real capital. The rate of depreciation (d) is measured by the proportion of value of the capital lost per period due to wear and tear, i.e., dP_K.

So the total cost of renting out a unit of capital for one period is thus:

$$\text{Cost of capital} = iP_K - \Delta P_K = P_K(i - \Delta P_K/P_K + d) \qquad \ldots (1)$$

So there are four determinants of cost of capital, viz., P_K, i, the rate at which P_K is changing and d. We put a negative sign before $\Delta P_K/P_K$ because P_K is assumed to be falling.

If we make the assumption that the price of capital goods rises with the price of other goods, as is the case during inflation, then $\Delta P_K/P_K$ is interpreted as the overall rate of inflation π. Since the real rate of interest (r) is the nominal rate of interest (i) less the rate of inflation (π), the cost of capital is

$$\text{Cost of capital} = P_K(i - p + d) = P_K(r + d) \qquad \ldots (2)$$

So there are three determinants of the cost of capital, viz., P_K, r and d.

The real cost of capital is written as

$$\text{Real cost of capital} = (P_K/P)\ (r + d) \qquad \ldots (3)$$

where P is the overall price index. It is the weighted average of all prices. Equation (3) expresses the cost of capital relative to other goods in the economy. The real cost of capital is the cost of acquiring and leasing out a unit of capital measured in units of GDP and has three determinants, viz., P_K/P, the relative price of capital goods, r and d.

THE DETERMINANTS OF INVESTMENT

Since all economic decisions are taken at the margin a rental firm, whose objective is profit maximisation, has to take decisions regarding whether to increase or decrease its capital stock on the basis of its own benefit-cost analysis. By renting out each unit of capital, the firm earns revenue R/P and incurs the real cost $(P_K/P)\ (r + d)$. So its real profit per unit of capital or the rate of profit is

$$\pi = R/P - (P_K/P)\ (r + d) \qquad \ldots (4)$$

Rate of profit = Real revenue from capital – real cost of capital.

Since the real rental price of capital equals the MPK, in equilibrium, the rate of profit may be expressed as:

$$\text{Profit rate} = MPK - (P_K/P)\ (r + d)$$

The rental firm makes a profit if MPK exceeds the real cost of capital. The converse is also true.

Net investment refers to absolute change in the capital stock of a firm ($I = \Delta K = K_t - K_{t-1}$). Equation (4) suggests that investment decision of the rental firm, i.e., decisions regarding whether to add to its capital stock or allow it to wear out completely depends on whether owning and leasing out capital is a profitable proposition. So long as MPK exceeds $(P_K/P)\ (r + d)$, firms find it profitable to make net investment, i.e., add to their existing stock of capital. The converse is also true. If MPK is less than $(P_K/P)\ (r + d)$ the firm will not care about even its existing stock of capital and just allow it to depreciate and shrink.

THE INVESTMENT FUNCTION

What is true for a firm that owns and rents out capital is equally true for a firm that both uses and owns capital. So we can write

$$\Delta K = I_n[MPK - (P_K/P)\ (r + d) \quad \ldots \quad (5)$$

where I_n depends on or is a function of the difference between the MPK and the real cost of capital which shows how much net investment responds to the incentive to invest. There is an incentive to invest if $MPK > (P_K/P)\ (r + d)$.

The investment function is

$$I = I_n[MP_K - (P_K/P)\ (r + d)] + dK \quad \ldots \quad (6)$$

where I is gross investment which is equal to net investment I_n plus depreciation dK. Thus total spending on business fixed investment depends on MPK, the real cost of capital and the amount of depreciation (i.e., the rate of depreciation times the amount of capital).

RELATION BETWEEN INVESTMENT AND INTEREST RATE

There is a close relation between investment and interest rate. A fall in the real rate of interest reduces the cost of capital and thus provides an extra incentive to accumulate more capital by raising the amount of profit from owning capital. The converse is also true. Firms reduce their investment when profitability falls due to a rise in real rate of interest which raises the real cost of capital. Thus there is an inverse relation between the real rate of interest (r) and the volume of investment.

Fig. 13.5(a) shows that business fixed investment increases when r falls. The reason is easy to find out. A lower rate of interest reduces the cost of capital and therefore makes it more profitable to own and use extra units of capital.

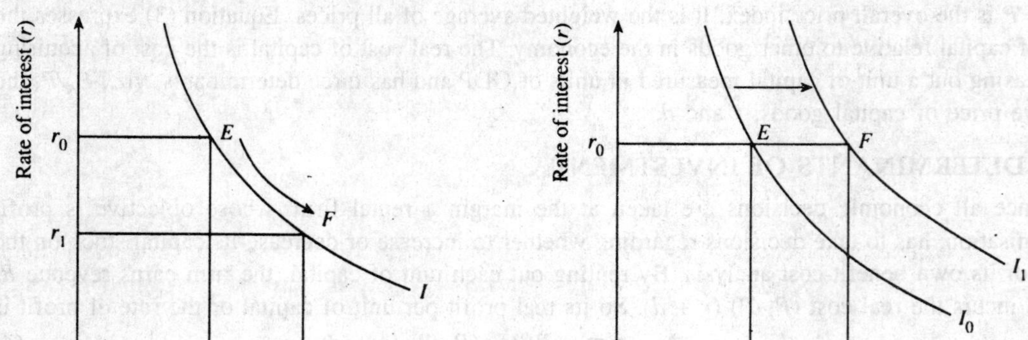

Fig. 13.5: Interest Rate and Investment

SHIFT OF THE INVESTMENT SCHEDULE

Any favourable development in the economy which raises the MPK increases the profitability of investment and causes the investment schedule of Fig. 13.5(b) I_0 to shift to the right to I_1. This implies that more investment takes place at the same real rate of interest. For example, a favourable technological change that raises the MPK increases the amount of capital goods that lease-renting firms' desire to buy at the same real rate of interest.

INTERTEMPORAL ADJUSTMENT OF CAPITAL STOCK

If *MPK* is initially above the real cost of capital, the capital stock will rise and the *MPK* will fall. If *MPK* is initially below the real cost of capital, the capital stock will fall and *MPK* will rise. So, ultimately as the capital stock adjusts, the *MPK* approaches the real cost of capital and the steady-state level of capital is expressed as:

$$MPK = (P_K/P)\ (r + d)$$

Since total profit from capital is maximum (constant) and marginal profit is zero, no addition is made to society's stock of capital, i.e.,

$$\Delta K = I = 0$$

because $MPK - (P_K/P)\ (r + d) = 0$. So there is no incentive to make further investment in fixed capital. Thus in the long run when the adjustment of capital stock continues over time *MPK* equals the real cost of capital. The speed of adjustment toward the steady state depends on the speed with which firms adjust their capital stock. This, in its turn, depends on the cost of building, delivering and installing new capital.

THE IMPACT OF INFLATION ON INVESTMENT

Investment decisions are largely influenced by the real rate of interest, if *MEC* remains constant. The real rate of interest(r) is written as:

$$r = i - \pi^e$$

where i is the nominal rate of interest and π^e is the expected rate of inflation. Thus if i remains constant as also the *MEC* or the investment demand schedule, the real rate of interest will fall if the rate of inflation increases. As a result the volume of investment will increase.

Much depends on whether inflation is anticipated by the economic agents or not. In case of unanticipated inflation, nominal wages lag behind prices. So real wages fall and profits increase. The rise in business profits stimulates investment. Unanticipated inflation promotes investment further by lowering real rate of interest.

On the other hand since unanticipated inflation redistributes income in favour of capitalists and against workers aggregate demand for goods and services is likely to fall. This will lead to a fall in *MEC* by reducing profit prospects and a fall in the volume of investment.

However, if inflation is anticipated by workers, money wages will be adjusted appropriately so as to keep real wages constant so new investment is unlikely to take place. Moreover since nominal interest gets adjusted to inflation, the real rate of interest remains unchanged. Thus new investment does not take place.

Investment may even fall for two reasons. Since rapid inflation acts as a disincentive to save, the supply of loanable funds will fall and the rate of interest will rise. The shortage of loanable funds will raise the cost of credit. Investment is bound to fall since credit becomes more costly and less readily available.

Secondly, in times of inflation people buy unproductive assets like gold, jewellery or even luxury goods like diamonds, costly cars, etc. Thus the potential saving of the community is converted into unproductive consumption, mainly luxury goods.

THE EFFECT OF MONETARY POLICY ON INVESMENT

The government of a country can stimulate investment by adopting expansionary monetary and fiscal policies. By reducing the bank rate, the central bank can reduce the cost of credit and by reducing CRR or SLR the central bank can increase the availability of credit. Any of these measures is likely to increase investment, assuming that *MEC* remains constant. However, the extent to which investment increases in response to a fall in the market rate of interest (due to a fall in the bank rate) depends on the interest elasticity of investment. If such elasticity is high, a small drop in the rate of interest will lead to a large increase in investment. The converse is also true.

This point is illustrated in Fig. 13.6. In panel (a) we see that an increase in the money supply shifts the money supply curve right from M_s to $M's$. As a result the rate of interest falls from r_0 to r_1. In panel (b), we see that the fall in the rate of interest from r_0 to r_1 increases the volume of investment from I_0 to I_2 along the investment demand schedule I from E' to F'. However, if the investment demand schedule is less elastic (I') investment will not increase that much. It will increase from I_0 to I_1 (point G').

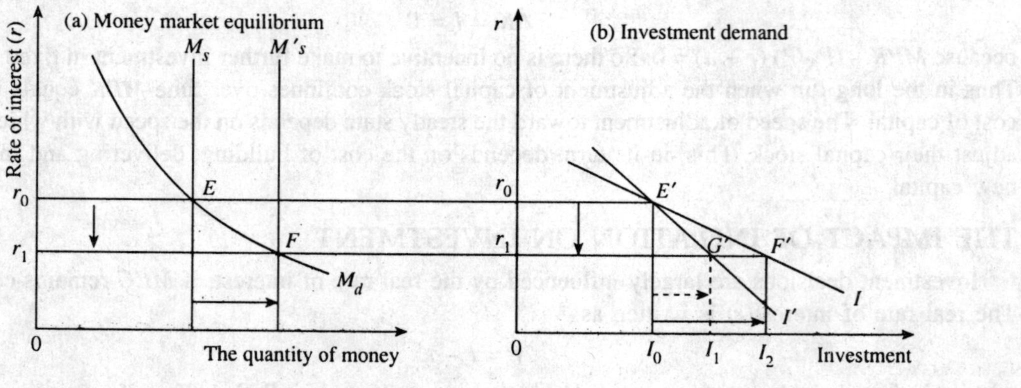

Fig. 13.6: Interest Rate-Investment Linkage

However, Keynes pointed out that monetary policy does not work in times of economic depression due to the existence of liquidity trap. Due to liquidity trap situation no change in the money supply can lead to a fall in the rate of interest. As a result new investment will not occur. However, empirical evidence in support of liquidity trap is weak.

Economic Insight: Liquidity Trap
Liquidity trap refers to a situation in which the real rate of interest cannot be reduced by any action of the central bank. Such a situation arises if the price level is expected to fall, i.e., if there is deflation. If the price level is expected to fall, holding money (cash balance) will generate real gain equal to the expected rate of deflation. The real rate of interest cannot be reduced beyond the point at which the nominal interest rate falls to zero, just by increasing the money supply even by a large amount. The central bank is thus unable to promote investment by cutting real interest rate(s), even if investment is likely to respond to such a move by the central bank.

THE EFFECT OF FISCAL POLICY ON INVESTMENT

An expansionary fiscal policy adversely affects investment in two ways. Firstly government borrowing to finance its expenditure generates crowding out effect. Government spending on public works might use scarce funds and divert them from private projects and raise interest rates. A rise in interest rate chokes off investment demand. Crowding-in occurs through favourable effects of an increase in government expenditure on infrastructure financed by printing new currency which increases the confidence of private investors. Thus a crowding-in effect is likely to occur, if investment tax credit is provided. This type of fiscal boost has increased investment in the USA and other advanced countries in the past by a huge amount. A cut in corporation income tax will also have a favourable effect on investment.

Secondly, a cut in personal taxes increases aggregate demand by raising the disposable income of the people. If people spend more, aggregate demand will increase, *MEC* will rise and investment will be stimulated. But there is an offsetting argument. A rise in demand for goods and services will also increase the transactions demand for money and thus the total demand for money. So the demand curve for money will shift to the right. If the supply of money remains constant, the rate of interest will rise. This will lead to a fall in investment. This point is illustrated in Fig. 13.7. Thus the indirect effect of fiscal policy is damaging for investment even though its direct effect is favourable.

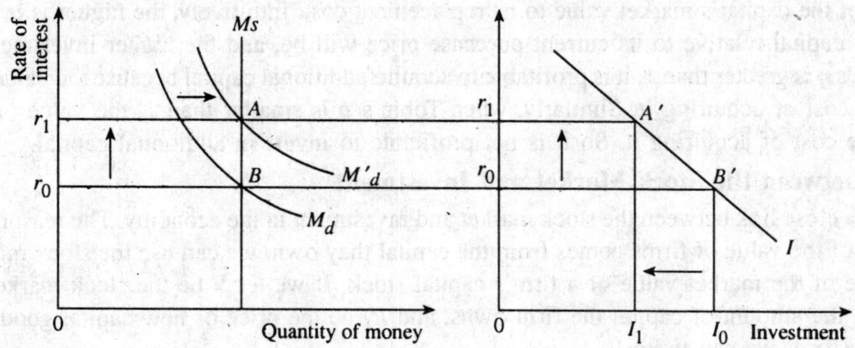

Fig. 13.7: The Indirect Effect of Fiscal Policy an Investment

However, the acceleration principle suggests that an expansionary fiscal policy which increases national income will increase the demand for consumption goods. This will stimulate private investment.

For example, if India's per capita income increases, there will be more demand for textiles and also of textile producing machines and the industry producing such machines will get more orders. Thus anything which increases consumption demand is always good for the industry producing capital goods. The reason is that the demand for capital goods is a derived (indirect) demand.

INVESTMENT AND STOCK MARKET: TOBIN'S *Q*-THEORY

There is a close relation between the stock market and investment. Fluctuations in the stock market can affect investment decisions of firms. The relationship between stock prices and firms' investment in physical capital is captured by the '*q*-theory of investment', developed by James Tobin.

Suppose a firm has 10 machines and 10 shares outstanding — one share per machine. Suppose the price per share is Rs. 100 and the purchase price of a machine is only Rs. 50. It is quite obvious that the firm should invest— buy a new machine—and finance it by issuing a new share. Each machine costs the firm Rs. 50 to purchase, but stock market participants are willing to pay Rs. 100 for a share corresponding to this machine when it is installed in the firm.

In effect, the stock price tells firms how much the stock market values each unit of capital already in place. So the investing firm has a simple exercise to perform. It has to compare the purchase price of an additional unit of capital to the price the stock market is willing to pay for it. If the stock value exceeds the purchase price, the firm should buy the machine; otherwise, it should not.

On the basis of that simple exercise Tobin constructed a variable corresponding to the value of a unit of capital in place relative to its purchase price, and examined how closely it moved with investment. Since he used the symbol '*q*' to denote the variable, it is called Tobin's *q*. Its construction goes as follows:

1. We have to take the total value of Indian corporations, as assessed by financial markets, that is, compute the sum of their stock market value (the price of a share times the number of shares). We also compute the total value of their bonds (debentures) outstanding. The reason is that firms finance themselves not only through stocks and shares but also through bonds and debentures. So we have to add together the value of stocks and bonds.

2. Then we divide this value by the value of the capital stock of Indian corporations at replacement cost (the price firms would have to pay to replace their machines, their plants, and so on).

The ratio gives us, in effect, the value of a unit of capital in place relative to its current purchase price. This ratio is Tobin's q.

Tobin argued that the rate of investment in any particular type of capital can be predicted by looking at the ratio of the capital's market value to its replacement cost. Intuitively, the higher is q, the higher the value of capital relative to its current purchase price will be, and the higher investment will be. When Tobin's q is greater than 1, it is profitable to acquire additional capital because the value of capital exceeds the cost of acquiring it. Similarly, when Tobin's q is smaller than 1, the value of capital is less than the cost of acquiring it. So it is not profitable to invest in additional capital.

The Link between the Stock Market and Investment

There is a close link between the stock market and investment in the economy. The reason is simple. Since much of the value of firms comes from the capital they own, we can use the stock market value as a measure of the market value of a firm's capital stock. If we let V be the stock market value of a firm, K be the amount of capital the firm owns, and P_k be the price of new capital goods, then for an individual firm we can write

$$\text{Tobin's } q = \frac{VK}{P_k V} = \frac{\text{Market value of installed capital}}{\text{Replacement cost of installed capital}}$$

where P_kK is the replacement cost of the firm's capital stock. If the replacement cost is not changing much, a boom in the stock market (an increase in V) will cause Tobin's q to rise for most firms leading to increased rates of investment. Essentially, when stock prices are rising, firms find it profitable to expand. So they invest more in physical assets. Thus Tobin's q establishes a relation between financial capital (share and stock) and real capital (plant, equipment and machinery). A boom in the stock exchange makes it easy for firms to raise more external capital for financing real investment.

Determinants of *q*

Three main factors affecting the desired stock of capital of a firm are the expected future marginal product of capital, the real interest rate and the purchase price of new capital. Each of these factors also affects Tobin's q. Let us give a more precise specification.

1. An increase in the expected marginal product of capital tends to increase the future earnings of the firm, which raises the stock market value of the firm and thus increases q.

2. A reduction in the real rate of interest also tends to raise stock prices (and hence q), as financial investors substitute away from low-yielding bonds and bank deposits and buy stocks instead.

3. A fall in the purchase price of capital reduces the denominator of the q ratio and thus increases q.

Since all three types of changes increase Tobin's q, they also increase the desired capital stock and investment, as predicted by the modern theory of investment.

Limitations

Empirical studies have revealed that investment in new capital goods tends to rise when the stock prices rise and fall when stock prices fall. Data show the strongest relation between investment this year and Tobin's q last year. In other words, movements in investment this year are more closely associated with movements in the stock market last year rather than with movements in the stock market this year. A plausible explanation for this is that it takes time for firms to make investment decisions, build new factories and set up new plants. However, the relationship is not always strong. The problem is partly attributable to the fact that, in practice, stock prices reflect many assets besides capital such as the patents a firm holds or the reputation of a firm's products. Thus changes in stock prices are imperfect measures of the changes in the market value of capital.

Conclusion

In spite of all these limitations there is a close relation between Tobin's *q* and investment. This is not so much because firms follow blindly the signals from the stock market, but because investment decisions and stock market prices depend very much on the same factors—expected future profits and expected future interest rates.

KEY POINTS

1. *Importance and meaning of Investment* : Investment is the most volatile component of GDP and is the proximate cause of business fluctuations or trade cycles which refer to short-run fluctuations in aggregate output (of goods and services). Investment refers to the change in the stock of capital of a firm in an accounting year. By adding up the investment demand schedules of firm, we arrive at aggregate investment.

2. *Keynes's theory of investment* : Keynes considered only autonomous investment. It has no relation to income. It varies directly with the expected rate of return on new investment or the marginal efficiency of capital (*MEC*) and the rate of interest *r* (or the price of loanable funds). It varies directly with the MEC and inversely with *r*. Modern economists, however, have drawn a distinction between marginal efficiency of capital and marginal efficiency of investment.

3. *Types of investment* : There are two main types of business investment: business purchase of new plant and equipment and addition to inventories. Another type of investment is residential construction, which is very much sensitive to interest rate changes and tax concessions given by government from time to time.

4. *Desired stock of capital* : According to the neoclassical theory, developed by D. Jorgenson a business firm determines its desired stock of capital by equating the marginal product of capital to the user cost of capital. A firm's desired stock of capital falls if user cost of capital rises. It rises if output or income rises. Thus Jorgenson's theory provides the microeconomic foundation of the aggregate investment function.

5. *The cost of capital* : The cost of capital depends on two variables, viz., the real interest rate and the rate of depreciation.

6. *Investment function* : Investment function indicates how much investment will occur in an accounting year depending on current conditions and expectations about the future.

7. *Induced investment and the acceleration principle* : In 1917 J. M. Clark developed the acceleration principle from the concept of induced investment. The principle refers to the accelerated effect on investment of a certain increase in the demand for and production of consumer goods. Thus anything which increases consumer demand is always good for the industries which produce capital (investment) goods. The key concept here is the accelerator or the acceleration coefficient which shows how much extra capital is required to produce an extra unit of output. Like the multiplier principle of Keynes, the acceleration principle also works in both the directions. Just as a small increase in the demand for (or output of) consumption goods leads to an accelerated increase in the demand for capital goods, a small drop in the demand for consumer goods leads to an accelerated drop in the demand for capital goods.

8. *Tobin's q-theory of investment* : Tobin explained the relation between stock market fluctuations and investment in fixed capital by using the *q*-ratio. It is the ratio of two things, viz., the market value of an economy's existing stock of capital and the market price (replacement cost) of the same capital stock. If the ratio is greater than one then only new investment is worthwhile.

KEY TERMS

Acceleration principle	User cost of capital
Autonomous investment	Monetary policy
Induced investment	Desired stock of capital
Tobins' *q*-theory of investment	Actual stock of capital
Fixed asset investment	Marginal efficiency of capital
Inventory investment	Marginal product of capital

ASSIGNMENTS

1. What is investment function? What are the two main determinants of the level of investment in a country?
2. (a) Distinguish between autonomous and induced investment. (b) What are the main types of investment?
3. What is marginal efficiency of capital (*MEC*)? How can you calculate it?
4. What is the essence of the accelerator theory of investment?
5. Explain the relation between investment and share price movements.
6. Discuss the neoclassical theory of investment.
7. Suppose that the demand for investment is given by the model $I = s(K^* - K_1)$ where K^* is the desired stock of capital given by $K^* = 0.1\ Y/r$ where Y is output and r is the interest rate. Assume that there is no depreciation and $r = 0.05$. Let = 0.25 to start.

   (i) Calculate the desired stock of capital in year if output is 200. Calculate the level of investment in the first year if the capital stock was 400 at the beginning of the first year.

   (ii) Suppose now that output sizes from 200 to 250 in year 2 and remains at this new level former. Calculate the level of investment and the capital stock in years 2, 3 and 4. What are the new long-run levels of investment and capital? Explain why investment reacts with a lag to the increase in output.
8. In the neoclassical model of business fixed investment, under what conditions will firms find it profitable to add to their capital stock?
9. Using the neoclassical model, explain why investment depends on the interest rate.
10. What is Tobin's q and what does it have to do with investment?
11. Describe how the accelerator model of inventories show a relation of inventory investment to economic fluctuations.
12. What are the reasons firms might hold inventories?
13. Suppose an investor wants to set up a factory. How does he decide whether it is worthwhile or not? Explain your answer with marginal efficiency of capital and investment.
14. Suppose there is a textile producer who annual sale of cloth now is Rs. 3 lakhs. His present capital stocks is Rs. 6 lakhs which consist of 20 machines of Rs. 30,000 each, are of which depreciates every year and has to be replaced. Now suppose his sale goes up by 50%. What will be the required increase in his investment? Now suppose after reaching this level, his sale remains constant. What will be the consequent fall in his gross investment?
15. What is the difference between the 'paper wealth' and the 'real wealth' of the economy? Does the increase in paper wealth indicate that the real wealth of the economy has increased?
16. How do social security, financial markets and a rapid growth in paper wealth influence the personal saving rate?
17. What are the major economic forces that determine business investment?
18. Distinguish between real and nominal interest rates. Explain the relation between interest rate and investment demand.
19. Use the neoclassical model of investment to explain the impact of each of the following on the rental price of capital, the cost of capital, and investment.

   (i) Anti-inflationary monetary policy raises the real interest rate.

   (ii) An earthquake destroys part of the capital stock.

   (iii) Immigration of foreign workers increases the size of the labour force.

CHAPTER 14

Employment and Unemployment

> *One of the most important questions in macroeconomics is why the economy does not provide work for the entire labour force. Even in the best of times, some people are unemployed.*
>
> R. Hall and D. H. Pappel

In this chapter we first discuss the classical and Keynesian theories of unemployment. Then we will discuss the modern theories of unemployment such as M. Friedman's and E. Phelps's theory of frictional (search) unemployment and structural unemployment. In this context we will discuss the issue of unemployment insurance. And we conclude with the efficiency wage theory. [In the appendix to this chapter we will discuss the nature and types of unemployment in India].

Most market-based economies of the Western World are subject to frequent and unpredictable fluctuations in output, prices and unemployment. Inflation and unemployment are the two main macroeconomic problems of the post-Second World War period. Now both the problems exist side by side and we face the problem of **stagflation** which refers to the co-existence of inflation and unemployment in a stagnant economy where output growth is virtually zero. While inflation affects most people both directly and indirectly, unemployment affects people most directly. So its effect is more severe than that of inflation. Those who are unemployed find that their living standards are going down day by day. They also suffer from psychological problems.

The burden of unemployment is more serious than that of inflation

Economists study unemployment for a twofold reason. The primarty objective is to identify its causes. But the ultimate objective is to suggest public policies for solving the problem.

The classical economists thought that full employment was the inevitable outcome of the free functioning of the market system and the classical theory was based on the assumption that the economy was always at full employment.

However, complete full employment does not exist today even in the best managed economies of the West. In other words, everyone in the labour force does not get a job all the time. All free market economies have to tolerate some unemployment even under normal functioning of their economies.

The problem of unemployment was not a matter of serious concern before the publication of Keynes's **General Theory** is 1936. The classical economists assumed full employment and thus ruled out the possibility of any type of unemployment. However, since the time of the Great Depression of 1929, the problem of unemployment has assumed serious proportions and has been a matter of considerable concern to the economists, the public and the policymakers. Unemployment means loss of some potential output or real GDP. As a result an economy is driven inside its production possibility curve (*PPC*) and is not able to operate efficiently and produce its maximum capacity output.

Unemployment is of different types. Moreover, the nature and causes of unemployment are not the same in developed and developing countries.

MEANING AND MEASUREMENT OF UNEMPLOYMENT

Unemployment means joblessness. It is said to exist when there are able-bodied persons of working age who are willing to work, but unable to get jobs at the prevailing wage rate. The unemployed are people looking for work and available for work but who have not found jobs. The total labour force of a country (L) can be divided into two parts: (1) those who are employed (E) and (2) those who are unemployed (U). So $L = E + U$ or $U = L - E$.

The *labour force* is defined as the number of people above 16 years of age who are either working or unemployed. The *unemployment rate* is the percentage of the labor force that is unemployed. Thus the rate of unemployment (u) is measured as follows:

$$u = \frac{L-E}{L} \times 100 = \frac{U}{L} \times 100\%$$

In every country there are millions of people who are not working but are not counted as unemployed. They are considered *out of the labour force* because they are retired, in school, at home looking after their own children, sick, or not looking for work for one reason or another. The *labour force participation rate* (LFPR) is the percentage of the working age (adult) population in the total labour force. It is expressed as

$$\text{LFPR} = \frac{\text{Adult population}}{\text{Total labour force}}$$

An important fact about the labour market is that, at any given time, not everybody who is in the labour force and available for work is actually employed. Unemployment is a feature of the economy even when supply and demand are in balance. Unemployment rises in recessions and falls in booms, but there is a certain level of unemployment called the **natural rate of unemployment.** The natural rate is the rate of unemployment which prevails even when the labour market is in equilibrium. One simple measure of the natural rate is the average rate of unemployment over several decades. The natural rate appears to lie between 5 and 6 percent in most industrially developed countries. The natural rate of unemployment is a limit on the amount of labour available as an input in production.

A related term is *underemployment*. If a person is capable of working for 40 hours a week (8 hours for 5 days) but gets job for 20 hours a week, he is said to be underemployed. Another variant of the concept is disguised unemployment, a term coined by Joan Robinson in 1934, and will be explained later is this chapter. We may now discuss the nature and causes of different types of unemployment.

TOTAL UNEMPLOYMENT

According to modern economists total unemployment in a country has two main components: natural unemployment and cyclical unemployment.

Thus we can write

$$U = U_n + U_c$$

$$\text{or, } U_c = U - U_n$$

Keynes was mainly concerned with U_c, while the modern economists like Friedman and Phelps were concerned with U_n. Natural unemployment has two components: frictional and structural.

THE CONCEPT OF FULL EMPLOYMENT

In this context we may refer to the concept of full employment. Full employment refers to a situation in which all those who are willing to work succeed in getting jobs at prevailing market-wage(s) and people have substantial choice of jobs. This means that those who lose their old jobs for some reason succeed in getting new jobs easily and quickly.

Complete full employment is a myth. There is no country in the world in which all willing workers succeed in getting gainful employment. Since the labour market is in a perpetual state of disequilibrium due to various frictions or imperfections, and since some people move among jobs all the time and others voluntarily quit jobs to put necessary search effort, some workers always remain unemployed, either voluntarily or involuntarily. So a more appropriate concept is 'near-full-employment' or 'almost complete full-employment' or 'virtual full employment.'

THE COSTS OF UNEMPLOYMENT

Five costs of unemployment are the following:

(i) ***Fall in GDP*** : Unemployment means a fall in national output (GDP). This implies a reduction in national income.

(ii) ***Idle capacity*** : When sales revenues of firms fall and firms have unused production capacity, profits decline.

(iii) ***Loss of income*** : When workers lose their jobs, they also suffer from a loss of income which they would have otherwise earned.

(iv) ***Fall in tax revenue*** : When income and business revenue fall during a recession, government also suffer because their tax revenues fall. So deficits are likely to arise in government budgets.

(v) ***Psychological cost*** : Unemployment has psychological costs also. Empirical evidence shows that increases in the rate of cyclical unemployment are associated with increased suicide, crime, mental disorder and physical illness. As David Hyman has put it "During recessions the average period of unemployment tends to double the normal two-month duration. During recession it is also more probable that in many families both spouses will lose their jobs. This tends to compound the stress and other social problems stemming from unemployment."

The loss in wages and profits is part of the costs of unemployment

THE MODERN THEORY OF EMPLOYMENT

The modern view is that virtual full employment exists if actual rate of unemployment does not exceed the natural rate or if total unemployment is equal to the natural unemployment and cyclical unemployment is zero. Thus we can write

Virtual full employment exists if actual unemployment is equal to natural unemployment and cyclical unemployment is zero

$$U = U_n \quad \text{and} \quad U_c = 0$$

Natural unemployment exists due to normal functioning of a dynamic economy which is characterised by both job loss and job creation. Thus if the number of old jobs lost is exactly matched by the number of new jobs created per period then there will be complete full employment. But this is unlikely to happen in reality. The truth is that in every economy there is both job vacancy and unemployment at the same time.[1]

Economic Insight: NAIRU

If the actual rate of unemployment does not exceed its natural rate, the rate of inflation will be stable, as Friedman has argued, while evaluating the Phillips Curve. This is why the natural rate of unemployment is also called, in terms of the modern Phillips Curve, inflationary-expectations-augmented Phillips Curve, and the natural rate of unemployment (NRU) the non-accelerating inflation rate of unemployment (NAIRU). In other words, NRU is consistent with reasonable price level stability.

1. Considerable research has been made on this point by C. Passeride of LSE who is one of the recipients of Noble Prize in Economics for 2010.

CLASSICAL AND KEYNESIAN UNEMPLOYMENT

Classical unemployment is equilibrium unemployment, Keynesian unemployment is disequilibrium unemployment

Economists often draw a distinction between voluntary and involuntary unemployment. This distinction is based on the views of two major schools of thought, viz., the classical school and the Keynesian school. While the classical economists considered only voluntary unemployment, Keynes introduced the term involuntary unemployment. According to Paul Samuelson, voluntary unemployment is equilibrium unemployment, while involuntary unemployment is disequilibrium unemployment". And because of voluntary unemployment, the classical labour supply curve tends to be vertical.

Economic Insight: Voluntary Unemployment in the Classical Model

The supply curve of labour in the classical model is assumed to be upward sloping as shown in Fig. 14.1. Here equilibrium in the labour market occurs at point E which corresponds to full employment. But the size of the labour force is $\bar{L}$. So $\bar{L} - L_f$ measures the magnitude of voluntary unemployment. Now if all those who are voluntarily unemployed joined the labour force, the labour supply curve will become vertical as shown by the segment $E'L_s$. Thus if the supply of labour is equated with the size of the labour force, the labour supply curve in the classical model tends to be vertical such as L_s at $\bar{L}$. This is an important insight provided by modern macroeconomists such as R. Barro and R. Lucas.

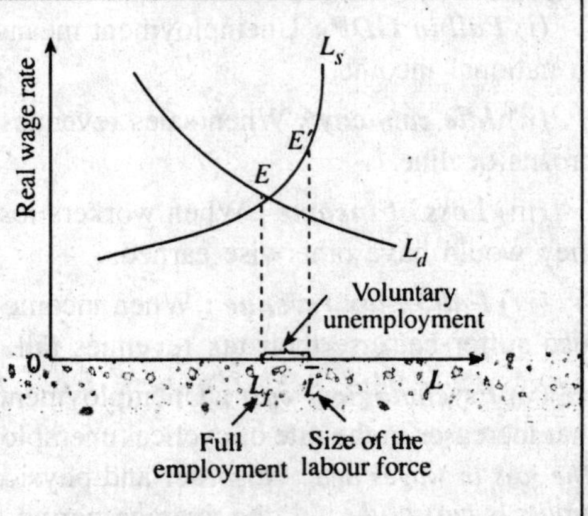

Fig. 14.1: Vertical Labour Supply Curve

THE KEYNESIAN VIEW OF INVOLUNTARY UNEMPLOYMENT

According to Keynes, the root cause of unemployment is deficiency of demand or purchasing power. Another cause is downward rigidity of nominal (money) wage. The Keynesian view of involuntary unemployment is explained in Fig. 14.2. The demand for labour, is a derived (indirect) demand. Thus, if aggregate demand for goods and services falls, the demand for labour will also fall. So the demand curve for labour will shift to the left from L_d to L_d'. As a result the level of employment will fall from L_1 to L_2. Thus $L_1L_2 = EF$ measures the magnitude of involuntary unemployment. Since the nominal wage does not fall below $\bar{w}$, this type of unemployment prevails in capitalist countries in times of recession or depression when aggregate demand falls.

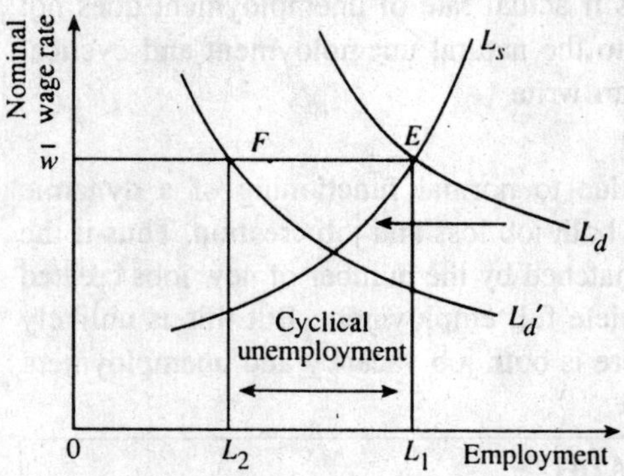

Fig. 14.2: Involuntary Unemployment

This type of unemployment does not exist in the classical world due to wage-price flexibility (or flexibility of real wage). But according to Keynes involuntary unemployment is a genuine possibility in a capitalist economy, characterised by nominal wage rigidity.

CAUSES OF MONEY WAGE RIGIDITY

There are four main causes of rigidity of money wage:

1. Worker resistance: Through trade unions workers strongly resist a cut in money wage because they normally suffer from money illusion. They take a cut in money wage as equivalent to a cut in real wage (or purchasing power of money wage).

2. Fixed wage contract: Since unions usually sign wage contracts with employees for a number of years, wages remain fixed during the period of the contract.

3. Fixation of minimum wage: Due to fixation of minimum wage by the government, employers cannot pay less than the legal minimum wage.

4. Efficiency of labour: Since high wages increase the efficiency of labour, employers do not want to reduce wage since wage cut will lead to a fall in efficiency (productivity) of labour.

Thus if the wage rate remains fixed at a certain level, a leftward shift of the demand curve for labour will create involuntary unemployment, as noted above.

Keynes' View on Wage Cut

However, Keynes pointed that wages are the main component of a country's national income. Thus an economy-wide cut in wages in times of depression will lead to a fall in the income of workers. So their consumption spending will fall. As a result aggregate demand will fall. And this will aggravate the problem of involuntary unemployment in times of low economic activity, i.e., mild recession or deep depression. So the cure may be worse than the disease.

A cut in money wage will make the problem of involuntary employment more serious in times of recession or depression

The Modern View of Wage Cut

In this context we may refer to the view of modern economists like E. Phelps and J. Stiglitz who **developed the theory of efficiency wage. The theory is explained below:**

The Theory of Efficiency Wage

A third cause of real wage rigidity and involuntary unemployment is associated with efficiency wage theories. This concept is based on the famous Marshallian concept— **the economy of high wages.** Marshall first hypothesised that high wages promote efficiency and low wages retard it. A high wage induces greater effort, as is shown by the effort curve in Fig. 14.3. The idea was put into effect in the American manufacturing industry by Henry Ford who followed the practice of giving higher than the prevailing market wage so that the rate of labour turnover came down to a minimum. Ford's basic objective was to ensure that his most productive workers did not leave the organisation after a short period.

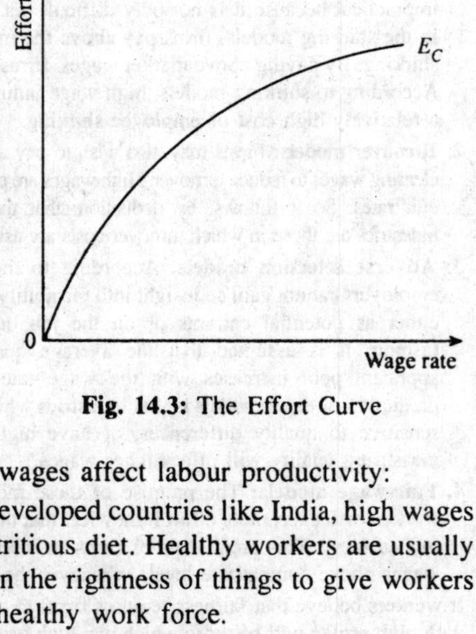

Fig. 14.3: The Effort Curve

The efficiency wage theory explains why firms do not cut wages even when there is excess supply of labour. The theory is based on the belief that a wage cut would lower a firm's wage bill no doubt, it would also reduce a firm's profits by lowering worker efficiency.

Various explanations have been offered to explain how wages affect labour productivity:

(i) *Improved health and enhanced productivity* : In less developed countries like India, high wages enable workers to improve their health by having a more nutritious diet. Healthy workers are usually found to be more productive than half-fed workers. So it is in the rightness of things to give workers a wage above the equilibrium level in order to maintain a healthy work force.

(ii) *Low labour turnover* : The higher the wage rate, the stronger the incentive of workers to stay with the firm. If the quit rate of workers can be reduced to a minimum, a firm can achieve economy in terms of the time spent on recruiting and training new workers.

(iii) *Reducing adverse selection* : The overall quality of a firm's labour force depends on the wages it pays to its employees. A wage cut will force a firm's best workers to take jobs elsewhere in other firms, leaving the firm with inferior employees who have hardly any opportunity outside the firm. This is an example of **adverse selection** since workers are more informed about their alternative opportunities outside the firm than the firm (the employer). This is also known as "hidden characteristics" problem. So by paying a low wage, a firm may take the risk of hiring inferior workers (who do not have any opportunity outside the firm). One way of reducing adverse selection is to pay a wage above the equilibrium level. This improves the average quality of the workforce. So labour productivity automatically improves.

(iv) *Overcoming the moral hazard problem* : High wages also improve worker effort. The truth is that it is not always possible to monitor the work effort of employees. It is the task of the employees themselves to decide how hard to work. This is known as **moral hazard**, also known as the "hidden action problem". This refers to the hidden tendency of workers to put sub-optimal effort if their activities are not perfectly monitored. One way of reducing this moral hazard problem is to pay a high wage. The higher the wage, the higher the cost of the worker of being dismissed. One way of increasing labour productivity is to pay a higher than market wage. This induces more and more of a firm's employees not to shirk.

The common theme of various efficiency wage theories (presented below in a summary form) is that by paying its workers a high wage, a firm can operate more efficiently. This is why many firms choose to pay more than the market clearing wage. This induces workers to stay with their firms and not to engage in job search activities. But efficiency wage increases the magnitude of involuntary unemployment and creates real wage rigidity.

Economic Insight: Four Models of Efficiency Wage

There are four models of efficiency wage. The common feature of all the models is that higher than competitive wage can be profitable. All the models are based on the hypothesis that output depends on worker effort in and effort, in its turn, varies directly with the wage rate. The more a firm pays, the more effort it gets. The models originating from the presumed source of positive effort-wage relationship are of the four types:

1. **Shirking models:** In most jobs, workers enjoy some discretion in deciding how hard they work. Piece rates are often impractical because it is not only difficult but virtually impossible to count the "pieces" and counting itself is costly. In the shirking models, firms pay above the market wages, engage in some monitoring and fire those workers caught shirking. By paying above market wages, firms decrease the incentive to shirk, since defection then entails loss of rents. According to shirking models, high wage industries are those with high monitoring costs and/or industries which bear a relatively high cost of employee shirking.
2. **Turnover models:** Firms may also wish to pay above market clearing wages to reduce turnover. High wages are paid to reduce quit rates. So it follows, by deduction, that the high-wage industries are those in which turnover costs are usually highest.
3. **Adverse selection models:** According to these models, employers cannot gain an insight into the ability of workers, either as potential entrants or on the job, in a costless fashion. It is assumed that the average quality of the applicant pool increases with the wage rate. The main prediction of these models is that industries which are more sensitive to quality differences, or have higher costs of measuring quality will offer higher wages.
4. **Fair-wage models:** The premise of these models is that workers will exert more effort if they feel that they are being treated fairly. This premise gives firms an incentive to pay wages above competitive levels whenever their workers' perceived fair wage exceeds the competitive wage.

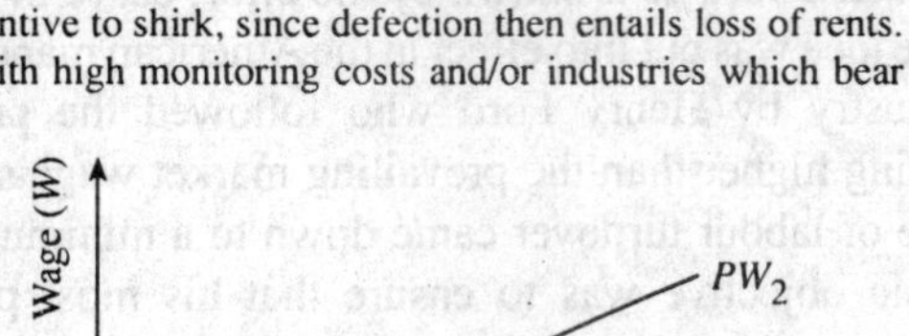

Fig. 14.4: Profit-Wage Trade-Off

If workers believe that fairness requires firms to share rents with employees, then fair wage models predict that industries with high profits will be those which pay high wages. In Fig. 14.4, we show profit-wage trade-off. In some industries high wages lead to low profits as is shown by the profit wage curve PW_1. If the wage rate is pushed up from W_1 to W_2, the rate of profit falls from π_2 to π_1. In other industries, high wages lead to high profit as is shown by the curve, PW_2. If the wage rate is pushed up from W_1 to W_2, the rate of profit goes up from π_0 to π_1.

The fair wage models also predict high wages in industries where teamwork and worker expectations are particularly important. However, the four models are not mutually exclusive. Firms might well pay above competitive wages to reduce shirking and thus, attract high quality applicants and improve worker morale.

Now we may pass on to a detailed discussion of the relation between wage cut and employment.

WAGE CUT AND EMPLOYMENT

There are two opposite views on the relation between wage cut and employment, viz., the classical view and the Keynesian view. These two views may be discussed one by one.

A. The Classical View

The classical economists virtually ruled out the possibility of involuntary unemployment. If there is any unemployment, according to the classicists, it will be of a purely temporary nature. Such unemployment may occur due to too high a real wage. However, such unemployment will not persist for long since the wage rate will fall automatically and the labour market will be cleared. The classicists believed in the automatic adjustment of the labour market (in the absence of any government intervention).

The classical unemployment is real-wage unemployment

The classical explanation goes as follows. A fall in wages will lead to a fall in cost of production of firms. As a result the prices of products will fall and larger quantities of products will be demanded and produced. Consequently the derived demand for labour will increase and full employment will be restored, sooner or later.

Keynes's Criticism

However, Keynes pointed out an economy-wide cut in wages will reduce aggregate demand for products since workers will now have less income to spend on consumption goods. As a result production will fall and the demand for labour will also fall. Thus, according to Keynes, unemployment occurs due to a fall in aggregate demand.

The effect of an economy-wide cut in wages on aggregate output is illustrated in Fig. 14.5. Here the economy is initially in macroeconomic equilibrium at point E, where real GDP is Y_1 and the aggregate price level is P_1.

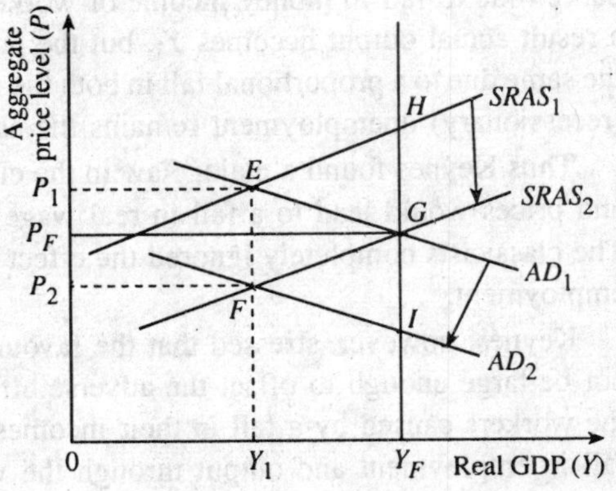

Fig. 14.5: The Effect of Downward Rigidity of Wage

Now actual output Y_1 is less than the full employment level of output Y_F. Therefore the gap between actual output and potential (full employment) output, i.e., $Y_F - Y_1$ measures recessionary gap. And there is involuntary unemployment in the economy.

Now the classical view is that a cut in wage will shift the short-run aggregate supply curve to the right from $SRAS_1$ to $SRAS_2$. So the economy attains a new equilibrium at point G. This implies that actual output increases to Y_F.

But the Keynesian view is that a cut in wage will reduce the income of the workers and shift the aggregate demand curve to the left (from AD_1 to AD_2). If the fall in aggregate demand is proportional to the increase in aggregate supply, then the economy will reach new equilibrium at point F, at which its actual output is Y_1. In addition, if the cut in wages leads to a proportional fall in the aggregate price level, then the real wage will remain unchanged. So there will be no change in the level of employment. Involuntary unemployment will exist in the economy due to output gap $(Y_F - Y_1)$ as is found in times of recession or depression.

The classical view is based on one hypothesis and one theory of microeconomics, viz., the law of diminishing (marginal) returns and the marginal productivity theory of wages. The law of diminishing returns states that as more and more workers are employed, keeping all other factors constant and production technology unchanged, marginal product of labour will fall (since each extra worker will gradually make less and less contribution to total output). And, according to the marginal product theory of wages in a competitive market each worker is paid the same wage which is determined by the value of the marginal product of labour (= the price of the product of a firm times the marginal physical product of labour). These two propositions conjointly imply that as more and more workers are employed the total wage bill will increase no doubt, but less than proportionately. This also implies that average wage will fall. Therefore a cut in wage will create more employment.

B. The Keynesian View

Keynes put forward an exactly opposite view. He argued that an increase in employment will lead to a fall in wage.

While the classicists argued that money wage (*W*) has to be reduced to bring real wage (*W/P*) down, Keynes argued that the level of employment has to be increased by raising aggregate demand (holding money wage constant). Due to diminishing marginal product of labour, an increase in employment will lead to an increase in marginal cost. As a result product price will increase and real wage (*W/P*) will fall. Thus, according to Keynes, an increase in aggregate demand is more effective in creating employment than a cut in real wage, as the classicists thought.

Thus employment is not created by cutting real wage. Real wage falls because new employment has been created by increasing aggregate demand. This point is also illustrated in Fig. 14.5. We see that due to rightward shift of the aggregate supply curve and leftward shift of the aggregate demand curve (due to fall in money income of workers), the economy attains new equilibrium at point *F*. As a result actual output becomes Y_1, but the price level falls from P_1 to P_2. Even if real wage remains the same due to a proportional fall in both the money wage and the price level, the magnitude of cyclical (recessionary) unemployment remains the same since output returns to the original level Y_1.

Thus Keynes found a major flaw in the classical theory that downward flexibility of money wages and prices would lead to a fall in real wage and enable the economy to reachieve full employment. The classicists completely ignored the effect of cut in money wage on aggregate demand and thus on employment.

Keynes, however, stressed that the favourable effect on employment of a cut in real wage would not be large enough to offset the adverse effect on employment of a fall in consumption demand of the workers caused by a fall in their incomes. In addition, a fall in consumption will lead to a faster fall in employment and output through the working of the reverse multiplier.

Keynes also realised that the higher consumption demand of the recipients of non-wage incomes in the form of rent, interest, profits and dividends would not be large enough to offset lower consumption demand of wage earners. So the net effect of any cut in money wages would be to depress output and employment.

The Effect of Wage Cut on Employment

According to Keynes, the effect of money wage cut on aggregate demand depends on its two main components, viz., consumption and investment.

1. Consumption: A cut in money wage is likely to reduce consumption demand by reducing aggregate propensity to consume. Due to cut in money wage and prices of products, there will be redistribution of income from wage-earners (having a high propensity to consume) to non-wage-earners (having a low propensity to consume). As a result aggregate consumption demand will fall.

Consumption expenditure also falls due to redistribution of income from debtors to creditors. Creditors spend a small part of their extra income generated through fall in prices. But debtors will be forced to reduce their consumption by a large amount so as to be able to pay high real interest, caused by a fall in price. (Recall that real interest = Nominal interest – the annual rate of inflation/deflation).

2. Investment: Private investment depends on the marginal efficiency of capital and the rate of interest. A cut in money wage and the consequent fall in price will have an adverse effect on *MEC*. However, if entrepreneurs expect that money wages will rise again in future, they will expect the demand for goods and services to rise also. This will improve their profit prospects and raise the *MEC*. So more investment is likely to take place.

In general, the effect of wage cut on *MEC* and investment is uncertain because there is uncertainty about the expectations of entrepreneurs.

However, Keynes pointed out that a cut in the rate of interest will increase investment demand which will increase aggregate demand, employment and output. However, this can be achieved by adopting an expansionary monetary policy. So a cut in wage is not a judicious policy for creating employment, as the classicists thought.

THE KEYNES EFFECT

According to Keynes, a cut in money wages and the consequent fall in prices is likely to reduce the rate of interest and thus stimulate investment. This is known as the Keynes effect. Keynes effect refers to a change in the demand for commodities as a result of a change in the aggregate price level. For example, a fall in the price level will increase the quantity of real money balances (M_d/P) and, therefore, more money will be available for speculative purposes. As a result the price of bonds will rise and the interest rate will fall. This, in its turn, will stimulate investment and increase the demand for goods and services.

Economic Insight: The Keynes Effect
The Keynesian economists regarded the money wage as inflexible in the short run and considered whether there existed any automatic mechanisms by which unemployment would be eliminated. The only such mechanism is the following: if wages fall in response to unemployment, labour costs fall and, therefore, prices fall; this increases the real money supply (*M/P*) and reduces the interest rate; and the lower interest rate leads to higher investment and, hence, higher income. In symbols $U \rightarrow W\downarrow \rightarrow P\downarrow \rightarrow M_2/P\downarrow \rightarrow r\downarrow \rightarrow I\uparrow\rightarrow Y\uparrow$

Keynes relied on this indirect mechanism for reducing the rate of interest since in times of depression monetary policy does not work to reduce the rate of interest below a certain minimum level due to the existence of liquidity trap, i.e., infinite elasticity of demand for money at a very low rate of interest. However, the extent to which a fall in the rate of interest will stimulate investment depends on interest elasticity of investment.

THE REAL BALANCE EFFECT

RBE refers to an increase in the demand for commodities as a result of a rise in real money balances caused by a fall in P

The indirect increase in the demand for commodities, as outlined by Keynes, and its effect on investment should be distinguished from the direct effects of a fall in the price level on the demand for commodities for consumption, as described by the Pigou effect.

The basic idea is simple. The real value of wealth would increase as prices fall. Thus wealthholders would seek to reduce their increasing real money balances, by spending the excess money thus raising aggregate demand towards the full employment level. This effect is also known as the real balance effect.

The modern view is that in times of recession, a fall in demand would lead to a fall in both prices and interest rates, raising the wealth of equity holders. Here wealth (*W*) is the capitalised value of income stream (*Y*), with the interest rate (*r*) acting as a discount factor. So we can write

$$W = \frac{Y}{r}$$

The real balance effect refers to the effect on spending of changes in the real value of money balances. In times of depression, as prices fall, the real purchasing power of the stock of money rises, which should eventually lead to increased spending[1]. However, the question is whether the effect will be strong enough to enable the depressed economy to reachieve full employment.

Economic Insight: Indirect Real Balance Effect Vs. Direct Real Balance Effect

Real balance effect (RBE) refers to a change in the demand for commodities as a result of a change in the quantity of real money balances. The direct RBE, as detailed by Don Patinkin, and earlier known as the Pigou effect, is the increase in the demand for consumption good as a result of portfolio adjustments by individuals in response to a change in real money balances.

The Keynes effect is essentially direct RBE and the Pigou effect is indirect RBE. The indirect change in the demand for commodities in response to price change is different from the direct effect of a change in the general price level on the demand for consumption goods as described by the direct RBE. The Keynes effect is illustrated by a shift in the *LM* curve while the direct RBE manifests itself *via* a shift in the *IS* curve. In practice, the term RBE is often used to describe both the effects.

STABILISATION POLICIES

Keynes suggested that demand management policies are to be adopted to lift the economy out of brief recession or even deep depression. Since deficiency of demand is the root cause of unemployment, the solution to the problem lies in increasing aggregate demand. Aggregate demand can be increased by adopting the following policies:

1. Deficit Spending

The classical economists were always in favour of balancing the government budget. They did not treat either budgetary deficit or budgetary supplies with favour. But it was Keynes who first suggested that in times of low economic activity, the government should deliberately incur a deficit in the budget to revive the economy and then lift the economy out of stagnation.

The government should spend more money on public works such as road construction, creation of railway network, digging canals, slum clearance, electrification of villages, expansion of irrigation facilities, schools, etc. The government should not borrow from the people or impose additional taxes but borrow from the central bank. As a result the money supply will increase and the aggregate demand curve will shift to the right. So more jobs and incomes will be created.

The initial increase in demand will lead to a multiple increase in national income and employment through the autonomous expenditure multiplier. However, the magnitude of such deficit should be kept within a safe limit so that the economy does not get overheated and there is no problem of demand-pull inflation.

2. Tax Cut

A tax cut stimulates the economy in two ways. Firstly, a cut in personal taxes will raise the disposable income of the people. This will stimulate consumption spending by the household sector. Similarly, a cut in corporate taxes will increase the net return on capital employed. As a result business firms will make new investment in fixed assets such as plant, equipment and machinery. Due to an increase in consumption and investment, the aggregate demand curve will shift to the right and the economy will move from depression to recovery and from recovery to prosperity.

Thus what can be achieved by an increase in government spending can also be achieved by cutting taxes. The famous U.S. Budget of 1964 presented under the Kennedy regime virtually did a miracle. Again in June 2003 the US Government announced a massive tax cut to revive the economy which was in recession.

1. The real balance effect (RBE) shifts the *IS* curve. This direct RBE is different from the indirect Keynes effect which shifts the *LM* curve.

3. Monetary Policy

Three main instruments of monetary control are the bank rate, open market operations and the reserve ratio. While the first affects the cost of bank credit, the other two affect the availability of such credit. Since bank credit is a major component of the total money supply of a country, the control of the money supply essentially amounts to controlling the volume of lending by commercial (and other) banks.

In times of depression, the central bank reduces the bank rate. As a result the market rate of interest falls. This stimulates investment and increases aggregate demand. So the economy is enabled to move out of depression and gradually to reachieve full employment.

During depression, the central bank buys back government securities (which it sold earlier) in the open market by paying cash. As a result the money supply with the public increases and people spend more. Again aggregate demand increases and the economy is enabled to move into the recovery phase of the business cycle.

Similarly, a cut in the cash reserve ratio (CRR) will leave more cash with banks. This will enable them to make more loans to business firms. As a result investment will increase and thus aggregate demand. The end result will be an increase in income and employment. In the same way the central bank can reduce the statutory liquidity ratio (SLR). This will have the same effect as that of a cut in CRR.

4. Export Promotion

Exports can be raised by adopting various organisational and fiscal measures such as improving the quality of export items, maintaining delivery schedules, participating in world trade fairs, advertising export items in foreign newspapers and commercial programmes, giving cash support to exporters, and excise duty concessions to exporters. It is also necessary to achieve export diversification—both country-wise and commodity-wise.

However, promotion of exports does not just depend on the adoption of the above domestic measures. It is also necessary to reach bilateral trade agreements with other countries (importers) for reducing various tariff and non-tariff barriers to exports.

An increase is exports, with imports remaining constant, will lead to an increase net exports. As a result the aggregate demand curve will shift to the right.

5. Import Control

A cut in imports is also likely to raise net exports. So there will be less leakage of money from the economy. Moreover, net exports will increase due to fall in imports, made possible by an increase in the domestic production of import-substitute items. As a result there will be more demand for labour and other factors. So, at the end, income and employment will increase since imports are a leakage from the circular flow of income.

THE MODERN THEORY OF UNEMPLOYMENT

As we have noted earlier in this chapter, complete full employment is a myth. In every economy there is some unemployment which is quite consistent with the normal functioning of the labour markets. This is known as *the natural rate of unemployment* (henceforth NRU). Economists differ in their views on what NRU is truly. The general view is that it is the average rate of unemployment around which the rate of actual unemployment fluctuates. Perhaps one of the most acceptable definitions of NRU has been suggested by Milton Friedman. In his words, it is "*the level that would be ground out by the Walrasian system of general equilibrium equations provided there is embedded in them the actual structural characteristics of the labour and commodity markets, including market imperfections, stochastic variability in demands and supplies, the cost of gathering information about job vacancies and labour availabilities, the cost of mobility and so on*". In simple terms, it may be regarded that the level of unemployment which nonetheless remains at full employment.

In truth, NRU is essentially a long-term phenomenon. It is the rate of unemployment toward which the economy gravitates in the long run, subject to the existing imperfections in the labour market which make it difficult for workers to find jobs easily and quickly.

JOB LOSS, JOB FINDING AND THE NATURAL RATE OF UNEMPLOYMENT

Most modern macroeconomists focus on the concept of *the natural rate of unemployment* (NRU). Since full employment is a myth, a country is said to have reached the full employment stage if the actual rate of unemployment is equal to the natural rate. According to Milton Friedman it is that rate of unemployment which is consistent with absolute price level stability. In the opinion of N. G. Mankiw, the NRU can be viewed as the steady-state rate of unemployment. It is the average rate around which the actual rate of unemployment fluctuates in the long run. It is calculated, for a particular year, by averaging all the unemployment rates from 10 years earlier to 10 years later.

There is always some unemployment even in highly developed countries like the U.S.A. or Japan. This is indeed the NRU which exists due to the fact that the labour market is in a perpetual state of disequilibrium due to job loss, job search and job finding. In other words, NRU measures frictional unemployment. We may now discuss the determinants of NRU.

Everyday some workers lose or quit their jobs, others look for new jobs and some unemployed are hired. This perpetual ebb and flow determines the proportion of the labour force that remains involuntarily idle.

Recall that the total labour force (L) of a country may be expressed as

$$L = E + U \quad \ldots (1)$$

where E = the number of workers employed and U = the number of unemployed workers.

So the rate of unemployment is $u = U/L$. $\quad \ldots (2)$

If the labour force remains fixed at L the transition of individuals in the labour force between employment (the rate of job finding) and unemployment (the rate of job loss) measures the unemployment rate, as shown in Fig. 14.6.

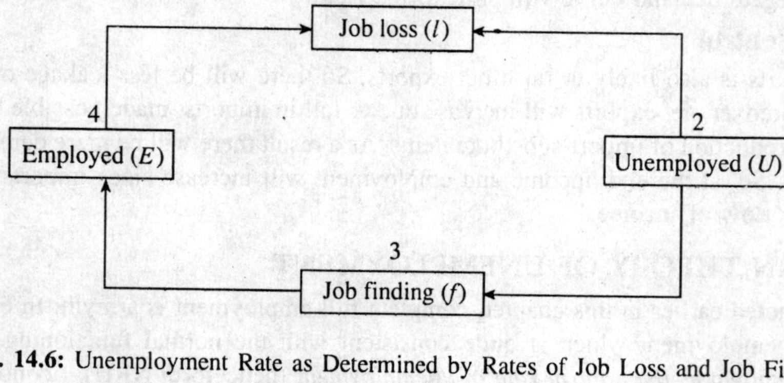

Fig. 14.6: Unemployment Rate as Determined by Rates of Job Loss and Job Finding

Let 'l' denote the rate of job loss, the proportion of employed individuals who lose their job every month. Let 'f' denote the rate of job finding, the proportion of unemployed individuals who find a job each month. The rate of unemployment is determined conjointly by the rate of job loss (l) and the rate of job finding (f).

If the number of people finding jobs equals the number of people losing jobs, then the unemployment rate remains constant and the labour market is said to be in a steady state. The number of people finding jobs is fU and the number of people losing jobs is lE. So in steady-state equilibrium

$$fU = lE \qquad \ldots (3)$$

Since $E = L - U$ from equation (1), i.e., the number of employed workers is equal to the labour force minus the number of unemployed we have

$$fU = l(L - U) \qquad \ldots (4)$$

Dividing both sides of this equation by L we get

$$f\frac{U}{L} = l\left(1 - \frac{U}{L}\right) \qquad \ldots (5)$$

Solving for the unemployment rate U/L we get

$$\frac{U}{L} = \frac{l}{l+f} \qquad \ldots (6)$$

Thus the steady-state rate of unemployment U/L depends on the rates of job loss 'l' and job finding 'f'. The higher the rate of job loss, the larger is the percentage of people unemployed. The higher the rate of job finding, the lower is the percentage of people unemployed.

Example 1

(a) In a particular month the labour force is 130 million. There are 9.1 million unemployed workes. The job-losing rate is 3% per month and the job-finding rate is 40% per month. How many people will be unemployed next month? (b) At what unemployment rate will the number of unemployed remain the same from one month to the next?

Solution: (a) Here $L = E + U$ (where L = labour force, E = the number of people employed and U = the number of people unemployed)

or, 130 = 120.9 + 9.1. So 3% of E (= 120.9) or 3.627 or approximately 4% of people will become unemployed next month.

Here 40% of U (= 9.1) is 3.640 or approximately 4% of people will get job next month. So virtually no one will remain unemployed next month.

(b) The steady-state rate of unemployment (or the NRU) is

$\frac{U}{L} = \frac{l}{l+f} = \frac{0.03}{0.03+0.4} = 0.06977$, where l is the rate of job loss and f is the rate of job finding.

At this rate of unemployment, the number of unemployed will remain the same from one month to the next.

Example 2

Suppose 1% of the employed lose their jobs each month and 20% of the unemployed find job each month. Find out the steady-state unemployment rate.

Solution: Here the rate of job loss (l) is 0.01 and the rate of job finding (f) is 0.20.

So the steady-state unemployment rate is

$$\frac{U}{L} = \frac{l}{l+f} = \frac{0.01}{0.01+0.20} = 0.0476$$

Thus the rate of unemployment is approximately 5%.

Prediction

The above analysis of the natural rate of unemployment has an obvious implication from the policy point of view. Any policy which seeks to lower the natural rate of unemployment has to either reduce the rate of job loss or increase the rate of job finding. Likewise any policy which affects the rate of job loss or job finding changes the natural rate of unemployment.

JOB SEARCH AND FRICTIONAL UNEMPLOYMENT

One proximate cause of unemployment is the mismatch between workers and jobs. Since labour is not homogenous, a job loss does not immediately lead to job finding. Workers who are laid off do not find a job easily and quickly.

Job finding itself is a resource-consuming and time-consuming endeavour. The unemployment caused by the time required by a worker is called **frictional unemployment.** Such unemployment occurs because we do not live in the wonderful world of the classical economists. It occurs because information about job availability is not freely available to workers and, even when it is available, it is imperfect. Moreover, workers are not geographically mobile. There are various barriers to labour mobility. These two factors conjointly reduce the rate of job finding. Moreover, since workers differ in their skill, ability, efficiency and performance and jobs also differ in their characteristics (in terms of rewards and sacrifies), different jobs require different skills and offer different wages. This is why an unemployed worker prefers to spend time and money to search out a job of his liking rather than accepting any job that comes along the line.

Frictional unemployment is also related to **shift unemployment**. Some unemployment occurs due to shifts in demand for consumer goods used by households and producer (capital) goods used by firms. Since the demand for labour is an indirect (derived) demand, any change in the pattern of demand for goods leads to a change in the demand for labour that is required to produce those goods. Likewise since different regions of a country produce different goods, the demand for labour may rise in one region (such as Maharashtra or Gujarat) and fall in another region (such as Orissa or Bihar). Such unemployment caused by a change in the composition of demand among industries or regions is called **shift unemployment.** This is another type of frictional unemployment. Since sectoral shifts are occurring all the time in a dynamic economy and since workers take some time to move from one sector to another due to lack of marketable skill or inadequate information frictional unemployment is a rule rather than an exception.

Frictional unemployment is inevitable due to the normal functioning of a market-based economy

Frictional unemployment occurs for various other reasons, for example, when old firms face problems of demand recession (such as the workers of Hindustan Motors), when workers' job performance is considered inadequate by any standard, and when workers of particular skills are not in demand any more. This has happened in cases of silent movie actors or typists or tram drivers in most parts of the world.

Frictional unemployment also occurs when workers voluntarily leave their jobs or move from one part of the country to another part (and try to search out better jobs).

Frictional unemployment occurs due to inter-sectoral imbalance between demand and supply forces, i.e., where there is excess supply of labour in one sector offering higher wages due to the fact that some workers from numerous low-paying sectors have crowded the few high-paying sectors.

REAL WAGE RIGIDITY AND FRICTIONAL UNEMPLOYMENT

Unemployment may occur if the real wage rate is not flexible but is fixed above market-clearing level. Thus wage rigidity—the failure of wages to adjust until labour supply equals labour demand—causes frictional unemployment.

As Fig. 14.7 shows if the real wage rate is fixed above the market-clearing level, there will exist excess supply of labour or unemployment (measured by the distance *FG*). In such a situation scarce jobs (L_a) are rationed among jobseekers (L_e). Rigidity of real wage rate raises the level of unemployment by reducing the rate of job finding.

The unemployment arising from wage rigidity and job rationing is known as **wait unemployment**. Workers are unemployed because, at the prevailing wage rate, the supply of labour exceeds its demand, not because they are actively searching for the jobs that are quite suitable for their individual skills. Such unemployment arises because workers are waiting for jobs to become available sooner or later. Such unemployment persists because firms are not able to reduce wages even in the presence of excess supply of labour.

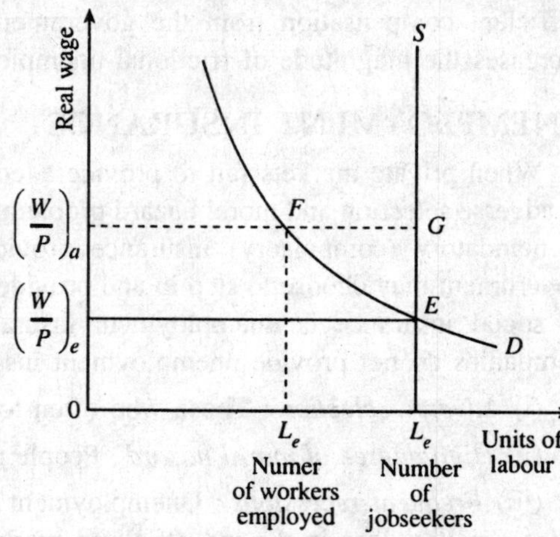

Fig. 14.7: Wage Rigidity and Job Rationing

There are three causes of wage rigidity, viz., minimum wage laws, monopoly power of trade unions, and efficiency wages. These three causes explain why the labour market does not clear, i.e., why wages do not fall despite an excess supply of labour.

UNIONS AND COLLECTIVE BARGAINING

The monopoly power of strong and well organised trade unions also cause wage rigidity. Since trade unions demand and succeed in getting higher wages, there is an increase in structural unemployment. Some firms voluntarily pay higher than the market wage as a preventive measure so that the workers feel happy and do not form unions.

The magnitude of structural unemployment also depends on another factor, viz., the conflict between two different groups of workers— *insiders* (who are in employ) and *outsiders* (who are out of employ). Insiders always try to keep the wages of their firms as high as possible. Outsiders are willing to work at lower wages. So they bear a portion of the cost of higher wage. The effect of collective bargaining on wages and employment depends on the relative power of the two groups. With an increase in unemployment the insiders become outsiders and their bargaining power becomes weaker. So unionisation benefits only the insiders and not the outsiders.

Insider-Outsider Model

The term 'hysteresis', is used to refer to the property that, when a variable is shocked away from an initial value, it shows no tendency to return even when the shock is over.

An interesting explanation for hysteresis in the unemployment process is the insider-outsider model. This model, like the sticky price models, is based on the assumption of imperfect competition.

According to this model, insiders (e.g., workers in unionised firms or industries) are the only group that affects the real wage bargain. Outsiders (e.g., the unemployed) seek jobs but cannot bargain for higher real wage. They cannot exert downward pressure on real wages because they are irrelevant to the wage-bargaining process.

In fact, the insiders are assumed to use their bargaining power to push the real wage above the market-clearing level, resulting in an unemployed group of outsiders. During recessions when workers are laid off insiders become outsiders.

PUBLIC POLICY TOWARDS FRICTIONAL UNEMPLOYMENT

Many public policy programmes such as retraining workers for new jobs and disseminating information about job vacancies in order to match the number of jobs and job seekers more efficiently have been adopted in a number of countries. Public expenditure on retraining workers seeks to absorb the workers displaced by declining (the so-called sunset) industries into emerging (sun-rise) industries.

Some government programmes increase the magnitude of transitional unemployment. One such programme is unemployment insurance. Many workers prefer to remain unemployed if they get sufficient compensation from the government rather than accept low-paid jobs. This programme increases the magnitude of frictional unemployment and raises the natural rate of unemployment.

UNEMPLOYMENT INSURANCE

When private markets fail to provide adequate insurance to individuals in times of distress (due to adverse selection and moral hazard problems) there is likely to be a role for social insurance, which is mandatory (compulsory) insurance provided by the government. In such circumstances, the government may choose to step in and provide broad and universal coverage. One important example of social insurance is unemployment insurance which seeks to promote social welfare. Private companies do not provide unemployment insurance for *three* reasons:

(i) *Adverse selection* : Those who often lose jobs are more likely to participate.

(ii) *High degree of moral hazard* : People may choose to remain unemployed if benefits are high.

(iii) *Frequent recessions* : Unemployment always occur during recessions which are so frequent now-a-days in the industrialised world.

For all three reasons most industrial countries have unemployment insurance (UI) systems that provide income support to the unemployed. UI refers to the payment of unemployment benefits to workers who lose their jobs. There are very good reasons why society should provide some insurance to workers who lose their jobs and find it difficult to get new jobs. The UI system is based on the basic economic philosophy that people should have '*a safety net*' under them as and when they lose their job. For this reason governments often take the initiative in providing unemployment insurance. The government cannot solve the moral hazard problem but can avoid the adverse selection through universal coverage.

Objective of the Scheme

The basic objective of the scheme is to reduce the economic hardship associated with unemployment. But UI benefits create a problem. Since unemployed workers who receive UI benefits can be more selective while searching for a job, the availability of benefits is likely to increase the duration of unemployment. In other words, UI may increase the natural rate of unemployment in two ways: (i) by increasing the time that the unemployed spend looking for work, and (ii) by increasing the incentives for firms to lay off workers during slack seasons.

UI increases the magnitude of NRU

The Rate of Job Finding

Statistical studies show that when unemployed workers become ineligible for benefits, they are more likely to search out and find new jobs. To be more specific the probability of an unemployed person finding a new job increases when his/her benefits go away. The main reason for this is that an absence of benefits increases the search effort of unemployed workers. It is also possible for workers without benefits to accept job offers that they would normally refuse to accept because of low wages and bad (unhealthy and unsafe) working conditions.

It is normally found that when unemployment benefits are stopped, workers put more effort to job search. Thus it logically follows that the incentives provided by the UI system affect the rate of job finding.

Criticism

Critics feel that by making the effects of unemployment less painful more generous unemployment benefits increase wages at a given unemployment rate. If UI did not exist workers would be virtually penniless and would be willing to accept very low wages to avoid remaining unemployed. But unemployment benefits give workers an opportunity to get higher wages. So at a given unemployment rate, higher employment benefits increase wages.

Conclusion

Some economists have suggested reforms to UI to achieve the best of both the worlds, viz., performing its function of supporting the unemployed, while, at the same time, reducing incentives for increased unemployment. For example, some employers frequently lay off their workers, on a temporary basis. More taxes should be imposed on employers so that they bear a greater portion of the unemployment benefits that their workers receive.

> **Economic Insight: Unemployment Insurance and Increase in NRU (or Steady-State Unemployment Rate)**
>
> UI policies slaken the job searching effort of unemployed individuals. In fact, the period alloted to individuals, during which they receive the insurance payment, is not utilised by workers fruitfully to look for new jobs. The beneficiaries remain idle and look jobs only after the expiry of the benefit.
>
> Secondly, the workers who are covered by UI generally do not press employers for providing guaranteed and secure jobs, through contractual agreements. So they are vulnerable to a greater chance of being laid off.
>
> Thus it is quite obvious that UI reduces the rate of job finding (f) by inducing workers to put less effort to find out jobs. It also increases the rate of job loss (l) by providing workers with a safety net. They live in a world of illusion. They feel that they are virtually employed. We know that the natural (steady-state) rate of unemployment is expressed as
>
> $$\frac{U}{L}=\frac{l}{l+f}$$
>
> A decrease in 'f' and an increase in 'l' conjointly raise $\left(\frac{U}{L}\right)$. Thus UI increases the NRU.

A NOTE OF STRUCTURAL UNEMPLOYMENT

It involves a mismatch between worker qualifications and job requirements. It often arises when changes take place in the methods of production and in the types of goods and services produced. It also arises from changes in the conditions of demand and supply for the products of particular industries. It persists over long periods of time and cannot be cured easily. New automatic banking machines may mean unemployment for bank tellers and book-keepers, and a switch in consumer preference from golf to tennis implies unemployment for golf-stick and golf-ball makers. Such unemployment also arises due to job discrimination and other barriers in the job market.

A close scrutiny reveals that structural unemployment is more serious than frictional unemployment because workers are not leaving their old jobs voluntarily in order to search out better ones. Their old jobs have disappeared owing to circumstances beyond their control.

Structural unemployment could persist even at a time when the overall demand for labour in the economy was high, and the removal of the unemployment requires a structural change in the economy.

In order to solve this complex problem some special programmes have to be undertaken—programmes that not only retain people but also help them discover and move to where new jobs are available. It is, however, felt that some structural unemployment is always present because workers cannot keep up with constant changes in the economy.

KEY POINTS

1. ***Natural rate of unemployment*** : The natural rate of unemployment (NRU) is often called the steady-state rate of unemployment because it depends on the rate of job loss and the rate of job finding.

2. *Frictional unemployment* : Some frictional unemployment is the consequence of the functioning of the labour market because workers devote some time to search out the jobs which best suit their individual tastes and skills.

3. *Structural unemployment* : Structural unemployment is the inevitable consequence of mismatch in the labour market. It results when the real wage remains above the market clearing level.

4. *Real wage rigidity* : Three causes of real wage rigidity are minimum wage legislation, the existence of powerful trade unions and the threat of unionisation.

5. *Efficiency wage* : Four efficiency wage models conjointly suggest that, for various reasons, firms often find it profitable to pay higher wages in spite of the existence of excess supply of labour.

6. *Periodicity of unemployment* : The duration of unemployment varies from country to country and period to period. Most spells of unemployment are short run in nature.

7. *Unemployment insurance* : One government programme which increases the magnitude of frictional unemployment, without intending to do so, is unemployment insurance in a dynamic economy. It refers to a government programme that partially protects workers' incomes when they become unemployed. This programme seeks to offer workers partial protection against unemployment and loss of income. The unemployed who quit their jobs, were fired for genuine reasons, or just entered the labour force are not eligible. Benefits are paid only to the unemployed who were laid off because their skill are no longer in demand in a dynamic economy.

KEY TERMS

Joblessness	Full employment
Structural unemployment	The Pigou effect
Frictional unemployment	The real balance effect
Cyclical unemployment	Keynes effect
Labour force participation rate	Real balance effect
Voluntary unemployment	Wage cut
Involuntary unemployment	Unemployment insurance
Equilibrium unemployment	Tax cut
Disequilibrium unemployment	Deficit financing
Wage rigidity	NAIRU
Natural rate of unemployment	Efficiency wage

ASSIGNMENTS

1. Why does the labour supply curve tend to be vertical in the classical model?
2. Why does the payment of efficiency wage create real wage rigidity and involuntary unemployment?
3. Discuss Keynes's theory of involuntary unemployment.
4. Explain why there is unemployment and job vacancy in an economy at the same time.
5. What is natural rate of unemployment?.How is it related to the concept of full employment?
6. Why is NRU called NAIRU?
7. Distinguish between indirect and direct real balance effect.
8. Define full employment. How can this be attained? Show diagrammatically.
9. Distinguish between (i) job creation and job loss, (ii) unemployment and job vacancy, (iii) frictional and structural unemployment, and (iv) the Keynes effect and the Pigou effect.
10. Let the total population of a country be 255 million and the number of people under the age of 16 who are not considered adults be 61.2 million. Let those who are retired, voluntarily idle, work in households, and are in schools number 65.5 million. The number of people who are employed is 118.4 million.

    Find out:

    (i) total labour force, (ii) total unemployed, (iii) unemployment rate and (iv) labour force participation rate.

11. True, False and Uncertain (explain your choice)
    (i) Both the insiders and outsiders gain from unionisation.
    (ii) Efficiency wage theory explains that firms pay workers equilibrium wage rate.
12. What are the determinants of the natural rate of unemployment?
13. What is unemployment insurance (UI)? Is it really effective in reducing the magnitude of natural rate of unemployment (NRU)?

[**Hint:** While (UI) unemployment insurance reduces the hardship of unemployment, it also increases the magnitude of unemployment. Since unemployment benefits stop when a worker takes a new job he puts less search effort and is more likely to reject unattractive jobs. In addition, because unemployment insurance makes unemployment less distressing and painful, workers are less likely to seek job security when they negotiate with employers over the terms and conditions of employment.

The design and pattern of the UI system influences the effort which the unemployed put to job search.

When the unemployed become ineligible for benefits, the probability of their finding a new job rises markedly. Thus, receipt of UI benefits reduces the search effort of the unemployed.

Even though unemployment insurance reduces job search effort and raises unemployment the programme achieves its main objective of reducing the income uncertainty which workers face. In addition when workers turn down unattractive jobs, they get the opportunity to search out better jobs which suit their individual tastes and skills. UI improves the ability of the economy to match each worker with the most appropriate job.

The study of UI shows that the unemployment rate is an imperfect measure of a nation's overall level of economic well-being. Eliminating UI would reduce the magnitude of unemployment in the economy. Whether economic well-being would be enhanced or diminished by this change in policy is, of course, debatable.]

14. What happens to the demand for labour if labour productivity falls, due to, say, an adverse shock to the production function? How will this affect employment and real wages if the labour market is in a perpetual state of disequilibrium? Will a productivity decline affect the labour market if unions resist employers' attempt to cut wages?
15. Explain briefly why frictional unemployment is inevitable in a modern economy.
16. In a particular month, the labour force is 130 million, there are 9.1 million unemployed workers, the job-losing rate is 3 per cent per month, and the job-finding rate is 40 per cent per month. How many people will be unemployed next month? At what unemployment rate would the number of unemployed remain the same from one month to the next?
17. Suppose that a country experiences a reduction in productivity—that is, an adverse shock to the production function.
    (a) What happens to the labour demand curve?
    (b) How would this change in productivity affect the labour market — that is, employment, unemployment and real wages — if the labour market were always in equilibrium?
    (c) How would this change in productivity affect the labour market if unions prevented real wages from falling?
18. Explain the factors which determine the natural rate of unemployment. What kind of unemployment does the natural rate capture?

14A THE MEASUREMENT OF UNEMPLOYMENT AND UNDEREMPLOYMENT IN INDIA

The problem of surplus labour (or labour redundancy) in LDCs like India gets reflected in (a) open unemployment, (b) underemployment and (c) disguised unemployment.

Raj Krishna suggested the following four criteria for measuring unemployment in India.

(a) **Time criterion:** This criterion suggests that only those who should be identified as unemployed who are engaged in gainful work for less than some standard normal hours in a week or less than a certain normal standard days in a month or a year.

(b) **Willingness criterion:** This criterion suggests that a person should be called unemployed when he is either having a job or is available for work at the prevailing wage rate.

(c) **Income criterion:** According to this criterion, only those persons whose income is less than a criterion 'minimum level' (based on a certain 'poverty norm') are to be treated as unemployed or underemployed. This poverty level of income is fixed on the basis of minimum calories required for subsistence.

(d) **Productivity criterion:** According to this criterion only those persons who are gainfully employed but have less than some normal standards of productivity are considered as unemployed or underemployed[1].

Since 1972-73 the following three approaches have been used to measure open unemployment as also underemployment by using time and willingness criteria. These approaches were recommended by the Dantwala Committee.

(i) **Usual status approach:** According to this approach only those persons who did not remain engaged in any gainful work (occupation) during the major part of the 365 days preceding the date of survey but were seeking jobs and were available for work are to be treated and recorded as unemployed. Thus this approach seeks to estimate the magnitude of long-term open unemployment.

(ii) **Weekly status approach:** This approach records only the current activity status of work relating to the week preceding the date of survey. So only those persons who are not gainfully employed even for an hour on a single day in the preceding week but were desparately looking for jobs or were readily available for work are to be classified as unemployed.

Comparing the Two Approaches

If we compare the above two approaches we find that those who may be treated as employed on the basis of the usual status approach may, however, become unemployed every now and then during some seasons or parts of the year. Thus weekly status approach also captures seasonal unemployment. In addition, this approach gives an estimate of weekly average rate of unemployment.

While the usual status approach estimates long-term open unemployment, the weekly status approach also captures seasonal unemployment

(iii) **Daily status approach:** A close look reveals that the weekly status approach tends to underestimate unemployment in the economy. The reason is that it is not judicious to treat all those who have been unemployed for the whole week except even for a single hour as employed. In truth, the demand for labour in rural areas—both in farming and in non-farming activities—often fluctuates for short spells of time even within a week. This is why there is need to use the daily status approach for measuring the magnitudes of unemployment and underemployment in India.

1. Amartya Sen has referred to three aspects of employment, viz., production aspect, income aspect and recognition aspect and defined unemployment accordingly. See his *Employment Technology and Development* (Oxford, 1973). See also *Economic Essays* by the author.

According to the daily status approach the current daily status of a person as to whether he is employed or unemployed or outside the labour force is recorded for each day in a particular **reference week.** Furthermore, 'half-day' has been used as a yardstick (or a unit of measurement) for estimating the magnitude of employment and unemployment. To be more specific, a person who works for 4 hours or more up to 8 hours on a day is recorded as employed for the whole day. Likewise, a person who works for an hour or more but less than 4 hours on a particular day is recorded as employed for 'half-day'. This means that only those persons who had no gainful work even for a single hour on a single day are treated as unemployed for the full day provided they are either looking for jobs or are readily available for work (i.e., not voluntarily unemployed).

Comparison with the Other Two Approaches

The daily status approach gives a more accurate measure of unemployment than the other approaches. The reason is simple. The daily status approach records not only the days of unemployment of those persons who are usually unemployed but also the days of unemployment of those who are recorded as employed on weekly status basis. Therefore the daily status approach to unemployment is more inclusive and, therefore, accurate than the other two approaches. In addition, it would give an estimate of an average number of unemployed persons per day in a year. These are also referred to as person days unemployed instead of persons unemployed. Therefore it gives a clear picture of the magnitude of both open unemployment and underemployment.

The daily status approach to unemployment is more accurate and inclusive than the other two approaches

The official estimates of unemployment in India on the basis of the above three approaches are presented in Table 14A.1.

Table 14A.1 the Magnitude of Unemployment in India (as percentage of the labour force)

Approach	1977-78	1983	1987-88	1993-94	1999-2000	2004-05
Usual Principal Status	4.23	2.77	3.77	2.58	2.78	3.06
Current Weekly Status	4.48	4.51	4.80	3.6	4.4	—
Current Daily Status	8.8	8.28	6.01	5.95	7.3	8.3

Source: Planning Commission and Tenth Five Year Plan and Eleventh Five Year Plan Documents

From Table 14A.1 we see that since 1993-94, all types of unemployment (in terms of percentage of the labour force) as per the three approaches, discussed above, increased in 1999-2000 and 2004-05. According to estimates made by the Planning Commission the magnitude of current daily status unemployment increased from 34.7 mn. in 2004-05 to 36.7 mn. persons in 2006-07 (assuming, of course, the same unemployment rate, just to make the comparison meaningful). So it is clearly evident that various economic reform measures adopted since 1991 have led to the worsening of the unemployment situation in the country. India virtually achieved jobless growth. The unprecedented increase in national and per capita incomes (and the surpassing of the so-called 'Hindu Growth Rate') did not get translated into employment generation in a labour surplus country. While India's average annual growth rate in the past decade has been slightly over 8%, the rate of employment generation was less than 2%.

It may also be noted that both the usual status approach and the weekly status approach cover a tiny fraction of the surplus labour (or disguisedly unemployed people in India). The reason is that both the approaches measure only the magnitude of open unemployment.

In addition, even the daily status approach, much like the other two approaches, fails to capture the disguisedly unemployed people with very low intensity of work and low productivity due to work stretching.[1] The work, which can be done by 3 persons, each working for 8 hours a day is normally done by 4 persons, each working for 6 hours a day. So each one is underemployed, and none is unemployed. If 3 of them become fully employed, the other will become totally unemployed. In spite of these limitations, it appears that daily status unemployment is a fairly accurate and acceptable measure of the magnitude of surplus labour in India since it is the most comprehensive measure of unemployment. It is better than the other two because it seeks to cover both open unemployment and the magnitude of underemployment as much as possible. This simply suggests that in order to make a proper and correct assessment of the magnitude of surplus labour which exists in India, the measurement of unemployment on the basis of daily hourly status is not enough. The measurement of disguised unemployment based on an acceptable norm such as the intensity of work (which gets reflected in labour productivity) is equally vital.

1. In fact, according to Amartya Sen, disguised unemployment usually gets reflected in lower intensity of work. In his **'Choice of Techniques'**, Sen cited the example of a farmer who was watching birds while sowing seeds, because he did not have enough work to do on a family farm where almost always there is overcrowding.

Part-III

Business Cycles and Fiscal Policy

15. Theories of Business (Trade) Cycles

16. Fiscal Policy for Economic Stabilisation

CHAPTER 15

Theories of Business (Trade) Cycles

> *A trade cycle is composed of periods of good trade characterised by rising prices and low unemployment percentages with periods of bad trade characterised by falling prices and high unemployment percentages.* J. M. Keynes

Most of free enterprise economies such as the USA, the UK, Germany, etc. have achieved rapid economic growth since the time of the first Industrial Revolution (which started around 1740). As a result their standard of living and level of economic welfare have improved considerably which get reflected in the improvement of the physical quality of life of their people. But economic growth, which is a long-term phenomenon, did not follow a steady and smooth upward trend. These countries have experienced periodic short-term fluctuations in the level of economic activities, with GDP, national income, the level of employment and the aggregate price level as key variables. Such fluctuations are known as business (trade) cycles. In the language of P.A. Samuelson "Business cycles are economywide fluctuations in total national output, income and employment, usually lasting for a period of 2 to 10 years, marked by widespread expansion or contraction in most sectors of the economy." Economic history shows that the period of good trade is followed by a period of bad trade, or prosperity yields place to mild recession or even deep depression. The periods of prosperity is characterised by rising income, output, employment or even the price level. By contrast the period of recession or depression is characterised by falling income, output, employment and the general price level. Such alternating periods of expansion and contraction in economic activity are known as business cycles. Business cycles refer to the fluctuations of economic activity around the long-term growth path. Statistical studies show that short-term economic fluctuations occur periodically with some degree of regularity. Of course, the duration or periodicity of business cycles varies.

Business cycles refer to the fluctuations of economic activity around the long-term growth path

Business fluctuations have traditionally been called *business cycles*. This name arose because at times there appears to be a regular alternation of expansions and contractions. Business fluctuations are not self-generating, with each phase caused by the preceding one. Nevertheless the use of the term 'cycle' for 'fluctuation' is well established in macroeconomics.

TYPES AND PERIODICITY OF BUSINESS CYCLES

Cycles of various lengths have been identical. Long cycle(s) in economic activity are known as Kondratieff's long waves. These are very long period cycles with a duration of 45 to 60 years. These cycles are thought to be associated with, *inter alia*, the major flourishes of investment activity consequent upon some fundamental innovation. However, economic records in most countries do not go back far enough on a reliable basis to allow this theory to be properly used. If it is correct, the remarkable spurt of growth in world incomes and trade from 1950 to 1980 may turn out to have been a boom phase in a long cycle.

The longest cycle usually identified is the Kondratieff wave (45-60 years)

But major cycles are of quite shorter length. These are called Juglar investment cycles (7-11 years) which average 9 years in length (from one peak to another) and they occur with pretty good regularity. This 9-year cycle is usually termed as trade cycle. (Actually most of the business theories are in regard to these waves.) The shortest cycle is the Kitchen inventory cycle (3-5 years). The Kuznets infrastructural investment cycle is even longer (15-25 years).

Business cycles also differ in their severity. In same cycles there are large swings away from the trend. In others these swings are of a mild (moderate) nature.

ECONOMIC COSTS

Business cycles involve huge economic costs. In times of recession or depression many people become unemployed. As a result there is a loss of potential output. In addition, due to fall in demand and fall in prices many businesses suffer huge losses. Some firms even go out of business or become bankrupt.

During depression the standards of living of people go down. In fact, depression and unemployment make the life of the people miserable and increase the incidence of poverty. At the same time, there is loss of output and wealth due to the existence of unemployed labour and idle production capacity.

During economic expansion, an economy experiences inflation. And inflation has various economic and social costs. Inflation reduces the real income (purchasing power) of the people and increases the incidence of poverty. It distorts the pattern of allocation of resources by diverting them from productive to unproductive uses (such as speculation, hoarding, black marketing, etc.). Inflation increases inequality by making the rich richer and the poor poorer. And high rate of inflation acts as obstacle to economic growth. [See Ch. on 'Inflation' for a detailed discussion of this point.]

Worse still, fluctuations in economic activity create a lot of uncertainty about the future. It makes it difficult for the economic agents to take correct decisions regarding production, consumption, saving, and investment.

THE PHASES AND THE TURNING POINTS

Business cycles, much like a year have their own seasons. The traditional view was that business cycles have four phases. But the modern view is that business cycles have two phases, viz., depression and prosperity and two turning points, viz., recovery (upper turning point) and recession (lower turning point).

A cycle involves a period of above-trend growth of output (recovery and prosperity) and a period of below-trend stagnation on or decline (contraction or recession).

In the language of P.A. Samuelson and W.B. Nordhaus, "Economists typically divide business cycles into two main phases; *recession* and *expansions.* Peaks and troughes mark the turning points of the cycles. The downturn of a business cycle is called a recession. A *recession* is a recurring period of decline in total output, income, and employment usually lasting from 6 to 12 months and marked by contractions in many sectors of the economy. A recession that is large in both scale and duration is called a *depression.*"[1]

Figure 15.1 shows the successive phases of a typical business cycle. We see that business cycles are irregular expansions and contractions in economic activity. This means that any two business cycles are not the same.

1. *Economics* (19th edn., 2010), p. 551

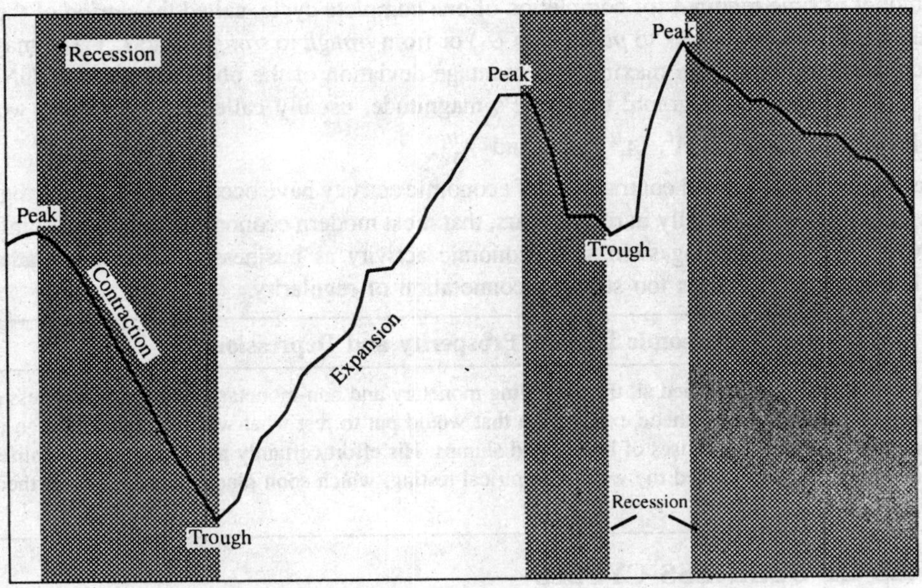

Fig. 15.1: A Business Cycle, like the Year, has its Seasons

One of the major reasons for studying macroeconomics is that there are times when just about everything seems to go wrong. Real income drops quarter after quarter and so does employment. The only thing that goes up is the unemployment rate. This general reversal of the normal growth of the economy is called a *contraction* or, more popularly, *a recession*. A particularly severe contraction is known as a *depression*. The more usual case of general growth in economic activity is called an *expansion*.

In a sense, a typical business cycle has *two* important phases.[1] During the *expansion* phase, GNP as a key variable grows more rapidly than its long-term trend growth rate and more rapidly than the rate of growth of productive capacity, with the proportion of productive capacity utilised increasing. At some point, the GNP series reaches its *upper turning point* and the *contraction phase* of the cycle starts. J. Poindexter has pointed out that "in the contraction, GNP may grow more slowly than its trend rate or may even fall in absolute value. During this phase, the proportion of productive capacity utilised falls". Finally, the GNP series reaches its *lower turning point* and expansion begins. In the idealised cycle in Fig. 15.2 two upper turning points (U and U_1) and two lower turning points (L and L_1) are labelled.

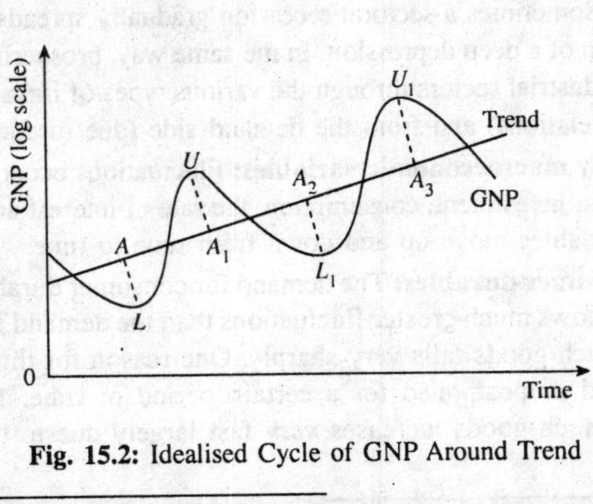

Fig. 15.2: Idealised Cycle of GNP Around Trend

1. See G. Haberler: *Prosperity and Depression*: A Theoretical Analysis of Cyclical Movements (Harvard University Press, 1958).

The amount of time required for completion of one complete cycle, called the *period* of the cycle, can be measured from cycle *peak* to *peak* (U to U_1) or from *trough* to *trough* (L to L_1). The magnitude of the cycle is measured by the maximum percentage deviation of the observed value of GNP from its trend value. In the above graph, the cycle's magnitude, usually called its *amplitude*, would be reflected in vertical distances A^L, A_1^U, $A_2^{L_1}$, and $A_3^{U_1}$.

Business cycles are recurrent

The periodic expansions and contractions of economic activity have occurred with such irregularity, especially in recent years, that most modern economists feel more comfortable labelling swings in economic activity as business '*fluctuations*' rather than '*cycles*'. The latter term carries too strong a connotation of regularity.

Economic Insight: Prosperity and Depression
G. Haberler reviewed and classified all the prevailing monetary and non-monetary theories of business cycles with the aim of producing a synthetic explanation that would put to rest what was then becoming an almost endless controversy about the causes of booms and slumps. His effort certainly put a stop to the proliferation of alternative theories and pointed the way to empirical testing, which soon placed business cycle theory on a more secure footing.

FEATURES OF BUSINESS CYCLES

No doubt, business cycles differ in periodicity and intensity[1]. To quote Samuelson: "No two business cycles are quite the same; yet they have much in common. They are not identical, but they are recognisable as belonging to the same family." Therefore, *no exact formula* can be found and used to predict the *timing* of future (or past) business/trade cycles. Yet they have some common features. These are the following:

1. Regularity: Business cycles differ in duration. But they occur regularly, i.e., as a matter of routine, so to say. But all cycles do not have the same regularity.

Recession or prosperity in one sector spreads quickly to other sectors

2. Diverse moments: All sectors of the economy do not move up or down in step with aggregate output. Construction, for example, generally fluctuates in a distinctly countercyclical pattern. Again industrial production is often out of step with aggregate final sales. At such times the economy suffers the undesired consequences of growing unemployment of labour and capital but no peak in output is identifiable. Clearly, the economists' scheme for labelling cycle turning points—hence expansion and contraction periods —is somewhat arbitrary.

3. Synchronic nature: Sometimes a sectoral recession gradually spreads quickly to other sectors and ultimately takes the form of a deep depression. In the same way, prosperity in a particular industry or sector spreads to other industrial sectors through the various types of linkages both from the supply side (through input-output relations) and from the demand side (due to complementaries).

4. Fluctuations in all key macroeconomic variables: Fluctuations occur in all key variables such as the real GDP, employment, investment, consumption, the rate of interest and the general price level at the same time. These variables move up and down from time to time.

5. The demand for consumer durables: The demand for consumer durables such as cars, houses, refrigerators, TV sets, etc. shows much greater fluctuations than the demand for non-durables. During recession the demand for such goods falls very sharply. One reason for this is that the purchase of such goods can be deferred or postponed for a certain period of time. In times of recovery or prosperity the purchase of such goods increases very fast largely due to the existence of pent-up demand.

1. As P.A. Samuelson has put it, "Business cycles are members of the same family but they are not identical twins."

6. Consumption of non-durables: Empirical studies show that consumption of non-durables and services does not vary much in the two phases of the business cycle, viz, depression and prosperity.

7. Investment fluctuations: Since investment depends on the animal spirits of capitalism (i.e., the waves of entrepreneurial optimism and pessimism), it shows much greater fluctuations than any other component of aggregate demand. According to Keynes, investment fluctuates because its main determinant, viz., marginal efficiency of capital (or the profit expectation of entrepreneurs) is most volatile.

8. Inventories: In times of depression, there is usually a huge accumulation of undesired inventories of finished goods. This leads to a sharp fall in production. On the contrary in times of recovery or prosperity there is a reduction of inventories. Actual inventories fall below the desired level. This encourages traders to place more orders for goods with manufacturers. This stimulates production and induces business firms to make new investment in fixed capital.

9. Fluctuations in profit: Profit shows much greater fluctuations than any other factor income. During depression profits may even become negative. As a result many firms go out of business. In times of prosperity, since costs do not rise as fast as prices, profits rise.

10. Uncertainty: Business cycles create much uncertainty about the future. So business firms cannot forecast future economic conditions accurately and cannot take long-term decisions such as investment in fixed capital in the form of plant, equipment and machinery.

11. International transmission: Business cycles get transmitted from one country to another through price effects and income changes. A recession in the USA or any other country leads to a fall in the demand for goods and services of the developing countries like India. So exports of such countries fall and they are forced to reduce their imports from advanced countries. Thus a chain reaction is triggered.

In fact, cyclical fluctuations (especially inflation) may be internationally transmitted. And a country may face the problem of 'imported inflation'.

Economic Insight: Characteristics of a Recession

A recession is defined as "a significant decline in economic activity spread across the economy, lasting more than a few months, normally visible in real GDP, real income, employment, industrial production, and whole sales-retail sales"

Simply put, a recession occurs when real GDP has declined for two consecutive calendar quarters.

Paul Samuelson has referred to the following *five* characteristics of a typical recession:

(i) **Fall in investment:** As soon as recession starts, investment first falls quite sharply. To start with there is decline in investment in housing. This happens mainly due to a financial crisis or a rising interest rates by the central bank to slow inflation. In addition, purchases of consumer goods often fall quite sharply. As businesses reduce production due to low demand real GDP falls.

(ii) **Job loss:** In the initial stage of recession, employment falls. It does not recover even when the economy moves to the next (recovery) phase. So all displaced workers do not get an opportunity to go back to work.

(iii) **Decelerating inflation:** With a fall in demand for consumer goods as also for raw materials, prices fall in the face of falling production. Wages and the prices of services do not fall, but they rise less rapidly in economic downturns.

(iv) **Decline in profits and share prices:** Business profits fall quite sharply in recession. In anticipation of this, prices of ordinary shares fall as investors apprehend the possibility of a business downturn.

(v) **Cuts in interest rates:** In general, as business condition deteriorate and employment falls, the central bank reduces short-term interest rates to stimulate investment. Consequently all other interest rates fall as well.

THEORIES OF BUSINESS CYCLE

Since the time of Alfred Marshall and W.S. Jevons several theories of business cycles have been presented by economists. These theories seek to identify the causes of business cycles.

EXTERNAL AND INTERNAL CYCLE THEORIES

Basically economists can distinguish between two broad classes of business cycle theories. The first class attributes cycles to forces *external* to the systematic interactions of the component parts of the economic system. Historically the focus of attention has been on wars, discovery of gold mines and major innovations (like the railroad, the automobile and the computer). As an interesting alternative source of fluctuations in business activity, Jevons, a 19th century economist, attributed trade cycles to changes in the level of sunspot activity. According to the sunspot theory, changes in sunspot activity affected the earth's climate which, in its turn, affected crop yields. Fluctuations in agricultural output and prices resulted in fluctuations in the overall level of economic activity.

The second class of theories, called the *internal* theories, ascribe business fluctuations to endogenous forces— forces within the economy that automatically reverse cumulative expansions and contractions in economic activity. The common point of all these theories is that the majority ascribe a pivotal role to movements in investment. The theories may now be discussed one by one.

1. Sunspot Theory

W. S. Jevons (1835-82) theorised that the sunspot cycle influences the weather, which affects the size of crops. Large crops occur when sunspots are at a minimum, and the resulting low prices of agricultural product stimulate the economy. Thus the theory predicts that economic activity can be co-ordinated with events outside the economic system. Jevons provided evidence that economic cycles could be linked to regular occurrence of the solar flares or spots. Sunspot theory now refers to the proposition that it is possible for the economic activity of individuals to be endogeneously coordinated and hence appear to be correlated with some outside activity (such an sunspot).

The sunspot theory of the business cycle did not get much empirical support. So it has been virtually rejected.

2. Pure Monetary Theory

According to R.G. Hawtrey money plays a dominant role in causing cyclical fluctuations in economic activities.[1] Variations in the supply of money, or in its velocity of circulation, are necessary conditions for changes in the monetary value of the nation's output.

Hawtrey postulates that expansions begin when traders, i.e., basically those who hold inventories of raw materials and finished goods borrow from the banks at low rates of interest. Banks, having excess reserves, reduce bank rates in order to encourage businesses to borrow more funds. This extra bank lending leads to an increase in the money supply. As a result business spending increases without an offsetting reduction of spending in other sectors. As long as the increase in the money supply continues, income and spending will also keep on growing. However, sooner or later the banks' excess reserves get depleted. In such a situation banks raise interest rates in order to reduce lending. This, in its turn, leads to reductions in the money supply. Thus a liquidity crisis arises in the economy since bank credit is costly and less readily available. So the economy moves into the contractionary phase of the business cycle, characterised by a fall in the money supply and the consequent fall in spending and income.

During the downswing (contraction) excess reserves build up, making the system ready for a new expansion. Monetarists, i.e., the followers of M. Friedman and A. Schwartz still hold the view that money is the only cause of business cycles. But the truth is that business cycles have both monetary and real causes.

An Overall Assessment of the Theory: Hawtrey's analysis correctly identifies inventory investment as the most volatile component of aggregate demand. Also, his concern with financial considerations broadens our perspective on the sources of economic fluctuations. But his failure to

1. In Hawtrey's theory an important role has been assigned to the wholeseller and his sensitivity to changes in interest rate (i.e., the cost of borrowing).

provide for any accelerator mechanism and his emphasis on the response of just inventory investment to changes in credit conditions limit the usefulness of his theory.

Economic Insight: Hawtrey on Business Cycles
R.G. Hawtrey's book, *Good and Bad Trade*: An Inquiry into the Causes of Trade Fluctuations (1913) expressed the view that business cycles are essentially a monetary phenomenon. They must, therefore, be controlled by regulating credit to wholesalers and retailers *via* the bank (interest) rate and not by raising public expenditure. Hawtrey never contemplated direct control of the money supply as advocated by M. Friedman and other monetarists. But he was quite right in his view since in the 1930s, monetary policy always meant, rightly or wrongly, a policy about the rate of interest and not a policy about the money supply targets. Hawtrey also suggested that expenditure on public works financed by the sale of government bonds do nothing to remedy a depression because they only 'crowd out private investment.' He also held the view that the demand for idle money balances is a key element in any policy designed to stabilise the level of total economic activity.

3. Underconsumption Theory

Following the Malthusian view, John A. Hobson, developed the underconsumption theory of business cycles. The theory gets ample support from J. M. Keynes and A. H. Hansen.

Underconsumption is the same using as oversaving. This means that at times saving is excessive in relation to the need for investment. This also means that the level of consumption may be too low to ensure full utilisation of the total productive capacity of the economy. This will result in unemployment and lower incomes, and less supply of consumption goods than the economy is capable of producing.

According to this theory, during the upswing of the business cycles household consumption does not increase as fast as their incomes rise. At the same time due to increase in the stock of capital (through an act of investment) it becomes possible to increase output of consumer goods and services. Even if income increases at the same rate as output, the demand for consumption goods grows slowly. Consequently business firms are left with increased productive capacity and some potential profit is lost. Therefore a fall in investment demand is inevitable even when saving is increasing. This means that total private demand (which is the sum of household consumption demand and business investment demand) is not strong enough to buy the amount of goods and services which firms are willing and able to produce and offer for sale in the market(s). So a contraction and crisis are soon to appear. Underconsumption theories have considered the following two main causes of business cycles:

(i) **Lags in economic behaviour:** According to Hobson, consumption habits are developed over the years. So people respond to increase in their incomes with a time lag. The reason is that they take some time to learn how to improve their standard of living when they experience an increase in income. By contrast, producers are very skilled at developing new and improved produces and introducing new techniques of creating and meeting new demand. Thus production lag is shorter than consumption lag. In other words, in production there is instantaneous adjustment and in consumption lagged adjustment.

(ii) **Inequitable distribution of income:** Another source of trouble lies in unequal distribution of income which is one of the common characteristics of the market-driven economies. During business expansions, non-wage (property) incomes such as profit, interest and rent grow much faster than wage. However, the wage earners have a stronger propensity to consume than other income recipients. Therefore, even in the expansionary phase of expansion of business cycles, consumption does not rise as fast as national income.

Economic Insight: Karl Marx on Business Cycles

According to Karl Marx, the underconsumption of the masses is the root cause of all capitalist crises. With an increase in the scale of production due to the ploughing back of profits by capitalists, there is an increase in the supply of mass consumption goods in capitalist countries. But wages remain fixed at the subsistence level. Workers are paid a minimum wage which is just sufficient for their survival and maintenance of their productive capacity. Capitalists exploit workers by depressing wages. Moreover due to growing mechanisation in the production process, there is a fall in the demand for labour and thus in the level of employment. As a result there exists a huge reserve army of unemployed in capitalist countries.

Workers consume the major portion of the income. So a fall in wage income for the above two reasons leads to the fall in the demand for consumption goods. Consequently capitalists are unable to realise the profits embodied in already produced goods. Thus the capitalist economy faces realisation crisis and ultimately collapses for want of markets.

4. The Non-monetary Overinvestment Theory

There is wide agreement among economists that one of the main causes of business cycles is investment fluctuation. The reason is that investment is the most volatile component of national income and thus aggregate demand (desired expenditure). The term 'overinvestment' refers to the observed tendency of investment to increase to such a level that is considered to be excessive in relation to demand for the output of goods and services it is capable of producing.

In this theory the economy moves up and slides down due to investment fluctuations. The expansion in economic activity occurs when business investment increases in response to improved profit opportunities at the beginning of the upturn since the rate of interest (cost of capital) is low due to an abundant supply of loanable funds. In truth, economic expansion follows a period of depression during which the capital has deteriorated in value, when there is an abundant supply of loanable funds (liquid money), interest rates are low and costs are also low due to low prices of resources.

When investment in plant and equipment increases, the incomes of those involved in producing capital goods (machines and equipment) also increase. This, in its turn, leads to an increase in demand for consumer goods.

However, business expansion and economic upturn cannot continue for long. Expansion comes to a halt due to rise in prices of resources. Resource prices rise due to growing competition among business firms. At this stage two developments occur in an economy: (i) The economy's capital stock grows. (ii) The supply of investible resources, which increases steadily in the initial stage of expansion, gets exhausted in a later stage. And the consequent shortage of loanable funds leads to a rise in interest rates. This makes further investment unprofitable. At the same time, the larger stock of capital is still capable of producing larger quantities of consumer goods. But the demand for such goods is not adequate to ensure full utilisation of installed production capacity. The reason is that when investment declines income falls due to creation of inadequate job opportunities. At this stage the producing units will discover that they have overinvested. The economy now moves into the contractionary phase of the business cycle which continues until the need for new investment arises and the supply of loanable funds increases so much that interest rates fall. The stage is now set for the economy to experience an upturn.

5. The Monetary Overinvestment Theory

The monetary overinvestment theory developed by F. A. Von. Hayek is based on the divergence between the natural rate of interest and market rate of interest, a distinction originally drawn by Knut Wicksell. The natural or equilibrium rate is the one which would prevail when the volume of household saving is equal to planned business investment. The market rate is determined by the impersonal forces of supply (which includes saving, increase in stock of money, an increase in the velocity of money and 'dishoarding' of funds) and demand (which includes investment, a decrease in velocity and 'hoarding'). The equality of the two rates of interest ensures that national income has attained its equilibrium level and has no tendency to move up or down. Thus the possibility of income fluctuations (business cycles) is ruled out. However, national income equilibrium is likely to be disturbed by an increase in the money supply due to the central bank purchase of government securities from the open market, lowering of legal reserve ratio or cash reserve ratio or even decrease in the bank (discount) rate. Due to any of the events (actions), the excess reserves of banks will increase. So they will be eager to make more loans and advances. Therefore they have to reduce the rate of interest so that bank credit becomes cheap. When this happens the market rate of interest will fall below the natural rate. So business firms will now be eager to invest more. This initiates the upturn and the expansionary phase of the cycle starts. On the other hand, households lose the incentives to save. So they increase their consumption spending. Due to an increase in both consumption demand and investment demand, in the absence of a corresponding increase in output to satisfy those demands, the price level will increase. Hayek assumes that due to business borrowing, the money supply will increase. This will lead to a flow of resources away from the production of consumption goods to the production of investment goods. This is a form of forced saving since consumers are forced to consume less, in real terms, than they wish to do, because of inflation. This expansion will continue as long as the money supply increases. However, this process cannot continue for long. As soon as the excess reserves of banks get exhausted, they will be forced to raise their lending rate (which is indeed the market rate of interest) and reduce their loans and advances. As a result the money supply growth will come to a halt. Now the economy moves into the contractionary phase in which business firms find it difficult to finance their new-investment plans. Consequently unemployment increases and prices fall. Overinvestment has indeed occurred.

6. Phychological Theory

Since almost all economic decisions involve the future and the future is uncertain (since it is characterised by an element of doubt), entrepreneurial optimism and pessimism may play an important role in causing business cycles. Waves of optimism and pessimism (or what Keynes calls the animal spirits of capitalism) may prevail the business community and as a consequence economic fluctuations do occur and often become serious. And A. C. Pigou and J. M. Keynes placed a disproportionate emphasis on psychological factors in their theory of business cycles.

> **Economic Insight: Hayek on Business Cycles**
>
> In his book *Prices and Production* (1931) R.G. Hawtrey argued that rising prices in a boom lead to fall in real wages. This then leads to the substitution of labours for machines and a general shortening of production periods. As a consequence the interest rate rises, investment falls, and the economy turns down. Conversely in a slump the rising level of real wage revives investment as labour is displaced by machines and periods of production are lengthened. In Hayek's view a rising level of consumption after a certain point reduces, rather than increase investment, and vice versa for a falling level of consumption. This is quite contrary to the usual Keynesian reasoning.

7. Keynes' Theory of Investment Fluctuations

Business cycles, according to Keynes, are caused by variations in the rate of investment consequent upon the volatility of the marginal efficiency of capital (*MEC*). Keynes thus assigns a major role to business person's profit expectations from new investment. Linked with fluctuations in *MEC* are movements in investment, output and employment. Business people are generally optimistic during expansionary phase as *MEC* is high. The rate of investment is high; so are the rates of income and employment. The prosperity period comes to an end when high *MEC* suffers a setback, due to two adverse forces: (i) as shortages and bottlenecks of raw materials and labour force arise due to high rate of production, production cost of new capital assets increases, and (ii) as the market becomes flooded with products, prices fall, leading to reduction of profits below expectation. Thus business optimism yields place gradually to pessimism. So *MEC* starts falling, leading to a fall in investment, employment and income in a cumulative fashion. Ultimately the lower turning point appears. Thus Keynes's theory is one of investment fluctuations. When the capital goods have worn out and excess supply (stock) of consumer goods has been exhausted, scarcity of capital and consumer goods again increases profits and profit opportunities. This invites expansion.

The transition from prosperity to recession (depression) occurs when the marginal efficiency of capital falls sharply and all of a sudden. As a result the investment demand schedule shifts to the left from I_0 to I_1. So investment falls from I_0* to I_1* as shown in Fig. 15.3. This leads to a fall in aggregate demand. As a result national income falls. This, in its turn, leads to a fall in consumption expenditure which leads to a further fall in income. And the process of income contraction continues due to the operation of the reverse multiplier. The fall in income (ΔY) due to the initial fall in investment (ΔI) will be equal to $-\Delta Y = m(-\Delta I)$, where $m = \frac{1}{1-b}$, and b is the marginal propensity to consume. Thus if $b = 0.80$, m will be 5. So a drop in investment of Rs. 100 crores will lead to a fall in income of Rs. 500 crores.

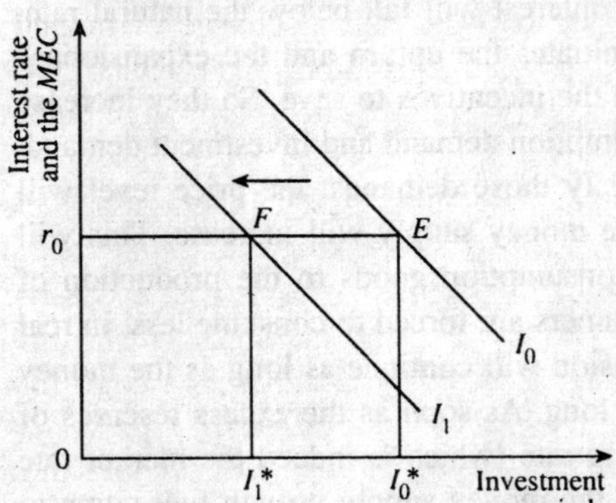

Fig. 15.3: Fall in an Autonomous Investment Due to a Fall in *MEC*

Criticism: The only criticism to Keynes's theory is that it laid too much stress on the role of multiplier only, while a complete explanation of trade cycles requires the interaction of both multiplier and accelerator.

8. Samuelson's Multiplier-Accelerator Interaction Theory (Model)

In order to acquire a basic understanding of what is involved in modern business cycle analysis, as our next task, we will take a close look at one prominent, post-Keynesian example of an internal cycle theory, viz., the multiplier-accelerator interaction theory. Interaction between the income multiplier and the accelerator mechanism has played a central role in virtually all modern business cycle models.

To start with, we may recall that the multiplier is the number by which the change in investment must be multiplied in order to present us with the resulting change in income. The implication is that *an increase in (autonomous) investment leads to an expansion of income and employment and* vice-versa *for a decrease in investment.*

The Acceleration Principle once again

The simple multiplier theory does nevertheless throw light on the aggregate economic process by which income and output change in the real world. Inequality of intended saving and investment causes the level of income to change. But observations from past data suggest that income fluctuations correspond to a regular cyclical pattern. The multiplier by itself does not explain this phenomenon; but it can help to explain it. We noted earlier that the positive effect of an investment stimulus on income may have a feedback effect in that the increased spending out of additional income may further stimulate investment. The 'acceleration principle' suggests that investment is related to changes in the level of output or sales.

The acceleration principle bears out the fact that fluctuations in industries producing capital goods are much greater than in the consumer goods industries. The acceleration principle suggests that this is because the level of investment depends not on the absolute level of demand but on its rate of change, so that investment may fall even when absolute demand is rising if the rate at which demand is changing begins to fall.

The acceleration principle can work in both directions. As Samuelson puts it: "Should sales now drop below a certain level, gross investment would drop away to nothing for a long time; in fact, the firm might want to disinvest by selling off some of its machinery. On the contrary a tremendous increase in investment spending is possible as a result of a moderate increase in consumption sales." According to the acceleration principle, "consumption has to keep on increasing in order for investment to stand still".

The accelerator principle relates the level of *net* investment to the rate of change of output.[1] According to the simple accelerator with output growing continuously net additions to the capital stock are required. For net investment to take place at a uniform *level* over time, the rate of growth of output must stay constant. As soon as it declines, even if it remain positive, investment falls.

The interaction of the multiplier and the accelerator provides some idea of how the business cycle occurs. Assume consumption expenditure increases, sales increase, and the demand for capital equipment increases, i.e., investment for expansion. The increased output both of consumer goods and of investment goods causes income to rise, and part of this will be spent on consumption, again causing sales to increase. In this expansionary phase the multiplier and accelerator reinforce each other. But when the rate of change of demand falls, net investment will be zero and replacement investment may even fall. Output of investment goods falls, which means that the income of factors of production in those industries falls. This will mean less consumption expenditure and so the multiplier will transmit itself in the reverse direction, and a contraction will set in until investment for replacement becomes necessary. Then the multiplier effect of increased investment spending and subsequently the combined multiplier-accelerator interaction will trigger off a new expansionary phase.

A simple example will make the idea clear. Suppose there is a textile producer who buys machines to produce cloth. Let us assume that he always keeps his stock of capital goods equal to 2 times the value of his yearly sales of cloth. So when his sales amount to Rs. 3 lakhs, he will be having machinery worth of Rs. 6 lakhs. He may possess 20 machines of different types and ages, one of which wears out each year and needs to be replaced. So each machine costs Rs. 30,000. There is thus no net investment since replacement is just balanced by depreciation and there is no net addition to his stock of capital.

Suppose now there occurs a sudden rise in his sales of 50% in the fourth year from Rs. 3 lakhs to Rs. 4.5 lakhs. The number of machines must then rise by 50%—from 20 to 30 machines. So, in the fourth year, he will have to order 10 machines instead of 1, i.e., 10 extra machines will have to be installed to meet the new demand.

In our example, sales grew by 50%. But as a result his demand for machines and so machine purchase grew 1000% — from 1 to 11. The acceleration principle just refers to the accelerated effect on investment of a small change in the demand for sales of consumption goods. If sales continue to rise by 50% every year machine production would go on rising by 1000% as a result. *So there can occur a substantial increase in investment spending due to a small (moderate) change in sales of consumption goods.* Thus consumption must keep on increasing in order for investment to occur steadily. If consumption of cloth remains unchanged at the old level, net investment will fall to zero. It is because no new machines need be installed to meet the existing demand. In our example, if sales stop growing after reaching Rs. 7.5 lakhs (50% every year) in the seventh year, gross investment will fall back to only 1 machine and this state of affairs will persist for a long time. Thus we see that a levelling off of sales at the original level (i.e., 0% drop in sales) results in 90% drop in gross investment (from Rs. 3.3 lakhs, i.e., 11 machines at Rs. 30,000 each to Rs. 30,000) and 100% drop in net investment (i.e., gross investment is just undertaken to replace one machine, i.e., to pay for depreciation).

1. This is also called *induced* investment.

The acceleration principle works *both* ways. *An increase in sales/production leads to an accelerated rise in investment. A levelling off sales makes investment zero.* In our above example, if sales drop down below Rs. 7.5 lakhs, gross investment may drop to zero or may even become negative in which case the firm might disinvest by selling off some of its machine which are currently underutilised. Thus, a great element of volatility is hidden in the core of the acceleration principle. The principle tells us, to quote Samuelson, "a prosperity period may come to an end, not simply because consumption sales have gone down, but merely because sales have *levelled off* at a high level (or have continued to grow at a lower rate than previously)".

So fall in the production of machine will reduce the income and employment in the machine-producing industry and its expenditure on food and clothing. An economy-wide recession may occur through the multiplier effect of a cut in spending in only one sector. This may, in its turn, cause further drop in investment due to further fall in demand for textiles.

The volatility of acceleration principle, if mingled with the multiplier, can generate a cumulative inflationary (or deflationary) spiral. The interaction model can explain how the end of a recession (and the consequent onset of a revival) and the end of an expansion (and the consequent onset of a downturn) come.

When the boom is reached and ultimately the full employment ceiling, output will not grow any further. And here acceleration principle tells us that the high level of investment (supporting the boom) will plummet to zero. The multiplier will then reduce income to a greater extent. Again accelerator will reduce investment and so on and so forth.

Now, when sales or output plummets downward at a fast rate, the acceleration principle calls for negative investment (or disinvestment) at a greater rate than the rate of depreciation. And the "wearout rate of capital puts a floor on how fast disinvestment can take place". As soon as the floor is touched, the disinvestment process stops, since one cannot disinvest beyond the amount of depreciation. At the lower limit, the economy then needs to maintain even the lower income level and thus there will be a revival of replacement demand to maintain the needed stock of capital. Thus some investment will take place. The multiplier then pushes up the level of income, which through accelerator, enhances investment. The upswing is set on.

To quote Samuelson again, "In the acceleration principle, we have a powerful factor making for economic instability. If business sales go up and down, the acceleration principle can intensify their fluctuation. It induces net investment on the upswing, but causes about the same amount of net *disinvestment* on the downswing."

In Fig. 15.4 we show how national income increases by a very large amount when the acceleration effect reinforces the Keynesian multiplier effect.

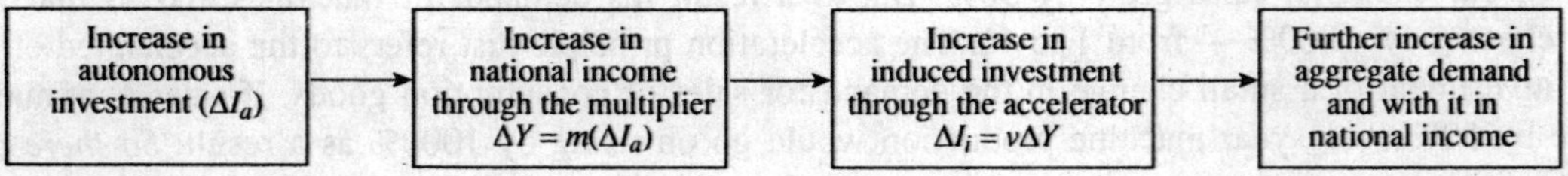

Fig. 15.4: The Combined Effect of the Multiplier and the Acceleration on National Income

Here $m = \dfrac{1}{1-b}$ is the multiplier, ΔI_i is the increase in induced investment and v is the acceleration coefficient, i.e., $v = \dfrac{\Delta Y}{\Delta I_i}$.

Thus we see that the acceleration principle, where one variable (consumption, for example) is a function of the rate of change rather than absolute level of another variable (for example income) interacts with the multiplier in explaining business cycles.

Ceilings and Floors

In the basic M-A model there is no limit on the rate of expansion until output has reached the full capacity level. But at that point output is constrained by the ceiling of productive capacity and can grow only as fast as productive capacity grows— say, 4 to 5% per annum in a typical capitalist economy. This rate of growth must be less than the rate at which output was growing prior to contracting or that contraction would never have occurred. To quote J. Poindexter. "With annual growth of sales slowed (to the rate of growth of productive capacity) the volume of induced investment called for by the accelerator falls and a contraction would be initiated. Thus, the production ceiling provides an upper turning point to the time path of output even if the observed values of the propensity to save and the accelerator imply a dynamically unstable (explosive) adjustment path for the basic multiplier-acceleration model. The ceiling not only limits the expansion of output but also provides for an automatic switch to the contraction phase of the cycle."

Now let us turn to the contraction phase of the cycle. And the question is: what provides a floor under output once contraction starts? According to the simple model, a fall in sales induces disinvestment in the next period, which lowers income inducing more disinvestment, and so on. However, it is unlikely that investment and income would ever fall to zero in actuality. As a contraction proceeds, income ultimately falls to the level where all income is consumed. At that point, even if there were no gross investment, the minimum level of gross income would have been reached. While *negative* net investment could, in theory, be so large that net income ($C + I_n$) was zero or negative in reality disinvestment is likely to be limited to the amount of depreciation. However the disinvestment could never fall to zero since that would require zero gross investment for every firm. There is a minimum value of autonomous investment that takes place independent of the level of income or its rate of change as business firms try to modernise their capital stock. In reality we get ample historical evidence to support the view that "in most contractions the volume of autonomous investment has been substantially lower than the volume of depreciation so that the floor on income has strictly limited the extent to which a contraction could proceed."

Once the floor value of output is reached, the contraction process comes to an end. With income no longer falling, the volume of induced investment called for by the simple accelerator (which was negative during the contraction) is increased to zero and we are back to the expansion phase of the cycle. In short, the basic M-A model fails to explicitly incorporate the required floor of minimum output and ceiling of maximum productive capacity.

The Model's Shortcomings

Samuelson's model offers a highly simplified explanation of business fluctuations. However, it has enjoyed prominence in modern business cycle analysis because, as well as being one of the first of the post-Keynesian breed of dynamic models, it clearly shows an interaction between the multiplier and the accelerator that is surely a basic ingredient of all endogenously generated cycles. Still, its extreme simplicity has compromised its validity as a complete cycle model. And some modifications to the basic M-A model are necessary in the interest of realism. If, for example, the simple accelerator is replaced with an investment function that calls for extended lags in the response of investment to changes in the level of sales, the probability of explosive adjustments in income is moderated. But even if the simple accelerator is retained, with no lag in the response of investment to sales changes, there are logical reasons for expecting a ceiling on the upswing of income, which can halt a potentially explosive expansion and lead automatically to contraction, as well as a floor under which these contractions lead to subsequent expansions. This deficiency was remedied by Hicks. And we may now turn to Hicks's theory.

9. Hicks's Theory of Explosive Cycles: Ceilings and Floors

According to J. R. Hicks, the trade cycle is generated within a growing economy. In his book: *A*

Contribution to the Theory of the Trade Cycle (1950) investment is classified as induced if it depends primarily on the rate of increase of income and as autonomous if it depends primarily on other factors. Hicks also assumes that the accelerator only operates in the expansion and not in the contraction when the actual rate of disinvestment depends on the rate of depreciation.

Autonomous investment continues to exist even during depression. It thus provides a floor to the trade cycle by setting a level below which aggregate output will not fall. Since autonomous investment is increasing over time this floor will be rising so that output in one depression is likely to stop falling before it reaches the lowest level attained in the previous slump.

As long as autonomous investment is positive society's stock of capital must be decreasing more slowly than its rate of depreciation. If autonomous investment is sufficiently large the aggregate capital stock will be increasing despite the fact that some firms are not replacing their capital stock during the contraction.

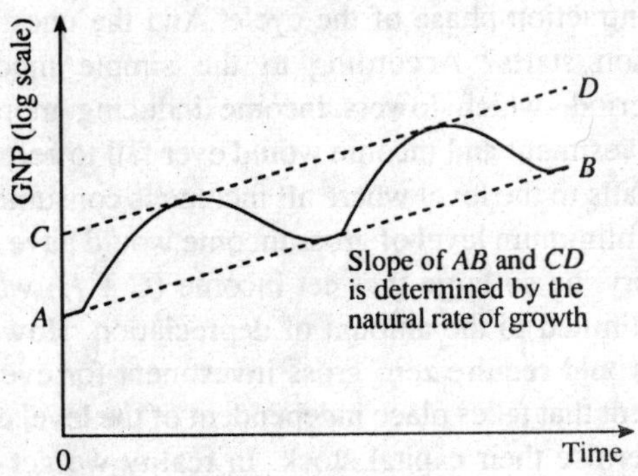

Fig. 15.5: Explosive Cycle Contained by Floors and Ceilings

The floor level of output, determined by autonomous investment sets a limit to which the capital stock can fall in industries which undertake induced investment. Once the capital stock has reached this level, firms need to replace capital equipment. Investment and hence output rise, the accelerator mechanism is set in motion and the economy moves into its expansion phase. [See Fig. 15.5 which is self-explanatory.]

Criticisms

Hicks's theory can be criticised on three main grounds. (i) The existence of an effective ceiling which does bring about the downturn has been put to question. (ii) The reliance on autonomous investment to provide a floor is felt to be unsatisfactory. The increase in the marginal propensity to consume in the downturn has been alternatively suggested as a factor preventing the continued decline in output and thus setting the floor. Since consumption is based on past income, this floor is rising in a growing economy. (iii) The multiplier-accelerator relationship can generate an upper turning point before the ceiling is reached; it can and often does produce explosive cycles. The existence of a floor is sufficient to put an end to an explosive adjustment path. The floor only allows the cycle one full period before it is brought to an end and a new set of initial conditions starts off a new cycle.

Kaldor has criticised Hicks's theory on the ground that it is based on the rigid form of the acceleration principle. If this form of the principle is not valid, then the Hicksian theory of business cycles will not hold.

According to Kaldor investment varies directly with the level of income and inversely with the stock of capital. This investment function is written as

$$I_t = I_a + gY_{t-1} - hK_t$$

where I_t is investment in the current year (t), I_a is autonomous investment, Y_{t-1} was last year's income, K_t is current year's stock of capital, and g and h are constants.

Thus an increase in income, with capital stock remaining constant, will lead to an increase in investment. And an increase in investment amounts to an increase in the economy's stock of capital. By contrast, if the stock of capital increases, income remaining constant, investment will fall (since it varies inversely with the capital stock). Thus in Kaldor's approach, current investment, as determined by the level of output of the last year, will cause the actual capital stock to expand towards the desired level. Kaldor's views have been supported by Goodwin as well.

However, in spite of this weakness of Hicks's approach, it is a valuable contribution to the theory of business cycles.

10. Modern Business Cycle Theory

Most modern theories of business cycles are based on time lags and lay stress on the dynamics of the macroeconomy. The lags are in the time required to adjust production to changes in demand, or, in the time required for consumption or investment activities to react to changes in incomes, prices, interest rate and other key macroeconomic variables.

Recall that the monetarists believe that the cycle is necessarily a monetary phenomenon. But Edward Prescott and Finn Kendall have developed real business cycle (RBC) theories.

REAL BUSINESS CYCLES

Real business cycle theorists differ from new classical economists on the causes of output and employment fluctuations. Real business cycle theorists see economic fluctuations as arising from variations in the real opportunities of the private economy. Factors that might cause such changes include supply-side variables such as shocks to technology, variables in physical environment, changes in the real (relative) prices of imported items (e.g., crude oil), changes in individual's preferences (such as a change in the preference for goods relative to leisure) and changes in tax rates in the short run. No doubt these factors determine long-run output growth in the classical model. But the classical economists assumed that these factors changed very slowly over time. So in the short run they were taken as given. In contrast, the real business cycle theorists argue that these supply-side variables are also the source of short-run fluctuations in output and employment.

The RBC theory developed by Kydland and Prescott uses the *AS-AD* framework. Business cycles are propagated partly because prices are sticky. Since prices adjust slowly to shocks, shifts in nominal demand have real effects. This does not mean that business cycles are impossible when prices are completely flexible. The RBC theorists argue that fluctuations can be seen, to a first approximation, as a market-clearing equilibrium phenomenon.

To be more specific, in an economy with flexible prices, the only shocks which affect the real economy are supply shocks. Such shocks shift the *AS* curve either to the right (if favourable) or to the left (if adverse). To the extent that monetary and fiscal policies do not affect the *AS* curve they are irrelevant. At the same time if the economy is always at full employment the propagation mechanism of the *AS-AD* world does not work. Real GDP simply moves up or down randomly in response to random supply shocks. So it would be quite reasonable to assume that such an economy would normally be free from cyclical upswings and downswings.

Productivity Shocks

The hallmark of RBC theory is its emphasis on propagation mechanism other than price stickiness and dynamics of underlying inflation. The stress is on supply shocks related to the production technology. And the main sources of impulses are new discoveries, inventions, product innovations and process improvements. These shocks alter the productivity of resources and induce changes in the behaviour of economic agents in response to changes in macroeconomic environment.

In the RBC framework shifts in the aggregate production function lead to change in total factor productivity (TFP) and are called technological shocks (which may be adverse or favourable.) These are the sole exogenous impulses that take the economy away from its smooth growth path.

Role of Technology (Productivity) Shocks in Causing Business Cycles

There are two channels in the RBC approach through which technological shocks cause business cycles:

1. Physical capital: The first is physical capital. The increase in marginal product of capital (MP_K) provides an incentive to invest. The building up of capital takes time but it leads to an increase in output. However, the technology shock is temporary and will lead to a fall in MP_K in the short run. As a result there will be an act of disinvestment and the productive capacity of the economy will return to the initial level.

2. Labour supply: The second propagation mechanism involves the response of labour supply in the short run to a temporary opportunity (created by rise in the wage rate). This is known as inter-temporal substitution of labour.

In Fig. 15.6 we illustrate the initial impact of a favourable temporary productivity shocks. It initially raises both marginal product of capital (MP_K) and marginal product of labour (MP_L). Since the stock of capital remains constant the rate of return on capital has to rise. This is shown by the upward shift of the MP_K curve.

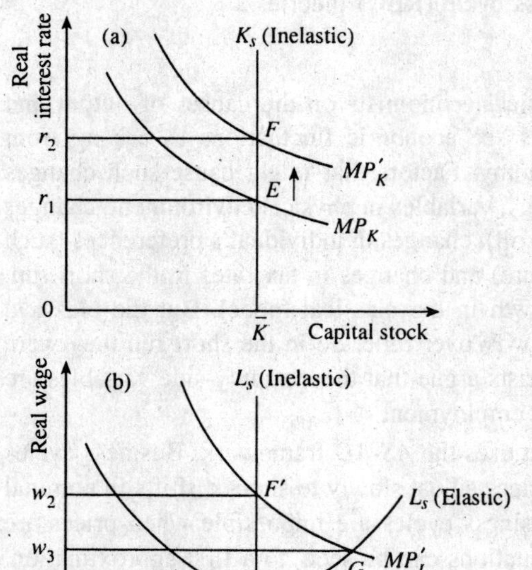

Fig. 15.6: The Initial Impact of a Favourable Productivity Shock

In panel (b) the labour supply curve is vertical implying that the supply of labour is completely inelastic. So a rise in MP_L leads to a rise in the real wage from w_1 to w_2. So aggregate output (real GNP) goes up since productivity of both K and L go up, i.e., the same amount of capital and the same number of labourers now produce more output. On the other side income increases because workers and producers both gain (in the form of higher wages and profits). So consumption also increases.

In panel (b) the supply curve of labour is inelastic. This implies that there is no change in employment over the cycle. But in reality employment fluctuates considerably. However, the supply curve of labour will be fairly elastic like L_s if there is the possibility of intertemporal substitution of labour, i.e., intertemporal choice between leisure today and leisure tomorrow.

The RBC approach stresses the possibility of taking less leisure —working harder in those periods when wages are high and rising. If the technological shock is a short-lived one, a worker will put more effort and substitute leisure for work. A favourable temporary productivity shock raises today's wage and the real interest rate. This generates both substitution and income effects.

(i) Substitution effect: *Prima facie*, a higher wage and a higher interest rate make work effort more rewarding today relative to tomorrow. And due to substitution effect a worker works harder today.

(ii) Income effect: By contrast, the income effect implies that a worker works less today than tomorrow, since he can enjoy more leisure in both periods by putting the same effort. If the substitution effect is stronger than the income effect, the labour supply curve in panel (b) will be elastic. So a very large amount of labour is supplied. Consequently there is a further rise in GDP, i.e., GDP rises over and above the level achieved by direct effect of the productivity shock. In later periods after the boom is over workers feel rich, enjoy more leisure and work less. A fall in labour supply leads to a fall in GDP. GDP fluctuates even in the absense of any friction in the economy such as any wage or price rigidity. So the RBC approach initially appeared very appealing since it was very difficult to explain wage and price stickiness.

In short, the RBC approach is an extreme version of the *AS-AD* model. It assigns no role to nominal variables nor to the nature and composition of aggregate demand. However, the approach is not free from defects. So we may now discuss why the RBC challenge to orthodox business cycle theories has failed.

Failure of RBC Challenge

The *AS-AD* or the sticky price explanation of business cycle relies on disequilibrium in product and labour markets. To be specific, prices do not adjust immediately to changing demand and supply conditions. By contrast, the RBC theory views short-term economic fluctuations as an equilibrium response to productivity shock. It ignores the forces of demand and supply since technology shocks affect both and economic agents know this fact very well.

One disturbing prediction of the RBC approach is that it is impossible to use demand-management policies to stabilise the economy. Another implication of the RBC theory is that it is not even desirable to smooth out the business cycle. The reason is that households and businesses are doing the best they can, given changing constraints. Deep recessions, for example, are seen as the economy's best response to remove productivity shocks.

There are two main problems with the RBC approach which led to its failure. These are:

1. Suspicion about cyclical behaviour of TFP: Productivity shocks are usually measured as the Solow residual, i.e., growth in total factor productivity (TFP). Economists are suspicious about the extreme volatility and cyclical behaviour of TFP growth. It is known that neither labour recruited nor capital installed by firms is always fully employed or utilised. With high costs of dismissing workers and firm-specific human capital, businesses avoid firing employees immediately in downturns. Even if production is reduced, workers perform subsidiary and supplementary jobs such as maintenance, cleaning, painting and improvement of office and factory buildings. As the economy gradually moves into the expansionary phase, and there is shortage of labour, a reserve of labour is available which can be utilised without paying any extra wage.

The same argument holds as far as the utilisation of the capital stock is concerned. Capital stock does not remain constant over the entire business cycle.

Total factor productivity is likely to remain steady due to a faulty measure of inputs. In recessions labour is employed no doubt but not in directly productive activities. Labour is hoarded and it is gradually put back to more directly productive use in the upturn of the business cycle.

In the same way, capital is used less in downturns leading to underestimation of its productivity in these periods. It is quite possible that the procyclical behaviour of the Solow residual largely reflects similar behaviour of the utilisation of hoarded factors of production.

2. Irrelevance of monetary policy: Perhaps the most serious problem with the RBC theory is its refusal to assign any role to monetary policy in the business cycle. This view challenges the role of central bank and monetary policy since the *AS* curve is always vertical and money is neutral— even in the short run. However, the real money stock is procyclical. But the RBC theory takes money and credit demand as passive, expanding with the economy but without having any causal effect on real variables. The theory supports this argument with the strongly procyclical behaviour of interest rates.

Empirical evidence indicates that consumer and producer price indices are rigid in the short run. It is this element of realism which is lacking in the RBC theory of macroeconomic fluctuations. This particular detail has far-reaching implications. So it is essential to include the indices in any acceptable theory of business cycles.

Critics are also sceptical about whether employment fluctuations occur due to intertemporal substitution of labour, whether changes in technology cause most business cycles, whether money is neutral in its effects (on real variables) and whether the short-term stickiness of wages and prices have any relevance in explaining short-term economic fluctuations.

11. New Keynesian Explanation of Business Cycles

New Keynesian economics uses the model of aggregate demand and aggregate supply. It seeks to suggest a more clear-cut explanation of stickiness of wages and prices in the short run. One version of the new Keynesian theory even goes to the extent of suggesting that small costs of price adjustment may have widespread ramifications due to aggregate demand externality. Another new Keynesian view is that recession is the result of the failure of the price system to perform its coordination function. Finally, the theory suggests that staggering price adjustment makes the overall price level slow to adjust in response to changing economic conditions.

Since the real business cycle theory is a modified version of the original classical economics, it recommends non-interventionist policy. The new Keynesian economics explains unemployment in terms of menu costs, efficiency wage considerations or bargaining models and advocates a potential role of stabilisation policy in preventing involuntary unemployment. It seeks to improve the microeconomic foundations of the original Keynesian models, not to challenge their major premises.

In the Keynesian theory aggregate demand is all the more important in determining output and employment in the short run. In contrast, in real business cycle models, changes in real (supply-side) values determine short run fluctuations in output and employment. Of course, Keynesian models are flexible enough to accommodate the effects of supply-side shocks. [See Ch. 28B for a detailed discussion]

12. New Classical Explanation of Business Cycles

In the real business cycle theory real supply-side factors are more important than nominal demand-side influences. In this sense real business cycle models are versions of the new classical model which can also incorporate supply-side shocks. Real business cycle theorists differ from new classical models on an important point—that is, monetary and other demand-side shocks have no significant effect on output and employment.

The new classical economists treated unanticipated changes in aggregate demand, resulting, for instance, from 'monetary surprises', as the main source of business cycles. They did not rule out the important role that supply-side variables play in causing fluctuations in output and employment. But to them unanticipated changes in demand were viewed as the major source of short run fluctuations in output. They paid relatively less attention to technology shocks or changes in individual preferences. [See Ch. 28C for a detailed discussion]

Final Comments

Before considering the role of government in business fluctuations in later chapters we can provide a summary description of the different sorts of cycle models that have enjoyed prominence. To that end, cycle models can be subdivided into monetary cycle theories, non-monetary demand theories, and supply theories, though some explanations of the cycle may overlap these categories. In the monetary theories, fluctuations in the interest rate and in the availability of loanable funds are held responsible for fluctuations in investment and, hence, in overall activity. Hawtrey's explanation of the business cycle fits this category quite well.

As for non-monetary demand theories of the cycle, expansions and contractions are generally prompted by an inconsistency between consumer demand and the existing capital stock. The investment component of aggregate demand fluctuates to provide turning points in the cycle.

Finally, there are the supply-side theories. In this category, it is fluctuations in operating costs and profit margins which bear the responsibility for propagating business fluctuations. Typically, changes in profit margins are held responsible in generating cycle turning points through the effects on expectations and thus on investment.

KEY POINTS

1. *Meaning of business cycles* : While long-run trend growth in productive capacity has been a characteristic feature of most developed economies, the growth in economic activity has not been smooth. Instead, economic history shows that all industrial economies have been plagued by sizable fluctuations—periods of expansion followed by recession in a seemingly endless cycle. This boom-bust sequence is termed as the 'business cycle'.

According to Keynes 'a trade cycle' is composed of periods of good trade characterised by rising prices, low unemployment percentages, alternating with periods of bad trade characterised by falling prices and high employment percentages. Cyclical movements can be observed in any number of macroeconomic variables, such as consumption, investment, unemployment and output. All these show cyclical fluctuations. However,since GNP is a comprehensive measure of the overall level of economic activity, movements in it may be the best indicator of business cycle fluctuations.

2. *Features of business cycles* : A typical business cycle has *four* important features: (i) Cycles are members of the same family, but they are not identical twins.

(ii) All the sectors of the economy are to some extent affected by the cyclical fluctuations.

(iii) All sectors of the economy donot expand and contract in step with aggregable output.

(iv) Cyclical fluctuations are internationally propagated though the extent of undulations varies among countries.

3. *Causes of business cycles* : There are various causes of business cycles. And various theories have been developed from time to time to explain these causes. Some important theories are Hawtrey's monetary theory, Keynes's theory of investment fluctuations and the multiplier-acceleration interaction theories of Samuelson, which was refined and modified by Hicks later. In recent years the theory of real business cycles has been presented by a number of economies.

4. *Real business cycles* : The theory of real business cycles suggests an explanation of short-term economic fluctuations on the basis of the classical assumptions such as the dichotomy of the commodity and money markets and wage-price flexibility. According to this theory, mainly due to technology shocks at periodic intervals, economic fluctuations are the natural and inevitable outcome of the adjustment of the economy to changing economic conditions.

KEY TERMS

Overinvestment	Intertemporal substitution of labour	Depression
Underconsumption	Multiplier-acceleration interaction	Recovery
Investment fluctuations	Kuznets cycles	Kondratieff cycles
Monetary theory	Recession	Juglar cycles
Accleration effect	Prosperity	Kitchin cycles

ASSIGNMENTS

1. What is a business cycle? Briefly describe the characteristics of a business cycle.
2. What are the different phases of a business cycle? What are its turning points?
3. What is recession? What are its characteristics?
4. Critically discuss Hawtrey's theory of business cycles.
5. Discuss critically the underconsumption theory of business cycles.

6. Discuss briefly the overinvestment theory of business cycles.
7. Give a brief account of Keynes's theory of business cycles.
8. Show how the simultaneous operation of the multiplier and the acceleration causes business cycles.
9. Critically examine Hicks's theory of business cycles. What determines the floor and ceiling of this model?
10. Discuss the theory of real business cycles.
11. Briefly discuss new classical and new Keynesian explanations of business cycles.

15A ADVANCED TREATMENT OF SAMUELSON'S MODEL

Paul Samuelson was stimulated by Alvin Hansen to work out in rigorous form as early as in 1939 what has become the best known of the multiplier-accelerator interaction models. We present it briefly before indicating some of its analytical limitations.

Samuelson's model is a non-accelerator interaction model with both consumption and investment endogenous and with both functions taking a dynamic form. The equations of the model are:

$$C_t = a + bY_{t-1} \qquad 0 < b > 1 \qquad \ldots \quad (15A.1)$$

$$I_t = v\,(C_t - C_{t-1}) \qquad v > 0 \qquad \ldots \quad (15A.2)$$

$$Y_t = C_t + \overline{I}_t + \overline{G} \qquad \ldots \quad (15A.3)$$

Equation (15A.1) indicates that consumption is à linear function of income of the previous period. Investment, as equation (15A.2) shows, is proportional to the change in the level of consumption between the previous and current periods. Here v is the accelerator, i.e., the ratio of investment to the change in consumption. It is assumed to be positive. It is also assumed that spending plans in period t are realised, so that the income definition is given by equation (15A.3). In this model, which we may call no-policy model, government expenditure (G) is exogenous and constant. No attempt is made to use G as an instrument for controlling the time path of income. Substituting for G_t and $\overline{I}_t$ from equations (15A.1) and (15A.2) in the income equation (15A.3), we have the expression for Y_t:

$$Y_t = a + \overline{G} + bY_{t-1} + v\,(C_t - C_{t-1})$$

$$\text{or, } Y_t = b\,(1 + v)\,Y_{t-1} - vb\,Y_{t-2} + (a + \overline{G}) \qquad \ldots \quad (15A.4)$$

This is a second-order difference equation which can easily be solved.

The equilibrium level of income Y^e is found by setting for equilibrium $Y_t = Y_{t-1} = Y_{t-2}$ in equation (15A.4), so that

$$Y^e = \frac{a+\overline{G}}{1-b} \qquad \ldots \quad (15A.5)$$

Investment is now entirely endogenous so that there is no I in equation (15A.5). Equilibrium income is the product of exogenous expenditure and the multiplier. The reason for the equivalence is that in equation $Y_t = Y_{t-1} = Y_{t-2}$ which means (from equation (15A.1) that $C_t = C_{t-1}$. With C constant, there is no *induced* investment (from equation (15A.2).

In disequilibrium, however, consumption plans change as the multiplier effect of a change in exogenous expression works itself out. With $C_t \neq C_{t-1}$, the multiplier-accelerator model displays several characteristics. Investment reacts to the change in consumption, and the change in investment expenditure in turn feeds back, via income, to consumption. There is an interaction between induced consumption changes and induced investment changes which gives rise to the possibility of cycles in the time path of income. We may now establish the conditions under which cycles will occur.

Equation (15A.4) can be written as:

$$Y_t - (b + v)\,Y_{t-1} + vb\,Y_{t-2} = 0 \qquad \ldots \quad (15A.6)$$

We may try a solution of the form $Y_{t-j} = Ak^{t-j}$, for $j = 0, 1, 2$ where $Ak^{t-j} \neq 0$. Thus substituting Ak^t for Y_t, Ak^{t-1} for Y_{t-1}, and Ak^{t-2} for Y_{t-2} in equation (15A.6) we have:

$$Ak^t - b(1 - v)\,Ak^{t-1} + vb\,Ak^{t-2} = 0 \qquad \ldots \quad (15A.7)$$

But since $Ak^t = (Ak^{t-1})k = (Ak^{t-2})k^2$

By definition, we can rewrite equation (15A.7) as:

$$Ak^{t-2}\,[k^2 - b\,(1 + v)k + vb] = 0 \qquad \ldots \quad (15A.8)$$

Therefore, with $Ak^{t-2} \neq 0$ we find

$$k^2 - b\,(1 + v)\,k + vb = 0 \qquad \ldots \quad (15A.9)$$

Here k is dependent on both b and v, as equation (15A.9) shows. It will be found, therefore, that the income path varies with different combinations of parameters b and v.

Because (15A.9) is quadratic there is no single solution for k. There are two roots k_1 that k_2 of equation (15A.9), which are found from

$$k_1, k_2 = \frac{b\,(1+v) \pm \sqrt{[b(1+v)^2 - 4vb]}}{2} \qquad \ldots \quad (15A.10)$$

The values of k_1 determine whether the system is stable and converges on Y_e, and whether the path towards, or away from, equation will be smooth or cyclical. Since k_1 and k_2 depend on b and v, the conditions for convergence and for cycles can be expressed in terms of b and v. The outcome is a classification of all possible combinations of b and v, first into those producing cycles and those yielding smooth income paths; and second into combinations leading to convergence on equilibrium and those which produce explosive (divergent) income paths.

The requirement for cycles to occur is that

$$b < \frac{4v}{(1-v)^2}$$

In Fig. 15A.1 all combinations of v and b which are below boundary [1] meet this requirement and produce cycles. Those on or above this boundary represent smooth growth or smooth decline of income.

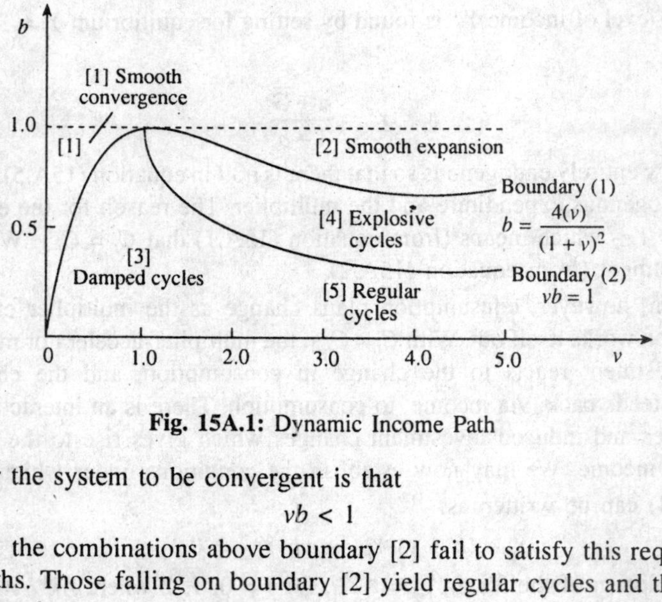

Fig. 15A.1: Dynamic Income Path

The condition for the system to be convergent is that

$$vb < 1$$

In this Fig. 15A.1 the combinations above boundary [2] fail to satisfy this requirement and yield explosive income paths. Those falling on boundary [2] yield regular cycles and those below it yield (convergent) income paths.

These two divisions create four areas of combinations of v and b, plus the special case of a fifth 'area' on the boundary [2]. The characteristics of the resulting income paths following a disturbance from equilibrium are summarised by means of Fig. 15A.1 and Table 15A.1.

Table 15A.1

	Parameter Values			
Area No.	**Boundary (1)**	**Boundary (2)**	**Description**	**Illustration**
[1]	$b > \frac{4v}{(1+v)^2}$	$vb < 1$	Smooth convergence	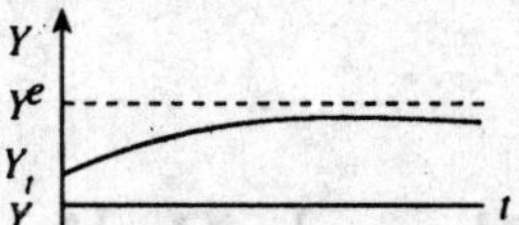
[2]	$b > \frac{4v}{(1+v)^2}$	$vb > 1$	Smooth explosion	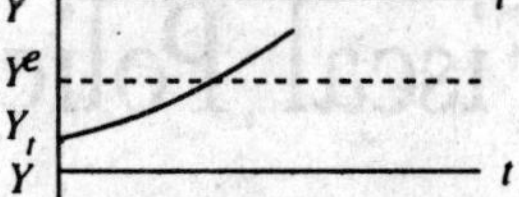
[3]	$b < \frac{4v}{(1+v)^2}$	$vb < 1$	Damped cycles	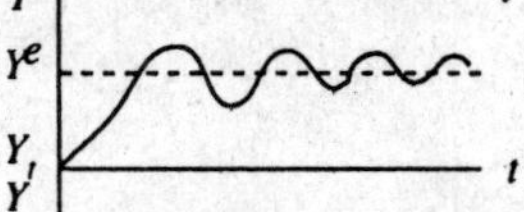
[4]	$b < \frac{4v}{(1+v)^2}$	$vb > 1$	Explosive cycles	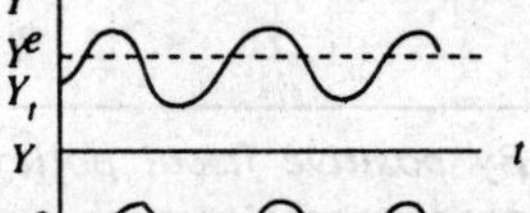
[5]	$b < \frac{4v}{(1+v)^2}$	$vb = 1$	Regular cycles	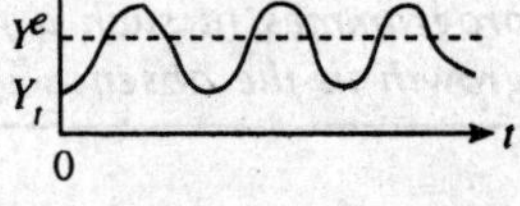

In Table 15A.1 the first column gives the number of the corresponding areas in Fig. 15A.1. The second and third columns show the relationship of each area to the two boundary conditions. In the case of area [3], for example, both the conditions for convergence and that for cycles are met, and the result is damped (convergent) cycles as shown in words in the fourth column and diagrammatically in the fifth column. In these illustrative figures Y^e is the equilibrium income level and Y_t an initial disequilibrium income.

Criticisms: There are four important limitations of the model as an explanation of the business cycle:

(1) It is built on a very simple explanation of the determinants of aggregate demand since the expenditure sector used contains no monetary factors.

(2) It does not impose any restrictions on variations in income and therefore in output. The combination of u and b determines the time path of aggregate demand, and the model assumes that none of the resulting demand levels exceeds full employment output.

(3) It produces symmetrical cycles, that is, cycles with upswings and downswings of similar duration.

(4) It does not explain the *trend* of equilibrium income about which cycles may occur in practice because the equilibrium level of income is exogenous to the model.

Conclusion: Nevertheless this Hansen-Samuelson model has had great appeal for economists, as offering a simple yet logical explanation of the essential mechanism of the business cycle. In fact, in an interesting experiment, G.H. Fisher showed how this cycle model would produce a synthetic 'time series' that looks convincingly like the familiar series used to show the business cycle, and with no apparent tendency for the cycle to die out, even after several hundred successive periods.

CHAPTER 16

Fiscal Policy for Economic Stabilisation

> *By positive fiscal policy we refer to the shaping of the government's taxation and expenditure programmes in such a fashion that a modern mixed economy is able to achieve full-employment growth in the absence of demand-pull inflation.*
> P. A. Samuelson

In the last chapter we noted that a market-based economy does not work smoothly all the time and does not steadily grow over time. It is characterised by cyclical fluctuations or business cycles which refer to periodic fluctuations in the level of economic activity. At times when there are idle production capacity and unemployed workers the economy has to face mild recession or even a deep depression. Consequently national income, output and employment fall much below their potential levels. At other times when factories are running to full capacity and all workers are fully employed the economy reaches the stage of maximum prosperity(boom). In such a situation, since the economy is producing its potential output, an increase in aggregate demand due to an increase in public expenditure (financed by money creation) often overheats the economy and generates a high rate of inflation. Thus a market-based economy is inherently unstable. In this chapter we discuss the role of fiscal policy in achieving economic stability, i.e., to overcome recession and control inflation.

The twin objectives of fiscal policy are the maintenance of price level stability and full employment. By a positive fiscal policy we mean the process of shaping *taxation* and *public expenditure* in order (a) to help dampen down the swings of the business cycle and (b) to contribute towards the maintenance of a growing, high-employment economy free from excessive demand-pull inflation or demand-deficient deflation. The generally accepted goals of fiscal policy is that of attainment of greater economic stability, that is, the maintenance of a reasonably stable rate of economic growth without development of substantial unemployment, on the one hand, or of upward or downward movements in the general price level, on the other. This implies that real national product should go up continuously and steadily with the passage of time and reach the maximum level permitted by changes in technology and factor supplies, while at the same time the price level should remain stable. Stability presupposes comparable rates of increase in aggregate demand and productive capacity. If aggregate demand goes up faster than the rate of increase in output, inflation will occur. In the converse case, there will be unemployment (since employment depends upon aggregate demand and deficiency of demand often aggravates the problems of unemployment). The actual growth rate will fall short of the expected (targeted) level.

A. AUTOMATIC STABILISERS

There are often some automatic tax and outlay changes that act to dampen fluctuations in income — automatic in the sense that they occur in response to a change in the level of GNP without any deliberate (discretionary) action by the government. Logically these automatic changes in taxes and revenues are called 'automatic stabilisers' or 'built-in stabilisers.'

The automatic stabilisers are supposed to provide what is called 'built-in-flexibility' with automatic adjustments in expenditures and revenues taking place in such a manner as to bring about economic stability without deliberate discretionary government intervention. And there is a long-run tendency for the budget to balance itself.

The Major Automatic Stabilisers

The three major automatic stabilisers are the *income tax* and the *government income transfer programmes* particularly unemployment compensation and welfare payments.

(i) Personal income taxes: During the contraction phase of the business cycle, tax revenues fall with a fall in GNP. This is, of course, the direction in which tax collections should move to counter a contraction in economic activity. The converse happens in the expansionary phase of the cycle. Once again tax revenue moves in the direction required for stabilisation.

(ii) Unemployment compensation: On the transfer side the most important stabiliser is unemployment insurance. During a contraction of business activity, those workers who become unemployed are eligible for unemployment benefits or compensation. Such transfers help to maintain disposable income (and thus, consumption spending) as GNP falls. By contrast during an expansion of business activity employment increases and unemployment compensation declines. Other forms of transfer payments (including old age insurance, pensions and other welfare payments) also tend to vary counter-cyclically, with government outlays rising when GNP falls and falling when GNP rises.

(iii) Dividend policies of corporations: Progressive corporations pay steady dividend even in the face of fluctuating earnings. The entire net profit earned in good times (recovery or prosperity) is not distributed as dividend among shareholders. A certain portion is retained for paying reasonable amount of dividend even when profits are low (as in recession). Thus the prudence observed by corporation in distributing dividends in prosperity enables it to create a reserve fund from which dividend distributed in times of recession.

The existence of automatic stabilisers makes cyclical fluctuations in GNP smaller than they otherwise would be. (In fact, the size of any multiplier is reduced by the existence of a budget structure that includes tax and transfer programmes). But while built-in stabilisers act to reduce the size of cyclical fluctuations in GNP, they clearly cannot prevent such cycles since the automatic changes in taxes and transfers are *induced*— they occur only if and when GNP has already changed.

DISCRETIONARY FISCAL POLICY

Automatic stabilisers can never fully stabilise an economy. So there is need for deliberate government action to offset the instabilities of an economy. A government that deliberately alters tax rates and planned outlays in an effort to stabilise the economy is practising what is termed 'discretionary fiscal policy.' Discretionary fiscal policy can take the shape of: (a) varying public works and other expenditure programmes, (b) varying transfer-expenditure (payment) programmes and (c) varying tax rates cyclically.

Discretionary fiscal policy entails a change in the *structure* of the government budget. A discretionary change in tax schedules alters the volume of tax revenues collected at any selected level of economic activity. By comparison a discretionary change in government transfer programmes results in a changed level of transfer payments at any level of business activity.

B. A DETAILED DISCUSSION OF DISCRETIONARY MEASURES

Fiscal policy seeks to stabilise the economy by controlling aggregate demand. This is why it is called demand-management policy. Two types of fiscal policy are adopted by the government, viz., expansionary and contractionary (restrictive) in two different phases of business cycles.

(i) Expansionary Fiscal Policy in Times of Recession

In times of recession, or low level of economic activity, there exists a deflationary gap in the economy. So the government has to adopt an expansionary fiscal policy to remove the gap. This is done either by reducing its expenditure or by cutting taxes or even by adopting both the measures at the same time. As a result the budget of the government shows a deficit. This point may be explained briefly.

In times of recession aggregate demand is too low to support a full-employment level of output. Since the problem is one of deficiency of demand, fiscal policy seeks to create additional demand or purchasing power which is likely to stimulate production and create more employment. Aggregate demand can be increased either directly—by increasing government spending (G) or indirectly—by cutting taxes which increases household consumption expenditure (C).

The effect of an expansionary fiscal policy is shown in Fig. 16.1. The economy is initially in equilibrium at point E where $Y = C + I + G$ and Y_F is the equilibrium level of national income. But

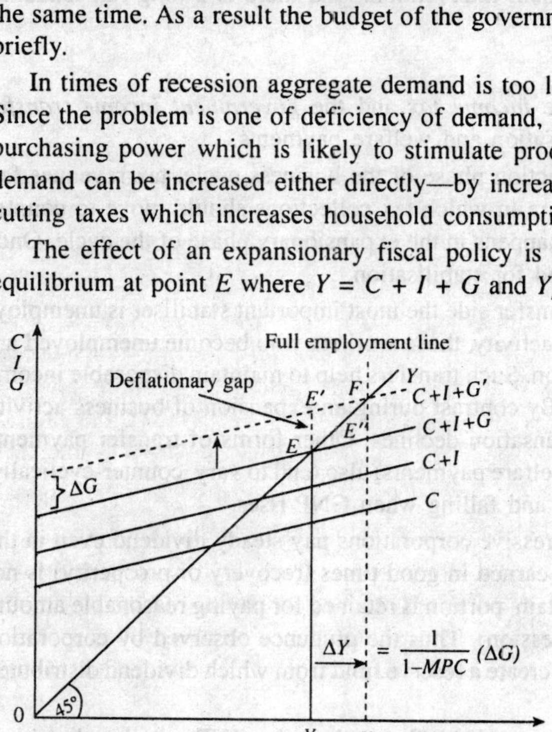

Fig. 16.1: The Effect of an Expansionary Fiscal Policy

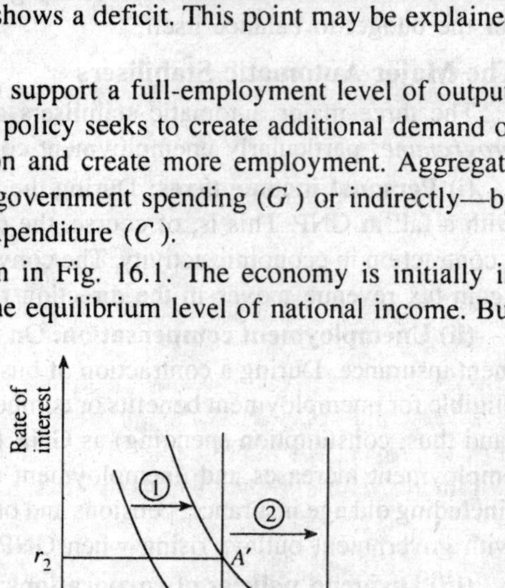

Fig. 16.2: Accommodating Monetary Policy

point E shows underemployment equilibrium or equilibrium at less-than full employment. Actual output is less than full-employment output Y_F, as shown by the vertical (dotted) full employment line. Now if the government increases its own expenditure by ΔG, the $C + I + G$ schedule will shift upward to $C + I + G'$ where $G' = G + \Delta G$. This new desired expenditure schedule intersects the 45° income line at point F which is on the full-employment line. As a result national income increases from Y_E to Y_F and the economy is enabled to reachieve full employment. Thus by increasing its own expenditure, the government has succeeded in eliminating the deflationary gap $EE' = E''F$. And the resultant increase in national income is a multiple of the increase in G due to the operation of the multiplier. Thus

$$\Delta Y = \frac{1}{1 - MPC}(\Delta G) \;= m(\Delta G), \text{ where } m \text{ is the multiplier.}$$

The same effect can be achieved by cutting taxes. The only difference between the two policies is that while an increase in government expenditure has a direct effect on Y, a cut in taxes has an indirect effect through an increase in consumption. This point may now be explained. A tax cut will lead to an increase in disposable income of the people. As a result they will spend more. So consumption spending will now increase. And the $C + I + G$ schedule will shift upward (in the same way) to $C' + I + G$ where $C' = C + \Delta C$. However, since $MPC < 1$, a much higher cut in taxes will be needed to achieve full employment than the increase in government expenditure needed to achieve the same result, i.e., full employment output.

The reason is that the tax multiplier is always one less than the government spending multiplier. Thus if $MPC = 0.75$, the government expenditure multiplier is 4 and the tax multiplier is 3. Thus if a deflationary gap of Rs. 600 crores is to be eliminated, the government is left with two alternatives, i.e., either to increase government expenditure by Rs. 150 or to cut taxes by Rs. 200. There are various historical evidences of the merit of tax cut.

ACCOMMODATING MONETARY POLICY

It may be noted that monetary and fiscal policies often complement each other in achieving the desired degree of economic stability. An increase in national income due to an increase in government expenditure or a cut in taxes will increase the transactions demand for money and thus the total demand for money. As a result the demand curve for money will shift upward from M_{d_1} to M_{d_2}, as shown in Fig. 16.2. Consequently the rate of interest (r) will initially rise from r_1 to r_2 as shown by point A and A'. This is likely to choke off investment demand and thus lead to a fall in income (Y) through the reverse multiplier. Now the government can instruct the central bank to increase the money supply so as to prevent the interest rate from rising. This point is also illustrated in Fig. 16.2. If the central bank increases the money supply from Ms_1 to Ms_2, the new money supply curve Ms_2 will intersect the new money demand curve M_{d_2} at point B. Thus the interest rate (r) will come back to the original level and the income contractionary process (due to a fall in investment) can be avoided.

Thus we see that by making appropriate use of fiscal and monetary measures (i.e., by supporting an expansionary fiscal policy by an expansionary monetary policy) it is possible to achieve the best of both the worlds—the full multiplier effect, without permitting the rate of interest to rise so as to generate crowding-out effect (which normally occurs when the government covers the deficit by borrowing).

FINANCING THE INCREASE IN GOVERNMENT EXPENDITURE AND COVERING THE BUDGET DEFICIT

The government can cover its budget deficit in one of the two ways, viz., (a) by market borrowing and (b) by creation of new money. These two alternative methods of financing government expenditure will be discussed in detail in a later chapter.

(ii) Contractionary Fiscal Policy

When an economy is threatened by the problem of demand-pull inflation (arising out of an inflationary gap, i.e., an excess of desired expenditure over full-employment output) an exactly opposite type of fiscal action is called for. Since the problem is one of eliminating excess demand pressure from the economy, the government has to adopt a contractionary fiscal policy which works through a cut in government expenditure or an increase in taxes or both at the same time.

The effect of an expansionary fiscal policy is illustrated in Fig. 16.3. The economy is initially in equilibrium at point A at which actual income (Y_A) exceeds full employment income (Y_F). And there is an inflationary gap EE' at the full employment level of income. This gap arises due to excessive government expenditure which is AH. Now if this expenditure is reduced by ΔG, the $C + I + G$ schedule will shift downward to $C + I + G'$ where $G' = G - \Delta G$. It now intersects the 45° income line at point E at which the inflationary gap EE' no longer exists. It has been eliminated by cutting government spending (G).

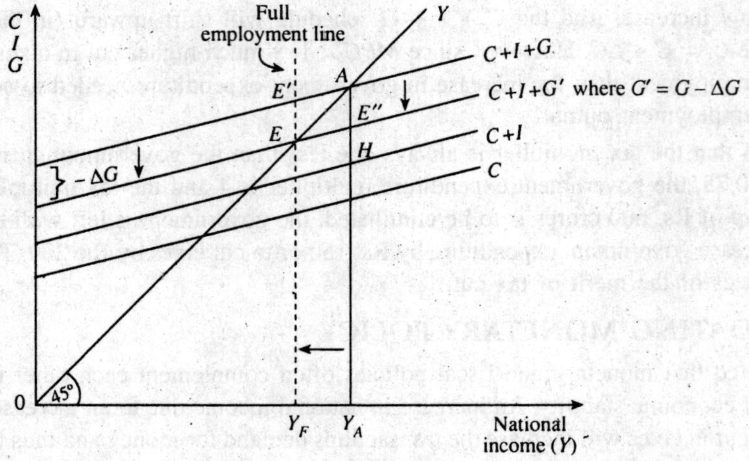

Fig. 16.3: The Effect of a Contractionary Fiscal Policy

The same effect can be achieved by raising taxes. Again the rise in the level of taxes has to exceed the cut in government expenditure to achieve the same effect. For example, if there is an inflationary gap of Rs. 600, and the value of the expenditure multiplier is 4, then a cut in government expenditure of Rs. 150 is sufficient to eliminate the inflationary gap. However, if the government follows the policy of raising the level of taxes in order to achieve the same goal, then an additional tax of Rs. 200 crores has to be imposed. The reason is that this will reduce disposable income by the same amount no doubt. But consumption will now fall by only Rs. 150 since $MPC = 0.75$ and $MPS = 0.25$.

UTILISING THE BUDGET SURPLUS

When the government cuts its own expenditure (G) or raises taxes (T), the budget of the government is likely to show a surplus[1]. And the effect of the government's anti-inflationary fiscal policy depends on how the surplus in the budget is utilised. And the surplus can be utilised in the following two ways:

1. Retiring public debt: The government can pay back its past debt. However, this will weaken the anti-inflationary effect of its fiscal policy. There are two reasons for this. When the government pays off its debt the money supply with the public will increase. This will stimulate consumption spending. Again an increase in the money supply will lead to a fall in the interest rate. This will stimulate private investment. Thus the favourable effect of a cut in government expenditure or a rise in taxes will be partly offset by the increase in consumption or investment or both at the same time and the anti-inflationary impact of public debt will be partly lost.

2. Impounding of public debt: To realise the benefit of an anti-inflationary fiscal policy as much as possible the budget surplus has to be kept idle. This implies that the government will have to withdraw some income or purchasing power from the circular flow of income. This is a preferable alternative to debt repayment and is thus more effective in controlling inflation.

The Crowding-Out Effect

The favourable effect of an expansionary fiscal policy is offset, at least partially, by the crowding out effect or capital displacement effect. This occurs for two reasons. An increase in income increases

1. If initially there was a large deficit in the budget, then the deficit will now fall. And if there was a balance in the budget, then there will now be a surplus.

the demand for money and pushs up the interest rate. As a result investment falls. In addition, if the government borrows from the market for loanable funds, there is a shortage of such funds for the private sector. This also raises the interest rate and chokes off investment demand. So in each case an income contractionary process starts, as is illustrated in Fig. 16.4 and Fig. 16.5.

Under the stimulus of an expansionary fiscal policy (i.e., an increase in government expenditure) the aggregate desired expenditure schedule shifts upward from $(C + I + G)$ to $(C + I + G')$ where $G' = G + \Delta G$. And as a result, as the economy moves from point E to point E'', national income rises from Y_1 to Y_3. Now if the interest rate increases due to an increase in demand for money or shortage of loanable funds due to competition between the private sector and the government, private investment falls. Consequently the $C + I + G$ schedule shifts downward to $C + I' + G$ where $I' = I - \Delta I$. Now the economy attains the new equilibrium point E' at which national income (Y_2) is lower than what it was immediately after the fiscal boost (Y_3). The subsequent fall in income after its initial increase is due to the crowding-out effect which is illustrated in Fig. 16.5. The size of the effect depends on

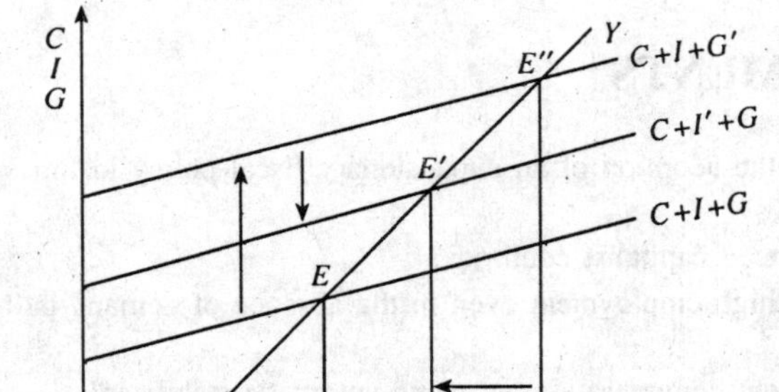

Fig. 16.4: Fall in Y due to fall in I

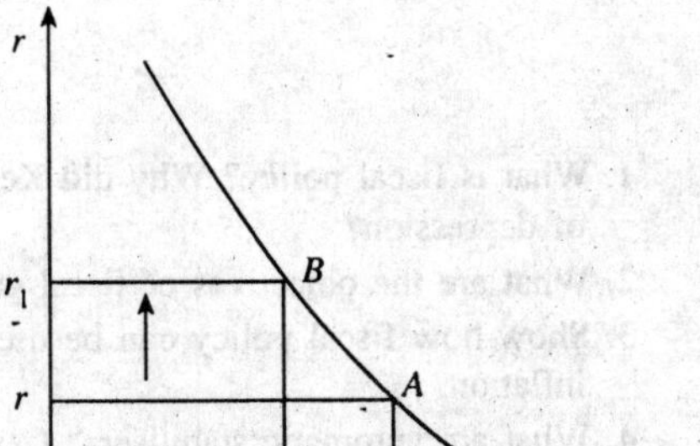

Fig. 16.5: Crowding-Out Effect

the interest elasticity of private investment and the magnitude of the fall in income depends on the numerical value of the multiplier.

AN OFFSETTING CONSIDERATION

There is, however, an offsetting consideration. An increase in income due to an increase in government expenditure or a cut in taxes stimulates the demand for consumption goods. This, in its turn, gives the incentives to business firms to invest more through the acceleration effect. So the investment schedule shifts to the right. When these two effects work in opposite directions we see that the net fall in income is not very large. In other words, the crowding-out effect is not really so strong as it appears at the first sight.

KEY POINTS

1. *Positive fiscal policy* : By positive fiscal policy we refer to the shaping of the government's taxation, expenditure and borrowing programmes in such a fashion that a modern mixed economy is enabled to achieve high employment growth in the absence of demand-pull inflation.

2. *Automatic stabilisers* : The fiscal system of a modern market-based economy has certain inherent properties which help to stabilise the economy even in the absence of any government intervention. These are known as automatic or built-in stabilisers. Examples of such stabiliser are automatic changes in tax revenue over the upswings and downswings of the business cycles, unemployment compensation and dividend policies of corporate enterprises.

3. *Discretionary measures* : Although automatic stabilisers are useful they are not fully effective in fully stabilising an economy, these are to be supported by certain discretionary measures. The government of a country has to make certain delibrate adjustments in its taxation and expenditure programmes so as to ensure the desired degree of macroeconomic stability. Three such measures are (i) public works programmes, (ii) state employment projects and (iii) a policy of tax cut. It was Keynes who first advocated the use of such policy to fight depression and unemployment.

KEY TERMS

Automatic stabilisers	Discretionary measures
Unemployment compensation	Tax cut
Public works programmes	State employment projects
Expansionary fiscal policy	Accommodating monetary policy

ASSIGNMENTS

1. What is fiscal policy? Why did Keynes suggest the adoption of an expansionary fiscal policy in times of depression?
2. What are the objectives of fiscal policy in advanced capitalist countries?
3. Show how fiscal policy can be used to achieve high employment even in the absence of demand-pull inflation.
4. What are automatic stabilisers? Can unemployment compensation act as an automatic stabiliser?
5. Discuss the effectiveness of fiscal policy in lifting an economy out of stagnation.
6. What is effective demand? How is it affected if the government covers its budgetary deficit (a) by raising additional taxes and (b) by printing new currency?
7. What are the basic components of anti-inflationary fiscal policy? How effective are they?
8. Discuss how fiscal policy can be used to control cyclical fluctuations in economic activity.
9. What is crowding-out effect? Do you think that the effectiveness of fiscal policy is reduced to a large extent due to this effect?
10. Does government borrowing from the open market generate crowding-out effect? Does it always occur?
11. Show how by making appropriate use of monetary and fiscal means it is possible for a modern mixed economy to achieve high employment in the absence of demand-pull inflation.

Part-IV

The Role of Money in the Macroeconomy

17. The Theories of Demand for Money
18. The Supply of Money and Its Determinants
19. Money Market Equilibrium
20. Monetary Policy for Economic Stabilisation
21. Monetary Policy in a Developing Economy with Particular Reference to India

CHAPTER 17

The Theories of Demand for Money

> *The need to have money to pay for purchases, or transactions of goods, services, and other items constitutes the transactions demand for money.*
>
> P. A. Samuelson and W. D. Nordhaus

PREVIEW

It has to be noted at the outset that the money market like any other market has two sides—the supply side and the demand side. In the last chapter we discussed the various concepts of supply of money as also the proximate determinants of the money supply. In this chapter we will discuss the other side of the money market, viz., the demand side. The money market reaches equilibrium when the fixed supply of money, determined by the central bank, is equal to the demand for money. When the money market is in equilibrium the rate of interest (the price of money) is determined. The general price level is also determined to a considerable extent by the demand for money.

Moreover the demand for money affects real variables such as investment and national income. For instance, if the demand for money increases, the supply of money remaining the same, the rate of interest rises, investment falls and income falls.

Since the time of Adam Smith the great classical economists showed interest in finding out the factors affecting the desire to hold money (cash). According to later classicists like Irving Fisher, A. Marshall and A.C. Pigou money is held only for the purpose of transactions, i.e., for buying goods and services. They treated money as a medium of exchange or a means of payment. However, Keynes pointed out that people hold money also for speculative purpose, i.e., for buying bonds at a low price with the objective of selling the same at a higher price later. By doing this they make capital gains (which is the difference between the selling price and the buying price of bonds). In other words, there is an asset demand for money since it is also a store of value. Thus the demand for money depends on the functions of money. See Fig. 17.1 where we show three different types of demand for money associated with two main functions of money.

Money as a Medium of Exchange	Money as both Medium of Exchange and Store of Wealth	Money as a Store of Wealth
↓ 1. Transactions Demand	↓ 2. Precautionary Demand	↓ 3. Speculative Demand

Fig. 17.1: Functions of Money and Demand for Money

NOMINAL VS. REAL BALANCES

People hold real balances and not nominal balances due to inflation

It may be noted at the outset that money is wanted not for its own sake but because it is used to buy goods and services. So what people really demand is real money balances or simply real balances and not nominal balances. Real balances, i.e., nominal balances divided (deflated) by the price index is the true indicator of the purchasing power of money. If, for instance, there is 10% increase in people's nominal balances and 10% increase in the price level at the same time in a year, their real balances will remain unchanged. It people take an increase in nominal balances in times of inflation as equivalent to an increase in real balances, they are said to be suffering from money illusion.

THE CONCEPT OF DEMAND FOR MONEY

The demand for money is different from saving

It may also be noted that the demand for money is not saving. When a person saves money by depositing it in a bank he earns interest. But if he holds money, he loses interest. The demand for money refers to the desire to hold money in liquid form (cash) as an alternative to purchasing income-earning assets like bonds or equities.

Different Approaches to the Theory of Demand for Money

Till the late 1940s there were three approaches to the demand for money, viz.,

1. the transaction balance approach of Fisher
2. the cash balance approach of Cambridge economists (such as Marshall and Pigou) and
3. the Keynesian approach (with focus on the speculative demand for money).

However, these approaches have been extended by W. J. Baumol, James Tobin and Milton Friedman in the 1950s. See Fig. 17.2.

Transactions demand for money	Restatement of the Quantity Theory of Money	Speculative demand for money
↓ W. J. Baumol (1952) James Tobin (1956)	↓ Milton Friedman (1958)	↓ James Tobin (1958)

Fig. 17.2: Post-Keynesian Extensions of the Theories of Demand for Money

In this chapter we discuss the original classical and Keynesian theories of demand for money. In the next chapter we will discuss the post-Keynesian developments in the theory of demand for money.

FISHER'S TRANSACTIONS BALANCE APPROACH TO THE DEMAND FOR MONEY

Fisher's quantity equation of exchange presented in 1911 implicitly recognises the concept of transactions demand for money. His equation of exchange is presented as follows:

$$MV = PT \qquad \ldots \quad (1)$$

where M = the quantity of money in circulation,

V = the velocity of circulation (or transactions velocity, indicating the number of times a unit of money circulates in the process of transactions),

P = the average price of different goods and services, and

T = the total number (volume) of transactions.

Equation (1) is an identity. It is always true. The volume of transactions depends on national income. Since Fisher, like all other classical economists, assumed that the economy is always at full employment, T was assumed to remain fixed, at least, in the short run.

Fisher also took the velocity of circulation (V) as constant because it is determined by various institutional and technological factors associated with purchase of goods and services. Since these factors remain more or less unchanged in the short run, V was assumed to remain constant.

Now the money market is in equilibrium when the nominal quantity of money demanded is equal to its supply which is fixed by the central bank. So we can write:

$$M_d = M_s = \overline{M}$$

where M_d is the transactions demand for money and $\overline{M}$ is its fixed supply.

As soon as the above two assumptions are made, the quantity equation of exchange (1) can be expanded as

$$M = \frac{P\overline{T}}{\overline{V}}$$

$$\text{or} \quad M_d = \frac{P\overline{T}}{\overline{V}} = \frac{1}{\overline{V}} . P\overline{T} \quad \ldots (2)$$

where M_d is the demand for money. It depends on three factors:

1. the number of transactions (T),
2. the average price of transactions (P) and
3. the velocity of circulation or transactions velocity (V)

Since (1) and (2) are assumed to remain constant in the short run, the transactions demand for money will increase if the average price of transactions increases.

Criticisms

Fisher's theory of demand for money has been criticised on the ground that it shows a mechanical relation between the demand for money and the value of transactions (PT). It does not depend on people's spending behaviour. The reason is that if P increases, PT will increase, with T remaining constant (due to the assumption of full employment). So even if people spend more money, they will get the same volume of goods.

Secondly, due to changes in the prices of capital goods such as machines and financial assets such as bonds and stocks, PT will not remain constant even if real GNP (Y) remains constant at full employment.

Finally, it is difficult to arrive at the general price level because it also covers prices of capital goods. However, prices of such goods change quite frequently even in the short run and cause a variety of measurement problems. So the measurement of P is not an easy task.

THE CAMBRIDGE CASH-BALANCE APPROACH TO THE THEORY OF DEMAND FOR MONEY

While Fisher emphasised the role of money as a medium of exchange, the cash balance approach of Cambridge economists such as Marshall and Pigou laid stress on the function of money as a store of wealth. According to them people hold money as a store of value now so that they can buy goods and services in the future. Their main point is that people's demand for nominal money or cash balance is proportional to nominal income. So the aggregate demand for money can be expressed as

$$M_d = kPY \quad \ldots (3)$$

where Y = real national income,

P = the current average price level,

PY = nominal national income, and

k = the fraction (proportion) of nominal income which is held by people in the form of cash.

Thus from (3) as also from Fig. 17.3, it is clear that there is a proportional relation between nominal national income (PY) shown on the horizontal axis and transactions demand for money (M_d) shown on the vertical axis. This is the money demand function. It is a straight line through the origin.

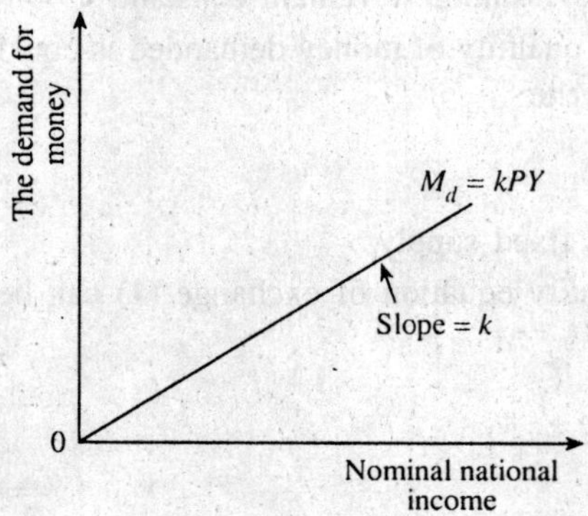

Fig. 17.3: Proportional Relation between Nominal Income and Transactions Demand for Money

Here k may be interpreted as the average propensity to hold money and thus the slope of the money demand function, i.e., $k = \frac{M_d}{Y}$. Thus the demand for money is a function of nominal income alone. This approach is a slight improvement over the Fisher approach for a simple reason. It brings into focus the behavioural relation between income and the demand for money. If income increases, the demand for money will increase proportionately (since the proportionality factor k remains constant by assumption). By contrast, Fisher's approach relates the demand for money to total value of transactions in a mechanical way. No doubt, the Cambridge economists implicitly recognised the role of interest rate, expected changes in interest rate and the price level as also wealth in influencing k. However, it was left to Keynes (and other Cambridge economists) to do the unfinished job of the predecessors by explicitly recognising and incorporating these variables in the theory of the demand for money. Keynes highlighted the influence of interest rate on the demand for money.

Elasticities of Money Demand

Two concepts emerge from the Cambridge version of the transactions demand for money, income elasticity of demand for money and price elasticity demand for money. Since the demand for money is proportional to PY, it is proportional to both P and Y. This implies that the price elasticity of demand for money (the proportional increase in demand for money divided by the proportional increase in the price level) is unity. Similarly, the income elasticity of demand for money (i.e., proportional increase in demand for money divided by proportional increase in income) is unity.

Criticisms

The Cambridge version of the theory of demand for money has been criticised mainly due to its inability to take into account various non-income determinants of the demand for money.

Secondly, the Cambridge economists failed to suggest an economic rationale for unitary income and price elasticities of money demand. Even empirical evidence shows non-proportional relation between changes in the price level and changes in the demand for money.

THE KEYNESIAN THEORY OF DEMAND FOR MONEY

Much like consumption function, the Keynesian theory of demand for money is some sort of innovation in macroeconomic theory. It is not just important for its own sake; it also has implications for the effectiveness of the central bank's monetary policy, as we will see in a later chapter.

Liquidity preference refers to the preference of an individual for cash

Keynes used the term 'liquidity preference' to refer to the demand for money. The term 'liquidity preference' refers to an individual's preference for cash. It gets reflected in his (her) desire to hold money in liquid form, as opposed to buying income-earning assets like government bonds. What is true of an individual is equally true of the whole economy. Liquidity preference for the country as a whole refers to the public's desire to hold cash instead of buying bonds.

Three Motives for Money Holding

According to Keynes, it costs money to hold money and the rate of interest is the opportunity cost of holding money (i.e., by holding money people lose the opportunity to earn interest). In spite of this, people hold money for three reasons, viz., (i) the transactions motive, (ii) the precautionary motive and (iii) the speculative motive. These are known as the motives for money holding.

1. The Transactions Demand for Money

Transactions demand for money arises because people have to bridge the interval between income receipt and income payment

The transactions demand for money arises primarily because money is used as a means of payment. Everyone needs some money to buy goods and services regularly. Such demand for money arises mainly because people want to reduce the time gap between receipt of income and its expenditure on goods and services. Most people receive income only once a month (or once a week as in England). But they have to make payments almost every day. In short, people hold transaction balances to reduce the time gap between two pay days or to strike a balance between uneven flow of income and a fairly constant flow of expenditure. The income stream is discontinuous but the expenditure flow is continuous[1]. So everyone has to hold a certain amount of cash all the time to be able to make necessary payment for goods and services.

Three Factors Affecting Transactions Demand for Money

Three factors affect transactions demand for money, viz., (i) the income of an individual, (ii) the time lag between two income receipts, and (iii) the existing method of making payments (i.e., whether in cash or in cheques or credit cards).

(i) **Income:** A rich person normally spends more money than a poor person. So the former holds more cash than the latter. This is true of the country as a whole. For example an average person in the USA will hold more money than an average Indian (due to differences in the per capita income levels between the two countries).

(ii) **Time lag:** Similarly an individual who gets his salary every month will hold more money than a person who receives wages on a weekly basis. And a daily wage earner need not hold any money for the purpose of transactions[2].

(iii) **Method of making payment:** Moreover people always hold money in cash mainly in the rural areas of Asia and Africa where cheques and credit cards are not accepted for most small transactions. In Britain people hold very little cash because cheques are used in all types of transactions—small, medium and large.

Like individuals businesses also hold cash. This is because money is a form of capital. It is used to buy raw materials, hold inventories of both raw materials and finished goods, pay wages to casual workers as also to workers in most small establishments. Cash is also used to cover other daily expenses

1. This point will be more clear when we discuss the Baumol-Tobin model of transactions demand for money in the next chapter.
2. Of course, he will hold some money for precautionary purposes since he may have negative transitory income due to sickness or accident or temporary loss of job.

such as purchase of certain raw materials and transportation charges. In general, large firms hold more cash than small and medium-sized firms.

In short, for individuals transactions demand for money arises because money is used as a medium of exchange (i.e., means of payment). For business firms cash is needed to cover current expenses. Just as an individual's transactions demand for money depends on his income, a business firm's demand for money for the purpose of transactions depends on its sales turnover (i.e., total revenue).

Apart from income, transactions demand for money depends on two other factors, viz., the price level and the interest rate.

If the price level rises, an individual holds more nominal balance

The price level: We have noted at the beginning of this chapter that people hold money for buying goods and services. This is why the demand for money is essentially a demand for real balances and not nominal balances. Thus, if the price level rises, an individual's nominal balance will remain the same, but his real balance will fall. So if he has to buy the same amount of goods and services, he has to hold more nominal balance in order to keep his real balance unchanged.

The rate of interest: According to Keynes, transactions demand for money does not depend on interest rate. But two post-Keynesians, viz., W.J. Boumol and J. Tobin have shown that even transactions demand for money depends on the interest rate. The reason is that the rate of interest is the opportunity cost of holding cash. So at a higher interest rate, households and businesses hold as less money as possible at each level of income in order to minimise the loss of interest associated with money holding. And if the interest rate increases there is transfer of funds from money to other short-term interest bearing financial assets.

2. Precautionary Demand for Money

People also hold cash to be able to overcome unforseen contingencies such as temporary unemployment, sickness, accident or, of course, sudden arrival of guests on holdings (when most banks remain closed)[1]. Such demand for money depends on an individual's foresight and his family circumstances. Precautionary demand for money serves two purposes. It acts as a medium of exchange and store of value.

3. Speculative Demand for Money

Although the classical economists referred to transactions and precautionary demand for money, the concept of speculative demand is a Keynesian innovation. According to Keynes, people also hold money for speculative purposes, i.e., to make gains arising from rise in the price of bonds (in the event of a fall in the market rate of interest). Speculative demand arises because money acts as a store of value. It varies inversely with the rate of interest.

Focus on Terminology: Speculation

Speculation refers to the profit-motivated response to expected but uncertain price (market) changes over time. Speculators are guided by expectations but expectations are uncertain. If an individual's speculation about the future price movements is correct, he will make capital gain. Capital gain occurs when the sale price of an asset such as bond is greater than its purchase price. If, on the other hand, his speculation appears to be perverse, he will end up making capital loss. Capital loss occurs when the sale price of an asset such as a bond is less than its purchase price.

In this context two points are to be noted. Firstly, an individual's wealth, according to Keynes, consists of money and bonds. So more money holding implies less bond[2] holding and vice-versa.

1. In recent years, the demand for cash for both transactions and precautionary purposes has come down to a very low level due to ATM facilities given by most banks. In a sense, ATM stands for 'all-time money.'
2. In those days all government credit instruments and special papers which yielded a fixed interest over a period of time were known as bonds.

Secondly, the price of existing bond is the reciprocal of the market rate of interest. If the rate of interest rises, price of bonds will fall. The converse is also true. A simple example will make the point clear. Suppose Mr *X* receives a bond (say, an annuity[1]) as gift from his friend. And it is written on the face of the bond that he will receive a fixed sum (say Rs. 10 p.a) as interest in perpetuity, (i.e., so long as he wants to hold it). Now Mr *X* has two options— either to receive Rs. 10 p.a. in perpetuity or to sell the bond now and get a certain sum only once. Suppose he wants to sell it. So he will first like to know what is its current market price. The price of the bond is calculated by using the following formula:

$$\text{The price of the bond} = \frac{\text{Annual income}}{\text{The current market rate of interest}}$$

Suppose the market rate of interest is 5%.

Then the price of the bond will be $\frac{\text{Rs. }10}{5\%}$ = Rs. 200. This is known as the capitalised[2] value of the bond. If the rate of interest is likely to rise, to, say 10% next year, then price of the bond will fall to Rs. 100 $\left(=\frac{\text{Rs. }10}{10\%}\right)$. So he will sell it now. The reason is that he will try to avoid capital loss of Rs. 100. On the other hand, if the rate of interest is likely to fall to $2\frac{1}{2}\%$ next year, the price of the bond will rise to Rs. 400. In this case a halving of interest rate implies a doubling of the market price of bonds (from Rs. 200 to Rs. 400). So Mr *X* will gain by selling the bond. So it will be judicious on his part to hold it for at least one year since he will be eager to make a capital gain of Rs. 200.

Economic Insight: Liquidity Preference

Liquidity preference refers to a preference for holding money instead of investing it in bonds. Keynes identified three motives for holding money:

(a) **transactions motive:** money held on a daily basis to finance current purchases of goods and services,

(b) **precautionary motive:** money held to meet unexpected future outlays, and

(c) **speculative motive:** money held in anticipation of a fall in the price of assets, mainly bonds.

The amount of money held for these three purposes depends on two main factors:

(i) the level of national income, and (ii) the rate of interest.

Here we assume that the price level remains constant. Otherwise transactions demand for money will also depend on the price level. Keynes pointed out that the speculative demand for money depends both on the current rate of interest and expected changes in it in the future.

Inverse relation between Interest Rate and Speculative Demand for Money

In this context Keynes suggested that there is an inverse relation between the rate of interest and the speculative demand for money. The relation is explained in Fig. 17.4.

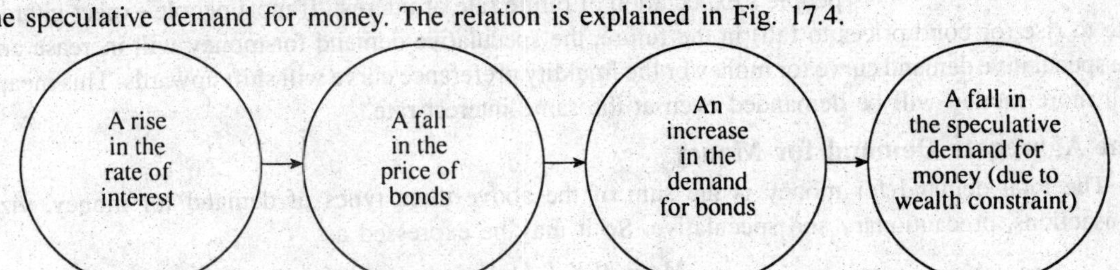

Fig. 17.4: Inverse Relation between Interest Rate and Speculative Demand for Money

1. An annuity is one which has no maturity period.
2. Capitalisation means conversion of income (a flow variable) into asset (a stock variable).

The basic point to note is that when the rate of interest is fairly low, people hold more money than when it is quite high. The reason is that at a low rate of interest people do not lose much interest by holding money. They do not earn much interest by holding bonds either. This inverse relation between interest rate and speculative demand for money is illustrated in Fig. 17.5.

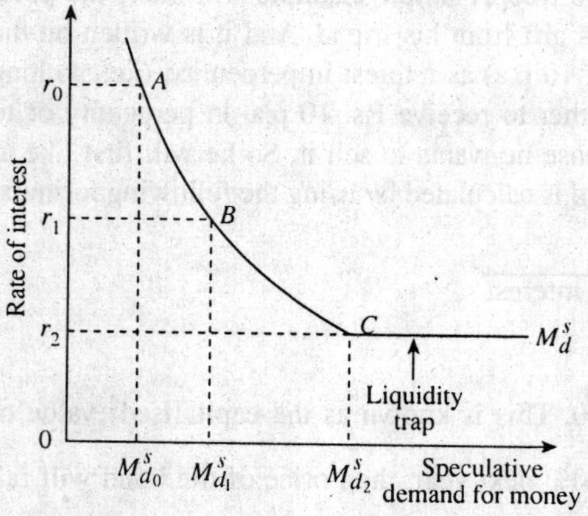

Fig. 17.5: Speculative Demand Curve for Money and the Liquidity Trap Situation

Here we measure the speculative demand for money on the horizontal axis and the rate of interest on the vertical axis. When the rate of interest is high (r_0), the speculative demand for money is low i.e., $M^s_{d_0}$. If the rate of interest falls to r_1, the speculative demand for money increases to $M^s_{d_1}$ and further to $M^s_{d_2}$. when interest rate falls to r_2. Thus the speculative demand curve of money (M^s_d) is downward sloping upto point C which corresponds to a very low rate of interest (r_2). However, the rate of interest does not fall further. Therefore the speculative demand curve for money or the liquidity preference curve becomes horizontal (or completely elastic). The completely elastic segment of the liquidity preference curve at a very low rate of interest is known as the liquidity trap.

Focus on Terminology: Liquidity Trap
'Liquidity trap' refers to a situation in which the rate of interest is so low that people prefer to hold money rather than invest it in bonds. At a very low interest rate, the money demand schedule becomes infinitely elastic. In such a situation an increase in the money supply does not have any effect on the interest rate. An additional money created by the central bank is absorbed by the people and businesses in the form of liquid balance. And this prevents the rate of interest from falling further.

The liquidity trap[1] situation describes *absolute liquidity* preference for the people. It seems as if the interest rate has fallen in a trap. In such a situation an increase in the supply of money has no effect on interest rate. So it is not possible to stimulate investment by using expansionary monetary policy. This type of situation is expected in times of recession or depression[2].

In a liquidity trap situation, any attempt by the central bank to lower interest rate to stimulate investment will be futile, and will simply result in more money being held

Expectations about Future Rate of Interest

Keynes also pointed out that speculative demand for money depends on people's expectation of future rate of interest. If most people expect interest rate to rise (or bond prices to fall) in the future, the speculative demand for money will increase and the speculative demand curve for money or the liquidity preference curve will shift upwards. This means that more money will be demanded even at the same interest rate.

The Aggregate Demand for Money

The total demand for money is the sum of the above three types of demand for money, viz., transactions, precautionary and speculative. So it may be expressed as

$$M_d = kPY + L(r) \quad \ldots \quad (4)$$

1. The term 'liquidity trap' was coined by D. Robertson and not by Keynes.
2. The Japanese economy is now in such a situation.

where M_d is the total demand for money, kPY is the sum of transactions and precautionary demand and $L(r)$ is speculative demand. Equation (4) may also be written as

$$M_d = M_{dt}(Y) + M_{ds}(r)$$

Thus if the price level remains constant the transactions and precautionary demand for money (taken together) M_{dt} is a function of national income and speculative demand for money M_{ds} is a function of interest rate. While M_{dt} varies directly with income (depending on income elasticity of demand for money), M_s varies inversely with interest rate (depending on the interest elasticity of demand for money)[1].

Criticisms of Keynes' Theory of Demand for Money

There are three main criticisms of Keynes's theory of demand for money.

1. *All-or-nothing choice* : First Keynes argued that people make all-or-nothing choice. They hold either money or bonds. But in reality, we find that people hold both money and bonds in their wealth portfolio (in different proportions depending upon their expectations of future return and attitude towards risk). Modern economists have gone further and suggested that an individual's wealth portfolio may consist of money, bonds, equities, or even physical assets like houses or land.

2. *Interest elasticity of transactions demand* : Baumol and Tobin have shown that even transactions demand for money is interest elastic. [This point will be taken up in the next chapter.]

3. *The modern view* : According to modern macroeconomists money represents a single asset. So the same unit of money may serve diverse motives. So it is not judicious to divide the total demand for money into three different types of demand, as Keynes has done.

POST-KEYNESIAN THEORIES

While the classical economists referred to transactions demand for money Keynes highlighted the concept of speculative demand for money and thus made a major breakthrough in the area of monetary economics. However, the Keynesian approach has been challenged by W.J. Baumol (in 1952), J. Tobin (in 1956) and M. Friedman (in 1958). Tobin, one of the followers of Keynes, developed the portfolio approach to the demand for money. He found one major flaw in the Keynesian theory. Keynes argued that an individual will hold all his wealth either in money or in bonds. But Tobin has postulated out that a wealth-holder can have both money and bonds in his asset portfolio. The proportion will vary from person to person and from time to time, depending on one's attitude towards risk. According to Friedman, an individual is likely to have a diversified portfolio of assets. His portfolio of assets may consist of money, interest-bearing bonds, equity shares, physical assets and even storable commodities (such as durable and semi-durable goods). Thus an individual's demand for money will depend on the relative rates of return of all these non-monetary assets and goods.

W.J. Baumol has pointed out that even transactions demand for money depends on the rate of interest. He developed the inventory-theoretic approach and the theory threw a challenge to both classical and Keynesian economics. We may now discuss these post-Keynesian theories of demand for money one by one.

1. TOBIN'S PORTFOLIO APPROACH TO SPECULATIVE DEMAND FOR MONEY

Money is a riskless asset but yields no return

Tobin refined and modified the Keynesian theory of speculative demand for money. He argued that a rational individual will hold an optimum proportion of money and bonds in his portfolio of assets. In his view, an individual is faced

1. According to Baumol and Tobin, even transactions demand for money depends on the interest rate. Others have argued that even speculative demand for money is an increasing function of total asset or wealth and Friedman has used permanent income as a proxy for total wealth. This means that even speculative demand for money depends on income.

with risk-return trade-off. He has to choose the right proportion of two assets — money (which yields no return) and interest-bearing bonds. Money is a safe asset and bond is a risky asset. The return on money is zero but the return on bonds is the fixed interest *plus* any capital gain (which may arise due to a rise in its price).

According to Keynes, an individual holds all his wealth either in money or in bonds depending on his expectation about the future rate of interest. But, according to Tobin, there is uncertainty about the future interest rate. And this leads to changes in bond prices. If bond prices fall, the bondholder will incur capital loss. By contrast, money is a safe asset but the return on money is zero. So an individual, faced with a choice between a safe and a risky asset, will diversify his portfolio by holding a judicious mix of money and bonds.

The choice of the balanced portfolio of assets depends on an individual's attitude towards risk. A risk-averse person will hold more money and less bonds in his asset portfolio. But a risk-taker will do just the opposite. He will hold very little money in his portfolio and the maximum number of bonds.

Liquidity Preference Function

In Fig. 17.6 we show Tobin's liquidity preference curve M_d which is downward sloping from left to right, as is the case in the Keynesian theory of demand for money.

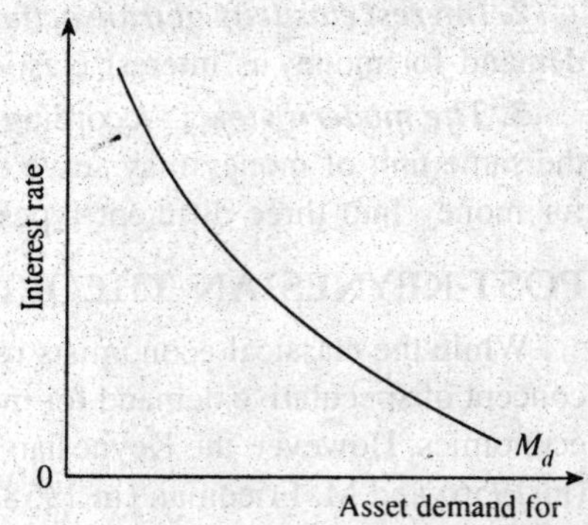

Fig. 17.6: The Demand Curve for Money in Tobin's Theory

The downward sloping money demand (or liquidity preference) curve M_d shows an inverse relation between the rate of interest (shown on the vertical axis) and the demand for money (shown on horizontal axis). Tobin argues that as the rate of interest rises, the price of bonds will fall. So people will buy more bonds and hold less money. This explains the inverse relation between the rate of interest and speculative demand for money. On the basis of this inverse relation, Tobin arrives at the aggregate liquidity preference (or money demand) curve. Tobin's approach gets much empirical support and interest elasticity of speculative demand for money is found to be quite high. Tobin's approach, known as liquidity preference as behaviour toward risk, may now be discussed in detail.

With a rise in the rate of interest an individual will increase the proportion of bonds and reduce the proportion of money in his asset portfolio

The main problem with the Keynesian approach to the demand for money is that it suggests that individuals should, at any given time, hold all their liquid assets either in money or in bonds, but not some of each. This is obviously not true in reality. Tobin's approach to liquidity preference deals with this problem by showing that if the return on bonds is uncertain, that is, if bonds are risky, then the investor, worrying about both risk and return, is likely to do best by holding both bonds and money.

Portfolio theories like the one presented by Tobin emphasises the role of money as a store of value. According to these theories, people hold money as part of their portfolio of assets. The reason is that money offers a safe (nominal) return, whereas the prices of stocks and bonds may rise or fall. Thus Tobin has suggested that households choose to hold money as part of their optimal portfolio.

Speculative Demand for Money as Behaviour Toward Risk

The focus in Tobin's theory is on an individual's portfolio (optimal) allocation between money holding and bond holding, subject to the wealth constraint, i.e., $\overline{W} = M + B$, where $\overline{W}$ is the total fixed wealth, M is money and B is bond.

Tobin's theory is explained in Fig. 17.7. On the vertical axis of the upper quadrant we measure the expected return to the portfolio; on the horizontal axis we measure the riskiness of the portfolio. The expected return on the portfolio is the interest which can be earned on bonds. This depends on two things: (i) the interest rate and (ii) the proportion of the portfolio held in bonds. The total risk faced by an individual depends on (i) the uncertainty concerning bond prices —that is, the uncertainty concerning future movements in market rate of interest and (ii) the proportion of the portfolio held in bonds.

Let us denote the expected total return by R and the total risk of the portfolio as σ. If an individual holds all his wealth (W) in money and none in bonds, i.e., $W = M + 0$, both R and σ will be zero, as shown by the origin (point 0) in Fig. 17.7. With an increase in the proportion of bonds, R and σ will both rise. The opportunity line $0C$ in panel (a) is a locus of points showing the terms[1] on which the individual investor can increase R at the cost of increasing σ. A movement along $0C$ from left to right shows that the investor increases his bond holding only by reducing his money holding.

Part (b) of Fig. 17.7 shows alternative portfolio allocations, resulting in different combinations of R and σ. The vertical axis measures bond holding. The amount of bonds (B) held in W increases as the investor moves down the vertical axis to a maximum of $\overline{W}$. The difference between $\overline{W}$ and B is the asset demand for money (M). The line $0K$ in the lower part of the diagram shows the relationship between σ and B. As the proportion of B in W increases, σ also increases. This means that as the proportion of bonds in the portfolio increases, the total risk of the wealth portfolio increases, too.

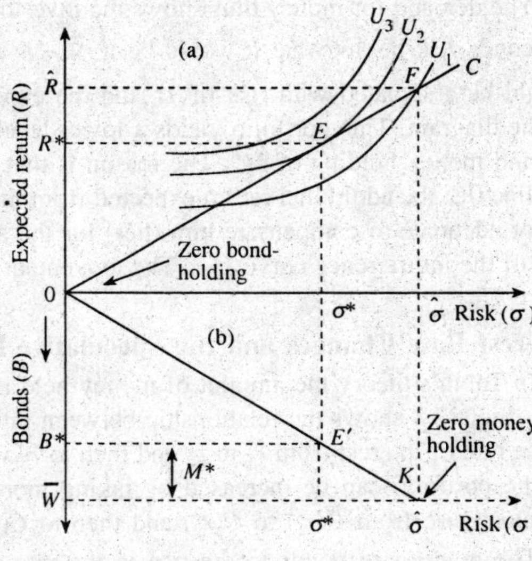

Fig. 17.7: Determination of the Optimal Portfolio

Preference of the Investor: Risk-Aversion

The optimal portfolio allocation depends on the preferences of the investor. Here we assume that the investor is risk-averse. He wants the best of both the worlds — a high return on the portfolio by reducing risk. He will accept more risk if he is compensated by an increase in expected return. Each indifference curve shows the risk-return trade-off, i.e., the terms on which the investor is desirous of taking more risk if he is compensated by a higher expected return. All the points on any such indifference curve yield the same fixed level of utility. Any movement from U_1 to U_2 and from U_2 to U_3 implies higher level of utility, i.e., higher levels of R and the same or even lower levels of σ. The indifference curves are upward sloping because the investor is risk-averse. He will take more risk only if he is compensated by a proportionately higher return. Moreover, the curves become steeper as the investor moves to the right, implying *increasing risk aversion.*

If we make this assumption, then the more risk the individual has already taken, the greater will be the increase in expected return required for the investor to be exposed to a greater degree of risk. We may now determine the optimal portfolio allocation of a risk-averse investor.

1. If σ measures the uncertainty about the price of a given bond, then the total risk on the portfolio is $\sigma = \sigma_b$.

Total expected return on bonds is $R = rB$. So the slope of the line $0C$ is $\frac{\Delta R}{\Delta \sigma}$.

Optimal Portfolio Allocation

A risk-averse investor will move to that point along the line $0C$ which enables him to reach the highest attainable indifference curve. At that point he ends up choosing that portfolio which he intends to choose and, thus, maximises his utility. The reason is obvious. At the tangency point E, with $R = R^*$ and $\sigma = \sigma^*$, the terms on which the investor is able to increase expected return on the portfolio by taking more risk, as shown by the slope of the line $0C$, is the same as terms on which he (she) is willing to make the trade-off, as is measured by the slope of the indifference curve. From the lower part we see that this risk-return combination is achieved by holding an amount of bonds equal to B^*, and by holding the remainder of wealth $(\overline{W} - B^* = M^*)$ in the form of money.

The demand for money thus shows the investor's behaviour towards risk, i.e., the result of seeking to reduce risk below what it would be if $\overline{W} = B$ and $M = 0$. In Fig. 17.7 such an all-bonds-portfolio would be associated with risk of $\hat{\sigma}$ and the expected return of $\hat{R}$, as shown by point F in part (a) of the diagram. This portfolio yields a lower level of utility than that represented by bond holding of B^* and money holding of M^*. The reason is that as the investor moves to the right of point E along the line $0C$, the additional return expected from the portfolio by holding more bonds (and less money) is not adequate to compensate him (her) for the additional risk (the slope of the line $0C$ is less than that of the indifference curve U_2). The movement to point F takes the investor to a lower indifference curve U_1.

Interest Rate Changes and the Speculative Demand for Money

In Tobin's theory the amount of money held as an asset depends on the interest rate and changes in it. Fig. 17.8 shows the relationship between interest rate and asset demand for money. An increase in the rate of interest from r_1 to r_2 and then to r_3 will improve the terms on which the expected return on the portfolio can be increased by taking more risk. So the line $0C$ becomes steeper.[1] It rotates anticlockwise from $C(r_1)$ to $C(r_2)$ and then to $C(r_3)$.

The investor responds to the rise in the rate of interest by taking more risk and earning higher expected returns by moving from E to F and then to G. It may be noted that each point is one of portfolio optimisation. In this case his holding of bonds (risky asset) increases (from B_1 to B_2, and then to B_3) and money holding falls (from M_1 to M_2, then M_3). In short, as the interest rate rises, a given increase in risk, which corresponds to a given increase in the amount of bonds in the portfolio, will result in a greater increase in expected return on the portfolio.

Comments

In Tobin's theory, like that of Keynes, the speculative demand for money varies inversely with the interest rate. The reason is that an increase in the rate of interest implies an increase in the payment received for taking more risk. When the interest rate increases, the investor is eager to put a larger proportion of his portfolio into the risky asset—bonds and thus a smaller proportion into the safe asset—money.

Tobin's approach generates a smooth and continuous liquidity preference function. In addition, Tobin postulates, and, quite realistically, that liquidity preference shows people's behaviour towards risk since it is not possible to know whether the rate of interest will rise or fall in the future.

From Tobin's portfolio theory, we can look at the money demand function $(M/P)_d = f(Y, i)$ as a useful simplification. First, it uses real income Y as a proxy for wealth W. Secondly, the only return variable it includes is the nominal interest rate (i) which is the sum of the real return on bonds and expected inflation (that is, $i = r_b + \pi^e$). Tobin's portfolio theory suggests that the demand function for money should also include the expected returns on other assets as well.

---

1. Since the slope of the line $0C$ is r/σ, an increase in r will increase the slope of the line.

Is Tobin's portfolio theory really useful for studying the demand for money? It depends on which measure of money we are considering. If we consider only narrow money (M_1), it is to be treated as a dominated asset, in the sense that as a store of value, it exists along with other assets that are always better. Thus, it is not judicious for people to hold money as part of their portfolio, and Tobin's portfolio theory cannot explain the demand for these dominated forms of money.

It may also be added that Tobin's portfolio theory is more plausible as a theory of demand for money if we adopt a broad definition of money. Although the portfolio approach to money demand may not be plausible when applied to M_1, it can suggest a clear explanation of the demand for M_2 or M_3.

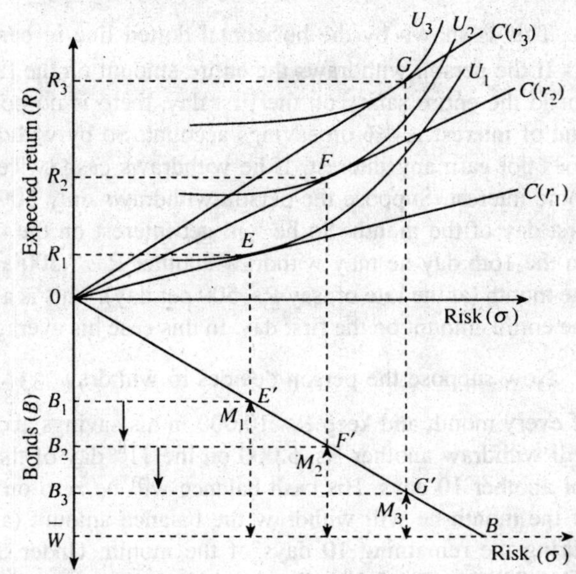

Fig. 17.8: Speculative Demand for Money and the Rate of Interest

2. BAUMOL'S INVENTORY-THEORETIC APPROACH TO TRANSACTIONS DEMAND FOR MONEY

First Baumol and then Tobin explained the transactions demand for money in terms of inventory management. In their view, people hold inventories of money for the same reason that companies hold stocks of finished goods. Companies hold inventories because production and sales do not always coincide. Similarly, individuals hold money because income and expenditure do not occur simultaneously. Individuals hold money because they buy goods and services every now and then. So people want to enjoy the convenience of money holding. They hold money for transaction purposes to bridge the gap between the receipt of income and its spending.

Money is held since it facilitates transactions

However, there is some cost of holding money. Firstly, there is the opportunity cost in terms of loss of interest. Secondly there is the transaction cost— cost of transport and loss of earning due to time lost in withdrawing money from bank. So while holding money for transaction purposes, people make a cost-benefit analysis. They compare the benefit of holding money which yields no return and the cost of holding money and withdrawing it for the purpose of spending. How do people take decision regarding cash management in such a situation? The answer to the question was given by both Baumol (in 1952) and Tobin (in 1956). Here we present Baumol's theory.

Baumol's Analysis in Detail

Baumol analysed the transactions demand for money of an individual who receives income, say, once a month and spends it gradually over the entire month. His spending behaviour and transactions demand for money are shown in Fig. 17.9.

We assume that he receives a salary cheque of Rs. 15,000 on the first day of every month. Since it is directly credited to his bank account, it is encashed on the same day. He spends Rs. 500 everyday throughout the month and at the end of the month his cash balance is zero. So his average money holding is:

$$\frac{\text{Cash balance at the beginning of the month} + \text{cash balance at the end of the month}}{2}$$

or, $$\frac{15,000+0}{2} = \text{Rs. } 7,500$$

This is shown by the horizontal dotted line in panel (a) of Fig. 17.9.

If the person withdraws the entire amount on the first day, he will lose interest. Since he does not spend the entire salary on the first day, there is no point in withdrawing it on that day. Suppose the rate of interest is 4% on savings account. So by withdrawing Rs. 15,000 on the first day, the person does not earn any interest. If he withdraws cash twice or thrice to meet his cash needs, he can earn some interest. Suppose the person withdraws only 50%, i.e., Rs. 7,500 from his bank account on the first day of the month. So he will get interest on the remaining 50% of his salary for 15 days. Then on the 16th day he may withdraw another Rs. 7,500 and spend it gradually over the next 15 days of the month (at the rate of, say Rs. 500 per day). This is a better way of managing cash than withdrawing the entire amount on the first day. In this case his average cash holding will be Rs. 7,500/2 = Rs. 3,750.

Now suppose the person decides to withdraw $33\frac{1}{3}\%$ of his salary (or Rs. 5,000) on the first day of every month and keep Rs. 10,000 in his savings account. He will spend the money in 10 days and will withdraw another Rs. 5,000 on the 11th day of the month. So he will get interest on Rs. 10,000 for another 10 days. His cash balance will be zero on the 20th day of the month. So on the 21th day of the month he will withdraw the balance amount (another Rs. 5,000) which he will spend evenly during the remaining 10 days of the month. Under this scheme, his average cash holding will be Rs. 5,000/2 = Rs. 2,500. But his interest income will he higher in this case.

However, apart from the loss of interest involved in cash withdrawal there are other costs also such as transport cost and loss of wage income (due to time spent on making trips to bank). So the larger the number of trips to the bank, the higher will be the cost.[1]

The less the number of cash withdrawals, the less will be transaction cost but greater will be the loss of interest

If he withdraws a large amount at a time, transaction cost will he low but interest loss (opportunity cost) will be high. Thus, the individual faces a trade-off. According to Baumol the optimum amount of cash-holding by a rational individual is determined by minimising total cost (i.e., interest loss and transaction cost) associated with cash withdrawal from bank. This point may be explained further.

Suppose we denote the salary of the person by Y, the average amount of cash he withdraws each time he goes to the bank by C, the number of trips he makes to the bank by N and transaction cost he incurs each time by t. Under the first scheme, $N = 1$, since he withdraws his entire salary on the first day. In this case, $N = \frac{Y}{C} = \frac{\text{Rs. } 15,000}{\text{Rs. } 15,000} = 1$, $C = Y$. In the second case, $N = \frac{\text{Rs. } 15,000}{\text{Rs. } 7,500} = 2$ and in the third case, $N = \frac{\text{Rs. } 15,000}{\text{Rs. } 5,000} = 3$.

The interest lost by the person by holding money is the average amount of money holding times the current rate of interest. Since the average amount of money held is half of cash withdrawn each time $\left(\text{i.e., } \frac{C}{2}\right)$, the loss of interest under the first scheme is $\frac{r.C}{2} = \frac{4}{100} \times \frac{15,000}{2} = \text{Rs. } 300$; in the second case it is $\frac{4}{100} \times \frac{7,500}{2} = \text{Rs. } 150$ and in the third case it is $\frac{4}{100} \times \frac{5,000}{2} = \text{Rs. } 100$.

1. An alternative way of interpreting these transport cost and loss of wage income is to refer to the brokerage fee incurred by an individual every time he converts interest-bearing bonds into money. Interest loss is the same in each case of withdrawing money from savings account or encashing interest-bearing bonds.

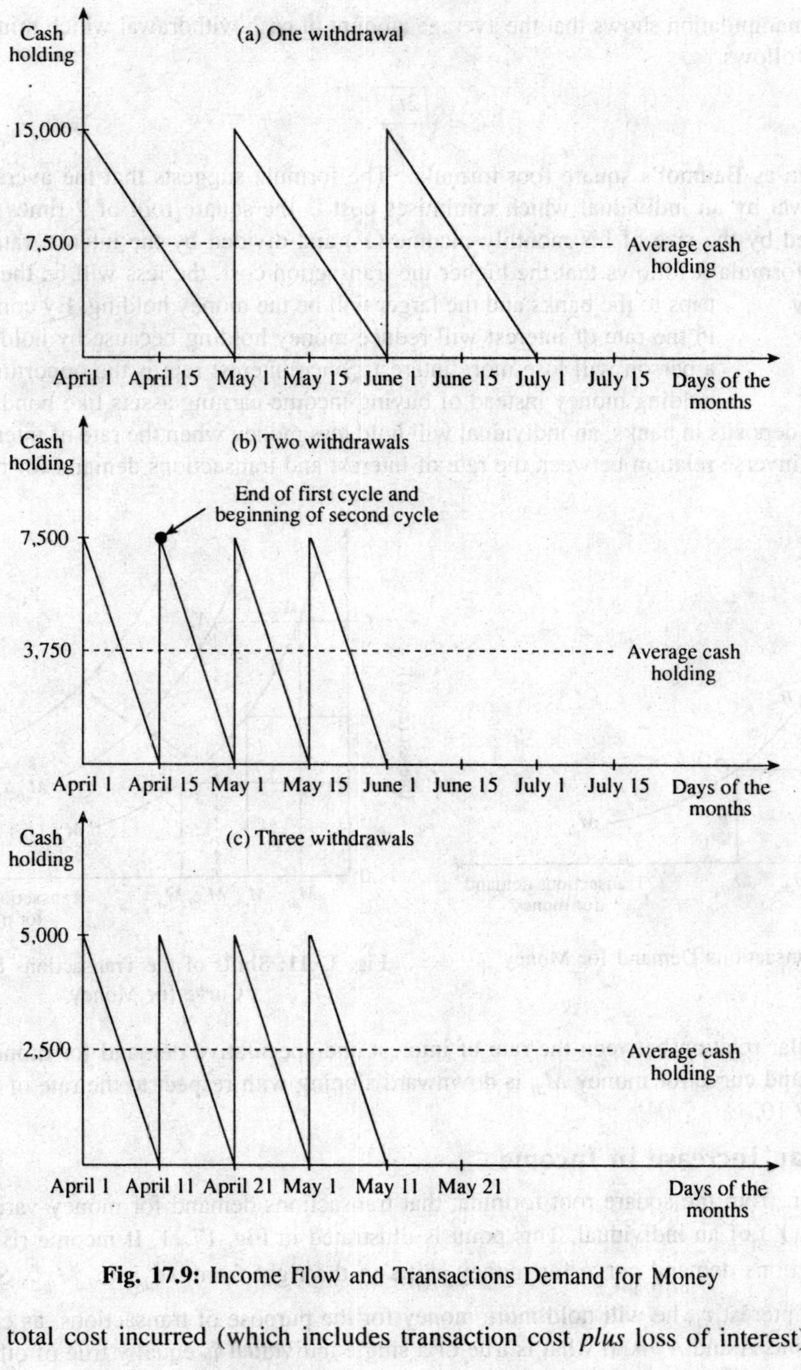

Fig. 17.9: Income Flow and Transactions Demand for Money

Thus the total cost incurred (which includes transaction cost *plus* loss of interest) is written as:

$$\text{Total cost } = tN + \frac{r.C}{2}$$

where t stands for transaction cost.

$$\text{Since } N = \frac{Y}{C}, \text{ total cost } = \frac{Y}{C}.t + \frac{r.C}{2}.$$

Now a little manipulation shows that the average amount of cash withdrawal which minimises cost is expressed as follows

$$C = \sqrt{\frac{2tY}{r}}.$$

This is known as Baumol's square root formula.[1] The formula suggests that the average amount of cash withdrawal by an individual which minimises cost is the square root of 2 times transaction cost (t) multiplied by the size of his monthly income (Y) and divided by the interest rate (r). From this square root formula it follows that the higher the transaction cost, the less will be the number of trips to the banks and the larger will be the money holding. By contrast, a rise in the rate of interest will reduce money holding because by holding money, a person will lose more interest. Since interest rate is the opportunity cost of holding money instead of buying income-earning assets like bonds or having saving and fixed deposits in banks, an individual will hold less money when the rate of interest is high. Thus there is an inverse relation between the rate of interest and transactions demand for money (just

By holding money people lose the opportunity of earning interest

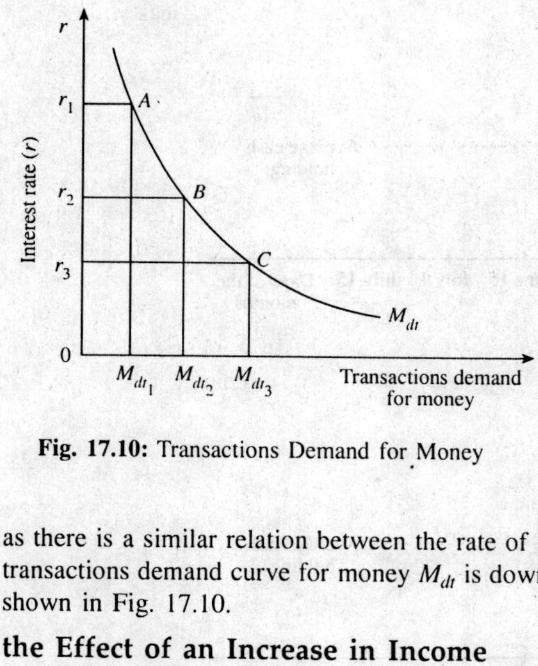

Fig. 17.10: Transactions Demand for Money

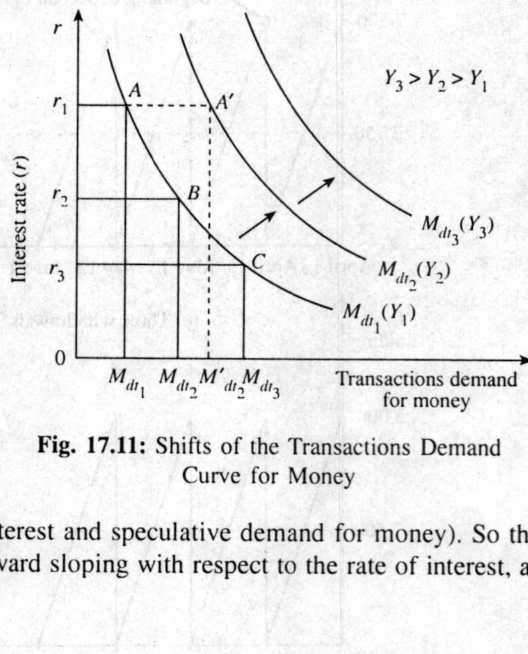

Fig. 17.11: Shifts of the Transactions Demand Curve for Money

as there is a similar relation between the rate of interest and speculative demand for money). So the transactions demand curve for money M_{dt} is downward sloping with respect to the rate of interest, as shown in Fig. 17.10.

the Effect of an Increase in Income

It is also clear, from the square root formula, that transactions demand for money varies directly with the income (Y) of an individual. This point is illustrated in Fig. 17.11. If income rises from Y_1 to Y_2, his transactions demand curve for money shifts to the right from M_{dt_1} to M_{dt_2}. So even, at the same rate of interest r_1, he will hold more money for the purpose of transactions, as can be seen by comparing points A and A'. And what is true of a single individual is equally true of other people.

It should also be clear from the square root formula that optimum money holding by an individual for the purpose of transactions will increase less than proportionately to the increase in income. In fact, there are economies of scale in money holding. If eight people live in a joint family, their total demand for cash will be less than what it would be if each one of them lived separately.

1. A similar type of formula is used to find out the minimum cost of holding a certain amount of inventory.

Thus transactions demand for money is a function of not only income, as the classicists and Keynes thought, but also a function of the rate of interest. So the transactions demand function for money may now be expressed as

Transactions demand for money varies directly with Y and inversely with r

$$M_{dt} = f(Y, r),$$

where M_{dt} depends on or is a function of Y and r.

3. FRIEDMAN'S THEORY OF DEMAND FOR MONEY

In 1958 Milton Friedman, the leader of Chicago (monetarist) school presented a new type of money demand function on the basis of which he made a restatement of the classical Quantity Theory of Money. In his view the money demand function is fairly stable. He treats money as just one type of asset in which people hold a certain portion of their wealth. Business firms hold money because they treat money as a form of capital goods which is the creater of consumer goods. For these two reasons the theory of demand for money is essentially an aspect of capital theory. We may now briefly discuss the return on different types of assets in which people hold their wealth.

(i) **Money:** Like any other capital goods, money yields return. Money also provides services. It may be noted at the outset that the real yield of money is the value of goods and services which can be purchased with money. This value depends on the price level.

(ii) **Bonds:** Bonds are another type of asset in people's wealth portfolio. Bonds generate a flow of fixed income (in terms of interest, called the coupon rate of interest). People also hold bonds if they anticipate capital gain due to expected changes in the market rate of interest.

(iii) **Equities:** People also hold equity and preference shares as part of their total wealth. Equity refers to ownership interest in a corporation in the form of equity capital. Three factors affect the return from equity, viz., the annual rate of dividend, expected capital gain or loss and expected change in the price level.

(iv) **Commodities:** People can also hold their wealth in capital (producer) goods and durable consumer goods (assuming that people are the owners of businesses). The return from holding commodities is *implicit* rather than *explicit*. The return takes the form of expected rate of change in their prices per period.

The Nominal Demand Function for Money

The nominal demand function for money may now be presented as follows:

$$M_d = f[W, h, r_m, r_b, r_e, P, \left(\frac{\Delta P}{P}\right)^e, U] \qquad \ldots \quad (1)$$

The demand for real balances is expressed as:

$$\frac{M_d}{P} = f[W, h, r_m, r_b, r_e, \left(\frac{\Delta P}{P}\right)^e, U] \qquad \ldots \quad (2)$$

where M_d stands for *nominal* money demand and $\frac{M_d}{P}$ is the demand for *real* money balance, W is wealth of the individuals, h is the proportion of human wealth to the total wealth held by people, r_m is the rate of return or interest on money, r_b is the rate of interest on bonds, r_e is the rate of return on equities, P is the price level, $\left(\frac{\Delta P}{P}\right)$ is the expected change in price level (i.e., the expected rate of inflation) and U stands for various institutional factors over which wealth-holders have no control.

These factors may now be explained one by one.

1. Wealth (W): An individual's total stock of wealth is the most important determinant of his demand for money. The greater the wealth of an individual, the more money he will demand for transaction and other purposes. For the same reason as a country continues to grow, the total demand for money for all purposes will also increase, though not proportionately.

Wealth has two main components—non-human and human. Non-human wealth consists of financial assets such as bonds, shares and money. Human wealth refers to the sum of an individual's present and future earnings or his permanent income. There are two main differences between non-human and human wealth. Non-human wealth can easily be converted into money. So such wealth is highly liquid. But human wealth (such as an individual's knowledge, skill and superior ability to perform a certain task) is not liquid. It cannot be used as security to borrow money. So the proportion of human wealth to non-human wealth is included as an independent variable in the money demand function. Friedman argues that as the proportion of human (or liquid) wealth to total wealth increases, the demand for money will increase to offset the illiquidity of human wealth.

2. The relative rates of return (r_m, r_b, r_e): In equation (1), r_m is the rate of interest on savings and fixed deposits. People compare all the three rates of interest while taking decision on how much wealth to hold in the form of money. If rates of return on bonds (r_b) and equities (r_e) increase, the opportunity cost of money holding will increase. This will reduce the demand for money [i.e., the desire to hold money either in liquid form (currency)] or in the form of demand (current) deposits on which no interest is paid. In short, the demand function for money varies inversely with the rate of interest (or return) on bonds and equities.

3. The price level (P): If the price level rises, people require more nominal balance to keep their real balance intact so that they can buy the same amount of goods and services. This means that as the price level goes up (down) the demand for money will increase (fall).

4. Expected rate of inflation $\left[\left(\frac{\Delta P}{P}\right)^e\right]$: If people expect a higher rate of inflation, they will reduce their money holding, since inflation will reduce the value (purchasing power) of their money holding. If the rate of inflation exceeds the nominal rate of interest, the real rate of interest will be negative. Therefore, when people expect a higher rate of inflation, they become eager to convert their money holdings into goods or real assets (like houses or land) which act as inflation hedges. The converse is also true. A fall in the expected rate of inflation will induce people to hold more money since its value is likely to increase in the future.

5. Institutional factors (U): Various institutional factors such as the method of wage payment and payment of bills affect the demand for money. If, in India, the method of weekly payment of wages and salaries is introduced as in Britain, the aggregate demand for money will fall. If there is more and more vertical integration in the corporate sector, business demand for money will fall. Similarly, if cheques are used in all types of transactions, the demand for money will fall. But if there is a wave of credit card fraud, the demand for money will increase since credit cards will not be widely accepted.

If people anticipate a major war or revolution, they will try to buy more goods, the prices of which are likely to rise sharply due to acute scarcity. So the demand for money will increase. Similarly a major global financial crisis will increase the demand for money and reduce the demand for bonds and equities. Finally, the demand for money varies in two different phases of the business cycle. It increases in times of depression or recession. In such times, unemployment is high and there is uncertainty about future income. All these institutional factors are included in the variable U.

A Simple Form of the Money Demand Function

Since it is difficult to measure the value of wealth (W) due to lack of reliable data, Friedman takes the present value of wealth which is $\frac{Y_p}{r_m}$, i.e., the discounted value of permanent income as a proxy for wealth. So his money demand function becomes

$$M_d = f(Y_p, h, r_m, r_b, r_e, \frac{\Delta P}{P}, U)$$

If we assume reasonable price level stability and constancy of institutional factors as also the ratio of non-human to human wealth and a uniform rate of interest (r) as returns on money, bonds and equities, then the demand function for money becomes

$$M_d = f(Y_p, r)$$

Once again we find that M_d is a function of two key variables, viz., Y and r.

KEY POINTS

1. *The concept of demand for money* : The demand for money refers to the desire to hold money as an alternative to purchasing income-earning assets like government bonds. In the true sense, the demand for money refers to people's desire to hold real balance (i.e., nominal balance devided by the price level). Two main theories of the demand for money are the classical theory and the Keynesian theory.

2. *Fisher's transactions balance approach to demand for money* : Fisher's Quantity Theory of Money contains an implicit idea of the demand for money. According to Fisher's transactions balance approach, the demand for money depends on three factors, viz., (a) the number of transactions, (b) the average price of transactions, and (c) the velocity of circulation of money, called transactions velocity.

3. *The Cambridge cash-balance approach to demand for money* : According to the Cambridge approach an individual's demand for nominal cash balance is proportional to his nominal income. While in Fisher's approach the demand for money is related to total transactions in a mechanical way, in the Cambridge approach, the same relation is behavioural, i.e., it depends on people's spending behaviour. However, critics have commented that any change in the price level may lead to non-proportional change in the demand for money.

4. *Keynes's theory of demand for money* : Keynes used the term 'liquidity preference' to refer to the demand for money. Liquidity preference means preference for cash. People's desire to hold money (in liquid form, i.e., in the form of cash) arises from three motives: (i) the transactions motive, (ii) the precautionary motive, and (iii) the speculative motive. Transactions demand for money arises because money is used as a means of payment (i.e., a medium of exchange). It depends on two main factors: (a) national income and (b) the price level. If the price level remains constant the transactions demand for money varies directly with income. Like individuals businesses also hold money for transaction purposes. People also hold money for precautionary purposes to be able to tackle unforseen contingencies. The speculative (asset) demand for money arises because people want to make capital gains by buying bonds at low price now and selling the same bonds at a higher price later. The speculative demand for money depends on the existing rate of interest as also on expected changes in the rate of interest in the future.

According to Keynes the rate of interest is the opportunity cost of money holding. By holding money people lose the opportunity to earn interest. So people hold less money when the interest rate is high and more money when interest rate is low. Thus the speculative demand for money varies inversely with the interest rate. This relation holds because there is an inverse relation between the rate of interest and the market price of old bonds. The total demand curve for money is downward sloping with respect to the interest rate due to the speculative component.

5. *Liquidity trap* : In times of depression the rate of interest falls to a very low level. It cannot fall further because the demand curve for money or the liquidity preference curve becomes completely elastic in such a situation. So any increase in the money supply by the central bank is absorbed by the people in the form of liquid (cash) balance. And this prevents the rate of interest from falling further. The completely elastic portion of the money demand curve is called liquidity trap. And because of liquidity trap, monetary policy of the central bank loses its effectiveness. This usually happens in times of recession or depression.

6. *Determinants of money demand* : There are two main determinants of the money demand, viz., the level of income and the rate of interest. While the transactions-cum-precautionary demand for money varies directly with income, the speculative demand for money varies inversely with the interest rate, due to the inverse relation between the rate of interest and market price of old bonds.

7. *Tobin's portfolio balance approach to speculative demand for money* : According to Tobin, an individual faces a risk-return choice while deciding how much of his wealth to hold in the form of money and what proportion of it to utilise in buying bonds. Money is a risk-free asset and yields no return. Bond is a risky asset and yields two types of return —fixed interest and capital gain (in case of price rise). A rational individual having a fixed amount of wealth seeks to choose an optimum mix of money and bond and, in the process, the most desirable combination of risk and return. Tobin's explanation of Keynes's liquidity preference theory is essentially one of liquidity preference as behaviour toward risk.

8. *Baumol's inventory management approach to transactions demand for money* : Initially Baumol and then Tobin have presented an inventory management approach to transactions demand for money. According to Baumol, apart from income transactions demand for money also depends on the rate of interest and varies inversely with it. While taking decision regarding optimal cash holding, an individual makes a cost-benefit analysis of money holding.

9. *Friedman's capital theory approach to the demand for money* : According to Friedman, the demand for money is an aspect of capital theory. It depends on various factors. However, the most important determinant of the demand for money is an individual's wealth. Other determinants are the ratio of non-human to human wealth, the rates of return on money, bonds, equities and commodities, the price level, the expected rate of inflation and the various institutional factors. Since wealth cannot be accurately measured, Friedman takes the present value of expected income (or permanent income) as a proxy for wealth and the rate of interest acts as the discount factor. In truth, Friedman made a restatement of the classical quantity theory of money.

KEY TERMS

Real balance
Nominal balance
Money illusion
Fisher's transactions balance approach
Cambridge cash balance approach
Transactions demand for money
Precautionary demand for money
Speculative demand for money
Liquidity preference
Business demand for money
Human wealth
Square-root formula
Portfolio choice
Institutional factors
Opportunity cost
Capital gains
Price of bonds
Income elasticity of demand for money
Interest elasticity of demand for money
Absolute liquidity preference
Thriftiness
Real factors
Monetary factors
Capital gain(s)
Liquidity trap
Inventory-management approach
Risk-aversion
Non-human wealth
Transaction cost
Permanent income
All-or-nothing choice
Risk-preference

ASSIGNMENTS

1. The classical economists treated money as a means of payment. Examine the statement.
2. Make a comparison between the two classical versions of the theory of demand for money. Which one is more acceptable to you and why?
3. (a) What are the motives for money holding?
   (b) What are the determinants of the demand for money?

4. What do you mean by the statement that the rate of interest is the opportunity cost of money holding? In this context show the relation between the price of bonds and rate of interest. How does this relation affect the demand for money?
5. Make a comparison between the Keynesian theory of demand for money and the classical theory.
6. Explain why the speculative demand for money is interest elastic.
7. In what way is the Keynesian theory of demand for money a departure from the classical theory? Discuss in detail.
8. Explain why the demand for money is considered to be a declining function of the rate of interest.
9. How does the Keynesian theory of interest differ from the classical theory?
10. Show how the rate of interest is determined if we take income as fixed.
11. The Keynesian theory of interest is not only inconsistent but also indeterminate and incomplete as well, Explain.
12. When does monetary policy lose its effectiveness completely? Explain with a diagram.
13. In what sense is Tobin's portfolio approach an improvement over Keynes's theory of speculative demand for money? How does Tobin explain the inverse relationship between the rate of interest and speculative (asset) demand for money?
14. How does Baumol's approach explain the inverse relation between the rate of interest and transactions demand for money?
15. What according to Tobin, are the determinants of the speculative demand for money?
16. How does Friedman's theory of demand for money differ from Keynes's theory of demand for money?
17. What, according to Friedman, are the main determinants of the demand for money? How do the composition of wealth and the rate of interest influence the demand for money?
18. Do you think that cash management model of money demand is an improvement on Keynesian model? If there is due improvement in cash availability through new banking facility, what will be the impact on cash demand?
19. Suppose that an epidemic of street crime sweeps the country, making it more likely that your wallet will be stolen. Using the Baumol-Tobin model, explain (in words, not equations) how this crime wave will affect the optimal frequency of trips to the bank and the demand for money.
20. Distinguish between the portfolio and transaction theories of money demand.
21. According to the Baumol-Tobin model, what determines how often people go to the bank? What does this decision have to do with money demand?
22. In what way does the existence of near money complicate the conduct of monetary policy?
23. What will be an economy's speculative demand for money if people are certain about their future expenditures? Explain.
24. Consider a risk lover. How will his indifference curve look like in the risk-return plane? How will he allocate his wealth between money and perpetuity in Tobin's model?
25. The RBI announces that it intends to increase money supply sometimes in the future. What will be the effect of this announcement on real demand for money? And on the price level today?
26. Suppose that an epidemic of street crime sweeps the country, making it more likely that your wallet will be stolen. Using the Baumol-Tobin model, explain (in words, not equations) how this crime wave will affect the optimal frequency of trips to the bank and the demand for money.
27. (i) Elucidate the difference between transaction and speculative demand for money. (ii) Credit market decision making is based on nominal interest rate. Explain your agreement or disagreement.
28. What is Liquidity Preference theory? Explain the effect of money supply expansion in that theory? What does the explanation assume about the price level?
29. (i) Define interest rate. (ii) What is the role of interest rate in liquidity preference theory?

CHAPTER 18

The Supply of Money and Its Determinants

There have been three great inventions since the beginning of time: fire, the wheel and central banking.

Will Roger

PREVIEW

Money exerts considerable influence over macroeconomic variables such as the rate of interest and the price level. It keeps the wheels of trade and industry moving. It also influences family budget and thus household consumption and saving. There is flow of money from the household sector to the business sector through the financial system of a country. This enables business firms to convert money into real assets— capital goods which are the creators of mainly consumption goods.

Money also affects business investment and national income indirectly. An increase in the money supply (M) leads to a fall in the rate of interest (r). This leads to an increase in investment (I), and through the multiplier, to a multiple increase in national income (Y).

Four Preliminary Observations

The concept of money supply is of crucial importance from the point of the whole economy. Four basic points are to be noted in this context.

1. Inside money and outside money: The money supply of a country is determined not only by the central bank but also by the commercial banks and the public. In fact, the ability of commercial banks to create money (credit) depends not only on their own cash requirements, but also on cash requirements of the public. In this context, we may draw a distinction between inside money and outside money.

Any money that is a net asset of the private sector of an economy is called *outside money*. Currency and bank reserves, high-powered money or base money constitute outside money. However, most money in modern economies is inside money, which is simultaneously an asset and a liability of the private sector. Inside money refers to the forms of money which are based on private sector debt such as commercial bank deposits, which are matched by bank lending to private sector borrowers. By contrast, outside money is money which is a direct debt of the public sector, e.g., circulating currency, or is based on such débt, e.g., commercial bank deposits matched by bank holdings of public sector debt. The terms were coined by John Gurley and Edward S. Shaw in *Money in a Theory of Finance* (1960) and a prime significance of the distinction is the contention that changes in the real amounts of the two types of money held by the private sector will have differing wealth effects, with further implications for the neutrality or otherwise of the money stock. It is argued that a fall in the real value of the inside money stock, caused by a rise in prices, will leave the net real wealth of the private sector unchanged, since the matching debts will be equally devalued and the net real wealth of the debtors increased. A similar change in the value of outside money will decrease the private sector's net real wealth, while the balancing change in the public sector's real wealth may be ignored if we assume that its economic behaviour will remain unaffected by the change. Even in this case the public, perceiving that its future real tax liability for debt interest and repayment has fallen, may regard its net wealth as unaffected. Inside money takes the form of bank deposits, which are an asset to their holders and a liability of the banks. Outside money is net wealth for the private sector, whereas inside money is not.

2. Different measures of money supply: In India, there are at least four different definitions (measures) of the money supply depending on which types of bank deposits and other financial instruments are included in it.

3. Functional classification of money: It is possible to classify different types of money on the basis of functions of money.

4. Effectiveness of monetary policy: The effectiveness of monetary policy depends on the concept (components) of money supply which we adopt. In fact, the concept of money supply varies from country to country and period to period.

CONCEPTS AND MEASUREMENT OF THE MONEY SUPPLY

The money supply is a stock variable

The term 'money supply' refers to the total stock of money (as a medium of exchange) in circulation in country per period. It is a stock variable because it refers to the total money available to the public at a fixed point in time. Two main elements of money supply are the following:

(i) currency in circulation (notes and coins) and

(ii) bank deposits of the public[1] (withdrawable on demand).

While commercial banks are creators of money, the central bank is both a creator and a controller of money

It may also be noted that the money supply refers to the quantity of money held by the public, viz., households, firms and non-banking institutions which are the users of money. The government and the banks are creators of money. In addition, the government or the central bank is the controller of a country's money supply. The distinction between creators and users of money is important from the point of view of the conduct of a country's monetary policy.

We may now discuss the two main components of the money supply in detail. Here, we give Indian examples to make the relevant terms and concepts clear.

(i) **Currency with the public:** The total currency with the public in India has the following two components:

(a) Currency notes of different denominations (such 2, 5, 10, 20, 50, 100, 500 and 1000) which are issued by the RBI for circulation.

(b) One rupee notes[2], ten, five, two and one rupee coins and coins of smaller denominations (such as 50 paise coins).

1. The term 'public' here refers not only to households but also business firms and other entities except banks and the government.
2. One rupee notes are issued by the secretary of the Department of Treasury and not by the RBI and 50 paise coins have just been removed from circulation.

Cash reserves with the banks have to be deducted from the money supply. The reason is that these reserves are held by the banks and cannot be used by the public for making payments for purchase and sale of goods and services. These cannot be used for making any transactions by commercial banks either.

FIAT MONEY AND LEGAL TENDER MONEY

As noted in Ch. 14 currency notes and metallic coins are fiat money. This means that these serve as money on the basis of the fiat (i.e., order of the government). These are also called legal tender money because anyone in India is under the legal obligation to accept such money for all types of transactions. Such money has legal backing due to the authority of the government and its official declaration on every currency note.

A related point may be noted in this context. Money has value not due to the guarantee given by the Governor of the RBI. It has value because we have less money than we need. If money becomes a free good and its supply exceeds its demand, then money will have no value in spite of the guarantee of the RBI[1]. This is why the supply of money in any country is not privately controlled.

DEMAND DEPOSITS WITH THE PUBLIC

Bank deposits are of two main types: demand (current and savings) deposits and time (fixed) deposits. The demand deposits in banks can be withdrawn for spending purposes by drawing cheques on them. By using cheques it is possible to transfer money to others. For example, if Mr. *X* has purchased a car from Jalan Distributors, he can pay the required amount of money by drawing a cheque on his demand deposit (held in, say, UCO bank). Thus a cheque makes demand deposit a medium of exchange and enables it to serve as money.

A cheque is not money

Demand deposits are called fiduciary money. Such money is accepted only on the basis of trust—the trust of Jalan Distributors in Mr. *X*. In most cases, however, cheques are not accepted from unknown persons or even companies for supplying goods immediately. So goods are delivered or services are rendered only after encashment of cheques.

It may be noted that a cheque is not money because it may be dishonoured. However any demand deposit withdrawable by cheque is money.

Bank deposits are initially created when people deposit their money in banks. And people make loans from such deposits after keeping a certain portion of it as legal reserve. Due to the present fractional (proportional) reserve system of commercial banking, it is possible for the banking system of a country as a whole to do what an individual bank cannot—converting a small increase in initial deposit into a multiple increase in bank credit and thus in a country's money supply. We have already discussed the process of multiple credit creation in detail in Ch. 15.

PRIMARY AND SECONDARY MONEY

For the sake of analysis, we may refer to primary money and secondary money. Bank deposits are received, loans are made and money is created by banks on the basis of the initial currency notes and coins issued by the central bank. So the money supplied by the central bank is primary money and the money created by the banking system as a whole is secondary money.

Secondary money is the most important component of the money supply in advanced countries but not in developing countries

In most advanced countries where cheques are widely used for all types of transactions, secondary money (i.e., bank deposits withdrawable by cheques) is the main component of the money supply (about 80%). But in developing countries like India, with underdeveloped money markets, cheques are not accepted for small

1. This is exactly what happened in Germany in 1923 when people used currency notes for making tea by burning paper currency instead of using kerosene which was scarce and highly expensive.

transactions as also in rural areas (where the majority of the people live). In such countries, most transactions are made mainly with notes and coins. So the proportion of bank deposit to total money supply is less than 50%. See Fig. 18.1 which shows the two components of a country's money supply.

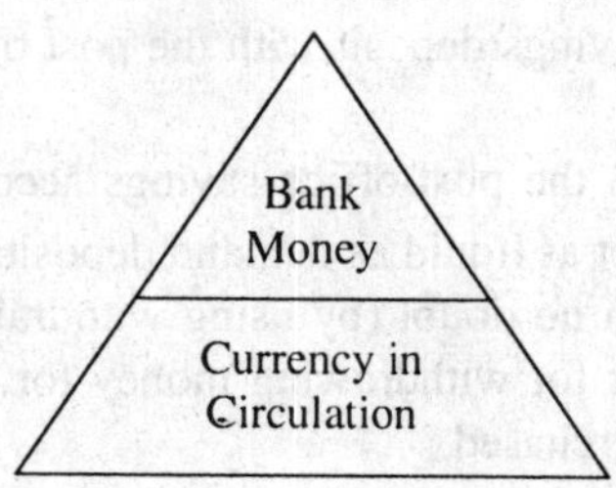

Fig. 18.1: The Reverse Pyramid of the Money Supply once Again

FOUR MEASURES OF MONEY SUPPLY

The most commonly accepted measure of money supply is M_1 which includes currency in circulation and demand deposits. Another concept of money supply is M_3 which adds time deposits to M_1. While people use M_1 mainly as a medium of exchange, i.e., for purchasing goods and services they use M_3 for the purpose of storing value (saving). Thus, while an increase in M_1 implies that people are spending more on consumption goods, an increase in M_3 implies that people are saving more. For these reasons, different concepts of money supply are used for different purposes. In other words, for theoretical analysis as also for formulation of monetary policy a single measure of the money supply is both inadequate and misleading.

Various measures of the money supply are used for different purposes

Since April 1977, the RBI has adopted four concepts of the money supply for both monetary management and policy formulation. It publishes weekly data on the quantity of and changes in money supply on the basis of this methodology. We may now explain these four measures of the money supply.

Narrow Money (M_1): This narrow measure of money supply has the following three components:

(i) currency in circulation(C),

(ii) demand deposits with the public in commercial and co-operative banks (D) and

(iii) other miscellaneous deposits held by the public with the RBI[1] (M).

So we can write:

$$M_1 = C + D + M$$

It may be noted that M_1 is the most liquid measure of the money supply and thus acts as a medium of exchange. It is the measure for making different types of payments or carrying out all types of transactions.

Now currency in circulation includes (a) currency notes in circulation with the public, (b) circulation of rupee coins as well as 50 paise coins and (c) cash reserves with all banks (also called cash-in-hand)[2].

The other deposits of RBI which constitute even less than 1% of India's total money supply include the following three items:

(a) deposits of public financial (term-lending) institutions such as IFCI, UTI, NABARD, IDBI, etc.,

1. In India, people keep their deposits with the RBI by purchasing interest-free bonds for saving capital gains tax as also by purchasing various other government bonds. After all, the central bank is the agent for the purchase and sale of government bonds and securities.
2. Inter-bank deposits, i.e., deposits held by a bank in other banks are excluded from D.

(b) demand deposits of foreign central banks and foreign governments.

(c) demand deposits of the IMF and the World Bank[1].

Broad Money (M_2)

We arrive at M_2 just by adding savings deposit with the post office savings accounts to M_1. Thus, we can write:

$M_2 = M_1$ + savings deposits with the post-office savings accounts.

Post office savings deposits are not as liquid as demand deposits with commercial and co-operative banks. It is possible to withdraw cash no doubt (by using withdrawal slips). But cheque facilities are not available from post offices, either for withdrawing money for transaction purposes or for making payments to others against goods purchased.

Broader Money (M_3)

As mentioned earlier, we arrive at M_3 by adding time deposits to M_1. So we can write:

$M_3 = M_1$ + time deposits with the banks.

So it is a broader concept of money supply than M_1.

No doubt, it is not possible to withdraw time (fixed) deposits by drawing cheques on them. However, it is possible to get loans against time deposits. Such loans can be used for transaction purposes. Moreover, time deposits can be fully encashed any time by foregoing some interest. For these reasons, time deposits are included in the broad definition of the money supply.

Till April 1977, M_3 was called by the RBI aggregate monetary resources (AMR). On the basis of the recommendations of the Chakraborty Committee, the GOI has been using M_3 for monetary planning and fixing targets of the growth of the money supply. By using this broad measure of the money supply the RBI makes a periodic analysis of growth of the money supply and its effects on the macroeconomic variables, mainly the price level.

Broadest Money (M_4)

This last measure of the money supply adds the total deposits held in post office savings accounts to M_3. So we can write:

$M_4 = M_3$ + total deposits with post office savings accounts.

However, the national saving certificates (NSCs) sold by the post offices are excluded from this measure.

The four concepts of the money supply as used by the RBI are summarised below.

Money Supply

M_1	M_2	M_3	M_4
= currency (C) + demand deposits (D) + other miscellaneous deposits of RBI (M)	$= M_1$ + savings deposits with post office savings accounts	$= M_1$ + time deposits with the banks	$= M_3$ + total deposits of post office savings accounts (excluding public deposits in NSCs)

In most countries, M_1 is taken as the most fundamental concept of the money supply and is used for both theoretical study and policy formulation.

1. Deposits held by the Central and State Governments as also RBI Employees' Pension and Provident Funds are excluded.

A NOTE ON CREDIT CARDS

No doubt the growing use of credit cards in recent years has reduced the demand for cash. But, as we noted in Ch. 14, credit cards are not money. These can be used as a *limited* and *restricted* medium of exchange, i.e., limited in the sense that if the credit limit is touched, a credit card cannot be used to exercise purchasing power and restricted in the sense that it is not universally accepted as a medium of exchange.

No doubt, credit cards such as Visa, Master Card, and American Express are 'plastic money'. Credit cards are widely accepted and serve as a means of payment in exchange for goods and services.

Moreover, the credit card statement, and not the card itself, serves as a unit of account. One of the advantages of credit cards is that one receives a statement listing exactly the price in rupees paid for each item charged. One's credit card statement clearly records the rupee amount one spent for petrol, a dinner, or a trip.

Moreover, credit cards cannot act as store of value (wealth). Therefore, they are not money. The word *credit* means receiving money today to buy goods in return for a promise to pay it back in the future. Credit cards only represent a prearranged short-term loan up to a certain limit. If the credit card company goes out of business, or for some reason decides not to honour one's card, a credit card is totally useless. Hence credit cards do not store value and are not money. If credit cards were money an individual would be indifferent between receiving Rs. 1,000 in cash and an equal rupee increase in one's credit limit.

The Effect on the Money Supply

The introduction and use of credit cards reduces the demand for money. As a result the rate of interest falls. So the central bank has to reduce the money supply to restore money market equilibrium and bring the rate of interest back to its old level. Therefore the supply of money has to fall.

The Determinants of the Money Supply

There are various determinants of a country's money supply. From now onwards we will use the narrow definition of the money supply since it is the most commonly (widely) used concept of money supply (M_1) and we use the symbol M rather than M_1. So we can write:

$$M = C + D \quad \ldots (1)$$

where M is total money supply with the public,

C is currency in circulation, and

D is demand deposits held by the public in banks.

The two proximate determinants of the money supply, as described in (1), are:

(i) the supply of high-powered (base) money and

(ii) the size of the money multiplier (i.e., the number by which the supply of high-powered money has to be multiplied to find out the total increase in the money supply).

We may now discuss the role of these two factors in determining a country's total money supply.

(i) **High-powered money (*H*):** The supply of high-powered money (H) refers to currency notes and coins issued by the RBI on behalf of the Government of India (GOI). A portion of the currency is held by the public (C) and a part is held by the banks in the form of reserves (R). Banks keep a portion of reserves in their vault to be able to meet the demand for withdrawal. Everyday some depositors withdraw a portion of their money. A bank should have sufficient cash in hand to be able to meet such demand. Banks also keep some deposits with the RBI. Thus banks keep a part of their reserves in their vaults and a part with the RBI[1]. Thus we can write:

$$H = C + R \quad \ldots (2)$$

1. In India, these are known as the CRR and SLR, respectively as already noted earlier.

where H is supply of high-powered money,

C is currency held by public (non-banks), and

R is cash reserves with the banks.

The RBI creates primary (base) money, known as high-powered money. And, commercial banks also create money by accepting deposits from the people which are also used as medium of exchange. However, for creating demand deposits from which loans are made, banks have to keep a certain portion of their deposits as reserves (denoted as R above).

High-poweredness of money issued by the RBI implies that its cash reserves with the banks serve as a basis for the multiple creation of demand deposits which constitute the major component of total money supply. In truth, it is against these cash reserves (R) that banks are able to increase the money supply through multiple credit creation (through the bank or deposit or credit multiplier). Due to the operation of the bank multiplier, discussed in detail in Ch. 15, a small increase in initial cash deposits leads to a multiple increase in bank (deposit) money.

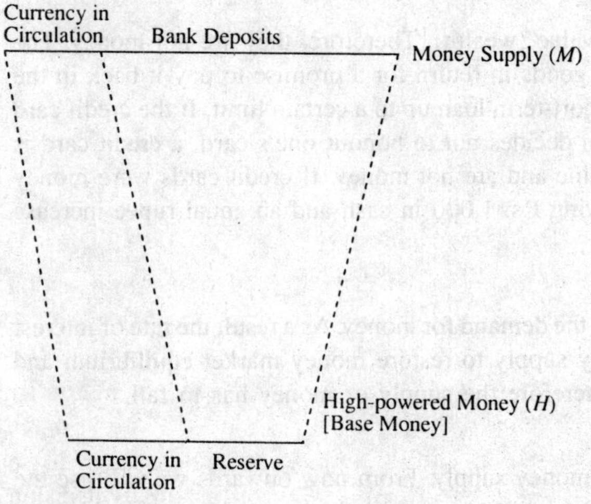

Fig. 18.2: The Relation between H and M

In truth, the money supply of a country is largely, if not, entirely determined by the supply of and demand for high-powered money. The relation between the high-powered money (H) and the total money supply (M) is shown in Fig 18.2. The base of the figure shows the supply of high-powered money (H) while the top shows the total stock (supply) of money. It is clear that $M > H$, since $D > R$, C being the common element of both M and H. Since bank deposits (D), which are a part of M, are a multiple of cash reserves (R) of banks which are a part of high-powered money (H), every rupee of H kept as R generates much more D. But how much more? This depends on the money multiplier, which shows the relation between the money supply and the high-powered money. It is expressed as:

$$mm = \frac{M}{H}$$

where mm is money multiplier,

M is the total money supply and

H is the supply of high-powered money.

The size of the money multiplier depends on

(i) the currency-deposit ratio of the public $\left(c = \frac{C}{D}\right)$ and

(ii) the currency-reserve ratio of the banks $\left(r = \frac{R}{D}\right)$

Here, 'c' shows the preference of the public to hold cash relative to bank deposits and 'r' is banks' both desired and required ratio of cash reserves to deposits.

Two Interesting Points

Two related points may be noted in this context. These are the following:

1. An increase in M: Suppose there is an increase in public's demand for cash for transaction purposes. Even if their demand deposits in banks remain unchanged, there will be an increase in the money supply with the public.

2. An unchanged M: If instead, there is an increase in bank reserves there will be no direct and immediate increase in M. But if reserves of bank increase and legal reserves remain the same, excess reserve of banks will increase. This will enable the banks to make more loans to businesses and households (or create more credit). So the process of multiple credit creation is likely to start. In spite of this, the money supply or the composition of high-powered money will remain unchanged. The reason is that both the components of H (i.e., C and R) are fixed by the RBI through its own actions.

3. The money multiplier: The money multiplier shows the extent to which the money supply increases as a result of the increase in the supply of high-powered money. It is the ratio of M to H and is expressed as:

$$mm = \frac{M}{H} \quad \ldots (3)$$

where mm is the money multiplier. Eqn. (3) can be rewritten as

$$M = mm.H$$

$$\text{or, } \Delta M = mm\, \Delta H \quad \ldots (4)$$

This means that mm is the number by which an increase in H has to be multiplied to find the resulting increase in M.

Two points are to be noted here:

1. From eqn. (3) we see that the money supply is determined by the value of the money multiplier (mm) and the quantity of high-powered money (H).

2. From eqn. (4) we see that if we know the value of mm, we can predict what will be the increase in M, following an increase in H. Since the RBI determines and controls H, the effect of any decision of the RBI to change H or M depends on the size of the money multiplier. We may now make an insightful analysis of the money multiplier.

The Size of the Money Multiplier

The size of the money multiplier depends on two important ratios: (1) the ratio of currency to bank deposits $\left(c = \frac{C}{D}\right)$ which depends on people's spending behaviour and (2) the ratio of bank reserve to bank deposit or the reserve-deposit ratio $\left(r = \frac{R}{D}\right)$ which depends on the monetary policy of the RBI.

We write down eqn. (1) once again

$$M = C + D \quad \ldots (1)$$

Recall that the money supply (M) has two broad components— currency with the public (C) and demand deposits (D) of public with the banks. The public maintains a certain proportion (c) of currency (they hold) to their demand deposits in banks. Since $c = \frac{C}{D}$, we can write:

$$C = cD$$

Now if we substitute cD for C in eqn (1), we have

$$M = cD + D = (c + 1)\, D \quad \ldots (5)$$

Again, in eqn. (2) of high-powered money $H = C + R$, R represents cash (currency) reserve of banks. It is a certain ratio of bank deposits and is called the reserve-deposit ratio or surplus cash-reserve ratio (r). Thus,

$$R = rD$$

Now if we substitute rD for R and cD for C in eqn. (2), we have:

$$H = cD + rD$$
$$= (c + r)\,D \qquad \ldots (6)$$

Finally, if we substitute the values of M and H from eqn. (5) and eqn. (6) in eqn. (3), we get

$$mm = \frac{M}{H} = \frac{(c+1)D}{(c+r)D} = \frac{c+1}{c+r}$$

$$\text{or, } mm = \frac{M}{H}\left[\frac{c+1}{c+r}\right] \qquad \ldots (7)$$

where r = the reserve ratio of banks

c = the currency-deposit ratio of the public[1].

THREE DETERMINANTS OF *M*

So the three determinants of M are the following:

1. the supply of H, i.e., high-powered money,
2. the currency-deposit ratio (C) of the public and
3. the reserve-deposit ratio (r) of the banks.

The size of the money multiplier depends on the value of r. The smaller the r, the higher is *mm*. The smaller the c, the larger is *mm*.

So we can make the following predictions:

1. If H increase, M will increase.
2. If c falls, M will increase.
3. If r falls, M will increase.

It may be noted that the rapid increase in M in India during the entire plan period has occurred due to an increase in H, with *mm* remaining fairly constant.

A numerical example will make the concept of *mm* and its role in determining M clear.

NUMERICAL PROBLEMS

Problem 1: Suppose we have the following information about an economy.

$C = 20$, $D = 100$, $R = 10$, $c = \frac{1}{5}$ and $r = \frac{1}{10}$

(i) Find out the size of the money multiplier as also the value of M.

(ii) What happens if R increases to 15, c falls to $\frac{1}{10}$ and r increases to $\frac{1}{5}$?

1. A much simple proof of the *mm* is available. We know that, $M = C + D$ and $H = C + R$ or, $\frac{M}{H} = \frac{C+D}{C+R}$. Now if we divide all the four terms on the r.h.s. of this eqn. by D, we have $\frac{M}{H} = \frac{\frac{C}{D}+1}{\frac{C}{R}+1} = \frac{c+1}{c+r}$, which is indeed the *mm*, derived in the text. Thus $M = \left(\frac{1+c}{1+r}\right)H$ or $\Delta M = \left(\frac{1+c}{1+r}\right)\Delta H$.

Solution:

(i) Here $M = cD + D = (c + 1)D = \left(\frac{1}{5}+1\right)100 = 120$ and $H = C + R = 20 + 10 = 30$

So $M = H\left[\frac{1+c}{c+r}\right] = 30\left[\frac{1+\frac{1}{5}}{\frac{1}{10}+\frac{1}{5}}\right] = 30 \times 4 = 120$

(ii) Now if R increases to 15, H will also increase from 30 to 35, M will now be

$$M = 35\left[\frac{1+\frac{1}{10}}{\frac{1}{5}+\frac{1}{10}}\right] = 117 \text{ (approx.)}$$

Thus we see that due to these three changes occurring simultaneously the money supply has fallen from 120 to 117, in spite of an increase in the supply of H.

Now let us consider two other examples related to the money supply.

Problem 2: Suppose that reserve deposit ratio is 0.1, currency-deposit ratio is 0.5. Now suppose that the central bank purchases government bonds worth Rs. X = Rs. 100. What will be the increase in the money supply? What will be the change in the money supply if the value of foreign asset in local currency increases by Rs. Y and the central bank sells government bonds the value of which is also Rs. Y?

Solution:

It is to be noted that the increase in the supply of high-powered money is $H = DC + FA$ where DC is domestic currency and FA is the value of the foreign asset in local currency.

Let $\Delta DC = \Delta H = X; M_S = \left(\frac{1+c}{r+c}\right)H$

$$\Delta M_S = \left(\frac{1+c}{r+c}\right)\Delta H$$

$$\Delta M = \left[\frac{1+c}{r+c}\right]X \text{ (which is the same as } H)$$

$$= \left[\frac{1+0.5}{0.1+0.5}\right]100 = (2.5)\,100 = 250$$

So the total increase in the money supply is the money multiplier times the increase in the money supply by the central bank which makes loan to the government.

If the value of the foreign asset increases by Y and the central bank also sells government bonds of the same amount, there will be no net increase in the money supply. This is known as sterilisation.

We know that $\Delta H = \Delta DC + \Delta FA$.

Here $\Delta H = 0$ because, while on the one hand DC falls by Y, and, on the other, FC increases by Y. So there is no change in the quantity of high-powered money and, therefore, no change in the money supply.

Problem 3: (a) Suppose cash-reserve ratio of commercial banks is 0.2 and the currency-deposit ratio of the public is also 0.3. Under these conditions if the government takes a loan of Rs. 100 from the central bank and spends it, then by how much will money supply, commercial banks' credit, commercial banks' deposit and currency with the public increase? Explain the process.

(b) If initially there existed excess demand for bank credit of only Rs. 100, what will be the effect on the money supply?

Solution

Government takes a loan of Rs. 100 from the central bank. This implies that $\Delta H = 100$.

The government spends this amount.

1st round: The recipient of this amount keeps 0.2 portion of this in the form of currency and deposits the rest in a bank. So C increases by 0.2×100 and D increases by $(1 - 0.2) \times 100$ in the 1st round.

The bank in which the deposit is made keeps 0.3 fraction of it in the form of reserves and loans act the rest.

So loans (L) increase by $\{(1 - 0.3) \times (1 - 0.2) \times 100\}$ in the 1st round.

2nd round: The recipient of the loan keeps 0.2 fraction of it (i.e., $0.2 \times \{(1-0.3) \times (1-0.2) \times 100\}$ in the form of currency. He deposits the rest in a bank.

So C increase by $0.2 \times \{(1 - 0.3) \times (1 - 0.2) \times 100\}$

and D increase by $(1 - 0.2) \times \{(1 - 0.3) \times (1 - 0.2) \times 100\}$

The bank in which the deposit is made keeps 0.3 fraction of the deposit in the form of reserves and loans out $(1 - 0.3)$ fraction of it.

So loan (L) increases by $(1 - 0.3) \times (1 - 0.2) \times (1 - 0.3) \times (1 - 0.2) \times 100$

This is equal to $(1 - 0.3)^2 \times (1 - 0.2)^2 \times 100$.

3rd round: Once again, the recipient of this loan keeps 0.2 fraction of it in the form of currency and deposits the rest in the bank.

So C increases by $0.2 \times \{(1 - 0.3)^2 \times (1 - 0.2)^2 \times 100\}$

and D increases by $(1 - 0.2) \times \{(1 - 0.3)^2 \times (1 - 0.2)^2 \times 100\}$

The bank in which the above deposit is made keeps 0.3 fraction of the deposit in the form of reserves and loans out $(1 - 0.3)$ fraction of it.

So L increases by $(1 - 0.3) \times [(1 - 0.2) \times \{(1 - 0.3)^2 \times (1 - 0.2)^2 \times 100\}]$

All other rounds

This is equal to $(1 - 0.3)^3 \times (1 - 0.2)^2 \times 100$.

Now, if we add up the increases in C in each round, we get the following infinite series:

$$0.2 \times 100 + 0.2 \times \{(1 - 0.3) \times (1 - 0.2) \times 100\} + 0.2 \times \{(1 - 0.3)^2 \times (1 - 0.2)^2 \times 100\} + \ldots$$

$$= 0.2 \times 100\ [1 + 0.7 \times 0.8 + 0.7^2 \times 0.8^2 + \ldots]$$

$$= 0.2 \times 100 \times \frac{1}{1-0.7\times0.8} = 20 \times \frac{1}{0.44} = 45.45$$

So C increases by 45.45

If we add up the increases in D in each round we get the following infinite series:

$$(1 - 0.2) \times 100 + (1 - 0.2) \times \{(1 - 0.3) \times (1 - 0.2) \times 100\}$$
$$+ (1 - 0.2) \times \{(1 - 0.3)^2 \times (1 - 0.2)^2 \times 100\} + \ldots$$

$$= (1 - 0.2) \times 100\ [1 + (1 - 0.3)(1 - 0.2) + (1 - 0.3)^2 (1 - 0.2)^2 + \ldots]$$

$$= 80 \times [1 + 0.7 \times 0.8 + 0.7^2 \times 0.8^2 + \ldots]$$

$$= 80 \times \frac{1}{1-0.7\times0.8} = 80 \times \frac{1}{0.44} = 181.82$$

So D increases by 181.82

If we add up the increases in L in each round, we get the following infinite series:

$$(1 - 0.3) \times (1 - 0.2) \times 100 + (1 - 0.3)^2 \times (1 - 0.2)^2 \times 100 + (1 - 0.3)^3 \times (1 - 0.2)^3 \times 100 + \ldots$$

$$= (1 - 0.3) \times (1 - 0.2) \times 100\ [1 + (1 - 0.3) \times (1 - 0.2) + (1 - 0.3)^2 \times (1 - 0.2)^2 + \ldots]$$

$= 0.7 \times 0.8 \times 100\ [1 + 0.7 \times 0.8 + 0.7^2 \times 0.8^2 + \ldots]$

$= 56 \times \frac{1}{1-0.7\times0.8}$

$= 56 \times \frac{1}{0.44} = 127.27$

So L increase by 127.27

To calculate the increase in money supply, we have to first calculate the money multiplier:

$mm = \frac{1+0.2}{0.3+0.2} = \frac{1.2}{0.5} = 2.4$

Now $M = mm \times H$

So $\Delta M = mm \times \Delta H$

$= 2.4 \times 100$

$= 240.$

Thus, M increases by 240.

The Reserve Ratio and the Bank (Deposit) Multiplier

In chapter 15 we have already discussed how the banking system of a country creates the money. We saw that under the present fractional reserve system of commercial banking with a small increase in initial cash deposit by a single bank, the banking system as a whole can generate a very interesting outcome, viz., a multiple increase in total demand deposits. And such demand deposits, as we have already noted in this chapter, are a part of the total money supply of a country. The extent to which this multiple deposit (credit) creation occurs depends on the value of the deposit multiplier (m_d) which is the reciprocal of the reserve ratio (r), i.e., $m_d = \frac{1}{r}$, where m_d is the deposit multiplier. If $r = \frac{1}{10}$, then an initial increase in cash deposit of Rs. 1,000 will lead to a ten-fold increase in the bank money assuming that there is no cash leakage from banks to the public[1].

And if $c = 0$, i.e., if the public do not hold any cash, then the bank (deposit) multiplier and the money multiplier will be the same.

Two Related Points

Two important and related points may now be noted.

1. Cash Leakage

In reality people do not hold all their money in the form of bank deposits. They hold a certain portion of it in the form of cash for transaction purposes. To the extent people's transaction demand for cash increases less money will be deposited in banks or more money will be withdrawn from deposit (current and savings) accounts. Thus if cash leakage from banks increases the value of the deposit multiplier will fall. So the whole process of deposit creation will slow down. [This process has already been discussed in detail in Chapter 15.]

2. Excess Reserves

If the demand for bank loans is not adequate due to lack of profit prospects, banks may be left with excess reserves. In some countries like the U.K., banks are also required to hold excess reserves

1. In India the currency reserve ratio is called cash reserve ratio (CRR) which is altered from time to time by the RBI in the context of its policy of achieving price stability and faster economic growth.

in time of inflation. And there is a feeling among bankers that it is a tax on them. As a result the bank reserve ratio (r) will increase and the value of the bank multiplier will fall.

These two points have greater relevance in case of deposit multiplier than in case of money multiplier. We may now make a comparison between the two types of multiplier.

The Deposit Multiplier Vs. the Money Mulitplier

If c = 0, the two multipliers are indistinguishable from each other

The deposit multiplier ignores the cash leakage from banks and, therefore, exaggerates the actual increase in M originating from a given rise in cash reserve of a single bank. But the money multiplier takes this factor into account and thus measures the actual increase in M following an initial increase in bank deposits. The m_m shows the increase in M for every rupee rise in H, taking into account cash leakage from banks for transaction purposes. For this reason the value of m_m is less than that of the bank multiplier. Since $c > 0$, $m_m > m_d$. If $c = 0$, the two are the same.

Stability of the Money Multiplier

In reality the money multiplier is fairly stable in the long run. It fluctuates only in the short run, causing large and unpredictable variations in the money supply in the absence of any change in the central bank's monetary policy. This very fact makes it difficult for the central bank to control the money supply to the desired extent.

MONEY SUPPLY IN INDIA

The main source of increase in the money supply in India in the past has been the increase in the supply of H. This has occurred over the entire plan period because the budget of the government showed a deficit all the time and the government had to borrow money from the RBI to cover its budgetary deficit. And the RBI made loans to the government by printing new currency notes. As a result new money came into circulation.

In India the money supply has been controlled by the RBI by using the bank rate, open market operations and reserve ratio of banks. However, the last technique did not achieve much success since many banks held excess reserves for two main reasons: (1) to remain liquid even in times of an increase in public demand for money and (2) to be able to make more profitable investment.

Factors Determining Money Supply in India

The RBI adds H with the ordinary money to arrive at the total money supply in India. According to the RBI the following four factors determine the money supply in India:

1. ***Bank credit to the government*** : The RBI makes loan to the government to enable the latter to cover its budgetary deficit. This method of financing government expenditure was earlier known as deficit financing. Now it is known as **monetisation of deficit** and is an important source of change in money supply in India. In 1995 the Fiscal Responsibility and Budget Management (FRBM) Act was passed. Since then the government's fiscal deficit is largely, if not entirely, financed by borrowing from the commercial banks and other financial institutions by selling government bonds and securities to them.

Commercial banks also lend money to the government for procurement of foodgrains from the farmers through the Food Corporation of India. The creation of credit by banks for lending to the government has the same effect as making loan to the private sector. The money supply with the public increases since the government uses the bank credit to meet its expenditure. And expenditure of the government becomes income of the private sector. In fact, government expenditure adds to private expenditure in determining aggregate demand and national income, as discussed in chapter 6 in the context of the Keynesian theory of income and employment determination.

2. ***Bank credit to the private (mainly commercial) sector*** : When banks make loans to the private sector to cover their consumption and investment expenditures, the money supply with the public

increases. Thus an increase in the supply of credit to the private sector has the same effect on the money supply as an increase in loan made to the government either by the central bank or other banks and financial institutions in times of fiscal deficit. However, the central bank can reduce the supply of credit to the private sector by increasing the reserve ratio. But the central bank does not impose any restraint on itself while making loan to the government.

3. *Change in net foreign exchange assets* : The deficit in the current account may occur due to excess of imports over exports. There will be greater outflow of foreign exchange than inflow (just as a surplus in the current account implies a net inflow of foreign exchange in the country). Now importers will require more foreign exchange, such as US dollars, to pay for their imports. They will buy it from the RBI by selling rupees. So the rupee reserves of the RBI will increase and thus a portion of domestic money supply will be immobilsed. As a result the supply of H and M will fall. The sequence is clearly presented in Fig.18.3.

A current account deficit reduces domestic money supply just as a current account surplus increases it

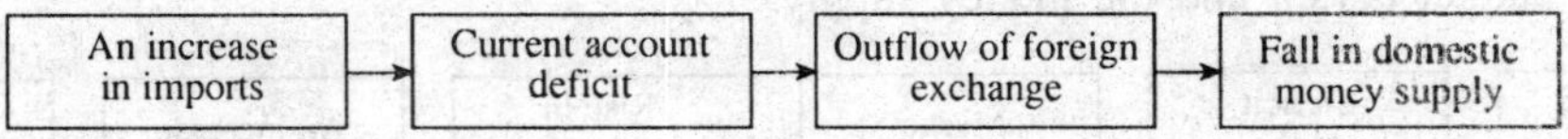

Fig. 18.3: External Component of the Money Supply

An exactly opposite result will follow if there is a surplus in the current account. The reason is that it will increase the foreign exchange assets and, in the process, will lead to an expansion in reserve money and thus the total money supply in the economy.

A country's foreign exchange reserves may also increase if there is a net inflow of financial capital (mainly in the form of foreign currencies). Capital inflows may occur through four channels, viz., foreign aid, deposits in Indian banks by non-resident Indians (NRIs), international portfolio investment by foreign institutional investors, such as investment companies, insurance companies, mutual funds, etc. and foreign direct investment made by multinational corporations (MNCs). This is exactly what had happened in India in 1977 as also during the three-year period from early 2005 to August 2008 (before the global financial crisis occurred in September 2008). Many people have described this event as the problem of plenty in the sense that an increase in foreign exchange reserves leads to an increase M and poses the threat of inflation. This was the problem of imported inflation which occurred due to income effect. As a result there was a sharp increase in the money supply in India. This was offset by the RBI through a matching open market sale of government securities to the banks.

As soon as the world financial crisis started in September 2008, there was a huge outflow of foreign exchange from India because foreign institutional investors sold their shares in Indian stock market and repatriated US dollars abroad. Since the demand for dollars increased, the rupee depreciated. To maintain exchange rate stability, the RBI had to sell dollars from its existing reserves and received rupees in exchange. As a result the money supply with the public fell (since a portion of the currency in circulation was immobilsed by the RBI).

4. *Government's currency liabilities to the public* : One rupee notes and coins constitute the government's currency liabilities to the public. If the government's currency liability increases, the money supply increases *pari pasu*. However, changes in M from this source is marginal and thus of not much significance either for monetary analysis or for the conduct of the RBI's monetary policy.

Budget Deficit and the Money Supply

Since there is a link between monetary policy and fiscal policy a deficit in government budget is also an important source of an increase in the supply of money. There are two links between government budget deficit and domestic money supply— one is indirect and the other is direct.

1. Government's borrowing

Government borrowing from the market may crowd out private investment

Suppose the government's budget is initially in balance, with government expenditure equal to its tax revenue. Now suppose the government increases its expenditure without increasing taxes. As a result there will be a deficit in the government budget. The government may cover this deficit by borrowing from the market by selling bonds. So there will be competition for loanable funds between the government and the private sector. And the resultant shortage of loanable funds will raise the market rate of interest and obstruct private investment. The fall in private investment due to government borrowing from the market for loanable funds is known as **the crowding-out effect**. If the objective of the central bank is to maintain the same rate of interest (i.e., if it fixes an interest rate target as part of its monetary policy), then it will have to increase the money supply in order to prevent the rate of interest from rising. Thus government borrowing from the open market can be an important source of an increase in the money supply. See the sequence presented in Fig.18.4 which shows an indirect link between government budget deficit and the money supply.

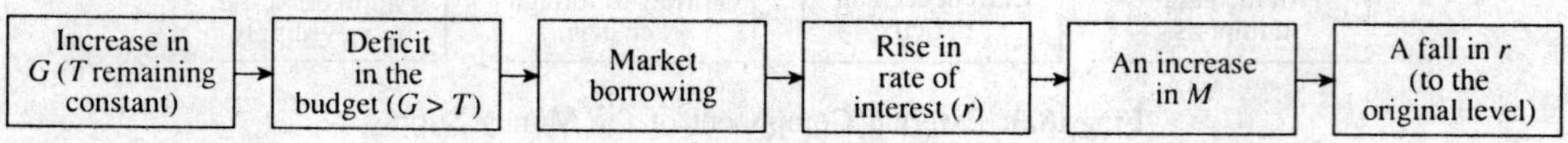

Fig. 18.4: The Effect of Government Borrowing on M

2. Deficit financing

There is also a direct link between budget deficit and an increase in the money supply. This occurs when the government borrows from the central bank by selling securities and the central bank prints new currency notes to make loan to the government and thus monetises the deficit in government budget.

A Dilemma Situation

In choosing the right course of monetary action the central bank faces a dilemma. If the objective of the central bank is to allow an expansion in income without a rise in the interest rate, it will have to increase the money supply. By doing this it can avoid the crowding-out effect.

By contrast, if the central bank monetises the government budget deficit, there is a danger of demand-pull inflation, if, of course, the economy is operating at or near full employment. But there is no such danger if the economy is in deep depression with huge idle production capacity and unemployed labour.

A tight monetary policy can lend support to loose fiscal policy in achieving price stability

So the central bank faces a dilemma in the matter of choosing the right type of monetary action in times of budgetary deficit. It has to decide whether to increase the money supply to prevent the rate of interest from rising so that the crowding-out effect can be avoided or whether to adopt a tight monetary policy along with an expansionary fiscal policy in order to hold the price line (i.e., to control inflation). The government of India adopted the second method before 1995 when a major portion of its high fiscal deficit was monetised.

THE MONEY SUPPLY IN AN OPEN ECONOMY

An open economy has not only trading relations (i.e., exporting and importing activities) but also financial transactions with the rest of the world (ROW) as shown by inflows and outflows of financial capital. The effect of such transactions on the domestic money supply can easily be understood by referring to the standard national income accounting identity. Such an identity for an open economy is written as

$$Y = C + I + G + NX \quad \ldots (1)$$

$$\text{Or, } NX = Y - (C + I + G) \quad \ldots (2)$$

Here *NX* refers to net exports or the balance of trade or even the balance on current account if we include trade (export and import) in services (i.e., invisible items). All other terms in equation (2) have their usual meaning.

If aggregate expenditure $(C + I + G)$ exceeds national income (Y), there will be a deficit in the current account (since *NX* will be negative). This implies that imports are greater than exports. The converse is also true. If $(C + I + G) < Y$, *NX* will be positive. This implies that exports will be greater than imports.

The Effect of Current Account Balance on the Money Supply

The effect of current account balance on the money supply depends on exchange rate system of the country. There are two main types of exchange rate systems – flexible and fixed. We will now see the effect of each on *M*.

A. Flexible Exchange Rate System

Suppose India is having a flexible (floating) exchange rate system under which the equilibrium rate of exchange between the Indian rupee and the US dollar is determined by the impersonal market forces of demand and supply (in the absence of any central bank intervention in the foreign exchange market). [After all the foreign exchange market is a real life example of a perfectly competitive market.]

Suppose the rate of exchange between Indian rupee and US dollar is Rs. 55 = $1 when Indian exports are equal to its imports. Now suppose there is a deficit in India's current account since its imports exceed its exports.

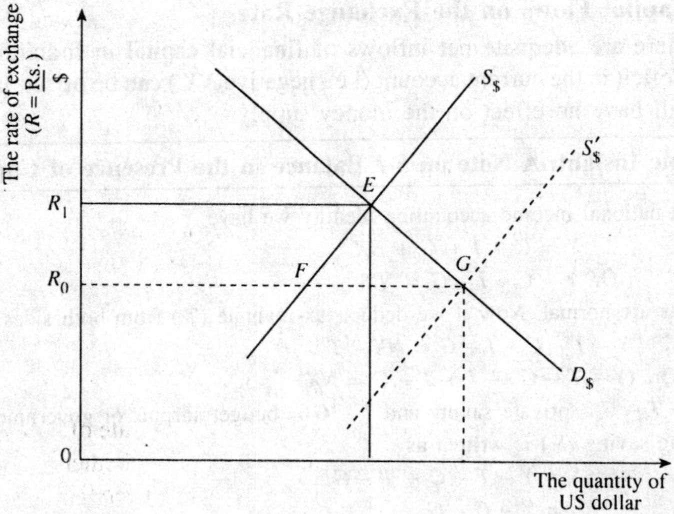

Fig. 18.5: The Effect of Current Account Deficit on the Exchange Rate

In Fig.18.5 the demand and supply curves of its dollar are shown as $D_\$$ and $S_\$$. When there is a deficit in the current account of *FG* the exchange rate is $0R_0$. Under the flexible exchange rate system, the rate of exchange will automatically move up to $0R_1$ (say to Rs. 60 = $1). Thus the rupee will depreciate in terms of the dollar. But there will be no change in India's money supply.

Under the floating exchange rate system a current account deficit has no effect on the domestic money supply

If, on the other hand, there is a surplus in India's current account, the exchange rate will move up, say Rs. 55 = $1 to Rs. 50 = $1 to restore equilibrium in the foreign exchange market. The whole mechanism will now work in reverse and there will be no change in the money supply.

B. The Fixed Exchange Rate System

Now suppose the government of India wants to maintain the original exchange rate $0R_0$. Now it has to pay for the excess of imports over exports by selling rupees in the foreign exchange market and buying dollars. So the demand for dollars in India exceeds its supply at the current rate of exchange. Now the government has to supply more dollars amounting to FG from its accumulated reserves. As a result the supply curve of dollar will shift to the right and intersect the original demand curve at G. This is how the deficit in the current account is covered (in the absence of any inflow or outflow of financial capital). When the RBI pays out dollars, it will receive rupees in the foreign exchange market (from importers of Indian goods and services). So some domestic currency (rupees) will flow to the RBI and will be withdrawn from circulation. Thus we see that central bank intervention in the foreign exchange market to pay for the current account deficit, while, at the same time maintaining the existing exchange rate, leads to a fall in the money supply. However, due to limited foreign exchange reserves, the central bank cannot do this every time there is a current account deficit and thus prevent the resultant downward pressure on the rupee in the foreign exchange market.

Under the fixed exchange rate system, government intervention in the foreign exchange market to pay for a deficit in the current account will lead to a fall in the domestic money supply

Now let us consider an opposite situation. Suppose there is a surplus in the current account (i.e., NX is positive). This means that the supply of dollars in India exceeds its demand. Now the RBI has to purchase this excess supply of dollars to maintain the original exchange rate (or to prevent an appreciation of the rupee in terms of dollar). How will the RBI buy this extra dollars? It will have to print new currency notes to pay for this extra dollars. So India's money supply will increase.

The Effect of Capital Flows on the Exchange Rate

However, if there are adequate net inflows of financial capital in India due to capital account surplus, then the deficit in the current account (i.e., negative NX) can be offset. In this case the current account deficit will have no effect on the money supply.

Economic Insight: A Note on *S-I* Balance in the Presence of Capital Flows

From the standard national income accounting identity we have

$$Y = C + I + G + NX \quad \text{... (a)}$$

$$\text{Or, } Y - C - I - G = NX \quad \text{... (b)}$$

where all the terms are normal. Now if we deduct tax revenue (T) from both sides of equation (b) we get

$$Y - T - C - I - G = NX - T$$

$$\text{Or, } (Y - T - C) - I + T - G = NX$$

We know that $Y - T - C$ = private saving and $T - G$ = budget surplus or government saving.

Thus total domestic saving (S) is written as

$$S = Y - T - C + T - G$$

$$= Y - C - G$$

Now if we substitute $S = Y - C - G$ in equation (b) we have

$$S - I = NX \quad \text{... (c)}$$

where S and I are domestic saving and investment, respectively.

Now if NX is negative, $I > S$. This means that the excess of domestic investment over domestic saving is financed by inflows of financial capital. By contrast, if NX is positive (since $X > M$), or if there is a surplus in the current account, $S < I$. This means that a part of domestic saving will be invested abroad.

The Effect of Capital Inflows on the Money Supply

A deficit in India's balance of payments (i.e., on the current account and capital account taken together) under flexible exchange rate system implies that capital inflows are not adequate to offset the deficit in the current account. This has to be covered by using the RBI's accumulated foreign exchange reserves. Under the flexible exchange rate system, the deficit in BOP will lead to the depreciation of the rupee. But under the fixed exchange rate system, the RBI is to buy US dollars to offset the deficit. Since it sells dollars and buys rupees, rupee currency flows into the RBI. As a result India's money supply will fall, as noted earlier.

The Effect of a Surplus in the Balance of Payments (BOP) on the Money Supply

We may now examine the effect of a surplus in BOP arising from an excess of capital inflows over the deficit in the current account. This has happened in India in 2000-01 and again 2007-8. In the absence of strong intervention by the RBI, rupee had appreciated by 15%. As a result exports fell. This had adversely affected output growth and employment generation. At the same time a fall in prices of imports increased the volume of imports of both final goods and raw materials and has done considerable damage to India's manufacturing industries.

To prevent unsustainable appreciation of the rupee in terms of the dollar, the RBI had to buy dollars by selling rupees in the foreign exchange market. So the RBI had to print more money. As a result new currency came into circulation. Thus every time the RBI intervenes in the foreign exchange market to prevent appreciation of the rupee, India's money supply increases.

In Fig. 18.6 we illustrate the effect of huge capital inflows and its effect on the external value of the rupee as also on India's money supply. Here we measure the quantity of US dollars on the horizontal axis and the rate of exchange between the rupee and the dollar on the vertical axis.

Suppose initially the rate of exchange between the rupee and the dollar is R_0, as is shown by point *E* where the original demand curve for dollars $D_\$$ intersects its supply curve $S_\$$. The initial rate of exchange is Rs. 60 = \$1. Due to huge inflows of financial capital (from all sources) the supply curve of the dollar shifts to the right to $S'_\$$. The horizontal distance *EF* measures the magnitude of such flows at the original exchange rate. Now in the absence of RBI intervention in the foreign exchange market the exchange rate will rise to Rs. 48 = \$1. Now if the RBI wants to maintain the original exchange rate, it will be required to buy US dollars equal to *EF* from the foreign exchange market. This amounts to shifting the demand curve for dollars to the right to $D_\$$. The new demand curve intersects the new supply curve at point *F*. So the appreciation of the rupee is prevented and the original exchange rate is restored.

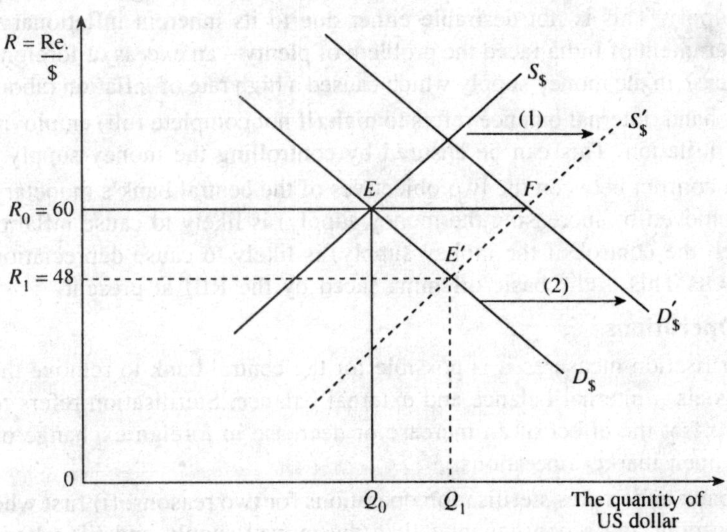

Fig. 18.6: The Appreciation of the Rupee Due to Capital Flows

However, in order to buy US dollars amounting to *EF*, the RBI has to print new rupee notes. Thus more high-powered money would come into circulation and India's money supply would increase.

But in reality the RBI did not intervene much and the rupee appreciated to some extent. The RBI felt that too much intervention would lead to a sharp increase in *M* and would cause double-digit inflation. In order to avoid such intervention, the RBI had to achieve an uneasy compromise between two goals – exchange rate stability and price stability. The RBI could not aim at exchange rate stability at the cost of price inflation. In fact, the RBI was faced with a dilemma situation, to which we turn now.

RBI's Dilemma

The RBI knows that if it does not intervene in the foreign exchange market when the rupee is appreciating (due to huge inflows of financial capital), India's export will also be hampered. And this will lead to a fall in the rate of growth of GNP and, of course, employment generation. On the other hand, if it intervenes to the extent necessary to prevent any undesirable appreciation of the rupee, then the money supply will increase to such an extent that there would be a high rate of inflation. Since the RBI's top priority is achieving price stability it has to strike a compromise between the two conflicting objectives.

The RBI has been intervening in the foreign exchange market from time to time to prevent large appreciation of the rupee. But it is not desirable for the RBI to buy foreign exchange with newly created money all the time since this easy method of intervention in the foreign market is not painless. It is likely to cause demand-pull inflation which also is a serious obstacle to India's planned economic development.

However, the RBI has engaged in *sterilisation* operations to offset the increase in the money supply due to inflows of foreign currency through open market sales of government securities from its reserves. But the RBI does not have an unlimited amount of government securities to sell to the banks. This means that it cannot undertake sterilisation operation any time it is needed for controlling the money supply and thus preventing inflation.

External Balance and Internal Balance

External balance refers to balance of payments equilibrium. When there is a deficit in the BOP, a country will be losing foreign exchange. As a result the rupee will depreciate. This is not desirable. On the other hand, a surplus in BOP implies inflow of foreign exchange and a corresponding increase in the money supply. This is not desirable either due to its inherent inflationary potential. In fact, in 1977 the government of India faced the problem of plenty – an excess of foreign exchange reserves and a sharp increase in the money supply which caused a high rate of inflation (about 16% per annum).

On the other hand, internal balance refers to high (if not complete full) employment in the absence of demand-pull inflation. This can be ensured by controlling the money supply.

So there is a conflict between the two objectives of the central bank's monetary policy. Exchange rate stability (achieved by increasing the money supply) is likely to cause inflation. And price level stability (through the control of the money supply) is likely to cause depreciation of the rupee and deficit in the BOP. This is the basic dilemma faced by the RBI at present.

Sterilisation Operations

Through sterilisation measures it is possible for the central bank to remove the conflict between the above two goals – internal balance and external balance. Sterilisation refers to the action of the central bank to offset the effect of an increase or decrease in foreign exchange on domestic money supply through open market operations.

The central bank undertakes sterilisation operations for two reasons: (i) first when there is a deficit in the current account and a consequent fall in the money supply and (ii) when there is a surplus in the current account and an increase in the money supply.

A. Deficit in the BOP and Sterilisation

The sale of foreign exchange in case of deficit in BOP causes domestic money supply to fall. This exerts a deflationary pressure on the economy. The central bank can avoid this by buying government securities in the open market by paying money. This is done by printing new currency. The increase in the money supply offsets the fall in it brought about by the central bank by selling foreign exchange for preventing depreciation of the domestic currency. This is known as sterilised foreign exchange market intervention. However, only if the central bank has sufficient foreign exchange, a country can manage a persistent deficit in BOP through sterilisation operations. The reason is that this policy insulates the changes in domestic money supply from the central bank's intervention in the foreign exchange market.

B. Surplus in BOP and Sterilisation

If there is huge capital inflow into a country a surplus is likely to be generated in its BOP. If this happens, the currency of the surplus currency (rupee in our example) will appreciate. This will adversely affect India's exports and hamper India's growth. This happened in India during a short period of two years (2006-08). The RBI intervened in the foreign exchange market by selling dollars. The RBI's purchase of dollars led to an increase in the money supply which, in turn, created inflationary pressures in the economy.

In such a situation the RBI had to intervene in a different way. It sold government securities to banks and got money in exchange from banks. So banks' excess reserves fell and at the end the money supply with the public fell since banks had to reduce their lending to firms and households.

In this way a certain portion of rupee currency had been withdrawn from the economy and the initial increase in the money supply through government purchase of foreign exchange and the consequent inflationary pressures had been offset by the RBI. The whole sequence is illustrated in Fig.18.7.

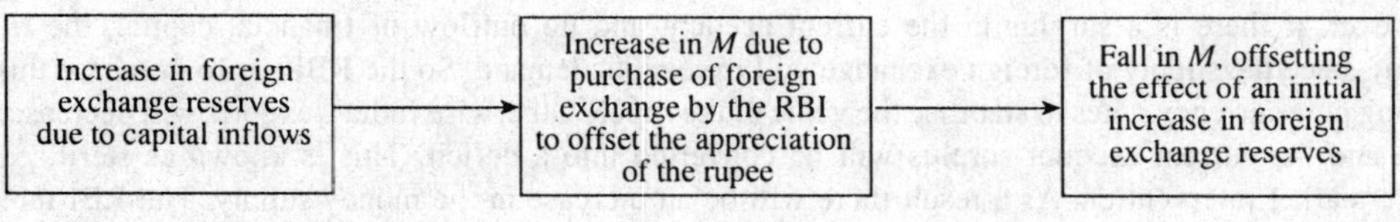

Fig. 18.7: The Effect of Sterilisation

KEY POINTS

1. *Importance of money* **:** Money plays an important role not only for ensuring short-run price level stability but also for ensuring high rate of growth in the long run. So there should be controlled expansion of money supply – not too much so that there is high rate of inflation and not too little either so that the much needed economic growth is hampered.

2. *The concept and measurement of the money supply* **:** The term 'money supply' refers to the total quantity of money in circulation in an economy per period. In a narrow sense, the money supply of a country includes currency in circulation and bank (demand) deposits withdrawable by cheques. Currency in circulation is called fiat (legal tender) money since it has legal backing of the government.

3. *Four measures of the money supply* **:** In India four different measures of money supply are used, viz., M_1 (currency + demand deposits + other deposits of the RBI), M_2 (= M_1 + time deposits with post office savings accounts), M_3 (= M_1 + time deposits with the banks) and M_4 (= M_3 + total deposits of post offices, but excluding public deposits in NSCs).

It may be noted that credit card is not money. Similarly, a cheque is not money but any deposit withdrawable by cheque is money. The concept of money supply varies from country to country and period to period. And the effectiveness of monetary policy depends on how money supply is measured.

4. *Determinants of the money supply* : There are two determinants of the money supply, viz., the supply of high-powered (base) money and money multiplier. High-powered money consists of currency in circulation and bank reserves. The money multiplier is the ratio of the money supply (which consists of currency in circulation and demand deposits of the public, withdrawable by cheques) to the high-powered money. The size of the money multiplier depends on (i) the currency-deposit ratio and (ii) the reserve-deposit ratio. Thus there are three determinants of a country's money supply, viz., the supply of high-powered money, the currency-deposit ratio and the reserve-deposit ratio.

5. *Factors determining the money supply in India* : According to the RBI, four main factors affecting the money supply in India are the following :

(a) Government's current liabilities to the public, (b) bank credit to the private (commercial and non-commercial) sector, (c) bank credit to the government and (d) changes in net foreign assets held by the RBI arising from changes in the BOP position of the country.

6. *Budget deficits and the money supply* : If the government borrows funds from the market to cover its budget deficit, the supply of money falls. So the rate of interest increases, and economic growth is hampered due to crowding-out effect (fall in private investment resulting from government borrowing.) But if the government borrows from the RBI for deficit spending, new money comes into circulation. Therefore the supply of money increases. The second method of financing the deficit, now called monetisation of deficit, often creates inflation by overheating the economy.

7. *The RBI's dilemma* : So the RBI faces a basic dilemma which makes a policy choice. An inadequate supply of money slows down the growth rate and an excessive increase in the money supply leads to price inflation.

8. *Money supply in an open economy with no capital flows* : Under the system of flexible exchange rate, a current account deficit will have no effect on its money supply. But under the fixed exchange rate system a current account deficit will lead to a fall in the money supply due to the RBI intervention in the foreign exchange market to stabilise the value of the rupee in terms of US dollar or any other foreign currency (as soon as the rupee depreciates).

9. *The effect of capital flows on the money supply* : If the deficit in the current account is met by net inflows of financial capital, then the money supply will remain unchanged.

However, if there is a surplus in the current account and no outflow of financial capital, the rupee will appreciate since the supply of foreign exchange will exceed its demand. So the RBI has to purchase this surplus by printing new currency notes to stabilise the value of the rupee. Otherwise India's exports will decrease, imports will rise and the current account surplus will be converted into a deficit. This is known as sterilised foreign exchange market intervention. As a result there will be an increase in the money supply. The RBI intervention in the form of issue of new currency notes to buy foreign exchange is needed when the rupee appreciates due to net inflow of foreign exchange. This also leads to an increase in the money supply.

10. *Sterilisation* : An increase in money supply caused by net inflow of financial capital is offset by the RBI by making open market sale of government securities of the same amount. This is known as sterilisation. An exactly opposite type of sterilisation operation is also needed in case of a deficit in BOP due to net inflow of financial capital.

11. *Saving and investment in the presence of capital flows* : An excess of domestic investment over domestic saving is to be financed by capital inflows. If, on the other hand, domestic saving exceeds domestic investment, a part of the saving will be invested abroad.

12. *Internal balance and external balance* : The objective of a government is to achieve internal balance (price stability and full employment) and external balance (equilibrium in the BOP). However, there is often a conflict between the two objectives. This conflict can be resolved by making appropriate use of monetary, fiscal and exchange rate policies as has been pointed out by James Meade and Jan Tinbergen.

KEY TERMS

Money supply	Monetisation of deficit
High-powered money	Fiscal deficit
Currency-deposit ratio	Excess reserves

Reserve-deposit ratio	Bank (deposit) multiplier
Sterilisation	Balance of trade
Current account balance	Balance of payments
International balance	External balance
Narrow money	Fiat(legal trade) money
Crowding-out effect	Sterilised foreign exchange market intervention
Bank money	Money multiplier
Bank multiplier	Currency in circulation
Broad money	Outside money
Intervention	Inside money

ASSIGNMENTS

1. Explain any three measures of money supply with which you are familiar. What are the determinants of a country's money supply?
2. Show how an increase in the supply of high-powered money leads to an increase in the money supply.
3. What is money multiplier? What is the economic significance of the concept?
4. How does a country's fiscal deficit affect its money supply?
5. How does an inflow of foreign exchange affect a country's money supply?
6. What is sterilisation? How far is it effective if there is a deficit in BOP and there is a large inflow of financial capital into a country?
7. What is the effect of a rise in the rate of interest on current account and on the BOP?
8. Why is there a conflict between internal balance and external balance? Why is the central bank often faced with a dilemma situation while seeking to achieve both internal balance and external balance?
9. Show that an excess of domestic investment over domestic saving is to be financed by capital inflow. What does a country do when domestic saving exceeds domestic investment?
10. Is currency account deficit necessarily bad for a country? Argue logically.
11. What are the determinants of money supply in an economy? What is the difference between inside money and outside money?
12. (a) Explain briefly how high-powered money may be created by a central bank.
    (b) Why does this result in an even greater increase in the money supply?
13. Give three alternative definitions of the supply of money. Which one is most acceptable to you and why?
14. (a) Is cheque money?
    (b) Is credit card money?
15. Who control the money supply controlled and how?
16. (a) Show how money supply is determined in an economy where public's demand for currency is already satisfied, banks do not hold any excess reserve and the required reserve ratio is fixed at $\overline{Z}$.
    (b) Suppose that commercial banks are not forced to hold reserves but do so voluntarily. Show that this behaviour of commercial banks frustrates the efforts of the central bank to control the money supply.
    [**Hint:** (a) Money supply = currency + demand deposits, i.e., $M = C + D$
    High-powered money = currency + reserves, i.e., $H = C + R$

$$\frac{M}{H} = \frac{C+D}{C+R} = \frac{C/D+1}{C/D+R/D} = \frac{c+1}{c+r} \text{ where } \frac{C}{D} = c \text{ and } \frac{R}{D} = r$$

This is the standard result.

If the public's demand for currency is already satisfied, then $\frac{\Delta C}{\Delta D} = 0$. Any additional supply of high powered money is held only as demand deposits, given the reserve-deposit ratio r.

$$\therefore \frac{\Delta M}{\Delta H} = \frac{1}{r} \text{ when } c = \frac{\Delta C}{\Delta D} = 0, \text{ with } r = \frac{\Delta R}{\Delta D}.$$

There is no cash leakage from the banks.
If the public do not need any currency, then

$$M = 0 + D, \text{ i.e., } M = D$$
$$H = 0 + R, \text{ i.e., } H = R$$
$$\therefore \frac{M}{H} = \frac{D}{R} = \frac{1}{R/D} = \frac{1}{r}$$

or, $M = H.\frac{1}{r}$.

(b) The smaller the value of r, the larger the credit creation multiplier. We know that

$$\Delta M = \underset{\substack{\uparrow \\ \text{Initial increase in } H \text{ in commercial bank 1}}}{\Delta H} + \underset{\substack{\uparrow \\ \text{Deposit in commercial bank 2}}}{(1-r).\Delta H} + \underset{\substack{\uparrow \\ \text{Deposit in commercial bank 3}}}{(1-r)^2.\Delta H} + \ldots = \frac{\Delta H}{1-(1-r)} = \frac{\Delta H}{r}$$

If commercial banks want to hold more reserves then r increases. Therefore, credit creation decreases. The central bank has to supply more H to attain a desired rise in M. This means that the central bank's control over the money supply decreases.]

17. (a) What are the determinants of the money supply in an economy? Outline the process through which the money multiplier operates.

(b) Comment on the use of cash reserve ratio as an instrument of credit control.

18. How is the money supply of a country related to the monetary base?

[Hint: The liabilities of the central bank create a base for the entire commercial banking system by providing reserves on which commercial banks build additional liquid assets.

Apart from bank notes the central bank's liabilities consist of reserves of the commercial banks, held by the central bank in it. These deposits are denoted by the symbol R (which stands for reserves). Commercial banks can access them at short notice to provide loans to their customers.

Eqn. (1) asserts the equality between the assets and liabilities of the central bank. The liabilities are referred to as the high-powered money or the monetary base:

$$H = C + R \quad \ldots (1)$$
$$M = C + D \quad \ldots (2)$$

Eqn. (1) divides the high-powered money into two components: currency in circulation, C (i.e., the RBI currency notes) and the reserves of the commercial banks, R. These reserves are held partly as cash in vaults of commercial banks and partly by the central bank in its own account.

Eqn. (2) defines the money supply, M, as the sum of the currency C, in the hands of the public, and chequable deposits D with the commercial banks.

The Money Supply and the Monetary Base

The money supply can be described as a multiple of the high-powered money, called the *money multiplier*. The main idea behind this concept is that the ratio of currency to deposits is fairly stable. If we treat this ratio as fairly constant, then the money multiplier remains constant and the money supply is exogenously controlled by the central bank. The money multiplier is based on two definitions: the currency-deposit ratio (c) and the reserve-deposit ratio (r):

$$c = \frac{C}{D} \text{ and } r = \frac{R}{D}$$

It follows from the definition of the money supply [eqn. (2)] and the definition of the money multiplier that the money supply is a fixed multiple of the high-powered money. Since the central bank can control the amount (quantity) of high-powered money through its open market operations, it can also control the entire money supply, as long as the money multiplier remains stable.]

CHAPTER 19

Money Market Equilibrium

> *Over all history, money has oppressed people in one of two ways: either it has been abundant and very unrealiable, or reliable and very scarce.*
> J. K. Galbraith

Money plays a crucial role in the life of each of us. And the price of money — the rate of interest — affects the functioning of the whole economy in various ways. So it is interesting to study how the market rate of interest is determined. Regarding interest rate determination there are three theories. According to the classical theory the rate of interest is determined by saving and investment. From the households' point of view, the rate of interest is the reward for saving. From the business firms' point of view it is the cost of using financial capital (which is borrowed for a certain period and converted into physical capital for producing and selling goods and services and making profits therefrom). According to the neo-classical theory the rate of interest is determined by the demand for and the supply of loanable funds. The demand for loanable funds depends on the marginal revenue product of capital (i.e., the extra revenue earned by a firm by selling the output produced by one extra—the last—unit of capital). And the supply of such funds comes mainly from private savings.

However, according to J. M. Keynes, the rate of interest is a purely monetary phenomenon and is determined by the demand for and the supply of capital. It is not the reward for saving but the reward for parting the liquidity (cash) for a certain specific time period. And the equilibrium rate of interest is determined when the money market is in equilibrium, i.e., when the demand for money (or 'liquidity preference', a term coined by Keynes) is equal to its supply. Keynes's basic point is that if national income remains fixed and the central bank of a country fixes the supply of money (i.e., the quantity of money in circulation), the rate of interest is determined by the demand for money (liquidity preference) and the fixed supply of money. In other words, the money market is said to be in equilibrium when at a particular rate of interest the demand for money is equal to its fixed (pre-determined) supply. It is against the backdrop that we now discuss money market equilibrium.

THE PHYSIOLOGY OF THE MONEY MARKET

We have already noted that the supply of money is a policy variable. It is determined exogeneously—by the central bank which is the central monetary authority. By comparison, the demand for money depends on peoples' behaviour — their spending habits, their attitude towards risks as also their expectations regarding future movements in the rate of interest. Thus so long we were concerned with the anatomy of the money market. Now we will be concerned with its physiology.

Two Basic Keynesian Propositions

According to Keynes, the total wealth of an individual ($\overline{W}$) has two components: money (M) and bond (B)[1]. So if the total wealth of an individual remains fixed ($W = \overline{W}$) more money holding implies less bond holding and vice-versa. Thus excess demand for money implies excess supply of bonds. The converse is also true — excess supply of money implies excess demand for bonds.[2] Thus $\overline{W} = M + B$. This means that if M increases B falls. The converse is also true.

The second Keynesian proposition is that the market price of existing bonds is the reciprocal of the rate of interest. Thus if the rate of interest rises, the price of old bonds fall. A simple example will make the point clear. Suppose you receive a fix-interest bond from your friend as a gift. It is written on the face of the bond that you will receive a fix-sum (say Rs 10) per annum in perpetuity, i.e., as long as you hold it. As a student of economics or management, you will surely be interested in knowing the current market price of the bond (more so, if you are interested in capitalising[3] it). Suppose the current market rate of interest is 5%. In this case the current market price of that bond (B_p) will be :

$$B_p = \frac{\overline{A}}{i} \quad \text{... (1)}$$

where $\overline{A}$ is the fixed sum receivable from the bond which is Rs 10 in this example. Since the nominal rate of interest (i) is 5%, the price of the bond is

$$B_p = \frac{\text{Rs } 10}{5\%} = \frac{\text{Rs } 10}{1/20} = \text{Rs } 200.$$

If the rate of interest rises to 10% the market price of the bond will be

$$B_p = \frac{\text{Rs } 10}{10\%} = \frac{\text{Rs } 10}{1/10} = \text{Rs } 100.$$

Thus we see that a doubling of the market rate of interest leads to a halving of the price of an old bond. If, on the other hand, the market rate of interest falls to, say, 2.5% per annum, the price of the bond will rise to Rs 400. Thus a halving of the nominal rate of interest implies a doubling of the price of an old bond. And price changes of income-earning financial assets such as bonds give rise to capital losses and capital gains. If the sale price of a bond falls below its purchase price, the bond-holder incurs capital loss (of Rs 100 in this example). If, on the other hand, the sale price rises above the purchase price, the bond-holder makes capital gain (of Rs 200, in this case). Both are equi-probable events. This means that bond-holding is a risky proposition. But money holding is always a safe option for a wealth holder, if of course, we rule out the possibility of a high rate of inflation — now or in near future.

The price of an old bond is the reciprocal of the nominal rate of interest

1. In those days, the financial market of a country was not much developed and so diversified as it is now. So people had only two alternatives — either to hold money or to hold bonds. However, one of the post-Keynesian economist, viz., James Tobin developed the portfolio approach and suggested that people can have both money and financial assets such as bond in their asset portfolio.
2. It may be noted that in the money market people increase or decrease their money holding by selling short-term fixed-interest bonds. These may be private (corporate) bonds or government bonds (securities), called gilt-edged securities or treasury bills (or, in short, T-bills).
3. Capitalisation means conversion of income (a flow variable) into an asset (a stock variable).

Money as a Financial Asset

Private wealth, i.e., the wealth of a household or a business firm is of two types, viz., real and financial. Real wealth consists of residential houses, and buildings as also factory buildlings and warehouses. Financial assets include (1) fixed interest (corporate or government) bonds, (2) equity shares of corporate forms of business (or public limited companies) and (3) money. Money obviously is a *financial asset*. But it can be converted into real asset such as a house or a machine.

In an earlier chapter we noted why people demand money or hold their wealth in liquid form. It is to be noted at the outset that money is different from income or wealth. In macroeconomics, the term 'money' is used in a narrow sense. By contrast, the term 'wealth' or 'income' is used in a broad sense. The demand for money refers to the desire to hold money (which is a part of an individual's or a society's wealth) in liquid form as an alternative to buying bonds or other financial assets. How much of their total wealth to hold in the form of money determines people's desire to hold money.

Transactions and Speculative Demand for Money

The demand for money is of two main types: (a) transactions and (b) speculative. If the general price level remains constant, the main determinant of transactions demand for money is the level of income. Transactions demand for money is proportional to national income or output. As national income of a country increases, people buy more goods and services. Therefore, they require more money (or want to have more cash in hand).

Households hold money to make payments for different goods and services which they buy every now and then. Similarly, business firms also hold transactions balance (or keep cash in hand) because goods are produced and distributed at different stages before reaching final buyers. And money is used by business as *circulating capital*. Businesses keep money to buy raw materials, to pay wages and to hold inventories of both raw materials and finished goods. As the volume of business increases more money is required to carry out the necessary transactions at both production and distribution stages.

The people of a country hold a certain portion of the national income in liquid form to be able to carry out necessary transactions. The higher the level of national income, the larger the demand for money. Thus transactions demand for money may be written as:

$$M_{dt} = kY \qquad \text{... (2)}$$

where M_{dt} is transactions demand for money, Y is the level of national income and k is the fraction (or proportion) of income held by people in the form of liquid balance (cash). Obviously, $0 < k < 1$. If, for example, Y = Rs 4,000 crores and $k = \frac{3}{4}$, then M_{dt} = Rs 3,000 crores. Since one person's expenditure is another person's income, the same unit of money is used again and again for exchanging various different types of goods and services produced in an economy per period. In this context, we introduce a new concept, viz., income velocity of money.

Income Velocity of Money

Income velocity of money refers to the number of times a unit of money is used for buying goods and services and thus receive as income. From equation (2) we get

$$kY = M_{dt}$$

$$\text{or, } k = \frac{M_{dt}}{Y}$$

$$\text{or, } \frac{1}{k} = \frac{Y}{M_{dt}} = V$$

where V is the income velocity of money and is thus the reciprocal of liquidity preference. In fact, k denotes the propensity (tendency) to hold money. An increase in liquidity preference (or the desire to hold cash balance) implies a fall in income velocity of money. If, for instance, most people hold cash with them for a long period or in the form of demand deposits in banks and do not spend their money quickly, income velocity will fall and the process of income generation will slow down.

The converse is also true. If people and business firms spend their liquid balance quickly, income velocity of money will increase and the process of income generation will be faster.

The Speculative Demand for Money

People hold money mainly because money is the most liquid of all assets. With money, you can buy anything, any time, you like. This is why people want to enjoy the convenience of money holding. However, Keynes pointed out that people hold money for another reason. With money they can buy bonds when bond prices fall. The objective to sell the bonds later at higher prices in order to make capital gains. From this motive arises the asset (speculative) demand for money.[1] After all money is a financial asset like bonds with the difference that by holding money people lose interest. Keynes pointed out that it costs money to hold money and the rate of interest is the opportunity cost of holding money. This means that by holding money people lose the opportunity to earn the current market rate of interest. In spite of this people hold money for speculative purpose, i.e., to take advantage of changes in future rate of interest which lead to changes in prices of old bonds. In this context, we refer to a new concept, viz., portfolio choice, a term coined by James Tobin, a follower of Keynes. And it was Tobin who extended the Keynesian theory of speculative demand for money in situations involving risk.

Portfolio Choice

Usually a rational individual does not keep all his eggs in the same basket. He keeps a portion of his wealth in liquid form and the balance in the form of income-earning financial assets like bonds, or even real assets like land or houses. When people take decision regarding how much money to hold for speculative purpose (i.e., buying bonds), they are said to be making a portfolio choice. This is not a once-and-for-all decision. People can adjust their portfolio by changing the mix of money and bonds even when their total wealth remains constant. Some people may increase their money holding by selling bonds and others may buy more bonds by reducing their money holding.

The Cost of Holding Money and Portfolio Choice

If people hold money with them, they lose interest. Even if they keep their money in the form of demand deposit, they earn very low rate of interest. By contrast, by buying bonds they can earn high interest. However, both money holding and bond holding have advantages and disadvantages. If people want to enjoy the convenience of money holding they have to lose interest. Thus they face a trade-off. By comparison, if people hold bonds in their asset (investment) portfolio, they earn high interest. But bonds cannot be used to pay for goods and services or for carrying out necessary transactions. In addition, people have to incur transaction costs (like brokerage fees) while converting bonds into money, apart from time and effort involved in this process.

Portfolio choice is essentially a decision about how much money to hold as an asset. An individual's portfolio choice is influenced by his own assessment of the advantages and disadvantages of holding money as an asset compared to those of other financial assets. At a particular rate of interest on bonds, an individual takes decision about portfolio choice after comparing the benefits and costs of holding money and bonds. And what is true for an individual is equally true of a society. If the interest on bonds rises, people will hold less money and buy more bonds. In this case the 'proportion' of money will fall and that of bonds will increase even within the same asset (wealth) portfolio.

---

1. Speculation refers to expected but uncertain price (market) changes over time.

The Relation between the Speculative Demand for Money and the Rate of Interest

The speculative (asset) demand for money depends on the rate of interest on bonds and it varies inversely with it. This point may be briefly explained. If the rate of interest on bonds rises the prices of old bonds fall. So people will buy more bonds and hold less money. They will do it to make capital gains by selling bonds at higher prices in the future. Follow the sequence:

The rate of interest on bonds increases.

↓

The prices of bonds fall.

↓

The demand for bonds increases.

↓

The demand for money for speculative purposes falls.

The whole sequence works in the reverse also. Thus we find that there is an inverse relation between the rate of interest and speculative demand for money. Therefore the speculative demand curve for money slopes downward from left to right as shown in Fig. 19.1. Suppose the nominal rate of interest is initially i_1 and speculative demand for money at this rate is M_1. Now if the rate of interest falls to i_0, the speculative demand for money increases from M_1 to M_0. By contrast, if the nominal rate of interest rises from i_1 to i_2, the speculative demand for money falls from M_1 to M_2.

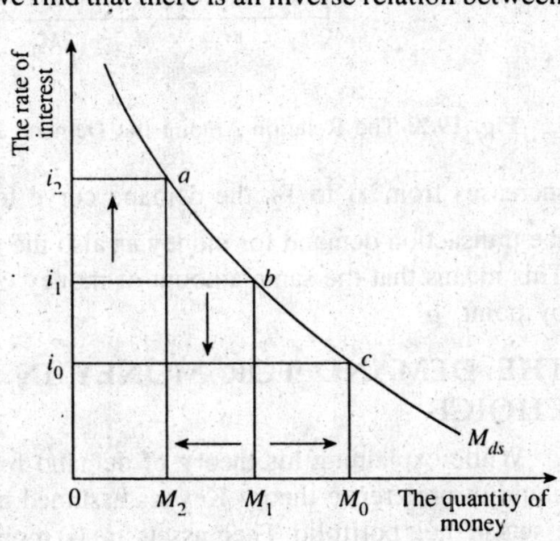

Fig. 19.1: The Speculative Demand for Money as a Function of the Rate of Interest

The speculative demand function for money may be expressed as

$$M_{ds} = f(i) = -hi \quad \ldots \quad (3)$$

where h is the sensitivity of asset demand for money to changes in the nominal rate of interest (i). Here 'h' is negative because there is an inverse relation between the nominal rate of interest and speculative demand for money.

THE TOTAL DEMAND FOR MONEY

Since the demand for money has two components, viz., transactions and speculative, the total demand for money depends on the level of national income and the nominal rate of interest. Thus by adding up the two money demand equations (2) and (3), we arrive at the following equation:

$$M_d = M_{dt} + M_{ds}$$

$$\text{or, } M_d = kY - hi \quad \ldots \quad (4)$$

Thus we see that the total demand for money depends on national income (Y) and the nominal rate of interest (i). It varies directly with Y and inversely with i. This means that the income elasticity of demand for money is positive but interest elasticity of demand for money is negative.

Movement Vs. Shift

We may now draw a distinction between movement along the same demand curve for money and the shift of the demand curve for money to a new position. This point is illustrated in Fig. 19.2. If the rate of interest rises from i_1 to i_2, there is movement along the same money demand curve M_{d_1}, from point 'b' to point 'a'. As a result the demand for money falls from M_1 to M_2. The money demand curve M_{d_1} has been drawn by taking a fixed level of national income Y_1. Now if national income

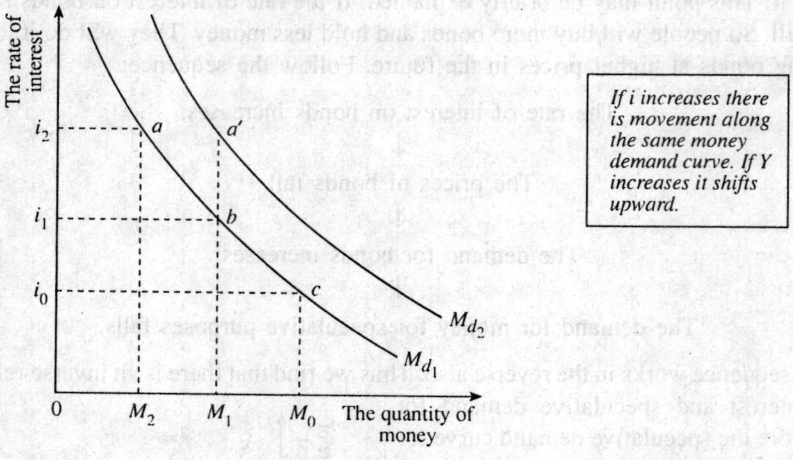

Fig. 19.2: The Relation Among the Demand for Money, the Level of Income and the Rate of Interest

increases from Y_1 to Y_2, the demand curve for money shifts upward from M_{d_1} to M_{d_2}. As a result the transaction demand for money as also the total demand for money increases at all rates of interest. This means that the same amount of money (M_1) is held at a higher rate of interest i_2, as is indicated by point 'a'.

THE DEMAND FOR MONEY IN A TWO-ASSET ECONOMY: PORTFOLIO CHOICE

While explaining his theory of demand for money as also interest rate determination in terms of liquidity preference theory Keynes assumed a very simple economy in which people keep only two assets in their portfolio. Their assets are (i) money in the form of currency (notes and coins) and demand deposits in banks on which no interest is paid and (ii) long-term bonds.

The aggregate demand for money depends on how people balance their portfolio between money and bonds. Two factors influence people's portfolio choice.

(i) ***Nominal income*** **:** The higher the level of national income, more money people will hold in their portfolio for transaction purposes. The reason is simple. With an increase in income people will buy more goods and services to meet their day-to-day needs. So they will need more cash also.

(ii) ***Nominal interest rate and expected changes therein*** **:** The higher the nominal rate of interest, the lower the demand for money for speculative purposes.

We have already noted that speculative demand for money varies inversly with the nominal rate of interest. The reason has been explained earlier in this chapter.

In addition, expected changes in the rate of interest also play an important role in determining speculative demand for money as also total demand for money of an individual or a society.[1]

If people expect the rate of interest to fall in the future or bond prices to rise, they will hold less money now and buy more bonds in order to make capital gains. By contrast, if people expect the rate of interest to rise in the future or bond prices to fall, they will hold as much money as possible and

1. In fact, according to Keynes, people's expectations about future rate of interest do exert influence on the actual rate of interest.

buy less bonds. There are two reasons for this. Firstly they will try to earn higher interest on bonds. Secondly, they will try to avoid capital loss due to fall in bond prices.

According to Keynes, transactions demand for money has no relation to nominal interest rate, as shown in Fig. 19.3. So, if nominal national income remains constant people will hold a fixed amount of money for transactions purposes as shown by the vertical straight line kY_1. However, the total demand for money will vary inversely with the nominal rate of interest due to its speculative component. This is why the total demand curve for money is downward sloping as shown by Fig. 19.3.

The shaded area in Fig. 19.3 indicates speculative demand for money. Thus when nominal income is Y_1, transactions demand for money is kY_1 at all nominal rates of interest. When the nominal rate of interest is i_2, the speculative demand for money is aa' and total demand for money is $i_2a + aa' = i_2a'$. As the nominal rate of interest falls from i_2 to i_1 and from i_1 to i_0, the total demand for money increases due to an increase in speculative demand from aa' to bb' and from bb' to cc'.

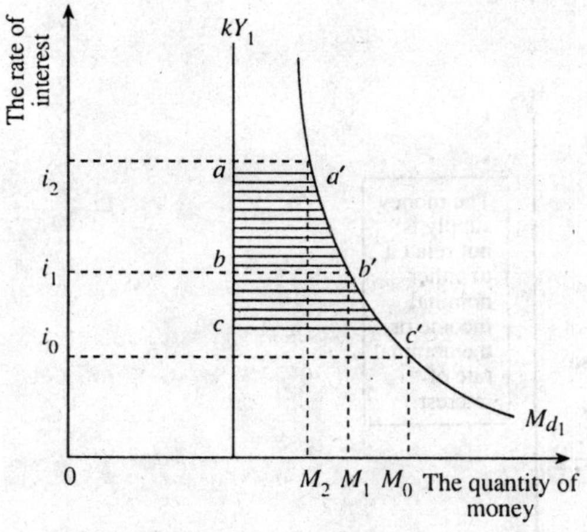

Fig. 19.3: The Transactions Demand and Total Demand for Money

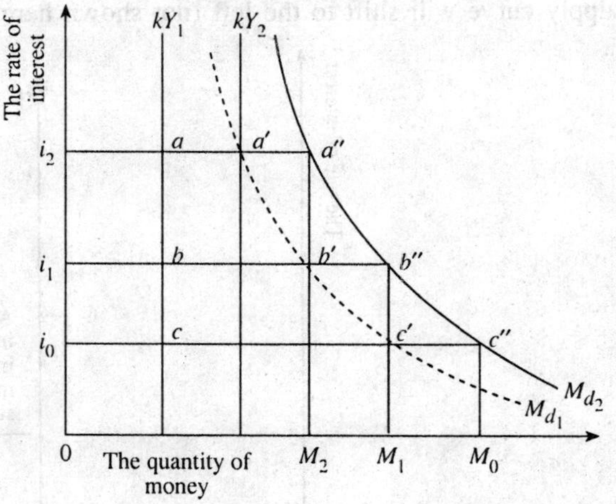

Fig. 19.4: The Effect of an Increase in National Income on the Demand for Money

Now, if national income increases from Y_1 to Y_2, transactions demand for money increases from kY_1 to kY_2 as shown by a rightward shift of transactions demand curve for money. As a result the total demand curve for money shifts to the right from M_{d_1} to M_{d_2}. Thus once again we see that in case of changes in interest rate, there is movement along the same money demand curve. But, in case of changes in national income the whole demand curve shifts to a new position.

THE SUPPLY OF MONEY

Money is a universally accepted medium of exchange and is used to carry out day-to-day transactions. It is also used as an asset. However, money has value only if it is scarce.[1] This is why the supply of money at a particular point in time or per period is fixed by the central bank and the central bank varies (increases or decreases) it within a specified limit. In times of inflation the central bank reduces the supply of money. In every country the central bank (such as RBI) is given the monopoly power to issue money and exclusive right to control the supply of money.

In India, the money supply is controlled by the policy actions of RBI. Since commercial bank credit is an important component of India's money supply, the control of the money supply implies control of commercial bank credit. The RBI exercises control over creation of bank credit by using three main

1. Money has value not due to the guarantee given by the RBI but because we have less money than we need. If money becomes a free good like air or water it will have no value. That is why the supply of money is controlled by a central monetary authority, viz., the central bank of a country.

techniques, viz., repo rate (the rate at which member banks borrow from the RBI), open market operations and changes in the cash reserve ratio (CRR) of banks.

In addition, in an open economy like India the money supply also increases under the influence of foreign exchange. When the RBI buys more foreign exchange from the market, it issues new currency to make payments for it.[1] So the money supply with the public (or domestic money supply) increases. Similarly when an individual earns foreign exchange such as the US dollar, he surrenders it to a domestic bank which pays rupees in exchange at the current rate of exchange.

In Fig. 19.5 we have drawn the two money supply curves. Since the money supply does not vary either with national income or nominal rate of interest, the initial money supply curve M_{s_1} is a vertical straight line.[2] If the central bank increases the money supply, the original money supply curve M_{s_1} shifts to the right to M_{s_2}. On the other hand, if central bank reduces the money supply, the money supply curve will shift to the left (not shown here).

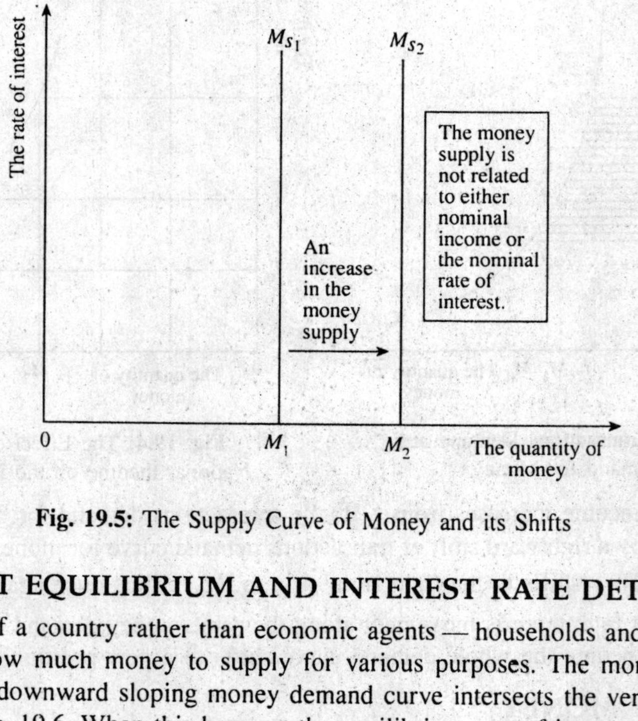

Fig. 19.5: The Supply Curve of Money and its Shifts

MONEY MARKET EQUILIBRIUM AND INTEREST RATE DETERMINATION

The central bank of a country rather than economic agents — households and businesses — take decisions regarding how much money to supply for various purposes. The money market reaches equilibrium when the downward sloping money demand curve intersects the vertical money supply curve, as shown in Fig. 19.6. When this happens the equilibrium rate of interest (i_0) is determined.

The Logic of the Equilibrium

We may now explain why no other interest rate except i_0 can be an equilibrium rate of interest. If, for instance, the actual rate of interest goes above, i_0, a disequilibrium arises in the money market. In Fig. 19.6, if the actual rate of interest is i_g, there is excess supply of money of *AB*. This means that people and businesses want to hold less money than what is being supplied by the central bank. So the question is: what will people do with the extra money? Obviously they will buy bonds. As a result

1. This may be offset in times of inflation through an act called *sterilisation*. It refers to open market sale of government securities to the public for offsetting an increase in domestic money supply caused by an inflow of foreign exchange.
2. The money supply is a policy variable. It depends on the monetary policy of the central bank.

the demand for and prices of bonds will rise. This implies a fall in the rate of interest. Thus the rate of interest will come back to the original (equilibrium) level (i_0).

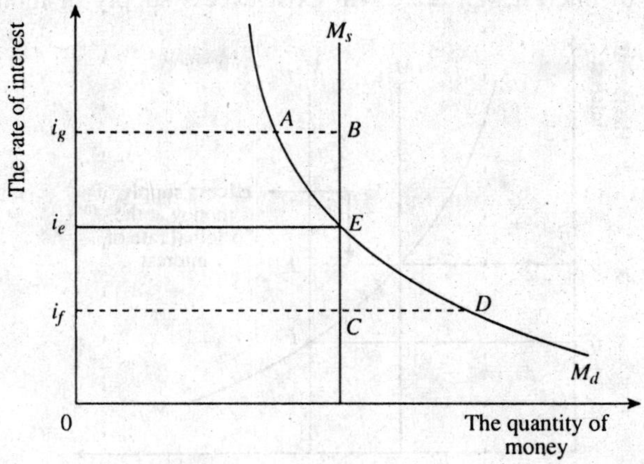

Fig. 19.6: Money Market Equilibrium

By contrast, if the rate of interest falls below the equilibrium level to, say, i_f, an exactly opposite type of disequilibrium situation will arise in the money market. There will exist excess demand for money of *CD*. This means that people and businesses now demand more money than is being supplied by the central bank. How will people meet this extra demand for money? Obviously, in a two-assest model, by selling bonds. Thus excess demand for money implies excess supply of bonds. This will lead to a fall in bond prices and thus to a rise in the rate of interest. So the rate of interest will return to the equilibrium level (r_e). This is how the money market adjusts in response to changes in the rate of interest which initially creates a disequilibrium situation.

A Mathematical Note (Optional)

The money market is in equilibrium when

$$\overline{M}_s = M_d \qquad \ldots (5)$$

We know that

$$M_d = kY - hi \qquad \ldots (6)$$

This means that the money supply is an exogenously determined (or policy) variable. And it remains fixed per period (unless there is any change in the central bank's monetary policy). We also know that the demand for money varies directly with nominal income (Y) and inversely with the nominal interest rate (i).

Equation (6) may now be expressed as

$$i = \frac{1}{h}(kY - M_s) \qquad \ldots (7)$$

This is indeed the equilibrium condition of the money market. This equation makes it clear that if the level of nominal income (Y) remains fixed, we can determine the nominal rate of interest (i).

The Equilibrium Rate of Interest

Thus according to Keynes' liquidity preference theory, the equilibrium rate of interest is determined by the demand for and the supply of money.

THE EFFECT OF AN INCREASE IN THE MONEY SUPPLY

If the objective of government policy is to reduce the rate of interest in order to stimulate private investment, the government can instruct the central bank to increase the money supply. As a result the money supply curve will shift to the right from M_{s_1} to M_{s_2} as shown in Fig. 19.7. This means that at the original rate of interest, (i_e) there will exist excess supply of money of EE'.

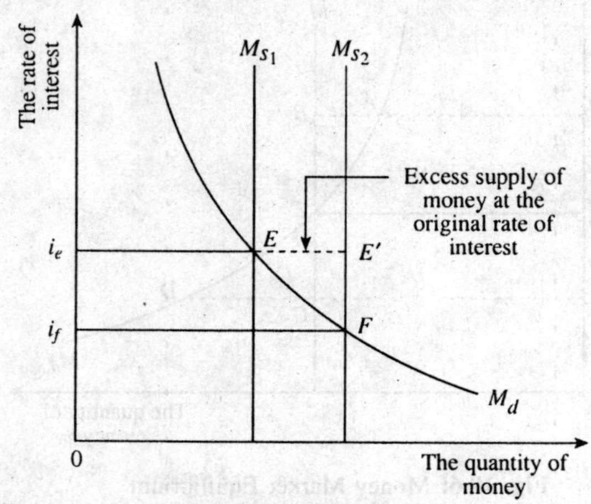

Fig. 19.7: The Effect of an Increase in the Money Supply on the Rate of Interest

This is equivalent to an excess demand of bonds. As a result bond prices will rise. This implies a fall in the rate of interest from i_e to i_f.

The Effect of an Increase in the Demand for Money (or Liquidity Preference)

If nominal income increases, the transactions demand for money will increase and thus the total demand for money will also increase. As a result the demand curve for money (or the liquidity preference curve) will shift to the right from M_{d_1} to M_{d_2} as shown in Fig. 19.8.

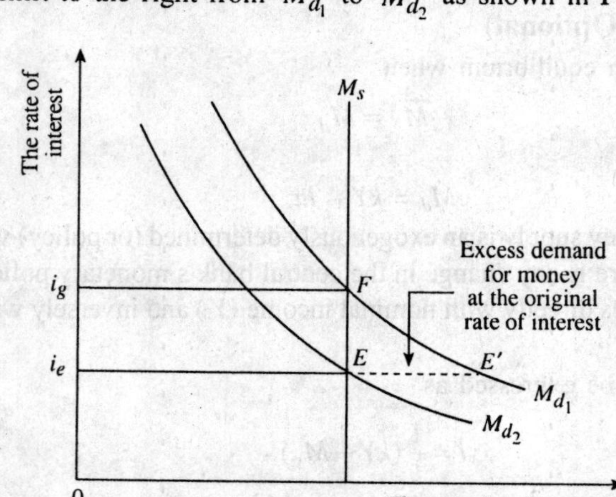

Fig. 19.8: The Effect of an Increase in the Demand for Money on the Rate of Interest

The demand curve for money may also shift to the right if there is a change in people's expectations about interest rate movements (caused by a rise or fall in bond prices). If most people expect bond prices to fall in near future or the rate of interest to rise, the demand for money for speculative purposes is likely to increase. The reason is that people will hold money more now to be able to buy more bonds in near future. As a result the demand curve for money will shift to the right and the rate of interest will rise.

So there will now exist excess demand for money of EE' at the original rate of interest (i_e). This means excess supply of bonds and a fall in the prices of bonds. And this is equivalent to an increase in the rate of interest. Thus the rate of interest rises from i_e to i_g by the full amount by which the demand curve for money or the liquidity preference curve shifts to the right.[1]

The point may be explained little further. If the money supply remains fixed and the demand curve for money shifts to the right, there will exist excess demand for money (which cannot be met at the original rate of interest). So there will be shortage of liquidity in the economy. In such a situation only one outcome is possible. The rate of interest will move up to enable the money market to reattain equilibrium.

Critical Appraisal

According to Keynes, if national income remains constant, the total demand for money will depend only on its speculative component. So the speculative demand for money along with (exogenously determined) supply of money determine the equilibrium rate of interest.[2]

Circular Reasoning

According to Keynes, when national income increases, the demand curve for money will shift to the right. Given the fixed supply of money, a new equilibrium rate of interest is established. Thus it is not possible to know the rate of interest unless we know the liquidity preference curve. In the same way we cannot draw the liquidity preference curve unless we know the level of income. Since at different levels of income, there will exist different demand curves for money and thus different interest rates, given the fixed supply of money, J. R. Hicks and A. H. Hansen have derived the *LM* curve or the liquidity preference-money supply curve. This curve is a locus of point showing alternative combinations of nominal rate of interest and nominal income which bring about money market equilibrium. [The actual process of derivation of the *LM* curve will be discussed in a later chapter].

Thus Keynes's analysis does not enable us to determine any specific rate of interest. And, therefore, much like the classical theory of interest rate determination, the Keynesian theory is also indeterminate. In short, in the Keynesian theory, the supply curve of and the demand curve for money cannot fix the rate of interest unless we already know the level of income.

Commentary: Interest Rates and Money Demand

Empirical studies have shown that if interest rates do not affect the demand for money, velocity is likely to remain constant—or at least predictable—so that the quantity theory view that aggregate spending is determined by the quantity of money in circulation is likely to be true. However, the more sensitive the demand for money is to interest rates, the more unpredictible velocity will be, and the less clear the link between the money supply and aggregate spending is likely to be. Indeed, there is an extreme case of ultrasensitivity of the demand for money to interest rates, called the *liquidity trap* in which case monetary policy has no effect on aggregate spending because a change in the money supply has no effect on interest rates.

The modern view is that the demand for money is sensitive to interest rates. But there is little evidence that a liquidity trap has ever existed. At present the Japanese economies appear to have fallen in a liquidity trap situation.

NUMERICAL PROBLEMS AND SOLUTIONS

Problem 1: The following demand for money function is given:

$$M_d = 0.4Y - 60i$$

where income Y is in crores of rupees, and interest rate i is in percentage.

(a) Calculate the demand for money when income is 5,000 crores and the interest rate is 5%.

1. The reason is that the money supply curve is vertical and the reason has already been explained.
2. According to the classical economists, the equilibrium rate of interest is established by saving-investment equality. But according to Keynes, saving-investment equality is brought about by income changes.

(b) Suppose that the level of income remains fixed at Rs. 5,000 crores. (i) Now the rate of interest falls to 2%, how will it affect demand for money? (ii) If the rate of interest rises to 8%, what will be the demand for money?

Solution:

(a) $M_d = 0.4Y - 60i$ . . . (1)

By putting the values of Y and i in (1) we get,

$$M_d = 0.4 \times 5{,}000 - 60 \times 5$$
$$= 2{,}000 - 300$$
$$= 1{,}700$$

(b) When the rate of interest is 2%, we have

$$M_d = 0.4 \times 5{,}000 - 60 \times 2$$
$$= 2{,}000 - 120$$
$$= 1{,}880$$

Thus we see that if the rate of interest falls from 5% to 2%, the demand for money increases. If the rate of interest is 6%, we have

$$M_d = 0.4 \times 5000 - 60 \times 6$$
$$= 2{,}000 - 360$$
$$= 1{,}640$$

Thus at a higher rate of interest the demand for money falls.

Problem 2: Suppose the demand function for money of an economy is given below:

$$M_d = 0.6Y - 50i$$

where Y is national income and i is nominal rate of interest. Suppose the central bank fixes the supply of money at Rs. 1,000 crores. Now calculate the equilibrium rate of interest. Assume that the equilibrium value of national income is 2,000 crores.

Solution: In money market equilibrium we have,

$$M_d = M_s$$

$$\text{Or, } 0.6Y - 50i = 1{,}000$$

Since, $Y = 2{,}000$ crores we have

$$0.6 \times 2{,}000 - 50i = 1{,}000$$
$$\text{Or, } 1{,}200 - 50i = 1{,}000$$
$$\text{Or, } 50i = 1{,}200 - 1{,}000$$
$$\text{Or, } 50i = 200$$
$$\text{Or, } i = \frac{200}{50} = 4\%$$

Problem 3: Suppose the demand function for money of an economy is given below:

$$M_d = 0.6Y - 50i$$

The national income of the economy is Rs. 2,000 crores and the central bank has fixed the money supply at Rs. 900 crores. Will the money market be in equilibrium at the prevailing rate of interest of 5%? Will the rate of interest increase or fall if it has not already attained its equilibrium value?

Solution: The money market reaches equilibrium when the demand for money is equal to its supply:

$$M_d = M_s$$

When the rate of interest is 5% and income is 2,000 crores

$$M_d = 0.6 \times 2{,}000 - 50 \times 5$$
$$= 1{,}200\text{-}250$$
$$= 950 \text{ crores}$$

Thus when the money supply remains fixed at Rs. 900 crores at the prevailing rate of interest of 5%, the demand for money (Rs. 950 crores) exceed the supply. This excess demand for money will push up the rate of interest so as to restore the money market equilibrium.

KEY POINTS

1. ***Money market*** **:** Like any then market the money market has two sides—the demand side and the supply side. And the price of money—the rate of interest — is determined when the demand for money is equal to its supply.

2. ***Interest rate*** **:** According to the neo-classical theory the rate of interest is determined by the supply of and the demand for loanable funds. According to the Keynes' liquidity preference theory the rate of interest is a purely monetary phenomenon and is determined by the demand for and the supply of money. Thus Keynes' theory is known as the monetary theory regarding interest rate determination.

3. ***Two basic Keynesian propositions*** **:** (a) Keynes pointed out that the total wealth of an individual has only two components — money and bonds. So if total wealth of an individual remains constant, more money holding implies less bond holding and vice-versa. It also implies that the excess demand for money is the same as the excess supply of bonds and vice-versa.

(b) Keynes also pointed out that the price of an old bond is the reciprocal of the existing rate of interest.

4. ***Money as a financial asset*** **:** Money obviously is a financial asset. But it can be converted into a real asset such as a machine or a house.

5. ***Transactions and speculative demand for money*** **:** The demand for money is of two main types: transactions and speculative. While the former varies directly with national income, the latter varies inversely with the nominal rate of interest.

6. ***Income velocity of money*** **:** Income velocity of money refers to the number of times a unit of money is used for buying goods and services and thus received as income.

7. ***Portfolio choice*** **:** Usually a rational individual keeps a portion of his wealth in liquid form and the balance in the form of income-earning financial assets such as bonds or even real assets like land or houses. Portfolio choice is essentially a decision about how much money to hold as an asset. Two factors affect people's portfolio choice, viz., (i) nominal income and (ii) nominal interest and expected changes therein.

8. ***Speculative demand for money and the rate of interest*** **:** Speculative demand for money is essentially the demand for money as an income-earning asset. It varies inversely with the market rate of interest.

9. ***Total demand for money*** **:** Total demand for money is the sum of transactions demand and speculative demand. The total demand curve for money is downward sloping due to speculative component.

10. ***The supply of money*** **:** The supply of money is a policy variable. It is fixed by the central bank of a country. So the money supply curve is a vertical straight line implying that it has no relation to the market rate of interest.

11. ***Money market equilibrium*** **:** The money market is in equilibrium when the demand for money is equal to its supply. These happens when the downward sloping money demand curve intersects the vertical money supply curve. And the rate of interest is automatically determined.

12. ***Changes in the rates of interest*** **:** If the demand for money increases, the rate of interest will increase. But if the supply of money increases the rate of interest will fall provided the demand curve for money is downward sloping throughout. It has no horizontal or infinitely elastic segment (as is found in a liquidity trap situation).

KEY TERMS

Portfolio choice	Transactions demand for money
Speculative demand for money	Capital gains and losses
Financial asset	Liquidity preference
Liquidity trap	Supply of money
Interest elasticity of demand for money	Income elasticity of demand for money

ASSIGNMENTS

1. What do you mean by money market equilibrium? How is the equilibrium rate of interest determined?
2. Define the demand for money. Why do people hold money?
3. What are the determinants of demand for money? Does the transactions demand for money depend on the rate of interest?
4. Do you agree with the view that money is an asset? In spite of the fact that money earns no interest, people hold money. Explain why.
5. Is the demand for money the same as saving? If not, explain why do people save money and why do people hold money.
6. What is the opportunity cost of holding money? If bond prices rise, how will the rate of interest be affected?
7. Explain how the demand for money is related to the nominal rate of interest and real income.
8. Suppose that the central bank of a country increases the money supply. What will be its effects on the rate of interest and other macroeconomic variables?
9. Suppose the demand for money of an economy (M_d) is represented by the following equation:

$$M_d = 0.8Y - 150i$$

   where Y is national income and i is the nominal rate of interest.

   Find out the equilibrium rate of interest if the money supply is Rs. 1,500 crores and national income is Rs. 5,000 crores.
10. Critically examine Keynes' theory regarding the determination of the rate of interest. Is the theory indeterminate? Does the theory involve circular reasoning?
11. The rate of interest is a purely monetary phenomenon. Does this mean that real factors such as saving and investment do not play any role in interest rate determination?
12. Suppose that the money demand function is $(M/P)^d = 1{,}000 - 100\,r$, where r is the interest rate in per cent. The money supply M is 1,000 and the price level P is 2.
   (i) What is the equilibrium interest rate?
   (ii) If the Central Bank wishes to raise the interest rate to 7 per cent, what money supply should it set?

CHAPTER 20

Monetary Policy for Economic Stabilisation

> *The essence of monetary policy is to control the release of resources in a manner which stimulates bank lending and investing in support of consumer and business spending, as well as government outlays in order to promote faster economic growth without contributing to inflationary pressures. Consequently monetary policy has the capacity to exert enormous impact on the level of employment, the volume of output and serves as a major policy tool for influencing economic activity.*
>
> I. M. Averbach

MONETARY AND FISCAL POLICY: AN OVERVIEW

A government's policy is akin to a strategy in game theory. It specifies a function at each date that maps two forms. First, includes endogenous variables such as past prices, past quantities or past actions of the government. Second, the government's information includes *exogenous* variables like the realisations of shocks to productivity or money demand.

Simply put, the term 'policy' is commonly used to refer only to the *current* choice of the government. Whether a policy is 'monetary' or 'fiscal' or 'neither' depends on the nature and type(s) of the actions specified by that policy. A policy is said to be *monetary* if the relevant actions are those generally undertaken by the central bank. These may include the size of monetary injections, reserve requirements by banks, the discount rate, or the scale of interventions in bond or foreign exchange markets. A policy is said to be *fiscal* if the relevant actions are tax rates and/or expenditures on various commodities.

Like fiscal policy, monetary policy is a demand-management policy and can be used to achieve certain common macroeconomic goals such as high employment and high level of output even in the absence of demand-pull inflation. Monetary policy seeks to stabilise the economy by changing the supply of money and, through it, the rate of interest, which affects mainly investment spending (and, to some extent, consumption spending also). This is how monetary policy influences the level of aggregate demand.

TWO TYPES OF MONETARY POLICY

For stabilising the economy, the central bank adopts two types of monetary policy, viz., (1) an expansionary monetary policy in times of low level of economic activity, viz., depression (recession) and unemployment and (2) a contractionary (restrictive) monetary policy in times of inflation. In times of depression and unemployment the central bank seeks to increase aggregate demand by promoting investment spending. Such monetary policy is called cheap money policy since such a policy seeks to make credit cheap and readily available mainly for investment and, to a lesser extent for consumption purposes. And in times of inflation the central bank tries to reduce consumer demand by reducing the money supply raising the rate of interest and discouraging businesses to make new investment in fixed assets. Such a policy is called dear money policy since credit is made more costly and less readily available.

Contractionary monetary policy is also called a policy of tight money

In developing countries like India monetary policy seeks to achieve economic stability and faster economic growth. This is why the Reserve Bank of India's (RBI) monetary policy is known as 'controlled expansion'. We have already discussed the proportional role of monetary policy in developing countries like India in an earlier chapter. In this chapter we will discuss the role of monetary policy in stabilising the economy.

TOOLS OF MONETARY POLICY

Some important tools of monetary policy which can be used to achieve price stability and full employment are open market operations (OMOs), changes in the bank rate, changes in cash reserve ratio (CRR) and statutory liquidity ratio (SLR) as also selective credit control (SCC). Since SCC is used only in developing countries like India and not in industrially advanced countries we will not discuss this technique of credit control in detail in this chapter.

A. EXPANSIONARY MONETARY POLICY IN TIMES OF DEPRESSION (RECESSION)

When an economy faces mild recession or deep depression the central bank of the country adopts an expansionary monetary policy for increasing aggregate effective demand and thus, through it for stimulating protection and employment. And the central bank adopts the following three types of monetary policy measures:

1. Open market purchase of securities

In times of recession or depression, when there is unemployment due to low demand, the central bank buy securities from the public, but mainly from commercial banks. As a result the reserve of commercial banks increases. This enables these to extend more to businesses which borrow extra funds for investment purposes. Since private investment increases, the aggregate demand curve shifts upward. Consequently national income and employment rise.

2. Lowering the bank rate

The bank (discount) rate is the rate of interest at which a commercial bank receives funds from the central bank. In times of depression the central bank reduces the bank rate. As a result the market rate of interest falls. This creates the impression among businesses that credit is cheap and more readily available. So firms take more loans from banks to make fresh investments. Consequently investment demand increases and the aggregate demand curve shifts upward and national income and employment rises through the multiplier.

3. Reducing CRR and SLR

Commercial banks have to keep a certain portion of their deposits in the form of cash so that they are able to meet the day-to-day demand for withdrawal. In times of depression the central bank reduces the cash reserve ratio (CRR) so that the excess reserves of commercial banks increase and commercial banks are able to make more loans and advances to the private sector. Consequently aggregate demand increases national income and employment rise.

In India there is another instrument of monetary control, known as the statutory liquidity ratio (SLR). This is used by the RBI from time to time to change the lending capacity of commercial banks and thus the flow of funds and the money supply in the economy. As mentioned in an earlier chapter, commercial banks in India have to keep a certain minimum portion of the deposits in the form of liquid assets such as government securities. This is known as SLR. In times of depression the RBI reduces the SLR in order to increase the amount of loanable funds of the banks. This increases the credit availability and thus the money supply.

All these measures increase the excess reserve of banks from which loans are made. So the result is the same in all cases—an increase in the money supply, a fall in interest rate, an increase in investment, an increase in aggregate demand and an increase in national income and employment through the multiplier.

How an expansionary monetary policy results in increasing income and employment is illustrated in Fig. 20.1 by using the Keynesian framework.

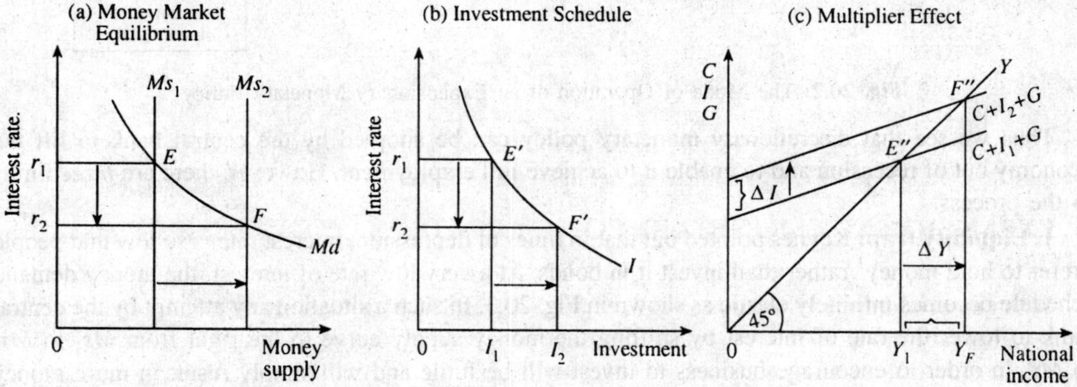

Fig. 20.1: The Multiplier Effect of an Expansionary Monetary Policy

In panel (a) we see that the money market is initially in equilibrium at point *E*. The initial rate of interest is r_1. At this rate of interest initial investment in panel (b) is I_1 and the initial level of national income is Y_1, in panel (c). However national income is less than its full-employment level.

Now suppose the central bank adopts an expansionary monetary policy. It increases the money supply from M_{s_1} to M_{s_2}. As a result the money supply curve shifts to the right and the rate of interest falls from r_1 to r_2 in panel (a). Consequently private investment increases from I_1 to I_2, as shown in panel (b). An increase in investment shifts the $C + I + G$ schedule upward as shown in panel (c). The new schedule $C + I_2 + G$ intersects the 45° income line at point F''. As a result national income rises from Y_1 to Y_F. Thus by adopting an expansionary monetary policy the central bank ensures the desired outcome. The economy is enabled to reachieve full employment. From panel (c) we see that the increase in national income (ΔY) is greater than the increase in investment. This is due to the operation of the multiplier effect.

Economic Insight: Indirect Vs. Direct Link
In the Keynesian view there is an indirect link between the money supply and aggregate demand through the interest rate. According to monetarists, there is a direct link between the money supply and the level of aggregate demand. In short, an increase in the money supply directly leads to an increase in the demand for final goods and services, and not just for investment goods. This proposition is based on the assumption that when households and businesses have more money than they need to hold, they will spend the excess on currently produced goods and services.

The fall in the rate of interest can also be shown to lead to an increase consumption expenditure. The lower cost of borrowing encourages people to use more loan finance to buy cars, televisions, refrigerators etc. Thus an expansionary monetary policy can stimulate both consumption and investment spending and thus generate the multiplier effect by increasing aggregate demand.

Fig. 20.2 gives a summary view of monetary policy. It shows the money supply-spending-income linkage.

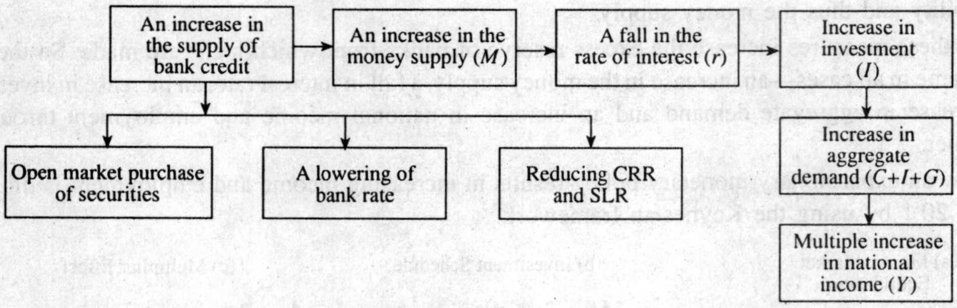

Fig. 20.2: The Mode of Operation of an Expansionary Monetary Policy

Thus we see that discretionary monetary policy can be adopted by the central bank to lift the economy out of recession and to enable it to achieve full employment. However, there are *three* limits to the process.

1. Liquidity trap: Keynes pointed out that in times of depression, interest rate is so low that people prefer to hold money[1] rather than invest it in bonds. At a very low rate of interest, the money demand schedule becomes infinitely elastic as shown in Fig. 20.3. In such a situation any attempt by the central bank to lower the rate of interest by shifting the money supply curve to the right from Ms_1 to Ms_2 to Ms_3 in order to encourage business to invest will be futile and will simply result in more money be held by people in the form of cash. In other words, whatever may be the increase in the money supply, it will be absorbed by the people in the form of liquid balance and thus will prevent the rate of interest from falling further. The rate of interest has fallen enough (to r_{min}). It cannot fall further.

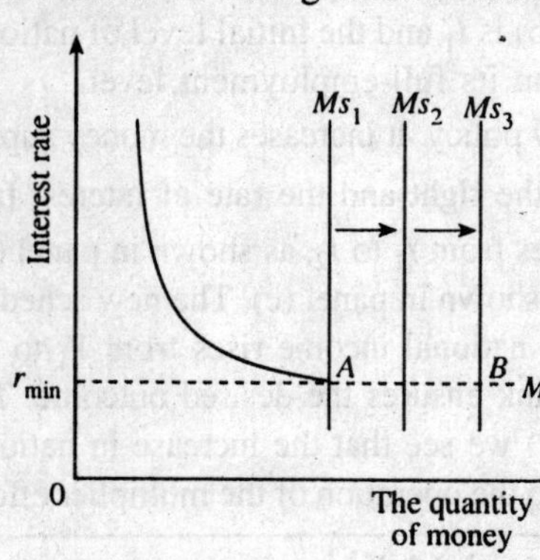

Fig. 20.3: A Liquidity Trap Situation

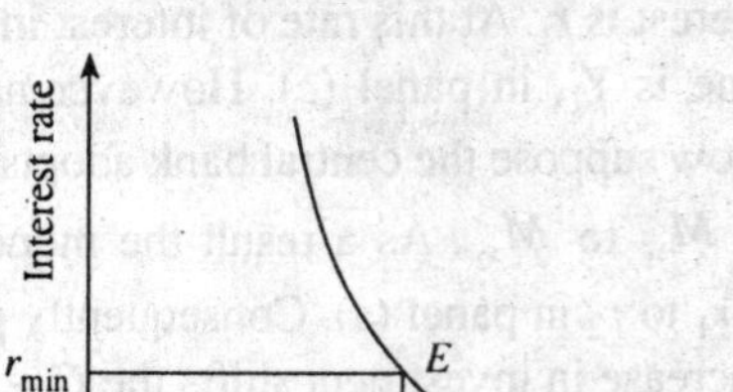

Fig. 20.4: Stagnant Investment Demand

In Fig. 20.4, we see that with the rate of interest remaining unchanged at r_{min} the volume of investment does not increase. With the level of investment remaining unchanged at I_1, there is no increase in aggregate demand.

1. This implies that they have a strong liquidity preference.

Consequently the economy remains in a state of depression with considerable idle capacity and widespread involuntary unemployment. Thus monetary policy cannot help a depressed economy to move to the recovery phase and reachieve full employment. Therefore expansionary fiscal policy has to be used in such a situation as has been suggested by Keynes and early Keynesians.

Keynes argued that in a depressed economy which is experiencing a liquidity trap situation, the only way to stimulate aggregate demand is to increase government spending or reduce taxes in order to increase aggregate demand and improve business confidence about future prosperity. This is likely to encourage businesses to invest more.

2. Low marginal efficiency of capital (*MEC*): Investment demand may not respond much to a fall in the rate of interest in times of depression due to low *MEC*. Keynes argued that whatever be the rate of interest, business people are unlikely to invest more if profit prospects are lacking. This happens in times of depression due to low *MEC*, caused by widespread business pessimism. Thus even if banks reduce the rate of interest, business firms will not be eager to take more loans to invest more[1]. In short, the interest elasticity of investment may be very low in times of depression due to low *MEC*.

3. Leakages from the multiplier: The effect of an increase in investment on national income and employment depends on the size of the multiplier. However, there are various leakages from the multiplier (such as debt repayment, taxes, imports, etc.). As a result an increase in investment will not lead to an appreciable increase in income and employment.

For all these reasons, monetary policy is not very effective in reviving a depressed economy. This, however, is the original view of Keynes. The new (modern) Keynesians believe that the liquidity trap situation does not exist in reality. There is hardly any empirical evidence on monetary policy for the existence of a liquidity trap. In addition, investment is very much sensitive to changes in interest rate. So monetary policy can be adopted to fight depression and unemployment and enable the economy to move to the recovery and prosperity phases of the business cycle and reachieve full employment.

B. CONTRACTIONARY MONETARY POLICY

Suppose now that an economy is threatened by the problem of demand-pull inflation. Such inflation occurs when aggregate demand increases sharply due to large increases in consumption investment and expenditures or, more importantly, a huge increase in government spending, financed by money creation, needed to cover the budget deficit. In such a situation an exactly opposite type of monetary action is called for. Such an action is known as contractionary monetary (tight) policy. A restrictive monetary policy works by making credit more costly and less readily available. In other words, it reduces the availability of credit and increases its cost.

Focus on Terminology: Monetary Overhang

In a market-based economy, the problem created by an excess of nominal money supply over nominal money demand is resolved through a combination of price, interest rate and real income changes. If these adjustment mechanisms are effectively blocked, a monetary overhang may emerge.

A pure monetary overhang requires three conditions. Individuals (a) face a binding upper limit on nominal expenditures on goods and services (typically reflecting rationing of goods at controlled prices), (b) face binding limits on the purchase of (non-monetary physical) assets and (c) are holding monetary balances that exceeds the levels they would choose to hold in the absence of restrictions on their purchase of goods and assets—financial and physical.

In practice, for a number of reasons these conditions are unlikely to bind absolutely for all individuals. So the term monetary overhang is also used more loosely to describe situations of excessive constraints on money spending.

1. In fact, it is easier to restrict the demand for bank loans than to raise it. This is why it is said that monetary policy is characterised by cyclical asymmetry.

In this case the whole sequence described earlier will be reversed and the tools of monetary policy will work in the opposite direction. Let us illustrate.

1. Open market sales of securities: In order to control inflation it is necessary to reduce the money supply with the public. This is done by the open market sale of government securities by the central bank to the commercial banks, non-banking financial institutions (which accept deposits from the public) and the general public. This will reduce reserves of the bank and of the public. As a result the lending capacity of commercial banks will be reduced. Instead banks will call in loans, i.e., ask for repayment of old loans. Consequently the total money supply in the economy will fall.

2. Raising the bank rate: In times of inflation the central bank raises the bank rate. This discourages member banks to take more loans from the central bank. So the quantum of their excess reserve or loanable funds falls. At the same time banks are forced to raise their lending rates. Consequently the demand for bank credit mainly for investment fall and the inflationary pressure is reduced.

3. Raising CRR and SLR: CRR is a very powerful instrument of credit control in developing countries like India. In times of inflation the central bank raises the CRR. As a result the excess reserve of banks falls. So banks are forced to reduce their lending. This reduces the supply of money and helps to control demand-pull inflation. The rate of inflation can be brought down further by raising the SLR. An increase in SLR serves the same purpose as an increase in CRR, i.e., one reinforces the other in ensuring reasonable price stability.

4. Selective credit control: In developing countries like India, the central bank also makes use of qualitative instruments of credit control such as raising the minimum margins as a pre-condition for getting loans from banks for holding stocks of sensitive items such as foodgrains, oilseeds, cotton sugarcane, raw jute, edible oil, etc. As a result business people have less funds for holding stocks of such goods. This measure indirectly helps in controlling inflation by checking speculation and hoarding of essential items of consumption.

GRAPHICAL REPRESENTATION OF THE MODE OF OPERATION OF MONETARY POLICY

Now the working of contractionary (or anti-inflationary) monetary policy is illustrated in Fig. 20.5.

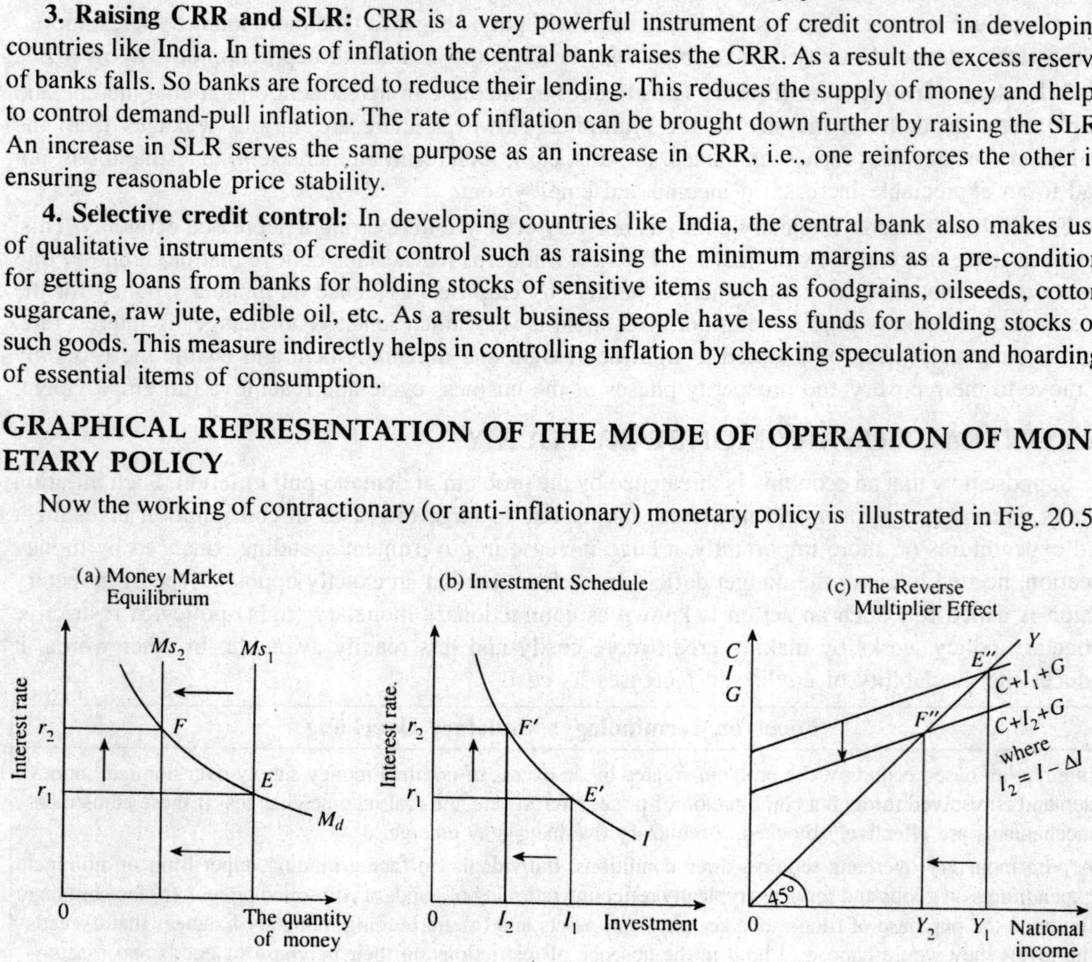

Fig. 20.5: The Working of the Anti-Inflationary Monetary Policy

In panel (a) we show money market equilibrium. The money market is initially in equilibrium at point *E*. The equilibrium rate of interest is r_1. At this rate, the level of investment is I_1, as shown by point *E*′ in panel (b). The initial equilibrium level of national income is Y_1, as shown by point *E*″ in panel (c). Now suppose the central bank reduces the money supply from M_{s_1} to M_{s_2} and the money supply curve shifts to the left. Consequently the rate of interest rises from r_1 to r_2 in panel (a). This reduces investment from I_1 to I_2 in panel (b). Consequently the aggregate demand schedule of panel (c) shifts downward from $C + I_1 + G$ to $C + I_2 + G$ where $I_2 = I_1 - \Delta I$. At the end national income falls from Y_1 to Y_2. This reduces inflationary pressure from the economy by eliminating the inflationary gap (i.e., the excess of desired expenditure over full employment output at the current price level). The whole sequence is summarised in Fig. 20.6.

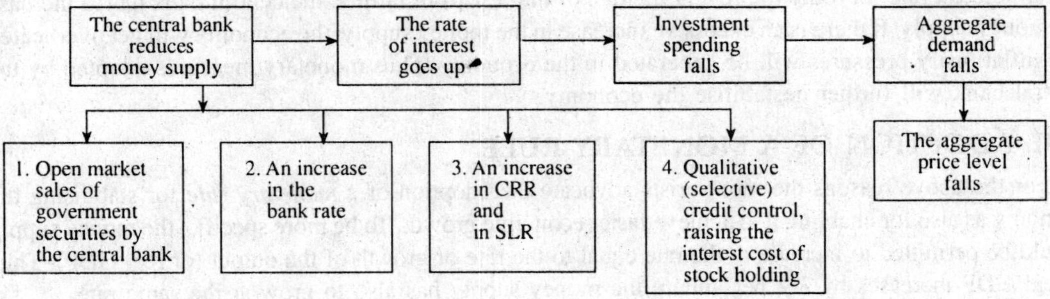

Fig. 20.6: The Working of the Anti-Inflationary Monetary Policy

THE MONETARISTS' VIEW

According to the monetarists any change in the money supply is the only determinant of the level of economic activity as also the general price level. Thus it is money which alone matters. They believe that while the demand curve for money is fairly inelastic, the investment demand curve is quite elastic. This implies that any change in the money supply will significantly affect investment demand and, through it, the equilibrium level of national income. However, Milton Friedman, the founder of the monetarist school, contends that the central bank control of the money supply and the consequent change in the rate of interest destabilise the economy. He blames the Fed for the Great Depression of 1929-33. In his view monetary mismanagement due to the adoption of discretionary monetary policy was the main cause of economic instability that characterised all free market economies. (This point has already been discussed in detail in the last chapter.)

SOURCES OF MONETARY MISMANAGEMENT

There are two main sources of monetary mismanagement. These are the following:

1. Variable time lags: There are large and variable time lags as far as the effectiveness of monetary policy is concerned. Changes in the money supply take long time to affect the key macroeconomic variables such as national income and the price level in desirable ways.

It is extremely difficult to predict such time lags. And it is virtually impossible for the monetary authorities to determine exactly when to adopt specific monetary policy measure, and which policy—expansionary or restrictive—is appropriate in a particular situation. In short, due to the uncertainty about the exact duration of the time lag involved, the use of discretionary monetary policy may actually destabilise the economy by intensifying cyclical fluctuations. In other words, the cure may be worse than the disease.

2. Wrong choice of the target variable: The central bank often chooses the rate of interest as a target variable. However, this action often proves to be wrong. The truth is that the central bank cannot stabilise the money supply and the rate of interest at the same time.

Suppose an economy is recovering from recession and is gradually approaching the state of full employment with aggregate demand, output employment income and the price level showing a steady upward movement. In such a situation the transactions demand for money and thus total demand for money will increase. Consequently the rate of interest will rise. But if the central bank decides to keep the rate of interest unchanged, it will adopt a restrictive monetary policy so as to prevent the rate of interest from rising. However, if the money supply is reduced, aggregate demand will fall and the recessionary situation will persist. In fact, a sudden reduction in the money supply may make the situation worse. A mild recession may become a severe one.

By comparison, when an economy is in the downhill, i.e., making a move from prosperity to recession, aggregate output and the price level will fall. This will lead to a fall in the demand for money and in interest rate. In order to prevent the rate of interest from falling, the central bank has to increase the money supply. If there is an excessive increase in the money supply, the economy will get overheated and inflationary pressures will be generated in the economy. Thus monetary measures adopted by the central bank will further destabilise the economy.

THE ADOPTION OF A MONETARY RULE

For the above reasons the monetarists advocate the adoption of a *monetary rule* for stabilising the economy as also for enabling it to achieve faster economic growth. To be more specific, the money supply should be permitted to increase at the rate equal to the rate of growth of the output (or real GDP). Thus if real GDP increases by 3% per annum the money supply has also to grow at the same rate.

So we can write

$$\frac{dP}{P} = \frac{dM}{M} - \frac{dY}{Y}$$

If $\frac{dM}{M} > \frac{dY}{Y}$, then $\frac{dP}{P} > 0$, i.e., there will be inflation in the economy. And if $\frac{dM}{M} < \frac{dY}{Y}$ then $\frac{dP}{P} < 0$, and there will be recession in the economy.

However if $\frac{dM}{M} = \frac{dY}{Y}, \frac{dP}{P} = 0$, i.e., there will be no inflation if M increases at the same rate at which Y is growing. The growth of output will fully absorb the extra money supplied by the central bank without generating any inflationary or recessionary pressure in the economy.

Thus the monetarists emphasise the need for a balanced relationship between the amount of money available to finance the purchases of goods and services on the one hand and the ability of the economy to produce such goods and services on the other.

Economic Insight: Monetary Accommodation
Monetary accommodation refers to the use of monetary policy to accommodate sudden supply-side changes in the economy, for example, an increase in nominal money supply to offset the inflationary impact of a rise in oil price or price of any other basic input. In the absence of monetary accommodation a cost-push inflation associated with an increase in oil prices would act to reduce the real money supply, increase interest rates and cause aggregate demand to fall. To avoid such recessionary tendencies, the central bank has to increase the rate of monetary growth to restore lost purchasing power.

The modern Keynesians have criticised the monetary rule. Since the velocity of money (V) is variable, it is difficult to predict the effect of an increase in the money supply (M) on aggregate demand (which is MV). Thus aggregate demand may sometimes exceeds the quantity of output or sometimes fall short of it. So the economy will face either demand-pull inflation or demand-deficient recession. Therefore the adoption of a monetary rule itself may destabilise the economy.

CHOICE BETWEEN MONEY SUPPLY AND INTEREST RATE TARGETS

1. *Uncertainty* : The main consideration affecting the choice between the money supply (monetary aggregate) target and the interest rate as an intermediate target is the uncertainty faced by the monetary authorities. If uncertainty is due to unpredictable shift of the *IS* curve caused by sudden and unexpected shift in private investment (in fixed assets and in residential construction) and consumer purchases of durable goods, a money supply target is superior to an interest rate target.

The interest rate target is preferable when there is uncertainty about shifts of the *LM* curve caused by unstable money demand. The *LM* curve shifts if there is a change in asset preference (shift of asset demand from money to one composite, non-money asset called 'bonds' or from 'bonds' to money), in which case the interest rate is the superior intermediate target.

2. *Credibility* : One extra advantage for a money supply target is that a strong commitment to keeping money supply growing in a target range ensures control of inflation for medium-term periods (3–5 years) in as much as sustained high inflation requires accommodating money supply growth. If money supply targets are strictly adhered, monetary accommodation is severely limited unless the targets are themselves high.

This means that by setting new, non-inflationary money supply targets, and hitting them, the central banks can build up anti-inflationary credibility. Reputation is a big factor here. If the public starts to believe that the central bank will carry out its announced policies, inflationary expectations can be kept at a low level.

No such anti-inflationary guarantee can be provided by an interest rate target. Even repeatedly hitting interest rate targets does not necessarily build up the credibility of the central bank's monetary policy. If the central bank targets the interest rate, it must increase the money supply to accommodate any increases in money demand. If a potential boom begins, money demand will increase (due to rise in transactions demand). The central bank may then be forced to fuel the inflationary fire, reluctantly though, by an accommodating increase in the money supply.

INFLATION TARGETING ONCE AGAIN

Many countries have gone for inflation targeting in recent years. Since low inflation has always been one monetary goal in industrial countries in the 1990s the central banks have been instructed to target inflation as the sole goal of monetary policy. There are two reasons for this:

(i) *Time inconsistency* : This concept grows out of the new classical macroeconomic perspective. It refers to problems that arise when monetary policy is conducted under discretion. Time inconsistency problems arise when a future policy is no longer optimal at a later date even when no new information has arrived in the mean time.

The control of inflation is associated with central bank independence

The time inconsistency problem creates an inflationary bias in monetary policy. If a monetary policy rule bound the policymaker to a zero inflation policy, society would be better off than with policy by discretion. The rule would give credibility to the policymaker's announcement. Since central bank independence is positively associated with lower inflation, inflation targeting is a way of giving the central banks independence for their instruments while keeping them accountable for goals.

(ii) *Anchor role* : As the relation between money and income becomes more unstable, central banks rely more on short-term interest rates in order to implement monetary policy. This approach leaves monetary policy without any anchor that serves as an anti-inflation guarantee. Such an anchor is provided by direct targeting of inflation rather than experimenting with monetary aggregate as intermediate targets. This policy has been followed in New Zealand recently.

KEY POINTS

1. *Monetary policy for achieving macroeconomic stability* : Monetary policy, much like fiscal policy is a demand-management policy. It can be used to achieve high employment and reasonable price level stability. Monetary policy seeks to stabilise the economy by changing the supply of money and, through it, the rate of interest which affect mainly investment spending and, to some extent consumption expenditure also. This is how monetary policy influences the level of aggregate demand.

2. *Two types of monetary policy* : For stabilising the economy the central bank adopts two types of monetary policy mainly, viz., (i) expansionary in times of recession or depression and (ii) contractionary in times of inflation.

3. *Tools of monetary policy* : The tools of monetary policy are of two main types; viz., quantitative (such as open market operations, changes in bank rate and varying the reserve ratio of commercial banks, i.e., CRR and SLR) and qualitative (selective) credit control.

4. *Monetary overhang* : It refers to that part of the money supply which people are holding mainly because they have not been able to spend it.

5. *The monetarits view* : According to monetarists any change in the money supply is the only determinant of the level of economic activity as also the general price level. Thus it is money which alone matters. The monetarists advocate the adoption of a monetary rule for stabilising the economy as also for enabling it to achieve faster economic growth. Modern Keynesians have criticised the monetary rule and have argued in favour of discretionary measures.

6. *Choice between money supply and interest rate targets* : Central banks cannot exercise control over the money supply and the rate of interest at the same time. They have to choose between the money supply targets and the interest rate target. In recent years, some countries have gone one step ahead of this mainly viz., for inflation targeting.

KEY TERMS

Variable lags	Discretionary monetary policy	Liquidity trap
Monetary policy rule	Open market operations	Bank rate
Selective credit control	Inflation targeting	Monetary overhang

ASSIGNMENTS

1. What is meant by monetary policy? What are the objectives of monetary policy?
2. What is monetary policy? What are the tools of monetary control?
3. How does monetary policy work? How does the Keynesian view of monetary policy differ from that of the monetarists?
4. What type of monetary policy has to be adopted (a) in times of recession and (b) in times of inflation?
5. Why does monetary policy fail to revive the economy in times of recession?
6. What, according to Milton Friedman, are the main defects of monetary policy for stabilising the economy?
7. What do you mean by lags in the effectiveness of monetary policy? Does monetary policy lose its effectiveness because of such lags?
8. Show how monetary policy can be used to achieve economic stability.
9. Write short notes on:
   (a) monetary overhang
   (b) cyclical asymmetry of monetary policy and
   (c) monetary mismanagement.

CHAPTER 21

Monetary Policy in a Developing Economy with Particular Reference to India

> *There is no subtler, no surer means of overturning the existing basis of society than to debauch the currency. The process engages all the hidden forces of economic law on the side of destruction, and does it in a manner which not one man in a million is able to diagnose.*
> John Maynard Keynes

A major instrument of a country's macroeconomic policy is monetary policy. The central bank, on behalf of the government, conducts monetary policy through managing a country's money, credit and banking system. Our central bank, the Reserve Bank of India (RBI), affects the economy by determining short-term interest rates. The RBI like any other central bank actually does this by changing the money supply (through buying and selling government securities) or by fixing short-run interest rates. Through its operations, the central bank influences many financial and economic variables such as interest rates, share prices, prices of houses and flats and foreign exchange rates. These variables affect spending on investment, particularly in housing, business investment, consumer durables and exports and imports.

Monetary policy is concerned with using certain official investments to control the cost and availability of bank credit and, with it, the supply of money. It is also concerned with the allocation of credit among different uses and various users, and, of course, both the lending and borrowing rates of interest of commercial banks. In industrially advanced countries it has been mainly used as an anti-cyclical measure, i.e., for lifting the economy out of depression and for controlling inflation. This is known as the **regulatory** role of the monetary policy. But in developing countries like India, monetary policy has an additional role to perform, i.e., the **promotional (developmental)** role. Since a high rate of inflation acts as an obstacle to growth, the main objective of monetary policy in developing countries like India is price stability in the short run and faster economic growth in the long run. In fact, growth with stability is the common objective of monetary policy in India.

The developmental role of monetary policy supplements its regulatory role

OBJECTIVES, TARGETS AND INSTRUMENTS OF MONETARY POLICY

The goals of monetary policy refer to its objectives such as reasonable price stability, high employment and faster rate of economic growth. The targets of monetary policy refer to such variables as the supply of bank credit, interest rate and the supply of money. These are to be changed by using the instruments of monetary policy for attaining the objectives (goals). The instruments of monetary policy are variation in the bank rate, the repo rate and other interest rates, open market operations (OMOs), selective credit controls and variations in reserve ratio (VRR). See Fig. 21.1.

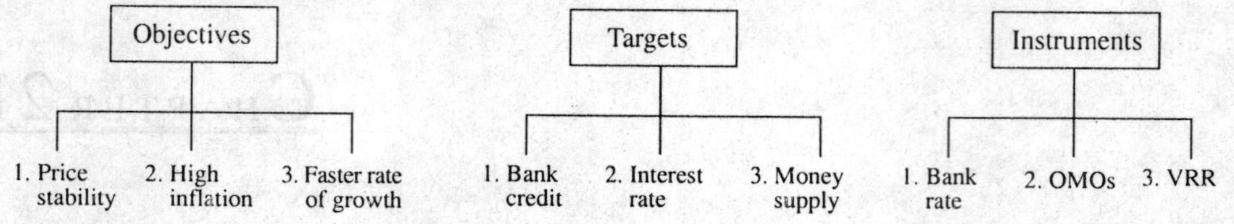

Fig. 21.1: Various Objectives, Targets and Instruments of Monetary Policy

[The targets are to be changed by using the instruments to achieve the objectives.]

We have already discussed in detail the various instruments of monetary control in the last chapter. In this chapter we first explain the goals or objectives of monetary policy in developing country like India.

OBJECTIVES OF MONETARY POLICY

Four most important objectives of monetary policy are the following:

1. Stabilising the business cycle

Monetary policy has an important effect on both actual GDP and potential GDP. Industrially advanced countries rely on monetary policy to stabilise the economy by controlling business. But it becomes impotent in deep recessions. Keynes pointed out that monetary policy loses its effectiveness during economic downturn for two reasons: (i) the existence of liquidity trap situation (i.e., infinite elasticity of demand for money) and (ii) low interest elasticity of (autonomous) investment.

2. Reasonable price stability

Price stability is perhaps the most important goal which can be pursued most effectively by using monetary policy. In a developing country like India the acceleration of investment activity in the face of a fall in agricultural output creates excessive pressure on prices. The food inflation in India is a proof of this. In such a situation, monetary policy has much to contribute to short-run price stability.

Due to various changes in the structure of the economy in a developing country like India some degree of inflation is inevitable. And mild inflation or a functional rise in prices is desirable to give necessary incentive to producers and investors. As P. A. Samuelson put it, mild inflation at the rate of 3% to 4% per annum lubricates the wheels of trade and industry and promotes faster economic growth.

Price stability is also important for improving a country's balance of payments. In the opinion of C. Rangarajan, "The increasing openness of the economy, the need to service external debt and the necessity to improve the share of our exports in a highly competitive external environment require that the domestic price level is not allowed to rise unduly". This is more so in view of the fact that India's major trading partners have achieved notable success in recent years in achieving price stability.

3. Faster economic growth

Monetary policy can promote faster economic growth by making credit cheaper and more readily available. Industry and agriculture require two types of credit—short-term credit to meet working capital needs and long-term credit to meet fixed capital needs. The need for these two types of credit can be met through commercial banks and development banks. Easy availability of credit at low rates of interest stimulates investment or expansion of society's production capacity. This in its turn, enables the economy to grow faster than before.

4. Exchange rate stability

In an 'open economy'—that is, one whose borders are open to goods, services, and financial flows—the exchange-rate system is also a central part of monetary policy. In order to prevent large depreciation or appreciation of the rupee in terms of the US dollar and other foreign currencies under the present system of floating exchange rate the central bank has to adopt suitable monetary measures. How this is done in India by the Reserve Bank has already been discussed in detail in the last chapter.

Conflicts among Objectives

In the long run there is no conflict between the first two objectives, viz., price stability and economic growth. In fact, price stability is a means to achieve faster economic growth. In the context of the Indian economy C. Rangarajan writes, "It is price stability which provides the appropriate environment under which growth can occur and social justice can be ensured."

However, in the short run there is a trade-off between price stability and economic growth. Faster economic growth is achieved by increasing the availability of credit at a lower rate of interest. This amounts to an increase in the money supply. But an increase in the money supply and the consequent rise in consumer demand tends to generate a high rate of inflation. This raises the question of what is the minimum acceptable rate of inflation which does not act as a growth-retarding factor. The question still remains unanswered.

There is also a conflict between exchange rate stability and económic growth. If the rupee depreciates in terms of the dollar, then RBI has to tighten its monetary screws, i.e., it has to raise the interest rate and reduce excess liquidity of banks (from which loans are made). On the other hand in order to promote faster economic growth the RBI has to lower interest rate and make more credit available for encouraging private investment. Thus the RBI often faces a dilemma situation.

We may now discuss in detail how monetary policy can be used for promoting faster economic growth in a developing country like India.

ULTIMATE VERSUS INTERMEDIATE TARGETS

The ultimate target over which the central bank of a country wants to exercise control are **three** major macroeconomic variables such as the rate (level) of employment, the general price level (or the rate of inflation) and the rate of growth of the economy which is measured by the annual rate of increase of real GDP. Now the question is how effectively does the RBI act on such targets? The truth is that RBI is not in a position to act on them directly. The main reason for this is its imperfect monitoring of the operation of the economy. This is attributable to lack of adequate, necessary and timely information about the key variables.

Changes in the rates of interest alter the incentives for investment in physical capital and financial assets

So what does the RBI do then? It has no other option but to control intermediate targets exert indirect influence on the ultimate targets and, of course, in a predictable manner. Important intermediate targets are the three money supply concepts (aggregates), viz., M_1, M_2 or M_3 and, of course, the interest rate. While the RBI seeks to control the rate of inflation by controlling the money supply, it exerts influence on economic growth by altering the interest rate structures which alter the incentives to invest in physical capital as opposed to that in financial (liquid) assets. See Fig. 21.2.

Intermediate targets		**Ultimate targets**
(a) Money supply changes	→	(c) Control of inflation
(b) Interest rate changes	→	(d) Promoting faster economic growth (by altering investment incentives)

Fig. 21.2: How the RBI's Intermediate Targets Exert Influence on its Ultimate Targets

Mode of Operation

The RBI's mode of operation as far as intermediate targeting on monetary aggregate is concerned is simple. At the start of each quarter, the Bank fixes the rate of growth of the money supply which, it thinks, is quite consistent with its ultimate target, viz., reasonable price level stability and faster economic growth. The RBI takes decision on the basis of data on past performance as also forecast about the next quarter or over a full financial year. The RBI makes an appropriate choice of its policy action with a view to meeting this fixed target. At the start of the next quarter, the RBI makes a review of its money supply target and adjust it appropriately on the basis of actual experience of the past.

In 1998, the RBI made a sudden switch from a money supply targeting to a list of certain broad policy indicators. In spite of this broad monetary aggregate (mainly M_3) is now perhaps the most important of its policy stance. There are two reasons for this.

(i) **Correct prediction of inflation:** In India the rate of inflation is measured by the wholesale price index (WPI). And in the intermediate run (covering a period of 3 to 5 years), M_3 is fairly accurate predictor of inflation.

(ii) **Transparency:** Most people in India have a fairly good idea of money supply targeting. With money supply targeting, the policy stance of the RBI is quite transparent and performs a signalling function. It gives a clear signal to the public and policymakers. The control of inflation depends much on the RBI's credibility reputation is a big factor here. If the RBI does exactly what it announces people will believe in the RBI's commitment to achieve price stability by keeping the growth of the money supply within a target range. This is perhaps the best way to achieve anti-inflationary credibility by keeping people's inflationary expectations at a low level. Interest rate targeting is not that effective as an anti-inflationary measure.

THE ROLE OF MONETARY POLICY IN PROMOTING FASTER ECONOMIC GROWTH

Economic growth refers to a sustainable or a continuous increase in national and per capita incomes. This occurs when there is an increase in an economy's capital stock through an increased investment. As a result there is expansion of the economy's production capacity. This enables the economy to produce more goods and services every year.

In truth, faster economic growth can be attained by an economy largely if not entirely, by increasing the rate of saving and investment[1]. How this can be achieved by using monetary policy may now be discussed.

1. Increasing the Rate of Saving

If monetary policy is to promote economic growth, it has to raise the rate of saving. In a developing country like India, the central bank should raise the rate of interest to a reasonable level to induce people to save more. So larger and larger volume of resources will be available for investment (particularly in fixed assets). In times of inflation the nominal rate of interest has to be raised so that the real rate of interest remains constant. In fact in order to mobilise more and more saving through the banking system for investment purposes, it is absolutely essential to maintain reasonable price stability so that people have less incentive to buy gold, real estate or goods for hoarding and speculation. If due to excessive rise in price the real rate of interest becomes negative, people will have less incentive to save.

However, the rate of interest affects only people's desire to save. But their capacity to save depends, apart from income, on the existence of banks and other financial institutions. So the governments of developing countries should build a strong financial infrastructure by setting up banks, post offices, insurance companies, stock exchanges, mutual funds, and pension funds mainly in rural areas where the majority of the people live.

1. In fact, investment and the way in which it is financed by domestic and foreign saving are the two main determinants of economic growth.

2. Monetary Policy and Investment

Even if the rate of interest is very low, private enterprises may not be willing to make new investment in time of depression due to lack of profitable business opportunities. This, of course, is Keynes's view. But in normal times an increase in the supply of money due to an increase in bank credit leads to an increased investment. In addition in a developing country public (government) investment plays an important role in economic development. So monetary policy should also make adequate funds available for public investment.

(a) **Monetary Policy and Public Investment**

The monetary policy of a developing country like India has to be such as to ensure that a large portion of deposits mobilised by banks is invested in government and other approved securities so as to enable the government to finance its planned investment. Infrastructure building is so important for economic development. So public investment has to be made to set up power plants, build roads, highways and ports. Such investment promotes industrial development directly and indirectly (by establishing backward and forward linkages). As a result there is a tremendous increase in demand for industrial products. Each industry purchases inputs from other industries and sells its products to both households and other businesses. The operation of multiplier stimulates private investment further. Thus public investment on social overhead capital will crowd in, rather than crowd out, private investment. Moreover, construction of irrigation dams promotes agricultural growth by raising both production and productivity.

In India, a new tool of monetary control has been introduced for taking out large resources from the banking sector for financing public investment, viz., statutory liquidity ratio (SLR). Now in addition to keeping cash reserves commercial banks are to keep a minimum portion of their total demand and time deposits in some specified liquid assets, mainly in government and other approved securities[1].

(b) **Monetary Policy and Private Investment**

Since both large-scale and medium-size industries require funds for investment in fixed capital, working capital as also for holding inventories (of both finished goods and raw materials) monetary policy has also to ensure that the need for bank credit for investment and production in the private sector is fully satisfied. Adequate bank credit is necessary for two purposes: (i) to utilise the existing production capacities in the private sector and (ii) to create additional capacity. Banks must also provide adequate credit to meet the minimum working capital needs of agriculture and industry.

(c) **Allocation of Investment Funds**

The mobilisation of savings is not enough. Savings are to be utilised for productive investment. So monetary policy should be discriminatory in nature. It should restrict the flow of credit in unproductive sectors and wasteful activities which are inimical to economic growth. At the same time it should direct the flow of credit in productive channels. So there is need for much stricter application of selecting credit control (SCC) mainly with a view to influencing the pattern of investment. SCC also helps the process of development indirectly by checking price rise and thus avoiding the distortion created by double digit inflation. However, it has to be supported by proper credit rationing.

In addition, measures such as lengthening the periods of repayment of loans, lowering of margin requirements, provision of rediscounting facilities at rates below the market rates, interest and provision of special loans to entrepreneurs setting up labour-intensive industries in backward areas are to be adopted for promoting faster industrial growth.

Monetary policy should provide the necessary incentives to channelise saving in the desired direction. This is supposed to widen the horizons of development in accordance with the pre-determined goals of planning.

1. However, if adequate loanable funds are to be obtained from banks, CRR has to be kept at a low level.

MONETARY POLICY TO ACHIEVE PRICE STABILITY

Mild inflation or a functional rise in prices helps the process of economic development. By giving incentives to producers; it leads to an increase in the volume of output (GDP). As mentioned earlier mild inflation is good for the economy because it keeps the spirit of producers alive and gives them the incentive to invest more and take more risks. But hyperinflation leads to the breakdown of the monetary system of the country and acts as a growth- retarding factor. This is why the RBI followed a policy of **controlled expansion.** Under this policy adequate credit is supplied to agriculture, industry and other priority sectors of the economy so that no genuine productive activity is hampered due to inadequate availability of institutional finance. At the same time bank credit is restricted to unproductive and socially harmful activities such as speculation, hoarding, black marketing, etc.

It may be noted that in developing countries the method of varying the CRR is more effective than the bank rate or open market operations for controlling credit and thus the rate of inflation. By raising the CRR the central bank can exercise effective control over commercial banks so that they restrict their credit expansion in times of inflation.

However, for controlling food inflation in India, the SCC measures have proved to be far more effective than the traditional measures. This has to be supported by credit (loan) rationing and direct measures such as physical control for achieving the desired degree of price stability.

It may also be noted that the root cause of persistent inflation in India over the plan period has been the rising budget deficit of the Government, financed by new money creation. And the monetary policy of the RBI was not very effective in controlling inflation mainly due to slow growth of the economy. In other words, the main cause of inflation in India is imbalance between aggregate demand and aggregate supply. Aggregate demand has increased much faster than the economy's capacity to produce more goods and services to meet the excess demand pressure.

There is no denying the fact that the RBI has adopted various positive measures to deepen and widen the financial system with a view to promoting saving and investment activities. The RBI was instrumental in setting up various term lending (public financial) institutions so as to ensure that the credit needs of agriculture, industry and exports are fully met.

MONETARY POLICY OF THE RBI

The monetary policy of the RBI during the plan period has been changing from time to time depending on the needs of development.

Two main objectives of the R.B.I's monetary policy in the pre-reform period were: (i) to secure price level stability and (ii) to ensure the supply of adequate bank finance to productive sectors and activities in order to support growth.

However, various other objectives are also being considered during the reform period. These are: (i) broadening and deepening the financial market, (ii) strengthening productive and supervisory norms of banks, (iii) improving credit delivery system, (iv) developing technological and institutional infrastructure to make the financial sector as efficient as possible (in a highly competitive environment), (v) ensuring financial stability and (vi) improving the payment and settlement system.

The Mode of Operation of Monetary Policy

From the mid of 1980 to 1997-98 the mode of operation of the monetary policy followed by the RBI was 'monetary targeting with feedback'. It envisaged formulation of monetary policy in terms of broad money (M_3) as the target. In India, two measures of money supply are commonly used, viz, M_1 and M_3. M_1 includes mainly (i) currency notes and coins in circulation with the public (but not those held by banks), (ii) deposits in current account and (iii) about 80% of the deposits in the savings bank accounts. Note that M_3 includes M_1 and in addition, (i) the fixed deposits and (ii) the remaining 14% of savings bank deposits with banks.

The money supply target is fixed by the RBI on the basis of three factors, viz., (i) growth of expected real output, (ii) expected income elasticity of demand for money and (iii) acceptable (tolerable) rate of inflation.

There is a provision for changing money supply target during a year in response to the changes in the above variables. A crucial assumption of the existing framework of monetary policy is the existence of a stable (and predictable) relation among money supply, real GDP and the aggregate price level, which are captured by the demand function for money under this framework. M_3 was taken as the operating instrument of monetary policy. However, from 1998-99 the RBI has been following a new approach as far as the operation of monetary policy is concerned, known as the Multiple Indicator Approach (MIA). The adoption of this new approach was necessitated due to the adoption of various liberalisation policies in the financial sector, the opening up of the economy, and short-term deviation in the relationship among the money supply, real GDP and the aggregate price level. Since it also became clear over time that apart from real income, the interest rate also influences the demand for money, the MIA was adopted by taking into a number of macroeconomic variables, other than M_3, while conducting monetary policy. See Table 21.1. In spite of this change in approach, M_3 is still used as an important indicator of monetary policy, although the RBI deemphasised the exclusive use of M_3 as an intermediate target. The most important thing to be said in favour of this approach is that it provides the needed flexibility to the RBI so that it can respond to changes in domestic and international economic and financial market conditions more effectively.

Table 21.1: The Current Framework of Monetary Policy in India

Attribute	Present Position
Objectives	(a) Ensuring reasonable price level stability (b) Ensuring steady flow of credit to productive activities
Intermediate target	Broad money(M_3)
Operating method	Multiple indicator approach (MIA)
Operating target	Reserves of banks
Major policy instruments	(a) CRR (b) Bank rate (c) Reserve ratio (d) Liquidity adjustment facility (e) Open market operations (f) Market stabilisation scheme

Source: P. D. Jeromi, 'Reforms in Monetary and Credit Policy in India', in B. A. Prakash (ed.): *The Indian Economy since 1991* (Pearson, 2009).

It is against this background that we discuss the major changes in monetary and credit policy in India during the reform period.

1. Break on automatic monetisation of fiscal deficit

The undesirable practise of automatic[1] monetisation by issuing *ad hoc* Treasury bills (without any limit), which led to the acceleration of inflation and thus destabilised the economy, was discontinued since 1997. This was replaced by a new system through which the RBI would provide Ways and Means

1. Under the earlier system when the GOI's balance with the RBI fell below the minimum level, the GOI could freely issue *ad hoc* T-bills on the RBI and the latter in its turn, was supposed to supply money to the GOI.

Advances (WMA) with a fixed limit for every year to enable the Government of India (GOI) to meet the temporary imbalance between its current revenue receipts and current expenditure. In addition, in 2009, the GOI formulated Fiscal Responsibility and Budget Management Rules which prohibited the GOI from borrowing directly from the RBI.

2. Deregulation of interest rates

From October 18, 1994 the system of administered rate of interest has been abolished. Now banks are free to fix their own rates of interest on both fixed deposits as also on savings bank deposits.

From April 19, 2001, the prime lending rate (PLR), or the minimum rate of interest charged by banks from their most creditworthy borrowers has been converted into a benchmark rate. This means that the lending rate of banks can go below the PLR in case of more creditworthy customers and it can go up in case of sub-prime borrowers.

3. Interest rate signal through Bank Rate

From April 1997, the bank rate was reactivated as a signaling and reference rate. The reason was simple. The quantum of funds which member banks could get from the RBI (mainly refinance) at the bank rate was low. Hence the bank rate could not influence the interest rates in the economy directly.

4. Less reliance on CRR and SLR

During the reform period both cash reserve ratio (CRR) and statutory liquidity ratio (SLR) were brought down to the minimum levels so as to improve the stability and profitability of banks. The reason is easy to find out. Due to the adoption of this measure there would be lower preemption of resources of banks.

Focus on Terminology: CRR and SLR

Banks are under the legal obligation to keep a portion of their assets in a certain specified form. The amount of money and liquid assets which the member banks must hold in gilt-edged (long-term government) securities or cash with the RBI, usually a specified percentage of their demand and time deposits, is called the reserve requirement. In India a distinction is drawn between CRR and SLR. Cash reserve ratio (CRR) consists of cash, money market instruments and Treasury Bills. It is the legal obligation on all scheduled commercial banks (having deposits of more than Rs. 50 crores) to maintain certain reserves in the form of cash with the RBI over a fortnight. The reserves are computed as a percentage of a bank's net demand and time liablities. Banks earn interest on eligible cash balances thus maintained. So they make some profits. However, such interest payment tends to dilute money control and hence these outflows are to be moderated, if so needed. A preferable alternative is to fix lower level of reserves and pay a minimum interest.

Statutory liquidity ratio (SLR) refers to the portion of net demand and time liabilities which scheduled commercial banks must invest in specified financial assets such as Treasury Bills, and government securities. The SLR acts as an instrument of credit control (indirectly though) by rendering the monetisation of the deficit which would have taken place if funds from the banking system were not statutorily preempted by the government sector.

However, it is a pity that, in spite of the relaxation offered by the RBI, banks continue to voluntarily maintain SLR securities worth more than 25% (in case of few banks, even more than 40%). The reason is that interest rates on govt. securities become competitive even without associated risk.

5. Liberalisation of directed credit

In the pre-reform period, banks had to take prior permission of the RBI under the credit authorisation scheme (CAS) for making big loans. During the reform period, the scheme has been discontinued. At the same time selective credit controls on trading in agricultural commodities have been done away with.

However, a few items have been included in the list of priority areas, for enabling banks to meet their credit targets. However, this diluted the concept of targeted lending to priority areas, at least partly.

The liberalisation of directed lending has given the banks an opportunity to finance activities taken up by the relatively efficient people.

6. Open market operations

In the 1990s the market for governor securities has widened because the Government offered market-determined interest rates on its securities. From 1992-93 the RBI was holding a large volume of government securities (placed with the RBI in the past). This enabled the RBI to conduct OMOs as a matter of routine, so to say, depending upon its liquidity position. However, due to a huge inflow of foreign exchange into the country, and the need for stabilisation[1], RBI's stock of government securities has almost got exhausted. This has restricted the ability of the RBI to conduct OMOs.

7. Liquidity adjustment facility

The liquidity adjustment facility (LAF) is a new monetary policy instrument. It was put into effect in June 2000. The scheme operates through repo and reverse repo auctions of securities. The repo rate is virtually the borrowing rate of the RBI. The RBI sells securities when there is excess liquidity in the economy, with the provision to repurchase the same at predetermined date and rate (repo rate). The repo rate is the rate at which banks perk their surplus funds with the RBI. By contrast, the RBI purchases securities with a commitment to sell at a pre-determined date and rate (the reverse-repo rate). The objective is to inject new liquidity into the economy. Repo transaction is usually undertaken when the call money rate goes below the repo rate. By contrast, reverse repo (or purchase) is undertaken when the call money rate goes above the reverse repo rate.

Repo relates to RBI sale of govt. securities and reverse repo rate to purchase

Focus on Terminology: Repos and Reverse Repos
A 'repo' is a shorthand expression of a repurchase agreement in which the RBI buys bonds by signing an agreement with the seller that the latter will repurchase them within a short period (ranging from 1 to 15 days). In the reverse repo, the RBI sells bonds and the buyer signs an agreement with the RBI to sell them back within a short period. So the effects on bank reserves of the initial purchase or sale is reversed on the date of repurchase or resale. For this reason repos and reverse repos are much more flexible instruments of short-term defensive OMOs and are extensively used now-a-days by the RBI as a part of its discretionary monetary policy.

The repo is undertaken for short-term adjustment of liquidity and the transaction is reversed after a specified number of days. By comparison, OMOs are undertaken for long-term adjustment of liquidity (without there being any provision for reversing the transaction).

The LAF scheme was revised from November 1, 2004. As per the revision the RBI would be conducting overnight fixed rate repo (at 4.75%) and reverse repos (at 6%), thereby leaving an interest rate corridor of 125 basis points.

8. Market stabilisation scheme

From April 2004, the GOI introduced market stabilisation scheme (MSS). The scheme enables the GOI to issue T-bills and dated securities for absorping excess system from the economy. This means that the GOI's cash balances with the RBI will go up correspondingly. However, since the GOI cannot withdraw the money, there is no possibility of market expansion which is likely to lead to a rise in the rate of inflation. Instead, securities provided for the MSS will be auctioned by the RBI on the basis of a fixed time table. The proceeds from the auction will be kept in a seperate MSS account maintained and seperated by the RBI, and utilised only for redemption of T-bills and/or dated securities issued under the MSS.

1. Sterilisation refers to absorption of liquidity generated through an increase in the money supply caused by an increase in foreign exchange reserves.

9. Structural and institutional reforms

Since 1992-93 the monetary policy of the RBI has been addressing certain key issues relating to structural and institutional reforms. However, what always has been a cause of concern of the RBI was the defective credit delivery mechanism especially to priority areas like agriculture and small-scale industries. The monetary policy has been addressing the issue on a continuous basis. In truth, most of the financial sector reform measures have been announced as part of the RBI's monetary policy. The reform measures included (i) fixing capital adequacy ratio (CAR) or prudential norms, for banks, (ii) classification of assets of banks, (iii) knowing the customer policy, (iv) risk-based supervision, (v) taking prompt corrective action and (vi) measures for strengthening urban cooperative banks.

The monetary policy of the RBI also deals with certain positive and constructive measures for widening, deepening and strengthening the money market, the government securities market and the foreign exchange market.

Finally, the monetary policy of the RBI is now addressing issues relating to upgradation of the technology in the financial sector and payment and settlement system.

Concluding comments

Reforms in monetary policy ensured effective for control of excessive and undesirable monetisation of fiscal deficit and preemption (earmarking) of resources from banks. The main focus of the RBI's monetary policy during the reform period was on market-oriented adjustments.

The 1990s paved the way for the emergence of monetary policy as an independent instrument of economic policy. It was fairly successful in achieving its twin objectives, viz., faster growth of the economy and reasonable price level stability. In recent years monetary policy has played an important role as an anti-inflationary measure to some extent, although it has failed to bring two new types of inflation under control, viz, food inflation and asset price inflation. And other macroeconomic policies such as fiscal policy and exchange rate policy, monetary policy have conjointly contributed to improved overall performance of the economy. This gets reflected in increase in foreign exchange reserves and a fall in current account deficit.

KEY POINTS

1. ***Monetary policy*** **:** Monetary policy refers to the policy of the central bank in exercising its control over the money supply, interest rates, banking system and, through it, credit conditions. The three main instruments of monetary policy are the discount rate, open market operations and reserve requirements.

2. ***Effect of monetary policy*** **:** The central bank's monetary policy determines short-run interest rates. It thereby affects bank credit conditions, and, through this, asset prices (such as prices of stocks and bonds) and exchange rates. Interest rate changes affect business investment, consumer spending on durables and exports and imports. Monetary policy exerts influence both on actual GDP and potential GDP.

3. ***Objectives of monetary policy in India*** **:** The RBI's monetary policy seeks to achieve economic stability in the short run and faster economic growth in the long run. Of course, at times there is a conflict between the two objectives.

4. ***Recent changes in RBI's monetary policy*** **:** During the period of economic reforms various changes have occurred in RBI's monetary policy such as abolition of the system of administered rate of interest and selective credit control, introduction of repo and reverse repo rates greater reliance on open market operations.

KEY TERMS

Cash reserve ratio (CRR)	Regulatory role of monetary policy
Statutory liquidity ratio (SLR)	Development role of monetary policy
Open market operations	Controlling inflation

Price stability	Intermediate targets
Exchange rate stability	Ultimate targets
Controlled expansion	Growth with stability
Selective credit control	Trade-off between
Repo rate	inflation and economic growth
Reverse repo rate	Liquidity adjustment

ASSIGNMENTS

1. 'Growth with stability is the primary objective of India's monetary policy'.—Discuss.
2. What is meant by price stability? Discuss the role of monetary policy in achieving price stability.
3. What measures can be taken by the RBI to ensure exchange rate stability (i.e., the external value of the rupee)?
4. Do you agree with the view that the objective of achieving price stability through monetary policy clashes with its objective of achieving faster economic growth?
5. Discuss the role of monetary policy in promoting economic growth in a developing country.
6. Discuss the tools of monetary policy used by the RBI to control inflation in recent years and comment on their relative effectiveness.
7. Do you agree with the Keynesian view that monetary policy is ineffective in times of recession and depression?
8. Discuss the likely trade-off between inflation and growth in the context of the adoption of monetary policy in developing countries which seeks to regulate the economy and promote faster economic growth at the same time.
9. Make an overall evaluation of the monetary policy adopted by the RBI during the reform period.
10. What is crowding-in effect of monetary policy?
11. What are repo and reverse repo rates?
12. Briefly discuss how monetary policy can promote saving and investment. How can it control inflation?
13. Define CRR and SLR and explain their role in banking business.

Part-V

The Synthesis of Monetary Analysis and Income Analysis

22. The IS-LM Curve Model

CHAPTER 22

The IS–LM Curve Model

> *Much, but not all, of the wisdom of post-Keynesian macroeconomics can be neatly depicted in the Hicks-Hansen diagram.*
> P. A. Samuelson

In the two-sector Keynesian model of income determination (Ch. 9), the equilibrium value of income *Y* is determined by aggregate demand or total spending which is equal to *C + I*. This shows goods market equilibrium. Keynes also discussed behaviour of the money market. The money market reaches equilibrium when the demand for money is equal to its supply. According to his liquidity preference theory the equilibrium rate of interest (*r*) is determined by the demand for money (liquidity preference) and the supply of money.

The goods market and money market can be in equilibrium at the same time

However, one year later (1937) J. R. Hicks[1] has showed that the goods market and the money market cannot be treated separately. The reason is that the people who take decisions regarding the purchase of the goods are the same people who take decisions regarding the purchase of income-earning assets like bonds. So people's behaviour in the good market affect their decision in the money market. For this reason the equilibrium level of national income (*Y*) and the equilibrium rate of interest (*r*) are to be determined simultaneously. In other words, the goods market and money market are not separated from each other but can be in equilibrium at the same time. The simultaneous determination of *Y* and *r* is shown by *IS-LM* model of the macroeconomy, initially developed by Hicks and then extended by A. H. Hansen. This is why the model is also known as Hicks-Hansen model. The model shows the synthesis of monetary analysis and income analysis or what P. A. Samuelson calls 'the great neoclassical synthesis'.

Two important points are to be noted in this context.

1. Demand-side model

The first point to note is that the *IS-LM* curve model is essentially a demand-side model. The model provides a comprehensive framework for analysing the factors determining the level of demand in an economy. It became the standard framework for studying macroeconomics, primarily because it was able to include widely differing views on the functioning of economy. The strength of the model is that it combines events in the money market with those in the goods markets to establish an equilibrium level of overall demand. Two variables—aggregate expenditure (*C + I + G*) and the interest rate (*r*)—determine (a) whether an equilibrium exists in the two markets, (b) whether the demand for investment

1. J. R. Hicks 'Mr. Keynes and the Classics', *Economica* (1937). See also D. Laider: *The Demand for Money.*

goods matches the supply of saving and (c) whether the demand for money matches its exogenously determined supply.

One central element of the Keynesian theory is the effect of changes in aggregate demand on real output and employment. Keynesian economics asserts that aggregate demand is the main driving force in the economy; in particular, during a recession the government can boost economic activity by increasing its spending, thereby inducing the private sector to increase consumption and investment.

2. Fix-price model

The *IS-LM* curve model is a fix price model. In this model there is only output adjustment, no price adjustment. Of course, we will relax the assumption and use the variable price *IS-LM* model to derive the aggregate demand curve later in this chapter. To start with we present the basic structure of the model and then go into a detailed analysis of the model.

THE STRUCTURE OF THE MODEL

The *IS-LM* curve model emphasises the interaction between the goods market and the assets markets. The Keynesian model looks at income determination by arguing that income affects spending, which, in its turn, determines output (GNP) and income (GNI). Hicks and Hansen add the effects of interest

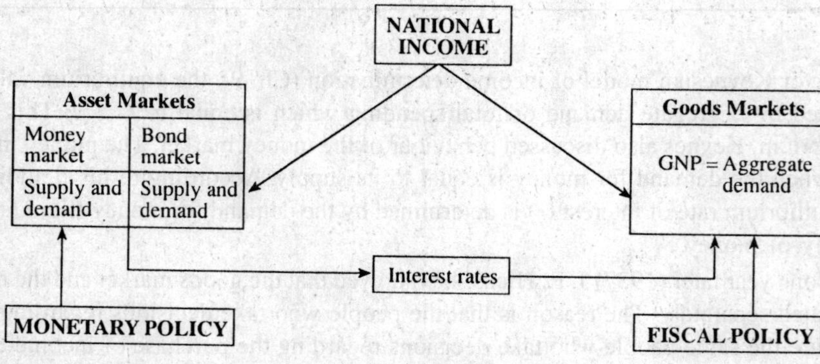

Fig. 22.1: The Basic Structure of the *IS-LM* Curve Model

rates on spending, and thus on income and the effect of any development of asset markets on income. Higher income raises the demand for money and thus interest rates. Higher interest rates lower spending and thus income. Spending, interest rates and income are determined jointly and simultaneously by equilibrium in the goods markets and assets markets as shown in Fig. 22.1.

A THREE-STEP EXERCISE

In this chapter, we initially proceed in three steps:

Step 1: First we derive the *IS* curve.

Step 2: Then we derive the *LM* curve.

Step 3: And finally we combine the two curves to show macroeconomic general equilibrium, i.e., equilibrium of both the markets simultaneously i.e., at the same time.

Step 1: The Derivation of the *IS* Curve

The *IS* curve is investment-saving curve. At any point of the curve, $I = S$ and the goods market is in equilibrium. The *IS* curve is derived on the basis of the following three by points:

1. If the rate of interest falls, investment increases. This is because the cost of borrowing loanable funds falls.

2. If investment increases aggregate demand $(C + I)$ increases. The aggregate demand curve intersects the income line at a higher point. As a result national income increases.

3. Therefore we find an inverse relation between r and Y. This relation is shown by the *IS* curve. In fact by combining these three points we get the *IS* curve.

The derivation of the *IS* curve is shown in Fig. 22.2, which has three panels.

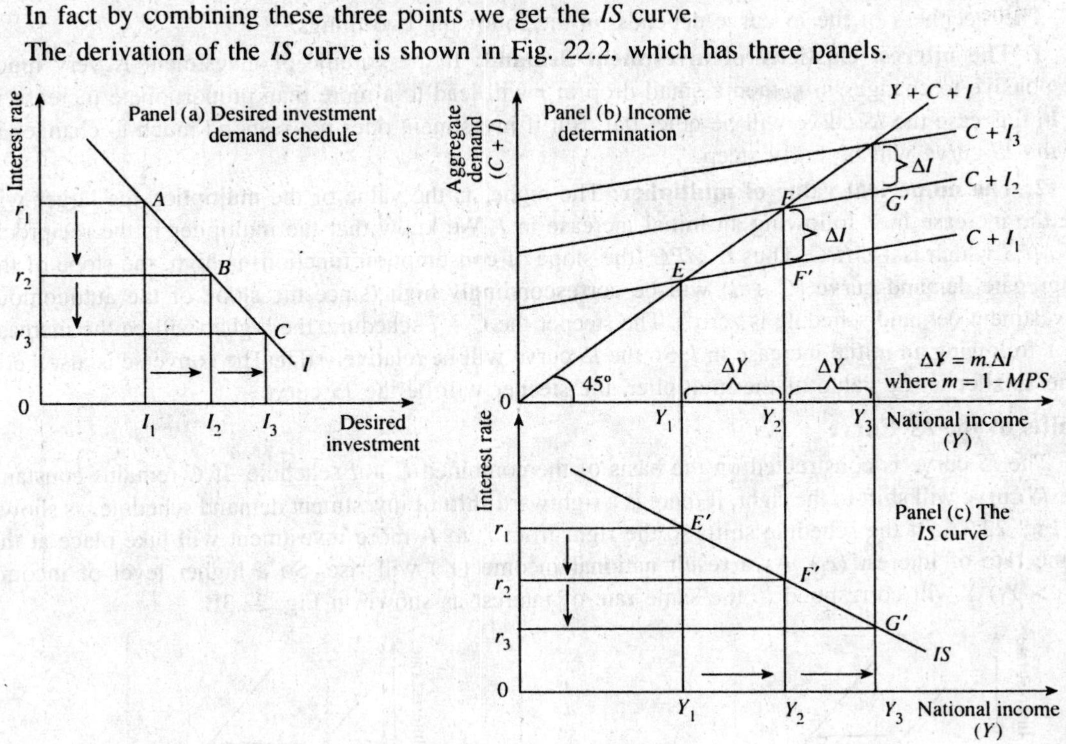

Fig. 22.2: Detailed Derivation of the *IS* curve

In panel (a) we show the planned investment demand schedule I. It is downward sloping due to inverse relation between r and I. If r falls, I increases. In panel (b) we present the Keynesian cross diagram. National income is initially in equilibrium at Y_1, (point E), when the rate of interest is r_1, and investment is I_1. Now if the rate of interest falls from r_1 to r_2, investment increases from I_1 to I_2 and the aggregate demand schedule $C + I$ shifts upward from $C + I_1$, to $C + I_2$ and intersects the 45° guideline (or income line) at point F. As a result Y increases from Y_1 to Y_2. Thus we see that if r decreases, I increases and if I increases Y also increases. In panel (c) we show this inverse relation between r and Y. Every time r decreases, I increases and as I increases, Y also increases. Thus in panel (c) we find three alternative combinations of r and Y (corresponding to three points, E', F' and G'). The locus of these points is the *IS* curve.

Definition of *IS* Curve

At any point of the IS curve I = S and the goods market is equilibrium

The *IS* curve is a locus of points showing alternative combinations of r and Y which bring about goods market equilibrium. And the goods market is in equilibrium when $I = S$. And at any point of the *IS* curve $I = S$ and when $I = S$, $Y = C + I$ as shown in panel (b).

Thus the *IS* curve shows that the two alternative ways of determining equilibrium value of Y are different but interrelated: $Y = C + I$ and $I = S$. Thus the saving-investment approach is a logical deduction from the income-expenditure approach.

The Slope of the *IS* Curve

The *IS* curve links the rate of interest with national income through investment and aggregate demand. It is downward sloping since a higher level of income is associated with a lower rate of interest.

The Steepness of the *IS* Curve

The steepness of the *IS* curve depends on the following two things:

1. The interest elasticity of investment demand: If the volume of investment is very much responsive to changes in *r*, then a small drop in *r* will lead to a more than proportionate increase in *I*. In this case the *IS* curve will be quiet flat. But if investment does not respond much to changes in *r*, the *IS* curve will be fairly steep.

2. The numerical value of multiplier: The higher is the value of the multiplier, the larger will be the increase in *Y* following an initial increase in *I*. We know that the multiplier is the reciprocal of *MPS* which is 1–*MPC*. Thus if *MPC* (the slope of consumption function) is high, the slope of the aggregate demand curve ($C + I$) will be correspondingly high (since the slope of the autonomous investment demand schedule is zero[1]). The steeper the $C + I$ schedule, the higher will be the increase in *Y* following an initial increase in *I*. So the *IS* curve will be relatively flat. The converse is also here. The smaller is the value of the multiplier, the steeper will be the *IS* curve.

Shifts of the *IS* Curve

The *IS* curve is constructed on the basis of the combined $C + I$ schedule. If *C* remains constant, the *IS* curve will shift to the right, if there is a rightward shift of investment demand schedule, as shown in Fig. 22.3A. If the schedule shifts to the right from I_1 to I_2 more investment will take place at the same rate of interest (r_1). As a result national income (*Y*) will rise. So a higher level of income ($Y_2 > Y_1$) *Y* will correspond to the same rate of interest as shown in Fig. 22.3B.

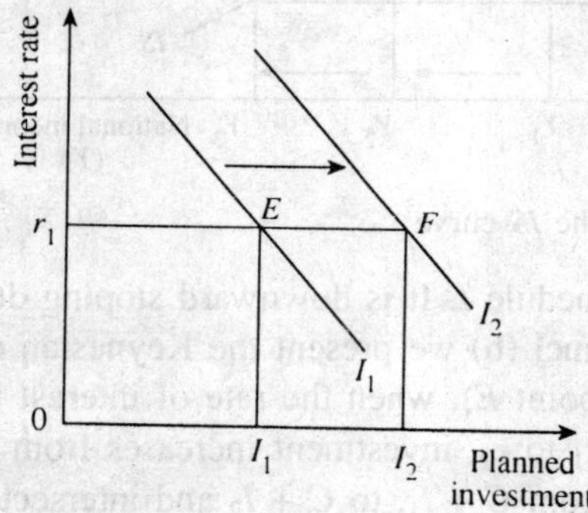

Fig. 22.3A: Shift in the Investment Demand Schedule

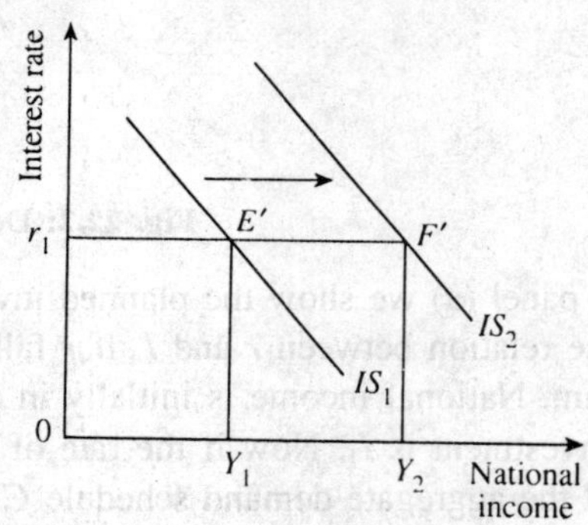

Fig. 22.3B: Shift in the *IS* Curve

The investment demand schedule may shift to the right if the profit prospect of investment increases. This may happen for a number of reasons.

Firstly due to population growth the demand for consumption goods may increase. This will stimulate investment demand.

Secondly, technological progress in the form of process innovation may reduce cost, increase profit prospects and thus give producers the inducement to invest in new machines and to set up new plants.

Thirdly, if the government spends more money in developing new economic and social infrastructure, such as roads, hospitals, educational institutions etc., the private sector will get the inducement and the motivation to invest more.

---

1. Recall that if investment is autonomous and is independent of income, the investment demand schedule is horizontal at all levels of *Y* and thus has zero slope since $\frac{dI}{dY} = 0$. For this reason the slope of the $C + I$ schedule is the same as that of the *C* schedule, i.e., the *MPC*.

In short, investment increases even at the same rate of interest if the expected rate of return on new investment (or the *MEC*) increases. An increase in consumption spending is also likely to shift the $C + I$ schedule upward (even if I remains constant). The consumption schedule will shift upward if the disposable income of the people increases. This happens when the government cuts taxes.

LOANABLE FUNDS INTERPRETATION OF THE *IS* CURVE [OPTIONAL][1]

It is possible to suggest an alternative interpretation of the *IS* curve by referring to the *dual role* of the rate of interest in the circular flow model of national income. *Prima facie*, the interest rate affects the supply of and demand for goods and services. It also affects the supply of and the demand for loanable funds. These are two different sides of the same coin.

Equilibrium in the Product Market

Now we include government spending (G) and taxes (T) in an analysis. The product market or the market for goods and services is in equilibrium when the supply of and the demand for the economy's output are equal:

$$Y = C + I + G \quad \ldots (a)$$

$$C = C(Y - T) \quad \ldots (b)$$

$$I = I(r) \quad \ldots (c)$$

$$G = \overline{G} \quad \ldots (d)$$

$$T = \overline{T} \quad \ldots (e)$$

These equations represent the demand side of the economy where the demand for the economy's output comes from C, I, and G [equation (a)]. Where all the terms are standard. And each component of aggregate demand has its own determinants.

The supply side of the economy is represented by the aggregate production function:

$$Y = F(\overline{K}, \overline{L}) \quad \ldots (f)$$

$$= \overline{Y} \quad \ldots (g)$$

Since factors of production K and L are assumed to remain constant the quantity of output produced (supplied) is always at its potential level [equation (g)].

By substituting the consumption function and the investment function into the national income accounting identity, we have

$$Y = C(Y - T) + I(r) + G \quad \ldots (h)$$

Since the variables G and T are exogenously determined, and the factors of production as also the production function determine the quantity of output supplied to the economy, we get

$$Y = C(\overline{Y} - \overline{T}) + I(r) + \overline{G} \quad \ldots (i)$$

Thus the supply of output equals its demand.

In equation (i) only r remains undetermined. The reason is that it must adjust to ensure that the demand for goods equals its supply. The higher is r, the lower the volume of I and thus the lower the demand for goods and services ($C + I + G$). If r is very high, I is too low and the demand for output falls short of its supply:

$$C + I + G < \overline{Y} \quad \ldots (j)$$

The converse is also true. If r is too low, I is too high, and

$$C + I + G > \overline{Y} \quad \ldots (k)$$

At equilibrium r, therefore, we have

$$C + I + G = \overline{Y} \quad \ldots (l)$$

1. This portion may be skipped without any loss of continuity.

In order to get a clear picture of how r adjusts (moves up or down) to balance the supply and demand for goods and services, we have now to consider the equlibrium in the financial market.

The Equilibrium in the Financial Market

The financial market reaches equilibrium when the supply of and the demand for loanable funds are in balance. In the context of the financial market in which r is both the cost of borrowing and the return to lending we can now present the national income identity as

$$Y - C - G = I \qquad \ldots (m)$$

The term $(Y - C - G)$ is saving (S). So $S = I$, i.e., saving equals investment.

National saving has two components — private saving $(Y - T - C)$ and government saving $(T - G)$. So we get

$$S = (Y - T - C) + (T - G) \qquad \ldots (n)$$

Thus the inflows into the financial market (private and public saving) must balance the outflows from the financial markets (investment).

Now by substituting $C(Y - T)$ and $I(r)$ into the national income accounting identity we get

$$Y - C(Y - T) - G = I(r) \qquad \ldots (o)$$

Or, supply of loanable funds = demand for loanable funds.

Since $G = \overline{G}, T = \overline{T}$ (by policy) and $Y = \overline{Y}$ (by fixed supplies of factors of production and the production function), we get

$$\overline{Y} - \overline{C}(\overline{Y} - \overline{T}) - \overline{G} = I(r)$$

$$\overline{S} = I(r) \qquad \ldots (p)$$

Thus $\overline{S}$ depends on Y, G and T. Since all the three variables have fixed values, S also remains fixed and does not depend on r (by assumption). But I is a function of r, i.e., I varies inversely with r since a rise in r reduces profitable investment opportunities.

In Fig. 22.4 the curve S is the supply curve of loanable funds and I is the demand curve. The equilibrium rate of interest r_e is determined by the saving-investment process. At the equilibrium rate of interest (r_e), the households' desire to save balances the firms' desire to invest, and the quantity of loanable funds demanded (here I) equals the quantity supplied (S). If $I > S$, r will rise, and, if $S > I$, r will fall.

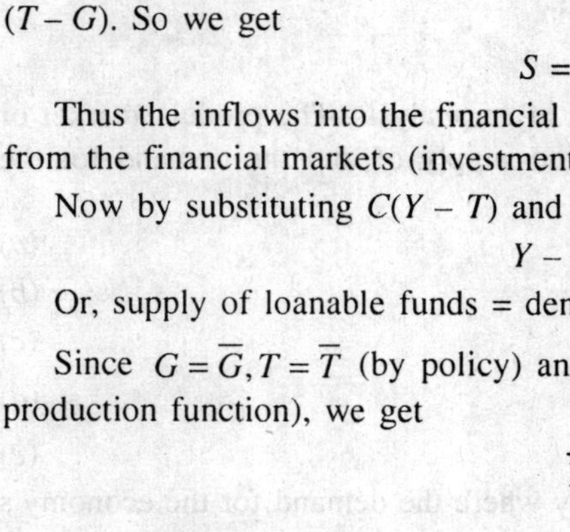

Fig. 22.4: Interest Rate Determination by Fixed Saving and Variable Investment

Thus both from national income accounting system of a country and from the Keynesian model we find an equivalence between supply of and demand for goods and services and those of loanable funds. This equivalence enables us to suggest an alternative interpretation of the *IS* curve.

Equation (p) shows that the supply of loanable funds depends on income and fiscal policy. The demand for loanable funds depends on r. Here r moves up or down to bring about equilibrium in the market for loanable funds.

We may now derive the *IS* curve from the equilibrium condition in the market for loanable funds. The *IS* curve shows the interest rate that brings about equilibrium in the goods market, income remaining constant. See Fig. 22.5. When national income rises from Y_1 to Y_2, national saving $(S) = Y - C - G$ increases but by less than Y since $MPS < 1$.

Fig. 22.5(a) shows that the increased supply of loanable funds pushes down the rate of interest from r_1 to r_2. As a result investment and income increase. Fig. 22.5(b) shows that an increase in income (which implies higher saving) implies a low equilibrium rate of interest. Due to this inverse relation between *r* and *Y*, the *IS* curve slopes downward from left to right.

In this case a change in fiscal policy will also shift the *IS* curve. If *G* increases, or *T* falls, *S* will fall if *Y* remains constant since

$$S = \overline{Y} - C(Y - T) - G = I$$

A cut in *T* will increase *C* and reduce $\overline{Y} - C - G$. The consequent fall in the supply of loanable funds raises *r* and equilibrates the market for loanable funds. Since *r* is now higher at a fixed level of *Y*, the *IS* curve shifts upward in response to the expansionary fiscal policy (which works through an increase in *G* or a cut in *T* or both at the same time).

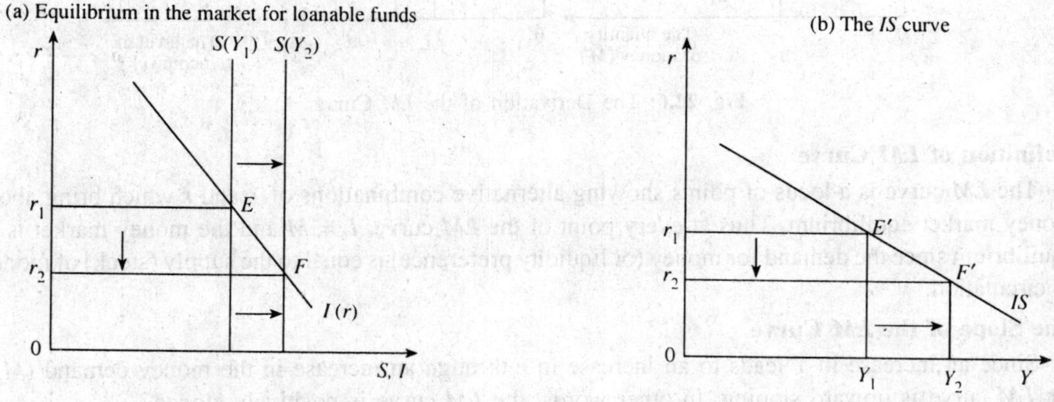

Fig. 22.5: The Derivation of the *IS* Curve from the Market for Loanable Funds

Thus the *IS* curve is a relationship between *Y* and *r* arising from either the commodity market or the market for loanable funds.

Step 2: The Derivation of *LM* Curve

The *LM* curve is liquidity preference (*L*) and money supply (*M*) curve. At any point on the *LM* curve the demand for money or liquidity preference is equal to the supply of money ($L = M$) and the money market is in equilibrium. The *LM* curve is derived on the basis of the following three key points:

1. If national income increases, the transactions demand for money (*kPY*) and therefore the total demand for money [$M_d = kPY + L(r)$] increases, the supply of money remaining constant (by being determined exogeneously by the central bank).

2. If M_d increases, with $Ms = \overline{Ms}$, the rate of interest will rise.

3. Thus an increase *Y* leads to an increase in *r*.

Now by combining these three points we derive the *LM* curve.

In Fig. 22.6 we show the derivation of the *LM* curve. In panel (a) we show money market equilibrium. The money market is initially in equilibrium at point *A*. The rate of interest initially is r_1, which corresponds to the level of income Y_1, as shown by point *A′* in panel (b). Now if national income increases from Y_1 to Y_2, the demand for money increases and the demand curve for money shifts from $M_{d_1} = kPY_1 + L(r)$ to $M_{d_2} = kPY_2 + L(r)$. Since the money supply remains fixed, the rate of interest rises from r_1 to r_2. Thus every time *Y* increases *r* also increases due to an increase in liquidity preference caused by an increase in the transactions demand for money. So we have various alternative combinations of Y and r, as indicated by points A', B', C', etc. in panel (b) of Fig. 22.6. The locus of all such points is the *LM* curve.

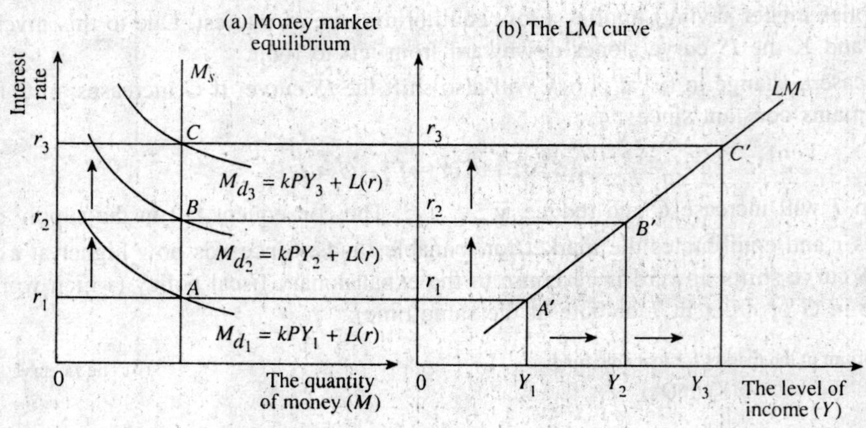

Fig. 22.6: The Derivation of the *LM* Curve

Definition of *LM* Curve

The *LM* curve is a locus of points showing alternative combinations of Y and r which bring about money market equilibrium. Thus at every point of the *LM* curve, $L = M$ and the money market is in equilibrium since the demand for money (or liquidity preference) is equal to the supply (stock) of money in circulation.

The Slope of the *LM* Curve

Since an increase in Y leads to an increase in r through an increase in the money demand (M_d), the *LM* curve is upward sloping. In other words, the *LM* curve is positively sloped.

The Steepness of *LM* Curve

Whatever the *LM* curve will be steep or flat depends on two factors, viz., (i) income elasticity of demand for money and (ii) the interest elasticity of demand for money. The higher is the interest elasticity of transactions demand for money, the steeper will be the *LM* curve. Likewise, the lower (higher) the interest elasticity of speculative demand for money the steeper (flatter) will be the *LM* curve.

Shifts of the *LM* Curve

If the money supply increases, the rate of interest will fall even at the same level of income, as is shown in panel (a) of Fig. 22.7(a). This means that speculative demand for money[1] and thus the

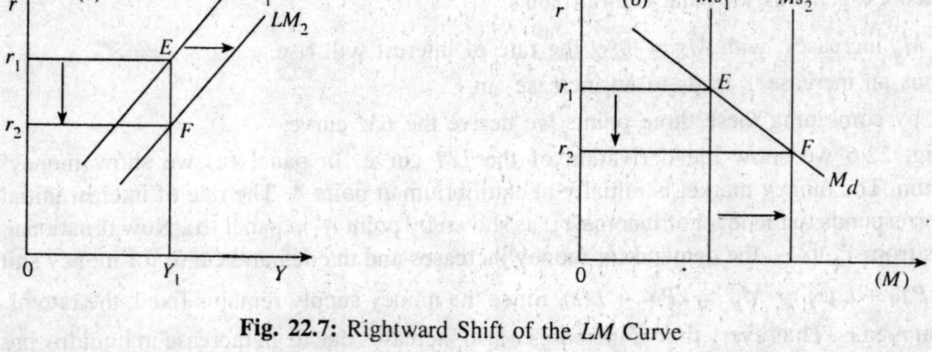

Fig. 22.7: Rightward Shift of the *LM* Curve

1. Speculative demand for money increases because it is inversely related to r.

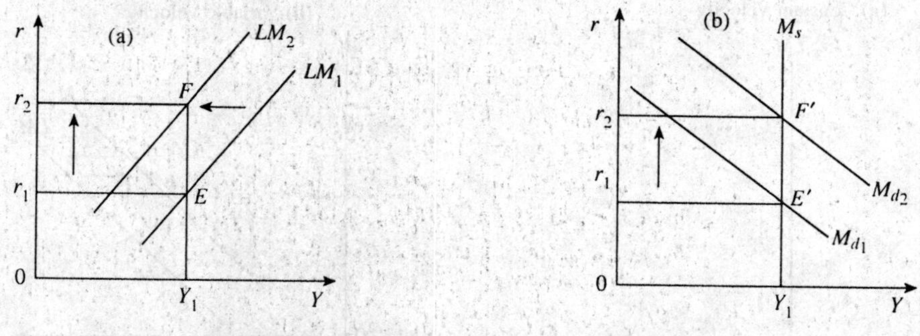

Fig. 22.8: Leftward Shift of the *LM* Curve

total demand for money has to increase to ensure that the money market is in equilibrium once again, as shown by point F in panel (a).

The *LM* curve will shift to the left as shown in Fig. 22.8(a) if the money demand curve shifts upward in Fig. 22.8(b) due to an increase in liquidity preference even at the same level of income. This will happen if the propensity to hold speculative balances increases due to expectation about a rise in r in future. Thus the rate of interest will rise immediately due to change in people's expectations about a rise in r in the future.[1]

THE QUANTITY THEORY INTERPRETATION OF THE *LM* CURVE [OPTIONAL][2]

We know that the real force behind the upward sloping *LM* curve is Keynes's liquidity preference theory of interest. But it is also possible to derive the *LM* curve by adopting the classical quantity theory approach. The quantity equation of exchange $MV = PY$ gives us the equilibrium condition of the money market. If V is assumed to remain constant, the equation is converted into the quantity theory of money. The assumption implies that, for any given price level P, the supply of money M itself is determined by the level of national income (Y):

$$\frac{dM}{M} + \frac{dV}{V} = \frac{dP}{P} + \frac{dY}{Y}$$

$$\text{or,} \quad \frac{dM}{M} = \frac{dY}{Y}$$

Since the level of income does not depend on the rate of interest (r), the *LM* curve derived from the quantity theory is vertical. See Fig. 22.9(a).

However, if we relax the assumption of constant V, we get the more familiar upward sloping *LM* curve from the quantity equation. The assumption that $V = \overline{V}$ suggests that the demand for real money balances depends only on Y. However, in Keynes's theory, the demand for real money balances also depends on r : a high r raises the cost of holding money and reduces the demand for money. If r rises, people reduce their money holding. So they use each rupee more frequently to buy a certain fixed amount of goods and services (or to support a given volume of transactions). Thus V increases when r rises. So we now express velocity as a function of r :

$$MV(r) = PY \qquad \ldots (a')$$

Here V is positively related to r. Since an increase in r raises V, it also raises Y, if M and P are assumed to remain constant. In this case the *LM* curve will be upward sloping due to a positive relationship between r and Y that originates from the money market. See Fig. 22.9(b).

1. In fact, Keynes himself recognised the fact that people's expectations play important role in interest rate determination.
2. This portion may be skipped without any loss of continuity.

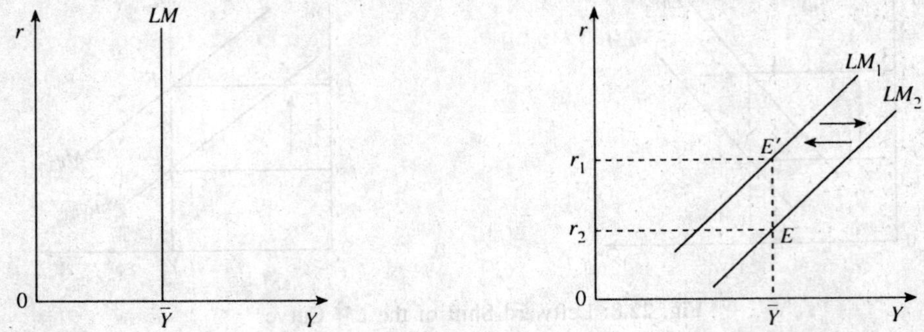

Fig. 22.9: Two Types of *LM* Curves

Equation (a') also shows that any change in *M* will shift the *LM* curve. Thus for any given interest rate and price level, the money supply and the level of income move up or down at the same time. Thus increases in *M* shift the *LM* curve to the right and decreases in *M* shift the *LM* curve to the left.

Step 3: Equilibrium of both the Goods Market and the Money Market

The most interesting feature of the Hicks-Hansen *IS-LM* curve model is that the goods market and money market can be in equilibrium at the same time. This happens when the *IS* and *LM* curves intersect as shown by point *E* in Fig. 22.10. As a result both the equilibrium level of income (Y_E) and the equilibrium rate of interest (r_E) are simultaneously determined.

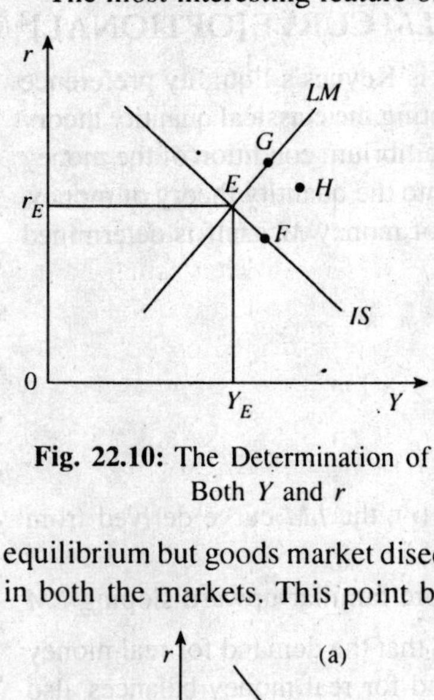

Fig. 22.10: The Determination of Both *Y* and *r*

We know that any point on the *IS* curve shows goods market equilibrium and any point on *LM* curve shows money market equilibrium. So when the two curves meet at point *E*, both the markets are in equilibrium.

Points On and Off the Two Curves

Any point on *IS* curve such as *F* in Fig. 22.10 shows goods market equilibrium but money market disequilibrium. Similarly any point such as *G* on the *LM* curve shows money market equilibrium but goods market disequilibrium and a point like *H* off both the curves shows disequilibrium in both the markets. This point becomes clear when we discuss the stability of *IS-LM* curve model.

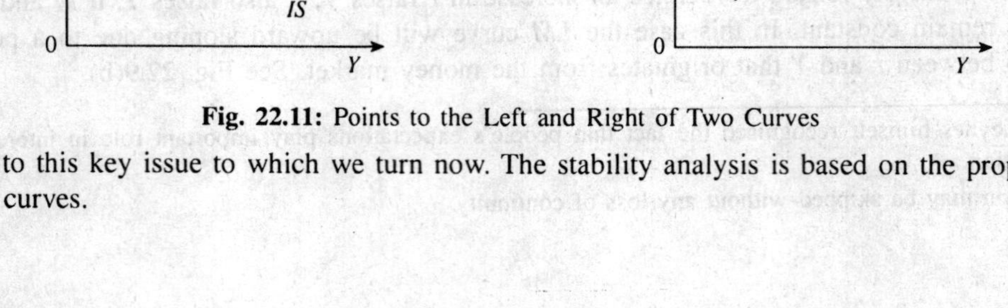

Fig. 22.11: Points to the Left and Right of Two Curves

It is to this key issue to which we turn now. The stability analysis is based on the properties of the two curves.

STABILITY OF THE MODEL

At this stage it may be noted that to the right of the *IS* curve there is excess supply of goods (*ESG*) and to the left of the *IS* curve there is *ESG*. See Fig. 22.11(a). Since it is a fixed-price model, *EDG* will lead to output expansion and *ESG* will lead to output contraction. To the left of the *LM* curve, there is excess supply of money (*ESM*) which will cause *r* to fall and to the right of the *LM* curve there is excess demand for money (*EDM*) which will cause *r* to rise. See Fig. 22.11(b). In Fig. 22.12 we show four points off the *IS* and *LM* curves (*A, B, C* and *D*). We see that if there is any deviation from point *E*, and the economy moves to, say, point *F*, it will come back to point *E*, in a cyclical manner though, as is indicated by the arrows in quadrant IV. The stability property of the *IS-LM* curve model may be explained further.

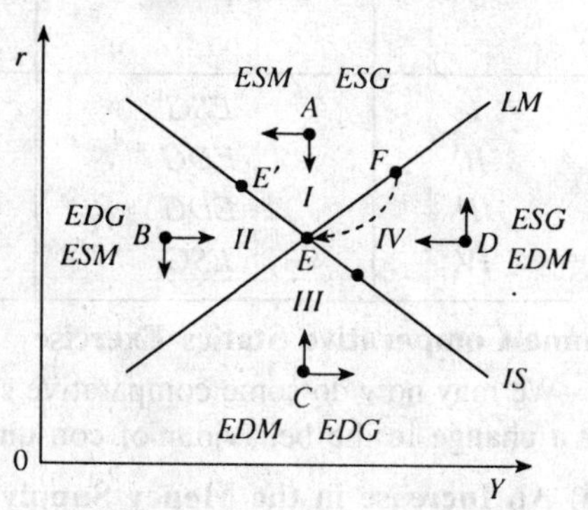

Fig. 22.12: Stability of the *IS-LM* Model

First, let us consider points *A* and *B* above the *LM* curves. There is *ESM* because, the corresponding *r* is too high for money market equilibrium. As a result *r* has to fall and there is a tendency for the macroeconomy to move toward the *LM* curve. Conversely, at points below the *LM* curve, such as *C* and *D*, there is *EDM* which will cause *r* to rise, as is shown by the two upward pointing arrows.

Now we consider two points *A* and *D*, lying above the *IS* curve, where there is *ESG*, i.e., output exceeding aggregate demand or saving plus taxes exceeding investment plus government expenditure ($S + T > I + G$). As a result *Y* will fall. Furthermore, at point *A* there is *ESM* which will cause *r* to fall, as is shown by the downward pointing arrow. The converse is also true. At points such as *B* and *C*, which also lie below and to the left of the *IS* curve, there is *EDG*. This means that actual output is less than the level that clears the goods market. So output (income) has to rise to meet the excess demand[1], as is indicated by the rightward pointing arrows. At interest rate indicated by either *B* or *C*, the corresponding output is below the level that will equate $I + G$ with $S + T$, as given by any point along the *IS* curve. Since at point *B* there is *EDG*, *Y* will rise. Moreover the *ESM* will cause *r* to fall. At point *C* there is *EDM* which will cause *r* to rise, as is shown by the upward pointing arrow.

However, a point like *F* on the *LM* curve shows money market equilibrium, but since it is not on the *IS* curve, it shows commodity market disequilibrium. This point may be compared with point *A* or point *D* which is off both the curves and shows disequilibrium in both the markets. Since point *F* is off the *IS* curve and lies above and to the right of the *IS* curve, there is *ESG*. This will cause output to fall, aggregate price level remaining the same. Similarly, any point on the *IS* curve other than *E* such as *E′* shows goods market equilibrium, but money market disequilibrium since it is off the *LM* curve. Since this point lies above and to the left of the *LM* curve, there is *ESM*. This will cause *r* to fall. Only at point *E* both the markets are in equilibrium at the same time. The equilibrium condition of the *IS-LM* model is satisfied only at this point where there is neither excess demand nor excess supply in any one of the two markets — the goods market and the money market. So there is neither upward nor downward pressure on the level of income or on the rate of interest. The nature of disequilibrium and the types of adjustment in the two markets are summarised in Table 22.1.

The equilibrium condition of the IS-LM curve model is satisfied if and only if their is neither excess supply nor excess demand in any of the two market

1. It may be recalled that in the Keynesian model there is no price adjustment. It is a fix-price model. Thus, if aggregate demand increases, for any reason, output will increase and not the aggregate price level.

Table 22.1: The Nature Disequilibria and the Processes (Types) of Adjustment

Goods Market			Money Market	
Region	Disequilibrium	Adjustment: Output	Disequilibrium	Adjustment: Interest Rate
I	*ESG*	Falls	*ESM*	Falls
II	*EDG*	Rises	*ESM*	Falls
III	*EDG*	Rises	*EDM*	Rises
IV	*ESG*	Falls	*EDM*	Rises

Some Comparative Statics Exercise

We may now do some comparative statics exercise and examine the effect of either policy change or a change in the behaviour of consumers or business firms, holding everything else constant.

(a) An Increase in the Money Supply

If the central bank increases the money supply the *LM* curve shifts to the right from LM_1 to LM_2 See Fig. 22.13. As a result new macroeconomic equilibrium now occurs at point *F* at which *r* is lower and *Y* is higher. The reason is that as the money supply increases, the rate of interest falls and investment increases. So *Y* also increases through the multiplier. The converse is also true. Here we consider only the effect of an increase in the money supply, holding everything else constant. In case of a decrease in the money supply, the *LM* curve will shift to the left. As a result *r* will increase and *I* will fall and *Y* will decrease through the reserve multiplier. A diagram similar to Fig. 22.13 may be drawn to show this.

If LM curve shifts to the right, r falls but Y increases

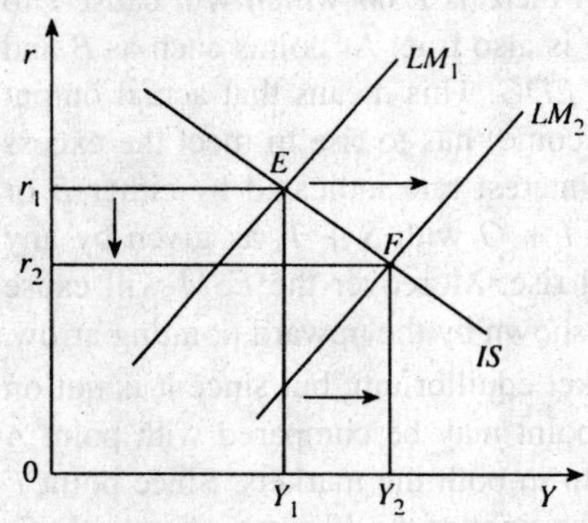

Fig. 22.13: The Effect of an Increase in the Money Supply on *r* and *Y*

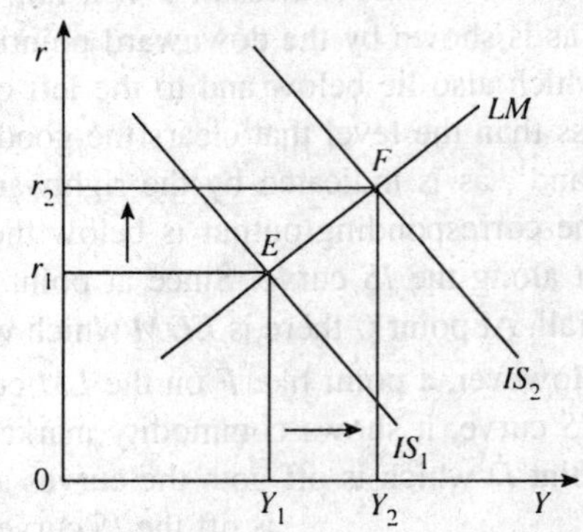

Fig. 22.14: The Effect of an Increase in the Propensity to Consume on *r* and *Y*

(b) An Increase in the Propensity to Consume

If there is increase in the propensity to consume or a fall in the propensity to save due to fall in *r*, consumption expenditure will increase even at the same level of *Y*. As a result the aggregate demand (*C* + *I*) schedule will shift upward. This implies that the *IS* curve will shift to the right from IS_1 to IS_2 as shown in Fig. 22.14. Consequently the level of income will increase. This, in its turn, will lead to an increase in the transactions demand for money and thus the total demand for money. Consequently the rate of interest will rise from r_1 to r_2 assuming that the money supply remains constant. Thus an increased desire to consume (or a decreased desire to save) will lead to rise in *Y* and *r* as shown in Fig. 22.14. The converse is also true. An increase in thriftiness will lead to a fall in both *Y* and *r*.

(c) An Increase in Autonomous Investment

If due to fall in r or due an increase in *MEC* autonomous investment increases, the $C + I + G$ schedule will shift upward. As a result the *IS* curve will shift to the right. Consequently Y and r will both increase as shown in Fig. 22.14. The converse is also true.

The same effect will be generated if government spending increases. This point will be discussed in detail in the context of effects of the policy changes in the *IS-LM* curve model later in this chapter.

Criticism of the *IS-LM* Curve Model

A serious limitation associated with the use of the basic *IS-LM* curve model in analysing economic events is the requirement of a constant price level which reflects the failure of the model to deal explicitly and convincingly with the production or supply side of the economy. Indeed, if we allow the price level to change, we can use the *IS-LM* curve model by using our earlier *AS-AD* framework, to derive the aggregate demand side, presented in ch. 11.

DERIVING THE *AD* CURVE FROM THE *IS-LM* CURVE MODEL

If we assume that the aggregate price level is variable (rather than fixed, as we assumed in the original *IS-LM* curve model), then we can derive the *AD* curve. This is an interesting exercise to which we turn now.

For any given money supply, if the price level falls, the supply of real money balances (M_s/P) increases and the *LM* curve shifts to the right from LM_1 to LM_2 (corresponding to the price curve P_2) as shown in Fig. 22.15.

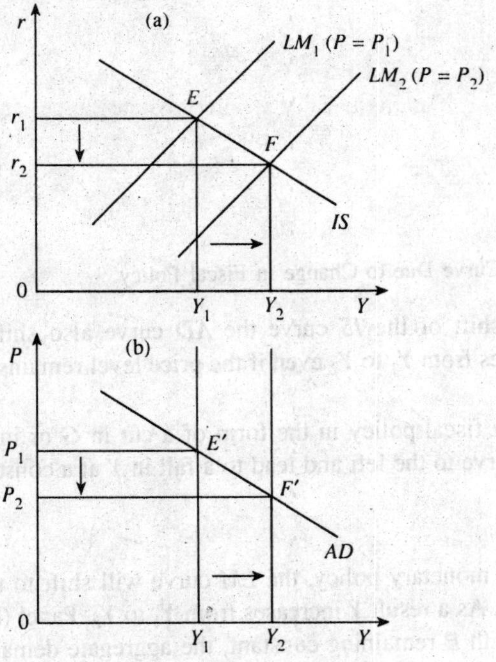

An increase in the supply of real balance due to a fall in P shifts the *LM* curve to the right and leads to a fall in r and an increase Y. So we find an inverse relation between P and Y which is shown by the downward sloping *AD* curve

Fig. 22.15: Deriving the *AD* Curve with the Variable Price Level

As the new *LM* curve intersects the *IS* curve at point *F*, Y increases from Y_1 to Y_2 and r falls from r_1 to r_2, as shown in panel (a). In panel (b) we show Y on the horizontal axis and the price level (P) on vertical axis. As Y increases from Y_1 to Y_2 the price level falls from P_1 to P_2 , as shown in panel (b). The locus of the alternative combinations of r and Y is the aggregate demand curve (*AD*). This is downward sloping due to the inverse relation between *P* and *Y*. A fall in *P* leads to an increase in *Y* by increasing real money balances and thereby shifting the *LM* curve to the right.

SHIFT OF THE *AD* CURVE

A. Fiscal Policy

A change in *G* or *T* or both at the same time will change the short-run macroeconomic equilibrium. As a result the *AD* curve will also shift as shown in Fig. 22.16. In panel (a) the *IS* curve shifts to the right due to the adoption of an expansionary fiscal policy in the form of an increase in *G* or a cut in

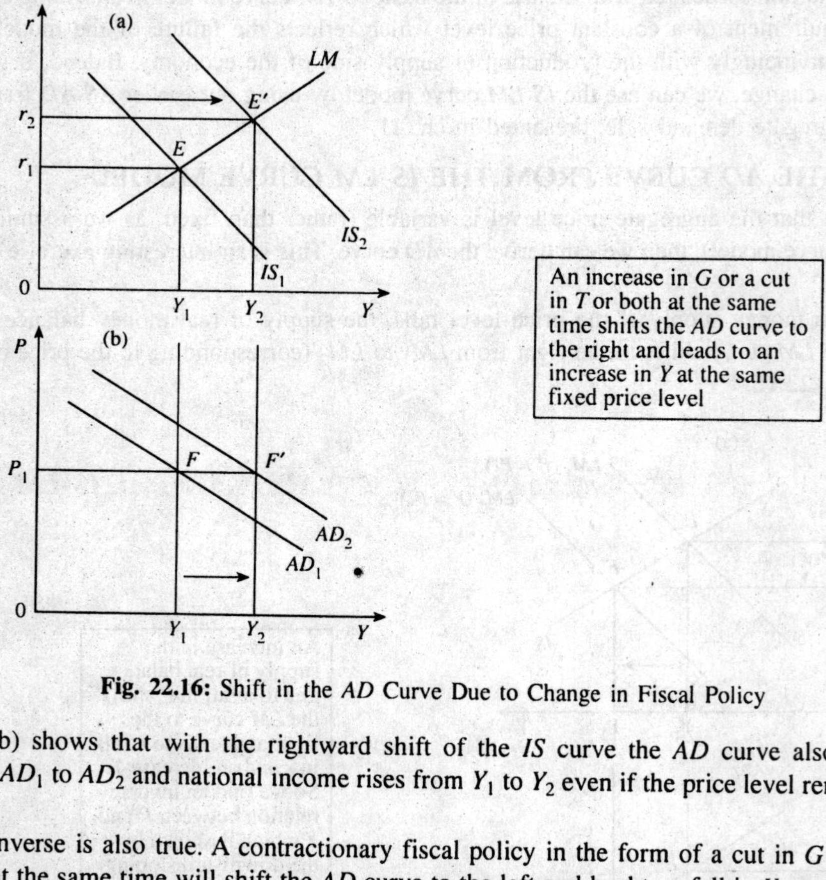

Fig. 22.16: Shift in the *AD* Curve Due to Change in Fiscal Policy

T. Panel (b) shows that with the rightward shift of the *IS* curve the *AD* curve also shifts to the right from AD_1 to AD_2 and national income rises from Y_1 to Y_2 even if the price level remains constant (at P_1).

The converse is also true. A contractionary fiscal policy in the form of a cut in *G* or increase in *T* or both at the same time will shift the *AD* curve to the left and lead to a fall in *Y* at a constant price level.

B. Monetary Policy

If the central bank adopts an expansionary monetary policy, the *LM* curve will shift to the right, as shown in panel (a) of Fig. 22.17 (next page). As a result *Y* increases from Y_1 to Y_2. Panel (b) shows that with a rightward shift of the *LM* curve, with *P* remaining constant, the aggregate demand curve also shifts to the right from AD_1 to AD_2. This means that a constant price level (P_1), aggregate output produced (or real GDP) and demanded (or aggregate desired expenditure) will increase from Y_1 to Y_2.

If the central bank adopts a contractionary monetary policy, an exactly opposite effect will be observed. The *LM* curve will shift to the left and *Y* will fall. In this case the *AD* curve will shift to the left. And *Y* will fall even at an input price level. A diagram similar to the previous one can be drawn to indicate this.

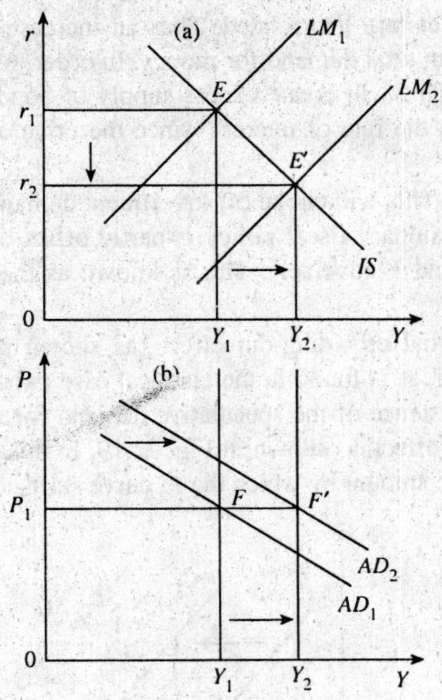

An expansionary monetary policy also shifts the aggregate demand curve to the right and leads to an increase in Y at the same price level

Fig. 22.17: Rightward Shift in the *AD* Curve due to Change in Monetary Policy

THE EFFECT OF FISCAL AND MONETARY POLICIES IN THE *IS-LM* CURVE MODEL

A. Fiscal Policy

(a) An increase in G: In Fig. 25.18 we show the effect of an expansionary fiscal policy. If government increases its own expenditure the *IS* curve shifts to the right from IS_1 to IS_2. As a result

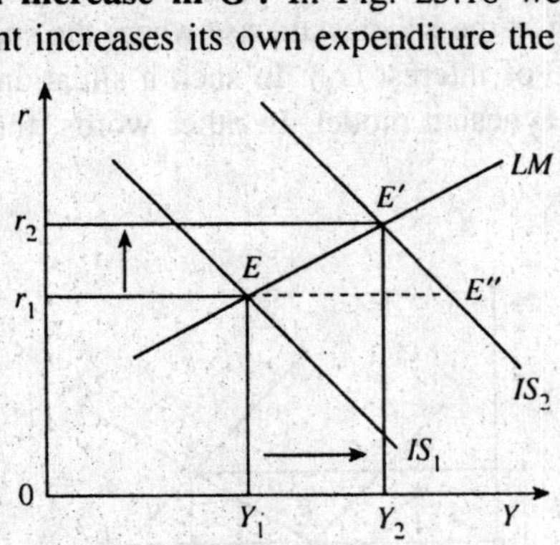

The multiplier effect in *IS-LM* curve model is less than that in the simple Keynesian model due to money market effects

Fig. 22.18: The Effect of an Increase in G on Y and r

national income increases from Y_1 to Y_2 and the rate of interest also rises from r_1 to r_2. In the Keynesian model an increase in government spending (ΔG) raises national income by $\Delta Y = \frac{1}{1-b}(\Delta G) = EE''$. So there is full multiplier effect. But in the *IS-LM* curve model, Y increases by less than this, as shown in Fig. 22.18. In this case $\Delta Y = Y_1Y_2$ which is less than EE''. In other words, $\Delta Y < \frac{1}{1-b}(\Delta G)$. The reason is that in the Keynesian model any development in the goods market does not effect the money market. But in the *IS-LM* curve model the two markets are interrelated. Thus an increase in *Y* leads to an increase in transactions demand for money and in total demand for money. In order to meet their extra demand for money the public will sell bonds. This will create excess supply of bonds and will lead to a fall in the prices of bonds or an increase in the rate of interest (since the price of bonds is the reciprocal of the rate of interest).

If the money supply remains constant, *r* increases. This will choke off investment demand and lead to a fall in *Y*. Thus the favourable effect of an expansionary fiscal policy is partly offset by a rise in *r* in the money market which, in its turn, affects *I* and *Y* adversely. This is known as the crowding out effect. There is partial crowding out in this case.

The crowding-out effect is of two types: (a) partial crowding-out effect (as shown above) and (b) full crowding-out effect. If the *LM* curve is vertical, as is found in the classical case (where interest elasticity of demand for money is zero due to non-existence of the speculative demand for money) an expansionary fiscal policy will have full crowding-out effect, as shown in Fig. 22.19. In this case fiscal policy has no effect on *Y*. But *r* increases exactly by the amount by which the *IS* curve shifts to the right.

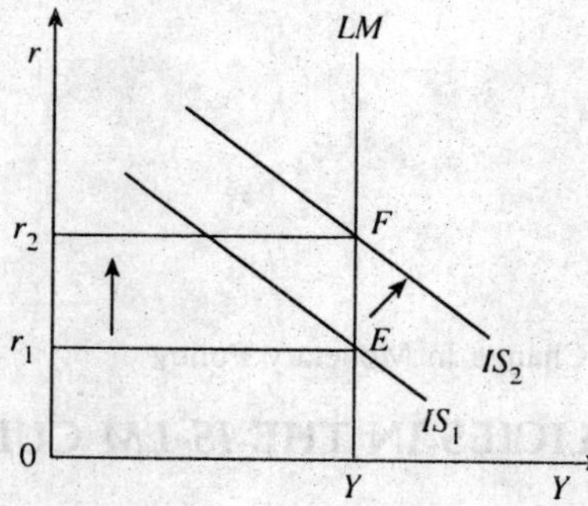

Fig. 22.19: Full Crowding-Out Effect

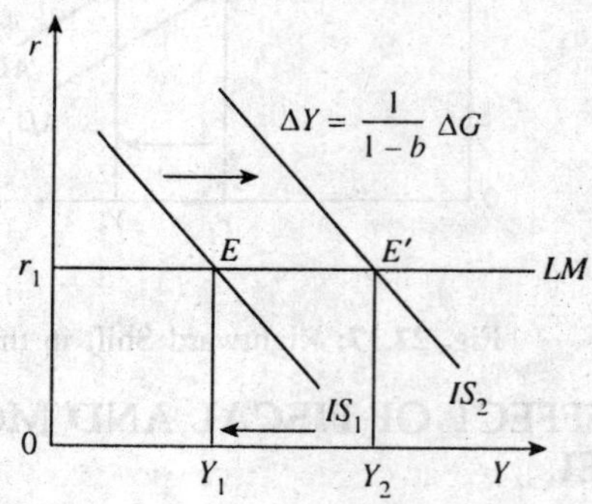

Fig. 22.20: No Crowding-Out Effect

In Fig. 22.20 the *LM* curve is horizontal. This is known as the Keynesian case where the speculative demand for money is infinitely elastic at a very low rate of interest (r_1). In such a situation a fiscal expansion has full multiplier effect, as in the original Keynesian model. In other words, there is no crowding-out effect. Here $\Delta Y = \dfrac{1}{1-b}(\Delta G)$.

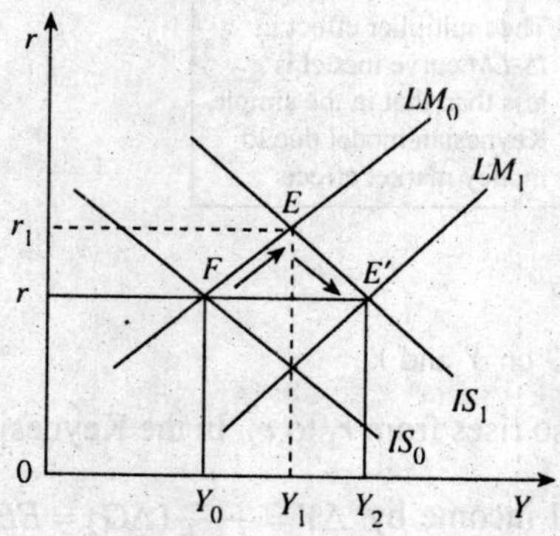

Fig. 22.21: The Effect of Tax Cut on *Y* and *r*

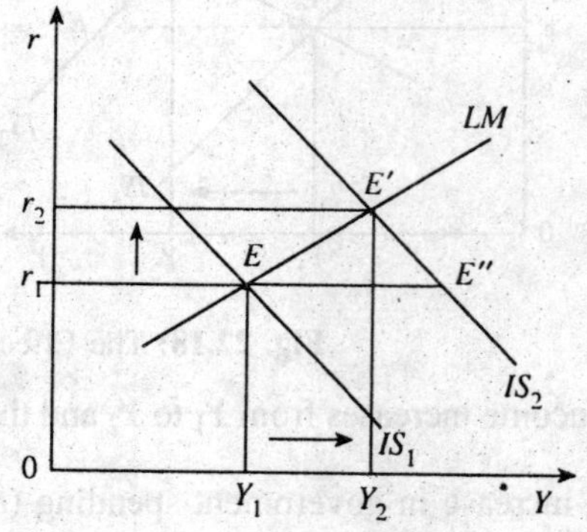

Fig. 22.22: The Effect of an Expansionary Monetary Policy on *r* and *Y*

(b) A cut in *T* : A cut in *T* will have same effect on *Y* and *r*, as is the effect of increase in *G*. The only difference is that the tax multiplier is one less than the government spending multiplier. In this case also $\Delta Y = \frac{-b}{1-b}(-\Delta T) = \frac{b}{1-b}(\Delta T) < EE''$ due to partial crowding-out effect, as shown in Fig. 22.21. Here $\Delta Y = Y_1Y_2 < EE''$. The converse is also true.

B. Monetary Policy

By using monetary policy, instead of fiscal policy, it is possible to affect aggregate economic activity. The type of monetary policy to be adopted depends on the state of the economy. Suppose the economy is in recession. In such a situation the central bank is likely to increase the money supply. As a result the *LM* curve will shift to the right from LM_1 to LM_2 as shown in Fig. 22.22. Consequently the economy will move from original equilibrium point *E* to new equilibrium point *E′*. Consequently *r* will immediately fall from r_1 to r_2. This will stimulate investment. As investment increases national income rises from Y_1 to Y_2 through the multiplier.

If the economy is threatened by the problem of demand-pull inflation, an exactly opposite type of monetary action is called for. The central bank will have to reduce the money supply. As a result the *LM* curve will shift to the left. So the rate of interest will increase and investment will fall. Finally *Y* will fall through the multiplier.

FISCAL-CUM-ACCOMMODATING MONETARY POLICY

By making appropriate use of monetary and fiscal measures it is possible to achieve the best of both the worlds—an increase in *Y* without permitting *r* to rise. The effect of such a policy mix is illustrated in Fig. 22.23.

Fig. 22.23 shows that a tax cut or an increase in government expenditure shifts the *IS* curve to the right from IS_0 to IS_1. As a result equilibrium income will rise from Y_0 to Y_1 and equilibrium rate of interest from r_0 to r_1. However, if expansionary fiscal policy is accompanied by an expansionary monetary policy the *LM* curve all also shift to the right from LM_0 (M_0) to LM_1 (M_1). This will offset the rise in *r* that would occur in the absence of monetary policy change. In this case we have illustrated the Keynesian pre-sumption of fiscal policy actions such as income tax cuts to expand the economy supported by an accommodating monetary policy—an accompanying increase in the money supply that will prevent the rate of interest from rising and preventing crowding out of investment.

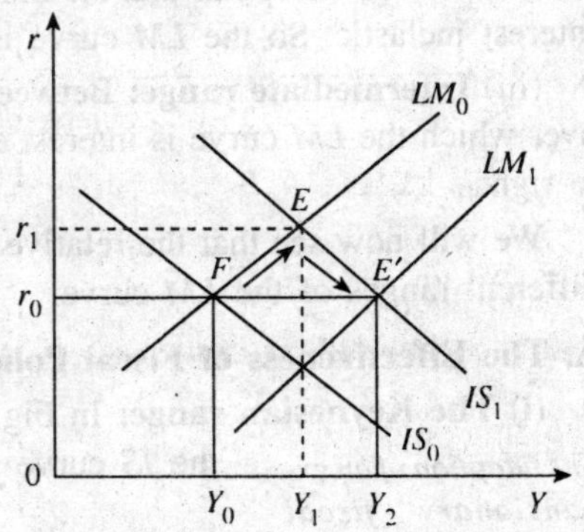

Fig. 22.23: Coordination of Fiscal and Monetary Policy

In Fig. 22.23 at the same time the *IS* curve is shifted to the right by a tax cut, the supply of money is increased sufficiently so that the *LM* curve also shifts far enough to the right so as to prevent a rise in the rate of interest, which is not considered as desirable by the policymakers.

Table 22.2 summarises the effects of changes in fiscal and monetary policy variables on *Y* and *r*.

Table 22.2: Effects of Fiscal and Monetary Policy Variables

Effects of changes in	*M*	*G*	*T*
On *Y*	+	+	–
On *r*	–	+	–

If the money supply (*M*) increases, *Y* also rises, but *r* falls. If government expenditure (*G*) increases, *Y* and *r* both rise. If tax total (*T*) rises, *Y* and *r* both fall.

THE SHAPE OF THE *LM* CURVE AND THE RELATIVE EFFECTIVENESS OF FISCAL AND MONETARY POLICIES

There is disagreement among the Keynesians and the monetarists on the relative effectiveness of fiscal and monetary policies. The reason is that Keynesian and monetarists differ in their opinion regarding the shape of *LM* curve. And the shape of *LM* curve, in its turn, depends on interest elasticity of the demand for money. And this again depends on the interest elasticity of speculative demand for money. The reason is that the real transactions demand for money is not related to the rate of interest either in the Keynesian model or in the *IS-LM* curve model. We can resolve the controversy by referring to the following three segments of the *LM* curve which are shown in a single diagram. See Fig. 22.24.

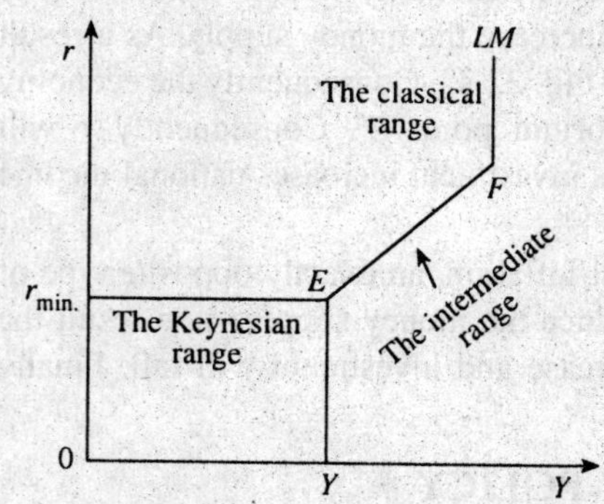

Fig. 22.24: Three Ranges of the *LM* Curve

(i) **The Keynesian range:** Since at very low rate of interest ($r_{min.}$) as shown in Fig. 22.24, the liquidity preference curve becomes horizontal, as is found in liquidity trap situation, the *LM* curve is also horizontal. This means that the demand for money is infinitely elastic at this rate of interest. In such a situation the central bank cannot influence *r* by changing the supply of money. This is why the horizontal segment of the *LM* curve is called the Keynesian range of the curve.

(ii) **The classical range:** Another extreme view has been expressed by the monetarists who believed in the classical viewpoint that the money is demanded only for transaction purposes and is completely interest inelastic. So the *LM* curve is vertical from point *F* onwards.

(iii) **Intermediate range:** Between these two extreme ranges there is the intermediate range (*EF*) over which the *LM* curve is interest elastic. Thus in this range the *LM* curve slopes upward from left to right.

We will now see that the relative effectiveness of fiscal and monetary policies varies in the three different ranges of the *LM* curve.

A. The Effectiveness of Fiscal Policy

(i) The Keynesian range: In Fig. 22.25 we see that as a result of an increase in *G* or a cut in *T*, the *IS* curve shifts to the right from IS_1 to IS_2. As a result national income increases from Y_1 to Y_2. In this case $\Delta Y = \frac{1}{1-b}(\Delta G)$

The adoption of an expansionary fiscal policy has full multiplier effect in the Keynesian range. So there is no crowding-out effect

$$\text{or} \quad \Delta Y = \frac{-b}{1-b}(-\Delta T) = \frac{b}{1-b}(\Delta T)$$

Thus we have the full multiplier effect or no crowding-out effect.

(ii) The classical range: In the classical range of the *LM* curve an expansionary fiscal policy has no effect on *Y*. But *r* increases exactly by the extent by which the *IS* curve shifts to the right. The rise in *r* reduces private investment (*I*) so much that the expansionary effect of an increase in *G* (or a cut in *T*) is fully offset. This is also the belief of the monetarists.

In the classical range fiscal policy is totally ineffective. An increase in G does not lead to an increase in Y. So there is full crowding-out effect or no multiplier effect

(iii) Intermediate range: In the intermediate range (*FI*) of Fig. 22.25 an expansionary fiscal policy (in the form of an increase in *G*) leads to a rightward shift of the *IS* curve from IS_3 to IS_4. As a result *Y* increases from Y_3 to Y_4 and the rate of interest also increases from r_3 to r_4. So there is partial crowding-out effect since $\Delta Y < \frac{1}{1-b}(\Delta G)$. We have described an exactly this type of situation in the previous section of this chapter. Here we present a more complete picture.

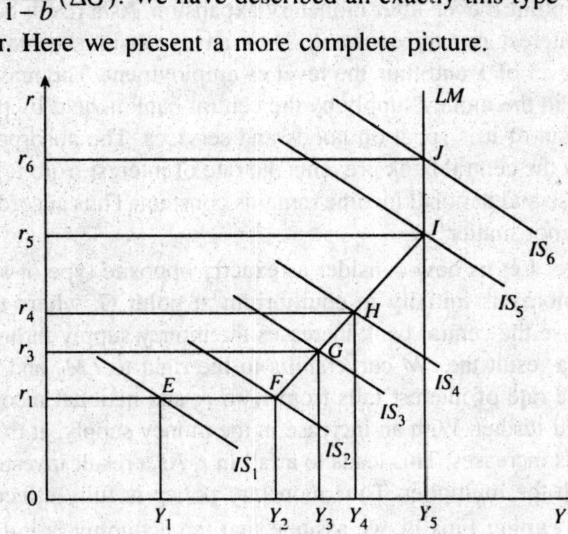

Fig. 22.25: The Effectiveness of Expansionary Fiscal Policy on the Three Ranges of the *LM* Curve

Even a policy of tax cut will generate partial crowding-out effect. A cut in taxes will raise disposable income of the people. As a result the demand for money will increase and the rate of interest will rise. This will crowd out some private investment and will, therefore, offset the expansionary effect of fiscal policy, at least partly.

B. Effectiveness of Monetary Policy

The effect of an increase in the money supply on the rate of interest and the level of income depends on the range of the *LM* curve over which the economy operates.

(i) **The Keynesian range:** In Fig. 22.26 the economy is initially at point *E* at which the IS_1 curve intersects the LM_1 curve, with equilibrium national income Y_1 and equilibrium interest rate at r_1. Now

> Monetary policy is totally ineffective in the Keynesian range due to the existence of a liquidity trap situation. Such a situation normally arises in times of depression when the *r* is too low and cannot fall further

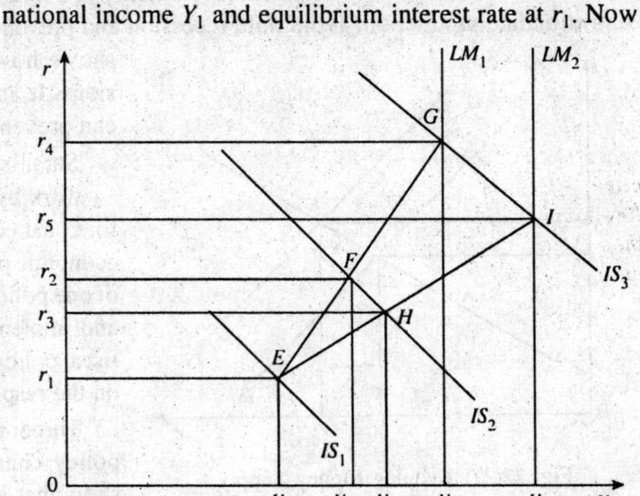

Fig. 22.26: The Effectiveness of Monetary Policy over the Three Ranges of the *LM* Curve

if the central bank increases the money supply the LM_1 curve now shifts to LM_2. The new LM_2 curve coincides with the original LM_1 curve in the Keynesian range r_1 *E* due to infinite elasticity of the liquidity preference curve (i.e., the prevalence of the liquidity trap situation). So the IS_1 curve intersects the LM_2 curve at the same point E even after monetary expansion. As a result both the level of national income and the rate of interest remain constant. Thus an expansionary monetary policy is totally ineffective in raising the level of Y and thus the level of employment. The reason is that in a liquidity trap situation any increase in the money supply by the central bank is held by people as liquid balance and not even a small portion of it is spent on goods and services. The absorption of the extra money injected in the economy by the central bank prevents the rate of interest from falling further. As a result investment does not increase and national income remains constant. Thus according to the view of early Keynesians, 'money does not matter'.

(ii) **The classical range:** Let us now consider as exactly opposite type of situation, where the LM curve is vertical. The economy is initially in equilibrium at point G, where the IS_3 curve intersects the LM_1 curve. Now suppose the central bank increases the money supply through open market sale of government securities. As a result the LM curve shifts to the right to LM_2 and intersects the IS_3 curve at point I. Consequently the rate of interest falls from r_4 to r_3 and national income rises from Y_4 to Y_5. This point may be explained further. With an increase in the money supply, at the same level of income, the supply of loanable funds increases. This leads to a fall in r. As a result investment increases and this, in its turn, raises Y through the multiplier. Thus monetary policy is fully effective in this case.

(iii) **The intermediate range:** Finally, we assume that the economy is initially operating at point F in the intermediate range with national income Y_2 and the rate of interest r_2. With an increase in the money supply by the central bank the LM_1 curve now shifts to the right to LM_2 and intersects the IS_2 curve at point H. As a result the rate of interest falls from r_2 to r_3 and national income increases from Y_2 to Y_3. This point may be briefly explained.

As the money supply with the public increases, people buy more bonds. As a result there is excess demand of bonds which raises bond prices. And a rise in the price of funds implies a fall in r. The fall in r stimulates investment and as a result Y increases. In the intermediate range, an increase in M reduces r and increases Y. But Y rises by less than the amount by which it rises in the classical range.

THE MONETARY-FISCAL LINK

It is the declared policy and true responsibility of a modern government to pro.note full employment and stimulate production, avoid mild recession and prevent deep depression. The model of AS and AD shows how shocks to the economy can cause recessions. It also shows how monetary and fiscal policies can prevent recessions by responding to these shocks.

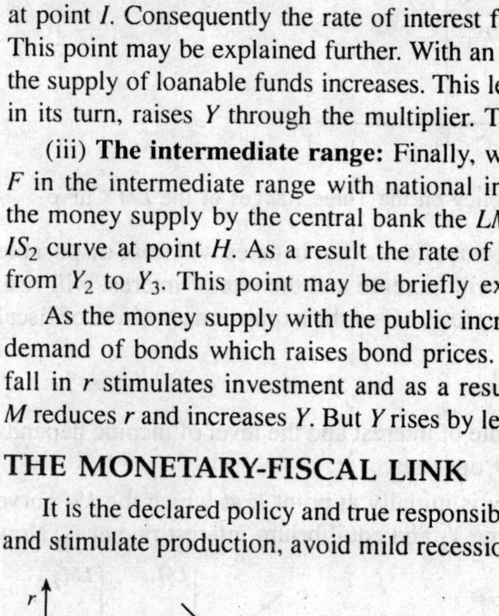

Fig. 22.27: Keeping Money Supply Constant

Stabilisation policies — such as monetary and fiscal — work by affecting aggregate demand and are, therefore, called *demand-management policies*. However, economic policies do not work in a vacuum. The success of one policy depends on how the other policy is directed and implemented. To be more specific, the effect of a fiscal policy in the form of raising taxes depends entirely on the response of the central bank to the fiscal policy.

Three possible outcomes of interdependence of policy changes are illustrated here. In each case we show that effectiveness of fiscal policy in the form of tax increase depends on how the central bank responds to it:

Situation* 1. *Mild recession : Recessions are periods of high unemployment, low incomes and increased economic distress and hardship. While depressions have economywide impact, recessions may be mild or deep. Suppose a tax increase shifts the *IS* curve to the left. Income falls due to a fall in consumption caused by a fall in disposable income. Since the demand for money falls at a lower level of income, the rate of interest falls, too. The fall in income causes a recession. The central bank remains neutral and allows the rate of interest to fall. The fall in *Y* is less than that in case of a deep recession due to crowding-in effect (as *r* falls, *I* increases, and *Y* increases, thereby partly neutralising the fall in *Y*). See Fig. 22.27 where both *Y* and *r* fall when money supply remains constant.

Situation 2. Deep recession : Now in Fig. 22.28 the central bank reduces *M* to keep *r* constant at its initial level in the face of a tax increase which shifts the *IS* curve to the left as in Fig. 22.27. The fall in *M* shifts the *LM* curve to the left. Now *r* does not fall but *Y* falls by a larger amount than in the situation where the central bank holds *M* constant. Whereas in Fig. 22.27 the lower *r* stimulated *I* and partly offset the contractionary effect of tax increase, in Fig. 22.29 the central bank deepens the

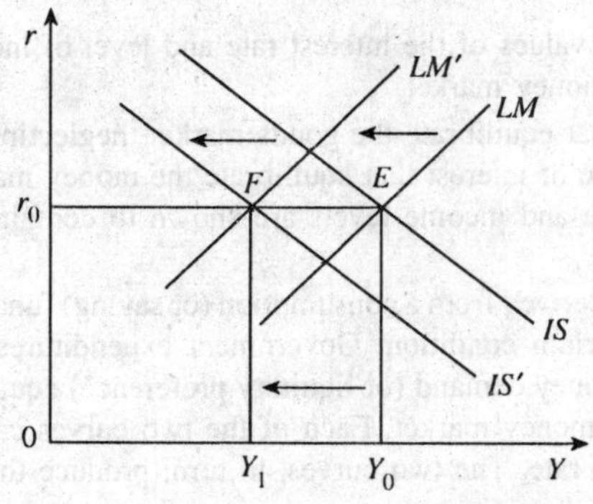

Fig. 22.28: Keeping Interest Rate Constant

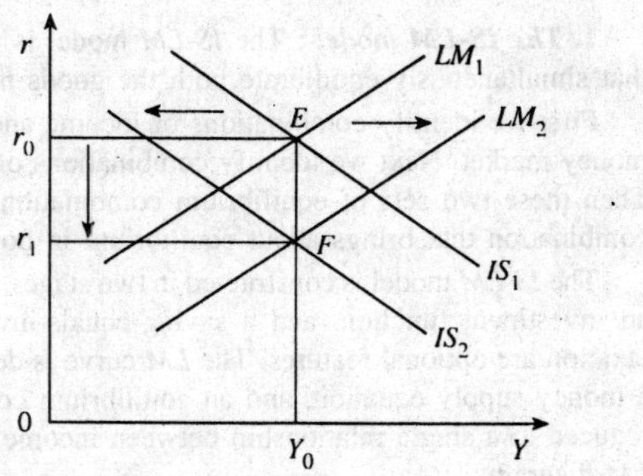

Fig. 22.29: Keeping Income Constant

recession by keeping *r* high. Here we have the worst mix of policies—fiscal contraction accompanied by monetary contraction to keep *r* constant.

An Application of the IS-LM Curve Model —The Effect of Credit Card Fraud

Suppose due to widespread credit card fraud, the government restricts the availability of credit cards. How does this affect the economy?

Restrictions on credit card availability will increase the amount of money people choose to hold. If money supply remains constant a rise in liquidity preference due to an increase in transactions demand for money

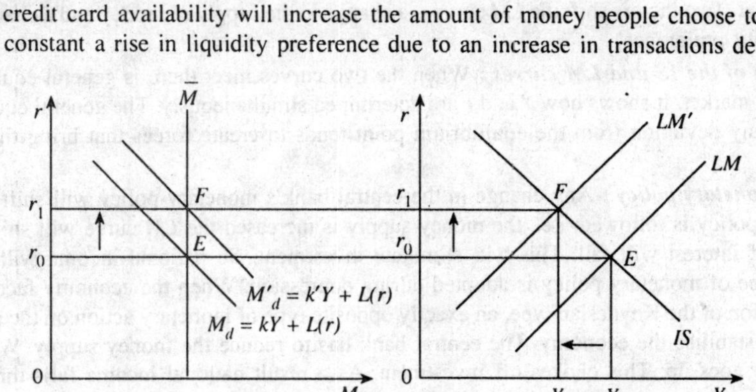

Fig. 22.30: Effect of Restrictions on Credit Card Availability in the *IS-LM* Framework

will raise the interest rate which is necessary to equilibrate the money market. Thus an increase in the demand for money shifts the *LM* curve upward and to the left. As a result *r* will rise and *Y* will fall (due to fall in investment in the goods market). See Fig. 22.30. An increase in liquidity preference (from *k* to *k'*) implies a fall in the velocity of money (*V*). So even in the classical framework, *Y*— which is determined by *V*— will fall.

Situation 3. No recession : Now we consider a situation of no recession ensured by the best mix of the two policies—fiscal contraction accompanied by monetary expansion. See Fig. 22.29. By shifting the *LM* curve to the right the central bank offsets the leftward shift of the *IS* curve. As a result *r* falls, but tax increase does not lead to a fall in *Y* as shown by a movement from *E* to *F*. So there is no recession. But *r* falls sharply. However, there is a change in the composition of *Y*. The higher taxes reduce *C*, but lower *r* stimulates *I*. Since the two effects exactly balance, *Y* remains unchanged, as shown in Fig. 22.29.

The last of the above three effects is the most desirable. It is because *Y* contraction (or recession) is avoided by making appropriate use of monetary and fiscal measures.

KEY POINTS

1. *The IS-LM model* : The *IS-LM* model is used to find the values of the interest rate and level of income that simultaneously equilibrate both the goods market and the money market.

First we identify combinations of income and interest rate that equilibrate the goods market, neglecting the money market. Next we identify combinations of income and rate of interest that equilibrate the money market. Then these two sets of equilibrium combinations of interest rate and income levels are shown to contain one combination that brings about equilibrium in both markets.

The *IS-LM* model is constructed in two stages. The *IS* curve is derived from a consumption (or saving) function, an investment function, and a saving-equals-investment equilibrium condition. Government expenditures and taxation are optional features. The *LM* curve is derived from a money demand (or liquidity preference) equation, a money supply equation, and an equilibrium condition for the money market. Each of the two curves can be reduced to a single relationship between income and the interest rate. The two curves, in turn, produce the *IS-LM* diagram.

2. *The IS curve* : The *IS* curve is defined as a locus of points showing alternative combinations of *Y* and *r* which ensure goods market equilibrium. Thus the *IS* curve is essentially investment-saving curve. The steepness of the *IS* curve depends on two things, i.e., (i) interest elasticity of investment and (ii) *MPS*, i.e., the slope of saving curve. The *IS* curve will shift if any or all of the components of autonomous expenditures (*T*, *I* and *G*) change.

3. *The LM curve* : The *LM* curve is a locus of points showing all combinations of *r* and *Y* which equilibrate the money market. The steepness or flatness of the *LM* curve depends on interest elasticity of demand for money. If the demand for money is interest inelastic the *LM* curve will be fairly steep. If it is fairly elastic, the *LM* curve will be relatively flat. Two factors shift the *LM* curve—a change in the supply of money and a change in the demand for money (liquidity preference).

4. *Intersection of the IS and LM curves* : When the two curves meet there is general equilibrium of goods market and money market. It shows how *Y* and *r* are determined simultaneously. The general equilibrium is stable in the sense that any deviation from the equilibrium point tends to create forces that bring the system back to equilibrium.

5. *Effect of monetary policy* : Any change in the central bank's monetary policy will shift the *LM* curve. If an easy monetary policy is followed, i.e., the money supply is increased the *LM* curve will shift to the right. As a result the rate of interest will fall. This will stimulate investment. So national income will rise through the multiplier. This type of monetary policy is adopted during depression. When the economy faces the problem of demand-pull inflation of the Keynesian type, an exactly opposite type of monetary action on the part of the central bank is needed to stabilise the economy. The central bank has to reduce the money supply. When this happens the rate of interest goes up. This chokes off investment. As a result national income falls through the reverse multiplier.

6. *Effects of fiscal policy* : Any change in the government's fiscal policy will shift the *IS* curve. An expansionary fiscal policy (i.e., a rise in *G* or a cut in *T* or both at the same time) will shift the *IS* curve to the right. As a result *Y* will increase. So the demand for money will also increase due to money market effects (an increase in transactions demand for money and the total demand for money) and the rate of interest will rise. This will choke off investment demand to some extent. So national income will rise by less than the increase in *G* or the cut in

T. This is why the government expenditure multiplier or even the balanced budget multiplier in the *IS-LM* model is less than that in the Keynesian model.

7. *Relative effectiveness of the two policies* : A fiscal policy alone is effective in two situations: (i) when there is a liquidity trap, i.e., when the demand for money is infinitely elastic with respect to r and (ii) when investment is completely interest inelastic. Monetary policy alone is effective when (i) the *LM* curve is vertical (i.e., the demand for money is completely interest inelastic) and (ii) the *IS* curve is horizontal (i.e., when investment is infinitey elastic with respect to changes in r).

8. *Monetary-fiscal policy mix* : The relative effectiveness of the two type of policies depends on the state of the economy. However, by making appropriate changes in monetary and fiscal policies it is possible to increase national income without permitting the rate of interest to rise and thus avoid the crowding-out effect. If the *IS* curve shifts due to a rise in G or a cut in T, there is need for an accommodating monetary policy (an increase in M by the required amount) to prevent r from rising, and I from falling and thus causing a fall in Y through the reverse multiplier.

9. *Crowding-out effect* : Crowding-out effect refers to fall in private expenditure due to the adoption of monetary and fiscal policies. There is full crowding-out if the *LM* curve is vertical. There is no crowding-out if the *LM* curve is horizontal. However, in the most normal situation where the *LM* curve is upward sloping there is partial crowding-out in which case the government expenditure multiplier in *IS-LM* model is less than that in the Keynesian model.

10. *Monetary-fiscal Link* : Whether a fiscal policy of raising taxes to reduce the budget deficit will lead to a recession, deep recession or no recession at all depends on the response of the monetary authority to the change in fiscal policy. What happens to output and the interest rate depends on whether the central bank holds (a) money supply constant, (b) interest rate constant or (c) income constant.

KEY TERMS

Goods market equilibrium	Excess demand for goods
Money market equilibrium	Excess supply for goods
Income elasticity of demand for money	Excess demand for money
Interest elasticity of demand for money	Excess supply for money
Liquidity trap	Monetary-fiscal link
The great neoclassical synthesis	Accommodating monetary policy
Crowding-out effect	Stability of the *IS-LM* curve model

ASSIGNMENTS

1. What is the *IS* curve? How it is derived? What are the determinants of the slope of the *IS* curve?
2. What is the *LM* curve? How it is derived? What are the determinants of the slope of the *LM* curve?
3. What are the equilibrium conditions of the goods market and the money market? Can both the markets be in equilibrium at the same time?
4. Show the effect of (i) as expansionary monetary policy and (ii) a contractionary fiscal policy in the *IS-LM* framework.
5. The relative effectiveness of monetary policy and fiscal policy depends on the elasticity of the *LM* curve. Discuss.
6. By making appropriate use of monetary and fiscal policies it is possible to avoid crowding-out effect. Explain.
7. Show that by using an accommodating monetary policy it is possible to derive the full multiplier effect.
8. Do you agree with the view that monetary policy is less effective at low level of Y and low r and fiscal policy is more effective when both Y and r are low?
9. The *IS-LM* curve model is a demand-side model. Explain.
10. Is the *IS-LM* curve model stable? Explain in detail.
11. Use the *IS-LM* curve model to show how fiscal policy can be used to overcome a recessionary situation.

12. Suggest a loanable funds theory interpretation of the *LM* curve and a quantity theory of money interpretation of the *LM* curve. Does velocity of circulation depend on the rate of interest?
13. (a) What are the properties of *IS* and *LM* curves?
    (b) Why is the *IS* curve negatively sloped and the *LM* curve positively sloped?
    (c) What factors determine the steepness or flatness of the *IS* and *LM* curves? Which variables will shift the two curves? Explain how a change in each variable will shift each curve either to the right or to the left.
14. Derive the *IS* curve for the case in which, rather than a fixed level of taxes (T), taxes depend on income, $T = t_1 T$, where t_1 is the marginal income tax rate. Will the *IS* curve be steeper or flatter in this case than when the level of taxes remains fixed?
15. (a) Derive *IS* and *LM* curves and explain their slopes.
    (b) What do the points off the two curves imply?
16. Examine the validity of the following statements:
    (a) The value of balanced budget multiplier may not be unity in a closed simple Keynesian model.
    (b) The value of balanced budget multiplier may be unity in an *IS-LM* framework.
17. The following equations describe an economy:

$$C = 0.9(1 - t)$$
$$I = 300 - 600r$$
$$G = 600$$
$$T = \frac{1}{3}Y$$
$$L(r, Y) = 0.25\,Y - 1500r$$
$$M = 375$$

    (a) Derive the equation for the *IS* curve.
    (b) Derive the equation for the *LM* curve.
    (c) What are the equilibrium levels of income and interest rates?
18. Compare the government expenditure multipliers in the simple Keynesian and the *IS-LM* models. Explain the economic significance of the difference between the two multipliers.
19. In a closed economy *IS-LM* model, show that a fiscal policy change may or may not produce a multiplier effect on income.
20. Consider the *IS-LM* model and explain the situation where
    (a) fiscal policy alone is effective and
    (b) monetary policy alone is effective.
21. Derive the *IS* curve by using the supply and demand schedules for loanable funds.
22. Explain why each of the following statements is true:
    (a) If investment does not depend on the interest rate, the *IS* curve is vertical.
    (b) If money demand does not depend on the interest rate, the *LM* curve is vertical.
    (c) If money demand does not depend on income, the *LM* curve is horizontal.
    (d) If money demand is extremely sensitive to the interest rate, the *LM* curve is horizontal.
23. If a change in the interest rate has no effect on planned investment spending, trace out what happens to the equilibrium level of aggregate output as interest rates fall. What does this imply about the slope of the *IS* curve?
24. Using a supply and demand diagram for the market for money, show what happens to the equilibrium level of the interest rate as aggregate output falls. What does this imply about the slope of the *LM* curve?
25. Explain the quantity equation $MV = PY$. Under what conditions will it give a positively sloped *LM* curve?
26. Consider the *IS-LM* model and explain the situation where
    (a) fiscal policy is alone effective and
    (b) monetary policy is alone effective.
27. How would an increase in tax rates alter the *IS* curve? Would this affect the effectiveness of monetary policy?

28. (a) Explain why the government expenditure multiplier in the *IS-LM* model is usually smaller than that in the simple Keynesian model.
    (b) Explain under what circumstances they will be the same in the two models.
    (c) Under what circumstances is the rate of interest constant and the multipliers equal in value?
    (d) Under what circumstances are the multipliers equal in value in spite of change in the rate of interest?
29. (a) Why does aggregate output increase by a smaller amount in the *IS-LM* model than in the simple Keynesian model following an increase in transfer payments? Explain.
    (b) Under what conditions does output increase by the same quantity in the two models? Explain.
30. (a) Consider an economy where the government considers two alternative programmes for contraction: (i) removal of investment subsidy, (ii) a rise in income tax rates. Can you use the *IS-LM* model to discuss the impact of these alternative policies on income, interest rates and investment?
    (b) Discuss briefly the circumstances where fiscal expansion leads to full crowding-out.
31. Examine the validity of the following statements:
    (a) The value of balanced budget multiplier may not be unity in a closed simple Keynesian model.
    (b) The value of balanced budget multiplier may be unity in an *IS-LM* framework.
32. Use the *IS-LM* curve model to show how income and interest rate are affected by each of the following changes:
    (a) An increase in the required reserve ratio for bank deposits.
    (b) An open market sale of securities by the central bank.
33. Does government expenditure financed by deficit spending necessarily crowd-out private investment in the *IS-LM* model?
34. Suppose that the government cuts income taxes. Show in the *IS-LM* model the impact of the tax cut under two assumptions: (a) the government keeps the interest rate constant through an accommodating monetary policy; (b) the money supply remains unchanged. Explain the difference in results.
35. In the framework of *IS-LM* curve analysis when will (a) fiscal policy be alone effective in increasing the level of national income and (b) monetary policy be alone effective in increasing the level of national income?
36. Within the *IS-LM* curve model, show how income and the interest rate are affected by each of the following changes:
    (a) an change in government spending,
    (b) an autonomous decline in investment spending,
    (c) an increase in taxes and
    (d) an change in the money supply.
37. Within the *IS-LM* curve model, analyse the effects of an increase in government spending financed by an equal increase in taxes. First consider the net result of a horizontal shift in the *IS* curve as a result of this balanced budget increase. Then consider the effects of an increase in the interest rate. Finally compare your result with the balanced budget multiplier.
38. Show, using the *IS-LM* model, whether a fiscal policy of raising taxes will lead to a recession, a deep recession or no recession at all depends on the response of the monetary authority to the fiscal policy. Is the last of the three above mentioned effects the most desirable?
39. In a less developed country (LDC) like India where economic growth is of paramount importance what kind of policy, monetary or fiscal, will you recommend to fight (i) recession and (ii) inflation? Use the *IS-LM* model to answer the question.
40. Explain the impact of the following policy options in the *IS-LM* model: in one the government raises G and finances it by taxes and in the other the government finances the increase in G by borrowing from the central bank. Make a comparative assessment of them from both the short and the long-run point of view. Which of the two policy options the government should adopt in times of recession and in the situation of full employment?
41. Indicate in which direction and why the *IS* curve would shift (a) if a subsidy is given to investment, (b) if the investors become pessimistic about the future of the economy and (c) if there is an increase in consumer confidence.

42. Show the impact of monetary and fiscal policies in the *IS-LM* model if transactions demand for money is interest sensitive.
43. Suppose the government cuts income taxes. Show in the *IS-LM* model the impact of the tax cut under two assumptions:
    (a) The government keeps interest rate constant through an accommodating monetary policy.
    (b) The money stock remains unchanged. Explain the difference in results.
44. Using the *IS-LM* model, discuss whether this change in the money demand function alters
    (a) the analysis of changes in government purchases and
    (b) the analysis of changes in taxes.
45. Does government expenditure financed by deficit spending necessarily crowd-out private investment in the *IS-LM* model?
46. Suppose that money demand depend only on income and not on interest rates.
    (i) What does the LM curve look like in this case?
    (ii) Show graphically that G has no effect on the level of output. What does G affect?
47. Show how the IS curve and the LM curve can be shifted to get an increase in output without a change in interest rates. What kind of mix of monetary annd fiscal policy is needed to do this? Will a reduction in interest rates, while holding output constant, do this?
48. Suppose that consumption function is $C = 220 + 0.63Y$, investment function is $I = 1000 - 2000R$, net export function $X = 525 - 0.1Y - 500R$ and money demand $M = (0.1583Y - 1000R)P$, where income Y, consumption C, investment I, net exports X, interest rate R, are endogenous variables, government purchases G and money supply M are exogenous variables and price level P is predetermined variable.
    (i) Find the numerical equations of *IS* curve and *LM* curve?
    (ii) Solving for Y, find the level of income that satisfies the *IS-LM* model? Supposing that money supply M is Rs. 900 billion, government spending G is Rs. 1200 billion and the price level is 1, find the *GDP*.
49. (i) Which assumption of Keynesian cross is dropped in case of IS relation.
    (ii) In dropping the assumption, how is the move from Keynesian Cross to the IS curve made possible?
50. Describe the effect of a tax cut on IS curve and the output.
51. Using the IS-LM framework, explain the effect of a tax rise on income and interest rate?
52. What is monetary transmission mechanism? Using the IS-LM framework, explain the effect of an expansionary monetary policy on output and interest rate.
53. (i) In terms of the IS-LM framework, briefly explain the phenomenon of crowding out effect resulting from fiscal expansion.
    (ii) Do you think that the IS-LM framework violates neutrality of money? Briefly explain.
54. True, false, uncertain (with explanation)
    (i) IS-LM explains the demand side of economy.
    (ii) Increase in money supply shifts the aggregate demand curve to the left.

[Guide to Students: Some of the questions can be answered only by reading the appendix to this chapter.]

22A THE IS-LM CURVE MODEL FOR AN OPEN ECONOMY

We now extend our analysis of a closed economy *IS-LM* model to an open economy and the only new variable to be taken into account here is net export $NX = X - M$.

THE EQUATION OF THE *IS* CURVE

We know that a currency depreciation (increase in the exchange rate e) raises X and reduces M and thus increases NX. Since M varies directly with Y (because the marginal propensity to import is positive), NX varies inversely with Y. India's export (which is import of the USA) varies directly with foreign income Y^f. Since NX varies directly with e and Y^f and inversely with Y, the equation of the *IS* curve is:

If Y increases M will increase and NX will fall

$$Y = C(Y - T) + I(r) + G + NX(Y, Y^f, e) \quad \ldots (1)$$

Now apart from C, I and G an increase in NX brought about by a rise in Y^f or rise in e (depreciation) will shift the *IS* curve to the right. Under a fixed exchange rate system, e can be raised through the policy of devaluation.

The Equation of the *LM* Curve

Since foreign trade or the exchange rate has no effect on either the demand for or supply of real balances, the equation of the *LM* curve is the same as that in a closed economy and is written as:

$$\frac{M_s}{P} = KY - br \quad \ldots (2)$$

General Equilibrium for an Open Economy

In Fig. 22A.1 we show how Y and r is determined simultaneously in an open economy under fixed exchange rate in the absence of any capital movement (taking G, T, X, Y^f and e as constants initially).

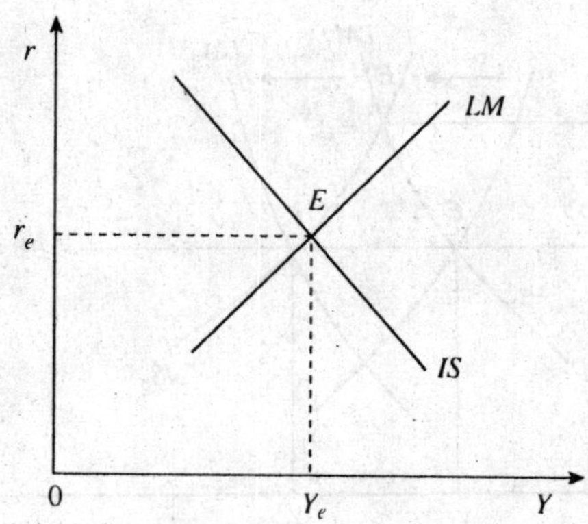

Fig. 22A.1: Determination of Y and r in an Open Economy

Policy changes under fixed exchange rate in the absence of International Capital Flows

(i) *Expansion of Fiscal policy* : If the Government cuts T or raises G, the *IS* curve shifts to the right. As a result a new equilibrium is established at which both Y and r are higher. A rise in Y raises M and reduces NX. It may be noted that an increase in foreign income Y^f shifts the *IS* curve to the right by raising NX. So both Y and r will increase. Thus while fiscal expansion reduces NX, an increase in foreign income increases it.

An expansionary fiscal policy has adverse effect on NX

(ii) *Expansionary monetary policy* : An increase in the money supply shifts the LM curve to the right reduces r, promotes I and raises Y. So increases and NX falls.

(iii) *Devaluation* : If the government devalues its currency (i.e., e is raised) NX will increase. The IS curve will shift to the right and both Y and r will increase.

An Open Economy with Capital Flows: The Mundell-Fleming Model

The Mundell-Fleming model explains the implications of inflows and outflows of financial capital among countries under alternative exchange rate systems. This model of an open economy model shows, how to make an appropriate use of monetary and fiscal policies to achieve both internal balance and external balance at the same time. The model focuses on the type of policy adjustments which are to be made by the government so as to resolve the conflict between internal balance and external balance.

Assumptions

Here we assume, and quite realistically in an era of globalisation or external liberalisation, perfect capital mobility. Capital is said to be perfectly mobile across national borders when domestic and foreign assets (bonds) are perfect substitutes and investors with complete information are free to transfer their funds from one country to another at zero transaction costs.

Economic Policy under Perfect Capital Mobility

Due to absence of transaction costs the rates of returns on bonds will be the same at the international level. Thus the domestic rate of interest will be the same as foreign rate of interest (r^f). It is also assumed that the foreign rate of interest remains unaffected by domestic policy changes.

(i) The Effect of an Expansionary Fiscal Policy under Fixed Exchange Rate

In Fig. 22A.2 the economy is initially in equilibrium at point E. The IS and LM curves intersect each other twice on the horizontal BB line. This shows that due to perfect capital mobility the domestic rate of interest (r_1) cannot deviate from the fixed foreign interest rate (r^f) except momentarily.

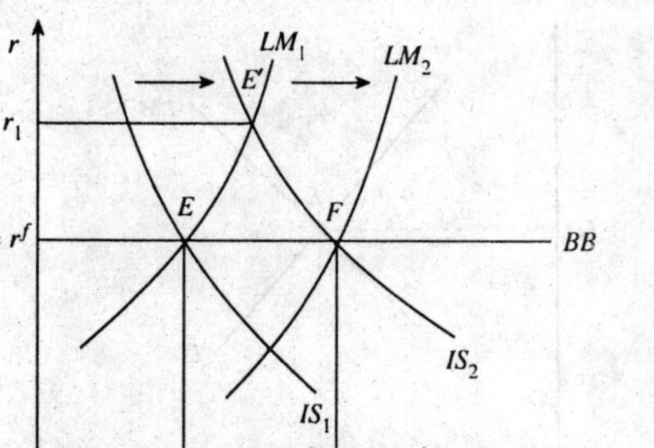

Fig. 22A.2: The Effect of Expansionary Fiscal Policy under Fixed Exchange Rate

Now suppose, due to the adoption of an expansionary fiscal policy (rise in G or a cut in T) the IS curve shifts to the right from IS_1 to IS_2. And due to a temporary rise in the interest rate from $r = r^f$ to r_2 (as shown by point E') there is a huge inflow of financial capital. In fact, financial capital is the most mobile of all assets and capital always has an extra temptation to go abroad in search of high return. Foreign investors now buy Indian bonds on a very large scale. As a result the demand for rupees increases in the foreign exchange market and rupee appreciates (or the exchange rate e falls). In order to keep the exchange rate unchanged the RBI will have to sell rupees and buy dollars. As a result India's money supply will increase and the LM curve will shift to the right from LM_1 to LM_2 and the economy will attain a new equilibrium at point F, at which the domestic rate of interest is equated to r^f once again. So the rightward shift of the LM curve reinforces the initial forward push given to the economy by a fiscal boost and, therefore, we will have a full multiplier effect (or no crowding-out effect). This increases that Y increases exactly by the magnitude by which the two curves shift.

(ii) The Effect of an Expansionary Monetary Policy under Fixed Exchange Rate

In Fig. 22A.3, we see that an increase in the domestic money supply shifts the LM curve to the right. As a result, the domestic rate of interest falls below the foreign rate ($r_0 < r^f$).

Consequently, there will be huge outflows of funds from India as investors will sell Indian bonds on a large scale and demand dollars in exchange. In order to keep the exchange rate fixed, the RBI will now have to sell dollars from its foreign exchange reserves and buy rupees. As a result the domestic money supply will fall and the process will continue until the LM curve shifts back to the initial position, as is indicated by the leftward pointing arrow. As soon as the rate of interest (r) is equated to r^f once again, outflow of capital and fall in money supply will stop. However, in this case Y will also go back to the original level implying that there is no multiplier effect of monetary policy. Under a system of fixed exchange and the perfect capital mobility expansion monetary policy is completely ineffective.

Under the fixed exchange rate system monetary policy cannot generate income expansion effect.

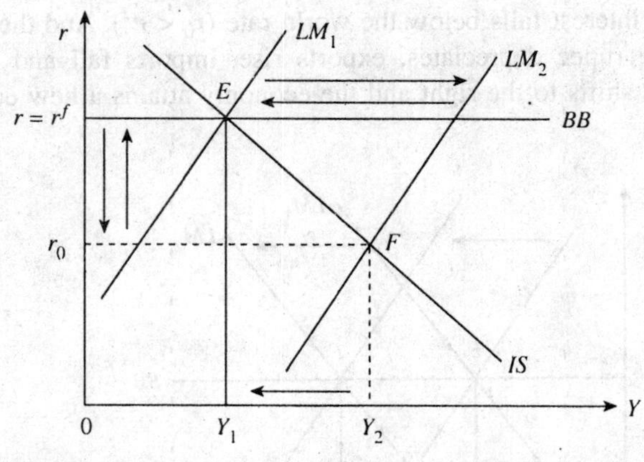

Fig. 22A.3: The Effect of an Expansionary Monetary Policy under Fixed Exchange Rate

(iii) The Effect of an Expansionary Fiscal Policy under Flexible Exchange Rate System

In the absence of any RBI intervention in the foreign exchange market, the domestic rate of interest goes above the foreign rate (r^f) due to a rightward shift of IS curve. Note that Y also increase from Y_1 to Y_2 In response to fiscal expansion under a flexible exchange rate system, there will be a massive inflow of capital into India in response to this difference in interest rates.

Under the flexible exchange rate system with perfect capital mobility, fiscal policy loses its effectiveness completely

So the demand for rupees will increase and the rupee will appreciate in terms the US dollar. Consequently, X will fall and M will increase and NX will fall. So the IS curve will shift back to its original position. Consequently r will be equated to r^f and capital in flow will stop and the exchange rate will be stabilised. Output will return to its original level (Y_1). So there is full fiscal crowding out effect or zero multiplier effect. This is in sharp contrast to the case of fixed exchange rate. However, in this case, crowding-out occurs due to a fall in *NX*, induced by currency appreciation, even if the rate of interest remains unchanged.

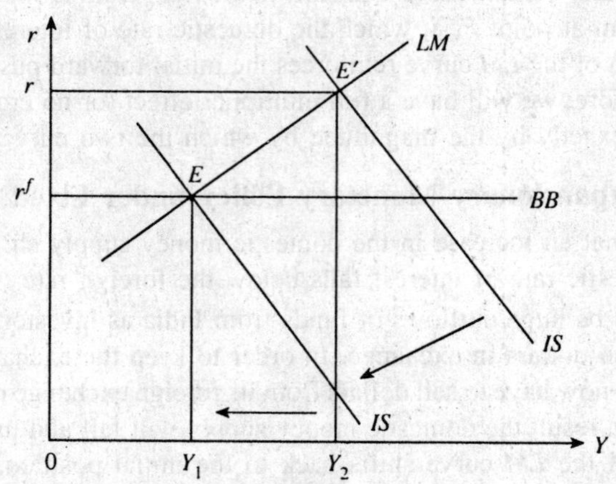

Fig. 22A.4: The Effect of an Expansionary Fiscal Policy Under the Flexible Exchange Rate System

(iv) The Effect of an Expansionary Monetary Policy under Flexible Exchange Rate System

An increase in the money supply shifts the *LM* curve to the right, as shown in Fig. 22A.5. As a result the domestic rate of interest falls below the world rate ($r_0 < r^f$). And there is huge outflow of capital from India. So the rupee depreciates, exports rise, imports fall and net exports increase. Consequently, the *IS* curve shifts to the right and the economy attains a new equilibrium at point *F*, with $r = r^f$ once again.

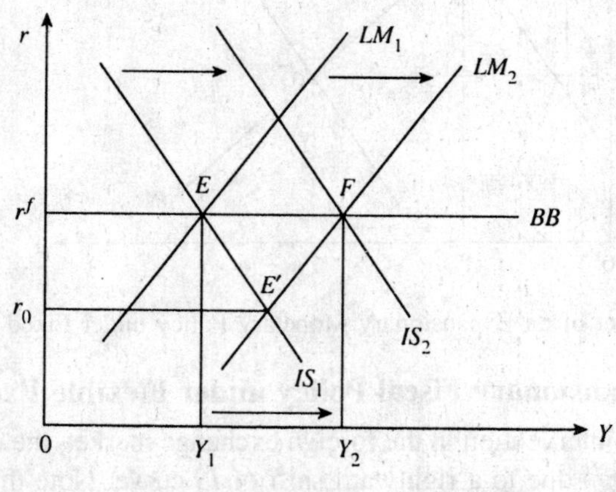

Fig. 22A.5: The Effect of an Expansionary Monetary Policy under Flexible Exchange Rate

A comparison of points *E* and *F* shows that monetary expansion has generated full multiplier effect. Here *Y* has increased exactly by the magnitude of shifts of the *LM* and *IS* curves along the horizontal *BB* line from Y_1 to Y_2.

In an open economy, monetary policy does not operate through the domestic *r*, since it is fixed by the foreign rate. The transmission mechanism is to be found elsewhere, in *NX* and in *e*. In short, assuming perfect capital mobility, fiscal policy has maximum (zero) effect under fixed (flexible) exchange rate. Monetary policy has maximum (zero) effect under flexible (fixed) exchange rate.

The Mundell-Fleming model demonstrates a paradox: in a fixed exchange rate system, fiscal policy is powerful and monetary policy completely ineffective, while the reverse is true in a floating exchange rate system. The paradoxical result is explained by the fact that with a floating exchange rate, fiscal policy operates through, for example, extra government borrowing which either pushes up the interest rate (and thus reduces private investment) or simply leads to inflow of foreign capital, which drives up the exchange rate (and thus reduces exports). Either way, any stimulatory effect is neglected. Monetary policy can work through changing interest rates by increasing the money supply and by affecting the exchange rate. Under the fixed rate system, money is powerless, as it has to accommodate any exchange rate target. Fiscal policy can work, no doubt, as no offsetting exchange rate or interest rate can undermine it.

Three Key Points

1. The Mundell-Fleming model shows how a nation can use monetary and fiscal policies to achieve both internal and external balance without any change in the exchange rate.

2. Within fixed exchange rates, monetary policy is completely ineffective if international capital flows are highly elastic as they are likely to be for most industrial nations in today's world of highly integrated capital markets.

3. By using monetary or fiscal policies to achieve internal balance, the nation will have to allow the exchange rate to vary or engage in expansion-switching policies such as devaluation and tariffs and quotas to achieve both internal balance and external balance simultaneously.

Criticisms of the Model

One serious criticism of the model is that it mixes stock and flow variables. On particular, the *LM* curve is based on the *stock* of money, while the *BB* curve is based on the *flow* of capital.

The model assumes that a rise in domestic interest rates will lead to a continuous capital inflow from abroad to finance the nation's BOP deficit. The capital outflow, however, is likely to be of a once-and-for-all type and will come to an end after investors have readjusted their portfolios following the increase in the domestic interest rate.

Part-VI

Macroeconomic Instability

23. Inflation and Unemployment: The Great Trade-Off
24. Inflation: Causes, Consequences and Remedies

CHAPTER 23

Inflation and Unemployment: The Great Trade-Off

The correlation between money prices and aggregate economic activity has long been of interest to macroeconomists. In the 1950s, A. W. Phillips observed that there was a negative relationship between the rate of change in money wages and the unemployment rate in the UK, a relationship that came to be known as the Phillips curve.
S. D. Williamson

In the simple Keynesian model of income and employment the short-run aggregate supply curve (with variable price level), is horizontal up to the level of full employment and vertical thereafter as shown in Fig. 23.1. This implies that the aggregate supply curve is infinitely elastic in times of depression when the economy is having huge excess production capacity with huge idle capital stock and massive involuntary unemployment. As soon as the full employment level of output is reached, the *AS* curve becomes completely inelastic (as shown by point *F*). So an increase in aggregate demand and a rightward shift of the aggregate demand from AD_0 to AD_1 in times of depression leads to an increase in aggregate output or real GDP and employment with the aggregate price level remaining unchanged at P_1. However, once the economy reaches full employment, no further increase in aggregate output and a rightward shift of the aggregate demand curve curve, say, from AD_1 to AD_2 will only cause the price level to rise from P_1 to P_2. Thus according to Keynes, the end of full employment is the beginning of inflation. Thus inflation occurs only when no further increase in aggregate output is possible. So there is no trade-off between inflation and unemployment.

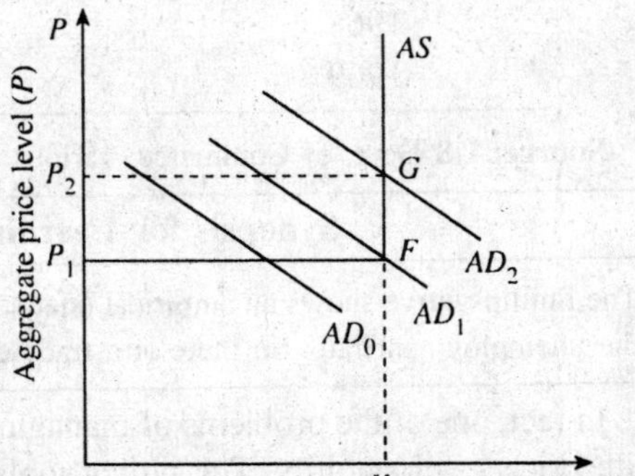

Fig. 23.1: The Keynesian Aggregate Supply Curve

INFLATION-UNEMPLOYMENT TRADE-OFF: THE PHILLIPS CURVE

In 1958 A. W. Phillips carried out an extensive study on the relationship between unemployment and the rate of change of money wages in Great Britain for a long period of time and found that there was indeed an inverse relationship between the rate of unemployment and the rate of inflation. A ready explanation of the connection between the two variables seemed at hand. On the basis of his own statistical studies of the relationship between unemployment and changes in wage rates in the U.K. between 1861 and 1957, Phillips proved conclusively, that wage rates tended to rise when unemployment rates were low and *vice versa.* This provided an empirical verification of an old hypothesis about labour markets— that labour unions are able to raise wages adequately when there is high demand for labour, but do not succeed in raising wages much when the magnitude rate or the of unemployment is high.

On the basis of Phillips's original study. American economists like Milton Friedman, Paul Samuelson, James Tobin and others explained price behaviour during the inflation of the 1960s, under the name 'the Phillips curve'. They argued that wages are the most important component of total costs. Therefore Phillips curve relationship between wages and unemployment can be readily translated into a relationship between prices and unemployment: the rate of inflation accelerates as the percentage of people unemployed falls. This argument was particularly appealing during the 1960s, when statistics seemed to verify the hypothesis, as Table 23.1 shows.

Table 23.1: Inflation and Unemployment in the USA

Year	*Price Increase* (%)	*Unemployment* (%)
1960	1.6	5.5
1961	1.0	6.7
1962	1.1	5.5
1963	1.2	5.7
1964	1.3	5.2
1965	1.5	4.5
1966	2.9	3.8
1967	2.8	3.8
1968	4.2	3.6
1969	5.4	3.5

Source: US Dept. of Commerce, various issues.

Synopsis for Learning: The Phillips Curve Relationship

The Phillips curve shows an empirical (statistical) relationship between two variables: the rate of inflation and the unemployment rate. So there is a trade-off between the two variables.

In fact, one of the problems of managing a modern mixed economy is to reconcile full employment with price level stability. The policy tools at the disposal of government for creating new jobs and incomes tend to generate inflation; and measures to reduce inflation tend to create unemployment.

It has been an empirical reality that an inflation, which raises money wage offers, may permanently reduce unemployment below the so-called natural rate (long-term trend or accepted rate of, say, 4 to 5%) by reducing the real wage (with labour, not fully perceiving the price level increase, thinking that the real wage increased, i.e., labour suffering from money illusion). If price adjustments are perfectly perceived in the long run, then changes in the inflation rate can only produce temporary, short-run changes in employment.

The empirical nature of the true link between the inflation rate and the level of employment has been the subject of intensive debate since the late 1950s. As an outgrowth of an investigation reported in 1958 by A. W. Phillips, economists have generated a large body of empirical evidence on that link. In Fig. 23.2 we have sketched a schedule, called the Phillips curve, named after its inventor.

The Phillips curve seemingly shows that full employment and price stability are not compatible goals— that there is a trade-off between unemployment and inflation (In Fig. 23.2) wage-change scale on the right side vertical axis is higher than the left hand price-change scale by an assumed 2%. The greater is unemployment on the horizontal axis, the lower is the rate of price inflation. As people fear price inflation they move upward along their Phillips curve and bring on *stagflation*: unemployment and inflation at the same time. This is a new economic term which refers to a stagnant economy with high unemployment, underutilised production capacity and chronically high inflation. In fact, we live in an era of *creeping inflation*. Paul Samuelson argues that this is a new kind of inflation. Now prices and wages start rising much before full employment of labour and full utilisation of capacity are reached. In fact, under modern cost-push (or sellers') inflation a mixed economy may experience stagflation—stagnation of output growth and employment, at the same time that prices rise. To have restricted inflation to an inconsequential rate of, say 1 to 2% annually it appears that the society will have to accept 5 to 6% unemployment rate. To reduce unemployment, it appears that the society must tolerate an increased rate of inflation. For example, to bring unemployment down to 3% of the labour force the Phillips curve may suggest that we would have to tolerate an annual inflation rate of 4%. The main point is that a modern mixed economy must tolerate a relatively high level or rate of unemployment if price stability is to be maintained.

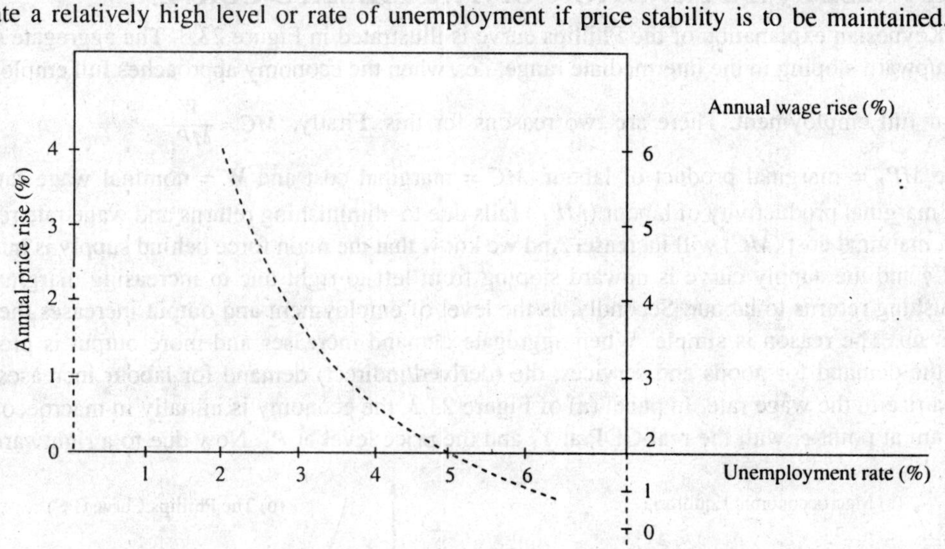

Fig. 23.2: The Phillips Curve

There are two reasons for this. The extent to which the wage rate will rise depends on the state of the labour market. Second, wage cost is the main part of total cost. So it is impossible in practice to realise the twin goals of price stability and full employment simultaneously. In other words, a policy of full employment is not possible without inflation. Similarly, a policy of price stability is not possible without unemployment.

The Phillips curve is a locus of points showing alternative combinations of two social evils: inflation and unemployment

The basic point is that higher is the percentage of people unemployed the less is the wage rise and the less is the price rise. By contrast, as an economy approaches the state of full employment and the wage rate keeps on rising, the price level also keeps on rising. Thus there is an inverse relationship between inflation and unemployment. This inverse relation implies a short-run trade-off between inflation and unemployment. This means that for reducing unemployment, an economy will have to tolerate a higher rate of inflation. And for reducing the rate of inflation, a higher rate of unemployment has to be accepted. The inverse relation between the rate of inflation and the rate of unemployment is presented in the form of a curve, called the Phillips curve[1], as shown in Figure 23.2.

1. In fact, with the appearance of the Phillips curve, the distinction between demand-pull and cost-push inflation disappeared.

A STABLE PHILLIPS CURVE RELATION IN THE 1950S AND 1960S

Actual data for the US economy collected in 1950s and 1960s showed a stable Phillips curve which indicated a predictable inverse relationship between inflation and unemployment. This implies that policymakers faced an uncomfortable situation due to the existence of a perplexing dilemma—the coexistence of inflation and unemployment. The Phillips curve shows the society's menu of choice between two social evils, viz., inflation and unemployment. If an economy has to achieve price stability it has to tolerate inflation. And if it seeks to achieve full employment then it has to tolerate inflation. So no society can achieve price level stability and full employment at the same time. However, during the 1970s and early 1980s both the USA and the UK experienced a high rate of inflation and a high rate of unemployment (at the same time) and that led to a low level of real GDP. This strange thing is known as stagflation. This phenomenon is a sharp contrast to the Phillips curve relation as also the simple Keynesian theory of income determination.

THE KEYNESIAN EXPLANATION OF THE PHILLIPS CURVE

The Keynesian explanation of the Phillips curve is illustrated in Figure 23.3. The aggregate supply curve is upward sloping in the intermediate range, i.e., when the economy approaches full employment or is near full employment. There are two reasons for this. Firstly, $MC = \frac{W}{MP_L}$.

[Here MP_L = marginal product of labour, MC = marginal cost and W = nominal wage rate]

So if marginal productivity of labour (MP_L) falls due to diminishing returns and wage rate remains constant, marginal cost (MC) will increase. And we know that the main force behind supply is marginal cost (MC) and the supply curve is upward sloping from left to right due to increasing marginal cost or diminishing returns to labour. Secondly, as the level of employment and output increases the wage rate goes up. The reason is simple. When aggregate demand increases and more output is produced to meet the demand for goods and services, the (derived/indirect) demand for labour increases. This leads to a rise in the wage rate. In panel (a) of Figure 23.3, the economy is initially in macroeconomic equilibrium at point e, with the real GDP at Y_1 and the price level at P_1. Now due to a rightward shift

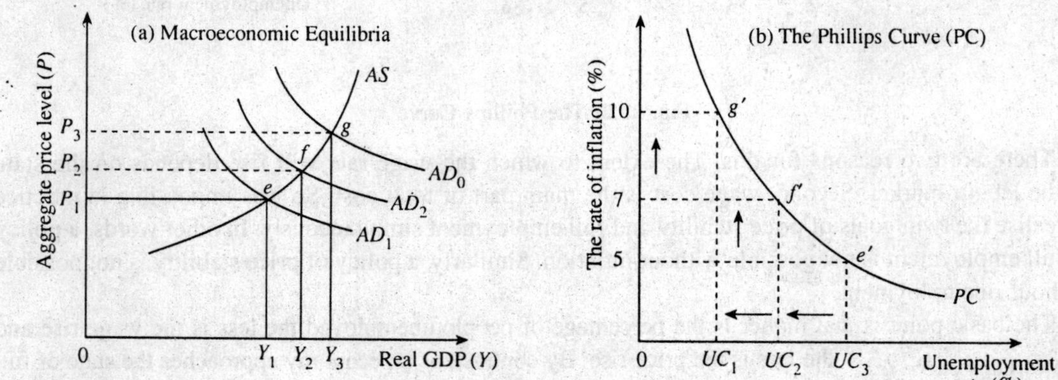

Fig. 23.3: The Keynesian Explanation of the Phillips Curve

of the aggregate demand curve from AD_1 to AD_2 and then from AD_2 to AD_3, both real GDP and aggregate price level rises from P_1 to P_2 and then from P_2 to P_3. Now an increase in output means an increase in the demand for labour. And an increase in the level of output implies a decrease in the level (rate) of unemployment. This point is illustrated in panel (b) of Figure 23.3. Every time aggregate price level (P) and real GDP (Y) increase in panel (a), the rate of unemployment falls in panel (b) from UC_3 to UC_2 and then from UC_2 to UC_1. This means that the rate of inflation increases from 5% to 7% and then from 7% to 10%. So we find an inverse relationship between inflation and unemployment. This relation is shown by the downward sloping Phillips curve (PC) in panel (b) of Figure 23.3.

THE SUBSEQUENT COLLAPSE OF THE PHILLIPS CURVE IN THE UK AND THE USA

In the two decades (1971-91) the stable short-run Phillips curve had disappeared in the USA. This means that both the rate of inflation and the rate of unemployment increased at the same time. So there was no trade-off between inflation and unemployment since a high rate of inflation was associated with a high rate of unemployment. See Fig. 23.4 which plots relevant data for two and a half decades (1971-96).

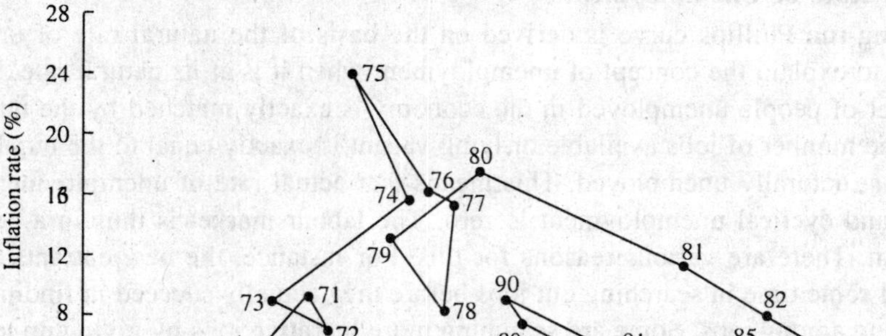

Fig. 23.4: Shift in Phillips Curve: United States

CAUSES OF SHIFT IN PHILLIPS CURVE

The main cause of the shift of the Phillips curve was adverse supply shock in the form of oil price hike by the OPEC cartel. Due to sharp increase in the price of crude oil, both production cost as also distribution (shipment/transportation) cost of almost all industries increased in October 1973. The price of oil has been raised several times since then. The oil price hike raises unit cost of production in those industries which use oil as the main or subsidiary input or as a source of energy. This point is illustrated in Figure 23.5.

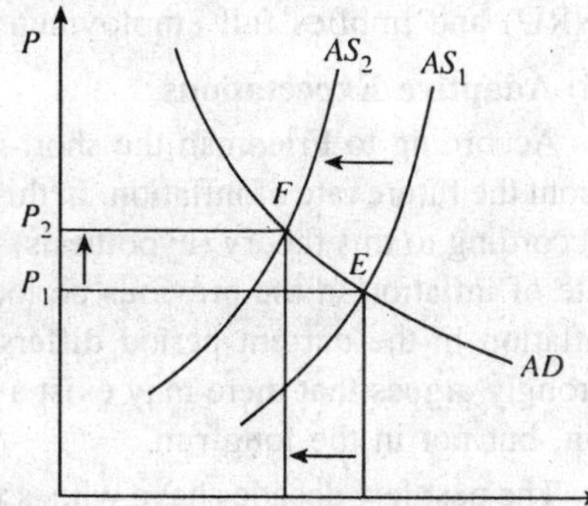

Fig. 23.5: Shift of the Phillips Curve Due to Adverse Supply Shock

Due to adverse supply shock the aggregate supply curve has shifted to the left[1] from AS_1 to AS_2. As a result equilibrium output fell from Y_1 to Y_2 and the price level rose from P_1 to P_2. A fall in output meant a fall in the level of employment or a rise in the level of unemployment and a rise in the price level implied an increase in the rate of inflation. Thus both unemployment and inflation increase at the same time. This amounted to a leftward shift of the Phillips curve or even a collapse of the original Phillips curve relation.

1. In truth, modern economists have derived the short-run Phillips curve from the short-run aggregate supply curve. So a leftward shift of the aggregate supply curve implies a corresponding shift of the Phillips curve. This implies breakdown of the short-run Phillips curve relation, or, the disappearance of inflation-unemployment trade-off.

THE NATURAL RATE OF UNEMPLOYMENT AND ADAPTIVE EXPECTATIONS

According to Milton Friedman and E. Phelps the inflation-unemployment trade-off exists only in the short run. But the relation between inflation and unemployment is not stable even in the short run since the Phillips curve may shift either to the right or to the left. However, in the long run since actual unemployment returns to its natural rate (which includes only frictional unemployment) and cyclical unemployment is zero, the long-run Phillips curve is vertical. This means that there is no trade-off between inflation and unemployment. So an expansionary monetary or fiscal policy will result in an accelerating rate of inflation with actual output coinciding with its potential level. This implies that money has a neutral effect on aggregate output and employment in the long run.

(i) The Natural Rate of Unemployment

Since the long-run Phillips curve is derived on the basis of the natural rate of unemployment (NRU), it seeks to explain the concept of unemployment when it is at its natural rate. This happens when the number of people unemployed in the economy is exactly matched by the number of jobs available, i.e., the number of jobs available or lying vacant is exactly equal to the number of people frictionally and structurally unemployed. This means that actual rate of unemployment is equal to its natural rate and cyclical unemployment is zero. The labour market is thus in a perpetual state of disequilibrium. There are various reasons for this. For instance, the new entrants in the labour force may spend some time in searching out jobs before they actually succeed in finding jobs. Some people are moving among jobs. Some are searching more lucrative jobs by giving up low paid jobs. Existing jobs may disappear in the declining industries like coal mining and expand in expanding industries like mobile phones. So there is both job creation and job loss at the same time. The unemployed workers are to be given sufficient training before they are absorbed in the expanding industries which offer new job opportunities only to skilled workers. Thus it is the sum of frictionally and structurally unemployed which constitutes the natural rate of employment (NRU). Since an equivalent number of jobs is available to the unemployed people, virtual-full employment or almost-complete-full employment exists. Thus an economy is in a situation of near-full employment, if the actual rate of unemployment does not exceed its natural rate. Since complete full employment is a myth, 4% to 5% unemployment constitutes the natural rate of employment (NRU) and implies full employment.

Full employment is said to exist if the actual rate of unemployment does not exceed its natural rate

(ii) Adaptive Expectations

According to Friedman the short-run Phillips curve shifts due to change in people's expectations about the future rate of inflation. In this context Friedman presented the theory of adaptive expectations. According to this theory (hypothesis) people form their expectations on the basis of past inflation (i.e. rate of inflation in the previous period). They change their expectations only when the actual rate of inflation in the current period differs from its expected rate. On the basis of this theory Friedman strongly argues that there may exist a trade-off between inflation and unemployment only in the short run, but not in the long run.

The past few decades have witnessed a synthesis of the old and new theories. Economists had come to realise that they must pay careful attention to expectations. In this context, a distinction may be drawn between the adaptive expectations (or backward-looking) approach and the rational expectations (or forward-looking) approach. The former approach holds that people form their expectations simply and mechanically on the basis of past information; the latter approach is based on the assumption that forecasts are unbiased and are based on all available information. For this reason, economists now realise the crucial importance of forward-looking expectations in understanding the behaviour of rational economic agents.

The expectations-augmented Phillips curve allows for the existence of a short-run trade-off between unemployment and inflation, but not for a long-run trade-off. The reason for this is that inflationary expectations are revised on the basis of actual rate of inflation in the past.

This assumption concerning the formation of expectations is called the adaptive expectations hypothesis.

Adaptive expectations hypothesis states that the expected rate of inflation is determined from observations of past rates of inflation

According to the **adaptive expectations hypothesis**, the expected rate of inflation is revised each period by adding on some proportion (say, λ) of the observed error in the previous period, where w lies between zero and one. For example, suppose that last year people expected a rate of inflation this year of 10%; if the actual rate turns out to be 16%, the expectation will have been in error by 6%. According to the adaptive expectations hypothesis, this year's expectation will be equal to last year's expectation (10%) plus some proportion (λ) of the error. So if $\lambda = 0.5$, this year's expected rate would be 13%; if $\lambda = 1$, this year's expected rate would be 16% (in this case, the expectation is said to have been fully adjusted); if $\lambda = 0$, the expectation would be 10% (that is, it would not have been adjusted at all). The proportion w is sometimes referred to as the *adjustment parameter*.

One result of this method of expectation formation is that the expected rate of inflation always lags behind the actual rate, though if the actual rate should remain constant the expected rate would eventually come to equal it. From this result we can predict that a short-run trade-off between unemployment and inflation exists, but that (so long as w is greater than zero) no long-run trade-off exists unless a continually rising rate of inflation is tolerated.

One problem with the adaptive expectations hypothesis is that it presumes that people do not learn from their past mistake. It was this criticism of the adaptive expectations hypothesis that led to the development of the rational expectations hypothesis.

No doubt, new classical approach to macroeconomics has brought many interesting and fruitful insights. What is crucially important is that most economic agents possess relevant and accurate information and act intelligently. They react to and often anticipate policy. This implies that their reaction and counteraction can change the actual behaviour of the real economy.

The theory of Friedman is illustrated in Figure 23.6. The economy is initially at point e on the short-run Phillips curve $SRPC_1$. This point shows that the natural rate of unemployment is 6.5% and the rate of inflation is 6%. Since the natural rate of employment (NRU) remains fixed, the rate of inflation depends on the level of aggregate demand. Here we also assume that the nominal wage has been fixed on the basis of the expectations that the rate of inflation will continue at 6% in the future, too.

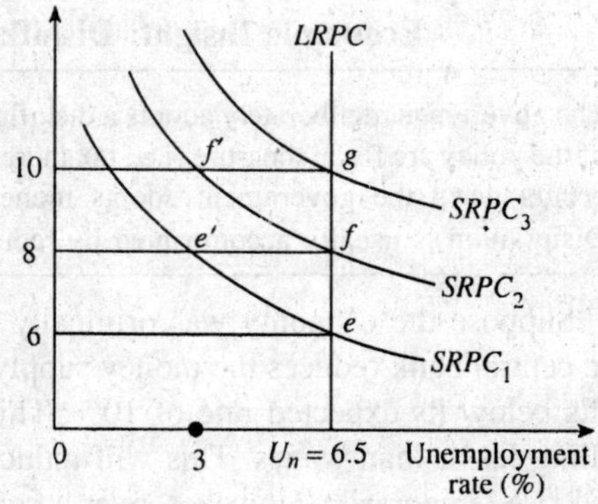

Fig. 23.6: Vertical Long-run Phillips Curve

Now if the government adopts expansionary monetary and fiscal policies to stimulate aggregate demand, the rate of inflation will rise to say 8%. Since the nominal wage rate has already been fixed, the higher rate of inflation would raise the profits of most firms. So they will get an incentive to increase their output of good and thus employ more workes. Consequently the economy will move to point e' on $SRPC_1$. This point corresponds to less unemployment (3%) since output has increased even at the high rate of inflation (8%). Thus we see that in making a transition from point e to point e' on $SRPC_1$, the economy has to tolerate a higher rate of inflation for reducing the rate of unemployment. So there is an inverse relation between inflation and unemployment, as has originally been postulated by the Phillips curve. However, the lower rate of unemployment is only a short-term phenomenon. Actual unemployment may deviate from its natural rate only in the short run. In the long run, unemployment will come back to its natural rate.

THE LONG-RUN PHILLIPS CURVE

In the long run workers will realise that since the actual rate of inflation has exceeded its expected rate, their real wage and real income have fallen. They will, therefore, demand higher nominal wage in order to prevent their real income from falling. If nominal wage rises the profits of businesses will fall to the original level. So they will employ less labour and unemployment will return to its natural rate of 6.5%. Thus with an increase in nominal wage the economy will move from point *e′* to *f*, i.e., from $SRPC_1$ to $SRPC_2$. At this point the rate of inflation remains the same (8%) in spite of an increase in unemployment rate (from 3% to 6.5%). Thus the higher rate of inflation caused by an increase in aggregate demand still persists. This means that at point *f*, which corresponds to 8% inflation, workers will expect the inflation rate to continue in the future. So the short-run Phillips curve shifts from $SRPC_1$ to $SRPC_2$.

Therefore the movement along the same Phillips curve is a purely temporary phenomenon. With the passage of time, nominal wage gets fully adjusted to the change in the rate of inflation. Consequently unemployment returns to its natural rate and a new short-run Phillips curve appears at the higher expected rate of inflation.

The same process described above will continue. In Fig. 26.6 economy will move from *f* to *f′* and then to *g* and another Phillips curve ($SRPC_3$) will appear, at a higher rate of inflation (10%) even at the natural rate of unemployment. In other words, as the economy makes a transition from one Phillips curve to another the rate of inflation rises even if unemployment remains the same. By connecting points such as *e*, *f* and *g* we derive the long-run Phillips curve, *LRPC* which is vertical. Since it is constructed on the basis of the expectations about the future rate of inflation, it is called inflationary-expectations augmented Phillips curve and the natural rate of unemployment (NRU) is called the non-accelearating inflation rate of unemployment (NAIRU). Thus there is no trade-off between inflation and unemployment in the long run.

Painless Disinflation

Friedman has also applied the theory of adaptive expectations to explain disinflation. Deflation is said to occur when the government adopts measures to bring the rate of inflation down.

Economic Insight: Disinflation — the Reduction of the Rate of Inflation
The government deliberately adopts a disinflationary policy in order to combat inflation. Two main instruments of the policy are fiscal measure (i.e., tax increase) and monetary measure (e.g., higher interest rate). Disinflation occurs when the government adopts monetary and fiscal measures to bring the rate of inflation down. Disinflation is usually accompanied by reduction in the level of national income.

Suppose the economy was originally at point *g*, with the rate of inflation at 10%. Now suppose the central bank reduces the money supply. As a result aggregate demand falls and the rate of inflation falls below its expected rate of 10%. This will lead to a fall in business profits since prices will be falling faster than wages. This will induce firms to employ less workers. So the unemployment rate will rise temporarily. However, over a period of time firms and workers will revise their expectations and unemployment will return to its natural rate. This process will be repeated and the economy will move along the vertical *LRPC*. This implies that the rate of inflation will fall even at the same natural rate of unemployment. This is known as painless disinflation, i.e., reduction in the rate of inflation without a rise in the rate of unemployment.

The basic message of Friedman's hypothesis is clear. Actual unemployment may deviate from its natural rate only in the short-run. In the long-run unemployment returns to its natural rate, irrespective of the rate of inflation.

THE THEORY OF RATIONAL EXPECTATIONS AND THE LONG-RUN PHILLIPS CURVE (*LRPC*)

When actual rate of unemployment is equal to its natural rate actual output is equal to its potential level

According to the theory of rational expectations, which is a variant of the natural rate hypothesis, nominal wages tend to lag behind the rate of inflation. However, since nominal wages get adjusted quickly to any expected change in the price level, there is no trade-off between inflation and unemployment. Since workers and businesses fully and correctly anticipate the rate of inflation arising from an increase in aggregate demand, the price rise gets fully and correctly incorporated into the wage agreements. As wages rise, firms raise the prices of products, too. This point is illustrated in Figure 23.7, where we see that everytime an increase in aggregate demand leads to a rise in the price level. But real GDP remains unchanged at the level. Thus the long-run aggregate supply curve (*LRAS*) is vertical as shown in panel (a). So the long-run phillips curve (*LRPC*) is also vertical, as shown is panel (b).

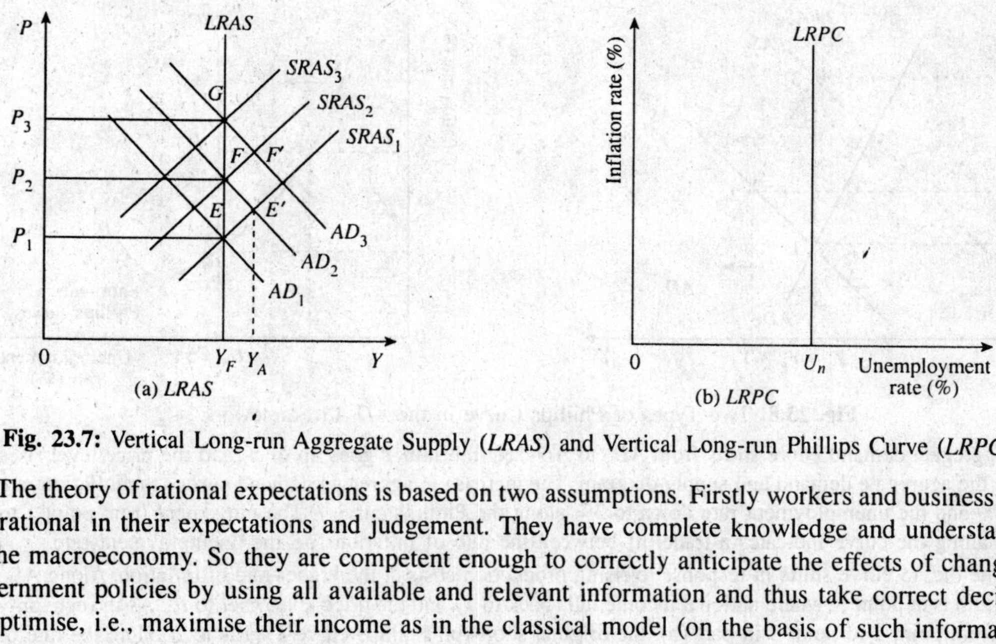

Fig. 23.7: Vertical Long-run Aggregate Supply (*LRAS*) and Vertical Long-run Phillips Curve (*LRPC*)

The theory of rational expectations is based on two assumptions. Firstly workers and business firms are rational in their expectations and judgement. They have complete knowledge and understanding of the macroeconomy. So they are competent enough to correctly anticipate the effects of changes in government policies by using all available and relevant information and thus take correct decisions to optimise, i.e., maximise their income as in the classical model (on the basis of such information).

New commodity prices are established on the basis of new information about the economy

Secondly, much like classical economists the rational expectations theorists assume that all product and factor markets are fairly competitive. Accordingly wages and prices of the products are completely flexible and, therefore, move up or down in response to changes in economic situations. The theory of rational expectations postulates that all new information about the economy due to the changes in technology or supply shocks (such as crop failure or oil price hike) or changes in government policy gets quickly incorporated in the market demand and supply curves. So new equilibrium prices adjust to new economic events and policies immediately.

The Phillips curve relation, on the basis of rational expectation hypothesis, is illustrated in Fig. 23.7. The economy is initially in equilibrium at point E where the aggregate demand curve AD_1 intersects both the short-run aggregate supply curve $SRAS_1$ and the long-run aggregate supply curve $LRAS$. So the price level is P_1 at the full employment level of output Y_E. Now suppose the government increases the money supply. The adoption of this expansionary monetary policy will increase aggregate demand (expenditure). So the aggregate demand curve shifts to the right to AD_1. Now workers, savers and businesses will correctly anticipate this policy change and adjust their behaviour accordingly. Workers will demand higher wages and succeed in getting it. The suppliers of loanable funds will raise the rate of interest. And business firms will raise the prices of their products. All these things will happen immediately. As a result the short-run aggregate supply curve will shift to the left from $SRAS_1$ to $SRAS_2$. Consequently the price level will rise to P_2. Since the increase in aggregate demand gets fully reflected in nominal wages, interest rates and prices, real wages, real interest rates and real GDP will remain unchanged. Thus any anticipated changes in government policy has neutral effect on these key macroeconomic variables.

Economic Insight: Aggregate Demand and Aggregate Supply Curves and the Phillips Curve

The movement from point 1 to point 2 to point 3 in Fig. 23.8 shows the adjustment of the economy to an increase in aggregate demand. Point 1 is the initial equilibrium in both diagrams. At this point potential real GDP is $Y_1 = Y_F$ and the price level is P_1 in the aggregate demand and supply-diagram or in panel (a) and the inflation rate is 3% with an unemployment rate of 5% (the natural rate) along the short-run curve *I* in the Phillips curve diagram or in panel (b).

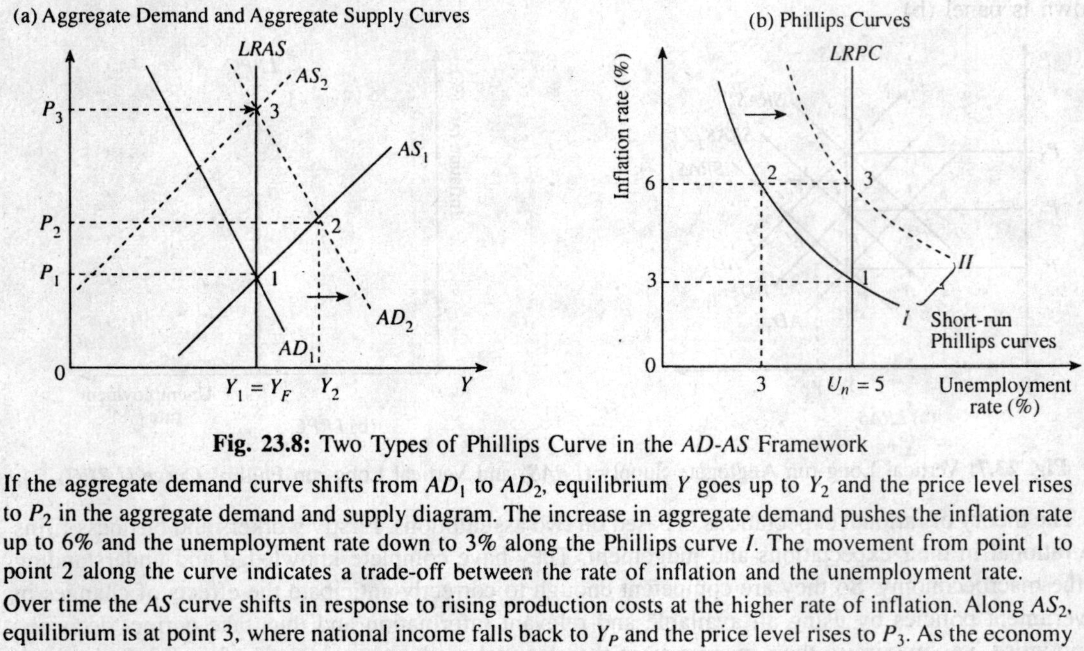

Fig. 23.8: Two Types of Phillips Curve in the *AD-AS* Framework

If the aggregate demand curve shifts from AD_1 to AD_2, equilibrium *Y* goes up to Y_2 and the price level rises to P_2 in the aggregate demand and supply diagram. The increase in aggregate demand pushes the inflation rate up to 6% and the unemployment rate down to 3% along the Phillips curve *I*. The movement from point 1 to point 2 along the curve indicates a trade-off between the rate of inflation and the unemployment rate.

Over time the *AS* curve shifts in response to rising production costs at the higher rate of inflation. Along AS_2, equilibrium is at point 3, where national income falls back to Y_P and the price level rises to P_3. As the economy moves from point 2 to point 3 in part (b), the original short-run Phillips curve *I* shifts to *II*. Here the rate of inflation remains high (at 6%), while the unemployment rate rises and returns to up to 5%, i.e., its natural rate or the rate which is consistent with real GNP at Y_P. In the long run, then, there is no trade-off between inflation and unemployment. The vertical long-run aggregate supply curve at the potential level of real GNP is associated with the vertical long-run Phillips curve at the natural rate of unemployment.

In the theory of rational expectations the economy does not move from point *E* to *E′* along the same short-run aggregate supply (*SRAS*) curve. Instead when the aggregate demand curve shifts to the right, the short-run aggregate supply curve shifts to the left due to instantaneous adjustment of prices, wages as also interest rates. The reason is that fully informed economic agents can anticipate the rate of inflation correctly. As a result the new macroeconomic equilibrium is attained at point *F* which corresponds to a higher price level P_2 in Fig. 23.7(a). The process is repeated every time such changes occur.

Economic Insight: The Relevance of Rational Expectations Hypothesis

According to the rational expectations hypothesis, workers and business firms can quickly incorporate the changes in the expected rate of inflation in fixing wages and prices. So there is no trade-off between inflation and unemployment and the long-run Phillips curve (*LRPC*) is vertical. This means that the short-run Phillips curve (*SRPC*) showing trade-off between inflation and unemployment does not indicate the correct options which are available to policy-making authorities.

This means that if any change in government policy is correctly anticipated by economic agents it will not be effective and may have neutral effect on the economy. If economic agents get adjusted completely to the expected rate of inflation, a policy change will have no effect on investment, employment and real GDP. This is why the long-run aggregate supply curve (*LRAS*) is vertical at potential GDP. This implies that there is no trade-off between inflation and unemployment in the long run. Thus an increase in aggregate demand will only cause inflation. It will fail to reduce unemployment.

According to rational expectations hypothesis, the long-run Phillips curve (LRAS) is vertical at the full level of GDP due to correct anticipation of the rate of inflation by workers and other input suppliers

If the actual rate of inflation exceeded the expected rate, the actual unemployment rate would have fallen below the natural rate and actual real GDP would have exceeded the potential level. It would be Y_A as is indicated by point *E′* in panel (a) of Figure 23.7.

Thus the long-run Phillips curve (*LRPC*) is vertical because it is derived from long-run-aggregate supply (*LRAS*) curve which is vertical at full employment. The *LRPC* shows the relationship between inflation and unemployment when the actual rate of inflation equals the expected rate. The vertical *LRPC* shows that macroeconomic equilibrium is always reached at the natural rate of unemployment whatever may be the expected rate of inflation.

THE RELATIONSHIP BETWEEN SHORT-RUN PHILLIPS CURVE (*SRPC*) AND LONG-RUN PHILLIPS CURVE (*LRPC*)

It is interesting to know the relationship between the two types of Phillips curve—*SRPC* and the *LRPC*. In Figure 23.9 we see that the $SRPC_1$ passes through point *E* on the *LRPC*. The position of the *SRPC* depends on the expected rate of inflation. The *SRPC* is drawn with a given expected rate of inflation. However, it will shift if there is a change in the expected rate of inflation. Thus if the expected rate of inflation is 9% per annum, then $SRPC_1$ passes through point *E* on the *LRPC* with natural rate of unemployment (*NRU*) at U_n. We know that any movement along a *SRPC* occurs due to a change in aggregate demand. If there is an anticipated increase in aggregate demand then the actual rate of inflation will exceed its expected rate and real GDP will increase. As a result unemployment will fall and the economy moves upward to the left from point *E* to *E′* on the same $SRPC_1$. The converse is also true. If there is an unanticipated fall in aggregate demand then actual rate of inflation will fall below its expected rate. So unemployment will increase above its natural rate. Consequently the economy will move downward to the right from point *E* to point *E″* along the same $SRPC_1$.

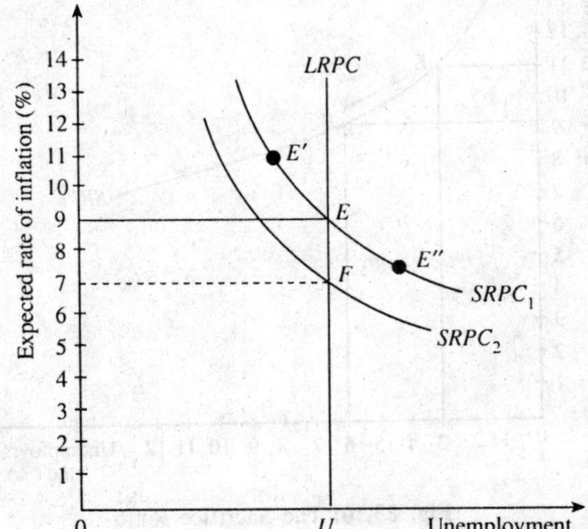

Fig. 23.9: Shifts in the *SRPC* along the same *LRPC*

SHIFTS IN THE SHORT-RUN PHILLIPS CURVE (*SRPC*)

However, if there is a change in the expected rate of inflation, the *SRPC* shifts to a new position. For example, if the expected rate of inflation is 9% per annum, the short-run Phillips curve is $SRPC_1$. If the expected rate of inflation falls to 7%, there is a downward shift of the short-run Phillips curve to $SRPC_2$. The new *SRPC* curve intersects the vertical *LRPC* curve at point *F*. The vertical distance between point *E* and *F* depends on the change in the expected rate of inflation. This point may now be explained.

Suppose initially the expected rate of inflation is 10%. In order to slow down the rate of inflation, the central bank adopts a contractionary monetary policy. If it reduces the money supply, the aggregate demand curve shifts downward. Consequently the rate of inflation falls to, say, 7% per annum. It is to be noted here that initially people are unable to anticipate the inflation rate. So wages and other input prices continue to rise at the expected inflation rate of 10%. And there is a rightward movement along the same *SRPC*. Consequently the unemployment rate rises and goes above the natural rate and as a consequence the real GDP falls.

However, when the rate of inflation remains steady at 7% per annum, people expect this rate to continue in the future, too. When this happens, increase in wages and factor prices slows down and with the increase in aggregate demand, actual unemployment rate falls to the natural rate and the real GDP increases. Consequently, the *SRPC* shifts downward to the new position $SRPC_2$ which corresponds to a lower expected rate of inflation of 7% per annum.

THE SACRIFICE RATIO AND THE POLICY OF DISINFLATION

One of the main objectives of macroeconomic policy is to reduce the rate of inflation. This is known as disinflation. However, economic life is full of trade-offs. To get something a society has to give up something else. There is no free lunch in economics. In truth, if an economy seeks to reduce the rate of inflation, it will have to tolerate more unemployment. This means that some output or potential GDP will be lost. As Figure 23.10 shows if the society has to reduce the rate of inflation from 11% to 9%, unemployment increases from 3% to 6%. As a result real GDP will fall. The amount of output lost due to every 1% fall in inflation rate is measured by the sacrifice ratio. To be more specific, it is the ratio of cumulative loss of GDP (as a result of disinflation policy) to the reduction of inflation that is actually achieved. Suppose every 1% fall in the rate of inflation leads to 2% increase in cyclical unemployment. And every 1% increase in cyclical unemployment leads to $2^1/_2$% fall in real GDP. So if the rate of inflation has to be reduced to 1%, the society has to tolerate (sacrifice) an output loss of 5%. So we can write:

Fig. 23.10: The Sacrifice Ratio

$$\text{Thus } s = \frac{\text{Percentage fall in real GDP}}{\text{Percentage fall in the rate of inflation}} = \frac{5\%}{1\%} = 5, \text{ where } s \text{ is the sacrifice ratio.}$$

Focus on Terminology: The Sacrifice Ratio

To reduce inflation, tight monetary and fiscal policies are to be used to slow the growth rate of aggregate demand. However, if economic agents fail to anticipate these policies perfectly, they will also cause employment and output to fall below the full employment levels at least for a time. This loss of employment and output is an important cost that must be weighed against the benefits of inflation-reducing policies.

The sacrifice ratio measures the cost of lowering the inflation rate. It is the amount of output lost when the inflation rate is reduced by one percentage point.

However, it is not very easy to determine exactly how much output loss can be attributed to a particular set of anti-inflationary policies. For example, to calculate the loss of output owing to disinflation it is necessary to measure the volume of output if there had been no disinflation. This is not an easy task. If the calculation of output loss is wrong, the sacrifice ratio will also be wrong. Factors such as supply shocks, which affect both output and inflation, can also distort the calculation of sacrifice ratio. Thus, at best, the sacrifice ratio is a rough and ready (or a crude) measure of the cost of reducing inflation.

The sacrifice ratio for any economy will be lower if disinflationary pressure is applied steadily. In addition, the ratio is likely to be lower if the authorities' commitment to reducing inflation is regarded as credible.

THE CHANGE IN THE SACRIFICE RATIO

Inflation reduction invariably causes a recession. The costs of disinflation are measured by the sacrifice ratio. It is the ratio of the cumulative percentage loss of GDP (as a result of a disinflation policy) to the reduction in the rate of inflation which is actually achieved. Thus suppose a policy reduces the rate of inflation from 10% to 4% over a three year plan at the cost of loss of output which is 10% below potential in the first year, 8% below potential in the second year, and 6% below potential in the third year. The total loss of GDP is therefore 24% (= 10 + 8 + 6), the reduction in inflation is 6% (10 – 4) and the sacrifice ratio is 4%.

Now-a-days economists pay careful attention to expectations. A useful distinction is between adaptive (or 'backward-looking') approach and the rational (or 'forward-looking') approach. The adaptive expectations approach holds that people form their expectations simply and mechanically on the basis of past information. The forward-looking or rational expectations approach holds that people use all available information before taking decisions.

The sacrifice ratio is low if the inflation rate is low. And the inflation rate is low if the economy benefits from the credible policy of the central bank as inflation fighter.

Creditability always plays a role in stopping hyperinflation. The central bank is able to establish creditability by keeping its promises. No doubt, credibility is an important aspect of policy-making. But its role has been exaggerated by the proponents of rational expectations hypotheses. In spite of this the major European hyperinflations had, as a result of a credible reform of monetary and fiscal policies, ended rapidly and at very little cost in terms of foregone (lost) output. Thus as an economy makes a transition from adaptive to rational expectations, the sacrifice ratio is likely to fall if, of course, the central bank is able to establish its credibility regarding contractionary monetary policy. This will reduce people's inflationary expectations. So the Phillips curve will shift to the left, unemployment rate will fall and not much output will be lost in the process.

TWO ALTERNATIVE STRATEGIES TO REDUCE INFLATION

Suppose the rate of inflation in the economy is 7% and the government decides to fight high inflation, intending to try to get the economy down to the inflation rate of, say, 2%. Governments often face this problem of how to deflate. This is known as *inflation targeting*. Under this rule the central bank would announce a target for the inflation rate (usually a low one) and then adjust the money supply when the actual inflation deviates from the target. Inflation targeting has the advantage that it insulates the economy from the effects of changes in the velocity of circulation of money.

The key questions for any government contemplating disinflation is how to disinflate in a virtually painless fashion—that is, with as small a recession as possible. Two alternative strategies for disinflation, i.e., reducing the growth rate of aggregate demand by cutting back on the money supply growth and thus shifting the *AD* curve to the left are the following:

(i) **Gradualism**

A policy of gradualism, shown in Fig. 23.11(a), attempts a slow and steady return to low inflation. The gradualist policy starts with a small reduction in the money supply growth rate that shifts the aggregate demand curve down from *AD* to *AD′*, moving the economy along the short-run aggregate supply curve, *SRAS*, from *e* to e_1. In response to lower inflation rate at e_1, the short-run supply curve shifts downward to *SRAS′*. A further decline in the money supply growth moves the economy to e_2, the aggregate supply curve shifts down again to *SRAS″* and the process continues.

Ultimately output returns to its full employment level at point *e′*, i.e., at a lower inflation rate. There is not much recession during the adjustment process, although actual unemployment exceeds its natural rate through the entire adjustment process (implying positive cyclical unemployment).

(ii) **Cold Turkey**

The alternative— cold turkey— solution to inflation is shown in Fig. 23.11(b). It seeks to cut the inflation rate very fast. For example, a rapid disinflation would lower output by 10% for 2 years. The strategy starts with an immediate sharp cut-back in the money supply growth, shifting the aggregate demand curve from *AD* to *AD′* and moving the economy from *e* to e_1. There is a deep recession, but because the aggregate supply curve is relatively flat, the reduction in inflation is small to begin with.

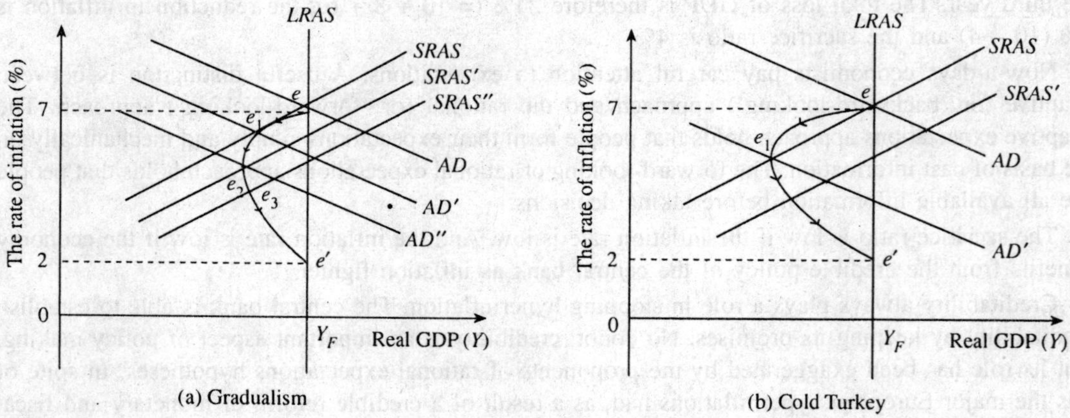

Fig. 23.11: Two Alternative Disinflation Strategies

By creating a large fall in the inflation rate than when gradualism is used, the cold turkey strategy causes the short-run supply curve to move down faster than it does. The cold turkey strategy keeps up the pressure by holding the rate of money supply growth low. Ultimately the rate of inflation falls so fast that output and employment gradually start rising. The economy returns to point *e′* with full employment and lower rate of inflation.

Gradualism Vs. Cold Turkey

We may now make a comparison of the above two scenarios. Fig. 23.12 presents the gradualist and cold turkey strategies in an alternative form. In the gradualist strategy the growth rate of money (*m*) is initially reduced only slightly, and the economy never moves away from the natural rate of unemployment. But the inflation rate (π) comes down only slowly. The cold turkey strategy, by contrast, starts with a huge cut in growth rate of money supply and a deep recession. The recession is much worse than it ever is in the gradualist strategy, but the reduction in inflation rate is much rapid.

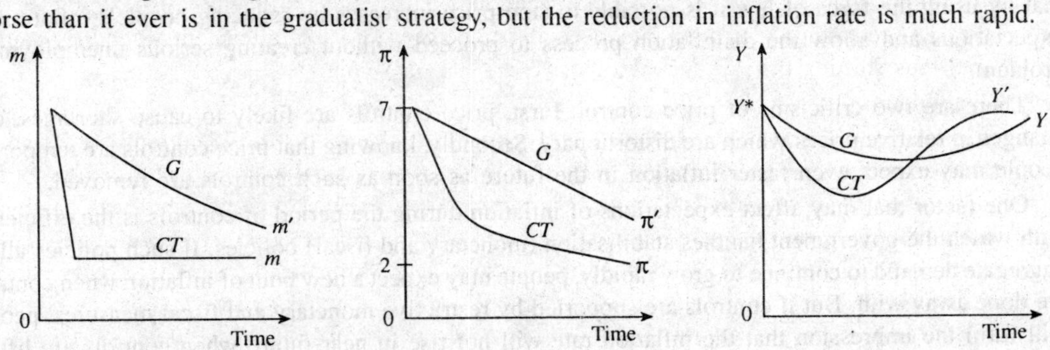

Fig. 23.12: Comparing Two Disinflation Strategies

The choice of the correct strategy is a complex task. It depends on the costs of the two social evils—inflation and unemployment.

Theory and Evidence

Historical evidence suggests that the reductions in inflation always come at the cost of temporarily lower output. Yet the size of the output loss varied from country to country and period to period. Rapid disinflations usually had smaller sacrifice ratios than slower ones. That is, in contrast with what the Phillips curve with adaptive expectations suggests, a cold-turkey approach is less costly than the gradualist one.

STRATEGIES TO REDUCE INFLATIONARY EXPECTATIONS

The policymakers can adopt various ways of reducing people's inflationary expectations. Three suggested approaches for reducing both inflation and inflationary expectation are the following:

1. Rapid Vs. Gradual disinflation

Disinflation can be implemented quickly by a rapid and drastic reduction in the growth rate of the money supply. This strategy, as already noted, is known as *cold-turkey* approach. This is the classical view. Since a cold-turkey disinflation is dramatic and clearly visible to the public, the supporters of this approach argue that it will quickly and substantially reduce peoples' inflationary expectations, particularly if the policy is announced well in advance. If expected rate of inflation falls sufficiently, the *LRPC* suggests that the costs of disinflation in terms of lost employment (increased unemployment) can be minimised.

The opponents, viz., Keynesians, however, argue that the cold-turkey strategy may not lower inflationary expectations, since people may expect the government to abandon the policy if the resulting unemployment is not politically acceptable. So Keynesians recommend a policy of *gradualism*, i.e., reducing the rate of money supply growth and inflation slowly and gradually over a number of years. It is suggested that a gradualist approach—which gives prices, wages and expectations more time to adjust to the disinflation—will raise the unemployment rate by less than the cold-turkey strategy. However, the time period during which unemployment exceeds the natural rate (i.e., implying positive cyclical unemployment) may be longer. It is also argued that, since the policy will be taken as politically sustainable, gradualism will be as effective as the cold-turkey approach in reducing inflationary expectations.

2. Incomes policy (wage and price controls)

Due to various costs and difficulties associated with money supply reduction for controlling inflation some countries like Great Britain and Sweden have adopted a more direct approach to inflation control in the form of imposition of wage and price controls. Acts have been passed to limit the ability of firms to raise wages and/or prices. Supporters of wage-price controls (also called incomes policy) argue that by using the force of law it is possible to stop price increases by reducing people's inflationary expectations and allow the disinflation process to proceed without creating serious unemployment problem.

There are two criticisms of price control. First, price controls are likely to cause shortages, and changes in relative prices which are distortionary. Secondly, knowing that price controls are temporary people may expect even faster inflation in the future as soon as such controls are removed.

One factor that may affect expectations of inflation during the period of controls is the efficiency with which the government handles stabilisation (monetary and fiscal) policies. If such policies allow aggregate demand to continue to grow rapidly, people may expect a new bout of inflation when controls are done away with. But if controls are supported by restrictive monetary and fiscal measures, people will form the impression that the inflation rate will not rise in near future when controls are lifted.

3. Credibility and reputation

Finally, for achieving disinflation without high unemployment costs, it is absolutely essential to reduce people's expected inflation rate. And, perhaps, the most important factor determining how quickly expected inflation adjusts is the credibility or believability of the government's announced disinflationary policy. If the government or the central bank announces a policy to reduce the inflation rate—and if workers, consumers and firms believe that the government will surely do what it says—the expected rate of inflation should fall fairly rapidly.

The easiest way for the government to improve its credibility with the public is to develop a reputation for carrying through its promises. Then when it announces a disinflation programme, people are likely to take this announcement at face value. They will believe what the government says.

One way of achieving credibility is to give autonomy to the central bank so that it is not required to function as a government department. A strong and independent central bank is likely to have credibility with the public when it announces a disinflationary policy. So long as the central bank acts as a government organisation, it will always be under political pressure when unemployment rises. So an announced disinflationary programme is likely to be less credible.

RATIONAL EXPECTATIONS AND THE POSSIBILITY OF PAINLESS DISINFLATION

An alternative approach to adaptive expectations has been suggested, viz., rational expectations. The rational expectations hypothesis (REH) was popularised by J.F. Muth and R. Lucas. The basic idea is simple enough. One might reasonably assume that people make optimal use of all the available information—including information about current government policies—to forecast the future. Since the current rate of inflation is considerably influenced by monetary and fiscal policies, expected inflation should also depend on the effectiveness of current demand-management policies. The theory of rational expectations suggests that a change in monetary or fiscal policy will change expectations. So an evaluation of any policy change has to be based on the effect of such change on people's expectations. And, therefore, any policy change has to be evaluated by taking into account the effect of policy change(s) on people's expectations. If people do form their expectations rationally, then the inflation inertia will be less intense than it appeared at the first sight.

The REH states that individuals take into account all available information in determining the expected rate of inflation

The supporters of rational expectations argue that the short-run Phillips curve fails to represent clearly and accurately the options open to the policymakers. If people see that the policymakers always keep their commitments, then people will reduce their expectations of inflation as soon as the policymakers are credibly committed to keep the inflation rate down. If the policymakers have the reputation of keeping their commitments, the inflation rate may fall without a rise in unemployment or fall in output. Under a credible policy, the sacrifice ratio will be very small, or negligible.

The problem of maintaining price stability in the face of price shocks is inseparably linked up with an alternative type of price stabilisation programme, viz., bringing down the rate of inflation when it has become too high and has become incorporated into people's expectations and price-setting behaviour. This, as noted above, is known as the problem of *disinflation*, that is, bringing down the rate of inflation. Developing a disinflation policy requires close attention to the role of expectations in the Phillips curve.

The Phillips curve tells us that, if the policymakers consider the inflation rate as too high and has to be brought down, then some sort of a recession is inevitable. The basic policy question related to disinflation is: How deep and prolonged the recession should be? So the pertinent question here is: How strongly should the policymakers use the policy instruments to bring about such a path for real GDP which is fairly consistent with the desired reduction in inflation?

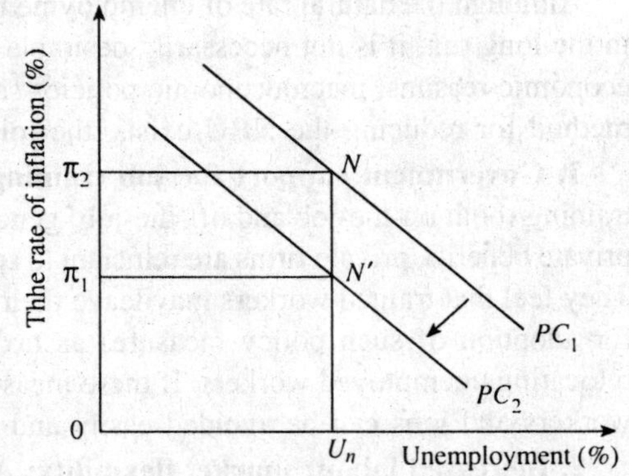

Fig. 23.13: Painless Disinflation and Irrelevance of Sacrifice Ratio

There are two requirements of painless disinflation. First, the policymakers should announce their plan to bring inflation down before workers and business firms, who set wages and prices, have formed their expectations. Secondly, the workers and firms have to take the announcement at face value. Reputation is a big factor here. Otherwise, they are unlikely to revise their inflationary expectations downward. If both requirements are fulfilled, the short-run Phillips curve will shift downward. This implies that the inflation rate will fall from π_1 to π_2 even at the same rate of unemployment as Fig. 23.13 shows.

Economic Insight: Rational Expectations and the Phillips Curve

The rational expectations hypothesis states that individuals take into account all available information in determining the expected rate of inflation. According to the hypothesis, individuals (and all other economic agents) take all the information available to them into consideration in forming their inflationary expectations, not just past inflation rates. This means that they take into account such information as what is happening to the money supply (since by assumption they believe that money supply growth is the cause of inflation) and what is happening to such factors as world oil prices, trade union militancy and the exchange rate (depending on which of these are perceived as major determinants of inflation). As long as people believe that policy-makers are committed to reducing inflation, then changes in economic policy variables (if announced beforehand) will be anticipated by adjustments in inflationary expectations which will then cause a shift in the short-run Phillips curve.

With rational expectations formation there will be no *systematic prediction errors and the inflation rate is likely to be predicted more accurately and more quickly.* This implies that a trade-off between unemployment and inflation may exist only in the very short term. Indeed, some New Classical economists (who subscribe to the rational expectations hypothesis) claim that even the short run Phillips curve may be vertical, in which case there is no trade-off.

The New Classical version of the theory implies that a change in an economic policy variable which is believed to affect inflation (or simply the *announcement* of a change in such a variable) will be anticipated *immediately* by an adjustment of inflationary expectations. To show this, suppose that unemployment is initially at the 'natural rate' and that both the actual and expected rates of inflation are zero. Now let the government announce that it plans to increase the money supply by 6% over the coming year. Economic agents will take this information into consideration and immediately adjust the expected rate of inflation to 6%. This suggests that both the short-and long-run Phillips curves are vertical at the natural rate of unemployment (NRU). It also means that the anticipated monetary policy will be totally ineffective in influencing output and employment, in either the short run or the long run. Rational expectations theory has been criticised for assuming that economic agents are able to form expectations as if they knew. the 'correct' model of the economy. This is clearly an unreasonable assumption.

Since expectations of inflation influence the short-run trade-off between inflation and unemployment, the credibility of monetary or fiscal policy to reduce inflation largely affects the social cost of the policy change. However, the sad truth is that most people do not view the announcement of a new policy as credible.

GOVERNMENT POLICIES TO REDUCE THE NATURAL RATE OF UNEMPLOYMENT

Although the natural rate of unemployment (NRU) is the rate toward which the economy gravitates in the long run, it is not necessarily desirable or optimal. So it is often argued that, for various socio-economic reasons, macroeconomic policies should be used to lower the NRU. Although no foolproof method for reducing the NRU exists, the following strategies may be suggested:

1. Government support for job training and worker relocation: Since worker education and training (both on-the-job and off-the-job) generates positive externalities (i.e., social benefit exceeding private benefit), private firms are reluctant to spend much money for educating and training the workers. They feel that trained workers may leave their companies and join rival organisations. So there is need for adoption of such policy measures as tax concessions (exemptions) or subsidies for training or relocating unemployed workers. If these measures are effectively implemented, the mismatch between workers and jobs can be avoided easily and quickly and the NRU will fall.

2. Increased labour market flexibility: At present, due to various types of government interventions in the labour market and regulations in the form of minimum wage laws, fixation of hours of work, and workers' fringe benefits, dismissing a worker is difficult, if not impossible.

These regulations are imposed with good intentions. But they have undesirable effects. They increase the cost of hiring additional workers, particularly workers with inadequate skills and lack of experience. So there is need to review new and existing labour market regulations carefully to ensure that benefits outweigh the costs they impose on society in terms of job loss.

3. Reform of unemployment insurance scheme: Unemployment insurance (UI) lengthens the period over which the unemployeds search for jobs. It also increases the incentives for employers to retrench workers in slack seasons. So there is need for reform of UI. For example, additional taxes may be imposed to force employers, who use temporarily unemployed workers extensively, to bear a greater portion of the unemployment benefits that their workers receive. This will automatically reduce the incentives of employers to lay-off workers during slack seasons.

4. Creating a high-pressure economy: Supporters of the hysteresis theory argue that if monetary and fiscal policies are used aggressively to keep unemployment as low as possible — a 'high-pressure' economy — then, following the principles of hysteresis, the NRU will ultimately fall. So, for example, if current employment is stimulated by monetary expansion, workers may be able to acquire more on-the-job training. This will surely reduce mismatch and lower NRU in the long run. Critics, however, apprehend that a high-pressure strategy would add fuel to the existing inflationary fire.

Conclusion

Whether minimising the NRU is a universal goal is not yet clear. Minimum wages, unemployment benefits, and taxes have other important implications besides their effect on NRU. So these variables should not be assessed solely in terms of their effect(s) on unemployment.

KEY POINTS

1. ***Inflation-unemployment trade-off*** **:** In the Keynesian model there is no trade-off between inflation and unemployment, because the end of full employment is the beginning of inflation. However, in 1958 A. W. Phillips showed in the context of the UK economy, an inverse relationship between inflation and unemployment. So the distinction between demand-pull and cost-push inflation disappeared.

2. *The Phillips curve* : The trade-off between inflation and unemployment is shown by the Phillips curve. The original Phillips curve relationship was derived on the basis of the inverse relationship between unemployment and rate of change of money wages. Modern economists have reinterpreted the Phillips curve by showing an inverse relationship between unemployment and inflation.

3. *The long-run Phillips curve* : The trade-off (or inverse relation between employment and inflation) holds only in the short run. There is no such trade-off in the long run when people form and revise their expectations about inflation. So the long-run Phillips curve is vertical and is called inflationary-expectations-augmented Phillips curve. It is based on the concept of natural rate of unemployment and the natural rate hypothesis, a term introduced by Milton Friedman and revised and modified by E. Phelps.

4. *Adaptive expectations* : Friedman's long-run Phillips curve is associated with an important hypothesis, viz., adaptive expectations. The hypothesis is backward looking in nature. Due to incorporation of the expectational hypothesis, the trade-off between inflation and unemployment disappears completely in the long run.

5. *Disinflation* : Freidman has also applied the theory of adaptive expectations to explain disinflation. Disinflation occurs when the government deliberately adopts monetary and fiscal measures to bring the rate of inflation down.

6. *Rational expectations* : According to the rational expectations hypothesis, presented by T.F. Muth and Robert Lucas, workers and business firms can quickly incorporate the changes in the expected rate of inflation in fixing wages and prices. So there is no trade-off between inflation and unemployment even in the short run. This is another explanation of the vertical shape of the Phillips curve.

7. *Sacrifice ratio* : The term 'sacrifice ratio' is used to refer to the amount of GDP which is lost due to an increase in unemployment rate needed to bring the rate of inflation down by every 1%. If an economy makes a transition from adaptive to rational expectations, the sacrifice ratio is likely to fall, if the central bank's committment to reducing inflation is regarded as credible.

8. *Strategies to reduce inflation* : Two alternative strategies to reduce inflation are (i) gradualism and (ii) cold-turkey. A policy of gradualism attempts a slow and steady return to low inflation. The cold-turkey solution seeks to cut the inflation rate very fast.

9. *Strategies to reduce inflationary expectations* : Three strategies to reduce inflationary expectations are (i) reduction in the money supply, (ii) wage and price controls and (iii) credibility and reputation.

10. *Painless disinflation* : Painless disinflation occurs when policymakers succeed in bringing the rate of inflation down without allowing the rate of (cyclical) unemployment to rise. When this is achieved, the sacrifice ratio becomes irrelevant. There are two requirements of painless disinflation.

11. *Government policies to reduce the natural rate of unemployment* : The macroeconomic policies are often used to lower the natural rate of unemployment. Four measures can be adopted by the government so as to achieve this goal, viz., (i) support for job training and worker relocation, (ii) increased labour market flexibility, (iii) reform of unemployment insurance scheme and (iv) creating a high-pressure economy.

KEY TERMS

Stagflation
Vertical Phillips curve
Cold-turkey approach
Disinflation
Credibility
Commitment
Adaptive expectations
Non-accelerating inflationary rate of unemployment (NAIRU)
Inflation-unemployment trade-off
Sacrifice ratio
Gradualist approach
Painless disinflation
Reputation
Natural rate of unemployment (NRU)
Rational expectations
Inflationary-expectations-augmented Phillips Curve

ASSIGNMENTS

1. Is a policy of full employment possible without inflation? Argue logically.
2. Discuss some meaning which can be adopted by the government to reduce the natural rate of unemployment.
3. Does unemployment insurance reduce NRU?
4. Can a modern mixed economy achieve full employment and price level stability simultaneously?
5. In what sense the Phillips curve shows the society's menu of choice? What are the policy implications of short-run Phillips curve (SRPC)?
6. Explain the short-run trade-off between inflation and unemployment. Why does the trade-off disappear in the long-run?
7. What is the essence of rational expectations hypothesis (REH)? How does the hypothesis show that the aggregate supply curve is vertical?
8. Explain why the SRPC is downward sloping and LRPC is vertical.
9. Does the trade-off between inflation and unemployment disappear both in the short-run and in long-run if the national expectations hypothesis hold?
10. Differentiate between adaptive and rational expectation. Under rational expectation, the Phillips relation fails to hold. Why? What is the implication of this failure for the supply curve?

CHAPTER 24

Inflation: Causes, Consequences and Remedies

> *An economy where goods and services are always bartered directly for each other would be spared of inflation and deflation. Such an economy would also be terribly inefficient.*
>
> James Tobin in D. Greenwald (ed.): *Encyclopedia of Economics*, p. 531

PREVIEW

Two major macroeconomic problems which have been harassing planners and policymakers and the public at large since the early 1950s are unemployment and inflation. While unemployment is known as public enemy number one, inflation is treated as public enemy number two. While inflation has redistribution effects, unemployed leads to deadweight losses. This is so because those who are unemployed have nothing else to lose. From the early 1970s, mainly due to oil price hike, these two problems were found to exist side by side in the midst of low rate of growth. The coexistence of inflation and unemployment in a stagnant economy is known as stagflation, i.e., inflation in the midst of stagnation and unemployment. In this chapter we will discuss the nature, causes, consequences and remedies of inflation. The inflation-unemployment trade-off is discussed in a separate chapter.

MEANING OF INFLATION

Inflation refers to a sustained rise in the general price level

Inflation refers to a phenomenon of constantly rising prices of goods and factors of production such as the prices of bread, cars, haircuts, raw materials, rent, wages and interest. For inflation to occur, the price rise has to be continuous. This simply means that a once-and-for-all in the price level is not inflation in the true sense. The distinction between price rise and inflation is shown in Fig. 24.1.

Inflation refers to a trend of constantly rising prices, and not just a once-and-for-all rise in prices

In panel (a) of Fig. 24.1 we see that with base price P_0 in the base year 0, there is no price rise up to the fourth year. However, there is a sudden rise in the price level from P_0 to P_1 in the fourth year, but there is no further price rise thereafter. This is known as a once-and-for-all price rise. This is not inflation in the true sense. By contrast, in panel (b) we see that starting from a base price of 100 in the base year 0, there is a continuous rise in the price level year after year. In times of inflation, one ten rupee note will buy less goods than it did last year and it will buy still less goods and services after one year than it does today. Thus in times of price inflation the value (purchasing power) of money falls.

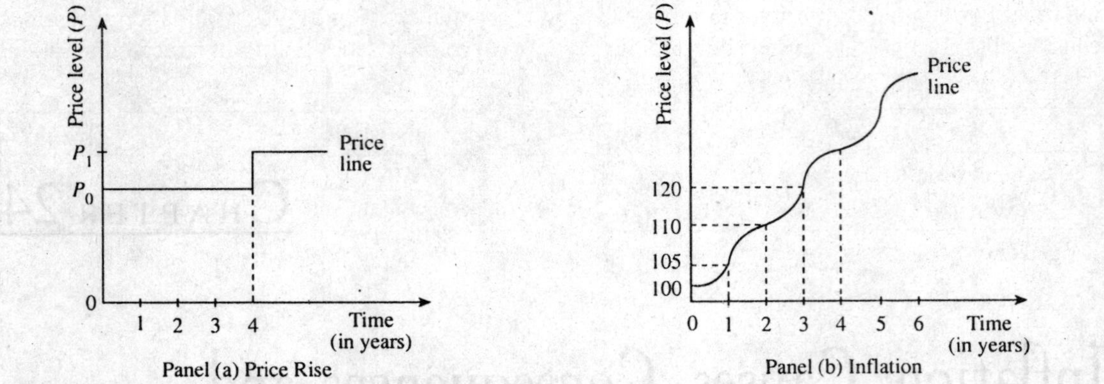

Fig. 24.1: The Distinction between Price Rise and Inflation

ABSOLUTE VS. RELATIVE PRICE

Inflation refers to a sustained rise in the overall (aggregate) price level. It does not refer to changes in relative prices. Relative prices always keep on changing. But such changes do not imply inflation. An opposite type of situation is known as deflation.

Deflation refers to a phenomenon of constantly falling prices of goods and factors of production.

MEASUREMENT OF INFLATION

While the quantity theory of money (QTM) shows a proportional relation between the money supply (*M*) and the price level (*P*) in a certain year, changes in the price level over a period of time or the rate of inflation is measured by the index numbers of wholesale and retail prices. There are three price indices which are used for measuring price level changes, viz., CPI, PPI and the GDP deflator. These concepts have already been briefly discussed in the context of national income accounting.

TYPES OF INFLATION

Inflation is like a disease (since it indicates ill-health of the economy) and, therefore, is of different types. We normally discuss the nature of different types of inflation on the basis of the causes. See Fig. 24.2. Here we classify inflation into three main categories, viz., demand-pull, cost-push and

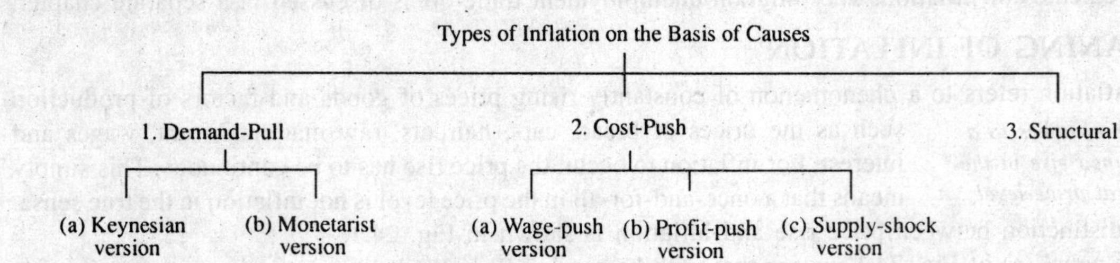

Fig. 24.2: Three Main Types of Inflation

structural. Two main theories are the theory of demand-pull inflation and the theory of cost-push inflation. Each has more than one variant. Which theory is correct? Probably all of these. That is, there is no simple answer. Inflation can be caused by a number of factors. Some of these factors are more important than others at any given moment.

Regarding demand-pull inflation there are two views, viz., the Keynesian and the monetarist. Similarly there are three variants of cost-push inflation, viz., wage-push, profit-push and (adverse) supply-shock. However, in reality it becomes very difficult to draw a line between the two types of inflation. For this reason we refer to mixed demand-cost inflation. A third type of inflation which has considerable practical relevance in developing countries of Asia and Latin America is structural inflation.

There are various other types of inflation also. These are listed below.

Economic Insight: Other Types of Inflation
Other types of inflation according to rates or patterns are (i) mild inflation (also called a functional rise in prices), (ii) hyperinflation, (iii) creeping inflation, (iv) runaway inflation and (v) galloping inflation.

We may now discuss three main theories of inflation.

1. DEMAND-PULL INFLATION

A. The Keynesian Theory

Demand-pull inflation occurs when there is an increase in aggregate demand (desired expenditure) but aggregate output cannot be increased further (i.e., when the economy is already at full employment).

Economic Insight: Two Versions of Demand-pull Inflation
The term 'demand-pull' implies that prices are said to be pulled up by a sudden increase in demand, or spending. Two explanations are given by two opposite schools of thought, viz., the Keynesians and the monetarists. Keynesians argue that an injection of new money in an economy will be spent on assets. But in their view the primary impact comes from the purchase of bonds. If the number of bonds remains constant, an increase in demand for bonds will bid up their prices which will lower interest rates. Lower interest rates, in turn, will encourage more investment spending and some consumer spending. The increase in demand for goods will pull prices up. According to monetarists demand-pull inflation occurs due to an increase in the money supply. The reason is easy to find out. When the central bank pumps out more money than is needed for transactions, the new money will be used to purchase both financial assets such as stocks and bonds and real assets such as television sets and cars. If the amount of assets in the economy remains constant, this new surge in demand will bid up prices. (More money chasing the same amount of goods causes higher prices).

According to Keynes for such inflation to occur there must exist an inflationary gap in the economy. It refers to the excess of desired expenditure over full employment output at the current price level. If there is an increase in any of the components of aggregate demand (such as government spending on goods and services) without a compensating fall in any of its other components, then aggregate demand will exceed aggregate supply of goods at current prices. Consequently there will be a rise in the price level.

We have already discussed the Keynesian concept of 'inflationary gap' in an earlier chapter. Here we repeat the concept briefly.

Economic Insight: Inflationary Gap
Inflationary gap refers to the excess of total spending (aggregate demand) at the full employment level of national income (potential GDP). Since it is not possible to increase output further, the excess demand will cause prices to rise. This means that since real output remains constant, the nominal value of output will get inflated. To counter this excess spending which creates an inflationary gap, the government can use monetary policy and fiscal policy to reduce aggregate demand.

Here it suffices to note that if government expenditure on different items such as public health, education and national defence increases and the government finances such expenditure by borrowing from the central bank, the money supply will increase. If the economy is already at full employment, more output cannot be produced to meet the extra demand. So too much money will be chasing too few goods and the price level will rise. Thus inflation occurs due to excess of desired expenditure over potential output at the current price level. Even if the economy is not at full employment, the price level is likely to rise if aggregate supply cannot be increased at the same rate at which aggregate demand is increasing. This imbalance between aggregate demand and aggregate supply is the root cause of demand-pull inflation.

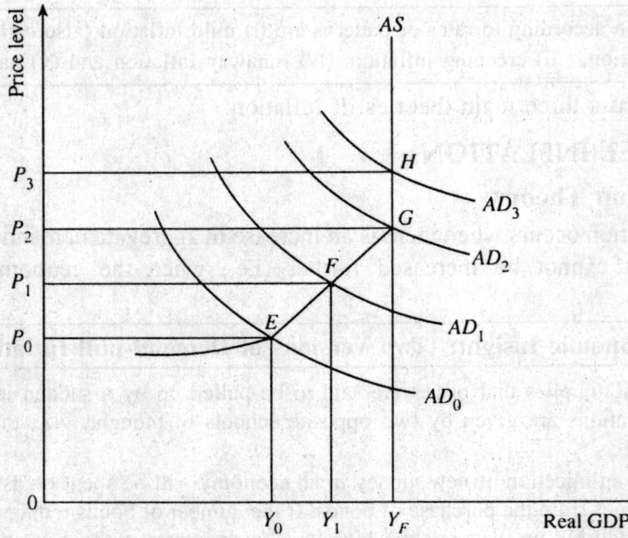

Fig. 24.3: Demand-Pull Inflation

The theory of demand-pull inflation is illustrated in Fig. 24.3. The economy is initially at point *E*, where real GDP is Y_0 and the price level is P_0. Now if aggregate demand rises to AD_1 due to an increase in government spending, the economy will move from point *E* to *F* along the rising portion of the *AS* curve. So real GDP will rise to Y_1 and the price level will increase to P_1. A further shift in aggregate demand curve AD_1 to AD_2 will have the same effects. However, the magnitude of increase in output and rise in the price level due to an increase in aggregate demand depends on the elasticity of the short-run aggregate supply curve. According to Keynes the rise in the price level associated with an increase in output cannot be treated as true inflation. Now, as soon as the full-employment level of output (Y_F) is produced, a further rightward shift of the aggregate demand curve will lead to only a rise in the aggregate price level from P_2 to P_3. In Keynes's view, this is inflation in the true sense — the end of full employment is the beginning of inflation. In other words, true inflation occurs only when the economy reaches full employment.[1] We now turn to the monetarist theory of demand-pull inflation.

Keynes explained inflation in terms of demand-pull forces

B. The Monetarist Theory

Like Keynes and Keynesians, the monetarists also explain demand-pull inflation in terms of an excess demand for goods and services, caused by an increase in the money supply. In the opinion of Friedman, inflation occurs only when the quantity of money increases faster than aggregate output.

In Friedman's view, when the central bank increases the money supply, there is an excess supply of money in the economy. As a result the macroeconomic equilibrium is disturbed since people have more money to spend than they need. So people will spend the extra money on goods and services and aggregate demand will increase. If aggregate output cannot be increased proportionately, the price

1. It may be noted that the classicists took a long-term view of the economy and, according to them, the economy reaches full employment in the long run. But Keynes took a short-term view of the economy.

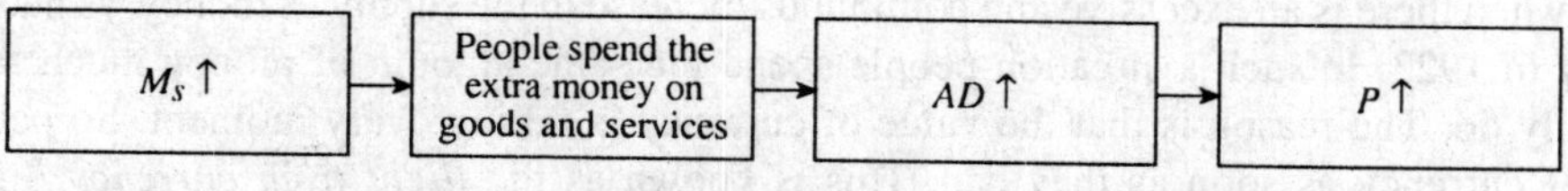

Fig. 24.4: The Inflationary Process in the Monetarist Theory of Demand-pull Inflation

level will rise. This is how inflation occurs. The generation of the inflationary process is shown in Fig. 24.4.

Since, according to Friedman, inflation is always and everywhere a purely monetary phenomenon, his theory of inflation is known as the monetarist theory. And the theory of inflation is a logical deduction from the quantity equation of exchange. If V is assumed to remain constant, then the equation of exchange is written as

$$\frac{\Delta P}{P} + \frac{\Delta Y}{Y} = \frac{\Delta M}{M}, \text{ with } \frac{\Delta V}{V} = 0$$

$$\text{or, } \frac{\Delta P}{P} = \frac{\Delta M}{M} - \frac{\Delta Y}{Y}.$$

Thus if M increases by 5% and Y increases by 2% per annum, there will be inflation from the demand side. Since in a modern economy M increases faster than Y, inflation is inevitable. An increase in M inflates the price level by increasing aggregate demand and creating excess-demand pressure. This point is illustrated in Fig. 24.5. A rightward shift of the aggregate demand curve from AD_0 to AD_1 caused by an increase in the money supply will cause real GDP to increase from Y_0 to Y_2 and the price level to rise from P_0 to P_2 as is shown by the movement along the fairly inelastic aggregate supply curve AS_0 from point E to F. But if the aggregate supply curve is more elastic, such as, AS_1, real GDP will increase from Y_0 to Y_1 and the price level will rise from P_0 to P_1 due to the same shift of the aggregate demand curve caused by an increase in the money supply by the same amount.

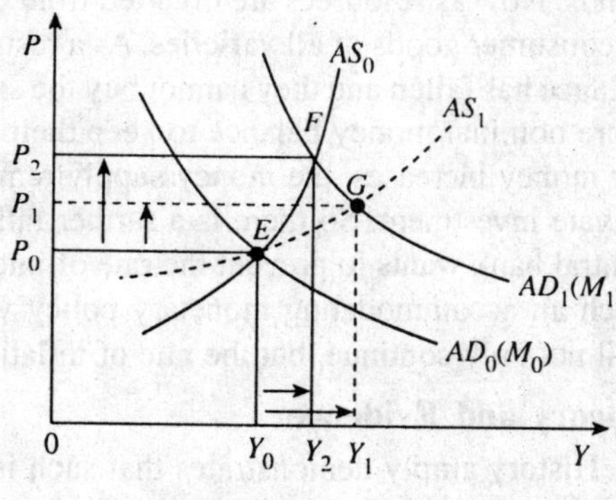

Fig. 24.5: The Effect of an Increase M on Y and P

Thus the more elastic the aggregate supply curve is, the faster will be the increase in real GDP due to an increase in aggregate demand and the slower will be the increase in the price level (or the rate of inflation). Thus the rate at which inflation occurs due to an increase in the money supply which shifts the aggregate demand curve to the right depends on the elasticity of the aggregate supply curve.

A Comparison

While the Keynesians explain demand-pull inflation in terms of increase in autonomous expenditure at full employment, the monetarists explain inflation in terms of faster growth of real GDP than in the money supply even at less-than-full employment. In each case an increase in the money supply plays an important role. But the causation is different. According to Keynesians an increase in government expenditure(G) will cause inflation only if the government prints more currency notes to finance it (provided the economy is already at full employment). So an increase in the money supply causes inflation indirectly—by inflating nominal spending at potential output. But according to monetarists, an increase in G causes inflation directly by generating extra spending even when aggregate output is increasing.

HYPERINFLATION

According to modern economists the monetarists' version of inflation, which emerges from the quantity equation of exchange, can only explain hyperinflation which occurs due to a war or an emergency when there is an excessive and continuous increase in the supply of money, as had occurred in Germany in 1923. In such a situation people spend the same amount of money much faster than they normally do. The reason is that the value of currency is falling every moment. So people want to get rid of currency as soon as they can. This is known as the *flight from currency*. In times of hyperinflation, the velocity of money approaches infinity and the value (purchasing power) of money falls to almost zero.

Economic Insight: Hyperinflation
Hyperinflation refers to a phenomenon of high and accelerating rates of inflation. In times of hyperinflation, people lose confidence in the currency which gradually becomes worthless due to rapid fall in its purchasing power. So people revert to barter. They demand commodities against commodities. This often leads to economic collapse mainly due to the breakdown of the monetary (currency) system. This type of inflation occurs due to the printing of excessive quantity of money to finance government spending (usually in times of war) or an acute shortage of goods and services combined with large pent-up demand, as is normally found in the period immediately after a major war or revolution. At present Zimbabwe is facing the problem.

The Mechanism

We may now briefly discuss how an increase in government spending causes hyperinflation. Suppose the government increases its expenditure to pay for a war. And the government issues war bonds. Now as resources are diverted from civilian production to military production, there is shortage of consumer goods of all varieties. As a result the price level rises. So people find that their real money balance has fallen and they cannot buy the same amount of goods and services. Therefore, they demand more nominal money balance to keep their real balance and consumption level intact. As the demand for money increases, the money supply remaining the same, the rate of interest rises. This crowds out private investment. So there is a further fall of output and a further rise in the price level. Now if the central bank wants to prevent the rate of interest from rising, it will have to increase the money supply. Such an accommodating monetary policy will lead to further price rise. And the process of inflation will not only continue, but the rate of inflation itself will accelerate. This is how hyperinflation occurs.

Theory and Evidence

History amply demonstrates that such inflation occurs due to an increase in the money supply by the central bank which either makes loans to the government to enable the latter to cover its budgetary deficit or it seeks to prevent rise in the rate of interest so as ensure that investment does not fall. And the only way to prevent hyperinflation is to stop the rapid growth of the money supply.

Role of Expectations

Expectations of economic agents mainly workers and business persons regarding future price movements also play an important role in causing demand-pull inflation. If a business firm anticipates that its rivals will raise prices of their products by 5% sooner or later, it will do the same now. Thus the actions of some firms will lead to price increases by others. So price expectations of some firms become self-fulfilling prophesies. The actual rate of inflation will be high if people expect it to be high. In fact, the current price level is high because in the past people expected it to be high and the future price level will be high because people now expect it to be high.

INERTIAL INFLATION

In this context we can refer to a new concept, viz., inertial inflation. In truth, since expectations can lead to an inertia, it is difficult to stop an inflationary spiral. Assume that the trend of rising prices continues. Also assume that the people's expectations are adaptive. This means that they form expectations about future prices on the basis of past price trends. In such a situation firms are likely to continue raising prices even if the demand for goods and services is increasing slowly. So the only way of slowing down the rate of inflation is by changing people's inflationary expectations. Thus inflation emerges as a self-fulfilling prophesy. This is known as inertial inflation.

2. COST-PUSH INFLATION

Rise in cost causes a fall in Y and a fall in Y causes a rise in P

Unlike demand-pull inflation, cost-push inflation occurs from the supply side. The critics of Keynes pointed out, on the basis of the actual experience of industrially advanced countries, that the assumption of full employment is not necessary to develop a theory of inflation. Inflation may well occur from the supply side even when the economy has unemployed labour and idle production capacity. We now discuss the theory of cost-push inflation.

Economic Insight: Three Forces behind Cost-Push Inflation
According to post-Keynesians cost-push inflation occurs because prices are pushed up by sudden increase in costs of production. Three causes of rise in costs are the following: (i) The wage-push view blames labour unions which negotiate wages higher than can be justified by workers' productivity. (ii) Companies then have to raise the prices of their products in order to cover their higher labour costs. The profit-push view is that companies simply raise their prices to increase their profits. (iii) The commodity-push view holds that an increase in commodity prices – due to political decisions by major producers (such as the OPEC), or bad weather (like a drought in the grain belt)—will spread throughout the rest of the economy, pushing up prices in general.

Cost-push inflation occurs when the aggregate supply curve shifts to the left due to an increase in cost of production which leads to a fall in real GDP. This, in its turn, cause a rise in the price level. This theory is illustrated in Fig. 24.6.

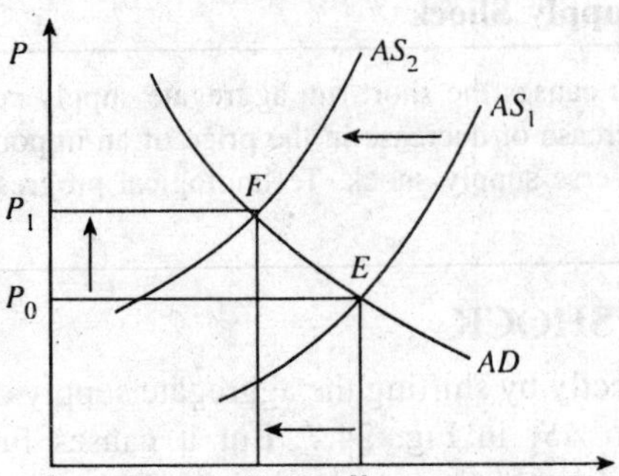

Cost-push inflation occurs even at less-than-full employment if the *AS* curve shift to the left due to an increase in cost of production which leads to a fall in aggregate output which, in its turn, leads to a rise in the price level.

Fig. 24.6: Cost-Push Inflation

The economy is initially in equilibrium at point *E* when the aggregate supply curve *AS* intersects the aggregate demand curve. So aggregate output is Y_0 and the aggregate price level is P_0. Now if, for some reason, cost of production increases, the aggregate supply curve will shift to the left from AS_0 to AS_1 and will intersect the aggregate demand curve at point *F*. Consequently aggregate output will fall from Y_0 to Y_1, and the price level will rise from P_0 to P_1 .

Since there are three variants of cost-push inflation it occurs for the following three main reasons:

(i) **Wage-push inflation:** Trade unions are normally held responsible for wage-push inflation. Trade unions often demand and succeed in getting higher wages even when there is no excess demand for labour. Instead, there may exist excess supply of labour. However, an increase in wage rate is not always the cause of such inflation. In fact annual price rise is the difference between annual wage rise and annual productivity (output) rise. So we can write:

$$\frac{dP}{P} = \frac{dW}{W} - \frac{dY}{Y}$$

where P is the price level, W is the wage rate and Y is the level of output (GDP). Now if wages rise faster than output, the price level will rise.

So we can write $\frac{dP}{P} > 0$ if $\frac{dW}{W} > \frac{dY}{Y}$

Thus if Y increases by 5% and W increases by 8%, then P will rise by 3%.

(ii) **Profit-push inflation:** Most real life markets are imperfectly competitive, i.e., either monopolistically competitive or oligopolistic in nature. In such markets firm set prices of their products by adding a margin of profit (or mark-up) to all costs (fixed and variable). Such mark-up may be fixed or variable (i.e., a percentage of unit cost). This is another cause of cost-push inflation, more so in view of the fact that the output of the industry (such as the steel or glass) is used as an input in many other industries (such as furniture, automobile, engineering, housing, etc.). So a rise in the price of steel (due to the addition of a profit margin to cost) will raise the cost of production and prices of furniture, cars, engineering goods and houses. This type of inflation is known as profit-push inflation.

(iii) **Supply-shock inflation:** Cost-push inflation also occurs due to adverse supply shock such as a rise in the price of petroleum products and various raw materials. This is exactly what happened in all oil-deficient countries since October 1973. In fact, supply-shock inflation became a global problem due to oil price hike. A rise in prices of oil and oil products causes inflation from the supply side because oil is used as the main or subsidiary input in a large number of industries. So one industry's price becomes a part of various other industries' cost-price structure.

Focus on Terminology: Supply Shock
The term 'supply shock' refers to an unexpected event which causes the short-run aggregate supply curve to shift. Supply shocks are often caused by an unexpected increase or decrease in the price of an important natural resource such as crude oil. This is an example of adverse supply shock. Technological progress is an example of a favourable supply shock.

INDIRECT EFFECTS OF ADVERSE SUPPLY SHOCK

An adverse supply shock no doubt causes inflation directly by shifting the aggregate supply curve from AS_0 to AS_1 in Fig. 24.7. But it causes further inflation, indirectly though. In fact, if the price level rises due to an increase in cost, real wage $\left(\frac{W}{P}\right)$ will fall. So workers will reduce the number of hours worked. As a result, there will be a further fall in aggregate output and a further rise in the price level, as shown in Fig. 24.7. As the aggregate supply curve shifts from AS_1 to AS_2 output falls from Y_1 to Y_2 and the price level rises from P_1 to P_2. Thus the rise in the price level from P_0 to P_2 due to an adverse supply shock occurs in two stages — first from P_0 to P_1 due to the direct effect of such a shock and then from P_1 to P_2 due to the indirect effect of the shock.

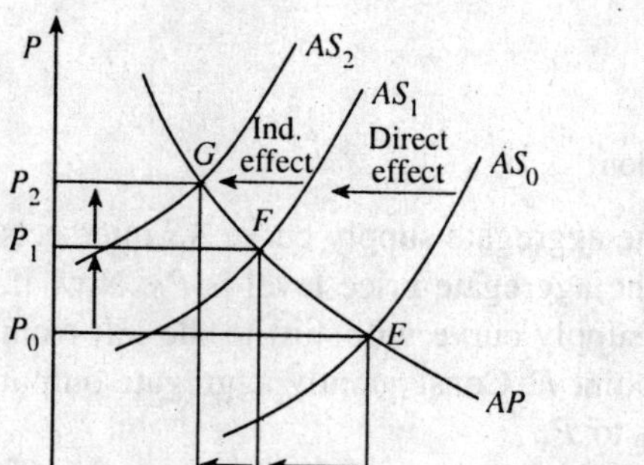

Fig. 24.7: Direct and Indirect Effects of an Adverse Supply Shock

MIXED DEMAND-COST INFLATION

According to modern economists such as G. Ackley and F. Machup, in reality it is very difficult to draw a distinction between two main types of inflation, viz., demand-pull inflation and cost-push inflation. The truth is that inflation is of the mixed demand-cost variety. This means that inflation occurs due to the interaction of demand-pull and cost-push factors or forces. Such interaction causes sustained inflation over time.

According to Machup, cost-push inflation cannot occur without an increase in purchasing power and demand. It is because cost increases usually create recession and unemployment, not inflation. Thus demand-pull inflation and cost-push inflation interact and excess demand pressure aggravates cost-push inflation. This point is illustrated in Fig. 24.8.

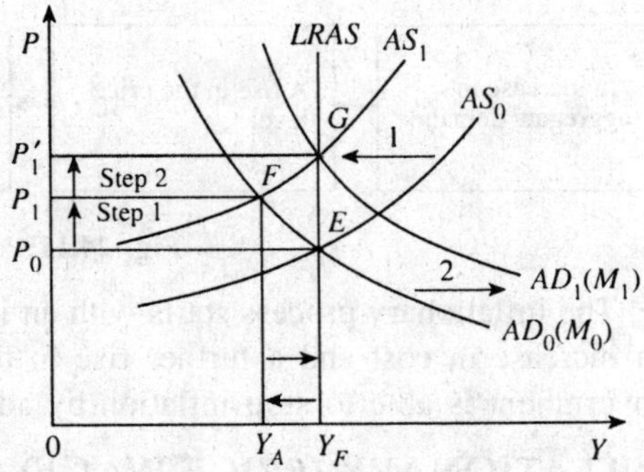

Fig. 24.8: Interaction of Cost-Push and Demand-Pull Forces in Causing Sustained Price Rise over Time

The economy is initially in equilibrium at point E. So real GDP is Y_F and the price level is P_0. Now due to an adverse supply shock the aggregate supply curve shifts to the left from AS_0 to AS_1. As a result, aggregate output falls from Y_F to Y_A and the price level rises from P_0 to P_1. Now the government adopts an expansionary monetary policy to increase aggregate demand so that the economy is able to reachieve full employment and actual output (Y_A) returns to its potential level (Y_F). Alternatively the government may adopt an expansionary fiscal policy in the form of an increase in its own spending (G) or a cut in taxes (T). As the aggregate demand curve now shifts to the right from AD_0 to AD_1 due to the adoption of an expansionary policy (monetary or fiscal), the economy reaches point G. So aggregate output returns to its potential level, but, at the same time, there is a further increase in the price level (from P_1 to P_1'). Thus we started from a situation of cost-push inflation but we end up with a situation of demand-pull inflation. This is known as mixed cost-demand inflation or hybrid inflation. The whole sequence is summed up in Fig. 24.9.

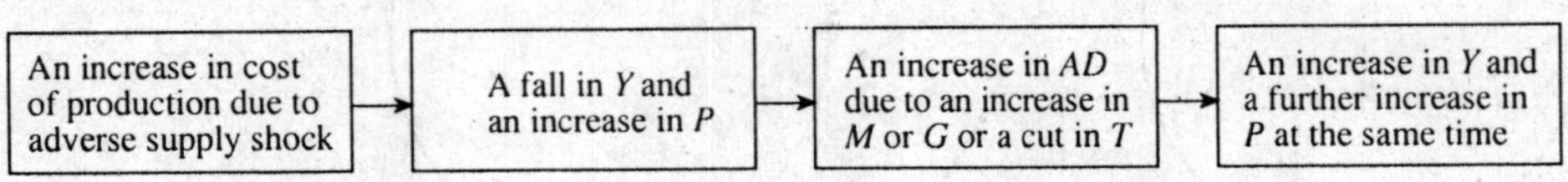

Fig. 24.9: Mixed Cost-Demand Inflation

Now we present an exactly opposite type of scenario. We now start with a situation of demand-pull inflation and will end up with a situation of cost-push inflation. In Fig. 24.10 we see that the economy is initially in equilibrium at point E with aggregate output Y_F and the price level P_0. Now the aggregate demand curve shifts from AD_0 to AD_1 due to the adoption of an expansionary policy by the government. So the economy attains a new equilibrium point F, at which actual output (Y_A) exceeds its potential level (Y_F) and the price level rises from P_0 to P_1.

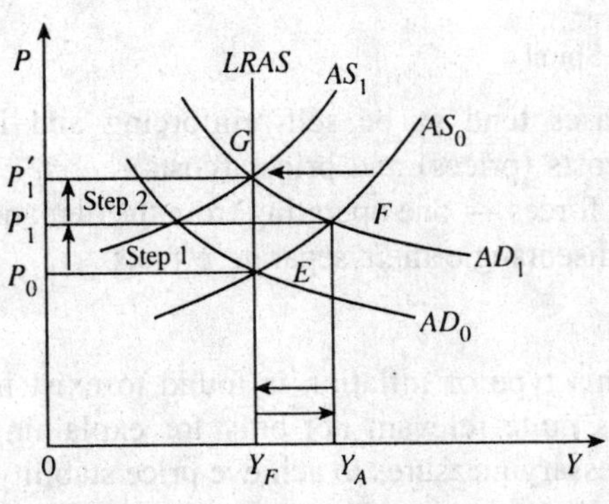

Fig. 24.10: Interaction of Demand-Pull and Cost-Push Forces in Causing Inflation

Now suppose due to higher price level, trade unions demand higher wages and get it. So cost of production will increase and the aggregate supply curve will now shift to the left for AS_0 to AS_1. Consequently, actual output returns to the full employment level. But the price level rises further from P_1 to P_1'. The whole sequence is summed up in Fig. 24.11.

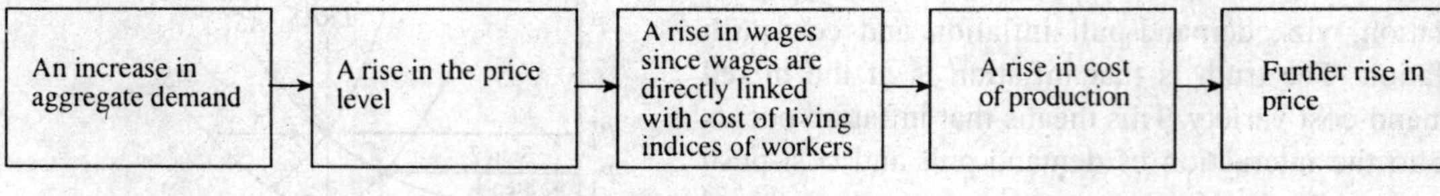

Fig. 24.11: Mixed Demand-Cost Inflation

The inflationary process starts with an increase in aggregate demand but gets its momentum with an increase in cost and a further rise in the price. The momentum continues until and unless the government is able to stop inflation by adopting both demand-side and supply-side policies.

INFLATIONARY (PRICE-WAGE) SPIRAL

Thus from Fig. 24.12 we see an inflationary spiral or price-wage spiral. It refers to a self-sustained increase in the rate of inflation brought about by the interaction of rising final prices and rising costs of raw materials and wages. For example, an initial sharp increase in prices of goods and services caused by an increase in prices of raw materials can lead to a demand for higher money wages by trade unions so as to prevent real wages from falling. If the wage rise occurs, higher wage costs force firms to raise prices of their products so as to maintain that profit margins. The higher prices, in turn, create demand for still higher wages, and the process goes on and on. It is just like a dog chasing its tail but is unable to catch it. See Fig. 24.12 which is self-explanatory.

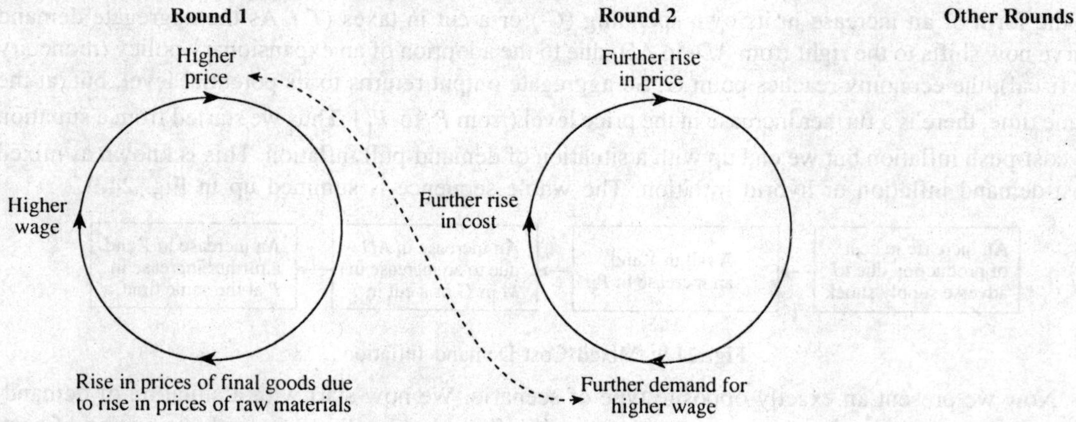

Fig. 24.12: A Price-Wage Spiral

Once it gets started, the process of price-cost increases tend to be self-reinforcing and is exacerbated by expectations of even further increases in costs (prices) and prices (costs).

Thus inflation occurs due to the interaction of two sets of forces — one operating from the demand side and the other from the supply side. It is difficult to disentangle their separate effects.

3. STRUCTURALIST INFLATION

The third type of inflation is structuralist in nature. This type of inflation is found to exist in developing countries. The structuralist view of inflation is quite relevant not only for explaining inflation in developing countries but for the adoption of necessary measures to achieve price stability. Such inflation occurs due to the very structure of developing countries. The main causes of such inflation are the following:

1. Agricultural stagnation: Although agriculture is the most dominant sector in developing countries like India, it itself is characterised by low productivity and low supply elasticity. There are various causes of low agricultural productivity such as sub-division and fragmentation of land holdings, growing pressure of population on land, inability of the farmers to use modern technology, dependence on nature and so on. Moreover, due to growing trend toward urbanisation and industrialisation, there is diversion of agricultural land for industrial and construction purposes. All these conjointly lead to a fall in food production. And this exactly what has happened in India in recent year. As a result developing countries like India have faced the problem of food inflation. And a rise in food prices leads to a rise in costs and prices of most other goods.

2. Bottlenecks: Various bottlenecks such as lack of adequate infrastructural facilities, shortage of power, coal, oil and inadequate availability of transport facilities also cause inflation by slowing down the rate of growth of the industrial sector. This point is quite relevant for India.

3. Shortage of foreign exchange: Due to excess of imports over exports developing countries face the problem of trade deficit. At times this creates acute shortage of foreign exchange. As a result such countries cannot import short-supply items like food, and industrial raw materials in order to meet domestic excess-demand pressure. And government measures such as currency devaluation makes things worse. Exports increase, imports fall and less goods are available for domestic absorption.

4. Excessive money creation: Due to sharp increase in government expenditure but inadequate revenue generation, the governments of developing countries often take resort to excessive money creation (i.e., deficit financing). This creates the problem of inflation, since the aggregate supply curve is fairly inelastic in such countries.

In truth, the excessive increase in the money supply in developing countries generates inflationary pressures, instead of causing inflation directly. In fact, this painless method of financing government expenditure has allowed inflationary spiral to manifest itself and become cumulative in nature.

In truth, various institutional and structural changes are needed in developing countries to ensure further economic growth with high employment in the absence of demand-pull inflation. The maximum priority has to be accorded to agriculture (the backbone of such economies) in planning in order to achieve price stability. We may now explain the causes of inflation in developing countries further.

INFLATION IN DEVELOPING COUNTRIES

In developing countries like India, inflation is not a purely monetary phenomenon. It occurs due to both demand-pull and cost-push factors (forces). The main reason for the emergence of inflationary gap in India during the entire plan period has been the rapid growth of government expenditure. This created budgetary deficit which had to be covered by printing new currency notes. Huge loans made by both Indian and foreign banks in recent years have also increased the money supply in India, increased aggregate demand in the process and caused inflation from the demand side.

From the supply side the factors generating inflationary pressures are the frequent rise in prices of petroleum, the hike in the prices of goods supplied by the government such as coal, steel, power, fertilisers (called administered prices), as also hike in railway fares, and freights at periodic intervals. The government has also increased procurement prices of foodgrains from time to time. In addition, the cascading effect (or cumulative burden) of indirect taxes has also increased cost of production and distribution and added fuel to the existing inflationary fire.

These two sets of forces cannot be separated from each other since they have conjointly created inflationary pressures in the economy. The joint operation of the two sets of forces – one from the demand side and the other from the supply side – is illustrated in Fig. 24.13. The economy is initially in equilibrium at point E where the aggregate supply curve AS_0 intersects the aggregate demand curve AD_0. The equilibrium real GDP is Y_0 and the price level is P_0. Now suppose aggregate demand increases due to an increase in government spending financed by printing new currency. As a result both real GDP and the price level rise as is indicated by point F (which is the new macroeconomic equilibrium point).

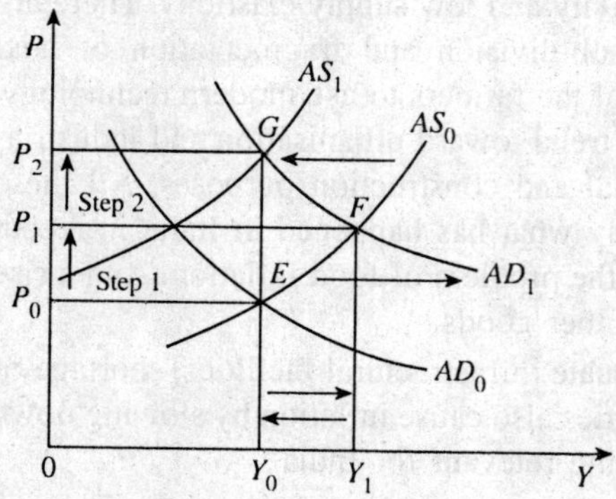

Fig. 24.13: The Inflationary Process in Developing Countries

Now if due to a rise in the price of oil or a rise in the wage rate the cost of production of firms increases, the aggregate supply curve will shift to the left from AS_0 to AS_1 and the economy will once again attain a new equilibrium point G. As a result real GDP will return to the original level (Y_0), but the price level will rise further from P_1 to P_1'. So the rise in the price level occurs in two stages — in stage 1 due to demand-pull factors and in the second stage due to cost-push forces. In addition, cost-push inflation occurs due to various bottlenecks such as shortage of power, coal, wagons, non-availability of critical raw materials, strikes in major industries and work stoppages due to political disturbances such as bandhs and hartals.

In India inflation has also occurred in the past due to the fact that production of foodgrains and other material items of mass consumption did not increase much. Since population increased rapidly, shortages have appeared in case of most consumer goods (both food and non-food). And the price level has continued to increase.

So the growth in the money supply alone is not the only cause of inflation in India. Therefore, the quantity theory of money cannot fully explain inflation in India. In other words, the monetarist theory of inflation is not a completely valid explanation of inflation in India.

INFLATION AND INTEREST RATE: THE FISHER EFFECT

In times of inflation the nominal rate of interest remains the same, but the real rate of interest falls. The real rate of interest is the difference between the nominal rate and the rate of inflation. The relation between the two rates of interest is shown by the following equation, called the Fisher equation:

$$i = r + \pi \qquad \ldots (1)$$

$$\text{or, } r = i - \pi$$

where r is the real rate of interest, i is the nominal rate and π is the actual rate of inflation, i.e., the rate of inflation over the period or duration of the loan.

The nominal rate of interest is the one which is paid by banks to its depositors. Suppose it is 9% on three-year time (fixed) deposits. Now if there is price stability, the real rate of interest will be same as the nominal rate. But if the annual rate of inflation is 5%, the real rate of interest will be (9% – 5% =) 4%. And if the rate of inflation is 10%, the real rate of interest will be – 1%.

The Fisher effect is an expression which allows for the effects of inflation upon the interest rate of a loan or a bond

Sometimes the nominal rate of interest is adjusted to make allowance for changes in the rate of inflation. Such adjustment is called the Fisher effect. If the real rate of interest required by lenders is 7%, then the nominal rate of interest has to rise exactly by the rate at which the rate of inflation increases from year to year. If initially the rate of inflation is 3%, the nominal interest rate has to be 10% to ensure that the real rate of interest is 7%. Now if the rate of inflation increases from 3% p.a. to 5% p.a., then nominal interest rate has to rise to 12% so that the real rate of interest remains unchanged at 7%. The inflation premium of 5% incorporated in the nominal interest rate serves to compensate lenders for the reduced value of money lent when it is returned by borrowers.

The Fisher effect suggests a direct relationship between inflation and nominal interest rates since changes in inflation rates lead to matching changes in nominal interest rates.

Another related concept is the expected real rate of interest. It is expressed as follows:

$$r^e = i - \pi^e$$

where r^e is the expected real rate of interest and π^e is the expected rate of inflation. If the actual rate of inflation (π) is the same as its expected rate π^e, then the actual real rate of interest will be the same as its expected real rate.

THE CONSEQUENCES OF INFLATION

The causes of inflation may be muddled, but its consequences are not. Inflation can be bad for some people and good for others. The problems created and inconveniences caused by inflation are known as its costs. In this context we may make a passing reference to the inflation fallacy.

INFLATION FALLACY

It may apparently seem that people make a living by earning fixed incomes. And income is earned by selling various factor inputs (services) just as business firms earn revenue by selling goods. People render different types of services and thus earn different types of income by using their brain power or muscle power. In times of inflation the prices of services rise as much as the prices of goods. For example, doctors, lawyers and business consultants raise their fees in times of inflation. Even barbers charge high prices for haircuts and laundries charge higher prices for washing clothes. Most people earn their incomes by selling services such as labour hours. So as wages rise in times of inflation, the incomes of the workers and other factor suppliers increase at the same time. This means that inflation does not reduce the real income (purchasing power) of these people. Trade unions demand higher wage and often succeed in getting it.

This view of inflation suggests that inflation is caused by an increase in the money supply. So only nominal incomes of firms and households increase, not their real incomes or purchasing power.

However, this argument is fallacious. In reality, prices of all services do not increase at the same rate as the prices of goods. This is why some people gain and others lose during inflation. This point becomes clear when we consider the effects of inflation in detail.

Economic Insight: Inflation as a Power Phenomenon
According to some economists, inflation is neither a demand-pull, nor a cost-push phenomenon. It is a power phenomenon. Since the size of GDP is like a cake, if the stronger groups in society are able to appropriate the major portion of it, the share of others will fall. If trade unions are very strong, the share of wage earners will be high. In this context J. K. Galbraith has referred to countervailing power. The capacity of firms to raise prices of their products is held in check by powerful trade unions which demand higher wages if they are able to anticipate any rise in the prices of the goods and services they produce and sell.

ANTICIPATED VS. UNANTICIPATED INFLATION

Inflation has various adverse and a few favourable effects on the economy. The adverse effects of inflation are called the costs of inflation. The effect of inflation depends largely, if not entirely, on whether it is anticipated by economic agents or not. In case of anticipated inflation, economic agents take into account the expected price rise while making negotiations regarding wages and fixing prices of products (both goods and services).

Inflation redistributes income in an undesirable way

Inflation redistributes income in favour of rich and against poor. It makes the rich richer and the poor poorest. So it increases income inequality and makes it difficult for the government to ensure distributive justice. Poor people find it extremely difficult to subsist in times of rapid inflation (as is occurring in India now due to rise in food prices). Many people go below the poverty line in times of double-digit inflation. However, the redistribution effect of inflation depends on whether it is anticipated by people or not.

Inflation creates uncertainty about the future. In the face of frequent price level changes, people cannot make anticipatory calculation about the future. So they cannot take long-term decisions, mainly decisions relating to purchase or acquisition of fixed assets.

Inflation also slows down the rate of growth of real GNP and acts as an obstacle to economic growth, especially in developing countries like India. These points will now be discussed one by one.

The Effects of Anticipated Inflation

If people can anticipate the rate of inflation, then they can make suitable adjustments in their contracts so as to avoid the adverse effects of inflation on their incomes and living standards. For example, trade unions can force employees to include an inflation clause in any labour agreement so that real wages remain constant even in times of rising prices.

Similarly lenders can include an inflation rate in the loan agreement so that the nominal rate of interest is adjusted appropriately to keep the real rate of interest unchanged.

If wages, rates of interest and rents are adjusted to the rates of inflation, then there will only the following types of costs of inflation:

1. Shoe leather costs: In times of inflation when the nominal rate of interest increases the opportunity cost of holding money also rises. So people economise their cash holding and make more frequent trips to the banks. As a result their costly shoes wear out quickly.

Focus on Terminology: Shoe Leather Costs of Inflation
Shoe leather costs of inflation refers to the presumption that one of the real costs of expected inflation is that it increases transaction cost by inducing people to economise on their money holdings. The shoe leather wears out quickly for making more frequent trips to banks to avoid carrying large amounts of cash and losing interest. This is an example of trade-off between earning interest and saving shoe leather costs.

2. Menu costs: Menu costs are the cost of changing prices. Such costs rise in times of rapid inflation. Changing prices is a costly affair. The reason is that firms have to print new catalogues (or new price list), distribute these among customers and make announcements through newspapers or TV advertising. From society's point of view, this is a total wastage. The time and resources devoted to making price changes could be more fruitfully utilised to produce desirable goods and services.

3. Inefficient allocation of resources: Firms having menu costs do not change their prices frequently. For this reason, the higher the rate of inflation, the greater the variability of the relative price, i.e., the price of the product of the firm compared to the overall price level. This creates distortion in production. The end result is inefficiency in resource allocation.

4. Inconvenience: People find it difficult to live in a world in which the price level is rising every now and then. In times of inflation, people and businesses become little confused (if not totally puzzled) and find it difficult to take rational decisions. Households do not know what is optimal saving for them. People develop a fear psychosis. Businesses do not know how to do rational investment and production planning for a long period of time.

THE EFFECTS OF UNANTICIPATED INFLATION

Unanticipated inflation has more damage effects on the economy than anticipated inflation. The reason is that people do not know what will be the actual rate of inflation in near future. So they cannot take any corrective measure to protect themselves from the adverse effects of inflation. The main effects of such inflation are the following:

1. Erosion of real income (purchasing power): Real income refers to the amount of goods and services which an individual can buy with his money income. It is the true indicator of the purchasing power of one's income.

Inflation reduces the purchasing power of money and thus people's real income. This means that with the same amount of money people are able to buy less goods and services or they require more money to be able to buy the same amount of goods and services.

2. Arbitrary redistribution of income and wealth: Perhaps the most serious consequence of unanticipated inflation is that it arbitrarily redistributes income and wealth among individuals. Some people gain at the expense of others in times of inflation. The reason is that during inflation all prices do not rise at the same time or in the same proportion. Some prices (such as those of food, petrol, etc.) rise faster than others. Some prices (such as house rent, metro rail fare, college tuition fee, etc.) remain constant. And some prices may even fall (such as the prices of computers, CDs, ball pens, readymade garments, pocket calculators, mobile phones, DVD players, etc.).

Gains and Losses from Inflation

Who are the gainers and who are the losers from inflation? Here we present the list of these two groups of people.

Table 24.1: The Losers and Gainers from Inflation

Losers	Gainers
1. Pensioners	1. Business people (who engage in profiteering activities)
2. Creditors	2. Professionals
3. Salaried people	3. Debtors
4. Holders of cash, government bonds and corporate debentures	4. Governments (both central and state) (as a major borrower from the market)

(i) **The creditors and debtors:** In times of inflation those who lend money at a fixed interest rate (the creditors) lose, while those who borrow money at the same interest rate (the debtors) gain. When the debtors repay the principal along with interest after a certain period, the creditors find that even with their extra income (i.e., principal plus interest), they cannot buy the same basket of goods and services which they could buy at the time of lending their funds. At times, the real rate of interest received by lenders is even negative. This is what we find in India now.

(ii) **Fixed income groups:** People with fixed income mainly the salaried people and the pensioners lose during inflation. Since their real income (or purchasing power of nominal income) falls, their level of living goes down in times of inflation. These two groups can be protected only through indexation, a concept to be discussed later in this chapter.

(iii) **Wealth-holders:** Those who hold their wealth in cash, fixed deposits in banks, corporate debentures or government bonds lose in times of inflation. Cash-holders are the worse sufferers during inflation. Lenders earn little or even negative real interest since the rate of inflation often exceeds the nominal rate of interest. This is why many people convert their financial assets into real assets in times of inflation. However, those who buy equity shares or risky assets often make capital gains.

(iv) **Business people:** Business people – both producers and traders – gain during inflation. The reason is that costs do not rise as fast as prices. Therefore profits increase faster than wages and other factor incomes.

Business people make further gains due to stock appreciation, i.e., rise in the prices of the finished goods which they hold as inventories. Such gains to producers and traders are known as windfall profits. These are not the reward for risk-taking but arise due to chance gains.

Thus inflation benefits people with variable incomes and hurts people with fixed incomes. However, the same person may hold more than one position in society. So he may lose as a fixed income earner (such as a college professor) and gain as a variable-income earner (such as a successful author of textbooks, the prices of which are revised upward in times of inflation).

Focus on Terminology: Inflation Tax
Inflation tax refers to the effects of inflation on the real value of money and government debt denominated in terms of money. Inflation is the cruelest of all taxes. It is not directly visible. This is why most people do not realise its true impact.

THE EFFECT ON OUTPUT

An increase in aggregate demand will increase both prices and output provided the economy has unemployed labour and unutilised production capacity. However, once the economy attains full employment, no further increase in aggregate output is possible, as shown in Fig. 24.3 (p 458).

Mild inflation or a functional rise in prices stimulates production by giving incentives to producers to invest more. So new jobs are also created. But in times of hyperinflation, only the price level rises, output remaining constant. Hyperinflation normally occurs in times of a major war when resources are diverted from civilian to military production. More arms and ammunitions are produced and less consumption goods.

The short-run Phillips curve shows that if a society wants to reduce unemployment and increase output, then it has to tolerate some inflation. But, this unemployment inflation trade-off does not exist in the long run.

However, cost-push inflation occurs because a fall in output leads to a rise in the price level. As we have noted earlier in this chapter, if the aggregate supply curve shifts to the left due to a rise in wages or in oil prices, aggregate output will fall and the price level will rise.

LOSS OF ECONOMIC EFFICIENCY

Inflation creates price distortions. This results in misallocation of resources and loss of economic efficiency. Inefficiency occurs due to abrupt changes in relative prices. As a result the price system fails to perform its signalling function. And variable rate of inflation is more damaging than high rate of inflation as far as efficient allocation of resources is concerned.

The shoe-leather cost of inflation, as discussed earlier in the chapter, indicates one type of economic inefficiency associated with inflation. In times of inflation people have to spend real resources in order to economise their cash holdings. Business firms have also to spend some resources to manage their cash-in-hand (which is a form of working capital).

BRACKET CREEP

In times of inflation people's nominal income increases. And under the present progressive tax system, people's tax liability increases faster than their income(s), since taxpayers move from a lower tax bracket to a higher one. This is known as *bracket creep*. A simple example will make the point clear. Suppose an individual's initial income is Rs.200,000 and he is paying a tax of 20% on his taxable income of Rs.50,000 (assuming that the exemption limit is Rs.150,000). So his tax liability is Rs.10,000 and his disposable income is Rs.190,000. Now if his income rises to Rs.210,000, his taxable income will be Rs.60,000 on which he is required to pay tax at the rate of 30%. So his tax liability is now Rs.18,000 and his disposable income is Rs.192,000. Thus even if his money income has gone up by Rs.10,000, his disposable income has gone up only Rs.2000, since he has moved to a higher tax bracket. If, as a result of this bracket creep, people reduce their work efforts, there is loss of potential output (real GDP). And this a genuine cost of inflation.

HYPERINFLATION AND CRISES

The true cost of inflation is the reduction in real income (purchasing power) of the people and the consequent drop in their standards of living. However, mild inflation is one thing and hyperinflation is another. If mild or creeping inflation is left unchecked for a long period of time, it may ultimately turn out to be hyperinflation. Hyperinflation is more damaging than mild inflation because the former leads to complete breakdown of the monetary (currency) system of the country which ultimately leads to collapse of the whole economy. Moreover, hyperinflation slows down the rate of economic growth. There are two main reasons behind this.

In times of hyperinflation, there is flight from currency

First, in times of hyperinflation people hold less currency and buy more of gold, jewellery, land and houses which give some protection against inflation. So the supply of loanable funds falls. And the shortage of such funds leads to a fall in investment. At the same time business people make more investment in hoarding and speculation of essential raw materials and consumer goods for making windfall gains. They do not want to make genuine productive investment. As a result both production and availability of essential items of consumption fall and the rate of inflation accelerates.

Hyperinflation affects the smooth functioning of a market-based economy. There is confusion regarding changes in relative prices and uncertainty about future prices. No one knows what is the correct price for a goods or service. So transactions always occur with a time lag. Due to rapid depreciation of the country's currency, money fails to act as a measure of value and a medium of exchange. Goods are demanded against raw materials and other inputs. So the money economy virtually yields place to the barter economy, in which commodities are directly exchanged for commodities.

The worst hyperinflation in recorded history occurred in Germany in 1923. Hyperinflation also occurred in Argentina and other Latin American countries in the 1980s and 1990s. And monetary reforms (mainly in the form of introduction of a new currency) were introduced.

Therefore only by taking timely action to control mild inflation, it is possible to prevent hyperinflation from occurring. And prevention is better than cure in this case.

INFLATION AND ECONOMIC GROWTH

Inflation has both favourable and adverse effects on economic growth. However, the adverse effects are stronger than the favourable effects.

A. Favourable Effects on Economic Growth

1. High rates of saving and investment: In times of inflation wages lag behind prices. Therefore profits go up. Since the capitalists have a high propensity to save, high profits lead to higher rates of saving and investment. So the rate of capital accumulation increases. And the end result is faster rate of growth of the economy.

No doubt high rate of economic growth is made possible by exploiting workers (who do not save much) and paying them low wages. However, even Karl Marx opined that, where there is no exploitation, there is no growth either.

2. Expansion of production capacity: By depressing wages capitalists earn more profits. As a result resources are diverted from the production of consumer goods to the production of capital goods. There are two reasons for this. Workers have a high propensity to consume and capitalists reinvest the major portion of their profits. Due to an increase in the production of capital goods there is an expansion of the society's production capacity. As a result labour productivity increases[1]. This ensures faster economic growth.

---

1. In fact, the productivity of labour depends on capital per worker. If more capital goods are produced, capital per worker will also increase.

B. Adverse Effects on Economic Growth

Critics have pointed out that inflation obstructs economic growth in a number of ways.

1. Fall in the rate of saving: In times of inflation people spend more money to buy the same amount of consumption goods so that they can maintain their standard of living. Some people buy more than what they need now since they apprehend further rise in prices of essential items. Moreover, people lose the incentive to save due to constant erosion in the value of their savings. So household savings fall and less funds become available for new investment in plant, equipment, machinery, etc. Thus inflation slows down the rate of capital accumulation and hampers economic growth.

Inflation reduces both the willingness and the ability to save

2. Unproductive investment: In times of inflation hardly any new investment is made in productive ventures due to rising costs of capital, time lags associated with fixed asset investment and uncertainty about future profits. Businesses indulge in unproductive activities such as speculation, hoarding, black marketing, etc. As a result there is not much addition to the economy's production capacity. So the rate of economic growth does not pick up.

3. Poverty: During rapid inflation more people go below the poverty line. And there is deficiency of demand or purchasing power. This also acts as an obstacle to growth, since consumption is the sole end and purpose of all production. Thus if consumption demand falls, aggregate demand will fall and aggregate output will fall.

4. Human capital formation: Economic development depends as much as on physical capital as on human capital. Human capital refers to investment in human beings. Inflation hampers human capital formation. In a country where people do not get sufficient food to eat they cannot spend much on health and education either. As a result their productive efficiency goes down.

5. The balance of payment crisis: Countries suffering from high rates of India have overvalued currency. The rupee is said to be overvalued in terms of the US dollar if there is an excess demand for dollars in India at the official rate of exchange. An overvalued currency decreases exports and encourages imports and leads to the deterioration of the BOP position of the country. In the long run this creates shortage of foreign exchange. As a result the deficit country cannot import either sufficient capital goods or essential raw materials which are needed for achieving industrialisation. The costs of inflation are summarised in Table 24.2.

Table 24.2: The Costs of Inflation: A Summary View

Anticipated	Unanticipated
1. Shoe leather costs	1. Erosion (partial loss) of purchasing power
2. Menu costs	2. Redistribution of income and wealth
3. Inefficient allocation of resources	3. Uncertain effect(s) on output and employment
4. Inconvenience	4. Speculation, hoarding and profiteering
	5. Fall in saving and investment (due to decision-making errors)
	6. Loss of economic efficiency
	7. Breakdown of the monetary (currency) system
	8. Balance of payments crisis
	9. Slower rate of economic growth
	10. Growing incidence of poverty

THE CASE FOR DEFLATION

Deflation refers to a phenomenon of constantly falling prices of commodities and factors of production. During deflation all the above mentioned effects of inflation are reversed since the shoe is on the other foot. In times of deflation workers gains and speculative activities are discouraged. Deflation also increases people's ability and willingness to save. More saving leads to more investment which, in its turn, ensures faster economic growth. In addition, exports rise, imports fall and there is greater and greater net inflow of foreign exchange which can be utilised for productive purposes and give support to the whole process of planned industrialisation.

However, during deflation profit expectations of businesses become bleak. So they lose the incentive to make new investment in fixed assets. As a result national income and employment fall. This is why some economists feel that falling prices are more damaging for the economy than rising prices.

NEED FOR PRICE STABILITY

Thus neither inflation nor deflation is desirable for the smooth and normal functioning of a modern economy. So what is called for is reasonable (if not absolute) price level stability. Relative prices always keep on changing in a market-based economy due to changes in demand and supply conditions in individual markets. Therefore steps should be taken to reduce the prices of those items which are going up by increasing their production or through imports so as to keep the price index constant.

Measures to Control Inflation

The control of inflation requires the adoption of various measures by the government. Since inflation can occur either from the demand side or from the supply side the control of inflation requires the adoption of two types of policies, viz., (1) demand-management policies (to eliminate inflationary gap) and (2) supply-management policies (to increase the production of those essential goods which are in short supply). These measures are listed in Table 24.3.

Table 24.3: Anti-inflationary Measures

Demand-management Policies	Supply-management Policies	Income Policies
A. Fiscal policy 1. A cut in government spending on currently produced goods and services (but not transfer expenditure such as pension and interest on government bonds which remain fixed) 2. An increase in direct taxes such as personal income tax and corporate income tax **B. Monetary policy** 1. An increase in the cost of credit 2. A decrease in the supply of money	1. Increase in domestic production (through the provision of incentives in the form of investment allowance, accelerated depreciation and cuts in indirect taxes) 2. Increase in imports of short-supply items, mainly food and industrial raw materials	1. Wage freeze 2. Ceiling on managerial remuneration 3. Productivity-linked bonuses 4. Wage indexation (partial or full), i.e., linking nominal wages partially or fully to the annual rates of inflation with a view to protecting real wages even in the face of rising prices (if necessary, through wage contracts.)

The measures listed above may now be discussed one by one.

A. Fiscal Policy

In India extra money created by the RBI to make loan to the government has not been matched by an increase in output of goods and services. So the price level has increased. Since demand-pull inflation occurs mainly due to an increase in government spending financed by new money creation, the government should reduce the magnitude of deficit financing in order to control such inflation. The magnitude of deficit financing should be kept within safe limits so that too much money does not chase too few goods.

In India the continuous increase in non-plan revenue expenditure of the government has caused inflation from the demand side. So there is need to reduce such expenditure as much as possible.

Economic Insight: Deficit Financing and Inflation

It may be noted that deficit financing is not always inflationary in its impact. Much depends on (1) the magnitude of deficit financing and (2) the utilisation of the newly created money. If deficit financing is kept within safe limits (say 2% to 3% of GDP), then there is likely to be only a functional rise in prices which is good for the economy. And if the newly created money is utilised for creating additional productive capacity in the economy in the form of infrastructure building or for setting up new factories producing mass consumption goods or for importing short-supply items, deficit financing may even promote faster economic growth instead of generating inflationary pressures in the economy.

There is huge scope for cutting down expenditure on defence, police force and general administration as also on subsidies provided on food, fertilisers and exports. It is also necessary to reduce inefficiency in resource use as much as possible and corruption involved in spending public money. At the same time there is need for resource mobilisation through (a) additional taxes (direct and indirect), (b) market borrowing and (c) raising small savings in the form of provident funds and national saving schemes (NSCs) by giving incentives (in the form of tax benefits and high interest rates.)

By cutting its non-essential and wasteful expenditure through greater resource mobilisation, it is possible to reduce budget deficit and control inflationary financing of government spending

B. Monetary Policy

Monetary policy influences aggregate demand by affecting the cost and availability of credit. Different techniques are used for the purpose. These are divided into two main categories, viz., quantitative and qualitative, as shown in Table 24.4. These techniques either affect the cost of credit or the availability of credit.

Table 24.4: Techniques of Monetary (Credit) Control

A. Quantitative (General)	B. Qualitative (Selective)	Effects on
1. Bank rate	1. Differential rates of interest	Cost of credit
2. Open market operations	2. Fixation of ceiling on specific types of advances	Availability of credit
3. Reserve ratio	3. Change in minimum margin requirement(s)	Availability of credit

A. Quantitative Techniques

The quantitative techniques of credit control are of the following three types:

1. Raising the Rate of Interest

In times of inflation, the central bank can raise the rate of interest. As a result the cost of credit will increase and business people will reduce their investment in inventories and fixed assets. So aggregate demand will fall.

At the same time a high rate of interest will encourage households to control consumption and save more. This will cause aggregate demand to fall further.

So to realise the full effect of restrictive monetary policy, it is not enough to raise the bank (discount) rate. It is also necessary to raise the deposit and lending rates of banks.

While the bank rate raise the cost of credit, other methods of monetary control reduce the availability of credit.

In recent years it has been realised that reduction of credit availability is more effective in reducing aggregate demand than an increase in the cost of credit. Credit availability can be reduced by using the following methods:

2. Open Market Operation

In times of inflation, the central bank sells securities mainly to the banks. Banks buy these securities from their excess reserves. So their excess reserves from which loans are made fall. So they are forced to reduce their lending to businesses. As a result business investment and aggregate demand fall and the rate of inflation comes down.

3. Variable Reserve Ratio

The cash reserve ratio (CRR) refers to a certain percentage of a bank's deposits which the bank keeps in cash, by law or convention, with the central bank as a reserve. The central bank can control the total volume of bank credit by raising or lowering this ratio. A rise in CRR causes a contraction of bank credit. It is because when the CRR is high, the banks are to keep larger reserves with the central bank and their power to give credit is reduced. The lowering of the CRR, on the other hand, causes an expansion of credit as the banks are to keep a smaller reserve with the central bank and so get a larger fund for lending.

Incremental CRR : For tightening credit restraint and for managing excess liquidity in the banking system, a central bank can ask for an additional CRR for excess deposit accumulated from a specified date. This technique is followed in India and is known as impounding of excess deposits through incremental CRR.

Limitations : J. M. Keynes lent his warm support to this weapon of credit control. Although this method can bring about a quick reduction in the bank credit by a mere stroke of pen, it is considered to be highly discriminatory. It affects the different banks differently. It affects smaller banks more adversely than the larger ones.

B. Qualitative (Selective) Methods of Credit Control

Selective credit control refers to qualitative method of credit control by the central bank. The methods aim, unlike general or quantitative methods of credit control, at the regulation of credit taken for specific *purposes* or *types of economic activity*. It aims at encouraging good credit, i.e., speculative credit. The techniques of selective credit controls generally are of two varieties: (a) minimum margins, higher or lower, for lending against specific securities, celings on the amount of credit for certain purposes, and differential rates of interest for certain types of loans and advances, and, above all, (b) regulation of consumer credit for purchasing durable goods.

The following are the major qualitative or selective methods of credit control:

1. Minimum Margin Requirements

This weapon is *selective* in respect of its field of application. The term '*margin*' refers to the amount of cash one must put up in addition to what one may borrow on his stock from a bank. Thus, if a loan of Rs. 9,000 is secured by a stock worth Rs. 10,000, the margin is said to be Rs. 1,000 or 10% of the value of the stock. Therefore, with a 10% margin requirement, one can borrow 90% of the value of the security. During inflation the central bank raises the margin in respect of loans taken against some sensitive commodities which are subject to seasonal price fluctuations. The Reserve Bank of India gives frequent instructions to other banks to keep higher margins for giving loans against essential commodities like paddy or rice, wheat, oilseeds, raw cotton, sugar, pulses, edible oils, etc. The objective is to restrict the supply of credit for hoarding such commodities and, thus, to curb speculative rise in their prices on account of their short supply. This method is highly effective (as is found in the underdeveloped money market of India) because it can strike at the strategic spot of the economy for controlling the inflationary rise in prices. But in reality it is difficult to select the commodities to be brought under such control as also to determine the proper margin for advances.

2. Consumer Credit Regulation

This technique originated in the U.S.A. during the Second World War (1939-45) and is based on the observation that the demand for durable consumers' goods is extremely unstable. Under this method, the central bank controls the bank advances intended for installment buying of durable consumers' goods like automobiles, household furniture, refrigerators, etc. This is done by regulating the amount of down payment as also the period of loan repayment.

C. Other Methods

There are some other methods of credit control. These minor methods are the following:

1. Rationing of Credit

The central bank, by using this method, introduces some sort of *quota system* of regulating bank loans or fixes the maximum limit of bank advances for different purposes.

2. Direct Orders

The central bank, being the supreme monetary authority, sometimes gives direct orders or instructions (e.g., Credit Authorisation Scheme as in India) to other banks to follow a particular policy of monetary control.

3. Moral Suasion

Moral suasion implies informal suggestions or recommendations through circulars which the central bank may make issue to other banks for credit regulation. The banks are persuaded to implement these suggestions.

Conclusion

It is to be noted that these methods of credit control do not have the same degree of effectiveness in all types of money markets. In underdeveloped money markets such as those in India all the methods of credit control, especially the traditional ones, have limited effectiveness. It is because a major segment of any money market in developing countries remains outside the influence and control of the central bank. So these minor instrument of credit control are not much effective as an anti-inflationary measure.

Economic Insight: Monetary Policy, Income and Spending
If the central bank wants to increase aggregate spending, it increases the money supply and people spend more since they now have more money. The converse is also true. The central bank increases the money supply by buying T-bills. The sellers of the T-bills, just exchange one asset — T-bills—for another asset—a cheque from the central bank. T-bills do not increase their income. No doubt, the money supply is now larger. But no one's income increases in the process of selling T-bills by the central bank. So no one's spending is affected. Therefore such action by the central bank has no effect on the price situation. In other words, this measure cannot be used to control inflationary price rise.

SUPPLY-MANAGEMENT POLICIES

The rate of inflation can be reduced by importing short-supply items— both consumer goods and industrial raw materials. This is possible by reducing import duties. The domestic supply situation can also be improved by imposing ban on exports of certain items or by fixing export quotas.

A policy of tax cut is essentially a supply-side measure

If the economy is having idle capacity, then it is possible to increase aggregate output by utilising the economy's existing production capacity fully. Full utilisation of production capacity is possible by removing various bottlenecks as also by giving tax concessions and subsidies to producers. Since a policy of tax cut makes the aggregate supply curve more elastic, it is treated as a supply-side measure for controlling inflation. In 1975 Arthur Laffter pointed out that a policy of tax cut imparts the needed dynamism to the economy and increases the supply of goods and services. If aggregate supply increases, the imbalance between aggregate demand and aggregate supply will gradually disappear and the price situation will be under control.

It is also necessary to create additional production capacity as quickly as possible so as to increase the production and availability of short-supply items and thus beat the price situation.

Incomes Policy

Finally to check the wage-price spiral, the government can impose controls over wages and other factor incomes. Such controls come under the heading 'incomes policy'. The inflationary effect of wage hike can be brought under control by linking wages to productivity. If wages are raised exactly at the rate at which labour productivity increases, there will be inflation since aggregate demand will not increase faster than the economy's capacity to produce goods and services.

Economic Insight: Prices and Incomes Policy
Prices and incomes policy is concerned with controlling inflation by *directly* attempting to halt or slow down the inflationary spiral of price-wage rises, in contrast to disinflationary monetary policy and fiscal policy, which work *indirectly* to bring inflation under control. The main rationale for such a policy is that whereas disinflationary monetary and fiscal policies can only control inflation by increasing the rate of unemployment, prices and income policy, if applied rigorously, can check inflation and maintain high levels of employment. Such policy links price increases to non-absorbable cost increases and wage increases to increases in productivity. It is a useful way of 'defusing' inflationary expectations. So it removes the danger of accelerating the inflation rate.

By adopting either demand-management or supply-management policies or both at the same time, it is possible to reduce excess demand pressure from the economy and achieve price level stability.

A NOTE ON INDEXATION

Indexation is a method of changing prices for goods and services by linking them to changes in the rate of inflation. It can be applied to wages, prices and taxes. General indexation has been used in some countries such as Brazil, Australia and New Zealand to help cope with inflation.

Economies facing very high rates of inflation often turn to indexing in order to protect people when prices for some goods and services rise more rapidly than others. The worst sufferers from inflation are those who have negotiated wages contracts or holders of long-term bonds, who feel helpless as the real value of their salaries (in terms of the amount of goods and services they can buy), or their bonds, is eroded by high rates of inflation. In this context we refer to wage indexation.

Wage Indexation: Partial and Full

Wage indexation refers to adjusting the nominal wage in times of inflation so as to protect the workers from the adverse effect of inflation, fully or partly. Suppose we have the following information about money wage and real wage:

Table 24.5: Money Wage Price Index and Real Wage

	(1)	(2)	(3) $= \frac{(1)}{(2)} \times 100$
Year	**Money wage**	**Price index**	**Real wage**
2012	Rs. 960	100	Rs. $\frac{960}{100} \times 100$ = Rs. 960
2013	Rs. 1,250	110	Rs. $\frac{1,250}{110} \times 100$ = Rs. 1,140

Here we see that due to 10% inflation in 2013 the increase in real wage from Rs. 960 to Rs. 1,140 is less than the increase in money wage from Rs. 960 to Rs. 1,250. In case of full indexation, real wage will be raised artificially to Rs. 1,250 in 2013. This virtually amounts to giving a compensation to workers of Rs. 110 (= Rs. 1,250 – Rs. 1,140). In this case workers get full protection of their real wage or purchasing power. Under partial indexation real wage may be raised to, say, Rs. 1,200. This means that workers are not much worse off due to fall in their purchasing power.

Indexation also seeks to protect taxpayers from the evil interaction between inflation and the progressive tax system— called bracket creep. Before indexation, when wages rose to keep pace with inflation, taxpayers found that their new, higher wages subjected them to a new, higher tax-rate bracket, even though their wages had not increased in real terms. Indexation now adjusts tax bracket for the impact of inflation.

In addition, indexation will make people insensitive to inflation (no pain, no anxiety) and thus less willing to fight it. This is why in those countries where there is total indexation of wages and taxes, inflation can skyrocket. While indexation reduces the costs of inflation, it raises people's inflationary expectations and makes it difficult to bring their expectations and rate of inflation down. (But supporters of indexation reply that even in countries without indexation, inflation often gets out of control.)

Criticisms

Indexation can apply to prices also. In practice, indexation means that the money value of a long-term loan would be increased in line with the retail prices index so that the borrower would be required to repay the loan in real terms. In the absence of indexation, unanticipated inflation, by eroding the real value of loans, shifts resources from lenders to borrowers and, therefore, disrupts the credit mechanism and the smooth functioning of the market for loanable funds. It also introduces various distortions in commodities and factor prices.

KEY POINTS

1. ***Meaning and measurement of inflation*** **:** Inflation refers to a phenomenon of constantly rising prices of commodities and factors of production. A one-time increase in the price level is not to be called inflation. Inflation is measured by the index numbers of wholesale and retail prices. Inflation may be slow or rapid. Slow inflation is called mild inflation and rapid inflation is called hyperinflation. It refers to a phenomenon of high and even accelerating rates of inflation.

2. ***Types of inflation*** **:** Inflation is of three main types — demand-pull, cost-push and structural. There are two versions of the theory of demand-pull inflation, viz., the Keynesian and the monetarist. Cost-push inflation has three variants, viz., wage-push, profit-push and supply shock. In developing countries like India it can be explained more clearly by referring to the structuralist theory. According to this theory inflation occurs due to various structural imbalances in the economy, especially various types of bottlenecks.

3. ***Mixed demand-cost inflation*** **:** In reality inflation occurs both from the demand side and from the supply side. This is why modern economists refer to mixed demand-cost inflation. Such inflation is illustrated by referring to inflationary spiral or price-wage spiral. Inflation may start either from the demand side or from the supply side. People's expectations also play an important role in causing inflation.

4. ***Inflation and interest rate*** **:** The real rate of interest is the nominal rate minus the annual rate of inflation. This is why, at times, the nominal rate of interest is raised in times of inflation to keep the real rate unchanged.

5. ***The costs of inflation*** **:** The adverse consequence or costs of inflation depend on whether it is anticipated or not. Four effects of anticipated inflation are (a) shoe-leather costs, (b) menu costs, (c) inefficient allocation of resources and (d) inconvenience associated with variable prices. The costs of unanticipated inflation are (a) erosion of real income (purchasing power), (b) arbitrary redistribution of income and loss of economic efficiency, and (c) bracket creep (increase in tax liability). Some people gain during inflation but most people lose. The output-cum-employment effect of inflation is uncertain. Hyperinflation leads to breakdown of a country's monetary (economy) system and ultimate collapse of the economic system.

6. *Inflation and economic growth* : Mild inflation helps the process of economic growth to some extent. But hyperinflation hampers economic growth in a number of ways: (a) by holding saving and investment, (b) hampering human capital formation, and (c) creating balance of payments problem.

7. *Price stability* : Price stability can be achieved by adopting demand-management (monetary and fiscal) policies and supply-management policies. A cut in the magnitude of deficit financing, an increase in direct taxes, a rise in the rate of interest and a fall in credit availability are all demand-management policies. The two types of policies are to be adopted simultaneously to achieve the desired degree of price stability. These may be supported by prices and incomes policies.

8. *Supply-management policies* : An increase in production, an increase in imports, a cut in indirect taxes, etc. are all supply-management policies.

9. *Indexation* : Indexation refers to the introduction of automatic linkage between monetary obligations and the price level. It is applied to wage, prices or taxes. The basic objective is to protect certain economic agents from the adverse effects of inflation. While indexation reduces the cost of inflation, it raises inflationary expectations of the people and makes it difficult to bring the rate of inflation down.

KEY TERMS

Inflation
Menu costs
Hyperinflation
Bracket creep
Wage-push
Wage-price spiral
Inflationary gap
Unanticipated inflation
Runaway inflation
Wage freeze
Shoe leather costs
Mild-inflation
Monetary policy
Cost-push inflation
Disinflation
Supply-shock
Anticipated inflation
Galloping inflation
Inflation tax
Supply-management policies
Deflation
Fiscal policy
Demand-pull inflation
Inflationary gap
Profit-push inflation
Structural inflation
Creeping inflation
Indexation
Prices and incomes policy
Price theory

ASSIGNMENTS

1. Show how an inflationary gap leads to a sustained rise in the price level. How can the gap be eliminated?
2. "Inflation is a purely monetary phenomenon."—Discuss.
3. "Direct taxes are anti-inflationary in nature, but indirect taxes cause inflation from the supply side." Critically examine the statement.
4. Discuss briefly the factors which create inflationary pressure in an economy.
5. What do you mean by inflationary spiral? How does it create high rate of inflation?
6. Discuss the economic effects of unanticipated inflation.
7. Does inflation hamper economic growth? Do you think that a functional rise in prices is good for the economy?
8. Write notes on (a) inflation tax, (b) selective credit control, (c) adverse supply shock, (d) shoe leather cost of inflation, (e) menu costs and (f) price-wage control.
9. What type of measures can be taken by the government to achieve price level stability?
10. What is indexation? How effective is it as an anti-inflationary measure?
11. (i) Suppose the expected inflation is 5% and real interest rate agreed upon by the borrower and lender 5%, what will be the nominal interest rate?
    (ii) If actual inflation turns out to be 7%, who will be the gainer and loser?
12. (i) Describe the role of demand for money in the quantity theory of money equation. (ii) Quantity theory of money reiterates the neutrality of money proposition. Do you agree?

Part-VII

International Business Environment

25. Theories of International Trade: Ricardian and Heckscher-Ohlin
26. The Multiplier in an Open Economy
27. International Linkages and the Mundell-Fleming Model
28. Free Trade vs. Protection
29. Trade Strategy for India: Import Substitution vs. Export Promotion
30. India's Foreign Trade
31. Foreign Exchange
32. International Financial Institutions: The IMF and the World Bank
33. The Balance of Payments and the Performance of India's External Sector
34. Foreign Investment and Multinational Corporations (MNCs)
35. Globalisation and its Impact on the Indian Economy
36. India and the WTO

CHAPTER 25

Theories of International Trade: Ricardian and Heckscher-Ohlin

> *Generally abundant factors are relatively cheap, scanty factors are relatively dear in each region. Commodities requiring for their production much of the former and little of the latter are exported in exchange for goods that call for factors in the opposite proportions. Thus indirectly, factors in abundant supply are exported and factors in scant supply are imported.*
>
> Bertil Ohlin

Two most important features of any modern economy is division of labour (DOL)[1] and specialisation. These two things become really meaningful only when there is scope for exchange.

Specialisation and exchange may occur at three different levels. Two different individuals may specialise. As a doctor, for example, may be a good car driver. But he prefers to keep a professional driver so that he can devote himself fully to medical profession which is his own area of specialisation. By doing so he can gain in terms of money and save time (apart from being free from tension). This type of personal specialisation originates from occupational division of labour.

Similarly two different regions of the same country may also specialise on the basis of natural and man-made advantages. For example, West Bengal has specialised in the production of jute goods and Maharashtra in textiles for obvious reasons. And both the regions have gained through inter-regional trade. Such trade is based on regional specialisation or location of industry in a particular region. An industry normally has tendency to concentrate in those areas which offer certain natural and man-made advantages.

Similarly two different countries may also specialise in production of different goods, for example India in cloth and America in machines. By doing this they stand to gain.

No country is self-sufficient today. For this reason no country can have a closed economy. Due to mutual interdependence among various nations, we find greater and greater degree of economic openness.

Countries engage in trade voluntarily simply because they gain from trade. Such gain arises mainly due to increase in productivity of labour and other resources as a result of specialisation which, in turn, is based on international division of labour and specialisation.

1. Although the concept of DOL was introduced by Adam Smith in 1776, the intellectual father of economics, it was put into practice by F. W. Taylor in 1911 in the context of the American manufacturing industries.

A country like India cannot meet all its needs through domestic production. So it has to import those commodities (such as crude oil, machinery and sometimes food even) which it needs but which it cannot produce cheaply or in adequate amounts or it cannot produce it all. Thus, in presence of international trade a country's domestic consumption is equal to its domestic production plus imports. However, in order to obtain imported items, a country needs foreign currencies, which are earned through exports. A country can export goods only by generating surplus of domestic production over domestic consumption. It is against this backdrop that we study the theories of international trade.

Any excess of domestic production of goods and services gets reflected in exports. In general, exports pay for imports

MEANING OF INTERNATIONAL TRADE

International trade refers to trade between two different countries of the world (such as India and the USA) or between one country and various other countries (or even the rest of the world). While the former is known as bilateral trade, the latter is called multilateral trade.

Difference between Domestic Trade and International Trade

International trade is the result of geographical specialisation and division of labour. It is fundamentally the same as trade between two regions within a country. As for domestic or inter-regional trade, each region tends to specialise in the production of that commodity for which it has necessary raw materials and equipment. For example, coal, tea and jute are produced in West Bengal while Maharashtra has specialised in the production of cotton textiles. This is also true in case of international trade, i.e., trade between two nations or two different geographical areas. Each country tries to specialise in the production of that commodity for which it has necessary facilities and exports that commodity. It imports the commodity which it cannot produce or produce cheaply. But still there are certain differences between domestic trade and international trade. As Friedrich List said long ago: "Domestic trade is among us; international trade is between them and us." The main points of difference between domestic and international trade are the following:

1. Factor mobility: Factors of production like labour and capital usually move freely between different regions of a country (say, from Bihar to West Bengal) in search of employment than between nations (say, India to Britain). Mobility of factors is mainly affected by returns to factors which differ both inter-regionally and internationally. Factors that restrict migration include differences in language, governmental regulations, customs and tradition.

2. Differences in price: The price of a commodity within a country is equal to its cost of production in the long run, especially its labour cost, if there is perfect competition. The tendency of wages toward equality within a country results in prices of goods being equal to their labour costs so as to equalise the return to labour in all occupations and regions. But there is always a difference between price and cost internationally, due to immobility of factors. Thus there may be a difference between the price of a commodity (say, jute) in one country (say, the UK) and its cost in another country (say, India) even in the long run. There is no automatic tendency for prices to equal costs between different countries. Sometimes transport costs become significant in this regard.

3. Natural advantages: Different countries have different natural resources. This is why a particular commodity can only be produced in a particular location, not in others. For example, gold is produced in South Africa, coffee in Brazil, oil in Venezuela and tea in India.

4. Commercial policy: Different regions within the same country are subject to the same sets of economic policies pursued by their government. However, as we shall see in ch. 28, different governments adopt different tariff quota and other trade policies.

In truth, restrictions are sometimes imposed on movements of particular commodities from one region to another. But they differ in nature from restrictions on commodities moving internationally.

5. Different currencies: International trade involves the use of different currencies. In different regions within the same country, the standard currency is the same. This implies that any change in the value of the currency would affect all the regions exactly equally. But it is not known whether a change in the value of a dollar would affect Indian or Pakistani exports equally favourably or equally adversely. It all depends. Moreover, as we will see in ch. 31, all currencies are not equally convertible in the foreign exchange market in dollars or other key currencies.

6. Capital movement: The above difference has a very important bearing on the mobility of capital internationally as compared to the same inter-regionally. One major reason why capital moves less freely internationally than inter-regionally is that a change in the internal value of a currency (say, over time) would affect the real value of a bond in all places equally irrespective of where (within the same country) it is held. But if the exchange rate of a particular currency moves, the value of capital held in that currency would surely be affected. This risk of a change in the value of foreign currencies tends to make people more inclined to keep their capital at home.

Need for a separate theory: So there are some very important differences between domestic trade and international trade. And this is why economists have developed a separate theory of international trade in terms of the principle of comparative cost or comparative advantage.

However, it may be noted that the difference between domestic and international trade is one of degree only. In general people tend to migrate within their own country more freely than they migrate abroad. The same is true of capital. Moreover, each country may be said to represent a separate market to its trade partners abroad, although the commodities involved and other terms and conditions may be the same. At times the reason for this separation may be interference by the state for achieving national goals. Markets may also be separated by language, customs, usance, habit, tastes and a host of other differentiating factors.

However, this distinction is rather vague. Even in different regions within a large country like India language, customs, usance, etc., do differ greatly. We may treat Indian market as a single market, but the market in Kolkata and that in Mumbai for the same commodity are quite different in respect of language, customs, etc. In conclusion, we can say that the circumstances governing the character and effects of international trade are more numerous, many-sided and difficult to describe in precise terms than those governing the nature, character and effects of inter-regional trade.

RATIONALE OF TRADE

The classical economists viz., Adam Smith and David Ricardo raised and answered two questions: (i) What is the basis of trade between two countries capable of producing the same two commodities? (ii) Why do countries engage in trade at all?

As an answer to the first question Adam Smith said that international trade is based on absolute advantage. However, Ricardo argued that the theory of absolute advantage does not provide a satisfactory explanation of the basis of trade between two countries. In his view, international trade is based on comparative advantage. Thus while Adam Smith developed the theory of absolute advantage to explain the gains from trade between two countries, Ricardo developed the theory of comparative advantage which, according to him, explains the gains from trade between two countries from the supply side.

As an answer to the second question both the economists argued that countries engage in trade voluntarily. The reason is that they gain from trade. And there are two sources of gains from trade, viz., (i) gains from specialisation and (ii) gains from exchange. Gains from specialisation arise due to increase in labour productivity in both countries after they open up their economies. Gains from exchange arise due to an improvement in the terms of trade[2] (or the international price ratio) after trade. We may now discuss the two classical theories of trade one by one.

1. In fact, the world Trade Organisation (WTO) was set up in 1995 mainly to promote free multilateral trade among its members by removing tariff and non-tariff barriers in a phased manner.

2. A rise in the price of exports or a fall in the price of imports or both at the same time implies an improvement in the terms of trade. And an improvement in the terms of trade is also a source of gains from trade.

A. SMITH'S THEORY OF ABSOLUTE ADVANTAGE

According to Adam Smith's theory of absolute advantage, different countries enjoy absolute advantage in the production of different goods. And trade between them is based on such advantage.

We may now illustrate the theory. In Table 25.1 we show the amounts of cloth and machine produced by one worker in the USA and India per week.

Table 25.1: Output of Worker in One Week

	USA	India
Machine	80	30
Cloth	20	60

We see that one worker in the USA produces 80 machines per week and one worker produces only 30 such machines in India. On the other hand one worker produces only 20 units of cloth in the USA. But one Indian worker produces 60 units of cloth. This simply means that the USA has an absolute advantage in the production of machine and India has a absolute advantage in the production of cloth.

Adam Smith argued that in such a situation both the two countries would gain and world output will increase if each country specialises in the production of only one commodity in which it has absolute advantage and trade with each other.

In Table 25.2 we show that such specialisation and trade would lead to an increase in output and ensure gains to both countries.

Table 25.2: Increase in Output after Specialisation

	USA	India	World Output
Gains in machines	+ 4	– 1	+ 3 machines
Gains in cloth	– 1	+ 2	+ 1 unit of cloth

Suppose in order to specialise in the production of machine, the USA withdraws one worker from the production of cloth and engages him in production of machines. In this case USA will lose 1 unit of cloth and gain 4 machines. In the same way in order to specialise in the production of cloth, India withdraws one worker from the production of machines and transfers him to the cloth industry. In that case, it will lose one machine but gain 2 units of cloth. Thus we see that transfer of labour from one industry to another in the two countries, on the basis of their respective areas of absolute advantage, will result in a net gain of 3 machines and 1 unit of cloth. This additional world output can be shared by the two countries through voluntary exchange.

Thus we see that without increasing the use of any one of the two countries' labour power, specialisation according to the principle of absolute advantage leads to a more efficient allocation of labour and thus an expansion of world output. According to Adam Smith the free play of competitive market forces (or the so-called *invisible hand* mechanism) and adoption of the principle of *laissez faire* (which also implies free trade between two countries) together would lead to specialisation and trade, from which the trading nations would gain.

From the theory of absolute advantage gains from trade are quite obvious. Now suppose a country such as USA can produce both machine and cloth more efficiently than India. The question now is: will the USA can still gain from specialisation and trading with India? This was, in fact, the question which was raised by David Ricardo who presented the theory of comparative cost (advantage) to explain the basis of trade between two countries from the supply side as also to explain the potential gain from international trade. And we now turn to Ricardo's theory.

B. RICARDO'S THEORY OF COMPARATIVE COST (ADVANTAGE)

International specialisation and trade occur mainly due to difference in costs of production. In fact, differences in costs determine what will be produced in different countries. According to Ricardo, who believed in the labour theory of value, differences in production cost occur due to differences in labour cost or labour productivity. And a country tends to specialise in the production that good in which it is relatively efficient. And comparative advantage refers to difference in relative efficiency between two countries in the production of the same two goods.

If each trading nation specialises in its own area of comparative advantage (relative efficiency) total supply of goods will increase. This means that international trade will increase the consumption possibility of each nation by enabling it to go beyond its production possibility curve (PPC).[1]

Ricardo's theory is based on the following two key assumptions:

(i) A perfectly competitive environment prevails in both countries.

(ii) Prices of both goods are equal to their respective labour costs.

The Theory of Comparative Cost in the Presence of Increasing Opportunity Cost

So we have noted that in case of constant opportunity costs, there is complete specialisation. This means that each country specialises in the production of only one commodity after trade. It imports the other commodity instead of producing it domestically. Opportunity costs remain constant when various resources are equally efficient in the production of any of the two goods. But this assumption is unrealistic. Resources (factor inputs) are not equally efficient in the production of both the goods. This is why we encounter the situation of increasing opportunity cost in which case PPC of each country, instead of being a straight line, is concave to the origin as shown in Fig. 25.1. This means that as resources are shifted from the production of machines to the production of cloth, marginal opportunity cost of cloth (i.e., the number of machines sacrificed for production of an extra unit of cloth) goes on increasing. The converse is also true.

In the presence of increasing opportunity cost the slope of the PPC is not the same as the domestic price ratio, as in the case of constant opportunity cost. Now the domestic price ratio (exchange rate) is also determined by demand conditions (and not just by supply conditions as Ricardo had postulated). In such a situation the production of two goods will be optimum when the following condition is satisfied:

$$MRT_{C,M} = \frac{P_C}{P_M} \qquad \ldots (1)$$

where $MRT_{C,M}$ is the marginal rate of transformation between the two goods (which is indeed the slope of PPC), P_C is the price of cloth and P_M is the price of machine.[2]

In Fig. 25.1 the domestic (pre-trade) price ratio between machine and cloth as determined by domestic demand and supply conditions is given by the dotted line (P_C/P_M). In pre-trade situation one country (say, India) produces at point S where the domestic price ratio is the same as the $MRT_{C,M}$. Now if the international price of cloth is higher than its domestic price, it will force India to engage in trade with another country (say the USA) or the rest of the world and increase the production of cloth and reduce that of machine. Suppose the terms of trade (or the international price ratio) is shown by the solid line tt'. The slope of the line indicates higher price for cloth and lower price for machine

1. Ricardo did not take into account the role of prices in his theory. According to him international trade is an organised system of barter.

2. The consumption of two goods in India depends on demand conditions which are determined by the tastes and preferences of Indian buyers. These are usually shown by social or community indifference curves (not presented here). We will make use of these curves later in the chapter in the context of the Heckscher-Ohlin theory of international trade which is essentially the modern theory of comparative advantage.

as compared to their respective domestic prices. This means that more machines can be obtained for the same amount of cloth.

In such a situation it will be advantageous for India to increase the production of cloth by transferring (diverting) some resources from machine. After trade India will reach equilibrium at T, where its PPC AZ is just tangent to the terms of trade line tt'. Thus India will now produce at T, but consume at point C. This means now it will export $Q'_C Q^{\circ}_C$ $(= BT)$ amount of cloth and import $Q^{\circ}_M Q'_M$ $(= BC)$ number of machines. And the triangle TBC is called India's trade triangle.

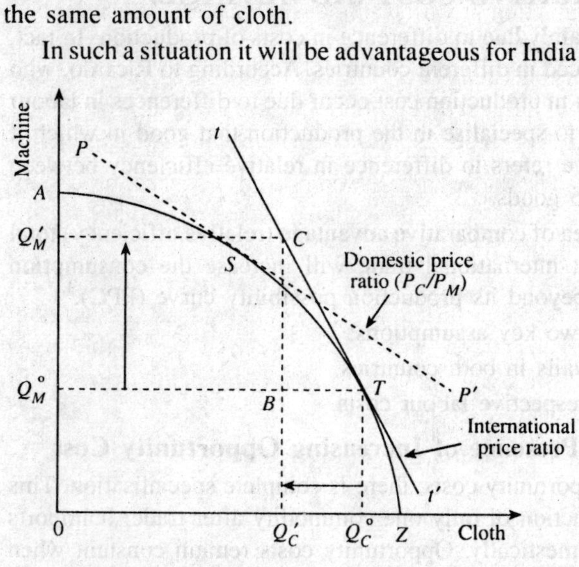

Fig. 25.1: Comparative Advantage in the Presence of Increasing Opportunity Cost

Thus we see that international trade has enabled India to consume more of both goods than in the absence of trade, i.e., under self-sufficiency (at point S).[1] This is clear from Fig. 25.1 where the consumption point lies above and to the right of point S.

We therefore see that in the presence of increasing opportunity cost, specialisation is, at best, incomplete. Ricardo failed to take note of this point which has validity in the real world. This point may be explained further.

Note that opportunity cost increases due to the operation of a fundamental technological law, viz., the law of diminishing returns. As India increases the production of cloth by diverting resources from the machine-producing industry marginal opportunity cost rises. This means that more and more machines are to be sacrificed to increase production of cloth by every extra unit. The reason is that as more and more labour is used in cloth industry marginal product of labour falls. In such a situation, it will be judicious on the part of India to stop at point T and end up producing both machines and cloth rather than move to point Z and end up specialising in the production of cloth completely.

The same thing holds for India's trading partner—the USA. The USA will encounter the operation of the law of diminishing returns as it increases the production of machines by transferring resources (manpower) from cloth industry to machine-producing industry. And opportunity cost (or transformation) ratios in the two countries may become equal even before either country ends up specialising completely in the production of only one commodity.

In short, in two-country, two-commodity world of the Ricardian type each country gains from trade since it is able to obtain a higher price for the commodity in which it specialises (due to its lower cost of production). It also gains because it pays a lower price for the commodity in the production of which it is less efficient.

Critical Review of Ricardo's Theory

The Ricardian theory of comparative cost is based on sound logic. Its basic contention that a country will gain by specialising in its own area of comparative cost (advantage) is still valid. As Paul Samuelson put it, the theory of comparative advantage contains an element of truth. The theory gives a satisfactory explanation of gains from trade. In spite of this Ricardo's theory has been criticised on the following grounds:

1. *The labour theory of value* : The Ricardian theory considers only labour cost to measure the comparative cost of producing various goods. However, labour is not the only factor of production, as Ricardo assumed. So total money cost incurred on labour and all other factors should be taken into account for estimation of comparative costs of production of various goods. However, G. Haberler and others reformulated the theory in terms of opportunity costs by taking into account all productive factors and these rescued the theory from the labour theory of value. And Haberler successfully reformulated the old classical theory of comparative cost in terms of general equilibrium theory. He also explained the classical theory in terms of opportunity costs, i.e., costs as alternative opportunities forgone.

2. *Causes of differences in comparative costs* : Ricardo argued that comparative costs of producing different commodities in various countries differed due to differences in efficiency (productivity) of labour. However, he failed to explain why the efficiency of labour varies from country to country.

According to the modern theories of comparative cost, developed by E. Heckscher and B.Ohlin comparative costs differ because different countries have different factor endowments. In addition, different production functions use the same factors in different proportions. In other words, the factor proportions are not the same in the production of different goods. [The Heckscher-Ohlin theory will be discussed in detail in the next section of this chapter.]

3. *Increasing opportunity cost and incomplete specialisation* : As already noted, if production takes place under conditions of increasing opportunity costs, specialisation in each country will be incomplete. This goes against the original Ricardian prediction that each country specialises completely in the production of only one commodity.

4. *The role of demand in determining the terms of trade* : The Ricardian theory fails to explain at what rate a trading nation will exchange its exports for its imports. In other words, the theory fails to explain what determines the terms of trade (or the international price ratio). However, the determination of the terms of trade is an issue of considerable importance to a nation. The reason is that an improvement in the terms of trade is also a source of gains from trade.

It was J. S. Mill, another classical economist, who removed this shortcoming of the Ricardian theory by explaining the determination of the terms of trade by introducing the theory of reciprocal demand. According to this theory the terms of trade are determined by the demand for one country's product by the other country and vice-versa.

5. *Trade based on general equilibrium theory of value* : Ohlin offered a satisfactory explanation of why comparative costs of producing different commodities vary among nations in terms of differences in factor proportions. In his view, the same two (or more) factors are to be used in different proportions in the production of different goods. He further improved the comparative cost theory by incorporating in his analysis the role of demand and thus based his theory on the general equilibrium theory of value.

6. *Two-country-two-commodity trade* : Ricardo's theory explains only bilateral trade. It also explains trade in only two goods. However, this is a serious (and a genuine) criticism of Ricardo's theory. In fact, F. Graham showed that the theory could be extended to cover more than two countries and two commodities. Thus it may explain multilateral and multi-commodity trade.

7. *Changing pattern of comparative advantage in a dynamic world* : The whole Ricardian theory was cast in a static analytical framework. However, in a dynamic world characterised by changes in factor supplies and improvements in technology, particularly in developing countries, we find changing pattern of comparative advantage. A country like India, for example, lost its comparative advantage in jute goods and cotton textiles to some extent and has acquired comparative advantage in software and consultancy services.[1] Similarly, the USA has lost its comparative advantage in shipbuilding and Singapore has gained it.

1. In fact, many developing countries protect their infant industries from foreign competition through import tariffs and import quotas. The main objective is to gain comparative advantage in the long run.

Conclusion

In spite of all these criticisms, the Ricardian theory still provides a simple and straightforward explanation of trade among nations. So it is used as a basic framework for studying trading patterns among nations.

THE HECKSCHER-OHLIN THEORY OF INTERNATIONAL TRADE

For nearly two hundred years since the publication of Ricardo's theory of comparative cost 1817 economists could explain trade based on comparative advantage, but they could not explain what caused comparative advantage. Heckscher and Ohlin explained the causes (or sources) of comparative advantage. Paul Samuelson later refined their basic idea, which is referred to as the factor proportions theory. The factor proportions theory states that a country's comparative advantage is determined by its initial resource endowments.

The Hickscher-Ohlin theory took into account the effect of differences in factor supplies (mainly land, labour and capital) on international specialisation. The theory also enables us to describe analytically the impact of economic growth on trade patterns and the impact of trade on the structure of national economies and on the differential returns or payments to various factors of production.

In fact the modern theory of comparative cost (advantage) developed by Heckscher and Ohlin suggests that differences in factor endowments of different countries and differences in factor proportions in production functions of different commodities account for differences in comparative cost. And the so-called Heckscher-Ohlin theory is known as the factor endowment theory as also the general equilibrium theory of international trade.

Contrary to the view of classical economists, Ohlin argues that there is no fundamental difference between domestic (inter-regional) trade and international trade. Both types of trade occur due to differences in factor endowments. Thus international trade is just a special case of inter-regional trade.

Synopsis for Learning: Inter-Regional and International Trade

Heckscher and Ohlin developed the thesis that both inter-regional and international trade are devices for the spatial exchange of the goods and services produced by factors of production since the factors themselves are to a greater or lesser extent incapable of being moved in space. Land is a classic example of an immovable factor. Consequently relative prices in different geographical locations depend on the relative scarcity of factor endowments in those locations.

According to the H-O theory comparative costs differ among nations for two main reasons:

(i) Different countries have different factor endowments.

(ii) Factor proportions or intensities differ in the production of different goods.

Focus on Terminology: Factor Intensity

Factor intensity refers to the relative properties of various factors of production used in producing goods and services. The factor intensity of the techniques of production chosen by a cost-minimising firm depends on the relative prices of different factors of production. For any given set of relative factor prices, some goods are produced with a low capital-labour ratio. Such goods are labour-intensive. Others are produced with a high capital-labour ratio. Such goods are capital-intensive. Agricultural goods may be produced by using a significant input of land and relatively few other inputs. Such products are land-intensive.

Factor Endowments

These are two definitions of factor endowments, viz., (a) the physical definition and (b) the price definition.

(a) ***The physical definition*** : If India has more labour and less capital than the USA then India will be called a labour-abundant country and the USA a capital-abundant country.

(b) ***The price definition*** **:** If the wage rate (i.e., the price of labour) is lower in India than in the USA and the price of capital (i.e., the rate of interest or the periodic rental) is lower in the USA than in India, then India will be treated as a labour-abundant country and the USA as a capital-abundant country.

It is quite obvious that factor endowments and factor prices are inseparably linked up with each other. Labour which is relatively abundant in India will have a lower price and capital which is relatively scarce will have a higher price. In the USA capital is an abundant factor and labour is a scarce factor. In India it is just the opposite. Due to this difference in factor endowments, capital will be relatively cheap in America and labour will be relatively expensive. In India it is just the other way round. So we can write:

$$\left(\frac{K}{L}\right)_A > \left(\frac{K}{L}\right)_I \quad \ldots (2)$$

$$\text{or, } \left(\frac{r}{w}\right)_A < \left(\frac{r}{w}\right)_I \quad \ldots (3)$$

where K is capital, L is labour, A stands for America and I for India, r is the price of capital or the interest rate and w is the price of labour or the wage rate.

Thus physical differences get reflected in price differences. In other words, the differences in factor endowments lead to differences in factor prices and hence account for differences in comparative costs of producing different commodities among trading nations.

In addition, differences in factor endowments and factor prices together account for differences in factor proportions (if, of course, we ignore the issue of technology[1]). And differences in factor proportions among different industries also account for differences in comparative cost. Since production functions differ from commodity to commodity and country to country, we also find differences in factor proportions or factor intensities. For example, the production of a good may require more capital than labour. It is, therefore, called a capital-intensive good. By comparison the production of another good may require more labour than capital and this is called a labour-intensive good. These differences in factor proportions (or factor intensities) in the production of different goods account for differences in comparative costs of producing them and lead to differences in their prices in different countries.

The Main Prediction of the H-O Theory

According to the H-O theory exports of a country are intensive in its abundant factor and imports are intensive in its scarce factor. This means that a capital-abundant country such as in USA will export a capital-intensive good such as machine and import a labour-intensive good such as cloth. This is because $\left(\frac{r}{w}\right)_A < \left(\frac{r}{w}\right)_I$. The reason is that a capital-abundant capital country has a comparative advantage in the production of a capital-intensive good and comparative disadvantage in the production of a labour-intensive good. The reverse is the case with India since the USA's comparative advantage[2] is India's comparative disadvantage and vice-versa. The reason is that $\left(\frac{w}{r}\right)_I < \left(\frac{w}{r}\right)_A$.

1. In reality differences in technology account for differences in factor proportions even if factor prices are the same in the two countries.

2. In fact, comparative advantage is a relative term. This simply means that comparative advantage in the production of one commodity implies comparative disadvantage in the other.

Economic Insight: Inter-Industry Trade

The H-O theorem explains inter-industry trade, i.e., trade between countries whose exports and imports consist of different types of goods. Such trade is based on differences in factor endowments. Countries tend to export goods which intensively use their abundant factors in production. They import goods which they cannot produce themselves or which they can only produce at high cost due to a scarcity of the factors intensively used in producing them.

Graphical Representation of the H-O Theory

We may now graphically represent the H-O theory of international trade. Here we assume that there are two countries – the USA and India. While the USA is a capital-abundant country, India is a labour-abundant one. So the USA will export a capital-intensive good (such as machine) to India and India will export a labour-intensive good (such as cloth) to the USA.

Due to differences in factor endowments the two countries will have different production possibility curves. The PPC of USA is *AZ* as shown in Fig. 25.2. Being a capital-abundant country, it can produce the more capital-intensive good machine than the labour-intensive good cloth. By contrast India, being a labour-abundant country, can produce more of the labour-intensive good cloth than the capital-intensive good machine. Each country will reach pre-trade equilibrium when the following condition holds:

$$MRT_{MC} = MRS_{MC} = \frac{P_M}{P_C} \quad \ldots (4)$$

where MRT_{MC} is the marginal rate of transformation of machine for cloth in production MRS_{MC} is the marginal rate of substitution of machine for cloth in consumption and $\frac{P_M}{P_C}$ is the ratio of the two prices, i.e., the price of machine divided by the price of cloth.

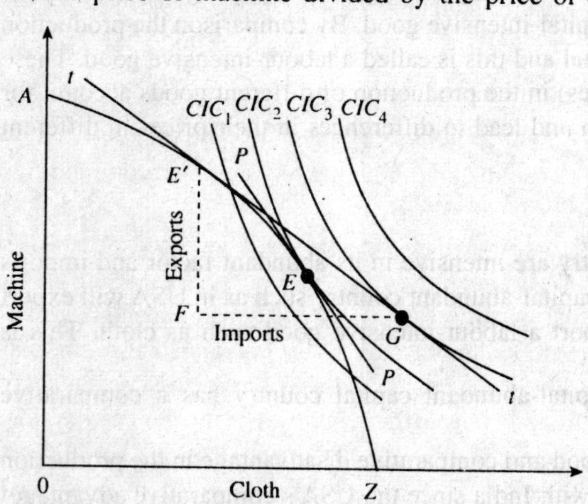

Fig. 25.2: Exports and Imports of USA

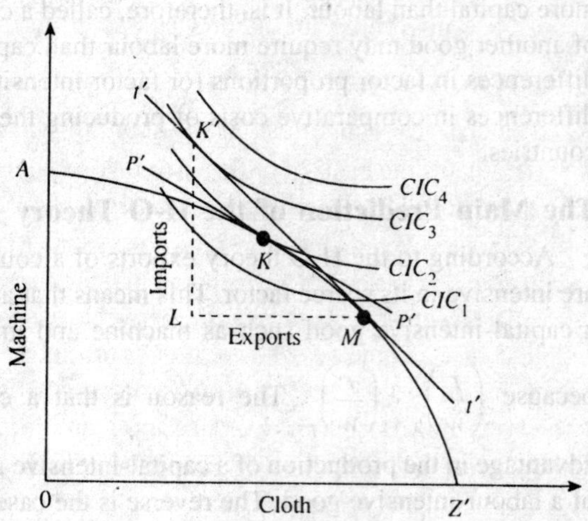

Fig. 25.3: Exports and Imports of India

The equilibrium condition given by equation (4) implies that under self-sufficiency both production and consumption in the two countries would take place at the point of tangency of the PPC with the highest attainable community indifference curve.

We see that under self-sufficiency the USA will be in equilibrium at point *E* where the PPC (*AZ*) is tangent to the community indifference curve (CIC_2). The tangency of the PPC and CIC_2 at point *E* indicates relative price, i.e., the ratio of the two domestic (pre-trade) prices.

By comparison, before trade when India is self-sufficient it produces at point *K*. This is India's (autarkic) equilibrium. At this point India's PPC (*A′Z′*) is just tangent to the community indifference curve CIC_2. The tangent passing through point *K* indicates the pre-trade (domestic) price ratio.

Since the domestic price ratios of the two commodities in the two countries differ as is indicated by the slopes of the tangents *PP* and *P′P′*, it will be judicious on the part of both the countries to engage into mutually beneficial trade with each other. Suppose the common international price ratio or the terms of trade (or the rate at which the two goods are exchanged between two countries) is given by the line *tt*. The USA will now produce at point *E′* at which the terms of trade line *tt* is tangent to the PPC (*AZ*). However, it will now consume a point *G* at which the terms of trade line is tangent to a higher community indifference curve CIC_3. This implies that the USA gains from trade. International trade enables it to increase its consumption possibilities by changing the composition of output even without augmenting its resources (factor supplies).

By comparing the production and consumption points before and after trade we see that the USA export *E′F* units of machine and imports *FG* units of cloth.

After trade India will produce at point *M* where its PPC (*A′Z′*) is tangent to the terms of line *tt*. India will now consume at point *K′* at which the terms of trade line *tt* is tangent to the community indifference curve CIC_3. Thus trade enables India to increase its consumption possibilities by being able to move from CIC_2 to CIC_3. And we see that after trade India produces *LM* units more of cloth and *LK′* less of machine than it consumes domestically. This means that India exports *LM* units of cloth and import *LK′* units of machine.Thus we see that USA specialises in the production of machine and exports it to India in exchange for its import of cloth from India, since it has a comparative disadvantage (relative inefficiency) in the production of cloth.

India will specialise in the production of cloth, export it to the USA in exchange for its import of machine, in which it has comparative disadvantage.

Trade Triangle

In short, before trade production and consumption in each country take place at the same point. After trade the two points differ, as is indicated in the trade triangle of each country. In Fig. 25.2 while *E′FG* is the trade triangle of the USA in Fig. 25.3, *K′LM* is India's trade triangle. The two trade triangles are identical since in a two-commodity two-country framework one country's export is the other country's import and vice-versa. Thus we see that due to differences in factor endowments in the USA and India as also due to differences in factor-incentives the production of the two goods in the two countries, there will always exist a basis of trade between two countries from both the supply side (as shown by the PPC of the two countries) and demand side (as shown by their respective community indifference curves). And both countries would gain from trade by specialising in the production of goods which make use of their abundant factors and by importing those goods which make use of their scarce factors. In short, exports are intensive in a country's abundant factors and imports are intensive in its scarce factors.

The differences between the production and consumption after trade is shown by trade triangle

Commentary: The Role of Demand
The mechanism whereby the benefits of trade are transmitted across national boundaries under the H-O approach is similar to that of the Ricardian theory. However, in the H-O case, with the possibility of different factor combinations for producing different commodities nations are assumed to be operating initially at some point on their concave (or increasing opportunity cost) production possibility frontier determined by domestic demand conditions. Thus one cannot say that demand has no role to play in the H-O theory. In other words, while Ricardo considered the supply side the H-O theory takes into account both the demand and the supply side.

In short, the H-O theory suggests that the capital-abundant countries will tend to specialise in such products as automobiles, aircrafts, sophisticated electronic communication goods and computers which have high capital intensity in their production technology. They will export some of these capital- intensive products in exchange for the labour- or land-intensive products like food, raw materials and minerals that can best be produced by countries which are relatively well endowed with labour or land. Due to increasing opportunity costs associated with resource shifting among commodities with different factor intensities of production complete specialisation will not occur as in the original Ricardian theory. Rising domestic costs and therefore domestic prices going above world prices will prevent complete specialisation.

Improvement of the H-O Theory over the Ricardian Theory

1. ***Equalisation of commodity prices*** **:** We have already noted, in the context of both the Ricardian theory and the H-O theory, that after trade and under free trade (i.e., in the absence of tariffs and quotas), the forces of international competition would lead to equalisation of commodity prices in the two countries — the USA and India. The reason is easy to find out. After trade the export of machine by the USA to India will lower their prices in India and raise their prices in the USA. Machines will be less abundant in the USA and machines will be less scarce in India than under autarky. This implies that prices of machines will rise in the USA and fall in India. Ultimately free trade between the two countries will lead to equalisation of the prices of machines. Exactly the same thing will happen in case of cloth. The price of cloth will rise in India and fall in USA and the trend will continue until and unless the two prices are equalised between the two countries.

2. ***Equalisation of factor prices*** **:** Paul Samuelson has proved conclusively that trade in commodities acts as a substitute for trade in factors. And free trade between two (or more) countries tends to equalise not only commodity prices but factor prices as well. The reason is easy to find out.

The export of machines by the USA using its abundant factor, capital will increase the demand for capital and thus make it relatively less abundant and, therefore, raise its price. By contrast, the import of cloth embodying large amounts of relatively scarce factor, labour would make it less scarce and therefore lower its price. The same thing will happen in India also. This simply means that changes in factor prices after trade between USA and India would result in the equalisation of factor prices (prices of capital and prices of labour) in them. The point may be explained further.

As a result of trade between the USA and India the demand for capital will increase in the USA and that of labour in India. As a result the price of capital in the USA and that of labour in India will rise. The reason is that with the import of labour-intensive good cloth by the USA and diversion of resources from the production of labour-intensive cloth to capital-intensive machines, the demand for labour and its price in the USA will fall. Thus, all other things remaining unchanged, the price of labour in India and that in the USA will tend to become equal after trade. The same argument holds in case of the price of capital[1].

In short, according to the H-O theory, free trade in goods between two countries would lead an equalisation of factor prices. Thus even if factors were not mobile between countries, free movement of goods from one country to another would equalise their prices.

Focus on Terminology: Factor Price Equalisation
Factor price equalisation refers to a tendency for international trade to reduce international differences relative factor prices. Imports of goods intensive in scarce factors lower the demand for them and their prices. By contrast, exports raise the demand for and thus the prices of abundant factors. Trade thus tends to reduce international differences in relative factor prices. In the absence of transport costs and restrictions on international trade (in the form of tariffs and quotas) complete factor price equalisation would result. In the presence of transport cost and trade barriers, trade tends merely to reduce international factor price differences and thus lead to only partial equalisation of such prices.

1. As India imports machines the demand for capital in India and its price will fall. And with the expansion of trade between the two countries, the forces of international competition would lead to equalisation of market prices of two goods.

In short, what would have been the case with free movement of factors between countries is indirectly achieved through movement of commodities differing in factor intensities. Thus according to Samuelson, who proceeded one step ahead of Ohlin, trade in commodities acts as a substitute for international mobility of factors.

According to the H-O theory countries (or regions) will export commodities which are produced with their relatively abundant factors of production and will import those which are produced with their relative scarce factors. Consequently international trade leads to an equalisation of factor prices between trading nations. This does not mean that they will be equalised in practice. There is at best a tendency toward equalisation of such prices.

Partial vs. Complete Factor Price Equalisation

In reality we find only partial equalisation of factor prices. However complete factor price equalisation can be achieved only under certain restrictive assumptions. These are the following:

1. The tastes and preferences of consumers or their patterns of demand remain same in each country even after trade.

2. There is no qualitative difference in factors of production. This means that factors do not differ in efficiency and productivity.

[By contrast, Ricardo assumed that differences in labour cost or labour productivity account for differences in comparative cost (advantage).]

3. The state of technology remains unchanged in each country.

4. The production function of each industry is the same in the two countries, i.e., it is either capital-intensive or labour-intensive. Such a simple type of production function permits limited substitution possibility between capital and labour.

5. There is no transport cost.

6. There are no barriers to trade in the form of tariffs and quotas in any of the trading nations.

7. Both the commodity markets and the factor markets are perfectly competitive. This means that factor prices remain constant even if the demand for one factor increases and that of another factor falls in each country after trade.

Since these are very restrictive assumptions and are not fulfilled in reality, complete factor price equalisation is not possible in reality. So we find just a tendency toward partial equalisation of factor prices.

Economic Insight: The Stopler-Samuelson Theorem
Another deduction the factor price equalisation theorem, originating from H-O theory is the Stopler-Samuelson theorem. The essence of the theorem is that free trade benefits a country's abundant factor and hurts its scarce factor. This theorem may now be briefly explained. As trade opens up, a country produces more of the good which uses its abundant factor more intensively and less of the good which uses its scarce factor most intensively. The reason is that exports are intensive in its scarce factor. With the expansion of trade the abundant factor becomes less abundant and the scarce factor becomes less scarce. As a result the price of the abundant factor (such as capital in the USA) rises and that of the scarce factor (such as labour in the USA) falls. Thus the owners of capital gain and the workers lose. An exactly opposite thing happens in India. In the context of developing countries, this generally labour means a rise in the share of national income going to labour. Under self-sufficiency share of the labour is likely to be small. Thus trade is supposed to promote greater equality in domestic income distribution.

Theory and Reality

The H-O theory predicts that international real wages rates and capital costs will gradually tend toward equalisation. In recent years, many highly paid manufacturing workers in the more developed countries apprehended that free trade and greater international competition would push their wages down to the levels of the developing countries.

But this has not happened except in a few Asian newly industrialising countries. In truth, the wage gap between developed and developing country workers remains persistently wide and in some cases has even increased.

A Critical Evaluation of the Heckscher-Ohlin Theory

The H-O theory has both merits and drawbacks. We first discuss the merits of the theory.

Merits of the Theory

There is no denying the fact that Heckscher and Ohlin have made an invaluable contribution to the theory of international trade. The theory does not deny that international trade is based on differences in comparative cost (advantage) between two (or more) countries. But it is a distinct improvement over the classical (Ricardian) theory for the following reasons:

(i) *General equilibrium approach* : Firstly the H-O theory rescued the theory of comparative cost from the shakles of the labour theory of value and reformulated it by adopting the general equilibrium approach. And according to this approach demand and supply conditions together determine the prices of goods and factors simultaneously in a much broader framework.

(ii) *Equivalence of inter-regional and international trade* : As soon as the H-O theory appeared, the distinction between inter-regional and international trade disappeared. The reason is that the basis of both types of trade is the same, i.e., differences in factor endowments.

(iii) *A more realistic explanation of the basis of trade* : Ricardo's explanation of the basis of trade between two countries (viz., differences in labour productivity) is not quite satisfactory. By contrast the reason mentioned by the H-O theory for differences in comparative costs between two countries, viz., differences in factor endowments between two countries and in factor proportions between two industries are quite valid.

The H-O explanation of the basis of trade is broadly true

(iv) *Present vs. future trade* : According to modern economists like K. Lancaster and Paul Krugman, the H-O theory presents a clear picture of the future of foreign trade. The Ricardian theory postulates that international trade exists due to differences in skill, ability and efficiency of labour or even technology (in the modern world)[1]. This means that with transmission of knowledge between two countries, trade between them comes to an end. By contrast the H-O theory suggests that even if there is complete transmission of knowledge between two countries international trade would not come to an end due to immobility of certain factors such as land and other natural resources.

Shortcomings of the H-O Theory

The H-O theory is not totally free from defects. It has the following shortcomings also:

(i) *The Leontief paradox* : In the H-O theory the forces operating from the supply side are much stronger than those operating from the demand side in determining factor prices. But if the forces operating from the demand side become stronger then the main prediction of the H-O theory may not hold. Suppose, for instance, there is high demand for capital in a capital-abundant country like the USA than in India. In such a situation the USA may export labour-intensive goods and import capital-intensive goods. This surprising result is a serious challenge to the H-O theory. In 1954 W.W. Leontief discovered that US exports were labour-intensive while US imports were capital-intensive. This finding contradicted the H-O theory, according to which a capital-abundant country like the USA would tend to export goods made with high capital-labour ratios and to import goods made with low capital-labour ratios. This surprising result has been called the Leontief paradox.[2]

---

1. In the modern world efficiency of labour depends also on technology.

2. Various attempts have been made to resolve the paradox. For details see any book on international economies.

(ii) ***Factor-intensive reversal*** : A production process is either capital-intensive or labour-intensive at a particular factor-price ratio. If there is a fall in the wage rate and thus a change in the factor-price ratio, the capital-intensive production process may become a labour-intensive one. Similarly in the event of a fall in the rate of interest (or the rental price of the capital) a labour-intensive production process may become a capital-intensive one. This is known as factor intensity reversal. And in the presence of factor-intensive reversal, the basic prediction of the H-O theory and its corollary, the factor price equalisation theorem will not hold.

Conclusion

The H-O theory presents a static supply-oriented interpretation of international trade which assumes that production functions are the same in all countries. The theory takes no account of the influence of dynamic technological change on comparative advantage nor does it consider the effect of demand and product differentiation on the pattern of international trade flows.

OTHER EXPLANATIONS OF TRADE

Over the years modern economists have modified and extended the H-O theory by dropping the assumptions that transport costs are zero, that there are no import duties, that economies of scale are absent, that the pattern of demand is identical everywhere, that capital as well as labour is immobile and that exchange rates are freely flexible. And various other explanations of the basis of trade between two or more countries have been suggested by modern economists. Some of these are the following:

1. Differences in Tastes and Preferences of Buyers (or in Demand Conditions)

The H-O theory has explained the basis of trade from the supply (production) side. Critics have pointed out that differences in the pattern of demand between two countries also give rise to mutually beneficial trade between them. And some modern economists have explained the basis of trade from demand (consumption) side.

According to the H-O theory, if two countries have the same factor endowments and cost ratios are also the same (due to the existence of the same production functions and the use of any two or more factors in the same proportion), then there would exist no trade between them. Modern economists have shown that trade between them is still possible if the patterns of demand or the preferences of the people of the two countries such as the USA and India for machines and cloth differ greatly.

Economic Insight: Demand Reversal

A strong assumption of the H-O model is that tastes and preferences are identical in all trading nations. If this is not true, it is not possible to predict the pre-trade (autarkic) prices and thus pattern of trade. The reason is that tastes and preferences in each country could cause it to treat (value) different products differently. An extreme example of this is known as demand reversal.

The difference in the nature of demand between any two trading countries, with each tending to prefer the good intensive in its physically abundant factor, may and often does cause them to trade in a manner opposite to that anticipated by the H-O analysis.

While demand patterns seem to be similar throughout the world, especially among similar economic (income) or social classes, differences in tastes and preferences certainly exist. If the differences are strong enough, then they can reduce the ability of the H-O model to predict the pattern of trade and the movement of factor prices (which have one-to-one correspondence with commodity prices).

2. Economies of Scale

Economies of scale also form the basis of trade between two countries. Economies of scale refer to the advantages of large-scale (or mass) production. With an increase in the demand for a good and expansion of its market, cost per unit falls. In other words, by expanding the size of the domestic market international trade allows a firm to increase its production. This increase in production can lead to greater efficiency and reductions in unit cost. And this gives domestic firms a distinctive advantage in overseas market. The reason is that while a high-cost firm cannot compete closely with its foreign counterparts, a low-cost firm can gain comparative advantage in the long run by becoming efficient. This point is illustrated in Fig. 25.4.

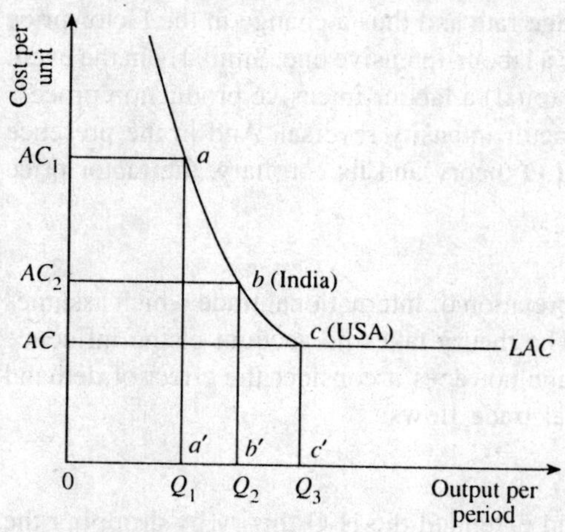

Fig. 25.4: Mass Production as the Basis of Trade

Suppose initially an Indian firm and an American firm face same cost conditions. So they have same average cost curve *LAC*. Cost per unit continues to fall with an increase in volume of production up to Q_3. After that cost remain constant and the *LAC* curve becomes horizontal. The level of output Q_3 indicates the minimum efficient scale of production.[1] The *LAC* of Q_1, say, computers is *aa′* and that of Q_2 is *bb′*. If the demand for computers per period (say, one year) is Q_2 in both the USA and India there would exist no trade between them. The reason is that cost per unit is the same. So price per computer will also be same.

Now suppose the demand for computers in India increases to Q_3 due to spread of education and computerisation of manual operations in most service-oriented industries such as banking, insurance, health care, and education. But the demand for computers remains constant in the USA at Q_2 per annum. So the Indian firms will now produce Q_3 units of computers and will be able to reduce cost further from *bb′* to *cc′* by taking advantage of economies of scale. As a result the price of computers will also fall. But cost per unit in the USA remains constant at *bb′*. Now the Indian firm can export a portion of its expanded output to the USA at a price which is lower than which prevails there. This simple example shows that economies of scale can be a realistic explanation of trade between countries.

3. Learning by Doing

Following K. J. Arrow, modern trade theorists have argued that cost per unit may fall in a country due to the knowledge and experience gained and accumulated by firms in producing a commodity over time. This is known as learning by doing or learning from experience. As a country produces larger and larger volumes of output over a period of time, its workers and managers gain experience through repetitive performance. As they gradually learn from experience less and less time is required to perform the same task. This virtually amounts to an increase in labour productivity and a fall in labour cost and thus fall in total cost. As cost per unit of the product falls it becomes profitable for a country to export it to other countries. So cost per unit becomes a function of the cumulative volume of output. The difference between economies of scale and learning by doing is shown in Fig. 25.5. In the presence of economies of scale, there is movement along the same *LAC* curve from *A* to *B*. This implies a fall in unit cost with an increase in the volume of output. In the presence of learning effect, the original *LAC* curve shifts downwards to *LAC′*. This implies fall in cost per unit of each level of output.

Learning by doing offers another explanation of trade between two countries from the supply side. And this simple hypothesis gets enough empirical support.

In short, the country which produces a good at a lower cost per unit by learning to use its labour and capital more efficiently can engage in trade. This is very much true for Japan and Korea which are resource-scarce countries.

1. It refers to the minimum level of output which has to be produced to minimise cost per unit.

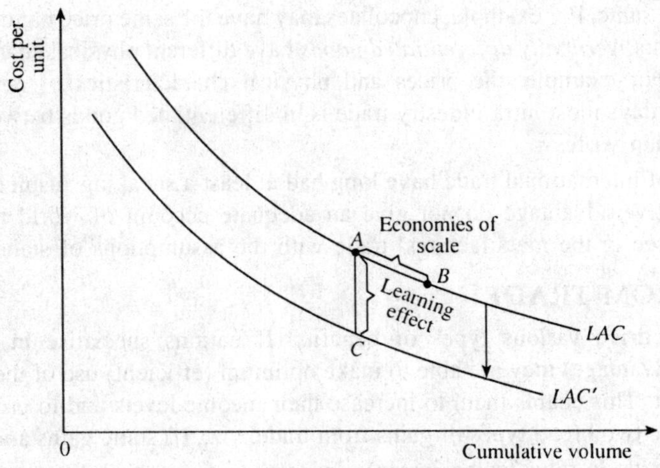

Fig. 25.5: Economies of Scale Vs. Learning Effect

Synopsis for Learning—Learning by Doing and Trade
Learning by doing is a valid explanation of trade for resource-scarce countries such as Japan and Korea.

The learning by doing explanation of comparative cost (advantage) is an example of gaining comparative advantage over time. In this case the whole causation is reversed. It is not lower cost per unit due to different factor endowments which induces a country to specialise and engage in trade. Instead it is specialisation which reduces cost per unit over time and forms the basis of trade. In the language of W. C. Sawyer and R. L. Sprinkle, "Learning curves have some important implications for international trade. The country that produces the largest quantity of products has the lower cost, not because of different resource endowments, but because it has learnt to use its labour and/or capital more efficiently. In this case, comparative advantage is something that is created. As such, it is not low costs that cause a country to specialise and trade; rather, it is specialisation that causes the low unit costs."

4. Intra-Industry Trade

Intra-industry trade refers to trade where goods of the same classification are both imported and exported. A large share of international trade is not based on comparative advantage that results from different factor endowments. Countries also trade essentially the same goods with one another. Intra-industry trade refers to international trade that occurs when a country exports and imports goods within the same industry or product group. For example, India exports certain varieties of steel and imports steel of certain other varieties. Similarly India exports Titan watches and imports Casio and Citizen watches[1].

Intra-industry trade is a consequence of imperfect competition. Firms with monopoly power sell to every country in which there is scope for making profits. In other words, intra-industry trade is a consequence of imperfect competition and often takes place between countries with similar factor endowments. By contrast, intra-industry trade arises from differences in factor endowments between countries. So a type of good is either exported or imported, but not both.

5. Monopolistic Competition

Monopolistically, competitive markets mostly explain intra-industry trade in differentiated products between (among) countries. *Horizontally differentiated goods* slightly differ among themselves but their

1. This is true in case of apples also. India exports certain varieties of apples and imports other varieties.

prices are almost the same. For example, chocolates may have the same price but often contain different flavours or ingredients. *Vertically differentiated goods* have different physical characteristics. And their prices also differ. For example, the prices and physical characteristics of new automobiles vary enormously. Now-a-days most intra-industry trade is in differentiated goods between countries. In this context Paul Krugman writes :

"Most students of international trade have long had at least a sneaking suspicion that conventional models of comparative advantage do not give an adequate account of world trade.... It is hard to reconcile what we see in the manufactures' trade with the assumptions of standard trade theory."

THE GAINS FROM TRADE

Trading nations drive various types of benefits. If nations specialise in their own areas of comparative cost (advantage) they are able to make optimum (efficient) use of their resource and thus produce more output. This enabls them to increase their income levels and to promote welfare of the people. Nations drive two broad types of gains from trade, viz., (i) static gains and (ii) dynamic gains.

Static gains from trade refer to the increase in consumption possibilities and thus in the utility (welfare) levels of the people of the trading nations as a result of specialisation and exchange. Such gains are thus decomposed into two parts viz., (i) gains from specialisation (ii) gains from exchange. The former arise due to an improvement in factor productivity after specialisation and the latter arise from an improvement in the terms of trade. These two types of gains are different but interrelated and are now illustrated graphically.

A DETAILED DISCUSSION OF STATIC GAINS

We go back to our earlier example of trade between the USA and India in machines and cloth. In Fig. 25.6 we see that before trade the USA produces and consumes at point *E* at which its PPC (*AZ*) is tangent to a community indifference curve CIC_1 and the slope of the PPC is equal to the domestic price ratio as shown by the tangent *pp*. Now suppose it specialises in machines and produces at point *T*. It exports *TB* number of machines to India and imports *BC* amount of cloth from India. So *TBC* is the USA's trade triangle. Now the USA consumes at point *C* which is on a higher community indifference curve (CIC_2). Since point *C* lies above and to the right of point *S*, the USA is able to consume more of both the goods than in the absence of trade. Now the international price ratio or the terms of trade is indicted by the line *tt* which is tangent to both PPC (at point *T*) and CIC_2 (at point *C*). Since after trade the USA is able to move to a higher community indifference curve, there is an improvement in welfare of the US people. In other words, the USA has gained from trade.

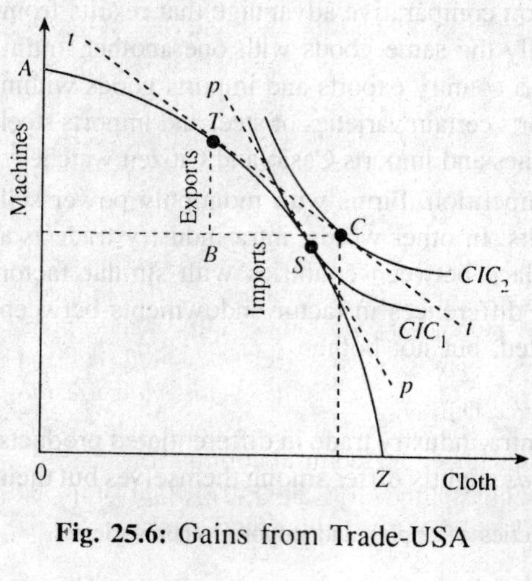

Fig. 25.6: Gains from Trade-USA

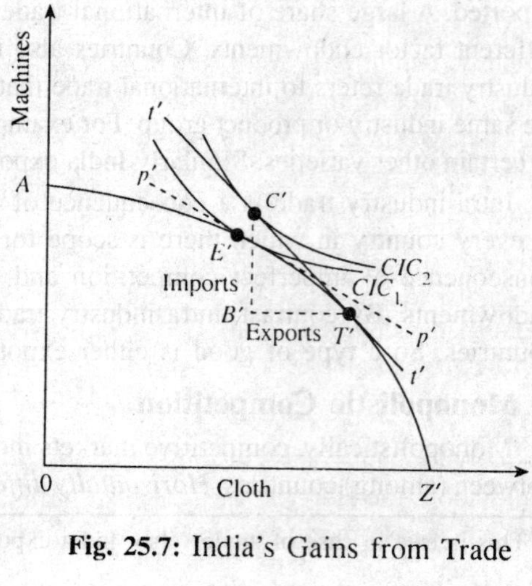

Fig. 25.7: India's Gains from Trade

By comparison under self-sufficiency India produces and consumes at point E', where its PPC ($A'Z'$) is tangent to the community indifference curve CIC_1. After it specialises in the production of cloth, it produces at point T' (which is on the PPC) but consumes at point C', which is on a higher community indifference curve CIC_2. Thus India is also able to consume more of both the goods than in the absence of trade. Since point C' lies above and to the right of point E', we see that international trade enables India also to increase its consumption possibility and improve the welfare of its people.

India now exports $B'T'$ amount of cloth and imports $C'B'$ units of machines. So its trade triangle is $C'B'T'$. Note that the trade triangles of both the countries, viz., the USA and India are the same; $TBC = C'B'T'$. The reason is simple. In a two-country two-commodity framework one country's export are the other country's imports and *vice versa*.

Thus we see that trade based on comparative cost (advantage) leads to an unambiguous improvement in economic welfare in both the trading nations. To quote G. Haberler, "International division of labour and international trade which enable every country to specialise and to export those things which it can produce cheaply in exchange for what others can provide at a lower cost have been and still are one of the basic factors promoting economic well-being and increasing national income of every participating country".

THE DYNAMIC GAINS FROM TRADE

While static gains from trade refer to the increase in national output and consumption levels of participating countries which accrue to a nation from efficient allocation of its resources on the basis of its relative efficiency (comparative advantage), the dynamic gains from trade refer to the positive contribution which trade makes to economic growth. Trade promotes faster economic growth. In this context we may refer to the vent for surplus theory, initially propounded by Adam Smith and subsequently refined and modified by Hla Myint.

Trade a Vent for Surplus

Trade can lead to a full utilisation of a country's idle and underemployed resources as Fig. 25.8 shows. In the absence of trade a developing country is operating at point I (an inefficient point). International trade enables it to operate at point E (an efficient point) and thus produce more of both consumption and capital goods. This is the essence of the *vent for surplus theory*. According to this

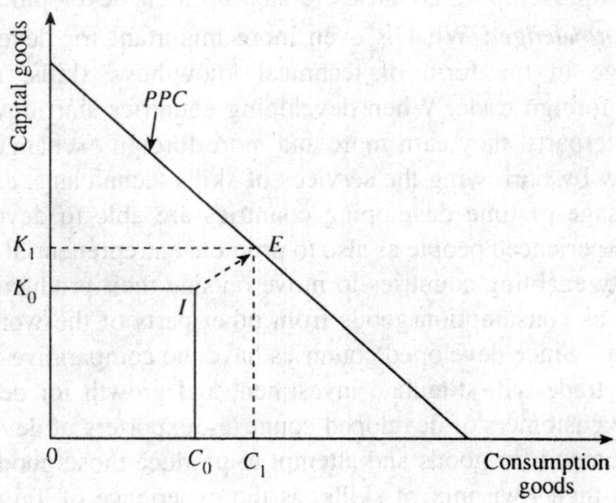

Fig. 25.8: The Effect of Trade on Resource Utilisation

theory, international trade represents an outlet for the potential surplus of agricultural commodities and raw materials of developing countries like India, Pakistan, Bangladesh and Sri Lanka. This has really happened in many developing countries, particularly those in South-east Asia and West Africa.

TRADE AS AN ENGINE OF GROWTH

Dennis Robertson treated trade as an engine of growth for the following reasons:

(i) *An increase in saving and investment* : Firstly with an increase in the volume of production and the level of national income made possible by specialisation and exchange, national savings and investment increase. This enables the trading nation to achieve faster economic growth.

(ii) *Import of capital goods and industrial raw materials* : By producing for exports developing countries are able to earn the much needed foreign exchange. This can be utilised to import capital goods and industrial raw materials which are so essential for developing countries at the early stages of economic growth when such countries do not have any basic or heavy industries.

If people have the desire to save and invest then a higher level of output will lead to faster economic growth. And the higher the rate of economic growth (as measured by the annual rate of increase in national and per capita incomes), the easier it is to escape the vicious circle of poverty and to move from the take-off stage into the stage of self-sustaining growth. Thus by raising the level of income trade promotes faster economic growth.

Other sources of dynamic gains from trade are the following:

(iii) *Acquiring new means of production* : As noted above international trade enables capital scarce developing countries to import the much needed capital goods so as to be able to expand their production capacity and thus step up their developmental effort. Resource-poor countries can also acquire industrial raw materials such as crude oil, raw cotton, iron ore, etc. through imports.

(iv) *Benefits of technological progress in advanced countries* : The past few decades have witnessed rapid technological progress in industrially advanced countries. As technology improves over time, cost per unit falls due to increase in labour productivity. In addition, technological progress leads to an increase in productivity of capital because advanced (superior) technology remains embodied in new machines and capital goods. Furthermore there are improvements in the quality of products also. These enable firms in developed countries to acquire sustainable competitive advantage.

By comparison the developing countries derive substantial gains by importing modern sophisticated technology from advanced countries even without developing such technology domestically at high costs. The import of machines, transport equipment, power generating equipment and road building machinery, etc. has enabled developing countries to step up their developmental efforts.

(v) *Transmission of knowledge* : What is even more important for developing countries is the transmission of knowledge in the form of technical know-how, skills, managerial talent, and entrepreneurship, through foreign trade. When developing countries start developing trade relations with their developed counterparts, they earn more and more foreign exchange. This enables them to import technical know-how by borrowing the services of skills technicians, engineers, managers and consultants. With the passage of time developing countries are able to develop their own pool of technically qualified and experienced people as also to promote entrepreneurial ability. As M.B. Todaro and S. C. Smith put it, "By enabling countries to move outside their production possibility frontiers and secure capital as well as consumption goods from other parts of the world, trade is assumed to stimulate economic growth." Since developed countries have the comparative advantage in producing higher-skill capital goods, trade will stimulate investment and growth for developing countries. By coming in contact with the customers of developed countries, exporters of developing countries come to know of the former's demand for goods and attempt to produce those goods which are in demand and can be produced with their own mix of skills, as the experience of Taiwan shows.

Trade also enables a developing country to import expensive raw materials and other inputs (such as knowledge, ideas, new technologies, etc.) with which it is less well endowed at lower world market prices. Trade can thus create the conditions for a more broadly based and self-sustaining growth of its industrial output. In this context, the following quote from Haberler is quite relevant:

"The late-comers and successors in the process of development and industrialisation have always had the great advantage that they could learn from the experiences of the successors as well as from the failures and mistakes of the pioneers and forerunners. Today the developing countries have a tremendous, constantly growing store of technical know-how to draw from. True, simple adoption of methods, developed for the conditions of the developed countries, is often not possible. But adaptation is surely much easier than the first creation.... Trade is the most important vehicle for the transmission of technological know-how."

TRADE AS A HINDRANCE TO GROWTH

Trade also acts as a hindrance to growth. Two points may be noted in this context:

(i) ***The deterioration of the terms of trade*** **:** R. Prebisch and H. Singer claimed that the terms of trade between primary products and manufactured goods deteriorate over time. There are various reasons for this. One reason is that the developing countries cannot bargain on equal terms with the developed countries in the international market. Another reason is that they cannot establish market power by forming cartels or by joining commodity agreements. As a result there is deficit in the balance of trade of developing countries. So the countries which export primary commodities should establish manufacturing industry to avoid the adverse effects of changes in the terms of trade.

(ii) ***Trade war*** **:** Intense competition among powerful trading nations often led to the adoption of unfair trade practices such as dumping which is injurious to trading nations. The present trade war between the USA and Japan reminds us of *mercantilism* and often is treated as *new mercantilism.*

KEY POINTS

1. ***Two classical theories*** **:** Adam Smith first explained the basis of trade between two countries by developing the theory of absolute advantage. David Ricardo refined and modified the theory and developed the theory of comparative cost (or comparative advantage). The theory explains the basis of trade between two countries by assuming that labour is the only productive factor. According to Ricardo differences in labour cost or labour productivity between two countries account for differences in comparative cost between them.

2. ***Two sources of gains from trade*** **:** Countries engage in trade voluntarily because they gain from trade. Gains from trade are of two types—gains from specialisation and gains from exchange. The first type of gain arises due to an increase in labour productivity after specialisation. The second type of gain arises due to an improvement in the terms of trade which is the ratio of the price index of exports to that of imports.

3. ***Increasing opportunity cost and incomplete specialisation*** **:** If the PPC of the country is concave to the origin and the opportunity cost of producing a good gradually increases then specialisation will be incomplete. This result is found when the Ricardian theory is presented in terms of the concept of opportunity costs.

4. ***Factor endowments theory*** **:** The modern theory of comparative advantage is known as the factor endowments or factor proportions theory. It was developed independently by E. Heckscher and B. Ohlin. According to this theory, a labour-abundant country like India will produce and export labour-intensive goods. Similarly, a capital-abundant country like America will produce and export capital-intensive goods.

5. ***Factor price equalisation*** **:** P. A. Samuelson has argued that free-trade among nations leads to equalisation prices of factors of production due to equalisation of commodity prices made possible by the forces of competition in the international market. Thus trade in goods acts as a substitute of (or proxy for) trade in productive factors in the presence of factor immobility.

6. ***Other causes of trade*** **:** Trade occurs for various other reasons such as economies of scale and learning by doing. Much of intra-industry trade takes place due to monopolistic competition (product differentiation). We also find inter-industry trade now-a-days.

7. ***Trade as an engine of and a hindrance to growth*** **:** International trade acts both as an engine of or as a hindrance to economic growth. It promotes growth by acting as a vent for surplus. It obstructs growth mainly by leading to a secular deterioration of the terms of trade of less developed (mainly primary commodity producing) countries.

KEY TERMS

Absolute advantage	Comparative advantage
Factor proportion	Factor endowments
Factor-intensity reversal	Economies of scale
Demand reversal	Learning effect
Static gains	Dynamic gains
Factor price equalisation	Gains from specialisation
Gains from exchange	Terms of trade
Free trade	Trade traingle
Labour theory of value	Division of labour
Specialisation	Exchange

ASSIGNMENTS

1. Explain how international trade enables a country to increase its consumption possibility beyond what is permitted by its production possibility curve (PPC).
2. Illustrate the Ricardian theory of comparative advantage in a two-country two-commodity framework by taking labour as the only factor of production.

   Or, Production is more efficient in developed countries than in developing countries. Still they are found to be engaged in mutually beneficial trade. Explain the basis of such trade.
3. Explain Ricardo's theory of comparative cost by using the opportunity cost approach.
4. Show that in presence of increasing opportunity cost specialisation is at best incomplete.
5. Distinguish between absolute advantage and comparative advantage.
6. Suppose that labour is the only factor of production and is homogenous in the USA and India which produce only two goods, viz., machines and cloth. USA is endowed with 50,000 units of labour and India is endowed with 5,000 units of labour. The amounts of labour required to produce one unit of a good in each country are given below:

Country	Labour Units Required USA	India
1 unit of machine	1	4
1 unit of cloth	2	3

Now answer the following questions:

(a) Which country has absolute advantage in the production of which good?

(b) Which country has comparative advantage over the other in the production of which good?

(c) Is trade possible between the USA and India ? If so, what is the basis of such trade?

(d) Before trade, what will be the price of machines in terms of cloth in the two countries?

(e) In which price range will international trade be beneficial to both the countries assuming that there is no transport cost?

(f) Draw the PPC of both the countries before and after trade.

[**Hint:** America has as absolute advantage in production of both the goods over India. However, India is relatively more efficient in production of cloth, whereas America is relatively less efficient in its production and America's comparative disadvantage is India's comparative advantage. Thus India has comparative advantage in the production of cloth and America has comparative advantage in production of machines. And comparative advantage forms the basis of trade between the two countries from the supply side not absolute advantage.]

7. Show that gains from trade arise partly from specialisation and partly from exchange. Show the two sources on a single diagram.

8. Identify the conditions that may give rise to trade between two nations. How can two countries gain from trade at the same time?
9. (a) There are two countries *A* and *B*, each producing two goods, *X* and *Y* will full employment of its resources. While country *A* can produce a maximum of 9 units of *X* or 6 units of *Y* country *B* can produce a maximum of 3 units of *X* or 6 units of *Y*. Both countries have straight line production possibility curves.
   (i) If they trade with each other, which country will specialise in which good?
   (ii) Under self-sufficiency, country *A* produces 8 units of *X* and 12 units of *Y*, and country *B* produces 8 units of *X* and 8 units of *Y*. With trade the international rate of exchange becomes $P_x = P_y$. Can you measure the gains from trade for each country?
10. What is the essence of the Heckscher-Ohlin theory of trade? Be explicit in the assumptions on which the theory is based.
11. In the context of the Heckscher-Ohlin model of trade show that free trade is better than no trade. Explain graphically the gains from trade to both the trading nations.
12. Does the factor price equalisation theorem follow from the Heckscher-Ohlin theorem?
13. Two nations *A* and *B* have the same production possibility curves. Can both of them still engage in mutually beneficial (gainful) trade.
    Or, Show that in a two-country, two-commodity, two-factor framework, trade can take place only if countries differ in their factor endowments.
14. "Trade in goods acts as a substitute for international mobility of factor of production and this leads to an equalisation of factor prices." Discuss.
15. What is meant by factor-intensity reversal? Does it invalidate the Heckscher-Ohlin theory?
16. Do you agree with the observation that differences in factor endowments are neither a necessary nor a sufficient condition for international trade? If so, give reason(s) for your answer.
17. (a) Free trade is better than no trade. True or False?
    (b) Do you also agree with the view that some trade is better than no trade ?
    [**Hint:** For answering the second part of this question, see Ch. 28 entitled 'Free Trade vs Protection'.]
18. Write short notes on the following :
    (a) factor-intensity reversal and Heckscher-Ohlin theorem
    (b) demand reversal and Heckscher-Ohlin theorem
    (c) economies of scale as the basis of trade
    (d) learning by doing as the basis of trade
    (e) intra-industry trade and
    (f) monopolistic competition as the basis of trade.
19. Does free trade hurt the abundant factor and benefit the scarce factor? What happens if an import tariff is imposed?
20. Export are intensive in a country's abundant factor(s) and imports in its scarce factor(s). Discuss.

CHAPTER 26

The Multiplier in an Open Economy

An open economy interacts with other economies in two ways. It buys and sells goods and services in world product markets, and it buys and sells capital assets such as stocks and bonds in world financial markets.

N. G. Mankiw

Keynes explained the process of income determination in a closed economy and used the theory of multiplier to explain how a small increase in autonomous investment leads to a multiple increase in national income. Now we extend the basic Keynesian model to show how national income is determined in open economy and how the multiplier process works in this extended framework, with exports and imports. In fact, exports, being autonomous in nature, also have a multiplier effect on national income. We will see that the value of open economy multiplier, called foreign trade (export) multiplier, depends not only on the marginal propensity to save (*MPS*) but also on the marginal propensity to import (*MPI*), a concept to be introduced in this chapter. We start with the import function.

THE IMPORT FUNCTION

In an open economy a part of income is spent on imported goods and services. The import function shows the relation of import and the level of national income and is expressed as

$$M = f(Y)$$

where M stands for import and Y for national income. Thus import depends on national income. The import function is represented graphically in Fig. 26.1. We show national income on the horizontal axis and import on the vertical axis.

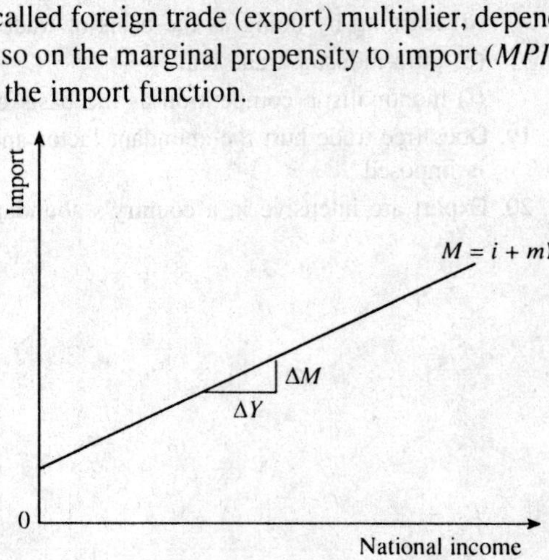

Fig. 26.1: The Import Function

The import function is $M = i + mY$, where i is autonomous import having no relation to Y and mY is induced import, which is related to Y. A country can import capital goods or essential items of consumption from its accumulated foreign exchange reserves or by borrowing from foreign countries or even from the IMF or the World Bank. Here m is the $MPI = \frac{\Delta M}{\Delta Y}$ or the ratio of the change in import to the change in national income which brings it about and the slope of the import function measures this.[1] Suppose, $i = 50$, $m = 0.10$ and $Y =$ Rs. 5,000. So M will be Rs. 50 + Rs. 500 = Rs. 550.

THE FOREIGN TRADE (OPEN ECONOMY) MULTIPLIER

While imports represent how much money goes out of the country, exports show how much money comes into the country

In an open economy imports, like savings and taxes, act as a leakage from the circular flow of the income. The reason is that, that part of Y (Rs. 550 in our above example) which is spent on import goes out of the country and does not come back to the circular flow of income. By comparison, exports, like private investment and government spending (net of transfer) act as injection into the circular flow. This means that exports refer to the expenditure made by foreigners on goods and services produced in the domestic economy (home country). Thus national income reaches equilibrium in an open economy when the sum of leakages is equal to the sum of injections:

$$S + T + M = I + G + X \qquad \ldots (1)$$

For simplicity we ignore T and G, assuming that the budget of the government is in balance and does not affect the equilibrium value of Y. So equation (1) can be rewritten as

$$S + M = I + X \qquad \ldots (2)$$

This does not mean that if $S = I$, M will automatically be equal to X. The truth is the sum of $S + M$ has to be equal to the sum of I and X. In other words S-I equilibrium does not imply trade balance.

Now if there is a change in any of the four variables, there will be a change in the other three variables as well so that the two sides of the equation (2) are equal once again. So we can write

$$\Delta S + \Delta M = \Delta I + \Delta X \qquad \ldots (3)$$

Here ΔS = change of saving and can be expressed as $s.\Delta Y$, where s is MPS. In the same way $\Delta M = m.\Delta Y$, where m is the MPI.

So equation (3) can be rewritten as

$$s.\Delta Y + m.\Delta Y = \Delta I + \Delta X$$

$$\text{or, } \Delta Y(s + m) = \Delta I + \Delta X$$

$$\text{or, } \Delta Y = \frac{1}{(s+m)}(\Delta I + \Delta X)$$

$$= \frac{1}{(s+m)}(\Delta A) \qquad \ldots (4)$$

where $\Delta A = \Delta I + \Delta X$.

If $\Delta I = 0$, then

$\Delta A = \Delta X$ and

if $\Delta X = 0$, then

$\Delta A = \Delta I$

Equation (4) shows that change in either import or export will lead to an increase in ΔY. But by how much? By a multiple of ΔI, or ΔX. Thus, in an open economy, if investment increases by ΔI, Y

1. A related concept is average propensity to import (API) which is expressed as $\frac{M}{Y}$, which is the ratio of total import to national income: $\frac{i + mY}{Y}$. However, this concept does not have any relevance for our discussion in rest of this chapter.

will increase by $\frac{1}{(s+m)}(\Delta A = \Delta I)$. Similarly, if exports increase by ΔX, Y will increase by $\frac{1}{(s+m)}(\Delta A = \Delta X)$. Here $\frac{1}{(s+m)}$ is the open economy multiplier (m_0). It may be expressed as:

$$m_0 = \frac{1}{(s+m)}.$$

The open economy multiplier is the reciprocal of *MPS* (*s*) *plus MPI* (*m*). Since import is the leakage from the circular flow of income, the open economy multiplier is less than the closed economy multiplier.

If $s = 0.3$ and $m = 0.1$ then,

$$m_0 = \frac{1}{0.3+0.1} = \frac{1}{0.4} = 2.5.$$

If $m = 0$, then we get the closed economy multiplier which is 3.3.

Now if $s = 0.4$ and $m = 0.1$, then

$$m_0 = \frac{1}{0.4+0.1} = \frac{1}{0.5} = 2.$$

The closed economy multiplier is 2.5 in this case.

Thus we see that multiplier for an open economy is less than that of a closed economy since import is a leakage from the circular flow of income.

GRAPHICAL REPRESENTATION OF OPEN ECONOMY MULTIPLIER WITHOUT INVESTMENT

The open economy multiplier is graphically represented in Fig. 26.2. Here we measure national income on the horizontal axis and saving, export and import on the vertical axis. Here we ignore G and I. The initial level of national income is Y_1. This is determined by the interaction of upward sloping saving-cum-import schedule $S + M$, with the initial export schedule X_1 at point E. Now there is an increase in autonomous export by ΔX. As a result the export schedule shift upward to X_2 and $X_2 = X_1 + \Delta X$. The new (higher) export schedule intersects the saving-plus-import schedule at point F. As a result national income increases from Y_1 to Y_2. This is greater than (or a multiple) of the initial increase in export due to the operation of the foreign trade multiplier (m_0). Here $m_0 = \frac{\Delta Y}{\Delta X} = \frac{EE'}{FE'}$, since $\Delta Y = m_0(\Delta X)$. The value of multiplier is the reciprocal of the slope of the combined $S + M$ schedule since $m_0 = \frac{1}{s+m}$, where $s = \frac{\Delta S}{\Delta Y}$ and $m = \frac{\Delta M}{\Delta Y}$.

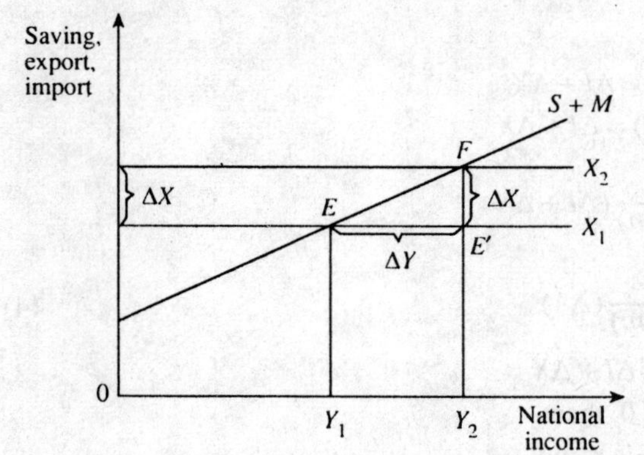

Fig. 26.2: Foreign Trade Multiplier without Investment

THE WORKING OF THE OPEN ECONOMY MULTIPLIER

The open economy multiplier works exactly in the same way as does the Keynesian investment multiplier. Suppose due to the change in taste and preference of foreigners for Indian goods (due to improved quality or lower prices), India's export increases. Initially this additional export may be made from inventories. This will lead to an initial increase in income of India's exporters. But if there is a further increase in foreign demand for Indian goods, there is a need to increase the production of exported goods. As a result more workers will be employed in export-oriented industries. These people will earn income. They will spend a portion of their income on other home produced goods and a portion on imported goods. The portion of income which is spent on import will leak out of the circular flow. But the portion which is spent on domestic goods will have an income-creating effect. So production of such goods will increase. Consequently income and employment will also increase in such industries. This is how increases in income will spread throughout the economy following an initial increase in export.

After all, export like investment, is a component of total autonomous expenditure and any increase in autonomous spending has a multiplier effect. In short, the increased expenditure on domestic goods following an initial increase in export will go on generating extra income at various rounds through a chain of secondary consumption spending and respending.

THE OPEN ECONOMY MULTIPLIER WITH INVESTMENT

A. National Income Equilibrium with Trade Balance

If we now consider investment along with export as two items of autonomous expenditure, the equilibrium condition of national income is

$$S + M = I + X$$

$$\text{or, } I + X - M = S$$

$$\text{or, } I + X = S + M$$

Here the sum of I and X (the two injections) have to be equal to the sum of S and M (the two leakages). The equilibrium condition is shown graphically in Fig. 26.3. The closed economy equilibrium is at point E. We now add import to saving to arrive at the combined $S + M$ schedule. The difference between S and $S + M$ schedules increases with increase in Y since M increases when Y increases. Similarly we add export to investment to arrive at the combined $I + X$ schedule. Here I and $I + X$ schedule are parallel since both I and X are autonomous and thus remain fixed at all levels of Y.

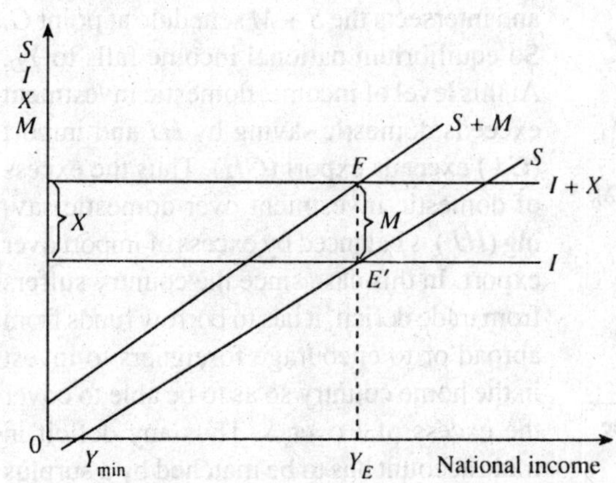

Fig. 26.3: National Income Equilibrium with Balanced Trade

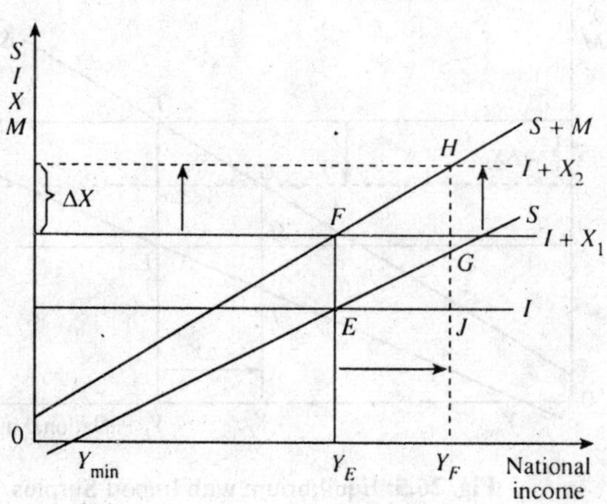

Fig. 26.4: National Income Equilibrium with Trade Surplus

The open economy equilibrium is at point F where $S + M = I + X$. In this case, since $I = S$ at point E', $X = M$. But this is just a coincidence. It is not necessary that at the equilibrium level of national income (Y_E), export (X) equals import (M) or that there is a balance in trade account. This point is illustrated in Fig. 26.4.

B. National Income Equilibrium with Trade Surplus

The closed economy equilibrium is at E where $S = I$, i.e., domestic saving equals domestic investment. The open economy equilibrium is initially at point F, where $S + M = I + X_1$ and national income attains its equilibrium value Y_F. Now suppose export increases from X_1 to X_2. As a result the combined $I + X$ schedule shifts upward from $I + X_1$ to $I + X_2$ and intersects the $S + M$ schedule at point H. So national income increases from Y_E to Y_F. Now at this level of income $S > I$ by the distance GJ. Here import is HG and is less than export which is HJ. So the excess of saving over investment (GJ) measures export surplus. Thus we see that the equilibrium level of national income can be reached even if export is greater than import. So it is not necessary to have a balance in the trade account in order to attain the equilibrium level of national income. Now the export surplus can be used to lend funds to foreigners or to invest in foreign countries. This point may be explained further. We know that

The excess of domestic saving over domestic investment has to be matched by an excess of export over import which is used to lend to foreign countries

$$S + M = I + X$$

$$\text{or,} \quad S - I = X - M$$

Thus we see that if $S > I$, X has to be greater than M. In other words, the excess of saving over investment has to be matched by an excess of export over import. Thus to achieve the equilibrium level of Y, it is enough to ensure that $S + M = I + X$. A simple example will make this point clear. Suppose $S = 120$, $M = 160$, $X = 180$ and $I = 100$. Then $S - I = 20$ and $X - M = 20$.

Thus any surplus in the trade account is to be offset by a deficit in the capital account so as to ensure that the balance of payments always balances.

C. National Income Equilibrium with Trade Deficit

In Fig. 26.5 we show an exactly opposite type of situation. The closed economy equilibrium is at point E, where $S = I$. The initial open economy equilibrium is at point F, where $S + M = I + X_1$ and the national income attains its equilibrium value Y_E. Now suppose there is a fall in autonomous export from X_1 to X_0 (Here $X_0 = X_1 - \Delta X$). As a result the $I + X$ schedule shifts downward to $I + X_0$ and intersects the $S + M$ schedule at point G. So equilibrium national income falls to Y_D. At this level of income, domestic investment exceeds domestic saving by HJ and import (GJ) exceeds export (GH). Thus the excess of domestic investment over domestic saving (HJ) is balanced by excess of import over export. In this case since the country suffers from trade deficit, it has to borrow funds from abroad or to encourage foreigners to invest in the home country so as to be able to cover the excess of I over S. Thus any deficit in trade account has to be matched by a surplus in the capital account so as to ensure that the balance of payments always balances, at least in the accounting sense (if not in the economic sense).

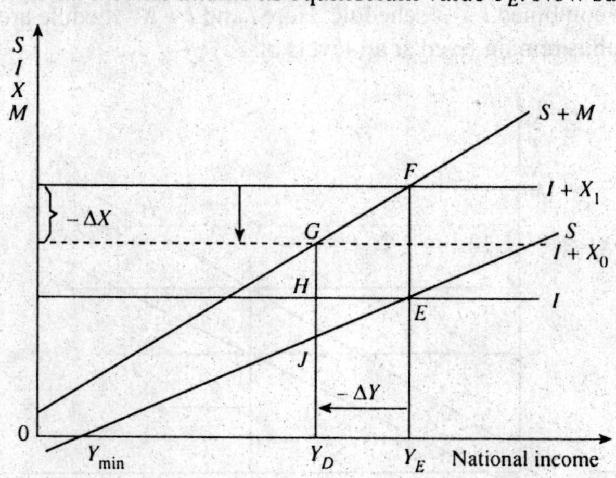

Fig. 26.5: Equilibrium with Import Surplus

AN INCREASE IN IMPORTS AND THE REVERSE MULTIPLIER PROCESS

Since import is a leakage from the multiplier process an increase in import will lead to a multiple contraction of income. In Fig. 26.6 we show the working of the process in absence of saving and investment. In this case national income attains its initial equilibrium value Y_E at point E where the import schedule M_1 intersects the export schedule. Now suppose due to a change in taste and preference of domestic consumers for foreign goods there is an increase in import and the import schedule shifts upward from M_0 to M_1. In this case import increases by ΔM (= EF) even at the same level of income (Y_E)[1]. Now the new higher import schedule (which is parallel to M_1) intersects the export schedule at point G. As a result national income falls from Y_E to Y_D. This happens because a rise in import leads to a

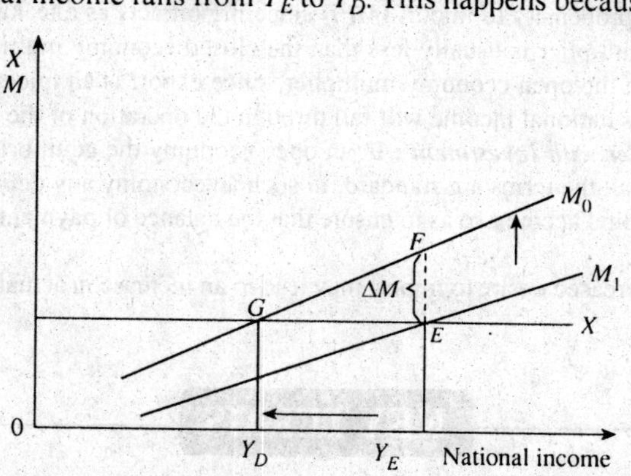

Fig. 26.6: Multiple Contraction of Income due to Rise in Import

fall in expenditure of consumers on domestic goods. Thus domestic expenditure is not reduced but is switched from home-made goods to foreign-made goods. The fall in expenditure leads to a fall in production, employment and income in several domestic industries. In fact there is multiple contraction of income due to a fall in expenditure on domestic goods in several rounds, following an initial decline in the demand for home-produced goods.

Import Paradox

Now we see that an increased desire to import leads to a fall in actual imports. The initial desire to import Y_EF amount of goods leads to a fall in national income[2]. As a result actual import (Y_DG) is less than desired import (Y_EF). This is known as the import paradox, which is comparable to the paradox of thrift, discussed in an earlier chapter.

Final Comment: the Value of the Keynesian Multiplier

We have noted that the value of the Keynesian investment multiplier is greater than 1. However, R.G. Lipsey has pointed out that if each component of autonomous spending, i.e., C, I, G, and X has an import content, then the value of the autonomous expenditure multiplier may even be less than one. This means that the multiplier effect is not only lost but is reversed as well. In this case rise in any component of autonomous spending will lead to a multiplier fall in national income.

KEY POINTS

1. *Open economy* : An open economy is one which has transactions with the rest of the world. Such transactions mainly include trade in goods and services and movements of financial capital. Most economies today are open for being involved in these types of transactions.

---

1. This implies an increase in *APS*. In this case there is a parallel upward shift of the import schedule with no change in its slope.
2. Since imports fall due to contraction of income this is known as *the income effect*. This is different from the fall in import after the imposition of an import tariff which reduces import by changing relative prices of home produced goods and imported goods. This is known as *the substitution effect*. In the first case, consumers reduce their expenditure on imported items (and possibly on home-produced goods) due to fall in income. In the second case consumers switch their expenditure from foreign to domestic goods.

2. *Import function* : The import function shows the relation of import and the level of national income. The slope of the import schedule is the marginal propensity to import (i.e., the ratio of the change in import to the change in national income).

3. *The open economy multiplier* : The open economy multiplier is the reciprocal of the marginal propensity to save (*MPS*) plus the marginal propensity to import (*MPI*) since import acts as a leakage from the circular flow of income. The open economy multiplier is usually less than the closed economy multiplier. If export increases national income will rise through the open economy multiplier, since export is an injection into the circular flow of income. But if import increases national income will fall through the operation of the reverse multiplier process.

4. *Open economy multiplier with investment* : In an open economy the equilibrium condition of national income is $S + M = I + X$, where all the terms are standard. In such an economy any deficit in trade account has to be matched by a surplus in the capital account so as to ensure that the balance of payments always balances, at least in an accounting sense.

5. *Import paradox* : An increased desire to import may lead to an increase in actual import. This is known as the import paradox.

KEY TERMS

Import function	Import leakage
Marginal propensity to import	Export injection
Average propensity to import	National income equilibrium in an open economy
Import paradox	Trade surplus (deficit)
Open economy multiplier	

ASSIGNMENTS

1. What is open economy multiplier? How is its value determined?
2. Why is the open economy multiplier usually less than the closed economy multiplier?
3. Can the balanced budget multiplier be less than one in an economy?
4. Show how the equilibrium national income is determined in an open economy (a) with trade balance, (b) with trade deficit, and (c) with trade surplus.
5. Explain why a surplus in the trade account is to be normally offset by a deficit in the capital account. Is the converse also true?
6. Explain the process of working of the open economy multiplier. Why is its value always less than that of a closed economy?
7. Show how an increase in imports affects the equilibrium level of national income. In this context discuss the paradoxical result which is normally encountered by an open economy.
8. Why is the investment multiplier usually different in an open economy from that in a closed economy? Will there be similar difference in the following two cases: (i) balance budget multiplier and (ii) investment multiplier when all imports are used as intermediate inputs for exports production?
9. Show that a given change in domestic investment or in export would have the same effect on national income but would have different implications for the balance of trade.
10. Consider the case where exports increase from Rs. 40 cr. to Rs. 80 cr. while imports also increase from Rs. 40 cr. to Rs. 80 cr. and another case where exports fall from Rs. 40 cr. to Rs. 30 cr. while imports fall from Rs. 40 cr. to Rs. 20 cr. What will be the effect on equilibrium national income in these two cases?

26A NUMERICAL EXAMPLES ON OPEN ECONOMY MULTIPLIER

Example 1

Suppose we have the following data about an open economy.

$$C = 50 + 0.8Y_d$$
$$I = 114 - 4r$$
$$G = 75$$
$$T = 25$$
$$T_R = 55$$
$$X = 6$$
$$M = 10 + 0.2\,Y.$$

(a) Derive the equation of the *IS* curve.

(b) Find out the equilibrium value of *Y*.

(c) What is the onen economy multiplier?

Solution

(a) $Y = C + I + G + X - M$ ... (1)

and $Y_d = Y - T + T_R$

Substituting the values of the variables and parameters in equation (1) we have

$$Y = 50 + 0.8\,(Y - 25 + 55) + 114 - 4r + 70 + 60 - (10 + 0.2\,Y)$$
$$= 50 + 0.8\,Y + 56 + 114 + 70 + 60 - 10 + 0.2\,Y - 4r$$

or $Y - 0.8\,Y + 0.2\,Y = (50 + 56 + 114 + 70 + 50) - 4r$

or, $0.4Y = 340 - 4r$

or, $\frac{2}{5}\,Y = 340 - 4r$

or, $Y = 340 \times \frac{5}{2} - \frac{5}{2} \times 4r$

or, $Y = 850 - 10r$ ... (2)

This is the equation of the *IS* curve.

(b) The equilibrium value of *Y* when $r = 5\%$ is

$$Y = 850 - 10 \times 5$$
$$= 850 - 50$$
$$= 800$$

(c) The foreign trade multiplier is

$$\frac{1}{1-b+m} = \frac{1}{1-0.8+0.2} = \frac{1}{0.4} = 2.5, \text{ where } b \text{ is } MPC.$$

Example 2

Suppose you have the following information about an open economy:

$$C = 100 + 0.9\,(Y - T)$$
$$T = 200$$
$$I = 300 - 5r$$
$$G = 200$$

$$M_d = L = 0.2\,Y - 20r$$
$$M_s = 200$$
$$X = 40$$
$$M = 20 + 0.1\,Y$$

where all the notations have standard meaning.

(a) Derive the *IS* and *LM* equations.

(b) Find out the equilibrium values of *r* and *Y*.

(c) What is the balance of trade?

Solution

(a) (i) **The derivation of the *IS* equation**

$$Y = 100 + 0.9\,(Y - 200) + 300 - 5r + 200 + 40 - 20 - 0.1\,Y$$
$$= 100 + 0.9\,Y - 180 + 300 - 5r + 200 + 40 - 20 - 0.1\,Y$$

or, $Y - 0.9\,Y + 0.1\,Y = 100 - 180 + 300 + 200 + 40 - 20 - 5r$

or, $0.2Y = 440 - 5r$

or, $Y = 2{,}200 - 25r$

(ii) **The derivation of the *LM* equation**

$$M_d = M_s$$
$$0.2Y - 20r = 200$$

or, $0.2Y = 200 + 20r$

or, $Y = 1{,}000 + 100r$

This is the equation of the *LM* curve.

(b) In macroeconomic equilibrium

$$IS = LM$$

or, $2{,}200 - 25r = 1{,}000 + 100r$

or, $125r = 1{,}200$

or, $r = \dfrac{1{,}200}{125} = 8.92 = 9\%$ (approx.)

Substituting the value of $r = 9$ in the *IS* equation we have

$$Y = 2{,}200 - 25 \times 9$$
$$= 1{,}975.$$

(c) The balance of trade $= X - M$

$$= 40 - 20 - 197.5$$
$$= -177.5$$

So there is a deficit in the balance of trade.

An Alternative Method

We can directly get the solution values by using the equation of the *IS* curve

$$Y = \frac{1}{1-b+m}(\bar{A}+dr)$$

where $\bar{A} = a - bT + \bar{I} + G + \bar{X} - \bar{M} - dr$

or, $Y = \dfrac{1}{1-0.9+0.1}$ $[(100 - 180 + 300 + 200 + 40 - 20) - 5r]$

$= 2{,}200 - 25r$

$$Y = 40 + 0.8\, Y_d + 140 - 5r + 120$$
$$= 40 + 0.8\,(Y - 100) + 140 - 5r + 120$$
$$= 40 + 0.8\, Y - 80 + 140 - 5r + 120$$

or, $Y - 0.8\, Y = 220 - 5r$

or, $0.2Y = 220 - 5r$

or, $Y = 1{,}100 - 25r$

Since the equation of the *LM* curve is

$0.2Y - 20r = 200$ we have

$0.8Y - 5r = 50$

or, $5r = 0.8Y - 50$

or, $r = \dfrac{0.8}{5} Y - 10$

$= 0.04\, Y - 10$

So $Y = 1{,}100 - 25\,(0.04Y - 10)$

$= 1{,}100 - 4\, Y - 250$

or, $2Y = 850$

or, $Y = 425.$

CHAPTER 27

International Linkages and the Mundell-Fleming Model

> *With no sterilisation, a fixed exchange rate will help to insulate the economy from domestic monetary changes. A floating exchange rate helps to reinforce the effect of a monetary change on national income and employment.*
>
> Phillip Hardwick

TRADE LINKS AND CAPITAL FLOWS

Different countries of the world are linked with one another in two ways: (1) trade in goods and services and (2) inflows and outflows of financial capital. Financial capital is the most mobile of all factors of production and it has always an extra temptation to go abroad in search of higher return(s).

From the late 1980s Globalisation led to greater and greater integration of all economies of the world and their financial markets. And due to removal of controls over capital movements capital now moves freely across national borders. Now not only banks but also households, corporate firms, insurance companies and mutual funds can hold financial assets such as bonds and equities of foreign companies as also bonds issued by foreign governments. For example, if the US Fed reduces the rate of interest below the rate which prevails in India, there will be an outflow of domestic funds from the USA and inflow of foreign funds into India. As a result India's foreign exchange reserves will increase and this, in its turn, will lead to an increase in India's money supply. The reason is that the money supply of a country has two components, viz., the domestic component and the foreign asset component.

It may also be noted that business cycles get transmitted from country to country. In the 1930s it was said that when the USA sneezes, the rest of the world catches cold. At that time the USA was occupying the preeminent position in the world economy. This is why the great world trade depression affected all the countries which had trading relations with the USA. Now we speak of the 'contagion effect'. Any financial crisis, originating in any country or in any part of the world, spreads to many other countries in no time. For example, the Thai currency crisis of 1997 affected most Asian countries. And the 2007-09 U.S. financial crisis adversely affected almost all other countries. Since international linkages in the area of financial capital has assumed considerable importance in the past two decades or so, growth and recession in one country have world-wide repercussions. In fact, the global financial crisis of

Contagion effect refers to the transmission of financial crisis from one country to another

2007-09 had its origins in the sub-prime housing crisis of the USA. It is in the context of such international linkages that we study open economy macroeconomics, with particular reference to the Mundell-Fleming model. However, to start with, we may briefly recapitulate the relation between national income and trade balance.

NATIONAL INCOME AND TRADE BALANCE

In an open economy national income, from the expenditure side, has four components:

$$Y = C + I + G + NX \qquad \ldots (1)$$

where all the terms have their usual meaning.

$$\text{Or, } Y - C - G = I + NX \qquad \ldots (2)$$

Here, $Y - C - G$ is national saving. It has two parts: private saving equal to $Y - T - C$ and public (government) saving equal to $T - G$. So we can write equation (2) as

$$S = (Y - T - C) + (T - G)$$
$$= Y - C - G. \qquad \ldots (3)$$

Substituting S for $Y - C - G$ in equation (2), we get

$$S = I + NX \qquad \ldots (4)$$

Subtracting I from both sides of (4) we get

$$S - I = NX \qquad \ldots (5)$$

Thus $S - I$ represents net capital inflow into the home country. This is equal to net export or the balance of trade. Thus equation (5) is the national income accounts identity for an open economy.

Equation (5) makes one thing very clear: international flows of capital ($S - I$) and international flows of goods and services ($NX = X - M$) are mirror image concepts. If we know the one, we can find out the other.

A surplus in the balance of trade (excess of export over import) implies net foreign investment. India can invest its funds in the USA, if it has an excess of exports over imports. In addition, Indians can buy foreign financial assets such as shares in the New York stock exchange or physical assets such as houses and factories in the USA. By buying US assets, Indians are making investment in and providing funds to the USA.

The Equation of the *IS* Curve in an Open Economy

The standard *IS-LM* curve model can be extended to analyse determinants of national income and of interest rate in an open economy.

The equation of the *IS* curve which shows goods market equilibrium in an open economy is expressed as follows:

$$Y = C(Y - T) + I(r) + G + NX(E) \qquad \ldots (6)$$

where C depends on disposable income ($Y - T$), I on the rate of interest(r) and NX on the rate of exchange (E). In reality NX depends on three factors: (i) foreign income (Y_f), (ii) domestic income (Y) and (iii) the real exchange rate (R). So the net export function can be written as

$$NX = X(Y_f, R) - M(Y, R)$$
$$= NX(Y_f, Y, R) \qquad \ldots (7)$$

where $R = E \times \frac{P_f}{P}$, where P is the domestic price and P_f is the foreign price level. In fact, R is often interpreted as the (commodity) terms of trade.

It has to be noted that national income (and expenditure) in an open economy is determined by spending on domestic goods both by the residents of a country and by foreigners(through exports). Domestic residents spend a portion of their income on foreign goods through imports.

Three important points emerge from the net export function (7).

1. An increase in domestic income will increase domestic spending on foreign goods. As a result imports will rise and the trade balance will show a deficit.

2. A rise in foreign income, such as that of the USA will increase India's exports and improve India's balance of trade. Consequently, aggregate demand in India will increase and India's national income (or expenditure) will rise.

3. A depreciation of the rupee (i.e., a rise in the exchange rate in real terms) will increase India's exports and reduce India's imports. As a result net exports will increase and, with it, India's national income and expenditure.

Net exports affect the *IS* curve by influencing total final expenditure.

The *IS* Curve for an Open Economy

Three points are to be noted about the *IS* curve in the context of an open economy.

1. ***Import leakage*** : In an open economy there is an import leakage. A portion of any increase in income is spent on imports. So the demand for domestically produced goods falls correspondingly. For this reason the *IS* curve is steeper than that in a closed economy. This implies that if the rate of interest falls by a certain percentage, a smaller increase in income is needed to achieve a new equilibrium in the goods market.

2. ***Depreciation of home currency*** : If the rupee depreciates in terms of dollar (and other foreign currencies), exports will increase, imports will fall and net exports will increase. As a result total final expenditure ($C + I + G + NX$) will increase and the *IS* curve will shift to the right.

3. ***An increase in foreign income*** : An increase in foreign income will be spent on imports. As a result there will be an increase in the demand for Indian goods. So India's exports will rise and the *IS* curve will shift to the right.

The Equation of the *LM* Curve

The *LM* curve remains the same in an open economy and is represented by the following equation

$$\left(\frac{M}{P}\right) = L(r, Y) \quad \ldots (8)$$

where $\left(\frac{M}{P}\right)$ is the supply of real money balances and $L(r, Y)$ is the demand for money which is a function of both r and Y.

GENERAL EQUILIBRIUM IN AN OPEN ECONOMY

As in a closed economy both the goods market and the money market can be in equilibrium at the same time in an open economy when the downward sloping *IS* curve intersects the upward sloping *LM* curve at point *E* as shown in Fig. 27.1. So the equilibrium level of income (Y_1) and the equilibrium rate of interest (r_1) are determined simultaneously. Thus point *E* shows macroeconomic general equilibrium.

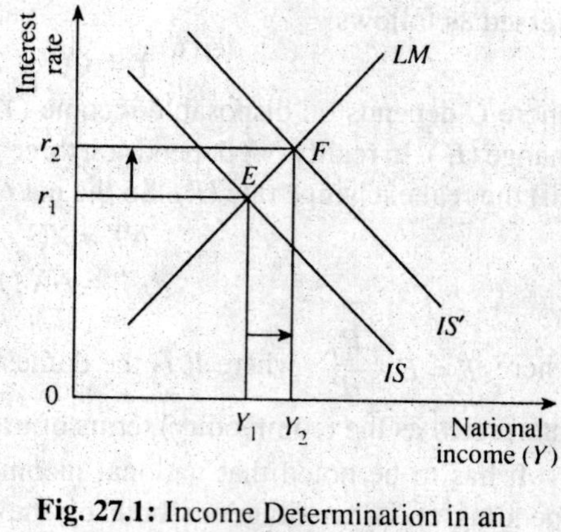

Fig. 27.1: Income Determination in an Open Economy

We may now do a few comparative statics exercises. To be more specific, we may have to examine the effect of an increase in net exports.

The Effect of an Increase in Net Exports

If foreign income increases, India's net exports will increase. As a result the *IS* curve will shift to the right from *IS* to *IS'*. Consequently the equilibrium level of income will increase to Y_2 and the rate of interest will also rise to r_2.

By contrast, if due to recession in a foreign country its national income falls, its imports (or India's exports) will also fall. Consequently the *IS* curve will shift to the left and both *Y* and *r* will fall.

The Effect of Currency Depreciation

If the rupee depreciates in terms of the US dollar or any other currency, India's net exports will increase. As a result the *IS* curve will shift to the right. So both *Y* and *r* will increase.

In truth, an increase in net exports raises aggregate demand for goods (and services) and thus increases India's national income through the multiplier. It is against the backdrop that we study the Mundell-Fleming model of open economy macroeconomics.

THE MUNDELL-FLEMING MODEL

We have noted earlier that due to greater and greater integration of the world's financial markets, households, corporations, banks of different countries try to get the highest return from their investment (both financial and real). This is why returns in capital markets in different countries are inseparably linked up with one another. For example, if the rates of return on bonds or equities in the USA rise, Indian investors will have a temptation to buy US bonds or invest their capital in the USA to derive higher returns from their financial assets. By contrast, US borrowers would turn to India to borrow funds from the Indian financial markets at low cost.

In the 1960s Robert Mundell and M. Fleming presented an interesting model to show that in the presence of perfect capital mobility, there is a tendency for the rates of return on financial capital to become equal in different countries. This occurs due to arbitrage which refers to transferring (switching) funds from low-return assets to high-return assets to take advantage of differences in return to capital.

Assumptions

The Mundell-Fleming model is based on three main assumptions. These are the following:

1. *Small country* : First, the model assumes a small open economy. It is a price taker in the world market and cannot exert any influence on the rates of returns on different types of investment. Such a country has to accept a fixed world rate of interest.

2. *Uniform tax rates* : Tax rates are assumed to be the same everywhere. This means that the after-tax return on investment will be the same everywhere in the world.

3. *Absence of political risks* : Foreign investors are not subject to any risk such as confiscation of foreign assets through sudden acts of nationalisation, imposition of restrictions on the transfer of assets across national borders and risk of default by domestic partners and foreign governments.

If these conditions are satisfied and financial capital is perfectly mobile, wealthholders will try to invest their funds in the country which offers the maximum return on investment. And due to financial arbitrage the rates of returns on the same type of assets will be the same throughout the world.

Arbitrage leads to equalisation of returns on the same types of assets everywhere

In fact, the equalisation of the rates of return will occur if capital is perfectly mobile internationally, in which case investors can purchase assets in any country of their choice any time at low transaction costs and in any amounts without exerting any influence on the world rate of interest. In short, under perfect capital mobility in their search of higher return or lower transaction costs investors can switch funds across national holders. And, for a small open economy, the domestic rate of interest is determined by the world rate of interest. So we can write

$$r = r_w$$

where r is the domestic rate of interest and r_w is the world rate of interest. In fact, free inflow and outflow of financial capital lead to equalisation of the two interest rates.

Two Key Points

Two important points may be noted now before we proceed further.

The behaviour of the macroeconomic variables in response to policy changes depends on the exchange system of the small country

1. The main focus of the Mundell-Fleming model is on the role of exchange rate in the determination of national income in the short run.

2. The behaviour of macroeconomic variables such as national income (Y), the rate of interest (r) and net exports (NX) in response to changes in government policy depends on whether the economy adopts the fixed exchange rate system or the flexible exchange rate system. This is a strategic issue.

THE MODEL IN EQUATION FORM

The model can be described by the two equations of the *IS* and *LM* curves presented earlier in this chapter.

The equation of the *IS* curve is:

$$Y = C(Y - T) + I(r_w) + G + NX \quad \ldots (9)$$

The equation of the *LM* curve is:

$$\frac{M}{P} = L(r_w, Y) \quad \ldots (10)$$

Here, G, T and M, r_w and P are all exogenous variables, i.e., given from outside the system.

Two important points are to be noted in this context:

1. *Income determination* : Since the interest rate is taken as given (a parameter rather than a variable), the level of national income is determined when both the goods market and the money market are in equilibrium, i.e., at the point of intersection between the *IS* curve and the *LM* curve.

2. *Exchange rate determination* : Under completely flexible exchange rate system, the equilibrium rate of exchange is determined automatically through the intersection of the *IS* curve with the *LM* curve.

A. ADJUSTMENTS UNDER THE FIXED EXCHANGE RATE SYSTEM

(i) The Role of Monetary Policy

In the Mundell-Fleming model under the fixed exchange rate system, the monetary policy of the central bank loses its effectiveness. However, there will be changes in balance of payments due to excessive inflows and outflows of capital in response to small difference(s) in interest rates among different countries. The changes in balance of payments will affect the exchange rate between two currencies and will eliminate any interest rate differential.

Under the fixed exchange rate system and perfect capital mobility no country can pursue its monetary policy independently. If it does that, there will be huge capital flows and interest rate movements. So the central bank has to intervene to bring the domestic rate of interest in line with the world rate of interest.

(a) The Effect of Expansionary Monetary Policy

In Fig. 27.2 we examine the effect of an increase in the money supply. In panel (a) along with the *IS* and *LM* curves, we have drawn a horizontal line *BP*. When the domestic interest rate is equal to the world rate, there is neither inflow nor outflow of capital from the home country and so the balance of payments is in equilibrium. There is neither a deficit nor a surplus in it (i.e., $BP = 0$).

If the rate of interest moves up (down) there will be huge capital outflows (inflows). As a result the balance of payments will show a deficit (surplus). So the exchange rate will increase (fall), and the central bank has to intervene to stabilise the exchange rate (i.e., maintain it at the original level).

In panel (a) of Fig. 27.2 we show the macroeconomic effects of the adoption of an expansionary monetary policy by the central bank. The economy was originally in equilibrium at point E, where the domestic rate of interest was equal to the world rate (r_w). Now if the central bank increases the supply of money, the *LM* curve shifts to the right from LM_1 to LM_2. Thus the economy reaches new equilibrium at point *E′*. This implies that the domestic rate of interest falls below the world rate ($r_2 < r_w$). So there is outflow of capital from the economy. As a result there will be a deficit in the balance of payments. This will cause the domestic currency (the rupee) to depreciate or the exchange rate to rise.

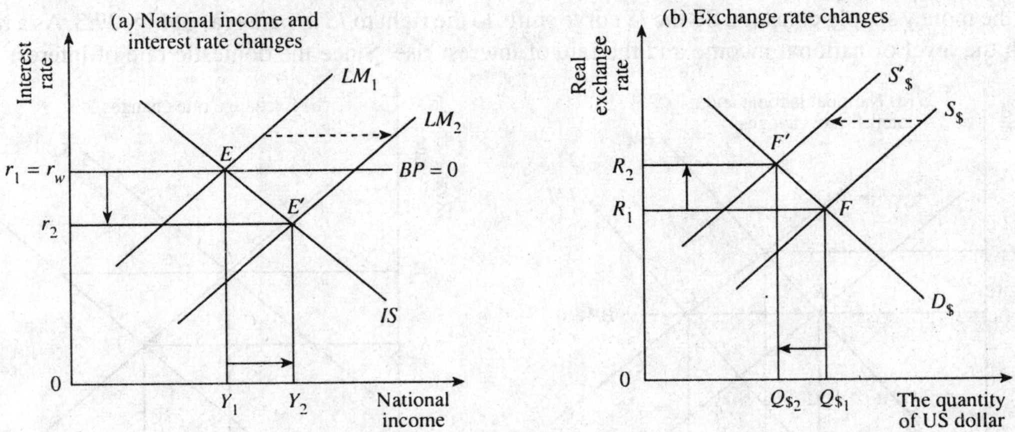

Fig. 27.2: The Effect of Monetary Expansion on *r*, *Y* and Exchange Rate

In panel (b) of Fig. 27.2 we show the movement in the rate of exchange between the rupee (the home currency) and the US dollar (the foreign currency). The initial equilibrium rate of exchange is R_1. It is determined by the demand for and supply of US dollars.[1] Now due to a fall in domestic interest rate to r_2 in panel (a), there will be huge capital outflows from India. This will reduce the demand for rupees and the supply of US dollars in the foreign exchange market. As a result the supply curve of US dollars will shift to the left to $S'_\$$ in panel (b). So the rupee will depreciate in terms of US dollar. A depreciation of the rupee implies, as noted earlier, a rise in India's foreign exchange rate. More rupees will now be exchanged for the same US dollar. To maintain the exchange rate, the RBI will have to intervene. It will be required to sell dollars (from its accumulated reserves) in the foreign exchange market. The outflow of dollar will lead to a fall in the money supply in India. As a result the *LM* curve will shift back to its original position in panel (a) and economy will return to the initial equilibrium point *E*. This is known as **sterilisation** i.e., offsetting action by the central bank, such as open market operation, to prevent a change in the money supply as a result of a balance of payments disequilibrium. Thus monetary policy is not effective in raising national income under the fixed exchange rate system.

(b) The Effect of a Contractionary Monetary Policy

An exactly opposite type of adjustment process (mechanism) will work itself out if the central bank adopts a contractionary monetary policy. In this case the *LM* curve will shift to the left (not shown here). So new macroeconomic equilibrium will be attained at a point which is to the left of point *E*. As a result the domestic rate of interest will go above the world rate. This will lead to huge inflow of capital and thus an increase in the demand for the domestic currency. Consequently the rupee will appreciate in terms of the US dollar. Now in order to maintain the original equilibrium rate of exchange the RBI will have to buy the foreign currency (the US dollar) by selling the domestic currency (the rupee). Consequently the domestic money supply will increase and the *LM* curve will shift to the right and the economy will return to the initial equilibrium point *E*.

Thus we see that with perfect capital mobility, under the fixed exchange rate system, monetary policy is not effective in a small open economy. It has no effect on national income (output) and employment.

1. Note that the demand curve for US dollars is the same as the supply curve of Indian rupees and the supply curve of US dollars is the same as the demand curve for Indian rupees.

This implies that the central bank of a country cannot adopt an independent monetary policy or insulate itself from the world economy.

(ii) The Role of Expansionary Fiscal Policy

Interestingly enough, fiscal policy is highly effective in the Mundell-Fleming model due to perfect capital mobility. Suppose the Government of India (GOI)) increases its expenditure, with the RBI holding the money supply constant. So the *IS* curve shifts to the right to *IS* in panel (a) of Fig. 27.3. As a result both the level of national income and the rate of interest rise. Since the domestic rate of interest goes

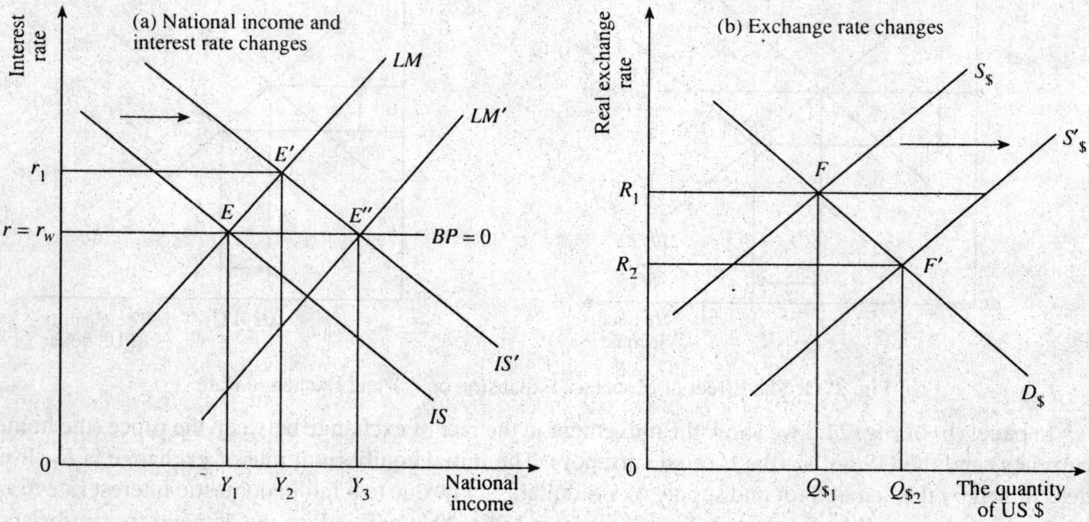

Fig. 27.3: The Expansionary Effect of Fiscal Policy

above the world rate ($r_1 > r_w$), there will be inflows of capital into the home country. As a result the demand for rupees will increase (since US investors will require more rupees to buy Indian assets).[1] So the rupee will appreciate (or the dollar will depreciate). In panel (b) we see that due to capital inflows, the supply curve of foreign currency (i.e., US dollars) which is the same as the demand curve of the domestic currency, will shift to the right from $S_\$$ to $S'_\$$ and will intersect the demand curve for dollars at point F'. So there is appreciation of the rupee or a fall in the exchange rate from R_1 to R_2.

Now to maintain the exchange rate at R_1 the RBI will have to expand the money supply. This will lead to a rightward shift of the *LM* curve, as shown in panel (b). As a result national income increases further from Y_2 to Y_3. But, at the new equilibrium point E'' (which is attained by the economy after the adoption of an expansionary monetary policy) the domestic rate of interest returns to the original level and is again equal to the world interest rate ($r = r_w$). And the original exchange rate (R_1) is restored. Thus by making appropriate use of fiscal and monetary policies it is possible to increase national income substantially without permitting the rate of interest or the exchange rate to rise. So there is no crowding- out effect due to the adoption of accommodating monetary policy to lend support to an expansionary fiscal policy.

Monetary policy is not effective under the fixed exchange rate system

Thus we see that the central bank's commitment to maintain a fixed exchange rate makes the changes in money supply **endogenous**. This is because the central bank has to intervene in the foreign exchange market to maintain the fixed exchange rate. This implies that the central bank cannot pursue an independent monetary policy (by insulating it from the rest of the world) to achieve domestic economic stability (or internal balance). However, the government can raise the level of national income (and, of course, employment) only by using expansionary fiscal policy.

1. They will do this by selling dollars in the foreign exchange market.

B. ADJUSTMENT UNDER FLEXIBLE EXCHANGE RATES

We now assume that domestic prices remain constant while the exchange rate is completely flexible. Under the flexible exchange rate system the exchange rate adjusts itself automatically to maintain equilibrium in the foreign exchange market even in the absence of government intervention. This also implies that the balance of payments is always in equilibrium. This happens because any deficit in the current account is financed by a surplus in capital account (i.e., by inflows of private financial capital). By contrast any current account surplus must be balanced by outflows of private financial capital.

Under the fully flexible exchange rate there is link between the money supply and the balance of payments

Under completely flexible exchange rate system, the central bank can pursue a discretionary monetary policy, i.e., it can increase or decrease the supply of money according to the needs of the situation. This implies that there is no link between the balance of payments and the domestic money supply.

In the Mundell-Fleming model perfect capital mobility ensures that there is only one rate of interest at which the balance of payments of a country is in equilibrium. This rate is the same as the world rate ($r = r_w$). Any other rate of interest will lead to capital movements and thus to a change in the real exchange rate. Assuming that domestic and world prices of goods (P and P_w) remain constant a fall in the domestic rate of interest below the world level (i.e., r_w) will lead to unlimited capital outflows from the home country. As a result the rupee will depreciate. So exports will rise and imports will fall and net exports (*NX*) will rise. Consequently the *IS* curve will shift to the right and national income will increase.

The converse is also true. If $r > r_w$, there will be continuous inflows of capital into the home country. The balance of payments will show a surplus. The rupee will appreciate. Exports will fall. Imports will rise and net exports (*NX*) will fall. So the *IS* curve will shift to the left and national income will fall.

THE SMALL ECONOMY IN EQUATION FORM

The small open economy under the flexible exchange rate system can be described by the following three simple equations:

$$Y = C(Y) + I(r) + NX(Y, Y_f, R) \quad \ldots \quad (11)$$

$$BP = NX(Y, Y_f, R) + CM(r - r_w) \quad \ldots \quad (12)$$

$$r = r_w \quad \ldots \quad (13)$$

Here (11) is the equation of the *IS* curve, *CM* stands for capital movements and all other terms have their usual meaning. Now we may do some comparative statics exercise and examine the effects of one exogenous change and two policy changes on *Y* and *r*.

1. Exogenous Increase in Exports

If there is an increase in India's exports, say, due to an increase in world demand for Indian goods the *IS* curve will shift to the right to *IS*′, as shown in Fig. 27.4. So national income increases from Y_1 to Y_2 as shown by the new macroeconomic equilibrium *F*. The domestic rate of interest also rises above the world rate ($r_1 > r_w$). This will lead to capital inflows. As a result the balance of payments will show a surplus and the rupee will appreciate. So India's exports will fall, imports will increase and *NX* will fall.

Consequently national income returns to its original level (Y_1), the rate of interest falls and is equated to the world rate (r_w) and capital inflow stops. This is how balance of payments equilibrium is restored.

Thus we see that an increase in exports has no long-term effect on the equilibrium level of national income in the Mundell-Fleming model with flexible exchange rate.

2. The Effect of an Expansionary Fiscal Policy

In the Mundell-Fleming model with flexible exchange rate an expansionary fiscal policy in the form of an increase in government spending or a cut in taxes has a neutral effect like that of an exogenous increase in export. The appreciation of the rupee induced by a higher interest rate and capital inflow leads to a fall in *NX*. This completely offsets the impact of fiscal expansion on national income. However, fiscal expansion changes the composition of domestic demand toward foreign goods and away from home produced goods and is thus an expenditure-switching, rather than an expenditure-reducing, policy.

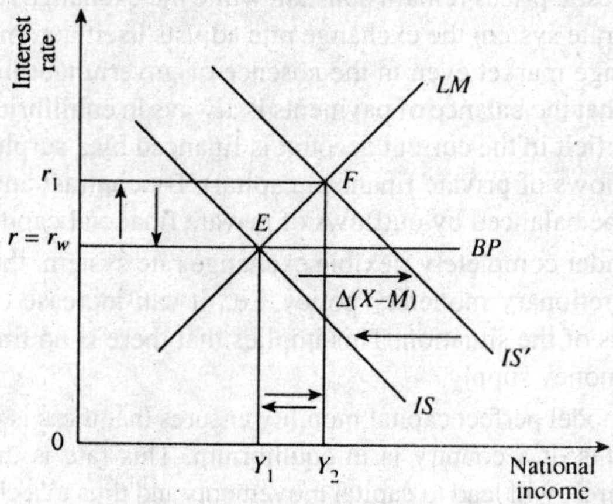

Fig. 27.4: The Effect of an Exogenous Increase in Exports on National Income and BOP

The Effect of Expansionary Monetary Policy

By contrast, an expansionary monetary policy is highly effective in raising the level of national income in this model. An increase in the money supply leads to an increase in national income due to depreciation of the rupee. This point is illustrated in Fig. 27.5.

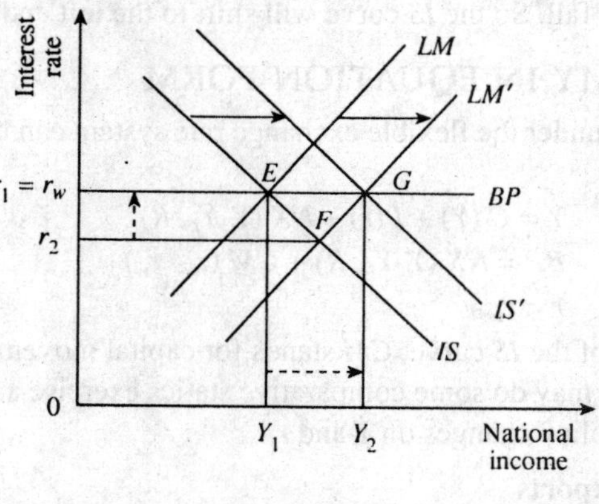

Fig. 27.5: The Effect of an Increase in the Money Supply on National Income

The economy is initially in equilibrium at point E, with national income at Y_1 and the domestic rate of interest (r_1) equal to the world rate (r_w). Now suppose the central bank increases the nominal money supply. Since the price level is assumed to remain constant, the real money supply (M/P) will increase. So, at point E, there will be an excess supply of real money balance. Therefore either the rate of interest has to fall or national income has to rise to restore equilibrium. Consequently the *LM* will shift to the right to *LM′* and intersect the original *IS* curve at point F. As a result the domestic rate of interest falls below the world rate ($r_2 < r_w$). This will lead to huge outflow of capital from the country, loss of foreign exchange (such as the US dollar) and depreciation of the rupee. Consequently net exports will increase (since exports will increase and imports will fall). Since aggregate final expenditure increases, the *IS* curve now shifts to the right to *IS′*. The final macroeconomic equilibrium for the small open economy is reached at point G at which the new *IS* curve intersects the new *LM* curve. So the domestic rate of interest rises from r_2 to r_1 and is equated to the world rate ($r_1 = r_w$). At the same time national income rises from Y_1 to Y_2.

Thus under the fixed exchange rate system an expansionary monetary policy cannot exert any influence on national income. But under flexible exchange rate system the central bank can change the supply of money to alter the rate of interest, exchange rate, net exports and national income.

Economic Insight: Competitive Depreciation

The depreciation of domestic currency is an expenditure-switching policy. It shifts demand from foreign goods (by reducing imports) towards domestic goods (by raising exports). As a result of a fall in imports and rise in exports, India's national income increases. But national income in the foreign country (the USA) falls. This is why such a policy is called beggar-thy-neighbour policy. This implies that an increase in national income and employment in the home country is at the expense of that in a foreign country (or various other foreign countries).

Beggar-thy-neighbour policy refers to a course of action which is taken by a country unilaterally to pursue its own interest even though this might adversely affect the position of other countries. The great danger with this type of policy, however, is that other countries may retaliate by depreciating their currencies. This is known as **competitive depreciation**. Every country depreciates its currency to increase its exports but no one can gain at the expense of others. This is exactly what had happened in 1997 in Asian countries which devalued their currencies after the lead was taken by Thailand. As a result every country in the Asian region suffered.

Criticisms of the Mundell-Fleming Model

The Mundell-Fleming model is based on certain restrictive assumptions. However, most of these assumptions are unrealistic. This is why the model has been criticised on the following ground:

(i) ***Different tax rates*** **:** Firstly, the tax rates of different countries are not the same. This adversely affects free mobility of capital among nations in response to inter-country differences in rates of interest.

(ii) ***Exchange rate changes*** **:** Secondly, substantial changes in the rates of exchange among different currencies affect return on capital invested abroad differently.

(iii) ***Control of capital movements*** **:** In addition, countries may impose various restrictions on capital movements.

(iv) ***Default*** **:** In some countries we may find default in making payments to foreigners.

For all these reasons free mobility of capital across national borders will be adversely affected and the rates of interest will not be the same in different countries of the world so as to ensure balance of payments equilibrium of the home country.

Critics have also pointed out that the main limitation of the model is the assumption of a fixed price level. If we relax the assumption, the model becomes quite complicated. This is why modern economists have presented a simple version of the monetarist approach to open economy macroeconomics. Monetarists argue that balance of payments problems are 'fundamentally monetary in nature.' They also emphasise the role played by a country's money market in determining its balance of payments position and exchange rate. The approach assumes that the total demand for money is a stable function of nominal national income and nominal rate of interest, based on a version of the quantity theory of money.

The Impossible Trinity of Finance of an Open Economy

While conducting monetary policy, a country seeks to achieve three goals;

(i) *a fixed exchange rate* where the value of currency is pegged to other currencies in order to stabilise international trade;

(ii) *international capital mobility* so that investor can move money in and out of the country, and

(iii) *control of the domestic monetary policy* so that a country can change interest rates to combat unemployment and inflation.

But R. Mundell and M. Fleming proved in 1962 that a country can only have two of the above — a principle known as the 'trilemma'.

Suppose India chooses a fixed exchange rate. It also has capital mobility, because today financial capital is the most mobile of all factors and it moves freely across borders. But if India tries to exercise monetary control — for example, by cutting interest rates to combat unemployment — it has to face a problem. If interest rates fall, investors will flee from the currency to find higher yields elsewhere. That means India has to defend the rupee — using up precious reserves — or admit defeat and raise interest rates again. In short, if India wants a fixed exchange rate and capital mobility, it cannot run an independent monetary policy. Governments are thus forced to make a choice: should they give maximum priority to macroeconomic management— the ability to respond to inflation or recession— or stable international trade?

If a country fixes its exchage rates and permits free mobility of capital, it cannot run an independent monetary policy

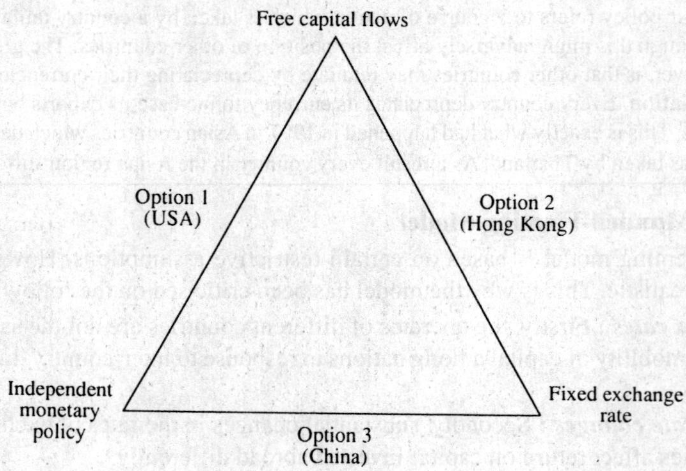

Fig. 27.6: The Effect of an Increase in the Money Supply on National Income

In Fig. 27.6 we see that it is impossible for a nation to have free capital flows, a fixed exchange rate, and an independent monetary policy. A nation must choose one side of this triangle, giving up the opposite corner.

KEY POINTS

1. *The Mundell-Fleming model* : The open economy general Keynesian model, known as the M-F model, shows that by making appropriate use of monetary and fiscal measures it is possible for a small country to achieve both internal balance and external balance.

2. *An increase in the money supply with a fixed exchange rate* : With no sterilisation, a fixed exchange rate will help insulate the economy from domestic monetary changes.

3. *An increase in government spending with a fixed exchange rate* : With no sterilisation, a fixed exchange rate helps to reinforce the effect of a change in domestic expenditure on national income and employment.

4. *An increase in the money supply with a floating exchange rate* : A floating exchange rate helps to reinforce the effect of a monetary change on national income and employment.

5. *An increase in government spending with a floating exchange rate* : A floating exchange rate helps to offset the effect of a change in domestic spending on national income and employment.

6. *Limitation of the model* : The main limitation of the Mundell-Fleming model is the assumption of a fixed price level. If this assumpton is relaxed, the analysis becomes complicated. This is why modern economists have adopted a simple version of the monetarist approach to open-economy macroeconomics.

7. *Impossible trinity:* Impossible trinity refers to the impossiblity of combining all three of the following: (i) monetary independence, (ii) full financial market integration, and (iii) exchange rate stability.

KEY TERMS

Small open economy
Monetary policy under flexible exchange rate
Fiscal policy under flexible exchange rate
Real money balance
Contagion effect
Monetary approach to open-economy macroeconomics
Monetary independence in an open economy
Monetary policy under fixed exchange rate
Fiscal policy under fixed exchange rate
Sterilisation
Capital movements
Beggar-thy-neighbour policy
Exchange rate stability
Full financial market integration
Monetary approach to open economy macroeconomics

ASSIGNMENTS

1. Develop a model for small open economy assuming perfect capital mobility and fixed prices. What are the limitations of the model?
2. Show how an open economy can achieve both (a) internal balance and (b) external balance by making appropriate use of monetary and fiscal policies (i) under the fixed exchange rate system and (ii) under the flexible exchange rate system.
3. Write short notes on:
   (a) sterilisation and
   (b) monetary approach to open economy marcoeconomics.
4. Explain why under the fixed exchange rate system monetary policy is not effective in the presence of perfect capital mobility. Why is fiscal policy effective?
5. What is mean by the impossible trinity in the context of the Mundell-Fleming model?
6. Suppose that a country has a capital account surplus of Rs. 20 million and a current account deficit of Rs. 14 million.
   (a) Calculate the Balance of Payment and state its situation?
   (b) If the Central Bank intervenes, does it buy or sell the home currency?
   (c) If the Bank does not intervene, what will be the impact on the home exchange rate?
7. Suppose that the rupee is appreciating steadily against the dollar. How would this affect (i) your US friend who wants to visit India, (ii) if you are an exporter of garments to the USA?
8. Decline is the price of oil in 1985-86 led to a sharp depreciation of the currency of Mexico, a major oil exporter. Explain this fact using a suitable diagram.
9. The Mundell-Fleming model takes the world interest rate as an exogenous variable. Let us consider what happens when the variable changes.
   (i) What might cause the world interest rate to rise?
   (ii) In the Mundell-Fleming model with a floating exchange rate, what happens to aggregate income, the exchange rate and the trade balance when the world interest rate rises?
   (iii) In the Mundell-Fleming model with a fixed exchange rate, what happens to aggregate income, the exchange rate and the trade balance when the world interest rate rises.
10. Suppose that money demand depends on disposable income, so that the equation for the money market becomes.
    $M/P = L(r, Y-T)$
    Analyse the impact of tax cut in a small open economy on the exchange rate and income under both floating and fixed exchange rates.
11. What are the important aspects of economic openness?
12. Describe the logic of speculative attack on currency.
13. Distinguish between flexible exchange system and fixed exchange system.

CHAPTER 28

Free Trade vs. Protection

> *International division of labour and international trade which enable each country to specialise and to export those things which it can produce cheaper, exchange for what others can produce at a lower cost have been and still are one of the basic factors promoting well-being and increasing national income of every participating country.*
>
> G. Harberler

In this chapter we discuss commercial or trade policy which is essentially concerned with whether a country should follow a policy of free trade or protection. The classical economists like Adam Smith, David Ricardo and J. S. Mill advocated the doctrine of free trade because it yields several advantages to a trading nation. However, in spite of the advantages of free trade, no country in the world has followed this policy. All countries have imposed restrictions on trade or have followed the policy of protectionism or simply protection. The policy of protectionism refers to any government interference with free trade. Since free trade and protection are the opposite sides of the same coin, the advantages of free trade are the disadvantages of protection.

Arguments for protection are essentially argument against free trade

The converse is also true. The disadvantages of free trade are the advantages of protection. This means that the arguments for protection are essentially arguments against free trade. Since free trade has some major drawbacks, no countries in the world trade follow the policy of free trade. And different countries have imposed different types of trade restrictions and thus imposed (erected) barriers to trade and restricted the volume of trade by imposing tariffs, quotas and other non-tariff barriers such as foreign exchange control, local content requirement and voluntary export restraint. Tariffs are used mainly to protect domestic industries from foreign competition and to raise revenue for the government.

Focus on Terminology: Free Trade Policy, Commercial Policy and Protectionism
Complete freedom from international trade is known as a free trade policy. Government policy towards international trade is known as commercial policy. Any departure from free trade designed to protect domestic industries from foreign competition is called protectionism. Protectionism refers to a deliberate policy on the part of a government to erect trade barriers such as tariffs and quotas in order to protect domestic industries from foreign competition.

Here we start with certain basic arguments in favour of free trade. Then we will examine the arguments in favour of protection (or protectionism).

THE CASE FOR FREE TRADE

The following arguments have been put forward in favour of free trade:

A. Static Gains

1. *Increase in productivity due to specialisation* : A country is able to produce more of a good through specialisation and export a portion of it to get those goods which it cannot produce at all or produce cheaply (at low cost per unit). Such gains from specialisation arises due to increase in factor (mainly labour) productivity after specialisation. Thus international trade increases a society's consumption possibilities by enabling it to go beyond its production possibility curve (PPC). Free trade leads to an efficient allocation of a country's resources; a high level of output and an improved standard of living then is possible under self-sufficiency (autarky).

2. *Gains from exchange* : An improvement in the terms of trade is also a source of gains from trade. A rise in the price of a country's exports or a fall in the price of a country's imports implies an improvement in its terms of trade. The gains from trade which arise from an improvement in its terms of trade is known as gains from exchange.

In fact, there are the two main sources of gains from trade: gains from specialisation due to increase in factor productivity and gains from exchange due to an improvement in the terms of trade. There is an other important source of gains from trade which is the following:

3. *Economies of scale* : The advantages associated with large-scale production can be derived when a country produces a good for the unlimited world market rather than for a narrow domestic market. The scope of division of labour and its corollary, specialisation depend on the size of the market for a product. International trade widens the market for a good and enables the trading nation to take full advantages of production on a very large scale. If the size of the market for a product is small, efficient production is not possible. Cost per unit will be high and the product cannot be exported at a competitive price.

For example, a small country such as Bangladesh cannot produce cars at a low cost due to the narrow size of its domestic market. But India is quite successful in producing cars which are both domestically used and exported to various other countries.

B. Dynamic Gains

In the long run, free trade stimulates economic growth. This is why Dennis Robertson and Hla Myint have described foreign trade as an engine of growth. So, it logically follows that trade restrictions hamper economic growth. Most Asian countries such as Japan, Taiwan, South Korea, Singapore, Hong Kong and China have achieved rapid growth through exports. They have achieved export-led growth. By contrast, India has achieved growth-led exports. Dynamic gains from trade arise from faster economic growth. Such gains are of the following three types:

1. *An increase in the rate of savings and investment* : Due to an increase in real national income through trade, there is an increase in the rate of saving. This, in its turn, leads to a high rate of investment and faster economic growth. Thus developing countries are able to break the age-old vicious circle of poverty to reach the 'take-off' stage initially and then achieve 'self-sustaining' growth.

Trade increases the rate of saving and capital formation and thus stimulates economic growth

2. *Import of (the much needed) capital goods* : A country can import capital goods which it cannot produce initially. This promotes faster industrial growth by adding to a country's stock of capital or by enabling the country to build additional production capacity. If domestic resources are not adequate, a country may even borrow from other countries to finance the import of capital goods.

3. *Transfer of technology* : A new technology developed in one country can be imported by another country which is technologically backward. This is possible through foreign trade and foreign investment which is associated with it. Developing countries can use modern improved technology without developing it, i.e., through imports. Trade among nations leads to international diffusion of technology or transfer of technology from developed to developing countries through licensing, joint ventures and multinational corporations (MNCs). Such technology transfer accelerates the rate of economic growth.

4. *Prevention of monopoly* : Under free trade domestic producers have to compete closely with their foreign counterparts. So as the volume of trade among nations expands, competition becomes more and more intense. This implies that free trade prevents the emergence of monopolies which normally emerge in narrow domestic markets under self-sufficiency. In addition, free trade acts as an anti-monopoly device. It forces monopolies to operate in a competitive environment and thus to expand output and reduce unit cost and price by being forced to operate efficiently in order to survive. In addition, free trade forces domestic firms to become more innovative and quality-conscious. They have to develop new products and processes as also to improve the quality of their products.

5. *Wider choice* : Free trade widens consumer choice. It offers consumers a wide range of goods to choose from. This, in its turn, promotes consumer welfare.

6. *Faster economic growth* : The increase in efficiency due to expansion of the scale of production and adoption of modern improved technology conjointly lead to lower cost and price, widens the market for a country's products and conduces to faster economic growth.

Lipsey and Crystal sum up the above advantages of free trade in the following words: "When countries protect their home markets with high tariffs, they reduce the amount of international competition faced by their domestic firms. This is particularly important when the countries are small so that there is room for only a few, possibly even just one, domestic firms to serve the local market. In these circumstances, international trade can increase competitive pressures that face domestic firms. This, in turn, may lead to more product and process innovation than which occurred under protection. Also because firms throughout the world are innovative in both product and production processes, an open trading regime allows consumers to benefit from the many technological changes that occur in other countries as well as locally".[1]

7. *Political stability* : Free trade promotes cooperation among nations and reduces the likelihood of war. Excessive protection and restriction on international transactions lead to trade wars, from which emerge strained political relations among nations. The recent trade war between the U.S.A and Japan is a case in point and reminds us of mercantilism. In fact, the frequent trade war between (among) nations is known as *new mercantilism*.

THE CASE FOR PROTECTION

In spite of certain advantages of free trade, it has a few disadvantages also. For instance, free trade creates uncertainty in times of war. In fact, in times of the last Gulf war, America refused to sell its products to its enemies (the Gulf countries). As a result there was an acute shortage of essential consumer goods in oil-rich Gulf countries and there was a very high rate of inflation.

Perhaps the worst consequence of free trade is that under unrestricted import of goods, a developing country's own industries never develop. Cheap imports often destroy its domestic industries. This had happened in India during the British period. Import of cheap, machine-made goods led to the decline of India's traditional industries, viz., handicrafts. In other words, the commercial policy adopted by the British Government led to deindustrialisation in India.

For these and other reasons governments of most countries imposed various types of restrictions on imports. Such restrictions are known as protectionism or simply protection. There are two aspects of protection, viz., methods or instruments of protection and arguments for protection. We first start with the methods of protection and then we will discuss the arguments for protection.

1. *Principles of Economics* (11th edition, Oxford, 2007), p. 616

A. Methods of Protection

Two most important methods of protection are tariffs and quotas. A tariff is a tax on exports or a tax on imports. Tariffs were earlier imposed on both exports and imports. Now only import tariffs are imposed by most countries. Export tariffs have been abolished. There are two types of import tariff, viz., (a) an *ad valorem* duty, which is levied as a fixed percentage of the value of the good and (b) a *specific duty* which is imposed as a fixed sum of money per physical unit of the good. A quota is an administrative device to limit the volume or value of imports. Under a quota system, the government directly restricts the volume of permissible imports to a specified maximum level. The basic objective, as under the tariff system, is to protect domestic industries from foreign competition.

The same reduction in imports and increase in domestic production can be achieved by imposing either an import tariff or an import quota. Here, for instance, we show import on horizontal axis and domestic and world prices on the vertical axis. In panel (i) of Fig. 28.1, domestic demand and supply curves are D and S, respectively and the world price is P_W. Under free trade domestic consumption q_4 exceeds domestic production q_1. So $q_1 - q_4$ represents imports.

In panel (ii), we initially show the effect of the imposition of an import tariff. If a specific tariff of 't' is imposed, domestic price P_d rises exactly by the amount of the tariff ($P_d = P_w + t$). As a result production increases from q_1 to q_2 since domestic producers now receive the higher import price. But consumption falls from q_4 to q_3. So $q_2 - q_3$ now represents the new level of imports. For purchasing q_3 amount consumers pay an extra amount, shown by the three areas A, B and C.

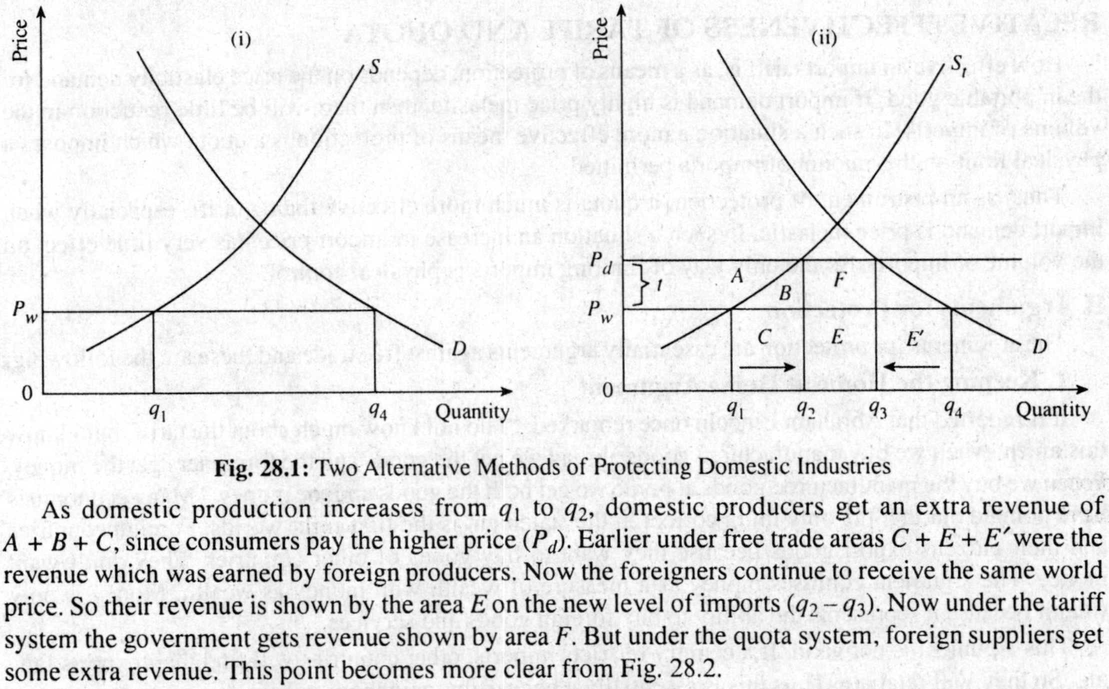

Fig. 28.1: Two Alternative Methods of Protecting Domestic Industries

As domestic production increases from q_1 to q_2, domestic producers get an extra revenue of $A + B + C$, since consumers pay the higher price (P_d). Earlier under free trade areas $C + E + E'$ were the revenue which was earned by foreign producers. Now the foreigners continue to receive the same world price. So their revenue is shown by the area E on the new level of imports ($q_2 - q_3$). Now under the tariff system the government gets revenue shown by area F. But under the quota system, foreign suppliers get some extra revenue. This point becomes more clear from Fig. 28.2.

Initially, India imports Q_f cars at the world price P_w. In fact, it is able to import any number of cars from Japan at the world price (which is the same as the domestic price under free trade) and the import supply curve S is completely elastic at the world price.

Now, if an import tariff of 't' per until is imposed, the world supply curve S shifts upward exactly by the amount of the tariff, as shown in panel (i). So domestic price is now P_d which is higher than the world price exactly by the amount of tariff (t). Now, imports fall from Q_f to Q_t. The revenue of foreign suppliers falls by the area (1). The government gets revenue, shown by area (3).

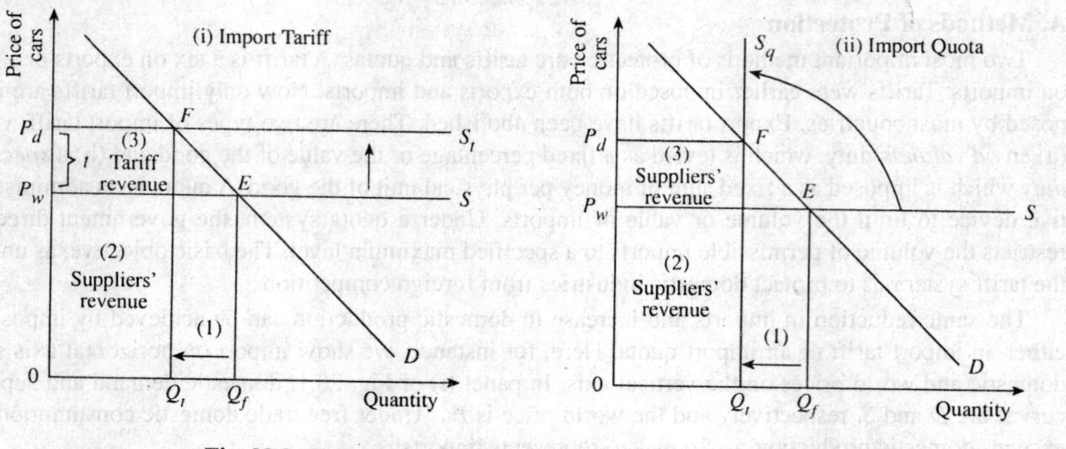

Fig. 28.2: Comparing the Revenue Effect of a Tariff and a Quota

By comparison, if an import quota is imposed, as shown in panel (ii), imports fall from Q_f to Q_t, as in the case of an import tariff. But the areas (2) and (3) now represent foreign suppliers' revenue. Although they lose the revenue area 1, they gain the area (3), which could be captured by the government under the tariff system. Thus we see that while an import tariff has both protective and revenue effects, an import quota has only protective effect.

RELATIVE EFFECTIVENESS OF TARIFF AND QUOTA

How effective an import tariff is, as a means of protection, depends on the price elasticity demand for the importable good. If import demand is highly price inelastic, then there will be little reduction in the volume of imports. In such a situation a more effective means of protection is a quota which imposes a physical limit on the amount of imports permitted.

Thus, as an instrument of protection, a quota is much more effective than a tariff, especially when import demand is price inelastic. In such a situation an increase in import price has very little effect on the volume of imports. So the only way of limiting imports is physical control.

B. Arguments for Protection

The arguments for protection are essentially arguments against free trade and these are the following:

1. Keeping the Home at Home Argument

It is reported that Abraham Lincoln once remarked: "I do not know much about the tariff, but I know this much: when we buy manufactured goods abroad we get the goods and the foreigners get the money. When we buy the manufactured goods at home we get both the goods and the money." Many economists have pointed out that the only thing correct in the statement is the first eight worlds. Foreign countries and their citizens export goods because they want to buy goods of other countries. They don't want money. The argument confuses money as a measure of wealth with money as wealth. Money is only wealth because it represents the ability to buy foreign goods and services.

This argument is not valid. If a country restricts imports, other countries will find their exports falling. So they will retaliate. Thus this is essentially a beggar-thy-neighbour policy.

Economic Insight: Beggar-Thy-Neighbour Policy

A beggar-thy-neighbour policy refers to a protective measure that is adopted by a country to promote its own interest in international trade even though this might adversely affect the trading position and welfare level of other countries. For example, country *A* might decide to impose tariffs or quotas on imports from other countries in order to protect certain domestic industries. The main drawback of this policy is that it can be self-defeating. The reason is that other countries may retaliate by imposing tariff or quotas of their own on country *A*'s exports, with the result that every trading country's exports suffer.

2. Income and Employment Argument

An important argument for protection is that it will lead to increase in domestic employment or at least preserve present domestic employment. It is often believed that imports of goods reduce domestic employment. Therefore, if instead of imports we produce those goods at home, domestic employment will increase. Besides, if prices of imported goods are lower, the domestic producers would not be able to compete with them and may be driven out of the market. This will destroy even present jobs in severed domestic industries. It is therefore suggested that protection of domestic industries will lead to their expansion. As a result more employment will be generated in domestic industries which are protected through tariffs and quotas.

3. Infant Industry Argument

From the point of developing countries like India the most forceful argument in favour of tariff is the infant industry argument. It is essentially an argument in favour of protection to gain comparative advantage.

Economic Insight: Infant Industry
According to Oxford Dictionary of Economics, an infant industry is a "new industry which during its early stages is unable to compete with estabilised producers abroad, often because of the lack of market reputation and small scale. Governments sometimes support the development of new industries either by direct subsidies or by protective tariffs or other methods of trade controls."

The Basic Argument

Protection can be an effective means of stimulating the development of an industry which is well suited to a country (in terms of potential comparative advantage), but finds it impossible to get started until it is protected from imports. However, if such an industry is initially protected for some time, it will be able to enjoy both internal economies of scale (i.e., fall in long-run average cost due to exploitation of a large domestic market) and to exploit various external economies (a well-trained work force or the 'learning-by-doing' effect). Sooner or later the new industry will be able to become equally or even more efficient and viable than its well-established rivals. When this happens the tariff can be removed and the country will now have an efficient industry which can compete with its foreign counterparts.

MERITS OF THE ARGUMENT

There is no conflict between infant industry argument and comparative advantage

It is believed that temporary protection of infant industries does not go against the goal of free trade: maximum specilisation on the basis of comparative advantage. In other words there is no conflict between are infant industry argument for protection and comparative advantage. It is only through the equalisation of competitive conditions or cost advantages that the infant industry is able to reach that stage of development which allows it to fully realise its true potential in the long run.

Drawbacks

There are three major drawbacks of the infant industry argument. These are the following:

(i) **Lack of Rationale**

Industries are often selected for protection not on the basis of favourable comparative advantage but for nationalist reasons (e.g., diversification of the economy).

(ii) **Lack of Merit**

Infant industry becomes a slogan to justify indiscriminate protection without regard to the promise or future growth potential of each industry.

(iii) **Excessiveness and Prolongation of the Waiting Period**

The protection attached may be excessive and continue for longer period than is truly necessary. So the tariff-imposing country has to wait for an indefinite period to gain comparative advantage. It may even appear that other alternative measures such as expansionary monetary and fiscal policies (such as loan at low rates of interest and subsidies) may be more effective in promoting industries which have a genuine chance of achieving sustainable comparative advantage.

(iv) **Anti-Dumping Argument**

The other important argument for protection is that foreign producers compete unfairly by dumping the goods in another country. Dumping is a form of price discrimination. This occurs when the producer of a country sells goods in another country at lower prices than those charged at home. Of course, the consumers of the importing country are the beneficiaries. But the industries of that country suffer as they are unable to compete with the 'dumped goods'. Besides there is more harmful 'predatory dumping' which implies that foreign firms try to sell goods in other countries even below cost to establish a world-wide monopoly by driving competitors out of the market. Once the local industries are competed out, they raise prices to obtain monopoly profits.

There is a strong evidence that firms of the USA and Japan often indulge in dumping of their goods in other countries to eliminate competition. But, instead of providing protection to domestic industries through tariffs or non-tariffs barriers, it is a judicious policy to pass laws against dumping. Dumping can be stopped by declaring it unlawful. In India such a law has been passed no doubt but is not being properly (effectively) implemented.

(v) **Revenue Argument**

In developing countries like India a tariff is imposed principlly as a source of government revenue. This is different from a protective tariff which is imposed mainly as a means of assisting domestic producers to compete with imports. Most tariffs have both effects. Though a country can impose tariff on goods which is not produced for raising revenue, a prohibitive tariff can stop imports altogether but it raises no revnue. In other words, a prohibitive tariff is one which is set so high that no trade in the good concerned can take place.

One important difference between an import tariff and an import quota is that while the former gives revenue to the government, the latter does not generate any revenue. So an import tariff and an import quota are not equivalent in their economic effects. However, both serve the basic purpose of protecting domestic industries from foreign competition (both fair and unfair).

(vi) **The Balance of Payments Argument**

Selective tariffs and quotas may assist in restoring a country's balance of payments (BOP) equilibrium but distort the ordering of industries according to a chain of comparative advantage. In addition, BOP equilibrium can be achieved more effectively by other measures such as monetary and fiscal policies as also exchange rate adjustments which affect all foreign transactions.

(vii) **The Terms of Trade Argument**

In some situations export tariffs can be imposed to improve a country's terms of trade. In October 1973, for example, the OPEC has raised the price of crude oil by 300% in one stroke and made substantial gains from trade by improving their terms of trade of their members. In fact, an improvement in the terms of trade is also a source of gains from trade. This is known as gains from exchange. For every barrel of oil which they exported to the rest of the world, they were able to get more of other goods in exchange.

Some importing countries impose tariffs to improve their terms of trade by pushing down prices in exporting countries. This applies especially to major importers who are large enough to exercise their bargaining power. However, the gains from lower-priced imports may be offset by two adverse effects of tariffs: the diversion of scarce and precious resources to less productive uses and retaliation by trade partners through the imposition of tariffs on their own.

Economic Insight: Optimum Tariff

An optimum tariff is one "which maximises a country's welfare, trading off improvement in the terms of trade against restriction of trade quantities. For a small economy which cannot affect world prices in the market in which it trades, the optimum tariff is zero. For a country with monopoly power in its export markets or monopsony power in import markets, the optimum tariff is positive, but not so large as to eliminate trade entirely." (*Oxford Dictionary of Economics*), p. 325

(viii) The Redistribution Argument

A case for protection has also been built up on the ground that a policy of protectionism can be adopted to make desirable redistribution of income from one section of society to another. Protection makes some people better off and others worse off. By giving protection to domestic producers it is possible to raise their profits at the expense of consumers. The reason is that they suffer welfare loss due to rise in domestic prices of imported goods. Thus, protection redistributes income in favour of domestic producers.

Economic Insight: The Stolper-Samuelson Theorem

The Stolper-Samuelson theorem (1941) postulates that free trade benefits the abundant factor of a trading cuts and protection benefits its scarce factor. According to the theory of comparative cost (advantage), known as the Heckscher-Ohlin theorem a country's exports are intensive in its abundant factor and its imports are intensive in its scarce factor. Thus, if an import tariff is imposed, imports will fall (provided the demand for imports is elastic) and domestic production of import-subsititute items will increase. Industries making such items will require more and more of the country's scarce factors. So the demand for and prices of such factors will increase and the returns to such factors will increase correspondingly. Thus an import tariff benefits a country's scarce factor(s).

ECONOMIC EFFECTS OF IMPORT TARIFF — LOSS OF EFFICIENCY AND WELFARE

It may also be noted that an import tariff reduces consumer surplus but increases producer surplus, as is shown in Fig. 28.3. Due to the imposition of a specific import tariff *t*, production increases from Q_1 to Q_2 and there is an increase in producer surplus measured by area P_wP_dAC, i.e., the area above the domestic supply curve but below the domestic price. But consumption falls from Q_4 to Q_3 and there is loss of consumer surplus, measured by the area $P_wP_d\,DF$, i.e., the area below the demand curve but above the

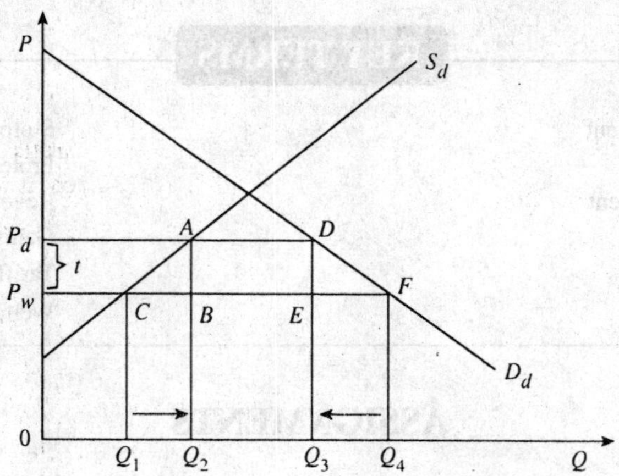

Fig. 28.3: Distorting Effects of an Import Tariff and DWL

world price. The area *ABED* measures government revenue and the sum of the two triangular areas—*ABC* and *DEF* measure deadweight loss (DWL) of an import tariff. It arises for the following two reasons:

1. Production Loss

Even if domestic production increases from Q_1 to Q_2 after the imposition of tariff, the triangle *ABC* measures production loss to the country. Under conditions of full employment of resources, production in the protected industries can be increased only by diverting resources away from others (non-protected) industries, which rank much higher in the order of productive efficiency. Thus, some resources are allocated less efficiently as a result of the tariff. Thus a tariff reduces efficiency in production.

A tariff reduces efficiency in production

2. Consumption Loss

The triangle *DEF* represents the 'consumption loss' to society. As a result of the tariff, some buyers are forced to switch to less desirable substitute products (such as margarine in place of butter). At the same time those consumers who continue to buy the imported good are now forced to pay a price for it which is in excess of the real economic cost of supplying it.

KEY POINTS

1. *Gains from free trade* : Free or unrestricted trade promotes economic welfare because a country makes two types of gains, viz., gains from specialisation and gains from exchange. Modern economists speak of two other types of gains, viz., static gains and dynamic gains. And trade often acts as an engine of economic growth.

2. *Protection* : However, in spite of the advantages of free trade no country in the world has given up protectionism. The reason is that there are various disadvantages of free trade And there are the advantages of protection. There are two aspects of protection, viz., instruments of protection and arguments for protection.

3. *Instruments of protection* : Two main instruments of protection are import tariffs and import quotas and tariff is a tax on imports. An imports quota is a physical limit on the volume of imports. Both the instruments protect domestic industries from foreign competition. But, unlike an import tariff, an import quota does not generate any revenue for the government of the quota-imposing country.

4. *Arguments for protection* : There are various arguments in favour of protection which are essentially arguments against free trade. These are (i) keeping the money at home argument, (ii) infant industry argument, (iii) terms of trade argument, (iv) balance of trade argument, (v) income and employment argument and (vi) revenue argument. However, the most relevant argument for protection in developing countries like India is the infant industry argument. This is essentially an argument in favour of protection to gain comparative advantage. By imposing a prohibitive tariff, it is possible to stop imports altogether. But there is no revenue for the government in this case.

KEY TERMS

Infant industry argument	Stolper-Samuelson theorem
Optimum tariff	Protective effect of tariff
Terms of trade argument	Revenue effect of tariff
Import tariff	Gains from protection
Import quota	Tariff-quota equivalence
Gains from free trade	Welfare effect of tariff

ASSIGNMENTS

1. What are the sources of gains from trade for a developing country like India?
2. What are the main advantages of free trade?
3. What are the disadvantages of free trade?
4. Explain why, in spite of the advantages of free trade, no country in the world has given up protectionism altogether.

5. What is the most powerful argument for protection in developing countries? What is the most forceful argument against tariff protection? Explain your answer.
6. Are tariffs and quotas equivalent in their economic effects? If so, when does the equivalence break down?
7. Discuss the economic effects of an import tariff.
8. Compare the effects of an import tariff with that of an import quota.
9. The policy of protecting domestic industries from foreign competition is essentially a beggar-thy-neighbour policy—critically examine the statement.
10. (a) Do tariffs lead to misallocation of a country's scarce economic resources?

    (b) What is optimum tariff?
11. When all countries impose optimal tariff, it is likely that everyone's economic welfare will decline as impediments to free trade become larger. All countries are likely to benefit if they abolish trade barriers. Critically examine the statements.

CHAPTER 29

Trade Strategy for India: Import Substitution vs. Export Promotion

> *A fundamental issue of economic development concern a country's stance toward international trade. Should developing countries attempt to be self-sufficient, to replace most imports with domestic production? Or should a country strive to pay for imports it needs by improving efficiency and competitiveness, developing foreign markets and keeping trade barriers low?*
>
> P. A. Samuelson and W. D. Nordhaus

PREVIEW

International trade plays an important role in promoting faster economic growth of developing countries like India and ensuring economic self-reliance (so that exports pay for imports and there is no balance of trade deficit). We have already explained both static and dynamic gains from trade in the last chapter. And the case for free trade or trade liberalisation has been made on the basis of both types of gains. The basic point to note here is that when a country specialises in its own area of comparative advantage (or relative efficiency) and determines its pattern of trade, (i.e., exports and imports) on the basis of such advantage it is able to allocate its productive resources optimally and use them efficiently. Consequently employment, output and income increase. And the end result is an improvement in the level of living of people or in social (community) welfare. The gains which arise from trade through improved (or efficient) allocation of resources are known as static gains.

International trade acts as an engine of growth

International trade also promotes further economic growth of a nation, since there are dynamic gains associated with it. D. H. Robertson described foreign trade as an engine of growth. Due to an increase in aggregate output and national income, through specialisation and trade, the savings and investment of a nation also increase. Consequently the rate of economic growth (as measured by a sustained or a continuous increase in national and per capita incomes) pick up. In addition, through larger export of goods and services, a developing country like India can earn the much needed foreign exchange which can be used to import capital goods, fertilisers and raw materials (mainly crude oil) which are so essential for raising agricultural productivity and promoting industrialisation which is so essential for achieving both faster economic growth and rapid economic development.

In addition, trade enables developing countries to import and use superior technology which is invented in developed (or industrially advanced) countries at huge costs and remains embodied in imported machines and capital goods. In other words, international trade leads to transfer of technology and thus transmission of knowledge and new technical know-how from developed to developing countries. All those factors conjointly conduce to faster economic growth. It is against this background that we study India's trade policy during the plan period. However, to start with it is necessary to know the pros and cons of two alternative trade strategies of less developed countries (LDCs), viz., import substitution and export promotion.

THEORETICAL BACKGROUND

Two alternative trade strategies for developing countries like India (as the opening quotation of this chapter indicates) are import substitution and outward orientation or openness.

An inward-looking policy such as that of import substitution seeks to impose tariffs at high rates on imported articles. The objective is not just to earn revenue but to protect domestic industries against foreign competition and enable such industries to produce import-substitute items so that foreign exchange can be saved.

By contrast, a policy of economic openness, with stress on export promotion, keeps trade barriers as low as practical. Such an outward-oriented policy relies primarily on tariffs rather than quotas and other non-tariff barriers.

Commentary: Import Substitution vs. Export Promotion

Having decided to industrialise, developing countries like India had to choose between industrialisation through import substitution or export promotion. Both policies have advantages and disadvantages. An import substitution industrialisation strategy offers two main advantages: (i) The market for the industrial products already exists, as shown by import of the commodity. So risks are reduced in setting up an industry to replace imports. (ii) It is easier for developing nations to protect their domestic markets against foreign competition in order to save foreign exchange than to earn foreign exchange by forcing developed nations to lower trade barriers against their manufactured exports.

Three disadvantages of such a strategy are the following: (i) Domestic industries become accustomed to protection from foreign competition and have an incentive to remain inefficient for ever. The reason is that as soon as they become self-sufficient, they apprehend that protection will be removed. So it pays high-cost domestic firms to remain inefficient for ever. Thus there is need for continuation of protection in order to enable inefficient firms not just to survive but even thrive under the tariff wall. (ii) Import substitution can lead to the emergence of inefficient industries due to the narrow size of the domestic market for industrial goods in many developing countries which does not allow firms to take advantage of economies of scale. Instead there is the problem of market saturation. (iii) After the simplier manufactured exports are replaced by domestic production, import substitution becomes more and more difficult and costly (in terms of the higher tariff and the resultant inefficiency) as there is need to replace more capital-intensive and technological advanced imports by domestic production.

Export-oriented industrialisation, by comparison, has the following advantages: (i) It overcomes the narrow size of the domestic market for manufactured goods and allows a developing nation like India to take advantage of economies of scale. This is more so for small developing countries with low income. (ii) Production of manufactured exports requires and promotes overall efficiency of the economy due to rational allocation of resources and cost reduction. This is more so when the output of one industry is used as an input of another domestic industry. (iii) The expansion of manufactured exports is not held in check (as in the case of import substitution) by the narrow size of the domestic market. After all, the world market is virtually unlimited.

On the other hand there are two serious disadvantages of outward orientation: (i) It may be very difficult for developing nations to set up export industries because of the competitive rivalry from the more established and efficient industries in developed nations. (ii) Developed nations often impose the high rates of tariffs or quotas on their imports of simple labour-intensive commodities in which developing nations already have or can soon gain a comparative advantage.

INDIA'S POLICY OF IMPORT- SUBSTITUTING INDUSTRIALISATION

At the very beginning of India's planning period in 1950-51, two options (or alternatives) were open to the policy-makers as far as its trade with the rest of the world was concerned. The first was *outward-looking* in nature, with stress on export-promotion for achieving faster economic growth by earning foreign exchange. The second one was *inward-looking,* with stress on import-substitution. The main objective of this strategy was saving foreign exchange and, in the process, achieving self-reliance (i.e., earning enough foreign exchange to pay for imports of raw materials and capital goods needed to achieve faster economic growth without external borrowing) rather than just self-sufficiency (i.e., stopping imports altogether by being able to balance domestic demand with domestic supply). And it was felt that one dollar saved through a cut in imports was as good for the country as the same dollar earned through exports.

In fact, due to bleak prospects of raising India's exports (or due to the so-called export pessimism) India was not in a position to earn sufficient foreign exchange to be able to pay for a large (and ever-increasing) volume of imports. Therefore, India's strategy of industrialisation was based on substitution of imports or replacement of imports through domestic production of import-substitute items.

Economic Insight: Export Pessimism

The term (export pessimism) was coined by Raul Prebisch who predicted a secular decline in the terms of trade of underdeveloped (developing) countries. Prebisch's prediction (or hypothesis) was based on three simple arguments. Firstly, the demand for primary products in which exports of underdeveloped countries were mainly concentrated were income-inelastic in nature. Secondly, technological progress in industrially advanced countries saved raw materials which were exported by underdeveloped countries. Thirdly, the prices of manufactured products exported by developed countries were fairly high, because these are set by large oligopolistic firms in imperfectly competitive markets. (In contrast, prices of primary products, mainly food and industrial raw materials were fixed in highly competitive markets). Thus, according to Prebisch, under such conditions or circumstances expansion of exports by underdeveloped countries was not treated as economically feasible.

Following almost the same line of reasoning as that of Prebisch, Ragnar Nurkse argued that for the newly industrialising countries like India, foreign trade could not act as an engine of growth. Such countries were not in a position to achieve export-led growth. Instead they achieved growth-led exports, i.e, exports were the by-products of growth. Nurkse's argument was simple. Since foreign markets could not absorb the products of developing countries like India on a sufficiently large scale, he suggested that in order to accelerate their growth process, developing countries should undertake the process of balanced growth. This could be achieved by making investment in a number of industries at the same time so that these could generate demand for one another's products and thus to lead to an expansion of the size of the domestic market for manufactured goods.

IMPORT SUBSTITUTION

It has to be noted at the outset that, up to the 1980s the Government of India (GOI) adopted an inward-looking trade strategy with stress on import substitution (IS). The choice of this policy was based on export pessimism, as noted above. This trade policy was implemented in two main ways: (1) by imposing complete ban on import of several items into India and (2) by fixing quotas (i.e., imposing quantitative restrictions) on certain other commodities. In addition, import tariffs (or customs duties) were levied on a number of items in order to discourage their imports by raising their prices. The main objective was to protect domestic industries (which were in their nascent stage) from foreign competition. The customs duties levied in India on certain imported items varied between 50% to 200% and were one of the highest in the world.

In addition, the GOI relied on the import licensing system with a view to regulating the quantities of several essential consumer and capital goods as also industrial raw materials. So licences for import quotas were issued by the Government. In case of certain other commodities a different scheme of import licensing was introduced in order to permit import of short-supply items, i.e., items the domestic demand for which could not be fully met through domestic production. In other words, imports of these items were permitted to the extent that domestic production fell short of domestic demand. Furthermore, strict and really stringent foreign exchange regulations were put into effect and foreign exchange was released only to the authorised agents or genuine licence-holders for importing certain specific items.

It is to be noted that India's policy of IS was indiscriminate in nature. And it remained effective for a fairly long period of time. We now make a brief review of the results of India's IS policy.

Result of IS Policy

No doubt the policy of IS made a genuine contribution to India's industrial growth between 1956 and 1966. However, with the passage of time several weaknesses of the policy of IS gradually appeared. The following points are worth noting in this context:

1. ***Fall in share of world trade*** : India's policy-makers underestimated the possibilities of expansion in exports. Consequently, India's share of world exports fell from 2% in 1951-52 to 0.53% in 1991-92.

2. ***Growing trade deficit*** : The policy of IS underestimated the import-intensity (or import content) of the process itself. The industries producing import-substitute items required huge imports of capital goods and raw materials. But this point was completely missed by Indian planners and policy-makers. Consequently restrictions imposed by the Government on imports of the much needed capital goods and industrial raw materials hampered the growth of import-substitute industries (and the production of import-substitute items for replacing imports). Consequently imports continued to increase sharply but there was no adequate growth in exports. This created balance of payments problem of a really serious nature. And, in spite of devaluation of the rupee in 1966, India's balance of trade deficit did not fall much. In other words, India's policy of IS was blamed for her increasing trade deficit.

POLICY SHIFT

In fact, the deficit in India's BOP arose mainly due to her inward-looking trade policy. This is why in the Third Plan (1961-66) and in the Fourth Plan (1969-74) various export promotion measures were adopted by the Government. However, in spite of this until the late 1970s, exports were primarily treated as a source of foreign exchange rather than as an efficient means of resource allocation. IS remained the basic premise of India's planned development strategy.

Since India pursued the policy of industrialisation based on IS, irrespective of considerations of relative efficiency or comparative cost, India emerged as a high-cost economy. Inefficiency in production and high costs accounted for her dismal export performance in spite of various concessions and initiatives offered by the Government for export promotion. We may now briefly discuss the various export promotion measures adopted by the GOI in 1980's.

EXPORT PROMOTION MEASURES OF THE 1980S

Because of mounting trade deficit in the early 1980s the issue of export promotion assumed great urgency and importance. And various export promotion measures were announced by the Government on the basis of the recommendations of the Tandon Committee. These were the following:

1. ***Rep. scheme*** : An incentive scheme to promote exports, called Replenishment (Rep.) Scheme was launched. It made provision for import of raw materials, machinery and capital equipment and accessories against exports.

2. ***Exim scripts*** : Exim scripts were introduced by replacing the Rep. Scheme. Exporters were given such scripts to the extent of 30% of the value of their exports. This revised scheme entitled exporters to import a certain specific amount of materials and machinery for increasing the volume of exports. This means that the main focus of India's trade policy was on import liberalisation for promoting exports.

3. ***Duty drawback scheme*** : An important fiscal concession, known as duty drawback scheme, was introduced. Under the scheme both excise duties and customs duties paid on domestic and imported materials used to make export items were refunded.

4. ***Tax concessions and tax holiday*** : A large proportion of profits or incomes earned from exports were exempted from income tax. In addition, a five-year tax holiday was announced in respect of the units set up in Special Economic Zones (SEZs) for financing exports.

5. ***Credit facilities*** : Liberal credit facilities, i.e., loans at concessional rates of interest were given to exporters by commercial banks.

6. ***Signing of trade agreements*** : Bilateral trade agreements were also signed with some countries.

7. ***Exchange entitlement scheme*** : In the second half of the 1980s the 'exchange entitlement' scheme was introduced. The objective was to enable exporters to utilise a part of their foreign exchange earnings for market development.

8. ***Cash compensatory support*** : A scheme for providing cash assistance to exporters was announced. Under the scheme cash assistance was given to exporters as compensation for taxes paid by them on the imported inputs used by them for the production of exportable items. This scheme was essentially a form of export subsidy, which was supposed to give necessary incentives to exporters.

9. ***Tariffication*** : Finally, in the second half of the 1980s the import quotas in respect of several items were replaced by tariffs for a twofold reason: (i) further liberalisation of imports and (ii) generation of revenue for the Government. This is known as tariffication.

In truth, in the 1980s, a progressively liberal trade policy was adopted by the GOI for two main reasons — (i) promoting exports and (ii) allowing larger imports of capital goods and technology. The main objective was to enable India to derive those gains from international trade which could not be reaped during the earlier years when the policy of import substitution was pursued.

AN OVERVIEW OF INDIA'S TRADE POLICY SINCE JULY 1991: IMPORT LIBERALISATION-CUM-EXPORT ORIENTATION

India had to face a crisis situation in 1991. The economic crisis originated from a persistent deficit in the BOP in the past several years. The Gulf War of 1990 raised India's import bill sharply. By March 1991, India's current account deficit reached a record level of about US $ 10 billion (which was more than 3% of India's GDP). Exports were falling. Foreign borrowing in the previous few years raised the ratio of short-term debt to foreign exchange reserves to an unusually high level of nearly 150%. The ratio of external debt to foreign exchange reserves crossed 35%. Consequently, India's foreign exchange reserves fell to such a low level that they were just adequate to pay for a few weeks' import bill. And in July 1991 there was a distinct possibility of India emerging as a defaulter for the first time. On the one hand, there was massive outflow of foreign capital from India (i.e., capital which was invested in India by foreigners in earlier years). What was worse, no fresh loan was made to India by foreigners since India lost its creditworthiness to them. And the severe economic crisis of 1991 forced India to introduce several drastic reform measures in respect of foreign trade (i.e., exports and imports).

Two notable features of India's new liberalised trade policy were (i) import liberalisation and (ii) export orientation. This new policy served two main purposes at the same time, viz., (i) allowing import of capital goods and essential raw materials and inputs needed for production of exportable items and (ii) stimulating exports. These two forces conjointly made India's transition to a globally-oriented economy faster by removing the anti-export bias (or, the so-called export pessimism) of the earlier policy. These two policies, were, in fact, recommended by both the IMF and the World Bank in the context of developing countries like India which were facing BOP problems for years together. These measures, it was felt, would serve a twofold purpose — (i) improving the external economic position of a deficit country like India in the short run and (ii) promoting faster economic growth in the long run. We now discuss the policy in detail.

Import Liberalisation

For achieving import liberalisation the following four measures were adopted by the GOI.

(i) ***Elimination of import quotas*** : Since 1991 India eliminated quantitative restrictions (import quotas) in a phased manner (i.e., in a step-by-step fashion) on most intermediate and capital goods. In addition, a short negative list of imports was published. The import of these items would be controlled and regulated by the Government. All other goods could be imported without taking permission from the Government (or obtaining approval of any authority), subject, of course, to payment of import duty. Earlier imports were regulated by means of a positive list of freely importable items.

(ii) ***Abolition of licensing*** : Most imported items were put under the Open General Licence (OGL). This means that for importing these items prior approval of any authority is not required. Earlier most imported items were subject to import-licensing restrictions (requirements).

(iii) ***Reduction in the rates of import tariff*** : The rates of import tariffs that were quite high (or even prohibitive in case of certain items) were drastically reduced. Such duties were supposed to give protection to India's infant industries (i.e., industries which were high-cost producers in their nascent stage). Since 1992-93 the maximum import duty has been reduced from 150% and brought down to 20% in 2004-05 in a phased manner.

It now seems that the reduction of import tariffs has increased productivity of resources and efficiency of domestic industries by exposing them to foreign competition.

(iv) ***Liberalisation of imports of gold and silver*** : Imports of gold and silver have been substantially liberalised. This has helped in preventing smuggling of these metals.

Export-Orientation of Trade Policy

Along with import liberalisation an outward looking trade strategy was adopted in 1991. In this context we refer to various export promotion measures adopted by the GOI. These are the following:

1. ***Reduction in customs duties*** : As noted earlier the rates of customs duties have been drastically reduced to remove the anti-export bias of India's trade policy and to promote the growth of exports.

2. ***Devaluation of the rupee*** : The rupee was devalued by 20% in July 1991. Along with this the cash compensatory scheme was abolished.

3. ***Market-determined exchange rate and convertibility of the rupee*** : In 1993 the GOI adopted the floating exchange rate system under which the external value of the rupee (i.e., the exchange rate of the rupee in terms of any other currency) would be determined by the market forces of demand and supply. The objective was to ensure at least a partial correction of disequilibrium in BOP. However, the RBI retained its power to influence the external value of the rupee through its intervention in the foreign exchange market (i.e., through buying or selling of the dollar or any other foreign currency). Thus India's present exchange rate system is one of managed (or dirty) floating rather than clean floating. Thus implies that the rupee has been made convertible on the current account of the balance of payments. To put it differently, importers can now get their rupee holding converted into dollars. Likewise, exporters can sell their dollars and acquire rupees any time at the prevailing market-determined exchange rate. This partial convertibility of the rupee (i.e., convertibility only on current account) has permitted liberalised imports and promoted exports at the same time and led to greater integration of the Indian economy with the rest of the world. In other words, currency convertibility has conduced to the globalisation of the Indian economy

4. ***Liberalisation of export control*** : Now any good can be exported from India without any restriction except for a few items mentioned in the negative list of exports. The items included in the list are regulated on a few important considerations such as protection of the country from foreign aggression, preservation (protection) of the physical environment, maintenance of ecological balance, generation of employment, and, of course, maintenance of the country's socio-cultural heritage.

5. ***Duty free import of capital goods needed for production of exportable items*** : Capital goods needed (or to be used) for the production of exportable items can now be imported without paying import duties.

6. ***Advance licences for imports against exports*** : Advance licences which are used to import certain specified raw materials without payment of any import duty against confirmed export order and/or letter of credit have been made transferable as soon as the export obligation is fulfilled.

7. ***Exemption from tax*** : Profits (income) from exports are now totally exempt from income taxes.

8. ***Subsidised credit*** : Exporters now have preferential access to credit from commercial banks, which now charge low rates of interest for both pre- and post-credit from exporters.

9. ***The duty drawback scheme*** : This scheme has been retained.

10. ***Incentives to exporters of services*** : For giving a major boost to exporters of services such as health care, entertainment, tourism and professional activities the Exim Policy of 2003-04 had introduced a new scheme, viz., duty-free import facility for those service sector units which succeed in earning a minimum foreign exchange of Rs. 10 lakh.

11. ***Scope for large-scale producers*** : For a large number of items the reservation policy of the GOI for small scale units has been abolished. So large-scale units can now produce these items at low-cost (due to advantages of mass production or economies of scale) and export them. The latest Exim Policy of the GOI covering the five-year period 2009-14 is discussed in the next chapter.

KEY POINTS

1. ***Trade and growth*** : International trade plays an important role in promoting faster economic growth of developing countries like India and ensuring economic self-reliance (so that exports pay for imports and there is no balance of trade deficit). And the case for free trade or trade liberalisation has been made on the basis of both types of gains. International trade also promotes further economic growth of a nation, since there are dynamic gains associated with it. In addition, trade enables developing countries to import and use superior technology which is invented in developed (or industrially advanced) countries at huge costs and remains embodied in imported machines and capital goods.

2. ***Two alternative trade strategies*** : Two alternative trade strategies for developing countries like India (as the opening quotation of this chapter indicates) are import substitution and outward orientation or openness. An inward-looking policy such as that of import substitution seecks to impose tariffs at high rates on imported articles. By contrast, a policy of economic openness, with stress on export promotion, keeps trade barriers as low as practical.

3. ***India's policy of import-substituting industrialisation*** : At the very beginning of India's planning period in 1950-51, two options (or alternatives) were open to the policy-makers as far as its trade with the rest of the world was concerned. The first was *outward-looking* in nature, with stress on export-promotion for achieving faster economic growth by earning foreign exchange. The second one was *inward-looking* with stress on import-substitution.

4. ***Export pessimism*** : In fact, due to bleak prospects of raising India's exports (or due to the so-called export pessimism) India was not in a position to earn sufficient foreign exchange to be able to pay for a large (and ever-increasing) volume of imports. Therefore, India's strategy of industrialisation was based on substitution of imports or replacement of imports through domestic production of import-substitute items.

5. ***Inward-looking strategy of the 1980s*** : Up to the 1980s the Government of India (GOI) adopted an inward-looking trade strategy with stress on import substitution (IS). The choice of this policy was based on export pessimism. The main objective was to protect domestic industries (which were in their nascent stage) from foreign competition. In addition, the GOI relied on the import licensing system with a view to regulating the quantities of several essential consumer and capital goods and industrial raw materials. India's policy of IS was indiscriminate in nature. And it remained effective for a fairly long period of time.

6. ***Result of IS policy*** : No doubt the policy of IS made a genuine contribution to industrial growth between 1956 and 1966. However, with the passage of time several weaknesses of the policy of IS gradually appeared.

7. ***Policy shift*** : In fact, the deficit in India's BOP arose mainly due to her inward-looking trade policy. This is why in the Third Plan (1961-66) and in the Fourth Plan (1969-74) various export promotion measures were adopted by the Government. However, in spite of this until the late 1970s, exports were primarily treated as a source of foreign exchange rather than as an efficient means of resource allocation. IS remained the basic premise of India's planned development strategy.

8. ***Export promotion measures of the 1980s*** **:** Because of mounting trade deficit in the early 1980s the issue of export promotion assumed great urgency and importance. And various export promotion measures were announced by the Government on the basis of the recommendations of the Tandon Committee. These were the following:

(i) rep. scheme,
(ii) exim scripts,
(iii) duty drawback scheme,
(iv) tax concessions and tax holiday,
(v) credit facilities,
(vi) signing of trade agreements,
(vii) exchange entitlement scheme,
(viii) cash compensatory support, and
(ix) tariffication.

9. ***An Overview of India's trade policy since July 1991*** **:** India had to face a crisis situation in 1991. And the severe economic crisis of 1991 forced India to introduce several drastic reform measures in respect of foreign trade (i.e., exports and imports). Two notable features of India's new liberalised trade policy were (i) import liberalisation and (ii) export orientation. This new policy served two main purposes at the same time, viz., (i) allowing import of capital goods and essential raw materials and inputs needed for production of exportable items and (ii) stimulating exports.

10. ***Import liberalisation*** **:** For achieve import liberalisation the following four measures were adopted by the GOI.

(i) elimination of import quotas,
(ii) reduction in the rates of import tariff,
(iii) duty drawback scheme, and
(iv) liberalisation of imports of gold and silver.

11. ***Export-orientation of trade policy*** **:** Along with import liberalisation an outward looking trade strategy was adopted in 1991. In this context we refer to various export promotion measures adopted by the GOI. These are the following:

(i) reduction in customs duties,
(ii) devaluation of the rupee,
(iii) market-determined exchange rate and convertibility of the rupee,
(iv) liberalisation of export control,
(v) duty free import of capital goods needed for production of exportable items,
(vi) advance licences for imports against exports,
(vii) exemption from tax,
(viii) subsidised credit,
(ix) the duty drawback scheme,
(x) incentives to exporters of services, and
(xi) scope for large-scale producers.

KEY TERMS

Import substitution	Export promotion	Cash compensatory support
Inward-looking trade policy	Outward-looking trade policy	Duty drawback scheme
Replenishment scheme	Negative list of imports	Open general licence
Exim scripts	Tariffication	Import liberalisation for export promotion
Export orientation	Export pessimism	

ASSIGNMENTS

1. What do you mean by import-substitution? Why did India adopt the strategy of import-substituting industrialisation in the initial stage of planning?
2. Make an overall evaluation of India's policy of import substitution.
3. Write a commentary on India's current trade policy which focuses on 'import liberalisation for export promotion'.
4. What do you mean by an export-led strategy of economic growth? Is it suitable for India?
5. What is meant by export-orientation of trade policy? Present your view on this.
6. Critically examine India's Exim Policy of the 1990s.
7. Make a comparison between two alternative trade strategies adopted by the Government of India during the plan period, viz., inward-looking strategy and outward-looking strategy.

29A RECENT TRADE LIBERALISATION AND GROWTH IN DEVELOPING COUNTRIES

Developing nations (such as India, Pakistan, and Argentina) which stressed industrialisation through import substitution fared much worse and grew at a much slower rate than those developing economies (such as Hong Kong, Korea and Singapore) that from the early 1950s followed an export-oriented strategy. This is why starting in the 1980s, many developing nations that had earlier followed an import-substitution industrialisation strategy began to liberalise trade and adopt an outward orientation. The reforms were spurred by the debt crisis which started in 1982 and the evident success of the outward-oriented countries. Table 29A.1 shows the trade-liberalising measures adopted by some developing countries in Latin America. Africa, and Asia during the 1980s and early 1990s. In general, the reforms involved a dramatic reduction and simplification in average tariff rates and quantitative import restrictions. These, in turn, resulted in a much higher degree of economic openness, as measured by the sum of

Table 29A.1: Trade Reforms in Selected Developing Countries

Country	Reforms
Argentina	Average tariff levels were reduced from 18% to 11% and import licensing restrictions were substantially eased in 1991. The highest tariff rate was cut further by another 15% points in 1992.
Brazil	Major trade reforms were announced in March 1990 to replace almost all quotas with tariffs. Average tariff rates were reduced from 37% to 25% in 1990, to 21% in 1992, and to 14% in 1994.
Chile	In 1973 all quotas were removed, and a uniform tariff of 10% was imposed on all goods except automobiles. The tariff was raised to 15% following the economic crisis of the early 1980s.
China	A 1992 agreement began significant import liberalisation, including a phaseout of almost 90% of all non-tariff barriers (NTBs) by 1998.
Egypt	The import quota on all tradable goods was reduced from 37% in 1990 to 23% in 1991 and 10% in 1992, and in 1993 the highest tariff rate was reduced from 100% to 80%.
India	Restrictive import licensing requirements covering 70% of all imports were eliminated in 1992, and the peak tariff was reduced from 110% to 85% in 1993.
Mexico	Quotas were substantially reduced starting in 1985. By 1988, tariffs were reduced to an average of 11%, with a maximum rate of 20%.
Philippines	Trade reform was adopted in 1991 to reduce the average tariff rate from 28% to 20% by 1995. Some quotas were also lifted.
Turkey	Quotas and other NTBs barriers have been substantially reduced starting in 1980 and tariff reduced substantially in 1992.

Source: D. Salvatore: *International Economics* (Wiley India, 10th edn., 2013), p. 382

exports plus imports as a ratio of GDP, a sharp increase in the ratio of manufactures in total exports and higher rates of growth for the liberalising economies. In this context D. Salvatore comments: "Trade reforms were most successful when launched in a single bold move rather than with a number of small hesitant steps over time and when accompanied by anti-inflationary measures."

CHAPTER 30

India's Foreign Trade

We must find ways in which trade aids development.	Manmohan Singh
What we must do is to build up new trade connections.	C. D. Deshmukh

PREVIEW

We live in an interdependent world in which no country is completely self-sufficient. This means that each country has to import certain goods and services. But this requires foreign currencies which are to be earned by exporting goods and services. And each country should specialise in the production and export of those goods in which it has comparative advantage (or relative efficiency).

However, in the past most countries imposed tariffs at high rates on imported items mainly to protect high-cost and inefficient domestic industries from foreign competition. However, the recent trend is toward freer multilateral trade. It is felt that growing trade among nations according to their respective areas of comparative advantage would enable them to achieve faster economic growth and thus to improve the living standards of their people. In short, foreign trade is supposed to act as an engine of growth. This is why the World Trade Organisation (WTO) had been set up in the mid-1990s and it started functioning from Jan. 1, 1995. And since then due to various arguments over the years among the member countries import tariffs have been substantially reduced and quotas (or quantitative restrictions on the volume/value of imports) have been completely removed. These measures are likely to promote freer multilateral trade and world trade is likely to grow much faster than before.

Since the very beginning of the planning process in 1951, India adopted an inward-looking trade strategy with stress on import substitution. It did not rely on an outward-looking strategy and thus ignored the importance of increasing exports for achieving faster economic growth. Consequently the share of India's exports was just 2% of global trade in 1951. And it fell to a meager 0.6% in 1995. However, it rose marginally to 0.85% in 2001.

The need to achieve planned economic development made it absolutely essential for India to import huge amounts of raw materials, crude oil and capital goods. And inadequate production of food, fertilisers and even various consumer goods made it necessary for India to import even these items. Therefore, over the last 63 years of planning India's imports grew quite fast. But exports did not increase proportionately. And the net result was a deficit in the balance of trade in most of the years. It is against this backdrop that we study the trends, composition and direction of India's foreign trade in recent years (since 2000-01, to be more precise).

THE VALUE OF INDIA'S EXPORTS, AND IMPORTS AND THE BALANCE OF TRADE

In Table 30.1 we present the value of India's exports and imports since 2000-01. We see that value of India's exports increased from $44,560 mn. in 2000-01 to $304,624 mn. in 2011-12. Imports increased from $50,536 mn. to $489,181 mn. in the same period. Consequently the balance of (merchandise) trade deficit increased from $5976 mn. to $184,558 mn.

Table 30.1: India's Exports, Imports and Balance of Trade

(US $ million)

Year	*Exports*	*Imports*	*Trade Balance*
2000-01	44560	50536	–5976
2001-02	43827	51413	–7587
2002-03	52719	61412	–8693
2003-04	63843	78149	–14307
2004-05	83536	111517	–27981
2005-06	103091	149166	–46075
2006-07	126414	185735	–59321
2007-08	163132	251654	–88522
2008-09	185295	303696	–118401
2009-10	178751	288373	–109622
2010-11	251136	369769	–118633
2011-12	304624	489181	–184558
2012-13 (April-Dec.)	214100	361272	–157172

Source: Economic Survey (2012-13), GOI

COMMODITY COMPOSITION OF INDIA'S EXPORTS

An important aspect of a country's foreign trade is its commodity composition. The composition of India's exports changed significantly over the 61 year period (from 1950-51 to 2011-12). In 2011-12, the major items of India's exports (in order of importance) were agriculture and allied products, ores and minerals, manufactured goods and mineral fuels and lubricants.

The main items of India's exports of agricultural and allied products were coffee, tea, oil cakes, tobacco, cashew kernels, spices, fish and fish preparations. The main article of export among ores and minerals was iron. As for manufactured goods, the major export items were textiles and readymade garments, jute manufactures, leather and leather products, handicrafts, gems and jewellery, chemicals and chemical products, metal products, iron and steel, and, last, but not the least, engineering goods, including machinery and transport equipment.

Changes in Composition of Exports

India's exports are classified into two broad categories — traditional and non-traditional. During the period under review India's exports of non-traditional items such as engineering goods, iron and steel as also chemical and chemical products have become more important than traditional items such as jute manufactures, tea, cotton textiles, mineral ores, hides and skins, cashew nuts, unmanufactured tobacco and spices. For example, the share of agriculture and allied products in India's exports fell from 44.2% in

1960-61 to 12.4% in 2011-12. Likewise, the share of primary products (i.e., ores and minerals) fell from 8.1% in 1970-71 to 2.8% in 2011-12. Thanks to industrialisation achieved, manufactured goods are now the most important items of India's exports.

The change in the commodity composition of India's exports is attributable to changing structure of the economy. The steady increase in the exports of engineering goods and chemical products is the result of industrial development achieved in the last six decades of planning.

DIRECTION OF EXPORTS

Though India has not succeeded in achieving much diversification in case of exportable items, it has achieved quite some success in diversifying its export markets geographically. The shift has been from developed world of the USA and Europe to the developing world of Asia and Africa. Apart from raising the value of exports, this has served a very useful purpose, viz., overcoming the global crisis of 2008-09 and the global slowdown due to the Euro Zone Crisis in 2008-09.

In short, as far as exports are concerned India has achieved considerable market (geographical) diversification. While exports to Europe and America have declined, exports to Asia and Africa increased.

COMPOSITION OF INDIA'S IMPORTS

Some notable changes have occurred in the composition of India's imports in recent years. The share of petroleum, oil and lubricants (POL) increased from 28.7% in 2010-11 to 31.7% in 2011-12. Likewise, the share of gold and silver imports increased from 9.3% in 2000-01 to 12.6% in 2011-12. However, due to slowdown of industrial activity the shares of capital goods, except electrical machinery and machine tools, transport equipment, as also project goods fell. The share of both types of electronic goods — consumer and capital — also fell in the past two years (2011-12 and 2012-13).

India's Import Growth

India's merchandise imports fell in 2009-10 due to slowdown in industrial activity. However, imports continued to increase since 2010-11, with a growth rate of 32.3% in 2011-12. This was largely attributable to increase in imports of POL by 46.2% and that of non-POL by 26.7%.

Imports of gold and silver (with a share of 12.6% of India's total imports) also increased by 44.5% in 2011-12.

THE PERFORMANCE OF INDIA'S FOREIGN TRADE SECTOR

In Table 30.2 we show the performance of India's foreign trade sector. We see that after initial setback during the short transition period of a couple of years (1990-91 to 1992-93), exports registered a growth of about 20% p.a. in the next three years (1993-94 to 1995-96). Then exports increased slowly during the next three years (1996-97 to 1999-2000) mainly due to slow growth of world trade and recession in the USA (which was India's major trade partner at that time). However, over the next 8-year period (2000-01 to 2008-09) there was more than 20% annual increase in exports, except for the year 2001-02.

In spite of slow growth of exports from 1996-97 to 1998-99 the deficit in the balance of trade was less than 4% of GDP due to equally slow growth of imports. However, due to strong growth momentum generated in the industrial sector during the 4-year period from 2004-05 to 2007-08, India's imports grew much faster than exports. Consequently the balance of trade deficit increased to 7.8% in 2007-08. In 2008-09 the rate of growth of exports was negative (–13.8%) due to global financial crisis and economic slowdown in the USA and Europe while imports grew at 26.7%. Consequently India's deficit in balance of trade increased to 12% in that year.

However, due to adoption of various measures by the Government to promote exports after the world recession of 2008, India's exports grew at an unprecedented rate of 40.5% in 2010-11. Then the growth rate suddenly fell to 21.3%, In the next year it became negative (–1.8%).

Table 30.2: The Post-Reform Performance of India's Foreign Trade Sector

	Annual Percentage Change		*As a percentage of GDP at market price*		
Year	Exports	Imports	Trade balance	Invisibles (net) as %	Current account balance
1990-91	9.0	14.4	−3.0	−0.1	−3.1
1991-92	−1.5	−19.4	−1.0	0.6	−0.3
1992-93	3.8	12.7	−2.3	0.6	−1.7
1993-94	20.0	6.5	−1.5	1.1	−0.4
1994-95	18.4	23.0	−2.8	1.8	−1.0
1995-96	20.8	28.0	−3.1	1.6	−1.7
1996-97	5.3	6.7	−3.8	2.7	−1.2
1997-98	4.6	6.0	−3.8	2.4	−1.4
1998-99	−5.1	2.2	−3.2	2.2	−1.0
1999-2000	10.8	17.2	−4.0	2.9	−1.1
2000-2001	21.1	4.6	−2.7	2.1	−0.6
2001-2002	−1.6	−2.8	−2.4	3.1	+0.7
2002-2003	20.3	19.4	−2.1	3.4	+1.3
2003-2004	21.1	27.3	−2.3	4.6	+2.3
2004-2005	30.8	42.7	−4.8	4.5	−0.4
2005-2006	23.4	33.8	−6.4	5.2	−1.2
2006-2007	22.6	24.5	−6.8	5.7	−1.0
2007-2008	29.0	35.5	−7.8	6.3	−1.3
2008-2009	13.6	26.7	−12.0	7.8	−2.4
2009-2010	−3.5	−6.0	−8.7	5.9	−2.8
2010-2011	40.5	28.2	−7.4	4.6	−2.8
2011-2012	21.3	32.3	−10.1	6.0	−4.2
2012-2013	−1.8	0.4	−10.8		−4.8

Source : *Economic Survey* (GOI), various issues

Note: 1. Exports and imports are estimated in US dollar.

2. Trade balance, invisibles and current account balance as percentage of GDP at market price are based on rupee equivalents of BOP.

Faster Growth of Trade in Services

A notable feature of India's trade is the sudden and rapid growth of trade in invisibles (services) since 1994-95. In truth, exports of commercial services have boosted India's exports considerably. The main categories in such exports are software and other miscellaneous services (which include professional, technical and business services). Consequently invisibles as a percentage of GDP varied between 2.2 and 5.2 from 1995-96 to 2005-06. It even rose to 5.8 in 2006-07. Such high growth of invisibles served a very useful purpose. It helped to keep India's current account deficit (CAD) below 2% of GDP throughout a 9-year period (from 1991-92 to 2000-01), compared to the deficit of 3.1% in the last pre-reform year (1990-91). In the next three years CAD was small. It varied between 0.4% to 1.2% of GDP. However, due to global financial crisis, the growth of exports slowed down and fell to 13.6% in 2008-09. And in spite of substantial increase in trade in invisibles CAD rose to 2.4% of GDP.

Contributory Factors

India's export performance improved since 2002-03 due to certain favourable factors — both internal and external. Global recovery led to expansion in world trade which helped to raise India's exports. Recent recovery of international commodity prices also helped India to achieve improved export performance. Likewise expansion of India's manufacturing sector conduced to an increase in exports of such items as engineering goods, textiles and readymade garments. Exports were also boosted by greater outward-orientation of the Indian economy and corporate restructuring which made India's export items more and more internationally competitive. Moreover, there is now a greater export orientation of domestic industries. In addition, the GOI took various policy initiatives for export promotion, such as giving incentives to exporters as also participation in world trade fairs and advertising India's products in foreign countries and giving publicity in foreign journals and newspapers, and market diversification. All these have gone a long way in promoting India's exports in recent years.

The depreciation of the rupee in 2006-07 helped a great deal in promoting exports. However, in 2007-08 the rupee suddenly appreciated by 11% against the US $ mainly due to huge capital inflows. This adversely affected the growth of India's exports. However, with global recovery in the second half of 2009-10, 2010-11 and 2011-12 the rate of growth of India's exports picked up.

INDIA'S RECENT EXPORT PERFORMANCE

India's exports suddenly fell in 2012-13 by 1.8% due to lack of sufficient orders. If this trend continues, exports would not grow by more than 10% in 2013-14. Imports also fell by 2.87% in 2012-13, leaving a trade deficit of $10.31 bn. Since imports cannot be curtailed much the only solution to the balance of trade problem lies in raising exports. And in order to achieve an accelerated growth of exports there is need to diversify the export market and make export items really competitive by improving product quality and cutting costs and prices.

Trade in Commercial Services

The trend towards globalisation, reinforced by the adoption and implementation of liberalisation measures as also removal of various controls and regulations, has conduced to the steady growth of trade in commercial services. In fact, the integration of telecommunication and computer technology has made most commercial services tradable across national borders.

India ranked among the first five countries in the export of commercial services, such as transport and travel, computerised information services, communication services, and personal, cultural and recreational services in 2009-10.

In India the share of commercial services other than transport and travel is higher than that of others. India's share of transportation is low due to her lower volume of merchandise trade as also fairly low participation of India's shipping in export trade. So there is need to pay special attention to developing India's shipping and travel services.

Import of Services

India's import of services fell by 2.9% in 2011-12, as against an increase of 34.2% in 2010-11. However, there was a resurgence of India's service imports in 2012-13. Such imports grew by 10.3%, as compared to a fall of 0.5% in 2011-12. The rise in imports of services was largely attributable to higher imports of software and business services.

Balance of Trade in Services

India's services trade surplus increased steadily in the past decade (2000-10) to reach its peak of $53.9 bn. in 2008-09. However it fell sharply to $35.7 bn. in 2009-10. This was largely caused by the global financial crisis, which led to virtual collapse of exports of non-software services, mainly business services, as also slow growth of software services and the increase in import of non-software services, mainly business and financial services. The surplus in services trade continued to be low in 2010-11. This was attributable to the sudden spurt in imports of non-software services, mainly business and financial services which far exceeded the rise in exports of these two types of services. If this trend continues in the years to come, then the extra support provided by the services sector to India's overall trade balance so far will no longer be available.

It is important to note that the surplus in India's services account has been a strong contributory factor in financing a major portion of her merchandise trade deficit.

POLICY INITIATIVES TAKEN

In the context of India's current account deficit in the wake of global recession, a few pragmatic measures were taken by the GOI to promote the services sector so that it could make larger and larger contribution to India's exports. Two such measures were: (a) extension of sunset clauses for Software Technology Parks of India (STPIs) and export-oriented units (EOUs) up to 2010-11 and (b) the doubling of duty-free entitlement to hotels under the 'served from India' scheme. However, experts feel that a much stronger and coordinated effort is needed toward the services sector.

There are also several barriers to trade in services at present. So it is of paramount importance, from India's point of view, to negotiate at both bilateral and multilateral fronts for removing such barriers, mainly the market access barriers to trade in services.

KEY POINTS

1. ***Inward-looking trade policy*** **:** Since the very beginning of the planning process in 1951, India adopted an inward-looking trade strategy with stress on import substitution. It did not rely on an outward-looking strategy and thus ignored the importance of increasing exports for achieving faster economic growth.

2. ***Huge imports*** **:** The need to achieve planned economic development made it absolutely essential for India to import huge amounts of raw materials, crude oil and capital goods. And inadequate production of food, fertilisers and even various consumer goods made it necessary for India to import even these items.

3. ***Trade deficit*** **:** Therefore, over the last 63 years of planning India's imports grew quite fast. But exports did not increase proportionately. And the net result was a deficit in the balance of trade in most of the years.

4. ***Change in commodity composition of exports*** **:** An important aspect of a country's foreign trade is its commodity composition. The composition of India's exports changed significantly over the 61 year period from (1950-51 to 2011-12) or from agricultural and allied products to manufactured goods. During the period under review India's exports of non-traditional items such as engineering goods, iron and steel as also chemical and chemical products have become more important than traditional items such as jute manufactures, tea, cotton textiles, mineral ores, hides and skins, cashew nuts, unmanufactured tobacco and spices.

5. ***Causes of change*** **:** The change in the commodity composition of India's exports is attributable to changing structure of the economy. The steady increase in the exports of engineering goods and chemical products is the result of industrial development achieved in the last six decades of planning.

6. ***Diversification of export market*** **:** Though India has not succeeded in achieving much diversification in case of exportable items, it has achieved quite some success in diversifying its export markets geographically.

7. ***Change in the commodity composition of imports*** **:** Some notable changes have occurred in the composition of India's imports in recent years.

8. ***Growth of exports*** **:** After initial setback during the short transition period of a couple of years (1990-91 to 1992-93), exports registered a growth of about 20% p.a. in the next three years (1993-94 to 1995-96). Due to adoption of various measures by the Government to promote exports after the global recession of 2008, India's exports grew at an unprecedented rate of 40.5% in 2010-11. Then the growth rate suddenly fell to 21.3%, In the next year it became negative (–1.8%). India's exports suddenly fell in 2012-13 by 1.8% due to lack of sufficient orders.

9. ***Trade in invisibles*** **:** A notable feature of India's trade is the sudden and rapid growth of trade in invisibles (services) since 1994-95.

10. ***Increase in CAD*** **:** Due to global financial crisis, the growth of exports slowed down and fell to 13.6% in 2008-09. And in spite of substantial increase in trade in invisibles CAD rose to 2.4% of GDP.

11. *Trade in commercial services* : The trend towards globalisation, reinforced by the adoption and implementation of liberalisation measures as also removal of various controls and regulations, has conduced to the steady growth of trade in commercial services. The rise in imports of services was largely attributable to higher imports of software and business services. The surplus in India's services account has been a strong contributory factor in financing a major portion of her merchandise trade deficit.

12. *Measures adopted by the GOI* : In the context of India's current account deficit in the wake of global recession, a few pragmatic measures were taken by the GOI to promote the services sector so that it could make larger and larger contribution to India's exports.

KEY TERMS

Market access	Trade in services
Merchandise trade	Visible items of exports and imports
Invisible items of exports and imports	Market access barriers
Market diversification	Comparative advantage
Traditional exports	Non-traditional exports
Trade as an engine of growth	Product-wise export diversification

ASSIGNMENTS

1. Why did India's imports grow faster than its exports in India during most years of planning?
2. Comment on the trend, composition and direction of India's exports and imports since 2000-01.
3. Write a note on the contribution of services exports to India's balance of trade.
4. Suggest measures for improving India's balance of trade position in the coming years.
5. How has India's trade pattern changed in the post-reform period?

30A SPECIAL ECONOMIC ZONES (SEZS) IN INDIA

Special economic zones (SEZs) are outward-oriented growth centres. These denote geographical areas which enjoy special privileges. Arvind Panagariya has described the concept of SEZ in the following wards: "Conceptually, SEZs operate like foreign entities within the territory of a country. They are usually separated by physical barriers from one another and from the rest of the country. They face no trade barrier. The countrys trade barriers apply strictly within the area excluding SEZs which is called the domestic tariff area (DTA). Any goods sold by agents within the DTA to agents inside the SEZs are treated as exports of the country and those purchased by agents in the DTA from those in the SEZs as imports subject to customs duty. Any trade between the SEZs and the outside world is allowed to bypass all custom requirements applicable to the DTA. That is, foreign goods enter the SEZs free of customs duty and exit abroad without being subject to any domestic taxes or customs regulations"[1].

The main motive behind setting up SEZs is to promote exports by concentrating resources in some pockets. They have been set up to serve two main objectives, viz., (1) promoting exports through the creation of a strong and integrated infrastructure and (2) attracting foreign direct investment (FDI) through the provision of various types of fiscal incentives(mainly tax concessions).

As early as in 1965 India established the first export processing zone (EPZ) in Kandla in order to promote exports. In fact it was Asia's first EPZ. After this seven more such zones have been set up. However, in order to remove various obstacles to export promotion which prevailed in India in the first four decades of economic planning (1950-51 to 1999-2000) such as multiplicity of controls and regulations, unstable fiscal regime, deficiency of world-class infrastructure and lack of adequate incentives required to attract large foreign capital the GOI decided to set up SEZs. The Government announced its policy relating to SEZs in April 2000 with a view to providing internationally competitive and hassle-free environment for exports.

In this context we may note that while a SEZ is an integrated township with fully developed infrastructure, an EPZ is just an industrial enclave. The SEZ Policy, 2000 sought to make SEZs an engine of growth by providing an integrated infrastructure, supported by fiscal concessions, both at the Central and State levels, with minimum possible controls and regulations. Accordingly the existing eight EPZs were converted into SEZs. Seven salient features of the new scheme are the following:

1. A designated duty-free enclave to be treated as a foreign territory for trading activities (operations) and import tariff.
2. No need for any import licence.
3. Domestic sales subject to normal customs duty and existing import policy.
4. Conduct of either manufacturing or services activities.
5. Compulsion regarding foreign exchange earning within three years.
6. Full freedom for doing sub-contracting business.
7. No routine of examination of import/export cargo by customs departments.

Any production unit may be set up in SEZs to manufacture either goods or to render services. However, any unit set up in the SEZ area has to be a net foreign exchange earner but no conditionality has been imposed or specification made so far regarding the minimum proportion of its output to be exported. A unit in SEZ can be set up by public sector, private sector, joint sector or even by a State Government in collaboration with any corporate enterprise.

As per the provisions of trade policy SEZs were supported to function initially from Nov. 1, 2000 to Feb.9, 2006. In the mean time, the SEZ Act (2005) was passed and it was put into effect on Feb. 10, 2006. The Act provided for drastic simplification of procedures for establishing SEZ,s and for getting

1. Arvind Panagariya: *India—The Emerging Giant* (Oxford, 2008), p. 271

clearance on all matters from both Central and State Governments through a single window. The SEZ rules specify certain minimum requirements for different classes of SEZ ventures.

Prior to the passing of the SEZ Act (2005), 7 Central Government and 12 State and/or public-sector SEZs were set up. Since then formal approval has been given to 579 proposals and of these 384 SEZs have already been notified.

SPECIAL PRIVILEGES FOR SEZs

SEZs are duty-free enclaves of development and are deemed as foreign territories as far as export-import trade, imposition of excise duties on domestic output and tariffs on import articles are concerned. Various fiscal concessions and incentives are offered to both developers of the SEZs and the units set up within these zones.

Corporate enterprises located in the SEZs will not be required to pay any income tax on their profit for the first five years. This is known as complete tax holiday. And such enterprises will be required to pay only 50% of their assessed tax for the next two years. This 50% tax concession can be extended for another three years if 50% of the profit of an enterprise is reinvested for productive purposes. In addition, units in SEZs can be exempted from various other taxes such as import duty, excise duty, service tax, value added tax and dividend tax.

Economic Insight: Enterprise Zones
One way to encourage entrepreneurship is enterprise zone, especially geographic areas to which governments attracts private business investment by offering tax concessions and other government support. These are also called empowerment zones or enterprise communities in the USA. The GOI could have a significant effects on entrepreneurship by offering tax brakes to businesses which make investments to create jobs. A new scheme, called payroll subsidy, can be introduced incase of highly labour-intensive industries to create new jobs.

PERFORMANCE OF SEZs IN INDIA

The performance of SEZs in India has been fairly satisfactory since their inception. The SEZs are becoming more and more important in India's export trade, in employment generation and in the area of investment. We now briefly review the role of SEZs in India on the basis of these three key indicators.

1. Exports: At present 160 SEZs are exporting their products, of which 93 are IT/IT enabled services, 17 multi-product and 50 others sector-specific entities. The total number of units in these SEZs at present is 3,308. Exports from SEZs rose to Rs. 2,20,271 crore in 2009-10 with a compound annual growth rate (CAGR) of 56.8% during 2003-04 to 2009-10 compared to the CAGR of 19.3% for total merchandise exports of India for the same period. And when the entire world including India was severely hit by the adverse effects of the global recession from 2008-09, the growth of exports from SEZs was 121% in 2009-10 compared to a meager 0.6% growth in total exports from India. The share of SEZs in India's total exports has increased consistently from 4.7% in 2003-04 to 26.1% in 2009-10 and 29.5% in 2010-11. Exports increased further to Rs. 3,15,868 crores in 2010-11 and to Rs. 3.64,478 crores in 2011-12.

2. Employment: Out of 9,45,990 persons employed at present in SEZs, 8,11,286 persons were absorbed after Feb. 2006. No less than double this number got indirect and subsidiary employment because of the linkage effects of SEZs. This is in addition to employment generated through the creation of infrastructure by the developers and the conduct of related activities.

3. Investment: Up to the end of Sep. 2012 a sum of Rs. 2,18,795 crore was invested in SEZs. This includes an investment of Rs. 2,14,000 crores in newly notified zones. The entire investment has been made by the private sector. The Government played the role of a facilitator by giving approval to proposed projects as quickly as possible. In SEZs 100% FDI is permitted through the automatic clearance route.

Five Issues Related to SEZs

Five important issues relating to SEZs are as follows:

1. Impact of direct tax code (DTC): As per the DTC, developers of SEZs would be allowed profit-linked deductions for all SEZs notified on or before March 31, 2012. Units in SEZs which would start commercial operations by March 31, 2014 would also be given profit-linked exemptions. Developers and units notified after this date would not be given any investment-linked exemptions. This was a cause for concern among developers and units particularly in big SEZs having long gestation time.

2. Goods and services tax (GST): Full and complete set-off would be available on the GST paid on import of goods and services.

3. Power generation and distribution: It is worth considering an appropriate policy to encourage generation and distribution of power by the SEZ developers and/or units.

4. Coordination: Since there are various authorities (having their own jurisdictions) to administer and control different SEZs, there is need for effective coordination of their activities.

5. Disinvestment: It is also necessary to examine whether some of the established SEZs can be privatised through an act of disinvestment. This measure, if taken, will serve three purposes: (i) It will bring extra revenue to the Government. (ii) More money can be spent for the development of India's social sectors. (iii) The SEZs would be able to improve their operational efficiency.

Comments

However, SEZs are not an unmixed blessing for India. There are concerns that SEZs primarily focus on real estate. In addition, there is a lack of level playing field between manufacturing units within SEZs and those in the Domestic Tariff Area. Finally there can be large loss of revenue on account of tax concessions for exports of goods and services which are already being exported without such concessions. These issues (concerns) should be properly addressed and, where necessary, adequate safeguards put in place.

CHAPTER 31

Foreign Exchange

The price of foreign exchange will, under a system of flexible exchange rates, fluctuate in such a way that the demand for foreign exchange equals the supply and the balance of payments is in equilibrium. There is no comparable mechanism that will keep the balance of payments in equilibrium under a system of fixed exchange rates. The normal situation is that the export of goods and services will not equal their import but that a surplus or a deficit will arise. A surplus in the balance of payments generally causes no problems...... A deficit in the balance of payments often entails difficult problems of economic policy.

Bo Sodersten

PREVIEW

In the last chapter we have discussed the various components of a country's transactions with the rest of the world. All these transactions are presented in the country's balance of payments. The money value of these transactions depends on the prices of the currencies of both home country and foreign countries. For example, in India the value of transactions is measured either in rupees or in US dollars[1]. The value of a certain fixed volume of transactions in rupees or in dollars depends on the rate of exchange between the rupee and the dollar. Thus there is a close relation between the balance of payments and the rate of exchange (in this case, between the rupee and the dollar).

Now the basic question is: How does international trade actually take place? If you want to import a printing machine from the USA you would like to pay in rupees. But the exporter in the USA would demand payment in dollars.

In truth, if we want to compare the value of a country's exports and imports a major difficulty arises. The value of a country's exports is usually calculated in terms of its own currency whereas its imports are priced in a wide range of different currencies. For example, India's exports are often calculated in terms of rupees and imports are first calculated in terms of currencies of different countries [US dollar ($), Japanese yen, British pound (£), German mark, French france, etc.] from where India imports. These again are converted into rupees to arrive at a comparable figure. In other words, the value of India's imports is to be recalculated in terms of rupees to compare import values with export values to find out whether India is enjoying a surplus or suffering from a deficit in the balance of trade.

1. In fact, the US dollar is an internationally accepted medium of exchange.

It is important to note that imports are to be financed by the currencies of the various supplying countries or by some means of payment (gold or reserve currencies like \$ or £ which are accepted in most international transactions) that can be readily converted into those currencies. So transactions between different trading countries can take place only if one currency (say, \$) can be exchanged for another (say, £), since each —whether in the form of inconvertible bank notes or bank deposits— can usually be spent only in the country of origin. A country's demand for foreign currency arises from its demand for imports. Foreign currency is, therefore, wanted only for the purpose of making purchases from foreign countries.

Economic Insight: Spot and Forward Exchange Rates

Most transactions in foreign exchange involve the payment and receipt of the foreign exchange within two business days after the day the transaction is agreed upon. The two-day period gives sufficient time for the parties to send instructions to debit and credit the appropriate bank accounts at home and abroad. This type of transaction is called a *spot transaction*, and the exchange rate at which the transaction takes place is called the **spot rate**.

In contrast, a *forward transaction* involves an aggrement today to buy or sell a specified amount of a foreign currency at a specified future date at a rate agreed upon today (the **forward rate**). For example, one could enter into an aggrement today to purchase £100 three months from today at \$2.02 = £1.

If the forward rate is below the present spot rate, the foreign currency is selling at a **forward discount** with respect to the domestic currency. On the other hand, if the forward rate is above the present spot rate, the foreign currency is said to be selling at a **forward premium**.

Forward discounts (*FD*) or premiums (*FP*) can be calculated by using the following formula:

$$FD \text{ or } FP = \frac{FR - SR}{SR} \times 4 \times 100$$

where *FR* is the forward rate and *SR* is the spot rate. The multiplication by 4 is to express the *FD* (–) or *FP* (+) on a yearly basis, and the multiplication by 100 is to express the *FD* or *FP* in percentages. Thus, when the spot rate of the pound is $SR = \$2.00$ and the forward rate is $FR = \$1.98$, we get

$$FD = \frac{\$1.98 - \$2.00}{\$2.00} \times 4 \times 100 = \frac{\$0.02}{\$2.00} \times 4 \times 100$$

$$= -0.01 \times 4 \times 100 = -4\%$$

Similarly, if $SR = \$2$ and $FR = \$2.02$, we get

$$FD = \frac{\$2.02 - \$2.00}{\$2.00} \times 4 \times 100 = \frac{\$0.02}{\$2.00} \times 4 \times 100$$

$$= 0.01 \times 4 \times 100 = +4\%$$

THE EQUILIBRIUM EXCHANGE RATE

The rate at which one country's currency is exchanged for that of another country is called the equilibrium rate of exchange

Foreign exchange refers to any foreign currency such as the US dollar or the British pound for India. The foreign exchange market refers to markets where foreign exchange is traded. This includes both spot markets for immediate delivery and futures market for delivery on future dates at pre-arranged prices. There is no particular place for this market, which operates via computer and telephone connections. The exchange rate is a relative price. It is the price of one country's currency in terms of that of another country. For example \$ 1 = Rs. 56, or £ 1 = Rs. 82.

The foreign exchange market is a highly competitive market. And the rate of exchange between two currencies is determined by the impersonal market forces, i.e., the forces of demand and supply. So the rate of exchange between any two currencies fluctuates every now and then. The daily movements of exchange rates are reported in newspapers. Such fluctuations give scope for speculation.

TYPES OF EXCHANGE RATE

Economists refer to three types of exchange rates, viz., (1) fixed exchange rate, (2) floating (or freely flexible) exchange rate and (3) managed floating exchange rate[1], which is a combination of (1) and (2). We may now discuss the three exchange rate systems or regimes one by one.

1. Fixed Exchange Rate

A completely fixed exchange rate system existed up to 1914 under the gold standard system.

Working of the Gold Standard

A country is said to be on the gold standard when its standard monetary unit can be freely exchanged for gold at a fixed rate without any restriction. Under full gold standard the monetary units consist of a fixed weight of gold of a definite fineness. In addition, there is no restriction on export and import of gold. Necessarily, under this system the exchange rate remains fixed and stable and adjustments in exchange rates are brought about by export and import of gold. Thus the value of a country's currency is fixed in terms of gold.

There are three essential rules of the gold standard. These must be observed by all the central banks if they are to operate and maintain the gold standard. The rules are the following:

(i) The central bank of each country must take step to fix the gold value of its own national currency.

(ii) There must be free import and export of gold into, and out, of each country which is operating the gold-standard system.

(iii) Finally, each central bank must make arrangements for the domestic supply of its own money such that the supply of the money goes up automatically with an inflow of gold into its territory, and, falls with an export of gold out of its territory.

If two countries, *A* and *B*, both fix the value of their currencies in terms of gold and if there is a free import and export of gold in both countries, the value of *A*'s currency (say, the dollar) will, within narrow limits, be fixed in terms of *B*'s currency (say, the pound).

Assume that the British pound is exchangeable for 113 grams of fine gold and the US dollar for 23.22 grams. Now suppose that the value of Britain's import from the USA exceeded the value of the exports. Therefore the demand for dollars will increase and, thus, the price of dollar would rise relative to that of pound in the foreign exchange market.

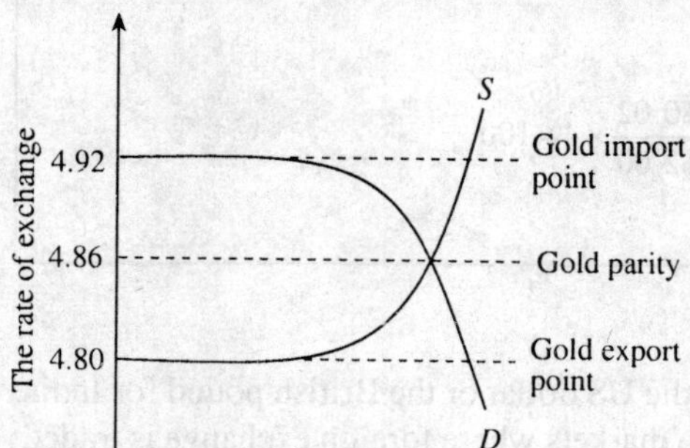

Fig. 31.1: The Gold Points

Now £1 would buy 113 grams of fine gold, and this quantity could be exchanged for $4.86. Therefore, £1 = $4.86. If, in the foreign exchange market, a British importer would obtain only $4.70 for £1, it would be cheaper for him to convert his pound into gold at the fixed price and then ship this gold to the US exporter in order to pay for the goods. Thus, in practice, £1 could never be exchanged for less than $4.86 minus the cost of buying gold and shipping it to the USA (about 1/2%). In a like manner, if exports exceeded imports, £1 could never be exchanged for less than $4.86 *plus* the cost of buying and shipping gold from the USA. Thus the rate of exchange between the £ and the $ could only fluctuate within very narrow limits—called the gold export and import points as shown in Fig. 31.1.

1. While (1) and (2) are two extreme forms of exchange rate systems, (3) takes an intermediate position since it is a combination of the two.

Years ago most governments (like the USA until the early 1970s) used gold to fix the rate at which their money would exchange with the monies of other nations. They did so by expressing their willingness to buy or sell unlimited amounts of gold at their official prices. Because each money was related to gold, gold became the standard on the basis of which they exchanged. For example, the exchange rate between the German mark and the US dollar would be 3 to 1 as long as the USA would buy and sell gold for, say, $ 35 an ounce and the German Government would buy and sell at 105 marks per ounce. Such a rate had to exist between such gold-related monies. Being able to buy and sell gold ensured that no one had to make an exchange at either place at 2 to 1. It was because, instead of giving up dollars to get only 2 marks, the dollar holders could exchange each dollar for gold and then sell the gold to the German central bank for 3 marks.

If we ignored the costs of mining and melting down, shipping across the ocean and recoining, all countries on the gold standard would have stable exchange rates. Under the system the par values, or parities between any two countries would be determined by the gold content of their coins or monetary units.

In short, under gold standard, the exchange rate remains fixed. The central banks of countries with such fixed rates then stand ready to exchange unlimited amounts of their monies at the fixed rates.

The Adjustment Mechanism

The adjustment mechanism under gold standard is simple enough. It was worked out in detail by David Hume. It is known as the *price-specie-flow-mechanism* or Hume mechanism. The mechanism is summarised below:

Suppose country *A* imports too much and begins to lose gold. This loss of gold reduces its price and cost levels thereby (i) decreasing its imports of foreign goods that have become relatively dear, and (ii) increasing exports of its now-cheapened home-produced goods.

The other country *B* is at first having a so-called 'favourable balance of trade'— as it sends more goods abroad than it imports, receiving gold in exchange. Now its price and cost levels of goods will rise *via* the Quantity Theory mechanism. This is the third reason (iii) for its now expensive exports to go down in physical amount and (iv) for its imports of the first country's now-cheapened goods to rise.

Advantages

The chief advantage of fixed exchange rates is that they give certainty to traders and investors

The first major advantage of gold standard was the encouragement given to international trade and investment. The second advantage was that it produced a mechanism of correcting balance of payments disequilibrium. Thirdly, fixed exchange rates reduce speculation. Fourthly, fixed exchange rates also impose discipline on domestic economic policies because, in the event of an adverse balance of payments, deflationary measures will have to be adopted to restore equilibrium in the balance of payments.

Disadvantages

On the contrary, if an exchange rate is fixed incorrectly, then this itself will cause intense speculation against the currency. Defending a fixed exchange rate can at times be very expensive requiring huge reserves of foreign exchange. Secondly, it may become necessary to raise interest rates for defending a currency. This can be both costly and damaging to the domestic economy. Therefore it is quite possible that a fixed exchange rate results in domestic policy being subordinated to the external situation.

DEVALUATION AND REVALUATION

Devaluation refers to an official reduction in the external value of a country's currency under the fixed exchange rate system, for example lowering of the rupee against the US dollar ($) from one fixed or 'pegged' level to a lower level, say, from Re 1 = $ $\frac{1}{45}$ to Re = $\frac{1}{50}$ [as shown in the vertical distance (*BC*) in figure 31.2.] A country devalues its currency to remove a deficit in the current account of the balance of payments. [This point will be discussed in detail later in this chapter.] Revaluation is just the opposite of devaluation.

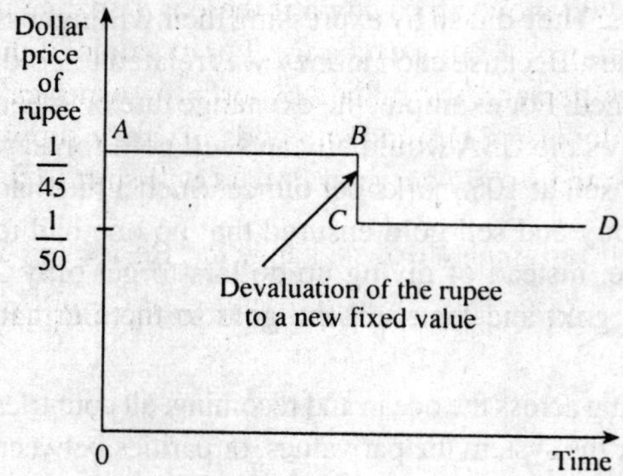

Fig. 31.2: Devaluation of the Rupee

2. Floating (Free Flexible) Exchange Rate

Under the present inconvertible paper currency system the rate of exchange between two currencies (such as the rupee and the dollar) is determined by the market forces of demand and supply. Indians sell rupee to buy US dollars (which is a foreign currency) and Americans sell dollars to buy rupees.

The Demand for Foreign Exchange (US dollar)

It has to be noted at the outset that the demand for a foreign currency is an indirect (derived) demand. There is demand for US dollars in India because Indians want to buy (import) American goods, to travel to the USA, to study in the USA, to buy US financial assets such as bonds and equity shares as also physical assets such as apartments, factories as also shops and establishments. The demand for dollar also arises because some Indians want to make loans or gifts to some people in the USA.

If the dollar depreciates in terms of rupee, fewer rupees will now be required to buy a dollar. So Indians will now be eager to buy more US goods and US assets. The converse is also true. If the dollar appreciates in terms of rupee, more rupees will be required to buy a dollar. So Indians will now be eager to buy less US goods and US assets. This means that more (less) dollars will be demanded in India at low (higher) price of dollar. This is why the demand curve for dollars is downward sloping, as shown in Fig. 31.3.

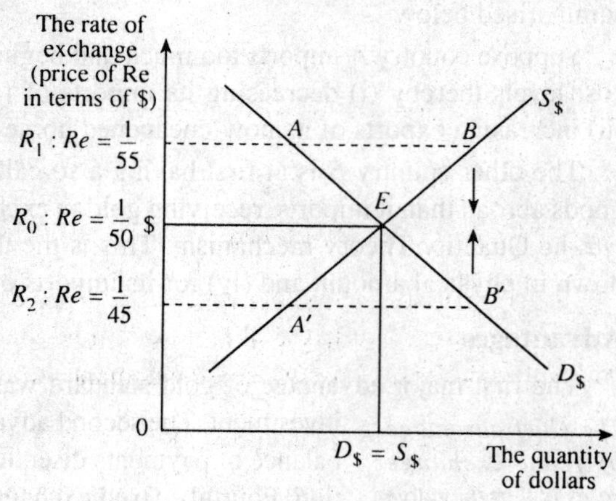

Fig. 31.3: Exchange Rate Determination

The Supply of US Dollar (Foreign Exchange)

By comparison, if the rupee depreciates (appreciates) in terms of dollar, Americans will be eager to buy more (less) Indian goods and Indian assets. So they will supply more (less) dollars in the foreign exchange market to buy more (less) rupees. For this reason the supply curve of dollars is upward sloping, as shown is Fig. 31.3.

The Equilibrium Rate of Exchange

The two curves meet at point *E* in Fig. 31.3 and the equilibrium rate of exchange is determined at \$ 1 = Rs. 50 or Re 1 = \$ $\frac{1}{50}$. At a higher price of dollar, say \$ 1 = Rs. 55 there is excess supply of dollar in India. As a result the rate of exchange will fall to Re 1 = $\frac{1}{50}$ \$ as is shown by the downward pointing arrow. At a lower price of dollar, say at Re 1 = $\frac{1}{45}$ \$, there is excess demand for dollars in India and the exchange rate will rise (as is shown by the upward pointing arrow). Thus the floating exchange rate moves up or down due to changes in the demand for and supply of goods, and services or assets—financial and physical.

CHANGES IN EXCHANGE RATE

The rate of exchange between the rupee and the dollar will move up or down if there is a change in any of the factors which determines the demand for and supply of foreign exchange. For example, if the American economy grows at a faster rate than before, the demand for India's exports (or America's imports) is likely to rise. So Americans well spend more dollars to buy Indian goods. As they supply more dollars in the foreign exchange market to buy rupees, the supply curve of dollars will shift to the right from $S_\$$ to $S_{\$'}$, as shown in panel (a) of Fig. 31.4. So at the original rate of exchange R_0 : Re 1 = $\frac{1}{50}$ \$, therle is excess supply of dollars of *EG*. This will lead to a depreciation of the dollar from R_0 to R_1 : Re 1 = $\frac{1}{45}$ \$.

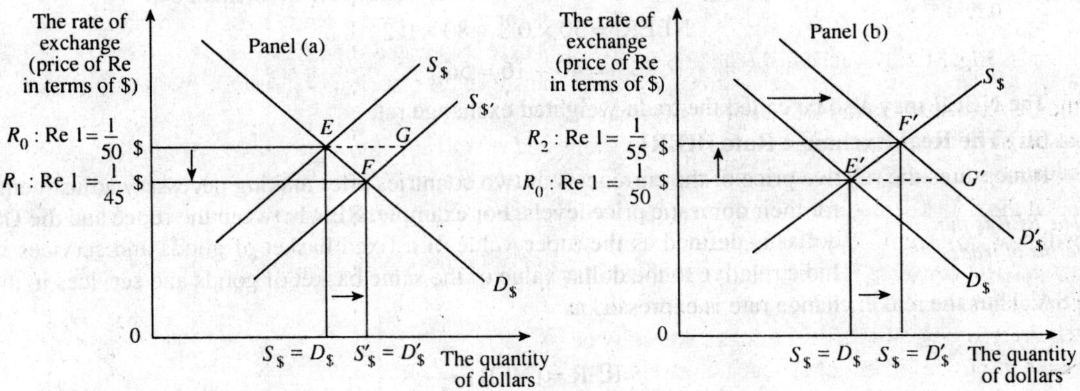

Fig. 31.4: Changes in the Rate of Exchange Due to Changes in Market Forces

By comparison, if India's national and per capita incomes increase, Indians will buy more of US goods and assets. So they will require more dollars. As a result they will sell rupees to get the required amount of dollars. Consequently the demand curve for dollars will shift to the right from $D_\$$ to $D'_\$$. Thus at the original rate of exchange R_0, Re 1 = $\frac{1}{50}$ \$ there will arise excess demand for dollars of *E′G′*. This will lead to an appreciation of the dollar or a depreciation of the rupee, as shown in panel (b) of Fig. 31.4. The new equilibrium rate of exchange now is R_2 = Re = $\frac{1}{55}$ \$.

Since all types of transactions—both in current and capital accounts— were taken into consideration in the supply-demand theory described above it is also known as the balance of payments theory regarding exchange rate determination.

VARIOUS CONCEPTS OF EXCHANGE RATES

The rate of exchange between the rupee and the dollar or between any two currencies is important from the point of competitive advantage of nations. To be more specific, the external value of the rupee determines the competitiveness of Indian goods and services in the international market. There are various different exchange rate concepts which have different implications for exports, imports and capital movements.

(i) The Nominal Exchange Rate (NER)

The usual practice is to quote foreign exchange rate as the number of units of a domestic currency (such as rupee) needed to purchase a unit of a foreign currency (such as the US dollar). Thus suppose \$1

= Rs. 50. This implies Rs. 50 can buy one US dollar in the foreign exchange market. This is known as nominal exchange rate (NER).

(ii) The Nominal Effective Exchange Rate (NEER)

It is the weighted average of different nominal exchange rates with the shares of different countries in the home country's exports and imports acting as respective weights. It may be expressed as follows:

The NEER is also called the trade-weighted exchange rate

$$NEER = (NER_1 \cdot w_1) + (NER_2 \cdot w_2),$$

where NER_1 and NER_2 are the nominal exchange rates of country 1 (say the USA) and country 2 (say the UK) in terms of Indian rupee and w_1 and w_2 are the respective shares of these two countries in India's foreign trade. Suppose $1 = Rs. 50 and the USA accounts for 80% of India's external trade while £ 1 = Rs. 80 and UK accounts for the remaining 20% of India's foreign trade. So the nominal effective rate of exchange is

$$NEER = 50 \times 0.8 + 80 \times 0.2$$
$$= 40 + 16 = 56.$$

The NEER may also be called the trade-weighted exchange rate.

(iii) The Real Exchange Rate (RER)

It measures the relative price of the currencies of two countries after making necessary adjustments for their domestic price levels. For example, RER between the rupee and the US dollar is defined as the rupee value of a fixed basket of goods and services in India relative to the dollar value of the same basket of goods and services in the USA. Thus the real exchange rate is expressed as

The RER is the terms of trade

$$RER = (NER)\frac{P_f}{P_d},$$

where P_f is foreign price level and P_d is domestic price level. It is another name of the terms of trade.

Difference between the Two Concepts

While the NER measures the rate at which one country's currency is exchanged for that of another, the RER measures the rate at which domestic goods (exports) can be exchanged for foreign goods (imports). Suppose, for example $ 1 = Rs. 50 at present. This is indeed the NER between the rupee and the dollar. If a fixed basket of goods cost Rs. 400 in India and the same basket costs $ 40, then the RER will be $(NER)\frac{P_f}{P_d} = 50\frac{40}{400} = 5$.

This implies that 5 units of Indian goods will buy one unit of US goods. The RER is the true measure of a country's international competitiveness. A rise in RER indicates that foreign (US) goods have become more expensive in terms of Indian goods. This implies that Indian goods have become more competitive in the international market.

(iv) The Real Effective Exchange Rate (REER)

It is a weighted average of real exchange rates of all trading partners, with the respective shares of different countries acting as weights. Thus, in India, REER is prepared by taking shares of five major trading partners, viz., the USA, the UK, Switzerland, France and Japan in India's exports and imports.

THE EXCHANGE RATE AND THE BALANCE OF PAYMENTS

The international status of a country's *currency* depends on its balance of payments position. If a country enjoys a surplus in its balance of payments, its currency appreciates and such a currency is usually called a *hard* or a (*convertible*) *currency*. The reason is that if India has a surplus in the current account of its balance of payments with the USA, US citizens will supply more dollars in the foreign exchange market to buy more rupees to pay for Indian goods. As a result the rupee will appreciate in terms of dollar (or the dollar will depreciate in terms of the rupee). By contrast, if Bangladesh has a continuous deficit in its current account with the USA, its currency taka, will depreciate in terms of dollar, and the currency of such a country is called a *soft* (or *inconvertible*) *currency*. We may now discuss the various factors which determine the rate of exchange between two currencies.

FACTORS AFFECTING THE RATE OF EXCHANGE

Changes in any of the factors which determine the demand for and/or the supply of a foreign currency in India will lead to upward or downward movement of the rate of exchange (i.e., the external value of the rupee). These factors may now be discussed in detail.

The Law of One Price (LOOP)

Under completely free trade, the rate of exchange between any two currencies will move up or down quite freely and, in the absence of transport costs, the exchange rate will show the differences in the domestic price levels of the two countries. The reason is simple. If, under the above assumptions, the price of a computer is lower in the USA than in India, then traders will find it profitable to buy computers in the USA and sell them in India. This is known as *international arbitrage*. Due to such arbitrage (i.e., transfer of computers from the USA to India), their prices in the USA will rise and their prices in India will fall. This process will continue for some time and will come to a halt, sooner or later, as soon as the two prices are equalised. Thus the same price for a good will prevail in both countries. This is known as the law of one price (LOOP). The law simply states that the price of an internationally traded good will be the same in two countries, when denominated in the currency of a single country. Thus, if the price of a computer is Rs. 5,000 in India, and \$1 = Rs. 50, then its price in the USA will be \$100. This implies that if the LOOP holds and each country consumes a fixed basket of goods, the rate of exchange between their currencies will be determined by their relative price levels (i.e., their price level in India ÷ the price level in the USA).

However, this does not happen in the short run. Only in the long run there is a tendency for relative prices in two countries to tend toward equality so as to ensure the equality of purchasing power of the two currencies.

The Rate of Inflation and the Exchange Rate

There is a close relation between the rates of inflation in two currencies and the exchange rate between their currencies. If the rate of inflation in India exceeds that of the USA, Indian goods will become more expensive in the USA and the US goods will become relatively cheap in India. This will lead to a fall in the demand for Indian goods in the USA and a consequent fall in the demand for rupees in the foreign exchange market. As a result the supply of dollars will fall and the supply curve will shift to the left from $S_\$$ to $S_\$'$. By contrast, India will now be induced to buy more of US goods. As a result the demand for dollars will increase in the foreign market as shown in Fig. 31.5 by the rightward shift of the demand curve for dollars from $D_\$$ to $D_\$'$. This means that the dollar will appreciate and the rupee will depreciate. The new supply curve of dollars $S_\$'$ intersects the new demand curve $D_\$'$ at point F. As a result the new equilibrium rate of exchange between the rupee and the dollar is Re 1

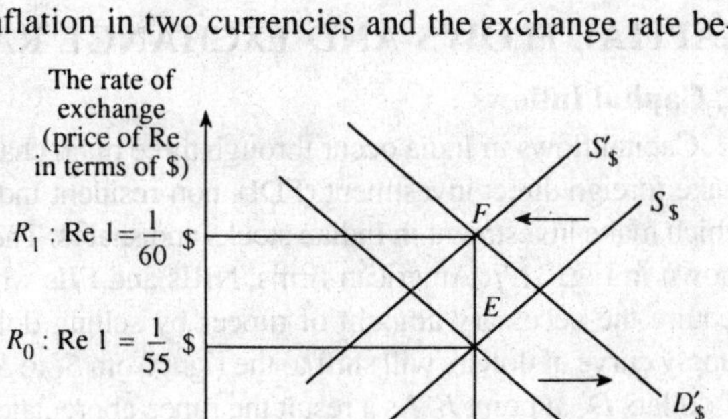

Fig. 31.5: The Effects of Differing Rates of Inflation on the Rate of Exchange

$= \frac{1}{60}$ \$. Thus the exchange rate in India rises and that in the USA falls. Thus one of the main causes of changes in exchange rate is differing rates of inflation. In fact, this is one of the deductions to be made by PPP theory to be discussed later in this chapter.

INTEREST RATES AND EXCHANGE RATES

Another factor causing a change in the rate of exchange between two currencies is the difference in the rates of interest between two countries. In the absence of any restriction on movement of financial capital there will always be an inflow (outflow) of funds in (from) the country where the return of capital is high (low)[1]. Suppose the interest on US bonds is 6% and that on Indian bonds is 10%. This will induce Americans to sell US bonds and utilise the funds received to buy Indian bonds. In order to buy Indian bonds, Americans will need more rupees. They will get it by supplying more dollars in the foreign exchange market. As a result the supply curve of dollar will shift to the right from $S_\$$ to $S_\$'$ in Fig. 31.6. The new supply curve intersects the original demand curve for dollars at point *F*. Consequently the rupee will appreciate in terms of dollar, or the dollar will depreciate in terms of rupee. In other words, the exchange rate, which is a relative price, will fall in India and rise in the USA.

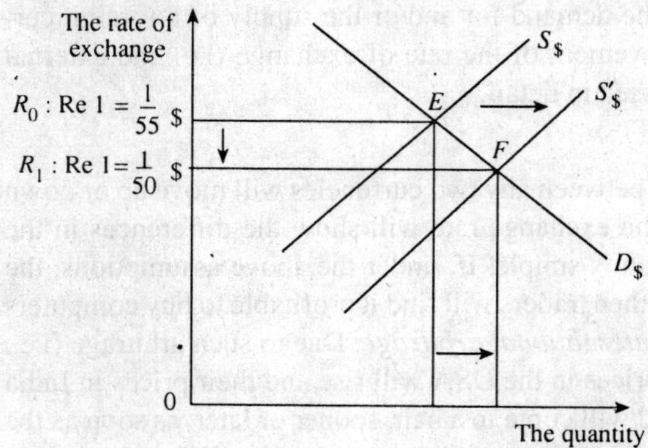

Fig. 31.6: The Effect of Interest Rate Changes on the Exchange Rate

This is exactly what happened in India in 2003 and 2004. And the Government of India (GOI) had to sell rupees in the foreign exchange market to stabilise the rupee-dollar exchange rate so as to prevent a fall in India's exports and a rise in India's imports and thus to avoid an increase in the current account deficit. Thus appreciation of a currency is not always a good thing for a country. And we see that the different rates of inflation and differing rates of interest can exert considerable influence on the exchange rate.

CAPITAL FLOWS AND EXCHANGE RATE

(i) Capital Inflows

Capital flows in India occur through three main channels, viz, multinational corporations (MNCs) which make foreign direct investment (FDI), non-resident Indians (NRIs) and foreign institutional investors (FIIs), which make investment in Indian stocks and shares. The effect of inflows of capital through these channels is shown in Fig. 31.7. American firms, NRIs and FIIs which want to invest in India will require rupees. They acquire the necessary amount of rupees by selling dollars in the foreign exchange market. As a result the supply curve of dollars will shift to the right from $S_\$$ to $S'_\$$. The new supply curve intersects the demand curve of dollars $D_\$$ at point *F*. As a result the rupee appreciates and the dollar depreciates.

Now Re 1 = $\frac{1}{45}$ \$ (or \$1 = Rs. 45) compared to Re 1 = $\frac{1}{50}$ \$ (or \$ 1 = Rs. 50).

However, the appreciation of the rupee creates a current account deficit of $E''F$ at the new exchange rate (by reducing imports and raising exports). But the deficit in the current account is totally offset by a

1. In fact, financial capital is the most mobile of all factors of production. And such capital has always a tendency or an extra temptation to move abroad in search of higher return(s).

surplus in the capital (financial) account as is shown by the magnitude of capital inflows (EE'). Here $E''F = E'E'$. So the overall balance of payments shows equilibrium;

Overall balance = current account deficit + capital account surplus = 0

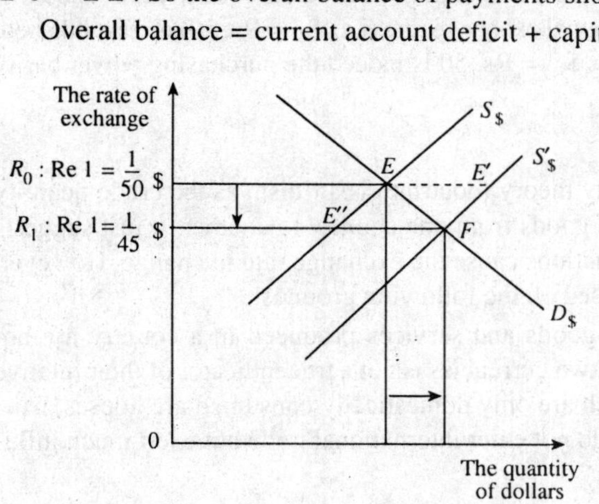

Fig. 31.7: The Effect of Capital Inflows on the Rupee-Dollar Exchange Rate

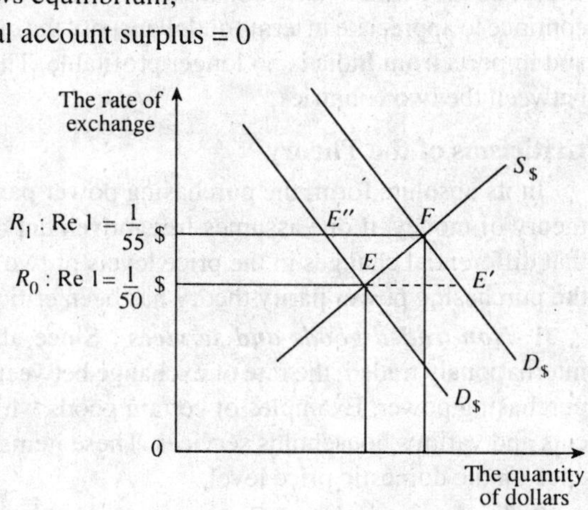

Fig. 31.8: The Effect of Capital Outflows on the Rupee-Dollar Exchange Rate

Thus our main prediction here is that any deficit in the current account implies matching capital inflows (i.e., foreign investment of the same amount.)

(ii) **Capital Outflows**

Outflows of financial capital from India will have an exactly opposite effect, as shown in Fig. 31.8. If Americans sell Indian bonds and securities, or MNCs, NRIs and FIIs withdraw a portion of their funds from India, they will be getting rupees. They will convert rupees into dollars. As a result the demand curve for dollars will shift to the right from $D_\$$ to $D'_\$$. Consequently, the rupee will depreciate in terms of dollar from \$ 1 = Rs. 50 to \$ 1 = Rs. 55. This will lead to a fall in India's imports and a rise in India's exports. So the current account of the balance of payments will show a surplus measured by horizontal distance $E''E$. This is just sufficient to offset the capital account deficit of EE', caused by outflows of capital from India. Thus our prediction here is the following:

Any surplus in the current account of the balance of payments will be balanced by a matching capital outflow due to sale of both paper wealth (securities) and real wealth (assets) in India. So the (overall) balance of payments is in balance, at least in an accounting sense.

THE PURCHASING POWER PARITY THEORY

The purchasing power parity (PPP) theory, developed by Karl Gustav Cassel (1866-1945), is a theory regarding the determination of the rate of exchange between two inconvertible paper currencies. According to this theory, the rate of exchange between two such currencies as the rupee and the dollar depends upon their relative purchasing power. The equilibrium rate of exchange will be the one which equates the purchasing power of rupee with that of the dollar.

Suppose a fixed basket of goods costs one dollar in the USA and the same basket costs Rs. 50 in India. Then the rate of exchange between the dollar and the rupee will be \$1 = Rs. 50. Now suppose the rate of exchange suddenly increases to \$ 1 = Rs. 55, the price level in the two countries remaining the same. This means that one dollar will still buy goods worth Rs. 50 in the USA. However, traders will now find it profitable to convert dollars in rupees at the new exchange rate (\$ 1 = Rs. 55), buy the same basket of goods from India and sell the same in the USA, and, by doing arbitrage operation, make a profit of Rs. 5 for every dollar worth of trading. As a result the demand for rupees in the foreign exchange market will increase but the supply of rupees will fall since American traders will now be less eager to export goods to India (and Indian traders will import less American goods)[1]. Consequently the rupee will continue to appreciate in terms of dollars until the original exchange rate (i.e., \$ 1 = Rs. 50) is reestablished, and imports from India is no longer profitable. Thus \$ 1 = Rs. 50 is indeed the purchasing power parity between the two countries.

Criticisms of the Theory

In its absolute form, the purchasing power parity theory (doctrine) is a truism as the crude quantity theory of money, if one assumes free movement of goods from one country to another. It just suggests that differential changes in the price levels of two nations cause the exchange rate to change. However, the purchasing power parity theory has been criticised on the following grounds:

1. *Non-traded goods and services* : Since all goods and services produced in a country are not internationaly traded, the rate of exchange between two currencies is not a true indicator of their relative purchasing power. Examples of certain goods which are only domestically consumed are houses, haircuts and various households services. These items do not enter international trade but exert much influence on the domestic price level.

2. *Trade restrictions* : Governments also impose restrictions on imports and exports of goods. If a country imposes an export tariff, the external value of its currency will rise, but its domestic price level will remain the same. And the PPP theory breaks down completely when there exists various restrictions on trade like tariffs and quotas, transport costs, exchange control, multiple exchange rates, etc. Under such situations the exchange rate hardly reflects the domestic purchasing power since an import price is the sum-total of the supply price of a foreign country *plus* the tariff imposed by the importing country. Says R.W. Waud: "Given a sufficient length of time, the exchange rate between the nations' currencies will tend to adjust to reflect changes in their price levels, all other things remaining the same. Of course, all other things typically do not remain same." Hence, it is usually difficult to observe real-world adjustments that are as simple as our hypothetical example, given above.

3. *Government controls* : In addition, the actual rate of exchange between two currencies may not indicate their true purchasing power due to government controls on prices or on foreign exchange.

4. *Index number problems* : The domestic purchasing power of a currency is usually measured by using index numbers. But there are various problems associated with the construction and use of index numbers (as have been discussed in an earlier chapter on inflation). The necessity of using index numbers for meaning price levels introduces all the defects of price indices. Thus this mechanism is a very imperfect means of calculating the equilibriuum exchange rate between two countries.

5. *Transport costs* : Prices of internationally traded goods are unlikely to be the same in two countries due to differences in transport cost. As Cassel himself admitted, "Differences in two countries' economic situations, particularly in regard to transport cost and customs duty, may cause the normal exchange rate to deviate to a certain extent from the quotient of the currencies' intrinsic purchasing power."

6. *Dynamic nature of the world* : In a dynamic world various factors such as changes in demand, technological progress, etc. lead to constant changes in domestic costs and prices. So it is difficult to predict the rate of exchange. For all these reasons, almost every day a new equilibrium rate of exchange between two currencies is established.

7. *Trade in services and capital movements* : The theory is applicable only to commodity trade which forms only a part of balance of payments. It excludes trade in services (invisible items) and capital transactions between countries which form an important item of a country's external transactions. Various items of the balance of payments such as insurance and banking transactions as also movements of financial capital are not much affected by changes in the general price level. But these items often exert

1. Recall that the demand for foreign exchange is a derived (indirect) demand.

influence on the exchange rate by altering the supply of and demand for foreign currencies. Capital movements often occur due to speculative motive. All these factors are ignored by the PPP theory.

8. *Two-way causation* : Just as changes in the domestic price level(s) lead to changes in the exchange rate, changes in exchange rate also exert some influence on the domestic price level(s). The theory predicts that differential rates of inflation lead to compensating exchange rate changes. It is also possible, however, for exchange rate changes themselves to lead to differential rates of inflation. If, for example, import demand is highly price inelastic, an exchange rate depreciation may lead to an increase in domestic inflation. There is thus a problem in respect of causalty, i.e., which one (hen) is the cause and which (egg) is the effect. This point was completely ignored by Cassel.

9. *Link between domestic and international prices* : The PPP theory makes a comparison between the aggregate price levels in two countries but it ignores the difference between the prices of domestically produced goods and that of internationally traded goods. In the absence of transport cost and trade restrictions, the forces of competition will lead to equalisation of prices of internationally traded goods. But domestic prices will be different in two countries or even between two parts of the same country (such as Kolkata and Mumbai).

10. *Structural changes in the economy* : The theory ignores the structural changes which occur in an economy from time to time. And, due to fundamental changes in the structure of trade between two countries, changes in national income and changes in tariffs or import controls throughout the period under consideration the theory is invalidated.

11. *Other influencing factors* : The PPP theory postulates that there is a direct link between the purchasing power of two currencies and the rate of exchange between them. But, in reality, we do not find any such link because the exchange rate is influenced by various other factors such as transport costs, tariffs, speculation and movements of financial capital.

12. *Quantity theory of money* : The PPP theory is based on the quantity theory of money. So it is subject to all the criticisms of the quantity theory.

DEVALUATION

A country often devalues its currency in order to improve its balance of trade (but only at the cost of the terms of trade). This is the issue to which we turn now. We have already returned to devaluation in the context of a country's balance of payments in the last chapter. Now we discuss the effects of devaluation in detail.

Recall that devaluation refers to an official reduction in the external value of a country's currency in terms of another currency under the fixed exchange rate system. But the depreciation of a currency such as the rupee refers to an automatic fall in its value in terms of another currency such as the US dollar through the market forces of demand and supply (in the absence of any government intervention in the foreign exchange market).

Effects of Currency Devaluation (Depreciation)

A successful devaluation or depreciation of the rupee is likely to stimulate the Indian economy. Devaluation makes Indian goods (exports) cheaper in foreign countries and foreign goods (imports) expensive in the home country. Thus if the demand for exports and imports is fairly elastic, India's exports will increase, imports will fall and the deficit in the current account will be removed either partly or fully. It has to be noted at the outset that devaluation affects only the current account of the balance of payments. It has no effect on the capital account. In addition, an increase in net exports will increase aggregate demand or desired expenditure in India and stimulate aggregate production. As a result India's national income (or real GDP) will increase. And more employment will be created in India in the process since it is an expenditure-switching policy. It shifts expenditure from foreign goods to domestic goods.

Devaluation affects only the current account of BOP

A devaluation increases import prices and makes imports less competitive against domestic products. This encourages domestic buyers to switch to locally produced substitutes.

Likewise, a fall in export prices is likely to induce foreign buyers to increase their demand for the devaluing country's exportable items in preference to locally produced items and the exports of other overseas products.

However, devaluation is a zero-sum game. One country's gain is the other countries' loss. If all countries attempt to devalue their currencies at the same time, there will be no net increase in national income for any of the devaluing nations. Such competitive devaluation is essentially a "beggar-thy-neighbour" policy. This point has already been discussed in detail in the context of the Mundell-Fleming model in chapter 27.

Devaluation and the Balance of Trade

The extent to which devaluation will succeed in affecting balance of payments depends on how it affects the magnitude:

Value of exports – Value of imports

which can be calculated either in terms of the domestic currency or in terms of any foreign currency.

Such calculations necessarily involve *two* sets of influences: firstly, the influence of the complex relationships of elasticities of demand for and supply of imports and exports and secondly, the influence of income effects which arise from changes in the demand for goods and services after devaluation. The former group of relationships comprises what is called, *the elasticity approach* to currency devaluation while the other comprises what is called, *the absorption approach*. Here we first discuss the elasticity approach and then pass on to the absorption approach.

THE ELASTICITY APPROACH

The success of devaluation in improving a country's current account depends on the price elasticities of demand for exports (e_x) and imports (e_m). Specifically, the elasticity values for a successful devaluation, for example, are the following:

the demand for imports is price elastic ($e_x \geq 1$) and
the demand for exports is price elastic ($e_m \geq 1$).

Assuming that we start from an equilibrium position initially, the trade balance will improve following a devaluation if $e_x + e_m > 1$.

This is known as the Marshall-Lerner condition. The condition may now be explained briefly.

The Marshall-Lerner Condition

How successful the devaluation is crucially depends on the reaction of import and export volumes to the changes in prices brought about by devaluation. If volumes of trade (i.e., exports and imports) are fairly elastic to price changes, then devaluation will be successful. This implies that an increase in import prices results in a more than proportionate fall in the volume of imports. This reduces the total import bill (in terms of foreign currency). At the same time a fall in export prices leads to a more than proportionate increase in the volume of exports. As a result export earnings (in terms of foreign currency) will increase.

By contrast, if the volumes of trade are fairly inelastic to price changes, an increase in import prices will lead to a less than proportionate fall in the value of imports. So the total import bill will increase. At the same time a fall in export prices will lead to a less than proportionate increase in the volume of export. So total foreign currency earnings on exports will fall. Therefore devaluation will not necessarily improve the balance of trade.

The *J* Curve Effect

Although it is very difficult to measure demand elasticities in international trade the existing evidence suggests that the sum of the elasticities is much greater than 1 in the long run. However, the Marshall-Lerner condition is unlikely to be satisfied in the short run. Firstly, it may take time for the devaluing country's importers to find alternative supplies in response to the rise in import prices. It may also take time for foreign (say American) buyers to raise their purchases of Indian goods after a fall in their prices. So a devaluation may at first cause the trade balance to deteriorate. Eventually, perhaps after a year, importers and exporters should respond to the changed prices and the trade balance will improve.

This point may now be explained. In the short run the demand for exports and imports is fairly inelastic. As a result the value of exports is unlikely to increase much in spite of fall in prices of exportables. This implies that export earnings will fall. Similarly the value of import is likely to remain more or less constant in spite of a rise in prices of imported goods. So the import bill is unlikely to fall much. Consequently the balance of trade, instead of improving, is likely to deteriorate further in the short run. However, things improve in the long run and devaluation yields the desired effect. This insight is given by the so-called *J* curve effect, illustrated in Fig. 31.9. Here we show trade deficit and surplus on the vertical axis and time on the horizontal axis. The *J* curve effect shows the tendency for a country's balance of trade to initially worsen following a devaluation of its currency before moving into a surplus subsequently.

The delayed improvement in the trade balance following a devaluation is referred to as the J curve effect

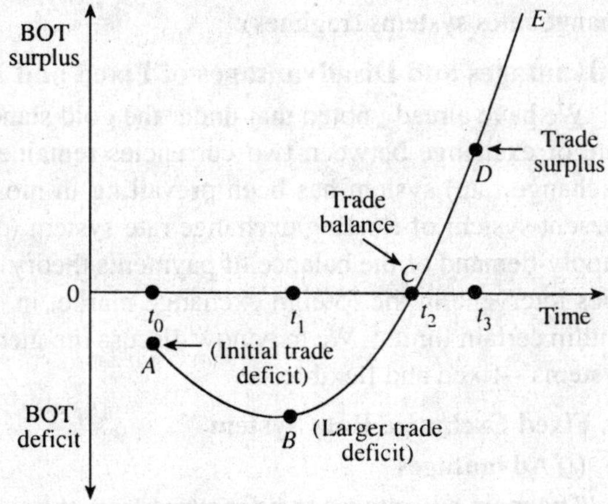

Fig. 31.9: The *J* Curve Effect

This is because the full adjustment of trade volumes to devaluation involves a time lag. There is an immediate fall in export prices and a rise in import prices. So current exports earn less foreign exchange and current imports absorb more foreign exchange. Thus the size of deficit in the current account increases, as is shown by the downturn of the *J* curve from point *A* (which shows initial trade deficit) in period t_0 to point *B* in period t_1 (when there is a larger trade deficit). Over time, however, the lower export prices will increase foreign demand and export earnings will increase. At the same time higher import prices will reduce domestic demand for imports leading to an improvement in the balance of trade. This is shown by the upturn of the *J* curve from point *B* to point *C* initially (where there is trade deficit) and then to point *D* in period t_3 (where there is trade surplus).

Thus we see that in the immediate post-devaluation period, since the volume of imports remain high and the volume of exports remain low, a country may experience a trade deficit. In the subsequent period, however, this will be eliminated and the current account slowly moves into surplus. This is likely to happen because the volume of exports and imports respond very slowly to the change in relative prices brought about by devaluation.

FIXED AND FLEXIBLE EXCHANGE RATES

One of the most important international decisions that national governments have to make is what kind of exchange rate system to adopt. In other words, they have to determine how their own currency should be related to other currencies in the world.

There are two main ways in which exchange rate systems can be arranged, viz., a completely fixed exchange rate system. The exchange rate system and a completely flexible exchange rate system of the IMF adopted through the Bretton Woods agreement is a mixture of the two and is called the adjustable peg system. It was devised in 1944 (as will be noted later in this chapter) and existed upto 1971.

Three Desirable Characteristics of the Exchange Rate System

The efficiency of any exchange rate system can be judged, at least partly, by the extent to which it achieves three desirable characteristics:

(a) ***Adjustment***: The exchange rate system should enable countries to correct balance of payments disequilibrium without putting much pressure on their domestic economies.

(b) ***Confidence***: The system should be such that traders have confidence in it so that international payments can be made efficiently and safely without the risk of huge losses.

(c) ***Liquidity***: If the adopted system requires central banks to intervene in the foreign exchange market to stabilise exchange rates, there should be a sufficient quantity of reserve assets to enable this to be done efficiently.

These three characteristics should be kept in mind while testing the efficiency of alternative exchange rates systems (regimes).

Advantages and Disadvantages of Fixed and Flexible Exchange Rate Systems

We have already noted that under the gold standard which prevailed over the period 1879-1914 the rate of exchange between two currencies remained fixed. Since 1971 the freely floating (or flexible exchange rate) system has been prevailing in most countries of the world. However, even under the present system of floating exchange rate system (discussed earlier in this chapter in the context of the supply-demand or the balance of payments theory) the governments or central banks of different countries intervene in the foreign exchange market in order to keep the external values of their currencies within certain limits[1]. We may now discuss the merits and demerits of the two alternative exchange rate systems—fixed and flexible.

A. Fixed Exchange Rate System

(i) Advantages

The main advantages to be secured from the fixed exchange rate are the following:

Exchange risk reduces the volume of trade

1. ***Exchange rate stability***: Fixed exchange rate ensures exchange rate stability which is so important for the smooth functioning of the world economy and for rapid growth of multilateral trade. Exchange rate fluctuations increase the risk of trading and thus reduce the volume of trade. Thus the fixed exchange rate system conduces to the smooth conduct of world trade by eliminating the uncertainties which exporters and importers face under floating exchange rate systems.

Since the developing countries suffer from persistent deficit in balance of payments, the fixed exchange rate system prevents continuous depreciation of their currencies which would otherwise occur under the flexible exchange rate system. So developing countries get an extra benefit from the fixed exchange rate system.

2. ***Encouraging capital inflows***: The fixed exchange rate system facilitates movements of private foreign capital by eliminating the possibility of capital loss due to currency depreciation every now and then.

3. ***Discouraging capital outflows***: Flexible or unstable exchange rates lead to excessive outflow of financial capital as had happened in case of Mexico in 1994 and Thailand in 1997, causing a serious balance of payments problem. But this does not occur under a stable exchange rate. By contrast under a flexible exchange rate system this is a genuine possibility in times of recession.

4. ***Absence of speculative attack on currency***: Under the fixed exchange rate system there is no scope for profitable speculation in the foreign exchange market. By contrast under the flexible exchange rate system there is always scope for destabilising speculation due to fluctuations in the rate of exchange every now and then. In fact, the speculators themselves cause exchange rate fluctuations through their own activities. If speculators expect the dollar to appreciate in terms of the rupee in near future they will buy dollars now by selling rupees in the foreign exchange market. As a result the dollar will appreciate

1. Thus the present system of floating exchange rate is treated by some economists as a type of managed floating system.

now.[1] By contrast, by eliminating the scope of speculation, the fixed exchange rate system ensures stability in the rate of exchange.

5. *A hedge against inflation*: In general, the government of a country often pursues expansionary monetary and fiscal policies to initiate economic expansion so as to reduce the rate of unemployment. The reason is that under the fixed exchange rate system, domestic inflation generates deficit in balance of payments and leads to loss of international reserves. This forces the government to adopt anti-inflationary measures so as to be able to achieve both internal balance (price stability) and external balance (balance of payments equilibrium).

6. *Promotion of world economic integration*: The fixed exchange rate system promotes economic integration among trading nations. The fixed exchange rate among different currencies virtually acts as a single currency in different countries and enables trading nations to form an economic union or a regional group. The euro was introduced precisely to serve the same purpose[2].

7. *Promotion of the growth of domestic financial markets*: Finally, the fixed exchange rate system promotes the growth of a country's money and capital markets. Due to risk of exchange rate fluctuations under the flexible exchange rate, households, firms and banking and non-banking financial institutions feel shy to borrow from and lend funds to the domestic financial market on a large scale.

(ii) **Drawbacks**

The main drawbacks of the fixed exchange rate system are the following:

1. *Loss of gold and international reserves*: Under the fixed exchange rate system countries with a large and persistent balance of payments deficit lose gold and foreign currencies. And the deficit countries run out of their accumulated international reserves.[3]

2. *Inflationary potential*: The dwindling international reserves of a deficit country under the fixed exchange rate system forces it to devaluate its currency. However, devaluation has a strong inflationary potential. Thus the fixed exchange rate system generates inflationary pressure in the economy, indirectly though.

3. *The problem of plenty*: A surplus country receives foreign currencies from other countries under the fixed exchange rate system. This leads to an increase in the domestic money supply and thus generates inflationary pressures in the economy. This problem of plenty is also embarassing since it has an inherent inflationary potential. A surplus country hesitates to revalue its currency since this is likely to reduce exports. So it has to solve the problem of domestic inflation by adopting other policies.

For all these reasons most countries have abandoned the fixed exchange rate system. Most countries of the world now have flexible or freely fluctuating (floating) exchange rate system for reason to be discussed now.

THE FLEXIBLE EXCHANGE RATE SYSTEM

Under the flexible exchange rate system the rate of exchange between two currencies is determined by the market forces of demand and supply. However, due to changes in economic conditions underlying demand and supply, the exchange rate will automatically move up or down even in the absence of any government intervention in the foreign exchange market.

(i) Merits

The flexible exchange rate system offers the following advantages:

1. *Automatic adjustment of balance of payments*: Under the flexible exchange rate system undervaluation or overvaluation of currencies is avoided. The reason is that in times of deficit in balance of

1. It is just like a self-fulfilling prophesy.

2. This virtually created the United States of Europe.

3. This is exactly what happened to India in May 1991 when the fixed exchange rate system prevailed. The problem was solved by abandoning the system and allowing the rupee to float in terms of five key currencies in July 1991.

payments, the currency automatically depreciates. This encourages exports, discourages imports and thus removes the deficit in balance of payments automatically.

On the other hand, if there is a surplus in a country's balance of payments, the currency of the country will appreciate. This will reduce exports, increase imports and the surplus in balance of payments will disappear automatically.

The flexible exchange rate system ensures equilibrium in the balance of payments

The automatic adjustment mechanism is the great virtue of a flexible exchange rate system. This implies that governments could concentrate their policies on the domestic problems of inflation and unemployment, leaving automatic exchange rate changes to deal with any external imbalances.

2. *No need for international reserves*: It follows as a logical corollary that governments would no longer be required to hold large quantities of international reserves. In truth, if central banks were not intervening in the foreign exchange markets to stabilise exchange rates, reserves would be unnecessary. Thus a completely flexible system should satisfy the criteria of *adjustment* and *liquidity*.

The flexible exchange rate system ensures rapid growth of multilateral trade without in any way affecting internal balance, viz., price level stability and full employment. Since under the flexible exchange rate system, the government of a country interferes as less as possible in the foreign exchange market, individuals and traders can pursue their own interests through exports and imports.

3. *Reducing exchange rate fluctuations*: We do not find undue and sharp fluctuations in exchange rates largely because random fluctuations around the normal rate of exchange are moderated by the actions of speculators. The reason is that if the currency of a country appreciates, i.e., its price falls in terms of foreign currency, speculators will buy it immediately. By contrast, if a currency depreciates, speculators will sell it. This is how they smooth out exchange rate fluctuations and help to keep the exchange rate stable.

(ii) Drawbacks

The main arguments against the flexible exchange rate system are the following:

1. *Violation of the Marshall-Lerner condition* : If the Marshall-Lerner condition (that $e_x + e_m > 1$) were not satisfied, a flexible exchange rate system would invite trouble. Suppose a deficit developed in a country. The excess supply of the deficit country's currency would lead to an automatic depreciation which would make the deficit bigger. Similarly, with a surplus, the excess demand for the currency would lead to an appreciation which could lead to an even bigger surplus. Thus a fully flexible exchange rate may be subject to extreme fluctuations in the rates in the short run (when the elasticity conditions are not favourable). So one may question the efficiency of the adjustment mechanism.

2. *Uncertainty* : Frequent changes in the exchange rate create uncertainty about export earnings and import payments. So traders are unable to take correct decisions about the volume of exports and imports. Therefore such uncertainty reduces the volume of trade.

3. *Loss of confidence* : Since the adjustment mechanism depends on automatic exchange rate changes, importers and exporters may be discouraged from trading because of the exchange rate risk. They can 'hedge' against this risk by operating on the 'forward' market. But this may involve those costs which would not exist if rates were fixed. The uncertainty introduced by flexible rates may cause traders to lose their confidence in the system to some extent.

However, empirical evidence does not support this allegation. The growth of world trade since 1971 has been fairly rapid in spite of widespread adoption of flexible exchange rate.

4. *Destabilising speculation* : The flexible exchange rate system gives scope for widespread speculation. Such speculation is most destabilising in nature and *accentuates* exchange rate fluctuations instead of reducing it.[1]

1. However, economists are still debating on this issue. As Milton Friedman, one of the supporters of the flexible exchange rate system, strongly believed that speculation had a stabilising influencing on the rate of exchange between two currencies.

5. ***Inflationary potential*** **:** A country with a persistent deficit in its balance of payments will experience a depreciation of its currency. Such a depreciation will raise the price of imports and, at the same time, increase the demand for the country's exports and import-substitute items. It may, therefore, exert both cost-push and demand-pull inflationary pressures on the domestic economy. Strong trade unions may, for example, resist any fall in real wages by demanding higher money wages as compensation. This may be really severe if the deficit country is operating at or near full employment.

For promoting freer multilateral trade and ensuring smooth capital flows among countries on larger and larger scale the convertibility of a currency is absolutely essential. Without full or at least partial convertibility of currencies trade and capital flows among countries are often obstructed. Perhaps the most important advantage to be secured from currency convertibility is that by ensuring expansion of trade among nations and smooth flow of financial capital across national borders currency convertibility conduces to faster economic growth. And this gets reflected in improved standards of living among people. This means that one of the pre-conditions for achieving faster economic growth through trade is to ensure convertibility of currency. As per the Bretton Woods Agreement (1944) the fixed exchange rate system was adopted by members of the International Monetary Fund (IMF). In order to maintain the exchange rate or the par value of their currencies in terms of the US dollar or gold the members of the IMF imposed various types of controls over the utilisation of their accumulated foreign exchange. This required the imposition of certain restrictions on the use of foreign exchange and its rational (judicious) allocation among different uses. And as per the rules (guidelines) of the IMF the currency of a nation could be converted into foreign exchange only at the officially fixed (declared) exchange rate.

With the collapse of the Bretton Woods System in 1971 due to the failure of the Smithsonian agreement many countries switched over to the freely flexible (or floating) exchange rate system. Under the system exchange rates were allowed to be determined through the market forces of demand and supply. In spite of this a number of countries still continued to impose foreign exchange control and were most reluctant to make their currencies convertible since they continued to face BOP crisis and at times of a really serious nature. And inconvertible currencies act as a safeguard against further deterioration of the external economic position of such countries through the operation of such destabilising forces as speculative attack on currencies.

With this introduction let us now move to a detailed discussion of currency convertibility. We start with the meaning of currency convertibility.

Meaning of Currency Convertibility

The convertibility of a currency means that the currency of a country can be freely converted into any foreign currency at the prevailing (market-determined) exchange rate, that is, the exchange rate is determined by the demand for and the supply of a currency. For example, the convertibility of the rupee means that those who have foreign currencies such as the US dollar or the British pound can get them converted into rupees at the market-determined exchange rate. The converse is also true. For a convertible currency there are authorised dealers of foreign exchange such as large international banks. The exporters and others who receive dollars, pounds and other hard currencies can approach these dealers and get their foreign currencies converted (exchanged) for rupees at the market-determined rates of exchange. In the same way, importers and others who require foreign exchange can go to these banks and get rupees converted into any foreign currency.

Current Account and Capital Account Convertibility of Currency

A currency may be convertible on only current account (that is, for exports and imports) only. Such a currency is also called a partially convertible currency. But currency is called fully convertible if it is convertible on both current and capital accounts.

Capital account convertibility of a currency means that it is freely convertible into foreign currencies in respect of all types of capital flows, viz., FDI, FPI, borrowed funds as also investment income, i.e., interests and dividends received and paid on them at the market-determined exchange rate. This simply means that those who are dealing in foreign exchange for purchasing stocks and bonds in Indian stock markets or for direct investment in various projects such as power plants, steel plants, infrastructure building (such as construction of roads and highways) can get them freely converted into rupees without obtaining any permission from the GOI. In the same way, the dividends and interest received on purchased equity , shares and debentures, capital gains made and profits earned on FDI in terms of rupees can be converted into US dollars, British pound, etc. at the current market-determined exchange rates and sent to foreign countries. However, capital account convertibility increases the risk of exchange rate movements and thus creates uncertainty. So it is to be introduced in the second phase of external sector reforms, i.e., after experimenting with current account convertibility for some time and after attaining a comfortable position and when the Central Bank the RBI is able to accumulate sufficient foreign exchange reserves.

The Convertibility of the Rupee

In the 1970s and the 1980s most industrially advanced countries switched over to full convertibility of their currencies. But India still continued to maintain the old exchange rate system.

In the post-reform period the rupee was made partialy convertible from March 1992 under the Liberalised Exchange Rate Management Scheme (LERMS) in which 60% of all receipts on current account (i.e., from exports of goods and services and other invisible items) could be converted freely into rupees at market-determined exchange rate, while the remaining 40% had to be surrendered to the RBI at the officially fixed (usually lower) exchange rate so as to enable the GOI to meet its own needs for foreign exchange as also for meeting the import bill of essential commodities. Thus partial convertibility of the rupee on current account led to the introduction of a dual exchange rate system. Under the system import of essential items could be made in adequate amounts so as to prevent their prices from rising much. In addition, the full convertibility of the rupee at that stage was treated as a very risky proposition in view of large current account deficit.

Since after partial convertibility of the rupee the external value of the rupee remained fairly stable, the GOI announced full convertibility of the rupee both only on the current account in the Union Budget for 1993-94 and from March 1993 the rupee was made convertible for all types of trade in goods (visible items). In March 1994 even services (invisibles) and inward remittances were allowed to be freely convertible into rupees at the then market-determined exchange rates.

Advantages of a Convertible Currency

A convertible currency offers the following advantages:

1. ***Incentive to exporters*** : Currency convertibility encourages exports by improving profit prospects since the market-determined rate of exchange is higher than the original officially fixed exchange rate. This implies that by exporting the same volume of goods, more rupees can be earned in terms of US dollars or any foreign currency. Currency convertibility gives special encouragement (or extra incentives) to those exporters whose products have low import-intensity.

2. ***Boost to import-substituting industrialisation*** : Since the market-determined exchange rate is higher than the original fixed exchange rate, imports become more expensive. This discourages imports and promotes import-substituting industrialisation.

3. ***Incentives to NRIs*** : The convertibility of the rupee provides greater incentives to NRIs and Indian workers doing jobs in foreign countries to remit larger sums in foreign exchange through the official channel. At the same time, it makes illegal remittance(s) such as 'hawala money' as also smuggling of goldless rewarding than before.

4. ***A balancing factor*** : A self-balancing mechanism lies embedded under the convertible currency system. Suppose the currency of a country is initially overvalued. Now if the currency initially depreciates it gives necessary boost to exports by lowering the prices of exportable items. At the same time it discourages imports by raising their prices. The operation of these two forces together ensures that the BOP deficit gets corrected automatically. An exactly opposite thing happens when the BOP is in surplus due to undervaluation of the exchange rate.

5. ***Specialisation in the areas of comparative advantage (relative efficiency)*** : In addition, currency convertibility ensures that the production pattern of different trading nations gets adjusted in accordance with their own areas of comparative advantage or relative efficiency (which is largely based on their relative factor endowments). The reason is that only under convertible currencies the market rates of exchange truly reflect the true purchasing powers of different currencies which, in turn, depend on different domestic prices of different traded goods. And international trade is based on differences in relative prices of goods in different countries. These prices, in turn, depend on differences in production costs arising from differences in factor endowments as has already been discussed in the context of the Heckscher-Ohlin theory in an earlier chapter. Thus currency convertibility leads to specialisation and exchange at the international level on the basis of comparative advantage. And trading nations tend to gain from such mutually beneficial exchange.

6. ***Acting as an integrating force in the world economy*** : Finally, currency convertibility conduces to the much needed integration of different economies of the world. In fact, it may be treated as the main force behind (or even an essential pre-requisite) for globalisation. In truth, an easy access to foreign currencies greatly helps the growth of trade and promotes faster flows of capital among trading nations. According to Nobel Laureate economist Paul Krugman currency convertibility may be treated as one of the main forces behind financial globalisation.

Capital Account(or Full) Convertibility of Rupee

For capital account currency convertibility no real transaction is necessary

In a sense capital account convertibility removes all the impediments to the smooth flows of funds into and out of India. While current account convertibility is effective only when there is some transaction such as importing and exporting of gods and services, inward and outward remittances, etc. involving conversion of one currency into another, capital account convertibility is effective even in the absence of any such transaction.

In 1997 the RBI appointed the Committee on Capital Account Convertibility with S.S. Tarapore as the Chairperson. The so-called Tarapore Committee defined capital account convertibility as the full freedom to convert or exchange local financial asset (such as equities and debentures) into or with their foreign counterparts and vice-versa at the market-determined rate of exchange. Simply put, under capital account convertibility any resident of India is at liberty to convert rupees into any foreign currency and reconvert the foreign currency into rupees any time he (she) likes. The main objective behind capital account convertibility is to give foreign investors an easy option to move in and move out of the foreign exchange market and to give a strong signal that the Indian economy is strong and vibrant enough and has sufficient forex reserves to tide over a difficult situation such as outflow of capital of any amount.

The Potential (Likely) Benefits of Capital Account Convertibility

The Tarapore Committee identified the following benefits of capital account convertibility:

1. Easy availability of large funds to bridge the domestic saving-investment gap and thereby promote faster economic growth;
2. greater access to the international financial markets and borrowing at low cost due to greater competitiveness among lenders of financial capital;
3. greater incentive for Indians to acquire and hold financial assets such as equities and bonds as also to purchase or acquire real assets abroad; and
4. improvement of the domestic financial system due to greater competition at the global level.

The Tarapore Committee strongly advocated capital account convertibility of the rupee and suggested the adoption of the following measures:

(a) Allowing Indian companies to issue foreign currency dominated bonds for absorption by Indian investors and issue of Global Depository Receipts (GDRs) without approval of the RBI or Government to enable Indian firms to go in for external commercial borrowings (of course, within certain prescribed limits).

(b) Permitting all-India financial (or term lending) institutions which fulfil certain regulatory requirements and certain prudential norms to participate in the foreign exchange market along with authorised dealers, viz., banks. The Committee also suggested that at a later stage, certain select non-bank financial companies (NBFCs) would also be permitted to act as authorised dealers in the foreign exchange market much like banks.

(c) Allowing banks and other financial institutions to operate both in domestic and international markets to buy and sell gold freely and attract gold-dominated deposits and make loans therefrom.

(d) Permitting resident Indians to have foreign currency denominated deposits with banks in India to make transfers of financial capital to other countries, of course within certain limits, to take loans (or borrow funds) from non-residents and others up to $1 million.

(e) Allowing Indian banks and NBFCs to borrow from global markets on both short-term and long-term basis up to certain prescribed limits, to invest in global money markets and to accept deposits and make loans.

Pre-conditions for Capital Account Convertibility

The Tarapore Committee recommended that, before going for capital account convertibility(CAC) of the rupee India has to fulfil the following three important pre-conditions:

(i) Fiscal deficit has to be kept at or below 3.5%. The GOI should also set up a Consolidated Sinking Fund (CSF)to reduce the quantum of public debt.

(ii) The GOI should fix a mandatory annual inflation target between 3 to 5%. And the RBI should be given the full power (or freedom) to use the necessary tools (instruments) of monetary control to achieve the target.

(iii) The financial sector of India has to be strengthened. For achieving this four measures have been specified by the Committee: (a) deregulation of all types of interest rates (already achieved), (b) reduction of non-performing assets (NPAs) to 5%, (c) reduction of average effective cash reserve ratio (CRR) to 3% and (d) liquidation of weak banks or their merger with strong banks.

Supplementary Measures

The Tarapore Committee also recommended the adoption of the following supplementary measures:

(a) The RBI should go for monitoring a permissible exchange rate band of 5% around the real effective exchange rate (REER) and should intervene only when the real exchange rate (RER) crossed the band.

(b) The current account deficit should be kept within manageable limits and the debt service ratio should be reduced from 25% to 20%.

(c) Forex reserves should be adequate and should lie in the range of $22 billion and $32 billion with a view to meeting import bill and meeting debt service obligations.

(d) The GOI should remove all restrictions on the inflows and outflows of gold into and out from India.

It was felt that for full convertibility of the rupee it was absolutely essential to achieve greater integration of the Indian economy with the rest of the world.

Unfortunately, it was not possible for the GOI to achieve CAC within a three-year period (1998-2000) as had been recommended by the Committee. The period was considered by the policymakers as too short to implement such a policy. Moreover, due to the emergence of Asian financial crisis and political instability in India the recommendations and suggestions of the Committee could not be put into effect.

The Second Tarapore Committee Report was submitted to the GOI in Sep. 2006. It had spelt out the details of the scheme and fixed 2011 as the target year for CAC of the rupee. However, economic events, especially the global financial crisis of 2007-09 hit the Indian economy very hard and there occurred huge capital outflows from India in 2008-09. And India would have been in deeper trouble if the recommendations of the Committee were implemented just before the onset of the crisis.

Problems

It is apprehended that CAC can give rise to certain problems. The following points are to be noted in this context:

(i) ***Generation of cost-push pressures*** **:** As noted earlier the market-determined exchange rate is normally higher than the pre-fixed (or officially announced) fixed exchange rate. This implies that a rise in the prices of essential imports is inevitable. This is likely to generate cost-push pressures in the economy.

(ii) ***Depreciation of the rupee*** **:** If a convertible currency like the rupee is not properly managed or monitored, the rupee will depreciate (or its external value will fall) through the normal operation of the market forces. If the rupee depreciates sharply people around the world will lose confidence in it and refuse to accept it for all types of transactions. This might adversely affect India's trade and capital flows.

(iii) ***Volatility*** **:** A convertible currency is highly volatile. In addition, operations of speculation in the foreign exchange market may make things worse and increase the degree of volatility further. In truth, the depreciation of Baht and other Asian currencies and the consequent loss of confidence of foreign investors in these currencies led to flight of capital from Thailand, Malaysia, Indonesia, Singapore and South Korea in 1997-98. This adversely affected their economic growth not just due to outflow of capital but also due to fall in real investment for at least three reasons: (a) less inflow of capital, (b) lack of confidence of foreigners in a depreciating currency (which could depreciate even further) and (c) lack of profit prospects of new projects in crisis-hit countries.

Managed Floating Exchange Rate System for India

At present flexible (or floating) exchange rate system prevails in India, as is found in most other countries of the world. In addition, like many other countries, India has not moved to a perfectly (or completely) flexible or floating exchange rate system. And changes in exports and imports as also, capital outflows and inflows bring about large fluctuations in the external value of the rupee. And sharp depreciation (or appreciation) of the rupee in terms of the US dollar (or any other currency) adversely affects the Indian economy mainly through exports and imports. In order to prevent sharp depreciation of the rupee, the RBI often intervenes to ensure that the exchange rate remains within reasonable limits. When there is undue depreciation of the rupee, the RBI sells dollars from its accumulated reserves of foreign currencies. This increases the supply of dollars in the foreign exchange market. As a result the depreciation of the rupee in terms of dollar is held in check.

In contrast, when the rupee appreciates sharply the RBI buys dollars from the foreign exchange market. This reduces the supply of dollars and thus prevents the appreciation of the rupee. Therefore through such interventions the external value of the rupee is not allowed to move beyond certain limits. Therefore the present exchange rate system in India is not fully flexible (or floating) in nature. It is essentially a system of managed float.

Focus on Terminology: Managed Float of the Exchange Rate

By the term 'managed floating' we refer to an exchange rate system in which the rates are determined mainly by the conditions of demand and supply, but in which central banks intervene at times to stabilise the rates or influence them in some way. With managed floating the fluctuations in country's exchange rates are smoothed out whenever the country's central bank regards the upward or downward movements as becoming excessive.

KEY POINTS

1. *The exchange rate* : The rate at which one country's currency is exchanged for that of another currency is called the exchange rate which is a relative price. A par exchange rate is one which is agreed between governments or is registered with the IMF. A market exchange rate is the actual price on the foreign exchange market.

2. *Spot and forward rates* : The foreign exchange rate which is quoted in day-to-day transactions is called the spot rate. Such a rate prevails in the spot market for immediately delivery. A forward exchange rate is one which is quoted today for delivery of a currency on a specified future date. The payment for the currency also occurs on the same future date.

3. *Nominal and real exchange rates* : The rate of exchange which is quoted in day-to-day transactions is called the nominal exchange rate. The real exchange rate compares the relative prices of different countries' products. A country's real exchange rate may change either through a change in its nominal exchange rate or through a domestic inflation rate faster or slower than that of its trading partners.

4. *Exchange rate systems* : To main exchange rate systems are: (i) the fixed exchange rate (which prevailed under the gold standard system) and (ii) the flexible (floating) exchange rate system which prevails today. Under the gold standard all countries are permanently committed to maintaining fixed exchange rate. Under the system every country makes its currency convertible into gold at a fixed price or the central bank controls buying and selling prices of gold which differ only by a very small percentage. The exchange rate between two currencies on the gold standard cannot move far from par. Under the freely floating exchange rate system no effort is made by governments or central banks to stabilise the exchange rate. These are left to be determined by the market forces. Both systems have advantages and disadvantages.

5. *Theories of exchange rate determination* : Regarding exchange rate determination under the present inconvertible paper currency system there are two main theories, viz., (i) the purchasing power parity theory and (ii) the supply-demand theory.

KEY TERMS

Managed floating	Price-specie-flow mechanism
Adjustable peg system	Exchange rate overshooting
Crawling peg	Devaluation
Confidence	Depreciation
Liquidity	J-curve effect
Adjustment	Marshall-Lerner condition
The elasticity approach to devaluation	Freely floating exchange rate

ASSIGNMENTS

1. How is the rate of exchange between two currencies determined (a) under gold standard and (b) under inconvertible paper currency system?
2. Discuss the advantages and disadvantages of the fixed exchange rate system.
3. "Exports pay for imports."—Discuss.
4. Briefly discuss the purchasing power parity theory regarding exchange rate determination.
5. "The floating exchange rate moves up or down in response to changes in the demand for and supply of goods and services as also financial capital." Explain this statement.
6. Show the relation between (i) the inflation rate and the exchange rate and (ii) the interest rate and the exchange rate.
7. Discuss briefly the factors which determine the rate of exchange between two currencies.
8. (i) Distinguish between nominal exchange rate and real exchange rate.

(ii) What is meant by a currency being at a three-month forward premium?

(iii) How are the spot and forward markets linked?

9. Write short notes on the following:

(a) forward market for foreign exchange,

(b) gold standard as an automatic adjustment mechanism, and

(c) case for a fixed exchange rate

10. Write short notes on working of fixed and flexible exchange rates system.

11. (a) Explain the difference between fixed and flexible exchange rates. Explain, in this connection, the meaning of an international gold standard.

(b) Derive the demand and supply curves of foreign currency of any country. When is such as a currency called 'hard' currency?

12. Explain how far devaluation is successful as an instrument for correcting a deficit in the current account of a country's balance of payments.

13. Define (i) Nominal Exchange Rate, (ii) Effective Exchange Rate, and (iii) Real Effective Exchange Rate.

14. Currency appreiation has adverse effect on trade balance by stimulating imports and reducing exports. Explain.

15. (i) What is the difference between depreciation and devaluation?

(ii) Explain the J-curve effect.

16. (i) Why are countries reluctant to explore the use of nominal devaluation to improve balance of payments?

(ii) Define purchasing power parity principle.

CHAPTER 32

International Financial Institutions: The IMF and the World Bank

> *Perhaps the greatest stumbling block to successful economic integration among groups of developing nations is the uneven distribution of benefits among members. Instead, benefits are likely to accrue mainly to the most advanced nations in the group. This leads lagging nations to withdraw, causing the attempt at economic integration to fail. One way to avoid this difficulty is to provide investment assistance through industrial planning.*
>
> D. Salvatore

In this chapter we discuss the role of certain international economic institutions which have emerged since 1944. The focus is on the role of the International Monetary Fund (IMF) and the World Bank.

THE IMF

The IMF the world's monetary system is governed by the IMF. It was set up in 1947 as a multinational institution to supervise the operation of a new international monetary regime — the adjustable peg exchange rate system. It is based in Washington, DC (USA) and currently has a membership of 181 countries. The Fund seeks to maintain cooperative and orderly currency arrangements among member countries, with the aim of promoting increased international trade and balance of payments equilibrium. The Fund is active in two main areas, viz., reducing variability in exchange rate and breaking down the barriers to international trade.

(a) **Exchange Rates**

Upto 1971, member countries established fixed exchange rates for their currencies which conducted to smooth flow of the trade among them. A member was initially required to declare a par value of its currency in term of US dollar or gold. It was allowed to alter its exchange rate upward (revaluation) or downward (devaluation) to a new fixed level only in a situation of fundamental disequilibrium in its balance of payment (BOP) — a situation of either chronic payments surplus or deficit. This procedure ensured that currency realignments were a decided by multilateral agreements. However, since the early 1970s, with a continued weakening of the US dollar and the onset of a world recession, a large number of currencies were 'floated' to provide a great degree of exchange rate flexibility. This resulted in the Fund losing control over exchange rate movements. However, the Fund instructs its members to avoid exchange controls.

(b) **International Liquidity**

The main role of the Fund now, as it had been the past, is to help a member country overcome its BOP problem by supplying it adequate international liquidity. From the very beginning the IMF was involved in lending money to its members scattered all over the world.

The Fund's loanable funds consist of a pool of currencies and international reserve assets (excluding gold) subscribed by its members according to their allocated 'quotas'. Each country pays 75% of its quota amounts in its own currency and 25% in international reserve assets. Countries are given *borrowing* or *drawing rights* with the Fund, which they can use together with their own accumulated international reserves, to finance a BOP deficit.

Ordinary Drawing Rights

Under the Fund's ordinary drawing right facilities, members with BOP difficulties may 'draw' (i.e., purchase foreign currencies from the Fund with their own currencies) up to 125% of their quota. The first 25% (the 'reserve tranche') may be drawn on demand; the remaining 100% is divided up into four 'credit trenches' of 25% each, and drawings here are 'conditional' on members' agreeing with the Fund's policies and programme (such as deflation and devaluation) for removing their payments' deficit. Members are required to repay their drawings over a three-to five-year period.

Special Drawing Rights

In 1967 the Fund created a new international reserve asset, the special drawing rights (SDRs), to augment the supply of international liquidity.

Focus on Terminology: Special Drawing Rights (SDRs) or Paper Gold
Special drawing right is a new form of international reserve asset, created by IMF in 1967. Its value is based on a weighted basket of five currencies: US dollar, German mark, UK sterling, French franc and Japanese yen. Unlike gold SDRs have no tangible life of their own and take the form of bookkeeping entries in a special account managed by the Fund. They are used as instruments for financing international trade and are often described as paper gold.

Special Programmes for Developing Countries

Over the years the IMF has introduced a number of 'special' funding arrangements mainly to assist developing countries suffering from acute foreign exchange crises, including Extended Fund Facilities (EFF), which were established in 1974 to make funds available for longer periods and in larger amounts to members experiencing severe BOP difficulties, particularly countries whose development policies have been held back due to shortage of foreign exchange. The Compensating Financing Facility (CFF), was established in 1963 to assist members, particularly primary commodity producing countries, experiencing balance of payments difficulties because of shortfalls in earnings from exports. (The Compensatory and Contingency Finance Facility superseded the CFF in 1988, adding 'contingency' support for adjustment programmes approved by the Fund). The Supplementary Financing Facility (SFF), was established in 1979 to provide assistance to members facing payments difficulties that are large in relation to their economies and their Fund quotas. The Buffer Stock Financing Facility (BSFF) was established in 1969 to provide assistance to members with a balance of payments need related to their participation in arrangements to finance approved international buffer stocks of primary products. The Systematic Transformation Facility (STF) was established in 1993 as a temporary facility to help member countries (such as eastern European countries) with severe payment problems arising from a shift away from trading at non-market prices to multilateral, market-based trade. The Enhanced Structural Adjustment Facility (ESAF) was established in 1988 to offer credit at concessional interest rates to developing countries that carry out Fund-supervised economic reform programmes. Some 73 countries are eligible for the 0.5% credits, which are paid back over a period of 10 years.

The Fund's increasing involvement in the provision of 'roll-over' credits to assist developing countries has led to criticism that it has become more of a *long-term* economic aid provider and that it now needs to get back to its core activity, namely, the provision of *short-term* liquidity to countries in *temporary* payment difficulties.

Synopsis for Learning: The Role of IMF
The IMF administers the international monetary system and operates a central bank for central banks. Members subscribe by lending their currencies to the IMF; the IMF then relends these funds to help companies in working their BOP problems. The main function of the IMF is to make temporary loans to countries which face BOP problems and external debt or under speculative attack in financial markets.

THE WORLD BANK GROUP

The major sources of multilateral assistance to developing countries are the World Bank or the International Bank for Reconstruction and Development (IBRD) and its two affiliates, viz., the International Development Association (IDA) and the International Finance Corporation (IFC). The World Banks is the world's foremost inter-governmental organisation concerned with the external financing of the economic growth of developing countries. The World Bank is an international organisation set up in 1947 (following the Bretton Woods Conference, 1944) to provide economic aid to member countries on a long-term basis.

The IBRD

Over the years the Bank has supported a wide range of long-term investments, including infrastructural projects such as roads, telecommunications and electricity and water supply; agricultural and industrial projects, including the establishment of new industries, as well as social, training and educational programmes. In general, the Bank operates according to 'business principles', lending at commercial rates of interest only to those governments it feels are capable of servicing and repaying their debts.

Economic Insight: Judging a County's Creditworthiness
Before recommending a bank loan, the staff of the Bank must be reasonably satisfied that the productivity of the borrowing country will be increased and the prospects of repayments are satisfactory. A country must be judged creditworthy. Engineering investigations are frequently carried out to determine the probable relation of the proposed project to its benefits and costs.

The total disbursement by the World Bank Group in 2007-08 was $ 72 billion of which $36 billion was on concessional terms.

The IDA

The International Development Association (IDA) is the 'soft' loan affiliate of the world bank and dispenses loans at very low rates of interest with long repayment periods. It is the most important provider of concessional multilateral assistance. The IDA gives liberal loans (i.e., at low interests rates with long repayment periods) mainly to third world and developing countries. Such countries have poor credit rating and are unable to get loans at reasonable interest rates.

The IDA offer loans to low income member countries repayable at 0.75% interest over 50 years (including a grace period of 10 years, during which no repayment has to be made). Note that the world bank charges 8.5%—just 0.5% over the costs of its borrowing. Loan funds are made available largely by the developed member countries.

The IFC

The International Finance Corporation (IFC) invests in the security of new and matured companies in developing countries. It aids in developing local capital markets. The money may be needed by businesses to buy property, set up plants and instal equipment.

Changing the Role of the World Bank

Up to the 1960s, the major emphasis of the Bank was financing infrastructure projects in the field of power generation and distribution, transportation, ports, telecommunication and irrigation. Programme loans were mainly made to developed countries. Agriculture and rural development, industry and tourism were almost completely ignored. These were neglected areas as far as Bank financing were concerned.

Increasingly, however, the Bank has shifted somewhat away from project lending (e.g., for a dam or a highway or a port); it has become concerned with education and other human services, the environment and, through structural adjustment loans, the modification of government policies which impeded long-term growth.

The current vision of the World Bank Group is to contribute to inclusive and sustainable globalisation—to overcome poverty, enhance growth with adequate environmental protection and achieving sustainable development. The Bank is committed to the Millennium Development Goal of halving the proportion of people in poverty by 2015 compared with the level in 1990.

At present, apart from programme assistance, the bulk of lending goes to transport and communication and education.

Structural Adjustment Lending

Since October 1979 the World Bank has taken a new initiative. It has started providing a different type of assistance in order to enable developing countries to overcome their debt crisis and improve their balance of payments. This new programme of assistance introduced to support balance of payments is known as structural adjustment lending. To qualify for structural adjustment loans, a country must adopt policies that are acceptable to the Bank and designed to achieve external balance (i.e., equilibrium in balance of payments) in the long run investment sacrificing growth. The stress is on improving the supply side of the economy. The main purpose of SAP is to improve the growth potential of countries.

Definition : The World Bank defines structural adjustment loans (SALs) as 'non-project lending to support programmes of policy instituted change to modify the structure of the economy so that it can maintain both its growth rate and viability of its balance of payments in the medium term'.

SALs are geared to the following:

1. Supply side reform, e.g., improving the efficiency of operation of the market system
2. Price reforms
3. Changing the price of tradable goods relating to non-tradeable
4. Setting the 'correct' terms of trade between agricultural goods and industrial goods
5. Reducing the size of the public sector through privatisation and cenationalisation
6. Financial sector reforms
7. Fiscal (tax) reforms.

Governments must commit themselves to policy reforms (or undertake structural adjustment programme) in order to qualify for a loan.

The common purpose SALs and structural adjustment programme (SAPs) is to improve the growth potential of its low-income member countries.

The Record

The World Bank group has had a significant positive effect on the flow of capital in the poorer countries of the world, both directly and indirectly. Still the record of the growth is mixed. In much of East Asia per capita income is raising rapidly, but in much of Africa, South Asia and Latin America, the growth of per capita income has been very slow.

Distinction between the IMF and the World Bank

No doubt balance of payments support has been the traditional preserve of the IMF. But there is a difference of emphasis between the IMF and the World Bank. Whereas the policies of the IMF focuses primarily on balance of payments management, the World Bank is more concerned with promoting policies to increase efficiency and providing incentives to raise export earnings and reduce import bill. The differences between the roles of the IMF and the World Bank are listed in Table 32.1.

Synopsis for Learning: The Role of the World Bank
The World Bank is funded by high-income countries which subscribe in proportion to their economic importance in terms of GDP and other key socio-economic indicators. The Bank makes long term low-interest loans to countries for projects which are economically feasible (or sound) but cannot get private sector financing. As a result of such long term loans goods and services flow from developed to developing countries.

Table 32.1: The Distinct Roles of the IMF and the World Bank

International Monetary Fund	The World Bank
1. Supervises the international monetary system, promotes international monetary co-operation and provides member countries with policy advice, temporary loans and technical assistance so that they can establish and maintain financial stability and external viability.	1. Seeks to promote long-term economic development and poverty reduction by providing technical and financial support and helping developing countries to undertake reforms in particular sectors to implement special projects—for example, building schools and health centres, providing water and electricity, fighting diseases and protecting the environment.
2. Promotes exchange stability and orderly exchange relations among its members.	2. Assists developing countries by providing long-term financing of development projects and programmes.
3. Assists members in temporary balance-of-payments difficulties by providing short-to medium-term financing, thus providing them with the opportunity to correct maladjustments in their balance of payments.	3. Provides special financial assistance to the poorest developing countries through the International Development Association (IDA).
4. Supplements the reserves of its members by allocating SDRs if there is a long-term global need.	4. Stimulates private enterprises in developing countries through its affiliate, viz., the International Finance Corporations (IFC).
5. Draws its financial resources principally from the quota subscriptions of its members.	5. Acquires most of its financial resources by borrowing on the international capital (mainly bond) market.

No doubt, the roles of the two institutions do overlap and will do so increasingly as the IMF itself insists on supply-side policies as a condition for assistance, as well as on the traditional demand-side policies of devaluation and deflation (monetary contraction).

The IMF and the World Bank collaborate in a variety of areas, particularly in supporting governments in implementing poverty reduction strategies in low-income countries, providing debt relief for low-income countries and assessing the financial sectors of countries. Now the two institutions complement each other.

KEY POINTS

1. ***International Monetary Fund (IMF)*** **:** International Monetary Fund is a multinational institution set up in 1947 (following the Bretten Woods conference 1944) to supervise the operation of a new international monetary regime—the adjustable-peg system. The Fund seeks to maintain cooperative and orderly currency arrangements among member countries, with the aim of promoting increased international trade and balance of payments equilibrium. The Fund is active into two areas, viz., (a) exchange rates and (b) international liquidity. Its main objective is to maintain an orderly exchange rate system. Its second objective is to extend short-term loan to members suffering from temporary BOP problem. Over the years, the IMF has introduced a number of "special' funding arrangements mainly to assist developing countries suffering from acute foreign exchange crises. It assists developing and third world countries to meet their external obligations. It promotes world trade partly through activities in foreign currencies markets. The IMF has an international paper currency called special drawing rights (SDRs) to increase international liquidity. In short, the IMF strives to minimise imbalances in the BOP of its member countries, promotes international trade, encourage monetary cooperation among countries and makes funds available to countries needing it.

2. ***World Bank (or the International Bank for Reconstruction and Development)*** **:** The World Bank is an international organisation which assists in making private investment and loans, particularly to developing countries. It supports international projects such as telecommunications, health and irrigation. It often requests recipients to make economic reforms.

3. ***International Finance Corporation (IFC)*** **:** Affiliated to the world bank, IFC invests in the securities of new and mature companies in developing countries. It helps in developing local capital markets. The money may be needed to buy property, plant and equipment for meeting capital needs.

4. ***International Development Association (IDA)*** **:** IDA is another affiliate of the World Bank which gives liberal loans (i.e., loans at low rates of interest and long repayment period), to Third World and development countries. IDA loans are often designated for specific purposes such as to develop education or to undertake public works projects.

KEY TERMS

Fundamental disequilibrium in BOP	Structural adjustment lending
Structural adjustment programmes	Infrastructure building
Poverty reduction	Soft (liberal) loan
Debt relief	Technical assistance
Multilateral assistance	Special drawing rights (SDRs)
Ordinary drawing rights	Quotas
Par value	Monetary cooperation

ASSIGNMENTS

1. (a) Why was the IMF set up?
   (b) What are two main areas of activity of the IMF?
2. (a) What were the initial objectives of the IMF?
   (b) How have these changed over the years?

3. (a) Why was the World Bank set up?
   (b) What are the main objectives of the World Bank Group?
   (c) Mention the areas (sectors) of the economy in which it has provided the maximum finance.
4. Make a comparison between the IMF and the World Bank. Are their activities gradually converging?
5. What are the three main sources of multilateral assistance to developing countries? Briefly discuss their activities.
6. Right an explanatory note on the special programmes undertaken by the IMF in recent years to assist developing countries.
7. Explain each of the following terms:
   (a) special drawing rights,
   (b) fundamental disequilibrium in BOP,
   (c) structural adjustment programme and
   (d) structural adjustment assistance.

CHAPTER 33

The Balance of Payments and the Performance of India's External Sector

> *In ordinary usage one speaks of countries that have a favourable balance of payments, or a surplus, and countries that have a negative or unfavourable balance of payments or a deficit. The most important question to be dealt with . . . is how a country with a deficit can cure it.*
>
> Bo Sodersten

PREVIEW

Every member of the IMF has to keep a consolidated official record of all its external transactions for a particular peri od, usually an accounting year. Such an account is known as the balance of payments. It is a systematic record of all economic transactions of the residents of a country with the rest of the world during a given period of time. The balance of payments account records all receipts and payments connected with export of goods and import of goods (or visible items) and services (or invisible items) and inflows and outflows of financial capital. The main purpose of keeping such records is to know the current international economic position of the country and thus to help the government in taking decisions on monetary, fiscal and other policies with a view to achieving both internal balance (price stability and full employment) and external balance (balance of payments equilibrium and stability of the exchange rate such as the rate of exchange between the Indian rupee and the US dollar).

THE BALANCE OF PAYMENTS ACCOUNTS

The ***balance of payments*** (henceforth BOP) is an account of all the transactions that take place between the residents of the home country and the rest of the world per period, usually one year. An international transaction refers to the exchange of a good, a service, or an asset (for which payment is usually required) between the members of the home country and those of the rest of the world. International transactions are in goods and services and in assets (capital). These two kinds of transactions give rise to a division of the balance of payments accounts. Trade in goods and services is recorded in the *current account*, and trade in capital is recorded in the *capital account*. Table 33.1 summarises the main components of India's balance of payments accounts.

The current account contains all sales and purchases of currently produced goods and services to or from the rest of the world. Specifically, it contains exports and imports of goods (merchandise) and services such as tourism, transport and communication, shipping, as also insurance and banking. The current account also contains transfers. Gifts and unilateral transfers (for which no payments are required) are also included in a country's BOP. So the current account includes three items:

(i) exports of goods and services,

(ii) imports of goods and services and

(iii) net unilateral transfers (unilateral receipts *minus* unilateral payments).

Services, investment income, and transfers are referred to as non-merchandise transactions or invisibles. Exports are entered as credit items (with *plus* sign). Imports are entered as debit items (with *minus* sign).

The difference between total exports of goods and total imports of goods is called the balance of visible (merchandise) trade. The difference between exports of goods and services and imports of goods and services is called the balance of trade (henceforth BOT). [Some authors, however, use the term BOT to refer to the balance of merchandise trade.] When net transfers are added to the BOT, we obtain the current account balance. A negative BOT, also called a BOT deficit is a debit owed by a country to the rest of the world. A positive BOT, also called a BOT surplus is a debit owed by the rest of the world to a country. Investment income includes interest profits and dividends. Transfers include personal and institutional remittances, official contributions and gifts — private and official.

Table 33.1: Structure of India's Balance of Payments

1. Current account

Visibles

- Exports of goods (monetary inflow)
- Imports of goods (monetary outflow)

Invisibles

- Services (financial; transport and travel; military services overseas) (inflow and outflow)
- Investment income (interest, profits and dividends) (inflow and outflow)
- Transfers (non-pecuniary) (inflow and outflow)

2. Capital account

Investment

- Foreign direct investment (FDI) in India (monetary inflow)
- FDI by Indian firms abroad (monetary outflow)
- Portfolio investment by overseas residents in India (monetary inflow)
- Portfolio investment by Indian residents abroad (monetary outflow)

→ Usually considered as long-term flows

Borrowings and lending

- By foreign banks to India (monetary inflow)
- By Indian banks abroad (monetary outflow)
- By foreign non-banking sector to India (monetary inflow)
- By Indian non-banking private sector abroad (monetary outflow)

Use of reserves of foreign currency (inflow and outflow)

Changes in other external general government assets and liabilities (inflow and outflow)

3. Balancing item

The capital account includes both long-term and short-term capital movements between India and the rest of the world. The long-term capital movements include *direct investments* (which involve the actual setting up and controlling of an enterprise in a foreign country), *portfolio investments* (which involve the purchase of securities of a foreign company or a government) and inter-governmental loan(s). The short-term capital movements include all forms of short-term private lending and short-term investments, caused by differences in the rates of interest existing in different countries. An increase in India's FDI and portfolio asset base is indicated by a negative sign (because it denotes a monetary outflow). Another type of capital account transaction covers borrowing and lending by the banking and non-banking private sector. Because it is associated with a monetary inflow, borrowing is usually recorded as a positive item, while lending outflow is usually recorded as negative item. However, at times the repayment of any liability can result in these signs being reversed. A third form of transaction recorded in the capital account concerns changes foreign exchange reserves of the Reserve Bank of India. The final items in BOP are *official reserves*. Official reserves are funds with which international payments can be made. They consist mainly of gold, US dollars, other foreign currencies, and special drawing rights (SDRs). SDRs are deposits with the International Monetary Fund (IMF). These can be used as international money to settle indebtedness among nations. An increase in reserves is recorded as a negative item and a decrease in reserves as a positive one. Finally, the capital account also includes changes in other external general government assets and liabilities. This category includes borrowing by central and state governments abroad (an inflow : recorded as a positive item) and lending abroad by central government (an outflow : recorded as a negative item).

Autonomous and Accommodating Transactions

Apart from both short-term and long-term capital movements between the home country and all other countries, the capital account includes those transactions which are necessary to cover any overall deficit or surplus in the rest of the accounts. These transactions include changes in the official reserves and foreign currency lending and borrowing. The inclusion of these transactions ensures that the BOP will always balance in an accounting sense.

This point may now be explained. In Table 33.1 investment is usually considered to be a *long-term capital flow* : and it is not subject to the same degree of variation as the other recorded capital flows.

The reason is that investment is an **autonomous transaction** in the balance of payments account. 'Autonomous' here refers to transactions undertaken spontaneously *for their own sake*. Both kinds of investment recorded on the capital account obviously originate in the profit-related activities of those who make them. All transactions on the current account are also autonomous in nature : an Indian resident, for example, buys an imported item because, he finds some personal benefit in doing so. But other items in the capital account are all *short-term* in nature. These are collectively known as **accommodating transactions**, and they are undertaken solely in order to make international trade possible and to make the balance of payments balance. Table 33.2 shows how they work.

Table 33.2: How the Balance of Payments Works

Current balance	
All are autonomous transactions	Net deficit of (–) Rs. 1 crore (outflow)
Capital balance	
Autonomous transactions (long-term investment)	Net deficit of (–) Rs. 1 crore (outflow)
Accommodating transactions	Borrowing of (+) Rs. 2 crores (inflow)
Balancing item	Zero

Because autonomous transactions show combined deficit of Rs. 2 crores, accommodating transactions must be made to cover the deficit. In order to cover the deficit India must borrow to cover the amount it owes to foreign residents. However, the deficit could alternatively be accommodated using currency reserves.

In Table 33.2 we show a hypothetical deficit of Rs. 1 crore for each of the current account and the long-term (LT) investment element of the capital account. Overall autonomous transactions show a deficit of Rs. 2 crores. This means that economic agents in India have sold goods, services, bonds shares and so on abroad worth Rs. 2 crores less than foreign agents have managed to sell in India over the period in question. The amount of Rs. 2 crores is in effect a collective debt owed by India to the rest of the world: a *net monetary claim* on Indian residents. How is this debt settled, bearing in mind that foreign residents will want to be paid in their own currencies rather than in Indian rupees? The answer is that payment is facilitated by (positive) accommodating transactions of Rs. 2 crores. India must either borrow the Rs. 2 crores equivalent of foreign currency that it requires, draw on the reserves of foreign currency that it already holds, or undertake some combination of both. This action leaves the balance of payments accounts as a whole *in balance* (that is, neither in surplus nor in deficit).

What happens if the situation is reversed, and India runs a surplus on its autonomous transactions? Here Indian residents have a *net monetary claim* on the rest of the world: foreign residents owe a debt, which must be settled normally in US dollar. In this case Indian(s) can conduct (negative) accommodating transactions, which involve lending the necessary dollars abroad. In addition, or alternatively, the Reserve Bank of India may supply dollars abroad in exchange for foreign currencies, thus increasing its reserves of foreign currency (but note that, as suggested, the increase must by convention be represented by a negative sign). Once again net autonomous transactions are balanced by equivalent net *accommodating transactions*. In the situation (and its inverse) depicted in Table 33.2 the balancing item must be zero. The balancing item, sometimes also referred to as 'errors and omissions', indicates any measurement discrepancies between autonomous and accommodating transactions. In our example there are none, but in reality this does not happen. Thus the balancing item permits the balance of payments to balance in an 'accounting' sense. The BOP always balances, since any imbalance in the current account is made good in the capital account.

The *balancing item* arises as follows. When all recorded capital transactions are added to the current balance, the total never adds up exactly to the amount of foreign currency the country has in fact gained or lost. Spending by Government of India overseas, for instance, is easier to record exactly than the (correctly) spending of people taking holidays abroad. Again goods may be exported in December, but payments for them may be made in the next February.

A 'balancing item' is therefore added to make up the difference between the total value of the transactions recorded and the precise accounts kept by the Reserve Bank of India. If the balancing item is '+', it means that more foreign currency has actually come in than the estimates of transactions have indicated. When there is a '–' balancing item, the opposite is the case.

EQUILIBRIUM AND DISEQUILIBRIUM IN THE BALANCE OF PAYMENTS

Equilibrium refers to state of balance which can be sustained even in the absence of government intervention. Before we analyse the causes of disequilibrium in the balance of payments, we would like to explain what is meant by equilibrium in the balance of payments. We have noted above that when we add up all the demand for foreign currency and all the sources from which it comes, these two amounts are necessarily equal and thus the overall account of the balance of payments necessarily balances or must always be in equilibrium.

What then do we mean by when we say that the balance of payments of a country is 'in equilibrium or disequilibrium'? As a matter of fact, when we speak of equilibrium or disequilibrium in the balance of payments we refer to the balance of those parts of the account which do not include the accommodating items such as borrowing from the IMF, use of SDRs and drawing from the reserves of foreign currencies held by the central bank. When we exclude these accommodating items, there is neither a deficit nor a surplus in the overall balance of payments. So it is said to be in equilibrium. When these are not excluded, there is either a deficit or a surplus, and the balance of payments is said to be in disequilibrium. The deficit in balance of payments can be financed by drawings from the IMF, use of SDRs, drawings from the reserves of foreign currencies and loan and aid received from abroad.

An equilibrium in balance of payments implies that the economy is in good health. By contrast, a persistent disequilibrium in the balance of payments implies that the country is about to face deep economic crisis and even financial bankruptcy.

THE BASIC BALANCE IN THE BALANCE OF PAYMENTS

The key concept in balance of payment equilibrium is basic balance. It is expressed by following equation:

$$(X - M) + LTCM = 0$$

where X stands for exports of both goods and services, M for imports of both goods and services and $LTCM$ for long-term capital movements.

If $X > LM$, then $(X - M)$ is positive. In such a situation the balance of payments will be in equilibrium if $LTCM$ is negative and offsets the positive value of $(X - M)$. Thus if there is surplus in the current account, there will be net capital outflow so that basic balance is achieved. The converse is also true.

If $M > X$, then $X - M$ is negative. In such a situation the balance of payments will be in equilibrium if $LTCM$ is positive. That implies that there will be net capital inflow to offset the deficit in the current account.

The Balance of Payments and the Exchange Rate

There is a link between the balance of payments and the foreign exchange market. When the balance of payments of a country is in equilibrium, the demand for its currency (say rupee) is equal to its supply in the foreign exchange market. This ensures stability of the external value of the rupee (i.e., the rate of exchange between the rupee and the dollar).

Equilibrium in the balance of payments is an indicator of the state of health of an economy.

CAUSES OF DISEQUILIBRIUM IN THE BALANCE OF PAYMENTS

It may be noted at the outset that disequilibrium in the balance of payments may arise either for a short period or for a long period. However, no country can be a perennial debtor, i.e., it cannot have an adverse balance of payments on a permanent basis. Total liabilities and total assets of a nation, like that of an individual, must balance in the long run.

This means that every country should try to achieve and maintain equilibrium in balance of payments by adopting appropriate measures. However, before proceeding further we have to first know the causes of disequilibrium in the balance of payments.

The main cause of disequilibrium in the balance of payments is the imbalance between exports and imports of goods and services. When, for some reasons, the value of exports falls short of the value of imports of both goods and services (i.e., the value of imports exceeds that of exports) a disequilibrium in the balance of payments is likely to arise. A country's exports may be low for internal factors such as its inability to generate sufficient export surplus (due to low volume of production and high costs) and prices of its products due to high rate of domestic inflation.[1] Exports may be low also due to external factors such as availability of cheaper substitutes or intense competition in the world market. If export earning is not adequate to pay the import bill, there will be a trade deficit. If this is not offset by accommodating capital movements, disequilibrium will arise in the balance of payments.

Symptoms of Disequilibrium

There are two symptoms of disequilibrium in the balance of payments. These are the following:

1. *Overvalued exchange rate* : An exchange rate becomes overvalued due to high rate of domestic inflation. This encourages imports and discourages exports.

2. *Excessive outflow of financial capital* : Financial capital is most mobile of all factors. It has always an extra temptation to move abroad in search of higher returns. Thus if the rate of return on financial capital is higher abroad than at home a huge amount of funds will be transferred from the domestic country to foreign countries. As a result there will be a deficit in the balance of payments.

Types of Disequilibrium

Disequilibrium in the balance of payments may be of the following *four* types:

1. *Cyclical disequilibrium* : Cyclical disequilibrium occurs due to trade cycles or short-run fluctuations in economic activities. In times of prosperity in other countries the demand for and prices of India's

1. Inflation makes domestic products expensive in foreign markets and imports cheaper in domestic markets. As a result exports fall and imports rise.

exports will increase. This will improve India's current account and the balance of payments. The converse is also true. In times of depression in other countries India's current account will deteriorate. This type of disequilibrium is short-run in nature.

2. *Secular disequilibrium* : If India is able to generate an export surplus, it will find that its domestic saving exceeds its domestic investment. So it will invest a portion of its saving abroad to get higher returns. A massive outflow of financial capital creates huge disequilibrium in the balance of payments. This is of long-term nature.

3. *Technological disequilibrium* : Technological change enables a country to gain comparative advantage in a new area. As a result its exports are likely to rise. As innovation may also lead to a fall in imports and production of import-substitute items. As a result there will be disequilibrium in balance of payments.[1]

4. *Structural disequilibrium* : Structural disequilibrium may occur either at the goods level or at the factors level. Such disequilibrium at the goods level occurs due to a change in demand for and supply of exports.

Suppose that foreign demand for Indian textiles falls. So the resources engaged in the production of textiles have to shift to some other line of industry or trade or India has to restrict imports in order to avoid a structural disequilibrium.

Structural disequilibrium may also occur from the supply side. Suppose the supply of sugar in India falls due to transfer of land to food crop in the wake of the current food inflation. So India's export of sugar will fall and a deficit in the balance of payments will arise.

A loss of service income from abroad may also create a deficit in the current account. Service income may fall due to failure of foreign investment made by Indians or nationalisation or outright confiscation of some company in foreign countries such as Iran's oil companies in the USA in the 1970.

Structural disequilibrium at the factors level occurs when factor prices are not in line with a country's factor endowments. If, for instance, the price of labour in India is high due to trade union pressure or government intervention in the form of fixation of minimum wages, more capital and less labour will be used by firms — both domestic and foreign. In addition, India will import more capital goods such as machinery and equipment. As a result a disequilibrium in the balance of payments is likely to arise.

Economic Insight: Balance-of-Payments Problem vs. BOP Crisis

A balance-of-payments problem or crisis means that the balance-of-payments situation is not sustainable. This means that foreign exchange reserves are falling rapidly, or are being maintained only by a level of foreign borrowing, leading to difficulties in obtaining further loans. This may happen because foreign exchange reserves are being run down, or because they are being maintained, but only by borrowing abroad at a rate that cannot continue for long before foreign lenders become too worried about the safety of their loans before providing any money. A balance-of-payments crisis may be ended by improving the balance of payments on current account, *via* a recession in domestic activity, or by a devaluation. It may alternatively be ended by changing policies so as to prevent capital flight and to induce inward capital movements. It may also help if a foreign loan can be obtained to allow time for the current account balance to improve. A balance-of-payments crisis differs from a problem only in the speed at which exhaustion of exchange reserves or borrowing capacity is approaching. While problem calls for action at some time in the future, a crisis calls for immediate action.

Comments

Prima facie, disequilibrium in the balance of payments may occur due to a fall in exports. India's export may fall due to recession in other countries (with consequent fall in the purchasing power of these consumers,) high costs and prices of Indian goods due to domestic inflation, or an appreciation of the rupee in terms of any other currency such as the US dollar or the British pound.

1. Correction of this type of disequilibrium requires either reduced exports or increased imports.

A disequilibrium in the balance of payments may also arise due to excessive import of goods and /or services which is not matched by increase in export inflow of financial capital.

If a country is in external debt and cannot repay it due to inadequate reserves of foreign exchange, it will have to service the debt by exporting more goods. So it has to generate an export surplus. This type of forced surplus leads to current account deficit.

Finally a country may face a deficit in the balance of payments if it has to make reparation payments after a war or has to pay indemnities to its creditors.

CORRECTION OF DISEQUILIBRIUM

Under the gold standard which existed upto 1914, exports used to pay for imports and the adjustment of the balance of payments occurred automatically through the price-specie-flow-mechanism in the absence of any government measure to correct a disequilibrium in the balance of payments. [See Ch. 31 for details.]

However, gold standard is a thing of the past. Now under the present inconvertible paper currency system as also the floating exchange rate system, the government of a country is required to adopt various measures to remove a deficit in the balance of payments, or even to generate a surplus in it. Four methods of correcting a disequilibrium in the balance of payments are the following:

1. Trade Policies

Trade policies refer to all the measures which can be adopted by a deficit country to raise exports and to reduce imports. There are various types of export promotion measures such as reduction or complete abolition of export duties and other taxes, giving export credit at low rates of interest and granting subsidies to exporters. By reducing excise duties on products which are exported, it is possible to make exports more competitive in the world market. This is likely to increase the value of exports. Certain organisational measures may also be taken to promote exports such as setting up of free trade zones, exports processing zones, advertising products in foreign countries, participation in world trade fairs and so on.

On the other hand, imports may be reduced by imposing or raising tariffs, imposing quotas or introducing a system of import licences. In addition, imports of certain non-essential items of consumption may be totally banned.

2. Expenditure-reducing Policies

For reducing deficit in the balance of payments it is necessary to adopt contractionary monetary and fiscal policies. Such policies aim at reducing aggregate expenditure. These two policies may now be briefly discussed.

(a) ***Tight monetary policy*** : Such a policy reduces mainly investment expenditure. If also reduces consumption expenditure (mainly on durable goods). By raising the bank rate, undertaking open market sale of government securities and raising the cash reserve ratio (CRR) of member banks, the central bank can make credit costly and less readily available. As a result both business investment and household consumption expenditure will fall. Since each form of expenditure has as import content, imports are likely to fall. This is likely to lead to an improvement in the balance of trade.

In addition, tight monetary policy seeks to reduce the rate of domestic inflation. This will discourage imports. This will also promote exports by making domestic products more competitive in the world market.

However, in times of recession, the use of tight monetary policy to reduce consumption expenditure will make things worse. It will deepen the recession. Therefore, monetary policy has to be supported by fiscal and trade policies to remove the deficit in the balance of payments.

(b) ***Tight fiscal policy*** : Aggregate expenditure can be reduced by raising direct taxes which reduce personal disposable income and thus household expenditure on both domestic goods and imports.

Aggregate expenditure can also be reduced by increasing excise duties and sales taxes, which raise prices of purchasable goods.

A cut in government expenditure, especially unproductive or non-developmental expenditure will reduce total expenditure both directly as also indirectly (through the operation of the multiplier).

A fall in imports and a rise in exports due to reduction in the rate of inflation will improve the balance of payments

If tight monetary and fiscal policies succeed in reducing the rate of inflation, a country's balance of payments position will improve. There are two reasons for this. Firstly, lower domestic prices will induce people to buy more of domestic (import-substitute) goods and less of imported items. Secondly, lower domestic prices will stimulate exports.

However, if reduction in aggregate expenditure occurs due to fall in investment caused by an increase in corporate taxes, the rate of economic growth will slow down. In addition, excessive taxes are likely to affect the incentive to work, save, invest and take risk.

3. Expenditure-switching Policies

When all the usual methods of removing a deficit in the balance of payments account fail, a country is said to be suffering from fundamental disequilibrium, a term first used by the IMF in 1944. In such a situation a country has to adopt expenditure-switching rather than expenditure-reducing policies. Expenditure-switching policies work through changes in relative prices. Such policies may lower the prices of domestic goods so as to increase their demand and, at the same time, reduce the demand for imports. Similarly such policies may reduce the prices of exports. This is likely to increase exports. Thus by changing relative prices, it is possible to improve the balance of payments.

Devaluation

Perhaps the most important form of expenditure-switching policy is devaluation. Devaluation refers an official reduction in the external value of a country's currency such as the rupee in terms of another currency such as the US dollar under the fixed exchange rate system.

However, no country can devalue its currency any time it likes. It has to obtain the formal permission of the IMF to take this measure. The IMF gives this permission only when a country suffers from a fundamental disequilibrium in its balance of trade. But the IMF has not given any specific or clearcut definition of fundamental disequilibrium. Such a situation is said to exist when a deficit country has tried all the possible measures to remove the deficit such as import tariff, import quota, foreign exchange control, multiple exchange rate system, etc., but has failed to achieve the desired goal. So it has to seek the permission of the IMF to devalue its currency as the last measure to remove its trade deficit. The policy of devaluation is indeed an expenditure-switching policy since, due to a fall in imports, the people of the country switch their expenditure from imports to domestically produced goods.

The coexistence of budget deficit and trade deficit is known as the twin deficits problem

However, the success of devaluation in improving a country's balance of trade position depends on the fulfillment of a condition, called the Marshall-Lerner condition. But this is just a necessary condition for the success of devaluation. It is not a sufficient one. The sufficient condition is that the devaluing country must be able to generate sufficient export surplus. However, in spite of this devaluation may not succeed in achieving its desired outcome, if, through competitive devaluation of their currencies, other countries retaliate. We will speak about devaluation in detail in the next chapter.

The Indian devaluation of July 1991 proved quite successful since exports grow rapidly since then. But imports remained within safe limits.

4. Control of Capital Movements and Exchange Control

The adverse effects of devaluation can be avoided if the government exercises control over foreign exchange. In addition, foreign exchange control enables a country to exercise control over movements of financial capital, i.e., borrowing from or lending to other countries.

Economic Insight: Exchange Control

Exchange control refers to a system under which holders of a domestic or a national currency require official permission or approval to convert it into foreign currencies. Exchange control may apply to all holders of a currency, or some holders, usually non-residents, may be exempted. Where non-residents are allowed convertibility, exchange control may be applied to transfer funds from resident to non-resident domestic currency bank accounts. Exchange controls may have different degrees of strictness; usually they are much more stringent on obtaining foreign currency for capital account than for current account transaction.

Under exchange control system all transactions in foreign exchange are made by the central bank of the country and the foreign exchange earned by the country is rationed out among the licensed importers. Thus the balance of payments deficit is corrected by keeping imports within limits.

Conclusion

No single tool should be used to correct all types of disequilibria in the balance of payments. Fiscal measures should be used to correct cyclical disequilibrium. Structural disequilibrium (both at the goods and at the factors level) can be corrected by adjustments in the economy which lead to desired changes in incomes and prices. The control of capital movements is needed to offset secular disequilibrium.

In 1944 the IMF was set up to maintain exchange rate stability as also to provide short-term loans to member countries in order to enable them to overcome deficit in balance of payments. The IMF also gives necessary advice to its member countries on how to correct a fundamental disequilibrium in the balance of payments.

DOMESTIC SAVING, DOMESTIC INVESTMENT, NET FOREIGN INVESTMENT AND GOVERNMENT BUDGET DEFICIT

One of the fundamental equations of a country's balance of payments account is the following:

Current account balance + financial account balance = 0

Or, current account balance = – financial account balance

Or, Net exports = net foreign investment

This equation tells us that a country which imports more than it exports must borrow from abroad rather than lend abroad. And if net exports are negative, net foreign investment will also be negative by the same amount. The converse is also true.

Domestic Saving, Domestic Investment and Net Foreign Investment

We know that

national saving = private saving + public saving and

private saving = national income – consumption – taxes.

Or, $$S_P = Y - C - T$$

Public saving is the difference between government saving and taxes. So we can write

$$S_G = T - G$$

We also know that the basic macroeconomic equation for GNP or national income is the following:

$$Y = C + I + G + NX$$

where net exports (NX) = exports – imports($X - M$)

Now we can use this equation, our definition of private saving and the fact that net exports (NX) = net foreign investment (NFI) to arrive at the following saving-investment equation:

National saving = domestic investment + net foreign investment

Or, $S = I + NFI$

This equation is an identity because it must always be true.

A country which has negative *NFI* must be saving *less* than it is investing domestically. So we can rewrite the above equation as

$$S - I = NFI$$

Thus if *NFI* is negative, then domestic investment (I) must be greater than national saving.

The Effect of a Government Budget Deficit on Investment

The link among saving, investment and *NFI* can help us to understand some of the effects of changes in government's budget deficit. When the government runs a budget deficit, national saving will decline unless private saving increases by the amount of the dèficit which is unlikely. As the saving-investment equation $S = I + NFI$ shows, the result of a decline in national saving must be a decline in either domestic investment or in *NFI*.

Twin Deficits

When a government budget deficit leads to a decline in net exports, the result is known as *twin deficits*. The result refers to the possiblity that a government budget deficit will also lead to a current account deficit.

The saving and investment equation shows that an increase in government budget deficit will not lead to an increase in current account deficit provided that either private saving increases or domestic investment declines. According to the twin deficits idea when the government runs a budget surplus the current account should also show a surplus or atleast the current acccount deficit should be small. In fact, the increase in national saving due to the budget surplus is more than offset by a sharp decline in private saving and the country runs very large current account deficit.

Due to external sector reforms CAD fell from 3.1% of GDP in 1990-1991 to 0.6% in 2000-01. This is no doubt an important benefit of external sector reforms. In fact, since 1991, CAD never exceeded 2% of GDP throughout the 1990s.

It is to be noted that in the next three years (2001-02, 2002-03 and 2003-04), the CAD was converted into a surplus. Since 2003-04 there was a small deficit in the current account up to 2007-08: However, CAD suddenly went up to in 2.4% in 2008-09 and 2.8% in 2009-10 due to global financial crisis and the consequent economic slowdown in industrial countries. In 2010-11 the CAD was 2.6%. It has to be note, however, that the CAD is not bad for a country. Instead it is good for a country if two conditions are satisfied: (i) CAD is small or is kept within safe limits, (ii) the deficit country has enough foreign exchange reserves and is having sufficient capital inflows. The fact is that CAD represents absorption of foreign capital by a capital-deficient country like India which is undertaking a comprehensive and, at times, on ambitious programme of industrialisation.

Commentary: In Defence of Current Account Deficit (CAS)

A current account deficit (CAD) for a country means that the country is spending more than its income, or alternatively, is saving less than what is needed to meet its investment needs. However, there is no reason to assume that a CAD is necessarily a 'bad thing' and that a country should always adopt policies to ensure balance in the current account or even generate a surplus in it.

In truth, a developing country like India may require a net investment outflow or a CAD in the initial stage of industrialisation. Even as the growth rate picks up and the country becomes less reliant on foreign funds, the interest and/or dividend payments in the accumulated foreign capital stock can result in a CAD. Ultimately, however, if repayment is needed on some or all of the initial foreign investment, the developing country will experience a current account surplus and a financial account deficit. This transition from a debtor (financial account inflow) nation to a creditor (financial account outflow) nation is no doubt a part of the process of economic development which is often equated with industrialisation.

Inflows of Foreign Capital

Another notable achievement of the external sector reforms is the steady inflows of foreign capital.

Net foreign investment flows increased from a modest $103 million in 1990-91 to $43.4 billion in 2007-08. Then it declined to $3.5 billion in 2008-09 due to global financial crisis which led to a sharp net outflow of portfolio capital. But this was just a transitory phenomenon. It again went up to $51.2 billion in 2009-10. In 2010-11 net foreign investment inflow in India amounted to $44.3 billion.

Industrial Growth and Exports

· Inflows of FDI served a very useful purpose. It stimulated industrial production and helped to accelerate the rate of industrial growth. Industrial growth, in its turn, led to increase in exports.

Accumulation of Foreign Exchange

Perhaps what was most significant was huge inflows of foreign exchange. India's foreign exchange reserves which were just $5.8 billion in 1990-91 continued to increase year after year and touched $304 billion on March 31, 2011. And such huge capital inflows created *the problem of plenty*. The planners were unable to decide how to utilise such huge resources for productive purposes. However, these served as a hedge against uncertainty caused by falling exports or as a cushion in case of unexpected capital outflows from India as had happened in 2011-12. It is interesting to note that India's foreign exchange reserves in 1990-91 was just sufficient to cover import bill for only 2.5 months. And such resources increased to $275 billion in Sep. 2013 and were enough to cover import needs for 70 months.

External Debt Burden

India's external debt was 28.7% of GDP in 1990-91. And it fell to 18% on March 31, 2010. But it again rose to 19.7% on March 31, 2012.

India's debt service ratio (i.e., the ratio of interest and principal amount payable on external debt to current export receipts) was 35% in 1990-91.This led to India's BOP crisis in 1991. But it was brought down to 17% in 1999-2000 and further to 4.3% on March 31, 2011. However, it again rose to 6% on March 31, 2012. Thus we see that economic reforms reduced India's external debt burden considerably.

Thanks to India's external sector reforms, the ratio of short-term debt to foreign exchange reserves was brought down from an abnormally high level of 146.5% in 1990-91 to a modest 10.3% in 1999-2000. With larger and larger inflow of foreign exchange in the next three years (2000-2003) and repayment of a portion of short-term debt, the ratio of such debt to foreign exchange reserves fell to a meager 3.9% on March 31, 2004 but rose again to 14.8% on March 31, 2008. This is no mean achievement. In fact, a judicious-cum-prudent external debt management policy has placed India in a comfortable position. Of late, the policy focus has shifted on concessional and relatively less expensive source of external funds. In this policy the preference is on loans with long maturity period, but the focus is on monitoring short-term debt as also on non-debt creating capital flows. The latest measures taken by the GOI for reducing the burden of external debt include repayment of high-cost external loans — both Government and non-Government, rationalisation of interest rates and structure of NRI deposits and making more precise and explicit specification of the end use of external commercial borrowing (ECB). All these measures are likely to improve India's external debt situation considerably in the years to come.

KEY POINTS

1. ***Balance of payments*** **:** The balance of (internal) payment is an overall statement of a country's economic transactions with the rest of the world over some period, often a year. A table of the balance of payments shows amounts received from the rest of the world and amounts spent abroad.

2. ***The current account*** **:** The current account includes exports and imports, that is, visible trade, and receipts from and spending abroad on services such as tourism. It also includes receipts of property incomes from abroad and remittances of property incomes abroad, and receipts and payments of international transfers, that is, gifts.

3. *The capital account* : The capital account of the balance of payments includes inward and outward foreign direct investment, and sales and purchases of foreign securities by residents and of domestic securities by non-residents. The third element in the balance of payments is changes in official foreign exchange reserves.

4. *Overall payments* : Overall payments, including changes in foreign exchange reserves must balance by definition. But this is not true for any one category of payments.

5. *The balance on current account* : The balance of payments on current account is the difference between total receipts and expenditures on current account: if receipts exceed spending, there is a current account surplus, and if spending exceeds receipts there is a current account deficit.

6. *The balance on capital account* : The balance of payments on capital account is the difference between receipts and expenditures on capital transactions with the rest of the world. Receipts come from the sale of securities or real capital assets to non-residents; expenditures are on loans to non-residents or purchase of real assets abroad.

7. *Changes in foreign exchange reserves* : Changes in foreign exchange reserves are equal to the sum of the current and capital account surpluses.

8. *The effect of government budget deficit on investment in an open economy* : When the government runs a budget deficit, national saving will decline unless private saving increases by the full amount of the budget deficit, which is unlikely. As the saving and investment equation — $S = I + NFI$— shows, the result of a decline in national saving must be to a decline in either domestic investment or net foreign investment.

KEY TERMS

Balance of trade	Balance of payments
Current account	Capital account
Fundamental disequilibrium	Expenditure-switching policy
Expenditure-reducing policy	Tariff and quota
Tight monetary policy	Tight fiscal policy
Cyclical disequilibrium	Secular disequilibrium
Overvalued exchange rate	Technological disequilibrium
Structural disequilibrium	Exchange control
External debt	External commercial borrowing
Debt service ratio	Debt trap
Foreign direct investment	Foreign portfolio investment
Trade-weighted basket of currencies	Expenditure-reducing policies
Expenditure-switching policies	Balance of trade
Balance on current account	Balance of payments
Current account of BOP	Capital account of BOP
Devaluation	Marshall-Lerner condition
Absorption approach to development	IMF conditionality
Disequilibrium in BOP	Correction of disequilibrium
Current account deficit	Current account surplus
Autonomous transactions	Accommodating transactions
Equality vs. equilibrium in BOP	Fundamental disequilibrium in BOP

ASSIGNMENTS

1. Distinguish between balance of trade and balance of payments. "The balances of payments always balances."—Discuss.
2. What are the items to be included in the balance of payments of a country?

3. Distinguish between 'equity' and 'equilibrium' in balance of payments. What are the causes of disequilibrium in the balance of payments?
4. Discuss briefly the various measures which can be adopted by a country to overcome disequilibrium in its balance of payments.
5. What type of fiscal policy helps to maintain equilibrium in the current account of the balance of payments?
6. Distinguish between expenditure-reducing and expenditure-switching policies to correct a deficit in the balance of payments.
7. (i) Explain the concept of equilibrium in the balance of payments account of a country. (ii) How would you relate the current account of the balance of payments with the budget deficit of the government and the domestic private saving and investment of a country?
8. Justify the statement: (i) 'the balance of payments always balances'. (ii) How do you explain the surplus and deficit in the balance of payments of a couuntry? (iii) Distinguish between 'current account balance' and 'capital account balance' in the system of international payments.
9. Define balance of payments equilibrium. How do you relate the current account deficit with the government budget deficit and the discrepancy between domestic private saving and investment?
10. Write short note on (a) concept of balance of payments equilibrium and (b) autonomous and accommodating transactions in the balance of payments.
11. Distinguish clearly between autonomous and accommodating transactions in the balance of payments accounting. Suggest as a definition of balance of payments disequilibrium in terms of these two transactions.
12. (a) Is the following statement true? Justify your answer.

    'The balance of payments always balances itself'.

    (b) Distinguish between the 'current account balance' and 'capital account balance' in the system of international payments, using illustrative numerical figures.
13. Define balance of payments equilibrium. How do you relate the current account deficit with the government budget deficit and imbalance between domestic private investment and saving?
14. What is the difference between BOT and BOP? 'The BOP always balances'. Critically examine this statement.
15. What are the items to be included in the BOP of a country? In this context draw distinction

    (a) between current account transactions and capital account transactions and

    (b) between autonomous transactions and accommodating transactions.
16. What is the difference between equality and equilibrium in BOP? When does a disequilibrium in BOP arise and what are the causes of such disequilibrium?
17. Suggest different measures which can be adopted by a country to correct disequilibrium in its BOP.
18. Distinguish between expenditure-reducing policies and expenditure-switching policies to correct a disequilibrium in its BOP.
19. What is currency devaluation? How far is it successful in correcting a country's current account deficit (CAD)? Does devaluation help to improve a country's capital account also?
20. Discuss the Marshall-Lerner condition which seeks to ensure the success of devaluation of a country's currency. Is it both a necessary and a sufficient condition?
21. Discuss the absorption approach to devaluation is a means of correcting a deficit in a country's current account.
22. Comment on the success and failure of various external sector reform measures adopted by the GOI since July 1991.
23. Comment on India's external debt position and briefly explain how India escaped from falling in a serious debt trap.
24. What is devaluation? Is it an expenditure-reducing or an expenditure-switching policy?
25. What is meant by IMF conditionality?
26. What have been India's steps in trade liberalisation? How has its external sector policy changed since the early 1990s?
27. Define (i) current account, (ii) capital account and (iii) balance of payments.
28. Current account deficit equals current account surplus. Explain.

33A INDIA'S BALANCE OF PAYMENTS AND EXTERNAL SECTOR REFORMS

The balance of payments of a country is a systematic record of all economic transactions between the 'residents' of a country and the rest of the world. It represents a classified record of all receipts on account of goods exported, services rendered and capital received by 'residents' and payments made by them on account of goods imported and services received from the capital transferred to 'non-residents' or 'foreigners'.

The Reserve Bank of India

PREVIEW

We have made a brief review of different aspects of a country's balance of payments (henceforth BOP) in this chapter. In context we have explained the basic concept of BOP as also equilibrium and disequilibrium in BOP. After analysing the causes of disequilibrium in BOP we finally discuss the measures which can be adopted to solve the problem of deficit (or surplus) in the BOP of a country. It is against this backdrop that we will now discuss India's BOP in the post-reform period (from July 1991 till March 2014). In this context we will also discuss India's external sector reforms.

In May 1991 India faced a severe BOP crisis. And due to an acute shortage of foreign exchange India was not in a position to service its external debt (i.e., pay the principal amount borrowed from the rest of the world along with interest). In fact, a default on payments became a genuine possibility since early July 1991. India lost its creditworthiness to foreigners and was not in a position to borrow more funds from abroad to tide over the difficult situation for a very simple reason. The rest of the world almost completely lost confidence in India's capacity to repay any loan (along with interest). It was at this time that the Government of India (GOI) adopted various measures of both short-term and long-term nature to overcome the crisis situation.

The costly and inefficient import-substitution (or inward-looking) strategy of industrialisation was abandoned. Various reform measures were adopted for improving India's BOP position. These measures worked wonders and became effective almost instantaneously. And India achieved a miracle, so to say. It succeeded in tackling the BOP problem mainly through faster growth of exports and larger inflows of capital (both FDI and FPI) and remittances by NRIs on a massive scale. However, India had also to take loan (special assistance) from both the IMF and the World Bank on a purely temporary (short-term) basis to be able to tide over the crisis situation.

INDIA'S BALANCE OF PAYMENTS

The Crisis of 1991

The crisis situation faced by India in early 1991 induced the policy-makers to adopt various liberalisation and structural adjustment measures. The crisis had roots in the serious BOP problem which emerged in 1990-91.

In fact, during the second half of 1980s (1985-86 to 1989-90) the average annual current account deficit (CAD) was 2.2% of GDP. It rose to 3.1% of GDP in 1990-91. And the Gulf War of 1991 was a severe blow to India's BOP. It made India's BOP problem more serious in two ways at least. Firstly, India's import bill suddenly increased substantially due to sharp rise in the prices of crude oil and petroleum products. Secondly, inward remittances by Indians working in Gulf countries, which were an important source of foreign exchange, suddenly dropped and subsequently stopped.

Another cause of CAD was the overvalued exchange rate. The rupee was overvalued in terms of the US dollar and other key (convertible) currencies which made India's export items costlier in other countries and imports cheaper. This led to a slow growth in exports and a sharp increase in imports. Apart from this, India's foreign trade policy was inward-looking in nature. It was tilted in favour of import substitution and was biased against exports.

In fact, the so called *export pessimism* prevented India from adopting strong and active export promotion measures. And this feeling was largely responsible for the slow growth of India's exports before the initiation of external sector reforms in July 1991.

The huge CAD in the second half of the 1990s was financed in two main ways: (i) through various types of external borrowing such as foreign assistance (i.e., loans taken from abroad at concessional rates of interest), commercial borrowing and NRI deposits and (ii) by running down of accumulated foreign exchange reserves. The huge external debt had to be serviced. And India's debt service burden (measured by the ratio of debt service charges in terms of interest and the principal amount payable to current export earnings) reached an all-time record of 35% in 1990-91. And this huge burden of external debt was the root cause of deterioration of India's BOP position.

Since the emergence of the BOP crisis from early 1991 various reforms in India's external sector have been undertaken. Firstly, the rupee was devalued to promote exports. Secondly, all export subsidies were withdrawn. Thirdly, imports have been reduced from 35% in 1990-91 to 10% in 2007-08. Fourthly, quantitative restrictions (or quotas) on import of intermediate and capital goods were withdrawn in 1991. The last two measures enabled India's export-oriented industries to acquire imported raw materials and capital goods at low prices. Consequently they were able to produce exportable items at low costs and achieve international competitiveness. In short, the *anti-export bias* in India's foreign trade policy was removed.

In addition, provisions relating to foreign direct investment (FDI) have been substantially liberalised and foreign institutional investors have been permitted to invest in equity shares and debt securities in the Indian stock markets.

All these measures of deregulation and liberalisation of foreign trade and investment improved India's BOP position considerably. And India was able to accumulate huge amount of foreign exchange. And the comfortable foreign exchange reserve position enabled India to import all items needed for export production in larger and larger quantities.

The Current Account of the BOP

Table 33A.1 shows the current account position of India's BOP for the 7-year period 2005-06 to 2012-2013. We see that there was a deficit over the entire period. Two main causes of India's CAD were (i) economic slowdown in advanced countries as also its spillover (spread) effects on emerging market-based economies and (ii) rise in prices of crude oil and gold. However, due to surplus in invisible accounts, there was a surplus in the current account for the first three years of the period under review.

However, a CAD is not always bad for a country. Sometimes it serves a very useful purpose. See box.

Commentary: Good Effects of a CAD

In the context of national income accounting, CAD for a country means that it is spending more than its income or, to put it from another side, is saving too little relative to its investment. However, a CAD is not necessarily a 'bad thing' for a newly industrialising country like India. So India should focus it attention on adopting policies to attain current account balance or even a current account surplus. In reality, a CAD for India can be viewed in a positive manner. To be more specific, a developing country like India may require a net investment inflow (and therefore a CAD) to assist it in its early efforts at industrialisation. Even as its growth picks and it becomes less reliant on foreign funds, the interest and/or dividend payments on the accumulated foreign capital stock can result in a CAD. Ultimately, however, if repayment is needed on some or all of the initial foreign investment, the developing country will experience a current account surplus and a financial account deficit. This transition from a debtor (financial account inflow) nation to a creditor (financial account outflow) is, in fact, a part of a natural sequence in the development process.

Table 33A.1: India's Balance of Payments on Current Account **(in Billion US $)**

Sl. No. Items	2005-06	2006-07	2007-08	2008-09	2009-10	2010-11	2011-12	2012-13
1. Exports	105.1	128.9	166.2	189.0	182.2	256.2	309.8	305.6
2. Imports	157.1	190.7	257.6	307.6	300.6	383.5	499.5	502.2
3. Trade Balance	– 52.0	– 61.8	– 91.5	– 118.6	– 118.4	– 127.3	– 189.9	– 195.7
	(– 6.2)	(– 6.5)	(– 7.4)	(– 9.8)	(– 8.6)	(– 7.8)	(– 10.1)	(– 10.6)
4. Invisibles (Net)	42.0	52.2	75.7	89.9	79.9	79.3	111.6	
(i) Non-factor Services	23.2	29.5	38.9	49.6	35.7	44.1	64.1	
(ii) Investment Income	– 5.9	– 7.2	– 5.1	– 4.0	– 8.0	– 17.9	– 16.0	–
(iii) Private Transfers (Net)	24.5	29.8	41.7	44.6	52.3	53.1	63.5	–
5. Goods and Services Balance	– 28.7	– 32.3	– 52.6	– 69.0	– 83.0	– 83.2	– 125.7	130.7
6. Current Account Balance (Net)	**– 10.0**	**– 9.6**	**– 15.7**	**– 28.7**	**– 38.4**	**– 48.1**	**– 78.2**	**– 87.8**
	(– 1.2)	(– 1.0)	(– 1.3)	(– 2.4)	(– 2.8)	(– 2.7)	(– 4.2)	(– 4.8)

Source: RBI Annual Report (various issues)

Note: Figures in brackets show per cent of GDP at market prices.

Two key points are to be noted here. A deficit on current account is beneficial for a developing country like India if two conditions are satisfied:

(i) it is kept within safe limits and

(ii) it is covered by non-debt-creating capital receipts.

The Effect of Global Financial Crisis

After initial slowdown India's exports fell sharply in 2008-09 due to global financial crisis. As a result there was large CAD. It was 2.4% of GDP in that year and could not be met by meager capital inflows ($ 8.6 billion). And the trend of rising CAD continued in the next four years (from 2009-10 to 2012-13). In 2012-13 it was 4.8% of GDP.

Weakening of the Rupee

Since July 1993, FIIs pulled out of both equity and debt markets leading to stock market crash (and sharp fall in share prices). This led to further increase in CAD and a sharp depreciation of the rupee by increasing the demand for dollars. High CAD weakened the rupee by increasing the demand for dollars. However, in 2012-13, it was possible to finance the CAD through capital inflows without running down the accumulated foreign exchange reserves.

Focus on Improving Trade Balance

Due to sudden reversal of capital flows on a number of occasions in recent past the CAD increased. Since undue dependence on volatile capital inflows through foreign institutional investors (FIIs) to meet CAD was found to be unsustainable, the priority has been shifted to improving trade balance, mainly by promoting exports. This was sought to be achieved by diversifying the commodity composition and country-wise destination of exports. The GOI has strongly encouraged software exports for earning foreign exchange.

The GOI has also raised prices of imported items, mainly crude oil to bring them to the international level. This is why petrol has been decontrolled and prices of diesel have been revised upward in Jan. 2013. The main objective behind this move has been to reduce the component of subsidy so that users bear the full landed cost of these two items which are produced from crude oil. The GOI also raised the customs duty on imported gold from 6% to 10% in two phases in order to discourage import of this item which was a major cause of CAD.

In addition, for improving CAD the GOI has given emphasis on facilitating remittances by NRIs. In recent years the surplus on the invisible account generated largely by this item has helped to reduce the magnitude of CAD.

In fact, remittances acted as the shock absorber when the country was hit by the global financial crisis of Sep. 2008. This is why various incentives have been given to NRIs to deposit their savings (denominated in foreign currencies) in India.

Commentary: Adverse Effect of CAD
Continual CAD cannot or should not be ignored by India's policy-makers. The concern here is not with the annual CAD as such, but with the potential growth in payments to foreign investors which accompanies the increasing holdings of assets in the country by foreign entities. Rapid growth of payments as returns to foreign investors not only worsens the current account balance further but can quickly lead to the emergence of a 'debt trap', where both the net debt position of the country and the CAD increase sharply.

The Capital Account of India's BOP

Table 33A.2 summarises the position of India on the capital account for the seven year-period 2004-05 to 2011-12. It may be noted that capital inflows are of two types: debt-creating and non-debt-creating. The former refers to both types of foreign investment — FDI and foreign portfolio investment (FPI). The latter includes external assistance (i.e., loans taken from abroad at low/concessional rates of interest), external commercial borrowing and deposits made in India's banks by NRIs.

Table 33A.2: India's Balance of Payments on Capital Account **(in Billion US $)**

Items	2005-06	2006-07	2007-08	2008-09	2009-10	2010-11	2011-12
1. External Assistance (Net)	1.7	1.8	2.1	2.6	2.9	4.94	2.3
2. Commercial Borrowing (Net)	2.5	16.1	22.6	7.0	2.8	12.16	10.3
3. Non-Resident Deposits (Net)	2.8	4.3	0.2	– 4.3	2.9	3.14	11.9
4. Foreign Investment (Net) of which	15.5	14.8	43.3	3.5	50.4	42.13	39.2
(i) FDI net	3.0	7.7	15.9	17.5	18.0	11.83	22.1
(ii) Portfolio Investment (Net)	12.5	7.1	27.4	– 15.0	32.4	30.3	17.2
(iii) Other capital flows (Net)	2.4	9.2	39.7	– 9.7	– 13.1	– 10.48	– 7.0
5. Capital Account Balance (Net)	**24.9**	**46.1**	**107.9**	**8.6**	**51.6**	**63.74**	**67.8**
6. Use of foreign Exchange (currency) Reserves (as also errors and omissions)	– 15.0	– 36.6	– 92.2	+ 20.1	– 13.4	– 13.1	+ 12.8

Source: RBI Annual Report 2012-13. As for use of foreign exchange reserves – indicates increase of reserves, and + indicates decrease of reserves.

From Table 33A.2 we see that in 2007-08 the net inflow of total foreign investment in India was US $ 43.3 billion. And there was a surplus in the capital account of US $ 107.9 billion in the same year. In spite of CAD of $ 157 bn. in 2007-08 there was a net accretion of foreign exchange reserves of $92.2 bn. However, due to reversal of capital flows after Sept. 2008 in the wake of the global financial crisis the GOI was forced to use $20.1 bn. of its accumulated foreign exchange reserves. At the same, due to increase in the flows of both FDI and FPI in 2009-10 the external economic situation improved to some extent. And net accretion to foreign exchange reserve was $13.4 bn since the current account deficit of $38 bn. was more than offset by capital account surplus of $51.6 bn. In 2010-11, the net accretion to foreign exchange reserves was $13.1 bn. due to the same reason — more than offsetting the CAD by the capital account surplus of $63.74 bn.

However, in the next year (2011-12) the situation virtually took a *U*-turn and it was not possible to meet the huge CAD through capital inflows alone. So there was need to withdraw US $12.8 bn. from accumulated foreign exchange reserves. However, in 2012-13 the external economic situation improved once again and it was possible to cover the CAD through capital inflows alone, by keeping foreign exchange reserves virtually intact.

THE PROBLEM OF GROWING CAD IN INDIA

In the past four years (2009-10 to 2013-14) India's CAD went from bad to worse, mainly due to growing merchandise trade deficit. Exports could not be raised much in the face of rising import bill for two main reasons: (i) lack of competitiveness of India's exportable items and (ii) the inability of the Government to diversify the market for exports. India's import bill was mainly due to continuous rise in the prices of crude oil and gold (which had both industrial and speculative demand). Gold was also in high demand from the household sector since it acted as a hedge against inflation. Many people tried to beat price inflation by holding a large stock of gold.

India CAD rose to 7% of the GDP as in 2012-13 as gold and oil imports increased. This was much higher than what it was during the 1991 crisis (3.4%). Slow growth of exports mainly of software as also of inward remittances due to weakening of the rupee and lower interest rates made things worse.

It has to be noted that CAD was high due to huge excess of import bill over export earning (even though net invisibles or net exports of services were positive all the time). Thus the overall deficit in the current account was due to huge deficit in merchandise trade (i.e., excess of imports of goods over exports).

In short, India's current account deficit was largely due to rising imports of three main items — crude oil, coal and gold. And this could not always be offset by generating surplus in capital account due to rise in the demand for US dollars which led to depreciation of the rupee. And the rupee continued to depreciate sharply, in spite of intervention by the RBI in Aug. 2013. This lead to huge capital outflows by eroding the confidence of foreign investors. Another cause of such capital outflows was the announcement of the US Federal Reserve Board (or Fed, in short) about the *quantitative easing* (QE) due to the recovery of the US economy, gradually though. This induced international portfolio investors to withdraw from India's capital market in May and June 2013 and reinvest the funds in the USA which they treated as safer and more rewarding.

The process of depreciation of the rupee continued in spite of the RBI's repeated efforts to bring the process to a halt, through sterilised foreign exchange market intervention. The process worked through RBI purchase of rupees by selling dollars in the foreign exchange market.

The Government, of course, adopted two pragmatic measures to reduce CAD which proved to be really effective, viz., (1) raising import duty on gold from 6% to 10%, as noted earlier and (2) by raising the upper limits on FDI in sectors such as telecom., oil refining, defence production and insurance.

SUGGESTED SOLUTIONS

The real solution to India's increasing CAD lies in raising exports on a sustainable basis. This can be achieved by making exportable items really competitive in the world market (both price-wise and quality-wise). So there is need to increase productivity of India's manufacturing sector so that costs and prices fall and exportable items become more competitive. However, for promoting exports of manufactured goods it is of paramount importance to remove certain bottlenecks such as power shortage and inadequate availability of coal. It is also necessary to provide adequate infrastructure facilities such as highways and ports. In addition, policy measures have to be taken to simplify and relax rigid labour laws, reduce transaction costs by reducing paper work and give environmental clearance to projects as quickly as possible (so that projects do not suffer from long gestation lags). Furthermore, the Government has also to give proper guidance to exporters so as to enable them to develop new markets, for example, in emerging economies such as several African nations which are now experiencing robust growth.

No doubt, the high current account deficit poses a great challenge for the Indian economy. If an adequate amount of foreign exchange is not available due to inadequate flow of both types of foreign investment – direct and portfolio, then there are only two ways of reducing CAD, viz., (i) raising exports and (ii) if exports can not be raised adequately, then by cutting imports. However, a drastic cut in imports is likely to have a damaging effect on the economy.

Two Types of Corrective Measures

Two types of measures may be suggested for solving the problem of CAD and to keep it within a safe level (such as 2.5% of GDP). The first type of measure is to reduce CAD by raising exports and reducing imports. The second type of measure refers to alternative ways of financing CAD.These two measures are now be discussed briefly.

(i) *Reducing CAD* : We have already referred to various export promotion measures. We may just add a few points here. India's export of iron has fallen sharply in recent years due to various restrictions imposed on mining of iron. For promoting exports of iron, these restrictions are to be relaxed, if not completely removed. Now we refer to certain measures which can be adopted to curtail imports. In recent time imports of gold have increased year after year and have reached a very high level and caused an increase in CAD.This is why the GOI raised import duty on gold from 6% to 10%, as noted earlier. But this measure alone is not enough. It is high time the RBI made imports of gold tougher. If may be noted that the RBI has recently announced that 20% of gold imported by a business person has to be exported in the form of jewellery. Otherwise, he(she) will not be allowed to import any more gold in the future. This measure is likely to promote export of gold and will help reduce CAD. Likewise, India's current account deficit has increased recently due to increase in import of coal. This is largely attributable to fall in domestic production due to allotment of quotas of coal mining to incompetent and inefficient persons. And this led to coal scam, involving the waste of crores of rupees. So import of coal has to be curtailed by increasing domestic production. This calls for a change in policy on coal mining.

Furthermore, a large amount of foreign exchange can be saved by curtailing imports of various electronic goods such as laptops, desktops, smart phones, mobiles, etc. by imposing high rates of import duties. It is also necessary to impose quantitative restrictions (or to fix import quotas) in case of such items as has been done in case of gold.

Now we pass on to the second option left with the government, i.e., exploring alternative ways of financing CAD.

(ii) *Financing CAB* : India's present level of foreign exchange reserves ($282 bn.) are not sufficient to cover the CAD. So we have to attract sufficient FDI by raising its limits in various industries and making its entry in India much easier than in the past. This can be achieved in two main ways: (i) by adopting proper policy measures and (ii) by restoring confidence among foreign investors. As noted earlier, the GOI has already raised the upper limits on FDI in various industries. It is also to be noted that the GOI has made its entry much easier by permitting a large percentage of FDI through the automatic route, i.e., without getting the approval of Foreign Investment Promotion Board (FIPB).

Finally the permission given by the RBI to raise interest rate on deposits made by NRIs in Indian banks is likely to lead to large inflows of dollars. This can be used to finance CAD.

EXTERNAL SECTOR REFORMS SINCE 1991

In order to overcome the BOP crisis as also to strengthen India's external sector various structural reforms and stabilisation measures have been undertaken by the GOI since July 1991. These are now briefly discussed.

1. Devaluation of rupee and related measures

For promoting exports and curtailing imports the rupee was devalued in terms of trade-weighted basket of five foreign currencies twice within a week's time in July 1991 on an average by 22.8%. However, the devaluation was followed by withdrawal of an important type of export subsidy, viz., cash compensatory support.

However, devaluation made imports costlier. This is why appropriate monetary and fiscal policies were adopted to check cost-push inflation, which could otherwise destabilise the economy.

2. Opening up the economy and reduction in import duties

In the context of globalisation (or external liberalisation) the Indian economy has been opened up. It may be noted that economic openness is measured by the percentage of exports and imports in GDP. The higher is the combined percentage, the greater is the degree of economic openness. And to achieve greater economic openess various trade liberalisation measures have been adopted. Firstly, the import-substitution strategy has been replaced by export-promotion strategy which was essentially an export-led growth strategy. To make the new strategy effective, customs duties on non-agricultural imports have been drastically cut so as to enable export-oriented industries to import raw materials and capital goods at low costs and thus produce exportable items at low (or internationally competitive) prices. In fact, the peak import tariff rate was lowered from 300% in 1990-91 to a modest 12.5% in 2006-07. This measure was supposed to serve at least three purposes, viz., (i) checking cost-push inflation which occurred due to devaluation of the rupee, (ii) reducing prices of exportable goods having a large import content (i.e., the production of which required a large quantity of imported raw materials and capital goods) and (iii) exposing Indian industries to foreign competition (for increasing the competitiveness of Indian exports).

3. Financial assistance from the IMF

In order to tide over the crisis situation, India had to obtain financial assistance from IMF by fulfilling certain stringent conditions such as devaluation of the rupee, liberalisation of imports by lowering import duties, introduction of several structural reforms through the announcement and implementation of various domestic liberalisation measures and opening up of the economy to foreign trade and investment. These measures were very effective and helped to restore the confidence of the foreign and domestic investors and hence enable India to tackle the BOP problem.

4. Cut in fiscal deficit

For achieving macroeconomic stabilisation the fiscal deficit of the GOI was reduced from 8.5% of GDP in 1987-88 to 4.7% in 1991-92. This was sought to be achieved in two ways: (i) by curtailing unnecessary expenditure and (ii) by introducing tax reforms. However, fiscal deficit initially increased to 6.4% in 1993-94, and was subsequently brought down to 4% in 1995-96 and 2.5% in 2007-08. The reduction of fiscal deficit led to a fall in aggregate demand which helped in reducing the rate of price inflation. And a lower rate of inflation led to an increase in exports and a fall in imports. In addition, a reduction in fiscal deficit created less need for external borrowing. This, in its turn, helped to lower the debt-service burden (i.e., measured by the amount of interest payable on external debt along with a certain portion of the principal amount) over a number of years.

However, in 2008-09 and 2009-10 the GOI adopted a package of fiscal measures to initially prevent economic slowdown and to stimulate the economy thereafter. Consequently fiscal deficit increased to 6% in 2008-09 and to 6.3% in 2009-10.

5. Changeover to market-driven exchange rate

The GOI, in its bid to tackle the BOP problem, abandoned the age-old fixed exchange rate system and allowed the exchange rate, i.e., the external value of the rupee in terms of dollar (and, of course, other key currencies) to be determined by the market forces of demand and supply (in the absence of any Government intervention in the foreign exchange market except in crisis situations). The rupee was also made convertible on current account, i.e., for carrying out all transactions relating to exports and imports of goods (visible items) and services (invisible items).

At present the RBI intervenes in the foreign exchange market just to prevent large fluctuations in the exchange rate. This is done by selling or buying dollars as the situation demands.

6. Elimination of the anti-export bias

Due to lowering import duties through the new liberalisation trade policy, the GOI virtually abandoned the policy of protecting inefficient (high-cost) industries from foreign competition. This measure was taken to enhance efficiency and productivity of Indian industries which so long operated in a sheltered market (or under the tariff wall). The lowering of import duties also removed the anti-export bias of India's trade policy and enabled India's export-oriented industries to acquire imported inputs (such as capital goods and raw materials) at low costs so as to be able to charge low prices for their products and compete effectively in export markets.

7. Liberalisation of foreign investment policy

Another notable reform in the external sector relates to foreign investment policy. [This is discussed in Chapter 34.]

8. Replacement of FERA by FEMA

The Foreign Exchange Regulation Act (FERA) was replaced by the Foreign Exchange Management Act (FEMA). Two main aims of FEMA are (1) to facilitate foreign trade and payments (i.e., transactions involving foreign exchange), and (2) to facilitate orderly functioning of the foreign exchange market.

The main provisions of the FEMA are the following:

(i) *Holding of real assets* : A resident of India can hold, own, transfer or invest in any foreign currency, any foreign security or any other immovable property situated outside India provided, of course, these were acquired, held or owned by him (her) when he (she) was a non-resident Indian.

(ii) *Holding of financial assets* : A non-resident Indian can now hold shares, securities and properties acquired by him while he was resident of India. A non-resident Indian is also permitted to hold such properties which have been inherited by him from a resident Indian.

(iii) *Transactions on current account* : Any Indian can sell foreign exchange to an authorised person (dealer) and draw it from such a person for any transaction in the current account without obtaining the permission of RBI. However, the Government is always at liberty to impose certain restrictions on such transactions, of course, in consultation with the RBI.

(iv) *Transactions on capital account* : A person can sell or draw foreign exchange to or from an authorised person for carrying out capital account transactions subject to a certain limit. However, the RBI has been empowered to regulate such transactions.

(v) *Furnishing details to RBI* : Every exporter of goods and services will have to give details regarding the value of exports of both goods and services to the RBI. He has also to realise and repatriate export proceeds within a stipulated period of time and in a manner as prescribed by the RBI.

(vi) *Foreign business and academic trips* : Indian residents going abroad for business purposes or for participating in conferences and seminars are not required to obtain the permission of the RBI to get necessary foreign exchange upto $25,000 per trip irrespective of the duration of stay.

(vii) Gifts and donations : The prescribed limit for making certain specified types of gifts and donations have been raised upto $5,000 in each case.

(viii) *EEFC and RFC accounts* : Transactions through the Exchange Earners' Foreign Currency (EEFC) accounts have been made simple. Holders of such accounts are now free to use the funds held in such accounts to carry out all permissible current account transactions. Similarly, holders of the

Residents' Foreign Currency (RFC) accounts are now free to use the funds held in such accounts for carrying out all permissible current account transactions and clearing other dues arising therefrom.

(ix) *GDR and ADR issues* : Indian firms of good market standing have been permitted, subject to government approval, to issue equity shares and convertible bonds through global depository receipts (GDRs) and American depository receipts (ADRs) in European and US capital markets, respectively up to prescribed limits.

(x) *Violation and penalties* : FEMA differs from FERA in respect of penalties and prosecutions in case of non-compliance of the Act. Under the FEMA, the recipient of illegal (laundered/hawala) money is to be made culpable, not the sender. Furthermore, the violators of FEMA would not be treated as criminals but just as civil offenders. They can be fined but cannot be imprisioned. The violation of FEMA provisions would attract monetary penalties amounting to a maximum of 3 times the sum involved. In addition, if an offender fails to pay the penalty, the Enforcement Directorate(ED) could move court, which could send him to jail. Finally, search and seizures can be conducted only if the ED has strong suspicions (or sufficient reason to believe) that the offender will not show up when summoned.

An Overall Evaluation of the Act

The provisions of FEMA have relaxed the conditions relating to dealings in foreign exchange to a large extent. This was exactly what was needed in the context of the changed economic environment created by the opening up of the economy in terms of exports, imports and inflows of foreign investment (both FDI and FPI). This Act has promoted India's exports, indirectly though and eased the process of procurement of imported raw materials and capital goods required for industrial production. It is largely due to FEMA that foreign institutional investors have put their funds in equity shares and debt instruments on a massive scale. This led to a boom in the Indian capital market up to Sep. 2008 when the global financial crisis hit the Indian economy.

The Success of External Sectors Reforms

External sector reform measures improved the performance of India's crisis-ridden economy and brought a number of benefits. Exports grew by 20.8% in 1995-96. After falling steadily in the next few years due to global slowdown, the growth rate again picked up and attained 21% and 20.3% in 2000-01 and 2002-03, respectively. And the high rate of growth of exports was maintained in the next three years (2003-06). In addition due to liberalisation of capital flows NRI deposits increased steadily from $1.5 billion in 1990-91 to $4.3 billion in 2006-07. However, such deposits were quite small in 2007-08 but rose to $9.3 billion in 2008-09. In the next two years these were $2.9 billion and $3.18 billion, respectively. Such deposits fell due to global slowdown, which led to withdrawal of funds from India, more so due to depreciation of the rupee.

CHAPTER 34

Foreign Investment and Multinational Corporations (MNCs)

> *It is not possible to buy development so cheaply. The provision of foreign capital may yield a more adequate infrastructure but rarely by itself generates rapid development unless there are already large investment opportunities going abegging.*
>
> A. C. Cairncross

PREVIEW

In the immediate post Second World War period (1939-45) the developed countries started making serious and concerted effort to achieve faster economic growth for creating more employment opportunities, and alleviating poverty. In addition, the period witnessed a steady growth of multilateral trade. However, developing countries like India faced the problem of capital scarcity more so in view of the fact that many of them, which were colonies for a long period, achieved independence and adopted the planning system to promote faster economic growth and rapid economic development. Their investment needs far exceeded their capacity to save. And to bridge the domestic saving-investment gap they invited foreign capital. As a result capital flows from the developed countries to the developing ones increased substantially in the past two decades (1992-2013), which coincided with the period of economic reforms and structural adjustment in India and other developing countries.

In the 1940s and early 1950s capital flows from the governments of developed countries to those of developing ones were mainly in the form of official development assistance or foreign aid. Developing countries also received funds from the international financial institutions such as the IMF and the World Bank. These two institutions provided loans only to the government.[1] In the last two decades foreign aid or official development assistance on government-to-government basis has virtually dried up. At the same time, it has become very difficult for developing countries to obtain funds from the IMF and the World Bank because both the institutions have imposed certain strict conditions on developing countries. For instance, only those countries which undertake certain specified structural

1. However, the International Development Association (IDA), the soft loan window of the Bank, also provided loans to the private sector, subject, of course, to guarantee given by the government of the country.

adjustment programmes and adopt economic reform measures are now eligible for obtaining concessional finance from these two institutions. In addition, the capital needs of the developing countries are so huge that the international financial institutions cannot alone fully meet their helds. So there is need for sufficient capital flows from private sources. Such capital flows have increased substantially in the past two to three decades.

Private capital flows are of the two types, viz., (i) international portfolio investment (IPI) and (ii) foreign direct investment (FDI).

We may now discuss briefly the nature of these types of private capital flows.

A. INTERNATIONAL PORTFOLIO INVESTMENT (IPI)

At present, IPI is the most important and the main form of private capital flow to developing countries like India. Such capital comes from foreign institutions such as banks, insurance companies, investment companies such as mutual funds and pensian funds which purchase stocks and shares of Indian companies in the secondary markets (i.e., stock markets). There are both advantages and disadvantages of such capital. These institutional investors get annual dividends. They also make capital gains under favourable conditions. But they do no directly exercise any managerial control over the companies in which they invest their capital. Due to the reduction or even removal of various types of restrictions on inflows of foreign equity capital by developing countries like India as also the adoption of the policy of economic liberalisation in such countries, flows of foreign portfolio capital in such countries has continued to increase of late. And foreign institutional investors have diversified their asset portfolio for reducing risk. And such capital has come to India in larger and larger amounts during the first two decades of economic reform (1991-2011).

Advantages

There are three main advantages of IPI. And these are the following:

(i) ***Higher return and lower risk*** **:** Investment in the stock markets of the developing countries enables the savers of developed countries to obtain higher returns on their financial capital as also to reduce risk through portfolio diversification.[1]

(ii) ***Supplying capital to domestic firms*** **:** In developing countries, international portfolio capital enables private companies to raise the much needed financial capital.

(iii) ***Increasing the flow of foreign exchange*** **:** Finally IPI brings the much needed foreign exchange in developing countries. This is very important at least in the early stages of economic development.

Disadvantages

The disadvantages of IPI are the following:

(i) ***Distabilishing effect*** **:** IPI has serious distabilishing effect on both the financial markets and on the entire macroeconomy of the developing countries. When the developing countries face troubles, there occurs net outflow of portfolio capital within a few days. This is exactly what happened in Mexico in 1994-95 and in Thailand in 1997-98. In fact the Thai currency crisis spread to the neighbouring countries through *financial contagion*. This refers to the fact that any sudden financial crisis in one country quickly gets transmitted to other countries due to faster mobility of capital and greater integration of world's financial markets.

(ii) ***Uncertainty*** **:** There is uncertainty regarding steady flow of portfolio capital in developing countries. Such capital flows are very volatile in nature and create serious problems in case of loss of confidence when funds are withdrawn. So developing countries cannot rely much on inflows of such capital for achieving faster growth or stepping up their developmental efforts.

---

1. After the Mexican currency crisis of 1994 there was net capital outflows from developing countries for a short period.

(iii) ***No real investments in the true sense*** **:** IPI does not result directly in 'real' investment in developing countries. Of course, it can help to increase the flow of financial capital which can be converted into real capital.

(iv) ***No role in bringing about desirable changes*** **:** No doubt IPI brings the much needed foreign exchange. But it should not be treated as a vehicle for achieving certain desirable macroeconomic goals such as maintaining exchange rate stability, removing deficits in the balance of payments (BOP), controlling price inflation and adopting an appropriate monetary policy which should maintain fairly high interest rates.

Comments

What developing countries truly need is the real capital such as plants, equipment, and machinery as also economic and social infrastructure and not equity fund (which is speculative in nature). Thus if developing countries are to ensure steady flow of portfolio capital on a sustained or a continuous basis, they will have to manage their exchange rates efficiently. This can be done by reducing current accounting deficit as also by keeping adequate foreign exchange reserves. Otherwise their currencies will remain overvalued. This is likely to lead to various adverse consequences in the long run.

B. FOREIGN DIRECT INVESTMENT (FDI)

Foreign direct investment (FDI) refers to real investment, i.e., investment in the construction of physical capital such as building private factories, socio-economic overheads and physical infrastructure (i.e., roads, highways, power plants, ports, telecommunication facilities, etc.) in the capital importing country. FDI comes in the following ways:

(i) ***Setting up of branches*** **:** An existing corporation can spread its business by setting up its branches in another country. For example, the Toyota Company of Japan has set up its branches in various other countries. Similarly, many foreign companies such as Nestle, McDonalds, Burger King, and KFC, etc. have set up their branches in India and produced various items such as chocolates and fast food.

(ii) ***Forming companies*** **:** Foreign firms can form companies and register them in a capital-receiving (host) country such as India without having any connection with the capital-investing (home) country. This is done by a foreign company primarily for avoiding high import tariffs charged by India. Another reason, of course, is to take advantage of various concessions offered by the GOI to national firms.[1]

(iii) ***Joint venture*** **:** Many foreign firms have set up industrial enterprises in collaboration with Indian firms such as the Hindustan Uniliver Ltd., or the Maruti Suzuki Ltd. This type of foreign investment offers a number of special advantages. These are the following:

(a) The long-standing reputation of foreign firms generates confidence in domestic entrepreneurs who become eager to invest funds in concerns with foreign partners. (b) Due to long experience and use of efficient techniques by foreign firms entrepreneurs of developing countries get wide opportunities for developing local skills. (c) In addition, a large proportion of profits is retained in a developing country. The foreign investor is also free from any discriminatory treatment by the government of the developing country.

Advantages of FDI

FDI, which comes through multinational corporation (MNCs), offer the following advantages to developing countries:

1. ***No fixed burden*** **:** FDI does not involve any fixed interest payment. Foreigners are rewarded in the form of profits. It does not involve rigid interest and amortisation requirements associated with external public debt (i.e., borrowing by a government from other countries).

2. ***Efficient utilisation of capital*** **:** Due to the inherent profit motive capital — both financial and physical — are most efficiently utilised.

1. Indian match industry is dominated by foreign (Swidish) firms, which are essentially old firms in new dress.

3. *Transfer of technology* : FDI is a vehicle for the transfer of technology in developing countries. FDI brings with it modern technology, improved skills and new ideas (which can be fruitfully utilised for product and process innovations). Thus FDI acts as an instrument for transferring modern technology to developing countries which are technologically backward and dependent on foreign countries.

4. *Ploughing back of profits* : A part of the profits of MNCs is ploughed back into business either for modernisation or expansion of existing firms or for diversification (i.e., establishing ancillary or subsidiary concerns in both related and unrelated fields). This gives developing countries a long-term (or sustainable) advantage.

5. *Favourable effect on the balance of payments* : FDI is likely to flow largely into export-oriented industries. By raising exports and reducing imports, it is likely to improve the balance of payments position of the developing countries. This is more so in times of recession when domestic sales fall. At the same time MNCs are guided by the profit motive since dividends paid to FDI is related to actual profits made.

6. *Activation of domestic investment* : FDI as a driving force behind domestic investment either in the form of joint ventures or in local ancillary industries. Thus FDI induces domestic entrepreneurs to overcome their shyness and venture out in new directions. In other words, FDI converts potential investment (idle capital) into actual investment (active capital).

7. *Creation of additional production capacity* : FDI makes a genuine addition to the productive capacity of the capital-importing country. Thus it acts as a growth-promoting factor by expanding a developing country's productive capacity and thus by enabling it to step up its developmental effort.

8. *Infrastructure building* : Most developing countries suffer from infrastructural deficiency. So MNCs can be given necessary inducement to invest in infrastructure such as power plants, telecom. facilities, setting up of new sea ports and airports. Infrastructural building by the MNCs enables developing countries to overcome supply-side bottlenecks and these induce domestic investors to venture out in new directions. MNCs have the financial resources, technology and technical know-how about how to participate in infrastructural building either solely or with local partners. For these reasons the GOI has been wooing MNCs to invest in the infrastructure sector.

9. *No distabilising effect on the economy* : It is very difficult to close down foreign concerns set up with FDI. FDI enters developing countries to set up factories. When foreigners decide to close such factories, these are purchased by local entrepreneurs. So even when foreigners exert an exit option, there is no destablising effect on the domestic economy.

Disadvantages

FDI is often criticised on the ground that it seeks to establish financial oligarchy or even imperialism. This is an unproved and probably a false belief. However, due to their strong economic power they enjoy political power also. They influence the government of developing countries as also the influential leaders of such countries[1] in order to enjoy various unfair advantages.

In order to encourage greater flow of FDI it is necessary for developing countries to assure higher returns and minimum risk of foreigners.

REFORMS IN INDIA'S FOREIGN INVESTMENT POLICY

Since the adoption of various economic reform measures in India from July 1991, both IPI and FDI increased steadily. The following measures have been adopted by GOI to encourage the inflows bothy types of capital:

1. *Greater equity participation* : FDI up to 51% of the equity share of are MNC is now allowed in 34 high priority industries through the automatic approval system. In addition, 100% equity holding is permitted in case of a production unit which is wholly export-oriented, i.e., which exports its entire output.

1. In this context mention may be made of the Bofors case of the 1980s as also the Lockheed scandal of the 1970s.

2. ***Automatic approval of infrastructure projects*** **:** Under the automatic approval route, 100% equity participation is permitted in case of certain infrastructure projects such as construction of roads, highways, ports and harbour and vehicular tunnels and bridges up to an upper limit of Rs 1,500 crores. In case of 100% equity participation in projects involving generation, transmission and distribution of electricity, the upper limit no longer holds.

3. ***Additional concessions for SEZs*** **:** FDI under automatic approval route has been allowed up to 100% for all manufacturing activities in Special Economic Zones (SEZs), except in certain specified activities.

4. ***Provisions for other sectors*** **:** FDI upto 100% in e-commerce, oil refining and drugs and pharmaceuticals, 49% in telecommunications, 50% in mining, 50% in hotels and tourism has been permitted.

5. ***Financial sectors*** **:** A large segment of the financial sector, which involves banking and insurance, has been opened up to FDI. This is why many foreign banks and insurance companies have opened branches in India. Some banks are reported to have even invested in other private banks.

6. ***Buying equity shares and debt securities*** **:** The registered foreign institutional investors (FIIs) have been permitted to buy equity shares and debt securities (such as bonds and debentures) directly from the Indian capital market.

7. ***Issue of equity shares and convertible bonds by Indian companies*** **:** Finally, Indian firms having good market standing and strong reputation have been permitted, subject to approval by the GOI, to issue equity shares and convertible bonds through Global Depository Receipts (GDRs) and American Depository Receipts (ADRs), respectively in the European and American markets. Of late, the GOI has permitted retail foreign investment in single foreign brands.

Thus the GOI followed a policy of economic liberalisation toward foreign capital. However, much remains to be done for improving India's investment climate. The adoption of the following measures may be suggested in this context:

1. Signing double taxation relief arguments with countries from which FDI is flowing.
2. Adopting friendly attitude toward foreign investors and not treating them as aliens.
3. Ensuring internal political stability.
4. Strongly defending the country from foreign aggression[1].
5. Giving adequate opportunity to MNCs to make profits.
6. Providing adequate facilities for the remittances of profits, dividends, interest and technical consultancy fees.
7. Removal of restrictions on the immigration of foreign technicians and engineers.
8. Giving permissions to MNCs to employ persons of their own choice and requirement.
9. Adopting no discriminatory measures against foreign firms in respect of corporate taxes and excise duties.
10. Giving adequate protection of private property rights.
11. Ensuring security of life.
12. Guaranteeing prompt payment of fair compensation and its remittance to the home country in the event of sudden nationalisation of a foreign firm in the host country.

FOREIGN DIRECT INVESTMENT FLOWS IN INDIA DURING THE REFORM PERIOD

Since the adoption of various reform measures and liberalisation of the policy towards foreign capital by the GOI since July 1991, inflows of FDI gently increased. The vast increase in investment by MNCs during the two decades of economic reforms was largely due to (1) the adoption of a new

1. After all, defence is no less important than opulence.

liberalised industrial policy which assigns a more crucial and strategic role of the private sector and (2) opening of the economy so as to permit greater flows of foreign trade and foreign investment. However, IPI increased much faster than FDI.

Table 34.1 shows gross foreign investment flows in India — both direct investment and portfolio investment — during the period of economic reforms.

Table 34.1: Gross Foreign Investment Inflows (Category-Wise)

	2011-12	2010-11	2009-10	2008-09
			U.S. $ Mn.	
Direct Investment*	**32,955**	**27,829**	**33,108**	**41,707**
SIA/FIPB	3,046	1,945	3,471	5,400
RBI	20,427	12,994	18,987	21,332
Acquisition of shares @	11,360	6,437	3,148	4,632
Portfolio Investment	**17,171**	**30,292**	**32,396**	**–14,032**
GDRs/ADRs+	597	2,049	3,328	1,162
FIIs#	16,813	29,422	29,048	–15,0117
Others	–	–	–	–
Total ....**	**39,177**	**41,597**	**50,361**	**8,311**

Note: Figures for 2009-10 onwards are provisional.

* Including acquisition of shares, equity capital of unincorporated bodies, reinvested earnings and inter-corporate debt.

@ Relates to acquisition of shares of Indian companies by non-resident Indians (NRIs).

\+ Represents the amount raised by Indian corporates through Global Depository Receipts (GDRs) and American Depository Receipts (ADRs).

\# Represents net inflow of funds by FIIs.

** Net of outward FDI.

Source: *Statistical Outline of India* (2012-13)

Table 34.2 shows country-wise FDI inflows in India.

Table 34.2: Country-Wise FDI Inflows in India

	2011-12*	2010-11*	2009-10*	2008-09	2007-08
			U.S.$Mn.		
Mauritius	8,142	5,616	9,801	10,165	9,518
U.S.A	994	1,071	2,212	1,236	950
Japan	2,089	1,256	971	266	457
Germany	368	163	602	611	486
U.K.	2,760	538	643	690	508
Netherlands	1,289	1,417	804	682	601
Total (including others)	**23,473**	**14,939**	**22,461**	**22,697**	**19,425**

Note: Excluding NRI direct investment routed through RBI since 1994-95

* Provisional

Source: *Statistical Outline of India* (2012-13)

Table 34.3 gives details of industry-wise FDI inflows in India.

Table 34.3: Details of FDI Flows in India (Industry-Wise)

	2011-12*	2010-11*	2009-10*
	U.S. $ Mn.		
Mining	204	592	268
Manufacturing	9,337	4,793	5,143
Electricity	1,395	1,338	1,877
Construction	2,634	1,599	3,516
Hotels & Restaurants	870	218	671
Transport	410	344	220
Financing, Insurance	2,603	1,353	2,206
Real Estate	340	444	2,191
Computer Services	736	843	866
Educational Services	103	56	91
Retail & Wholesale Trade	567	391	536
Communication Services	1,458	1,228	1,852
Business Services	1,554	569	1,590
Total (Incl. others)	**23,473**	**14,939**	**22,461**

Note: Data in table exclude FDI inflows by way of acquisition of shares by non-residents.
* Provisional

Source: SOI

Table 34.4 makes an international comparison of FDI flows for two years 2009 and 2010.

Table 34.4: An International Comparison of FDI Flows in India

	FDI Inflows		FDI Outflows	
	2010	2009	2010	2009
	U.S. $ Bn.			
World	**1,243.7**	**1,185.0**	**1,323.3**	**1,170.5**
Developed countries	**601.9**	**602.8**	**935.2**	**851.0**
Developing countries	**573.6**	**510.6**	**327.6**	**270.8**
Of which:				
India	**24.6**	**35.6**	**14.6**	**15.9**
China	105.7	95.0	68.0	56.5
Argentina	6.3	4.0	1.0	0.7
Mexico	18.7	15.3	14.3	7.0
Korea, Rep.	6.9	7.5	19.2	17.2
Chile	15.1	12.9	8.7	8.1
Malaysia	9.1	1.4	13.3	7.9
Indonesia	13.3	4.9	2.7	2.2
Venezuela	–1.4	–3.1	2.4	1.8
Hungary	2.4	2.0	1.5	2.7
Egypt	6.4	6.7	1.2	0.6
Colombia	6.8	7.1	6.5	3.1
Nigeria	6.1	8.7	0.9	1.5
Turkey	9.1	8.4	1.8	1.6
Philippines	1.7	2.0	0.5	0.4
Pakistan	2.0	2.3	0.05	0.07

Note: Year are calendar years, not financial years

Source: SOI

We have already noted that foreign capital is of two types — IPI and FDI. The former can have two sub-components: (i) foreign institutional investment (FII) and (ii) euro equities and others.

The Pattern of Foreign Investment

Although in recent years that flows of FDI have decreased to some extent (mainly because other countries are giving more attractive incentives to foreign investors), the flow of IPI in India has increased steadily. For various reasons India is rated higher than China, the Philippines, South Korea, Indonesia, Cambodia, Peru, Greece and Hungary by most fund managers.

Table 34.3 shows sectoral allocation of FDI in India. In 2011-12, the maximum FDI flows occurred in manufacturing (US $ 9.33 million), followed by construction financing and insurance (US $ 2,603) million) and insurance (US $ 2,634 million), business services (US $ 1,554 million) and computer services (US $ 1,736 million).

From Table 34.4 we see that there has occurred a huge increase in foreign investment flows in India. It is gratifying to note that due to sustained economic growth, India has become a favourable destination for private foreign investors. Foreign investors are attracted by one of the world's longest market for manufactured goods and services. Due to widening of the market for industrial goods, India now offers a high return on foreign investment.

We have already noted that the procedures for sanctioning FDI have been greatly simplified. The huge increase in FDI inflows in India in recent years is also attributable to improved investment climate and further opening of telecom., single brand retail and several other sectors such as real estate, petroleum refining, commodity exchanges, mining and civil aviation[1]. This is why outflows of FDI from India have also increased. So net FDI was lower than what it could have been otherwise.

Inflows of FDI in India have been much lower than those in China, as Table 34.4 shows. Past policies of GOI such as scrapping of the Enron Power Generation Project by the GOI are largely responsible for this. After suffering a setback in the late 1980s and early 1990s, inflows of foreign investment again picked up.

It is to be noted that some state governments are reviewing their earlier decisions and permitting MNCs to enter the power sector in a big way This is no doubt an encouraging trend.

Upto 2007 India's booming stock market gave a fillip to FDI inflows. Foreign equity investors mainly ventured in Information Technology and IT-enabled Services (IT and ITES), followed by HDFC, banking, financial services and insurance sectors.

It is expected that in the coming years most of the FDI will be made in infrastructure projects. This is likely to lead to faster growth of the Indian economy.

INDIA'S ENVIRONMENT

India offers certain special advantages to foreign investors, such as its vast domestic market for industrial goods, low wages and low cost of inputs, availability of skilled managers, easy repatriation facilities and a strong legal framework. All these have enabled India to steal a march over its rivals. If these features are supported by a stable macroeconomic environment, India will be able to attract more and more FDI.

However the global financial crisis of 2007-08 has created liquidity crunch in the US and European countries and this is likely to obstruct the flows of FDI into India now as also in the future.

It is felt that there is also need for adopting a holistic approach to attract more foreign capital. Regional disparities in attracting foreign capital have also to be taken care of.

The Role of Multinational Corporations

The multinational corporations (MNCs) are large international firms which have headquarters (or decision-making centres) in one country but branch offices as also production and distribution centers

1. Foreign investment up to 49% has been permitted in construction of new airports.

in various countries of the world. In this context we may draw a distinction between MNCs and transnational corporations. Any company operating in various other countries is called a transnational corporation. But an MNC is one which has FDI in other countries. MNCs own, control and manage their enterprises located in foreign countries.

Economic Insight: The Concept of MNC
A multinational firm is one which exercises managerial control over operations in more than one national market. A corporation, headquartered in one nation, holds managerial control over foreign branch operations or wholly owned (or even majority-owned) subsidiaries. An MNC refers to any firm which controls operations in a nation other than that which constitutes the firm's principal market, even if these operations are very small relative to its domestic operations. An MNC is a large firm for which non-domestic operations account for some significant portion of its total revenue.

Most US and Japanese firms are multinationals and they undertake diversified business activities. Ford, for example, produces motor cars, not only in the USA but also in Western Europe and Japan. This is true of Sony, National, Mitsubishi and Toyota.

As noted earlier, FDI flows occur through the MNCs and an MNC also act as a vehicle for the transfer of technology across national borders.

The Rationale of International Business: Worldwide Sourcing

It may be noted at the outset that a company goes international for world-wide sourcing. It seeks to buy cheap raw materials from other countries and to take advantage of low wages so as to achieve efficiency in production and gain competitive advantage by reducing cost and prices of its products through mass production. It also seeks to sell its products in wider international markets. The reason is that the size of domestic market is limited and it reaches the saturation point sooner or later.

Foreign direct investment (FDI) occurs through the MNCs. Firms become multinational by making FDI. FDI is the private capital flows resulting from an investor (usually a firm) in one nation gaining control of a firm in some other nation *via* acquisition or setting up of a separate establishment. And MNCs supply the much needed financial capital to developing countries where the return on such capital is higher than that in developed countries. And financial capital has always an extra temptation to go abroad in search of higher returns.

MNCs also develop production facilities in developing countries like India through international sub-contracting. For example, an MNC may buy raw cotton from India, produce textiles in Korea where the wage rate is low and sell finished textiles in the USA and European countries.

MNCs also operate in developing countries since environmental standards are not strictly enforced in such countries. The law enforcement authorities are weak.

Finally, MNCs try to avoid payment of high excise duties and import tariffs which prevail in developing countries. Rather than exporting a good to India from Japan, a Japanese firm can set up production units in India and thus escape all trade taxes.

A related point may also be noted in this context. The key word in multinational business is 'efficiency'. MNCs operate efficiently by internalising their production and distribution activities rather than contracting them out to other firms. Judicious management of a firm involves deciding which activities (associated with production and distribution of goods and services) it will perform internally and which ones it will contract out to other firms. This issue has assumed greater significance due to the emergence of a new business practice of late, viz., business process outsourcing.

The greater the economies of 'internalising' economic activities within an organisation, the larger the span of the organisation. When economies of internalisation of international activities are significant relative to use of the market mechanisms (e.g., licensing or exporting) the firm will become multinational.

Alternative Channels of FDI

In order to improve their profitability MNCs go for both types of integration — horizontal and vertical. This calls for judicious management of such firms. And management of an international firm is much more difficult and complex than that of a domestic firm. In addition, since such firms operate in various countries they have to control and manage their assets properly so as to be able to achieve growth and diversification. There are four methods of overseas operation by an MNC. These are the following:

1. Sales Agreement with Domestic (Local) Firms

This is the simplest way for an MNC to operate in another country. An MNC can enter into an agreement with local firms for selling its products in various countries. For example, an Indian firm may be given the franchise to sell its product both in India and abroad. In this case the Indian firm is able to control all aspects of its sales operations in certain specified territories such as Nepal, Bangladesh, Sikkim and Bhutan. An American MNC normally finds it difficult to conduct its sales operations in each small developing country from its headquarter.

2. Setting Up a Wholly-Owned Subsidiary

Alternatively an MNC can set up a wholly (1956) owned subsidiary in a foreign country such as India as per the Companies Act. The subsidiary derives the benefit of strong financial resources, long-standing international reputation and superior managerial skills of the parent company. In this case the MNC retains its complete control over its entire business — from production to distribution. However, the subsidiary enjoys some degree of freedom.

3. Setting Up Branches

MNCs can also set up branches in foreign countries. Such branches do not have any separate legal status. Instead they are directly linked with the parent company. So they do not enjoy much freedom.

4. Foreign Collaboration and Joint Ventures

An MNC can set up joint venture in a foreign country either to produce its product jointly with a local partner and for selling its product both in the host country as also in third countries. For example, the Suzuki Company of Japan has entered into partnership with Maruti Udyog Ltd. for production and sale of cars both in India and in other countries. Sometimes an MNC can enter into collaboration with foreign local firms to acquire raw materials which are not available in the home country.

In most cases, MNCs set up joint ventures with foreign firms to manufacture input components or sub-assemblies to produce the final product in the home country. For example, an American company can produce steel in India by using India's iron ore and then use the finished steel to manufacture cars or refrigerators in the USA. This strategy is followed to reduce production cost.

ALTERNATIVE FORMS OF INTERNATIONAL BUSINESS

No doubt business has been conducted on an international scale for a long time. But such business became more and more visible and assumed more and more importance due to the growth of large multinational corporations. The international businesses involves transactions across national borders and include the transfer of goods, services, technology, managerial knowledge, skill and financial capital to other countries — both developed and developing or from the home (parent) country to host country.

Global firms like Boeing, Ford, or IMB have large multinational accounts. However, getting started globally is often a matter of (i) being determined and (ii) taking risks.

The interaction of a global firm with the host country can take seven different forms as shown in Table 34.5. Thus in developing (and evolving) a global strategy an international firm enjoys several options. These are the following:

Table 34.5: Seven Main Forms of International Business

Types of Business	Nature of Transfer from Home Country to Host Country
1. Exporting	Both goods and services
2. Licensing agreement	Primary technical know-how
3. Managerial contracts	Management and technical know-how
4. Joint ventures and strategic alliances	Materials, services and personnel
5. Wholly-owned subsidiaries	Capital and know-how
6. International franchising	Business concept with corresponding operational guidelines to non-domestic parties for a fee
7. Wholly-owned ventures (a) Greenfield investment (b) Acquisition or merger	 Investment in a completely new facility with an already established local firm

1. Exporting

Exporting refers to the action by the global firm to send produced goods and services from the home country to other countries. Exporting does not require much resources. So it is less costly than setting up joint ventures. Moreover, it is also easier for the multinational firm to withdraw its operations with least damage. However, there is one major disadvantage of exporting strategy. Due to the physical distance, the multinational firm is not able to control its overseas operations.

2. Licensing

International licensing is the transfer of patented information and trademarks, information and know-how, including specifications, written documents, computer programmes and so forth, as well as information needed to sell a product or service, with respect to a physical territory.

There are two main benefits of licensing:

(i) ***Speed***: Licensing enables a firm, which lacks sufficient skills, capital or personnel to enter a foreign market quickly.

(ii) ***A step toward a joint venture:*** Licensing may also be used as a step towards a more committed mode of entry such as a join venture or a wholly-owned firm.

3. Management Contracts

A global firm may also engaged in management contracts for operating foreign companies. This method of conducting international business is on the rise now mainly due to various restrictions on FDI by developing countries.

4. Joint Venture and Strategic Alliance

Joint venture is a method of interaction of a global firm with a firm in the host country. One form of joint venture is the strategic alliance which is often formed in order to achieve geographical expansion of business. This is usually done by airlines and quite extensively at that.

Strategic alliance refers to strategic cooperative agreement or agreements, between two or more firms, to pursue a set of agreed upon strategic goals while remaining independent organisations. An *international strategic alliance* involves organisations from at least two different countries and has the following three characteristics:

(i) *Cooperative:* It is a partnership agreement between two or more firms, which remain independent organisations.

(ii) *Strategic:* It is a response to strategic challenges or opportunities that the partner firms face.

(iii) *International:* It is agreement between firms from at least two different countries.

Focus on Terminology: International Strategic Alliance
A strategic alliance is strategic cooperative agreement or agreements between two or more firms to persue a set of agreed upon strategic goals while remaining independent organisations. It is international when it involves organisation form at least two different countries.

5. Wholly-Owned Subsidiaries

Multinational coorporation may also set up wholly-owned subsidiaries or branches with production facilities in the host country.

6. International Franchising

International franchising is essentially a contract-based organisational structure for entering new markets. It involves a franchiser firm which undertakes to transfer a business concept that it has developed, with corresponding operational guidelines, to non-domestic parties for a fee. Franchisers are responsible for improving product/service mix, improving output quality and promoting the brand in the host country.

The franchising strategy has been increasingly and extensively deployed as a method of business expansion over the last four decades. For example MacDonalds has developed a successful international franchising network.

7. Wholly-Owned Ventures

In contrast to exporting, licensing and franchising, wholly-owned subsidiaries involve a high degree of risk. MNCs have two options: greenfield investment in a completely new facility, or acquisition of or merger with an already established local firm.

(a) The greenfield strategy

A greenfield strategy entails building an entirely new subsidiary in a foreign country from scratch to enable foreign sales and/or production.

In general, a greenfield investment signifies that the parent firm has decided to clone its strategy and structure in the foreign plant by transferring its technology, supply chain, organisational structure and corporate culture. Greenfield investments are usually preferred when specific technical and organisational skills define a firm's ability to compete.

(b) The mergers and acquisitions (M & As) strategy

An international merger is a transaction which combines two companies from different countries to establish a new legal entity. International acquisition refers to the acquisition of a local firm's assets by a foreign company. In an acquisition, both local and foreign firms may continue to exist.

It may be also be noted that for companies to go for acquisition rather than making a greenfield entry, the cost of constructing new facilities, installing equipment and hiring and training new labour force must exceed the costs of purchasing and recasting (renovating) existing properties.

---

1. This is exactly what happened in India during the British period. The establishment of modern manufacturing industries led to deindustrialisation in India, i.e., decline of handicrafts. As a result many artisans lost their traditional means of livelihood.

In the short run, cross-border M & As can have positive benefits for the shareholders of the acquired firm. In the long run, however, profit prospects are often limited or are even non-existent. In Table 34.6 we give a list of the world's leading MNCs, also known as international giants.

Table 34.6: Ten Largest Multinational Corporations in the World

Company	Country	Market Capitalisation (in $ billions)
1. Exxon Mobil	United States	406
2. Wal-Mart	United States	214
3. China Mobil	China	209
4. Industrial and Commercial Bank of China	China	183
5. General Electric	United States	178
6. Procter & Gamble	United States	177
7. Microsoft	United States	169
8. Volkswagen	Germany	168
9. Royal Dutch Shell	Netherlands	166
10. Petrochina	China	161

Source: *Business Week*, January 12, 2009

THE ROLE OF MNCs IN INDIAN ECONOMY

Since the announcement of the policy of economic liberalisation the GOI has recognised the importance of private foreign capital in India's economic growth. And since private foreign capital mainly comes through MNCs, they have been given wider opportunities to operate in the Indian economy subject to certain restrictions. The following are the main reasons for the adoption of the policy of liberalisation towards MNCs by the GOI:

1. *Bridging domestic saving-investment gap* : MNCs can close the gap between the need for investible resources and the supply of domestic savings in India, more so when official development assistance to India has been falling. It may be noted that foreign investment, much like domestic investment, has a multiplier effect on employment and income in India. For example, the selling up of Maruti Udyog Ltd., with investment of Japan Suzuki, has generated various types of multiplier effects in India. Apart from direct income and employment generation in the Maruti's plant many workers are employed by the company's dealers all over the India and abroad. Similarly, many small firms are now engaged in supplying various intermediate goods such as parts and components to the company. And many workers remain employed in such input-supplying firms.

2. *Non-debt creating capital flows* : By relying more and more on FDI through MNCs, a developing country like India can avoid its external debt servicing obligations. MNCs only repatriate a portion of their earning if and only if they make profits. Their operations in India do not involve any fixed interest obligations. Thus MNCs help to reduce strains and stresses on India's balance of payments.

3. *Transfer of technology* : MNCs usually transfer modern sophisticated technology to developing countries. This is so important for raising labour productivity and thus enabling developing countries like India to start new productive ventures which require the use of modern cost-effective technology. Along with physical capital (such as new machines) MNCs import skills and technical know-how needed to operate new machines and equipment. This enables Indian workers, technicians and engineers to learn the new art of production. In other words, by passing through a learning process Indians are able to use new superior technology developed in foreign countries. Thus MNCs can play a positive role in upgrading India's technology.

4. *Export promotion* : MNCs have strong worldwide links. In addition, they are able to reduce cost due to economies of scale and internal efficiency. So they can play an important role in raising exports of developing countries in which they invest. For instance, the Suzuki has made investment in India's Maruti Udyog Ltd. And Maruti cars are now sold not only domestically but exported in large numbers to other developing counties where there is high demand for small, fuel-efficient cars.

In fact, in its latest industrial policy (announced in July 1991) the GOI has declared that an MNC would be allowed to invest the India subject to the condition that it would export a certain portion of its product and earn foreign exchange for the country. This is a right step.

5. *Investment in infrastructure and crowding-in effect* : With their huge financial resources and enormous capacity to raise additional funds from both the Indian and the global financial markets MNCs make huge investment in infrastructure building. They can set up power plants, modernise airports and sea ports and improve telecommunication facilities which are of much importance to India for achieving faster industrial growth. This, in its turn, is likely to create income and employment in a labour-surplus country. Investment in infrastructure generates external economies as also linkage effects and will therefore crowd-in investment by domestic enterprises. This will stimulate overall economic growth.

For all these reasons the GOI has stressed the role of FDI in the Common Minimum Programme (CMP). The GOI will encourage FDI mainly in four areas, viz., (a) infrastructure, (b) high technology, (c) exports and (d) creation of domestic assets and employment opportunities on a large scale.

A Critical Review of MNCs

However, MNCs are not an unmixed blessing. Their operations in developing countries have created several problems, and generated tensions and anxieties both for the people of such countries as also the policy makers. The following are the main criticisms against the MNCs in developing countries like India.

1. *Deindustrialisation and joblessness* : It is alleged that with their vast resources and tremendous economic power MNCs capture the domestic markets of developing countries and establish virtual monopoly by driving small domestic firms out of business[1]. This is likely to lead to a fall in employment opportunities in India.

2. *Use of capital-intensive technicians in a labour-abundant country* : MNCs bring modern sophisticated technology when they invest in India. Such technology is capital-intensive in nature. As a result there is slow growth of employment opportunities in India's industrial economy. As A.P. Thirlwall has put it, "Perhaps the overriding factor that accounts for the relative capital intensity of the modern sector of developing countries is that many of the techniques of production are imported from abroad, with a heavy bias in the labour-saving direction."[2]

The labour-saving bias of the technology imported by the MNCs is to be explained by the labour-saving bias of technical progress in advanced countries where labour is relatively scarce and expensive.

3. *Last for conspicious consumption* : MNCs mainly produce non-essential items and luxury goods. These goods are mainly consumed by the upper strata of society. Examples of such goods consumed by the Indians elites are expensive cars (such as Honda City, Hyundai's Accent, Mercedes, Opel Astra, etc.), air-conditioners, washing machines, 32″ TV sets, costly refrigerators, etc. By generating

1. For instance, in 2004-05 and 2005-06 there was a huge inflow of capital in India through giant financial MNCs in India to take advantage of the higher interest rates prevailing at that time as also the booming Indian capital markets.
2. *Economics of Development* (9th edn., 2011), p. 247

international demonstration effect MNCs lure people in developing countries to consume such goods. And people in such countries have a tendency to emulate the consumption pattern of people in developed countries. Consumption of such goods leads to a wasteful expenditure and loss of potential saving of the community[1].

4. *Imports of outdated and obsolete technology* : Most MNCs import obsolete machines and outdated technology. Some of these are inappropriate to Indian conditions. Critics often allege that India has been made a dumping ground for obsolete technology. Such technology serves no useful purpose but puts a financial burden on India because payments are to be made for such technology whether used or not.

5. *Lack of adequate R&D efforts* : The MNCs do not make any investment on research & development (R&D) in India to develop indigenous technology which is suited to India's factor endowments. Instead, they make all investment on R&D at their headquarters.

6. *Capturing domestic markets* : MNCs make investment in developing countries such as India mainly for capturing domestic markets. They have very little interest in export promotion.

7. *Setting up of environmentally polluting industries* : In order to evade strict environmental control measures in their home countries, MNCs set up polluting industrial units in developing countries like India. Such units spell disasters for host countries. For instance, leakage of poisonous gas from the Union Carbide's Bhopal plant in 1984 killed thousands of people. Many others become handicapped due to serious ailments. In fact, with the tightening of environmental protection measures in advanced countries, there is a tendency among the MNCs to locate their highly polluting industries in the developing countries. The main reason for this is that in such countries environmental legislation is almost non-existent or that the law enforcement agency is very weak.

8. *Exchange rate fluctuations and the balance of payments crises* : A large inflow of FDI leads to an increase in the supply of foreign exchange, denominated in US dollars and leads to the appreciation of the rupee in terms of the dollar. This increases imports and reduces exports and thus generates a deficit in the balance of trade.

On the other hand, when the interest rates or rates of return on capital in the home country go up or when there is loss of confidence in the host country about its capacity to pay back the money invested by MNCs in local enterprises under the joint venture scheme, there is huge outflow of capital through MNCs. This leads to balance of payments crisis and sharp depreciation of the external value of the currency of the host country. This is exactly what happened in South-east Asian countries in 1997. Thus inflows and outflows of financial capital are often responsible for exchange rate fluctuations and the resultant BOP crisis in developing countries.

9. *Transfer pricing and tax evasion* : Most MNCs are vertically integrated firms. The production of a finished good by an MNC passes through various stages. The parts and components used in the production of a final good may be produced in the home country or by the subsidiaries in the host countries.

MNCs adopt transfer pricing practices to evade local taxes. This is detrimental to the interest of the governments of developing countries. They increase their R&D expenditure in India[2] where the tax rate is high and produce new items from Hong Kong where the tax rate is low. This goes against the interest of GOI. Thus MNCs bring profit to the Government of one country, at the expense of another. In this case, the GOI looses tax revenue and the Government of Hongkong gets it it. So the policy is discriminatory in nature.

1. An increase in income in such countries is not used for saving and investment for productive purposes but wasted by being spent on items of conspicuous consumption. The reason is that new rich class try to demonstrate their riches.
2. R & D expenditure is a deductible item from corporate tax in most countries.

Concluding Comments

FDI by MNCs have both advantages and disadvantages. So it is of paramount importance to control and regulate them. However, instead of following an open door policy, the GOI should permit FDI only in certain selected sectors. If the GOI is to achieve its declared objective of faster economic growth with reasonable price stability and equity (distributive justice) it should follow a discriminatory policy toward MNCs. The MNCs should be adequately controlled and properly regulated so that they serve useful purposes such as bringing capital and ensuring steady flow of foreign exchange which are non-debt creating in nature, promoting the development of modern sophisticated technology and raising exports. The governments of developing countries should eliminate the evils of the MNCs while at the same time permitting them to invest in infrastructure, high-tech. areas, in export-oriented industries as also in those industries which have tremendous employment potential in labour surplus countries like India.

KEY POINTS

1. *Private capital flows* : Private capital flows are of the two types, viz., (i) international portfolio investment(IPI) and (ii) foreign direct investment(FDI).

2. *International portfolio investment (IPI)* : At present, IPI is the most important and the main form of private capital flow to developing countries like India. Such capital comes from foreign institutions such as banks, insurance companies, investment companies such as mutual funds and pension funds which purchase stocks and shares of Indian companies in the secondary markets (i.e., stock markets).

3. *Foreign direct investment (FDI)* : Foreign direct investment (FDI) refers to real investment, i.e., investment in the construction of physical capital such as building private factories, socio-economic overheads and physical infrastructure (i.e., roads, highways, power plants, ports, telecommunication facilities, etc.) in the capital importing country.

4. *Advantages of FDI* : FDI, which comes through multinational corporation (MNCs), offer a number of advantages.

5. *Disadvantages of FDI* : FDI is often criticised on the ground that it seeks to establish financial oligarchy or even imperialism.

6. *Reforms in India's foreign investment policy* : Since the adoption of various economic reform measures in India from July 1991, both IPI and FDI increased steadily. The following measures have been adopted by GOI to encourage the inflows both types of capital:

(i) Greater equity participation,
(ii) Automatic approval of infrastructure projects,
(iii) Additional concessions for SEZs,
(iv) Provisions for other sectors,
(v) Financial sectors,
(vi) Buying equity shares and debt securities, and
(vii) Issue of equity shares and convertible bonds by Indian companies.

7. *Foreign direct investment flows in India during the reform period* : Since the adoption of various reform measures and liberalisation of the policy towards foreign capital by the GOI since July 1991, inflows of FDI gently increased. The vast increase in investment by MNCs during the two decades of economic reforms was largely due to (1) the adoption of a new liberalised industrial policy which assigns a more crucial and strategic role of the private sector and (2) opening of the economy so as to permit greater flows of foreign trade and foreign investment.

8. *The pattern of foreign investment* : There has occurred a huge increase in foreign investment flows in India. Due to sustained economic growth, India has become a favourable destination for private foreign investors.

9. *India's environment* : India offers certain special advantages to foreign investors, such as its vast domestic market for industrial goods, low wages and low cost of inputs, availability of skilled managers, easy repatriation facilities and a strong legal framework. All these have enabled India to steal a march over its rivals. If these features are supported by a stable macroeconomic environment, India will be able to attract more and more FDI.

10. ***The role of multinational corporations*** **:** The multinational corporations (MNCs) are large international firms which have headquarters (or decision-making centres) in one country but branch offices as also production and distribution centers in various countries of the world.

11. ***The concept of MNC*** **:** FDI flows occur through the MNCs and an MNC also act as a vehicle for the transfer of technology across national borders.

12. ***The rationale of international business*** **:** A company goes international for world-wide sourcing.

13. ***Alternative channels of FDI*** **:** In order to improve their profitability MNCs go for both types of integration — horizontal and vertical. This calls for judicious management of such firms. And management of an international firm is much more difficult and complex than that of a domestic firm. In addition, since such firms operate in various countries they have to control and manage their assets properly so as to be able to achieve growth and diversification. There are four methods of overseas operation by an MNC. These are the following:

(i) Sales agreement with domestic (local) firms,

(ii) The setting up of a wholly-owned subsidiary,

(iii) Setting up branches, and

(iv) Foreign collaboration and joint ventures.

14. ***Alternative forms of international business*** **:** No doubt business has been conducted on an international scale for a long time. But such business became more and more visible and assumed more a more importance due to the growth of large multinational corporations. The international businesses involves transactions across national borders and include the transfer of goods, services, technology, managerial knowledge, skill and financial capital to other countries — both developed and developing or from the home (parent) country to host country.

In developing (and evolving) a global strategy an international firm enjoys several options. These are the following:

(i) **Exporting:** Exporting refers to the action by the global firm to send produced goods and services from the home country to other countries.

(ii) **Licensing:** International licensing is the transfer of patented information and trademarks, information and know-how, including specifications, written documents, computer programmes and so forth.

(iii) **Management contracts:** A global firm may also engaged in management contracts for operating foreign companies.

(iv) **Joint venture and strategic alliance:** Joint venture is a method of interaction of a global firm with a firm in the host country. One form of joint venture is the strategy alliance which is often formed in order to achieve geographical expansion of business.

(v) **Wholly-owned subsidiaries:** Multinational corporation may also set up wholly-owned subsidiaries or branches with production facilities in the host country.

(vi) **International franchising:** International franchising is essentially a contract-based organisational structure for entering new markets.

(vii) **Wholly-owned ventures:** In contrast to exporting, licensing and franchising, wholly-owned subsidiaries involve a high degree of risk. MNCs have two options: greenfield investment in a completely new facility, or acquisition of or merger with an already established local firm.

15. ***The role of MNCs in Indian economy*** **:** Since the announcement of the policy of economic liberalisation the GOI. MNCs have been given wider opportunities to operate in the Indian economy. The following are the main reasons for the adoption of the policy of liberalisation towards MNCs by the GOI:

(i) Bridging domestic saving-investment gap,

(ii) Non-debt creating capital flows,

(iii) Transfer of technology,

(iv) Export-promotion, and

(v) Investment in infrastructure and crowding-in effect.

16. ***A critical review of MNCs*** **:** However, MNCs are not an unmixed blessing. The following are the main criticisms against the MNCs in developing countries like India.

(i) Deindustrialisation and joblessness,

(ii) Use of capital-intensive techniques in a labour-abundant country,

(iii) Lust for conspicuous consumption,

(iv) Imports of outdated and obsolete technology,
(v) Lack of adequate R&D efforts,
(vi) Capturing domestic markets,
(vii) Setting up of environmentally polluting industries,
(viii) Exchange rate fluctuation and the balance of payments crisis, and
(ix) Transfer pricing and tax evasion.

17. ***Concluding comments*** **:** FDI by MNCs have both advantages and disadvantages. So it is of paramount importance to control and regulate them.

KEY TERMS

Multinational corporation	Strategic alliance
Trans national corporation	Mergers and acquisitions
Foreign direct investment	Greenfield strategy
International portfolio investment	International franchising
Joint ventures	International sub-contracting
Exporting	Transfer of technology
Licensing	Management contracts
Wholly-owned subsidiaries	Foreign collaboration
Wholly-owned ventures	Franchise business

ASSIGNMENTS

1. Why has private foreign capital assumed so much importance in developing like India in recent years?
2. Distinguish between international portfolio investment and foreign direct investment. Why has the former increased in India and the later declined?
3. Discuss the role of private foreign capital in India's industrial economy.
4. What are the advantages of MNCs?
5. What are the main criticisms against MNCs?
6. Suggest some measures which may be adopted by the GOI to woo FDI? Are you in favour of an open door policy towards MNCs or a selective approach?
7. Why does a company go international?
8. What is the difference between an MNC and a transnational corporation?

34A FOREIGN CAPITAL FLOWS AND MACROECONOMIC STABILITY IN INDIA

Effects of Volatile Capital Inflows in India

Foreign capital inflows are needed in India for two main purposes, viz., (i) to finance the deficit in the current account of the BOP in the short run and (ii) to promote faster economic growth in the long run through fresh (new) investment. However, both capital inflows and outflows in India are very much volatile. And volatility of capital inflows creates macroeconomic instability in the form of fluctuating exchange rates and varying rates of inflation which conjointly affect exports and imports, domestic share prices as also domestic liquidity position (it flow of funds in the market). In fact, volatile capital flows have adversely affected India's BOP position during the entire post-reform period. Volatile capital inflows and outflows have caused the boom and bust cycle in the stock exchange and even led to stock market crashes in the past.

Both too much and too little capital flows are bad for an economy. In fact, the Indian economy was characterised by large net inflows of financial capital as well as sudden outflows of such capital in times of global financial crisis. So such flows are to be judiciously managed for stabilising the economy. An appropriate use of flexible exchange rate system, sterilisation of the impact of inflows of foreign currencies on domestic liquidity, adoption of a prudent approach to liberalisation of capital accounts and the drawing of accumulated foreign exchange reserves are several alternative ways of dealing with the adverse effects of foreign capital flows.

In recent past the volatility of capital inflows and outflows occurred mainly due to transfer (or switching) of portfolio capital into and out of India by foreign institutional investors (FIIs). And this caused macroeconomic instability. The total net FII flows to India was US $18.51 billion in 2009. Such flows increased to $39.71 billion in 2010 due to buoyancy in the capital market, strong domestic macroeconomic fundamentals and, of course, high rate of GDP growth. However, such flows were fairly low in 2011 and 2012.

Capital inflow leads to appreciation of the rupee. But it often overheats the economy by injecting excess liquidity and causes price inflation which depresses exports (by eroding India's competitive advantage) but raises he import bill. In contrast, capital outflow causes depreciation of the rupee and BOP crisis by destroying the confidence of foreign investors and thus leading to further capital outflows. So there is need for sterilised foreign exchange market intervention by the RBI in both situations. In times of capital inflows and appreciation of the rupee the RBI can buy some foreign exchange (mainly dollars) flowing into the country. And in times of large capital outflows the RBI has to sell dollars from its accumulated foreign exchange reserves to present undue depreciation of the rupee.

Larger capital flows no doubt helped the process of growth in India but led to financial instability also. So India is faced with a dilemma situation. It needs foreign portfolio capital through FIIs to cover its current account deficit (CAD). But such capital is highly volatile in nature. And for achieving faster economic growth it needs more stable and long-term capital flows in the form of FDI through the multinational corporations(MNCs).

However, the main problem created by volatile capital flows is that they are used cover widening CAD. So it is not judicious on the part of India to impose controls on foreign capital inflows.

Suggested Measures

In truth, the RBI has to be watchful of capital inflows and outflows as also the resultant exchange rate movements. It should actively intervene in the forex market to ensure exchange rate stability. It has also to encourage inflows of long-term capital through the MNC route. Stable FDI flows, which are so important for infrastructure building, has to be encouraged, without, at the same time, imposing any control on outflows of portfolio capital so badly needed at present to cover CAD and to stabilise the external value of the rupee and to reduce undue fluctuations of share prices.

A fall in inflows of portfolio capital due to sharp depreciation of the rupee in the past few months made financing CAD difficult in 2013-14. So the only way to make India's macroeconomic environment stable is to attract more FDI which is fairly stable.

Current Trend

It is interesting to note that due to the adoption of certain measures by both the RBI and the Government, capital inflows through FDI and NRI deposits have started picking up from July 2013. While several NRIs were taking their funds out of India to avoid loss of their wealth due to the depreciation of the rupee, the disquieting trend seems to have been partly reversed after a series of steps announced both by the Government and the RBI.

34B FDI IN MULTI-BRAND RETAIL SECTOR

After a long debate and strong opposition from various groups the GOI took a bold decision on Nov. 24, 2011 to allow FDI in multi-brand retail sector. This is no doubt a very big and fairly significant external sector reform measure which is supposed to benefit both consumers and farmers. By eliminating intermediaries it will ensure two things at least. Firstly, farmers will get higher prices for their products. Secondly, consumers will get necessary goods at lower prices. In addition, this scheme, if successful, is likely to generate additional employment to 10 million people within the next three years (i.e., by the end of 2014).

It is also felt that this new scheme will not only bring the much needed foreign capital in India but also modern (improved) technology and superior management skills and expertise.

As things stand today 100% FDI is permitted under the automatic route for wholesale trade subject to certain end-sale limitations and restrictions. However, the permissible limit in a single brand retail is 51%, subject, of course, to approval by the Government. The GOI's policy of allowing FDI in multi-brand retailing will open the door for global giants such as Wal-Mart, Tesco and Correfour to set up large stores in India with back-up infrastructure. And the Government's proposals make provision for certain safety clauses and the appointment of a regulator to protect various interest groups in India.

Conditionality

The Government has permitted entry of FDI in retail subject to the following conditions:

1. The minimum investment by a big global retailer setting up stores in India should be Rs. 100 crores.
2. At least 50% of the investment in a multi-brand retail giant has to be in back-end infrastructure such as supply chains, storage (warehousing) facilities, logical support and transportation.
3. At least 30% of goods purchased for resale in a multi-brand store must be acquired from small-scale and medium enterprises (SMEs).
4. At present these giant stores can only be opened in 43 cities with at least 10 lakh population.
5. The Government will have the prior claim as far as the right to procure agricultural products is concerned.
6. Each State in India is at liberty to permit or not to allow the setting up of retail shops by an international giant.

It is, however, apprehended that the opening up of multi-brand retail stores through FDI would adversely affect India's large unorganised retail sector which will not be able to compete closely with its foreign counterpart. This is why the Government proposal contains passing a law, called Multi-Regulation Act for protecting small retailers and setting up a centrally administered agency to monitor compliance with the rules.

Relaxation (Easing) of Rules Relating to FDI in Multi-Brand Retail Business

More than two years have passed since the Government has allowed FDI in multi-brand retail business. The investment limit has been fixed at 51%. In addition, the retail giants would have to purchase goods from small and medium enterprises for resale. Furthermore, each retail giant would have to deposit Rs. 100 crore with the Government and make 50% investment in building back-end infrastructure. But, so far no global FDI-based retail giant has made a pioneering endeavour to set up its supermarket in India. Therefore, to woo them the Government has eased rules for them.

In July 2013, the Government drastically relaxed the rules in multi-brand retail and eased the conditions for entry of global giants into India. Now a global giant will be required to procure 30%

of their merchandise for resale in India from local small firms and artisans. In addition, the Government allowed global chains to open stores in 53 smaller cities having a minimum population of 1 million. Goods purchased from companies which have invested at least $2 million in fixed capital will now be beneficiaries of the mandatory 30% sourcing requirement for big retailers. These retailers can now buy from such companies. Such suppliers will continue to qualify as small enterprises even if their fixed asset investment exceeds the lower level of $2 million.

In addition, farmers and agriculture cooperatives will be treated as small firms for fulfilling the mandatory sourcing requirement. This implies that the processing of fruits and vegetables procured from Indian farmers will be very much a part of the 30% local sourcing condition.

Retailers will have to meet at least 30% of their needs in the first five years. So if they acquired less than 30% in the first two or three years, they would have to make compensatory adjustments in the subsequent years.

However, in spite of these relaxations no retail giant has as yet shown willingness to set up supermarket shops in India. Some giant retailers are waiting for the new economic policy to be announced soon by the BJP Government which has assumed our at the centre from the end of may 2014. They are apprehending that the new Government may even ban the entry of multi-brand FDI retail giants into India on political grounds alone.

34C FRANCHISING—AN EMERGING BUSINESS VENTURE IN INDIA

A franchise agreement is an arrangement whereby someone with a good and a new idea for a business (the franchisor) sells rights to use the business name and sell a product or service (the franchise) to others (franchisees) in a certain area or a given territory.

Some people, who are not much confident or very comfortable with the idea of starting their own business from scratch, would prefer to join a business with a proven track record through a franchise agreement. A franchise can be formed as a sole proprietorship, a partnership or a corporation. Some of the best known franchises are McDonald's, KFC and Subway. McDonald's, the largest restaurant chain in the USA, is often considered the golden standard of franchising. One of the fastest-growing franchise sectors is medical care. Door-to-door dry cleaning franchises are also gaining popularity in the USA and Europe day by day.

In truth, franchising has penetrated every aspect of US and global business life by offering products and services which are reliable, convenient and competitively priced. And past record shows that the failure rate for franchising has been lower than that of other business ventures.

Most franchisers are not large systems like McDonald's and Subway. Many are small, rather obscure companies that prospective franchisees may know little about.

International franchising travels both ways. Just as McDonald's and Subway have golden arches and sub sandwiches worldwide, foreign franchisers are changing tastes in the USA. What makes franchising successful in international markets is what makes it successful in India also : convenience and a predictable level of service and quality. It is against this backdrop that we make a brief review of franchise business in India.

A recent survey carried out by Diptoshree Sengupta in *Business Economics* (April 01-15, 2014) finds that franchising is the most common and globally used technique for business expansion. It enables a company to put its own brand everywhere in the world. India is a destination for more than 3000 brands with franchise outlets. This kind of business is showing mushroom growth all over the world. In 2012 the value of the business was US $ 13.4 billion. According to KPMG by 2017 franchising business is likely to grow fourfold and reach US $ 50.4 billion. And the number of franchise outlets will increase from 45,000 to 1,68,000 during this five-year period(2012-17).

Employment Potential

Starting from footwear company Bata to watch making company Titan everyone is adopting the vitually painless franchise model. No doubt it is a convenient business concept to go for food-chain franchise like McDonald's. In this five-year period (2012-17), 11 million more people are expected to earn their livelihood from the sector. KPMG predicts that the growth will be so robust that the contribution of the franchise sector to India's GDP will increase from a modest 1.4% in 2012 to 4% by 2017. The contribution of the franchise sector to GDP in industrially advanced country varies between 10% to 25% at present.

Two-Person Positive Sum Game

Franchise business is not a two-person zero-sum game but a positive-sum game. The reason is that not only the franchiser but the franchisee also stand to gain from this type of business. It is a less risky way to start a new business than venturing out in a completely new area. The franchising industry has opened a wide window for many would-be and budding entrepreneurs. Basically it creates a win-win situation for both franchiser and franchisee by generating synergic effect. Buying franchise generates self-employment opportunity by enabling one to become his own boss in any field that the owner-entrepreneur is passionate about without the added worries about his own venture — generation of new ideas, brand building, laying down infrastructure and solving legal problems.

Demand and Supply-side Forces

The main reason for the growth of franchise business is increasing consumption and willingness to spend in recent past due to globalisation and urbanisation. The so-called 'middle class' in India has been growing by leaps and bounds, as also their purchasing power. Initially it was felt that only the affluent class goes to McDonald's or KFC. But at present children are taking their family members out to these outlets. The younger generation have turned brand conscious and are showing a lust for branded products. The increased global exposure and growing aspirations to adopt Western culture are creating demand for international brands and are acting as one strong driving force behind the opening of franchise outlets for tapping the unexploited market.

From the supply side, franchising businesses have been developed mainly from opportunity-driven competent entrepreneurs. Increasing awareness of franchising as a business opportunity and its relatively low risk profile have encouraged young managers and professionals to venture out in new directions and become this own bosses. A big factor behind the emerging business is the initiative taken by the Government of India such as the liberalisation of FDI in retail, which has made entry of foreign brands in India possible. It is not that only international brands open franchise outlets in India, but Indian brands have also opened franchise outlets abroad.

High prospects for the successful franchise opportunities in India exist in retail trade, food and beverage, health, beauty and wellness, consumer services, education and training. Food and beverage have proved to be a universally favourite business all the time. Today's younger generation's special likings are in coffee shops, quick service restaurants and kiosks. Health and beauty are two prospective areas and are dominated by saloons, spa, slimming and fitness centres. The educational sector has also a tremendous potential to grow. Starting from pre-school chain to a post-graduate computer training institute (centre), we find a common thread — the franchise link.

Quality as the Key to Survival

Like other businesses franchising bushiness also involves some risk. The probability of success of this businesses (in such sectors as apparel, consumer durables, electronics, food and grocery, jewellery, books, music and stationery, pharmacy and furniture and furnishing) depends to a large extent on the location of the shop or office. Arranging finance is also a challenge since it requires some extra amounts to buy the brand. But the most vital thing is quality assurance. Quality is the key to success of any brand. With an increase in the scale of production there is every possibility of deterioration of product quality. With a fall in product quality or standard the credential of the brand goes down automatically and this does considerable damage to the business. If the quality of the goods and services is not properly maintained and improved from time to time the brand as also the business are likely to the destroyed (since the whole image of the business is likely to be tarnished). This is why many successful brands like Wal-Mart never go for franchising.

Conclusion

However, on balance, it appears that the benefits are greater in franchise business compared to the challenges (if not threats). The franchise is essentially an act of buying a business with proven record of success and brand from the franchiser. By contrast, the franchiser is outsourcing the responsibility of running a branch not to a employee but rather to an aspiring businessperson. The investment and risks are also borne proportionately by franchiser and franchisee. This is why the trend is both increasing and encouraging.

CHAPTER 35

Globalisation and its Impact on the Indian Economy

> *There is a need for patent and copyright protection but such protection does constitute a restrain on trade.*
>
> George Soros

PREVIEW

Globalisation refers to the tendency for markets to become global, rather than national, as barriers to international trade (e.g., tariffs and quotas) are reduced and international transport and communication systems improve; and the tendency for large multinational enterprises to grow in order to serve global markets. So it implies the expansion of firms into all corners of the world both in terms of sales and sourcing of materials and components. Thus globalisation implies the greater and greater openness of an economy and its integration with the global economy through the following:

(i) free flow of goods and services among nations, (ii) free investment of financial capital among countries, (iii) free movement of labour across national borders, and (iv) free transfer of technology among different countries of the world.

In fact, three main markets have been globalised in the last two decades or so, viz., the product market, the capital market and the labour market. And largely due to globalisation two Asian countries, viz., India and China have achieved the fastest economic growth in the world. This is why these two countries are often cited as two models of globalisation.

Globalisation is external liberalisation. Two main factors leading to globalisation are (1) removal of various types of controls and regulations on the movement of goods, services and factors of production and (2) revolution in information technology which virtually brought about the third industrial revolution. It is against this backdrop that we discuss the pros and cons of globalisation.

GLOBALISATION OF INDIAN ECONOMY

Various economic reforms were introduced in India in July 1991. Since then various arguments have been put forward for integrating the Indian economy with the global economy.

Various tariff and non-tariff barriers have been either reduced or totally removed to promote free trade. The Government of India (GOI) invited foreign investment by removing various types of controls on multinational corporations (MNCs) and non-resident Indian (NRIs). It has also encouraged import of technology from the industrially advanced countries. In addition India has benefitted from liberalisation and globalisation in various other ways. These are the following:

1. *Shift from inward-looking to outward-looking growth strategy* : The import-substitution strategy adopted by India and other developing countries largely failed to achieve the desired objectives. So there was a shift from import-substituting (inward-looking) to export promotion (outward-looking) growth strategy. By specialising in production of labour-intensive goods in which India has comparative advantage and by exporting such goods India has achieved faster growth.

In addition, due to increase in production and export of such goods due to integration of the India's economy with the global economy, more employment opportunities were created.

The success of India's export promotion strategy was largely attributable to the reduction of import tariffs and removal of non-tariff barriers (mainly import quotas) after the setting up of the World Trade Organisation (WTO) on Jan 1, 1995.

Greater inflow of international portfolio capital removed the BOP constraint on economic growth

2. *Inflow of foreign capital* : The greater integration of capital markets of the world increased the flows of foreign capital in India. Foreign direct investment (FDI), through MNCs raised the volume of real investment in the economy and helped India to achieve faster economic growth. This had generated multiplier effect on output and employment.

Greater flow of foreign portfolio investment (FPI) enabled India to earn huge amount of foreign exchange. This not only solved India's balance of payments problem but removed one of the main constraints on economic growth, viz., foreign exchange crisis.

3. *Transfer of technology* : Due to high costs and low profit margins, Indian companies were not able to make adequate investment on R and D which was so important for technological progress and faster economic growth. And globalisation acts as a mechanism for the transfer of modern technology from the developed countries of the world. MNCs also act as the vehicle for such transfer. They enter into financial and technological collaboration with domestic enterprises. The technology upgradation of Indian industries is of considerable importance for raising labour productivity and achieving a faster rate of industrial growth.

Globalisation leads to faster spread of new ideas in the world

Globalisation leads to faster diffusion of modern technology throughout the world and enables the developing countries to catch up with the West in a short span of time and we now find convergence of growth race among various nations. So, in the context of globalisation, the widening gap hypothesis is not much relevant.

4. *Widening of the market* : Free trade resulting from globalisation widens the market for industrial products. As a result there is greater scope for division of labour and work specialisation. And the economies of scale associated with large-scale production lower unit cost(s). This leads to a fall in prices of exportable goods and thus increases the competitiveness of India's manufactured products in the world market. Thus globalisation increases gains from trade. Such gains arise due to the increase in labor productivity as a result of specialisation. In addition the widening of the market for industrial goods increases the incentives to invest in product and process development. The development and commercial introduction of new product increase the return to investment.

5. *Faster economic growth and poverty reduction* : Globalisation helps in reducing the incidence of poverty by accelerating the rate of economic growth. The newly industrialised countries like Hong Kong, Singapore, Republic of Korea and Taiwan have achieved significant reduction in poverty by achieving faster economic growth and by opening their economies to trade. These countries have proved that the greater the degree of economic openness, the faster is the rate of economic growth and the faster is the rate of poverty reduction. By contrast, India and other developing countries, which remained virtually closed for achieving economic self-sufficiency grew at less than 1.5% in per capita terms in the late 1970s, achieved hardly any reduction in the poverty ratio. Both India and China succeeded in alleviating poverty after dismantling autarkic policies and after achieving faster economic growth.

6. ***Employment generation*** **:** Trade liberalisation and greater capital flows generate more employment opportunities for two main reasons. Firstly, increase in the volume of exports due to widening of the market generates more employment opportunities. Secondly, the removal of restrictions on capital movements leads to greater inflows of foreign capital, mainly FDI. This initially creates employment not only directly but also indirectly through the multiplier effect.

DANGERS AND RISKS OF GLOBALISATION

However globalisation is not an unmixed blessing. There are various dangers and risks associated with it. These are the following:

1. ***Double standards*** **:** No doubt the USA and European countries preach the gospel of free trade and globalisation. But in practice they adopt protectionist policies in order to promote their own interests. They impose tariffs on imports of steel and provide subsidies on farm products and cotton textiles in order to protect their agriculture and industry. This is a real life example of setting double standards.

2. ***Fall in farm exports*** **:** The recent failure of multilateral talks held under the auspices of the WTO at Doha, Seattle, Singapore and Cancun to liberalise trade between the developed and developing countries largely failed since the USA and European Union (EU) countries were most reluctant to reduce the huge subsidies they were providing to their farmers as also subsidies on exports of farm products. This support by the developed countries to their farmers lead to sharp fall in agricultural exports for the developing countries in which they have comparative advantage. This, no doubt, is against the spirit of globalisation.

3. ***Anti-outsourcing campaign*** **:** Recently the US president B. Obama has withdrawn tax concessions from those corporations which outsource their jobs, i.e., get some jobs done or sub-tasks accomplished from developing countries such as India and China. In addition, he has imposed visa restrictions for foreign skilled workers (e.g., software specialists) with a view to giving job protection to the Americans. These protectionist measures are likely to go against the interests of Indian educated youth.

Focus on Terminology: Outsourcing
Outsourcing is the process whereby one firm contracts with other companies, often in other countries, to do some or all of its functions. In the USA companies have outsourced payroll functions, accounting and some manufacturing operations for many years. Recently there is a shift primarily to low-wage global markets, called *off shore outsourcing*.

4. ***Exchange rate fluctuations and economic instability*** **:** Perhaps the most serious consequence of economic reforms and globalisation is excessive fluctuation of the external value of the rupee. This has done considerable damage to the Indian economy. The huge inflow of international portfolio capital through foreign institutional investors (FIIs) during the period 2003-2004 to 2007-2008 led to appreciation of the rupee. In fact, from July 1991, the market-determined exchange rate system was introduced. This adversely affected India's exports. Moreover, huge inflow of US dollars led to a rapid increase in the domestic money supply which generated inflationary pressures in the indian economy. In addition, injection of huge international portfolio capital in the Indian stock market raised prices of shares of Indian enterprises rather artificially.

By contrast, in 2008-2009 the US banking sector faced a serious crisis due to defaults on sub-prime housing loans and mortgage failures on a massive scale. (For a detailed discussion of this point see chapter 45 of this book).

In such a situation there occurred a huge outflow of funds from India through the FIIs since they sold shares of Indian companies on a very large scale. This led to a depreciation of the rupee and made imports costlier. Depreciation also created an apprehension among FIIs of further depreciation of the rupee and thus induced further capital outflow. So due to increased pressure the rupee continued to depreciate. This compelled the RBI to intervene in the foreign exchange market. It sold US dollars from its reserves in order to prevent a further depreciation of the rupee against the US dollar.

Furthermore, huge outflows of capital from India by FIIs generated liquidity crisis in the Indian banking system in the second half of 2008-09. This led to a fall in aggregate investment.

MEASURES ADOPTED BY INDIA TO PROMOTE GLOBALISATION

The Indian economy faced a crisis situation in early 1991 due to sharp rise in oil prices in the wake of the Gulf War. In order to overcome the crisis and to restore the health of the economy a number of measures were adopted by the GOI. These measures, discussed below, promoted globalisation or external liberalisation.

1. *External liberalisation* : Import control through licensing was abolished on all items of capital goods, raw materials and intermediate goods in a phased manner. In addition, from 1995 all quantitative restrictions, including those on imports of consumer goods, have been removed in a number of phases. These two measures, no doubt, largely removed the anti-export bias of Indias earlier trade policies.

The GOI also liberalised the import of two precious metals—gold and silver. From January 2004 no commission had to be paid for importing gold. These measures reduced the incentive for illegal transactions in precious metals (i.e., smuggling) considerably.

2. *Market determined exchange rate* : In 1993, the market-determined exchange rate system was introduced. Now the external value of the rupee is freely determined by the forces of demand and supply in the foreign exchange market.

3. *Partial convertibility of the rupee* : The rupee was made convertible on the current account. This implies that importers can acquire the necessary amount of foreign exchange by converting rupees into dollars in the foreign exchange market. The exporters are no longer required to surrender their foreign exchange (US dollar and other foreign currencies) to the RBI. They can now sell them freely in the foreign exchange market.

4. *Liberalisation of foreign investment* : The reform measures adopted since July 1991 considerably widened the scope for both types of foreign investment in India —FDI and FPI. The new policy toward foreign capital provided for automatic approval of FDI up to 51% of the total equity capital of firms belonging to 34 top priority industries. In such cases no prior permission of the GOI is required. This limit was raised to 74% in 1996.

In addition, foreign equity participation in non-priority industries (which was earlier approved on a case by case basis after a close scrutiny) was liberalised with a view to attracting more foreign investment in India. Finally, the scrapping of industrial licensing restrictions, and the opening up of a number of industries, (which were previously reserved for the public sector) to the private sector also served to promote foreign private investment. The end result was faster industrial growth.

5. *International portfolio investment (IPI)* : The new economic policy laid stress on non-debt creating capital inflows such as FDI and IPI. The objective was to reduce the reliance on debt flow as the main source of external resource. Therefore, in addition to FDI, provisions relating to IPI have also been liberalised.

Economic Insight: Difference between FDI and FPI
FDI comes through MNCs and involves both financial capital and management control over enterprises set up with foreign capital. By comparison, IPI comes through foreign firms, FIIs and NRIs who invest their funds in the bonds, equities and securities of Indian firms. In this case foreign investors get returns in the form of interest, dividends and capital gains. But they do not exercise any managerial control in running these companies. Such capital provides the needed finance to the Indian firms and brings the much needed foreign exchange in addition. But such capital inflows are subject to greater volatility than FDI. The main reason is it is subject to speculative attack. The sudden outflow of IPI led to the Asian currency crisis of 1997-98.

6. *FEMA* : The Foreign Exchange Regulation Act (FERA) has been replaced by the Foreign Exchange Management Act (FEMA) which makes it easier for Indian companies to operate in foreign countries. The GOI has also considerably simplified the procedure for investment by Indian companies in foreign countries as also for raising funds from abroad through external commercial borrowing, i.e., through ADRs and GDRs.

Economic Insight: American Depository Receipt (ADR) and Global Depository Receipt (GDR)
ADR is a certificate of ownership issued to an individual or a corporate investor by a US bank which holds (on deposit) the investor's or the company's stocks and shares. The ADR serves as a proof of the ownership of the securities held by the bank and can be used as a negotiable instrument. GDR is a short-hand expression of global depository receipt. It is a certificate for shares of stocks traded abroad. Such a certificate is held by a bank in one country representing shares of stocks that are traded on an exchange in a foreign country but can be purchased through various banks worldwide.

GLOBALISATION AND ITS IMPACT ON INDIAN ECONOMY

There was an extra temptation on the part of foreign institutional investors (FIIs) to diversify their wealth portfolio and to reduce risks by investing in India's stocks. Foreign portfolio investment was attracted to India due to the operation of both pull and push forces. Examples of pull factors were the improvement in India's macroeconomic environment due to the abolition of the licensing system and reforms in the financial sector in general and banking sector in particular. By comparison, push factors were fall in interest rates and returns on investment in the wake of slowdown in economic growth in USA and some European countries. The two sets of factors conjointly induced foreign investors to put their funds in India's financial market. The reason is that financial capital is the most mobile of all factors and it has always an extra temptation to go abroad in search of higher returns.

Impact of Globalisation on India

Globalisation has had both favourable and adverse effects on the Indian economy. So we get a mixed picture. The following points are to be noted here:

1. Effect on economic growth : The main argument in favour of globalisation and liberalisation was that they would promote faster economic growth. Due to serious BOP crisis in 1991, growth in GDP became miserably low at 1.3% in 1991-92. But economy gradually gathered momentum in the next decade (1992-2001). And the annual growth rate picked up to 6.1%. And the growth momentum was maintained in subsequent years. In fact, during the Tenth Plan period (2002-07), the average annual growth rate was 7.8%. And in the last three years of the Plan (2005-06, 2006-07, 2007-08) the growth rate picked up to 9.5%, 9.6% and 9.3%, respectively. Thus the policy of globalisation and economic liberalisation undoubtedly accelerated the rate of economic growth in India.

However, due to the global financial crisis of 2008-09 the growth rate suddenly dropped to 6.7% in 2008-09. In spite of this the growth rate could be maintained at 8.6% in 2009-10 and raised to 9.3% in 2010-11 largely due to the financial stimulus given by the Government and the expansionary monetary policy adopted by the RBI. However, due to adverse developments in the global economy such as productivity slowdown and de-industrialisation in the USA, recession in the European countries and Eurozone crisis adversely affected the growth of India's exports as also the overall rate of growth. However, the growth rate dropped to 6.2% in 2011-12 and to 5% in 2012-13. Volatile capital flows did considerable damage to the economy by creating uncertainty and making the economic environment unstable. In 2013-14, the growth rate was expected to be around 5%. Thus the growth momentum could not be sustained in spite of globalisation. Greater volatility in capital flows as also financial contagion in the wake of globalisation due to greater integration of the world's capital markets and faster information transmission led to exchange rate fluctuations (i.e., appreciation and depreciation of the rupee), price level changes (inflation and deflation) and sharp fluctuations in share prices (creating some sort of boom and bust cycle). In short Indian economy showed volatility due to the adverse developments in the global economy.

2. Impact on foreign trade and BOP: Trade liberalisation and globalisation had favourable effects on foreign trade and BOP. Exports grew steadily since 1993-94. Imports also increased year by year. However, due to unprecedented growth in export of invisible items (services) the current account deficit (CAD) remained below 2% of GDP up to 2007-08, as compared to 3.1% in 1990-91 (the last pre-reform year). In fact, the current account showed a surplus in the three-year period 2001-04. And this was accompanied by a surplus in capital account. Hence there was a huge increase in foreign exchange reserves.

It is gratifying to note that, due to satisfactory growth in exports in the last three years of the Tenth Plan (2005-06, 2006-07, 2007-08) CAD was less than 2% of GDP which placed India in a comfortable position and was financed by capital inflows. In truth, globalisation not only helped to accelerate India's industrial growth but also led to an improvement in her balance of payments position. In short, liberalisation of trade and removal of restrictions on foreign investment conjointly led to an increase in capital inflows which conduced to faster economic growth.

However, globalisation has not been an unmixed blessing for India. There were various dangers and disadvantages of globalisation. It exposed India to a high degree of risk mainly due to the highly volatile nature of foreign portfolio capital flows and have destabilised the economy by exposing the country to a series of external shocks.

3. Impact on poverty: An accurate measurement of the impact of globalisation on poverty in India is difficult due to differences in the methodology used by different economists and institutions in defining the poverty line and in estimating the poverty ratio or the incidence of poverty. Data collected from National Sample Survey (NSS) showed that in 2004-05 about 37.2% of people in India lived below the poverty line. In 2011-12, the percentage fell to 21.9, indicating a decline in poverty by 15.3% over the seven-year period 2005-06 to 2011-12. This was attributed to higher average rate of economic growth of over 8% per annum achieved during this period. It was claimed by the Government that this was due to the policy of liberalisation and globalisation.

It may be noted that reduction in poverty was not necessarily due to higher rate of economic growth achieved by industry by using highly capital-intensive techniques of production. However, a large number of new employment opportunities were created in the export sector. At the same time liberalisation of imports due to globalisation and trade liberalisation displaced labour in a number of industries. However, whether there has occurred a net increase in employment due to the operation of these two opposite (pull and push) forces is not clear.

4. The employment effect of globalisation: It apparently seems that liberalisation and globalisation led to jobless growth in India. What is worse, the employment situation deteriorated or the unemployment problem became more serious. In fact, all the three unemployment rates, viz., usual status, weekly status and daily status, as National Sample Survey (NSS) data show, after initial decline up to 1992-93 increased during the period 1993-94 to 2004-05. The unemployment rate, on the basis of its main indicator, viz., current daily status (CDS), or average unemployment rate in a particular reference week increased from 6.1% in 1993-94 to 8.3% in 2004-05.

On the basis of NSS data, it is found that the rate of employment generation increase from 1.25% per annum during the six-period 1993-94 to 1999-2000 to 2.62% during the next five years (1999-2000 to 2004-05). However, the rate of new employment generation was largely in the earn organised and informer sector. In fact the rate of employment generation in the organised sector which was 1.2% during the pre-reformed period (1983-84) failed to a meagre 0.5% per annum in the post reform period (1994-2008).

However, according to NSS data, the rate of unemployment on capital CDS fail marginally to 6% and 5.6%, respectively for the years 2009-10 and 2011-12 from 8.3% in 2045. However, this was mainly attributable to the implementation of the Mahatma Gandhi National Rural Employment Guarantee Scheme (MGMREGA). The growth of the organised sector played hardly any role in new increation of new employment opportunities. Although employment generated under the scheme led to fall in unemployment in 2009-10 and 2011-12 on CDS basis the scheme generated only unproductive employment. Those who were employed under the scheme did not make any contribution to creation of productive assets like irrigation dams, all-weather rural areas or high ways connecting rural with urban areas. Therefore employment generated through the scheme was of a purely temporary nature and was not sustainable in the long-run.

In fact the increase in unemployment—both in absolute numbers and in percentage terms—was attributable to a number factors such as growing capital-intensity in the firm sector, lack of adequate investment in agriculture, poor implementation of land reform measures and rapid growth of the labour force (due to natural growth of population on the one hand and the carry out of the huge back lock of unemployment persons from one year to the next).

A related point may also be noted here. No doubt increase in exports laid to the creation of the new employment opportunities. In contrast, increase in imports, due to tariff cards and other trade liberlisation measures, laid to huge job loss mainly due to closures of some small and medium enterprises which could not compete with low-costs imports from both developed countries and China.

5. Foreign capital inflows: External sector reforms in a globalised era led to huge inflows of foreign private capital in India both in terms of FDI and IPI, as noted earlier and helped India to largely offset CAD. However, the global financial crisis of 2008-09 created a serious liquidity crisis in India by generating redemption pressure on securities held by FIIs. In fact, to meet the liquidity needs of their own countries FIIs pulled out of India's financial markets by selling Indian shares on a really massive scale and repatriated dollars. The consequent huge outflow of funds not only led to a crash of the Indian stock market but resulted in a sharp depreciation of the rupee. However, this adverse effect did not last for long. There was reversal of IPI flows in 2009-10 and 2010-11. However, this trend did not last for long. Capital inflows fell again in 2011-12 and 2012-13 due to Eurozone crisis and overall instability of the global financial market.

6. Effect on India's foreign reserves: Thanks to globalisation and liberalisation, India's foreign exchange reserves increased quite sharply. And accumulation of such reserves was made possible largely due to the bold policy initiative taken by the Government without which India would have faced a much deeper crisis situation. The major contributor to dollar inflows in India was FIIs which initiated huge sums in both equity and debt markets in India.

In addition, a fairly large part of foreign exchange inflows was due to deposits of funds by NRIs in Indian banks to take advantage of high rates of interest prevailing in India.

Furthermore, a large portion of these reserves was external commercial borrowing (ECB) by India's corporate enterprises. At the same time. Capital inflows through FDI also continued to increase during the reform period, more so after 2006-07.

In fact, four main factors contributed to huge inflows of foreign funds in India, viz., (1) booming stock market, (2) high rate of growth of GDP (of 9% or even more), (3) improved performance of India's corporate sector and (4) a high rate of return on investment in India.

Commentary: India's Achievement

In spite of global financial crisis and the Eurozone crisis (discussed in detail in another chapter of this book) India was able to accumulate huge foreign exchange reserves. The enabled the country to tide over the difficult BOP situation (because of which India was in real trouble from time to time). However, happily enough, the bulk of the increase in foreign exchange reserves was of the non-debt variety. In truth, India was able to repay a portion of her external debt much before schedule by utilising its accumulated foreign exchange reserves. The large reserves made India feel safe and secured against any future contingencies and permitted the authorities to take crucial policy decisions on various issues without being constrained by the conditionalities and bindings of the IMF and the World Bank (as was the case in pre-reform period).

GLOBAL FINANCIAL CRISIS AND ITS IMPACT ON INDIA'S GROWTH

Unlike the industrially advanced countries Indian economy was not really hard hit due to its less dependence on export markets and that the major contribution to India's overall growth rate (measured by the annual rate of increase in GDP) was made possible by domestic factors such as high rate of capital formation, technological progress, and, above all, rapid growth of the service sector. However, the deepening of the global crisis and the subsequent deleveraging and 'risk aversion' of banks to extend credit in the downswing of the business cycle led to loss of India's growth momentum to some extent and thus led to slowing down of India's growth rate. However, domestic demand in India was fairly strong and investment activities were largely financed from domestic saving. The global financial crisis had very little effect on India's GDP growth in the true sense.

Focus on Terminology: Deleveraging

The term 'deleveraging' is the opposite of leveraging (gearing). Leveraging refers to the relative importance of loans in the capital structure, or incurring of fixed costs to increase profitability.

No doubt, recession in countries where India exported its goods led to sharp fall in the growth of India's small organised segment of the manufacturing sector from the second half of 2007. However, since 2000-01, the Indian economy had witnessed slow growth of the commodity producing sectors and much faster growth of the services sector. Since the services sector was not much sensitive to demand fluctuations and exports of services made insignificant contribution to GDP, the growth momentum in this sector was maintained even in times of global economic crisis. In fact, the last one and a half decades saw a sharp increase in the growth of community, social and personal services in India. In 2009-10 India recovered quickly from the adverse effects of the global crisis and succeeded in achieving a growth of 8.6% and in the next year (2010-11) the growth rate picked up to 9.3%. This very fact makes one thing clear at least: Indian economy has a strong resilience against external shocks.

KEY POINTS

1. *Globalisation* : Globalisation refers to the tendency for markets to become global, rather than national, as barriers to international trade (e.g., tariffs and quotas) are reduced and international transport and communication systems improve; and the tendency for large multinational enterprises to grow in order to serve global markets.

Globalisation implies the greater and greater openness of an economy and its integration with the global economy. Globalisation is external liberalisation. Two main factors leading to globalisation are (1) removal of various types of controls and regulations on the movement of goods, services and factors of production and (2) revolution in information technology which virtually brought about the third industrial revolution.

2. *Globalisation of Indian economy* : Various economic reforms were introduced in India in July 1991. Since then various arguments have been put forward for integrating the Indian economy with the global economy. These are the following:

a. Shift from inward-looking to outward-looking growth strategy

b. Inflow of foreign capital

c. Transfer of technology

d. Widening of the market

e. Faster economic growth and poverty reduction and

f. Employment generation

3. *Dangers and risks of globalisation* : However, globalisation is not an unmixed blessing. There are various dangers and risks associated with it. These are the following:

a. Double standards

b. Fall in farm exports

c. Anti-outsourcing campaign and

d. Exchange rate fluctuations and the consequent economic instability

4. *Measures adopted by India to promote globalisation* : The Indian economy faced a crisis situation in early 1991 due to sharp rise in oil prices in the wake of the Gulf War. In order to overcome the crisis and to restore the health of the economy a number of measures were adopted by the GOI. These measures, promoted globalisation and are the following:

a. External liberalisation

b. Market determined exchange rate

c. Partial convertibility of the rupee

d. Liberalisation of foreign investment

e. International portfolio investment (IPI) and

f. FEMA

5. *Impact of globalisation on India* : Globalisation has had both favourable and adverse effects on the Indian economy. So we get a mixed picture. The following points are to be noted here:

a. Effect on economic growth

b. Impact on foreign trade and BOP

c. Impact on poverty

d. The employment effect of globalisation

e. Foreign capital inflows and

f. Effect on India's foreign reserves

KEY TERMS

Deleveraging	GDR	Transfer of technology
Leveraging	ADR	Outward-looking trade strategy
Outsourcing	FDI	Inward-looking trade strategy

ASSIGNMENTS

1. What do you mean by globalisation? Discuss the main forces behind globalisation.
2. Discuss the arguments put forward for integrating the Indian economy with the global economy.
3. Is globalisation an unmixed blessing? If not, discuss the risks (or dangers) of globalisation.
4. Discuss the impact of globalisation on the Indian economy.

CHAPTER 36

India and the WTO

> *The WTO is a chartered (permanent) trade organisation, not just a secretariat, as was GATT. In other words, while the GATT was just an agreement, the WTO is both an organisation and an agreement.*
>
> M. D. Levi

The GATT is a 1948 agreement which established an international forum for negotiating mutual reductions in trade restrictions

An important step in the area of global trading was the setting up of the World Trade Organisation (WTO) in Jan 1995 in order to promote free trade among nations. In 1948 government representatives from 23 nations formed the General Agreements on Tariffs and Trade (GATT) — a global forum for reducing trade restriction on goods, services, ideas and cultural programme. In 1986 the Uruguay Round of the GATT convened to renegotiate trade agreements. After eight years of meetings, 124 nations voted to lower tariffs, on average, by 38% worldwide and expand new trade rules to areas such as agriculture, services and the protection of patents.

The Uruguay Round also established the WTO. The WTO is an international organisation which replaced the GATT and was assigned the duty to mediate trade disputes among nations.

The setting up of WTO was necessary because the GATT was found to be weak and ineffective in lowering the rates of tariffs imposed by developing countries on imports of manufacturing goods from developed countries. The process of trade liberalisation suffered a major setback since 1974. No doubt, the trend towards tariff reduction continued but developed and developing countries increased non-tariff barriers substantially.

Unlike the GATT, the WTO is a permanent organisation. It is the principal international organisation entrusted with the responsibility of solving the trade problems of member countries and providing a forum for multilateral trade negotiations.

THE OBJECTIVES OF WTO

The main objective of WTO agreements is to establish a multilateral trade system in order to promote free and fair trade among its members. The key focus of the Dunkel Act, on which the WTO has been founded, is on liberalisation of trade on the basis of different nations' own areas of relative efficiency or comparative advantage. This is why the WTO provides an organisational framework for promoting multilateral trade in farm products, manufactured goods and services. In addition, it seeks to protect trade-related intellectual property rights (TRIPs). By commiting each member to give the most favoured nation (MFN) treatment to all its trading partners, it has sought to promote freer multinational trade.

Economic Insight: The Most Favoured Nation Clause
The most favoured nation (MFN) clause is underlying principle of the WTO whereby each country undertakes to apply the same rate of tariff to *all* its trade partners. This general principle of non-discrimination evolved out of earlier WTO endorsement of bilateral trade treaties, whereby if country *A* negotiated a tariff cut with country *B* and subsequently country *B* negotiated an even more favourable tariff cut with country *C*, then the tariff rate applying to the second case would also be extended to *A*.

At present WTO has 152 members which includes both developed and developing countries. Their purpose is to oversee (or supervise) cross-border trade issues and global business practices.

THE FUNCTIONS OF THE WTO

Five important functions of WTO are the following:

1. *Providing an organisational framework* : The WTO provides an organisational framework for administration and implementation of multinational trade agreement reached in the last round of the GATT in 1994, viz., the Uruguay Round.

2. *Providing a forum for negotiation* : The WTO provides a forum for negotiation among its members related to their multilateral trading issues, i.e., issues included in the agreement reached at the Uruguay Round.

3. *Settlement of trade disputes* : The WTO is responsible for the settlement of any trade dispute which may arise among its members. Such disputes normally arise due to different interpretations of the rules and procedures on which a member may have already reached an agreement. Trade disputes are presented by member nations for decision to be made within a year, rather than remaining pending for many years as in the past.

4. *Review of trade policy* : The WTO administers the 'Trade Review Mechanism.'

5. *Cooperation with other international bodies* : With a view to formulating an appropriate global economic policy to promote free and fair trade among its members, the WTO extends the necessary cooperation to other international bodies such as the IMF and the World Bank Group (which includes IBRD, IFC and IDA).

ADMINISTRATIVE BODIES

Two important bodies of the WTO have been set up to perform its various functions:

1. *Dispute Settlement Body (DSB)* : The DSB, which is represented by all member countries, usually meets its members twice a month to listen to the complaints of violations of WTO rules and agreements. It sets up export panels to study disputes and ascertain whether any rule has been violated. The DSB's decision on any issue is final and cannot be challenged.

2. *Trade Policy Review Body (TPRB)* : The TPRB is a forum to make a periodic review of trade policies of all member countries. The major trade policies are reviewed every two years and others every four years.

Three other bodies are the Council for Trade in Goods, the Council for Trade in Services and the Council for Trade-Related Intellectual Property Rights (TRIPs). TRIPs provide patent protection to products and processes in all areas of technology.

THE GUIDING PRINCIPLES

As an international body to promote multilateral trade, the WTO is guided by the following principles:

1. *Non-discrimination* : Non-discrimination is the most fundamental principle of the WTO. It implies two things. (i) Firstly, all trading nations (who are the members of WTO) will be granted the MFN status, that is, each member country will treat every other member equally. No discrimination will be made by a member country with any other member of WTO. (ii) Secondly, foreign goods, services, trade marks, patents and copyrights should be given the same treatment as is given to their domestic counterparts. There is a WTO rule that prohibits countries from treating physically similar products differently based on how they are made. This rule is designed to prevent countries from discriminating against foreign suppliers.

Economic Insight: Intellectual Property Rights
An essential feature of a tangible property is that its value is derived from the use that the owner makes of it, but intellectual property derives its value from the use that others make of it. Authors want their works read and inventors want their inventions used. Patents and copyright serve to ensure that the creators are rewarded. The establishment of patents and intellectual property rights has helped to turn intellectual activity into business activity and business is motivated mainly by profit. Patent protection is necessary to encourage investment in research and development (R & D).

2. *Promotion of free trade* : The objective of WTO, like that of GATT, is to promote free trade among nations through progressive reduction of rates of tariff and reduction of import quotas by member countries. This is to be achieved through negotiations. The objective of tariff reduction is to promote growth of trade in manufactures. Free trade is also promoted by agricultural trade liberalisation through reduction of tariffs and subsidies on both production for the home market and exports. Liberalisation of trade in services is sought to be achieved through the General Agreement on Trade in Services (GATS).

3. *Ensuring stability in the trading system* : Under the WTO contracts members are committed not to raise rates of tariff or erect non-tariff barriers suddenly and arbitrarily. This ensures stability and predictability to the global trading system.

4. *Promotion of fair competition* : The WTO provides for transparent, fair and undistorted competition among member countries through a policy of non-discrimination as also by discouraging unfair competition. Unfair competition among members exists when they adopt such devices as export subsidies and dumping[1].

5. *Market access commitment* : The WTO agreements, which seek to establish multilateral trading system require the member countries to ensure market access on a reciprocal basis by redistributing and abolishing non-tariff barriers. The understanding on market access requires each member to cut tariffs on both farm products and manufacturers by 37%. In addition, in order to provide market access to the products of developing countries to the USA, the latter agreed to cut down farm subsidies. The developing countries are also to reduce subsidies on farm products to 10%.

In the area of trade in services, market access has been ensured by according the suppliers of foreign services the same treatment as that received by domestic service suppliers.

THE GROUP OF 20

India and other developing countries have formed a group, called *G*-20. It makes the demand on the industrialised countries to reduce agricultural subsidies and allow free movement of skilled labour and highly specialised personnel. In its negotiating proposal, India has demanded substantial reduction in tariffs and elimination of trade-distorting domestic support and export subsidies to agriculture by the developed countries. The group has sought liberalisation of movement of professionals through the removal of various constraints.

AN ASSESSMENT OF WTO WITH RESPECT TO INDIA

While controversy arises regarding India's commitment to WTO guidelines and whether India stands to gain from these. The new trade arrangements are an established fact and are bound to have an impact

1. Dumping refers to charging a low price of a good in a foreign market and a high price of the same good in the domestic market.

on various aspects of India's foreign trade. So it is necessary to discuss and examine the nature and amount of impact of WTO negotiations on India.

To begin with, India's participation in international trade is very small at around 0.7%. If share in world trade is an indicator of the extent of globalisation then India is still a long way off from going global. However, important changes are imminent with respect to trade in agriculture, textiles and pharmaceutical industries in particular, as well as the services sector, to mention a few.

Impact on the Agricultural Sector

The impact of WTO on India's agricultural sector is to be felt through the following:

(i) **Reduction in subsidies on agricultural products.** This was done in the form of withdrawal of support prices beyond 10% of the gross value of agricultural output. This, however, will not have much effect in India as the subsidies provided are well below the stipulated figure.

(ii) **A minimum level of import content in total consumption.** This was stipulated to be at least 3% initially, and gradually raised to 5%. This clause too is not effective for India, as it is a country classified as one having balance of payments (BOP) problem and hence exempted from the clause.

(iii) **Disbanding on public distribution system (PDS).** According to the WTO stipulation, any agricultural product has to be procured, and sold at the market price. The Government of India's stand is that the PDS is for the benefit of the poor consumer and not for the poor farmer. Hence this clause too, is not binding for India.

(iv) **Seed patenting.** In response to the WTO rule that seeds must be patented, India enacted the Plant Breeders Right (PBR) Act in 2000, whereby a farmer does not use the seed for commercial purpose (farmer's privilege). The same Act also reserves the right of the agricultural researcher to experiment with any protected variety of seed (researcher's privilege).

Impact on the Textile Sector

The Multi-Fibre Arrangement (MFA) stipulates that the quota system fostered by the eight importing countries (Australia, Canada, European Economic Community (EEC), Finland, Norway, the USA, Japan and Switzerland) would have to be lifted within 10 years. This is supposed to benefit the developing countries' exporters of cotton textiles, India being one of them. This argument, however, does not stand ground for two specific reasons. Firstly, a 10-year period is a very long time during which developed countries like Portugal, Greece and Spain in the EEC and Mexico in North American Free Trade Association (NAFTA) block are likely to consolidate their textile industry. Secondly, India is not the only country that is going to benefit from the arrangement. In fact, competition is going to be more intense among the East Asian and South East. Asian countries and Indian products do not have high profile so far as price and quality are concerned.

Economic Insight: Multi-Fibre Arrangement (MFA)

The Multi-Fibre Arrangement (MFA) is a trade pact between some 80 developed and developing countries, introduced since 1974, which regulates internal trade in textile and clothing through the use of quotas on imports. The purpose is to give low income countries guaranteed and growing access to markets in Europe and North America but at the same time to ensure that this growth does not do any damage to the order established textile and clothing industries of the developing countries.

The MFA is a form of protectionism which discriminates against the interests of the developing countries, many of which are highly dependent on the textile industries as a leading sector in promoting their economic development. It goes against the principles of the WTO but has been tactfully 'exempted' from that body's rules of good conduct. Under an agreement reached in the 'Uruguay Round' of negotiations, however, the MFA was phased out in 2005.

Impact on the Pharmaceutical Sector

Patenting under trade-related aspects of intellectual property rights (TRIPs) has been extended to the large area of microorganisms like bacteria, algae, fungi and virus that serve as the basis for the pharmaceuticals industry. Patents on microorganisms have already been acquired, or likely to be acquired by the multinational firms sooner than the developing countries can lay claim to these. Thus, there remains little scope for developing countries like India to gain from the new arrangement.

Impact on the Services Sector

The opening up of trade in services like banking, insurance, telecommunications and shipping to foreign companies is likely to have an adverse effect on the services sector of the LDCs like India. The reason is that the development of services in these sectors in the developed countries far outstrips that in the developing world.

Commentary: Failure of the Doha Round
The success of the WTO and its predecessor the GATT can be assessed by a very simple fact. Compared to the situation which prevailed before 1947, tariffs imposed by developed countries have fallen from an average of approximately 40% to a modest 4%. In addition, the proportion of duty-free imports of manufactured goods made by developed countries has more than doubled. Such imports increased from 20% to 43%. However, progress in freer trade in agriculture (form) products has been limited. So the gains from liberalised trade have not been fairly shared by exporters of agricultural (primary) products which are mainly developing countries likes India, Pakistan, Nepal and Bangladesh. An extensive round of discussions between developed and developing countries referred to as, the Doha Round, which began in early 2008, to break up in July 2008.

TRIPs

Various types of policies aimed at the domestic market also have direct implications for trade flows. For instance, inconsistent treatment of intellectual property rights (through patents, copyrights trade marks etc.) across countries can distort international trade flows. This is why in the Uruguay Round of trade negotiations, completed in 1994, agreement was reached on harmonisation of such practices, commonly known as trade-related aspects of intellectual property rights (TRIPs).

In fact, action on TRIPs provided for minimum standards for trademarks, patents and copyrights. For example, patents are now in force for 20 years in the USA. The previous length of time had been 17 years.

However, the TRIPs features of the agreement reached at the Uruguay Round hurt the developing countries through the payments that were expected to be made by them in the future to the developed countries for the use of intellectual property.

TRIPs agreements cover the following areas: copyrights, trademarks, including service marks, geographical appellations (i.e., names or titles) of origin, industrial designs and products as well as process patents. Under the Indian Patent Act of 1970, only processes and not products are patented.

Under the new requirement, a transitional period of 10 years is allowed for the adoption of the product patent. A paper presented by the Federation of Indian Export Organisation (FIEO) titled Implications of WTO on India's Trade reveals that trade and non-trade barriers have not really disappeared following the setting up of WTO, but have remerged under fresh garbs in the developed countries. So the developing countries have been forced to open their economies and markets to international competition. The paper divides trade barriers into three categories: *tariff barriers, antidumping* and *safeguarding*.

For example, while agricultural sector has opened up and our farmers can export their grains and cut-flowers to the West, in practice, floriculture is subject to 15 to 20% duty by the EU countries on the plea that India is not a developing country. Besides, the EU has eracted safeguard measures by setting high standards for pesticide residues in case of fruit and vegetables exports resulting in stiff barriers against their entry in the West. Barriers have also been created on the issues of labour standard and environment. The use of child labour has been made a ground for blocking Indian carpet exports into the Western countries. Insistence on sanitary measures and eco-friendly technology are other forms of non-trade barriers used by the developed countries, besides several anti-dumping duties.

Trade-Related Investment Measures (TRIMs)

Trade-related investment measures (TRIMs) consist of various policy steps of a trade nature which are associated with foreign investment activity within a country. Examples would be 'performance requirements', whereby the foreign investor must export a certain percentage of output (and thus earn foreign exchange for the host country), and requirements mandating that a specified percent of inputs used in the foreign investor's final products of domestic origin.

Focus on Terminology: Local Content Rule
The local content rule or rule of origin refers to the stipulation by a country that for a product to qualify as a genuine domestically manufactured product (i.e., originating in the country) the product must be manufactured largely, if not entirely, from locally supplied inputs and components (as opposed to imported components). Local content rules are used by governments mainly to prevent the operation of the so called 'screwdriver' plants (i.e., plants producing final products from mainly imported components) set up to avoid tariffs, quotas and antidumping duties imposed on imported final products.

This measure is adopted quite frequently in developing countries like India and it distorts trade from the pattern dictated by comparative advantage.

Some TRIMs such as local content requirements for foreign investors were to be eliminated within two years by developed countries, five years by developing countries and seven years by 'least developed countries.'

Focus on Terminology: GATS
A general agreement on trade in services (GATS) calls for 'rational treatment' in services. This means that any country is to treat foreign service providers in the same fashion as domestic services providers.

THE FAILURE OF WTO TALKS

The WTO has not solved all global trading problems. Legal and regulatory differences often impeded trade expansion. And a wide gap separates developing nations (80% of WTO membership) and industrialised countries. The WTO meetings in Doha, Quatar began in 2001 to address dismantling protection of manufactured goods, eliminating subsidies on agricultural products and overturning temporary protectionist measures. Unfortunately the Doha Round ended in 2008 with no significant agreements.

In truth, the failure to reach agreement on whether to allow tariff protection for farmers in developing nations marked the end of the Doha Round of the trade talks among the members of the WTO. Some disappointed member countries apprehended that the failure could also endanger global agreements on other issues such as global warming.

In September 2003, trade ministers of developed and developing countries met at Cancun for the next stage of talks on the multilateral trading system. The *G*-20 countries, led by India, Brazil and China frustrated the attempts of the US and the European countries combined to pressurise the developing countries to accept the agenda which mostly suited them and was supposed to promote their interest against the interest of developing countries. This is why the Cancun meeting ended without reaching a final outcome. The main lesson from the failure of Cancun meeting is clear; unless the developed countries work beyond their own interests and try to promote a multilateral trading system which is just and fair to developing countries, nothing tangible is likely to follow. Another area of contension is the agreement on Trade-related Investment Measures (TRIMs). TRIMs are designed to provide a level-playing field between foreign and domestic enterprises. On the face of it, is a worthy objective. But the fact is that in a world in which capital is free to move about, the playing field is heavily tilted in favour of international investors and MNCs. TRIMs institutionalise and reinforce the bias, even thought TRIMs are designed to prevent trade-related bias against MNCs. This is why critics have interpreted the GATT as 'the gentlemen's agreement to talk and talk' and the WTO as the wrong trade organisation.

KEY POINTS

1. *The World Trade Organisation (WTO)* : On January 1, 1995 the day on which the Uruguay Round took effect, the GATT was transformed into the World Trade Organisation. This transformation turned GATT from a trade accord into a permanent membership organisation, responsible for governing the conduct of trade relations among its members, with the GATT obligations remaining at the core of the WTO. As of July 2013, the WTO had 153 members, including China which joined later. Through various councils and committees, the WTO administers the many agreements contained in the Uruguay Round, plus agreements on government procurement and civil aircraft. It oversees the implementation of various tariff cuts and reduction of non-tariff measures agreed to in the negotiations. It is also a watchdog of international trade, regularly examining the trade regimes of individual members. One of the main objectives of the WTO was strengthening the GATT mechanism for settling trade disputes. In addition, substantial institutional reform of the GATT process was sought under the GATT Uruguay Round for expediting the process for settlement of disputes and for launching a regular trade policy review mechanism.

2. *An assessment of WTO with respect to India* : While controversy arises regarding India's commitment to WTO guidelines and whether India stands to gain from these, the new trade arrangements are an established fact and are bound to have an impact on various aspects of India's foreign trade.

3. *Trade-related aspects of intellectual property rights (TRIPs)* : Various types of policies aimed at the domestic market also have direct implications for trade flows. For instance, inconsistent treatment of intellectual property rights (through patents, copyrights trade marks, etc.) across countries can distort international trade flows. This is why in the Uruguay Round of trade negotiations, completed in 1994, agreement was reached on harmonisation of such practices, commonly known as trade-related aspects of intellectual property rights (TRIPs).

4. *Trade-related investment measures (TRIMs)* : Trade-related investment measures (TRIMs) consist of various policy steps of a trade nature which are associated with foreign investment activity within a country. Examples would be 'performance requirements', whereby the foreign investor must export a certain percentage of output (and thus earn foreign exchange for the host country), and requirements mandating that a specified percent of inputs used in the foreign investor's final products of domestic origin.

KEY TERMS

GATT	Multi-Fibre Agreement	MFN treatment
Uruguay round	TRIPs	Local content rule
Doha talks	TRIMS	Trade review mechanism
Group of 20	GATTs	Reciprocity
Non-discrimination	Market access commitment	Dispute settlement

ASSIGNMENTS

1. What are the objectives of WTO? What are its guiding principles?
2. Make an assessment of WTO with respect to India.
3. Briefly discuss the functions of WTO.
4. Briefly discuss the causes of failure of WTO.

36A WTO AND AGRICULTURE

The WTO agreement on agriculture provides a framework for the long-term reform of agricultural sector over the years to come with the objective of introducing increased market orientation in agricultural trade. It provides for commitment in the area of market access, domestic support and export competition. The members have to transform their non-tariff barriers like quotas into equivalent tariff measures. (The tariffs resulting from this transformation, as well as other tariffs in agricultural products, are to be reduced on an average by 36% in the case of developed countries and 24% in the case of developing countries. The reductions were required to be undertaken over a 6-year period in the case of developed countries and a 10-year period in the case of developing countries. The least developed countries were not required to make any commitment for reduction).

The main benefit that less developed countries (LDCs) like India expect from the WTO provision relates to the improved prospects for agricultural exports as a result of likely increase in the world prices of agricultural products due to reduction in domestic subsidies and barriers to trade. While on the one hand earnings from agricultural exports are likely to increase, on the other hand LDCs have been ensured that all major programmes for the development of agriculture will be exempted from the disciplines in the Agricultural Agreement. Thus the operation of the public distribution system will not be affected by the provisions of the Agreement; agricultural subsidies granted by LDCs need not be withdrawn till such time they remain within the prescribed limits specified in the Agreement; and protection necessary for developing the agricultural sector in the LDCs might be continued. In fact, LDCs hope that the reduction of subsidies in the USA and the European Community will enable them to increase their earnings from agricultural exports.

Critical Review

There are a number of issues of concern to LDCs as far as the WTO Agreement on Agriculture (AOA) is concerned.

1. Discrimination: AOA has legitimised the various trade distorting practices of the developed countries in their favour.

2. Unfair advantage for DCs: AOA provides that countries not using any subsidies during the period 1986-88 (which has been identified as the 'base period' for the Agreement) are prohibited from introducing any new subsidies in the WTO regime. This automatically places a small number of rich countries, which have been using export subsidies, in an advantageous position as they have been provided the opportunities to use these subsidies. (It may be noted that while developed countries are allowed to retain 80% of their subsidies, the developing countries can subsidise their farmers not more than 10% of the total value of agricultural production.)

3. Green box and blue box subsidies: At present the position farmers in the USA and EU is in the form of Green Box and Blue Box subsidies and are thus exempted from reduction commitments. Non-or minimal-trade distorting subsidies are called Green Box subsidies and less trade-distorting subsidies are treated as Blue Box subsidies. India and other LDCs have objected to this and have argued that in the absence of specific discipline to ensure that farmers do not divert payment received for non-trade distorting objective to production-boosting investment, all subsidies can distort trade.

4. Peak tariff: The maximum tariff on agricultural commodities in LDCs is very high. And the most important areas for LDCs fall under the highest tariff rates and include the major agricultural staple foods, cereals, meat, sugar, milk, butter and cheese as well as tobacco and cotton. Moreover, tariff wedges will continue to be significantly high on account of tariff escalation, which is a major factor preventing LDCs from diversifying and increasing their share of processed agricultural exports.

5. Food security: Finally, an issue of specific concern to LDCs is food security. The AOA does not address itself adequately to this question and there is a line of thinking that views trade as providing the means for food security in these countries. This assumes that the existence of global surpluses of foodgrains would enable the LDCs to meet their food needs through trade. According to this view, it is not necessary for LDCs to target food self-sufficiency as global surpluses would enable these countries to meet their food needs. This view is wrong.

Furthermore this view is based on the belief that LDCs have sufficient foreign exchange at all times to meet their food import requirements. This again is not true. Accordingly, food self-sufficiency should remain the cornerstone of the food security system of the LDCs.

Comments

An important question has been asked in the context of WTO provisions relating to agriculture. The question is: do agricultural subsidies of developed countries hurt the Third World?

One of the major complains of LDCs during the Doha negotiations (2001) was the continuing existence of large agricultural export and production subsidies in rich countries. The US cotton subsidy, which depresses world cotton prices and, therefore, hurts cotton growers in West Africa, is the most commonly cited example.

On the other hand, China, which exports manufactured goods and imports food and other agricultural products is likely to be hurt by the removal of agricultural subsidies.

However, in Paul Krugman's view, LDCs may actually benefits from rich-country export subsidies. As he put it, "Some Third World farmers are hurt by low prices of subsidised food exports from Europe and the USA— but urban residents in the Third World benefit and so do farmers producing goods, such as coffee, that don't compete with the subsidised products."

As far as the effects of the Doha Round (2001) on low-income African countries is concerned, it appears that such countries would actually be made worse off. The reason is that the negative effects of higher food prices would more than offset the gains from higher prices for crops such as cotton.

Part-VIII

Macroeconomic Problems, Policies and Planning

37. India's Fiscal Situation and Fiscal Policy
38. Fiscal Deficit and Economic Growth
39. Financial Sector Reforms
40. Industrial Policy
41. The Public Sector and the Issue of Privatisation
42. Industrial Sickness in India
43. Consumer Protection
44. Planning in India
45. Global Financial Crisis, Eurozone Crisis and their Impact on Indian Economy
46. Environment, Climatic Change and Sustainable Environment

CHAPTER 37

India's Fiscal Situation and Fiscal Policy

> *The power to tax is not only the power to destroy but also the power to keep alive.*
>
> The US Supreme Court
>
> *A tax policy at lessening inequalities through reducing incomes at the higher levels is only one form which fiscal operations may assume in this sphere. An important complementary aspect lies in the part that public expenditure for economic development (e.g., agriculture and irrigation) and expansion of social services like education and health, may play in strengthening the position of the weaker sections of the community.*
>
> Report of the Taxation Enquiry Commission

PREVIEW

In this chapter we will discuss the role of fiscal policy not only for raising resources in order to enable an economy to achieve faster economic growth but also for ensuring macroeconomic stability (i.e., reasonable price stability with high employment) and equity (i.e., fairness or distributive justice). Fiscal policy refers to the shaping of government's expenditure, revenue and borrowing programmes in such a fashion that a modern mixed economy like India is able to achieve a faster rate of economic growth and high employment in the absence of demand-pull inflation. Since fiscal policy changes are announced through the (annual) budget of the government, fiscal policy is often equated with the budgetary policy. The budget is a consolidated statement of the estimated revenue and expenditure of the government for the coming fiscal year. Every year the budget of the Government of India (GOI), called the Union Budget, is announced on 28th Feb, but it becomes operational from the next fiscal year (which starts from April 1 and ends on March 31, next year). The GOI also announces its fiscal policy every year through its annual budget. Fiscal policy is mainly concerned with revenue-raising and revenue-spending activities of the government. So there are two sides of fiscal (budgetary) policy — the revenue side and the expenditure side. The budget makes proposals about what new taxes are levied, what changes are made in the existing tax rates, and how the government allocates its expenditures among different sectors or activities such as agriculture, irrigation, defence, education, health, physical capital formation (through the setting up of industries in the public sector), infrastructure building, etc.

The budget is of considerable importance to a nation. Households, businesses and financiers — all take interest in the budget. It affects the disposable income and the level of living of people. It also affects corporate profitability as also the returns on investment in financial assets such as dividends as also capital gains and losses.

THE CLASSICAL AND KEYNESIAN VIEW OF THE BUDGET

The classical economists like Adam Smith, David Ricardo and even J. S. Mill were all in favour of balancing the budget of the government. They feel that government's current expenditure should be fully covered by its current revenue (both from tax and non-tax resources). They did not treat budgetary deficit (i.e., excess of current expenditure over current revenue) with favour. The reason is that when the government borrows funds to meet its budgetary deficit, it is in debt and public debt not only imposes burden on the current generation but may also shift the burden on to the future generation.

However, in 1936 J. M. Keynes challenged the classical view and suggested that in times of recession or depression or low economic activity, the government should deliberately incur a deficit in the budget by lowering taxes or increasing its own expenditure to stimulate the economy. By increasing its expenditure, the government would add to private expenditure and this would have job-creating and income-creating effects through the multiplier process. This is known as expansionary fiscal policy which enables a depressed economy to reachieve full employment.

In times of demand-pull inflation the government should raise taxes (to reduce the disposable income of the people) or curtail its own expenditure so as to reduce excess demand pressure from the economy. This is known as contractionary fiscal policy. Thus, according to Keynes, budgetary deficits and surpluses could and should be used both to stimulate and stabilise the economy.

THE MODERN VIEW

According to modern economists, fiscal policy should not just be used as a revenue-raising device but as an instrument for achieving various socio-economic goals such as faster economic growth, macroeconomic stability and equity (distributive justice). The nature of fiscal policy to be adopted depends both on the state of the economy and the objectives of the government's macroeconomic policy. At present, India's fiscal policy seeks to raise resources for the government so as to enable it to carry out its ever-growing expenditure. However, it also serves as an instrument for promoting faster economic growth, generating high employment and ensuring price level stability. This modern view of using the budget as a tool for performing some economic functions or achieving certain economic policy objectives is known *as functional finance*, a term introduced by A. P. Lerner. According to the functional finance school of thought, fiscal policy should be concerned with performing six main functions, viz., taxing and spending, borrowing and lending, buying and selling. According to the principle of functional finance, the size of deficits and surpluses in the government budget are to be judged solely with reference to the levels of employment and prices in the economy and the public debt is in no sense as economic burden on future generations.

GOVERNMENT BUDGET IN INDIA

The budget of GOI has two parts:

1. the revenue account (or the revenue budget) and
2. the capital account (or the capital budget).

The Revenue Account

The revenue account of the budget has two sides. The receipts side shows revenue raised through taxes – both direct and indirect, fees, dividends and profits of public sector enterprises. Such receipts do not create any liability of the government since these are not to be repaid. So such receipts do not lead to any reduction in assets of the government. The expenditure side of the account shows government expenditures on purchase of goods, on social sectors such as health and education as also on defence, public administration and subsidies (on food, fertilisers, cooking gas and exports), as also payment of interest on public debt.

The Capital Account

The receipts side of this account shows (a) recovery of loans by the GOI from the state and local governments, (b) market borrowing (i.e., borrowing by the government from the public, banks and non-banks financial institutions), (c) small savings (i.e., postal savings, provident fund, national savings scheme, etc.), (d) proceeds from disinvestment of public sector enterprises and (e) foreign capital (both foreign aid and external public borrowing). Capital receipts either create a liability for the government or lead to disinvestment of government assets. Such expenditure is essentially consumption expenditure of the government.

The main items of expenditure in the capital account are infrastructure building (construction of roads, bridges, highways, power plants, etc.), loans to public enterprises for productive (developmental) purposes, loans to States and Union Territories. Capital expenditure is incurred for building durable assets such as machinery and equipment, roads and highways, irrigation dams, steel plants, power plants, etc. Thus such expenditure is investment expenditure and is supposed to promote faster economic growth and rapid development of the economy.

TAXES: DIRECT AND INDIRECT

Taxes are of two types: *direct* and *indirect*. On the basis of rates, taxes have been classified into three categories, viz., progressive, proportional and regressive. In addition, taxes may be either lumpsum (like licence fee) or specific (a fixed sum per unit of a good) and ad valorem (a certain percentage of the price of a product)[1].

Shifting, Incidence and Impact

The distinction between direct and indirect taxes is based on shifting, incidence and impact. A direct tax like a personal income tax cannot be shifted. So its incidence is on the assessee (i.e., the person on whom it is imposed). But an indirect tax such as a sales tax, or a value added tax (VAT) or an import duty is initially imposed on seller of a good but it is subsequently passed on to the buyer in the form of higher price of the final good. Such a tax can be shifted either fully or partly. So the incidence (or ultimate burden) is either fully on the buyer (seller) or partly on the buyer and partly on the seller.

As for impact, it is said that direct taxes reduce disposable income of the people and thus their consumption spending. So such taxes act as an anti-inflationary measure. By contrast, since indirect taxes are imposed both on inputs and intermediate goods as also on final goods, they generate cascading effect (i.e., create cumulative burden). Thus such taxes create cost-push pressure and generate inflation from the supply side.

Examples: Personal income tax, corporate tax, gift tax, wealth tax, expenditure tax and capital gains tax are examples of direct tax. In case of such taxes there is direct contact between the taxpayer and the tax-collecting authority.

Examples of indirect taxes are excise duties, sales tax, VAT, customs duty and service tax. While excise duty is imposed on the producer or the manufacturer of a good, sales tax or VAT is imposed on the seller of the good. And the seller subsequently passes the burden of the tax on to the buyer in the form of higher price of the taxed good. Therefore excise duties and sales tax are called *commodity taxes*. Similarly, service tax is imposed on the uses of telephone, insurance premia paid, use of credit cards and air travel. In case of all these indirect taxes, there is no direct relationship between the taxing authorities and taxpayers. The relation is indirect. The producers and sellers collect such taxes from buyers or users of goods and services and pass the money on to the central and state governments.

1. While in case of a specific tax, the revenue of the government depends on the number of units sold, in case of an ad valorem tax, it also depends on the price of the product sold.

OBJECTIVES OF FISCAL POLICY IN INDIA

In developing countries like India, fiscal policy in the form of taxes, government expenditure and borrowing is a powerful and an effective instrument through which the government can promote faster economic growth, achieve macroeconomic stability and distributive justice (i.e., an equitable distribution of income and wealth). The main objective is to create adequate employment opportunities, bring inflation under control, reduce inequality and alleviate poverty.

Four reasons: There are at least five reasons for adopting an appropriate growth-oriented fiscal policy in developing countries like India, viz., (i) existence of various unutilised natural resources, (ii) shortage of technical know-how, (iii) lack of adequate economic and social infrastructure and (iv) rapid growth of population which creates the problem of widespread unemployment and mass poverty.

The main objectives of an appropriate (positive) fiscal policy in India should be the following:

(i) to mobilise resources mainly for the public sector and for developmental purposes according to plan priorities and targets;

(ii) to provide necessary incentives to the private sector to save and invest;

(iii) to control price inflation in order to ensure macroeconomic stability;

(iv) to ensure equitable distribution of income and wealth so that the fruits of material progress are shared by all sections of society (so that with faster economic growth the rich people do not get richer and the poor people poorer).

(v) to promote balanced regional development (so as to avoid uneven growth and regional disparity in a federal country);

(vi) to discourage the consumption of harmful articles such as liquor, cigarettes, harmful drugs, etc. and to save scarce resources which can be utilised for producing mass consumption goods and thus ensure an optimum allocation of resources;

(vii) to protect domestic industries from unfair foreign competition and encourage import-substituting industrialisation (i.e., domestic production of import-substitute items); and

(viii) to achieve economy in government expenditure by curtailing wasteful and unproductive public spending (mainly non-plan revenue expenditure which is the root cause of inflation from the demand side).

In developing countries like India fiscal policy has a special but challenging role to play in promoting faster economic growth with a view to solving the twin problems of poverty and unemployment. Fiscal policy has also to control inflation for reducing the hardship of poor people as also to create a stable macroeconomic environment. The reason is that, inflation often acts as a major obstacle to economic growth. Finally, it has to reduce large inequalities in the distribution of income and wealth and thus ensure equity or economic justice. In short, the budget has to strike a fine balance among three mutually reinforcing objectives, *viz.*, growth, stability and equity. This accords with the functional finance doctrine of Lerner (mentioned earlier in this chapter).

FISCAL POLICY AND MOBILISATION OF RESOURCES FOR PLANNED ECONOMIC GROWTH

Fiscal policy plays an important role in mobilising resources for planned economic growth in developing countries like India. Since economic growth is largely a matter of physical capital formation a growth-oriented fiscal policy has to induce people and business firms to save more so that more investment is made in productive assets and there is an expansion of a society's production capacity and the economy achieves growth faster than before. The following points may be noted in this context:

1. *Raising the ratio of savings to national income*: For achieving faster economic growth, it is necessary to raise the ratio of savings to national income. Economic growth mainly depends on the rate of savings and capital formation. So tax incentives may be given to promote private investment.

An appropriate use of fiscal policy also helps to mobilise savings and convert the same into productive investment, which is so essential for achieving faster economic growth.

2. *Public investment* : Tax incentives can be given to raise aggregate savings for public investment. This is why GOI laid stress on the development of basic and heavy industries such as iron and steel, petrochemicals, coal, heavy engineering, etc. in the public sector since 1956.

3. *Infrastructure building* : Government expenditure plays an important role in the growth process. Without an adequate and an integrated infrastructure faster economic growth is not possible. In other words, infrastructure is key to economic progress. Since economic infrastructure generates positive externalities[1], and return on such investment is low and uncertain, private sector is unlikely to invest in infrastructure building.

In a developing country like India sufficient voluntary savings cannot generated for stepping up the rate of capital formation for at least four main reasons, viz., (i) low per capita income, (ii) high propensity to consume of the poor (who form the majority of population), (iii) conspicuous consumption due to international demonstration effect and (iv) purchase of unproductive assets such as gold, jewellary, real estate, etc. both for short-term speculation and long-term productive investment. So fiscal policy has to be to used raise private savings and encourage business people to invest more.

We now discuss how the various instruments of fiscal policy such as taxation, borrowing and Government spending can be used to mobilise resources for India's planned economic development.

The Mobilisation of Resources through Direct Taxes

By imposing progressive income tax at the personal level, the Government can raise a large amount of resources. Such a tax also helps to reduce income inequality.

However, high marginal tax rates encourage tax evasion and avoidance and lead to the emergence of the parallel economy. In addition, high taxes adversely affect private savings and investment by destroying incentives. This is why the US Supreme Court made the comment in 1964 that "the power to taxes is not only the power to destroy but also the power to keep alive."

The disincentive effects of personal income tax can be avoided by imposing other direct taxes such as capital gains tax, wealth tax, gift tax, estate duty or inheritance tax or death duty. Such taxes have tremendous revenue potential and thus help raise sufficient resources for capital formation. They also serve to reduce inequalities of income and wealth.

Economic Insight: Kaldor's Suggestions
N. Kaldor proposed the introduction of a comprehensive expenditure tax to replace the existing system of taxation in developing countries like India. Kaldor also suggested the imposition of agricultural income tax in countries like India. He felt that without raising sufficient resources from agriculture it would not be possible to active self-sustaining growth in resource-poor countries like India.

The Scope of Agricultural Taxation

The agricultural sector makes the maximum contribution to GDP (national income) of developing countries like India. And a substantial amount of economic surplus is generated from the agricultural sector. And this surplus is mainly appropriated by rich farmers, landowners, moneylenders and traders. And in the absence of an agricultural income tax this surplus is used for consumption of luxury goods by the rural rich and for buying unproductive assets. By imposing agricultural income tax, this surplus can be tapped for capital formation. Thus, according to Kaldor, "the taxation of agriculture by one means or another has a crucial role to play in accelerating the process of economic development".

Due to Green Revolution, since the mid-1960s, the income of the farming community has increased tremendously. This, therefore, has to be mopped up for promoting faster economic growth. There is

1. This means that the total social benefit from infrastructure exceeds private benefit.

need to tax the agricultural sector not only because it generates a surplus but also to ensure effective and efficient use of land. Agricultural tax can be imposed to penalise those people who make injudicious use of fertile land, so that they hand over their land to those who can use it properly. Tax may be imposed on total market value of land holding by an individual family as the Raj Committee had suggested in 1974. In addition, progressive agricultural income tax may be imposed on rich and affluent farmers, with a view to tapping resources. Of course, certain exemptions may be given in deserving cases.

There is no denying the fact that while there is excessive taxation on the industrial sector, the agricultural sector is quite undertaxed. However, if sufficient resources are to be mobilised for planned economic development, there is need to raise the level of agricultural taxation. Planners and policy-makers in India should take the note of this reality.

Advantages of Direct Taxes

As for resource generation and mobilisation for economic development direct taxes offer three advantages: (i) They raise resources without generating inflationary pressures in the economy. Instead by curtailing consumption by reducing the disposable income of the people, such taxes act as an anti-inflationary measure. (ii) They ensure equity by reducing inequalities of income and wealth. (iii) They reduce non-essential and wasteful consumption and thus generate larger surplus for capital formation.

Disadvantages of Direct Taxes

However, there are certain demerits of direct taxes. The yield is low due to narrow base, small coverage and widespread tax evasion and avoidance. The base is narrow due to high exemption limit in a country where per capita income (PCI) is low. While India's annual PCI at current prices were Rs 61,564 in 2011-12, the exemption limit was Rs 1,80,000 (raised) in 2012-13. So most people in India do not fall under the tax net. The low yield from personal income is also due to high marginal rates which encourage widespread tax evasion and tax avoidance. The yield from other direct taxes such as wealth tax, gift tax, capital gains tax is quite meager due to narrow coverage, low rates and tax evasion.

THE ROLE OF INDIRECT TAXES IN RESOURCE MOBILISATION

Due to low contribution of direct taxes there is undue reliance on indirect taxes in developing countries like India. In India almost all commodities — both consumption goods and capital goods — have been brought under the indirect tax net. Three main indirect taxes are the excise duties, custom duties (export and import duties) and sales tax (now replaced partly by value added tax at the state level). Indirect taxes are an important source of development finance in India. They lead to maximum resource mobilisation for economic growth. There are two main reasons for this:

1. The average propensity to consume is much higher in India than in developed countries.
2. Indirect taxes raise prices of consumption goods and reduce real consumption and thus raise the rate of saving which is so important for economic growth.

It is usually said that indirect taxes are regressive and thus create inequality by imposing the major portion of the burden on the poor people (who have a high propensity to consume). Indirect taxes at progressive rates can be imposed on luxury goods and non-essential items which are consumed mainly by the rich and affluent sections of society such as luxury cars, air conditions, 32″ TV sets, air travel, etc.[1] Thus indirect taxes can also promote equity.

In addition, by imposing indirect taxes at higher and higher rates on harmful articles such as cigarettes and liquor, the government can discourage the consumption of such goods and divert resources for productive investment.

In this context a quote from R. N. Tripathy is relevant: "High rates of taxes on commodities with a high income elasticity of demand are quite effective in siphoning a substantial portion of increase in output into the resources of the public sector needed for development financing and a stiff rate of

1. The demand for such goods is highly elastic.

commodity taxes on luxury articles tends to introduce an element of 1940 progressiveness in an otherwise predominantly regressive tax structure in developing countries".[1]

The revenue from indirect taxes that increased from Rs 227 crores in 1970-71 to Rs. 297,720 crores in 2011-12. Thus indirect taxes made an important contribution for mobilisation of resource for achieving faster economic growth. However, due to reduction in excise and custom duties since July 1991 and increase in resources from direct taxes, the share of indirect taxes to the GOI's total tax revenue fell to 56%.

Service Tax

In 2011-12, 70.2%, about of India GDP is derived from 'services'. Therefore to widen the indirect tax base, the GOI has imposed tax on more than 100 items. It is expected that in the coming years the service tax will make a substantial contribution to the mobilisation of resources for India's planned economic development.

Limitations of Indirect Taxes

There are a few disadvantages of using indirect taxes for raising revenue:

(i) *Cost-push pressures* : Indirect taxes generate inflationary forces from the supply side by creating cost-push pressures. Such pressures are very high in India due to the cascading effect (or the cumulative burden) of such taxes. The cascading effect is generated by the fact that in India indirect taxes are imposed both on inputs and on output. And the burden of taxes become cumulative as the output of one industry is used as an input in a large number of other industries and the same item passes through different stages of production and distribution.[2]

(ii) *Customs duty* : By imposing customs duty on industrial raw materials and capital goods the GOI itself has accelerated inflationary pressures in the economy by adding to the existing cost-push pressures.

(iii) *Breeding inefficiency* : In addition, by protecting domestic industries from foreign competition by imposing custom duties the GOI has encouraged the growth and survival of inefficient (high cost) firms and industries. These are not necessarily infant industries which have a genuine prospect of standing on their own feet in the long run by gaining sustainable comparative advantage.

(iv) *Regressiveness* : Indirect taxes are regressive in nature. Since the rich and poor pay such taxes at the same rates, equity cannot be ensured. The need for raising larger and larger amount of resources has forced the GOI to impose higher and higher taxes on almost all mass consumption goods such as sugar, kerosene, electric fans, matches, etc. Most poor people cannot buy these items. So they live under severe hardships.

(v) *Loss of competitiveness* : High indirect taxes have raised the prices of Indian goods above their international levels. As a result India has lost her competitiveness in most export markets. And in times of high rate of inflation Indian firms find it profitable to sell their products in domestic markets without putting any extra effort, i.e., taking the trouble of selling their products in overseas markets. Thus indirect taxes are responsible for slow growth of India's exports and loss of potential foreign exchange (i.e., foreign exchange which could be earned by stepping up exports)

For all these defects of India's indirect tax system the GOI has introduced various reforms in India's tax structure. The focus was on reducing undue reliance on indirect taxes and striking a proper balance between the two types of taxes.

Another objective of tax reform has been to rationalise the indirect tax system mainly with a view to eliminating the cascading effect and thus promoting greater competitiveness of the Indian industry.

For improving the indirect tax structure, broadening its base and rationalising the rates the GOI is planning to introduce a simple indirect tax called goods and services tax (GST). This is likely to

1. *Public Finance in Developing Countries* (1996), p. 200
2. However, this effect can be avoided by introducing a full-fledged value added tax.

replace the CENVAT (i.e., central excise duty levied on the basis of value added). Service tax will be imposed by the Centre and VAT levied by the States. We will discuss GST in detail later in this chapter.

THE ROLE OF TAXATION IN PROMOTING PRIVATE SAVING AND INVESTMENT

In a developing country it is of paramount importance to increase aggregate (national) savings which include both private and public savings. Public savings can be increased by the government through sound fiscal management, viz., by raising tax and non-tax revenues and by cutting public expenditure. At the same time, the tax system should be such as to give necessary incentives to the private sector—both households and businesses—to save and invest more. And a policy of tax cut is likely to impart the needed dynamism to the economy. So planners and policy-makers in developing countries like India face a dilemma situation. If they impose progressive taxes at the personal and corporate levels to raise more revenue, the private sector is likely to lose the incentive to save and invest more. High taxes reduce work effort, the desire to save and invest as also to take risk. So it is necessary to achieve a pragmatic compromise between the revenue needs of the Government and the growth needs of the economy. One way of overcoming the dilemma situation is to impose taxes at high rates and, at the same time, give subsidies and preferential tax treatment for genuinely productive and development-oriented economic activities. The tax system should be so designed as to avoid disincentive effects.

The fiscal system can promote savings in various other ways, indirectly though.

(i) *Tax concessions on private savings* : The return on financial investment can be raised by exempting interests or dividends on various types of private savings (such as bank deposits, contributions to provident fund, life insurance premiam, purchase of units of UTI and National Savings Certificates and various approved Government securities) either totally or substantially from taxation.

(ii) *Reducing progressivity* : By reducing the rate of progression of income taxes both on individuals and companies, it is possible to promote private savings and investment provided rich people who normally have a high propensity to save do not indulge in conspicuous consumption. If this happens, there will be double loss. The Government will lose revenue due to tax cut and for providing various types of incentives. At the same time the potential savings of the community will be wasted through unnecessary expenditure in luxury goods.

(iii) *Preferential treatment of retained profits* : Private investment can be stimulated by exempting retained profits from taxation or by taxing them at low rates. The surcharge on corporate tax has to be abolished for promoting faster industrial growth.

(iv) *Liberal provision for depreciation and investment allowances* : For growth-oriented firms making investments on new plant, equipment and machinery, there is need to give preferential treatment in the form of accelerated depreciation and investment allowances. In order to stimulate investment governments provide tax write-offs on plant and equipment. In the UK, for instance, there is provision for write-offs against corporation income tax when a firm invests in new plant and equipment.

Capital allowances seek to stimulate investment and thus increase the supply-side capabilities of the economy and thus the rate of economic growth. Investment incentives are also offered in many countries. These are essentially inducements provided by the Government to encourage capital investment by the private sector. Government inducements may take the form of capital grants towards the cost of equipment or tax relief on any profits earned. The main rationale behind these incentives is to promote faster economic growth and reduce unemployment by generating the multiplier effect. The GOI can adopt these measures for achieving its plan objectives.

(i) *Investment subsidy* : Investment subsidy or tax break/ rebate can be provided by the Government as is done in the USA. This measure generally proves to be very effective in promoting private investment.

(ii) *Payroll (wage) subsidy* : In Canada, payroll subsidy is given to promote the growth of backward regions. The GOI can also give wage subsidy to entrepreneurs who set up production units in backward areas or the growth centers. This fiscal incentive is likely to induce private entrepreneurs to set up labour-intensive units in rural and semi-urban areas. And such units have tremendous employment potential in a labour-surplus economy.

(iii) ***Tax holdings*** **:** Private investment can also be stimulated by granting of tax holidays. This means exempting profits of new entrepreneurs from taxes for few initial years when overheads are high and profits are low.

(iv) ***Excise duty concessions for expanded production*** **:** For giving extra incentives to the private sector, excise duty concessions may be given to firms which are able to produce goods above a certain specified amount. Suppose, the normal output of a firm is 1,000 units per period. If it succeeds in producing 1,200 units per period, it will be fully or partly exempted from the payment of excise duty.

(v) ***Indirect tax cuts*** **:** In addition, the GOI can totally exempt or lower the rates of sales tax or excise duty on some important raw materials. It can also lower import duties on raw materials and capital goods. All these measures are likely to boost private investment.

(vi) ***Export subsidy*** **:** Finally subsidies on exports are likely to have a favourable effect on investment in export-oriented industries.

Two Sufficient Conditions

Two other conditions have to be fulfilled to make the above fiscal measures really meaningful and effective. These are the following:

1. ***A simple scheme of incentives*** **:** The various incentives to promote savings and investment will bear fruit only if they are kept simple, transparent, certain and, of course, fairly stable. A complicated scheme of incentives itself generates complications and creates more problems than solve and often become self-defeating in nature.[1] Frequent and arbitrary changes in tax policy and tax rates create uncertainty and make it difficult for business people to make anticipatory calculations about the future. Therefore it is possible to take long-term decisions such as investment in fixed assets or expansion and diversification of existing enterprises (even through mergers and acquisitions).

2. ***Favourable macroeconomic environment*** **:** Finally, it may be noted that private investment depends upon numerous diverse factors such as the size of the market for industrial goods and services, costs and availability of raw materials and inputs, the existence of an integrated infrastructural facility in the form of adequate supply of power, coal, steel, oil, technical know-how, transpart facilities, and so on., Tax incentives will become really effective if these factors are favourable. Certain other preconditions have also to be fulfilled such as an efficient and competent system of tax administration. Otherwise the cure may be worse than disease. The tax incentives will be misused. Greedy and powerful business people will take undue advantage of these tax exemptions and turn things in their own favour without bringing any benefit to the community as a whole.

REVENUE MOBILISATION THROUGH GOVERNMENT BORROWING

Since the tax revenue of the GOI is not sufficient to meet its ever-growing expenditure, it has to face a deficit in its annual budget. This is covered in three other ways, viz., (i) small savings, (ii) market borrowing and (iii) borrowing from the Reserve Bank of India.

(i) ***Small savings*** **:** Small savings are collected by the GOI by issuing various types of credit instruments such as NSCs, National Infrastructural Bonds, Power Bonds, Kisan Vikas Patra, Rural Development Bonds, postal saving certificates, etc. Since these instruments are not negotiable; these are not offered for sale in the capital market.

(ii) ***Market borrowing*** **:** In case of market borrowing the government floats long-term bonds in the capital market for financing capital projects. These vary in yield and maturity. These types of bonds

1. Moreover, too heavy taxation leads to fall in tax revenue by destroying private incentives to invest and take risk.

are used for raising funds for development. By comparison, the current or short-term needs of the Government are met by issuing treasury bills. Sometimes new bonds are issued for servicing old bonds, i.e., repaying old debt along with interest.

(iii) ***Monetisation of deficit*** **:** Over the entire plan period the GOI has borrowed from the RBI against its securities and raised large amounts of funds for financing its various planned development projects. But this painless method of borrowing has led to new money creation because the RBI has printed new currency notes for making loan to the GOI[1]. As a result the economy got overheated. And the end result has been price inflation. And deficit spending by the GOI has been one of the main causes of price inflation in India throughout the plan period.

At present government deficit is measured by 'fiscal deficit' which indicates total borrowing requirements of the government. However, government borrowing from the RBI against its securities is now called monetisation of fiscal deficit since it leads to an increase in the supply of high-powered money. And excessive monetisation sets in motion strong inflationary forces by increasing aggregate demand (at least in the short run when aggregate output cannot be increased much). Sometimes interest paid on such bonds is free from taxes.

Advantages of Market Borrowing

(i) ***The easiest way to raise funds*** **:** The government can raise funds through borrowing easily and quickly. The issue of government bonds normally generates good response from the public because the subscribers are able to derive a minimum return in terms of interest without bearing any risk of default. At times the interest on such bonds is free from taxes. But changes in tax rates or tax total can be made only once in a year.

(ii) ***Avoidance of burden through judicious use of funds*** **:** If the funds raised through borrowing are used for genuine (productive) purpose, the burden of public debt can be largely avoided.

(iii) ***Creation of additional production capacity*** **:** The funds raised through market borrowing can be effectively utilised for building up economic infrastructure in the form of construction, of irrigation dams, transport network, power generation plants and communication system. These can help in building a strong agricultural and industrial base of the economy. All such investments promote savings and investment, which are the two most crucial determinants of economic growth.

Problems Associated with Market Borrowing

(i) ***Crowding-out effect*** **:** Public borrowing from the capital market makes it difficult for the private sector to borrow large sums for productive investment. The competition between the private and public sector for limited loanable funds creates shortage of such funds and raises the market rate of interest. This chokes off private investment to a considerable extent. Thus government borrowing is at the expense of private investment. In other words, government borrowing crowds out or obstructs private investment. This crowding-out effect is reinforced by the fact that banks and non-bank financial institutions prefer to invest in risk-free government securities and bonds. So the supply of loanable funds to private investment is reduced further.

Three Related Points

(i) ***Establishing strong financial network in rural areas and developing savings habit among the rural people*** **:** In order to ensure success of government's borrowing policy, it is absolutely essential to set up financial institutions in the rural areas where the majority of population lives. This is likely to help develop thriftiness among rural people and enable the government to utilise more and more rural savings for productive investment.

1. A nexus between the budgetary deficit of the GOI and the domestic money supply has all along operated in India and deficit financing shows the net indebtedness of the GOI to the financial sector.

(ii) ***Covering only capital expenditure with borrowed funds*** **:** The borrowed funds should not be used for covering the revenue expenditure of the Government which does not create any productive asset[1]. In other words, borrowed funds are to be utilised only for covering the capital expenditure of the GOI.

(iii) ***Devising suitable techniques of borrowing*** **:** There are three alternative methods of borrowing from which the government has to choose. These are the following:

- **(a)** ***Bonds*** **:** The Government should use suitable techniques of market borrowing to suit the needs of different types of investors. While bonds of large denominations and long maturity may be offered to institutional investors, small denomination and short-maturity ones may suit the need of non-institutional retail investors.
- **(b)** ***Small savings*** **:** The Government can also mobilise an adequate amount of résources by properly devising various small saving schemes.
- **(c)** ***Dishoarding*** **:** According to the neo-classical theory of interest, one of the sources of supply of loanable funds is dishoarding. By mobilising the hoarded gold and jewellary through new schemes, the Government can collect sufficient funds for development purposes.

REVENUE DEFICIT AS AN OBSTACLE TO GROWTH

India's revenue deficit in the budget continued to increase in the first decade of reforms (from 3.4% in 1990-91 to 4.4% in 2002-03). Revenue deficit implies public dissaving. It also implies that the revenue of the Government—both from tax and non-tax sources—were not sufficient to meet the current (consumption) expenditures of the Central Government So the revenue deficit has to be covered by utilising borrowed funds (i.e., capital receipts). These funds could have been more productively utilised to meet the capital (investment) expenditure. Thus revenue deficit has acted as an obstacle to economic growth. In other words, by reducing the amount of funds which could be utilised for investment purposes, revenue deficit slowed down the rate of capital formation and economic growth.

THE FRBMA

To overcome the drawback of India's fiscal system, the Fiscal Responsibility and Budget Management Act (FRBMA) was passed in 2003. It prescribed reduction of revenue deficit to zero by 2008-09. However, to counter the slowdown of the Indian economy and to keep the growth momentum alive, even in a situation of global financial crisis, the GOI had to increase its expenditure and cut both excise duties and customs duties in order to give the necessary fiscal boost to the economy. As a result the revenue deficit increased to 4.5% of GDP in 2008-09 and further to 5.7% in 2011-12.

FISCAL CONSOLIDATION

In order to achieve fiscal consolidation (i.e., reduction of fiscal deficit) with a view to making larger and larger resources available for planned economic development (with focus on employment generation as also for the control of inflation). The stress has been on two things: (i) raising revenue through taxes and (ii) improving the quality of public expenditure. The second objective was sought to be achieved by reducing non-plan revenue expenditure and by raising plan capital expenditure which was productive and growth-promoting in nature. Since the bulk of public expenditure is of a committed nature, such as payment on interest on public debt, defence spending, disbursement of wages and salaries and pensions of government employees there is not much scope for economy in public expenditure in the short run. So the objective of achieving faster economic growth and generation of additional employment opportunities had to be achieved by raising tax revenue and improving the quality of public expenditure. This is why various reform measures had been carried out in the areas of both direct and indirect taxes and in the area of public expenditure, keeping in view the need to

1. Otherwise the mobilisation of resources for economic development will not be meaningful.

achieve fiscal consolidation. It is against this backdrop that we make an overall assessment of India's fiscal reforms.

A BROAD OVERVIEW OF INDIA'S FISCAL REFORMS

(a) The First Decade of Reforms

Fiscal reforms were initiated in India since 1991 in order to achieve three main objectives of planning, viz., faster economic growth, reasonable price stability and equity. In order to achieve these objectives it was necessary to raise more resources through taxation and reduce the growth of non-plan revenue expenditure in first decade of economic reforms(1991-2001).

(b) The Second Decade of Reforms

Since 2001-02 the GOI continued to follow the same prudent fiscal policy. The Central Government evolved a balanced tax system based on moderate tax rates and minimum exemptions. In addition, the tax base was widened by including a large number of new taxpayers. While achieving economy in its non-plan revenue expenditure, the Government adopted a positive measure. It made adequate provision for meeting the infrastructural needs of the country — both economic and social. Although the Government laid stress on revenue-stretching fiscal strategy, it did not go for fiscal compression. Instead, it laid emphasis on re-prioritisation of public expenditure. The maximum stress was laid on plan capital expenditure for expanding the economy's production capacity. The following specific fiscal measures were adopted during the second decade of economic reforms:

(i) *Raising tax-GDP ratio* : The Government aimed at raising the tax-GDP ratio by making the tax system more productive (i.e., revenue yielding). The objective was to make more funds available for development purposes. And to fulfil the objective various tax reform measures have been carried out — in respect of both direct and indirect taxes. While the Government reduce tax rates, it widened the direct tax base by bringing more people under the tax net. As a result total tax revenue as a percentage of GDP increased from 15.4% in 1990-91 to 21.2% in 2008-09 (although it fell marginally to 14.5% in 2000-01).

By adopting various reform measures the Government attempted to bring about a change in the tax structure and succeeded in reducing its excessive dependence on regressive resource-distorting indirect taxes and increasing its dependence on progressive direct taxes. As a result more resources have become available for accelerating the rate of economic growth and for achieving price stability at the same time. The change in the tax structure led to an increase in revenue from direct taxes in spite of cuts in tax rates. While the contribution of indirect taxes to total tax revenue had fallen from 83.7% in 1990-91 to 57.1% in 2008-09, those of direct taxes increased from 16.3% to 42.9%.

(ii) *Incentive to exporters* : In order to raise exports it was necessary to increase the competitiveness of Indian products in the international market. This was sought to be achieved by cutting both excise duties and custom duties.

TAX REFORMS

One of the key elements of India's economic reforms has been the reform of the tax system[1]. It was recognised that a larger collection of tax revenues could not be achieved by high rates of taxation, which tended to encourage evasion. By contrast a tax system which is simple to administer, has moderate rates of taxation and relies upon a broad tax base is most appropriate for India.

With lower tax rates revenue buoyancy from direct taxes, mainly income taxes — both personal and corporate — could be achieved through better compliance and minimal exemptions. In fact, the long term fiscal policy announced in 1985 rightly emphasised that "a broader base of taxation, combined with moderate rates of taxes and strict enforcement, can yield better revenue results".

1. See J. D. Sachs [ed.]: *India in the Era of Economic Reforms* (Oxford).

Main Reform Measures

During the reform period, the Government has pursued the strategy of tax reforms which was largely based on the recommendations of the Tax Reforms Committee (TRC) or the Chelliah Committee[1]. Broadly, the TRC proposed that while the share of customs duties in total taxes should be reduced, the share of direct taxes be raised at the same time. In addition, larger revenues need to be mobilised *via* excise duties by transforming them into a system of value added tax (VAT). However, no realistic growth-oriented solution to India's fiscal problems could be achieved only by raising tax revenues as a percent age of GDP. For a country at India's levels, tax rates and revenues were both high up to 1996-97 compared to those in the faster growing economies of East and West. This is why the following tax reform measures were adopted:

A. Direct Tax Reforms

(i) *Tax cuts* : The Government announced a number of tax cuts in 1997-98. The maximum marginal rate of personal income tax was reduced from 40% to 30%. The corporate income tax[2] for domestic companies was reduced to 35% and the surcharge of 7.5% was abolished. Corporate tax on foreign companies was reduced from 55% to 48%.

Comments: In order to discourage tax evasion, raising India's competitiveness and to reduce tax arbitrage opportunities (through transfer pricing practices of multinational corporation or, in short, MNCs), the Government should reduce corporate tax rates further. And in order to attract foreign capital these rates need to be aligned with those prevalent in the neighbouring East Asian countries.

Economic Insight: Transfer Price

Transfer price is the internal price at which factor inputs and products are transacted between the branches or subsidiaries of an integrated firm. The transfer price may be set by reference to the prices ruling in the outside (external) markets for inputs and products (e.g., arm's-length pricing) or it may be administered according to some internal accounting convention (for example, a full-cost pricing).

Transfer pricing gives a firm added direction in pricing its products, and the danger is that it could well be tempted to employ 'manipulative' transfer pricing to harm competitors (for example, price-squeeze by a non-competitive firm).

(ii) *Introduction of Minimum Alternate Tax (MAT)* : The Central Government introduced a new tax —'Minimum Alternate Tax' (MAT) on companies.[3] In a case where the total income of a company, after all eligible deductions (and exemptions) is less than 30% of book profit, the total income of such a company would be deemed to be 30% of book profit and would be taxed accordingly. In order to raise revenue, MAT has been raised from 7.5% to 10% of book profit of corporate enterprises (limited companies). In addition, long-term capital gains have been included in the book profits. Thus the current base of the MAT is book profit. This is easily manipulated by various companies to generate zero tax.

If may be noted that MAT rate was 15% of book profits up to 2009-10. In the Union Budget 2010-11, the rate was raised to 18% and further to 18.5% in the Budget 2011-12.

1. The TRC laid out a two-pronged strategy to improve the yield of income tax— (i) widening the tax base combined with moderation in rates and (ii) strengthening tax administration.
2. In the same year, corporate tax rate in Singapore was 27%, Thailand 30% and Malaysia and South Korea 34%.
3. When a company pays MAT, the tax credit enjoyed by it can be carried forward for a period of five assessment years. And in the assessment year when regular tax becomes payable, the difference between regular tax and tax computed under MAT for that year will be set off against the MAT credit available. This implies that every company including zero tax companies would have to pay a minimum income tax of 10.5% of its book profits.

Focus on Terminology: Minimum Alternative Tax

Normally, a company is liable to pay tax on the income computed in accordance with the provisions of the Income Tax Act, but the profit and loss account of the company is prepared as per the provisions of the Companies Act. There were a large number of companies which had book profits as per their profit and loss account but were not paying any tax because income computed as per the provisions of the Income Tax Act was either nil or negative or insignificant. In such case, although the companies were showing book profits and declaring dividends to the shareholders, they were not paying any income tax. These companies are popularly known as zero-tax companies. In order to bring such companies under the income tax net, Section 115 JA was introduced with effect from the assessment year 1997-98.

According to this Section, if the taxable income of a company computed under this Act, in respect of previous year 1996-97 and onwards is less than 30% of its book profits, the total income of such company is chargeable to tax for the relevant previous year to an amount equal to 30% of such book profits.

A new tax credit scheme is introduced by which MAT paid can be carried forward for set-off against regular tax payable during the subsequent five-year period subject to certain conditions, as presented below:

- When a company pays tax under MAT, the tax credit earned by it shall be an amount which is the difference between the amount payable under MAT and the regular tax. Regular tax in this case means the tax payable on the basis of normal computation of total income of the company.
- MAT credit will be allowed the carry-forward facility for a period of five assessment years immediately succeeding the assessment year in which MAT is paid. Unabsorbed MAT credit will be allowed to be accumulated subject to the five-year carry forward limit.
- In the assessment year when regular tax becomes payable, the difference between the regular tax and the tax computed under MAT for that year will be set off against the MAT credit available.
- The credit allowed will not bear any interest.

(iii) *Other taxes* : Two other taxes have been imposed during the reform period. The fringe benefit tax (FBT) was levied on corporate employees. And securities transactions tax (STT) was levied on the purchase and sells of shares and securities.

Comments: In the last two decades, efforts have been made to reduce direct tax rates and broaden the direct tax base by withdrawing certain exemptions and concessions. This has improved tax compliance and resulted in revenue buoyancy. However, much larger revenues can be collected from direct taxes if a number of existing exemptions (which have lost their relevance) are withdrawn and the direct tax system is simplified further and made transparent, as has been suggested by the Kelkar Committee.

B. Indirect Tax

As for indirect taxes of the GOI, there has occurred quite some progress in the reform of customs duties and union excise duties. In addition, service tax has been introduced.

(i) *Customs duties* : Two main objectives of import tariffs reform have been (a) to reduce the cost of intermediate and capital goods to the economy and (b) to gradually lower the excessively high level of protection given to the Indian industry. Other objectives of such reform have been to promote domestic competition, make Indian exports more competitive and benefit domestic consumers through improved quality and lower price. No doubt the continued and rapid liberalisation of trade is crucial for improving India's growth prospects. However, in spite of lowering of rates in the last two decades of economic reforms, customs duties still remain high. These are much above the levels prevailing in India's competitor countries. Consequently they make India's labour-intensive capital goods less attractive in export markets.

The GOI has plans to reduce the maximum rate of customs duties to the Association of South-East Asian (ASEAN) level. No doubt, India is committed to reduce import duties under trade liberalisation agreement of WTO. However, there is the need to provide effective protection to agriculture and industries, such as textiles by fixing higher than peak rates.

(ii) ***Domestic commodity taxes*** **:** Reforms in the areas of domestic commodity taxation were initiated in the 1993-94 budget of the Union Government. The objective was to simplify and rationalise the then existing excise-modified value added tax(MODVAT) system. The MODVAT was introduced from March 1986 (through the 1986-87 Union Budget). Under the MODVAT scheme, credit of duty was allowed on inputs, which were used either for producing excisable finished products or intermediate goods. Over the years the coverage of the MODVAT has been extended to include more commodities and sectors.

The VAT was put into effect from April 2005. It is expected that through effective implementation of the VAT, it will be possible to eliminate the cascading effect (cumulative burden) of sales tax and excise duty as also to achieve price stability. The revenue of the governments — both central and State— is also likely to rise due to the cross-checking system which will avoid tax evasion.

Now there is a single excise duty, called CENVAT (which resembles VAT very closely) at the uniform rate of 16% on all items which pass through a production chain. And the Government is trying to transform it into a full-fledged VAT.

(iii) ***Service tax*** **:** During the reform period, the GOI has introduced service tax. And to collect more revenue from this tax, more and more services have been brought under the tax net. At present service tax is imposed on more than 100 items.

In short, the increase in the share of direct taxes and a fall in that of indirect taxes is one welcome feature of India's changing tax structure. This is attributable to the success of the strategy of tax reform followed since July 1991.

Suggestions for Improving India's Tax System

The following suggestions may be put forward for improving the yield from direct taxes, mainly income taxes from individuals and companies. These will surely lead to an increase in the tax-GDP ratio.

(i) ***Widening the tax base*** **:** In order to increase revenue from personal income tax, the Government must further broaden the base of the tax-paying population. Base widening can be done in two ways: (a) by bringing more and more potential tax-payers into the tax net and (b) by eliminating numerous exemptions and deductions provided in computing taxable income[1]. Due to these exemptions the effective rate of corporation tax is much less than its nominal rate. What is worse is that some of these exemptions are misused in order to evade taxes.

Commentary: Presumptive Taxes
Attempts have been made to broaden the base with a scheme of presumptive taxation for shopkeepers and other retail traders, persons engaged in a vocation or in the running of an eating house or restuarant, and small road transport operators, hiring, operating or leasing only one transport vehicle. Subsequently, a new estimated income scheme for contractors (with a turnover of up to Rs. 4 million) and for truck owners (who own up to ten trucks) was also introduced. In a view of the enormous size of India's unorganised sector, presumptive taxation is particularly suitable since tax evasion is rampant and enforcement costs are very high. Apart from its administrative ease, the presumptive approach can raise both equity and efficiency, by collecting taxes from those who never paid them earlier, but in an almost lump-sum manner. It is felt that the GOI should continue to improve the design and enforcement of the scheme.

Base broadening can also be achieved by widening the coverage of tax. It can be achieved by removing those exemptions and deductions which are allowed on various grounds of social and economic policy.

1. Sometimes these concessions are offered to serve non-tax objectives (or purposes).

A related point may now be noted here. The long-term capital gains from shares have been exempted from taxes since 2004-05. And the Government has introduced the Securities Transactions Tax. At the same time, the short-term capital gains tax has been reduced from 20% to 15%. This provision goes against broadening the tax base.

(ii) *Lowering tax rates* : The above mentioned measures would help provide a ground for further lowering of tax rates. In addition, there is a strong case for levying tax on the rent-free or the concessional-rent residential accommodation provided to the employees of the Government and the public sector. Similarly, since restrictions on salary levels in the private sector have been removed, fringe benefits provided to the employees in the private sector too needs to be taxed as well. In fact, the GOI has already introduced fringe benefit tax. However, the main difficulty with the tax is that it often becomes difficult to draw a line between legitimate business expenses and fringe benefit(s).

(iii) *Corporate tax reform* : In the area of corporate taxation, too there is need to increase the number of tax-paying companies. Still there exists a large number of companies which pay substantial dividends but do not pay any corporate income tax. These are often reported as 'zero-tax' companies. With continuing prevalence of such companies, there is need to introduce a minimum tax in order to ensure fairness and increase revenue buoyancy of the income tax.

(iv) *Tax on gross assets and not on book profits* : The introduction of MAT is no doubt a step in right direction. But it has one main drawback. It cannot tackle issues related to underreporting of profits due to manipulations through transfer pricing. Similarly, MAT will not be applicable if there is no taxable income or if companies show losses. Companies which have sufficient investment every year to allow for depreciation provisions can very well show a zero taxable income. MAT may serve its purpose better if levied on gross corporate assets as against being levied on book profits.

(v) *Tax on agricultural income* : With a view to mobilising large tax revenues, State Governments need to levy tax on agricultural income. Over the last five decades or so, incomes in the agricultural sector, especially for the large landowners, have increased considerably. The State Governments need to design tax systems which are simple to administer, have moderate rate structure and rely upon a broad tax base. However, small and marginal farmers, with little or no landholdings, should be exempted for paying income tax. For that purpose an exemption limit has to be set.

C. Reform of the Indirect Tax System

The following reform measures have been adopted in the area of indirect of taxes since 1991:

(i) *Further reduction of import duties* : India needs to reduce import duties much further and bring them in line with the levels still prevailing in other Asian economies. What is of paramount importance is that tariff rates on imported capital goods used for producing export terms and on imported inputs which go into export production should be duty free. High protection to the consumer goods industries tends to divert resources to inefficient areas and leads to higher prices. At the same time the absence of international competition leads to no quality upgradation in major industries producing consumer goods.

(ii) *Evolving a full-fledged VAT* : Further reforms in the area of domestic commodity taxes are required to transform the existing CENVAT system into a full-fledged VAT at the Central level covering all commodities and services. Quite some progress has been made in this direction. However, it is felt that, over a period of time, the VAT system would be instrumental in generating dynamic efficiency as have been made by China, Pakistan and Thailand.

(iii) *State taxes* : The transformation to a VAT at Central Government level needs to be supplemented by reform of indirect taxes at the State level, too. With a complex and inefficient State sales tax regime, and a lack of harmonisation between Central and State taxes, the indirect tax system as a whole remains complex in nature and distortionary in impact. VAT at a uniform rate has to be introduced at the State-level through mutual agreement among States so that some States do not gain at the expense of the others through arbitrage (i.e., transferring goods from one State with low tax to another with high tax).

D. Expenditure Reform

A distinct change in the pattern (composition) of public expenditure in India is observable. While there has occurred just a marginal drop in plan (developmental) expenditure (mainly on agriculture and rural development as also on infrastructural building) as a percentage of GDP, due to the inability of the Government to reduce growth of the revenue expenditure adequately, non-plan (non-development) expenditure[1] feel sharply. This is, no doubt, an encouraging trend. It implies a distinct improvement in the pattern and quality of expenditure. If this trend is accelerated, India will be able to grow faster during the Twelfth plan period (2009-10). This will become a reality if the Government can sustain its effort of shifting its resources away from revenue expenditure and toward capital expenditure. And this will become possible by raising more revenue through taxes while, at the same time, cutting non-plan expenditure. These two measures are conjointly likely to lead to a fall in revenue deficit, which is good for the economy. To put it from the other side, an increase in revenue deficit is bad for the economy because it does not lead to the creation of productive assets which are so essential for achieving economic growth.

In any case the GOI should not permit any decline in capital expenditure. The reason is that such expenditure represents investment in physical assets and creation of additional production capacity.

Subsidies: One of the main components of the Government's revenue expenditure is subsidy. The Government's present policy is to increase food subsidy and to target all subsidies at the weaker sections of the society, i.e., the poor and the needy, such as the small and marginal farmers, landless labourers as also the urban poor.

Commentary: The Developmental Nature of Revenue Expenditure
All the types of revenue expenditure are not non-developmental in nature. Some components of such expenditure such as those on social sectors (mainly elementary education and primary health care) are developmental in nature. In this context we may cite the examples of expenditure on Sarv Shiksha Abhijan and Mid-day Meals; health and family welfare (National Rural Health Mission), rural employment as also physical infrastructure such as rural roads. So it is not always possible to draw a line between non-developmental and developmental expenditure and the classification of public expenditure is largely arbitrary.

Fiscal Consolidation: Reduction in Fiscal Deficit

A large fiscal deficit is a perennial macroeconomic problem for India. Fiscal deficit is the excess of total Government expenditure including loans, net of repayment, over revenue receipts *plus* those capital receipts which are not borrowing and which finally accrue to the Government. It indicates the total borrowing requirements of the Government from all sources (i.e., market borrowing, net borrowing from the RBI or the monetisation of deficit, small savings and external assistance or borrowing from abroad at concessional rates of interest).

For achieving macroeconomic stability, fiscal deficit has to be reduced. This is known as fiscal consolidation which is supposed to promote faster economic growth with stability and equity. As noted above, this can be achieved by raising tax-GDP ratio and cutting non-plan expenditure at the same time.

Three Concluding Comments

1. India should adopt a comprehensive VAT, wherein there is sharing of the tax base by the Central and the States. The suggested tax regime would constitute a national-level value added tax whose revenue will be shared between the Centre and the States. For raising more revenue as also for achieving macroeconomic stability and distributive justice there is a need to look at the whole value addition chain covering both goods and services.

2. The MAT reform would lead to further liberalisation of trade taxation.

1. Non-developmental expenditure is incurred on interest payment, major subsidies and national defence.

3. The major source of budget balancing (or, fiscal consolidation) will have to be expenditure cuts. The Government should cut its non-plan (revenue) expenditure as much as possible, while at the same time maintaining or even stepping up its capital expenditure.

Fiscal Policy, Inclusive Growth and Equity

Fiscal policy can be used to achieve inclusive growth, i.e., growth with distributive justice. This can be achieved by reducing inequality and creating sufficient employment opportunities. However, high taxes reduce the incentive to save and invest and they act as an obstacle to capital formation and economic growth. Thus there is a trade-off between growth and equity. So it is absolutely essential to strike a balance between the two apparently conflicting objectives: (i) strengthening incentives to invest so as to accelerate the rate of capital formation and enable the economy to achieve a faster rate of economic growth and (ii) reducing economic inequalities (i.e., inequalities in income and wealth).

It is necessary to formulate a well-balanced fiscal policy in such a fashion that higher incomes are taxed at a progressive rate but the initiative and enterprise of the private sector are not destroyed. For promoting equity, the Government has to spend huge sums on anti-poverty programmes such as National Rural Employment Guarantee (NREG) Scheme, Antyodaya Anna Yojana, and Bharat Nigam Yojana. These have created gainful employment opportunities for 100 days in rural areas. Other employment-generating programmes include providing employment to one bread earner in each family at minimum wages and the food-for-work programme in 150 districts of the country. For improving the economic conditions of the poor, the Government has stepped up its expenditure on primary education and public health. The underlying objective is to ensure universal access to basic (primary) education and health. This is why adequate funds are raised for Sarv Shikhsa Abhijan, Mid-day Cooked Meal Scheme, basic health care and drinking water facilities in rural areas. In fact, for achieving the objective of universal elementary education, the Government has imposed 3% education cess on all central taxes such as personal income tax, corporation tax and excise duty.

Fiscal Policy and Price Stability

The main cause of demand-pull inflation in India has been the growing fiscal deficit of the Government. The deficit increased year after year because the Government has not been able to finance its mounting expenditure through taxes and surpluses of public sector units.

Therefore, under the new economic policy (NEP, 1991), attempts have been made to reduce fiscal deficit by reducing Government expenditure and raising more revenue through greater tax effort. It was thought that this measure would help reduce the rate of inflation.

However, fiscal deficit increased to 6.1% of GDP in 2008-09 and to 6.7% in 2009-10 due to global financial crisis. This has a strong inflationary potential. And to check inflation, the Government has to reduce fiscal deficit both by raising revenue and by cutting its non-plan (revenue) expenditure as much as possible.

It appears that, the present food inflation cannot be checked by fiscal policy. Other measures have to be adopted such as increase in food production through a second green revolution based on biotechnology research. This is why some economists have opposed tax on agricultural income.

THE MAJOR SOURCES OF REVENUE OF THE CENTRAL GOVERNMENT

We have already discussed briefly the main sources of revenue of the GOI earlier in this chapter. We now discuss these sources in detail. The major sources of revenue of the Central Government are the following:

A. Direct Taxes: Four important direct taxes levied by the Central Government in India are:

(a) Personal income tax (or tax on household income),

(b) corporation tax (or tax on corporate profit)

(c) expenditure tax and

(d) wealth tax.

B. Indirect Taxes: Three most important indirect taxes levied by the Central Government of India are:

(a) Union excise duties (at the manufacturing stage),

(b) custom duties (on imported articles) and

(c) service tax (on financial, insurance and other services).

C. Non-Tax Revenue: It is divided into two parts, viz.,

(a) ***Revenue receipts*** **:** Three main sources of such receipts are:

(i) Interest receipts from loan given to the States and public sector units (PSUs),

(ii) Trading surpluses (profits and dividends) from PSUs and

(iii) External grants.

b. ***Capital receipts*** **:** The main items of such receipts are the following:

(i) Recovery of loans,

(ii) Market borrowing (by selling bonds and other long-term credit instruments),

(iii) Borrowing from the RBI against its securities (and monetisation of deficits),

(iv) External assistance received from other countries also from the IMF and the World Bank,

(v) Disinvestment of government equity held in PSUs,

(vi) Small savings (such as post office deposits and NSCs, etc.), and

(vii) Public provident fund (PPF).

While items (i) and (v) are non-debt capital receipts, all other items of capital receipts are debt receipts. This means that they add to public debt — both internal and external. Item (iii) implies that the RBI issues new currency notes against Government securities to make loans to the Government.

We may now discuss the main sources of revenue of the Central Government in further detail:

A. Direct Taxes

1. Personal Income Tax: The revenue from personal income tax increased from Rs. 114 crores in 1970-71 to Rs. 1,250 crores in 1990-91 and to Rs. 119496 crores in 2011-12. And, in a federal country like India this revenue is shared between the Centre and the States on the basis of the recommendations of the Finance Commissions[1].

Personal income tax is imposed on individuals and Hindu undivided families (HUFs). The GOI has imposed income tax at a progressive rate in order to reduce inequality in the distribution of income and wealth. Under the progressive tax system an individual's tax liability increases faster than his income. This means that the marginal tax rate is higher than the average tax rate.

Up to 1976-77, the personal tax rate in India was the highest in the world (97.75%). So the tax was confiscatory in nature and led to widespread tax evasion and avoidance[2]. However, over the years the tax rate has been reduced. As a result tax revenue has increased, mainly due to greater tax compliance.

At present, income up to Rs. 180,000 is exempted from income tax. For working women exemption limit is Rs. 1,90,000 and for senior citizens Rs. 2,50,000.

The maximum rate of income tax at present is 30%. This rate is applicable on income above Rs. 8,00,000. The threshold for incidence of the peak income tax of 30% was increased to Rs. 10 lakh from Rs. 8 lakh.

1. Finance Commissions take decision on tax sharing for a five-year period. So far 13 such Commissions have been appointed by GOI. The awards of the Thirteenth FC is valid for the five-year period 2010-15.

2. As a result a parallel economy emerged in India.

The present rate structure is as follows:

Income	Tax rate
Up to Rs. 1,80,000	nil
Rs. 1,80,001 – Rs. 3,00,000	10%
Rs. 3,00,000 – Rs. 8,00,000	20%
Above Rs 8,00,000	30%

The union budget 2013-14 provided for tax credits of Rs. 2000 for persons having annual income between Rs. 2 lakhs and 5 lakh. A surcharge of 10% on income tax was imposed on persons having taxable income of more than Rs 1 crore per year.

At present there is 3% educational cess on personal income tax. However, additional exemption up to Rs. 1,00,000 is given to individuals under section 80C of the Income Tax Act to encourage people to save more. So contribution to PPF, premia on life insurance, equity-linked saving schemes (ELS) of mutual funds, an employee's contribution to pension funds and investment in fixed deposits in scheduled commercial banks (for a term of 5 years or more) are exempted from income tax. In addition, senior citizens' saving scheme and post office time deposit scheme have also been exempted under section 80C up to Rs. 1,00,000.

2. Corporation Tax: The corporation tax is a tax on the income (i.e., profits) of public limited companies. At present it is imposed at a flat rate of 30% of the net profits of corporate enterprises. Depreciation of plant and machines is partly (up to 15%) treated as a deductible expense for tax purposes (while calculating profits). There is an educational cess of 3% on corporation tax. There is also MAT at the rate of 18.5% on book profits of zero tax companies, as mentioned earlier. In addition, long-term capital gains arising out of shares/securities are included in book profits. At present there is no surcharge on income tax in case of small and medium enterprises with a taxable income of Rs. 1 crore or less. The rationale behind this provision is to leave more funds with such enterprises and encourage them to plough back a major portion of their funds for expansion and diversification. The revenue from corporation tax in 2011-12 was Rs. 230,682 crores.

3. Expenditure Tax: At present expenditure tax is imposed on people who stay in luxury hotels and pay rent of Rs. 400 or more per day as also on bills of restaurants providing extra facility such as air-conditioning. Revenue from the tax was only Rs. 82 crores in 1990-91.

4. Wealth Tax: The revenue from the wealth tax was Rs 603 crores in 2010-11. The exemption limit at present is Rs. 30 lakhs. Assets such as shares, bank deposits and one residential house are exempted from wealth tax. The tax is applicable for individuals, HUFs and companies. The rate varies between 0.5% to 2% of taxable wealth. It is levied on the basis of slab system. Although the revenue from wealth tax is small, it serves an important purpose, viz., distributive justice or social equity.

5. Securities Transaction Tax (STT): For those who pay capital gains tax, there is STT at the rate 1.5% of the value of transactions of equities delivered. The tax is shared by the buyer and seller on a 50:50 basis. For those who hold units in equity-linked assets the rate of STT is 0.15% of the value of transactions. For (a) intra-day trades and arbitragers of equities/securities and (b) traders of derivatives (futures and options — both call and put) the rate of STT is 0.015% and 0.011, respectively of the total value of transactions.

B. Indirect Taxes

Indirect taxes are a very important source of revenue of the Central Government of India. With an increase in the volume of production of goods and services, the revenue from such taxes is increasing year after year. Such taxes therefore give greater buoyancy to Indias tax system. Three most important types of indirect taxes are the following:

1. Union Excise Duties: Union Excise Duties are imposed on producers of goods or on manufactures. At present there is excise duty on a large number of goods such as sugar, cement, kerosene, matches, cigarettes, cloth and virtually every manufactured good. The Government has imposed central excise duty on a number of items at the rate of 14% on the basis of value added. This is called CENVAT. Every year more and more goods are brought under the CENVAT. The revenue from union excise duties was Rs. 120,905 crores in 2011-12.

2. Customs Duties: Customs duties refer to import and export duties. At present there is no export duty in India. So in the Indian context customs duties refer to only import duties. These duties are imposed on imports for two reasons: (i) raising revenue for the Government and (ii) protecting domestic industries from foreign competition and thus enabling domestic firms to produce import-substitute items[1].

At present the peak rate of customs duties for non-agricultural products is 10%. The rate has been reduced (over the years from 300%) since one of the objectives of GOI's trade policy is import substitution. The revenue from customs duties was Rs. 108,442 crores in 2011-12.

3. Service Tax: As the name implies it is a tax on services provided to the people such as specialised banking and financial services, portal services, telex services, video tape services, broadcasting services and servicing of vehicles at authorised stations. Thus while excise duties are imposed on goods, service tax is imposed on services. The tax is applicable to more than 100 items at present. The rate is 12%. In addition, there is educational cess of 2% on it. The revenue from service tax has yielded Rs. 133,000 crores in 2012-13.

4. Goods and Services Tax (GST): To simplify the indirect tax structure, to eliminate the cascading effect (cumulative burden), to generate more revenue for both the Central and State Governments and thus to resolve the conflict between the Central and the States, the Kelkar Committee suggested the introduction of a Goods and Service Tax (GST). If this tax is introduced, it will replace all multi-stage value added taxes such as CENVAT, service tax levied by the Centre and the VAT levied by the States. It is felt this tax will be appropriate for deepening the tax structure.

The GST is essentially a comprehensive consumption tax. The Kelkar Committee recommended the introduction of a 'dual' GST by both the Central and State Governments with a view to achieving a pragmatic compromise between fiscal autonomy of the Centre and the States and the need for harmonisation of the tax structure throughout the country. The Committee further recommended that Governments at both levels should give comprehensive coverage of the tax by including numerous goods and services belonging to the whole supply chain. At present such a tax exists in Singapore.

C. Non-Tax Revenue: It is devided into two parts, viz.,

(a) *Revenue receipts* : Three main sources of such receipts are:

(i) Interest receipts: Interest received by the GOI on loans given to States and public sector enterprises yielded Rs. 19,254 crores in 2010-11.

(ii) Dividend and profits: The GOI owns equity capital (i.e., shares) to the extent of 49% to 51% of paid-up capital of both public sector and joint sector units[2]. In addition, the GOI derives profits from wholly-owned financial institutions such as the LICI and the RBI. It also gets a share of dividends of financial institutions partly owned by it. Receipts from dividends and profits amounted to Rs. 51,309 crores in 2010-11.

---

1. If this happens the country will be able to achieve import-substituting industrialisation. The infant industry argument which is essentially an argument in favour of protection to gain comparative advantage is the most forceful one in the context of developing countries like India.
2. The revenue of the Government has increased due to an increase in the prices of petrol, cooking gas, steel, electricity, etc. which are produced largely by the Government or state-owned (public sector) enterprises.

(iii) External grants: External grants refer to certain portions of foreign aid which are not to be repaid receipts from this source was Rs. 21,636 crores in 2009-10.

(b) Capital Receipts

Capital receipts are the revenues raised by the GOI for creating a liability or by reducing assets to some extent. The main types of such receipts are the following:

(i) Recovery of loans net: Loan recording are a component of capital receipts because it reduces assets of the Central Government. It yielded Rs. 14,258 crores in 2011-12.

(ii) Borrowing: When the expenditure of the GOI exceeds its revenue (from both tax and non-tax resources), it is said to have a fiscal deficit. This is covered in the following two ways:

(a) *Market loans* : The Government covers a portion of its fiscal deficit by selling securities of various types and maturity dates to banks, insurance companies and other financial institutions, corporate enterprises and the public. The market borrowing programme of the GOI is managed by the RBI. However, as noted earlier, market borrowing generates crowding out effect. In 2011-12, market loans (net) amounted to Rs. 436,414 crores. This sum was the difference between gross borrowings of Rs. 510,000 crores and loan repayments of Rs. 73,585 crores.

(b) *Monetisation of deficit* : If market borrowing is not enough to cover the total borrowing requirement of the Government, it borrows from the RBI, which leads to new money creation. So the fiscal deficit is monetised.

(iii) Other sourcs of capital receipts:

(a) External assistance: The major portion of foreign assistance is repayable on a long-term basis. Foreign assistance (net) amounted to Rs. 10,311 crores in 2011-12.

(b) Small savings (net): The Government also accepts small savings of the people through such devices as NSCs, rural development bonds, post office savings deposits, etc. These are non-negotiable credit instruments. So these are not bought and sold in the open market. Small savings yielded Rs. 10,302 crores (net) in 2010-11.

(c) Provident funds: The yield from provident funds (net) was Rs. 10,000 crores in 2011-12.

(d) Disinvestment in equity holding of public sector enterprises: Receipts from this source amounted to Rs. 15,493 crores in 2011-12.

Comments: The GOI generates revenue from three main sources, viz., taxes, market borrowing and monetisation of deficit. Each method of raising revenue has one major drawback. Taxation, for instance, leads to loss of incentives to work, save, invest and take risk. Market borrowing generates crowding-out effect which, in the long run, acts as a growth-retarding factor. Monetisation of deficit generates inflationary pressure from the demand side. See Table 37.1. So there is need to make a pragmatic compromise among the three alternative ways of financing Government expenditure in India.

Table 37.1: Raising Plan Resources in India

Alternative Methods	Effects
1. Taxation	Loss of incentives
2. Market borrowing	Crowding-out effect
3. Deficit spending	Demand-pull inflation

TRENDS IN GOVERNMENT EXPENDITURE IN INDIA: REVENUE AND CAPITAL

Government expenditure is of two main types: revenue (recurring) and capital (non-recurring). Revenue expenditure is incurred every year on civil administration (i.e., police, jails, and judiciary), national defence, public health and education. By contrast, capital expenditure is incurred on building roads, highways, bridges, ports, steel plants, power plants, etc. as also for buying directly productive assets such as machinery and equipment. Only this type of expenditure creates new assets or reduces Government liabilities.

The GOI has to spend large sums on development schemes and projects according to plan priorities and targets in such diverse sectors or areas as agriculture, industry, power, transport, communication, science and technology (including biotechnology research) as also on social services such as education, health care, broadcasting, family welfare, supply of safe drinking water, sanitation, nutrition, etc. The GOI also spends money either directly or through various State Governments on various anti-poverty measures. In addition, it has given adequate budgetary support to losing public sector enterprises in order to prevent sickness and the consequent joblessness.

In a federal country like India there is inter-governmental transfer of financial resources, i.e., from the Centre to the States. The objective is to enable the State Governments to perform their assigned roles and fulfil their plan targets. Table 37.2 shows the trends in revenue and capital expenditure of the Government since 1990-91.

Table 37.2: Trends in Revenue and Capital Expenditure of the Central Government in India

(as per cent of GDP)

Expenditure	1990-91	1995-96	2000-01	2001-02	2002-03	2003-04	2004-05	05-06	06-07	07-08	08-09
Revenue expenditure	12.9	11.8	13.3	13.2	13.8	13.1	12.2	12.3	12.5	12.6	15.1
of which											
(a) Interest	3.8	4.2	4.8	4.7	4.8	4.5	4.0	3.7	3.6	3.6	3.6
(b) Major subsidies	1.7	1.0	1.2	1.3	1.8	1.6	1.4	1.2	1.3	1.4	2.3
(c) Defence	1.9	1.6	1.8	1.7	1.7	1.6	1.4	1.3	1.3	1.1	1.4
Capital expenditure	4.4	2.4	2.3	2.7	3.0	4.0	3.6	1.9	1.7	2.6	1.8

Source: Government of India, *Economic Survey*, 2008-09

In the initial years of economic reforms both types of expenditure as a percentage of GDP fell to some extent, as noted earlier in this chapter. However, from 2007-08 the capital expenditure mainly on infrastructure building has gone up. This is no doubt a desirable trend.

An alternative classification of public expenditure is adopted in India. It is divided into plan and non-plan expenditure. Each has revenue and capital components. Table 37.3 shows trends in recent years in which both plan and non-plan expenditure as percentage of GDP has declined compared to that in 1990-91.

Table 37.3: Plan and Non-plan Expenditure of the Central Government (In Rs. crores)

Category	1990-91	2003-04	2004-05	2005-06	2006-07	2007-08	2008-09 (RE)	2009-10 (BE)
Plan expenditure	28365	122,280	132,276	140,138	172,730	205,100	171,633	200,290
Non-plan expenditure	69907	348,923	365,406	363,770	408,907	475,421	617,996	695,689
				(As per cent of GDP)				
Plan expenditure	5.0	4.4	4.2	3.9	4.1	4.3	5.3	–
Non-plan expenditure	12.3	12.6	11.6	10.2	10.6	10.7	11.6	–

Source: Government of India, *Economic Survey*, 2008-2009, and Budget for 2009-10

The economic classification of public expenditure in India is different. Economists draw a distinction between consumption expenditure and investment expenditure.

Capital expenditure and plan expenditure are the closest approximation to investment expenditure. The reason is that such expenditure creates productive assets. However, public expenditure on productive assets as percentage of GDP has declined since 1990-91, except in 2008-09.

A. REVENUE EXPENDITURE

Plan Revenue Expenditure

Plan revenue expenditure includes expenditure on social services and anti-poverty programmes of the five year plans, which seek to create employment opportunities for the poor, mainly in rural areas. Two such programmes are the National Rural Employment Guarantee Scheme and the Bharat Nirman Scheme.

Plan revenue expenditure as a percentage of GDP increased in recent years, mainly due to increased budgetary support given to the social sector, mainly primary education and literacy through such schemes as Sarv Sikhsha Abhijan and a Mid-day Meal scheme, National Rural Health Mission and Integrated Child Development Scheme.

Non-Plan Revenue Expenditure

Non-plan revenue expenditure refers to the Government's annual expenditure on interest payments, national defence, subsidies, wages and compensation, pension, transfer and other types of consumption expenditure. These are now briefly discussed:

(i) *Interest payments* : Interest payments on public debt (arising from market borrowing) are the largest item of the GOI's revenue expenditure. It amounted to Rs. 248,664 crores in 2010-11. One key indicator of the fiscal situation of a country is primary deficit. It is fiscal deficit *minus* payment of interest on public debt.

It is possible to reduce the interest burden by relying less on market borrowing as also by adopting sound practice(s) as far as the management of public debt is concerned. The success of this scheme will help the Government to release sufficient funds for developmental purposes.

(ii) *Defence spending* : Due to constant threat from its two neighbours — Pakistan and China — India has to spend a large sum every year on defence. In addition, India is spending a huge amount to develop its nuclear power so as to be able to match that of its neighbours. As a result India's defence expenditure (which has both revenue and capital components) has been rising sharply. It amounted to Rs. 147,344 in 2010-11. India probably believes in Adam Smith's dictum that defence is more important that opulence (wealth and prosperity).

(iii) *Subsidies* : The GOI also incurs a huge expenditure on subsidies mainly on three items, viz., food, fertiliser and petroleum products. The main objective is to help in developing agriculture and small industries and thus to ensure social justice. The subsidy is mainly on food articles which are supplied by ration shops in order to help the poor to acquire the minimum amount of such articles.

Subsidy is given on fertilisers with a view to increasing agricultural productivity, i.e., yield per hectare. Similarly the GOI has given subsidy on petroleum products to check rise in its domestic prices in the face of rise in international prices. The expenditure on subsidies was Rs. 116,224 crores in 2010-11.

In addition, implicit subsidies are given on education, health care, postal services, rural electricity, irrigation and public transport by both the Central and State Governments.

Substantial increase in expenditure on subsidies has reduced the funds available for productive purposes. It has also increased the Government's fiscal deficit. And Government's plans to reduce deficit under various economic reforms measures could not be realised. So subsidies as a percentage of GDP, instead of falling, continued to increase year after year. The recent years have witnessed a rising trend in expenditure on major subsidies, mainly those on food.

B. CAPITAL EXPENDITURE

Capital expenditure, both plan and non-plan, is essentially investment expenditure. Since it creates productive assets, it is a crucial determinant of economic growth.

(i) Non-pan capital expenditure

The largest component of non-plan capital expenditure is on defence services. Other items of such expenditive are loans and advances to States and Union territories, loans to PSUs and foreign governments (mainly India's neighbouring countries at lower stages of development).

(ii) Plan capital expenditure

Inadequate provision had been made for total capital expenditure on the schemes of the Eleventh Plan. And marginal increase in plan capital expenditure was likely to adversely affect the achievements of the growth targets of the Plan.

Consequences of Growing Public Expenditure

Four consequences of growing public expenditure were the following:

(i) *Inflation* : Rising government expenditure created deficit in the budget. This was financed by borrowing from the RBI. The RBI made loan to the GOI by printing new currency notes. As a result the money supply with the public increased. And the end result was price inflation.

(ii) *Obstacle to economic development* : The GOI gave disproportionate emphasis on national defence. No doubt defence is more important than opulence. However, India's developmental effort has been largely held in check due to the necessity to divert scarce resources for meeting her defence needs.

(iii) *Persistent inefficiency of public sector units (PSUs)* : Since the GOI gave constant budgetary support to loss-making PSUs the managers of these units did not really put any serious effort to improve the operational efficiency of their enterprises and thus these units became a permanent burden on the Exchequer, at least before the initiation of the reform process in the form of disinvestment of PSUs. In fact, PSUs appeared to be models of inefficiency due to constant budgetary support. And one of the main causes of growing fiscal deficit of the Government of India (GOI) was the staggering losses of PSUs.

(iv) *Debt trap* : Due to growing public expenditure, mainly of non-plan revenue variety, the GOI was forced to borrow larger and larger amounts to meet the revenue gap and thus fall into an internal debt trap. In fact, the growing internal debt burden is the price the country is now paying partly for economic growth and partly for wasteful current expenditure.

Highlights of Interim Budget for 2014-15

In the interim budget planned by the Finance Minister for 2013-14 the fiscal deficit to GDP ratio has been brought down to 4.6%. The revised estimate was 0.2% point lower than the target set a year ago. This has been done by rolling over a big chunk of the subsidies to the next fiscal year (2014-15). The fiscal deficit was lowered not by increasing revenue but by cutting plan expenditure by 14.4% in the revised estimates over the budget estimates.

The Finance Minister (FM) is cutting capital expenditure which could promote further growth of the economy. At the same time the GOI's non-plan expenditure has increased to some extent in recent past.

Largely due to a sharp 5.4% fall in tax collection, the total receipts of the Government have fallen by 4.5% in the revised estimates over what was targeted.

The main focus of the budget has on faster economic growth. This is why the FM took measures to boost manufacturing production whose growth fell sharply in 2013-14.

To stimulate growth in the capital goods and consumer non-durables, the FM has proposed to reduce the excise duty from 12% to 10% upto 30.06.2014. Likewise to give relief to the automobile industry, which is showing negative growth, the FM has proposed to reduce the excise duty. In Table 37.4 we present the

Table 37.4: Highlight of the Interim Budget (2014-15)

Growth
• GDP expansion in third and fourth quarters of 2013-14 estimated at 5.2%. Growth for the whole year expected at 4.9%.
Fiscal Deficit
• Fiscal deficit projected at 4.1% of GDP in 2014-15. • Bring down the deficit to 3% of GDP by 2016-17.
Current Account Deficit
• Current account deficit for 2013-14 estimated at US $ 45 billion from last fiscal year's US $ 88 billion. • Forex reserves to rise by US $ 15 billion by end of 2013-14.
Subsidies
• Total spending on food, fertilisers and fuel at Rs. 2.5 trillion in 2014-15. • Food subsidy estimated at Rs. 1.15 trillion, fertiliser subsidy at Rs. 679.71 billion. Petroleum subsidy seen at Rs. 634.27 billion versus revised figure of Rs. 854.8 billion for 2013-14.
Defence
• Spending raised to Rs. 2.24 trillion in 2014-15, up 10% year on year.
Exports
• Merchandise exports seen at US $ 326 billion in 2013-14, up 6.3% year on year. • Agricultural exports expected to touch US $ 45 billion in 2013-14, up from US $ 41 billion in 2012-13.
Tax Proposals
• No major change in tax rates. • Factory gate tax to be reduced to 10% from 12% on some capital goods and consumer durables. • Cut excise duty on small cars, two wheelers and commercial vehicles to 8% from 12%.

Comments

1. Although the National Manufacturing policy has set the goal of increasing the share of manufacturing in GDP to 25% and to create 100 mn. jobs over a decade the Budget has not announced any new scheme of employment growth.

2. No new expenditure schemes were announced in the interim budget which is reassuring from the point of view of fiscal restraint.

3. On the revenue side, the specific reduction in excise rates, for a limited period though, will provide a boost to auto and manufacturing sectors. However, the extent of revival is likely to be dampened by the short time frame as well as sluggish investment and consumption sentiments. It was widely felt that the government should provide a big push to the manufacturing sector.

4. The quality of fiscal adjustment in 2013-14 was somewhat sub-optimal.

5. The budget fails to address the slow progress towards realisation of the additional capacity even though power shortage is open of the main bottlenecks for industrial growth.

6. The FM totally omits steel, coal and mining.

7. The FM's attempts of underprovisioning for subsidy payments in the interim budget for 2014-15 makes the issue of subsidy much tougher and complex for the next Government. He dismissed any rollovers for the 3Fs (food, fuel and fertiliser) for the next financial year on subsidy.

8. Finally, while the FM has highlighted the role played by the Cabinet Committee for Investment in clearing stuck (incomplete and temporarily suspended) projects, there is an urgent need for a comprehensive review of the entire mechanism for grant of clearances to industrial projects.

TRANSFER OF RESOURCES TO STATES

An important component of Central Government expenditure in a federal country like India is the transfer of financial resources from the Centre to the States. Such transfers are of three types:

(a) plan assistance to States and Union Territories (UTs),

(b) non-plan assistance to States UTs and

(c) States' share of taxes and duties.

The Central Government has to make outright grants to States (which are unconditioned and not repayable) since various schemes related to social services and natural calamities are not covered by five year plans.

In addition, as per the provisions of the constitution, Finance Commissions make certain recommendations regarding the allocation of tax revenue between Central and the States. It is against thus a backdrop that we will now study Central-State financial relations in the Indian context.

Centre-State Financial Relations

In a federal country like India, the assignment of expenditure responsibilities and division of tax powers form the basic foundation of inter-governmental fiscal relations. Restructuring of Central-State fiscal relations is absolutely essential in order to achieve sound fiscal consolidation.

Constitutional Provisions

The Constitution of India provides three lists: the Union list, the State list and the concurrent list. The Constitution gaves the Centre the power to levy income tax, both individual and corporate, customs duties and all excise duties except those on liquor and liquor products.

On the other hand, the States were allocated tax revenues related to land revenue, agricultural income tax (non-existent till date), sales tax except that on inter-State movement of traded goods (octroi), cess on liquor, taxation of inland transport, except railways, property (wealth and gift tax) and entry tax. Since the most important and productive taxes were assigned to the Centre, the Constitution provided for sharing of Central taxes between Centre and States on the basis of certain criteria such as (a) population (b) collection and (c) distance (i.e., the difference of the domestic product of one state and of the state having the highest SDP).

Three Channels of Transfer

One of the notable and significant features of financial transfers from the Centre to the States in India is that there existed three channels for such transfers to take place. While the Finance Commissions make recommendation for transfer which are restricted to the States' non-plan requirements in the current (revenue) account, the Planning Commission makes the recommendations for transfer to States through grants (unconditional transfers) and loans to meet their requirements. In addition, various cabinet ministers of the Central Government make specific-purpose transfers with or without matching requirements.

Accordingly income tax and excise duties collected by the Centre were to be shared with States on the basis of the recommendations of the Finance Commissions. Beginning in 1952, 13 such Commissions have been appointed far.

After the establishment of the Planning Commission, and with development planning gaining emphasis, the scope of the Finance Commissions recommendations was reduced. Over the years the Planning Commission has become a major fund transferring body to the States.

The Gadgil Formula

Since 1969, plan assistance is being made on the basis of Gadgil formula. According to this formula, 30% of the funds available for the distribution by the Planning Commission is earmarked for ten special category States[1] and is given on the basis of plan projects formulated by them, with 90% of assistance given by way of grants and the rest 10% as loans. The remaining 70% of funds available for the rest of the fifteen States (of which 70% of assistance is given by way of loans and rest as grants) is distributed in accordance with the following: 60% weight assigned to population, 25% to per capita SDP, 7.5% to fiscal management, and the remaining 7.5% to special problems faces by these States.

The third component of transfers from the Centre to the States is for specified purposes with or without matching provisions. These are called the central sector or centrally sponsored schemes. Grants for central sector schemes are given to States to undertake certain agency functions and are, therefore, entirely financed by the Central Government. Centrally sponsored schemes, on the other hand, are initiated with regard to services falling within States' jurisdiction to ensure that optimum levels of services are provided. These are shared cost programmes, and the matching ratios vary from project to project, but are uniform across States. These schemes have raised a great deal of criticism from States, and are seen by States as an unwarranted intrusion into their domain by the Central Government.

Concluding Comments

A favourable macroeconomic situation of low inflation along with high growth cannot be achieved on a sustainable basis unless substantial fiscal adjustments are made both by the Central and State Government in India. In truth fiscal deficits have remained high despite two decades of fiscal consolidation effort (1991-2011). There are two ways of reducing fiscal deficit and achieving fiscal consolidation.

1. Expenditure reduction

While both Central and State Governments have reduced their expenditure-GDP ratio, this is clearly not sufficient. Quite evidently, expenditure reform has lagged behind tax reform. Obviously, the ratio of internal public debt to GDP has continued to rise and the debt-service burden has risen even faster because of rising interest rates. The composition of Government spending is still skewed towards unproductive current expenditures and away from basic infrastructural as well as vitally needed human resource developmental needs (especially basic education and health care). To a large extent, the responsibility of reducing fiscal imbalances lies with States and a major effort on their part is called for in order to improve the fiscal situation.

The Central Government can reduce expenditures in the area of interest payments on domestic debt via privatisation of State assets; fertiliser and food subsidies; public administration, and grants to the States; and losses of public sector enterprises. On the other hand, by raising user charges on water on the basis of actual costs incurred and aligning tariff rates of the state electricity companies on the basis of their costs the State Governments could significantly reduct their budgetary losses.

2. Revenue mobilisation

There is a need for speedy implementation of the remaining tax reforms so as to simplify the tax structure and to evolve a competitive tax structure based on moderate tax rates with a broad base of tax collection. For the Central Government, needed reforms include further reduction in import tariffs and corporate taxes, a MAT based on gross assets of companies, and the transformation of the existing

1. These are: Arunachal Pradesh, Assam, Himachal Pradesh, Jammu and Kashmir, Manipur, Meghalaya, Mizoram, Nagaland, Sikkim and Tripura.

excise modvat system into a national-level value added tax. For the State Governments, on the other hand, there is need to replace sales tax with a shared portion of the national value added tax, and the extension of income tax to agricultural, income among currently untaxed areas.

The Recommendation of the Thirteenth Finance Commission (TFC)

In order to make the roll out of goods and services tax palatable to State Governments, the IFC has recommended a grant of Rs 50,000 crore to offset the losses of State Governments stemming from implementation of goods and services tax. The share of every State in all shareable taxes as suggested by the Commission is given in Table 37.5.

Prima facie, the Commission recommended a 'calibrated exit strategy from the expansionary fiscal stance of 2008-09 and 2009-10'. It has suggested that the revenue deficit of the Centre should be eliminated and the objective should be to have a revenue surplus from 2014-15 onwards. In the context of combined debt of the Centre and States, the Commission has suggested a target of 68% of GDP to be achieved by 2014-15.

Table 37.5: The Shares of States in Tax Revenue

	Share of all Shareable Taxes* (per cent)	Share of Service Tax (per cent)		Share of All Shareable Taxes* (per cent)	Share of Service Tax (per cent)
Andhra Pradesh	6.937	7.047	Maharashtra	5.199	5.281
Arunachal Pradesh	0.328	0.332	Manipur	0.451	0.458
Assam	3.628	3.685	Meghalaya	0.408	0.415
Bihar	10.917	11.089	Mizoram	0.269	0.273
Chhattisgarh	2.47	2.509	Nagaland	0.314	0.318
Goa	0.266	0.27	Orissa	4.779	4.855
Gujarat	3.041	3.089	Punjab	1.389	1.411
Haryana	1.048	1.064	Rajasthan	5.853	5.945
Himachal Pradesh	0.781	0.793	Sikkim	0.239	0.243
Jammu and Kashmir	1.551	Nil	Tamil Nadu	4.969	5.047
Jharkhand	2.802	2.846	Tripura	0.511	0.519
Karnataka	4.328	4.397	Uttar Pradesh	19.677	19.987
Kerala	2.341	2.378	Uttarakhand	1.12	1.138
Madhya Pradesh	7.12	7.232	West Bangal	7.264	7.379

Source: Report of Thirteenth Finance Commission, Government of India 2010.
Note: *Excludes service tax.

The following are some of the key recommendations of the Thirteenth Finance Commission:

1. The share of States in net proceeds of shareable Central taxes shall be 32% every year for the period of the award.
2. Revenue accruing to a State is to be protected to the levels that would have accured to it had service tax been a part of the shareable Central taxes, if the 88th Amendment to Constitution is notified and followed up by a legislation enabling States to levy service tax.
3. Centre is to review the levy of cesses and surcharges with a view to reducing their share in its gross tax revenue.
4. The indicative ceiling on overall transfers to States on revenue account may be set at 39.5% of gross revenue receipts of the Centre.
5. The Medium-Term Fiscal Plan (MTFP) should be a statement of commitment rather than intent.

6. New disclosures have been specified for the Budget/MTFP including on tax expenditure, public-private partnership liabilities and the details of variables underlying receipts and expenditure projections.
7. The Fiscal Responsibility and Budget Management (FRBM) Act needs to specify the nature of shocks that would require relaxation of the targets thereunder.
8. States are expected to be able to get back to their fiscal correction path by 2011-12 and amend their FRBM Acts to the effect.
9. State Governments are to be eligible for the general performance and special area performance grants only if they comply with the prescribed stipulation in terms of grants to local bodies.
10. The National Calamity Contingency Fund (NCCF) should be merged with the National Disaster Response Fund (NDRF) and the Calamity Relief Fund (CRF) with the State Disaster Response Funds (SDRFs) of the respective States.
11. A total non-plan revenue grant of Rs. 51,800 crore is recommended over the award period for eight States. A performance grant of Rs. 1,500 crore is recommended for three special category States that have graduated from a non-Plan revenue deficit situation.
12. An amount of Rs. 19,930 crore has been recommended as grant for maintenance of roads and bridges for four years (2011-12 to 2014-15).
13. An amount of Rs. 24,068 crore has been recommended as grant for elementary education.
14. An amount of Rs. 27,945 crore has been recommended for State-specific needs.
15. An amount of Rs. 5,000 crore each as forest, renewable energy, and water sector-management grants have been recommended.
16. A total sum of Rs. 3,18,581 crore has been recommended for the award period as grants-in-aid to States.

Source: *India Development Report* 2012-13

Debt: If the recommendations of the TFC are implemented and its suggestions are followed, then one can forsee an improvement in the fiscal situation of both the Central and the States.

KEY POINTS

1. *Government budget in India* : The budget of GOI has two parts:

a. the revenue account (or the revenue budget) and

b. the capital account (or the capital budget).

2. *Taxes: direct and indirect* : Taxes are of two types: *direct* and *indirect*. On the basis of rates, taxes have been classified into three categories, viz., progressive, proportional and regressive. In addition, taxes may be either lumpsum (like licence fee) or specific (a fixed sum per unit of a good) and ad valorem (a certain percentage of the price of a product).

3. *Objectives of fiscal policy in India* : In developing countries like India, fiscal policy in the form of taxes, government expenditure and borrowing is a powerful and an effective instrument through which the government can promote faster economic growth, achieve macroeconomic stability and distributive justice (i.e., an equitable distribution of income and wealth). The main objective is to create adequate employment opportunities, bring inflation under control, reduce inequality and alleviate poverty.

4. *Fiscal policy and mobilisation of resources for planned economic growth* : Fiscal policy plays an important role in mobilising resources for planned economic growth in developing countries like India. Since economic growth is largely a matter of physical capital formation a growth-oriented fiscal policy has to induce people and business firms to save more so that more investment is made in productive assets and there is an expansion of a society's production capacity and the economy achieves growth faster than before.

5. *The mobilisation of resources through direct taxes* : By imposing progressive income tax at the personal level, the Government can raise a large amount of resources. Such a tax also helps to reduce income inequality.

However, high marginal tax rates encourage tax evasion and avoidance and lead to the emergence of the parallel economy. In addition, high taxes adversely affect private savings and investment by destroying incentives.

6. *The scope of agricultural taxation* : The agricultural sector makes the maximum contribution to GDP (national income) of developing countries like India. And a substantial amount of economic surplus is generated from the agricultural sector. And this surplus is mainly appropriated by rich farmers, landowners, moneylenders and traders. And in the absence of an agricultural income tax this surplus is used for consumption of luxury goods by the rural rich and for buying unproductive assets. By imposing agricultural income tax, this surplus can be tapped for capital formation.

7. *The role of indirect taxes in resource mobilisation* : Due to low contribution of direct taxes there is undue reliance on indirect taxes in developing countries like India. In India almost all commodities — both consumption goods and capital goods —have been brought under the indirect tax net. Three main indirect taxes are the excise duties, custom duties (export and import duties) and sales tax (now replaced partly by value added tax at the state level). Indirect taxes are an important source of development finance in India. They lead to maximum resource mobilisation for economic growth.

8. *The role of taxation in promoting private saving and investment* : In a developing country it is of paramount importance to increase aggregate (national) savings which include both private and public savings. Public savings can be increased by the government through sound fiscal management, viz., by raising tax and non-tax revenues and by cutting public expenditure. At the same time, the tax system should be such as to give necessary incentives to the private sector—both households and businesses—to save and invest more. And a policy of tax cut is likely to impart the needed dynamism to the economy.

9. *Revenue mobilisation through government borrowing* : Since the tax revenue of the GOI is not sufficient to meet its ever-growing expenditure, it has to face a deficit in its annual budget. This is covered in three other ways, viz., (i) small savings, (ii) market borrowing and (iii) borrowing from the Reserve Bank of India.

10. *Revenue deficit as an obstacle to growth* : India's revenue deficit in the budget continued to increase in the first decade of reforms (from 3.4% in 1990-91 to 4.4% in 2002-03). Revenue deficit implies public dissaving. It also implies that the revenue of the Government—both from tax and non-tax sources—were not sufficient to meet the current (consumption) expenditures of the Central Government So the revenue deficit has to be covered by utilising borrowed funds (i.e., capital receipts). These funds could have been more productively utilised to meet the capital (investment) expenditure.

11. *The FRBMA* : To overcome the drawback of India's fiscal system, the Fiscal Responsibility and Budget Management Act (FRBMA) was passed in 2003. It prescribed reduction of revenue deficit to zero by 2008-09.

12. *Fiscal consolidation* : In order to achieve fiscal consolidation (i.e., reduction of fiscal deficit) with a view to making larger and larger resources available for planned economic development (with focus on employment generation as also for the control of inflation). The stress has been on two things: (i) raising revenue through taxes and (ii) improving the quality of public expenditure. The second objective was sought to be achieved by reducing non-plan revenue expenditure and by raising plan capital expenditure which was productive and growth-promoting in nature.

13. *A broad overview of India's fiscal reforms* :

(a) The First Decade of Reforms: Fiscal reforms were initiated in India since 1991 in order to achieve three main objectives of planning, viz., faster economic growth, reasonable price stability and equity.

(b) The Second Decade of Reforms: Since 2001-02 the GOI continued to follow the same prudent fiscal policy. The Central Government evolved a balanced tax system based on moderate tax rates and minimum exemptions. In addition, the tax base was widened by including a large number of new taxpayers. The following specific fiscal measures were adopted during the second decade of economic reforms:

(i) Raising tax-GDP ratio

(ii) Incentive to exporters

14. *Tax reforms* : One of the key elements of India's economic reforms has been the reform of the tax system. It was recognised that a larger collection of tax revenues could not be achieved by high rates of taxation, which tended to encourage evasion. By contrast a tax system which is simple to administer, has moderate rates of taxation and relies upon a broad tax base is most appropriate for India.

15. *Direct tax reforms* :

(i) Tax cuts : The Government announced a number of tax cuts in 1997-98. The maximum marginal rate of personal income tax was reduced from 40% to 30%.

(ii) Introduction of Minimum Alternate Tax (MAT) : The Central Government introduced a new tax — 'Minimum Alternate Tax' (MAT) on companies.

16. *Indirect tax* : As for indirect taxes of the GOI, there has occurred quite some progress in the reform of customs duties and union excise duties. In addition, service tax has been introduced.

(i) Customs duties

(ii) Domestic commodity taxes

(iii) Service tax

17. *Reform of the indirect tax system* : The following reform measures have been adopted in the area of indirect of taxes since 1991:

(i) Further reduction of import duties

(ii) Evolving a full-fledged VAT

(iii) State taxes

18. *Expenditure reform* : While there has occurred just a marginal drop in plan (developmental) expenditure (mainly on agriculture and rural development as also on infrastructural building) as a percentage of GDP, due to the inability of the Government to reduce growth of the revenue expenditure adequately, non-plan (non-development) expenditure feel sharply.

19. *Subsidies* : One of the main components of the Government's revenue expenditure is subsidy. The Government's present policy is to increase food subsidy and to target all subsidies at the weaker sections of the society, i.e., the poor and the needy, such as the small and marginal farmers, landless labourers as also the urban poor.

20. *Revenue expenditure* : Plan revenue expenditure includes expenditure on social services and anti-poverty programmes of the five year plans, which seek to create employment opportunities for the poor, mainly in rural areas. Two such programmes are the National Rural Employment Guarantee Scheme and the Bharat Nirman Scheme.

Plan revenue expenditure as a percentage of GDP increased in recent years.

21. *Non-plan revenue expenditure* : Non-plan revenue expenditure refers to the Government's annual expenditure on interest payments, national defence, subsidies, wages and compensation, pension, transfer and other types of consumption expenditure.

22. *Capital expenditure* : Capital expenditure, both plan and non-plan, is essentially investment expenditure. Since it creates productive assets, it is a crucial determinant of economic growth.

(i) Non-pan capital expenditure

The largest component of non-plan capital expenditure is on defence services. Other items of such expenditive are loans and advances to States and Union territories, loans to PSUs and foreign governments (mainly India's neighbouring countries at lower stages of development).

(ii) Plan capital expenditure

Inadequate provision had been made for total capital expenditure on the schemes of the Eleventh Plan. And marginal increase in plan capital expenditure was likely to adversely affect the achievements of the growth targets of the Plan.

23. *Transfer of resources to states* : An important component of Central Government expenditure in a federal country like India is the transfer of financial resources from the Centre to the States. Such transfers are of three types:

(a) plan assistance to States and Union Territories (UTs),

(b) non-plan assistance to States UTs and

(c) States' share of taxes and duties.

The Central Government has to make outright grants to States (which are unconditioned and not repayable) since various schemes related to social services and natural calamities are not covered by five year plans.

KEY TERMS

Presumptive taxes
Modvat
MAT
Fiscal consolidation
Agricultural tax
Cenvat
FRBMA
Market borrowing
Market borrowing
Revenue deficit
Transfer price
Export subsidy
Goods and services tax
Public expenditure
Service tax
Crowding-out effect

ASSIGNMENTS

1. What are the main sources of revenue of GOI?
2. What are different types of expenditure of the GOI?
3. Comment on the various tax reform measures adopted by the GOI during the first two decades of economic reform (1991-2011). Discuss the role of fiscal policy in financing India's economic development.
4. Discuss the role of fiscal policy in economic growth with particular reference to India.
5. "The tax system of a developing country like India should not be treated just as revenue-raising device but as an instrument of promoting faster economic growth."—Discuss.
6. Do taxes create distortions in an economy? Give you views.
7. Are taxes inflationary in their impact? Make your own comments.
8. Comment on the changes in the relative importance of direct and indirect taxes in India during the period of economic reforms.
9. Highlight the causes of increase in public expenditure in India in the last two decades. Analyse the impact of huge increase in public expenditure on India's macroeconomic environment.
10. "The power to tax is not just the power to destroy but also the power to keep alive."—Discuss.
11. Make a comparison between (a) taxation and borrowing and (b) borrowing and deficit spending as alternative methods of financing India's public expenditure as also for raising resources for her planned programme of development.
12. Does government borrowing generate crowding out effect? Does investment on infrastructure also generate crowding-out effect?
13. How does the tax system of a country affect the conduct of business behaviour? How does it affect business growth?
14. Comment on the changing pattern of Government expenditure in India in recent years.
15. Do high tax rates yield more revenue?
16. Are high taxes confiscatory in nature? How does the tax system of a country affect aggregate saving, investment and economic growth?
17. How does the tax system of a country ensure inclusive growth and lead to poverty alleviation?

CHAPTER 38

Fiscal Deficit and Economic Growth

> *Fiscal policy has two major roles in financing of development. The first is to maintain the economy at full employment so that the saving capacity of the economy is not impaired. The second is to design a tax policy to raise the marginal propensity to save of the economy as far above the average as possible without discouraging work effort and consistent with an equitable distribution of tax burden.* A. P. Thirwall

The main objective of fiscal policy in advanced capitalist countries is to achieve economic stability—high employment in the absence of demand-pull inflation. This is why the adoption of an expansionary fiscal policy is strongly recommended in times of depression like the one experienced by the USA and virtually the whole of the capitalist world during the period 1929-33. And following Keynes, all such countries deliberately incurred a deficit in the budget to increase aggregate effective demand and succeeded in stimulating their economies, and, in the process, creating jobs and incomes. However, in developing countries like India fiscal deficit may also be incurred to achieve faster economic growth while at the same time keeping the rate of inflation down. This poses a challenge to the policymakers who are often faced with a dilemma situation.

Fiscal policy can be used to promote faster economic growth along with reasonable price level stability. In recent years India's fiscal deficit has increased steadily since government expenditure has exceeded its revenue from tax and non-tax sources. This has created huge excess demand pressure in the economy and this, in its turn, has resulted in a high rate of inflation (i.e., sharp rise in the general price level).

Budgetary deficit occurs due to a deficit in revenue budget and/or in capital account and thus in general budget. In case of budgetary deficit the Government of India (GOI) has to borrow funds from either the market by selling bonds or from the RBI against its own securities. While market borrowing creates crowding-out effect (COE), borrowing from the RBI generates inflation. The newly created money (due to the issue of new currency notes against government securities and T-bills) leads to a rise in the income of the people. This creates excess demand, more so because aggregate supply is inelastic. The excess demand creates an inflationary gap and leads to price inflation. In this context we refer to four types of deficit.

1. REVENUE DEFICIT

Revenue deficit arises when total revenue receipts (from both tax and non-tax sources) exceed total revenue expenditures. The main sources of revenue are taxes (direct and indirect), interest received from loans made in the past and surpluses of public sector enterprises. The main types of revenue expenditure are (a) interest payment on the accumulated debt, (b) expenditure on general administration, (c) spending on national defence, (d) expenditure on various types of subsidies, i.e., on food, fertilisers, exports and (e) expenditure on social services such as education and health care.[1]

Revenue deficit occurs when there is an excess of revenue expenditures over revenue receipts. In India, there has existed a deficit in the revenue account of the budget for the past several years. This has created overall budgetary deficit ($G > T$). It amounts to negative saving (or dissaving) of the government. Therefore the government had to utilise a portion of its borrowed funds to meet revenue deficit. Two main causes of revenue deficit were the following:

(i) **Fall in tax revenue:** GOI's revenue deficit increased since 2008-09 due to the fiscal stimulus which had to be given by the GOI to prevent the slowdown of the Indian economy as a result of the global financial crisis. The GOI reduced excise and customs duties. This resulted in a fall in tax revenue.

(ii) **Increase in expenditure:** At the same time the government's revenue expenditure increased for two main reasons: (a) waiving of loans to farmers and (b) rise in salaries of Central Government employees after the implementation of the Sixth Pay Commission report.

2. FISCAL DEFICIT

Fiscal deficit is the excess of total expenditures (both on revenue and capital accounts) over revenue receipts and non-debt type of capital receipts such as loan recovery. So it can be expressed as

Fiscal deficit = Total expenditure on both revenue and capital accounts, revenue receipts and non-debt type of capital receipts.

Thus fiscal deficit is a broader measure of budgetary imbalance than budget deficit.

Covering a Fiscal Deficit

Fig. 38.1 shows how a fiscal deficit is covered. There are two ways of financing a fiscal deficit. First, the government can borrow either from its own citizens or from foreign countries. If the government borrows domestically by selling interest-bearing bonds, two problems are created. First, the government has to service the debt. And if the present generation escapes the debt burden, the burden is shifted to future generations. Additional taxes are to be imposed on them to service the past debt. Secondly, government borrowing creates crowding-out effect, with all its adverse consequences.

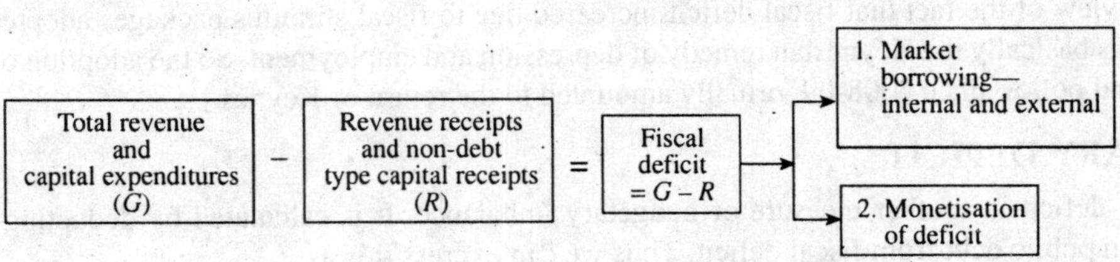

Fig. 38.1: Covering a Fiscal Deficit

If the government borrows from other countries, it has to pay interest along with a portion of the principal (loan amount) every year in foreign exchange. If the country does not have sufficient foreign exchange, then it has to export goods. If aggregate output remains constant, but a larger and larger

1. In the late 1980s and early 1990s Poland, Brazil and Mexico lived under severe hardships since they had to service a huge amount of external debt.

portion of it is to be exported, the domestic supply of consumption goods will fall.[1] This may not only reduce a society's consumption possibilities and put the country inside the production possibility curve (which is an inefficient point) but also lead to price rise by creating shortages of essential items of consumption.

Alternatively, a country may take a fresh loan to repay an old external debt, in which case it falls in a debt trap. If the fiscal deficit is covered by new money creation, there is the danger of demand-pull inflation.

ECONOMIC IMPLICATIONS

Four economic implications of fiscal deficit are the following:

1. *Increase in public debt*: Since a large part of the fiscal deficit is covered by borrowing—both internally and externally—the burden of public debt increases.

2. *Inflation*: The monetisation of a part of fiscal deficit creates inflation.

3. Slow rate of economic growth: Since the government has used a large portion of borrowed funds to cover its current consumption expenditure, a small part is left for productive investment such as building economic and social infrastructure in the form of roads, bridges, power plants, educational institutes and hospitals. As a result the rate of economic growth slows down.

4. Capital displacement (crowding-out) effect: Finally, due to crowding-out effect, less investment is made by the private sector. This slows down the rate of economic growth further.

For promoting faster economic growth with price stability it is necessary to reduce fiscal deficit. To achieve this goal the GOI passed the Fiscal Responsibility and Budget Management (FRBM) Act in 2008-09. The IMF and the World Bank had recommended that India's fiscal deficit should be reduced to 3% of GDP. This can be achieved by reducing unproductive (non-plan) revenue expenditure. However, in India attempts have also been made to curtail capital expenditure, i.e., expenditure on creating community assets and on various other developmental activities. This has adversely affected India's economic growth. Such practise, which India followed in the past, should be avoided as much as possible.

In order to promote faster economic growth, there is need to mobilise extra resources through taxation and to cut revenue expenditure as much as possible. Furthermore, borrowed funds should be used for productive purposes and should not be wasted by being spent on socially undesirable or wasteful projects.

However, in times of recession like these one faced by the country in times of global slowdown in 2008-09, an increase in government expenditure through monetisation of deficit was considered as highly desirable. This is why the GOI monetised its deficits[1] in the years 2008-09 and 2009-10 to some extent, more so in view of the fact that fiscal deficit increased due to fiscal stimulus packages adopted by the GOI. [This is basically the Keynesian remedy of depression and employment. So the adoption of expansionary fiscal policy since 2008-09 virtually amounted to the return of Keynes.]

3. PRIMARY DEFICIT

Primary deficit is another measure of budgetary imbalance. It is calculated by deducting interest payments on public debt from fiscal deficit. Thus we can express this as

Primary deficit = Fiscal deficit – debt interest payments

Primary deficit is lower than fiscal deficit

Alternatively stated, payment of interest on public debt incurred in the past gets reflected in the difference between fiscal deficit and primary deficit, or the excess of fiscal deficit over primary deficit. In recent years, India has fallen in an internal debt trap due to cumulative burden of such debt. Since interest payment is a liability on the revenue account of the budget, fiscal deficit can be reduced by reducing interest payment. This can be

1. If non-budgetary oil bonds issued by the GOI are taken into account the magnitude of fiscal deficit will be higher.

done by quickly retiring public debt or by mobilising more resources and curtaining the government's non-devel̃opmental expenditure (i.e., non-plan revenue expenditure).

Monetisation of Fiscal Deficit

Covering the fiscal deficit by using new currency through borrowing from the RBI against its own securities or T-bills is now called monetisation of fiscal deficit. Now the GOI publishes data on three types of deficit, viz., (i) revenue deficit, (ii) fiscal deficit and (iii) primary deficit.

Measures to Reduce Fiscal Deficit

We have noted that a large fiscal deficit, which is covered either by market borrowing or by new money creation, has one of the two adverse consequences, viz., crowding-out effect or price inflation. And for maintaining price stability fiscal deficit has to be reduced. This can be done in two ways, viz., (i) by reducing public expenditure and (ii) by increasing tax revenue.

(i) **Reducing Public Expenditure**

In the context of the present Indian economy the following measures may be taken to reduce public expenditure.

1. *Subsidy reduction*: A sharp cut in expenditure on subsidies on food, fertilisers, power and export is absolutely essential for curtailing public expenditure to a considerable extent.

2. *Reduction of unnecessary expenditure*: The government can reduce such unnecessary expenditure as LTC, bonus leave encashment, etc. At present the government spends a huge sum on these heads.

3. *Disinvestment*: At present interest payment on past debt account for 40% of the government's revenue expenditure. If the government utilises the major portion of funds raised through disinvestment of public sector enterprises to retire a portion of its accumulated debt, then payment of interest on such debt in the future can be reduced.

4. *Revised policy toward the public sector*: It is also absolutely essential to reduce continuous budgetary support to public sector enterprises except for infrastructural projects which help the process of economic development directly and indirectly (after a time lag, though).

5. *Economy in public expenditure*: Necessary austeriry measures should be adopted in all departments of the government with a view to curtailing non-plan revenue expenditure. The reason is that an increase in such expenditure has been the main cause of inflation in India over the years.

(ii) **Increasing Tax Revenue**

Fiscal deficit can be reduced by raising tax revenue. The following measures may be adopted to achieve this goal.

Excessive taxes should be avoided

1. *Tax simplification and rate reduction* : By imposing moderate taxes with simplified structure it will be possible to raise revenue. Since high marginal rates of taxes create disincentive effect[1] and encourage tax evasion, these should be avoided. If the tax system is elastic[2], a cut in the tax rate will lead to an increase in tax revenue. Planners and policymakers should take note of this reality.

2. *Broadening of the tax base* : India's existing tax base is narrow due to high exemption limit and complete absence of agricultural income tax. Very few people (less than 3% of the population) pay personal income tax. So tax revenue can be raised by broadening the tax base. This can be done by including incomes derived from agricultural, unorganised industries and different types of services. At the same time the various exemptions, concessions and deductions provided in respect of income and

1. In fact, high tax rates lead to loss of incentives to work hard, save, invest and take risk.

2. The elasticity of the tax system is measured by the following formula:

$$E_t = \frac{\%\text{ Change in } T}{\%\text{ Change in } Y} = \frac{\Delta T / T}{\Delta Y / Y} = \frac{\Delta T}{\Delta Y} \div \frac{T}{Y} = \frac{\text{marginal tax rate}}{\text{average tax rate}}$$

wealth taxes should be withdrawn. In short, while the policy of imposing moderate taxes are to be followed, the tax base has to be broadened. Progressive taxes lead to fall in revenue.[1]

3. *Unearthing black money* : At present a huge amount of black money is circulating in the Indian economy, in spite of partial success of the Voluntary Disclosure of Income scheme introduced in 1997-98. This is due to tax evasion, which has to be checked by strict enforcement of tax laws. In addition, various other steps are to be taken to unearth black money.

4. *Service taxes* : The revenue from commodity (indirect) taxes has virtually reached the stage of diminishing returns. The growth of such revenue has almost reached a vanishing point. So the only way to raise extra revenue from indirect taxes is to bring more services under the tax net.

5. *Withdrawal of tax concessions* : The central and state governments had given various tax concessions for promoting industrialisation in the backward areas. But these measure did actually serve the desired purposes. What is worse, these measures were used to evade taxes. So it is high time these concessions were withdrawn.

6. *Introduction of capital gains tax* : At present long-term capital gains are exempted from income tax. Keeping in view the revival of the capital market after the setback in 2008-09 (due to global financial crisis), this exemption should be withdrawn.[2]

7. *Public sector reforms* : Finally, there should be a thorough restructuring of public sector enterprises so as to enable them to generate surplus funds for their own development and they do not need government's budgetary support year after year. One major aspect of such reform is the adoption of an appropriate pricing policy. The pricing policy of such enterprises should be such as to cover user cost.

If the above measures are effectively enforced (or properly implemented), fiscal deficit is likely to come down to a very low level indeed and is unlikely to cross the safe limit. The reduction in fiscal deficit will prevent the emergence an inflationary gap in the economy and will thereby help in achieving reasonable price stability.

FISCAL DEFICIT AND ECONOMIC GROWTH

If the government incurs a large fiscal deficit for making productive investment, especially for the development of infrastructure and for promoting rural development, this will act as a growth-promoting factor. It will stimulate production and create additional employment opportunities. Such a policy will help the process of growth from both the demand side and the supply side. It will increase aggregate demand. It will also increase aggregate supply by expanding production capacity.

So the stress in India should not be on reducing fiscal deficit but revenue deficit by increasing tax revenue and reducing unproductive consumption expenditure of the Government. However, during the reform period the Government incurred a huge revenue deficit which had to be covered by borrowing. As a result capital expenditure in the form of investment on infrastructure projects (such as road building, construction of irrigation dams, etc.) and rural development as a percentage of GDP declined. This had adversely affected India's economic growth. The trend has to be reversed as soon as possible. If the present trend of increasing revenue deficit continues, there will be a shortage of funds for development of economic and social infrastructure and the whole process of economic growth will suffer a setback.

The government should borrow only for investment purposes or for increasing capital expenditure, i.e., financing infrastructure — both physical and social.

In short, there is need to reduce revenue deficit which is not only less productive but inflationary in its impact. This can be done not just by raising tax revenue but by improving the quality of public expenditure (i.e., curtailing the growth of non-planned revenue expenditure while raising planned investment expenditure).

1. The canon of equity also calls for introduction of such a tax, more so because capital gains represent unearned income.
2. This implies that the degree of progressiveness depends on the differences in ability to pay off different individuals.

KEY POINTS

1. *Objectives of fiscal policy* : Four main objectives of fiscal policy in developing countries like India are (i) mobilisation of resources for the public sector, (ii) providing individuals and firms necessary incentives to save and invest, (iii) achieving price stability and (iv) ensuring an equitable distribution of income and wealth.

2. *Tax policy* : More resources can be generated for economic development through direct taxes. Such taxes have neutral effect on the pattern of resource allocation. By imposing indirect taxes it is possible to increase saving by curtailing consumption of luxury goods. In addition, agricultural income tax may be introduced on a purely selective basis. However, tax revenue has to be judiciously spent.

3. *Public investment* : Public investment, mainly on infrustructure building, has a strong growth-promoting effect. However, crowding-out effect of such investment has to be avoided.

4. *Borrowing* : Resources for economic development may also be generated through borrowing for creating additional production capacity. Two main forms of borrowing are: (a) market loans and (b) then small saving. Public bonds may also be floated in the capital market for financing long-term projects.

5. *Deficit financing* : For covering a portion of the budgetary deficits, governments of developing countries have to take resort to deficit financing (money creation by the central bank for making loan to the central government). However, excessive reliance on this method of financing government expenditure is likely to generate inflation. So there is need to make judicious use of this easy method of covering budget deficit.

6. *Fiscal policy and income distribution* : Progressive taxes on individuals and firms may be imposed to reduce inequality of income and wealth. The tax system can also reduce poverty and inequality by generating additional employment opportunites in a labour-surplus country like India.

7. *Fiscal policy and price stability* : Direct taxes reduce disposable income of the people and thus help to control inflation by curtailing their consumption expenditure. Indirect taxes on inputs generate cost-push pressures and have to be avoided as much as possible. Such taxes are to be imposed at high rates on a few selected items (mainly luxury goods and non-essential items of consumption). Low rates should be applied in case of most mass consumption goods due to the regressive nature of such taxes.

KEY TERMS

Fiscal policy	Budget deficit
Direct taxes	Indirect taxes
Subsidies	Stabilisation role of fiscal policy
Economic growth	Economic equality
Market borrowing	Deficit financing
Developmental role of fiscal policy	Monetisation of deficit
Food inflation	Crowding-out effect

ASSIGNMENTS

1. Briefly discuss the objectives of fiscal policy in developing countries like India.
2. What, according to you, should be the objectives of tax policy in developing countries? What is the role of taxation in financing economic development?
3. What are the alternative methods of raising resources for economic development? Briefly discuss their merits and drawbacks.
4. What is the role of fiscal policy in reducing poverty and inequality? What role does it play in ensuring price stability?
5. (a) Deficit financing is inflationary in its effects.
   (b) Deficit financing promotes faster economic growth.
   How do you reconcile these two conflicting statements?
6. Write shortnotes on following:
   (a) monetisation of deficit, (b) crowding-out effect and (c) taxes and incentives.

38A FISCAL DEFICIT AND ECONOMIC GROWTH IN INDIA

Government expenditure is mainly financed through taxes. It is an important component of aggregate effective demand ($C + I + G$) in a closed economy. When the government spends more on goods and services than it is able to collect through tax and non-tax revenues, there is said to be a deficit in the budget. In recent years there has arisen huge deficit in the government budget. Such deficit is now called fiscal deficit which has generated huge excess demand pressure in the economy. Fiscal deficit arises either due to deficit in revenue budget or due to deficit in the capital budget or both at the same time. As a result the rate of inflation has increased year after year.

Focus on Terminology: Budget Deficit vs. Fiscal Deficit
Budget deficit refers to the excess of total budgetary expenditure (both on revenue and capital accounts) over total budgetary receipts (both on revenue and capital accounts) Fiscal deficit is the difference between revenue receipts plus certain capital receipts which are not borrowing (such as loan recovery) and which finally accrue to the government and the total expenditure including loans, net of repayment. It indicates the total borrowing requirements of the government from all sources.

Fiscal deficit of the GOI has to be financed either by borrowing from the market by selling bonds or by taking loans from the RBI against its own securities (since the RBI is banker to the government). And the RBI prints new currency notes to make such loans.

The newly created money increases the income of the people. As soon as they spend a portion of it excess demand pressure is generated in the economy. If aggregate supply is fairly inelastic, only one outcome is possible. The aggregate price level will rise.

Revenue Deficit

In India there has occurred deficit in the revenue account of the budget in the past two decades. Revenue deficit refers to the excess of revenue disbursement over revenue receipts (both from tax and non-tax sources).

Focus on Terminology: Revenue Deficit
The main sources of revenue receipts are taxes (both direct and indirect), interest on loans and profits and dividends of public enterprises. These are known as non-tax revenue. Revenue expenditure is made on public goods (mainly economic infrastructure) as also on social and community services, including transfer payments. The main components of such expenditure are (i) interest payments on public debt, (ii) civil administration, (iii) defence, (iv) subsidies on food, fertilisers and exports and (v) education and health. Revenue deficit is the excess of revenue expenditures over revenue receipts.

Causes

Revenue deficit increased for a number of reasons such as (i) reduction in excise duties and customs duties, (ii) waiving of loans of farmers and (iii) increase in wages and compensation of the central government employees on the basis of the recommendations of the different Pay Commissions. While revenue receipts fell due to (i), revenue expenditure increased due to (ii) and (iii). And funds from the capital account had to be diverted to meet a portion of revenue deficit.

Revenue deficit has slowed down the growth rate of the economy

Effects

A revenue deficit indicates negative saving of the government (or government dissaving). As a result government investment has fallen over the years and this has slowed down the growth rate of the economy.

Fiscal Deficit

Fiscal deficit is the excess of total expenditures (both on revenue and capital accounts) over revenue receipts as also non-debt type of revenue receipts such as loan recovery (i.e., recovery of past loans). So we can write:

Fiscal deficit = Total expenditures on revenue and capital accounts – revenue receipts + other types of capital receipts.

It has to be noted that fiscal deficit is a much more comprehensive measure of the government's budgetary imbalance than budget deficit.

FINANCING FISCAL DEFICIT

Fiscal deficit can be financed in following two ways:

(i) ***Market borrowing*** : The government can borrow from the market—both domestic and international (global). However, when the government borrows by selling bonds and securities, it has to service the debt, i.e., it has to repay the loan along with interest on time. This is true of both internal debt and external debt. Sometimes the burden of public debt is very high and the present generation is not in a position to repay it. And if the present generation escapes the burden, it is shifted on to the future generation(s) on which a huge tax burden will have to be imposed by the government for repayment of its debt.

(ii) ***Deficit financing*** : The GOI can borrow from the RBI and the RBI will make loan to the GOI by printing high-powered money. This means that the government budget deficit is absobed by the RBI by making new note issue. Such monetisation of deficit results in an increase in domestic money supply. And if the magnitude of budgetary deficit is high, there will occur an excessive increase in the money supply. And the end result will be price inflation.

EFFECT OF FISCAL DEFICIT

A large fiscal deficit has an adverse effect on economic growth. Due to large revenue deficit, the government has to borrow a huge sum mainly to finance its current consumption expenditure. So a very small amount is left for productive investment, mainly on economic infrastructure (such as roads, bridges, highways, etc.) and social services (mainly education and health). As a result the rate of growth of the economy slows down. Government borrowing from the market slows down the rate of growth in another way—by reducing the availability of investible resources.

In fact, there is shortage of funds for private sector investment due to competition between the two sectors—government and private—for a limited amount of funds. Private investment also falls due to rise in the rate of interest which makes various investment projects less profitable than they were initially (i.e., when the government did not appear in the capital market for raising funds).

The IMF has asked the GOI to reduce fiscal deficit to 3% of GDP in a phased manner. And in order to achieve this, the GOI has reduced its capital expenditure as much as possible because there was no scope for reducing the government's consumption expenditure. This has adversely affected economic growth. The following two important suggestions may now be put forward in this context:

(i) ***Maintaining capital expenditure*** : Since reduction of fiscal deficit by curtailing capital expenditure, as has been done in India so far, acts as an obstacle to growth, it should be avoided as much as possible. So only revenue expenditure has to be cut.

(ii) ***Reducing revenue deficit*** : For sound management of government finance, there is need to reduce revenue deficit. This can be acheived by cutting wasteful and unproductive revenue expenditure as much as possible. At the same time more revenue has to be generated through taxation for mobilising resources for productive investment and not for spending on wasteful and useless projects which serve no socio-economic purpose.

It is to be noted that the GOI passed the Fiscal Responsibility and Budget Management (FRBM) Act in order to impose discipline on its fiscal system and to reduce fiscal deficit so that there is not much inflation on the one hand and a huge increase in public debt on the other.

Primary Deficit

The last concept associated with government budget deficit is primary deficit. It is calculated by subtracting interest payments on public debt from fiscal deficit. It can thus be expressed as

$$\text{Primary deficit} = \text{Fiscal deficit} - \text{interest payments on public debt}$$

It may be recalled that government interest payments on public debt are government transfer payments and are not included in national income.

From the above equation it is obvious that the difference between fiscal deficit and primary deficit is payment of interest on accumulated public debt. And in recent past, the payment of such interest in India has increased sharply. And India has virtually fallen in an internal debt trap. India's fiscal deficit increased sharply in the initial few years of economic reforms mainly due to growing interest burden on public debt. This is why primary deficit was much lower than fiscal deficit.

India is now caught in an internal debt trap

Since interest payment is a major item on the liability side of the revenue account of the government budget, more and more interest payments created growing revenue deficit and, through it, fiscal deficit (because the capital account of the budget showed a surplus all the time). Therefore fiscal deficit can be reduced by reducing interest payments. This can be done by quickly retiring public debt or by generating more resources through greater tax effort and by curtailing the government's non-plan (or non-developmental) revenue expenditure.

Monetisation of Fiscal Deficit

Fiscal deficit can be covered by borrowing from the RBI. Earlier this was done by selling ad hoc treasury bills. When the GOI borrows from the RBI, the RBI makes loan to the government by printing new currency notes. This is known as monetisation of deficit. However, this practice has been stopped some time ago.

Measures to Reduce Fiscal Deficit

Growing fiscal deficit is undesirable for two main reasons: (i) it generates crowding-out effect, (ii) it causes inflation from the demand side. So it is absolutely essential to reduce fiscal deficit as much as possible. This can be achieved in two ways, viz., (i) by reducing public expenditure and (ii) by raising tax and non-tax revenues. These two measures may now be discussed one by one.

(i) **Reducing Public Expenditure**

The following measures may be adopted to reduce public expenditure:

1. *Subsidy reduction* : A drastic reduction of subsidies on major items such as food, fertiliser, export and electricity is absolutely essential at this stage of the economy. This will reduce public expenditure considerably.

2. *Curtailment of unnecessary expenditure* : Public expenditure can also be reduced by curtailing unnecessary and unproductive expenditure such as leave encashment, bonus, leave travel concessions (LTC), etc. A huge sum is spent on these heads every year and is no doubt an unnecessary burden on the Exchequer.

3. *Debt repayment through disinvestment* : Perhaps the best way to cut public expenditure drastically is to reduce payment of interest on past debt. This single item accounts for at least 40% of the revenue expenditure of the government at present. And funds raised through disinvestment of public sector enterprises should be used to repay a part of old debt. This will reduce future interest burden on public debt.

4. *Revised policy toward the public sector* : Fiscal deficit can also be reduced through public sector reforms. Budgetary support to all public sector enterprises, except those engaged in infrastructure building has to be reduced to a considerable extent. At the same time such enterprises should be asked to generate operative surplus which can be used for their own expansion and modernisation. So they will not need budgetary support year after year just to survive. For this it is necessary to adopt proper pricing policies so that costs are fully covered from user charges of providing public goods and services.

5. *Economy in government expenditure* : Economy drive should be initiated in all government departments for curtailing non-plan expenditure substantially. This can be achieved through the adoption of various austerity measures.

(ii) **Raising Tax Revenue**

Fiscal deficit can also be reduced by raising tax revenue. The following measures may now be adopted by the government to achieve this purpose:

1. *Tax cuts and simplification of the tax system* : By imposing taxes at low rates and by simplifying the tax structure considerably it will be possible to raise tax revenue to a large extent. Since high tax rates act as disincentives to work hard, save, invest and take risk, these should be avoided. In addition, high marginal tax rates should be avoided so that there is not much tax evasion and avoidance.

2. *Broadening the direct tax base* : India's direct tax base is narrow. Less than 3% of people in India pay personal income tax. There is a strong case for broadening the direct tax base by introducing agricultural income tax. Taxes may also be imposed on incomes derived from unorganised sector which includes both industries and services. The objective should be to raise the tax-GDP ratio. Various exemptions and deductons which are now offered in respect of income and wealth taxes should be withdrawn because they do not really serve any productive purpose. There should also less dependence on regressive (indirect) taxes and more on progressive (direct) taxes for raising more revenue which can be used for investment (capital formation) and for achieving faster economic growth. At the same time cuts in excise duties and customs duties are necessary for promoting exports by making Indian products more competitive in world markets.

3. *Unearthing black money* : Widespread tax evasion and avoidance in India has created a serious problem—generation of huge black money. Voluntary disclosure scheme (VDS), introduced in the past, failed to solve the problem. So there is need for strict enforcement of existing tax laws for unearthing black money.

4. *Service taxes* : More services are to be brought under the tax net for raising revenue from indirect taxes. This is so important because the yields from excise duty and customs duty have virtually reached the point of diminishing returns.

5. *Withdrawal of tax concessions* : In the past various concessions in respect of both direct and indirect taxes have been given for promoting industrial development in backward areas and for generating employment by setting up new industries. However, these concessions did not serve the purpose for which they were offered. Instead they encouraged tax evasion. These should, therefore, be removed so as to achieve budgetary saving.

6. *Capital gains tax* : At present there is no tax on long-term capital gains. There is strong economic rationale for taxing such gains because these are unearned incomes. Taxing such gains is strongly justified by Adam Smith's canon of equity.

If the above measures are effectively enforced or properly implemented fiscal deficit will come down to a low level and will not cross the safe limit. The reduction in fiscal deficit will ensure that excess demand pressure is not generated in the economy and the rate of inflation does not accelerate year after year.

Fiscal Deficit and Economic Growth

During the period 1997-2003 Indian economy was characterised by deficiency of demand. In such a situation there was not much danger of inflation through large budget deficit. So there was need to increase aggregate demand in order to stimulate the economy so that more output was produced and more jobs and incomes were created in the process. There was need to increase productive investment on infrastructure building with stress on roads, highways and irrigation projects. This would have served two purposes—stimulating demand and increasing aggregate output (i.e., supply of goods and services) by expanding the productive capacity of the economy.

Since in the early 1990s capital (investment) expenditure of the government for productive purposes as a percentage of GDP fell the rate of growth of the economy slowed down. And huge fiscal deficit due to deficit in the revenue account served no useful purpose. It just destablished the economy by adding fuel to the existing inflationary fire.

So the stress should now be on reducing only revenue deficit mainly by curtailing unproductive consumption expenditure of the government. An increase in fiscal deficit is not a bad thing for India provided it arises due to an increase in investment expenditure of the government, and that too for productive purposes.

To sum up, any amount of fiscal deficit and the consequent borrowing by the government is not good for achieving faster economic growth and generating adequate employment opportunities. The borrowing method of covering fiscal deficit involves not only payments of huge sums of money as interest, it also reduces the availability of investible resources for productive purposes and thus adversely affects economic growth. Fiscal deficit should be incurred only for financing productive public investment and not for meeting growing consumption expenditure of the government. The GOI's unproductive consumption expenditure should be reduced as much as possible.

CHAPTER 39

Financial Sector Reforms

The resources of the financial system are held by financial institutions in trust and have to be deployed for the maximum benefit of their owners—viz., depositors and investors. The safety of their funds should be primary concern of banks and regulatory authorities and ensuring solvency, health and efficiency of the institutions should, therefore, be central to effective financial reform.

Report of the Committee on Financial Reform, 1991
(Narasimham Committee)

PREVIEW

The financial sector includes both the money market and the capital market. It also includes the market for government securities. So financial sector reforms refer to reforms in all the three types of markets. Money market reforms mainly refer to reforms in the banking system.

Financial sector reforms are necessary for promoting faster economic growth. And economic growth is largely a matter of capital formation and productive investment. An efficient banking system and a well-functioning capital market are essential for mobilising household savings and channelising them to productive uses. And a high rate of saving and productive investment is necessary for achieving faster economic growth.

Prior to July 1991, when economic reforms were introduced, the first Narasimham Committee found a few major weaknesses of both the money market and the capital market. The main weaknesses were the following:

(i) *Regulation* : Certain areas of the banking system were regulated. But other areas remained unregulated.

(ii) *Administered rates of interest* : The system of regulated rates of interest prevailed. The RBI used to fix the rates of interest which could be charged by banks on different types of loans.

(iii) *High SLR and CRR* : A very high proportion of bank deposits was immobilised by the RBI by fixing high statutory liquidity ratio (SLR) and a high cash reserve ratio (CRR). As a result there was decrease in excess reserves of banks from which loans and advances were made to the private sector for investment purposes. Due to shortage of loanable funds banks were forced to charge high rates of interest on their loans and advances.

(iv) *Lack of transparency* : There was lack of transparency in accounting practices of banks. In addition, international norms had not been applied by banks. For these two reasons bank balance sheets did not reflect their true financial status. This anomaly got reflected in the 1992 security scam.

(v) *High proportion of NPAs* : Due to lack of transparency, the quality of investment portfolio of banks deteriorated and 'non-recovery' of loans became widespread in public sector banks. This increased the proportion of non-performing assets (NPAs). And this was a serious problem since it reduced bank profits.

Financial sector reforms sought to remove these drawbacks of the system and thus to make the Indian financial system more viable, operationally efficient and more prudent. The objective has been to improve allocative efficiency[1] of banks as also their profitability. Reforms have been undertaken in all the three segments of the financial system, viz., the money market, capital market and the market for government securities. We may now make a review of the various types of reforms made in these segments of the financial market since 1991.

A. MONEY MARKET REFORMS

Various money market (mainly banking sector) reforms have been introduced in India since July 1991. The most notable ones are the following:

1. Reduction in SLR

Since July 1991, both SLR and CRR have been reduced in a phased manner so as to make more bank credit available to agriculture, industry and trade. The SLR has been reduced from 39% to 25%. This implies that banks are required to maintain a minimum amount of liquid assets in the form of gold and approved government securities of not more than 25%.

It may be noted that reduction in SLR has been possible primarily because the Government had to reduce its fiscal deficit and thus its borrowing requirement, at the insistence of the IMF. In addition, this could be achieved due to the payment of market-related interest rates even on government (or gilt-edged) securities, which are free from any risk of default. Due to payment of interest at such rates, banks may become eager to invest their surplus funds in these securities, especially when the demand for bank loans from trade and industry was not adequate.

2. Reduction in CRR

The CRR has been reduced from 15% to 4.5% in June 2003. This became possible mainly due to reduction of the Government's budget deficit (which could till then be monetised automatically by taking loans from the RBI) and the discontinuation of the practice of financing budget deficit by issuing *ad hoc* treasury bills by the Central Government.

The reduction of both SLR and CRR made more loanable funds available to agriculture, industry and trade. This was made possible also because the RBI used both changes in the bank rate and open market operations as two main tools of monetary policy for promoting faster economic growth as also to ensure both domestic price stability and stability of the exchange rate[2].

3. Abolition of the System of Administered Rate of Interest

Upto 1993 both deposit rates and lending rates of commercial banks were fixed by the RBI from

1. Allocative efficiency refers to the efficiency of banks allocating their funds in such a fashion that there is maximum loan recovery so that high profit is earned.
2. In this context, the following quote from C. Rangaranjan, the former governor of the RBI is relevant: "As we move away from automatic monetisation of deficits, monetary policy will come into its own. The regulation of money and credit will be determined by the overall perception of the central monetary authority on what the appropriate level of expansion of money and credit should be depending on how the real factors in the economy are evolving."

time to time. The basic objective was to make adequate credit available to certain priority sectors, viz., agriculture and small-scale industries at concessional rates of interest. At the same time, high rates of interest were fixed for loans to be made to non-priority sectors like large and medium-sized industries, real estate, etc.[1] Since 1993, the system of administering (fixing) interest rates paid (for borrowing) and charged (for lending) by commercial banks has been done away with in a phased manner. The RBI no longer fixes or prescribes interest rates which can be paid by commercial banks on fixed (time) deposits. At present banks are also at liberty to determine their own terms and conditions for premature withdrawal of funds by depositors. Of late, interest paid on savings accounts has also been freed from RBI control.

Different types of bank lending rates which were earlier fixed by the RBI have also deregulated. This means that banks can now fix their lending rates on the basis of their perception of riskiness of loans as also the rewards they get in the form of interest. Banks also take into consideration the purposes for which loans are needed and given.

However, each bank is required to announce prime lending rates and the maximum spread[2] (i.e., the difference between a bank's borrowing rate or cost of fund and its lending rate). At present, loans upto Rs. 200,000 are to be provided at prime lending rates. Similarly, lending rates for exporters depend on the duration of loans.

4. Prudential Norms: High Capital Adequacy Ratio

Prudential norms in the form of high capital adequacy ratio have been introduced in accordance with international standards. The objective behind this move has been to ensure that the financial system operates on a sound and competitive basis.

Economic Insight: Capital Adequacy

Capital adequacy refers to the possession by a firm of sufficient capital for the business it is doing. This matters to the firm itself; if it is undercapitalised, a small adverse shift in the circumstances can impair its solvency. Capital adequacy, therefore, matters to a firm's creditors. In case of banks, it also matters to the regulatory authorities, whose concern is that the failure of a particular bank might cause a general financial panic. The level of capital adequacy is defined by the Basle Committee of the Bank for International Settlements.

Capital adequacy norm is fixed by referring to the ratio of paid-up capital and reserves to total deposits of banks. The capital base of Indian banks has been consistently low, at least by international standards. What is worse, it has declined steadily over the years.

During the post-reform period, capital adequacy ratio, based on risk-weighted asset ratio, has been introduced in India. Indian banks operating abroad were required to achieve this norm by March 31, 1994. Foreign banks operating in India had to achieve this norm one year earlier. Other Indian banks had to achieve this norm by March 31, 1996. Banks were instructed by the RBI to review their existing level of capital funds and compare the same to the prescribed norm and take steps to increase their capital base in a phased manner to 8% by the stipulated date.

Commentary: The Link between Capital Adequacy and Provisioning

Banks can meet capital adequacy norm only by making provision for adequate capital. To enable banks to achieve this norm, the GOI provided long-terms funds to some nationalised banks. The GOI also passed laws to enable public sector banks to raise funds from the capital market in order to improve their capital base. Some strong nationalised banks have already raised funds by selling equity. Banks have also been permitted to plough back a part of their retained earnings to strengthen their capital base.

1. Thus the system of administering the rates of interest involved cross subsidisation, i.e., the loss incurred by banks by giving loans to priority sectors was offset by high rates of interest charged from non-priority sectors.
2. This determines the profitability of banks.

5. Competitive Financial System

In the post-nationalisation period since July 1969 the GOI felt that there was an urgent need for making the Indian money market more competitive so that the entire financial market could operate more efficiently. This is why various other banks such as the HDFC bank, ICICI bank, the Corporation bank, the UTI bank (now the Axis bank) and the IDBI bank have been set up. These banks have led to diversification of banking business by providing non-traditional types of loans such as housing finance, car loan, and retail credit through the credit card system. They have ensured wider use of plastic money, namely, ATM cards, debit cards and credit cards. The GOI also permitted the entry of several foreign banks as also insurance companies such as the Citi bank, the Standard Chartered Banks, the Bank of America, the American Express, the Bank of Tokyo, and the HSBC bank to open branches in India, especially in four main metropolitan cities.

Another important step taken by the GOI is the liberalisation of foreign direct investment (FDI) in banks. In the budget for 2003-04, the limit of the FDI has been raised from 49% to 74% of the paid-up capital of foreign banks. However, this provision did not apply to the wholly-owned subsidiaries of such banks[1].

The above measures have served a number of purposes:

(i) setting up subsidiaries of foreign banks;

(ii) creating a competitive environment in the banking sector; and

(iii) enabling banks' transparency and (public) disclosure standards to reach international levels.

Banks have to appraise the RBI and the SEBI about the maturity pattern of their assets and liabilities, movements in the provisioning account and about non-performing assets (NPAs) from time to time. These are officially disclosed by the RBI in its annual publication: *Trends and Progress of Banking in India*. From this document it is possible to know about banks' financial position, that is, their profits, losses, assets, liabilities and net worth as also capital base and NPAs so that the operational efficiency of the banking system can be assessed at periodic intervals.

6. Non-Performing Assets (NPAs) and Income Recognition Norm

One major problem faced by the nationalised commercial banks in India is a high proportion of non-performing assets (NPAs). NPAs mean bad loans, i.e., loans which cannot be recovered easily and quickly. A high proportion of NPAs also lowers the profitability of banks. In this context, the RBI introduced a norm, viz., a norm of income recognition. According to this norm, income derived from assets of a bank cannot be recognised if a bank is unable to receive it within *two quarters* after the last date.

Various measures have been taken in recent years to recover bank loans quickly. The focus has been on reducing NPAs. Some specific measures to reduce NPAs include restructuring of bank assets, recovery of bad debts through Lok Adalats and civil courts, setting up of Recovery Tribunals as also compromise and mutual settlement. The recovery of bad debt became truly effective with the enactment of the Securitisation and Reconstruction of Financial Assets and Enforcement of Security Interest (SARFAESI) Act, which led to the setting up of debt recovery tribunals. Such tribunals have greatly facilitated the recovery of bad debts of banks. Due to the adoption of these measures gross NPAs of banks fell marginally from Rs. 70,861 crores in 2001-02 to Rs. 68,715 crores in 2002-03. So this is not a very impressive achievement. Banks still have huge NPAs which are yet to be recovered.

A related point may be noted in this context. Due to the introduction of risk-based supervision by the RBI, the ratio of gross NPAs to gross advances of scheduled commercial banks fell from 12.7 in 1999-2000 to 8.8 in 2002-03.

---

1. It may be noted that a foreign bank may operate in India through three alternative channels: (i) as a branch of a foreign bank, (ii) as a wholly-owned subsidiary of a foreign bank and (iii) as a subsidiary with FDI up to 74% of the paid-up capital.

7. Abolition of Selective Credit Controls

The GOI has also abolished direct or selective (qualitative) credit controls. By using this technique, the RBI used to control the provision of bank credit to traders (who used bank finance for holding stocks of sensitive commodities) as also to stock brokers (who used bank loans to buy shares). Due to abolition of the system, both banks and borrowers enjoy greater freedom as far as both disbursement and distribution of bank credit are concerned.

It may, however, be noted that banks are not totally free to determine their pattern of lending even now. They have to follow the RBI guidelines regarding lending to priority sectors such as small-scale industries and agriculture. The priority sectors are now eligible for getting more loans and advances at deregulated rates of interest. The RBI has made this provision since at present the main problem of commercial banks is excess liquidity rather than excess demand for bank loans. In June 2004, the GOI officially declared that credit to farmers would be available at 2% below the prime lending rates of banks. The GOI had also contemplated doubling of the volume of agricultural credit by May 2007 (i.e., within three years).

8. Abolishing the System of Automatic Monetisation of Budget (Fiscal) Deficit

In 1997 the GOI discontinued its age-old practice of automatic monetisation of the budget deficit by using ad hoc treasury bills. From April 1, 1997, the GOI has also abolished the system of issuing 91-days' T-bills. From the same date, the GOI introduced a new system, called Ways and Means Advances (WMA). These are advances to the government made by the central bank in the short run. These are made as and when necessary if government expenditure exceeds its receipts from taxation plus borrowing from the public. And market-related interest rate is charged on these advances[1]. Through mutual agreement, the RBI and GOI take decision on the upper limit of WMA and the rate of interest to be charged by the RBI on them.

With the introduction of the system of WMA, the traditional concept of budget deficit and deficit financing (spending) have lost their relevance in India. Instead, at present three key indicators of the GOI's fiscal position are the magnitudes of revenue deficit, fiscal deficit and primary deficit. Revenue deficit relates to the excess of revenue expenditures over revenue receipts. Fiscal deficit is the difference between revenue receipts *plus* those capital receipts which are not borrowings and which finally accrue to the government and the total expenditure including loans, net of repayment. It indicates the total borrowing requirement of the government from all sources. Primary deficit is fiscal deficit *minus* interest payment on public debt.

Commentary: WMA and Effectiveness of Monetary Policy
The introduction of the system of WMA has given more autonomy to the RBI for conducting its monetary policy. It has no doubt increased the effectiveness of RBI's monetary policy. In addition, since 2000, the RBI has not permitted the GOI to enjoy overdraft facilities for more than 10 days. This measure has ensured monetary stability to some extent.

9. Fiscal Responsibilities and Budget Management Act (FRBM)

One of the basic lessons of macroeconomics is that monetary policy depends, for its success, on fiscal policy. In fact, the link between monetary policy and fiscal policy is established through the government budget deficit. Earlier any budget deficit of the GOI was met by borrowing money from the RBI. And the RBI made loans to the GOI by printing currency notes. So new money came into circulation. And this often overheated the economy and caused inflation. This means that unless the GOI reduces its fiscal deficit, the money supply cannot be held in check and inflation cannot be brought under control. Realising this point, the RBI passed the Fiscal Responsibilities and Budget Management

1. Thus WMA virtually amount to lending by the RBI to the GOI for a short period of time.

(FRBM) Act, which has established a link between the GOI's fiscal stance and the RBI's monetary management. According to the Act, the GOI was supposed to take appropriate measures to reduce fiscal deficit to 2% of GDP and to eliminate revenue deficit completely by March 31, 2008. The Act also declared that the revenue deficit and the fiscal deficit may be allowed to exceed the limit only on grounds of national security, natural calamity or such other exceptional circumstances as may be specified by the GOI from time to time. The Act has also prohibited the GOI from borrowing from the RBI except through WMA. Finally, from 2006-07, the Act has stopped the RBI from subscribing to the primary issues of the GOI.

10. Market Stabilisation Scheme

The GOI introduced another notable reform measure known as market stabilisation scheme (MSS). The scheme was introduced since April 1, 2004 to stabilise the inflationary impact of huge foreign exchange inflows into the economy as also to prevent undue appreciation of the Indian Rupee. In fact, on March 31, 2004, the accumulated foreign exchange reserve of the RBI crossed $107 billion. So an undue and uncalled for appreciation of the rupee was apprehended. To prevent this from happening the RBI bought US dollars by selling rupees. As a result, the liquidity with the banking system and thus the money supply increased and this created inflationary pressures. The rate of inflation which remained low in the past few years (7.61% at the end of July 2004) suddenly rose to 8.33% in August, 2004. To prevent the growing inflationary pressures in the economy, the RBI sterilised much of the liquidity in the bank system by selling government securities (held by it) to the banks. As a result, the rupee reserves of the RBI continued to increase. At the same time the trend of growing inflows of foreign currencies continued. But further sterilisation was not possible through open market sale of government securities since the RBI had aheady exhausted its stock of such securities. So higher rates of inflation were apprehended.

Focus on Terminology: Sterilisation
Sterilisation is a method by which a central bank prevents a country's balance of payments surplus (or deficit) from affecting its domestic money supply. If there is a surplus in the balance of payments, this leads to a rise in the foreign exchange reserves, and an increase in the money supply. If the central bank does not want the money supply to increase, it can prevent this by selling securities so as to sterilise the cash inflow. The central bank buys securities in times of balance of payments deficit. The central bank can choose to sterilise some proportion rather than the whole of the monetary effects of changes in foreign exchange reserves.

To overcome this undesirable situation the RBI entered into an agreement with the GOI in April, 2004, which led to the emergence of a new scheme, called the Market Stabilising Scheme (MSS). Under the scheme, the GOI issued special treasury bills or dated securities in addition to what it normally issues. The main purpose of the scheme is to enable the RBI to absorb excess liquidity in the banking system. The upper limit for the issue of additional government securities for the purpose of stabilisation was fixed at Rs. 60,000 crores for the year 2004-05. These special securities were sold by the RBI to both member banks and non-banking financial institutions. The funds raised in the process were held in specific cash accounts of the RBI, and were not to be used by the GOI for any purpose.

B. CAPITAL MARKET REFORMS

A number of capital market reforms were introduced for improving efficiency, increasing transparency and preventing unfair practices regarding capital market transactions. The following measures have been introduced since 1991 for liberalising, regulating and developing India's capital market.

1. Establishment of SEBI

The GOI set up the Securities and Exchange Board of India (SEBI) for controlling and regulating India's equity market. The regulation of the stock markets is important for at least *three* reasons: (i) smooth and orderly functioning of the stock markets, (ii) giving a fair deal to customers by brokers and other professionals and (iii) providing all types of information by issuing firms about themselves so as to enable people to make intelligent investment decisions.

The following regulatory measures and guidelines have been introduced by SEBI over a period of time as far as issuing and selling of shares in the primary market are concerned:

(a) *Public disclosure through advertisements* : The SEBI has introduced a code of advertisement for companies making public issues. All companies making public issues are required to give insertions in newspapers disclosing all relevant facts and indicating risk factors associated with their projects. The main objective of the SEBI code is to ensure that companies make fair and honest disclosures.

(b) *Amendment of listing agreements* : The stock exchanges are under the legal obligation to amend their listing agreements from time to time. The objective is to ensure is that a listed company furnishes yearly statements to them, clearly indicating discrepancy between financial projections and actual utilisation of funds in a project. This will console and delight shareholders since they will be able to make comparisons between the promises made by a company and its actual performance (and thus its success in honouring its obligations to the equity-holders).

(c) *Bringing merchant banking under regulatory framework* : The SEBI has brought merchant banking also under its regulatory framework. Merchant banks are involved in stock broking and corporate finance. They arrange new stock and share issues on behalf of corporate clients and underwrite such issues.[1] The merchant banks are under the legal obligation to follow the code of conduct issued by the SEBI in respect of pricing and fixation of premium in the context of new issues by corporate enterprises.

(d) *Stopping preferential allotment of shares* : The SEBI has stopped the age-old practice of corporations of making preferential allotment of shares at arbitrary prices, having hardly any relation to the existing market prices. Now companies have to be transparent in their share allotment.

(e) *Stopping insider trading* : The SEBI has stopped insider trading. The objective is to ensure transparency in share transactions.

Focus on Terminology: Insider Trading
Insider trading refers to dealing in company shares with a view to making a profit or avoiding a loss while in possession of information that, if publicly known, would affect share prices.

(f) *Introduction of rolling settlement system* : As per SEBI guidelines those who are or have been connected with a company (e.g., the directors, the company secretary, employees and professional advisors) are prohibited from such dealing or, in certain circumstances, from entering the stock exchange if they acquire the information by virtue of their connection and in confidence. The prohibition extends to certain unconnected persons to whom the information has already been conveyed.

In order to establish transparent rules for stock trading, the pernicious (harmful/damaging) *badla system* has been totally banned. The rolling settlement system has been introduced in its place.

2. Promoting the Establishment of Private Mutual Funds

During the reform period the GOI granted permission to private sector to go into mutual fund business. This is why a number of business houses set up their mutual funds for raising funds from the public. Mention may be made of the Tata Mutual Fund, Reliance Mutual Fund, Birla Mutual Fund, Bajaj Allianz Mutual Fund, etc. Consequently the UTI, the first mutual fund in India set up in 1964, lost its preeminent position in mutual fund business. At the same time the UTI has been brought under regulation and control of the SEBI.

1. Underwriting refers to the acceptance by a financial institution of the financial risks involved in a particular transaction at an agreed fee. Merchant banks underwrite new share issues, guaranteeing to buy up any shares that remain unsold in the open market.

Focus on Terminology: Mutual Fund

A mutual fund is a financial institution which holds shares on behalf of investors. Investors buy shares, or units in the fund. The fund, in its turn, uses the money raised to buy shares in certain companies. An investor selling back the units gets the proceeds of selling a fraction of the fund's asset portfolio. The management of the fund benefits from appreciation of the shares the fund holds since management charges one per cent of the market value of its portfolio as fees.

A mutual fund raises money by selling shares or units to the public and it invests the funds in the shares and debentures of some selected and reputed companies. Mutual funds are of two types: open-end funds and close-end funds[1].

A mutual fund may be either equity-based or debt-based or a balanced one having a judicious mix of equities and debentures. By putting their savings in mutual funds investors are able to reduce risk.

Private mutual funds have also been permitted to open offshore funds so that they can invest in foreign equities.

3. Open Door for Foreign Capital

With a view to attracting private capital the GOI has also permitted foreign institutional investors (FII) to buy shares and debentures of private Indian companies from the stock exchange. They are also permitted to invest in government securities. For FIIs the rupee has been made a fully convertible currency.

4. Access to Global Finance

The Indian corporate sector has been given the permission to raise funds from the global financial markets through such instruments as American depository receipts (ADRs), global depository receipts (GDRs), foreign currency convertible bonds as also external commercial borrowing. At the same time, foreign corporations and non-resident Indians have been given the permission to invest in equity shares of Indian companies.

Focus on Terminology: ADRs

American depository receipt (ADR) is a receipt issued by a US bank to a member of the US public who has bought shares in a foreign country. The certificates are denominated in US dollars and can be traded as a security in US markets.

5. The Operation of Banks in Capital Markets

The GOI has permitted banks to lend against various capital market instruments such as shares and debentures to individuals, investment companies, trusts and endowments, share brokers, corporations as also SEBI-approved market-makers. However, banks have been instructed to follow certain norms which relate to purpose, capital adequacy, and transparency of transactions, upper limit and duration of the loan.

Focus on Terminology: Market-Maker

A market-maker is a trader in securities market who holds a stock of the security and is willing to buy or sell at a pre-announced price. This price only applies up to some limited quantity, but up to this limit they provide liquidity for other people or firms who want to buy and sell. For larger deals the market-makers will negotiate over price.

Bank lending against shares and debentures is likely to make scrips partly liquid and help reduce price fluctuations, encourage the presence of market-makers so as to reduce market concentration and help in both widening and deepening of trading in the secondary market.

1. See p. 303 Hobbard and Obryan: *Macroeconomics* (Pearson Education).

THE INTEGRATION OF MONEY AND CAPITAL MARKET

During the reform period we have seen some sort of integration of the money market with the capital market. The money market deals in short-term credit instruments such as cheques, bank drafts, pay orders, etc. which are valid for less than one year. And the money market provides short-term loans to meet the working capital needs of trade and industry. By contrast, the capital market deals in long-term credit instruments such as equity shares, debentures, bonds, etc. And the capital market meets the fixed capital needs of large and medium-sized industries.

The money market mainly consists of depository institutions such as banks and non-banking financial intermediaries. The latter resembles banks closely since they attract public deposits and make loans to the private sector but they are not directly under the control of the central bank.

The capital market mainly consists of the primary (new issue) market, the secondary market (stock exchanges) as also term-lending institutions such as IFCI, ICICI or development banks such as the IDBI. At the state level they are 18 State Financial Corporations (STCs) which are state counterparts of the Industrial Finance Corporation of India (IFCI). These institutions provide loans for a maximum period of 25 years and underwrite the shares and debentures of corporate enterprises.

Focus on Terminology: Underwriting
Underwriting refers to the provision by development banks of a guaranteed market for a new issue of shares, a job which was traditionally done by merchant banks. Firms making new issues cannot know in advance whether there will be sufficient demand for the shares they offer at the issue price, from public or institutional investors. An underwriter removes the uncertainty as to whether shares will sell by promising to buy those shares which remain unsold in the market. These shares then have to be sold, which may involve accepting a low price or a long wait. A commission is charged for this service.

During the reform period the commercial banks have been performing some of the functions of the development banks. Similarly the development banks have been performing some of the functions of commercial banks. So the distinction between the two types of banks is no longer valid. And we find convergence of the functions and activities of the two types of banks or financial institutions. This virtually amounts to the integration of the money market with the capital market. The following points may be noted in this context:

(i) *Capital market operation by commercial banks* : Some commercial banks have been operating in the capital market. Let us take the example of SBI Cap. Commercial banks are now providing not only housing loan but also long-term loans to industry.

(ii) *Money market operations by development banks* : Some development banks such as IDBI and ICICI have set up their banking institutions such as the IDBI bank and the ICICI bank. So they are now engaged in retail banking. They are making short-term loans, including car loans to individuals and households. Some of these banks have also entered insurance business and mutual fund operations in a big way. We can cite the example of ICICI Prudential Life Insurance.

Similarly, the UTI has also set up its own commercial bank, viz, the UTI bank which is now known as the Axis bank. It is also engaged in retail banking business like all other commercial banks. It is also involved in a big way in foreign exchange business.

Universal Banking

Since commercial banks are performing some of the functions of the development banks and development banks are also performing the functions of commercial banks, a new concept of the banking has emerged, viz., universal banking. And the ICICI Bank is the first universal bank of India.

The integration of the two markets has been made possible largely due to the abolition of the system of administered rates of interest. Now banks are having surplus liquidity. And they are eager to lend as much fund as possible at the market determined rate of interest. And individuals can borrow at low rates of interest through negotiation and bargaining in a highly competitive banking environment. Very recently the RBI has set interest rates even on saving deposits free from its control. Now commercial banks can pay any rate of interest on saving deposits.

C. REFORMS IN THE MARKET FOR GOVERNMENT SECURITIES

Since 1911 the following reform measures have been undertaken to both widen and deepen the market for government securities and to increase transparency in the sale of such securities.

1. *Reduction of SLR* : As noted earlier, the SLR has been reduced from 45% to 25% in a phased manner. As a result more bank resources have become available for private sector lending. Moreover banks have been permitted to invest more than 25% of their excess reserves in approved government securities[1].

2. *Sale through auction* : Due to the abolition of the system of administered rates of interest, these securities are now sold through the auction system and go to the highest bidder(s). This is why government securities are now sold at market-driven rates of interest.[1]

3. *Widening the market for government securities* : The government has given permission to foreign institutional investors (FII) to invest in a certain approved government securities. This has widened the market for such securities.

4. *Repurchase (Repo) agreement* : The Liquidity Adjustment Facility (LAF) scheme was introduced to facilitate trading in government securities. The scheme operates through repo and reverse repo operations for a very short period such as a day or a few days. In times of liquidity crisis, the RBI lends funds to banks at a fixed repo interest rate by purchasing securities from them for a very short period. On the other hand, in times of excess liquidity, banks park their surplus funds with the RBI at a fixed reverse repo rate and they get government securities in exchange. This is how the RBI is now able to adjust, control and regulate the liquidity of banks.

5. *Other reform measures* : Other reform measures related to the market for government securities are the following:

(i) permitting primary dealers to act as market-makers in case of government securities,
(ii) introducing Delivery versus Payment (DVP) settlement system to ensure transparency in the purchase and sale of government securities,
(iii) the termination of automatic monetisation of budget deficits and
(iv) the introduction of Market Stabilisation Scheme (MSS).

We can expect that due to the adoption of these measures the market for government securities will gradually emerge as a strong and vibrant segment of the Indian capital market.

THE PERFORMANCE OF THE FINANCE SYSTEM DURING THE REFORM PERIOD

We may now discuss how the three main segments of the Indian financial system have performed. We start with the banking sector.

(a) The Banking Sector

The banking sector reforms have sought to increase efficiency and productivity of banks through the creation of a more competitive environment. In addition, these reforms sought to achieve social objectives such as increase in lending to the priority sectors such as agriculture and small-scale industries. No doubt, banking sector reforms led to marked improvement in the financial health which gets reflected in capital adequacy norms and improved asset quality. In Table 39.1 we present the position of banks, classified according to the risk-weighted capital adequacy. A CAR below 10% implies the risk of default by a bank. This, therefore, implies poor financial health of a bank. In 1995-96 no

1. Many banks have considered this profitable since they have sufficient excess liquidity.

less than 50 commercial banks had CAR below 10%. The number of such banks fell sharply to 6 in 2002-03. This is no doubt a commendable achievement.

Table 39.1: The Distribution of Commercial Banks According to Risk-Weighted Capital Adequacy

Year	Below 4%	Below 4-9%	Below 9-10%	Above 10%	Total Number of Banks
1995-96	8	9	33	42	92
1999-00	3	2	12	84	101
2000-01	3	2	11	84	100
2001-02	1	2	7	81	91
2002-03	2	0	4	87	93

Note: The number of banks has declined due to merger of weak banks with strong ones.

Source: Rakesh Mohan: *Financial factor Reforms in India*, EPW, March 2005.

Progress of Nationalised Commercial Banks

During the 1970s and 1980s nationalised commercial banks made notable progress in terms of expansion of branches (especially in rural and semi-urban areas) as also expansion of credit, especially in the top priority sectors. However, the progress came to a halt since 1991. From Table 39.2 we see that there has not occurred much progress in banks' branch expansion programme. In addition, the number of people served by a particular branch of a nationalised commercial bank remained more or less unchanged at 15,000. This means that no further progress was made in the banking arena during the post-reform period. The reform process just maintained and consolidated the gains of the earlier years. This reminds us of a famous statement made by J.R.Hicks: "Maintenance is more important than expansion".

Table 39.2: Progress of Commercial Banking in India

Indicators	June 1969	June 1980	March 1991	March 1995	March 2000	March 2003
Number of commercial banks	73	154	272	284	298	292
Number of banks' offices	8262	34594	60570	64234	67868	68561
Rural and semi-urban bank offices	5172	23227	46550	46602	47693	47496
Population per office ('000s)	64	16	14	15	15	16
Per capita deposit (Rs.)	88	738	2368	4242	8542	12253
Per capita credit (Rs.)	68	457	1434	2320	4555	7275
Priority sector advances @(per cent)	15.0	37	39.2	33.7	35.4	33.7*
Deposits (per cent of national income)	15.5	36.0	48.1	48.0	53.5	51.8

@: Share of priority sector advances in total non-fund credit of scheduled commercial bank.

*: As at end-March 2002

Source: Reserve Bank of India

However, some definite gains were made in other areas, viz., in terms of deposits per head of population and issue of credit per borrower. Per capita deposits increased from Rs. 2,368 on March 31, 1969 to Rs. 12,253 on March 31, 2003 and per capita credit increased from Rs. 1,934 to Rs. 7,275 in the same period. There also occurred a marginal increase in bank deposits as a proportion of national income from 48.1 to 52 during the same period.

However, there has occurred a decline in priority sector advances during the post-reform period. This is no doubt a disquieting trend. During the period under consideration priority sector lending as a proportion of total advance remained unchanged at around 8. In order to increase the flow of such credit the RBI has given certain incentives to public sector banks. As a result the percentage increased from 10.8 in 2001 to 12.9 in 2008.

In spite of the reduction of SLR banks were compelled to make large investment in government securities, also known as gilt-edged securities (since these are free from the risk of default). The reason was that the demand for bank credit fell due to slowdown in industrial growth rate for five years (1997-2002). However, commercial banks provided more credit to industry and trade since 2003 to meet the growing demand for bank credit due to initial revival and subsequent acceleration in the rate of industrial growth. In truth, due to adoption of various liberalisation measures in the banking sector, including reduction in SLR, banks have attempted to strike a fine balance between making long-term investment and providing short-term loans and advances with a view to achieving their basic objective, viz., profit maximisation.

Non-Performing Assets (Loans)

There has occurred substantial improvement in the quality of bank assets during the period of reforms. Table 39.3 shows that non-performing loans (NPLs) of nationalised commercial banks as a percentage of both advances and assets (gross and net) declined steadily since 1996-97.

Table 39.3: NPAs of Nationalised Commercial Banks

Year	Gross NPL Advances	Gross NPL Assets	Net NPL Advances	Net NPL Assets
1996-97	15.7	7.0	8.1	3.3
1997-98	14.4	6.4	7.3	3.0
1998-99	14.7	6.2	7.6	2.9
1999-2000	12.7	5.5	6.8	2.7
2000-01	114	4.9	6.2	2.5
2001-02	10.4	4.6	5.5	2.3
2002-03	8.8	4.0	4.4	1.9
2003-04	7.3	-	3.0	-

Source: Reserve Bank of India

There are two reasons for this: (i) considerable improvement in the credit evaluation system of banks making loans and advances and (ii) faster recovery of NPLs of late.

Profitability of Banks

Due to greater intensity to competition, banks have been forced to improve their performance mainly by raising productivity of human resources. As a result profitability of both nationalised and non-nationalised banks has improved. In the pre-reform period most public sector banks used to make losses as a matter of routine, so as to say. During the post-reform period their losses have been converted into profits.

(b) The Capital Market

Financial sector reforms led to a healthy growth of the capital market, if we leave aside two major stock market scams (by H. Mehta in 1992 and Ketan Parikh in 1998). The equity market achieved substantial growth in terms of key parameters such as (i) resource mobilisation, (ii) the number of listed companies and (iii) trading volumes. See Table 39.4. However, the number of stock exchanges fell from 22 in 1991-99 to 20 in 2008-09.

Table 39.4: Some Stock Market Indicators in India

Year (end-March)	1961	1971	1980	1991	2000	2002	2003
Number of Stock Exchanges	7	8	9	22	23	23	23
Number of listed companies	1,203	1,599	2,265	6,229	9,871	9,644	9,413
Market capitalisation (Rs. billion)	12	27	68	1,103	11,926	7,493	6,318

Source: Rakesh Mohan: op. cit

The number of companies listed in Bombay Stock Exchange (BSE) increased from 4,898 in 2005-06 to 5,038 in 2008-09. Market capitalisation at BSE increased from Rs. 3022,189 in 2005-06 to Rs. 5,382,05 in 2009-10. And in National Stock Exchange (NSE) it increased from Rs. 4,858,22 crores in 2007-08 to Rs. 6,009,173 crores in 2009-10.

Thanks to the effective enforcement of the SEBI's strong regulatory framework the efficiency of stock exchanges improved considerably. This gets reflected in fall in transaction costs, improvement in transparency and safety in transactions. The efficiency of stock markets improved for four additional reasons, viz.,

(i) the introduction of rolling settlement system,

(ii) abolition of the dangerous Badla system,

(iii) implementation of improved risk management system and

(iv) introduction of trading in derivatives.

Due to introduction of various liberalisation measures FIIs has been induced to make more investment in both equity and debt instruments of the Indian corporations. FII investment[1] in India increased from \$9,363 million in 2005-06 to \$16,442 million in 2007-08. The amount[2] raised through GDRs/ADRs increased from \$2,552 million to \$6,645 million in 2007-08. This had led to sharp and consistent increase in portfolio investment in India which, in turn, led to huge increase in India's foreign exchange reserves. The BSE sensex went up from 1880 in 1991-92 to 4,659 in 1999-00 and to 12,366 in 2007-08. Then it fill suddenly in 2008-09 due to global financial crisis. It again increased to 15,585 in 2009-10.

(c) The Market for Government Securities

At present, the fiscal deficit of the government is financed through market borrowing. The government makes loan by selling securities to banks and many companies. The fiscal deficit of the GOI has varied between 6% and 6.4% since 1992. As a result the outstanding debt consisting of stock of central and state government securities has increased considerably over the period 1992 to 2004, as shown in Table 39.5.

Table 39.5: Outstanding Stock of Government Securities

	1992	1995	2000	2003	2004
Centre	769 (10.3)	1,375 (11.6)	3,819 (18.1)	6,739 (27.3)	8,243 (29.7)
States	190 (2.5)	312 (2.6)	739 (3.5)	1,331 (5.4)	1,795 (6.5)

Note: Figures in brackets show outstanding debt as per cent of GDP at current market prices.

Source: RBI.

1. However, FII investment was \$28,297 in 2008-09 due to global financial crisis.
2. It fell to \$1 162 million in 2008-09.

A related price may be noted in this context. The combined outstanding debt of the Central and State governments as a percentage of GDP at current market prices rose from 12.4 in 1992 to 36.2 in 2004. In spite of a sharp increase in borrowing by the GOI at two different levels to cover its fiscal deficit, the interest on government securities (or the cost of government borrowing) has fallen steadily. This is attributable to improved liquidity position of banks as also the decision of the government to reduce interest rates for keeping its cost of loans low. The yield on primary issues of government securities having maturity period of 5 to 10 years fell from a range of 13.25% to 14% in 1996 and 4.02% to 5.73% in 2004. In spite of a fall in yield rates on government securities the turnover increased sharply. This clearly indicates high demand for low-return, but completely risk-free government securities. This implies that the purchasers of government securities are essentially risk-averse people.

KEY POINTS

1. *Importance of financial sector reforms* : The financial sector includes both the money market and the capital market. It also includes the market for government securities. So financial sector reforms refer to reforms in all the three types of markets. Money market reforms mainly refer to reforms in the banking system.

Financial sector reforms are necessary for promoting faster economic growth. And economic growth is largely a matter of capital formation and productive investment. An efficient banking system and a well-functioning capital market are essential for mobilising household savings and channelising them to productive uses. And a high rate of saving and productive investment is necessary for achieving faster economic growth.

2. *Money market reforms* : Various money market (mainly banking sector) reforms have been introduced in India since July 1991. The most notable ones are the following:

a. Reduction in SLR, (b) Reduction in CRR, (c) Abolition of the system of administered rate of interest, (d) Prudential norms: High capital adequacy ratio, (e) Competitive financial system, (f) Non-performing assets (NPAs) and income recognition norm, (g) Abolition of selective credit controls, (h) Abolishing the system of automatic monetisation of budget (fiscal) deficit, (i) Fiscal responsibilities and budget management act (FRBM), (j) Market Stabilisation scheme.

3. *Capital market reforms* : A number of capital market reforms were introduced for improving efficiency, increasing transparency and preventing unfair practices regarding capital market transactions. The following measures have been introduced since 1991 for liberalising, regulating and developing India's capital market.

(i) *Establishment of SEBI*

The following regulatory measures and guidelines have been introduced by SEBI over a period of time as far as issuing and selling of shares in the primary market are concerned:

(a) Public disclosure through advertisements, (b) Amendment of listing agreements, (c) Bringing merchant banking under regulatory framework, (d) Stopping preferential allotment of shares, (e) Stopping insider trading, (f) Introduction of rolling settlement system

(ii) *Promoting the Establishment of Private Mutual Funds*

During the reform period the GOI granted permission to private sector to go into mutual fund business.

(iii) *Open Door for Foreign Capital*

With a view to attracting private capital the GOI has also permitted foreign institutional investors (FII) to buy shares and debentures of private Indian companies from the stock exchange. They are also permitted to invest in government securities.

(iv) *Access to Global Finance*

The Indian corporate sector has been given the permission to raise funds from the global financial markets through such instruments as American depository receipts (ADRs), global depository receipts (GDRs), foreign currency convertible bonds as also external commercial borrowing.

(v) *The Operation of Banks in Capital Markets*

The GOI has permitted banks to lend against various capital market instruments such as shares and debentures to individuals, investment companies, trusts and endowments, share brokers, corporations as also SEBI-approved market-makers.

4. *The Integration of Money and Capital Market* : During the reform period we have seen some sort of integration of the money market with the capital market.

During the reform period the commercial banks have been performing some of the functions of the development banks. Similarly the development banks have been performing some of the functions of commercial banks. So the distinction between the two types of banks is no longer valid. And we find convergence of the functions and activities of the two types of banks or financial institutions. This virtually amounts to the integration of the money market with the capital market.

5. *Universal banking* : Since commercial banks are performing some of the functions of the development banks and development banks are also performing the functions of commercial banks, a new concept of the banking has emerged, viz., universal banking.

6. *Reforms in the market for government securities* : Since 1911 the following reform measures have been undertaken to both widen and deepen the market for government securities and to increase transparency in the sale of such securities.

(a) Reduction of SLR, (b) Sale through auction, (c) Widening the market for government securities, (d) Repurchase (repo) agreement, (e) Other reform measures.

KEY TERMS

Repo rate	Reverse repo rate
NPS	CAR
Sterilisation	Mutual fund
Insider trading	Market-maker
Ways and means advances	Monetisation of fiscal deficit
Provisioning	Prudential norms
Competitive financial system	Income recognition norm
Risk aversion	Universal banking

ASSIGNMENTS

1. Write an explanatory note on the integration of the money market and capital market in the context of India's financial sector reforms.
2. Make a brief review of India's banking sector reforms since July 1991, with particular reference to (a) CAR and (b) NPAs.
3. Distinguish between SLR and CRR.
4. What is universal banking?
5. What is repo rate? What is reverse repo rate?
6. Account for the broadening of the market for government securities in India.
7. Make an overall evaluation of various capital market reforms undertaken in India since July 1999.
8. Comment on the integration of the money market and the capital market in India in the context of financial market reforms.

39A INDIA'S CAPITAL MARKET

The resources of the financial system are held by financial institutions in trust and have to be deployed for the maximum benefit of their ownes, viz., depositors and investors. The safety of their funds should be the primary concern of banks and regulatory authorities and ensuring solvency, health and efficiency of the institutions should therefore, be internal to effective financial reform.

Report of the Committee on Financial Reform, 1991
(Narashimham Committee)

IMPORTANCE OF AN INTEGRATED FINANCIAL INFRASTRUCTURE

The financial system of a country plays a crucial role in the process of economic growth. Finance is the lifeblood of industry and trade. Financial capital can be converted into real capital or productive assets. This is why economic growth in general and industrial growth in particular depends on the existence of an integrated financial infrastructure. In fact, a strong financial structure is an essential pre-requisite for initiating the process of economic growth as also for accelerating it.

An efficient financial network conduces to the process of economic growth in more ways than one. In fact, the growth of the financial infrastructure and economic growth complement each other. Just as the emergence and growth of financial intermediaries is a pre-condition for achieving faster economic growth, economic growth is characterised by various types of financial innovation in the form of emergence of new financial techniques such as disintermediation and securitisation and new products such as call and put options and futures (called derivative) and diversification of the whole financial structure. A diversified financial structure conduces to the process of economic growth by imparting the needed dynamism to the industrial sector.

THE MEANING AND COMPONENTS OF FINANCIAL INFRASTRUCTURE

The term 'financial infrastructure' is a broad one and includes financial assets (primary and secondary securities), financial markets (money and capital markets) and financial intermediaries (banks and non-bank financial institutions). Thus there are *three* ingredients of a country's financial system.

Financial Markets

It has to be noted at the outset that financial markets provide the basic mechanism for trading financial assets through financial intermediaries. Financial markets act as the link between surplus-generating units (households) and deficit-spending units (firms or corporate enterprises). Such markets provide institutional arrangements to facilitate the flow (transfer) of funds between them.

Money Market and Capital Market

Financial markets are divided into broad categories, viz., money market and capital market. While the money market provides short-term funds to meet the working capital needs of trade and industry, the capital market provides long-term funds to enable businesses to create or acquire fixed assets. Other differences between the two markets are the following:

(i) ***Short-term and long-term credit instruments*** : The money market deals in short-term credit (financial) instruments which are valid for less than one year such as bills of exchange, promissory notes, certificates of deposits (CDs), commercial papers, inter-bank participations and treasury bills. The capital market deals in long-term credit instruments such as equity shares, preference shares, bonds, debentures, hybrid convertibles or convertible bonds or debentures, gilt-edged (government) securities[1] and units of the UTI.

(ii) ***Components*** : The main components of the money markets are the inter-bank call money market; treasury bills market, commercial bills market, as also the discount and Finance House of India (DFHI). Two broad components of the capital market are the industrial securities market (which includes both the new issue market and stock exchanges) and the market for government securities (called the gilt-edged market).

(iii) ***Participants*** : The main players in the money market are commercial banks. In the capital market the main transactors are the non-bank financial intermediaries.

(iv) ***Direct and indirect roles of monetary policy*** : The current trends in interest and short-term flow of funds (liquidity) get reflected in the money market. This means that the money market provides necessary information to the central bank (the RBI) for formulation and management of monetary policy. So the role of monetary policy is direct. By contrast, in the capital market, monetary policy plays both direct and indirect roles — direct through RBI's open market operations in the market for government securities (or the gilt-edged market) and indirect through bridge loans provided by banks to the corporate sector.

Focus on Terminology: Bridge Financing (Bridging)

Bridge financing or simply 'bridging' refers to short-term lending needed by a borrower prior to the receipt of permanent finance. This financing is a popular way of making a big purchase such as a house, or of adjusting an investment portfolio. It is often necessary as purchases are financed by the delayed proceeds from the sale of another asset. This is a popular source of personal finance in industrially developed countries.

(v) ***Control and regulation*** : The money market is controlled and regulated by the central bank (such as the RBI) which is the central monetary authority. The capital market is controlled by an investment regulatory authority such as the Securities and Exchange Board of India (SEBI).

In short, in spite of their functional differences, the money market and the capital market conduce to the smooth flow of funds from one sector to another. This is so crucial for the process of capital formation and economic growth. This is why the RBI and the GOI have been constantly pursuing policies to establish a strong and integrated financial infrastructure, more so after the adoption of the policy of economic liberalisation since July 1991. And the policies have been truly effective.

THE SECURITIES MARKET IN INDIA

The capital market of a country is an amalgam of several diverse channels through which the savings of the households flow to industrial and commercial ventures, as also for public investment. Perhaps the main channel of the transfer of the community's savings to the investors is the purchase and sale of securities, i.e., financial claims held by investors against a corporation to which households place their funds. The corporate enterprises or joint stock companies raise funds by issuing three types

1. Long-term government bonds are called gilt-edged securities or simply 'gilts' since these are completely free from the risk of default.

of securities, viz., (i) equity (ordinary) shares[1], (ii) preference shares and (iii) bonds or debentures. These are known as industrials securities. By comparison, governments at different levels – central, state and local — raise funds by issuing gilt-edged securities. These are long-term government securities, free from the risk of default.

The securities market includes all the agencies and institutions which help in the sale and resale of securities. The main players in this market are obviously the buyers and sellers of securities.

The securities market of India was originally narrow and traditional in nature. However, during the reform period it has become broad and diversified. Fig 39A.1 gives a broad overview of India's securities market. We now discuss each segment of the market separately.

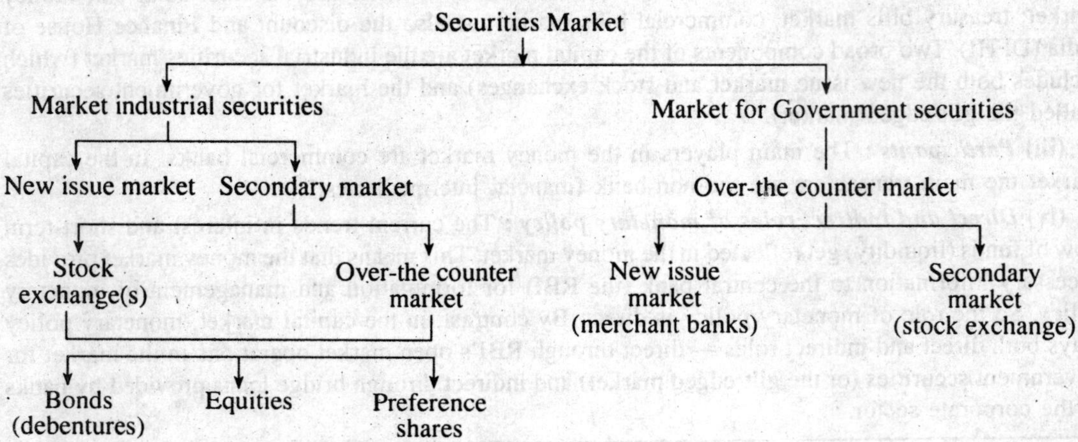

Fig. 39A.1: The Structure of India's Securities Market

1. Industrial Capital Market

The industrial capital market includes both the market for shares and that of bonds (debentures) of both existing and new companies. This market is sub-divided into new issue market (or the primary market) and the secondary market (or the stock exchange). While the former deals with 'new securities', issued to the public for the first time, the stock exchange deals with old securities, i.e., securities which have already been issued. However, there is functional interdependence between the two segments of the industrial capital market.

(a) The Primary Market

New shares and bonds are floated in the primary market so as to enable both new companies and existing ones to raise funds for expansion and diversification. A new issue is floated on the basis of the advice given by a merchant bank. And the marketability of the new issue is ensured by institutional investors like the IDBI, ICICI, LICI, UTI, etc. These institutions stand guarantee for the absorption of any unsubscribed share(s). This is known as underwriting. The underwriters buy securities from the new issue market and hold these for future sales at higher price(s).

Two main ways of floating new issues in India are the following:

(i) *Public issues* : A company floats securities in the new issue market through a legal document, known as the 'prospectus'. Through a prospectus a company gives an open invitation to the public to subscribe to the issue at par or at premium.

(ii) *Right issue* : An existing company whose shares are already listed in the stock exchange makes a right issue. Through such issue a company invites its existing shareholders to a part or the whole of the new issue in a fixed proportion to their shareholding.

1. In the USA these are called common stocks.

Table 39A.1 shows collection of financial resources by the Indian corporate enterprises from the primary market over a three-year period (from 2008-09 to 2010-11).

Table 39A.1: Capital Issues by Indian Private Sector

	2010-11*		2009-10		2008-09	
	No.	Rs. crs.	No.	Rs. crs.	No.	Rs. crs.
Type of Issues						
Equity shares	70	24,830	67	25,299	45	14,671
Pref. shares	–	–	–	–	–	–
Debentures	–	–	1	180	–	–
Total	**70**	**24,830**	**68**	**25,479**	**45**	**14,671**
Modes of Raising						
Issues through prospectus	51	19,678	39	17,160	25	2,673
Issues through rights	19	5,152	29	8,319	20	11,997
Total	**70**	**24,830**	**68**	**25,479**	**45**	**14,671**
New & Existing Cos.						
Issues by new cos	49	16,149	36	14,595	21	2,033
Issues by existing cos	21	8,681	32	10,883	24	12,637
Total	**70**	**24,830**	**68**	**25,479**	**45**	**14,671**

Source: *Statistical Outline of India* (2012-13)

Note: Data, based on RBI, exclude issues privately placed with financial institutions but include amounts raised by some of these institutions.

Total figures may not exactly tally with the components due to rounding off.

* Provisional.

(iii) ***Initial public offer (IPO)*** **:** Equity capital may be raised through initial public offer (IPO), which is the first issue of shares by a corporate enterprise to the general public. This method is used for raising financial capital for business expansion. Two alternative methods are used in making IPO, viz., the fixed price method and the book-building procedure. The issue of shares through IPO by Indian companies as also the fixation of prices of shares are regulated by the SEBI. The IPO is followed by a listing of the shares in the stock market.

(iv) ***Private placement*** **:** A huge amount of capital is raised in India through private placement[1]. Such private equity issue is not regulated by the SEBI. An unlisted company (whose name does not appear in the register of stock exchange) follows this method of fund raising. A company which wants to raise funds but is not yet ready to make an IPO may privately place its equity or related financial products with one or more term-lending institutions or institutional investor such as IDBI, IFCI, ICICI,

1. A firm issuing new securities has to get itself registered on a stock exchange by applying for listing of its shares. Such listing enables the firm to sell its shares in a competitive market which is governed by the forces of demand and supply.

mutual funds, venture capital funds and even commercial banks. A private placement can be made by a company to the investors at any agreed price and quantity.

Focus on Terminology: Venture Capital
Two main classes of investors in new and young private companies are value-added investors and others. One of the keys to raising risk capital is to seek investors who will make genuine addition to the venture well beyond the money initially raised. However, investors may add or deduct value in a new (young) company (enterprise). This is done by employing really talented managers, adding new customers or suppliers or making additional investment (if, of course, the initial investment appears to be profitable). The term 'venture' suggests that venture capital involves a degree of risk and even something of a gamble. This private risk capital acts as a fuel of today's entrepreneurial engine. Venture capitalists supply capital and other resources to entrepreneurs in business with high growth prospects (potential) with the expectation of getting a high rate of return on invested funds. Venture capitalists work as coaches and partners with entrepreneurs and innovators at a very early stage to help shape and secure the development of the company. The investing process begins with the conception of a new (target) investment opportunity (or a class of opportunities) which leads to a written proposal (prospectus) to raise a venture capital fund. Once the money is raised, the value creation process moves from generating deals to creating and executing harvest strategies and back to raising another fund. And another new venture capital cycle starts all over again. The process usually takes several (often upto 10) years to unfold, but there are often exceptions in both directions—restarting the process in case of profit or closing it altogether in case of loss.

In the past two decades or so the SEBI has introduced various types of reforms in the New Issue Market. These reforms led to improved disclosure standards, fixation of prudential norms and considerable simplification of issue procedures.

(b) The Secondary Market

The secondary market is the market for old or existing securities. Such a market facilities the purchase and sale of old securities. This market not only makes existing shares fairly liquid but also improves marketability of such securities. In this market a share can be bought or sold at a very low transaction cost.

Two segments of the secondary market are the following:

(i) *The stock exchange* : The stock exchange is a highly organised market for the purchase and sale of old (second-hand) shares and debentures of corporate enterprises which appear on the approved list of a stock exchange. Such securities are traded in the floor of stock exchanges.

An organised stock exchange is essentially an auction-type of markets where the prices of traded securities are settled by open bids and offers on the floor of the exchange. Stock transactions are of the following two categories:

(i) *Investment transactions* : An investment transaction refers to the purchase of securities and holding such securities for a long time with a twofold objective — (1) deriving income every year in the form of dividends and (2) making capital gains by selling these securities at higher prices. Such a transaction involves the actual delivery of the security and payment of its full price. And it enables the investor to derive a steady flow of income every year, while, at the same time, ensuring safety of investment. If the price of a share goes down an investor can hold the share for some time and sell it later when its price goes up.

(ii) *Speculative transactions* : A speculative transaction is concerned with the purchase or sale of securities for making capital gains. In such a transaction there is no physical delivery of shares. No immediate payment is made to cover the transaction. Instead the speculator only receives or pays the difference between the purchase price and sale price, whichever is higher. Such trading in securities without the intention of taking delivery or making payment is known as forward trading. The Securities

Contract (Regulation) Act, 1956 has suspended such trading in 1969. As a result a new vacuum has been created in the stock market. To fill in that vacuum, the stock-brokers introduced the *badla system*. This system, however, did not have a legal backing. Under the system, any security contract could be converted into a carry-forward contract between the same buyer and the same seller of a particular security. This implied that only the difference between the 'contract price' and the 'market price' would be paid by the buyer to the seller.

However, the badla system gave scope for excessive speculation and short-selling, which virtually amounted to gambling. This is why the SEBI has banned the system in December, 1993.

Trading in Derivatives

Since share price movements are often taken as the barometer of a country's economy[1], it may considered necessary to give necessary boost to the stock exchange. The objective was to meet an increasing demand for legistimate forward trading. Realising this point the SEBI reintroduced the badla (forward trading) system on July 27, 1995. Subsequently with the introduction of new financial instruments, the same purpose is now being served by *futures* which are one type of *derivatives*.

The Bombay Stock Exchange

The Bombay Stock Exchange (BSE) is the leading stock exchange in India. There are 14 other recognised stock exchanges in the country. The BSE handles more than 75% of the total trading in securities in India. As Table 39A.2 the number of companies listed on the BSE was 5,133 in 2011-12.

Table 39A.2: Bombay Stock Exchange and National Stock Exchange — Performance Indicators

	Bombay Stock Exchange		National Stock Exchange*	
	2011-12	2010-11	2011-12	2010-11
	Nos.			
Companies listed	5,133	5,067	1,646	1,574
Brokers	1,376	1,301	1,423	1,389
Corporate brokers	1,164	1,087	1,269	1,239
Sub-brokers registered ...	33,852	38,124	42,327	44,783
	Rs. crs.			
Turnover				
Cash segment	667,498	1,105,027	2,810,893	3,577,410
Derivative segment	808,476	154	31,349,732	29,248,221
Market capitalisation.......	6,214,941	6,839,084	6,096,518	6,702,616
Sensex+	17,404	19,445	–	–
S & P CNX Nifty ++ ...	–	–	5,296	5,834

* National Stock Exchange was set up in Nov. 1994.

\+ BSE Sensitive Index

++ S & P CNX Nifty for NSE

1. A rise in share prices implies that the economy is in the upswing of the business cycle. And a share market crash implies that the economy is on the downhill, i.e., it is facing recession or depression.

The Establishment of the National Stock Exchange

In July 1994, the National Stock Exchange of India (NSEI) was established with a twofold objective: (i) to promote efficient functioning of the 15 recognised stock exchanges and (ii) to ensure transparency of stock market transactions (by preventing insider trading).

The NSEI is spread to 13 cities including Bombay (now Mumbai). Functionally the NESI has two segments, viz., (i) wholesale debt market(WDM), (ii) capital market (CM). In the WDM there is trading in government (gilt-edged) securities, treasury bills, bonds of public sector undertakings, certificates of deposits, commercial papers and corporate debentures. For ensuring transparent and regulated deals the RBI has directed banks to use only the NSEI for all transactions in debt securities, instead of depending on the brokers (which practice is not much reliable).

Equities are traded in the capital market segment of NSEI. Thus the establishment of the NSEI can be regarded as a major development as far as reform of stock market is concerned. See Table 39A.2 which gives information about the performer indicators of NSE (as also of BSE).

In short, stock exchanges, as secondary market in industrial securities, impart the needed dynamism to the India's capital market by making shares highly liquid — perhaps as liquid as money. During the past two decades the SEBI has framed several rules and guidelines and imposed certain ligitimate regulations to ensure that India's stock exchanges function in accordance with the principle of safety of the market, ensure transparency of transactions and give necessary protection to investors. And, thanks to liberalisation, privatisation and globalisation (LPG) of the Indian economy there has occurred a phenomenal increase in transactions in industrial securities in both the New Issue Market and the Secondary Market (stock exchanges).

Recent Trends in India's Stock

In 2007-08, trading activity expanded very fast in the secondary market segment. Both BSE and NSE indices reached new highs in Jan 2008. Of course the upward trend was characterised by intermittent fluctuations due to change in market sentiments. But the rising trend was not reversed during the year. Two proximate reasons for this rising trend were: (i) larger inflows of funds through foreign institutional investors (FIIs) and (ii) greater and wider participation by domestic institutional investors. The upward trend in case of both Sensex and Nifty were also attributable to higher growth rates, improved profitability of Indian companies, higher rate of interest prevailing in India than in other countries, attractive returns on equities and, above all, a strong rupee (due a surplus in the capital account of the BOP).

Both Nifty and Nifty Junior indices showed record-high annual returns in 2007. Such return is calculated by using the following formula:

$$\frac{\text{Current year - end index}}{\text{Previous year - end index}} \times 100$$

The BSE Sensex (composed of top 30 stocks) also exhibited almost the same trend. It showed the fastest climb up to September, 2007 (crossing 19,000 mark). It crossed 20,000 mark in December 2007 and 21,000 in an intra-day trading in January 2008.

The size of the capital market is assessed by the ratio of market capitalisation to GDP.

With rise in stock indices, investors' wealth also increased correspondingly. This got reflected in market capitalisation, which almost doubled in 2007. Market capitalisation is an indicator of the size of the capital market, which is evaluated by the ratio of market capitalisation to GDP. Market capitalisation was 150% of India's GDP at the end of Dec. 2007.

In addition, turnover in the spot and derivatives market, both on NSE and BSE, continued to show an upward trend. This was no doubt an indication of the good health of the economy.

Institutional investors played an important role in 2007. Both domestic mutual funds and foreign institutional investors leveraged their activity.

Sharp Declines in Stock Indices

However, the momentum gained in 2007 could not be sustained in 2008. Market activity in the secondary segment started with bullish note at the beginning of 2008. Both BSE and NSE indices reached new highs of 20,873 and 6,287, respectively on Jan 8, 2008. But this euphoria did not last for long. In Jan 2008, both BSE and NSE declined sharply in the wake of the global financial crisis, which was triggered by the US sub-prime housing crisis. Due to US crisis all major international indices showed significant downward movement in the second half of Jan 2008 and this got reflected in Indian stock indices due to financial contagion. Now-a-days any financial crisis anywhere in the world get transmitted to all countries due to greater and greater integration of the world's financial markets.

Stock prices fell due to financial contagion

In fact, intraday fall of Sensex by 1968 points on Jan 21, 2008 was the highest ever recorded. In spite of intermittent corrections in the stock market, the market sentiment did not improve much for at least four reasons: (i) acceleration of inflation rate, (ii) increasing oil prices, (iii) volatility in international financial markets (due to US crisis which created uncertainties about US sub-prime mortgage market and credit market exposures) and (iv) negative flows of portfolio investment.

Market sentiments remained bearish during Feb-Manch 2008

Although the indices showed marginal improvement in April 2008 due to positive cues from the global market, the market sentiment turned extra-cautious for quite some time. There were at least five reasons: (i) increase in crude oil prices, (ii) steady downward trend in major international equity markets, (iii) increasing concerns about domestic inflation, (iv) widening trade deficit and (v) slow but steady depreciation of the rupee.

During Oct-Dec. 2008, the Sensex fell sharply due for at least three reasons: (i) volatility in international equity market, (ii) net outflow of funds from domestic capital market by FIIs and (iii) slowdown of domestic economic activity.

Both Nifty and Nifty Junior indices recorded negative annual equity returns.

THE GLOBAL FINANCIAL CRISIS OF 2008 AND VOLATILITY OF THE INDIAN CAPITAL MARKET

The year 2008 started with a highly bullish trend. This got reflected in both BSE and NSE indices which reached new highs of 20,873 and 6,288 points, respectively. But the euphoria did not last for long. The global financial crisis of 2008 was a severe blow to the Indian capital market. The global financial crisis adversely affected the market sentiments.

Mainly due to fall in prices of Indian shares market capitalisation of shares traded on BSE and NSE declined sharply in 2008.

After experiencing robust growth for almost two years—2007 and 2008—both the primary and the secondary markets received a severe jolt in 2008. Both the shares prices as also total amount of capital raised through equity issues fell sharply. The end result was a substantial decline in the market capitalisation of shares traded on BSE and NSE in 2008. In a single year — from end Dec 2007 to end Dec 2008 — market capitalisation fell by no less than 50%.

Stock Volatility

The volatility of weekly returns of Indian stock indices increased sharply in 2008. The volatility was much higher than that of overseas indices such Hangsen index (of Hong Kong), S & P 500 (of the USA) and Kospi (of South Korea).

It may be noted that market volatility is measured by the standard deviation of daily volatility. In case of BSE it increased sharply, from 1.5 in 2007 to 2.85 in 2008.

Another measure of market volatility is the price-earnings ratio (*P/E*). Since it discounts future corporate earnings to some extent, investors expectations of profits get reflected in it. The ratio showed almost uniform decline in all segments of the market reflecting a steady downward trend in stock prices. The volatility of weekly returns of Indian indices increased so sharply in 2008 that it far exceeded that of S & P 500 and Kospi.

However, the trend continued upto Jan-March 2009, when *P/E* ratio reached the bottom. Since then the BSE Sensex started rising.

Turnover in Spot and Futures Market

Now we find two markets for financial instruments or financial products, viz., the spot market and the futures market. On the spot market actual delivery of shares has to be taken immediately after purchase. By contrast, in case of derivatives (which are also known as futures) actual delivery of shares/securities is not taken (made) at the time of purchase. Just the difference between the actual price at a future date and the contracted price has to be paid.

It may be noted in 2008 two diverse trends were observed. On the one hand the turnover in the spot market on the NSE maintained its steady upward trend. By contrast, the BSE spot market turnover showed a marginal decline.

Transactions by Foreign Institutional Investors

Although there has been a slowdown in the flows of foreign direct investment (FDI) in India through multinational corporations in recent years, there has occurred a steady increase in the flow of financial capital due to international portfolio investment, i.e., investment made by foreign institutional investors (FIIs). In fact, they were setting the tune in the India stock market and other investors danced at it. In 2006 and 2007 there was huge capital appreciation of Indian stockholders due to rise in stock indices of India. This was the result of huge capital inflows through FIIs which made huge purchases of shares of Indian companies.

However, as some as the global financial crisis started in 2008 FIIs sold the shares in Indian stock market on a massive scale and repatriated the funds to their home countries. And this was the root cause of the crash in Indian stock market which caused huge losses of wealth of India.

Resource Mobilisation by Mutual Funds

In recent years resource mobilisation in India through mutual funds has assumed much more importance than in the past. The proximate reason is that mutual funds cater to the needs of numerous small (retail) investors. In spite of this, a study of the capital structure of mutual funds shows that, on average, about two-thirds of subscriptions to such funds still are made by corporate enterprises.

Quite in line with the rising trend in the volume of financial resources raised in the primary market, the net inflow of savings into mutual funds increased by 33% in 2007. This sharp increase in the flow of funds was partly due to buoyant equity markets and partly to the efforts made by the Indian mutual funds to introduce various new and innovative investment schemes.

As for resource mobilisation the private sector mutual funds performed much better than their public counterparts. However, the trend of rising net inflow of saving into mutual funds during the three-year period (2005-07) suddenly got reversed in 2008. The year 2008 saw net inflow of saving into mutual funds, due to huge net outflows of funds. Even the UTI recorded huge net redemption.

However, an interesting point may be noted in this context. In spite of global financial crisis and market volatility, the public sector mutual funds (other than the UTI) succeeded in mobilising a large amount of funds. Their success under such adverse conditions reflected changing attitude of investors toward risk. Most small (retail) investors preferred to invest in less risky public sector institutions in turbulent times.

2. THE MARKETS FOR GOVERNMENT (OR GILT-EDGED) SECURITIES

A gift-edged security (or simply gilt) is a fixed-interest security issued by the government. Gilt-edged securities are totally safe since they are free from the risk of default. However, their prices fluctuate inversely with current interest rates.

In the gilt-edged market the securities of the both the central and state governments are traded. In addition, the securities guaranteed (as for both the principal amount and interest) by the GOI are placed in this market for trading.

Importance

The gilt-edged market is an important segment of India's capital market. This market is of strategic importance since it provides mechanism for the GOI to manage public debt and the RBI to conduct open market operations. So the market exerts a strong influence on both fiscal policy of the GOI and monetary policy of the RBI. In addition, the market is important due to fiscal-monetary link. Monetary policy depends for its success on fiscal policy.

Segments

The gilt-edged market has two broad segments, viz., (i) the Treasury Bill Market and the (ii) Government Bond Market.

(i) *The Treasury Bill Market*

The Treasury Bill market (or the T-bill market) is a source of short-term funds for the Government. A T-bill is a type of processory note and a liability of the GOI. The maturity periods of T-bills are of 91,182 and 364 days. As the principal holder of these bills the RBI sells them on behalf of the Government. In addition, for getting higher return the RBI reduces its holdings of T-bills by converting them into dated-government securities at market-related interest rates. Furthermore, commercial banks hold these bills. This means that the T-bills market is a captive market[1], with a narrow base (without much spread — deepening or widening).

The Indian T-bills market is still in an underdeveloped state as compared to its US or British counterparts. However, in recent years the RBI has adopted certain reform measures in the T-bills market for making its base broader.

The 364 days' T-bills are held only by the market players and not by institutional authorities. In the past the GOI used to borrow from the RBI by issuing T-bills to meet its budgetary deficit. This is known as monetisation of government debt. However, during the reform period this practice has been totally discontinued. The basic objective behind this move has been to hold the price line (i.e., to control inflation and thus make the macroeconomic environment of the country stable).

(ii) *The Government Bond Market*

The Government Bond Market is one of the main sources of funds to both the Central and State Governments. Government bonds are essentially dated securities. These are floated for raising long-term funds from the open market. It may be noted that institutions, rather than individuals, are the main buyers of government bonds. Individuals are reluctant to invest their liquid funds in government bonds. There are three main reasons for this: (i) relatively low rate of interest, (ii) long maturity period and (iii) face value in large denominations (which are beyond the reach of small savers). Financial institutions such as commercial banks, LICI, and GICI are the main buyers of government bonds. The reason is that while building their asset portfolio they are under the legal obligation to invest a certain minimum proportion of their total funds in these bonds.

The RBI plays a key role in the government bond market. Since it has to manage public debt, it operates on the supply side of the market.

As soon as the subscription period is over the RBI undertakes underwriting business. It holds all unsold government bonds with a view to selling them on its own accord.

It may also be noted that the government bond market is also a capital market, with narrow base though. However, the RBI is planning to launch a new system, under which primary dealers would be able to actively participate in the market. The objective is to both widen and deepen the government

1. A captive market is one which is kept within bounds and held under control.

bond market. In 1993-94 the Securities Trading Corporation of India was set up to develop the secondary market in gilts.

Comments

A robust growth of the market for government securities is an essential pre-requisite for achieving faster growth in India's market-driven economy. For this reason both the RBI and the GOI have adopted various reform measures in both the new issue market and the secondary market which deals in both industrial and government securities.

A liquid and well-developed secondary market for government securities is absolutely essential for efficient and effective management of government debt. Of late due to the adoption of certain reform measures the volume of outright transactions in secondary market for government securities has increased steadily.

Finally, since 2009, the yield an the secondary market securities moved up, after showing intra-year variations in 2008. This is largely attributable to borrowing by the GOI on a massive scale.

3. THE CORPORATE DEBT MARKET

In 2007, the SEBI instructed the BSE, the NSE and the Fixed Income Money Market and Derivatives Association of India (FIMMDA) to set up and maintain corporate bond reporting platforms, for collecting all reliable and accurate information relating to trading in corporate bonds. In the next stage the BSE and the NSE put in place corporate bond trading platform in the same year (2007) so as to enable efficient price discovery in the market. The price discovery process refers to the continuous interaction between buyers and sellers to determine prices in the market. In response to these favourable developments, trading in corporate bonds increased sharply in terms of number and volume of trading.

GROWTH OF THE INDIAN CAPITAL MARKET

The process of planned industrialisation initiated in 1951 brought into focus the strategic importance of a strong, growing and vibrant capital market. It was realised that the growth and diversification of the capital market was an essential pre-condition for the growth of the private corporate sector.

In 1951, India's industrial economy was in a bad shape. And the capital market existed only in name. However, over the years the capital market has undergone a see change — a metamorphosis, so to say. It has become highly diversified in terms of financial assets traded in as also financial intermediaries operating in it. We now make a brief review of the major developments in the Indian capital market.

1. Growth in Financial Intermediation

Largely due to the introduction of an innovative scheme, viz., indirect financing, the Indian capital market has virtually achieved robust growth. This mechanism has conduced to a steady flow of funds from surplus-generating units (savers) to deficit-spending units, mainly businesses through such financial institutions and intermediaries as the UTI, the LICI and the GICI. The LICI has build up a 'life fund' by mobilising household savings. A part of the fund is deplayed to purchase the shares and debentures of the private corporate enterprises. In the same way, the UTI, the first mutual funds of the country, which was set up in 1964, has been mobilising savings of households by selling 'units'. And the bulk of the sales proceeds has been invested in securities of the so-called 'blue-chip' companies.

In truth, these financial intermediaries have hastened and activised the growth process of the Indian capital market, as is shown by the rising *intermediation ratio*. The intermediation ratio is the ratio of the volume of financial instruments issued (i.e., secondary-market securities) by financial institutions to the volume of primary securities issued by non-financial corporate enterprises.

2. Growth in Underwriting Business

The growth of the new issue market[1] depends largely on underwriting of securities by specialised financial institutions such as merchant banks, insurance companies like the LICI, mutual funds like the UTI and public financial (term-lending) institutions such as the IFCI, the ICICI and the IDBI. During the reform period (starting from July 1991) the number and volume of securities underwritten by these institutions have increased steadily and tremendously. The percentage of securities underwritten increased from 50 in 1955-56 to about 99 in 2011-12.

Economic Insight: Underwriting

Underwriting refers to the provision by merchant banks of a guaranteed market for a new issue of shares. Firms making new issues cannot know in advance whether there will be sufficient demand for the shares they offer at the issue price from the public or institutional investors. An underwriter removes this uncertainty as to whether shares will sell by promising to buy only a number of unsold shares. These shares then have to be sold, which may involve accepting a low price or a long wait. A commission is charged for this service.

3. An Increase in Response to Initial Public Offering of Shares and Debentures

Since July, 1991 people gradually developed an equity cult (culture) and initial public offerings of shares and debentures evoked tremendous response. There are various reasons for this such as rise in rates of return on industrial securities compared to those on non-marketable financial assets and real assets, adoption of liberal monetary and fiscal policies and all types of legal protection given to investors by the GOI. This has strengthened the Indian capital market in spite of the fact that 'equity-cult' has not yet been developed in rural areas where the majority of the people live.

4. Growth of Merchant Banking

A merchant bank is a bank which deals mainly with other firms rather than the general public. Merchant banks supply industrial finance, underwrite new issues, advise on project selection and mergers and takeover as also takeover bids as also managing investment for institutions.

In 1969 the Grindlays Bank established a special cell called the 'Merchant Banking Division'. Now almost all commercial banks in India have the 'Merchant Banking Division'. The main function of this division is to advise private companies about economic (financial) viability as also technical feasibility of potentially profitable projects. They do the initial feasibility study in order to ascertain, on the basis of an indepth and insightful analysis of the present investment climate of the country, whether a new issue would be oversubscribed or undersubscribed and thus advising the company (planning to make an initial public issue of shares or debentures) accordingly.

At present Indian merchant banks play a dual role. Firstly they so underwriting of shares and debentures. Secondly they manage new issues of securities. And by performing these two roles they have strengthened the institutional base of the Indian capital market. However, all the operations of merchant banks relating to issue of shares and debentures by companies are regulated by the Security and Exchange Board of India (SEBI).

5. Emergence of Credit Rating Agency

Credit rating means measuring the credit worthiness of a corporation. For corporations, the most famous rating is conducted by the US agency Standard and Poor (S & P). AAA is the top credit-rating of the securities issued by corporations and companies. This rating is based on the view that default is likely to be minimal.

An important and interesting development as far as the growth of India's capital market is concerned is the emergence of two leading credit rating agencies. The Credit Rating Information

1. New issues refer to the process of sales of newly issued shares in public companies. This is one of the main sources of finance for companies.

Services of India Ltd.(CRISIL) is a pioneer in credit rating business. It rates debt instruments of corporate enterprises, banks and non-bank financial intermediaries. The Investment Information and Credit Rating Agency of India (ICRA) rates bonds, corporate debentures, shares and commercial papers. The credit assessment of companies planning to make new public issues conduces to the growth of the new issue market, which is a very important segment of the capital market.

6. The Growth of Mutual Funds

A mutual fund is a financial institution which holds shares on behalf of investors. In India the first mutual fund, viz., the UTI was set up in 1964. Investors used to buy shares, or 'units' in the funds, which used their money to buy shares in companies. An investor selling back the units gets the proceeds of selling a fraction of the fund's portfolio.

In essence, mutual funds are investment trust companies. The essence of the mutual fund scheme is to mobilise funds from individuals and institutional investors. They get 'units' against their invested amounts. Such 'units' can be redeemed after a certain lock-in-period, at their net asset value (NAV). The mutual funds schemes offer a two-fold benefit, viz., (i) tax relief and (ii) buyback facility.

A number of commercial banks, insurance companies as also private companies have launched mutual fund schemes. Mention may be made of Canstock scheme of the Canara Bank and Dhanashree, Dhanaraksha, and Dhanabiddi schemes of the LIC. Bajaj Allianz, Tata, Reliance Industries have also formed mutual fund companies.

Mutual fund schemes help to mobilise small saving, i.e., savings of people with modest means. These are invested in shares and securities of companies with good track record. Total net assets of mutual funds companies increased from Rs. 66,272 crores in 1993-94 to Rs. 505,152 crores in 2007-08, which fell to Rs. 417,299 crores in 2008-09. So various mutual funds schemes contributed to the growth of the market. And investment by mutual funds are a potent force behind share price movements.

7. Stock Exchange Regulation Act

The GOI passed the Stock Exchange Act to ensure that only recognised stock exchanges are allowed to function. Two main objectives of the Act are (i) to protect the investors from fraud and/or default and (ii) to regulate the working of stock exchanges after proper enquiry into their day-to-day affairs. The Securities and Exchange Board of India (SEBI) has been established in 1988. Since 1991, SEBI has been introducing and implementing various measures and practices to ensure as much transparency in the mode of operation of the capital market as possible. Two main objectives of SEBI are to give adequate protection to investors and to ensure smooth and orderly development of the securities market through greater public participation and corporate diversification.

8. Liberalisation

Attempts have been made not only to broaden the Indian securities market but also to widen its area of operation through liberalisation. Investment norms for foreign institutional investors and NRIs have been liberalised. They have been given the permission to buy shares and debentures of Indian companies without taking prior permission from the RBI.

To sum up, the Indian capital market has achieved some sort of robust growth since 1951, more so since July 1991 after the implementation of various financial sector reform measures. The setting up of new institutions, introduction of new financial instruments and new (and much liberalised) regulatory measures have led to an unprecedented and some sort of spectacular growth of the Indian capital market. The Indian capital market got the real boost for achieving speedy growth after the adoption of various liberalisation measures under the New Economic Policy (NEP).

THE SECURITIES EXCHANGE CONTROL BOARD OF INDIA (SEBI) AND CAPITAL MARKET REFORM

In 1956 the Securities Contract (Regulation) Act was passed. It empowered the GOI to regulate the stock exchanges. In 1988 the Securities and Exchange Board of India (SEBI) was set up mainly with a view to promoting an orderly growth of the securities market. In 1992 SEBI was made a statutory body by an Act of Parliament. In 1995 this Act was amended to provide SEBI additional powers so that it could do its job more effectively and efficiently.

Objectives of SEBI

The SEBI operates with a two-fold purpose: (i) regulating the securities market in the interest of subscribers to securities, that is, investors and (ii) ensuring healthy development of the capital market. Its main focus is on the following two things:

(a) ***Investor protection*** **:** In order to safeguard the interests of investors in securities the SEBI has made it obligatory on the part of companies issuing securities to publicly disclose necessary information so as to enable the investors to perceive risks and returns correctly.

(b) ***Regulation*** **:** SEBI regulates not only the activities of brokers and sub-brokers, bankers to an issue, underwriters, merchant banks and mutual funds. The objective is to hold in check all types of shady activities relating to securities trading.

Capital Market Reforms by SEBI

Since its inception the SEBI has introduced no less than a dozen of reform measures in the capital market. These are the following:

1. Formation of governing body: *Prima facie*, the SEBI has issued detailed guidelines to stock exchanges for broad-basing their governing bodies. As per the guidelines, the governing body of a stock exchange must have five elected numbers, of which four members may be nominated by the GOI or SEBI itself and three members may be nominated as public representatives.

2. Registration: The SEBI has introduced the system of registration of market intermediaries, such as brokers and sub-brokers. The registration has to be made strictly on the basis of certain eligibility criteria. The main criterion, of course, is capital adequacy.

3. Framing rules: The SEBI has framed rules not only for making the relation between investors (clients) and brokers more transparent but also for keeping the accounts of investors and brokers separate.

4. Periodic inspection: The SEBI has also introduced the system inspection of stock exchanges at periodic intervals, as a matter of routine, so to say.

5. Public disclosure: The SEBI has made it obligatory for listed companies to furnish annual statements to stock exchanges showing discrepancies between financial protection in the offer documents and actual utilisation of funds. The objective is to enable shareholders to make a comparison between targets and achievements.

6. Vetting the offer document of listed companies: SEBI vets the offer document of every listed company. The objective is to ensure that the company has made all necessary disclosures at the time of applying for listing of its shares and debentures to a stock exchange.

7. Monitoring the operations of mutual funds: The SEBI has almost made it obligatory for mutual funds to get their offer documents (giving details of their proposed schemes) vetted. It has also introduced a specific method of calculating and declaring the net asset value (NAV) of each mutual fund scheme. The basic objective is to enable investors to assess the performance of mutual funds. It may be added that the mutual funds have been allowed to enter underwriting business. However, the SEBI does not give full freedom to mutual funds as far their operations are concerned. Instead the SEBI monitors the activities of mutual funds on a regular basis so as to ensure compliance with its regulations.

8. Guidelines for merchant banks: The SEBI also controls and regulates merchant banks. These banks are to follow the code of conduct issued by SEBI as far as pricing and fixation of premium(premia) on new issue(s) are concerned.

9. SEBI clearance: In spite of the abolition of control on capital issues, companies can approach the capital market for funds, only after getting due clearance from the SEBI.

10. Code of advertisement: Some time ago the SEBI has introduced a code of advertisement for public issues. The basic objective is to ensure fair and correct (truthful) disclosure. Companies are under the legal obligation to make all relevant facts and specific risk factors associated with their projects publicly known at the time of making public issues.

11. Allotment of new shares: The SEBI has issued detailed guidelines for allotment of new issues. As per the guidelines, preferential allotment of shares is to be made to the extent of 20% for mutual funds, 20% for domestic financial institutions, 24% for foreign institutional investors and 10% for the employees of the company making the issue (under the 'stock' option for employees scheme). After this, the remaining 25% will be offered to the general public, of which half has to be earmarked for small investors applying upto 1,000 shares. The unsubscribed portion in any category is fully interchangeable, i.e., can be placed into any other category.

12. Allotment of market-related prices: The SEBI has stopped the earlier practice of making preferential allotment of shares at *ad hoc* prices which were completely out of line with their market prices. Fresh guidelines have been issued for alloting shares at market-related prices.

13. Dematerialisation: The SEBI has adopted various measures to promote dematerialised trading of securities through the promotion of a strong and integrated network of depositories. The basic objective is to eliminate the risks of bond delivery and trading in fake (forged) shares. The depositories place before the public a system to officially record all details relating to ownership of securities.

14. Derivatives trading: Under the present SEBI guidelines 'derivatives contracts' are to be treated as 'securities' trading and trading in stock indices is likely to provide investors a 'hedging instrument' to protect themselves against risk and to help in injecting more liquidity in the secondary market.

15. Ban on short-sale of securities: The SEBI has put complete ban on short sale of securities from 15 June, 1998. The basic objective was to reduce the degree (range) of share price fluctuations.

16. Prescription of volatility margin: In addition, the SEBI prescribed additional volatility margins (AVM) from July 6, 1998. The daily price band was reduced from 10% to 8%. The weekly 25% band was replaced by the graded margin system.

17. Other positive measures: Nine other measures adopted by the SEBI are the following:

(a) The guidelines for the issue of bonus shares have been substantially liberalised.

(b) The SEBI has permitted foreign institutional investors to gain access to India's capital market after getting duly registered with it.

(c) The SEBI has brought primary and secondary market intermediaries within its regulatory framework.

(d) The SEBI has introduced new guidelines for substantial acquisition of shares as also for corporate takeovers.

(e) For making stock trading as transparent as possible, the SEBI has banned the *badla system* in 1993.

(f) The SEBI has exempted infrastructure firms from certain norms, while making an initial public issue (IPI), such as making a minimum public offer of 25% of equity, minimum subscription of 90% and five shareholders per Rs. one lakh of offer.

(g) The SEBI has adopted regulatory measures relating to buy-back of shares by Indians companies. This is to be permitted only for the purpose of capital restructuring and for no other reason.

(h) The SEBI has given complete freedom to companies to determine the par value of shares issued by them.

(i) Finally, with a view to encouraging the initial public offers (IPOs), SEBI has relaxed its norms. It has stipulated 'ability-to-pay' in place of 'actual payment of dividend'.

Comments

The SEBI made serious and sustained efforts to improve trading practices and to introduce greater transparency in both segments of India's securities market — primary and secondary. These were absolutely essential in the context of liberalisation, privatisation and globalisation (LPG) of the Indian economy. The numerous reform measures introduced in India's capital market are a step toward building up a strong financial mechanism for ensuring a smooth flow of funds and thus assisting the corporate enterprises to raise more funds so that they can go ahead with their expansion and diversification programmes. The public sector units are also likely to get sufficient funds from a strong and vibrant capital market. Thanks to the various promotional and regulatory measures adopted by the SEBI, the Indian equity market has become very much transparent and highly liquid. It has succeeded in attracting investors from all over the world. The National Stock Exchange (NSE) is now the third largest in the world in terms of yearly transactions.

However, the other side of the picture is not that rosy. Hardly any progress has been made outside the equity market. The corporate bond market in particular is still in its nascent stage. The investor base in corporate bonds is still narrow. The main reason for this is easy to find out. Strict and stringent regulatory guidelines severely restrict the ability of banks and other financial institutions to invest in corporate bonds. Without balanced development of all the segments of the capital market it will be difficult for India to emerge as a global financial centre. Furthermore, India's equity market has a major shortcoming. The frequent and wide fluctuations in share prices make stock market investing a risky proposition for small and retail investors who prefer other types of investment which are less risky and more rewarding.

A related point may also be noted in this context. Of late, retail investors have been running away from both the equity market and mutual funds mainly due to high degree volatility. This problem has to be tackled as soon as possible for improving the health of India's capital market.

CHAPTER 40

Industrial Policy

> *Taking a good hard look at what has happened in India over the last decade and a half, it is evident that public and private enterprises have not remained in the categories prescribed by the industrial policy resolution.*
>
> Gunnar Myrdal in *Asian Drama*

Every country in the world conducts what is known as *industrial policy*. An industrial policy is the effect of government regulation on the industrial structure of the country. In some cases this policy is very specific, as the government may want to clearly favour one industry over another. In other countries, the industrial policy is simply a part of the overall planning process. In fact, planning in market-based economies is carried out through industrial policy: selectively providing cheap credit, tax preferences (concessions) and trade protection to all sectors of the economy which are found to be protentially competitive in the world economy. All governments pass regulations that impact business even if the purpose of the regulation is not specifically aimed at favouring one industry over another. Since we cannot consider every possible governmental policy that influences the private sector, we will consider certain major aspects of industrial policy in the context of India's mixed economy.

INDIA'S INDUSTRIAL POLICY

The economic policy announced by the Government of India (GOI) at the time of formulation of the First Five Year Plan (1951-56) envisaged that the State would not only take the primary responsibility of providing an integrated infrastructure, but would directly take part in the production of a wide range of goods and services. The GOI recognised the need for state intervention in India's planned programme of industrialisation. And the public sector was entrusted with the responsibility of developing all basic and strategic industries, i.e., industries which were of national importance. Since the task before the country was really gigantic, a complementary role was assigned to the private sector and so a wide field of operation was left open to it. In the First Industrial Policy Resolution (IRP) of 1948, the GOI declared that it was going to have a 'mixed economy', in which the private and public sectors would exist side by side and take decisions, with the former stealing a march over the later and reaching the commanding heights of the economy.

The Industrial Policy Resolution of 1956

The 'mixed economy' principle was adopted in practice at the commencement of the Second Five Year Plan (1956-61) by announcing the Second Industrial Policy Resolution in April, 1956. Although the policy was revived and modified several times in the past, it all along provided the basic framework and policy direction for industrial development of the country.

The revised IPR declared that the public sector would gradually enter new fields and lay the foundation for India's economic development by strengthening its industrial base. This is why all industries of strategic importance to the country were nationalised. The life insurance business was first nationalised in 1956 user the LICI was set up. Then in June 1969 the top 14 scheduled commercial banks (with deposits of more than Rs. 50 crores) were nationalised. And in 1973 the coking coal industry was nationalised.

In order to expand the public sector the GOI made huge investment for providing infrastructure in the form of irrigation, power, transport and communications as also for the development of basic and heavy industries such as iron and steel, petro-chemicals, oil, fertilisers and machine building. These are essentially input-supplying industries. The GOI also provided finance, marketing facilities, technical advice and various other types of assistance to promote the development of the private industrial sector.

The IPR (1956) demarcated the respective roles of the private and public sectors. As the Resolution puts it, 'The need for planned and rapid development requires that all industries of basic and strategic importance or in the nature of public utility services should be in the public sector. Other industries, which are essential and require investment on a scale which only the State, in the present circumstances, could provide, have also to be in the public sector. The State has, therefore, to assume direct responsibility for the future development of the industries over a wide area."

Two schedules were prepared: Schedule 'A' consisting of 17 industries, the future development of which would be the exclusive responsibility of the State and schedule 'B' consisting of 12 industries which were to be progressively State-owned and in which the State would, therefore, generally take the initiative in establishing new industries. However, in this schedule the private sector was also expected to supplement the effort of the State. The development of all other industries were left to the initiative and enterprise of the private sector.

In 1951 the Industries (Development and Regulation) Act was passed. It introduced the industrial licensing system which was put into effect from 1952 and was mainly designed to channelise investment in the desired directions in accordance with plan priorities and targets. Other objectives of industrial licensing were to prevent undue concentration of wealth and economic power in private hands and to promote technological improvement in private sector industries.

No doubt, the licensing policy was amended, modified and liberalised from time to time so that it did not act as an obstacle to growth of the private sector. But the public sector continued to play a dominant role for 35 years (1955-90). However in July 1991, the industrial policy was thoroughly and drastically revised. In the new policy the GOI adopted a policy of economic liberalisation and the public sector lost its pride of place. Its role has been greatly diluted. In contrast the private sector has been assigned much greater role in India's industrial development.

THE NEED FOR DRASTIC REVISION OF INDUSTRIAL POLICY IN 1991

For a number of reasons the industrial policy of 1956 had to be revised in 1991. In the late 1980s it became quite clear that undue importance given to the public sector in the strategy of industrial growth and excessive controls and regulations over the private sector enterprises were acting as serious obstacles to India's economic growth and were breeding inefficiency. Furthermore, India faced two major problems: (i) a high rate of price inflation and (ii) a mounting deficit in the balance of payments.

To enable India to overcome these problems (and tide over the crisis situation that it had faced) some renouned economists advised India to adopt the policy of economic liberalisation. It was felt that greater reliance on free markets and on the private sector (including foreign investors) would foster efficiency by promoting competition.

In the 1956 Policy and various amendments made in it from time to time, the public sector was assigned a pivotal role in India's industrial development and the policy achieved astounding success at the initial stage of planning for industrialisation. Huge public sector investment on infrastructure pushed up industrial growth by creating various types of linkages — both backward and forward. A number of basic and heavy industries were built up.

Focus on Terminology: Backward and Forward Linkage
In 1958 A.O. Hirschman suggested that developing planning is only effective when it concentrates its efforts on key industries with ample backward and forward 'linkages' to other industries. A backward linkage refers to the inputs which an industry employs, and which connect it with the producers of raw materials, machines, and semi-finished goods. A forward linkage refers to the output which an industry sells to other industries rather than to final customers. Thus the leather tanning and hide industry is a key industry, but the shoe industry is not.

However from the mid-1980s several weaknesses of the public sector gradually surfaced. First, the public sector, instead of generating adequate resources for India's planning for development incurred huge losses mainly due to operational inefficiency and steady increase of the GOI's non-plan revenue expenditure. Secondly, macroeconomic imbalances — both internal and external — suddenly appeared and gradually became more and more serious in 1990-91. The huge budgetary deficits of the Government and the consequent increase in the money supply created the problem of double-digit inflation. At the same time the external position was not comfortable either. Instead it appeared to be a source of constant worry and tension. In fact, huge external commercial borrowing at high rates of interest created a persistent deficit in the balance of payments and the deficit went on increasing year after year. This lead to a sharp fall in India's foreign exchange reserves. The reserves fell to such a low level that these could meet the import bill for just few weeks. So for the GOI had no other alternative but to approach the IMF and the World Bank for adjustment assistance. The IMF in particular agreed to help India if and only if India adopted the policy of economic liberalisation as per its prescriptions (known as IMF conditionality). The IMF recommended public sector reforms as also budgetary (fiscal) reforms which were interrelated. So an important role was assigned to the private sector for boosting industrial investment, fostering competition and promoting faster industrial growth. It was felt that creation of a highly competitive environment would promote efficiency and stimulate industrial growth in particular and economic growth in general. It is against this backdrop that the New Industrial Policy was announced in July 1991.

THE INDUSTRIAL POLICY OF 1991

The main features of the New Industrial Policy (1991) are the following:

1. Abolition of Industrial Licensing

Upto 1984-85 India's industrial sector had to function under a system of tight controls and regulations imposed by the licensing system which was supposed to allocate resources rationally (i.e., according to plan priorities and targets) for building a strong industrial base. Once the industrial economy of India has achieved a rapid growth and wide diversification, the 1991 policy abolished licensing except for 18 specific industries of national importance. Again in April 1993, three more industries were de-served and left open to the private sector, viz., (i) motor cars, (ii) while goods (such as domestic refrigerators, washing machines, microwave ovens and airconditioners) and (iii) raw hides, skins and leather. The remaining 15 industries still remained reserved for the public sector for security and strategic reasons, safety purposes and environmental protection. And for granting licence to these residual industries, the administrative procedure has been greatly simplified. However, for obtaining licence, only certain vocational norms are to be fulfilled and some simple guidelines are to be followed. The basic objective was to ensure that polluting industries did not locate in densely populated metropolitan cities.

The 15 specified industries which continued to require licence were the following:

(i) Coal and lignite

(ii) Petroleum (other than crude) and its distillation products

(iii) Distillation and brewing of alcoholic drinks

(iv) Sugar

(v) Animal fats and oils

(vi) Cigars and cigarettes of tobacco and manufactured tobacco substitutes

(vii) Asbestos and asbestos-based products

(viii) Raw hides and skins, leather

(ix) Tanned or dressed furskins

(x) Paper and newsprint except bagasse-based units

(xi) Electronic aerospace and defence equipment (all types)

(xii) Industrial explosives, safety fuse, gun powder and matches

(xiii) Drugs and pharmaceuticals

(xiv) Plywood and other wood-based products and

(xv) Hazardeus chemicals.

The policy-makers expected that with almost complete removal of licensing control India's industries would become more competitive, more efficient and modern and thrive in a competitive environment.

2. Greater Freedom of the Private Enterprices

By abolishing the licensing system private industrial enterprises have been given the permission to expand their existing production capacity and to create new capacity if market conditions became really favourable. Furthermore, firms were given freedom to manufacture any article in response to market demand (except for the licensed items). Large industrial houses have been given permission to expand and diversify their operations. They have also been permitted to engage actively in merger and acquisition activities.

3. The Role of the Public Sector and Privatisation

A key role was assigned to the public sector in the 1956 industrial policy. As noted earlier, public sector was initially required to make adequate investment in infrastructure and heavy industries for laying the foundation for India's future industrial growth. In addition, the expansion of the public sector was considered essential to prevent undue concentration of wealth and economic power in a few private hands as also to ensure balanced region development.

However, gradually various problems arose in public sector enterprises such as operational inefficiency, low productivity of resources (so has labour and machines), poor project management, low rate of capacity utilisation, unrealistic pricing policies practices, overstaffing, top heavy administration, lack of modernisation and rationalisation and inadequate investment in R & D for technological upgradation. All these factors conjointly led to huge losses and yielded a very low rate of return on new capital employed. Thus, instead of generating investible surplus for industrial development, PSUs became a burden on the exchequer.

In addition, the public sector units (PSUs) drifted away from its original role considerably. First, for giving job protection, the GOI had to acquire a number of sick industrial units from the private sector. Such enterprises accounted for about 33% of the losses of all Central PSUs. Secondly, the public sector units had also entered industries producing consumer goods and services such as cars, watches, luxury hotels, shopping complexes, etc. These areas could be left completely open for the private sector.[1]

1. The reason is that the public sector does not have greater efficiency or comparative advantage in such areas.

For all these reasons the industrial policy adopted a new approach to the public sector. This approach fixed the following priority areas for future growth of PSUs:

(i) production of essential infrastructural goods and services,

(ii) exploration and exploitation of oil and mineral resources and

(iii) technological development and investment in manufacturing capacities in those areas which were essential for long-term development of the economy where the private sector was unlikely to make the required amount of investment.

4. Dereservation of Industries belonging to the Public Sector

The new industrial policy initiated far reaching structural reforms to enable industries to be free from exclusive direct controls and regulations and operate in a market-oriented economic system. This means that the 1991 policy expresses the Government's intentions to encourage larger and larger participation of the private sector in important areas of the economy. So the number of industries reserved for the public sector has been reduced from 17 to only 8. The new policy threw open many core industries, reserved earlier for the public sector, for the private sector such as iron and steel, power, air transport, ship building, heavy chemicals and heavy machinery such as telecommunication cables and instruments.

From March, 1993, two more industries, viz., (i) Mining of iron ore, manganese ore, sulphur, gold and diamond and (ii) Mining of copper, lead, zinc, tin, etc. were deserved. The remaining 6 industries continued to be reserved for the public sector mainly due to national security and strategic considerations. The resources generated by PSUs would henceforth be utilised for the development of strategic, high technology and highly essential infrastructural areas. The GOI will take necessary measures to strengthen only those PSUs which fall in the reserve category or belong to high-priority areas or are yielding a satisfactory return on net capital employed. Such enterrises would be granted much greater autonomy by signing Memoranda of Understanding (MOU). Competition would also be fostered in those areas by inviting private sector participation.

Economic Insight: Disinvestment of PSUs
The 1991 policy also declared that in some selected public sector enterprises which are non-essential and commercial in nature, part of the Government equity holding will be disinvested. So from 1991 an annual target of realising a certain amount through such disinvestment was set. The revenue raised was to be used to reduce budget (fiscal) deficit and help ease the internal debt burden. Another objective was to improve the operational efficiency of PSUs. So far the GOI has carried out disinvestment in BALCO, Modern Bread, Indian Tourism Development Corporation, Asoka Hotel, Hotel Corporation of India, Maruti Udyog Ltd and IPCL. [see ch. 41 for detailed discussion]

5. The MRTP Act and Large Business Houses

In the industrial policy the MRTP Act virtually lost its relevance since all monopolistic clauses of the act have been removed.[1] Under the Monopolies and Restrictive Trade Practices (MRTP) Act on 1969, as amended in March 1985, any firm having assets of more than Rs. 100 crores was treated as an MRTP company. It could enter only some selected industries and had to apply for a fresh licence in order to expand and diversity.

The approval from the MRTP Commission was required by any large firm for getting any important proposal sanctioned. This generated an adverse effect on large firms. They could not plan for growth and diversification since they did not have the freedom to enter areas of their choice. This is why the asset limit in case of large houses and dominant undertakings were removed. So these firms are now at liberty to invest in delicensed industries. Large firms will now be able to achieve (derive) economies of scale

1. Only some restrictive clauses have been retained.

and thus raise productivity of resources and gain sustainable competitive advantage. The 1991 policy has introduced the following changes as far as the MRTP act is concerned:

(i) There is no need to obtain the approval of the GOI for getting investment proposals (regarding expansion of existing undertakings and establishment of new undertakings by big industrial houses) clearance.

(ii) The provisions which prohibited a company to merge, or amalgamate with other firms or to acquire other firms have been withdrawn.

(iii) In the new policy the stress is on controlling monopolistic, restrictive and unfair trade practices. So the provisions of the MRTP Act was strengthened to enable the MRTP Commission to take appropriate action if a firm is found to indulge in such practices. Accordingly, the newly created Monopoly Commission has been instructed to investigate the complaints received from consumers of industrial goods.

6. Inflow of Foreign Capital and Transfer of Technology

The 1991 policy adopted a liberal attitude towards inflow of foreign capital and transfer of technology. With a view to enabling industries to upgrade their technology, the industrial policy has made provision for automatic approval of technology transfer agreements in high-priority industries subject to certain specified guidelines. Similar facilities have also been provided to other industries provided such agreements do not have any foreign exchange implication. Indian companies are now free to negotiate the terms of technology transfer with foreign companies on the basis of commercial (i.e., profit and loss) considerations.

The 1991 policy stressed that opportunities for foreign investment in India should also be utilised to ensure rapid industrial growth. It welcomed foreign capital to supplement the resources raised domestically. So the GOI liberalised its policy toward foreign investment. To attract FDI automatic approval was granted to private foreign investors so that they could have majority (51%) equity holding of a company in 34 high-priority industries. This facility would be available to those firms which are able to finance their import of capital goods by utilising their foreign equity (and not domestic resources). So no case-by-case approval of foreign investment is required now.

The priority sector industries include power generation and petroleum refining. In addition, the GOI has assured a minimum guaranted 16% return on foreign investment in priority sectors.

7. Further Liberalisation of Industrial Policy

While pursuing its 1991 industrial policy, with stress on liberalisation, privatisation and globalisation (LPG), the GOI has adopted the following additional measures in order to make both domestic and foreign enterprises free from undue and excessive controls and regulations.

(i) *Promotion of competition* : In order to prevent monopolistic practices and to promote Competition, the Competition Act was passed in 2002. The Act established the Competition Commission of India on October 14, 2003 in order to prevent anti-competitive forces as also to create and sustain competitive markets in the country. The Commission is expected to protect the interests of consumers and to ensure free and fair trade so that no pressure is created on either the buyer or seller in a competitive environment.

In 2004-05 the GOI announced its plan to set up a National Manufacturing Competitiveness Council with a view to advising the GOI for promoting and sustaining the growth of manufacturing indusries from time to time. The Council will also be asked to suggest measures to promote (increase) competitiveness in the manufacturing sector. The Council is also supposed to recommend industry-specific policies for enhancing competitiveness.

(ii) *Dereservation of items for small scale industrial (SSI) units* : The 1991 Policy declared that 887 items reserved for exclusive production in the SSI units since 1967 would be deserved so as to permit large-scale units also to produce them. This measure was introduced to enable large firms to derive economies of scale through mass production of those items as also to raise productivity of resources and compete closely in international markets. Thus the gains derived by large firms will enable them to achieve two goals simultaneously, viz., (i) boosting industrial production and (ii) raising exports. In June 2005, 75 items consisting of chemicals and chemical products, leather and leather products, paper products, laboratory reagents, etc. were deserved.

In addition, the investment limit (in fixed capital such as plant, equipment and machinery) for SSI units was increased from Rs. 1 crores to Rs. 5 crores to enable such units to achieve technological upgradation and to carry out their modernisation plans so that productivity of resources increases and these firms are able to compete in global markets.

In 2004-05, 85 more items have been added to the list. However, in order to promote technological upgradation of SSI units the capital subsidy scheme has been liberalised. This is likely to enable them to grow in a competitive environment.

(iii) *Liberalisation of policy toward FDI* : In the 1991 Policy, the GOI has been encouraging inflow of FDI, which also leads to transfer of technology. It is expected that the inflow of FDI will give Indian industries an opportunity to upgrade their technology and gain access to improved managerial skills. FDI was also supposed to lead to optimal utilisation of potential natural and human resources. More importantly since FDI comes through multinational corporations, it is the key to the integration of India's industrial economy with the global manufacturing network. Realising the importance of foreign capital in India's economic development the GOI set up the Foreign Investment Promotion Board (FIPB) to facilitate the inflow of FDI in India. It adopted a liberal policy toward FDI and transfer of technology associated with it. At present 100% FDI is permitted in most sectors, through the automatic approval route.[1]

It may be noted that, in spite of the adoption of a liberal policy framework, the inflow of FDI in India had been very small in the first decade of economic reform (1991-2001). However, it increased in recent years from US $2,320 million in 2004-05 to US $22,697 million in 2008-09 (excluding NRI direct investment routed through RBI since 1994-95). In fact, due to the adoption of a liberal policy toward FDI, India has emerged as a highly favourable environment for the operation of MNCs which are involved in world-wide sourcing.

A related point may also be noted in this context. The National Common Minimum Programme (NCMP) of GOI declared that the GOI would encourage the inflow of FDI, particularly in infrastructure and high-technology sectors. Realising the urgent need for injecting large doses of FDI, GOI raised the upper limit for FDI in telecommunication from 49% to 74%, in civil aviation from 40% to 49% and in insurance from 26% to 49%.

(iv) *Establishment of Investment Commission* : In order to make India's investment environment attractive, in 2004-05, the GOI announced to setting up of an Investment Commission.[2] It will have the authority to discuss with both the domestic and foreign business persons about the prospect of investment in India. It will also invite them to make more investment so as to promote faster growth and generate more employment in a labour-surplus country.

AN OVERALL EVALUATION OF THE NEW INDUSTRIAL POLICY (1991)

Largely due to the introduction of far-reaching changes made in industrial policy, India moved much away from a mixed economy with control (exercised through the planning system) towards a market-based (if not a completely free-market) economy. In such an economy the private sector, which is governed by market forces, plays a dominant role and the public has lost its pre-eminent position.

More than two decades have passed since the industrial policy was changed in July 1991. Largely due to industrial and trade reforms we no longer face any foreign exchange crisis in the true sense.

1. This implies that no prior approval is necessary for FDI. There is only need for post-entry notification.
2. Its functions are comparable to those of Private Investment Corporation of Asia (PICA) of the Philippines.

Foreign exchange reserves (consisting of foreign currency, gold and SDRs) which fell to a very low level in May 1991 to Rs. 11,416 crores increased to Rs. 1,506,130 crores in 2011-12. One may expect, with cautious optimism, that the much improved foreign exchange reserves position will enable the country to tide over any crisis situation that may arise in near future. However, this large amount of foreign exchange reserves led to a sharp increase in the money supply and generated inflationary pressures in the economy. The GOI has also faced the problem of utilisation of such huge reserves for developmental purposes. Thus the GOI has become aware of the fact that the problem of plenty is sometimes as embarassing as the problem of poverty.

The annual rate of inflation, measured by changes in wholesale price index (WPI), fell from 14% in 1991-92 to 4.5% in 1997-98. But it jumped up to 8.2% in January 2001. In 2007-08, the rate of inflation fell to 4.1% due to the adoption of three measures, viz., (i) tight monetary policy, (ii) increase in domestic supply of goods through import of short-supply items and (iii) restrictions on export of certain essential commodities. In spite of this, the rate of inflation, as measured by changes in CPI remains relatively high. In the past six years (2008-14) two new problems have arisen in the Indian economy, viz., the problem of food inflation and asset price inflation. The prices of food articles are rising much faster than the prices of other (non-food) items. This has become a matter of considerable concern for the common man and is harassing the planners and policy-makers.

In fact, since March 2008 the price situation worsened and the rate of inflation was about 13% in September 2008. And the GOI has failed to bring inflation down by using tight monetary and fiscal measures. In March 2014 the rate of inflation was like above 10%.

It is to be noted that inflation in India is the result of the operation of various diverse forces operating from both demand and supply sides. And originate both from both domestic and external factors. There is hardly any direct link between economic reforms and recent price inflation.

Economic Growth

A notable increase in the rate of growth of gross domestic product (GDP) has been achieved during the post-reform period. While the annual average growth rate of India's national income was 5.7% during the Seventh Plan (1985-90), it picked up to 7.8% during the Tenth Plan (2002-07). Agriculture production remained more or less stagnant during the same period at 4.2% per annum. In fact, it fell from 4.2% during the Seventh Plan to 0.1% during the two annual plans (1990-92). Then it rose to 3% during the Eighth Plan (1992-97) and again fell to 0.9% in the Ninth Plan (1997-02). Only in the Tenth Plan (2002-07), it increased to 4.2%.

In truth, economic reforms completely neglected the agricultural sector. This is why the performance of the agricultural sector was perhaps the worse in the immediate post-reform period.

However, the performance on the industrial front presents a mixed picture. The average annual rate of industrial growth during the eight-year period 1992-93 to 2002-07 fell to 6.4% from 7.1% achieved during the nine-year period 1981-82 to 1990-91.

Industrial Growth and Industrial Slowdown

The first decade of reform (1992-93 to 2001-02) presents a mixed picture as far as industrial growth is concerned. For the purpose of analysis, the whole period can be divided into two sub-periods. During the first sub-period (1992-93 to 1996-97), the average annual rate of industrial growth was 7.6%. But it fell to a modest 4.6% per annum in the second sub-period (1997-98 to 2001-02). Two main reasons for the slowdown in industrial growth rate during this period were (i) fall in public sector investment and (ii) slow growth of exports due to global slowdown. The fall in public sector investment affected industrial growth from both the supply side and the demand side. It adversely affected aggregate supply by creating infrastructural bottlenecks. It also affected aggregate demand for industrial goods. Due to slow growth of industries the actual growth rate, measured by the annual average rate of increase in GDP, was only 5.5% during the second sub-period.

Revival of Industrial Growth

However, the period since 2002-03 saw a revival of industrial growth. The rate of industrial growth rose to 7.1% in 2003-04, to 9.4% in 2003-04 and further to 9.8% in 2004-05 and then it fell marginally to 9.6% in 2005-06. In the Tenth Plan period (2002-07), the average annual rate of industrial growth has been 8.7% which is largely attributable to the policy of economic liberalisation. Other factors such as a huge increase in public sector investment in infrastructure and easy availability of cheap credit from 1997 to 2008 also contributed to the great revival and faster growth of the industrial sector. In fact, the recent acceleration in growth of industries producing consumer durables as also of the automobile industry in recent past was the result of availability of cheap credit. Another factor contributing to the higher rate of industrial growth has been the sustained annual growth of export at the rate of 20% or even more. The indusrial growth rate is likely to pick up further if infrastructural deficiency and other bottlenecks are removed.

Importance of the Services Sector

The overall growth of the economy from 1992-93 to 2000-01 was quite high, though it slowed down during the Ninth Plan period (1997-2002). However, 5.5% annual average growth in GDP during this period has been achieved largely due to higher growth rate achieved in the services sector during the Ninth Plan period. In fact, the two decades of economic reforms have witnessed slow growth of the commodity producing (primary and secondary) sectors and fast growth of the services (tertiary) sector. The reason is that the services sector, consisting of such activities as transport and communication, banking and insurance and retail and wholesale trade as also tourism promotes faster economic growth by creating various linkages — both from the supply side and the demand side. However, due to revival of industrial growth during the Tenth Plan period a high annual rate of GDP growth (7.8%) could be achieved. In fact, industrial growth rate fell from 3.6% during the Seventh Plan (1985-90) to 0.6 during the two annual plans (1990-92). Then again it picked up to 4.1% in the Eighth Plan (1992-97). It fell to 33% in the Ninth Plan (1997-02). But it again picked upto 7.8% in the Tenth Plan (2002-07).

Effect on Employment

After the adoption of the new industrial policy, the employment situation worsened. Employment in organised sector (inclusive of the private and public sectors) increased from 22.9 million in 1981 to 26.7 million in 1991 and to 27.8 million in 2001. Then it fell to 27.2 million in 2002, 27 million in 2003 and 26.4 in 2004. It increased marginally to 265 million in 2005 and to 27 million in 2006 and 27.3 million in 2007. The slow growth of employment in the organised sector of industry is attributable to rapid growth of industrial labour force and the inability of the industrial sector to absorb them.

Three main causes of unemployment were (i) the of labour-saving techniques of production, (ii) growing competition faced by domestic producers from cheap imports and (iii) large-scale disinvestment of the public sector.

The rate of unemployment at the all-India level (in urban and rural sectors taken together) on current daily status basis fell from 9.2% in 1983 to 6.1% in 1993-94. It again increased to 8.3% in 2004-05. The unemployment rate increased from 9.2% in 2001 to 9.8% in 2006-07.

Slowdown in Poverty Reduction

Economic reforms in the context of globalisation of the Indian economy has led to a slowdown in the rate of fall in poverty ratio (i.e., the percentage of people living below the poverty line) in spite of a high rate of economic growth achieved in the post-reform period.

Three main causes of slowdown in the rate of fall in poverty ratio were: (i) displacement of labour on a large scale due to the adoption of capital-intensive techniques of production, (ii) fall in the rate of labour absorption in small and medium enterprises due to their inability to compete with cheap imported products and (iii) drastic cut in the quantum of funds allocated to agriculture, leading to fall in rate of increase in food production and causing hunger and malnutrition mainly in rural areas.

NATIONAL MANUFACTURING POLICY

The acceleration in India's growth rates in recent past has been largely due to unprecedented growth of the services sector. And the contribution of the manufacturing sectors to GDP has been only 15-16% of late the GOI realised the there is need for greater focus on the manufacturing sector which acts as the engine of growth for atleast to reason. Manufacturing output is tangible and there is greater scope innovation in this sector. It is now felt that unless India's manufacturing sectors gathers real momentum it will not be possible to maintain the present high growth rate and to create adequate employment opportunities for Indias' growing labour force. All these consideration have induced the GOI to give renewed focus on industrial policy. Consequently the GOI realised the National Manufacturing Policy (NMP) statement on November 4, 2011.

.Objectives of NMP

Seven main objectives of NMP are the following:

1. Increasing the rate of the growth manufacturing sector to 12-14% over the medium term.
2. raising the contribution of manufacturing in GDP from 16%-25% by 2022.
3. Creating 100 million new jobs in the manufacturing sectors by 2022.
4. Formation of appropriate marketable skills among. Two classes of people—the rural migrants and the urban poor.
5. Increasing value addition of manufacturing in domestic output.
6. ensuring technological upgradation in the manufacturing sectors.
7. Enhancing global competitiveness of India's export-oriented industries.

Policy Initiatives

Auxcelitration the growth of the manufacturing sectors, the new policy envisages the creation of a proper and healthy macroeconomic environment so as to enable the sectors to grow and diversify. The NMP also six to simplify the regulatory framework of business, keeping in view the importants of small and medium enterprises (SMEs) in Indias' the policy gives due importance of SMEs through such measures as technological upgradation, adoption environmental friendly technology and equity investments. High priority has been according to skill formation among young people to make them employable. For this various fiscal concessions have to be given to private sectors. At the same time various gov ernment schemes have been announced.

Finally, due provision has been made for NIM National Investment and Manufacturing Zones (NIMZ) on degraded and uncultivable land areas. These will be use for creating integrated industrial townships with world-class physical and social infrastructure.

KEY POINTS

1. *Industrial policy resolution of 1948* : The Industrial Policy Resolution, 1948—divided the industrial structure into four groups. To ensure the supply of capital goods and modern technology, the IPR, 1948, encouraged the free flow of foreign capital. The Government ensured that there shall be no discrimination between Indian and foreign undertakings, facilities shall be given for remittance of profit and due compensation shall be paid in case a foreign undertaking is nationalised. The IPR also emphasised the importance of small-scale and cottage industries in the Indian economy.

The Industries (Development and Regulation) Act was passed in 1951 to implement the Industrial Policy Resolution, 1948.

2. *Industrial policy resolution of 1956* : On April, 30, 1956 the Government revised its first Industrial Policy (i.e., the policy of 1948), and announced the Industrial Policy of 1956. The Resolution classified industries into three categories having regard to the role which the state would play in each of them: The IPR, 1956, stressed the importance of cottage and small-scale industries for expanding employment opportunities and for wider decentralisation of economic power and activity. The Resolution also called for all efforts to maintain industrial peace; a fair share of the proceeds of production should be given to the toiling mass in keeping with the avowed objectives of 'democratic socialism'. Regional disparities in industrialisation should be reduced. The Government's attitude to foreign capital remained unchanged.

The features of the new policy that distinguished it from the previous one are:

(i) **Expansion of the role of the state:** This was in keeping with the Mahalanobis Strategy of large-scale industrialisation embodied in the Second Five Year Plan.

(ii) **Reduced threat of nationalisation:** The apprehensions of nationalisation contained in the previous policy was reduced to the bare minimum.

(iii) **More meaningful approach to our 'mixed economy':** The complementarity of the public and private sectors were made clear.

3. *The Industrial Policy, 1991* : The Government has announced a New Industrial Policy (NIP) on July 24, 1991, in Parliament. The policy proposes to substantially amend the licensing policy and offer a series of initiatives designed to unshackle Indian industry from the various administrative and legal controls. The main features of the New Industrial policy are the following:

(i) **Salient features of the NIP:** The NIP does away with licensing for all major industries, irrespective of the investment level, proposes liberal foreign investment, dispenses with MRTP clearances but curbs unfair trade practices and emphasises technological upgradation. While allowing a greater role for the private sector, it vests the Government with necessary control in key areas of industry as per the Industrial Policy Resolution of 1956.

(ii) **Abolition of licensing procedures:** The NIP has abolished the industrial licensing requirement irrespective of the level of investment in all industries except those 18 industries.

(iii) **Broad branding facility and FMP:** Existing and new industrial units have been provided with the broad branding facility to produce any article so long as no additional investment in plant and machinery is undertaken. The phases manufacturing programme (PMP) will no longer be applicable to new projects.

(iv) **Modifications in the MRTP Act:** The MRTP Act will be amended to remove the threshold limit of assets in respect of MRTP companies and dominant undertakings. This would eliminate the requirement of prior approval of the Central Government for establishment of new undertakings, merger, amalgamation, takeover and appointment of directors under certain circumstances.

(v) **Foreign investment:** While welcoming foreign investment with its attendant advantage of technology transfer, marketing expertise, introduction of modern managerial techniques and export promotion, the NIP provides for automatic approval of foreign equity participation up to 51 per cent in high priority industries.

(vi) **Foreign collaboration:** On foreign technology agreements, the Government intends to combine the need for updating technology in high priority areas with incentives for domestic sales and export promotion.

Foreign technology agreements in high priority areas with incentives for domestic sales and export promotion.

(vii) **Import of capital goods:** The NIP envisages automatic clearances for import of capital goods provided the foreign exchange requirement for such imports is ensured through foreign equity.

(viii) **Public sector:** The pre-eminent place of public sector will be continued in 8 core areas.

(ix) **Non-applicability of convertible clause:** In a significant step, the NIP has dispensed with the applicability of the mandatory convertibility clause which enabled financial institutions to convert loans into equity for the term loans extended by financial institutions for new projects.

(x) **Reservation for small-scale industries:** The reservation of items for small-scale sector will be continued to promote industrial and agro-industrial employment base. A package for tiny and small-scale sector will be announced by the Government separately.

(xi) **Locational policy:** In cities of less than 1 million population there will be no need for obtaining industrial approvals from the Central Government except for industries subject to compulsory licensing.

KEY TERMS

Mixed economy licensing system	Dereservation	Foreign portfolio investment
Disinvestment	Services sector	Manufacturing sector
Foreign direct investment	Globalisation	Inflow of foreign capital
Transfer of technology	Common minimum programme	Basic and heavy industries

ASSIGNMENTS

1. **Highlight the salient features of India's Second Industrial Policy Resolution announced in 1956. Why did it stress the role of basic and heavy industries?**
2. **Make a critical review of the Government of India's present industrial policy. How does it differ from earlier policies?**
3. **How did the industrial sector perform during the reform period? Did it show revival in terms of growth and diversification?**
4. **Comment on the growth of India's services sector during the reform period.**
5. **Comment on the effects of the New Industrial Policy on (a) employment generation and (b) poverty alleviation.**
6. **Write an explanatory note on changes in the pattern of industrialisation in India during the reform period.**
7. **What is industrial policy? Comment on the importance of industrialisation in the context of India's economic development.**

40A NOTE ON THE INDUSTRIAL LICENSING SYSTEM

In the pre-reform period, the private sector in India was closely controlled through the licensing system. In order to get an industrial licence an entrepreneur had to clear the following of hurdles.

1. **Letter of Intent:** Before making an investment, an entrepreneur had to obtain approval from the Ministry of Industry in the form of a Letter of Intent (LOI). This enabled the entrepreneur to tie up other requirements for setting up the project.

2. **Capital goods import licence:** If an entrepreneur needed to import a capital good, he had to obtain a capital goods import licence also from the Chief Controller of Imports and Exports (CCI & E).

3. **Foreign technological collaboration:** If there was also need for a foreign technological collaboration, the entrepreneur had to obtain a specific approval for this.

4. **Capital issue:** If an entrepreneur wanted to raise funds from the capital market for his project, he needed a separate approval from the Controller of Capital Issues.

5. **Import of raw materials and components:** For import of raw materials and components, separate licences had to be obtained on an annual basis from the CCI & E.

In each case, an 'essentially' and 'indigenous non-availability' clearance had to be given by the Directorate General of Technical Development (DGTD).

Once all the steps were completed and integrated with one another and the unit was about to start commercial production, the entrepreneur had to go back to the Ministry of Industry for an 'industrial licence'.

6. **MRTP clearance:** In addition, any large house having an asset of Rs. 20 crores or more had to obtain seperate MRTP clearance from the Department of Company Affairs.[1] Such a unit had to initially get one license for carrying on business. It had also to apply for a fresh licence in order to expand and diversify.

Performance of the Industrial Licensing System

(i) Negative Side

1. **Channeling investment into desired directions:** Since the early 1960s it became very clear that the licensing system was not quite suitable for directing investments in the desired channels which was its primary objective.

2. **Balanced Regional development and wide dispersal of industries:** The licensing system also largely failed to achieve its declared objective of achieving balanced regional development (through promoting industries in backward areas) and wider distribution of entrepreneurship.

3. **Follow-up action:** Hardly any follow-up action was taken to see that approved projects were completed on time. In most cases there were inordinate delays in project completion.

4. **Ranking and priority:** In attempting to cover virtually the whole range of large-scale industries, the licensing system invariably failed to realise the importance of different projects/products, i.e., whether they were critical to the economy or not. Since all applications had to undergo similar processing, licences were issued indiscriminately without ranking industries in order of plan priorities and targets.

Such indiscriminate issue of licences largely accounted for its failure on almost all fronts. The licencing system failed practically on all counts — whether it was regional dispersal, import substitution or prevention of undue concentration of wealth and economic power in private hands. Licencing also failed to ensure the development of industries according to plan priorities. In addition, licences were issued in excess of targeted capacity even in non-priority industries. Influential persons and large business houses

1. The asset limit was later raised to Rs. 100 cr.

were permitted to preemt capacities. The follow-up of licences was not systematic and licences remained unimplemented for long periods.

(ii) Positive Side

In spite of all these defects, the industrial licensing system was supported to play an important role in India's planned economic development. The following points are to be noted in this context:

1. **Growth of small scale industries:** Firstly, the industrial licensing system permitted the growth of small-scale industries through a list of reservations. The system has been virtually done away with in recent past.

2. **Ban on further capacity creation:** Secondly, ban on further capacity creation were supported to prevent the emergence of undersirable activities or lines of production directed toward the production of non-essential luxury goods in case of diversified enterprises.

A Summary View

Some economists have argued that the industrial licensing system had promoted rent seeking which is an example of Government failure. According to Oxford Dictionary of Economics, rent seeking refers to "spending time are money . . . to get the government to change the rules so as to make one's business more profitable" by keeping out competitors or by profit colusion and those firms which are already by changed in an activity. According to J. N. Bhagwati, the system provided the rationale behind the pursuit of directly unproductive activities. As well summarised G. Mier, "The promotion of a sheltered home market had a common appeal to the bureaucratic authoritarian State, urban manufacturers and multinationals that supplied technology and capital. Protection also met the State's objectives of pursuing revenue and expenditure maximising activities through maximum revenue tariffs and export tariffs."

In short, the interests of politicians, bureaucrats, multinationals, as well as domestic industrial houses all coincided to keep Indian industry sheltered through the operation of the licensing system.

From the end of 1970s Indian industry was exhibiting a slow-down in growth due to low productivity, high costs, low quality of products and obsolete technology. This is why several expert committees, appointed to review the industrial control system, recommended the following:

(i) an easing up of trade (export-import) policy,

(ii) the substitution of physical and quantitative controls by fiscal and other measures of macroeconomic managements.

(iii) the promotion of greater public sector autonomy in taking decisions in their day-to-day functioning, and

(iv) the need for additing necessary measures to enhance production efficiency and to promote modernisation.

CHAPTER 41

The Public Sector and the Issue of Privatisation

In view of the historical background of public enterprise in India, it is inconceivable that privatisation in this country will be accepted by the society as an end in itself, since there is no consensus in favour of market solutions and property rights, nor are these considered as prime movers for much needed social and economic change. The real issues centre on the alleviation of poverty and the upgrading of technology in a highly differentiated society of continental dimensions.
V. V. Ramanadham

I believe that the objective for disinvestment should be to benefit the public, the consumer and the investor, and, at the same time, to improve competitiveness and eliminate monopoly.
George Fernandes

The Second Industrial Policy Resolution (1956) assigned a very important role to the public sector in India's industrial development. At the time of independence, the Indian economy was in a bad shape. It was a predominantly agrarian (peasant) economy with hardly any industrial base. In addition, even the most essential and basic infrastructural facilities were conspicuous by their absence. In truth, the Indian economy was caught in a spreading vicious circle of underdevelopment and needed a big push or a critical minimum effort through the public sector to be able to move ahead and achieve self sustaining growth. In fact, the private sector was in moribund state. It had neither the capacity nor the desire to initiate the process of industrialisation in India by providing an integrated infrastructure or by developing certain basic and heavy industries. *Prima facie*, the private sector did not have adequate resources to develop such highly capital-intensive industries which required a huge amount of initial investment. Secondly in such input-supplying industries the gestation period was very long and the yield (measured by the rate of return on net capital employed) was supposed to be very low (compared to that in industries producing mass consumption goods). So the private entrepreneurs did not have either the desire and or the incentive to set up basic and heavy industries which required a huge amount of initial investment.

India's First Plan (1951-56) allocated the maximum amount of resources for agricultural growth and infrastructural development. However, from the beginning of the Second Plan (1956-61) and till the mid-1970s the public sector was assigned the strategic role of developing certain basic and heavy industries. So a large amount of funds was allocated to the public sector.

In addition, the Mahalonobis strategy of development laid emphasis on import-substituting type of industrialisation. So the public sector was entrusted with the responsibility of developing industries which would produce import-substitute items so as to enable the country to save foreign exchange and achieve economic self-reliance. It is against this backdrop that we study the role of the public sector in India's industrial economy as also in India's mixed economy.

THE ROLE OF THE PUBLIC SECTOR IN INDIA

It may be noted at the outset that a vital role was assigned to the public sector in India's mixed economy for promoting faster economic growth and for ensuring distributive justice. This, it was believed, would enable the country to move toward a socialistic pattern of society which was one of the declared objectives of the Directive Principles of India's State Policy.

The following points bring into focus the importance of the public sector in India's mixed economy:

1. Promoting faster economic growth: Only through an expansion of the public sector it would be possible to achieve faster economic growth and rapid economic development. This would enable the country to break the vicious circle of poverty and underdevelopment. This goal could not be achieved in a free enterprise and unplanned economy.

2. Infrastructure building: It was the task of the public sector to make adequate investment in economic infrastructure such as transport and communication, power, fuel, etc. Without an integrated infrastructure, the process of economic development could not be accelerated by removing various bottlenecks and ensuring an optimal utilisation of scarce resources. Since unfrastructure is an example of public good which generates positive externalities, it is essential that the government takes the lead in providing such good in which social benefit exceeds private benefit.

3. Setting up of basic and heavy industries: The public sector was supposed to expand basic and heavy industries such as steel, fertilisers, heavy chemicals, heavy engineering (e.g., machine making). Since such industries supplied inputs to a large number of other industries, investment in such industries was crucial for promoting industrialisation with a view to creating more jobs and incomes and enabling the country to achieve economic self-reliance. The setting up of such industries required a huge amount of resources which only the State could provide. Moreover, the private sector had hardly any incentive to invest in these (as also in infrastructure) industries due to low rate of return and long gestation period.

4. Reaching the commanding heights of the economy: The industrial policy resolution (1956) declared that the public sector would gradually reach the commanding heights of the economy such as finance and banking, life and general insurance, so as to strengthen the socio-economic infrastructure as also to regulate the functioning of the private firms in the public interest and in accordance with the plan priorities and targets.

5. Preventing undue concentration of wealth and economic power: An undue expansion of big business (both domestic and foreign) would be held in check by a parallel expansion of the public sector. Public sector enterprises (PSUs) exercise their countervailing power to hold in check undue concentration of wealth and economic power in a few private hands. Thus in order to prevent the emergence of monopolistic conditions in India's industrial economy PSUs would be required to make investment on a huge scale and produce mass consumption goods to take advantage of economies of scale so that consumers could get some essential items (such as coal, electricity, cement, steel, telephone services, watches, etc.) at low prices.

6. Balanced regional development: The public sector has to play an important role in setting up industries in notified backward regions of the country or the so-called growth centres, having sufficient natural resource endowments. This would help to generate income and employment opportunities for the poor all over the country and thus reduce regional inequality and imbalance.

7. Making investment on social sectors: The public sector had an important role to play in creating which needed social infrastructure by setting up educational institutions and health centres, constructing tubewells to provide safe drinking water in all parts of the country. These would certainly help to reduce the incidence of poverty. This is why Amartya Sen calls for more public sector investment in such areas as human capital formation and nutrition not only to promote faster economic growth but also to improve the quality of life of the people. Therefore the government and the public sector have an active role to play in India's socio-economic development. It was expected that the public sector would work efficiently so as to minimise cost of production and to generate surplus or savings which could be ploughed back for accelerating the rate of capital formation and thus promoting faster economic growth.

The Diluted Role of the Public Sector in the New Economic Policy

However, during the period of economic reforms (starting from July 1991), the role of the public sector has been greatly diluted. In the new economic policy, the private sector and foreign investment have been assigned more important role for promoting India's economic growth.

The Growth of India's Public Sector

Since 1956, there has occurred a steady and rapid growth of the public sector. Both the Central and State Governments set up a number of industrial enterprises for production of various goods and services. Both the number of enterprises as also the volume of investment in them increased year after year. Whereas there existed only 5 Central Government units with a total investment of Rs. 29 crores in 1951, the number went up to Rs. 232 in 1999-00 with an investment of Rs. 302,947 crores. See Table 41.1.

Table 41.1: Growth of Central Government Enterprises*

	2010-11	2009-10	2008-09	1999-00
Running enterprises (No.)	220	217	213	232
	Rs. crs			
Capital employed	949,499	908,007	792,232	302,947
Turnover	1,473,319	1,244,805	1,271,529	389,199
PBIT**	170,625	160,017	142,395	42,270
Loss : interest	38,998	36,060	39,300	20,233
Profit before tax	131,627	123,957	103,095	22,037
Profit after tax (PAT)	86,324	83,939	69,267	14,331
PAT to turnover (%)	5.9	6.7	5.4	3.7
PAT to capital employed (%)	9.1	9.2	8.7	4.7

*Excluding banks, insurance companies and financial institutions.

**Profit before interest and tax.

The Pattern of Investment

More than 20% public sector investment has been made by the Central Government on basic infrastructural industries such as power, coal, petroleum as also heavy (high capital-intensive) industries such as steel, fertiliser and heavy engineering (21%) in 2004-05. However, the maximum investment (22.4%) has been made in financial services (mainly in commercial banking and insurance companies). By contrast, only 5.5% of total investment was made in textiles and 1.2% in consumer goods.

A related point may be noted in this context. A number of sick units belonging mainly to textiles and consumer goods were taken by the Central Government from the private sector, mainly for the purpose of protecting jobs.

The Performance of the Public Sector

Profitability

Over the years most PSUs incurred loss for a number of reasons. In 1991-92, when the process of disinvestment or privatisation of PSUs was started, most such units earned very low profit. However since 1993-94 much improved profitability of central PSUs was observed.

A major portion (more than 40%) of the profits of PSUs was contributed by the oil sector. In 2000-01, 107 PSUs signed Memorandum of Understandings. The objective was to improve the efficiency and profitability of PSUs and to grant autonomy by the Government as far as decision making and day-to-day functioning were concerned.

Economic Insight: Three Other Efficiency Criteria

Apart from profitability, there are three other criteria by which PSUs can be judged, viz., (a) technical efficiency, (b) allocative efficiency and (c) dynamic efficiency.

Technical efficiency is measured by total factor productivity (TFP) which is the ratio of output produced by an enterprise to inputs used by it.

Allocative efficiency is achieved by making an optimal correction of market failure. Any PSU can do this by providing certain essential items on the basis of non-commercial considerations (i.e., not profit-and-loss considerations). Improved allocative efficiency is achieved by producing such goods. Dynamic efficiency is achieved by developing new products and process. In other words, it can be gained largely through product innovation which largely depends on expenditure on research and development (R and D). It can be partly achieved through process innovation which depends on upgradation of technology which enables PSUs to produce the same item at a lower cost so that most consumers can afford to buy it. If we evaluate PSUs on the basis of these non-profit criteria, we find that these units have performed quite well.

Contribution to India's Economic Growth

In addition, PSUs have made notable contribution to India's economic growth through new investment or by raising the country's overall rate of capital formation. This became evident from the fact that a sudden fall in public investment from the mid-1960s to mid-1970s as also during the late 1990s led to considerable slowdown in industrial growth. However, while some PSUs made positive contribution to India's economic growth, most of them had incurred losses in the first four decades of planning (1951-91).

Causes of Poor Performance

We may now discuss briefly the cause of poor performance of PSUs. These are the following:

1. *Lack of profit and loss consideration* : Initially the profitability criteria was not given due importance as far as the working of PSUs were concerned. Instead the stress was given on the social obligations of such enterprises. It is only in recent years that the profitability aspect of their operations has been given some importance.

2. *Wrong location* : One of the causes of low profitability of PSUs is the location of such enterprises at wrong places. The main reason is that most such units were set up here and there mainly on political considerations. The location decision was not based any rational economic canon.

3. *Underutilisation of installed capacity* : Low capacity utilisation has been one of the main reasons for the poor performance of several PSUs. Huge initial production capacity has been created by taking foreign loans and using foreign technical know-how on easy terms (i.e., at low rates of interest and long repayment period). But most PSUs failed to make full utilisation of their installed production capacity. This problem has arisen for a number of reasons such as overestimation of demand, administrative delays, choice of wrong production techniques, lack of proper work environment and culture, labour trouble, breakdown of machines due to lack of maintenance, reluctance to install balancing equipment and indifferent attitude of management toward upgradation of technology due to lack of incentives.[1]

4. *Lack of proper feasibility studies* : Most PSUs were set up without making proper feasibility studies which would take into consideration such factors as the production process to be used, the

1. Managers of PSUs get a fixed compensation. So like private monopolists they lead a quiet life without being bothered about improving production technology.

availability of essential raw materials such as fuel as also inputs such as power, skilled manpower, cheap credit, transport and communication facilities. These factors were not taken into consideration while launching projects. Hardly any calculation was made of the demand for the product of an enterprise and its production potential.

It is also surprising to note that in case of number of units such as Trombay Fertiliser Project, Hindustan Insecticides and Indian Telephone Industries, tenders were invited even though no project report was prepared.

5. *Delay in completion of project* : Hardly any consideration was given to the time schedule within which a public sector project had to be completed. Most projects were commissioned much later than the scheduled date. Consequently the cost of construction increased unnecessarily. For instance, Trombay Fertiliser Project was supposed to be completed within 3 years. But it took 6-7 years to complete the project. So there was a huge cost overrun (escalation).

6. *Lack of professionalism in management* : There occurred no spread of professionalism in PSUs. The members of the boards were appointed politically. There was domination of IAS officers most of whom had no professional background or managerial competence. This accounted for inefficient functioning of many such enterprises.[1]

Most PSUs were characterised by top heavy administrative structure in which there existed a disproportionate number of managers and board members. These people put extra burden on PSUs due to high cost (an account of deputation pay, leave-salary PF and pension contribution) and low efficiency.

7. *Defective recruitment procedure and faulty manpower planning* : Due to faulty manpower planning there was overstaffing in most organisations. More persons were recruited than needed to perform a particular task or sub-task. Most PSUs did not undertake proper human development programmes. Moreover the method of recruiting was wrong in most cases. In truth, defeated politicians and retired officials were damped into PSUs without assessing their ability and competence. This is why purely bureaucratic approach was followed in the administration of these undertakings.

8. Absence of rational pricing policy : Most PSUs failed to adopt a rational pricing policy for their products. This is why they failed to achieve an optimal utilisation of resources and improve their profitability.

9. Unnecessary political interference : Undue political pressure has forced the management of several PSUs to abandon sound commercial principles (based on profit-and-loss considerations) while taking investment, production, and pricing decisions.

Conclusion

Inadequate trading surpluses generated by PSUs are attributable to their long gestation period, shortage of trained and expert personnel, at least in the initial stage, faulty planning, wrong pricing policies and monopolistic nature of several PSUs which led to organisational slack or X-inefficiency (by making managerial staff lethargic). There is no doubt that there may be losses in the initial stage but PSUs should not be perennial losers. The PSUs make inefficient use of resources and productivity of resources is low in most cases due to lack of proper accountability.

DISINVESTMENT AND PRIVATISATION OF PSUs

The industrial policy of 1991 declared that the GOI would not operate PSUs on commercial considerations. For this reason the GOI decided to adopt the policy of disinvestment of the PSUs. The Government could either sell its enterprises completely to the private sector or disinvest a part of the equity held by it either to the private companies or offer a portion of its equity in the open market for absorption by

1. The reason is that these people acquired a different type of training and gained a different type of experience. So they developed a different type of attitude and worked in a different type of environment and culture. So they could not perform their tasks properly so as to conduce to the efficiency of their organisations.

the public or institutional investors — domestic and foreign. In this context we may note the difference between disinvestment and privatisation.

Distinction between Disinvestment and Privatisation

There are two alternative ways of diluting the stake of Government in a PSU. When the government sells less than 50% of its equity or stock in a PSU, it is called disinvestment. In this case the control and management of the PSU still remains in the hands of the Government. On the other hand, privatisation occurs when the Government sells more than 50% of its equity in a PSU. In this case the majority ownership and, therefore, control and management of the PSU is transferred to a private enterprise.

By following any of the routes of equity dilution, the Government can raise a reasonable amount of resources which can be used for four purposes:

(i) to improve the operational efficiency of PSUs[1];

(ii) to retire (pay back) a portion of internal public debt[2] and to reduce the interest burden of the Government;

(iii) to cover a portion of the Government's fiscal deficit; and

(iv) to make investment not only on economic infrastructure, but also on social infrastructure i.e., on education, health care, and water supply as also for employment generation, poverty alleviation and improvement of the physical quality of life of the people.

Reason for Disinvestment

There are various reasons for disinvestment. *Prima facie*, the Government needs resources for various reasons as just noted. In addition, when the government disinvests a substantial portion of its stake in a private enterprise or to the general public, the accountability of management of an enterprise is automatically improved. This is likely to have a favourable effect on the operational efficiency of the enterprise.

If the Government spends a portion of the proceeds from disinvestment on the social sector, the borrowing requirement of the Government will be less. So the Government will not face a huge debt burden.

However, critics comment that disinvestment virtually amounts to the sale of 'family silver' for meeting its current expenditure. The truth is everything depends on how the Government utilises the funds raised through disinvestment.

The Disinvestment Process and Asset Valuation

There are four types of disinvestment processes. These are the following:

1. *Privatisation* : A PSU can be sold to a private firm in it entirety. It is supposed to be sold to the highest bidder, i.e., to one who is willing to pay the maximum price. In this case both ownership and control (management) are transferred to the private firm. For example, Modern Food, a PSU was sold to Hindustan Lever. In the same way the Century Hotel in Bombay was sold to a private company.

2. *Strategic sale* : Alternatively, the Government can sell usually 26% of its stake to a strategic private company, i.e., an ideal investor having genuine strategic interest in a PSU and is competent enough to run and manage it efficiently. This is accomplished by the transfer of managerial control[3]. The strategic buyer is selected by inviting tenders from intending private companies. This method really worked wonder by enabling the Government to reap handsome dividends since a wide range of PSUs have been disinvested through this route.

---

1. This is normally done by restructuring and strengthening the potentially viable PSUs as also the loss-making ones.
2. Of late India has fallen in an internal debt trap.
3. There is at present a market for managerial control.

3. *Public offer for sale in shares* : The Government can offer its shares in a PSU for sale to the general public through jobbers and brokers (who act as intermediaries in stock markets).

4. *Auction of shares* : Finally, the Government can sell a certain number of shares which it holds in PSU through auction among a few select private companies. The minimum acceptable (or, a Marshallian reservation price) of shares of a PSU which are auctioned is determined by a consultant, preferably a merchant bank.

THREE ASPECTS OF PUBLIC SECTOR REFORMS

The three main aspects of reforms in PSUs are the following:

(i) The sale of at most 26% of Government equity in all non-strategic PSUs is the most important strategic move of the Government as far as its policy of disinvestment of PSUs is concerned.

(ii) The Government will take necessary step to revive and restructure those PSUs which appear to be potentially viable.

(iii) Those PSUs which have no chance of revival will have to be closed down as part of the Government's exit policy.

It is felt that there is need for evolving a fair, transparent and standard procedure for disinvestment in select PSUs. The success achieved by the Government with regard to disinvestment of PSUs which started in 1991-92 is shown in Table 41.2.

Table 41.2: Disinvestment of Equity in Public Sector Enterprises (Rs. crores)

	Target	Realisation	Cumulative
1991-92	2,500	3,038	3,038
1992-93	2,500	1,913	4,951
1993-94	3,500	–	4,951
1994-95	4,000	4,843	9,794
1995-96	7,000	168	9,962
1996-97	5,000	380	110,342
1997-98	4,800	910	11,252
1998-99	5,000	5,371	16,623
1999-00	10,000	1,860	18,483
2000-01	10,000	1,871	20,354
2001-02	12,000	5,658	26,012
2002-03	12,000	3,348	29,360
2003-04	14,500	15,548	44,908
2004-05	4,000	2,765	47,673
2005-06	*n.a*	1,570	49,242
2006-07	*n.a*	–	49,242
2007-08	*n.a*	4,181	53,424
2008-09	*n.a*	–	53,424
2009-10	*n.a*	4,260	57,684

Source: SOI (2012-13), p. 124

Public Sale of Shares

As an alternative to strategic sales approach which was challenged by the Supreme Court various PSUs went for a soft option — making public offer for sale of a part of Government equity. By using this method the Government realised Rs 15,547 crores in 2003-04.

Commentary: Strategic Sale vs. Public Sale

If the objective of disinvestment to change existing management, then strategic sale appears to be the most preferred route to Indian disinvestment under the present conditions. The reason is easy to find out. Disinvestment and privatisation occur in the true sense when a company is controlled and managed by professional managers. However, there is an offsetting argument. It is possible to appoint professional managers in PSUs which are controlled by the Government. In addition, even profitable PSUs can raise resources from the capital market through sale of equity to the public.

The GOI's Approach to PSU Disinvestment

As a part of the Common Minimum Programme (CMP), the GOI decided not to privatise profit-making PSUs. Instead the GOI decided to give full managerial and commercial (financial) autonomy to successful, profit-making PSUs which were operating in a competitive environment. Each proposal for privatisation would be considered on a transparent and case-by-case basis. The Navratnas will continue to remain in the public sector. However, they will be permitted to raise resources from the capital market.

Public Sector Reform

Apart from disinvestment, three major steps have been taken by the GOI while introducing public sector reforms. These are the following:

1. ***Delegation of power*** **:** Enhanced financial and operational power has been delegated to central PSUs with a view to professionalising the Board of Directors.

2. ***Corporate governance*** **:** The GOI has also issued guidelines to such enterprises on corporate governance.

3. ***Sale of closure of sick units*** **:** The GOI will put all possible efforts to modernise, restructure and revive sick PSUs. However, the perennial losers or chronically sick units which have no chance of revival will either be sold off or closed down after clearing the accumulated dues of workers.

Navratnas

In 1997 the GOI identified nine profit-making PSUs which were found to have the resources and the capacity to emerge as global giants, viz., IOC, ONGC, HPCL, IPCL, VSNL, BHEL, SAIL and NTPC. These were called Navratnas. However, due to political opposition, the GOI could not pursue its policy of disinvestment in these and other profit-making enterprises. It had to defer the implementation of the policy.

BRPSE

The Government will induce private investors to turn around those sick and loss-making enterprises that have a strong chance of (or potential for) revival. This is why the Government set up The Board for Reconstruction of Public Sector Enterprises (BRPSE). Its main task is to advise Government on revival of such units. The BRPSE has made recommendations in 47 cases including two for closure till Oct 31, 2007. The proposals for revival of 26 central public sector enterprises and closure of two have already got the approval of the Government. The total assistance approved by the Government upto Dec. 2007 for these units was 8,285 crores of which Rs. 1955 crore was cash assistance and the balance (Rs. 6,330 crore) non-cash assistance.

National Investment Fund (NIF)

Another notable aspect of the GOI's public sector reforms was the creation of the National Investment Fund (NIF). The objective was to deposit the sales proceeds of disinvestment of the GOI's stake in PSUs.

DISINVESTMENT OR PRIVATISATION: AN OVERALL EVALUATION

There are arguments both in favour of and against disinvestment and privatisation. So the debate on the issue is not yet over. The main arguments in favour of disinvestment or privatisation are as following:

1. ***Promoting operational efficiency and raising productivity of resources*** : Disinvestment of PSUs in general and privatisation in particular is expected to lead to the spread of professionalism in PSUs. Since professional managers are guided by F.W. Taylor's scientific management principles, they are competent enough to be able to improve the operational efficiency of such enterprises. Since the modern techniques of cost reduction and cost control can be introduced the productivity of resources and profitability of PSUs are likely to increase.

2. ***Closure of sick units*** : All sick and unviable PSUs will have close down as a result of privatisation. A private company which buys a sick PSU will make some money by selling the assets of the sick unit (such as land, factory buildings, staff quarters, etc.).

3. ***Low government savings*** : Disinvestment is also advocated on the ground that due to losses of PSUs or very little profits of a few of such enterprises, Government savings will be either very low or even negative. In fact, one of the main causes of Government budget deficit is marketing losses of PSUs.

4. ***Resource generation*** : Disinvestment is likely to generate a large amount of resources for the Government, which can be used for a number of purposes (as already noted).

5. ***Attracting private foreign investment*** : The conversion of PSUs into private companies will enable them to set up joint ventures by attracting private foreign investment. Inflow of funds through FDI is more fruit-bearing than funds raised through foreign aid or external commercial borrowing.

6. ***End of state monopoly*** : Privatisation will lead to an end of state monopoly which is as harmful and undesirable as private monopoly. The privatisation of PSUs would force the firms to operate in a highly competitive environment. As a result they will be able to operate efficiency by fully utilising their production capacity and succeed in raising productivity of resources. Consequently some loss-making companies are likely to be converted into profit-making ones.

Arguments against Disinvestment or Privatisation

The following argument have been put forward against privatisation of PSUs in India:

1. ***Emergence of private monopolies*** : Due to the absence of anti-trust laws in India in the true sense, privatisation of some PSUs would lead to emergence of private monopolies, which would lead to misallocation of resources. In addition, due to the adoption of monopolistic practices by these firms, output and employment will fall but product prices will rise.

2. ***Spread of professionalism and improved managerial efficiency*** : Professional managers can be appointed to improve operational efficiency of PSUs. Privatisation is not necessary for the spread of professionalism of management in such enterprises (units).

3. ***Concentration of economic power*** : Privatisation will lead to undue concentration of wealth and economic power in private hands. This can be used to exploit consumers on the one hand and workers on the other. In addition, it will lead to an increase in inequality of income and wealth. So privatisation will go against the GOI's declared objective of promoting growth with distributive (social) justice.

4. ***Growing unemployment*** : Privatisation will lead to retrenchment of workers. So they will go below the poverty line by losing their means of livelihood. Furthermore, profit-seeking private firms have a tendency to use capital-intensive techniques of production. So new employment opportunities will not be created. In other words, the problem of unemployment will go from bad to worse.

5. ***Industrial sickness*** : Privatisation is not a real solution to the problem of growing incidence of sickness in PSUs. In truth, the Government has taken over a number of sick private units, mainly in the field of textiles just for protecting jobs.

6. ***Social costs and benefits*** : Finally, since even some loss-making PSUs are socially desirable, they should not be privatised. In fact, without the growth of PSUs in industries such as machine-making, heavy chemicals, fertilisers, steel, power, and transport and communication, the country would not have a strong industrial base and rapid industrial development would not have been possible. Many PSUs are in the nature of public utilities which are not guided by commercial (profit-and-loss) considerations.

Their primary objective is promotion of social (community) welfare. Other objectives are of secondary importance.

Conclusion

In the ultimate analysis it seems that the GOI's need for resources is very urgent and pressing. Therefore it has decided to go for privatisation of PSUs. The policy of disinvestment will be effective and really fruit-bearing if some supportive measures are adopted such as control of private monopoly by the MRTP Commission and protection of the interest of workers while making strategic sale to an appropriate buyer. The Government should permit a private firm to reduce manpower only if voluntary retirement scheme (VRS) is introduced and sufficient compensation is paid to workers who have been made redundant by the privatisation move. Golden handshake may be an appropriate policy in this context. It refers to a generous upfront payment designed to persuade a person to leave his current employment and to join the organisation offering the payment.

KEY POINTS

1. ***Role of the public sector in India*** **:** A vital role was assigned to the public sector in India's mixed economy for promoting faster economic growth and for ensuring distributive justice. The following points bring into focus the importance of the public sector in India's mixed economy:

(i) promoting faster economic growth,
(ii) infrastructure building,
(iii) setting up of basic and heavy industries,
(iv) reaching the commanding heights of the economy,
(v) preventing undue concentration of wealth and economic power in private hands,
(vi) balanced regional development and
(vii) making investment on social sectors.

2. ***The diluted role of the public sector in the new economic policy*** **:** The private sector and foreign investment have been assigned more important role for promoting India's economic growth in the new economic policy of the GOI ammended in July 1992.

3. ***The growth of India's public sector*** **:** Since 1956 there has occurred a steady and rapid growth of the public sector in India's mixed economy. Both the Central and State Governments set up a number of industrial enterprises for production of various goods and services. Both the number of enterprises as also the volume of investment in them increased year after year.

4. ***The performance of the public sector*** **:** Over the years most PSUs incurred losses for a number of reasons. A major portion (more than 40%) of the profits of PSUs was contributed by the oil sector.

5. ***Causes of poor performance*** **:** There were various causes of poor performance of PSUs. These were the following:

(i) lack of profit-and-loss considerations,
(ii) wrong location,
(iii) underutilisation of installed capacity,
(iv) lack of proper feasibility studies,
(v) delay in project completion,
(vi) lack of professionalism in management,
(vii) defective recruitment procedure and faulty manpower planning,
(viii) absence of rational pricing policy and
(ix) unnecessary political interference.

6. ***Disinvestment and privatisation of PSUs*** **:** The industrial policy of 1991 declared that the GOI would not operate PSUs on commercial considerations. For this reason the GOI decided to undertake disinvestment of the number of PSUs. The Government can either sell its enterprises completely to the private sector or disinvest a part of the equity held by it either to the private companies or offer a portion of its equity in the open market for absorption by the general public or institution investors — domestic and foreign.

7. *The disinvestment process and asset valuation* : There are four types of disinvestment process. These are the following:

(i) privatisation,
(ii) strategic sale,
(iii) public offer for sale in shares and
(iv) auction of shares.

8. *The GOI's approach to PSU disinvestment* : As a part of the Common Minimum Programme (CMP), the GOI decided not to privatise profit-making PSUs. Instead the GOI decided to give full managerial and commercial (financial) autonomy to successful, and profit-making PSUs which were operating in a competitive environment. Each proposal for privatisation would be considered on a transparent and case-by-case basis. The Navratnas would continue to remain in the public sector. However, they would be permitted to raise resources from the capital market.

9. *Navratnas* : In 1997 the GOI identified nine profit-making PSUs which were found to have the resources and the capacity to emerge as global giants, viz., IOC, ONGC, HPCL, IPCL, VSNL, BHEL, SAIL and NTPC. These were called Navratnas. However, due to political opposition, the GOI could not pursue its policy of disinvestment in these and other profit-making enterprises.

10. *National investment fund (NIF)* : Another notable aspect of the GOI's public sector reforms was the creation of the National Investment Fund (NIF). The objective was to deposit the sales proceeds of disinvestment of the GOI's stake in PSUs.

11. *Debate on disinvestment* : There is on going debate in India on disinvestment vs. privatisation. The GOI's decision, however, is tilted in favour of privatisation.

KEY TERMS

Navratnas
Strategic sale
Exit policy
Golden handshake
Public sale of share

Disinvestment
Privatisation
Commanding heights of the economy
Professionalism in management

Mixed economy
Balanced regional development
Asset valuation
Nationall Investment fund
Industrial sickness

ASSIGNMENTS

1. Comment on the role of public sector enterprising in India as specified in the Second Industrial Policy Resolution (1956).
2. Briefly discuss the role of PSUs in India in the context of the present industrial policy (1991).
3. What is meant by disinvestment of public sector units? What are the different methods of disinvestment of such units?
4. What is the difference between privatisation of PSUs and disinvestment of such units? Comment on the GOI's policy toward such units since July 1991.
5. Outline the various reform measures adopted by the GOI for improving the operational efficiency (performance) of PSUs.
6. (a) What is strategic sale?
   (b) Which PSUs are called Navratnas and why?
7. Briefly explain why the GOI decided to go for disinvestment of PSUs.
8. Discuss the causes of poor performance of PSUs in India during the first four decades of planning (1951-91).

41A PSU DISINVESTMENT—ENDEMIC PROBLEMS

A Commentary by Professor Alok Ray, IIM, Calcutta

Public sector units across the globe are suffering from three major problems:

1. Soft Budget Constraint

Unlike private companies, many loss making PSUs are kept afloat by either direct goverment subsidy or by direct bank credit from state-owned banks. In the past, even 'sick' private companies have been taken over by the state, out of political consideration, which has been a major factor behind the near bankruptcy of many state governments and some public sector banks.

2. Multiple Objectives

PSUs were expected to promote social objectives such as generating guaranteed employment, taking industries to backward areas, buying inputs from other PSUs to support them, providing output at "reasonable" prices to people and so on. Their performance was not to be judged by commercial profitability.

Apart from the confusion created in the minds of managers as to what goals to be given priority, it provided convenient excuses to hide inefficiencies.

3. Multiple Control Authorities

The public sector manager is subject to control and scrutiny by different ministries, the Bureau of Public Enterprise, various parliamentary committees and investigating agencies. As a result, no bold decisions can be taken on modernisation, liberalisation or technological upgradation. The promotion and career prospects of the managers are not usually linked to his dynamism or entrepreneurship and often have more to do with keeping his political bosses in good humour.

The basic problems lie in the nature of ownership and the consecutive incentives. State ownership is ownership by an impersonal legal entity called state. Often, state-owned units are headed and managed by politicians and civil servants, rather than professional managers, as chairmen or managing directors.

Thus it is difficult to expect the PSUs with the above mentioned endemic problems to maintain their profit records in a highly competitive regime, and hence it is advisable for the government to sell them fast while they are still making profits, and the proceeds could be earmarked for specific development projects.

It is advisable to sell the profit making PSUs such as HPCL and BPCL, since no one would be willing to buy the loss making ones or the 'junk' ones first, whereas there are people still willing to buy the "family silver" like HPCL and BPCL at good prices before it loses its shine.

As for the junk PSUs, many of them have been sick for long. Given the opposition from the government, trade unions and other interests, and the long legal process for liquidation, no one wants to come forward to buy these perennial loss-makers.

Secondly, the government should sell the profit making PSUs to the private strategic investors because selling to a large number of widely dispersed individuals would mean that effective management and control would remain in the ministry's hand and nothing basically will change. Block sale of shares to public financial institutions would not change the basic quality of management either.

It is only by selling controlling interests to one major private investor who has the funds and the expertise to manage, and, if necessary, reconstruct the company that the government can hope to get the possible price. An investor would be willing to pay the maximum only when he gets effective control, and that sets the market price.

However, it is feared that strategic sales would lead to private monopolies. If an existing player such as Reliance buys a controlling interest in HPCL or BPCL, the chances of a private monopoly increase.

In today's world, a large number of players are not needed to maintain competition. Even two or three players can do it, for instance the Coke-Pepsi or the Indian Airlines-Jet-Sahara situations. Finally, the government's job is put in place independent regulators to curb anti-competition practices. Hence, the chances of creating a private monopoly in the present cases in India are slim.

It is however, worrying to think about what the Government would do with the divestment proceeds. If the government uses the money to maintain its consumption expenditure rather than to retire past high-cost loans or invest in creating physical and social infrastructure, it would just be postponing the day of reckoning by trying to sweep the fiscal mess under the carpet.

One practical problem could be earmarking of divestment proceeds for specific development projects, particularly in the regions where some people lose jobs as a result of privatisation. If the people of the region can clearly see that the new schools, hospitals or drinking water facilities are being built with these funds, then the political opposition would be less while, at the same time, the funds can be utilised in a productive manner.

CHAPTER 42

Industrial Sickness in India

The fault, dear Brutus, is not in our stars—but in ourselves.	William Shakespear *Julius Caesar*

PREVIEW

The health of the industrial sector largely determines the strength of an economy. Industrial sickness is a symptom of ill- health of the economy. Unfortunately, one of the major problems of India's industrial growth is the growing incidence of sickness, which leads to huge waste of natural, human and financial resources, even when the country faces the problem of resource scarcity. An industrial unit is treated as sick if it has incurred financial losses for past several years due to poor performance and has defaulted in its debt repayment obligations.

DEFINITION

A sick industrial unit is defined as an industrial company (being a company registered for not less than seven years) which has at the end of any financial year accumulated losses equal to or exceeding its entire *net worth* and has also suffered cash losses in such financial year and the financial year preceding such financial year. The RBI has defined a sick unit as one "which has incurred a cash loss for one year and is likely to continue incurring losses for the current year as well as in the following year and the unit has an imbalance in financial structure, such as current ratio[2] is less than 1 : 1 and there is worsening trend in debt-equity ratio." The State bank of India has defined a sick unit as one "which fails to generate an internal surplus on a continuous basis and depends for its survival upon frequent infusion of funds." According to the Sick Industrial Companies Act (SICA), 1985, as amended in 1992, a registered industrial company which has been in existence for at least 5 years can be declared as sick if it has, at the end of any financial year, accumulated losses equal to or exceeding its net worth.

1. Net worth refers to paid-up capital *plus* free reserves.
2. Current ratio is the ratio of a firm's current assets to its current liabilities (that is, its short-term loans and trade debts). The ratio is used as an indicator of a company's ability to pay its debt on time, and thus of its liquidity.

Criteria of Sickness of a Small-Scale Unit

The criteria of sickness for a small unit are different. A small-scale industrial (SSI) unit is treated as sick if it has (i) incurred a cash loss in the previous accounting year and was likely to continue with losses in the current year, and in addition, its cumulative cash losses are equal to 50% or more of its peak net worth during the last five years and (ii) if it has defaulted in paying four instalments of interest consecutively.

According to the Development Commissioner, a small-scale industrial (SSI) unit becomes sick if its:

(a) capacity utilisation is less than 50% of the maximum achieved in the past five years[1].

(b) there has occurred more than 50% erosion of net worth; and

(c) the unit has remained close for more than six months.

Symptoms of Sickness

In short, the main symptoms of industrial sickness are unbalanced financial structure, erosion of the bulk of its net worth, lack of generation of internal surplus, and underutilisation of capacity. In addition, the survival of the unit depends on fresh injection of funds on a regular basis.

The Incidence of Industrial Sickness

One of the most serious problems faced by India's industrial economy is the growing incidence of sickness. Undoubtedly, it is mater of serious concern not only for the shareholders and creditors of the sick unit, but also for the society. Sickness exists both in the large-scale sector as also in SSI units. Huge amounts of bank resources remain locked up in sick units. The problem of growing industrial sickness surfaced even before the adoption of the new economic policy of liberalisation, privatisation and globalisation (LPG) by the GOI in July 1991. The number of sick SSI units increased from 23,149 in December 1980 to 218,828 in March 1990 and to 306,221 in March 1999. Then it gradually declined to 114,132 in Mach 2007 and to 85,187 in March 2008.

Table 42.1 gives detailed information about the number of sick units in both the SSI and non SSI sectors as also the total outstanding bank credit in such units.

Table 42.1: Industrial Sickness—March 2008

Category	Number of units	Outstanding Bank Credits
1. SSI units	85,187	3,083
2. Non-SSI units (large and medium)	4,454	32,283
Total	89,641	35,366

Source: *Statistical Outline of India* (TECS): 2012-13, p.68

We see from Table 42.1 that even if the number of large and medium sick units in the non-SSI sector is much smaller than that in SSI units, the outstanding bank credit in the former far exceeds that in the latter.

As on March 31,2008, outstanding bank credit in 4,455 non-SSI industrial units was Rs. 32,283 crores. The major portion of bank credit remained blocked in five industries, namely, textiles, engineering, electrical, chemicals and iron and steel.

The incidence of industrial sickness continued to increase over the 20-year period 1980 to 1999. And sickness has been growing faster in SSI units than in large and medium-scale sectors. Since then the incidence has fallen. At the end of March 2000, there were 309,013 sick units. It gradually came

1. This is a case of incipient sickness.

down to 118,128 on March 31 2007. Of this 114,132 were in the SSI sector and 3,992 were in the non-SSI sector.

THE NATURE AND CAUSES OF INDUSTRIAL SICKNESS

Competition ensures the survival of the fittest. It is both a boom and a bane. It promotes efficient enterprises and helps them to survive and grow. But it hurts weak industrial units and makes them inefficient and sick. Since 1982-83, the GOI started liberalising its industrial policy, approved more foreign collaboration agreements (financial or technical or both) as a result industrial houses became bigger and bigger and started enjoying economies of scale. So consumers derived the benefits of lower price and wider choice. But due to growing intensity of competition, many weak firms became sick and had to struggle for survival. The worse suffers had to adopt the exit option. After all, the neglect of indirect effects is the common source of all fallacies.

Three Types of Sickness

Industrial sickness is of three types:

(a) **exogenous sickness** which arises due to external factors which are beyond the control of management;

(b) **endogenous sickness** which arises from non-viability of projects (largely due to lack of feasibility studies); and

(c) **self-created sickness** which arises due to managerial incompetence and inappropriate policies pursued by promoters deliberately to siphon off the assets and properties of the concern and to avoid repayment of loans taken from banks and public financial institutions.

Some cunning industrialists buy some losing or closed down concerns by giving the displaced workers a ray of hope just to pursue their own interests. There are so many instances of unscrupulous promoters who often adopt fraudulent practices to start a concern to create a good public image. But sooner or later, they run away with the funds acquired from public financial institutions by making their units unvaible and sick after some time.

Causes of Industrial Sickness

There are both internal and external causes of industrial sickness. The two sets of causes operate jointly to create some sort of spreading vicious circle. These causes may be briefly discussed.

A. External Causes

The external causes of industrial sickness are the following:

(i) *Economy-wide recession* : A sudden slowdown of economic activity affects the performance of individual firms, more so when demand forecasts go wrong. In fact, deficiency of demand is the main cause of industrial sickness.

(ii) *High prices of inputs* : When costs of production are high and the realisation of sales revenue is low, an industrial unit cannot survive for long. This happens due to new type of scissors crisis — rise in the prices of inputs such as fuel and energy due to adverse supply shock and a fall in the prices of finished products due to competitive pressure and easing of supply.

In panel (a) of Fig. 42.1, we see that due to leftward shift of the supply curve, the price of crude oil rises from P_0 to P_1, and this raises the cost of production of a competitive firm. But in panel (b), we see that due to rightward shift of the supply curve, the price of finished products falls from P_0 to P_1.

(iii) *Non-availability of raw materials* : When raw materials are not available as and when required or the materials are not of acceptable quality, some industrial units have to suspend production from time to time. This is because different production processes are linked with one another. If the production department cannot function, the packaging department will also be functionless.

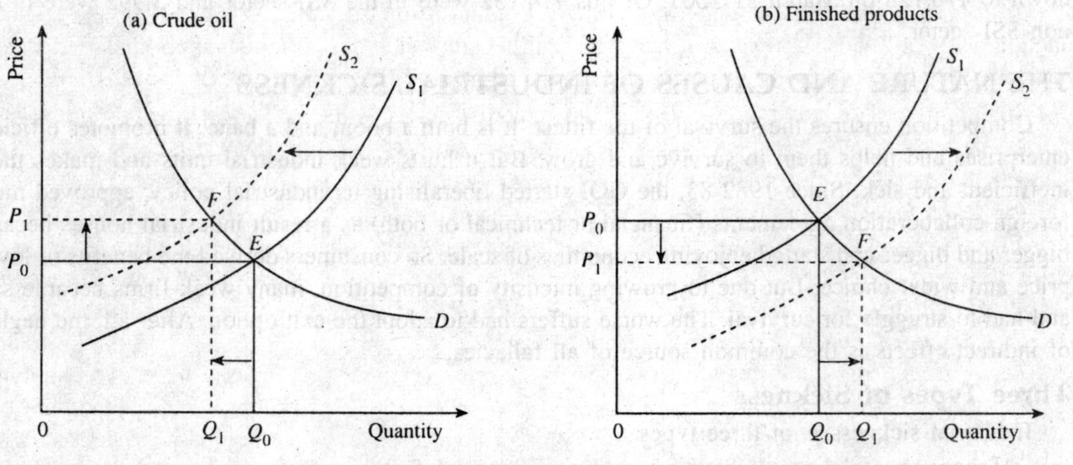

Fig. 42.1: Diverse Price Movements

(iv) *Changes in government policies* : Frequent changes in government policies affect a firm's long term production, financial and marketing plans and programme. Even viable units are likely to be sick due to changes in government policies regarding taxation, industrial licensing, taxation and imports. In truth, the GOI's policy of import liberalisation since 1991 has made many small scale units sick.

(v) *Infrastructural deficiency* : Inadequate availability of infrastructural facilities is one of the main causes of industrial sickness. No industrial unit can remain viable in the face of power shortage and non-availability of adequate transport facilities.

B. Internal Causes

Some of the internal factors leading to industrial sickness are the following:

(i) *Lack of project viability* : An industrial unit becomes sick when it is made operational without making a proper feasibility study. Without such study it is not possible to make a comprehensive appraisal of a project's economic, financial and technical viability.

(ii) *Adverse industrial relations situation* : No industrial unit can function smoothly and efficiently if it faces constant labour trouble. If management cannot motivate workers by giving proper incentives and cannot impose discipline on them, labor productivity is bound to fall. The main reason for this is that workers do not develop a sense of involvement and belonging in their organisation. They often adopt go-slow tactics. At other times strong and powerful trade unions lead to sudden work stoppages.

(iii) *Choice of wrong production techniques* : Most SSI units do not take the help of professional people in installing the right type of machinery and equipment. If the machines are found to be defective or unsuitable, losses are inevitable due to frequent work stoppages or production of defective items which cannot be sold in the market and the end result is financial loss and the consequent sickness.

(iv) *Wrong product line policy* : An industrial unit may become sick due to rapid technological progress which makes its product obsolete. Since there is no much demand for such a product, the market for this product reaches the saturation point sooner or later. An industrial unit becomes sick when it does not change its product-mix to meet the changing pattern of consumer demand. A company achieves long-term viability only when its product line policy is such that it drops an old product (which has become obsolete and the market for which has reached the saturation point). At the same time, it has to develop new products to remain viable.

(v) *Wrong location* : If an industrial unit is located at a wrong place, which has no proximity either to the market for its products or the supply of its inputs, its operations may remain suspended at times. So its costs will increase and it will gradually become unviable.

(vi) ***Lack of finance*** **:** Adequate and timely availability of finance is essential for the smooth functioning of an industrial unit. An industrial unit becomes sick due to non-availability of adequate finance or due to its inability to get finance at the right time (i.e., exactly when it needs is) .

(vii) ***Inappropriate capital structure*** **:** If the capital structure (which refers to the appropriate mix of fixed capital and viable capital) of an industrial unit appears to be unsound or inappropriate, say due to delayed construction or operation of a project, there will be cost overruns or huge borrowing. This will spell disaster for the company.

(viii) ***Managerial problems*** **:** Perhaps the proximate cause of industrial sickness is lack of professionalism in management or lack of experience of existing managers. In fact, the existence of hierarchial management results in inefficiency. Most managers are conservative in their outlook and treat organisational change and development with suspicion or apprehension. So they do not introduce necessary changes in methods of production by using modern (improved or sophisticated) technology or cannot introduce modern marketing methods due to lack of knowledge. They cannot motive employees through team work. They cannot build confidence of others since they take decisions on an *ad hoc* and autocratic basis. In fact, mismanagement by private business persons has been the main cause of industrial sickness.

(ix) ***Created (man-made) sickness*** **:** Sometimes entrepreneurs deliberately make their organisations sick for getting various types of concessions from the government or aid from financial institutions.

Thus industrial sickness, like human disease, has many causes. However, these causes are not mutually exclusive. It occurs due to a number of reasons or a combination of several inter-related factors.

GOVERNMENT POLICY TOWARD SICKNESS

Various of measures have been taken by the GOI to tackle the problem of industrial sickness. The importance of detection of sickness at the incipient stage has been emphasised by the RBI. The policy framework in respect of measures to deal with the problem of industrial sickness has been laid down in the guidelines issued on October 1981 (which were subsequently modified in February 1982) for giving necessary guidance to administrative ministries of the Central Government, State Governments and financial institutions.

The salient features of these guidelines are the following:

(a) The administrative ministries in the Government will have specific responsibility for prevention and remedial action in relation to sickness in industrial sector within their respective charges. They will have a central role in monitoring sickness and co-ordinating action for revival and rehabilitation of sick units. In suitable cases, they will also establish standing committees for major industrial sectors where sickness is widespread:

(b) The financial institutions will strengthen the monitoring system so that it is possible to take corrective action on time to prevent incipient sickness. They will obtain periodical returns from the assisted units and from the Directors nominated by them on the Boards of such units. These will be analysed by the Industrial Development Bank of India and results of such analyses conveyed to the financial institutions concerned and the Government.

(c) The financial institutions and banks will initiate necessary corrective action for a sick or an incipient sick unit on the basis of a diagnostic study. In case of growing sickness, the financial institutions will also consider taking of management responsibility where they are confident of restoring a unit to health. The Ministry of Finance will have to issue suitable guidelines for management;

(d) Where the banks and financial institutions are unable to prevent sickness or ensure revival of a sick unit, they will deal with their outstanding dues to the unit in accordance with the normal banking procedures. However, before doing so, they will report the matter to the Government which will decide whether the unit should be nationalised or whether any other alternative — including workers' participation in management — can revive the undertaking.

(e) Where it is decided to nationalise the undertaking, its management may be taken over under the provisions of the Industries (Development and Regulation) Act, 1951, for a period of six months to enable the Government to take necessary steps for nationalisation.

(f) Finally the industrial undertakings presently being managed under the provisions of the Industries (Development and Regulation) Act, 1951, will also be dealt with in accordance with the above principles.

Concessions

The Government has also provided certain concessions to assist revival of sick units without direct intervention. (i) *Prima facie*, the Government has amended the Income-tax Act in 1977 by addition of Section 72A by which tax benefit can be given to healthy units when they take over the sick units by amalgamation, with a view to reviving them. The tax benefit is in the form of carry forward of the accumulated business losses and unprovided depreciation of the sick companies by the healthy companies after amalgamation. (ii) A scheme for provision of margin money to sick units in the small-scale sector at soft terms to enable them to obtain necessary funds from banks and financial institutions to implement their revival scheme has been introduced from January 1, 1982. (iii) In addition, financial assistance in the form of long-term equity up to Rs. 15 lakhs to units with a project cost not exceeding Rs. 10 lakhs at a nominal service charge of 1% is available to potentially viable sick SSI units from the National Equity Fund.

Establishment of BIFR

The Central Government has set up a Board for Industrial and Financial Reconstruction (BIFR) with effect from 12 January, 1987 in pursuance of enactment of the Sick Industrial Companies (Special Provisions) Act, 1985. This is a major step for intervening at an early stage and detecting, preventing, as well as taking ameliorative, remedial and such other measures which need to be taken with respect to sick and potentially viable companies.

The role of the Board for Industrial and Financial Reconstruction (BIFR) needs a relook in the face of a steep rise in the number of industries turning sick. The BIFR was constituted to facilitate the revival of industries deemed sick. When an industry turns sick, the BIFR acts as an operating agency (generally the lead financial institution having the largest loan exposure among the creditors) to devise a revival strategy proposal.

Progress in the right (proper) disposal of sick company cases registered with BIFR has been slow on account of the conflicting interests between the companies and the creditors (banks and financial institutions, government bodies/agencies) and certain lacunae in the SICA Act. The rehabilitation schemes met with 40-45% failure, as a result of which many of the cases had to be reopened.

The rate of registration/sickness increased substantially during 1997-98 due to (a) the recessionary trends prevalent in industry, (b) poor financial market conditions, and (c) the tough stance taken by banks/financial institutions (FIs) towards defaulters/potentially sick companies under their non-performing assets (NPAs) accounts for rescheduling of repayments, etc.

The problem appears even more acute if we take note of potentially sick BIFR companies, as also the NPAs of FIs and banks. In fact, the NPAs of banks and others have continued to rise.

Upto 1997-98 the outstanding bank credit against sick companies has reached an abnormal proportion of over Rs. 23,658 crores, in March 2000. Over 15 lakh workers have been affected by companies turning sick.

The Setting Up of IRBI (IIBI)

The Industrial Reconstruction Bank of India (IRBI) set up in 1985 has initiated various steps for checking the growth of industrial sickness and helping in industrial revival. From April 1997 the name of IRBI has been changed to Industrial Investment Bank of India (IIBI). By March 2000, cumulative financial assistance sanctioned and disbursed by it stood at Rs. 10,090 crores and Rs. 7,353 crores, respectively.

A significant measure taken during 1986 was the setting up of Small Industries Development Fund (SIDF) in the IDBI. This was meant to provide special financial assistance to the small-scale sector. The Fund would be used for providing refinancing assistance not only for development, expansion and modernisation, but also for the rehabilitation of the small-scale sick industries.

Modernisation Fund

The Government has set up two funds, namely the Textile Modernisation Fund and the Jute Modernisation Fund, for modernisation of the textiles' and jute sectors. Under these two funds, assistance is provided not only to the healthy units for modernisation at 11.5% rate of interest, but also to sick but potentially viable units. Special loans are given to the weak units for meeting a part of the promoters' contribution.

Goswami Committee Report

The Committee on Industrial Sickness and Corporate Restructuring under the chairpersonship of Dr. Omkar Goswami submitted its report in July 1993. The main recommendations of the Committee with respect to sick companies are the following:

(a) For early detection of sickness the definition of sickness should be changed to: (i) default of 180 days or more on repayment of loans to term lending institutions, and (ii) irregulatities in cash credits or working capital for 180 days or more.

(b) The Urban Land (Ceiling and Regulation) Act, 1976 had to be unended improve generation of internal resources of sick companies.

(c) The BIFR should be empowered for speedier restructuring, winding-up and sale of assets of companies.

(d) A sick company's own reference of BIFR should be voluntary, not mandatory.

SICA Amendment Act, 1994

The modifications brought in the Sick Industrial Companies (Special Provisions) Act, 1985 by the 1994 Amendment Act pertain to the changes in the definition of SICA, expansion of the term *operating agency*, clarification that an enquiry as to sickness shall be deemed to have commenced on receipt of a reference by the BIFR, complete in all respects, scope for reverse merger, "deemed consent" after the lapse of 120 days, "single window concept" for release of funds by banks/financial institutions to the sick company, monitoring implementation of sanctioned revival schemes by BIFR, holding on operations by financial institutions/banks/State Governments, empowering the Central Government, State Governments, banks, institutions, etc., to report cases of potential sickness, etc.

In the definition of sickness the period for the registration of an industrial company as sick has been reduced from seven to five years. Furthermore, the condition of incurring cash losses during the preceding two years has been waived. This means that an industrial company would be considered a sick industrial company once its net worth is completely eroded and has been registered for not less than five years.

The Companies (Second Amendment) Act, 2002

This Act, passed in Dec 2002, replaced the Sick Industrial Companies (special provisions) Act, 1985. The new Act redefined a sick industrial company. According to the Act, a sick industrial company means one which has (i) the accumulated losses in any financial year which are equal to 50% or more of its average net worth during four years immediately preceding such financial year; or (ii) failed to repay its debt within any three consecutive quarters on demand made in writing for its repayment by a creditor or creditors of such company.

National Company Law Tribunal

The Act provides for the setting up of a National Company Law Tribunal (NCLT) to perform the functions of BIFR for revival and rehabilitation of sick companies. The BIFR will be woundup.

Reference to NCLT by a Sick Company

In case an industrial company becomes sick, its Board of Directors will have to make a reference to NCLT and prepare scheme for its revival and rehabilitation. This is no doubt step in the right direction. In truth, in the new atmosphere of liberalisation and openess which has emerged during the post-reform period there is clear and strong case in favour of liquidition of sick industrial companies rather than their revival and rehabilitation.

SUGGESTED REMEDIES

Some of the effective measures which may be taken for revival of sick units are technical help, professional counselling and improved management. Also, the role of professionals and experienced management becomes more important in times of sickness.

In addition to technical and professional consultants, no sick industry will ever be able to recuperate without sufficient, timely and soft finance. Bankers are the key to the problem. The role of the bankers needs to be redefined and a new direction needs to be given to support, aid and lift sick industrial units from the situations that befall them. It is also the level of service and support in terms of financial advice, assistance in related matters of insurance, release of hypothecated assets and timely finance.

The Sick Industrial Companies (Special Provisions) Bill, 1997, passed by Lok Sabha, introduced encouraging changes. It suggested that a time-bound procedure was to be adopted within which the scheme has to be sanctioned and BIFR would play the role of a mediator and not a court.

Technical obsolescence and financial mismanagement are also important factors that lead to industrial sickness. As per the new provisions, an opportunity will be given to get an unanimous consent to a scheme from all concerned, failing which secured creditors will attempt to form a scheme and, if all these fail, the undertaking would be sold off. Only if it is not possible to do that, the BIFR may order winding up of the company.

KEY POINTS

1. ***Definition of industrial sickness*** **:** A sick industrial unit is defined as an industrial company (being a company registered for not less than seven years) which has at the end of any financial year accumulated losses equal to or exceeding its entire *net worth* and has also suffered cash losses in such financial year and the financial year preceding such financial year.

2. ***Symptoms of sickness*** **:** The main symptoms of industrial sickness are unbalanced financial structure, erosion of the bulk of its net worth, lack of generation of internal surplus, and underutilisation of capacity. In addition, the survival of the unit depends on fresh injection of funds on a regular basis.

3. ***Causes of sickness*** **:** There are both internal and external causes of industrial sickness. There are: (i) economy-wide recession; (ii) high prices of inputs; (iii) wrong location; (iv) lack of finance; (v) inappropriate capital structure; (vi) managerial problems; (vii) created (man-made) sickness.

4. ***Government policy*** **:** Various type of measures have been taken by the GOI to tackle the problem of industrial sickness. The Government has also provided certain concessions to assist revival of sick units without direct intervention. The Central Government has set up a Board for Industrial and Financial Reconstruction (BIFR) with effect from 12 January, 1987 in pursuance of enactment of the Sick Industrial Companies (Special Provisions) Act, 1985. The Industrial Reconstruction Bank of India (IRBI) set up in 1985 has initiated various steps for checking the growth of industrial sickness and helping in industrial revival. The Government has set up two funds, namely the Textile Modernisation Fund and the Jute Modernisation Fund, for upgradation and modernisation of the textile and jute sectors.

KEY TERMS

Sick industrial unit
Net worth
Current ratio
Exogeneous sickness
Endogeneous sickness
Self-created sickness
Single window
Incipient sickness
Exit option

ASSIGNMENTS

1. What is industrial sickness? What are the causes?
2. Briefly discuss the internal and external causes of grossing industrial sickness in India. Suggest remedial measures.
3. Define a sick industrial unit. Comment on the incidence of industrial sickness in India.
4. What are the three different types of industrial sickness? What measures have been adopted by the Government of India to reduce the incidence of such sickness?

CHAPTER 43

Consumer Protection

> *Despite unanimous acceptance of Adam Smith's dictum that "consumption is the end purpose of all production", mainstream economics has taken little note of consumerism and its highly visible institutions. The few exceptions would include a new literature on the economics of information, informationaly imperfect markets, issues of regulation and deregulation, and the economics of safety.*
>
> E. S. Maynes in The McGraw-Hill *Encyclopedia of Economics* (ed.) D. Greenwald

PREVIEW

Now-a-days we find growing consumer awareness about their legitimate rights. Consumer protection movement was launched in the USA by Ralph Nadar in view of the exploitation of consumers as buyers of goods and services as compared to all powerful manufacturers (producers) and traders (sellers) and the powerlessness of consumers to do much about it. Then the movement it spread virtually to most parts of the world. In a market-based economy, where firms compete with one another to sell goods and services to consumers, the former are supposed to promote the interests of the latter in the best possible way. But in reality consumers are more often than not exploited by firms through the adoption of various unfair, unethical and restrictive trade practices. Due to aggressive advertisement by firms and lack of knowledge and bargaining power of consumers the concept of 'consumer sovereignty' has largely lost its relevance and has yielded place to the concept of 'producer sovereignty'. Now producers do not produce those things which consumers are eager to buy. Instead consumers are induced to buy those goods which are offered for sale by producers and promoted through advertising and other selling techniques.

Thus even in a free market economy, the powerless consumer requires legal protection of his legitimate rights. Even in centrally managed (planned) economy, where the state is very powerful, the consumers are often denied of their legitimate rights. So even in such economies they need protection.

This is an age of industrialisation. Most consumers buy goods and services on the basis of false advertising which means giving incorrect information to buyers. Through such advertising firms exaggerate the attributes and quality of the goods and services which they offer for sale. But buyers often find that the goods or not well to the original specification of sellers. So to protect the consumers, legal action against erring vendors is absolutely essential. Otherwise consumers cannot be protected from the exploitation and deception by the greedy and dishonest manufacturers and traders. Due to this realisation of the virtual powerlessness and helplessness of consumers in 1985 the United Nations General Assembly recommended to its member States to adopt corrective measures to prevent the unethical business practices and thus to protect the legitimate rights of consumers. The resolution required all member States to set up appropriate agencies for adjudication of consumer claims so as to create a proper environment for consumer protection. To be more specific, the UN recommended the setting up of consumer councils with a view to redressing the genuine complaints, grievances and legitimate claims of consumers.

CONSUMER RIGHTS

Since most people in industrially advanced countries are literate and knowledge they are quite conscious of their rights. By contrast, in India and other developing countries most consumers are poor, illiterate and quite ignorant of their legal rights. For this reason manufacturers and suppliers often exploit them by adopting unfair and restrictive trade practices. However, with the gradual spread of education among almost all sections of society in India, consumers are becoming more and more aware of their legal rights. And the Government of India has set up several consumer forums or councils for redressal of the complaints and grievances of consumers as also for peaceful settlement of their claims in case of loss or damage. And more and more consumers who had been deceived or exploited in the past are now approaching such organisations for necessary guidance, help and assistance.

In this context we have to know about the right of consumer.

Six important consumer rights are the following:

1. The Right to be Heard

If a consumer has any complaint or grievance regarding goods and services he (she) has the legal right to be heard. This means that his complaint and grievance has to receive due attention and genuine (and sympathetic) consideration at an appropriate forum.

2. The Right to Product Safety

A consumer is entitled to protection of his health and safety from a good or a service which he buys. So producers or manufacturers should not supply products which are unsafe or cause health hazards.

3. The Right against Exploitation

A consumer has the right to protect himself from unfair trade practices and exploitation by greedy and dishonest (unscrupulous) traders who charge exorbitant prices of goods or services, even by violating legal barriers.

4. The Right to Information

Consumer protection laws specify that a consumer should be given correct and full information about the quality of goods that he buys. This obviously includes information about the ingredients of the product, freshness as also the side-effects which are likely arise due to the consumption of the product[1]. The same thing is true for any essential service.[2]

5. The Right to Choose

In some countries sellers are under the legal obligation to offer a wide range of products (goods and services) to consumers to choose from. By deliberately offering a narrow range of goods and services firms often restrict their choice.

---

1. For example, on every packet of medicine information is given about the maximum retail price or, in short, MRP (inclusive of all taxes), the date of manufacturing and the date of expiry. Similarly on every packet of cigarettes or every bottle of wine there is statutory warning that cigarette smoking is a cause of cancer or that consumption of alcohol is injurious to health.
2. For example, in the letterhead of a doctor (medical practitioner), his (her) registration number has to be printed.

6. The Right to Get Redress

There are legal provisions regarding the redressal of consumers' complaints and grievances about the product offerings and in ease of genuine damage or loss suffered, they should be adequately compensated.

In India the Consumer Protection Act was passed in 1986. It was amended in 2002. In this revised Act, adequate provision has been made for most of the consumer rights mentioned above. [We will discuss the Act in detail later in this chapter]. However before we proceed further, we may briefly discuss the need for consumer protection in a developing country like India.

THE NEED FOR CONSUMER PROTECTION

The sad truth is that in developing countries like India consumers are often denied of their due rights. So they need protection for a number of reasons. These are the following:

1. Reducing Consumer Exploitation

The manufacturers and suppliers often exploit consumers by adopting various unfair and restrictive trade practices. For example, large firms with considerable market power often merge and collude with other firms to restrict output jointly and raise price of even highly essential items such as baby food or life saving drugs[1]. For instance, most drug manufacturers charge exorbitant prices which are much higher than their costs of production. Some pharmaceutical companies even misuse their patent rights to exploit helpless and ignorant consumers. So it is needless to say that consumers need protection from such unfair and restrictive trade practices.

2. False Advertising

False advertising means giving incorrect information to buyers. And through such misleading advertisements, producers deceive the consumers. Consumers often find that the products they have purchased do not meet the original specification of buyers. This means that they have not got their money's worth.

What is worse still through persuasive advertisement, firms take away customers from their rivals by deceiving them. And prices of products rise due to high cost of advertisement.

Excessive and often wasteful advertising enables firms to protect their market shares. But total demand for an industry's product or even its output does not increase. There is just shift of demand from one firm's product to that of another firm (or other firms). So consumers need protection from such deceptive or persuasive advertisement.

3. Controlling Adulteration of Commodities

Another trading practice of suppliers, which is highly injurious to consumers especially in India, is adulteration of commodities. And this practice is quite widespread in India since the law enforcement machinery (agency) is weak. Such adulteration takes place at almost all stages of production and distribution of a good. For example, stone particles are found even in packed biscuits or in pulses. This often leads to tooth injury or even breaking of a portion of a tooth. This practice of mixing small pebbles and dust with wheat and coarse grains such as jowar, bajra and maize to increase weight is quite common. Similarly sand is mixed with cement and leaves and barks of some trees and mixed with tea leaves. In addition, vanapati is often mixed with ghee, or green banana with butter and margarine. All such practices of food adulteration are not only hazardous to human health but pose a threat to human life. What is most distressing is that many patients die every year due to consumption of spurious drugs. Needless to say, consumers need legal protection from these unethical trade practices.

4. Use of Short Weights

The use of short weights particularly in the market for vegetables and fish is quite common. This is more widely practised in small areas. Consumers need protection from the government in all such cases. Only the government can force the traders to use correct weights and measures.

1. This is done by forming tacit cartels.

For all these reasons the consumer protection movement, called consumerism gradually gained momentum in the past four decades or so. This movement has forced the government to pass laws to protect the consumers. We may now briefly discuss the meaning of consumerism before we pass on to important methods of consumer protection.

CONSUMERISM

Consumerism refers to the social movement which seeks to augment the rights and powers of consumers. The objective is to protect the consumers from unfair and unhealthy restrictive trade practices by manufacturers and distributers, wholesalers and retailers. It may be defined as the monitoring and control of those activities of both private and public organisations which are designed to protect individuals from practices which impinge upon their rights as consumers.

There are two views on consumerism — those of moralists and activists. According to moralists, consumerism is the 'articulation' of consumer discontent and the 'furtherance' of corrective measures. It is a diverse and evolving social movement seeking to enhance the economic well-being and political power of consumers.

By contrast, activists such as Ralph Nadar have a narrower focus, tending to restrict consumerism to efforts directed toward government intervention on behalf of consumers.

Consumerism and the Price Mechanism

Consumerism attracts the attention of economists because it responds to the failures and helps to improve the functioning of the price mechanism that lie at the heart of the modern market-based economy.

Fundamentally the price system is a system of motivation and error correction. A price rise signals that the economic agent is performing well and should do more of it; a price fall, the opposite. The main motivation for responding to the signal is self-interest in the form of high wages, rent, profits. Over time, the market economy becomes a system of error correction.

The organisations of the consumer movement improve the functioning of the price mechanism in several ways. First, they provide information that helps consumers make better choices for basic necessities.

Second, consumer organisations can express discontent in a strong and commanding way. For instance, the Consumers' Guidance Society of India seeks to give protection against food and drug adulteration. Similar efforts abound in many countries.

Third, within businesses, consumer affairs professionals seek to anticipate and avoid consumer problems and to respond quickly and effectively to problems that occur. The nature of business response is indicated by the activities in which the consumer affairs professionals engage: complaint resolution (their dominant activity), consumer education, employee training, monitoring consumerism, their firms' response to consumeralism, their firms' advertising and consumer policies. The information feedback to firms from these activities clarifies the market signal and thus improve the functioning of markets.

The Causes of Consumerism

Consumerism can be more than just widely shared feelings of consumers that they are ill-served by their economy (i.e., their interest are not promoted in a desirable way). In its most vigorous form, it produces outrage, sometimes stemming from the abuses of power by sellers, a situation which still holds in many developing countries. Often this discontent arises from market failures, arising from (1) unsafe products, (2) dishonest promises, misrepresentation, deceptive advertising, fraud, failures of communication between buyer and seller, (3) performance failure ("it does not work" or does not work as it should, e.g., repairs that are done badly or not at all), delivery failures (not delivered, delivered late, or not delivered as specified), (4) price gouging, (5) all these, amplified by the rising expectations of consumers. Even this list of causes is incomplete when we recognise the frustrations arising from the information problems which consumers face in assessing quality, understanding complex products and services (e.g., life insurance), even in conceptualising their problems as consumers. Finally, most consumers have yet to recognise and learn to deal with the near zero correlation of price and quality in local consumer markets.

It is difficult to organise consumers, because consumer interest is a 'thin interest', approved by many, while primary to hardly anyone. It stands in strong contrast to the producer interest of, say, farmers, which is primary, commanding strong support.

IMPORTANT METHODS OF PROTECTING THE CONSUMER

Three important ways of protecting the consumer are the following:

1. Imposition of Self-Regulation and Discipline by Manufacturers and Dealers

Perhaps the most effective way of protecting the consumer is through the voluntary imposition of self-regulation and discipline by manufacturers and others involved in the whole chain (or channel) of distribution. If they are self-enlightened, they will pay the needed attention to consumer rights, remembering all the time what Adam Smith said in 1776: "Consumption is the sole end and purpose of all production." In his text, *The Practice of Management* (1954), P.F. Drucker opined that there is no business without a customer. This implies that if consumers are dissatisfied all the time, business firms cannot survive in the long-run.

Profit should be made by enhancing operational efficiency and improving the quality of products rather than by deceiving consumers and exploiting them in various ways. Morality and business ethics demand that the socially responsible producers and distributors do not form cartels and jointly restrict supply to raise prices and exploit the consumers.

Restraint is best exercised voluntarily. Otherwise the government will be forced to pass legislation to protect consumers. Advertising agencies and market organisations have a very important role to play in this respect. However, this is earlier said than done.

2. Formation of Voluntary Organisations of Consumers

In most industrially advanced countries the consumers have organised themselves on a purely voluntary basis and succeeded in forming consumer groups and councils. These groups and councils protect consumer rights in three main ways. These are the following:

1. They supply necessary information with a view to educating consumers on matters which affect their interest(s).

2. They put strong pressure on manufacturers' associations so that manufacturers adopt certain measures which promote consumer interest such as proper labelling of products on which information is printed about the maximum retail price of a product, the nutritional contents of the product, and adverse effects, if any, of the product, as in the case of drugs.

3. They organise consumer protection movements, i.e., movements against the malpractices of manufacturers and traders such as raising prices of products arbitrarily and charging different prices for the same product from different buyers.

In the 1960s and 1970s several voluntary consumer organisations emerged in four metropolitan cities of India, with Delhi and Mumbai taking a lead in the matter. In fact, the whole concept of Super Bazzar, based on cooperative principles, emerged from the resistance given by consumer associations against arbitrary and unannounced price hikes by traders. In this context, mention may be made of an organisation, named 'Common Cause' set up in Delhi which succeeded, to some extent, in protecting the rights of consumers.

In addition, in order to protect the consumers from various types of malpractices of traders, the consumers cooperative movement had been started in India long ago. A consumer cooperative is a voluntary organisation of consumers set up not for protecting but for promoting consumer interests in various ways. These are the following:

(i) *Prima facie*, it has given a fair deal to consumers by opening an opportunity before them to buy certain essential goods and services at less than market prices. This has been possible for two reasons. First cooperatives make bulk purchase on behalf of some members and thus get price concessions. Secondly, they do not seek to maximise profit. It may be noted that in India consumer cooperatives are engaged mainly in distributing certain essential goods at fair prices.

(ii) Moreover since the cooperatives are controlled by insiders, consumers are assured of quality goods and unadulterated products.

(iii) Consumers are not deceived through the use of short weights and measures.

However, in spite of certain good intentions and their best efforts, the voluntary organisations have largely failed to protect consumers and safeguard their legitimate rights. Such societies have grown only in the areas of housing cooperatives.

3. Government Intervention

In both developed and developing countries, the governments have protected consumers by passing various laws. In India the state governments have passed laws relating to cooperative society.

Various other acts have been passed in India from time to time to protect the consumers. In this context mention may be made of (1) Prevention of Food Adulteration Act, 1954, (2) the Essential Commodities Act, 1955, (3) Agricultural Produce (Grading and Marketing) Act, (4) Drugs Control Act, (5) Drugs and Cosmetics Act, (6) Standards of Weights and Measures Act, (7) Drugs and Magic Remedies (Objectional Advertisement Act), (8) Water (Prevention and Control of Pollution) Act, (9) Prevention of Black Marketing and Maintenance of Essential Commodities Act, and (10) Air (Prevention and Control of Pollution) Act.

In addition, an economic legislation, viz., the Monopolies and Restrictive Practices (MRTP) Act was passed in 1969 mainly with a view to creating a competitive environment in the country by controlling monopolies and preventing the formation of mergers by large industrial houses. The second objective of the Act was to protect the consumers by preventing monopolistic and restrictive trade practices. It was thought that expansion of output and the resultant advantage of large-scale production (in the form of economies of scale) in a truely competitive environment would provide benefits to consumers due to lower price and wider choice. In addition, 12B of the MRTP Act has empowered the MRTP Commission to compensate consumers in case of unfair trade practices.

Last, but not the least, the GOI passed the Consumer Protection Act in 1986. Under this Act, consumers enjoy the legal right to approach the appropriate consumer forum or commission set up under the Act to get their complaints redressed. The main provisions of the Act may now be discussed.

THE CONSUMER PROTECTION ACT (1986)

In 1986 the Indian parliament passed the Consumer Protection Act to protect consumer rights, redress consumer complaints and grievances and resolve consumer disputes. Since every person is a consumer of goods and services he (she) expects a fair deal against unfair and restrictive trade practice. The Act applies everywhere in India but not in the State of Jammu and Kashmir. It is a comprehensive legislation and covers all goods and services purchased by the consumers and all sectors — private, public and cooperative. The basic objective of the Act is to protect the intersects of consumers in the best possible way. For achieving this purpose, the Act makes provision for the establishment of Consume Councils and the other authorities for the settlement of consumer disputes and for related matters. It protects the consumers from unfair trade practices and exploitation.

The Consumer Protection Act seeks to protect the following rights of consumers:

(a) the right to be heard and to be assured that consumers' interests are given due consideration at an appropriate forum;

(b) right to seek redressal against unfair, restrictive and unethical trade practices or undue exploitation of consumers; and

(c) right to consumer education.

The Act was amended in 2002. The revised Act makes the following additional provisions:

(d) the right to be assured, wherever possible, of access to a wide variety of goods and services at fair (reasonable) prices;

(e) the right to be informed about the quality, potency, purity standard and prices of goods or services with a view to protecting consumers against unfair trade practices; and

(f) the right to be protected against the making of goods (and services) which are injurious to health and hazardous to human life and tangible assets (property).

Redress Agencies

As per the Consumer Protection Act (1986) the following authorities have been set up for protecting the consumers:

1. Consumer Protection Councils

The Act has made provision for setting up of a Central Consumer Protection Council by the GOI. It has also made provision for the setting up of a State Consumer Council by each state.

The objectives of both the Central and the State Consumer Councils are to protect the rights of consumers and promote their interest as listed above from (a) to (f).

Consumer Disputes Redressal System

The Consumer Protection Act (1986) set up a three-tier consumer disputes redressal system by establishing the following agencies:

1. District Consumer forum in each district of a state (through the State Government)
2. State Consumer Commission in each state (by the state itself) and
3. National Consumer Commission (by the Central Government).

As per the amendment of the Act in 2002, a district forum has been empowered to deal with complaints if the value of good or service and compensation claimed, if any, does not exceed Rs. 20 lakhs. A complaint by a consumer will be filed in a district forum if one of the opposite parties or both reside or carry on business in the same district at the time of filing the complaint.

The State Consumer Commission has been empowered to entertain complaints where the value of goods or services and compensation claimed, if any, exceeds Rs. 20 lakhs but is less than Rs. 1 crore.

Any complaint regarding the values of goods and services and compensation claimed in excess of Rs. 1 crore has to be made to the National Consumer Commission. It has also been empowered to hear appeals against the order of any State Consumer Council. And, in case of necessity, it can call for the records from any State Commission.

Remedial Action

A complaint to a redressal agency in relation to goods sold or delivered or services rendered may be filed by (a) an individual consumer or (b) a group of consumers (having common interest), (c) recognised consumer association and (d) the State or Central Government.

In case of a genuine complaint, the redressal agency will issue an appropriate order to the opposite party. The order may be of any of the following types:

1. to remove the defect, if found genuine, by the appropriate laboratory or testing house in the good(s) in question;
2. to replace defective goods with new (defect-free or flawless) goods;
3. to return to the complainant price of the defective good or payment made by him;
4. to pay compensation to the complainant for the loss suffered by him on the basis of decisions of the redressal agency;
5. to remove the defects or deficiencies in the service rendered to consumers;

6. to prevent unfair or restrictive trade practice or give undertaking in writing not to indulge in such practices in the future;
7. not to supply any hazardous good;
8. to withdraw the hazardous goods being offered for sale; and
9. to compensate the parties concerned for any cost incurred.

Penalties

In case a trader or a person fails to comply with the order of the redressal agency the Consumer Commissions are authorised to impose penalties. While punishment may involve imprisonment for a maximum period of three years, a maximum fine of Rs.10,000 may be imposed. Both may be imposed, in some cases, if considered necessary.

THE CONSUMER PROTECTION AMENDMENT ACT (2002)

As per the Consumer Protection Act (2002), the three redressal agencies have been given powers of a first class judicial magistrate for trial of offences within their respective jurisdictions, with the provision that a lower redressal agency can appeal to a higher one, if necessary. The notable changes made by the amended Act are the following:

1. Restrictive Trade Practices

'Restrictive trade practices' now also include delay in the supply of goods or services and rise in prices between placing orders and taking delivery.

2. Unfair Trade Practices

An advertiser will be held responsible for giving incorrect information to buyers and thus misleading or (misguiding) the consumer. If a buyer finds that a product or a service is not according to the original specification of the seller, then the seller will be held responsible for taking corrective measures at his own cost.

3. Raising the Upper Limit of Compensation

The District Forums have been empowered to deal with cases involving the payment of compensation up to Rs. 20 lakhs. At the same time, the State Consumer Commissions have been empowered to deal with cases involving a maximum compensation of Rs. 1 crore. Finally, the National Consumer commission can deal with cases involving compensation of Rs. 1 crore or even more.

4. Provision for Surviving Representatives of the Complainant

In case of death of the complainant, his (her) surviving legal representatives can file complaints or enjoy an alternable arrangement in place of the existing one as a substitute.

5. Liability of Suppliers for Deceiving Consumers

If it can be proved that any seller has consciously and knowingly supplied a good which is hazardous to life or safety of the public, then he will be liable to pay compensation to the affected parties. In addition, the Act has clearly specified the liability of suppliers of spurious products and services.

6. Redefination of the Term 'Manufacturing'

The term 'manufacturing' has been redefined to include either assembling parts of goods made by others or putting one's own trademark or brand name on any good manufactured by others.

7. Broadening of the Term 'Restrictive Trade Practices'

The term 'restrictive trade practices' has been widened by including such practices as the manipulation of price or conditions of delivery of goods. Such practices also include those practices which affect the flow of supplies of goods in the market such that either undue cost is imposed on the consumers or inconvenience is caused to them. Finally, such practices also include inconvenience caused to consumers by rise in prices due to delay in the delivery of goods and services beyond the period mentioned in the sales agreement (document). Thus we see that the restrictive trade practices have been made more stringent by the Amendment Act (2002).

8. Redefining Unfair Trade Practices

The Amendment Act specifies that misleading or deceptive business practices of both traders and suppliers would be treated as unfair and thus unlawful.

Those who mislead consumers by giving incorrect information or false advertising and induce them to buy goods or services would fall within unfair trade practices and thus would have to face legal consequences, if found guilty.

The Act also covers the unfair treatment of consumers who have suffered by being lured by the schemes offering attractive gifts, concessional prices or some items free of charge as prizes on the basis of the publication of official results of a competitive scheme. The Act makes it obligatory on the part of the sponsors to make correct information regarding the result of a scheme publicly known through newspapers or TV programmes.

An Overall Evaluation of the Consumer Protection Act

The amended Consumer Protection Act is no doubt a very comprehensive piece of legislative inasmuch as it seeks to protect consumers against unfair and exploitative practices of manufacturers, traders and suppliers of various different goods and services. In fact, suppliers of goods and services in knowledge-intensive sectors such as information technology and electronic commerce (e-commerce) are also covered under the Act in order to protect consumer interests as much as possible.

Apart from manufacturers and suppliers of goods, suppliers of insurance and medical services as also of loanable funds (such as lending and recovery of bank loans) are also covered by the Act. Three case examples may now be given in this context.

1. Consumer Protection Act and Medical Practioners

For various acts of negligence such as operating a wrong eye, removing a kidney of a person without his knowledge and consent, leaving foreign elements (such as screw, scissors and cotton in the abdomen of a patient), giving a wrong injection, leading to sudden death of a patient, adequate compensation can be claimed from doctors and hospitals. In addition, penalties can be imposed on them.

2. Consumer Protection Act and Insurance Companies

The Act is also applicable in case of claims against insurance companies. There are instances of several insurance companies (both private and public) delaying mediclaims to the insurers on the flimsy ground that they did not disclose the pre-existing diseases, i.e., disease that they were suffering from before getting insured. In a number of cases consumer commissions have rejected the arguments of insurance companies and have made the insurers liable for the damages and forced them to fulfil the contractual obligation by paying adequate compensation and settling the issue to the (full!) satisfaction of the victims or affected parties.

Consumers Protection act and Recovery of Bank Loans

Many banks make use of the muscle power of hired goons for recovery of loans, often by seizing vehicles. The State Consumer Commissions intervene in such matters and hold banks guilty for any deficiency in service and for indulging in unfair trade practices. Seizing of any vehicle illegally, as has happened many times in the past, amounts to breach of terms of contract of hire purchase and a loan agreement.

Conclusion

Thanks to the effective implementation of the Act an average consumer gets protection in virtually all areas involving sale of goods and services for due consideration. The machinery is effective for a consumer, but awesome to the delinquent trader. Let us hope, with cautious optimism, that with the passage of time, the law will apply with greater force and consumers will get greater and greater protection and will no longer feel helpless.

KEY POINTS

1. *Consumerism* : Consumerism refers to the view that economic life should be organised for the benefit of consumers, rather than producers. Because consumers are individuals and while produces are mostly organised in firms and consumers spread their purchases over a much wider variety of goods and services than most firms produce, consumers are mostly less informed and less organised than producers. Consumerism takes the view that where the interests of consumers and producers are often in conflict with each other, the law should take the side of consumer protection against firms' profits or their workers' job security.

2. *Need for consumer protection* : A consumer needs protection against various types of exploitation and cheating by both producers and traders such as the following:

(i) adulteration of food articles such as vegetable oil, rice, butter, pulse, milk powder and various types of spices,
(ii) supply of poor quality products (both goods and services),
(iii) use of short-weights and measures,
(iv) false advertisement by sellers, i.e., giving wrong information to buyers and making fantastic promises (which sellers cannot fulfil).

3. *Rights of consumers* : Indian consumers have the following rights:

(i) right to safety,
(ii) right to be informed,
(iii) right to choose,
(iv) right to be heard,
(v) right to seek redressal,
(vi) right to education,
(vii) right to basic needs and
(viii) right to healthy environment.

4. *Different ways of protecting consumers* : Consumers are protected in the following ways:

(i) self-regulation by business,
(ii) formation of business associations for promoting consumer literacy,
(iii) formation of consumers' self-help groups and active participation of members,
(iv) setting up of consumers' associations and
(v) government intervention in various ways.

Perhaps self-regulation seems to be the best method of protecting consumers.

5. *Methods of protecting consumers* : Indian consumers are protected through a number of forums and schemes such as the following:

(i) Lok Adalats
(ii) Public Interest Litigation (PIL)
(iii) Redressal Forums
(iv) Consumer Protection Councils
(v) Eco-Mark Scheme
(vi) National Youth Award on Consumer Protection
(vii) Publicity Measures and
(viii) Consumer Welfare Fund.

6. *The existing legal machinery for redressal of consumers' grievances* : The Consumer Protection Act (1986) provided for the setting up of Consumer Disputes Redressal Agencies at three different levels: (i) District level, (ii) State Level, and (iii) National Level.

(i) **District Forum.** One such forum is established by each State Government in each district, for filing complaints in all cases involving goods or services as also the compensation claims not exceeding Rs. 20 lakhs.

(ii) **State Commission.** Such a Commission is set up by the State Government for hearing grievances of consumers in a particular State. In deals with those cases where the value of compensation claimed varies in the range of Rs. 20 lakhs and Rs. 1 crore.

(iii) **National Commission.** Set up by the Central Government, this Commission will hear those complaints whose value is to exceed Rs. 1 crore.

KEY TERMS

Non-governent organisation
District forum
Eco-mark scheme
Right to choose
Consumer protection
National Commission
Lok Adalats
Right to protection
Right to be heard
Consumer awareness
State Commission
Public interest litigation
Right to information
Consumerism
Consumer Welfare Fund

ASSIGNMENTS

1. What do you mean by Consumer Protection? What type of protection does the consumer need?
2. What are the main provisions of the Consumer Protection Act (1986)?
3. Highlight the features of the Consumer Protection Act as amended in 2002.
4. Briefly discuss the main functions of different consumer protection agencies set in India from time to time.
5. Comment on the effectiveness of various consumer protection measures adopted in India in recent years.
6. Define the term 'consumer protection' and state the importance of the concept.
7. Explain the importance of consumer protection in India.
8. What is meant by consumer protection? State the importance of consumer protection from the consumers' point of view.
9. Explain the following rights of consumers:
   (i) The right to be informed,
   (ii) The right to choose and
   (iii) The right to healthy environment.
10. Explain the following rights of consumers:
    (i) The right to safety,
    (ii) The right to consumer education, and
    (iii) The right to be heard.
11. Explain, in brief, the rights of consumer as provided under the Consumer Protection Act (1986).
12. Briefly explain the functions of consumers' organisations and NGOs for protecting and promoting the interests of consumers.

CHAPTER 44

Planning in India

> *A plan organises consistent thinking, helps to clarify what we expect, reveals its inconsistencies, and therefore improves the process of making decisions.*
>
> W. Arthur Lewis

At the time of Independence Indian economy was in a bad shape. It was a backward economy and the level of living of most people was low. There was a few industries since there was a shortage of entrepreneurs. So India which was rich in natural resources could not achieve high rates of growth so as to create adequate employment opportunities and remove mass poverty.

Immediately after Independence it was felt that only by accelerating the rate of economic growth, it would be possible to improve the living standards of the people (provided, of course, the fruits of progress were shared by all section of society — both rich and poor). It was also realised by Indian leaders that the private sector did not have either the resources nor the enthusiasm to make adequate investment for expanding India's production capacity and thus enable it to grow faster than was possible during more than two centuries of alien rule. Taking a leaf from book of the then Russia, India adopted the planning system through which it sought to move in the desired directions. So the Indian Planning Commission was set up to guide the economy appropriately and enable it to move on the right growth path.

Economic Planning

Economic planning is the process of consciously and systematically organising economic and technical information into an internally consistent conceptual framework within the context of economic and non-economic constraints toward the realisation of a prescribed goal. An economic plan—the blue print for an economy—is a particularly useful tool to bring certain predetermined goals such as full employment at relatively stable prices or the desirable economic and social development of a country into fruition.

Definition

According to Jan Tinbergen, "Planning should be seen as a manifestation of the ever-growing tendency consciously to organise human activity. In this process there is a continuous search for efficiency in its broadest sense". A plan, as W. Leontief has said, "is not a forecast. The whole idea of planning assumes the possibility of choice between alternative feasible scenarios".

Development planning is the main focus of planning activities in developing countries like India. It concentrates on laying the foundation for achieving the general goal of increasing per capita incomes. These efforts include establishing a data bank (containing social and economic statistics) and providing the appropriate economic infrastructure, road networks, power facilities and educational institutions toward the desired goal of industrialisation.

Planning in India

From 1950-51 India adopted the planning system for two main purposes (i) to control and to regulate the private sector and (ii) allocate resources among different sectors and activities as also between the Centre and the States.

The initial focus of planning in India has been on poverty alleviation by generating adequate employment opportunities with a view improving the level of living of the people. It is against this backdrop that we will discuss the role of planning in India (a) in the pre-reform period and (b) in the post-reform period.

A. The Role of Planning in the Pre-reform Period

The role of planning in India during the pre-reform may first be discussed briefly. The following point are worth noting in this context.

(i) *Accelerating the rate of economic growth* : The most important role of planning in India, at least in the first three decades (1950-51 to 1980-81) was to raise the rate of saving and capital formation so as to enable the economy to achieve faster rate of economic growth. Since the private sector did not have sufficient resources to undertake a hust among of investment the expansion of the public sector was found to be the only way to break the spreading vicious circle of poverty and underdevelopment. And the state had to raise resources on a very large scale through the planning system to supplement the effort of the private sector.

(ii) *Industrialisation* : N. Kaldor and B. Yamey have equated economic development with industrialisation. And following the then Soviet methodology, the GOI adopted the Mahalanobis growth model during the Second Five Year Plan. The model laid stress on the development of basic and heavy industries as also industries producing capital (investment) goods. [We have already discussed the model in detail in an earlier chapter.]

(iii) *Economic self-reliance* : It was soon realised by that shortage of wage goods mainly food, rather than capital goods such as machines, could act as a major constraint on Indias economic growth.[1] This is why in the Third plan (1961-66) the GOI laid greater stress on raising food production with a view to achieving economic self-reliance. So the maximum priority was accorded to agricultural growth. This was sought to be achieved by the state through such measures land reforms, supply of adequate institutional credit to small and marginal farmers and development of rural infrastructure in the form of irrigation dams, power plants and roads.

(iv) *Making an optimal correction of market failure* : Since in the 1950s and 1960s, the market system failed to ensure intertemporal allocation of resources, the state had to make adequate investment, through the planning system, in infrastructure which generated substantial external economies and promoted the growth of industries in the private sector. The private sector was neither capable nor desirous of investing in infrastructure for two reasons—(1) high initial expense and (2) inability to appropriate the full benefits of such investment (which generates positive externalities), i.e., social benefit exceeds private benefit.

1. In fact, India faced a severe food crisis in 1956 along with foreign exchange crisis which restricted the ability of the country to import adequate food to bridge the domestic supply-demand gap. This mainly occurred due to almost complete neglect of agriculture.

(v) *Regulation of the private sector* : Although the private sector was assigned an important role in India's mixed economy, it was not given complete freedom as is the case in free enterprise economies like the USA or Japan. Through industrial policy the GOI specified the area of operation of the private sector. Moreover, the private sector had to be controlled through the licensing system with a view to reducing undue concentration of wealth and economic power in a few big business houses. While foreign trade was subjected to control in order to pursue the strategy of import substitution, industrial production and investment were subjected to control with a view to directing resources according to plan priorities and targets.

(vi) *Poverty alleviation* : Finally, there was need for planning in order to solve the problem of unemployment and alleviate poverty with a view to helping the poor and weaker sections of society. A faster rate of economic growth was not enough to eradicate unemployment and poverty. There was also need to adopt various special programmes such as the food-for-work programmes and employment guarantee schemes through the planning process. The last scheme seeks to provide one member of a family living below poverty line employment for 100 days in a year.

B. The Role of Planning in the Post-Reform Period

Even in the era of privatisation and economic liberalisation planning had an important, though different role to play. We may now discuss the role of planning in the post-reform period.

(i) *Improving the quality of life of people* : According to A. K. Sen and his supporters, planning is needed for creating social infrastructure and achieving human development. Both are of crucial importance for promoting faster economic growth and improving the physical quality of life of people. So there is need for planning for building up educational institutions, research centres and hospitals so as to increase India's stock of human capital. By setting up technical training institutes the State can train[1] the youth and make them skilled workers and thus help raise their productivity.

(ii) *Poverty alleviation* : As in the pre-reform period, planning has an important role to play for generating employment and for alleviating poverty. The reason is that much dent could not be made on the poverty problem in spite of four decades of planning (1951-91). It is through planning that adequate credit can be supplied to farmers to enable them to make improvement in their land and develop irrigation facilities. Planning can also help build other assets so as to increase the productivity of resources, mainly manpower.

The private sector and the market mechanism cannot be expected to generate productive assets for the poor, increase their income and lift them above the poverty line.

(iii) *Special anti-poverty schemes* : For various reasons such as factor price distortions, overvalued exchange rates etc. the private sector has an extra temptation to use capital-intensive techniques of production. This practice acts as an obstacle to sufficient employment generation.

At present the price of capital in a surplus country is low due to various fiscal concessions and the price of labour is high due to payment of minimum wages to workers in spite of low productivity. Only through planning it is possible to remove such factor market distortions and encourage business firms to use more labour and less capital in the production process. This can be achieved by raising the cost of labour by giving subsidies.[2]

(iv) *Building an integrated physical infrastructure* : Since economic growth is held in check due to lack of adequate infrastructural facilities there is need to make further investment in economic infrastructure within the framework of a well-designed plan. This is of strategic importance for achieving faster economic growth on a sustainable basis.

---

1. The private sector can recruit the required number of trained workers without actually bearing the cost of training.
2. The scheme of payroll subsidies can be introduced to encourage the growth of labour-intensive industries select in backward areas with a view to absorbing India's huge surplus labour.

(v) *Need for more investment in agriculture* : Economic reforms in India almost completely neglected agriculture. However, the Government provided huge subsidies to farmers. But agriculture suffered from capital starvation since the early 1990s. And the average annual rate of agricultural growth has been very low in the last two decades. As a result the employment situation worsened. What is still worse, many farmers in Andhra Pradesh, Maharashtra, Karnataka and Orissa committed suicide after prolonged distress and perennial indebtedness.

Now the country is facing food crisis. And it appears that unless there is a second green revolution in near future, the food problem will become more serious. So more investment has to be made on agriculture. Only the Government can expand irrigation facilities and undertake flood control measures on a large scale. The Government should also make available sufficient institutional credit to farmers at low rate of interest.

(vi) *Regional balance* : There is also need for planning to remove large disparities in the levels of development of different regions. Considerable planned efforts and resources are needed to develop backward regions (growth centres) and thus enable the country to achieve balanced regional development which is one of the declared objectives of industrial policy. Plans should therefore make provisions for increasing the productivity of agriculture as also for setting up new agro-based industries in backward areas. Planned efforts are also needed for integrating the backward areas with the rest of the country. This is possible by developing adequate transport and communication—facilities.

(vii) *Protecting the physical environment and maintaining ecological balance* : Environmental protection and maintenance of ecological balance are absolutely essential for achieving sustainable growth. Since the private sector makes reckless and irrational use of India's scarce and non-renewable natural resources, such resources are likely to get depleted very soon in the absence of adequate and effective state intervention. So the Government has to intervene through the planning system to ensure that resources are judiciously used and inter-generational equity is maintained.

(viii) *Transfer of resources from the centre to the states* : Finally, in a federal country like India planning is also necessary for allocating financial resources between the Centre and the States. [This point has already been discussed in chapter 37 under the heading 'Centre-State Financial Relations in India']

Indicative Planning

During the reform period the GOI has relied on indicative planning. In such planning we see the uses of centrally determined targets to coordinate private and public sector investment and output plans.

Economic Insight: Indicative Planning
The use of centrally determined targets to coordinate private and public sector investment and output plans. Decision-making remains decentralised but sectors of the economy are encouraged to meet agreed targets. There are two approaches to indicative planning. The first is to ask firms in all sectors of the economy to submit output and investment intentions for the forthcoming planning period; these plans are scrutinised for possible bottlenecks and if identified attempts to resolve the inconsistencies are made by persuading the relevant sectors to raise targets. The second takes as its starting point a target national growth rate which is then used as the basis for detailed sector targets which are compatible with this growth rate. If the resources are available and the sector targets are believed then the plan can be expected to induce the investment necessary to satisfy the plan. A major rationale of indicative planning is improvement in the flow of information within a market economy, and reduction in the uncertainty surrounding decision-making. By doing so business confidence is improved and stability and cohesion within the national economy promoted. The French have been major proponents of indicative planning, while Britain experimented with it during the 1960s.

Indicative planning takes as its starting point a target national growth rate which is then used as the basis for detailed 'sector-specific' target which are compatible with this growth rate. If the resources are aquitable and the sectoral targets are realistic (achievable), then the plan can be expected to induce the investment necessary to well the plan target. A major rationale of indicative planning is improvement in the flow of information within a market economy and reduction in uncertainty surrounding decision-making. Such planning improves business confidence and promotes stability and cohesion within the national economy.

Indicative Planning in India

Under indicative planning, the Planning Commission has to outline the broad directives in which the economy should be growing. So planning has to (a) provide a clear vision of the future, (b) make medium-term economic projections for the whole economy, (c) evolve a system of information gathering and transmission, (d) identify strengths of the economy as also its weakness and (e) formulate appropriate measures to achieve national goals and objectives. [We will discuss the issue of indicative planning in detail later in this chapter.]

THE STRATEGIES OF DEVELOPMENT IN INDIA'S FIVE YEAR PLANS

The Second Plan and the Mahalanobis Model

From the Second Five Year Plan (1951-56) till the Fourth Plan (1969-74) the main constraint on India's economic growth was acute scarcity of physical capital which was responsible for low productive capacity of the economy. P.C. Mahalanobis, one of the earlier architects of Indian planning, was of the opinion that in a virtually closed economy facing a serious foreign exchange constraint and an acute shortage of physical capital, the only way to achieve faster economic growth and self-reliance was to make adequate investment in basic heavy industries. According to the Mahalanobis model, on which the Second Five Year Plan was based, the "proper development strategy would be to bring about a rapid development of industries producing investment goods in the beginning by increasing appreciably the proportion of investment in basic and heavy industries. As the capacity to manufacture both heavy and light machinery and other capital goods increases, the capacity to invest in home produced capital goods would also increase steadily and India would become more and more independent of imports of foreign machinery and capital".

Employment Implications of the Model

The Mahalanobis strategy of development also suggested that productive employment could be guaranteed by increasing the production of capital good. According to this strategy, "the only way of eliminating unemployment in India is to build up a sufficiently large stock of capital which will enable all unemployed persons being absorbed in productive activities. Increasing the rate of investment is, therefore, the only fundamental remedy for unemployment in India".

Import-Substituting Industrialisation

Another important aspect of the development strategy adopted in India's Second and Third Five Year Plans was the stress on import-substituting type of industrialisation. This is why an inward-looking development strategy was adopted. This strategy was supposed to generate sufficient employment opportunities. So surplus rural labour could be transferred to more productive employment in industries. The expectation was based on the Mahalanobis hypothesis that agriculture was subject to diminishing returns to labour. So it had limited capacity to absorb surplus labour since such labour could not be productively employed. By contrast, production in industries was subject to increasing returns to scale.

Thus excessive dependence on agriculture was treated as economic underdevelopment and industrial growth was equated with the development of heavy industries. This was the basic approach of Second Five Year Plan. To quote the Second Plan, "Low or static standard of living, underemployment and unemployment and, to a certain extent even the gap between the average income and the highest income are all manifestations of the basic underdevelopment which characterises an economy depending mainly on agriculture. Rapid industrialisation and diversification of the economy is thus the core of development. But if industrialisation is to be rapid enough, the country must aim at developing basic industries and industries which make machines to make the machines needed for further development".

The above quote from the Second Five Year Plan indicates a clear shift of priorities from agriculture to industries and within the industrial sector to basic heavy industries. It was thought that the growth of such industries would lead an acceleration the rate of capital formation and thus enable the Indian economy to achieve a faster rate of economic growth.

In fact, the Second Plan equated the rate increase in investment with the rate of growth of capital of the sector producing capital goods.

The Mahalanobis Four-Sector Model

In order to ensure adequate employment opportunities in India's labour supply economy, it was also necessary to set up numerous labour-intensive industries. Keeping thus important issue in mind, Mahalanobis presented a four-sector model. In this model he divided the consumption goods sector (or *C*-sector) into three slube sectors, i.e., C_1, C_2 and C_3. Sector C_1 represented factory enterprises producing consumer goods and was supposed to use mechanised techniques of production. Sector C_2 represented household and small-scale enterprises producing consumer goods using labour-intensive technique of production and sector C_3 represented provision of servive. Thus only sector C_2 would create employment opportunities because of its labour-intensive character. By adopting this approach, the Second Plan imposed restrictions on the expansion of capacity in factory enterprises engaged in the production of consumer goods. However, due to lack of adequate financial resources and low labour productivity the household and cottage industries could neither generate adequate employment opportunities nor supply an adequate amount of consumer goods.

The Strategic Role of the Public Sector

Another notable aspect of Indian development strategy pursued up to the end of 1980s was the strategic role assigned to the public sector. This was based on the belief that an undue reliance on the private sector and market mechanism would lead to maximum production of luxury goods and non-essential items of consumption for the rich. At the same time there would be underinvestment in industries producing mass consumption goods which was so essential in a low-income country for reducing the incidence of poverty by ensuring an abundant supply of wage goods or mass compaign goods.

THE THIRD PLAN AND ECONOMIC SELF-RELIANCE

The Third Five Year Plan also laid stress on the development of basic industries such as steel, fuel, power, chemical and machine building because these were of strategic importance to the nation. These industries were supposed to largely determine the pace at which the economy could become economically self-reliant.

No doubt, two main objectives of the Third Plan were achieving self-sufficiency in foodgrains and increasing agricultual production to meet the requirements of industry and exports. In spite of this, there was not much difference in the actual allocation of resources between agriculture and other sectors between Second and Third Plan.

Growth Orientation

Essentially a growth-oriented development strategy was pursued in India till the end of the Third Plan. The plans also mentioned two other objectives viz., increasing employment and reducing income inequalities.

Economic Crisis

During this period, due to war with China in 1962 and with Pakistan in 1965 Indian was constrained to raise its defence expenditure sharply.

The inflow of foreign aid started falling. As a result there was a services foreign exchange crisis. The devaluation of the rupee in June 1966 failed to stimulate exports, reduce imports and increase the net inflow of foreign exchange.

The overall economic situation turned from bad to worst due to successive droughts in 1966 and 1967.

Two Shortcomings of the Developing Strategy

The deteriorating economic situation brought into focus two main shortcomings of the development strategy. The first was relative neglect of agriculture which resulted in serious food crisis. The Second was undue reliance on foreign aid for stepping up India's development efforts in the subsequent plans. The Government soon realised that for achieving the cherished goal of planning, viz., economic self-reliance, it was of paramount importance to reduce dependence on foreign aid.

Plan Holiday (1966-69)

In late 1960s the resource position of the public sector became so critical and uncertain the Government had to abandon planning for three years (1966-69) and declared a plan holiday. Due to that shortage of plan resources, public sector investment had to be cut drastically. So the system of five-year plans was replaced by annual plans.

THE FOURTH PLAN (1969-74) AND POVERTY ALLEVIATION

In the Fourth Five Year Plan (1969-74) there was shift of emphasis on poverty alleviation by helping the weaker sections of society mainly in rural areas, such as small and marginal farmers and landless workers. This is why the Fourth Plan raised the allocation of the plan outlay to agriculture and irrigation from 20% in the Second Plan and in the Third Plan to about 23%.

Green Revolution and Self-Sufficiency in Foodgrains

More resources were allocated to agriculture in the Fourth Plan in order to achieve self-sufficiency in foodgrains. At the same time a new agriculture strategy was adopted. It involved the use of high yielding varieties (HYV) seeds, fertilisers, pesticides and the supply of irrigation water in a few selected districts of Punjab, Haryana and Western UP. This brought about green revolution which raised India's wheat output appreciably.

Export Promotion

In addition, much importance was given to export promotion. At the same time the policy of import substitution remained intact.

Slowdown of Industrial Growth

However, in spite of drastic increase in food output, economic growth slowed down due to deficiency of demand or purchasing power created by a fall in public sector investment from the mid-1960s. The average annual growth in net national product (NNP) was only 3.3%. The overall growth rate fell mainly due to the slowing down of industrial growth over the period 1966-67 to 1978-79. Some economists like I. J. Ahluwalia have ventured to call this slowdown in industrial growths as *industrial stagnation*.

THE FIFTH PLAN (1974-78)[1]

At the time of formulation of the Fifth Plan it was realised that economic growth alone would not lead to the solution of the problem of poverty and unemployment in India in near future. In fact, 321 million people lived below the poverty line in 1973-74 and unemployment problem was becoming more

1. Although the original time span of the Fifth Plan was five years (1974-79), it was terminated in one year earlier (in 1978).

and more serious and alarming with the completion of each plan. So the Fifth Plan adopted a strategy of making direct attack on poverty by formulating and implementing some special employment programmes such as Jawahar Rozgar Yojona for giving wage employment to the poor and integrated rural development programme (IRDP) for providing self-employment opportunities to the unemployed youth.

According to the Approach to the Fifth Plan, 'The strategy for elimination poverty ...... rested on two major factors —a rising rate of growth of domestic product combined with declining rate of population growth."

20-Point Programme

During the Fifth Plan period, the Prime Minister's 20-Point Programme was accorded higher priority than the implementation of the plan programmes and meeting plan targets.

THE SIXTH PLAN (1980-85)

The development strategy of the Sixth Plan laid stress on ensuring efficiency in the use of resources and increase in resource productivity. It set a growth target of 5.2% per annum. As for resource allocation, the maximum priority was accorded to infrastructure sector. In addition higher priority was given to employment generation and poverty alleviation. To be more specific, the Plan fixed a target of generating additional employment 46 mn. persons through three scheme, viz., IRDP. National Rural Development Programme (NRDP) and Rural Landless Employment Programme (RLEP). The Sixth Plan also fixed a target of reducing the percentage of people living below the poverty line to 30. Like the earlier plans, agriculture, rural development and special employment programmes received an allocation of 13% of total plan outlay.

THE SEVENTH PLAN (1985-90)

Four notable feature of the Seventh Plan strategy were the following:

(i) ***Full capacity utilisation*** **:** The Seventh plan was guided by the Hicksian dictum, that maintenance is more important than expansion. This is why the development strategy of the Seventh Plan focused on the utilisation of existing production capacity rather than creating new capacity. So it aimed at the best possible utilisation of the production capacity created over the years.

(ii) ***Direct attack on unemployment and Poverty*** **:** In addition, the Plan laid stress on making a direct attack on the problem of unemployment and poverty by making provision for larger outlay on special employment programmes.

(iii) ***Maximum production of wage (mass consumption) goods*** **:** The Seventh Plan gave high priority to the production of wage (mass consumption) goods such as foodgrains, edible oil, sugar and textiles. So it adopted non-inflationary growth strategy.

(iv) ***Economic liberalisation and greater scope for the private sector*** **:** In fact, it was during the Seventh Plan period that the process of economic liberalisation was initiated. The licensing system was liberalised. Various stringent procedures were relaxed. In addition, the Government allowed the private firms to achieve diversification through broad banding. This, it was thought, would enable them to utilise their production capacity fully. All these implied that the private sector was given much wider scope to operate in India's mixed economy.

INDIA'S ECONOMIC PERFORMANCE IN THE PRE-REFORM PERIOD (UPTO 1990-91)

A study of India's performance in the first four decades of planning—known as the pre-reform period—presents a mixed picture. The following points are worth noting in this context:

1. However during 1980s and 1990s the growth rate picked up due to high rate of growth of real GDP on the one hand and slowing down of the rate of growth of population on the other.

(i) *Structural change* : Indian economy achieved structural transformation during this period. The share of agriculture in GDP fall and that of industry increased.

(ii) *Self-sufficiency in foodgrains* : Since food production increased faster than the rate of growth of population India achieved self-sufficiency in foodgrains.

(iii) *Industrial growth* : The industrial sector grew very fast in the first 15 years of planning for various reasons. There was no shortage of critical raw materials during this period. However, industrial growth slowed down since 1966 and the trend continued up to 1978. In spite of this India became self-sufficient in consumer goods and almost self-sufficient in capital goods.

In fact, India was able to meet its entire need for consumer goods and about 85% of its need for capital goods through domestic production.

India also succeeded in building a strong industrial base due to development of basic and heavy industries.

India also achieved quite some success in building a huge reserve of technically and managerially qualified people. Thus there was not only physical capital formation but human capital formation as well.

In truth, in the first three decades of planning the average annual growth rate (as measured by annual rate of income in real GDP) was 3.5%. However, the overall growth rate slowed down due to setback on both agricultural and industrial fronts.

Since population grew at the rate of 2.25% per annum during this period per capita income (PCI) increased[1] at the rate of only 1.25%.

Poverty Alleviation

However, whatever little economic growth was achieved during the first three decades of planning it did not have any notable impact on the incidence of poverty. In fact the poverty ratio fluctuated between 50% and 58% of the population during this period. This simply means that the benefits of economic growth did not trickle down to the poor.[2]

During the Sixth Plan period (1980-85) the average annual growth rate was 5.4%. It increased marginally to 5.6% during the Seventh Plan (1985-90). The growth rate of the industrial sector was 8% during the 1980s. And, due to slowing down of the rate of growth of population, a high rate of growth of PCI—3.2% and 3.6%, respectively was achieved. As a result there was decline in the poverty ratio from 51.3 in 1977-78 to 44.5 in 1983 and further to 38.9 in 1987-88.

Sources of Growth

(i) *Pick up of public sector investment* : The acceleration in growth rate in the late 1970s and the whole 1980s was mainly attributable to the pick up of public sector investment which virtually stagnated fill the and of the 1970s. 5.6% to 6% per annum, respectively. In aaddition, some special.

(ii) *Economic liberalisation measures* : Other growth promoting factors were the liberalisation measures adopted by the government, especially the removal of certain licensing restrictions and relaxations of various controls and regulations with a view of encouraging greater capacity utilisation in the private sector and creating a more competitive business environment.

(iii) *Export promotion* : Export promotion measures were given greater emphasis than import substitution. As a result exports increased quite fast in the second half of the 1980s. This pushed up the overall growth rate of the economy. And outward-looking trade policy proved to be more effective than inward-looking policy.

---

1. However, during the 1986s and 1990s the growth rate picked up due to high rate of growth of real GDP on the one hand and slowing down of the rate of population growth on the other.
2. Only in 1980s and 1990s the economic growth rates picked up to employment schemes were launched which led to a decline in the incidence of poverty. These points will be discussed later.

High Rate of Domestic Inflation

However, the high growth rate achieved in the 1980s was not sustainable. The reason was simple. The increase in the public sector investment was achieved by incurring more and more deficits in the budget. This overheated the economy, generated high rates of inflation and made the micro-economic environment unstable. Inflation definitely acted as a growth-retarding factor in a number of ways.

Growing External Debt

A portion of public sector investment was covered by external commercial borrowing. Since the volume of such borrowing continued to increase over the years, there occurred a sharp increase in India's external public debt. And India was saddled with a huge debt service burden. Here debt-service ratio continued to increase. External debt service (i.e., payment of interest along with a certain portion of the principal amount) consumed about one-third of India's export earning in the 1980s. As a result India faced a severe foreign exchange crisis and was about to become a defaulter.

Focus on Terminology: Debt Service Ratio
Debt service ratio refers to a country's repayment obligations of principal and interest for a particular year on its external debt as a percentage of its exports of goods and services. i.e. its current receipts in that year.

Unemployment

In spite of the adoption of various special job-creating programmes, employment opportunities increased only marginally. However, due to adoption of capital-intensive techniques of production for accelerating the growth of both agriculture and industry, labour redundancy was inevitable and it was not possible to absorb even the annual new entrants into the labour force, not to speak of the huge backslog of unemployed. So there was more unemployment at the beginning than at the end of each plan.

Trends in Saving and Capital Formation

The rates of gross savings and domestic capital formation as a percentage of GDP showed an upward trend during the first three decades of planning (1951-80). Of course, there was fluctuations in some of the years. The excess of gross domestic investment over gross domestic saving was covered by foreign aid, i.e., concessional foreign assistance.

Upto 1965 foreign aid was adequate to bridge domestic saving investment gap. However, after war with Pakistan in 1965 on the Kashmir issue and then again in 1971 on the Bangladesh issue the flow of foreign aid continued to be diminish. This slowed down the overall rate of capital formation (investment).

In the second half of the 1980's (1986-90) there was a sharp increase in external foreign debt which put pressure on India's balance of payments and created foreign exchange crisis. And due to widening gap between gross domestic saving and gross domestic capital formation there was capital inflow to the extent of 3.2% of GDP.

ECONOMIC CRISIS (1991) STRUCTURAL REFORMS AND PLANNING IN THE POST-REFORMS PERIOD

Due to maintenance expenditure on defence, food and fertilisers and rising import in the 1980s the budget of the central Government showed growing deficit year by year. The Government had to take resourse to external commercial borrowing on a large scale. This resulted in excessive debt burden and increased debt service charges. As a result India faced a serious balance of payments crisis in 1990-91. And to tide over the difficult situation India had to adopt fiscal stabilisation and structural adjustment programme as suggested by the World Bank and the IMF. The following adverse developments forced India to adopt the following reform measures:

1. Losses of Public Sector Units (PSUs)

Mainly due to operational inefficiency most public sector units (PSUs) incurred huge losses. And the Government had to give them central budgetary support. As a result the expenditure of the government increased quite sharply.

2. Macroeconomic Imbalances

Macroeconomic imbalances both internal and external became truly serious in 1990-91.

(a) ***Double-digit inflation*** **:** Growing deficit in successive Union budgets due to excess of Government expenditure over revenue led to the creation of more money. This caused double digit inflation. The rate of inflation crossed 15% in 1991. Thus to reduce budget deficit, which was the main cause of inflation, the Government was forced to adopt a contractionary fiscal policy.

(b) ***Deficit in balance of payments*** **:** Due to ever rising imports and slow growth of exports, the balance of payments showed a huge deficit. In the whole of the 1980. And to meet the deficit the Government had to take resort to external commercial borrowing at high rates of interest.

Moreover due to persistent deficit in the current account the foreign exchange reserve position became very critical in May 1991. India's foreign exchange reserves were just sufficient to pay for a few weeks', worth of imports. This forced the government of India to approach the International Monetary Fund (IMF) for loans to each the deficit in the current account and to accumulate a minimum foreign exchange reserves.[1]

New Economic Policy (New) of Structural Adjustment

To overcome the economic crisis of 1991 and in order to achieve a higher rate of growth in the long run along with price stability as also to improve the balance of payment position the GOI adopted the new economic policy (NEP) at the insistence of the IMF and the World Bank. The first step taken by the Government, while implementing the policy, was to cut down its expenditure with a view to reducing its fiscal deficit which generated inflationary pressures in the economy by increasing the money supply.

However, what is more important is that NEP adopted various structural adjustment reforms which sought to establish a market-based system even within the mixed economy framework by removing various restrictive and strignent controls on industrial production and investment, exports and imports.

Three Main Aspects of Economic Reforms

No doubt, the reforms heralded a major change in India's development strategy. Three notable features of the reform measures were the following:

1. gradual abandonment of the quantitative controls in economic management in favour of market-based instruments.
2. a decisive move away from inward-orientation and forward outward-orientation and greater integration with the global economy; and
3. a distinct and clearly visible shift away from an overstretched, overextended, rigid and inefficient public sector and toward greater reliance on the private sector.

Changing Role of Public and Private Sectors

As a part of structural adjustment programme the role of the public sector got diluted and that of the private sector expanded. Thus the industrial strategy of 1956 (i.e., expansion of public sector and contraction of private sector) was reversed. This is why two measures have been taken by the Government viz., disinvestment of the public sector on an expanded scale and abolition of physical controls and relaxation of licensing provisions. The private sector was assigned a pivotal role in

1. To avoid the risk of default and to establish its creditworthiness to the international community and win the confidence of the business world, the Government sold a part of its gold to IMF. A certain portion of gold stock was also pledged as collateral security to obtain foreign exchange for meeting external obligations.

promoting faster economic growth by being guided by the market forces and working in a more competitive business environment so as to achieve improved efficiency.

In addition, imports have been liberalised through drastic tariff cuts. And foreign investment has been given much greater importance for bridging India's domestic saving-investment gap and various incentives (mainly fiscal concessions) have been offered to attract it. In addition, with a view to achieving economic self-reliance there was shift of emphasis from import-substitution to export-promotion.

During the past two decades of economic reforms four five-year plans have been launched. We may now discuss them one by one.

THE EIGHTH PLAN (1992-97) AND ITS DEVELOPMENT STRATEGY

The final version of the Eighth Plan (1992-97) was formulated in the context of the new economic policy (NEP) which put stress on liberalisation, privatisation and globalisation (LPG). The public sector, which was assigned a dominant role in earlier plans, lost its pre-eminence.

Role of the Public Sector

The following two roles have been assigned to the public sector in the Eighth plan:

(i) *Infrastructure building* : The public sector was instructed to make investment only in the infrastructure sector (such as irrigation, power, transport and communication) where adequate private sector investment was not likely to occur for obvious reasons: (a) high initial cost, (b) low rate of return, (c) long generation period, and (d) inability to apply the exclusion principle[1].

(ii) *Operation on the basis of commercial considerations* : Public enterprises were expected operate on commercial (profit and loss) considerations except in case of commodities and services which were produced and distributed specifically for the benefit of the poor and the weaker sections of the society.

Indicative Planning

In the Eighth Plan document, it was declared that planning in India would be indicative in nature. Indicatives Planning is a method of controlling the economy which involves the setting of long-term objective using techniques of input output analysis. Unlike a centrally planned economy, indicative planning works through the market (price) system rather than replaces it. To this end the planning process specifically brings together both sides of industry (the trade unions and management) and the government.

Indicative planning is also a very useful way of transmitting information to the private sector.

In addition, indicative planning enabled the Government to adopt selective approach in its plan for industrialisation. By using various fiscal and monetary instruments the Government could encourage industry having bright prospects (called *sunrise industries*) and discourage others (called *sunset industries*) since they face an uncertain future and bleak prospect.

Promotion of Competition

The main thrust of the Eighth Plan was on creating a more competitive environment as a means of improving the efficiency of private enterprises and raising productivity of resources. This was sought to be achieved by removing the barriers to entry of new firms into the industry and restrictions on the expansion and diversification of existing firm in the private sector.

Export Orientation

The Eighth Plan adopted an export-oriented growth strategy. The stress was on promoting exports with a view to achieving economic self-reliance. The Plan set a target of achieving 13.6% annual rate of growth in exports and only 8.6% annual rate of growth in imports.

1. In fact, the public sector was supposed to withdraw itself from these areas where it did not serve any public purpose.

Saving Investment and Economic Growth

The Eighth Plan fixed a target of achieving an annual growth rate of 5.6%. Assuming an incremental capital output ratio (ICOR) of 4.1, the Plan fixed the investment rate at 23% of GDP which would be covered largely by domestic saving (21.6%) and foreign saving or current account deficit (1.4%).

With an actual investment rate of 23.3% and ICOR at 3.5, the country was able to achieve a growth rate of 6.7% per annum which exceeded thePlan target.

THE NINTH PLAN (1997-2002) AND ITS DEVELOPMENT STRATEGY

The Roles of Private and Public Sector

In the Ninth Plan the private sector was assigned a key role in raising the rate of growth and creating adequate employment opportunities. It was felt that a vibrant private sector, operating in an environment of free markets and active competition would be able to make efficient use of scarce resources. At the same time the Government and public sector were entrusted with the task of providing essential social services such as health care, education and safe drinking water, especially in the rural areas.

Infrastructure Building in Both Urban and Rural Areas

In the Ninth Plan high priority was accorded to public investment and mainly in economic infrastructure for promoting faster growth by stimulating private investment. Furthermore, for promoting broad-based agricultural growth laid stress on constructing rural roads, irrigation dams, promotion of agricultural research and setting up of growth markets for farm products.

Export-Led Growth

The Ninth Plan also laid emphasis on promoting exports as part of its export-led growth strategy. The focus was on raising exports of agriculture products with a view to increasing the incomes of the farmers.

More stress was given on export promotion than in the earlier plans not only to enable the economy to achieve economic self-reliance but also achieve faster growth. The economy was opened up and integrated with the rest of the world. To enable domestic industries to compete with their foreign counterparts the Government planned to strengthen its anti-dumping measures with a view to promoting domestic industries from unfair foreign competition.

Disinvestment

The Ninth Plan also stressed that the proceeds from disinvestment of public sector enterprises in non-strategic enterprises would be used for mainly the much needed investment in the social sector, especially health and education.

Reduction of Fiscal Deficit for Holding the Price Line

Finally the Ninth Plan highlighted the need for reduction of combined fiscal deficit of the Central and State Governments. This was mainly sought to be achieved through larger tax collection, subsidy reduction and cut in non-plan expenditure. Importantly enough, the subsidies were to be targeted to specific groups—the really needy and economically weaker sections of the society.

Achievement of the Plan

The Ninth Plan did not achieve much success in the true sense. Instead it failed on two main fronts—economic growth and employment generation. The Ninth Plan achieved a growth rate of 5.5% per annum against the target of 6.5%. This was due to slow growth of the agricultural sector – 2.5% per annum against the target of 3.9% per annum and sharp fall in industrial growth. The industrial sector grew at the rate of only 3% per annum as against the target of 8.2%. Two main causes of lower industrial growth were: (i) demand recession emerging from fall in public sector investment, (ii) setback on the agricultural front (which not only created shortage of raw materials but acted as an additional demand constraint).

Employment Generation

The Plan failed to generate employment for 50 million persons as per the target. The sad truth is that the unemployment rate on the current daily status basis which was 7.32% in 1999-2000 jumped during the plan period. Consequently the backlog of unemployment reached 35 million persons at the end of the Plan. This was no doubt an alarming figure and a cause for much concern.

THE TENTH PLAN (2002-2007)

Objectives and Targets

The Tenth Plan set a fairly ambitious growth target of 8% per annum. However, the main stress was on human development. This is why it also sets the targets for other aspects of all-round development. The focus was on the following:

1. ***Reduction of poverty*** : The Tenth Plan envisaged to reduce the poverty ratio from 26.1 in 2000 to 21 in 2007.

2. ***Increase in literacy rate*** : The overall literacy rate (of 7 years +) was to be increased from 65 to 75 over the five-year period.

3. ***Employment generation*** : A really notable objective of the Tenth Plan was to generate 50 million jobs over the five-year period. However, the Plan did not suggest the adoption of any specific measure for making this ambitious target a success.

4. ***Balanced development of States*** : The Tenth Plan laid stress on the importance of achieving balanced development of different states and thus avoid uneven development. For this reason it gave a Statewise break-up of broad development targets which included growth rates and social developments in line with national targets.

5. ***Equity and social justice*** : Finally, the Tenth Plan emphasised the goal of achieving equity and social justice. This is why various employment generation programmes such as Swarnajayanti Gram SwarozgarYojana (SGSY), Sampoorna Grameen Rozgar Yojana (SGRY), Antyodaya Anna Yojana have been included in the Plan. In addition, the Plan included various projects for supplying clean and safe drinking water and housing for the poor. The programmes were supposed to reduce poverty and generate gainful employment opportunities.

Development Strategy

Five notable aspects of development strategy of the Tenth Plan were the following:

1. ***Redefining the role of the state*** : The Tenth Plan defined the role of the state in the context of the emergence of a strong and vibrant private sector. So the Plan made provision for greater participation of the private sector in the process of growth. It was supposed to raise its investment level appreciably. At the same time there was a renewed emphasis on the role of the public sector in building economic infrastructure. In addition, monetary and fiscal policies have been given due importance in influencing private firms and channelising investment in proper directions as also for raising resources for infrastructure building.

2. ***Improving the quality of life*** : For improving the quality of life of the people, the Tenth Plan laid stress on much greater access to basic social services such as education, health, clean drinking water and basic nutrition. It recognised the paramount importance of improvement in these key areas. In this context the plan set following specific targets:

1. Universal access to primary education by 2007.
2. Increase in literacy of 75% population by 2007.
3. Reduction of infant mortality rate to 45 per 1,000 live birth by 2007.
4. Reduction of maternal mortality ratio to 2 per 1,000 live birth by 2007.
5. Improving ecology by increasing forest and tree cover to 25% by 2007.
6. Supplying clean drinking water to the people in all villages by 2012.
7. Cleaning all major polluted rivers by 2007.

In order to achieve the above targets additional resources have been allocated to the social sectors.

3. *Stress on agricultural development* : The development strategy of the Tenth Plan also laid stress on the acceleration of agricultural growth, through diversification. This implied not only crop diversification but also diversification of rural economic activities. In addition to growing disverse crops farmers were supposed to venture out in such areas as horticulture, fisheries, and vegetables for improving their economic conditions.

4. *Employment generation through growth of the services sector* : In addition, for creating more employment opportunities an important role has been assigned to the services sector which includes tourism, transport and communication, trade, IT-enabled services, computer software as also construction of houses and hotels. However, it has been correctly pointed out that rapid growth of the services sector could not be achieved in the absence of faster industrial growth.

5. *Special poverty alleviation measures* : Finally, it was recognised by planners that faster economic growth alone was not enough to create employment opportunities for 50 million workers and thus bring the poverty ratio (i.e., the percentage of people living below the poverty line) to 21% of the population by 2007. So it was planned to undertake certain special anti-poverty programmes.

Growth Target

One of the causes of slow growth of the Indian economy over the years has been high incremental capital-output ratio (ICOR). And Indian planners thought that it could be brought down from 4.53 in the Ninth Plan to 3.58 in the Tenth Plan. Keeping this point in view the Plan sought to utilise the installed production capacity of the economy fully rather than creating new capacity. So the focus of the Tenth Plan was on completion of on-going projects as also privatisation of those private sector enterprises which were having idle production capacity (i.e., which were unable to utilise their installed capacity fully).

Macroeconomic Parameters

Two main macroeconomic parameters of the Tenth Plan were the following:

(i) *Outlay* : The total outlay envisaged for the Tenth Plan was Rs. 19,68,815 crores (which included provisions for both Central and State plans).

(ii) *Fiscal and revenue deficit* : Fiscal deficit and revenue deficit had been projected at 4.7% and 2.9% of *GDP*, respectively.

Achievements and Failures of the Tenth Plan

The Tenth Plan achieved success in most areas but failed in others. The following points are to be noted in this context:

A. Areas of Success

(i) *Faster economic growth* : During the Tenth Plan the Indian economy made notable progress at least in terms of growth of GDP. The actual growth rate (7.6%) fell short of the Plan target (7.8%) only marginally. This was much higher than the growth rate of 5.5% achieved in the Ninth Plan. Two main causes of this faster rate of growth of the economy were (1) an increase in the rate of domestic saving and investment (from 28.4% in the Ninth Plan to 31.4% in the Tenth Plan) on the one hand and (2) fall in the ICOR (which depressed per capita GDP growth during the entire plan period) on the other. The achievement of the overall growth rate induced the planners to set a target of average growth rate of 9% p.a. during the Eleventh Plan period.

(ii) *Increase in foreign exchange reserves* : There occurred a significant increase in India's foreign exchange reserves during the Tenth Plan period mainly due to continuation of the reform measures. Three main sources of a large increase in foreign exchange reserves were the following:

(i) increase in inflows of financial capital through foreign institutional investors (FIIs),

(ii) large flow of foreign direct investment (FDI) through multinational corporations and

(iii) greater flow of funds through deposits made by non-resident Indians (NRIs). India's accumulated foreign exchange reserves which crossed US $100 bn. in December 2003 reached $192 bn. at the end of March 2007.

Commentary: The Pattern of Capital Inflows and its Consequences

The inflows of international portfolio investment (IPI) as a proportion of total capital flows increased much faster than FDI flows. Thus the pattern of foreign capital inflows was tilted in favour of IPI which is invested in speculative activities such as shares and debentures of private companies. By comparison, FDI flows, which help to create productive capacity slowed down during the Tenth Plan period.

In short, the rate of growth of the Indian economy accelerated during the Tenth Plan. This was made possible mainly by higher rate of saving and investment and faster rate of industrial growth as also growth of exports.

B. Areas of Failure

However, there were three important areas where failure was observed, viz., agriculture, employment generation and poverty reduction (alleviation).

(i) *Agriculture* : The average annual rate of growth of agriculture was only 2.5% against the target of 4%. In fact, the main drawback of the Tenth Plan was the dismal performance on the agriculture front. And fall in production of foodgrains created a new problem, viz., food inflation. In other words, food inflation was caused by supply-side constraints.

(ii) *Jobless growth* : Secondly, the Tenth Plan could not make any dent on the unemployment problem. The rate of unemployment on current daily status basis for the economy as a whole increased from 7.3% in 1999-2000 to 8.3% in 2004-2005. While rural unemployment increased from 7.2% to 9.1%, urban unemployment increased from 7.2% to 8.8% during the Tenth Plan period. A matter of really serious concern was a sharp increase in unemployment among agricultural labour households which represent one of the poorest sections of society.

Economic Insight: Unemployment in Organised and Unorganised Sectors

It has to be noted that not much employment was generated in the organised sector during the 10th Plan period. In truth, employment has increased mainly in the unorganised sector characterised by low labour productivity.

In short, one of the major failures of the Tenth Plan is its achievement of jobless growth. And faster economic growth has virtually been anti-developmental in nature.

(iii) *Persistence of poverty* : Finally, the Tenth Plan could not achieve the targeted reduction in poverty ratio. It was envisaged that faster rate of economic growth and effective implementation of the employment guarantee scheme would conjointly lead to a fall in the poverty ratio to 19% in 2006-2007 from 26.1% in 1999-2000. But the 61st Round of NSS reports, on the basis of uniform recall period of 30 days indicate that the poverty ratio was 27.5 in 2004-05 (compared to 36 in 1993-94).

This means that during this period there was a fall in the poverty ratio by 8.5 percentage points or 0.74% p.a. Thus, in spite of a higher rate of growth achieved during the Tenth Plan period, not much reduction in the incidence of poverty could be achieved.

Synopsis for Learning: The Tenth Plan Scorecard
Thus an overall evaluation of the Tenth Plan presents a mixed picture. While the targets of faster GDP growth and greater inflows of foreign capital and foreign exchange were achieved, two important objectives, viz., the targeted fall in rate of poverty and generation of adequate employment opportunities could not be achieved.

THE ELEVENTH PLAN (2007-12)

The Eleventh Plan (2007-12) envisaged faster economic growth. The stress was on inclusive growth. Such growth implies that all sections of society have to derive the benefits of whatever GDP growth the country is able to achieve. Such growth is essentially growth with equity or distributive justice. The main objectives of the Eleventh Plan were the following:

1. *Faster economic growth* : The Eleventh Plan laid stress on achieving faster economic growth for two main reasons, viz., (1) raising the income levels of the masses so as to ensure an improvement in their living standard and (2) generating adequate resources for providing basic services such as health care, education, safe drinking water and sanitation facilities to all. The basic objective was to ensure that the fruits of progress were shared by all sections of society.

Economic Insight: Inclusive Growth
Q1. What does inclusive growth imply?
Ans. Empowerment of the people and expansion of the opportunities to extract the maximum benefit from state-provided services and facilities.
Q2. What inclusive growth does not imply?
Ans. Marginalisation.

The Eleventh Plan set a target of 9% annual growth rate, compared to 7.6% achieved during the Tenth Plan. It was projected that with 1.5% growth of population p.a. and 9% growth of GDP, real per capita income (PCI) would get doubled within the next ten-year period.

It was also specified that the higher growth rate would be achieved by stepping up the rate of investment to 36%, with an unchanged ICOR of 4%. This was sought to be achieved by increasing the domestic saving rate to 39.8% of GDP and inflow of foreign capital to 1.88% of GDP. Even though the target rate of investment had been achieved in the very first year of the Eleventh Plan (2007-08), the rate of growth of GDP was revised downward to 7% due to the impact of global financial crisis.

Realistic targets have also been fixed for different sectors of the economy. For example, the target for agricultural growth has been fixed at 4% p.a. while for industry and services the target has been fixed at 10.11% and 9.11% p.a., respectively. These may be compared with the actual growth rates achieved during the Tenth Plan period. See Table 44.1.

Table 44.1: Achievement of Key Macroeconomic Targets during the Eleventh Plan Period

Indicator	*Tenth Plan (Actuals)*	*Eleventh Plan (Targets)*	*2007-08*	*2008-09*	*2009-10*	*2010-11*
A. Growth Rate GDP at market prices (%)	7.8	9.0	9.2	6.7	8.0	8.5
1. Agriculture and Allied Sectors	2.5	4.0	4.7	1.6	0.4	6.6
2. Industry	8.6	10.11	9.3	3.1	10.4	7.3
3. Services	9.0	9.11	10.4	9.3	8.3	9.3
B. Investment Rate (as % of GDP) of which	31.4*	36.7*	37.7	34.9	36.5	36.4
1. Public sector	6.9	8.0	9.1	N.A	–	–
2. Private sector	22.9	28.7	28.5	N.A	–	–
C. Gross Domestic Saving Rate (% of GDP)	31.4	34.8	36.4	32.5	33.7	33.8
D. Current Account Deficit that is, foreign savings (as % of GDP),	0.0	–1.88	–1.3	–2.4	–2.8	2.6
E. Government Fiscal Deficit (both Centre and States Combined, as % of GDP)	8.0	6.0	2.6*	6.0*	6.7*	5.1*

Source: (1) Planning Commission, *Eleventh Five Year Plan*, 2007. *indicates figures of the Centre only
(2) GOI, *Economic Survey:* various issues

The actual growth rate was just a modest 2.5% p.a. in agriculture. In industry the actual growth rate was 8.6% during the Tenth Plan. So the increase is just a modest one. In case of services the actual growth rate achieved was 9% p.a. and the target for the Eleventh Plan was 9.11% p.a. This shows just a marginal increase.

2. *Spread of educational opportunities* : For achieving inclusive growth it is not enough to raise agricultural production and productivity and generation of additional employment opportunities. A spread of educational opportunities is equally vital. Without minimum education people will not get the opportunity to achieve their goals. Education is absolutely essential for empowering people with skills and knowledge and for giving them adequate employment opportunities in the future. Keeping this point in view, the Eleventh Plan proposed to raise public expenditure on education to 6% of GDP. The objective of the Plan was to fulfill the constitutional obligation of providing free and compulsory elementary education of good quality to all children up to age 14.

For expanding educational opportunities the Eleventh Plan suggested the following measures:

1. All children had to complete 8 years of schooling. This could be achieved by reducing the drop-out rates in primary school from 45%in 2007-2008 to 20% in 2011-2012.
2. The Plan aimed at raising the literacy rate to 85%.
3. The Plan also aimed at reducing the gender gap in literacy rate by 10%.
4. Finally, the Plan sought to raise the percentage of youth receiving higher education from 10% to 15% over the five-year period.

3. *Improvement of public health* : Like education health is also a part of human capital and is an important socio-economic indicator of development. As regards promotion of health of the people, the Eleventh Plan fixed the following targets:

1. The primary aim was to reduce infant mortality rate to 28% and maternal mortality rate to I per 1,000 live births.
2. The Plan also aimed at reducing total fertility rate to 2.1% by 2011-2012 with a view to slowing down the rate of growth of population.
3. The Plan sought to provide safe (clean) drinking water facilities tó all people of the country by 2009-10.
4. Finally, the Plan sought to reduce malnutrition among children of age group 0–3 years by at least 50%.

4. *Provision of adequate infrastructural facilities*: For providing infrastructural facilities the Eleventh Plan made the following provisions:

1. *Prima facie*, it sought to connect all villages and households below the poverty line (BPL) by the terminal year of the Plan (2011-12).
2. The Plan proposed to establish all-weather road connections to all habitations with a population of 1,000 persons and above (500 and above for hilly areas) by the year 2009-10.
3. The Plan also proposed to ensure connectivity of every village by telephone as also to provide broad-band connectivity to all villages by 2011-12.
4. Finally, the Plan proposed to provide homestead sites to all by 2011-12 and to accelerate the pace of construction of houses for all the poor by 2016-17.

Sectoral Allocation of Resources

In the Eleventh Plan the total outlay on various schemes has been fixed at Rs. 36,44,718 crores, compared to Rs. 16,18,460 crores in the Tenth Plan.

Total outlay on agriculture and allied activities has been more than doubled, though the percentage increase was just marginal (from 3.7 in the Tenth Plan to 3.8). The expenditure on spread of irrigation facilities and flood control has been raised from Rs. 1,12,000 crores in the Tenth Plan to Rs. 2,10,000 crores, though in terms of percentage of total output it fell from 6.9 to 5.8. It was felt that more funds should have been allocated under these heads since there were identified as two main forces behind faster agricultural growth.

Keeping in view the social dimensions of economic development, the outlay on social services (such as education, health and supply of safe drinking water) has been increased substantially — both in absolute and in percentage terms. At the same time more resources have been allocated to energy generation, with its percentage share raised from 22.4 in the Tenth Plan to 23.6 in the Eleventh Plan.

Population, Labour Force and Employment Generation

The Planning Commission estimated that India's population would increase from 1,128.1 mn. in 2007-08 to 1,208 mn. in 2011-12. During the same period the labour force would grow from 438.9 mn to 483.6 mn. And employment opportunities would be created for 460.3 mn., compared to 402.2 mn., i.e., by 58.1 mn. This implied that the number of persons employed would fall from 36.7 mn. to 23.3 mn. during the five-year period. Consequently, the daily status unemployment (DSU) was supposed to fall from 8.36% to 4.83% during the same period.

An Overall Evaluation of the Eleventh Plan

No doubt the Eleventh Plan set a few highly ambitious objectives and targets. However, most of the objectives remained largely unfulfilled. The following points may be noted in this context:

(i) *Economic growth*: In the first year (2007-2008) of the Eleventh Plan the rate of growth of GDP (at market price) was 8.7%, which was near the target set (9%). However, from the second year (2008-09), the rate of growth slowed down mainly due to global financial crisis originating from the US sub-prime crisis. The crisis (turmoil reduced not only India's exports but decreased inflows of financial capital, especially FDI. At the same time the depreciation of the rupee raised the cost of imports. And these factors adversely affected India's BOP. Thus economic growth during the whole Plan period fell short of the target of 9%.

(ii) *Employment generation* : During the Eleventh Plan period no specific policy measure was adopted to ensure gainful employment opportunities to India's growing labour force. So the magnitude of surplus labour (including the so-called disguisedly unemployed people) did not fall much. Most new employment opportunities were created in the informal (unorganised) sector. In truth, during one and half decades of economic reforms (1994-2009) there was a net fall in employment in the organised sector (both private and public). The reason was negative growth of employment in the public sector against a marginal (0.58% p.a.) increase in employment in the private sector. And the employment situation is likely to deteriorate further in the near future.

(iii) *Inclusive growth* : Furthermore, the objective of achieving inclusive growth was not realistic. The Plan almost completely neglected the issue of land reforms and subsistence farming. Instead it shifted emphasis on contract farming which was highly capital-intensive in nature. In fact, the Eleventh Plan did not have any concrete plan to create gainful employment opportunities in agriculture. For all these reasons the goal of achieving inclusive growth remained unfulfilled. In fact, the objective of achieving inclusive growth itself was an unrealistic one.

No doubt some special programmes have been launched (or schemes undertaken) for achieving the ambitious goal, viz., inclusive growth. In this context mention may be made of a few major social programmes undertaken during the Eleventh Plan period to achieve inclusive growth, viz., The Bharat Nirman Programme, Mid-day Meal Scheme, National Rural Health Mission, Jawaharlal Nehru National Urban Renewal Mission and the National Rural Employment Guarantee Scheme (NREGS). Central support for such programmes has supplemented efforts made by the States for achieving the maximum possible effectiveness.

Of these the NREGS is perhaps the most notable. Under the scheme more than 4 cr. households were provided employment in 2008-09, showing a notable increase over the 3.39 cr. households covered under the scheme a year ago.

Finally, the agricultural debt waiver and relief scheme implemented during the Eleventh Plan served a very useful purpose. It made institutional credit available to farmers and helped to generate consumer demand, which, in its turn, stimulated investment in the rural sector.

Macroeconomic Performance during the Post-Reform Period

In the first two decades of economic reforms (1991-2012) India made notable progress in raising the levels of income and improving the standards of living of the people. India succeeded in surpassing the so-called Hindu rate of growth (3.5%) which it just managed to achieve during the first two decades of planning (1951-70). In the 1980s India succeeded in achieving an annual GDP growth of 5.6%. However, due to the serious BOP crisis faced by the country in 1991, the planners changed the development strategy from import-substitution (or inward-orientation) to export promotion (or outward-orientation). No doubt, the performance of the Indian economy was quite satisfactory (and much better) due to the initiation of economic reforms after the adoption of the new economic policy (NEP). We now discuss the different aspects of India's economic performance since the implementation of various reform measures in July 1991. See Table 44.2.

Table 44.2: Macroeconomic Trends in the Post-Reform Period

Indicator	8th Plan	9th Plan	10th Plan	Eleventh Plan Period					
	(1992-93) to 1996-97)	(1997-98 to 2001-02)	2002-07 (Average)	2007-08	2008-09	2009-10	2010-11	2011-12	Average
GDP growth (% a year)	6.7	5.5	7.8	9.3	6.7	8.6	9.3	6.2	8.0
Agriculture & Allied Sectors	4.7	1.8	2.5	5.8	0.1	0.8	7.9	3.6	3.7
Industry	7.6	4.5	8.6	9.7	4.4	9.2	9.2	3.5	7.2
Services	7.5	8.1	9.28	10.4	9.3	8.0	9.4	7.9	9.7
Investment rate (% of GDP) at current market prices	23.3	22.5	31.4	38.1	34.5	36.5	36.4	35.0	–
Public Sector	–	8.0	6.6	8.9	9.5	9.2	–		
Private Sector	–	15.3	15.9	28.1	24.6	24.9			–
Central Govt. Fiscal Deficit (% of GDP)	–	–	4.4	2.6	6.0	6.7	5.1	5.7	–
Fiscal Deficit of Centre and States combined	7.2	9.3	8.0	5.5	8.0	10.0	8.5	8.7	–
Inflation (Average WPI % change in year)	8.7	4.9	5.1	4.6	8.4	3.6	9.6	5.9	–
Current account balance (% of GDP)	1.2	–0.7	+1.3	–1.3	–2.3	–2.8	–2.8	– 4.2	–

1. Economic Growth

As is seen from Table 44.2, the rate of growth of GDP was 6.7% p.a. during the Eighth Plan (1992-93 to 1996-97). However, the growth momentum could not be maintained and the growth rate fell to 5.5% during the Ninth Plan period (1997-98 to 2001-02). Again it picked up to 7.8% p.a. during the 10th Plan (2002-07). During the Eleventh Plan (2007-12), the average annual growth rate was 8% p.a.—the highest so far in any Five Year Plan. This was achieved in spite of global financial crisis of 2008-09 which lasted for a number of years. At present India is the second fastest growing nation in the world, next only to China.

Two Notable Points

Two important points are to be noted now:

(i) *Inclusive growth* : In spite of fall in rural demand for manufactured goods and decline in public sector investment, industrial growth had been quite high during the Tenth Plan period (2002-07). The rate of growth of industrial production was 8.6% p.a.

(ii) *Structural change* : India's industrial growth in the 1990s was led both by industry and services. And the first two decades of economic reforms (1991-2011) saw a change in the structure of the economy, with services acting as a leading sector and agriculture as a lagging sector. While the share of agriculture in GDP fell to 14%, that of services increased to 55% during this period.

Slowdown of Economic Growth

The economic growth achieved by India during the period of economic reforms has been largely attributable to steady increase in both gross domestic saving and gross domestic investment. Growth rates achieved in 2005-06, 2006-07 and 2007-08 were 9.5%, 9.6% and 9.3%, respectively. However, due to the adverse effect of global financial crisis of 2008, the growth rate suddenly fell to 6.7% in 2008-09. However, in the next two years — 2009-10 and 2010-11 — the growth rate picked up and rose to 8.6%, and 9.3%, respectively. But it again fell to 6.2% in 2011-12 and to 5% in 2012-13. This happened even though the rate of gross capital formation was quite high (32% of GDP in 2012-13).

Growth Retarding Factors

Both domestic and international factors accounted for the slowdown of the growth rate. Fall in inflows of FDI in the wake of the global financial crisis was a severe blow to India. It was largely responsible for holding India's growth in check or even for causing a decline in the growth rate.

Fall in FDI adversely affected India's growth rate

In addition, huge deficit in the current account made it difficult for the GOI to pay for even essential items in foreign exchange (mainly US$) as also to meet its external debt obligations. In fact, there emerged a distinct possibility of default by India in paying its debt.

Furthermore, the huge fiscal deficit (4.8% of GDP in 2012-13) also adversely affected foreign investors' confidence in India. The reason was simple. Most investors thought that a cut in plan expenditure was inevitable, which would reduce the demand for various goods and services produced by the private sector. Moreover, a cutback in government spending also implied less expenditure on infrastructure building. And infrastructural deficiency was no doubt a major constraint on industrial growth in particular and economic growth in general.

2. Inflation

In the face of falling growth rate, the economy faced the problem of double-digit inflation. The annual rate of inflation, as measured by the wholesale price index(WPI), crossed 9.6% in 2010-11. The root cause of inflation was sharp rise in food prices which made the life of most people miserable. In fact, two new types of inflation emerged, viz., food inflation and asset price inflation. Apart from rise in food and fuel prices, prices of land, flats and houses virtually skyrocketed. Even though the rate of increase in prices of manufactured goods was comparatively low, the annual rate of inflation was near the double-digit level. The inflation rate fell marginally from 9.6% in 2010-11 to 8.4% in 2011-12 mainly due to sharp fall in the rate of food inflation.

In fact, inflation in India during the Eleventh Plan period occurred due to both demand-pull and cost-push factors. Cost-push forces became very strong from Sep. 2011 due to sharp fall of the external value of rupee, i.e., depreciation of the rupee in terms of US $ and other key currencies. The fall in the external value of the rupee raised the cost of imports of raw materials and fuel needed for industrial production. Consequently overall costs of production of manufactured goods increased. So India faced the problem of imported inflation. This means that inflation in India did not just have domestic sources; it had international roots also. And anti-inflationary measures adopted by the GOI did not achieve much success(because there were not really strong).

3. Employment Generation

The Eleventh Plan could not make much dent on the unemployment problem either. The rate of employment generation was less than 1% p.a in spite of fairly satisfactory growth rate achieved. Thus India virtually achieved jobless growth.

4. Imports and Exports

Both imports and exports of India increased quite fast since the opening up of the economy since July 1991 and greater and greater integration of the Indian economy with the rest of the world. Exports also increased for another reason, viz., the depreciation of the rupee after the 1991 crisis. Imports increased due to relaxation of import control and permission given by the GOI for importing more goods. Imports increased due to the adoption of various trade liberalisation measures such as removal of quantitative restrictions on imports and large reduction in tariffs.

The GOI adopted various positive measures to promote exports. Consequently the rate of growth of India's exports in 2010-11 was 4.5%. But the momentum could not be sustained and the rate of growth of exports fell sharply to 21.3% in 2011-12. The rate of growth of exports fell sharply in 2012-13. And since the growth of exports fell far short of that of imports, there was a huge deficit in the current account.

5. Capital Movements

Economic reforms led to larger and larger inflows of foreign capital. This improved India's BOP position considerably. In fact, the increase in exports and greater inflows of foreign capital together made India's BOP position comfortable. However, due to global financial crisis there occurred huge outflow of financial capital from India since 2008-09. This led to a deficit in India's BOP (current account and capital account taken together).

The Effect of Global Financial Crisis

Financial globalisation was not an unmixed blessing for India. In fact, the free flow of international portfolio capital led to lot of volatility in the external value of the rupee and adversely affected not only India's trade in goods but also inflows and outflow of financial capital (which was the most mobile of all factors). To be more specific, due to global financial crisis, there occurred huge outflow of capital from India. This led to depreciation of the rupee. And since May 2010 the rupee continued to depreciate quite sharply. The process was largely initiated by the announcement of the US Federal Reserve Board (FRB) that it would start relaxing its quantitative easing (QE) programme from Sep. 2013 in view of the recovery of the US economy. Consequently it was apprehended that India would become capable of paying for its imports and the end result would be an increase in current account deficit (CAD). In addition, the sharp depreciation of the rupee led to huge outflows of financial oapital through foreign institutional investors (FIIs). They first, pulled out of the corporate debt market and then from the equity market. This, in its turn, led to further depreciation of the rupee.

Moreover the global financial crisis deepened in 2008, creating liquidity crisis in the USA and leading to capital outflows from India. This was another cause of depreciation of the rupee. The reason was simple. To cure the liquidity crisis of the home country FIIs sold shares of Indian companies in large quantities and got rupees which they converted into dollars for repatriation to the USA. So the supply of rupees and the demand for dollars increased in the foreign exchange market . Consequently the rupee depreciated in terms of the dollar. This made India's imports, mainly of crude oil, expensive and adversely affected her balance of payments. At the same time India faced a new problem, viz., imported inflation since rise in price of imported inputs, mainly capital goods and metals, raised domestic costs and prices.

Poverty Alleviation

According to the 55th round of NSS (1999-2000) for all-India (covering both rural and urban areas), the percentage of people below the poverty line fell from 36 in 1993-94 to 26 in 1999-2000. However, the rate of reduction in poverty ratio slowed down over the 12-year period, 1993-94 to 2004-05, as compared to the pre-reform period. In 2004-05, the rural poverty ratio fell to 28.3. In spite of this the incidence of poverty in rural areas was higher than that in urban areas in the same year.

Another point to note is that a secular decline in rural poverty ratio occurred in every Indian state, to a varying extent though.

There was also a secular decline in the urban poverty ratio in every State, although there was a lot of inter-State variation in the ratio.

Latest Estimates of Poverty

The poverty estimates made by the Planning Commission on the basis of special 68th round of NSS in June 2013 shows that during the 7-year period 2004-05 to 2011-12 there has occurred a large decline in poverty ratio — from 37.2 to 21.9. This shows a total decline of 15.3% or an annual decline of 2.2% (approx.). Furthermore there was a much further decline in poverty ratio in rural areas (by 16.1%) than in urban areas (12%). By using the poverty line cut-off ratio it was found that there were 270 mn. poor in India in 2011-12 compared to 407 mn. in 2004-05. So, around 137 mn. people were lifted above the poverty line.

In short, poverty declined at the rate of 2.2% per annum over the 7-year period (2004-05 to 2011-12) as against 0.74% during 1993-94 and 2004-05.

According to the Planning Commission, the incidence of poverty fell during the reference period for a simple reason. The benefit of high average growth (of 8.5% p.a.) trickled down to the poor in spite of the worst droughts of 2009-10 and the slowing down of growth rate in 2008-09 due to global financial crisis.

Another factor contributing to decline in poverty during this period was larger government spending on social welfare programmes. Perhaps the most notable programme is the Mahatma Gandhi Rural Employment Guarantee Scheme (MGREGS), which was started in 2006. The scheme guarantees employment of 100 days for one person in each rural family at a daily minimum wage of Rs. 100. Apart from providing employment to the rural poor, the scheme helped to push up wages in rural areas by increasing the demand for labour and thus led to a fall in the incidence of rural poverty.

Over the 7-year period under consideration about 138 mn. people were lifted above the poverty line (from 326 mn. to 217 mn. in rural areas and from 81 mn. to 53 mn. in urban areas).

High Level of Malnutrition

It has to be noted that in spite of reduction of poverty, malnutrition still remained high during the period under review, as was indicated by the high percentage of underweight children below 3 years of age. No doubt poverty is the main cause of malnutrition. But malnutrition cannot be explained only (or fully) in terms of poverty. So it is high time Indian planners gave greater focus on the issue of malnutrition.

Social Indicators of Development

Amartya Sen and Jean Dreze have shifted their focus on poverty estimates based on the headcount ratio to certain broad social indicators such as real agricultural wages, infant mortality rate and illiteracy rate. And due to greater stress on development of social services for achieving inclusive growth by Sen and others, GOI has increased its expenditure on social services. The share of the Central Government expenditure on social services (such as education, health, and rural development) in the total expenditure of the Government has increased from 11.23% in 2002-03 to 19.44% in 2008-09. Such expenditure by both the Central and State Governments increased from Rs. 1,53,454 crores in 2003-04 to Rs. 3,57,381 crores in 2008-09, showing an increase of 132%.

Agriculture

Perhaps the most serious drawback of planning in the 15-year period (1997-2012) was almost complete failure on the agricultural front. The rate of growth of the agricultural sector picked up marginally from 1.8% p.a. in the Ninth Plan (1997-2002) to 2.5% in the Tenth Plan (2002-07). And slow growth of the farm sector held in check the progress on the industrial front since industrial growth depends on generation of demand for manufactured goods from the farm sector. Therefore, it may be suggested that investment for building adequate agricultural infrastructure in the form of expansion (or spread) of irrigation facilities, rural roads, and flood control measures has to be given much greater priority and has to be stepped up in the next and subsequent plans.

Employment Generation

Perhaps the most dismal performance of planning during the post-reform period has been in the area of employment. And due to the inability of the planners to create sufficient employment opportunities, the rate of unemployment, instead of falling, has remained more or less constant, or even increased in some of the years. In fact, data show deterioration on the employment front. To be more specific, the rate of growth of employment in the organised sector has been a measure 0.05% per annum in the 14-year post-reform period(1994-08), compared to 1.2%p.a. in the 11-year pre-reform period (1983-94).

Price Inflation

Another major failure of Indian planning is found in the area of price stability. Planners failed to bring the rate of price inflation down for ensuring macroeconomic stability. High fiscal deficit of the Government (at around 5% of GDP) in recent years was the main cause of high rate of inflation (exceeding 10% p.a.) in recent years. Apart from causing distress to millions of poor people in India, double-digit inflation acted as a serious constraint on economic growth.

Current Account Deficit

The high rate of inflation also increased the CAD by raising imports and slowing down the rate of growth of exports. The CAD was 4.8% in 2012-13 which was quite unsustainable and was the main cause of a sharp depreciation of the rupee.

Comments

Two needs of the hour are (i) to promote agricultural growth and (ii) to build a strong and integrated infrastructure. Agricultural growth can be promoted through new investment by both public and private sectors. A faster growth of the farm sector by improving the supply situation will help to bring the rate of food inflation in particular and rise in industrial costs and prices in general down. In addition, agricultural growth is likely to promote industrial growth through both demand and supply linkages.

The country is now faced with food problem which is likely to assume serious proportions day by day. And there is a genuine threat to India's food security system. This is why many economists and agricultural researchers have felt the need for a Second Green Revolution which alone can solve India's food problem.

Finally, it may be suggested that to achieve faster economic growth on a sustainable basis public investment in infrastructure building has to be increased. New investments by the private sector are also needed for expanding existing production capacity. This is the essential pre-requisite for achieving faster industrial growth, which is the main source of overall growth of the economy, as measured by GDP at market price.

KEY POINTS

1. ***Economic planning*** **:** Economic planning is the process of consciously and systematically organising economic and technical information into an internally consistent conceptual framework within the context of economic and non-economic constraints toward the realisation of a prescribed goal.

2. ***Planning in India*** **:** From 1950-51 India adopted the planning system for two main purposes: (i) to control and to regulate the private sector and (ii) allocate resources among different sectors and activities as also between the Centre and the States.

The initial focus of planning in India has been on poverty alleviation by generating adequate employment opportunities with a view improving the level of living of the people.

3. *The role of planning in the pre-reform period* : The role of planning in India during the pre-reform may first be discussed briefly. The following points are worth noting in this context:

(i) *accelerating the rate of economic growth,*

(ii) *accelerating the rate of economic growth,*

(iii) *economic self-reliance,*

(iv) *making an optimal correction of market failure,*

(v) *regulation of the private sector, and*

(vi) *poverty alleviation.*

4. *The role of planning in the post-reform period* : Even in the era of privatisation and economic liberalisation planning had an important, though different role to play. Regarding the role of planning in the post-reform period the following points are to be noted:

(i) *improving the quality of life of people,*

(ii) *poverty alleviation,*

(iii) *special anti-poverty schemes,*

(iv) *building an integrated physical infrastructure,*

(v) *need for more investment in agriculture,*

(vi) *regional balance,*

(vii) *protecting the physical environment and maintaining ecological balance, and*

(viii) *transfer of resources from the centre to the states.*

5. *Indicative planning* : During the reform period the GOI has relied on indicative planning. In such planning we see the use(s) of centrally determined targets to coordinate private and public sector investment and output plans.

6. *The Second Plan and the Mahalanobis model* : From the Second Five Year Plan (1951-56) till the Fourth Plan (1969-74) the main constraint on India's economic growth was acute scarcity of physical capital which was responsible for low productive capacity of the economy. According to the Mahalanobis model, on which the Second Five Year Plan was based, the "proper development strategy would be to bring about a rapid development of industries producing investment goods in the beginning by increasing appreciably the proportion of investment in basic and heavy industries. The Mahalanobis strategy of development also suggested that productive employment could be guaranteed by increasing the production of capital good. According to this strategy, the only way of eliminating unemployment in India is to build up a sufficiently large stock of capital.

7. *Import-substituting industrialisation* : Another important aspect of the development strategy adopted in India's Second and Third Five Year Plans was the stress on import-substituting type of industrialisation. This is why an inward-looking development strategy was adopted. This strategy was supposed to generate sufficient employment opportunities.

8. *The strategic role of the public sector* : Another notable aspect of Indian development strategy pursued up to the end of 1980s was the strategic role assigned to the public sector. This was based on the belief that an undue reliance on the private sector and market mechanism would lead to maximum production of luxury goods and non- essential items of consumption for the rich.

9. *The Third Plan and economic self-reliance* : The Third Five Year Plan also laid stress on the development of basic and heavy industries such as steel, fuel, power, chemical and machine building. Two main objectives of the Third Plan were achieving self-sufficiency in foodgrains and increasing agricultual production to meet the requirements of industry and exports.

Essentially a growth-oriented development strategy was pursued in India till the end of the Third Plan. The plans also mentioned two other objectives viz., increasing employment and reducing income inequalities.

10. *The Fourth Plan (1969-74) and poverty alleviation* : In the Fourth Five Year Plan (1969-74) there was shift of emphasis on poverty alleviation by helping the weaker sections of society mainly in rural areas, such as small and marginal farmers and landless workers.

At the same time a new agriculture strategy was adopted. It involved the use of high yielding varieties (HYV) seeds, fertilisers, pesticides and the supply of irrigation water in a few selected districts of Punjab, Haryana and Western UP. This brought about Green Revolution which raised India's wheat output appreciably.

11. ***The fifth Plan (1974-78)*** **:** At the time of formulation of the Fifth Plan it was realised that economic growth alone would not lead to the solution of the problem of poverty and unemployment in India in near future.

During the Fifth Plan period, the Prime Minister's 20-Point Programme was accorded higher priority than the implementation of the plan programmes and meeting plan targets.

12. ***The Sixth Plan (1980-85)*** **:** The development strategy of the Sixth Plan laid stress on ensuring efficiency in the use of resources and increase in resource productivity. It set a growth target of 5.2% per annum. As for resource allocation, the maximum priority was accorded to infrastructure sector. In addition higher priority was given to employment generation and poverty alleviation.

13. ***The Seventh Plan (1985-90)*** **:** Four notable feature of the Seventh Plan strategy were the following:

(i) *full capacity utilisation,*

(ii) *direct attack on unemployment and poverty,*

(iii) *maximum production of wage (mass consumption) goods, and*

(iv) *economic liberalisation and greater scope for the private sector.*

14. ***India's economic performance in the pre-reform period (upto 1990-91)*** **:** A study of India's performance in the first four decades of planning—known as the pre-reform period—presents a mixed picture. The following points are worth noting in this context:

(i) ***Structural change*** **:** Indian economy achieved structural transformation during this period. The share of agriculture in GDP fell and that of industry increased.

(ii) ***Self-sufficiency in foodgrains*** **:** Since food production increased faster than the rate of growth of population India achieved self-sufficiency in foodgrains.

(iii) ***Industrial growth*** **:** The industrial sector grew very fast in the first 15 years of planning for various reasons.

However, whatever little economic growth was achieved during the first three decades of planning it did not have any notable impact on the incidence of poverty. This simply means that the benefits of economic growth did not trickle down to the poor.

However, the high growth rate achieved in the 1980s was not sustainable. The increase in the public sector investment was achieved by incurring more and more deficits in the budget.

A portion of public sector investment was covered by external commercial borrowing. Since the volume of such borrowing continued to increase over the years, there occurred a sharp increase in India's external public debt.

In spite of the adoption of various special job-creating programmes, employment opportunities increased only marginally.

The rates of gross savings and domestic capital formation as a percentage of GDP showed an upward trend during the first three decades of planning (1951-80). The excess of gross domestic investment over gross domestic saving was covered by foreign aid, i.e., concessional foreign assistance.

15. ***The Eighth Plan (1992-97) and its development strategy*** **:** The final version of the Eighth Plan (1992-97) was formulated in the context of the new economic policy (NEP) which put stress on liberalisation, privatisation and globalisation (LPG). The public sector, which was assigned a dominant role in earlier plans, lost its pre-eminence.

The main thrust of the Eighth Plan was on creating a more competitive environment as a means of improving the efficiency of private enterprises and raising productivity of resources.

The Eighth Plan adopted an export-oriented growth strategy. The stress was on promoting exports with a view to achieving economic self-reliance.

16. ***The Ninth Plan (1997-2002) and its development strategy*** **:** In the Ninth Plan the private sector was assigned a key role in raising the rate of growth and creating adequate employment opportunities. At the same time the Government and public sector were entrusted with the task of providing essential social services such as health care, education and safe drinking water, especially in the rural areas.

The Ninth Plan also laid emphasis on promoting exports as part of its export-led growth strategy. The focus was on raising exports of agriculture products with a view to increasing the incomes of the farmers.

The Ninth Plan also stressed that the proceeds from disinvestment of public sector enterprises in non-strategic enterprises would be used for mainly the much needed investment in the social sector, especially health and education.

Finally the Ninth Plan highlighted the need for reduction of combined fiscal deficit of the Central and State Governments. This was mainly sought to be achieved through larger tax collection, subsidy reduction and cut in non-plan expenditure.

The Ninth Plan did not achieve much success in the true sense. Instead it failed on two main fronts— economic growth and employment generation. The Plan failed to generate employment for 50 million persons as per the target.

17. ***The Tenth Plan (2002-07)*** **:** The Tenth Plan set a fairly ambitious growth target of 8% per annum. However, the main stress was on human development. This is why it also set the targets for other aspects of all-round development. The focus was or the following:

(i) *reduction of poverty,*

(ii) *increase in literacy rate,*

(iii) *employment generation,*

(iv) *balanced development of states, and*

(v) *equity and social justice.*

18. ***Development strategy*** **:** Five notable aspects of development strategy of the Tenth Plan were the following:

(i) *redefining the role of the state,*

(ii) *improving the quality of life,*

(iii) *stress on agricultural development,*

(iv) *employment generation through growth of the services sector, and*

(v) *special poverty alleviation measures.*

19. ***Achievements and failures of the Tenth Plan*** **:** The Tenth Plan achieved success in most areas but failed in others. The following points are to be noted in this context:

(i) *faster economic growth, and*

(ii) *increase in foreign exchange reserves.*

20. ***The eleventh plan (2007-12)*** **:** The Eleventh Plan (2007-12) envisaged faster economic growth. The stress was on inclusive growth. The main objectives of the Eleventh Plan were the following:

(i) *faster economic growth,*

(ii) *spread of educational opportunities,*

(iii) *improvement of public health, and*

(iv) *provision of adequate infrastructural facilities.*

No doubt the Eleventh Plan set a few highly ambitious objectives and targets. However, most of the objectives remained largely unfulfilled.

21. ***Macroeconomic performance during the post-reform period*** **:** In the first two decades of economic reforms (1991-2012) India made notable progress in raising the levels of income and improving the standards of living of the people. India succeeded in surpassing the so-called Hindu rate of growth (3.5%) which it just managed to achieve during the first two decades of planning (1951-70). In the 1980s India succeeded in achieving an annual GDP growth of 5.6%. However, due to the serious BOP crisis faced by the country in 1991, the planners changed the development strategy from import-substitution (or inward-orientation) to export promotion (or outward-orientation). No doubt, the performance of the Indian economy was quite satisfactory (and much better) due to the initiation of economic reforms after the adoption of the new economic policy (NEP).

KEY TERMS

Indicative planning	Green revolution
Inward-looking policy	Outward-looking policy
Economic self-reliance	Market failure
Plan holiday	Structural change(s)
Inclusive growth	Empowerment
Marginalisation	Food security
Food inflation	Asset price inflation
Regional balance	Poverty alleviation
Import-substituting industrialisation	Promotion of competition
Disinvestment	Hindu growth rate

ASSIGNMENTS

1. Make an overall assessment of India's planning experience.
2. What are the major accomplishments of the process of planning in India.
3. Discuss some areas where Indian planning exercise has failed miserably.
4. Make a critical assessment of the Eleventh Five Year Plan (2007-12).
5. Discuss the new role of planning in the new liberalised era.
6. "Indian plans are good on paper but suffer from implementation failure". Discuss.
7. Discuss the perennial conflict between growth and equity in the context of Indian planning.
8. Comment on the following two statements:
   (a) Indian planning has neglected the agricultural sector almost completely, at least during the post-reform period.
   (b) India has achieved virtually jobless growth during the post-reform period.
9. Write short notes on the following:
   (a) indicative planning and
   (b) plan holiday
10. Why did the Mahalanobis strategy of developing basic and heavy industries got into trouble and how it was modified in the fifth and subsequent plans?

44A THE TWELFTH FIVE YEAR PLAN (2012-17)

The Twelfth plan became operational at a wrong time — when the global economy was passing through a second financial crisis, known as the sovereign debt crisis of Euro zone. The crisis surfaced in the terminal year of the Eleventh plan and affected most, if not all, countries of the world, including India. Consequently India's GDP growth rate fell to 6.2% in 2011-12. The falling trend continues in 2012-13 which was the first year of the Twelfth plan. The growth rate in that year was only 5%. The focus of the Twelfth plan was on achieving higher rate of growth. The objective was to make growth both *inclusive* and *sustainable.*

The focus of the Twelfth Plan is on 'faster, sustainable and inclusive growth'. This is why it has given necessary emphasis on poverty alleviation, ensuring mass access to both economic and social infrastructure which comprises roads, highways, irrigation water, electricity, etc. as also health care and educational opportunities. It also lays stress on reducing regional/social/gender inequalities and making a special case in favour of the marginalised and the weaker sections of society. This is why the Plan is tilted in favour of allocating more resources to the priority sectors/areas with a view to ensuring inclusiveness. This means that all sections of society, mainly the poor and marginalised get the maximum benefits of the fruits of the progress and thus making the concept of inclusiveness becomes really meaningful.

As noted earlier, India faced two main macroeconomic imbalances, viz., (i) high fiscal deficit (which was 4.8% of GDP in 2012-13) as a result of global financial crisis and (ii) widening deficit in the current account of the BOP (which rose to 4.8% of the GDP in 2012-13).

Two-Pronged Strategy

Keeping in view the above two constraints, the Twelfth Plan proposed a two-pronged strategy. The initial focus was on bringing the macroeconomic imbalances under control. The subsequent focus was on reversing the slowdown of the growth rate, and pushing structural reforms in many areas which were growth-promoting in nature. So reform measures were undertaken in those areas which were found to be crucial for maintaining the medium-term GDP growth rate.

Overall and Sectoral Growth Targets

The Twelfth Plan (2012-17) has set a target of average annual 8% GDP growth over the five-year period, which is equal to the actual average growth rate achieved in the 11th plan. The target rate of growth for agriculture has been fixed at 4 % p.a., for industry (which includes mining and quarrying, manufacturing, power generation, gas and water supply and construction) at 7.6% p.a. and for services at 9% p.a.

It may be noted that in the first two years of the Twelfth Plan (2012-13 and 2013-14), the actual rate of economic growth achieved was only 5% and fell far short of the target. So a very sharp acceleration of the growth rate to 10% would be needed in the next three years of the Plan to recover the lost ground and achieve the Plan target. Since this does not seem to be quite feasible the planners are now thinking of revising the average growth rate target downward, as also the target growth rates of different sectors. Thus the whole 12th Plan growth targets seem to be fairly uncertain.

The Growth Trajectories

Recognising the uncertainty of achieving 8% growth rate per annum, the Planning Commission has recommended the following three growth trajectories:

Trajectory 1: Robust inclusive growth

This is supposed to ensure 8% growth per annum, with focus on the objective of 'inclusiveness' by implementing a well-designed strategy addressing the key growth-retarding factors, i.e., the obstacles to growth. This, of course, requires to start with, an identification of those factors which are holding India's economic growth in check.

Trajectory 2: Inadequate effort (or insufficient action)

While the overall direction of policy may be sound, if the policy action (implementation) is weak or policy implementation is poor (ineffective), then the outcomes are likely to be weaker than anticipated. This is clearly visible in one controversial area of the economy at least, viz., the subsidies. Till date the policy conflict between subsidies and financial stability of the economy is very much there (or is yet to be resolved).

Trajectory 3: Policy ineffectiveness

If structural bottlenecks or critical supply constraints relating to energy and transport are not overcome, then hardly anything can be done to build (regain) the growth momentum (which has been partly lost).

Investment

Economic growth is largely a matter of investment or physical capital formation. And to achieve the growth rate of 8% or even 10% in the terminal year, it is estimated that the rate of fixed investment will have to increase by 1.5% of GDP per annum over the level of that in 2011-12. It is projected that the fixed investment rate has to increase to 35% of GDP for the whole Plan period. However, the increase in investment is just a necessary condition for accelerating the rate of growth. The sufficient condition is that there should be relaxation in the physical constraints or bottlenecks which hold economic growth in check. This, of course, requires removal of various types of infrastructural deficiencies.

Composition. The rate of investment in the public sector is assumed to remain unchanged at 8.4% during the Twelfth Plan period. Household fixed investment (which includes investment by unincorporated businesses) is projected to reach an average rate of 12.3%. Private corporate investment is projected to increase from 11.3% in 2012-13 to 15% in 2016-17, showing an average of 13.5%. This will be the most important component of aggregate investment during the Twelfth Plan period.

The private sector is assumed to play an important role in infrastructure building, viz., power generation, construction of roads, ports, airports and establishment of telecommunication facilities. This focus in the area of infrastructure building will be on private-public partnership. It is felt that allocation of more investible resources in the infrastructure sector is absolutely essential for reviving investment climate and for encouraging business people to make more investment in the manufacturing sector.

Financing the 12th Plan

As for the financing pattern of the public sector in the Twelfth Plan, it has to be noted that the balance from current revenue (BCR) of the Centre as a percentage of GDP is estimated to be 1.88 for the Twelfth Plan. Note that BCR refers to the excess of tax revenue and other non-tax revenue over the current expenditure of the Central Government. With sufficient (growing) buoyancy in tax revenue and a cut in non-plan expenditure, the estimate of BCR (i.e., 1.88%) seems to be quite realistic. The Plan document projects higher tax collection including that from goods and service tax (GST). The gross tax revenue as a percentage of GDP is estimated to increase from 7.60 of GDP in 2012-13 to 8.79 in 2016-17, showing an average of 8.27% during the entire Twelfth Plan.

The Twelfth Plan has fixed the target of fiscal deficit at 3% for 2016-17. This suggests that the target of borrowing including net miscellaneous capital receipts (MCR) has to fall from 5.06% in the Eleventh Plan to 3.55% of GDP in the Twelfth Plan.

Domestic Saving Rate

The projection of the average level of domestic saving for the Twelfth Plan period is 33.6% of GDP. This is marginally higher than the 33.5% recorded in the Eleventh Plan.

Current Account Deficit

On the basis of its projections of exports and imports of goods (visible items) and services (invisibles), the Planning Commission estimates the current account deficit to be 3.4% of GDP for the Twelfth Plan. This is the average figure for the Plan as a whole.

However, to achieve this target the capital account of the BOP has to be managed in such a way that there is greater and greater inflow of financial capital.

Subsidies

Total subsidies, as a proportion of GDP, are projected to decline to 1.5% by 2016-2017. It is apprehended that the inability of the Government to pass an increase in global oil prices to the consumers through reduction of subsidies would have a telling effect on Plan resources. If the desired reduction in subsidies is not achieved, there is likely to be a resource crunch during the Plan period.

Resources of the Centre

The GBS available for the Twelfth Plan is estimated at Rs. 35,68,626 cr. at current prices. Central assistance (CA) to the States, and plans of Union Territories stands at Rs. 8,57,786 cr. Resources of Central public sector enterprises including borrowed resources, is estimated to be Rs. 16,22,899 cr. Thus the total resources available for meeting Central Plan outlay are, therefore, projected at Rs. 43,33,379 cr.

Borrowing

It is projected that borrowing by the GOI for financing its projects for Twelfth Plan will rise initially but is planned to fall gradually. The Centre's net borrowing which was 5.9% of GDP in 2011-12 was estimated to decline to 5.1% of GDP in 2012-13. Projected figures for the subsequent years have not yet been worked out or released.

Comments

The total resources for both the Central and State plans have to increase from an average of 10.96% of GDP in the 11th Plan to an average of 11.80% of GDP in the Twelfth Plan. The planned increase in resources mobilisation has to be achieved, keeping borrowing within the limit set and reducing fiscal deficits of both the Centre and the States to the projected level (3%). Keeping in view the resources mobilised by the public sector, the combined BCR of the Centre and the States has to increase faster than that projected in the Plan document. In fact, the Planning Commission admits that its assumptions regarding the increase in tax revenues of both the Centre and the States during the Twelfth Plan is not realistic, more so in view of sharp fluctuations in recent past mainly due to two major global crises — the US sub-prime crisis and the Eurozone crisis (also known as the sovereign debt crisis). So efforts have to continue during the Twelfth Plan for achieving the targeted tax-GDP ratios.

Now we pass on the issue of subsidies (or negative taxes). The increase in expenditure on subsidies is inevitable due to rise in prices of food (due to proposed food security legislation), fertiliser and petrol (due to increasing international price of crude oil from time to time). There is an urgent need to review the whole issue of subsidy and to introduce necessary reforms in this area so that the level of subsidy does not cross the ceiling of 1.5% of GDP by the end of the Twelfth Plan. Otherwise it will be difficult to generate the necessary resources for undertaking different plan activities as projected.

Allocation of Resources in the Public Sector

The total allocation of resources for the public sector during the Twelfth Plan has been fixed at Rs. 80,56,123 crores at current prices, of which the Centre's share is Rs. 43,33,739 crores as also that of Union Territories (UTs) States is Rs. 37,16,385 crores.

In fact, the Plan projects an increase of 132.12% in the GBS for the Centre. Central Assistance (CA) to State/ UT Plans for State sector/ UT programmes is almost 105.53% higher than that in the

Eleventh Plan. In absolute terms the Plan proposes to provide Rs. 8,57,786 crores at current prices as CA or grant to State/ UT Plans.

The total plan outlay for all the States and UTs is projected to increase from Rs. 17,25,848 crores in the Eleventh Plan to Rs. 37,16,385 crores in the Twelfth Plan (both at current prices), showing an increase of 115.34%. Three sectors would get the maximum allocation in State plans, viz., social services (41.68%), transport (11.53%) and agriculture and allied activities (6.85%).

An Overall Review of Objectives and Targets

We now summarise the objectives and targets of the Twelfth Plan.

1. Economic growth

The overall growth target (in terms of real GDP) has been fixed at 8% p.a. The target of growth for the manufacturing sector has been fixed at 10% p.a. On the basis of current trend and policy ineffectiveness, it seems that the higher projected growth rate is unlikely to be achieved.

2. Employment generation

The Twelfth Plan proposes to generate 50 mn. new employment opportunities in the non-farm sector. The Plan also incorporates a comprehensive scheme to promote skill certification to an equivalent number of people.

3. Poverty alleviation

The Twelfth Plan has also set a target of reducing absolute poverty, as measured by the headcount ratio, by 10% from 21.9% to 11.9% over the five-year period.

4. Education

The following three provisions have been made in the area of education:

(i) The mean years of schooling has to increase to 7 years by 2016-17.

(ii) The access to higher education will be enhanced by creating two million additional seats for each age group keeping in view the economy's need for different types of skills.

(iii) Finally the Plan seeks to eliminate both social gap and gender gap in school enrolment (i.e., gap among SCs, STs, Muslims and the rest of the population on the one hand and gap between girls and boys on the other hand).

5. Health

In the area of health the following three provisions have been made:

(i) Bringing down infant mortality rate (IMR) to 25 per 1,000 and maternal mortality rate (MMR) to 1 per 1,000 live births and improving child sex ratio (0-6 years) to 950.

(ii) Reducing the total fertility rate to 2.1%.

(iii) Reducing undernutrition among children aged 0-3 years to half of the existing level.

6. Infrastructure — both urban and rural

The Twelfth Plan has set the following targets for infrastructure building:

(i) Increasing investment in infrastructure as a percentage of GDP to 9%.

(ii) Increasing the gross irrigated area from 90 mn. hectare to 103 mn. hectare.

(iii) Providing electricity connection to all villages and reducing AT & C losses to 20%.

(iv) Establishing connection of all villages through metalled and all-weather roads.

(v) Upgrading the national and state highways to the minimum two-lane standard.

(vi) Completing Eastern and Western Dedicated Freight Corridors.

(vii) Increasing rural tele-density to 70%.

(viii) Ensuring access to at least 50% of rural population to 40 lpcd piped drinking water supply and giving Nirmal Gram Status to 50% of gram panchayats.

It is important to note that the Planning Commission has hinted at private-public partnership in infrastructure building so as to generate synergic effect. Otherwise infrastructure deficiency is likely to arise. And this will hold economic growth in check.

7. Environmental protection and sustainable development

Finally, the Twelfth Plan makes the following provisions for ensuring two things — protection of the environment and achievement of sustainable growth.

(i) Increasing green cover (as measured by satellite imagery) by 1 mn. hectare every year.
(ii) Adding 30,000 MW of renewable energy capacity.
(iii) Reducing emission intensity of GDP in line with the target of 20% to 25% over the 2005 level by the year 2020.

Concluding Comments

In the context of the present policy framework and macroeconomic parameters it appears that various targets regarding expansion of economic (infrastructural) and social (mainly education and health) facilities are unlikely to be reached by the end of the Twelfth Plan. Perhaps the most serious drawback of the Twelfth Plan is that it has not taken the problem of inflation seriously and has not chalked out an early strategy to tackle the problem. Inflation is now a more serious problem for the economy as a whole than it was a decade ago. Thus is causing severe hardship to most people by eroding their real income (or purchasing power) and pushing many people below the poverty line. Critics have pointed out that the Government should have devised an effective strategy to tackle the problem of inflation. But it is quite surprising that it has not done so.

CHAPTER 45

Global Financial Crisis, Eurozone Crisis and their Impact on Indian Economy

Business cycles may be transmitted from one country to another both through the price mechanism and the income effect.
W. M. Scammel

PREVIEW

From October 2007 the US economy faced a serious financial crisis. It started with a burst of housing bubble which led to large-scale mortgage defaults. Consequently banks and non-banking financial institutions incurred huge financial losses. The crisis occurred due to huge sub-prime housing loan made by American banks in the past few years. However, the crisis had its roots in burst of the IT bubble in the 2000s, which created some sort of mini-recession in the US economy. To enable the economy to recover from recession the Fed. reduced interest rates. Since banks were flushed with funds they wanted to dispose of their surplus liquidity by making as much loan as possible at low rates of interest. Since bank credit became cheap and readily available, loan was made even to less credit-worthy borrowers, who did not have the capacity to repay their loans even at the prime lending rate.[1]

So millions of sub-prime households borrowed huge sums of money to buy both cars and houses without taking into consideration their capacity to repay their loans. So Americans experienced a real estate boom. Prices of houses started rising sharply due to pent up demand. And both banks and households expected that prices would continue to rise.

However, the building of houses much in excess of real demand caused prices of houses to fall in 2006. And the housing bubble, much like the IT bubble, burst in the second half of 2007. With the fall in prices of houses, which were held as mortgage by banks, the poor households started defaulting on a large scale. They failed to make their installment payment on time. As a result banks suffered huge losses. Consequently the sub-prime market for bank loans collapsed.

---

1. Note that the minimum rate of interest at which a commercial bank makes loan to its most creditworthy borrower is known as the prime lending rate.

Earlier, in the 1920s, it was said that 'when America sneezes, the rest of the world catches cold'. Now-a-days we refer to the 'contagion effect' or the 'financial contagion'. This refers to the fact that any financial crisis anywhere in the world affects all other countries immediately mainly due to greater and greater integration of the world's capital markets.

SECURITISATION OF SUB-PRIME LOANS

Most banks succeeded in transferring their sub-prime mortgage loans to other banks and investors through a new type security called collateralised debt obligations (CDOs) which were backed by various types of mortgage assets.[1]

Financial intermediaries in the USA and Europe such as banks, hedge funds, pension funds, mutual funds, etc. invested huge sums in CDOs on the basis of sub-prime mortgage loans, without knowing how much risk was involved in it. The situation turned from bad to worse due to leverage. Those who bought these securities borrowed heavily from banks and various other financial institutions.

LIQUIDITY CRUNCH AND RECESSION

Banks and investment funds which had bought billions of dollars worth of these complex securities, on the basis of sub-prime mortgages, suffered huge losses. As a result there was liquidity crunch in the whole of the US economy. Many securities held by banks lost their value almost completely since there was no market for such securities to recover the capital embodied in them. So banks incurred huge losses. Consequently a large number of banks and investment institutions including the Leham Brothers went bankrupt. Other banks were also on the verge of bankruptcy due to liquidity crisis. So they suddenly stopped lending to firms and households. Instead they started calling in loans, i.e., asked their borrowers to repay loans as soon as possible. Due to such credit crunch both consumption and investment demand fell. This led to a slowdown in the rate of economic growth in the USA. In truth, the US economy experienced a drop in GDP in the second half of 2008 and had to face a recession. Paul Krugman sums up the causes of the crisis thus: "The crisis started with a burst of housing bubble which led to widespread mortgage defaults and hence to large losses of many institutions. The initial shock was compounded by secondary shocks as lack of capital forced banks to pull back, leading to further decline in the prices of assets, leading to more losses and soon a vicious circle of 'deleveraging'. Pervasive loss of trust in bank reinforced the vicious circle."[2]

Due to credit crunch the US economy faced recession in 2008

STOCK MARKET CRASH

The liquidity (credit) crunch due to financial crisis led to crash of the stock markets in the USA and Europe. Share prices of most companies fell to very low levels. This led to sharp fall in the capitalised value of companies. As a result the investors incurred huge losses and were reluctant to make more investment due to almost complte loss of confidence.

EFFECT ON ECONOMIC GROWTH

Due to erosion of capital base both banks and non-banking financial institutions faced a serious liquidity crisis. This adversely affected the smooth flow of loanable funds to companies which needed such funds for meeting their fixed and working capital needs. The shortage of funds to meet working capital needs made it difficult for companies to make payments to workers and suppliers of materials. And the shortage of long-term funds forced many companies to abandon their on-going (and half-finished) projects. As several banks and companies laid off their workers, there was a strong apprehension that such banks and corporations would sooner or later go bankrupt.

1. This is why CDOs are also called 'mortgage-backed securities'.
2. P. Krugman : 'Moment of Truth', *New York Times*, Oct. 2, 2008.

Consumers also found it virtually impossible to obtain loans to buy durable goods such as cars and houses. Consequently, both investment and consumption demand fell and the rate of economic growth in the USA and Europe slowed down.

A few years ago the USA achieved consumption-led growth fueled by the wealth effect resulting from the stock exchange boom. By contrast due to negative of wealth effect caused by a fall in share prices from the second half of 2007, there was a sudden fall in the demand for consumer goods. This choked off investment demand in both the USA and Europe through the acceleration effect.

In short, due to liquidity crunch, the financial crisis spread to the real sector of the US economy. As a result the process of economic growth virtually came to a grinding halt.

INTERNATIONAL TRANSMISSION OF THE CRISIS

When the strong and powerful US economy faced a severe financial crisis, banks, non-banking institutions of other countries as also individuals, which (who) invested their surplus funds in the USA, suffered huge losses. The reason was that their funds were used to finance the housing credit bubble. So they gave a call for being bailed out (rescued) by their governments or central banks.

In addition, due to crash in stock prices in the Wall Street, share prices in all European and Asian countries (including India) fell sharply. This led to huge losses to investors.

The US financial crisis led to international transmission of business cycle

Finally, the recession in the US economy led to decline in exports of European and Asian countries, including Japan. As a result production of exportable goods fell, leading to huge job losses. These countries had also to face recession. Thus there was international transmission of business cycles.

THE IMPACT OF GLOBAL FINANCIAL CRISIS ON INDIA

The global financial crisis affected India in more ways than one. The following points are to be noted in this context.

1. Stock market crash

When share prices in the USA and European countries started falling sharply, the problems of liquidity and credit crunch assumed serious proportions. And its effect spread to India. In order to meet their cash needs or their liabilities to creditors, foreign institutional investors (FIIs) started selling the shares of the Indian companies held by them and thus pulled out capital from India. Due to a strong selling pressure, the Sensex of the Bombay Stock Exchange (BSE) started falling sharply—from 21,000 in January 2008 to 9000, in Nov. 2008—by 60% in less than one year's time. As a result Indian companies and investors —both individual and institutional—incurred huge losses. Their life-time savings (wealth) had virtually been wiped out in no time.

2. The depreciation of the rupee

By selling shares in India, the foreign institutional investors got rupees. They converted rupees into dollars to repay their loans. As a result the demand for dollars increased and the dollar appreciated in terms of the rupee. In other words, the rupee depreciated and more dollars were required to buy for the same volume of imported goods. So India's import bill increased. Moreover, the Indian banks, located in other countries, also purchased dollars in India to carry on their foreign exchange business since foreigners were unable to lend to them by depositing them money. These two factors further raised the demand for dollars, causing further depreciation of the rupee.

3. Liquidity crunch in the banking sector

In order to maintain stability of the rate of exchange between the rupee and the dollar, the RBI had to intervene. It had to supply dollars from its accumulated foreign exchange reserves. As a result the quantity of rupee with the banking system fell since the RBI withdrew huge sums from the banking system. So banks had to face a serious liquidity crisis. This, in its turn, adversely affected the flow of credit to industry for meeting both working capital and fixed capital needs. As a result many potentially profitable investment projects had to be cancelled.[1]

Thus the proximate cause of liquidity crisis and credit crunch was the sale of billions of dollars by the RBI by withdrawing rupees from the banking system. As a result the inter-bank call rate touched a peak of 23%, much above the repo and reverse repo rates.

4. Impact on economic growth

The effect of US recession spread to Europe, Japan and most Asian countries. The growth rate of India's GDP fell to 6.4% in 2008-09 from 9% a year ago. In 2009-10, the Indian economy recovered slightly and its growth rate was marginally higher at 7.2%.

In 2008-09 the rate of growth of output in the manufacturing sector fell to 3.2% from 10.3% in 2007-08 and 14.9% in 2006-07. There was a drastic fall in the output of automobile, aviation and shipping industries as also in export-oriented industries such as textiles, leather goods, gems and jewellery. There occurred huge job loss in these sectors.

The rate of growth of agriculture fell from 4.9% in 2007-08 to 1.6% in 2008-09. And in 2009-10, the growth rate was virtually negative.

Perhaps the most serious consequence of the global financial crisis on India was fall in the rate of growth of output in the manufacaturing sector from 10.3% in 2007-08 to 3.2% in 2008-09. Both domestic demand and export demand for manufactures fell. Domestic demand fell since banks were reluctant to give consumer credit. Export demand fell due to recession in the USA and other countries. Consequently the employment situation worsened in 2008-09. Large job losses were reported in such labour-intensive sectors as textiles, metals, leather goods and gems and jewellery.

The rate of inflation, as measured by the CPI, increased to more than 11% in 2008-09. What was worse was the food inflation the rate of which touched around 18% in February 2010. All these were the causes of slow growth of the Indian economy.

5. Exports and BOP

India's exports fell sharply due to recessionary conditions in the USA and Europe. Moreover, India's import bill increased in 2008-09 due to sharp depreciation of the rupee, in spite of a fall in world commodity prices, including the price of crude oil. So India's balance of trade position worsened in 2008-09.

INDIAN RESPONSE TO THE CRISIS

Various measures have been adopted by the Government of India (GOI) to overcome the crisis situation faced by the country in the wake of the global financial crisis. These were the following:

A. Monetary Measures

The RBI adopted various measures to prevent the sharp depreciation of the Indian rupee.

In order to increase the quantum of liquidity of the banking system, the RBI cut the CRR during October 2008 and January 2009 from 9% to 5% in four steps. This enabled banks to acquire Rs.20,000 crores from the RBI against government securities for lending to mutual funds. In addition, the RBI released Rs.25,000 crores to banks in connection with the Government of India's farm loan waiver scheme. Moeover, unwinding of some marketing stabilisation schemes was also undertaken to increase the liquidity of banks. Through all these measures a sum of about Rs.200,000 crores had been injected into the Indian money market.

---

1. The problem became so serious that the inter-bank call money market virtually ceased to operate. No bank was willing to lend to other banks since every bank needed liquidity to overcome the crisis situation it faced. So the flow of credit to industries was obstructed. The flow of credit to both consumers for purchase of durable goods and to companies for making investment was further restricted due to the risk-averse attitude of most Indian banks.

In addition, the repo rate at which banks borrow from the RBI for a short period was cut five times from 9% to 4% in 2008. Due to the adoption of all these measures by the RBI, most Indian banks reduced their prime lending rate to around 12.5%. Since November 2008, the rate of inflation came down, mainly due to an increase in the supply of manufactured goods under the monetary stimulus.

The RBI also cut the reverse repo rate[1] to 4%. The objective was to provide more credit to both businesses for investment and consumers for purchase of durable goods.

In spite of all these, most banks have surplus liquidity now. The reason is that banks have become more risk averse and are reluctant to lend indiscriminately in order to avoid default risk.

B. Fiscal Package

In 2008-09 the Government of India introduced a fiscal package of Rs.30,700 crores. It comprised both an increase in government expenditure and a cut in taxes. The object was to help the growth of infrastructure industries, export-oriented industries, housing, automobiles as also small-scale and medium-scale industries. It was thought that this fiscal package would increase both consumer demand for goods and services and investment demand, which, in its turn, would stimulate economic growth.

We may now briefly discuss the various items of this first fiscal package one by one.

(i) Financing infrastructure development

The first fiscal package permitted Indian Infrastructure Finance Company Ltd. (IIFCL) to raise Rs.10,000 crores by issuing tax-free bonds. The IIFCL supplies fund to refinance low-interest long-term bonds provided by banks for undertaking infrastructure projects, especially those relating to highways, power and ports under public-private partnership. Such projects not only create the much needed social overhead capital but also increase the demand for steel, cement and various items and thus generate new employment.

(ii) Cut in central excise duty

The first fiscal package also sought to raise the demand for all commodities by cutting excise duties by 4% and thus leading to fall in their prices. As a result the demand for consumer durables such as cars, refrigerators, washing machines, etc. increased.

(iii) The textile sector

An additional allocation of Rs.1,400 crores has been made for upgrading of technology and thus achieving cost reduction in the textile sector. The objective was to make textile producing units, which were hit by falling export orders, to become viable domestically and more competitive in the international market.

(iv) Housing

With a view to giving a boost to the housing sector, which is highly labour-intensive, the RBI extended a credit of Rs. 4,000 crores to the National Housing Board (NHB) to enable it to lend to housing finance companies like HDFC and HUDCO. In addition, public sector banks announced a package for those who take housing loans in two categories – upto Rs.5 lakhs and between Rs.5 lakhs to Rs.20 lakhs. The basic objective was to create greater demand for houses and generate multiplier effect[2] due to the linkages of the housing industry with a number of other industries such as cement, steel, transport and communication, etc. An increase in demand for housing was supported to create employment. And the backward and forward linkage of the housing sector was likely to create indirect employment. So the total increase in employment and income would be a multiple of the initial increase in investment.

(v) Export promotion

In order to prevent the fall in exports due to global financial crisis, the government subsidied interest costs of exporters to the extent of 2 percentage points, subject to a minimum interest rate of 7% per annum. The low interest cost was supposed to make Indian exports more competitive by helping such

1. The reverse repo rate is the overnight rate of interest at which banks park their surplus funds with the RBI.
2. The multiplier effect includes both direct and indirect effects.

sectors as handlooms, textiles, leather goods, gems and jewellery as also small and medium enterprises. The Government ensured full refund of duties including service tax paid on inputs by providing an additional fund of Rs.1,100 crores.

(vi) Small and medium enterprises

The upper limit of unsecured loan to small, medium and micro-enterprises has been raised from Rs.50 lakhs to Rs.1 crore. In addition, the lock-in period for loans to such enterprises under the existing credit guarantee scheme was reduced from 24 months to 18 months in order to encourage banks to give more loans to this sector.

In addition, the RBI earlier announced an increase in refinance facilities to the Small Industries Development Board of India (SIDBI) which lends to small enterprises. These measures were likely to generate adequate employment opportunities in these highly labour-intensive units.

THE SECOND FISCAL STIMULUS PACKAGE

On January 2, 2009 the Government of India announced its second fiscal package to boost demand and increase real GDP. The focus was on increasing the supply of credit. Special attention was given to the housing and infrastructure sectors so that there was multiplier effect on employment and income[1] through an increase in demand for cement, steel, glass etc.

In order to ensure an increase in expenditure on infrastructure, finance was provided to non-banking finance companies (NBFCs) which specialise completely in financing of infrastructure. For this the Indian Infrastructure Finance Company Ltd (IIFCL) was allowed to borrow Rs.30,000 crores from the market by issuing tax-free bonds. This measure was supposed to assist in financing project worth Rs.75,000 crores.

Moreover, the depreciation rate for commercial vehicles purchased during January-March 2007 was raised to 50%. In addition, an extra line of credit was given to NBFCs so that they could assist the purchase of commercial vehicles. These measures were supposed to raise the demand for commercial vehicles which was severley hit by the global recession.

In order to stimulate the real estate and infrastructure sectors, the GOI reintroduced countervailing duties (CVs) on two basic inputs, viz., steel and cement in order to protect domestic industries from foreign competition.

In addition, the GOI increased the upper limit on investment by foreign institutional investors (FIIs) in rupee-denominated corporate bonds from \$8 mn. to \$15 mn. The objective was to ensure greater flow of cheap line of credit to the Indian corporate enterprises.

The NBFCs which supply funds to the infrastructure sector(s) were permitted to follow the route of external commercial borrowing. The GOI also permitted real estate companies to utilise ECB funding for development of integrated townships. The objective was to help Indian corporate enterprises to raise funds for carrying on their were investment activities.

THE THIRD FISCAL STIMULUS PACKAGE

In the third fiscal stimulus package announced on January 24, 2009 the GOI sought to increase aggregate demand by cutting central excise duty, customs duty and service tax.

1. The central excise duty was reduced from 10% to 8%. In addition, the earlier 4% cut in excise duty announced in December 2008 was extended beyond March 31, 2009.
2. In order to give relief to the power sector, import of naptha[2] was fully exempted from basic customs duty beyond March 2009.
3. The GOI also announced across the board cut in service tax from 12% to 10%.

1. This was likely to happen due to an increase in consumption demand following an increase in income.
2. Naphtha is required for power generation.

THE RECOVERY OF THE INDIAN ECONOMY

The Indian economy gradually recovered from the slowdown caused by the global financial crisis from the second half of 2009-10, mainly due to the initial increase in government expenditure under the fiscal stimulus and to the increase in household consumption expenditure and business investment demand later.

It is gratifying to note that the fundamentals of the Indian economy are still strong. As a result of high rates of saving and investment India has emerged as the second fastest growing nation in the world, next only to China. India's exports have also increased in 2009-10. Since global investors are getting higher returns from India, FDI has increased steadily since 2009-10.

EUROZONE CRISIS AND ITS IMPACT ON INDIA

In 2010 the world economy had a second financial turmoil. Consequently developed countries were threatened by another recession, especially in the European Euroland (consisting of all those countries which adopted the common currency Euro) even when the effects of global financial crisis (2007-09) completely subsided. The new crisis emerged due to the threat of defaulting on payment of its debt by governments of most European countries, especially, the Greek Government. In a sense this new crisis is a continuation of the earlier one. The reason is that in order to overcome recession or slowdown following the financial crisis of 2007-09, governments of most European countries increased their public expenditure through excessive external borrowing. Consequently their sovereign debt increased sharply. And these countries faced the problem of debt servicing. The huge debt service burden (involving payment of annual interest along with the repayment of the principal amount borrowed) created the risk of default on the part of the debtor nations.

The huge debt burden of Euroland shied away foreign investors by creating uncertainty about the returns for their investments in Euroland bonds. Consequently stock prices crashed not only in Europe but also in the USA and larger parts of Asia due to the contagion effect. In addition, fears of deep recession were widespread. These two factors — of which one was real and the other was much expected — led to fall in world prices of commodities, crude oil and petroleum. In fact the price of crude oil fell quite sharply.

Causes of Eurozone Crisis

The main cause of the Eurozone crisis was huge external debt burden. The Eurozone countries incurred huge external debt to lift their economies out of the deepest slump in 2007-09 and had to face the genuine possibility of defaulting on external debt. Asian countries including India had to suffer due to certain wrong steps taken by the European countries. The European countries had to incur huge debt which was not sustainable, since there was genuine possibility of default. However, there was need to borrow huge sums of money because these countries were living beyond their means.

While Greece, Ireland and Spain incurred huge fiscal deficit in the past and added to their debt every year, Greece experienced negative growth of GDP which made her burden more serious. Greece virtually received a double blow — mounting fiscal deficit in the midst of negative growth of GDP.

The external debt problem of 2010, which virtually reached a crisis proportion, was also faced by Spain, Portugal, Ireland, Italy and even the UK (which did not surrender its currency, viz., pound sterling to the European Central Bank). In order to avoid the likely contagion effect of the default on its external debt by Greece, the EU and IMF jointly announced $1 trillion bail-out package for Greece and other Eurozone countries to enable them to overcome the crisis situation by being able to service their debt (so that they did not fall in a debt trap). In addition, the European Central Bank (ECB), being an independent institution, was persuaded by members of the EU to buy Greek Government bonds with a view to easing the pressure on redemption of such bonds. This measure was supposed to help the Government of Greece to overcome the crisis. And the ECU, while announcing this measure, imposed the condition that Greece and other Eurozone countries would have to reduce their fiscal deficit. For achieving this the debtor nations had to raise taxes and reduce public expenditure at the same time.

The Debt Crisis of 2011

A more serious debt crisis again arose in Greece in 2011, putting the global financial markets in turmoil. The ECB again came to its rescue and purchased its bonds by imposing some stringent conditions that Greece would adopt more severe austerity measures for reducing its debt burden.

Spread of the Sovereign Debt Crisis

The sovereign debt crisis of 2011 spread to Italy, Spain and other countries of the region including Ireland, Portugal, UK and even Hungary, putting the whole Eurozone under tremendous pressure. They are all on the razor's edge and faced the risk of default on their external debt. In truth, the spread of the crisis to most European countries frightened investors who tried to pull out of sovereign bonds of the countries. This led to sharp fluctuations in share prices as also in exchange rates throughout Europe, the USA and Asia. There was huge outflow of funds from the whole Eurozone to the USA in both 2010 and 2011. However, in 2011 the USA itself was dragged into the zone of instability. As a result there was a great turmoil in financial markets in Europe, the US and even in Asia. In Aug. 2011, ECB purchased Italian and Spanish debt bonds to the value of 22 billion Euro as an emergency measure. In addition, in Sep. 2011 private banks which lent huge sums to Greece and other Eurozone countries agreed to write off 50% of their debt to three countries. This was no doubt a great source of relief to all debt-ridden European countries.

Eurozone Treaty

In Dec. 2011 the EU summit was held in Berlin to solve the Eurozone debt problem and in this summit a Eurozone Treaty was signed by member countries to pursue the EU to lend up to $ 200 billion to the IMF to enable it to aid Eurozone countries facing debt crisis. In addition, European Stability Financial Fund (ESFF) with $440 billion had already been established. Finally, a permanent facility, called the European Stability Mechanism with 500 billion Euro was established in 2012. However, it appears that the best way to solve the sovereign debt problem is to achieve greater and deeper integration of the economies of the Eurozone.

Impact on India

European debt crisis and slow economic recovery in the USA conjointly led to the slowdown of the Indian economy by hurting its exports and reducing capital inflows. In fact, if the austerity measures became much too stringent, these could have more adverse effects on India. In truth, huge outflows of funds from India through FIIs led to recurring crashes in stock market by hurting the sentiments of the investors, as had happened in 2008. The huge outflows of portfolio capital from India also led to the intense depreciation of the rupee which was subsequently aggravated by domestic speculative activity. No doubt, at the root of depreciation of the rupee is the ongoing sovereign debt crisis in Europe which still remains unresolved.

Due to this new global crisis India's exports to European countries and the USA fell sharply. This increased India's current account deficit (CAD). The growing CAD proved to be unsustainable and has been a cause of serious concern to India's policymakers, including the Governor of the RBI. And the large CAD in 2011-2012 and 2012-2013 put excessive downward pressure on the rupee. All these have adversely affected India's industrial growth. In fact, the current slowdown in India's economic growth is partly a result of Eurozone debt crisis, stagnation in European countries and a slow recovery in the USA. Of course, the rise in interest rates by the RBI to fight inflation also led to a fall in the demand for and production of capital goods which adversely affected her growth momentum to some .

KEY POINTS

1. ***Global financial crisis*** **:** From Oct. 2007 the US economy faced a serious financial crisis and recession. It started with a burst of housing bubble which led to widespread mortgage defaults. Since banks, making sub-prime loans, suffered huge losses, the sub-prime market collapsed. The credit crunch due to financial crisis led to the crash of the stock markets in the USA and Europe. This choked off investment demand in both the USA and Europe through the acceleration effect. There was international transmission of business cycles.

2. ***Effect on Indian economy*** **:** The global financial crisis affected the Indian economy in more ways than one. It led to stock market crash, the depreciation of the rupee, liquidity crunch in the banking sector and slowing down of the rate of economic growth, and fall in exports.

3. ***Indian response to the crisis*** **:** The GOI adopted a number of monetary and fiscal measures to revive the economy. And quite some success has been achieved in lifting the economy from recession and short-term sluggishness.

KEY TERMS

Prime lending rate	Sub-prime crisis
Mortgage-backed securities	Contagion effect
Securitisation of sub-prime loans	Liquidity crunch
Consumption-led growth	International transmission of business cycles

ASSINGMENTS

1. Highlight the causes of global financial crisis which started from October 2007.
2. Discuss the effects of global financial crisis of 2007-08 on the Indian economy.
3. Highlight the measures adopted by the Government of India to overcome the recessionary situation faced by India from October 2007. Comment on the effectiveness of the measures.
4. Do you agree with the observation that business cycles are transmitted from country to country? If so, briefly discuss how this happens.
5. Write short notes on:
   (a) Contagion effect and
   (b) International transmission of business cycles.

CHAPTER 46

Environment, Climatic Change and Sustainable Environment

> *Environmentalism ... sees humanity as a biological species tightly dependent on the natural world ... Many of Earth's vital resources are about to be exhausted, its atmospheric chemistry is deteriorating and human populations have already grown dangerously large. Natural ecosystem, the well-springs of a healthful environment, are being irreversibly degraded ... I am radical enough to take seriously the question heard with increasing frequency: Is humanity suicidal?*
> E. O. Wilson, the distinguished Harvard Biologist

PREVIEW

In the past two decades there has been growing concern over different types of pollution, deterioration of the environment and climatic change since all these are likely to affect the future development of all countries — both developed and developing. In 1992 a meeting called the Earth Summit or the United Nations Conference on Environment & Development (UNCED) was held at Rio in Brazil. Representatives from more than 150 countries participated in meeting. This Conference first brought into focus the link between the physical (natural) environment and economic development. It also introduced a new concept, viz., sustainable development. And the Conference generated greater awareness about environmental issues and sought to promote cooperation among different countries to avert environmental degradation, mainly by reducing the emission of greenhouse gases (GHG) such as carbon-dioxide. The main objective is to prevent adverse climatic change or global warming which is threatening the world at present. If this is not prevented, people all over the globe are going to face disastrous consequences.

There has always has been a conflict between faster economic growth and protection of the physical environment. The conflict is becoming more and more serious day by day, particularly in developing countries like India, mainly due to population explosion and mass poverty. Most developing countries are putting serious efforts to strike a balance between their need for achieving faster economic growth and keeping their natural base intact. In India and most other developing countries deterioration (degradation) of the physical environment is largely attributable to the adoption of a development strategy with primary focus on large-scale industrialisation. This is sought to be achieved by adopting energy-intensive techniques of production. In some countries bio-chemical based agricultural techniques are also in use.

At present India is achieving fairly rapid economic growth no doubt. But at what cost? At the cost of its environment. So there is need to control environmental pollution, clean rivers and avert climatic change as much as possible.

Causes of Environmental Degradation

There are three main causes of deterioration of the natural environment. These are the following:

1. Population Growth

There is concern about environmental issues mainly because sooner or later the size of the global population is likely to exceed the earth's carrying capacity. The needs of a rapidly growing population cannot be adequately met by the earth's finite resources. As a result a fall in the standard of living of the people in the future is inevitable. Rapid growth of population leads to excessive exploitation of natural resources such as forests, water, fisheries and minerals much faster than their capacity to regenerate themselves and thus lead to deterioration of the physical environment.

In addition, due to growing pressure of population on land, the same plot of land has to be cultivated more intensively by using chemical fertilisers and pesticides which often lead to soil pollution. Furthermore due to growing population there is overgrazing of grassland and forest land by domesticated animals. This leads to topsoil erosion or even desertification (conversion of fertile land into deserts). Finally, growing population leads to deforestation in two ways. Rural people cut trees for timber and firewood. Urban people destroy forests for constructing houses and townships. As a result there is increase in carbon dioxide content of the atmosphere which causes air pollution.

In short the growth of population itself generates more and more pressure on arable land and causes various environmental problems such as air, water and soil pollution as also biodiversity loss. And polluting environment spreads various types of diseases which are harmful to human health.

Furthermore overexploitation and overuse of land and water resources and the consequent deforestation and loss of biodiversity adversely affect sustainability of agriculture. Consequently food security is threatened, particularly in developing countries like India. The truth is that the Earth's capacity to support even the existing human and animal population has already been far exceeded in many parts of the world. It is felt that if the rate of growth of population is not slowed down or held in check, the food security system in most countries of Asia and Africa will be threatened. In addition, the increase in income in recent years is likely to increase the demand for fish and animal products. However, due to deforestation, water pollution and habitat loss the growing demand for such products in the face of an increase in purchasing power of the people cannot be met.

In addition, due to lack of adequate infrastructural facilities population growth has also created shortage of clean water in urban areas. Furthermore, there has occurred mushroom growth of slums with poor sanitation. This has increased the risk of various diseases.

So our main prediction is that slowing down of population growth is of paramount importance to protect the physical environment. In other words, environmental degradation has to be held in check to prevent future disaster.

2. Poverty

The second reason for environmental degradation in developing countries like India is mass poverty, particularly in rural areas where the majority of the people live. Poor people in rural areas depend heavily on common resources because they do not have adequate private property. So for survival they are constrained to cut forests for timber and firewood.

In addition, rural people use pasture land for grazing of their domesticated animals. These natural resources are exploited much faster than the rate at which they can be regenerated. Moreover when arable land becomes more and more scarce, poor people are forced to make a living by cultivating fragile land on hills and mountains.

Consequently there is large scale erosion of the topsoil which virtually amounts to converting fertile (arable) land into barren land. The growing incidence of poverty leads to degradation of the soil which, in its turn, increases the incidence of rural poverty. Thus there is some sort of vicious circle of poverty. Furthermore poverty results in malnutrition and reduces the poor people's capacity to earn more income by putting adequate and, times, streneuous effort. Poverty is thus self-perpetuating rather than self-destroying.

The rural people can survive only by exploiting and destroying natural resources on which property rights are not clearly assigned (or defined). So a basic paradox is encountered, known as *the tragedy of commons*. The basic point is that there is a conflict between private interest and community's benefit. What is good for an individual is not good for the society.

The poor people encroach upon large remote areas of forests and grassland to subsist. The pressure on the poor to push cultivation frontiers into ecologically fragile land leads to growing incidence of flood and soil erosion. And any attempt by the government to prevent such encroachment is strongly opposed by the poor, particularly in tribal areas. In many parts of India, stiff resistance has been put by these people.

Environment problem can be solved through poverty alleviation

Thus it is quite obvious that the environmental problem can be solved only through poverty alleviation. This case be achieved in various ways such as land reforms, generation of employment opportunities in the off-season and an increase in yield per hectare of land already in use. The productivity of land can be improved by making traditional (inadequate resource-based) agriculture to modern science-based agriculture. This is why suggestions have been put forward to introduce *organic farming*.

3. Green Revolution

The green-revolution technology has no doubt achieved quite some success in raising yield per hectare. But it has been criticised on environmental grounds. *Prima facie*, the use of fertilisers and pesticides has increased soil salinity. The problem has been compounded by spread of irrigation facilities which, in the absence of adequate drainage facilities, has resulted in soil degradation through salinity and water logging. So the time has come for taking adequate and appropriate steps to make the green-revolution technology clean and environment-friendly through the development of less poisonous chemicals, pest and insect control, application of less chemicals and improvement of drainage facilities.

BUSINESS AND THE NATURAL ENVIRONMENT

Business firms have the following two types of links with the natural environment:

(i) *Dependence on nature and natural resources*

On one hand, businesses require natural resources such as land for setting up plants and factories and using energy based on petroleum products (fossil fuels), coal, natural gas, wood and water for carrying on production. However, due to development of modern sophisticated technology in recent years most industries do not depend so much on natural resources.

(ii) *Generation of pollution*

On one hand industrial production generates various types of pollution and leads to environmental degradation. At present industries and vehicles in urban areas generate air, sound and water pollution. Such pollution causes considerable damage to human health and thus imposes costs on society. Thus the need to regulate the polluting industries is urgent. The Union Carbide's Bhopal plant is an infamous example of a polluting firm which did immesurable damage to health and life of the local people. Since the multinational company operated in an urban area without taking proper safeguards, leakage of gas from its pesticides plant claimed the lives of thousands of poor. It also posed a threat to the health of numerous others. Many people became blind and others became physically handicapped and thus permanantly disciplined.

In December 2011 about hundred people died in the AMRI hospital in Kolkata due to billowing toxic gas from the basement.

In all the major cities, numerous unauthorised polluting production units have been set up in most congested residential areas even by violating master plans and environmental laws. These units have got environmental clearance from the government and managed to thrive due to rampant corruption in the bureaucracy.

The Basic Dilemma

Economic development cannot be achieved without industrialisation. At the same time rapid industrial growth pollutes the environment in various ways. Industrialisation and urbanisation conjointly lead to deterioration of the physical environment since most modern industries use the environment as the waste sink. Thus if we are to achieve faster economic growth, the environment will also deteriorate very fast. If, on the other hand, we want to protect the physical environment, we have to sacrifice the much needed industrial growth which is the *sine qua non* of all-round economic development. Herein lies the dilemma and is illustrated by the environmental Kuznent's curve.[1]

Industrialisation, Urbanisation and Environment

According to N. Kaldor and others economic development is equated with industrialisation and in the wake of industrialisation there is a trend toward urbanisation. Realising the need to achieve rapid economic development in India, the maximum priority was accorded to industrialisation from the very beginning of the Second Five Year Plan (1956-61). The objective was to achieve rapid economic growth and in the process, generate adequate employment opportunities in a labour-surplus economy. No doubt new industrial plants and factories have been set up since 1956 in various metropolitan cities and semi-urban areas. As a result the material standards of living of the people have improved over the years but industrialisation and urbanisation led to the deterioration of the physical environment through air and water pollution and generation of huge quantities of hazardous wastes. Households and firms have used the environment as a waste sink, as mentioned earlier.

Air and water pollution are a serious health hazard to the present population. It is also a serious threat to future generations since it leads to global warming with all its disastrous consequences.

It may also be noted that India's urban population has been increasing much faster than the rate of industrial growth. This is not only polluting the environment but putting more and more pressure on existing sanitation facilities and creating shortage of clean water. As a result the urban population is exposed to serious health hazards. The urban people suffer from various types of air-borne and water-borne diseases. As a result their health deteriorates. There has also occurred mushroom growth of slums due to lack of adequate housing facilities. Those who live in slums do not get adequate supply of water. And since they live under unhygenic conditions they are exposed to various types of diseases.

The governments of developing countries like India are unable to supply adequate clean water and sanitation facilities to their rapidly growing urban population. Urban population is increasing not so much due to natural growth but mainly due to migration of people from rural to urban areas in search of jobs and opportunities.

Air and Sound Pollution

Two root causes of air pollution are use of energy from fossil fuels in industrial production and continuous increase in the number of vehicles which are run by petrol and diesel. Both are man-made sources of air pollution.

As the share of industry in GDP and employment increases, the consumption of energy also increases very fast — at times even faster than the rate of growth of GDP. This is exactly what has happened in India since the beginning of the Second Plan which accorded the maximum priority to basic heavy and chemical industries. As a result the pollution level has been increasing day by day.

1. See the author's *Contemporary Development Economics* (NCBA, 2nd Edn., 2011)

Industries cause air pollution by emitting smoke and dirt containing carbon dioxide, carbon monoxide, and methane gas in the atmosphere. Such toxic emissions by the factories cause a serious health hazard. Toxic gases are also emitted from vehicles plying in urban areas. Motor vehicles such as cars, buses, trucks and two-wheelers generate pollutants such as carbon monoxide, hydrocarbon and nitrogen oxide and these result in air pollution. Such pollution does considerable damage to human health. In addition, such vehicles cause tremendous noise pollution which tells on the nerves of the people. Due to unnecessary honking by most drivers either due to ignorance or due to habit persistence, the problem gets from bad to worse. In all metropolitan cities of India air pollution due to vehicular movements has virtually crossed tolerance limits.

Air pollution leads to deterioration of people's health conditions by causing tuberculosis, asthma and other respiratory diseases. As a result their working capacity and productivity fall. This is a social cost or negative externality which is ignored by most private entrepreneurs while making their own profit and loss calculations. So the persons affected by such diseases have to spend lots of money for their treatment. What is more serious is that a high level of lead emitted by motor vehicles go into the blood of youth children and expose them to various health problems, including neurological deficiencies. A higher level of lead in the air expose even adults to high blood pressure and great risk of heart attack or even brain stroke.

Notwithstanding its adverse consequences the consumption of energy has been increasing day by day in India and other developing countries for a very simple reason. Environmental regulations are not very strong in such countries. Even though many environmental regulation laws have been passed at the Central and State levels from time to time and pollution control boards have been set up, the enforcement machinery is very weak.

Marginal Improvement in Environment

Due to legal actions taken by high courts and the Supreme Court for improving the environment, some success has been achieved toward the use of lead-free fuels and in fixing better emission standards for cars and buses running in urban areas. Some buses and three-wheelers have already started using less toxic CNG gas instead of diesel and petrol. In addition, the Government has taken some measures to reduce emission of lead by motor vehicles. These are no doubt encouraging trends and these measures are to be adopted on a wider scale as soon as possible.

Water Pollution

Apart from air and sound pollution, there is another type of pollution which often goes unnoticed, viz., water pollution. It is a serious problem in both urban and rural areas. The problem arises in urban areas mainly due to contamination of underground water from industrial wastes. Most urban industries throw toxic chemicals and heavy metals such as lead and mercury into nearby rivers, lakes and ponds. This leads to contamination of water. The main rivers of India, viz., Ganga and Yamuna have become highly polluted over the years. As a result two problems have arisen. (i) There is acute scarcity of safe drinking water. (ii) Fish stocks have decreased due to limited capacity of rivers to support aquatic life.

Industrial pollutants thrown into rivers lead to contamination of surface water near towns and cities. In addition, ground water has become polluted due to seepage of chemical wastes, heavy metals and other hazardous industrial wastes which are thrown into rivers and drains. In the Behala area of Kolkata some people developed skin disease due to disposal of waste material by a soap factory which led to contamination of drinking water.

Contamination of drinking water is a very serious problem for urban slum dwellers who do not get adequate clean water to drink and proper sanitation facilities either. These urban poor suffer from water-borne diseases which claim lives of a large number of people, mainly children. It is a pity that over the years the number of people without access to clean water and proper sanitation has increased steadily in spite of faster growth of the economy.

Agricultural and Rural Development and the Environment

The steady increase in food production in India, in the face of fall in per capita land availability has led to degradation of land and loss of ecological balance. The main reason is that since the late 1960s the stress has been on intensive rather than extensive cultivation which relies on the use of chemical fertilisers and pesticides. If the trend is not reversed the country's food security system is likely to be threatened.

Land degradation occurs due to top soil erosion[1], salinisation of soil and water logging and it reduces yield per hectare. This is a genuine threat to the survival of rural people. In addition, the diversion of arable land for non-agricultural purposes and the depletion and pollution of water resources result in loss of rural livelihood. This also leads to unplanned migration of rural people to towns and cities, resulting in the proliferation of urban slums, with all its adverse effects.

In order to ensure food security through sustainable agriculture, while at the same time protecting the means of subsistence of the rural poor, land and water resources ought to be protected from pollution and degradation. As M. S. Swaminathan writes: "The future of food security depends on the conservation and care of arable land through attention on soil health and replenishment of fertility and the conservation and careful management of all water resources so that more crops can be produced. Improvement of production in perpetuity without associated social or ecological harm is vital to safeguard food security". So it is high time the Government integrated the use of appropriate technology for protecting soil fertility with its programme and strategy of agricultural growth.

Deforestation

Another important cause of land degradation is deforestation, that is, cutting of trees for fuel, timber (mainly commercial logging) as also for extending area under cultivation for growing both food and non-food crops.

Deforestation leads to an increase in the quantity of CO_2 in the atmosphere which leads to climatic change. It also leads to floods, water logging and soil erosion on a wide scale and this, in its turn, leads to land degradation. Even deforestation in India causes flooding in Bangladesh. This is known as *transboundary externality,* i.e., externality generated in one country crossing its national boundary.

So deforestation has to be stopped for protecting the natural environment. During the process of photosynthesis forest trees absorb carbon dioxide from the atmosphere and release oxygen which is so important for human existence[2]. By contrast, afforestation reduces CO_2 in the atmosphere which prevents the increase in temperature of the Earth's surface. This is why there is so much stress on *social forestry* in recent years.

Overgrazing on Common Land

Another important cause of land degradation is overgrazing on common land and shift from extensive to intensive cultivation which relies on the extensive use of irrigation water, chemical fertilisers and pesticides. However, the main cause of land degradation is over-exploitation of this scarce natural resource by poverty-stricken people.

Economic Insight: The Tragedy of Commons

Common property, like trees in forests on common land, belong to everyone. No one user has a strong incentive to conserve it. As population increases, village pasture that is open to all local farmers tends to get exhausted by the first ones to place their livestock upon it. "Use it or lose it" is the maxim.

If property rights are absent or weakly enforced, excessive exploitation is bound is take place. This is more so in rural India where most people are poor and do not have much private property. This is the 'tragedy of the commons'. Mass poverty is the root cause of exhaustion of common resources and consequent deterioration of the physical (natural) environment.

---

1. It may be noted that top-soil erosion occurs due to rain water being drained away from the top-soil of arable land. The end result is loss of fertility, fall in the rate of agricultural growth and a threat to food security.
2. This point is realised by tourists who suddenly visit Ladakh.

Water Scarcity

Another serious environmental problem facing India at present is diminishing underground water resources. This is mainly attributable to demand-supply forces. Water is being pumped out mainly for irrigation purposes, faster than the rate at which acquifiers can be replenished by rainfall. The problem of water scarcity is a serious threat to sustainable agriculture. The problem can be solved by adopting a number of measures at the same time, viz., (i) scientific delivery and judicious use of irrigation water, (ii) use of drought-resistant seeds, and (iii) change in the cropping pattern, as and when necessary through proper crop rotation. Some countries are also making use of dip irrigation. Under the system water is supplied in measured doses through slender pipes close to the plants. Thus waste from spillover and overflow is largely avoided. This method can be used in India, where water is becoming more and more scarce day by day. It is also necessary to grow water-intensive crops like rice and sugarcane in rain-fed areas — areas where these crops are grown traditionally.

There is also need for enough ground water reservours. The reason is simple. There is almost complete dependence on ground water reserves not only for carrying out agricultural operations but also for meeting domestic water requirement. The possibility of harvesting in rain-fed areas should be fully exploited. Numerous small dams, instead of a few large (mega) dams, may be constructed to provide water locally.

Shortage of Clean Drinking Water and Lack of Sanitation Facilities

Most rural people are poor and they do not get adequate clean and safe water to drink. They do not enjoy adequate sanitation facilities either. For these two reasons they suffer from various water-borne diseases such as typhoid, cholera, amoebic infections, bacillary dysentery and diarrhea. These diseases claim the lives of a large number of people, mainly children every year. They also lead to deterioration of the health of the rural people and a consequent fall in labour productivity. Since health is an aspect of human capital, the rate of growth of the economy slows down.

Air Pollution in Rural Areas

It is normally believed that rural areas are free from air pollution. But this is not true. The rural people also face pollution due to excessive dependence on biomass fuels such as wood, straw and manure. This is largely attributable to their poverty. As a result their health deteriorates. To be more specific, the burning of biomass fuels for cooking and boiling of water create very high levels of indoor pollution from which mostly women and children suffer. Smoke and fumes from indoor stores account for a large number of childhood deaths each year from respiratory diseases and to more and more chronic respiratory illness.

Economic Insight: The Pollution Pays Principle

A soap factory, as a result of its production process, releases toxins into a nearby river. These waste materials kill the fish and make the swimmers sick. The factory, however, does not compensaes any of the victims. This means that the factory's private cost of production fails to reflect the true social cost of its operation. It is in this context that environmentalists have presented a principle, called the polluter pays principle (PPP). The basic idea behind the principle is that the soap factory should bear the full cost of its actions. This implies that the damages caused by the pollution — the lost value to potential fishermen and swimmers—should be included in the cost of production. The PPP puts a price on pollution and attributes the responsibilities for it to the polluter. The principle in based on a fundamental tenet of economic efficiency — that prices should reflect all the cost of production and is thus quite congruent (consistent) with ethical principles of equity and responsibility. Various statutory (legal) measures (instruments) can be used to apply the PPP, and prevent or regulate pollution such as taxes, pollution permits, quotas, technology standards and so on.

SUSTAINABLE DEVELOPMENT

The Rio Conference held in 1992 in Brazil first defined the term 'sustainable development'. Economists and environmentalists have used the term in the context of the urgent and pressing need of the hour to strike a balance (or to achieve a pragmatic compromise) between achieving faster economic growth on one hand and conserving and protecting the natural environment. The term sustainable development was defined by Brundland Commission as development which "meets the needs of the present generation without compromising with the ability of future generations to meet their own needs." Thus economic growth will be sustainable if the stock of both physical capital and natural capital (i.e., land and natural resources) remains intact or increases over time. In this context the famous Harvard environmentalist E. O. Wilson has sounded a note of caution in the following words. "Many of Earth's vital resources are about to be exhausted, its atmospheric chemistry is deteriorating and human populations have already grown dangerously large. Natural ecosystems, the well-springs of a healthful environment, are being irreversibly degraded." [This is a portion of this opening quotation of this chapter]

Believers in this dismal picture argue that humans must practise sustainable economic growth and learn to live within the limitations of the Earth's scarce natural resources or they will suffer dire and irreparable consequences.

The society like an individual faces an intertemporal choice problem

Thus the society as a whole is facing an intertemporal choice problem. Future economic development as also the physical quality of life largely depend on the present natural resource base and, of course, the quality of the physical environment, i.e., the quality of land, water and air. No doubt, faster economic growth and improved living standards can be achieved in the short run by making reckless use of non-renewable resources and by overexploiting renewable ones. But this will lead to a fall in the growth rate in the long run due to diminishing quantity and quality of natural resources. At the same time the quality of life of the people will also be adversely affected due to deteriorating quality of the environment. So planners and policy-makers should take note of this reality. They should give due consideration to the environmental issues while fixing growth targets for the present and the future. They should ensure that there is no net loss of natural capital at present in the process of achieving faster economic growth. This can be ensured if, in the event of destruction or depletion of natural capital in one area, there is replenishment or regeneration of an equal or even a greater amount of such capital so that future growth is sustained and inter-generational equity is maintained.

Economic Insight: Intergenerational Equity

Any type of economic development is based to some extent on the exploitation of natural resources. These include non-renewable environmental assets such as fossil fuels, and renewable resources such as fish stocks and wild life and certain borderless assets which are capable of regeneration, though with a certain loss of uniqueness, such as rain forests.

The pertinent question is: what price is acceptable in trading-off present exploitation for the future? Paying too high a price to protect the environment means condemning present population—and unborn future generations—to low levels of consumption and hardship; too low a price means depriving our children and grandchildren of the environmental opportunities we ourselves inherited. It is a matter of inter-generational equity.

A Simple Model of Sustainable Development

D. W. Pearce and J. J. Warford have presented a simple model of sustainable development. In their view, sustainable growth can be achieved through the protection and preservation of the environment. In this context they have taken a broad view of society's capital stock. It includes (i) man-made physical capital (such as plants, equipments, machinery, roads etc.), (ii) human capital (education, health and skill levels of the people) and natural capital (such as arable land, minerals, soil quality, forests, water and climate).

In their view sustainable development implies that the overall (total) capital stock remains intact during the growth process. To be more specific, the sustainable level of net national product (NNP^*) is the one which is absorbed during the process of economic growth without any decrease in the existing stocks of all the three types of capital during a year. Thus the basic equation of Pearce-Warford model is written as

$$NNP^* = GNP - D_m - D_n - E_r - E_c$$

where NNP^* is sustainable *NNP* (in the sense that it does not diminish during an accounting year), *GNP* is actual gross national product, D_m depreciation, i.e., reduction in the value of man-made physical capital due to its contribution to the production process, D_n is the fall in the value of natural capital in a year, E_r is the expenditure required to replenish natural capital used (destroyed) during a year and E_c is the expenditure required to conserve natural capital by preventing their destruction.

The Present Challenge

Due to rising consumption levels both in developed and developing countries in the face of rapidly growing population in low-income countries, achieving sustainable development is not an easy task. Instead it is a major challenge facing the whole world today. The growth of population in the future will lead to a rise in consumption levels and to meet the growing demand for goods and services there will be the need to increase production. As a result more and more pressure will be put on natural resources. And achieving sustainable development will be a complex task.

The truth is that most developed countries not only use highly energy-intensive techniques of production but exploit huge quantities of natural resources in the process of production. The end result is emission of greenhouse gases in the atmosphere. This pollutes the environment.

Sustainable development can be achieved only through international policy coordination

By importing western technology developing countries are also following the same path of development, which is unsustainable. This path of development not only pollutes the environment on a large scale but leads to loss of ecological balance as well. In such a situation sustainable development can be ensured only through international policy coordination. Both developed and developing countries have a role to play in achieving this common goal. The goal can be achieved by adopting appropriate environment-friendly measures.

CLIMATIC CHANGE

The Basic Issue

Climatic change or global warming has become one of more serious environmental issues facing the people of both developed and developing countries. The problem arises mainly due to the burning of fossil fuels in different type of production activities. Such activities often disturb the planet's heat and radiation balance. These activities are likely to lead to an increase in the earth's temperature (i.e., warmer climate) in the coming years and are likely to adversely affect both the process of economic growth and the physical quality of life of people (which depends so much on a clean environment). So the time has come for halting global warming through reduction in emission of greenhouse gases such as carbon dioxide (CO_2). Otherwise the pursuit of a strategy of achieving rapid growth will spell disaster for the humanity.

Meaning of Climatic Change

For quite some time scientists all over the world have observed that greenhouse gases such as carbon dioxide, methane, nitrogen oxide and water vapour in the atmosphere trap the incoming heat from the sun. And the most important source of carbon dioxide emission is burning of fossil fuels in the wake of industrialisation and urbanisation in both developed and developing countries. As a result there is an increase in the Earth's temperature. This is known as global warming. And this is likely to lead to sudden, abrupt and adverse changes in weather patterns and even in such serious events as cyclones, hurricanes, floods and rise in sea levels.

Nature and Dimension of the Problem

Global warming is a serious environmental problem. However, it is a global problem and is treated as a transboundary externality. The reason is that air and winds have no national boundaries. The emission of toxic gas into the air by some polluting industries in one nation pollutes the whole global atmosphere. Thus the emission of greenhouse gases by polluting industries of the West leads to climatic change in India and other developing countries. In addition, the flow of water in seas and oceans has no national boundaries. Thus a rise in sea levels due to climatic change often affects the people of coastal areas of many countries. This is why coordinated activities of different nations and global cooperation are needed to avert climatic change. It is gratifying to note that negotiations are going on since 1992 to avert climatic change (or global warming).

Durban Conference on Climate Change (December 2011)

To reach a concensus to deal with global warming representatives of 194 countries met at Durban in South Africa from December 1-14 to find ways of achieving carbon emission cuts by various countries as also to review Kyoto Protocol. A major achievement of the Durban agreement is the extension of the commitment period from 2013 to 2017.

Doha Climate Change Conference 2012

The 18th session of the Committee of Parties to the UNFCCC, which started on November 26 and concluded on December 8, 2012 in Doha, Qatar succeeded in carrying out amendments to the Kyoto Protocol to ensure a second commitment period which would last for 8 years from January 1, 2013.

INDIA'S CONCERN ABOUT CLIMATIC CHANGE

Climatic change is no doubt a threat to environmentally sustainable development and thus to the future generations. India is worried about climatic change for a number of reasons. These are the following:

1. Fall in agricultural production

An increase in temperature is likely to affect the timing and volume of water flows from rivers and thus adversely affect crop production in certain areas as the Tibetian Plateau, the Himalayas and the Hindu Kush. In general climatic change slows down the rate of agricultural growth in developing countries.

2. Rise in sea level

It is apprehended that due to global warming a large coastal area will come under sea. This will cause migration from coastal areas. The migrants will initially face a lot of hardship and will subsequently create various problems until and unless they are properly resettled elsewhere.

3. Human misery

Due to environmental disasters in the wake of climatic change such as acid rains, cyclones and hurricanes there will be human suffering in form of death and loss of the means of subsistence. Such human misery occurs not only in developed but also in developing countries.[1]

4. Slowing down the growth rate

A policy of deliberately reducing the emission of greenhouse gases in developing countries like India means deliberately sacrificing the much needed economic growth. Consequently the incidence of absolute poverty will increase. So such countries find it very difficult to reduce the emission of such gases to meet the global target.

By contrast, it is easier for advanced Western countries to reduce the emission of such gases. There are two reasons for this. Firstly, they have reached the stage of self-sustaining growth and managed

1. Deforestation also leads to climatic change and flooding. And flooding causes lots of human suffering.

to eliminate the incidence of absolute poverty largely, if not entirely. Secondly, they have both adequate finance and necessary technology to avert climatic change.

Measures to Mitigate Climatic Changes in India

Considering the disastrous consequences of climatic change India has adopted the following environmental friendly policies to mitigate climatic change:

1. Conservation of the sources of energy

Greater efficiency in energy use in order to reduce greenhouse gas emissions has been achieved in India as a result of governmental efforts. But India is yet to achieve much success as far as energy conservation is concerned.

2. Increased efficiency in energy use

Due to removal of import controls various firms and joint venture enterprises producing consumer durables such as cars, televisions, refrigerators, air-conditioners, micro-ovens, washing machines, electric stoves, etc. have been facing strong competition from imported items. So these firms and enterprises have been constrained to become more fuel-efficient. This is more so in view of the fact that the removal of subsidy has raised the electricity tariff.

3. Production of non-commercial sources of energy

Steps have been taken in India to develop and exploit non-conventional sources of energy which are clean and renewable. For this wind farms, micro-hydroelectric plants, biomass and cogeneration power plants and solar photovoltic systems have been set up.

4. Reduction in air pollution

Due to the adoption of certain measures to increase efficiency in the use of fossil fuels local air pollution has been reduced to a considerable extent. It has been possible to achieve abatement in emission of greenhouse gases. In addition, by prescribing pollution levels for urban vehicles, it has been possible to achieve further reduction in air pollution through an improvement in fuel quality.

5. Afforestation and development of wasteland

Of late, the Government has launched the programme of afforestation and wasteland development. The objective is not just to stop deforestation but also to plant more trees as part of the social forestry programme, in order to increase green cover and maintain ecological balance. This policy, if properly framed and effectively enforced, is likely to reduce the emission of CO_2 ,which leads to degradation of both forests and soils, as also to improve soil fertility. An increase the fertility of the soil will surely provide renewable sources of fuel and forest products — both timber and non timber — which are a source of livelihood of India's farming millions residing in rural areas.

6. Substitution of coal by oil and gas

Since 1991, when the policy of economic liberalisation was introduced in India coal has been increasingly substituted by oil and gas in both industries and power plants. Most power plants in India now use natural gas. Fertiliser plants also do not use coal now. They use other fuels instead. Finally railways no longer use coal.

Climatic Change Negotiations

In the past many negotiations have been made at the international level to reduce the severity of climatic change or global warming. As noted earlier the Earth Summit held in Rio in May 1992 has imposed some binding rules to be pursued by more than 150 participating nations regarding emission of greenhouse gases. It was recognised that global climate was a common resource and aversion of climatic change is a common responsibility.

Due to inadequacy of the measures taken by Rio Summit to reduce emission of greenhouse gases, a convention on climatic change was held at Berlin in Germany in 1995. The third convention was held at Kyoto in Japan in Dec. 1997. But the Kyoto protocol did not achieve much success due to opposition from the USA, which refused to sign it, keeping in view its need for achieving faster economic growth which results in huge emission of greenhouse gases. Finally, a convention on climatic change was held in Copenhagen in Dec. 2009, under the auspices of the UN with a view to reaching a consensus among participating nations on averting climatic change. But it failed to agree on new targets. In the mean time the World Meteorological Panel on Climate change (IPCC) warned in 2007 that global temperatures could rise by between one and six degrees centrigrade during the 21 century.

The Stran Review (2006) on the economic of climatic change, commissioned by the UK government, concludes on the scientific evidence that climate change is a serious threat, with many of the impacts being irreversible. So it requires an urgent global response. According to this report, the importance of climate change to future economic development requires expensive decision to be made by the world community in the short term. The Review suggests that economic growth in developing countries can still be achieved in the face of climate change. However, for this to become a reality, it is necessary for both the government of a developing country and international organisations to intervene and improve the operation of markets with regard to the environment and in particular with regard to the impacts of climate change on developing countries.

The World Bank sees poverty as a major cause of environmental damage and the poor are found to be heavily dependent on the environment. This is why the Bank now lends explicity for environmental projects and through the Global Environmental Fund makes grants to protect the physical environment.

Similarly, the IMF has gradually begun to recognise the need to take account of the environment in its structural adjustment programmes (SAPs).

Finally, the World Trade Organisation (WTO) has framed rules for the adoption of trade-related measures in order to protect the environment. However, it is felt that such measures are best managed through multilateral environmental agreements.

Current Focus: Global Climate Change
No doubt, the most pressing ecological problem today is global climate change. And this is causing considerable concern to every conscious citizen in the whole world. The Inter-governmental Panel on Climate Change was established in 1983 by the World Meteorological Office and the United Nations Environment Programme to provide an objective and reliable source of information about climate change. From its 4th Assessment Report published in Nov. 2007 it is confirmed that global climate change is occurring, that 'anthropogenic' activity is a contributing factor and that there is a need to reduce the GHGs that are the cause of global warming. With the publication of the report the debate about the exact role of human beings in increasing the threats posed by climate change (IPC) has virtually ended.

KEY POINTS

1. *Environmental problems* : Environmental problems arise because of externalities which stem from production or consumption. An externality is an activity which imposes involuntary costs or benefits on others and whose effects do not get fully reflected in market prices.

2. *Growth and environment* : Economic growth and development in the past has caused serious environmental damage and the present state of the environment will constrain future economic development in developing countries like India.

3. *Efficient use of resources* : The efficient use of both renewable and non-renewable resources over time depends upon their social value, the growth of renewable resources and the reserves of non-renewable resources. The market often fails to make an efficient use of both types of resources.

4. *Adjusting national income* : International agencies have attempted to adjust measures of national income for environmental degradation by increased economic activity. The relation between economic development and environment is complex.

5. *Sustainable development* : Since the 1980s, the idea of sustainable development has emerged. The idea is based on the belief that the well-being of future generations is not to be compromised by meeting the material needs of the present generation. The idea lays stress on the natural environment supporting economic activity and suggests that caution has to be observed at the global level in depleting natural capital.

6. *Climate change* : Climate change is the serious threat at present, with many of its impacts being irreversible, and requires an urgent global response. It is high time nations worked together to devise new tools to enforce international agreements to ensure that global warming does not threaten the natural ecosystem and standard of living of the people.

7. *Responsibility of businesses* : An unregulated market economy will produce two much pollution and too little abatement. The efficient use of environmental resources requires that businesses bear the full social costs (negative externalities) of their activities.

KEY TERMS

Climatic change	Transboundary externality
Sustainable development	Water pollution
Tragedy of commons	Air pollution
Natural capital	Soil pollution
Organic farming	Sound pollution
Environmental degradation	Urban pollution
The polluter pays principle	Rural pollution

ASSIGNMENTS

1. Discuss the importance of protecting the natural environment.
2. How is the protection of the environment related to industrial growth?
3. What are the arguments for and against keeping the stock of natural capital fixed?
4. How do industrialisation and urbanisation lead to deterioration of the environment?
5. (a) Faster industrial growth increases the level of pollution.
   (b) A clean environment slows down the growth rate.
   How do you resolve the conflict between industrial growth and environmental protection in the light of the above two statements?
6. How does rapid population growth lead to deterioration of the environment?
7. How does a growing incidence of absolute poverty lead to deterioration of the environment?
8. How do business activities lead to deterioration of the environment?
9. Why should the business firms be concerned about the environment?
10. (a) What are the causes of urban pollution?
    (b) What are the causes of rural pollution?
11. Do you advocate organic farming for reducing the problem of rural pollution?
12. Define and explain the idea of sustainable development. How can it be achieved?
13. Comment on the importance of achieving sustainable development. What are the obstacles to the achievement of environmentally sustainable development?
14. What is climatic change? What are its adverse effects in developing countries like India?
15. Suggest measures for averting climatic change or global warming.
16. Highlight the measures adopted in India to mitigate climatic change.
17. Explain the causes of the tragedy of the commons.
18. How have international organisations responded to the ideas of sustainable development and the economic importance of the environment?
19. How are the poor in developing countries affected by climatic change?
20. What are the physical and economic impacts of climatic change?

46A ECONOMIC EXTERNALITIES

Market forces, properly redirected, are often the best remedy for market failure. N. G. Mankiw

An efficient functioning of the market system ensures an optimal allocation of an economy's scarce resources. However, sometimes a market fails to perform its allocative function efficiently. When this happens we say that there is market failure. So it becomes necessary for the visible hand of the government to ensure an optimal correction of market failure. Thus while the market organises economic activities efficiently, the government is likely to improve market outcomes.

The Nature and Sources of Externality

The market failures come under the broad heading 'externalities'. An externality arises when a person's activity affects another person either adversely or favourably but for which neither any compensation is paid to the sufferer nor any reward is received from the beneficiary. If Mr. X's activity adversely affects Mr. Y, it is called a negative externality. If Mr. X's activity benefits Mr. Y, it is called a positive externality. In the presence of *externalities*, there are divergence between private cost and social cost on the one hand and private benefit and social benefit on the other. In truth, in the presence of externalities any transaction involving a buyer and a seller affects a third party, indirectly though. This is why an externality is also known as the *third party effect* or the *neighbourhood effect*.

Since buyers and sellers take into account only their own private benefits and costs and neglect the external effects of their actions, when deciding how much to buy and sell of different goods and services, the market economy is not efficient in the presence of externalities. This means that in competitive economy, total benefit to society (measured by the sum of consumer surplus and producer surplus) is not maximised. So maximum economic welfare is not promoted. The release of smoke and dirt from the chimney of a steel plant such as that of TISCO in Jamshedpur is an example of a negative externality. A profit-seeking firm is always guided by self-interested behaviour. So it does not take into account the full cost of the pollution it creates. And it pollutes the environment too much in the absence of any government control and regulation. Since an individual consumer or a firm fails to take into account the external effect of his (or its) action, the government has to take certain corrective measures to protect the interest of third parties (i.e., those who are not involved in a transaction but are indirectly affected by it).

Externalities and Loss of Market Efficiency

We now examine why in the presence of externalities markets fail to allocate resources efficiently.

In fact, the absence of externalities the equilibrium price of a good such as soap refers both to the marginal private benefit (MPB) to consumers and marginal private cost(MPC) of producers, as shown in Fig. 46A.1. At the equilibrium quantity(Q_E) and equilibrium price(P_E) there is maximum consumer surplus (AP_EE) and producer surplus (BP_EE). So resources are efficiently allocated since the actual quantity produced and sold ($0Q_E$) is the socially desirable one. Now we may examine what happens to market outcomes in the presence of externalities — negative and positive. We start with the effect negative externality. We also discuss how it is taken care of, i.e., internalised.

In the presence of a negative externality such as pollution, it is possible to evaluate a market outcome only by taking into account the loss of welfare of third parties. In the presence of externality resources are allocated inefficiently even in a free market.

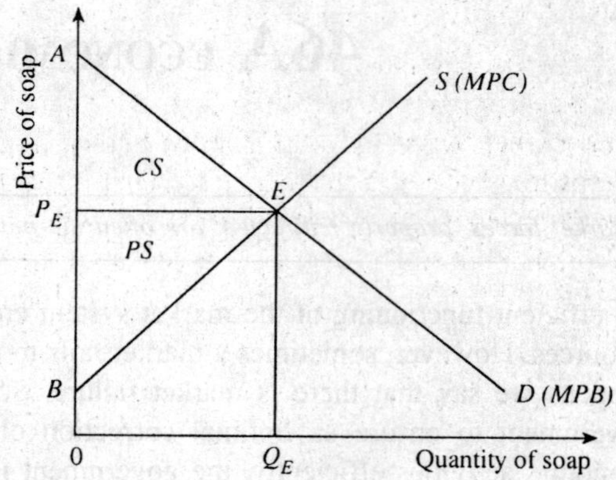

Fig. 46A.1: The Market for Soap

NEGATIVE EXTERNALITIES

Let us suppose that the soap factory emits smoke. For each unit of soap produced, a certain amount of smoke enters the environment. As a result there is air pollution. So people residing in the locality face a health risk by breathing the polluted air. This smoke is a negative externality. And it affects the market outcomes adversely.

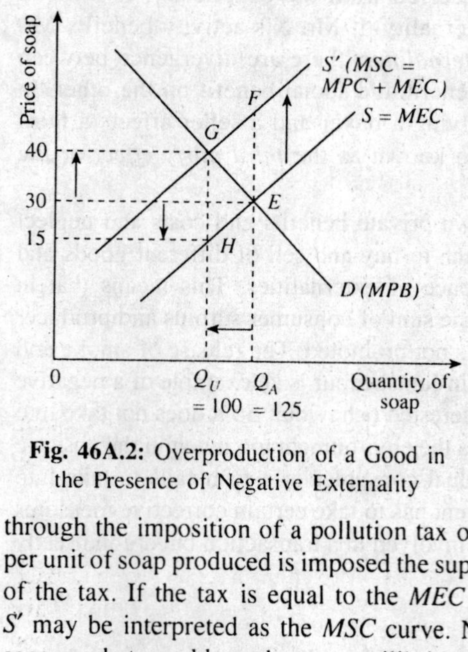

Fig. 46A.2: Overproduction of a Good in the Presence of Negative Externality

In presence of a negative externality the marginal social cost (*MSC*) of production of a good exceeds its *MPC*. The difference between the two is marginal external cost (*MEC*). So we can write

$$MSC = MPC + MEC$$

$$\text{Or, } MEC = MSC - MPC$$

And the good generating negative externality is overproduced, i.e., actual output (Q_A) of 125 units exceeds its socially desirable (or optimal) level (Q_0) of 100. How can actual output be reduced to the optimal level units? This can be done by the government through the imposition of a pollution tax of *EF* which is equal to *MEC* in Fig. 46A.2. If a tax of *EF* per unit of soap produced is imposed the supply curve of soap would shift upward exactly by the amount of the tax. If the tax is equal to the *MEC* of the smoke released into the air, the new supply curve *S′* may be interpreted as the *MSC* curve. Now the output of soap will fall from 125 to 100 and the soap market would reach new equilibrium at point *G* at which actual output of soap is the same as its optimum output.

Internalisation of Externalities

The imposition of such a tax leads to internalisation of externality. The reason is that the tax induces buyers and sellers in the market to take into account of the external effects of their actions. In this case a tax of Rs. 25 per soap creates a wedge (or a divergence) between the price consumers pay (Rs.40) and price soap producers receive (Rs. 15). Since the tax forces producers to pay for external costs they impose on society, they will reduce the supply of soap. And since the market price of soap (Rs.40) now includes the tax on producers, consumers will now buy a smaller quantity of soap. Thus we see the real life application of one of the basic principles of economics: people respond to incentives.[1]

1. In this case the incentive is negative.

POSITIVE EXTERNALITIES

Some activities such as education and health care generate positive externalities. This means social benefit exceeds private benefit. An educated person usually is more productive than an illiterate worker. So the former earns more in form of higher wages and compensation. In addition, education yields benefits to other members of society in various ways. Firstly, with spread of education, people become more knowledgeable[1] voter. This means more efficient and acceptable government for every citizen of a country. Secondly, the spread of education among people create another social (community) benefit. There is a fall in the incidence of crime and violence. Thirdly, with the spread of education there is continuous development and transmission of technological knowledge. This raises labour productivity and wages. As a result the standard of living of the people of a country improves. For these reasons, a rational individual prefers to stay in a community where most people are educated.

In the presence of positive externalities the demand curve is shown by *MPB*. Since marginal social benefit (*MSB*) exceeds marginal private benefit (*MPB*), the *MSB* curves lies above the *MPB* curve of a good. The vertical distance between the two curves measures marginal external benefit (*MEB*).

In Fig. 46A.3 initial market equilibrium occurs at point *E*, where 75 students get enrolled in a college at a monthly fee of Rs. 30. However, the optimal number of students is 100. Now the actual number can be increased from 75 to 100 by giving subsidy equivalent to *MEB* of Rs. 25. If this is done, the college gets Rs. 45 from the students. But each student pays only Rs. 20 per month. So there is a subsidy of Rs. 25 per student which is just sufficient to bring the actual number of students to the optimal (or socially desirable) level. And in this case Rs. 2500 (= Rs 25 × 100) is the total cost of government subsidy.

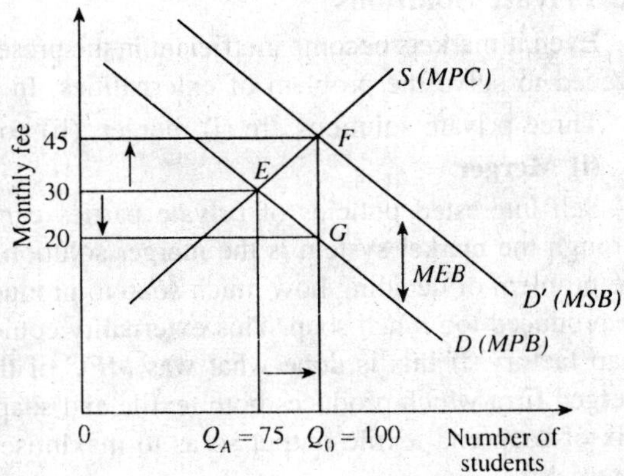

Fig. 46A.3: Positive Externality Generated by Education

In India and most other countries education is subsidised at almost all levels. The reason is that it generates positive externalities.

Some Case Examples

Dissemination of Technology

Another real-life example of positive externality is a technology spillover. This refers to the impact of one firm's research and production activities on other firms' access to technological advance. This is why governments often give subsidy to those who produce new capital goods like industrial robots to spread technology. This is how externality is internalised. It may apparently seem that if a subsidy equal to the value of the technology spillover is given, actual output will be equal to its optimal level. However, there is disagreement among economists on this issue. In this context we refer to the following two relevant points:

1. *Industrial policy* : Some economists suggest that the government should identify those industries who yield the maximum spillover and should subsidise them. Technology-enhancing industries can be promoted through industrial policy.

2. *Patent protection* : Other economists argue that a better way to ensure technology spillover is patent protection. The patent laws protect the rights of inventors for a certain period of time by giving

---

1. Education + information = knowledge.

them an opportunity to make exclusive use of their innovations. If a firm succeeds in achieving a technology breakthrough, it can get the idea patented (or legally protected) and reap the major portion of the benefit for itself. Differently put, the patent seeks to internalise the externality by giving the inventor an intellectual property right over its invention. If other firms want to use the new technology, they have to take the official permission of the inventor and pay it some royalty. For these reasons a patent system gives firms a greater incentive to engage in research and development(R & D) activities which lead to development of technology.

SOLUTIONS TO EXTERNALITIES

There are two solutions to externalities: private solutions and government solutions. All the solutions have a common goal: moving the actual allocation of resources closer to the social optimum. We now discuss private solutions to start with.

A. Private Solutions

Even if markets become inefficient in the presence of externalities, government action is not always needed to solve the problem of externalities. In some situations, private solutions work fairly well.

Three private solutions are (i) merger, (ii) contract and (iii) private negotiation and bargaining.

(i) Merger

Self-interested policies of private parties can solve the externality problem. One such solution through the market system is the merger solution. Initially when the owner of the soap factory faced the problem of deciding how much soap to produce, he neglected the negative externality. As a result he produced too much soap. This externality could be internalised if a nearby textile plant bought the soap factory. If this is done what was *MEC* of the soap factory will now become *MPC* of the new merged firm which produces both textile and soap. So the owner of the firm will choose an optimum mix of soap and textile output so as to maximise his overall profit. This is one way of internalising externality.

The converse is also true. If the textile plant is doing damage to soap output by emitting pollution the owner of the soap factory may buy the textile plant. And once again the output of textile will be brought to the socially desirable level.

(ii) Contract

Another way to solve the externality problem is to enter into a contract. A contract between the soap factory and the textile plant can solve the externality problem by specifying the optimal quantity of soap and the optimal quantity of textile, and a payment from one firm to the another. Through the contract, both firms may agree on the optimal amounts of soap and textile output and remove the inefficiency associated with these externalities and make both the firms better off.

(iii) Private Negotiation and Bargaining—the Coase Solution

According to Ronald Coase, at times and in some situations the private market can prove to be very effective in internalising externalities and ensuring an efficient allocation of resources. This is possible if two conditions are satisfied: (i) private property rights are clearly defined and (ii) there are no transaction costs (i.e., costs of negotiations and bargaining).

In 1960 Coase first pointed out the reciprocal nature of the externality problem. Suppose there are two parties *A* and *B*. Each can do harm to each other by selfishly pursuing its own interest. To avoid the harm to *B* would inflict harm to *A*. The real question here is should *A* be allowed to harm *B* or should *B* be allowed to harm *A*? The problem is to avoid the more serious harm[1].

Coase explained that when either of two parties has property rights that are adversely affected by the action of the other, both parties will have an incentive to negotiate an acceptable outcome. Coase gave the example of cattle from a ranch entering a neighbour's land and destroying crops.

1. R.H.Coase, "The Problem of Social Cost", *Journal of Law and Economics* (Oct., 1960).

If the property right is assigned to the farmer (the law assigns liability to the cattle-rancher) there will be an incentive for the cattle-rancher to offer a payment to the farmer to take some adjacent land out of corn production. The farmer would have an incentive to negotiate with the rancher because the foregone payment that could be obtained from the rancher is a cost of raising crops. Thus the farmer will want to see if he can receive a payment from the rancher that exceeds the loss of corn output on the adjacent land.

If the property right is assigned to rancher (i.e., if his cattle can roam anywhere), then the farmer has an incentive to offer payment to the cattle-rancher to reduce the size of his herd. The rancher now has an opportunity cost. If he increases the size of his herd he loses the potential payment from the farmer. In either assignment of property rights, a negotiated settlement is likely and there is no need for any government intervention. Coase's ideas have come to be known as the Coase theorem.

According to the Coase theorem, the affected party can bargain with the inflicting agent and agree on an efficient solution. This means that economic agents can solve the problem of externalities through voluntary negotiation and bargaining

Thus the Coase theorem suggests that the clear assignment of property rights can eliminate the need for taxes and subsidies if transaction costs are negligible. The Coase theorem suggests that voluntary negotiation and bargaining by the private parties can solve the problem of externalities. Whatever the initial assignment of property rights, the interested parties can always reach a mutually beneficial and economically efficient bargaining due to the reciprocal nature of the problem. However, the Coase theorem fails in case of a large externality problem (i.e., when the number of parties involved in a bargain is very large).

Problem with Private Solutions

The problem with the Coase theorem is that many real world externalities such as air and water pollution affect a large number of people, making negotiation and activity of bargaining not only difficult but costly as well. Suppose, for example, a soap factory throws its waste material in a nearby pond. As a result there is water pollution and it is a threat to the livelihood of a washerman. According to the Coase theorem the washerman and the factory could reach a bargain in which the washerman pay to the factory not to pollute. However, if there are numerous washermen in a nearby take or river it is virtually impossible to bring them at one place and coordinate them all to collectively bargain with the factory.

When private economic agents cannot solve the problem of externalities themselves the government has to intervene

In fact, negative externality is no longer a local problem. It has a true global character. It is called transboundary externality. For example, the global warming problem involves thousands of firms and millions of individuals in various nations. In such cases, bargaining costs are substantial and government intervention — both at domestic and international levels — may prove to be really effective.

The government is responsible for the collective actions

Thus when private bargaining fails the government can take corrective actions on behalf of an affected party such as the washerman in our example. We may now discuss how the government can try to remedy the problem of externalities.

Public Policies for Solving Externality Problem

There are two measures through which the government can control externalities so as to enable the market to ensure an efficient allocation of resources. These two methods are presented in the chart below:

It may be noted at the outset that command-and-control policies regulate the behaviour of polluters directly. Market-based policies control externalities indirectly by creating an incentive system so that private agents are induced to solve the problem voluntarily in order to promote their own interest.

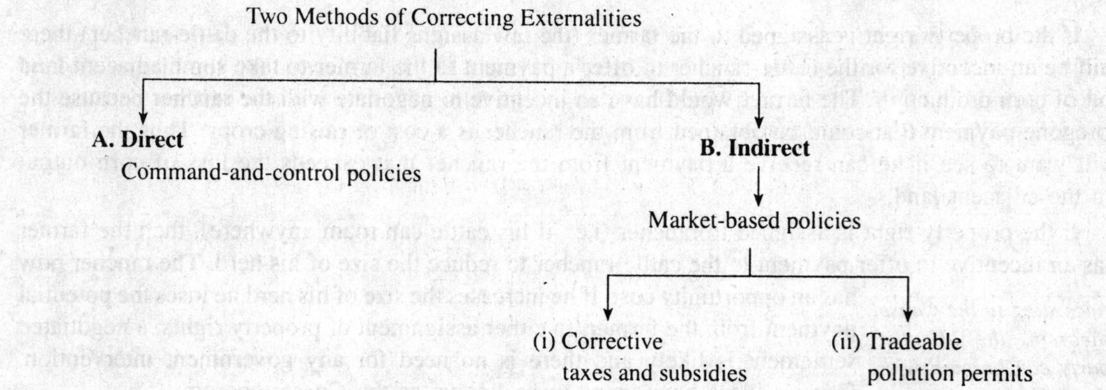

Command-and-Controls Policies

Command and control policies are essentially an act of regulating the private economic agents. By using such a policy the government either regulates the private parties to behave or not to behave in certain ways. For example, it is crime to smoke at public places in many countries. In Singapore it is a punishable offence. However, in India even the order of the Supreme Court goes unheaded by most people since the law enforcement authorities are not strong. Similarly in the USA it is a crime to dump poisonous chemicals into a lake or a river. The reason is that the *MEC* to society far exceeds the *MEB* to the smoker (or the polluter). In Gujarat school students are not permitted to use mobile phones for the same reason. In each case the governments prohibits a society to perform an undesirable act by announcing and enforcing a command-and-control policy. However, there is one major drawback of the policy. Due to lack of adequate and reliable information about specific industries and about alternative techniques of production, which those industries could adopt, it is virtually impossible for the government authorities to design proper regulatory policies.

Market-Based Policy 1: Corrective Taxes and Subsidies

The government can regulate the behaviour of pollutants through certain market-based policies in order to achieve a judicious mix of private incentive and social efficiency. One such policy is known as Pigouvian taxes and subsidies, named after A.C. Pigou. A corrective tax would equal the *MEC* in case of a negative externality, and a corrective subsidy would equal the *MEB* in case of positive externality. Taxes are advocated on the ground that they reduce pollution at lower cost to society and the desirable outcome can be achieved under government regulation.

Whereas regulation would specify a level of pollution, the tax would give the pollutants an economic (negative) incentive to reduce pollution. In fact, the higher the tax, the larger the reduction in pollution. If the tax is raised to a very high level, pollution may even fall to zero. The reason is that some factories will close down their operations completely. Such a tax may be called a prohibitive tax. However, it is easy to suggest this policy, but it is difficult to implement it in practice.

Even with government intervention it is not possible for an economy to abandon the market forces completely. Instead the government is required to bear the social costs of these activities.

Taxes are advocated on the ground that they reduce pollution more efficiently than regulations. However, any type of regulation is not very effective because it imposes the same restriction(s) on all firms. But in reality all firms do not pollute the environment equally. So a reduction in pollution by the same amount by all firms is not the cheapest way to reduce pollution. For instance, a soap factory can reduce pollution at a lower cost than a textile plant. So the soap factory would have an extra incentive to reduce pollution as much as it can for avoiding the tax. By contrast, the textile plant would prefer to pay the tax and reduce pollution by the minimum amount.

In truth, the corrective tax puts a price tag on the right to pollute. It induces firms having the minimum cost of reducing pollution to avoid paying the tax and the firms having the highest cost of reducing pollution to pay the tax. This is how such a tax allocates pollution among the two types of firms. See Table 46A.1 which shows the strategic choice of two types of firms.

Table 46A.1: Strategies of Two Types of Firms

A. Firms with low cost of reducing pollution	Reduce pollution as much as possible	Pay less tax
B. Firms with high cost of reducing pollution	Pay more tax	Reduce pollution as much as possible

Whatever the level of pollution as specified by the pollution control authorities a firm can achieve the target at the minimum possible cost by using the tax system rather than the regulatory method.

Under the regulatory method the polluting firms have no incentive to reduce pollution further once they reach the target. By comparison, the tax gives the polluting firms an incentive to use a clean technology so that they can avoid their tax liability as much as possible.

Corrective taxes in fact, serve two purposes. Firstly they raise revenue for the government. Secondly, they move the allocation of resources near the socially desirable level and thus promote greater economic efficiency than command-and-control policies.

Market-Based Policy 2: Tradable Pollution Permits

Corrective taxes on emissions and pollution permits internalise the externality of pollution

The government can also create a new scarce resource: pollution permits. Suppose the government issues 100 such permits and these are sold in the open market. The permits will be acquired by firms which are inclined to pay the maximum amount for them[1]. A firm's willingness to pay, in its turn, will depend on its cost of reducing pollution. The higher is a firm's cost of reducing pollution, the larger is the amount it will be ready to pay for a permit.

Adam Smith's 'invisible hand' will ensure that this new market for pollution rights will allocate the right to pollute efficiently. To be more specific, those firms which are able to reduce pollution at a low cost will sell whatever permit they get. By contrast, firms which can reduce pollution at a high cost will buy the required number of permits. So whatever the initial allocation of 100 permits by the government, the permits will ultimately be efficiently allocated among firms if there exists a free market for pollution rights.

Similarity between Corrective Taxes and Pollution Permits

In case of both corrective taxes and pollution permits, firms pay for their pollution[2]. However, while in case of taxes polluting firms must pay a tax to the government, in case of pollution permits polluting firms must pay to buy a permit either from the government (at the initial price) or from another firm (at a higher price later). In spite of their differences, the two policies are, therefore, similar at least in one respect. Both seek to internalise externality by imposing costs on the polluting firms.

1. The logic behind this method of the allocation of permits is comparable to that of the Coase theorem.
2. If a firm is already having a permit it must pay to pollute. The opportunity cost of polluting is the maximum price it could obtain from the open market by selling its unused permits. Suppose the firm has a permit from the government at Rs. 5,000. However, this is not the true cost of its polluting activity. If it can sell the permit to the highest bidder, who is to ready to pay Rs. 15,000, this is the true opportunity cost of polluting the environment.

In Fig 46A.4 we show the equivalence of the two policies. In panel (a), the regulatory authority fixes a price of pollution by imposing a corrective tax per unit. The supply curve for pollution rights

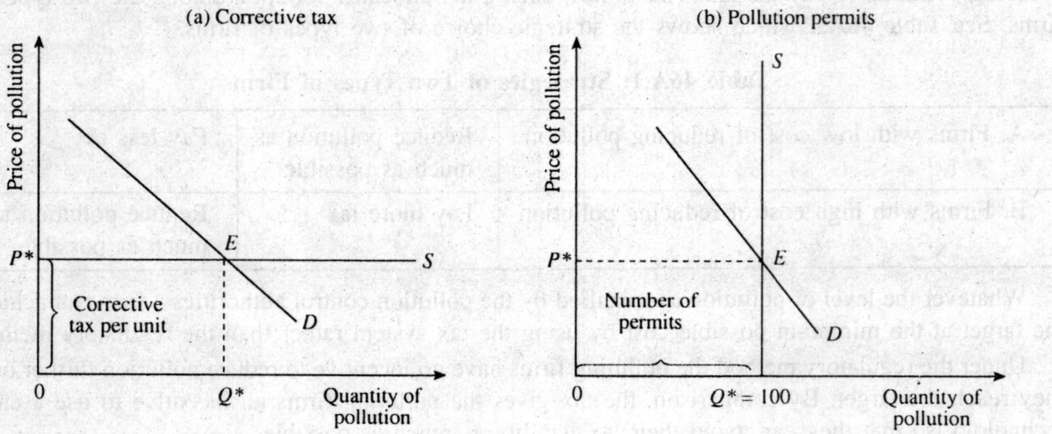

Fig. 46A.4: A Comparison of Corrective Taxes and Pollution Permits

is completely elastic. As a firm can pollute as much as it likes by paying the unit tax. However, the demand curve shows that the lower the price of polluting the larger will be number of firms willing to pollute. So the demand curve for pollution rights determines the quantity of pollution. In panel (b) the supply curve is completely inelastic because the number of pollution permits being used is limited. Again the demand curve determines the price of the pollution.

In each case a firm is a price taker and a quantity adjuster as in a competitive market. In addition, the price and quantity of pollution are the same in both situations. So there is hardly anything to choose from the two corrective measures. Mainly for this reason the pollution permits, much like corrective taxes, are now extensively used in many countries of the East and the West for keeping the environment clean at low cost.

Concluding Comments

It may be noted that one of the basic principles of economics is that people face trade-offs. All of us put high value on clean air and water. But their value has to be compared with their opportunity cost. Any attempt to eliminate all types of pollution would lead to technological advances and thus enable us to enjoy a high standard of living. However, most people will be reluctant to accept low-quality diet, poor medical care or unsafe houses to make the environment as clean as possible. So elimination of all types of pollution completely is neither technically possible nor socially desirable.

A clean environment has the characteristics of both a private good and a public good

A clean environment has the characteristics of both a private good and a public good. It is enjoyed by all people of a country whether they pay for this or not (non-excludability). And one person's enjoyment of it does not reduce the enjoyment of the others (non-rivalry). Again like most private goods it has a positive income elasticity of demand. The affluent society can afford a clean environment than a poor nation. For this reason we find a more vigorous protection of the environment in the USA than in India. Finally, the law of demand applies in case of environmental goods (such as clean air and clean water) also. The lower the price of environmental protection, the greater is its demand. In recent years the public's demand for a cleaner environment has increased due to a fall in cost of environmental protection brought about by pollution permits and corrective taxes. Thus if market forces are perfectly redesigned and redirected they may prove to be the most effective way of ensuring an optimal correction of market failure.

ASSIGNMENTS

1. Give two examples of economic externalities — one positive, one negative.
2. Use the supply-demand apparatus to show the effect of a negative externality in production.
3. What are the private solutions to the externality problem? Can the problem be solved by using the patent system?
4. Suppose a smoker shares a place of accommodation with a non-smoker. Can the Coase theorem be applied in this case to reach an efficient outcome?
5. What are Pigouvian taxes? Do you think that these are better than government regulations as a way to protect the physical (natural) environment?
6. Examine whether the following statements are true, false or uncertain, giving reason(s) in each case:

   (a) The government should impose tax on consumers or producers, depending on which side of the market (the buyers' side or the sellers' side) is generating the externality.

   (b) The welfare (deadweight) losses from Pigouvian taxes far exceeds the benefits of corrective taxes as a way to reduce pollution.
7. Susan plays Hindi music at high volume. Ravi hates it. They live in two adjacent rooms of the same apartment.

   (a) Is there any externality here?

   (b) Can the landlord ensure an efficient outcome by using the command-and-control policy?

   (c) Suppose the landlord is indifferent to the tenants. Can the Coase solution make things better? Is there any hindrance to an efficient outcome?
8. The Government of Holland subsidises cattle farming and gives maximum subsidy to the areas which attract the maximum number of tourists. Why does the Government do this? Is the policy efficient?

   [**Hint:** The main reason for giving subsidy is to promote the sale of cheese and milk chocolates.]
9. An increase in the consumption of alcohol leads to more car accidents and these impose costs on those who do not drink and drive.

   (a) Illustrate the market for alcohol, showing the demand curve, the social value curve, the supply curve, the social cost curve, the market equilibrium level of output and the efficient level of output.

   (b) Can you show the deadweight loss of the market equilibrium on the same diagram?

   [**Hint:** The DWL occurs because some units of alcohol are consumed for which the social cost exceeds the social value.]
10. The levels of pollution in Kolkata are now too high.

    (a) If the West Bengal Government wishes to reduce overall pollution by a certain amount, why is it efficient for different firms to reduce pollution by different amounts?

    [**Hint:** Because some firms can reduce pollution at lower costs than others.]

    (b) Why do the command-and-control approaches fail to target the firms which should achieve bigger reductions the pollution levels?

    [**Hint:** The reason is that such approaches often rely on uniform reductions among firms.]

    (c) How do Pigouvian taxes and tradable pollution rights seek to achieve an efficient pollution reduction? Can both the approaches discriminate among firms planning to undertake smaller and bigger reductions?
11. Suppose the Government of Britain decides to issue tradable pollution permits for reducing air pollution.

    (a) Should it distribute or auction the permits if its objective is to achieve economic efficiency?

    (b) Suppose the Government decides to distribute the permits. Does the allocation of the permits among different firms affect economic efficiency?
12. There are three business firms in Richland:

Firm	Initial level of pollution	Cost of reducing pollution by 1 unit
A	40 units	Rs 500
B	60 units	Rs 800
C	80 units	Rs 1,000

The Government of Richland wants to reduce pollution by 120 units. So it gives each firm 40 tradable pollution permits.

(a) Which firms sell the permits and how many do they sell? Which firms buy the permits and how many do they buy? Why are some firms willing to sell and others willing to buy permits?

(b) Can you calculate the total cost of pollution reduction in this case?

(c) What would be the cost of pollution reduction if the permits were not tradable?

EPILOGUE

New-Economic Policy of the BJP Government

Attributing the present economic woes to a "decade of jobless growth", finance minister Arun Jaitley underlined the need to contain price rise and hasten economic reforms to boost, low-cost manufacturing.

"Reviving the growth momentum, containing inflation and altering the pattern of growth to gainful employment are today over-riding priorities", he said in his *Facebook* post summing up his one week in office.

India's economic growth stayed below 5% for the second year in a row at 4.7% in financial year 2013-14, mainly due to decline in manufacturing and mining output. Growth remained subdued at 4.6% in the fourth quarter of the last fiscal.

"There is a need to boost domestic low-cost manufacturing and hasten the pace of reforms. Price stability and growth are intertwined, but may require a different strategy. This will require a combination of monetary policy and fiscal policy", he said.

Many key economic reforms, including increasing foreign direct investment in the insurance sector, implementation of Goods and Services Tax, and the Direct Taxes Code, remained in limbo in the last UPA government.

Hinting at immediate measures to be taken to strengthen the economy, he said: "short-term (fiscal) disciplining till we reverse the present trend will give us long-term benefits".

He emphasised that there is a need to move towards an era of fiscal discipline with the objective of reduce fiscal deficit, contain inflation and improve growth rate.

"We must commit ourselves to this discipline in order to strengthen the Indian economy which can improve the quality of life of every Indian and pull out the deprived ones from the state of poverty", he said.

Noting that the investment cycle has been disturbed, he said the manufacturing sector has had an abysmal performance last year. The negative sentiment has affected trade, hotels and transportation sectors which are poised for a slower growth compared to last year.

"The slowdown in economic growth, coupled with high inflationary pressure, poses a challenge to the macroeconomic environment .... India can ill afford this trend. This has serious social consequences since slowdown comes with a decade of jobless growth", he said.

As per the CSO estimates released in May, inflation continues to be rising with April figure at little more than 8.9%.

Mr Jaitley said tax collections have come down to 10.1% of the gross domestic product compared to the initial Budget estimates of 10.9%. "Slower GDP growth will imply lower tax buoyancy and higher fiscal deficit", he said.

Mr Jaitley's remarks came two days ahead of the Reserve Bank's monetary policy review which reduced the SLR marginally in its bid to fight inflation.

BIBLIOGRAPHY

1. Anderson, Marlin and Others (ed.): *Innovation and Growth* (Oxford, UK, 2012)
2. Trebilcock, Michael and Others (ed.): *The Regulation of International Trade* (Routedge, New York, 2013)
3. Clark, Thomas and Branson Douglas (ed.): *The SAGE Handbook of Corporate Governance* (Sage, New Delhi, 2012)
4. Carroll, Archie B. and Others (ed.): *Corporate Responsibility* : the American Experience (Cambridge University Press, 2012)
5. Bliss, Christopher: *Trade Growth & Inequality* (Oxford, UK, 2007)
6. Kapila, Uma: *Economic Development and Policy in India* (Academic Foundation, New Delhi, 2009)
7. Jefferson, Phillip N. (ed.): *The Oxford Handbook of the Economics of Poverty* (OUP, 2012)
8. S. Kumar, Sentlin, A. and Ramakrishnan, L.: *Emerging Paradigms in Insurance Industry and Management* (Serials Publications, New Delhi, 2012)
9. Alvesson, Mats: *Understanding Organisational Culture* (Sage New Delhi, 2nd edn., 2013)
10. Singh, Anita and Others (ed.): *Governance and Poverty Reduction* (PHI, 2009)
11. Galor, Oded: *Unified Growth Theory* (Princeton University Press, Princeton & Oxford, 2011)
12. Kunjukunju, Berson & Mohanan, S. (ed.) *Financial Markets & Financial Services in India* (New Century, N. D. 2012)
13. Brooks, Ian and Weatherston J.: *The Business Environment* — Challenges and Changes (Prentice Hall/Pearson, England, 2000)
14. Seitz, John L.: *Global Issues* — An Introduction (Blackwell, 1995)
15. Griffiths, Alan and Wall Stuart (ed.): *Applied Economics* (8th edn., Reason, 1999)
16. Kalirajan, K. and Others (ed.): *Strategies for Achieving Sustained High Economic Growth* (Sage, 2010)
17. Dixit, Avinash K. and Nalebuff, Barry J.: *Thinking Strategically* : The Competitive Edge in Business Policy and Everyday (W. W. Norton & Co., New York, 1995)
18. Nickels, W.G. and Others: *Introducing Business* (McGraw-Hill, 2011)
19. Sen, Amartya: *Development as Freedom* (Oxford, 1998)
20. Bhaduri, Amit: *An Intelligent Person's Guide to Liberalisation* (Oxford, 2001)
21. Jalan, Bimal: *The Future of India* (Penguin, 2011)
22. Thirlwall, A. P.: *Economics of Development* (9th edn., 2011, Palgrave, UK)
23. Srinivasan, S.: *Microfinance India* — State of the Sector Report 2011 (Sage, New Delhi, 2012)
24. Samuelson, William and Marks, Stephen: *Managerial Economics* (5th edn., 2008, John Wilay & Says)
25. Ghoshal, Sumantra and Others: *Managing Radical Change* (Portfolio Penguin, 2000)
26. Chappelli, Peter and Others: *The India Way* (Havard Business Review Press, Boston Mass., 2011)
27. Miskin, F. S.: *The Economics of Money, Banking and Financial Markets* (Addison Wesley, Longman, 6th edn., 2000)
28. Savas, E. S.: *Privatisation and Public-Private Partnership* (EWP, N. Delhi, 2000)
29. Anderson, Chris: *Makers — The New Industrial Revolution* (Random House, London, 2012)

INDEX

A

Absolute advantage, 490
Absolute income hypothesis, 221-22
Acceleration principle, 254-57
Accountability, 71
Adaptive expectations hypothesis, 445
Adverse selection, 272
Aggregate supply, 162
Amazon, 29

B

Balance of payments, 53-58, 62-63, 593
Balanced budget multiplier, 198
Baumol's inventory theoretical approach, 35-39
Business cycle, features of, 294-95
Business cycle, theories of, 295-325
Business cycles, 291-313
Business strategy, 26

C

Capabilities approach, 39
Circular flow of income, 109-11, 112-15
Climatic change, 824, 832
Coco Cola, 29
Comparative cost (advantage), 491
Competitive depreciation, 529
Consumer protection, 77
Consumption demand, 160-61
Consumption function puzzle, 223
Controlled expansion, 396
Convergence hypothesis, 38
Corporate culture, 19-20
Corporate governance, 64-72
— OECD guidelines, 69
Corporate social responsibility, 74-75
Corporate strategy, 25
Credit card, 349
Current account deficit, see BOP

D

Deflationary gap, 188-89
Deleveraging, 650
Demand for money, theories of, 323-41
Demographic environment, 13
Disinvestment, 752
Doha Round, 652
Drucker, P. F., 21-29

E

East-Asian Miracle, 44
Economic development, 38
Economic growth, 36
Economic reforms, basic rationale of, 94
Effective demand, 165
Efficiency wage, theory of, 271-72
Environment, 824
Ethics, 16
Eurozone crisis, 821
Exchange rate, 58-59
Export pessimism, 544
Export promotion, 545
External environment, 9

F

Factor price equalisation, 498
FEMA, 639
Financial sector reforms, 703
Ford Motor Company, 29
Foreign direct investment (FDI)
— See MNCs
Foreign direct investment in retail, 635
Foreign exchange, 314-20, 562
Foreign trade multiplier, 511
Franchising, 637
Frictional unemployment, 280-81
Friedman's theory of demand for money, 339-41
Full employment, 267, 268
Functional strategy, 26

G

GDRs, 639
General environment, 4
Global warming,
— See climatic change
Globalisation, 639

Group of 20, 650

H

Harrod-Domar model of economic growth, 82-86
Heckscher-Ohlin theorem, 494
High-powered money, 349

I

Import substitution vs. export substitution, 542
Import-substituting industrialisation, 89, 544
Income determination in a three-sector model, 186-88
Income determination in an open economy, 201
Income determination, 168
Induced imports and income determination, 203
Industrial licensing, 10
Industrial policy, 731
Industrial sickness, 761
Inflation, 45-48, 459
Inflationary gap, 167-68, 187, 189
Injection, 173, 191, 210
Integration, backward and forward, 32
Intellectual property rights, 650
Internal environment, 15
International environment, 15
International linkages, 520
International Monetary Fund (IMF), 586
Investment, 248
Investment, Keynesian theory, 250-52
Involuntary unemployment, 210
IS-LM curve model, 405
IS-LM model for an open economy, 431

J

J-curve effect
— See foreign exchange
Jobless growth, 51

K

Keynes effect, 275
Keynesian consumption function, 217
Keynesian model of income determination, 159-184
Koontz, Harold, 22
Kotler, P., 31-32
Kuznets' consumption function, 223-24

L

Leakage, 173, 191, 210
Learning by doing, 502
Life cycle hypothesis of consumption expenditure, 226-28
Liquidity adjustment facility (LAF), 399
Liquidity preference, 329
Liquidity trap, 262, 330
Local content rule, 653

M

Mahalanobis model, 86-92
Management by objectives (MBO), 31
Marginal efficiency of capital, 248-52
Market stabilisation scheme (MSS), 399
Marketing mix, 21
MFN clause, 649
Microsoft, 18
Mission statement, 17, 18, 29
Monetary accommodation, 388
Monetary policy for development, 391-401
Monetary policy of the RBI, 396, 400
Monetary policy, 381-90
Money market equilibrium, 374-75
Money multiplier, 350
Money supply, 345-50, 373-74
Moral hazard, 272
Morality, 16
Multi-fibre arrangement, 647
Multinational corporations, 615
Multiplier effect, 115
Multiplier, theory of, 238-47
Mundell-Fleming model, 523

N

NAIRU, 269
National income, 107-08
National Manufacturing Policy, 743
Natural environment, 14
Natural rate of unemployment, 277-78
Neo-classical theory of investment, 257
Net export function, 203
New economic policy, 98-103
Non-price competition, 8

O

Open market operations, 399
Open system, 3
Organisational structure, 18
Outsourcing, 26, 641

P

Permanent income hypothesis of consumption, 228
Phillips curve, 439
Planning in India, 781
Portfolio theory of Tobin, 331
Privatisation and disinvestment of public sector units, 199, 748
Productivity, 41
Public sector, 748
Purchasing power parity, 59

Q

Q-theory of investment, 263-65
Quota, 534

R

Ratchet effect, 225
Rational expectations, 447
Real balance effect, 275-76
Real business cycles, 305-309
Real multiplier effect, 239
Recession characteristics, 295
Relationship marketing, 7
Relative income hypothesis, 224-26
Reliance Industries Limited, 18
Rental price of capital, 257-58
Repos and reverse repos, 399
Residual factor of growth, 42

S

Saving-investment equilibrium, 177-78
Say's Law of market, 48
Sen, Amartya, 103
Stagflation, 267
Stiglitz, J., 103
Strategic business units (SBUs), 26
Strategic management, 28
Strategic planning, 27
Strategy, 25
Structural adjustment programmes, 98
Structural adjustment reforms, 96
Structural change, 38
Structural unemployment, 283
Style of management, 19
Sustainable development, 831

T

Tactics, 25
Tariff and quota, 534
Tariffication, 546
Task environment, 4
Technological environment, 12
Technology, 12
Thrift, paradox of, 243-44
Total factor productivity, 40
TOWS matrix, 22
Trade as a hindrance to growth, 507
Trade as an engine of growth, 506
Trickle-down hypothesis, 38
TRIMs, 653
TRIPs, 649, 653

U

Underemployment equilibrium, 166
Unemployment insurance, 282-83
Unemployment, 48-53, 286

V

Vent for surplus, 505
Vertical integration, 6
Voluntary unemployment, 270

W

Washington Consensus, 96-97
World Bank, 588
World Trade Organisation (WTO), 10, 648

x. Name and address of the bookseller from whom you have purchased this book:

....

....

....

xi. Name and address of the library where you would like to find the book:

....

....

xii. Name and address of your institution (Please mention the University or Board):

....

....

xiii. Your name, e-mail, and complete postal address:

....

....

....

xiv. A few other titles published by us that you would like to read:

....

....

The best assessment will be rewarded half-yearly. The award will be in the form of our publications, as decided by the Editorial and Marketing Operations Division, amounting to Rs. 1000/- (Rupees one thousand) only.

....

Please mail the filled up coupon at your earliest to :

Editorial & Marketing Operations Division

NEW CENTRAL BOOK AGENCY (P) Ltd

8/1 Chintamoni Das Lane, Kolkata 700 009

West Bengal, INDIA

Phone + Fax: 033 + 2241 8411, 2241 8573, 2241 9094

e-mail: ncbapvtltd@eth.net, ncba@cal2.vsnl.net.in

Website: www.centralgroup.com

Some exciting gifts are up for grabs with this book!!

ECONOMIC ENVIRONMENT OF BUSINESS

Sampat Mukherjee

FREE Gifts Rs. 1000/-

DEAR READERS

By now you must have gone through this book in the entirety. So we invite your assessment on this title with absolute impartiality and candid observations. After all, we publishers blindly depend on your benchmarking. Friends, please fill up the open spaces below with CAPITAL LETTERS. You may add some extra sheets of paper if the space provided is not sufficient for you.

i. What are the important topics of your syllabus which are not adequately covered in this book?

ii. In which chapters and on what topics the treatment of the subject-matter by the author is not satisfactory and why?

iii. Have you come across the typos, factual inaccuracies, inconsistencies, and other forms of mistakes in the book? If yes, then please specify the mistakes and page numbers.

iv. Name top three books on the same subject, which, in your consideration, are better than this book. Could you provide some reasons?

Your 1st Preference: ....

Your 2nd Preference: ....

Your 3rd Preference: ....

v. Any suggestion to improve the quality of illustrations, diagrams, etc.?

vi. How did you like the cover design? Any suggestion on colours?

vii. Suggestions for further improvement of production-standard:

viii. Who recommended you this book:

☐ Teacher ☐ Friend ☐ Parents ☐ Bookseller ☐ Librarian

ix. Name of the person who has recommended:

Designation: ....

Address: ....

Phone No.: ....

e-mail: ....